F. H. Hall

An
Introduction
to
Literature

An
Introduction
to
Literature

Mary Rohrberger

OKLAHOMA STATE UNIVERSITY

Samuel H. Woods, Jr.

OKLAHOMA STATE UNIVERSITY

Bernard F. Dukore

QUEENS COLLEGE OF THE CITY UNIVERSITY OF NEW YORK

RANDOM HOUSE New York

Acknowledgments

THE SHORT STORY

"The Secret Sharer," by Joseph Conrad. Reprinted by permission of J. M. Dent & Sons Ltd. and the Trustees of the Joseph Conrad Estate.

"The Infant Prodigy," by Thomas Mann, from *Stories of Three Decades*. Copyright 1936 by Alfred A. Knopf, Inc. Reprinted by permission of the publisher.

"The Egg," by Sherwood Anderson, from *The Triumph of the Egg*. Copyright 1921 by Eleanor Anderson, copyright renewed. Reprinted by permission of Harold Ober Associates Incorporated.

"Araby," by James Joyce, from *Dubliners*. Originally published by B. W. Huebsch, Inc., in 1916. All rights reserved. Reprinted by permission of The Viking Press, Inc.

"A Hunger Artist," by Franz Kafka, from *The Penal Colony*. Copyright © 1948 by Schocken Books, Inc. Reprinted by permission of Schocken Books, Inc.

"The Rocking-Horse Winner," by D. H. Lawrence, from *The Complete Short Stories of D. H. Lawrence*, Vol. III. Copyright 1933 by the Estate of D. H. Lawrence, © 1961 by Angelo Ravagli and C. Montague Weekley, Executors of the Estate of Frieda Lawrence Ravagli. Reprinted by permission of The Viking Press, Inc.

"The Fly," by Katherine Mansfield, from *The Short Stories of Katherine Mansfield*. Copyright 1922 by Alfred A. Knopf, Inc., and renewed 1950 by John Middleton Murry. Reprinted by permission of Alfred A. Knopf, Inc., and by The Society of Authors as the literary representative of the Estate of the late Katherine Mansfield.

"The Catbird Seat," by James Thurber, from *The Thurber Carnival*, published by Harper and Row. Copyright © 1945 James Thurber. Originally printed in *The New Yorker*. Reprinted by permission of Helen Thurber.

"Wash," by William Faulkner, from *Doctor Martino and Other Stories*. Copyright 1934 and renewed 1961 by William Faulkner. Reprinted from *Collected Stories of William Faulkner* by permission of Random House, Inc.

"The Short Happy Life of Francis Macomber," by Ernest Hemingway, from *The Short Stories of Ernest Hemingway*. Copyright 1936 Ernest Hemingway; renewal copyright © 1964 Mary Hemingway. Reprinted with the permission of Charles Scribner's Sons.

"Flight," by John Steinbeck, from *The Long Valley*. Copyright 1938, 1966 by John Steinbeck. Reprinted by permission of The Viking Press, Inc.

"My Oedipus Complex," by Frank O'Connor, from *Stories of Frank O'Connor*. Copyright 1950 by Frank O'Connor. Reprinted by permission of Alfred A. Knopf, Inc., and A. D. Peters & Co.

"Petrified Man," by Eudora Welty, from *A Curtain of Green and Other Stories.* Copyright, 1939, renewed, 1967, by Eudora Welty. Reprinted by permission of Harcourt, Brace & World, Inc.

"A Good Man Is Hard to Find," by Flannery O'Connor, from *A Good Man Is Hard to Find and Other Stories.* Copyright, 1953, by Flannery O'Connor. Reprinted by permission of Harcourt, Brace & World, Inc.

"The Black Prince," by Shirley Ann Grau, from *The Black Prince.* Copyright 1953 by Shirley Ann Grau. Reprinted by permission of Alfred A. Knopf, Inc.

THE NOVEL

"Hardy's Cosmic Vision," from the book *The English Novel* by Walter Allen. Copyright, ©, 1954 by Walter Allen. Reprinted by permission of E. P. Dutton & Co., Inc., pp. 285–304, by J. M. Dent & Sons Ltd., and by David Higham Associates, Ltd.

The extracts quoted by Walter Allen in this selection are from *The Return of the Native, Far from the Madding Crowd, The Mayor of Castorbridge,* and *Jude the Obscure* by Thomas Hardy. Reprinted by permission of the Trustees of the Hardy Estate and Macmillan & Co. Ltd.

"Multivalence in *The Trial*," from the book *Hawthorne and the Modern Short Story* by Mary Rohrberger. Copyright 1966 by Mouton & Company, The Hague. Reprinted by permission of the publisher.

In this selection, quotations from *The Trial,* by Franz Kafka. © Copyright, 1937, 1956, by Alfred A. Knopf, Inc. Reprinted by permission of Random House, Inc. Quotations from *Franz Kafka: Parable and Paradox,* by Heinz Politzer. © 1962 by Cornell University. Reprinted by permission of Cornell University Press. "Give It Up!" by Franz Kafka, from *Description of a Struggle.* Reprinted by permission of Schocken Books Inc. Copyright © 1958 by Schocken Books Inc.

In "Theme and Structure in *Absalom, Absalom!*" Quotations from *Absalom, Absalom!* by William Faulkner. Copyright, 1936, by William Faulkner. Copyright, 1951, by Random House, Inc. Reprinted by permission of Random House, Inc.

"The Theme and the Narrator of *The Great Gatsby*," by Thomas Hanzo, *Modern Fiction Studies,* II (Winter, 1956–1957). Reprinted by permission of the Purdue Research Foundation, Purdue University, and Thomas Hanzo.

"The Eyes of Dr. Eckleburg: A Re-examination of *The Great Gatsby*," by Tom Burnam, *College English* (October, 1952). Reprinted by permission of the National Council of Teachers of English and Tom Burnam.

POETRY

"Edward," "Sir Patrick Spens," "The Twa Corbies," "The Unquiet Grave," from *English and Scottish Popular Ballads,* ed. F. T. Child, abridged by H. C. Sargent and G. L. Kittredge. Reprinted by permission of Houghton Mifflin Company.

"They Fle from Me" by Sir Thomas Wyatt, from *Sir Thomas Wyatt: Collected Poems,* ed. Kenneth Muir, Cambridge, Mass.: Harvard University Press. Copyright, 1949, by Routledge and Kegan Paul Ltd. Reprinted by permission of Routledge and Kegan Paul Ltd.

959 by Holt,
Symons. Re-
"Epitaph on
lected Poems
Winston, Inc.
sion of Holt,
ve poems has
representative
an Cape Ltd.,

eprinted with
Helmet and
cmillan Com-
Villiam Butler
any from *Re-*
llan Company
ans of Coole"
he Macmillan
 Yeats. Copy-
ertha Georgie
eprinted with
s by William
ewed 1952 by
 Butler Yeats.
om *Collected*
ompany 1928,
Villiam Butler
any from *The*
ompany 1928,

ems of W. B.
agents to Mr.
nada Ltd. and

ar," "Bantams
t 1923 and re-
of Alfred A.

 Woods on a
It," by Robert
6, 1923, 1930,
, 1942, 1944,
y Lesley Frost
Winston, Inc.
nd, from *Per-*
permission of

n Crowe Ran-
opf, Inc., and
sion of Alfred
of Literature,"
927 by Alfred
 Reprinted by

ve," by Christopher Marlowe, and "The
," by Sir Walter Ralegh, from *England's*
 Cambridge, Mass.: Harvard University
edge and Kegan Paul Ltd. Reprinted by
n Paul Ltd.
 Drayton, from *Poems of Michael Dray-*
, Mass.: Harvard University Press. Copy-
an Paul Ltd. Reprinted by permission of

re," "The Baite," "The Flea," "A Vale-
"Death Be not Proud," "At the Round
 Donne, from *The Complete Poetry and*
printed by permission of Random House,

tar," "Vertue," "Love," by George Her-
hinson. Reprinted by permission of The

' "Upon Julia's Clothes," "To the Vir-
To the Rose," by Robert Herrick, from
 Reprinted by permission of The Claren-

ve Bestowes," by Thomas Carew, from
inted by permission of The Clarendon

he Rose," by Richard Lovelace, from
rinted by permission of The Clarendon

 Light Is Spent," "Methought I Saw My
ilton, from *Complete Poems and Major*
v York: Odyssey Press, 1957. Copyright

by Mistress," by Andrew Marvell, from
rgouliouth. Reprinted by permission of

n *Poems and Fables*, ed. James Kinsley.
arendon Press, Oxford.
ldsmith, from *The Vicar of Wakefield*
)55, Random House, Inc. Reprinted by

wed," Poem #280 "I felt a funeral in
came down the walk," Poem #465 "I
m #712 "Because I could not stop for
rinted by permission of the publishers
ege from Thomas H. Johnson, Editor,
ambridge, Mass.: The Belknap Press of
t, 1951, 1955, by The President and

eauty," "Spring and Fall: to a young
, from *Poems of Gerard Manley Hop-*
iversity Press, Inc. Reprinted by permis-

erence, this is stupid stuff,' " by A. E.
," Authorised Edition, from *The Col-*

lected Poems of A. E. Housman. Copyright 1939, 1940, ©
Rinehart and Winston, Inc. Copyright © 1967 by Robert E
printed by permission of Holt, Rinehart and Winston, Inc.
an Army of Mercenaries," by A. E. Housman, from *The Cc
of A. E. Housman.* Copyright 1922 by Holt, Rinehart and
Copyright 1950 by Barclays Bank Ltd. Reprinted by permi
Rinehart and Winston, Inc. Permission to reprint the abo
also been granted by The Society of Authors as the literary
of the Estate of the late A. E. Housman, and Messrs. Jonath
publishers of A. E. Housman's *Collected Poems.*

"No Second Troy" and "The Mask" by William Butler Yeats. F
permission of The Macmillan Company from *The Gree
Other Poems* by William Butler Yeats. Copyright The Ma
pany 1912, renewed 1940 by Georgie Yeats. "The Magi" by
Yeats. Reprinted with permission of The Macmillan Comj
sponsibilities by William Butler Yeats. Copyright The Macm
1916, renewed 1944 by Bertha Georgie Yeats. "The Wild Sv
by William Butler Yeats. Reprinted with permission of T
Company from *The Wild Swans of Coole* by William Butle
right The Macmillan Company 1919, renewed 1946 by P
Yeats. "The Second Coming" by William Butler Yeats. F
permission of The Macmillan Company from *Later Poem.
Butler Yeats.* Copyright The Macmillan Company 1924, rei
Bertha Georgie Yeats. "Sailing to Byzantium" by William
Reprinted with permission of The Macmillan Company f
Poems by William Butler Yeats. Copyright The Macmillan C
renewed 1956 by Georgie Yeats. "Leda and the Swan" by
Yeats. Reprinted with permission of The Macmillan Comp
Tower by William Butler Yeats. Copyright The Macmillan C
renewed 1956 by Georgie Yeats.

    Permission to reprint the above poems from *Collected P
Yeats* has also been granted by A. P. Watt & Son as literary
M. B. Yeats and on behalf of The Macmillan Co. of Ca
Mr. M. B. Yeats.

"Peter Quince," "The Emperor of Ice-cream," "Anecdote of the
in Pine-Woods" by Wallace Stevens, from *Poems.* Copyrigh
newed 1951 by Wallace Stevens. Reprinted by permissioi
Knopf, Inc.

"After Apple-Picking," "The Road Not Taken," "Stopping by
Snowy Evening," "Departmental," "Design," "The Most of
Frost, from *Complete Poems of Robert Frost.* Copyright 19
1939 by Holt, Rinehart and Winston, Inc. Copyright 193
1951, © 1958 by Robert Frost. Copyright © 1964, 1967 t
Ballantine. Reprinted by permission of Holt, Rinehart and

"Ancient Music" and "Ballad of the Goodly Fere," by Ezra Po
sonae. Copyright 1926, 1953 by Ezra Pound. Reprinted by
New Directions Publishing Corporation.

"Here Lies a Lady," "Philomela," "Captain Carpenter," by Joh
som, from *Selected Poems.* Copyright 1924 by Alfred A. K
renewed 1952 by John Crowe Ransom. Reprinted by permi
A. Knopf, Inc. "Piazza Piece," "Janet Waking," "Survey
by John Crowe Ransom, from *Selected Poems.* Copyright
A. Knopf, Inc., and renewed 1955 by John Crowe Ransom

newed 1964 by W. H. Auden. Reprinted from *The Collected Poetry of W. H. Auden,* by permission of Random House, Inc.

"Musée des Beaux Arts," "In Memory of W. B. Yeats," "Edward Lear," "Herman Melville," "Oh what is that sound that so thrills the ear," by W. H. Auden, from *Collected Shorter Poems.* Reprinted by permission of Faber & Faber Ltd. "Anthropos apteros for days," by W. H. Auden, from *New Year Letter.* Reprinted by permission of Faber & Faber Ltd.

"Dolor," by Theodore Roethke. Copyright 1943 by Modern Poetry Association, Inc.; "My Papa's Waltz," by Theodore Roethke. Copyright 1942 by Hearst Magazines, Inc.; "I knew a Woman," by Theodore Roethke. Copyright 1954 by Theodore Roethke. From *The Collected Poems of Theodore Roethke.* Reprinted by permission of Doubleday & Company, Inc.

"August" and "The Stranger," by William Everson (Brother Antoninus), from *The Residual Years.* Copyright 1948 by New Directions. Reprinted by permission of New Directions Publishing Corporation.

"University," by Karl Shapiro, from *Person, Place and Thing.* Copyright 1940 by Karl Shapiro. Reprinted from *Poems 1940–1953* by permission of Random House, Inc. "Jew," by Karl Shapiro, from *V-Letter and Other Poems.* Copyright 1943 by Karl Shapiro. Reprinted from *Poems of a Jew* by permission of Random House, Inc.

"The force that through the green fuse . . . ," by Dylan Thomas, from *Collected Poems.* Copyright 1939 by New Directions Publishing Corporation. Reprinted by permission of New Directions Publishing Corporation. "And Death Shall have no Dominion," by Dylan Thomas, from *Collected Poems.* Copyright 1943 by New Directions Publishing Corporation. Reprinted by permission of New Directions Publishing Corporation. "A Refusal to Mourn . . . ," by Dylan Thomas, from *Collected Poems.* Copyright 1945 by the Trustees of the Copyrights of Dylan Thomas. Reprinted by permission of New Directions Publishing Corporation. "Fern Hill," by Dylan Thomas, from *Collected Poems.* Copyright 1946 by Dylan Thomas. Reprinted by permission of New Directions Publishing Corporation.

"The force that through the green fuse . . . ," "And Death Shall have no Dominion," "A Refusal to Mourn . . . ," "Fern Hill," by Dylan Thomas. Reprinted by permission of J. M. Dent & Sons Ltd.

"After Sunday Dinner We Uncles Snooze," by John Ciardi, from *39 Poems.* © 1959, Rutgers, The State University. "Vodka," "English A," "Suburban Homecoming," by John Ciardi, from *In Fact.* © 1962, Rutgers, The State University. Reprinted by permission of John Ciardi.

"Children of Light" and "Mr. Edwards and the Spider," by Robert Lowell, from *Lord Weary's Castle.* Copyright, 1944, 1946, by Robert Lowell. Reprinted by permission of Harcourt, Brace & World, Inc.

#15 ("Constantly risking absurdity") and #28 ("Dove sta amore"), by Lawrence Ferlinghetti, from *A Coney Island of the Mind.* Copyright © 1955, 1958 by Lawrence Ferlinghetti. Reprinted by permission of New Directions Publishing Corporation.

"The Death of a Toad," by Richard Wilbur, from *Ceremony and Other Poems.* Copyright 1948, 1949, 1950, by Richard Wilbur. Reprinted by permission of Harcourt, Brace & World, Inc.

"For W. A. Mozart" and "The Wise Men," by Edgar Bowers, from *The Form of Loss.* Copyright, 1956 by Edgar Bowers. Reprinted by permission of the publisher, Alan Swallow.

"Abraham's Madness" and "Afternoon for a Small Boy," by Bink Noll, from *The Center of the Circle.* Copyright, 1960, by Bink Noll. Reprinted by permission of Harcourt, Brace & World, Inc.

Preface

This book differs from the usual introduction to literature text in that it neither attempts to analyze all the selections nor omits analysis altogether. Several of the selections are analyzed with some care but never to the point where the student is led to believe that the meaning of the selection has been exhausted. All the analyses are designed to lead to further exploration and discussion of meanings. The teacher using this apparatus should be able to carry on the Socratic method as begun in the introductory sections.

A second major difference is that while this book is designed to be chiefly analytical, it uses analysis in connection with insights and perspectives from other varieties of criticism besides the New Criticism. The very arrangement of the selections should do a great deal to give the student a historical framework in which to place what he has learned. The failure of most types-anthologies to present material chronologically, within the genre sections, means that class time can be wasted orienting the student historically. Much of this information can be conveyed to the student painlessly and almost unconsciously by the historical arrangement we have adopted within each genre section. For the teacher who wants to orient his students historically, such an arrangement is invaluable. And the teacher who wants to ignore historical considerations is free to do so.

An introductory section, discussing literature as an art form, has been devised to provide the student with a rational basis for a critical approach. This section also includes a discussion of the varying critical approaches currently in fashion: formalist, historical, biographical, anthropological, psychological, etc. When the student begins more independent study of literary history and criticism, he soon becomes aware that many of the books he reads are radically unlike what he has been taught. So that he may use such books with some profit and without necessarily becoming by turns a disciple of each school of criticism, we try to let him understand the principal approaches that he is likely to meet and to show by means of comments and questions the kinds of perspectives each school can offer.

Each genre section is in line with our over-all purpose. Each includes introductory material that defines the particular genre, discusses its origins and development, and explains techniques employed, either similar to or different from those used in other genres. Selections, arranged chronologically but not meant to survey historical periods, are varied enough to include a sampling of different devices and themes. Brief biographical notes precede the selections, and short comments follow most.

The section on the novel does not include the text of a novel, since the inclusion of one would limit the length of other sections in the book unnecessarily and since inexpensive editions are easily obtainable. The section does include discussions of five well-known novels, each discussion approaching a different novel from a different critical perspective.

After the genre sections, we have included a section dealing with writing about literature that is devised to show the student how to find a subject, isolate it, and develop it. The need for a section like this in a text of this kind seems to us to be amply demonstrated by the many paperback supplements now available. This section has the advantage of offering assignments coordinated with the selections and with the other analyses in the book.

A brief glossary of important critical terms, cross-referenced to the introductory material, ends the book.

We should mention that it has not been our purpose to present an exhaustive inquiry into any selection or critical approach. This book is an introductory text, and our desire has been to acquaint the student with the subject in as broad a manner as possible, while giving him basic information which he will need in any further pursuit of the subject, whether independently or in the classroom.

We take great pleasure in recording our thanks to all those who have helped in bringing this book to conclusion. We should like to thank Professor Harry M. Campbell, former Head of the Department of English, Oklahoma State University, for his encouragement and for permission to use student papers belonging to the department. We particularly thank the following students for permission to use their work: Oma Jean Baldwin, Joseph Hepp, John Lanier, Norah Loftiss, Elizabeth A. Loudenback, Diana Mehring, Barry Ross, and Lana Vandever. Ernestine Hill assisted by typing an early draft of the manuscript.

We owe an especial debt to those who helped during the latter stages: Elmer Lawson, for much good advice; David Dushkin, for helpful assistance at critical stages throughout work on the book; Mrs. Anne Olin, for much patience during the editing; Ruby Cohn, who read an early draft of the section on the drama and made invaluable suggestions; Dorothy Heiderhoff Petty, whose questions and comments helped to provide the approach we take here; and Clara Belle Woods, who rendered invaluable assistance from beginning to end.

MARY ROHRBERGER

SAMUEL H. WOODS, JR.

BERNARD F. DUKORE

Contents

§ THE NOVEL

Introduction

❧ *Literature as an Art Form*

A critical approach to literature necessitates an understanding of its nature, function, and positive values. One must know what literature is, how to read it, and how to judge it. The critic is involved in what is called applied esthetics, a branch of philosophy devoted to a study of art and the nature of beauty. As one of the arts, literature is said to have esthetic value; the response to literature as an art form is called the esthetic response, and the response is to its beauty.

The esthetic response is somewhat hard to define, but everyone knows what it is. It is an experience that can be isolated from other experiences, being different in character from them. It is a pleasurable response, but the response to all positive values is pleasurable, and all positive values are not esthetic values. Receiving an A on a quiz or smelling a steak cooking over burning coals elicits pleasurable responses but not esthetic ones.

In his book *Perception and Aesthetic Value*, Harold N. Lee gives a graphic example. We are to suppose that there are four laborers working in a field at sunset on a summer day. A bell begins to ring, and all four men hear the bell. One of them gathers up his tools and prepares to go home; the bell has reminded him that it is time for dinner. This man is *not* having the esthetic response. A second man hears the bell and kneels down to pray; the bell is the Angelus and calls him to worship. This man is *not* having the esthetic response. The third man thinks the bell might be a fire alarm and hurries off to see if he can help those in distress. This man is *not* having the esthetic response. But the fourth man hears the bell and listens to the sound of it, for the music gives him pleasure. This man *is* having the esthetic response.[1]

All of us have had such a response to a beautiful sunset, perhaps, or to a perfectly shaped rose, or to the experience of standing by the ocean on a gray day with the wind blowing the surf. And most of us have had this response to beautiful man-made objects—to symphonies, ballets, paintings, stories, or poems. Most people, also, have a physical response to an esthetic experience, although the nature of the response varies. Some people de-

[1] Harold N. Lee, *Perception and Aesthetic Value* (New York: Prentice-Hall, 1938), p. 15.

scribe a tingling sensation; others feel a gripping in the pit of the stomach; and still others experience what are called goose bumps. But whatever the response, it is characteristic and unique.

In order to participate in the esthetic response, however, it is necessary that we be *in a position to apprehend* the beautiful object; we must be properly distanced from the object. This concept is called *psychic distance,* and it is not difficult to understand. If you have ever been to a ballet and sat in the front row or to a movie and sat way up front or far off to the side, you will know what it means to be *improperly* distanced. At the ballet your attention would very likely be drawn to the muscles in the dancers' legs, and you would find it difficult to respond to the total experience of the dance. At the movie the figures and objects on the screen would be distorted and this (together with your physical discomfort) would prohibit the esthetic response. If in a symphony hall you are seated within five feet of the drums, or if you are either too close or too far away from a Frank Lloyd Wright building, or if you are tone deaf at a string quartet, or color blind at an art exhibit, or unable to read German and presented with a volume of Rilke's poems, or if you are a ten-year-old and given a copy of William Faulkner's *Absalom, Absalom!* your esthetic response will, in each case, be blocked or incomplete.

Physical and psychic factors might also inhibit the esthetic response. Even though you are properly distanced from the art object you may not be in a right relationship to it. If your neck is strained at a movie, or if you are at the seashore and getting a cold so that your health is endangered, or trying to read a poem while you have a raging headache, or viewing a painting of a snake when you have an irrational fear of snakes, the chances are good that you will not have an esthetic response.

When can you have an esthetic response? Simple—when you are in the proper relationship to the art object, when you are properly distanced from it both physically and psychically.

What has all this to do with literature and your response to it? Literature, as we have said, is one of the arts, distinguished from the other arts in that it is a *verbal structure.* Commonly defined as that part of the total of preserved writings belonging to a culture which is notable for *literary form,* as distinguished from works of a merely technical or erudite, journalistic or ephemeral nature, literature is *shaped* content, significant *form.* It is a structure of words composed in such a way that there is a harmony of all related parts to the whole. When there is this harmony of parts in the whole, the literary object is said to be beautiful, and if the reader is properly distanced from the object, it will act as a stimulus to elicit the esthetic response. The esthetic response is an emotional response and is immediate, occurring at that moment when the reader apprehends the totality. *One cannot be taught the esthetic response, but one can be given information which will put him in a better position to receive the stimulus.*

Consider, for example, the primary problem of words. Literature is a *verbal* structure. In the first place, one has to be able to read words, and, in the second place, one has to be able to understand them as they are used together to shape meaning. Consequently, a study of how words are used in specific literary objects is necessary if one is to experience esthetic values.

But why bother? Because, in esthetic terms, the response is pleasurable and is a positive value in itself. (There are, however, other values, not equal but tangential to the primary value.) We have defined literature as *shaped* content, as *significant* form. Besides being a verbal structure, literature is a meaningful structure; it involves one in experiences that he values; it provides knowledge that he values; it enables him to participate vicariously in an immense variety of experiences; and, in so doing, it provides a means toward greater knowledge and eventual wisdom. Because there is value in what literature offers, it is to one's advantage to prepare oneself to participate in its values.

It is relatively easy for anyone to respond to a simple structure. Small children take delight in nursery rhymes and adventure stories. They respond at a primary level to the beat of the patterned lines or the suspense of the chase; but the more complex the structure, the greater the knowledge and experience we need to respond to it. Indeed, there are some structures that are shaped in such a way that they can afford pleasure at level after level to varying readers at different times in their experience. *Gulliver's Travels,* for example, can be read to the four-year-old and by the fourteen-year-old, and each will have, at his own level, a pleasurable response. And it can be read again at twenty-four, when one's additional knowledge and experience will make Gulliver's adventures more meaningful and again at forty-four or sixty-four when increased wisdom will provide greater pleasure in an increased understanding of the complexity of the form. Indeed, with the great works of art it seems necessary that each generation bring its knowledge, its insights, and its experiences into the task of understanding and evaluating, for a true appreciation of their complexity derives from the same deep level of the human mind from which they were created, and that level encompasses not only the whole past history of human development but also has within it the seeds of the future. The purpose of a course such as this is to put you in a position to receive some of the positive esthetic values, to provide the means whereby you may understand how literature is shaped, and something of what it means.

❈ The Critical Approaches to Literature

The problem, as we have said, is to apprehend the *totality* of the literary object. This is not as easy as it may at first appear. Indeed for hundreds of years critics have been disputing the proper approaches to take to the art form, and their efforts may be broadly categorized into several frames of reference. In recent times, by far the most dominant critical method is that practiced by a group known variously as "New Critics," "formalists," or sometimes "textual," "esthetic," or "ontological" critics. They appear to follow the injunction of Ernst Cassirer, who said in *An Essay on Man*, "In our study of language, art, and myth the problem of meaning takes precedence over the problems of historical development." [2] These critics insist on the total integrity of the literary piece. Concentrating entirely on its esthetic value, they are concerned with demonstrating the harmonious involvement of all the parts to the whole and with pointing out how meaning is derived from structure and how matters of technique determine structure.

The formalist critic examines the literary piece without reference to biographical facts of the author's life, without reference to the genre of the piece or to its place in the development of the genre or in literary history, and without reference to its social milieu. A vigorous movement, the New Criticism revolted against the traditional scholarly approach to literature, which was concerned with the ideas, personality, and development of the author and with the conception and dissemination of ideas through literary pieces in historical context. Objecting that the esthetic value of the piece was lost in a focusing of attention on peripheral matters, the New Critics sought to put the emphasis where they felt it belonged—on the literary object itself and its esthetic meanings.

But a movement so vigorous and so opposed to the traditional approach brought much opposition in its wake. Critics of other schools pointed out limitations of the formalist approach and asserted the validity

[2] Ernst Cassirer, *An Essay on Man* (New Haven: Yale University Press, 1944), p. 69.

Bough documented the extent of myth-making and the effect myths have on human behavior, and from the works of Carl Gustav Jung, which in part express the theory that myths are retained in social memory by the "collective unconscious" of a people. The anthropological critics claim that cyclic patterns of withdrawal and return and of death and rebirth, patterns involving guilt and expiation and sacrificial suffering, propitiation rites, fertility rites, initiation rites—among others—are common to all people and that themes concerning them find their way into all significant literature whether the author makes conscious or unconscious use of them. The validity of many of their claims cannot be denied. The frequency of the so called "initiation theme" in literature can be documented by a quick look at the stories collected in this text. "My Kinsman, Major Molineux," "The Secret Sharer," "Araby," "Flight," to mention only a few, take the introduction of a youth into the realities of the world as central subject matter. Further, the extensive use that authors have made of patterns of behavior basic to Christian theology hardly needs demonstrating. Most medieval literature has as its basis some aspect of Christian doctrine for both themes and structural patterns in the works. The relationship between primitive rites and primitive art and Greek myth and Greek art can also be easily seen. Perhaps not so easy to see, however, is the use modern authors make of ancient myths and rites. The student, however, need only look to such stories as "The Old People" by Faulkner or "Death in the Woods" by Sherwood Anderson. In "The Old People," Faulkner drew heavily upon the folk belief that by eating the flesh of an animal (or by being anointed with a substance from its body), one acquires certain physical, moral, and intellectual qualities characteristic of that animal. So, for example, he who feeds on venison is swifter and more sagacious than he who lives on the flesh of the clumsy bear. Similarly, he who eats of the body of a god (or an animal elevated to the status of a god) shares in the god's attributes and powers. In "The Old People," the mystical relationship of Sam Fathers to his totem animal becomes the basis for the initiation rites (a tribal ceremony) of young Isaac MacCaslin. In "Death in the Woods," Anderson made use of certain primitive taboos that are expressed as ceremonial rites to ward off death, and he also made extended use of the Demeter-Proserpine myth with its patterns of death and rebirth. Fairy tale motifs can be easily located in such stories as E. T. A. Hoffmann's "The History of Krakatuk," Edgar Allan Poe's "Hop-Frog," and D. H. Lawrence's "The Rocking-Horse Winner"; and Shirley Ann Grau has made extensive use of devil lore in her story "The Black Prince."

The question as to whether an author is always fully aware of these patterns in his fiction is as difficult to answer as the larger question of whether he is aware of the total implications of his work. Certainly it is possible that certain themes and structural patterns might appear in a narrative without the author's conscious awareness, and certainly, also, a writer calls upon certain primordial responses which the reader brings to the art form. Denying a conscious awareness of certain symbolic identifications in his own works, Faulkner said: "What symbolism is in the books is evidently instinct in man, not in man's knowledge but in his inheritance of his old dreams, in his blood, perhaps his bone, rather than in the storehouse of his memory." [6] Such a view would seem to bear out Jung's opinion that these patterns and figures are common to all men, primitive or civilized, however far removed they may appear to be from this highly technological, mechanized, automated life.

Still, as valuable as the anthropological approach might be, certain dangers should be avoided. The student should be aware that in locating and demonstrating widely recurrent patterns there is some danger that a critic might place too much emphasis on merely identifying them and overlook how they are used or whether other themes are present. In other words, there is a danger in reducing a work of literature to a mere statement of a pattern. To do this is to take a part for the whole and thus lose the whole. The student should also be careful that there is sufficient evidence in the piece of literature before he makes statements concerning the location and use of such patterns. Not every thirty-three-year-old man is a Christ-figure, nor is every tree the Tree of Knowledge, nor every dance a ceremonial rite.

THE PSYCHOLOGICAL APPROACH

Like the anthropological approach to literature, the psychological involves the effort to locate and demonstrate certain recurrent patterns. It is different in that it draws on a different body of knowledge—most often on that offered by Sigmund Freud and his followers. This is not to say that all psychological criticism postdates Freud. Many theories of human motivation predated his—the theory of humors, for example, or the associationist psychology prevalent in the late eighteenth and early nineteenth centuries. But the modern psychological movement received its greatest impetus from Freud, especially after the English translation and publication of *Three Contributions to the Theory of Sex* (1910) and *The Interpretation of Dreams* (1913). Freud's exploration of the unconscious area of the human mind led him to the conclusion that it was this area that was the wellspring of man's rich imagination, his capacity for creation, and the complexity of his thought and behavior, and that the contents of this region of the mind found expression in symbolic words, thoughts, or actions. Through analysis of the structure and content of dreams he was led to believe that there existed a set of symbols which were common to all men and which could be interpreted. The human personality (which he divided into three parts— the ego, the superego, and the id—all residing within the mind of man and often in conflict with one another) developed from infancy through childhood until adolescence. One of the most powerful of these conflicts which

[6] *Faulkner at Nagano*, ed. Robert A. Jellife (Tokyo: Tuttle, 1956), p. 68.

occurs early in childhood, Freud called the Oedipus complex after the protagonist of the Greek tragedy *Oedipus the King*. In the thirteenth lecture of a series called *A General Introduction to Psychoanalysis*, Freud explained the Oedipal situation in this way:

> The son, when quite a little child, already begins to develop a peculiar tenderness towards his mother, whom he looks upon as his own property, regarding his father in the light of a rival who disputes this sole possession of his; similarly the little daughter sees in her mother someone who disturbs her tender relation to her father and occupies a place which she feels she herself could very well fill. Observation shows us how far back these sentiments date . . . because in the Oedipus myth the two extreme forms of the wishes arising from the situation of the son—the wish to kill the father and to marry the mother—are realized in an only modified form.[7]

These subconscious incestuous desires of the son for the mother (or the daughter for the father) cause simultaneous feelings in the child of guilt, fear, and anxiety. In normal growth the child must release his libidinal desires from his parent in order to employ them in the quest of an external love-object so that he can establish his own identity.

The influence of Freud's psychology on modern writers has been immeasurable. One cannot fail to detect Freudian themes in the works of Lawrence, Anderson, Thomas Mann, Eugene O'Neill, Franz Kafka, to name just a few; and many critics have located these themes in their works. Some critics, however, hesitate to use Freudian ideas to interpret the works of authors who predate Freud. Still, if Freud's theories have any validity they should be applicable to human behavior in any time or place. Followers of Freud insist that he did not invent behavior patterns; he analyzed what he believed had always existed.

In applying these theories, however, the student must once again be careful that he does not take the part for the whole and reduce a piece of literature to a mere statement of a behavior pattern. One more caution is perhaps in order. The student should avoid reading a piece of literature as though it were a case study which might be used as a basis for psychoanalysis of the author. Such activity is outside of the province of the student of literature.

THE IMPRESSIONISTIC APPROACH

"Impressionistic criticism" is the term often applied to the subjective response the reader makes to a work of art. Since this kind of criticism can, and often does rest upon preference, whim, or prejudice, it does not seem to the editors to have the same kind of objectivity that the approaches already discussed do. It is as valuable or as worthless as the taste of the individual

[7] Sigmund Freud, *A General Introduction to Psychoanalysis* (New York: Perma-books, 1953), p. 217.

critic, and assumes that any opinion trained or untrained, is as valuable as any other.

The five approaches described all have their values and their limitations. It seems likely to the editors that no single approach will serve for every piece of literature. But each one has its proper insights to give, and part of the task of the critic and reader of literature is to find the approach or approaches that will best lead to a just appreciation of the particular work of literature. An anthropological approach can do much to help us understand Faulkner and Ernest Hemingway but relatively little to understand James Thurber. A purely formalist approach will probably lead us to misunderstand the importance of Lawrence as a writer. No one of the theories seems to the editors to offer a foolproof system of understanding literature. If we keep in mind that our aim is to understand literature as an art form and that virtually any of these can contribute to that end, we shall not go far wrong.

🮥 *The Symbolic Content of Literature*

One reason why it is possible to approach literature from so many different directions and by many readers of different generations is its symbolic nature. It is widely recognized that the art form, because it has a reference beyond itself, is fundamentally symbolic. *Agamemnon* is not merely about one king in Bronze Age Mycenae, or even only about kings, but about all proud, unheedful men. Anderson's "The Egg" has real meaning for us only if we recognize our own origins as being in a certain sense similar to that of the chicken. In this broad sense we can say that all literature is symbolic.

But authors use symbols, also, in a more specific sense. Objects, details, characters, places, even actions may be endowed with a meaning beyond themselves so that ideas and feelings, intangible things, may be given a concrete reality and meanings be made visible. Symbols are not something invented by an author to confuse the reader, not strange objects with far-fetched meanings arbitrarily attached to them; but they are, in literature as in life, a vital part of our experience. A cross on a building says that it is in some way connected with Christianity. All federal buildings fly the American flag, and schools fly American and state flags, and these symbolically tell us that these buildings are devoted to public purposes. In Great Britain, the symbol of the crown similarly marks national or "crown" property or officials. A driver stops when the traffic light at an intersection is red, another form of symbolic communication. Pins, lapel buttons, or watch-keys show that their wearers belong to various organizations, and usually these symbols of membership are so distinctively shaped as to be recognizable beyond reading distance.

All these are called public, common, or conventional symbols. Just as their meanings are understood in life, so are literary symbols. If, in a story, a military officer is wounded and then sheathes his sword, this action probably has symbolic importance. Without actually having the officer say, "I am wounded, and I relinquish my command," the author makes the reader understand just this, probably more effectively and economically than an explicit statement could. The sword is a common symbol of military authority, and once sheathed, it is neither an effective weapon nor an instrument of authority.

This use of the symbol in literature does not offer many difficulties, even for the untrained reader. But occasionally authors use symbols in a more complex way. The symbol, by definition, stands for something beyond itself and often for many things. The figure of a woman mending the strings of an apron as she sits by a fireside might suggest the pleasures, comforts, and securities of home and mother; or the same figure might arouse feelings of anxiety and hostility over the ties that bind one to home and family, restricting one's freedom. In a piece of literature the author might wish to use both sets of associations, or he might wish to limit the reader's response to one or the other. The only way one can tell what symbolic identification the author wishes him to make is by reference to the author's use of his symbol within his text. In "The Fly," by Katherine Mansfield, for example, the reader must understand that flies are created in multitudes, live their brief existences often in sordid or dirty surroundings, and appear to be subject to a fate greater than their own will to survive. But one must also understand that humans are like flies not only in this way but also in their ability at times to rise above their surroundings in metaphorical flights through the heavens. To fly, to soar through the skies, is to escape, if only for a time, earth-bound reality. By presenting a situation where the reader sees the fly's struggle to escape and its destruction at the hands of a power greater than itself, Miss Mansfield presents the first set of associations; then by extending her symbol to identify all humans with flies, including the one human who destroys the fly, she leads the reader to the second set of associations. His task is to identify the symbol and to discover what it means. In this identification and discovery the reader can usually trust the story or poem, for when an author wishes to endow an object or detail with symbolic significance, he will indicate, either explicitly or implicitly, his intended meaning or meanings.

Another kind of symbolism that could cause the reader some problem is what is called "private" or "personal" symbolism. This nomenclature is possibly somewhat misleading since no symbol is altogether private or personal. If it were there would be no possibility of communication. Nevertheless, there has been a tendency, particularly during the last hundred years, for writers to endow objects with certain symbolic aspects that are not a part of the public domain. In "Sailing to Byzantium," for example, William Butler Yeats uses Byzantium, the capital of the Eastern Roman Empire during the Middle Ages, as a symbol of the heaven of the intellectual mind. He describes Byzantium as "the holy city" and alludes to the mosaics that are among the best Byzantine art and to the intricate clockwork birds built for the emperors. By noticing the features of the city and its life that are emphasized within the poem and the fact that the speaker considers it a desirable place to go, the reader comprehends some of the meanings Yeats wants his symbol to convey. In leading one to his meaning, Yeats uses some relatively public information in that details about Byzantium are readily available in reference books. He also uses some private meanings—for example, the idea that Byzantium is an ideal state of existence, an idea made clear within the poem.

Literary symbolism accounts for much of the complexity, intricacy, and richness of many great works of art. This is not to say that all authors use symbols to the same extent or in exactly the same way. But if symbols are present, if through emphasis, repetition, implications, or recurring patterns, the author indicates that he is saying one thing in terms of another, these hints should never be neglected, for they lead to eventual understanding.

The
Short Story

❈ *Origins and Development*

For a long time the short story was assigned a somewhat inferior status, being popularly thought of as some little piece an author tossed off between major productions. To some extent this view is still with us, but as those knowledgeable in the area have examined the modern short story they recognize that it is an exceedingly complex form, making up in depth what it lacks in length.

As we know it today, the short story is the most recent literary genre, coming into existence as a separate form of fiction early in the nineteenth century. The novel, which dates from the early eighteenth century, is a hundred years older. Unlike the novel, which arose from the realistic movement in literature, the short story had its beginnings in the romantic tradition—in fairy tales, myths, and legends, like those written by the Germans, Tieck and Hoffmann, and the brothers Grimm. This influence can be clearly seen in Washington Irving's "Rip Van Winkle" and "The Legend of Sleepy Hollow," and in Nikolai Gogol's collection of pieces based upon Ukrainian folklore, *Evenings on a Farm Near Dikenka*. Perhaps the influence is not so easily seen in Gogol's St. Petersburg stories, which combine the element of fantasy with a surface realism. But if one remembers that one of the basic tenets of the romantic movement was the assertion that there is more to the world than that which can be discovered through the senses, that there is what might be called an under- or inner-world no less real than the world of material fact, and if one recognizes that the early practitioners of the short story moved beyond the bounds of the observable, then it is not hard to realize the connection these writers sought to make between the seen and the unseen. Irving, Gogol, Edgar Allan Poe, and Nathaniel Hawthorne (each of whom has been called at one time or another the originator of the short story) presented the supernatural as though it is real, and, in so doing, they asserted its reality.

This is not to say that all short narrative fiction has so recent a history, for the brief tale is as old as literature itself, and the brief tale in prose is as old as the history of prose fiction. But early in the nineteenth century something happened to the form of the brief tale which caused certain men to recognize a difference between what was being written by such authors as Irving, Gogol, Poe, and Hawthorne and what had been written earlier.

Poe is considered the first writer to attempt to theorize upon the new form. In a review of Hawthorne's *Twice Told Tales*, Poe set down statements that are now so well known that they have become a part of the basic knowledge of all students of literature:

> A skillful artist has constructed a tale. He has not fashioned his thoughts to accommodate his incidents, but having deliberately conceived a certain single effect to be wrought, he then combines such events, and discusses them in such tone as may best serve him in establishing this preconceived effect. If his very first sentence tends not to the outbringing of this effect, then in his very first step he has committed a blunder. In the whole composition there should be no word written of which the tendency, direct or indirect, is not to the one pre-established design.

Poe wrote in the 1840's. In the 1880's Brander Matthews, using Poe's statement as a basis, proclaimed the birth of the new genre and formulated the now generally accepted conditions of the form.[1] Matthews said that the short story has a unity of impression which the sketch or tale does not have and which the novel cannot have. The short story, he continued, deals with a single character, a single event, a single emotion, or the series of emotions called forth by a single situation.

As with all definitions there are some problems inherent in this one. The most important thing that Poe did in his critical statement was to give the short story the status of a verbal art form, since in all perfectly realized art an inner consistency—a total integration, a unity—is basic to the form itself. And Matthews' statement is somewhat limited, since anyone familiar with a number of short stories knows that they can deal with more than one important character and often contain several situations. Still, for our purposes, the statements that we have are valid (if loose) and workable (even if exceptions occur). The short story is commonly defined as a piece of short prose fiction characterized by a unity of effect, freedom from irrelevance, and a closely wrought texture; and it deals with a single character in a single situation at a single moment in time.

The standard of excellence achieved by the early practitioners of the new form, especially by Poe and Hawthorne, is equaled by the short pieces of Herman Melville, Stephen Crane, Henry James, Joseph Conrad, Anton Chekhov, and Katherine Mansfield. Structurally, Melville's short pieces closely follow the symbolic pattern developed by Hawthorne, in which symbols extend meaning to many levels. But Melville was able to manipulate narrative point of view to better advantage than Hawthorne. Crane, James, and Conrad add a dimension of surface reality not before achieved, and Chekhov and Miss Mansfield move away from stories with a strong

[1] Brander Matthews, *The Philosophy of the Short Story* (London: Longmans Green, 1901).

plot line to the presentation of brief moments where atmosphere, mood, exact detail, and precise and evocative phrasing help to expand the moment and give it universal significance.

Almost every first-rate author of our century has tried his hand at the writing of short stories and many of them are considered masters at it. An interesting and correlative fact is that of all the practitioners of the short story in English, a great majority have been American, to the extent that some people have considered the short story to be peculiarly American in origin, development, and standard of achievement. Perhaps Wallace and Mary Stegner are correct when they say that as a literary form it most expresses us as a people, being nervous, formal, concentrated, brief, and penetrating.[2] But in America the first two decades of this century almost saw the demise of the short story. Writing for the *Atlantic Monthly* in July, 1915, Henry Seidel Canby said that contemporary efforts were sketchy, anecdotal, and mechanical. He put the blame on editors who desired nothing more than these "made to order" stories and on a proliferation of textbooks variously called *Selling the Short Story* or *How to Write the Short Story*. In an article in the *Dial* for May, 1917, Herbert Ellsworth Cory found the short story to be on its last legs because it was being written by a mob of imitators whose efforts lacked high seriousness, whose techniques had grown more and more self-conscious, and whose final products were contrived. But a vital form does not usually just disappear. More often it waits for a new master to revitalize it, and in the early 1920's Sherwood Anderson came along to insist in his autobiographical *A Story Teller's Story* that people were constantly spoiling the tale in telling it:

> There was a notion that ran through all story telling in America, that stories must be built about a plot and that absurd Anglo-Saxon notion that they must point a moral, uplift the people, make better citizens, etc. The magazines were filled with these plot stories . . . "The Poison Plot," I called it in conversation with my friends as the plot notion did seem to me to poison all story telling. What was wanted I thought was form, not plot, an altogether more elusive and difficult thing to come at.[3]

Like Miss Mansfield, Anderson was greatly influenced by Chekhov, but Anderson was also acquainted with the experimental writings of Gertrude Stein and with the psychoanalytic theories of Sigmund Freud. These influences combine in the impressive collection *Winesburg, Ohio* and perhaps form a cornerstone for the monumental achievements of later short story writers not only in America but also on the Continent.

There are reasons to begin a study of the critical approach to literature with an examination of the short story. In the first place the prose form is

---

[2] Wallace and Mary Stegner, eds., *Great American Short Stories* (New York: Dell, 1957), p. 10.

[3] Sherwood Anderson, *A Story Teller's Story* (New York: The Viking Press, 1924), p. 352.

more familiar to modern day students, and the narrative gives it a special appeal. Everybody responds at a basic level to the storyteller's art. But there is also the length of the short story which makes it more convenient to handle in the classroom where time is often at a premium. The relative brevity of the short story makes it easier for teacher and student to examine every aspect of the story in relationship to the total unity. Further, the number and variety of short stories make it possible for a range of techniques and ideas to be displayed.

The Devices of Fiction

An understanding of what a story communicates and how it achieves that communication is vital to a critical approach. Before communication can be achieved, however, a reader must be drawn into the story in such a way that he participates vicariously in the experience. Only then will the experience have meaning for him. Because of his own humanity a reader is able to identify with certain characters, and because a reader performs certain actions in his own life he is able to understand a character's interaction with his environment. In the story an author presents an illusion of reality which must be credible and which the reader must accept as credible. Even in fantasies and science fiction, in which the reader knows what is being described is not literally true, what is described must seem believable in light of the reader's ideas of probability. The participation in the experience which the author presents is a participation in a total action where the characters and events have been rigorously selected by the author to dramatize a central idea about life. This idea is called the *theme* of the story. The theme controls the author's selection—consciously or unconsciously—of characters, plot, setting, conflict, point of view, and style.

Analysis involves a study of the various elements of the story in an effort to understand the theme of the story. The successful story combines all the elements in such a way that there is a complex interaction among them. For this reason it is difficult to separate single elements—to talk, for example, about character without talking at the same time about plot, or setting, or conflict, because characters often determine plot, and setting helps to define characters, and conflict results from the placing of characters in situations. Before we can talk about any of these elements, however, we need to define them.

A good place to start is with the term *narrative*. A narrative, of course, is a story, and stories involve persons, called *characters*, who act out in a particular time and place (*setting*) some kind of *conflict* in a pattern of events. This pattern of events is called *plot*. The most important character in a story, the central character, the one to whom all the events in the story have relevance, is called the *protagonist*. In the short story there is usually a single protagonist; however, some stories have more than one person central to the action.

Characters must be credible; that is, readers must accept them as believable people. Characters can be described as *flat* or *round:* Flat characters are one-sided; round characters are many-sided. In fiction either kind can be credible. This is not to say that real people can be one-sided, but it is possible to know only one side of a person. Characters have particular personalities and physical attributes that distinguish them from other characters. The process by which an author creates a character is called *characterization*. There are two principal ways an author can characterize. He can use *direct* means to describe physical appearance. He can say, for example, that Sally is five feet, four inches tall, weighs 110 pounds, and has blond hair and blue eyes. Or he can describe her intellectual and moral attributes or explain the degree of her sensitivity. He can say that she is a bright girl who respects her parents and feels their disapproval strongly. Or he can use *dramatic* means and place her in situations to show what she is by the way she behaves or speaks.

A character's behavior must be consistent with his nature; a particular character put in a situation should react in a particular way. His actions must be motivated in terms that a reader can accept. Henry James put it well when he said: "What is character but the determination of incident? What is incident but the illustration of character?"

In the short story characters are usually both individuals and types. Unlike the novelist, the short story writer has little space in which to develop a character fully. Therefore, to get greater meaning or to universalize his theme, he often makes a character symbolic. In "My Kinsman, Major Molineux," for example, Robin is both an individual and a symbol of youth. In "The Fly," the symbolic role of the protagonist is emphasized by his title, the Boss.

When a protagonist is involved in conflict with another character, this other character is called the *antagonist*. But conflict is, of course, not confined to a struggle between people. The protagonist may be in conflict with fate or the gods or environment, or his struggle may be an inner one whereby he does battle with a part of himself or with conflicting value systems or desires, or his inner conflict may be objectified in a conflict with someone or something outside himself.

The protagonist acts out his conflict through a sequence of events that make up the plot or *narrative structure* of the story. There are various ways the author may arrange the events. He can begin at the beginning of the struggle and proceed to order episodes chronologically, or he can begin with a chronological arrangement and then by means of a flashback reveal an episode or episodes that took place at an earlier time, or he can begin in the middle (*in medias res*) and then go back to pick up earlier events before moving to the end of the narrative. Narrative structure usually takes a certain pattern. The author begins by giving the reader information which he must have before he can understand the conflict to follow. This necessary information is called *exposition*. The author then proceeds to introduce the *complication* or conflict. This section of the narrative is often called *rising action*. The *climax* is the turning point of the action which leads to the *resolution* (sometimes called *falling action*). The resolution or *denouement* usually involves recognition or discovery by the protagonist, or if not by the protagonist, by the reader who is led to an understanding by some kind of disclosure.

In his presentation of the action the author chooses to delineate some events by means of direct dramatic *scenes* and some by *summaries* of the action. The relative importance of events can often be discovered by reference to whether or not the author chooses to present them by scene or summary.

In fiction the plot, or certain actions which are part of the plot, can become symbolic and are hence known as *symbolic action*. If a character raises a shade to let light into a darkened room, he may also be shedding light on a problem. Whether he raises the shade quickly or slowly or in a sweeping gesture or hesitantly may indicate his feelings about finding the solution to the problem. Acts are sometimes made symbolic by repetition. In "My Kinsman, Major Molineux," Robin repeats essentially the same behavior three times. This repetition forces the reader to look for symbolic content in the act. Often the entire narrative structure of a story is symbolic. This is especially true in stories whose plots follow a dream pattern or repeat a universal human pattern.

A reader's natural interest in what happens next in the story, together with the tension that has been built up by previous events or the author's skillful use of *foreshadowing* (hints of what is to come), create *suspense* (a certain expectancy concerning forthcoming events). In the successful story there is a subtle balance of suspense and foreshadowing—suspense used to keep the reader, at a conscious level, uncertain about the plot's resolution, foreshadowing functioning at a level below that of conscious awareness to tell the reader what will happen next. Foreshadowing never interrupts the natural flow of events; it seems sometimes only incidental, but it helps to control the reader's response, allowing him to experience at the end of the story a sense of the inevitability of the outcome. When one rereads a story he becomes conscious of the ways in which the author has led him to expect the events that actually occur.

The events of the plot take place at a particular time and place. The setting of a successful story is as functional as any of the other elements of a story, and, like the other elements, it never exists by itself. Setting can help to explain both characters and situation; it can contribute to the *atmosphere* or predominant *mood*, it can be active in foreshadowing, and it can be symbolic. The first paragraph of John Steinbeck's story "Flight" shows the setting acting in all these ways. Pepé is a product of his environment. His conflict and eventual end are foreshadowed by the ominous mood and by the symbolic identification of the people with the houses which are like aphids clinging to the skirts of the mountain.

Stories involving characters in conflict must be told from a particular *point of view*. This term has special significance when used in the analysis of fiction that should not be confused with everyday usage. Point of view signifies a position from which something is considered or evaluated; ordinary usage identifies it with opinion. If someone were to ask you your point of view concerning poetry, for example, you would probably answer either that you like or dislike it or you would reveal some of your thoughts about it. In the analysis of fiction, however, *point of view always refers to the particular vantage point from which a story is told.* There are two broad categories from which the author may choose—first person and third person. The first-person point of view involves a *narrator* who tells the story in his own voice and manner. A story told this way is sometimes called a *first-person narration*. The narrator may be the protagonist, or he may be a minor character, or he may be an observer who is outside the action.

First-person narrative has a built-in advantage. It enables the reader to make a fairly close identification with the observer since the first-person narrator observes the action in a manner similar to that of the reader. He is conscious of his own thoughts and can express them, but, of course, he does not know what other people are thinking unless they tell him. What he sees and can report is therefore limited by his point of observation and by his sensitivity and his ability to understand what he observes and experiences. Any possible disadvantage imposed by these limitations may be balanced by the immediacy and authority the narrative gains by telling it in the first person.

The reader should never confuse the narrator with the author. The narrator is a character, created and manipulated by the author who is able to reveal to the reader information beyond the ken of the narrator who is limited by his own personality and biases. Suppose, for example, one is reading a story told by a narrator who, in the opening paragraphs, describes himself as a tactful fellow who always knows how to handle himself in polite society. Then, a few paragraphs later, the narrator reports his experiences at a party by means of a dramatic scene whereby the reader is able to see him in action. At the party the behavior of the narrator reveals him to be both rude and boorish. Clearly there is inconsistency here between what the narrator says he is (or what he thinks he is) and what he actually is (or appears to be). The author has manipulated his character and situation to show the reader that the narrator cannot be altogether trusted in what he says. The reader should always be careful to notice whether the narrator can be completely trusted or whether he is limited or biased so that he is unable to report accurately. Whether he can be trusted or not affects the meaning of a story.

A *third-person narration* involves several possibilities. The author may assume a position of omniscience whereby he is able to reveal the thoughts of all the characters and to shift scenes at will. Or the author can choose to limit his view to that of a single character who is the *central observer* of the action. Finally, the author can choose a completely *objective view* whereby he apparently operates much like a camera reporting only what is visible to the eye.

Stream of consciousness is a device sometimes employed in a third-person narrative. It is a means by which the author attempts to reproduce thoughts and sensations that flow without apparent logic. People do not ordinarily think in sentences nor are their thoughts as carefully controlled as paragraphs. Often thoughts follow a process of association of which a person is not consciously aware. In reproducing this state, the author attempts to set down random thoughts that appear to be chaotic. But the reader must remember that in fiction the effect of chaos is only apparent and not real. The author is manipulating the thoughts of his characters for a purpose which is ultimately significant. Indeed, point of view in any piece of fiction is relevant to the total effect of the story. An author chooses the particular point of view which he feels will best reveal his theme.

Stories are told in words that are formed into sentences and paragraphs. An author's vocabulary and syntax, his words and his use of words, form the basis of his *style*. The good writer tries to find a style that best expresses what he means to say. Styles vary from writer to writer. They range from the relatively uncomplex to the very complex, from the simple words and simple sentences employed by a writer like Ernest Hemingway to the multisyllabic words and involved syntax of a writer like William Faulkner. Faulkner's style is one of the most famous in modern literature. Every stylistic device that he employs can be directly related to his attempt to convey his impression of reality. In his writings he makes use of devices to accomplish an almost complete merging of past and present time. Long sentences, word lists, adjective-filled clauses, the repetition of words and phrases, parenthetical expressions and parentheses within parentheses, and the frequent use of the past participle combine with shifting points of view and contrapuntal plots to convey the unrelenting continuity of experiences, the intensity and complexity of life itself.

Tone, the voice or attitude of the author that emerges from the work, cannot be separated from style, any more than it can be separated from the other materials of fiction. Thus a reader must be aware of the tone of the comments and interpretations made by the narrator or author. If one fails to grasp an ironic tone, for example, he may miss the whole point of the story. The tone is controlled by the demands of the theme in the same way that the other elements are controlled. The unity of the total work demands internal consistency.

In other words, the identification of characters, conflict, plot, setting, atmosphere, point of view, and style does not in itself constitute interpretation. Interpretation is the process of deriving meaning from the facts. In the interpretation all the facts must be considered and none ignored. A valid interpretation is suggested by the story and based upon evidence found in the story. Thus in making a legitimate interpretation of a story, one does not read meaning *into* a story. Instead, he should draw his interpretation *out of* the story, basing it upon the things which are said and done in the story.

In the analysis of fiction it is necessary to examine the elements (the parts or what we might call the facts of the story) not as entities in themselves, but as they are related to the whole. Such an interpretation is not really seeking what is often called a "hidden meaning" so much as it is developing a set of meanings from the implications of speeches and actions within the story. Like life itself, stories make people think and interpret and compare evidence so that they understand the point of what has happened without being told explicitly what it all means. Broadly speaking, readers nearly always agree about the main meaning of a story, though of course they have different interpretations of the smaller points. Most real life experiences do not end by teaching a neat moral lesson. Likewise most stories do not tell the reader how to lead his life either, though they may well help him to understand something of the complexity of the human condition and thus broaden his sympathies and enlarge his imagination.

The evaluation of a piece of literature is directly related to interpretation; an interpretation that emerges from an examination of all the facts is a demonstration of the totality of the work and as such implies its esthetic value. Such an interpretation is also a means by which one can judge the significance of the experience. Thus after the totality of a piece has been demonstrated the reader goes a step further to comment on the experience he has undergone and to consider its implications, its complexity, the universality, and profundity of its statement. Great art mirrors our complex world and comments on it.

The stories that follow will each be an experience, and each experience will need interpretation and evaluation. In forming your interpretations you should be careful to examine all the facts. To do this you might need to read the story more than once, and you might need to test a variety of interpretations before you decide on one that seems to you most valid. The stories are arranged in chronological order so that you can see something of the development of the short story. Brief biographical notes should help acquaint you with the author. Comments that follow should help you to interpret the stories. When one or another of the various critical approaches mentioned earlier seems a valid entry into the story, questions have been devised in such a way as to lead you to examine that validity.

❧ E. T. A. Hoffmann § 1776–1822

Hoffman was an author, a musician, a composer, and a gifted music critic. Although his literary productions caused him to be rated as a major figure in the German Romantic Movement, he is nevertheless best known to the rest of the world as the author of the three stories on which Offenbach's opera Tales of Hoffmann *is based. Hoffmann's fiction, although not as widely known as Offenbach's opera, has had tremendous influence on many important writers. Hans Christian Andersen, Victor Hugo, Alexandre Dumas, Robert Louis Stevenson, the Brontës, Hawthorne, Longfellow, and Poe were familiar with Hoffmann's fabulous and often grotesque tales, which at their best embody man's fears, tensions, anxieties, and desires. "The History of Krakatuk" exhibits Hoffmann's considerable skill in the form of the fairy tale. This translation is by Thackeray.*

The History of Krakatuk

Perlipat's mother was the wife of a king—that is, a queen; and, in consequence, Perlipat, the moment she was born, was a princess by birth. The king was beside himself for joy as he saw his beautiful little daughter lying in her cradle; he danced about, and hopped on one leg, and sang out, "Was anything ever so beautiful as my Perlipatkin?" And all the ministers, presidents, generals, and staff-officers, hopped likewise on one leg, and cried out, "No, never!" However, the real fact is, that it is quite impossible, as long as the world lasts, that a princess should be born more beautiful than Perlipat. Her little face looked like a web of the most beautiful lilies and roses, her eyes were the brightest blue, and her hair was like curling threads of shining gold. Besides all this, Perlipat came into the world with two rows of pearly teeth, with which, two hours after her birth, she bit the lord chancellor's thumb so hard that he cried out, "O gemini!" Some say he cried out, "O dear!" but on this subject people's opinions are very much divided, even to the present day. In short, Perlipat bit the lord chancellor on the thumb, and all the kingdom immediately declared that she was the wittiest, sharpest, cleverest little girl, as well as the most beautiful. Now, everybody was delighted except the queen—she was anxious and dispirited, and nobody knew the reason; everybody was puzzled to know why she caused Perlipat's cradle to be so strictly guarded. Besides having guards at the door, two nurses always sat close to the cradle, and six other nurses sat every night round the room; and what was most extraordinary, each of these six nurses was obliged to sit with a great tom-cat in her lap, and keep stroking him all night, to amuse him, and keep him awake.

Now, my dear little children, it is quite impossible that *you* should know why Perlipat's mother took all these precautions; but *I* know, and will tell you all about it. It happened that, once on a time, a great many excellent kings and agreeable princesses were assembled at the court of Perlipat's father, and their arrival was celebrated by all sorts of tournaments, and plays, and balls. The king, in order to show how rich he was, determined to treat them with a feast which should astonish them. So he privately sent for the upper court cook-master, and ordered him to order the upper court astronomer to fix the time for a general pig-killing, and a universal sausage-making; then he jumped into his carriage, and called, himself, on all the kings and queens; but he only asked them to eat a bit of mutton with him, in order to enjoy their surprise at the delightful entertainment he had prepared for them. Then he went to the queen, and said, "You already know, my love, the partiality I entertain for sausages." Now the queen knew perfectly well what he was going to say, which was that she herself (as indeed she had often done before) should undertake to superintend the sausage-making. So the first lord of the treasury was obliged to hand out the golden sausage-pot and the silver saucepans; and a large fire was made of sandal-wood; the queen put on her damask kitchen-pinafore; and soon after the sausage soup was steaming and boiling in the kettle. The delicious smell penetrated as far as the privy-council-chamber; the king was seized with such extreme delight, that he could not stand it any longer. "With your leave," said he, "my lords and gentlemen"—jumped over the table, ran down into the kitchen, gave the queen a kiss, stirred about the sausage-brew with his golden scepter, and then returned back to the privy-council-chamber in an easy and contented state of mind. The queen had now come to the point in the sausage-making, when the bacon was cut into little bits and roasted on little silver spits. The ladies of honor retired from the kitchen, for the queen, with a proper confidence in herself, and consideration for her royal husband, performed *alone* this important operation. But just when the bacon began to roast, a little whispering voice was heard, "Sister, I am a queen as well as you, give me some roasted bacon, too"; then the queen knew it was Mrs. Mouserinks who was talking. Mrs. Mouserinks had lived a long time in the palace; she declared she was a relation of the king's, and a queen into the bargain, and she had a great number of attendants and courtiers underground. The queen was a mild, good-natured woman; and although she neither acknowledged Mrs. Mouserinks for a queen nor for a relation, yet she could not, on such a holiday as this, grudge her a little bit of bacon. So she said, "Come out, Mrs. Mouserinks, and eat as much as you please of my bacon." Out hops Mrs. Mouserinks, as merry as you please, jumped on the table, stretched out her pretty little paw, and ate one piece of bacon after the other, until, at last, the queen got quite tired of her. But then out came all Mrs. Mouserinks' relations, and her seven sons, ugly little fellows, and nibbled all over the bacon; while the poor queen was so frightened that she could not drive them away. Luckily, however, when there still remained a little bacon, the first lady of the bedchamber happened to come in; she drove all the mice away, and sent for the court mathematician, who divided the little that was left as equally as possible among all the sausages. Now sounded the drums and the trumpets; the princes and potentates who were invited rode forth in glittering garments, some under white canopies, others in magnificent coaches, to the sausage feast. The king received them with hearty friendship and elegant politeness; then, as master of the land, with scepter and crown, sat down at the head of the table. The first course was polonies. Even then it was remarked that the king grew paler and paler; his eyes were raised to heaven, his breast heaved with sighs; in fact, he seemed to be agitated by some deep and inward sorrow. But when the blood puddings came on, he fell back in his chair, groaning and moaning, sighing and crying. Everybody rose from table; the physicians in ordinary in vain endeavored to feel the king's pulse: a deep and unknown grief had taken possession of him.

At last—at last, after several attempts had been made, several violent remedies applied, such as burning feathers under his nose, and the like, the king came to himself, and almost inaudibly gasped out the words, "Too little bacon!" Then the queen threw herself in despair at his feet: "Oh, my poor unlucky royal husband," said she, "what sorrows have you had to endure! but see here the guilty one at your feet; strike—strike and spare not. Mrs. Mouserinks and her seven sons, and all her relations, ate up the bacon, and—and——" Here the queen tumbled backwards in a fainting-fit! But the king arose in a violent passion, and said he, "My lady of the bedchamber, explain this matter." The lady of the bedchamber explained as far as she knew, and the king swore vengeance on Mrs. Mouserinks and her family for having eaten up the bacon which was destined for the sausages.

The lord chancellor was called upon to institute a suit against Mrs. Mouserinks and to confiscate the whole of her property; but as the king thought that this would not prevent her from eating his bacon, the whole affair was entrusted to the court machine and watchmaker. This man promised, by a peculiar and extraordinary operation, to expel Mrs. Mouserinks and her family from the palace forever. He invented curious machines, in which pieces of roasted bacon were hung on little threads, and which he set round about the dwelling of Mrs. Mouserinks. But Mrs. Mouserinks was far too cunning not to see the artifices of the court watch and machine-maker; still all her warnings, all her cautions, were vain; her seven sons, and a great number of her relations, deluded by the sweet smell of the bacon, entered the watchmaker's machines, where, as soon as they bit at the bacon, a trap fell on them, and then they were quickly sent to judgment and execution in the kitchen. Mrs. Mouserinks, with the small remnants of her court, left the place of sorrow, doubt, and astonishment. The court was rejoiced; but the queen alone was sorrowful; for she knew well Mrs. Mouserinks' disposition, and that she would never allow the murder of her sons and relations to go unrevenged. It happened as she expected. One day, whilst she was cooking some tripe for the king, a dish to which he was particularly partial, appeared Mrs. Mouserinks and said, "You have murdered my sons, you have killed my cousins and relations, take good care that the mouse, queen, does not bite your little princess in two. Take care." After saying this, she disappeared; but the queen was so frightened, that she dropped the tripe into the fire, and thus for the second time Mrs. Mouserinks spoiled the dish the king liked best; and of course he was very angry. And now you know why the queen took such extraordinary care of princess Perlipatkin: was not she right to fear that Mrs. Mouserinks would fulfill her threat, come back, and bite the princess to death?

The machines of the machine-maker were not of the slightest use against the clever and cunning Mrs. Mouserinks; but the court astronomer, who was also upper-astrologer and star-gazer, discovered that only the Tom-cat family could keep Mrs. Mouserinks from the princess's cradle; for this reason each of the nurses carried one of the sons of this family on her lap, and, by continually stroking him down the back, managed to render the otherwise unpleasant court service less intolerable.

It was once at midnight, as one of the two chief nurses, who sat close by the cradle, awoke as it were from a deep sleep; everything around lay in profound repose; no purring, but the stillness of death; but how astonished was the chief nurse when she saw close before her a great ugly mouse, who stood upon his hind legs, and already had laid his hideous head on the face of the princess. With a shriek of anguish, she sprung up; everybody awoke; but Mrs. Mouserinks (for she it was who had been in Perlipat's cradle), jumped down, and ran into the corner of the room. The tom-cats went after, but too late; she had escaped through a hole in the floor. Perlipat awoke with the noise, and wept aloud. "Thank heaven," said the nurses, "she lives!" But what was their horror, when, on looking at the before beautiful child, they saw the change which had taken place in her! Instead of the lovely white and red cheeks which she had had before, and the shining golden hair, there was now a great deformed head on a little withered body; the blue eyes had changed into a pair of great green gogglers, and the mouth had stretched from ear to ear. The queen was almost mad with grief and vexation, and the walls of the king's study were obliged to be padded, because he was always dashing his head against them for sorrow, and crying out, "O luckless monarch!" He might have seen how that it would have been better to have eaten the sausage without bacon, and to have allowed Mrs. Mouserinks quietly to stay underground. Upon this subject, however, Perlipat's royal father did not think at all, but he laid all the blame on the court watchmaker, Christian Elias Drosselmeier, of Nuremberg. He therefore issued this wise order, that Drosselmeier, should before four weeks restore the princess to her former state, or at least find out a certain and infallible means for so doing; or, in failure thereof, should suffer a shameful death under the ax of the executioner.

Drosselmeier was terribly frightened; but, trusting to his learning and good fortune, he immediately performed the first operation which seemed necessary to him. He carefully took Princess Perlipat to pieces, took off her hands and feet, and thus was able to see the inward structure; but there, alas! he found that the princess would grow uglier as she grew older, and he had no remedy for it. He put the princess neatly together again, and sunk down in despair at her cradle; which he never was permitted to leave.

The fourth week had begun,—yes, it was Wednesday! when the king, with eyes flashing with indignation, entered the room of the princess; and, waving his scepter, he cried out, "Christian Elias Drosselmeier, cure the princess, or die!" Drosselmeier began to cry bitterly, but little Princess Perlipat went on cracking her nuts. Then first was the court watchmaker struck with the princess's extraordinary partiality for nuts, and the circumstance of her having come into the world with teeth. In fact, she had cried incessantly since her metamorphosis, until some one by chance gave her a nut; she immediately cracked it, ate the kernel, and was quiet.

From that time the nurses found nothing so effectual as to bring her nuts. "O holy instinct of natural, eternal and unchangeable sympathy of all beings; thou showest me the door to the secret. I will knock, and thou wilt open it." He then asked permission to speak to the court astronomer, and was led out to him under a strong guard. These two gentlemen embraced with many tears, for they were great friends; they then entered into a secret cabinet, where they looked over a great number of books which treated of instincts, sympathies, and antipathies, and other deep subjects. The night came; the court astronomer looked to the stars, and made the horoscope of the princess, with the assistance of Drosselmeier, who was also very clever in this science. It was a troublesome business, for the lines were always wandering this way and that; at last, however, what was their joy to find that the princess Perlipat, in order to be freed from the enchantment which made her so ugly, and to become beautiful again, had only to eat the sweet kernel of the nut Krakatuk.

Now the nut Krakatuk had such a hard shell that an eight-and-forty-pound cannon could drive over without breaking it. But this nut was only to be cracked by a man who had never shaved, and never worn boots; he was to break it in the princess's presence, and then to present the kernel to her with his eyes shut; nor was he to open his eyes until he had walked seven steps backwards without stumbling. Drosselmeier and the astronomer worked without stopping three days and three nights; and, as the king was at dinner on Saturday, Drosselmeier (who was to have had his head off Sunday morning early), rushed into the room, and declared he had found the means of restoring the princess Perlipat to her former beauty. The king embraced him with fervent affection, promised him a diamond sword, four orders, and two new coats for Sundays. "We will go to work immediately after dinner," said the king in the most friendly manner, "and thou, dear watchmaker, must see that the young unshaven gentleman in shoes be ready with the nut Krakatuk. Take care, too, that he drink no wine before, that he may not stumble as he walks his seven steps backwards like a crab; afterwards he may get as tipsy as he pleases." Drosselmeier was very much frightened at this speech of the king's; and it was not without fear and trembling that he stammered out that it was true that the means were known, but that both the nut Krakatuk, and the young man to crack it, were yet to be sought for; so that it was not impossible that nut and cracker would never be found at all. In tremendous fury the king swung his scepter over his crowned head, and cried, with a lion's voice, "Then you must be beheaded, as I said before."

It was a lucky thing for the anxious and unfortunate Drosselmeier that the king had found his dinner very good that day, and so was in a disposition to listen to any reasonable suggestions, which the magnanimous queen, who deplored Drosselmeier's fate, did not fail to bring forward. Drosselmeier took courage to plead that, as he had found out the remedy and the means whereby the princess might be cured, he was entitled to his life. The king said this was all stupid nonsense; but, after he had drunk a glass of cherry-brandy, concluded that both the watchmaker and the astronomer should immediately set off on their journey, and never return, except with the nut Krakatuk in their pocket. The man who was to crack the same was, at the queen's suggestion, to be advertised for in all the newspapers, in the country and out of it.

Drosselmeier and the court astronomer had been fifteen years on their journey without finding any traces of the nut Krakatuk. The countries in which they were, and the wonderful sights they saw, would take me a month at least to tell of. This, however, I shall not do: all I shall say is, that at last the miserable Drosselmeier felt an irresistible longing to see his native town Nuremberg. This longing came upon him most particularly as he and his friend were sitting together smoking a pipe in the middle of a wood; in Asia. "O Nuremberg, delightful city! Who's not seen thee, him I pity! All that beautiful is, in London, Petersburg, or Paris, are nothing when compared to thee! Nuremberg, my own city!" As Drosselmeier deplored his fate in this melancholy manner, the astronomer, struck with pity for his friend, began to howl so loudly that it was heard all over Asia. But at last he stopped crying, wiped his eyes, and said, "Why do we sit here and howl, my worthy colleague? Why don't we set off at once for Nuremberg? Is it not perfectly the same where and how we seek this horrid nut Krakatuk?" "You are right," said Drosselmeier; so they both got up, emptied their pipes, and walked from the wood in the middle of Asia to Nuremberg at a stretch.

As soon as they had arrived in Nuremberg, Drosselmeier hastened to the house of a cousin of his, called Christopher Zachariah Drosselmeier, who was a carver and gilder, and whom he had not seen for a long, long time. To him the watchmaker related the whole history of Princess Perlipat, of Mrs. Mouserinks, and the nut Krakatuk; so that Christopher Zachariah clapped his hands for wonder, and said, "O, cousin, cousin, what extraordinary stories are these!" Drosselmeier then told his cousin of the adventures which befell him on his travels: how he had visited the grand duke of Almonds, and the king of Walnuts; how he had inquired of the Horticultural Society of Acornshausen; in short, how he had sought everywhere, but in vain, to find some traces of the nut Krakatuk. During this recital Christopher Zachariah had been snapping his fingers, and opening his eyes, calling out, hum! and ha! and oh! and ah! At last, he threw his cap and wig up to the ceiling, embraced his cousin, and said, "Cousin, I'm very much mistaken, *very* much mistaken, I say, if I don't myself possess this nut Krakatuk!" He then fetched a little box, out of which he took a gilded nut, of a middling size. "Now," said he, as he showed his cousin the nut, "the history of this nut is this: Several years ago, a man came here on Christmas Eve with a sackful of nuts, which he offered to sell cheap. He put the sack just before my booth, to guard it against the nut-sellers of the town, who could not bear that a foreigner should sell nuts in their native city. At that moment a heavy wagon passed over his sack, and cracked every nut in it except one, which the man, laughing in an extraordinary way, offered to sell me for a silver half-crown of the year 1720. This seemed odd to me. I found just such a half-crown in my pocket, bought the nut, and gilded it, not knowing myself why I bought it so dear and valued it so much." Every doubt with respect to its being the nut which they sought was removed by the astronomer, who, after removing the gilding, found written on the shell, in Chinese characters, the word Krakatuk.

The joy of the travelers was excessive, and Drosselmeier's cousin, the gilder, the happiest man under the sun, on being promised a handsome pension and the gilding of all the gold in the treasury into the bargain. The two gentlemen, the watchmaker and the astronomer, had put on their night caps and were going to bed, when the latter (that is, the astronomer) said, "My worthy friend and colleague, you know one piece of luck follows another, and I believe that we have not only found the nut Krakatuk, but also the young man who shall crack it, and present the kernel of beauty to the princess; this person I conceive to be the son of your cousin!" "Yes," continued he, "I am determined not to sleep until I have cast the youth's horoscope." With these words he took his night cap from his head, and instantly commenced his observations. In fact, the gilder's son was a handsome well-grown lad, who had never shaved, and never worn boots.

At Christmas he used to wear an elegant red coat embroidered with gold; a sword, and a hat under his arm, besides having his hair beautifully powdered and curled. In this way he used to stand before his father's booth, and with a gallantry which was born with him, crack the nuts for the young ladies, who, from this peculiar quality of his, had already called him "Nutcrackerkin."

Next morning the astronomer fell delighted on the neck of the watchmaker, and cried, "We have him,—he is found! but there are two things, of which, my dear friend and colleague, we must take particular care: first, we must strengthen the under-jaw of your excellent nephew with a tough piece of wood, and then, on returning home, we must carefully conceal having brought with us the young man who is to bite the nut; for I read by the horoscope that the king, after several people have broken their teeth in vainly attempting to crack the nut, will promise to him who shall crack it, and restore the princess to her former beauty,—will promise, I say, to this man the princess for a wife, and his kingdom after his death." Of course the gilder was delighted with the idea of his son marrying the Princess Perlipat and becoming a prince and king; and delivered him over to the two deputies. The wooden jaw which Drosselmeier had fixed in his young and hopeful nephew answered to admiration, so that in cracking the hardest peach-stones he came off with distinguished success.

As soon as Drosselmeier and his comrade had made known the discovery of the nut, the requisite advertisements were immediately issued; and as the travelers had returned with the means of restoring the princess's beauty, many hundred young men, among whom several princes might be found, trusting to the soundness of their teeth, attempted to remove the enchantment of the princess. The ambassadors were not a little frightened when they saw the princess again. The little body with the wee hands and feet could scarcely support the immense deformed head! The hideousness of the countenance was increased by a woolly beard, which spread over mouth and chin. Everything happened as the astronomer had foretold. One dandy in shoes after another broke teeth and jaws upon the nut Krakatuk, without in the slightest degree helping the princess, and as they were carried away half-dead to the dentist (who was always ready), groaned out—that was a hard nut!

When now the king in the anguish of his heart had promised his daughter and kingdom to the man who would break the enchantment, the gentle Drosselmeier made himself known, and begged to be allowed the trial. No one had pleased the princess so much as this young man; she laid her little hand on her heart, and sighed inwardly, Ah! if *he* were the person destined to crack Krakatuk, and be my husband! Young Drosselmeier, approaching the queen, the king, and the princess Perlipat in the most elegant manner, received from the hands of the chief master of ceremonies the nut Krakatuk, which he immediately put into his mouth,—and crack! crack!—broke the shell in a dozen pieces; he neatly removed the bits of shell which yet remained on the kernel, and then with a most profound bow presented it to the princess, shut his eyes, and proceeded to step backwards. The princess swallowed the kernel; and oh! wonderful wonder! her ugliness disappeared, and, instead, was seen a form of angel beauty, with a countenance like lilies and roses mixed, the eyes of glancing azure, and the full locks curling like threads of gold. Drums and trumpets mingled with the rejoicings of the people. The king and the whole court danced upon one leg, as before, at Perlipat's birth, and the queen was obliged to be sprinkled all over with eau de Cologne, since she had fainted with excessive joy. This great tumult did not a little disturb young Drosselmeier, who had yet his seven steps to accomplish: however, he recollected himself, and had just put his right foot back for the seventh step, when Mrs. Mouserinks, squeaking in a most hideous manner, raised herself from the floor, so that Drosselmeier, as he put his foot backwards, trod on her, and stumbled,—nay, almost fell down. What a misfortune! The young man became at that moment just as ugly as ever was the princess Perlipat. The body was squeezed together, and could scarcely support the thick deformed head, with the great goggling eyes and wide gaping mouth. Instead of the wooden roof for his mouth, a little wooden mantel hung out from behind his back. The watchmaker and astronomer were beside themselves with horror and astonishment; but they saw how Mrs. Mouserinks was creeping along the floor all bloody. Her wickedness, however, was not unavenged, for Drosselmeier had struck her so hard on the neck with the sharp heel of his shoe, that she was at the point of death; but just as she was in her last agonies, she squeaked out in the most piteous manner, "O Krakatuk, from thee I die! but Nutcracker dies as well as I; and thou, my son, with the seven crowns, revenge thy mother's horrid wounds! Kill the man who did attack her, that naughty, ugly wicked Nutcracker!" Quick with this cry died Mrs. Mouserinks, and was carried off by the royal housemaid. Nobody had taken the least notice of young Drosselmeier. The princess, however, reminded the king of his promise, and he immediately ordered the young hero to be brought before him. But when that unhappy young man appeared in his deformed state, the princess put her hands before her and cried out, "Away with that nasty Nutcracker!" So the court marshal took him by his little shoulder and pushed him out of the door.

The king was in a terrible fury that anybody should ever think of making a nutcracker his son-in-law: he laid all the blame on the watchmaker and astronomer, and banished them both from his court and kingdom. This had not been seen by the astronomer in casting his horoscope; however, he found, on reading the stars a second time, that young Drosselmeier would so well behave himself in his new station, that, in spite of his ugliness, he would become prince and king. In the meantime, but with the fervent hope of soon seeing the end of these things, Drosselmeier remains as ugly as ever; so much so, that the nutcrackers in Nuremberg have always been made after the exact model of his countenance and figure.

§ FOR COMMENT

In its attempt to explain the origin of the Nuremberg nutcracker, "The History of Krakatuk" might more properly be called a legend, although it exhibits most of the characteristics of the Märchen or fairy tale. In nearly all fairy tales the ordinary laws of nature are suspended. The story operates in a realm outside of known reality. The reader must put his knowledge of the real world out of his mind and accept the assumptions of the story. In most fairy tales there is some kind of conflict involving people, animals, or strange creatures who, nevertheless, behave in human ways. Characters are often only sketchily presented as either good or evil, handsome or ugly. Settings are often remote, landscapes sometimes unfamiliar; and details of the setting often exhibit a curious mixture of the particular and the vague. Miraculous adventures take place, but plots often ramble without orderly arrangement of incidents. Sometimes the storyteller wanders from his narrative path to tell another story (called tale within a tale) which may or may not be closely tied to the major action. Although the typical fairy tale is often filled with violent actions involving horrible consequences (Hansel and Gretel, for example, being fattened for a witch's meal), it usually ends happily, being in essence wish-fulfilling. The hero, for example, kills the dragon and wins the hand of the beautiful princess; or the heroine, who has been transformed into an ugly creature by a wicked witch, is restored to her former shape by the hero who has successfully completed his quest.

List the characteristics of the Märchen as they are used in "The History of Krakatuk." What are the initial assumptions of the story? Who are the principal characters? How fully are they characterized? How much setting does the story contain? Are some parts of the setting better than others? What is the main conflict, and how is it resolved? How is the tale within the tale related to the principal action? Does this story end happily or unhappily? The requirements of the legend, of course, make it necessary that at the end young Drosselmeier look like the figure of the Nuremberg nutcracker. But how delightful is the notion that the commonplace nutcracker is in reality an enchanted young man who will ultimately be prince and king!

The fairy tale belongs to the oral tradition in literature. Properly speaking it is the recounting of a story which has been handed down from generation to generation by word of mouth or in writing. Its long life attests its popularity. In occidental culture there are some fairy tales that are three or four thousand years old. It is easy to see the fascination that tales of wonder and adventure hold for children. But what pleasure is afforded an adult audience? Are there elements of the fairy tale in our popular novels and television programs? Give examples.

Reread "The History of Krakatuk," noticing some of the details and complications that might give a mature reader pleasure. Notice how the narrator at times uses irony to suggest symbolic meaning. The first paragraph, for example, presents a delightful picture of all the ministers, presidents, and generals hopping on one leg in imitation of their king.

Edgar Allan Poe § 1809–1849

*From the time that he was orphaned at three, through his marriage
to his thirteen-year-old cousin, up to his premature death, presumably caused by excessive drinking, Poe's life was filled with experiences that appeal to the sensational minded. However, in spite of
these experiences and his continual struggle to make his writing pay,
his achievements cause him to be acknowledged today as one of the
geniuses of American letters. A gifted poet and short story writer and
a respected critic, he was the first to theorize upon the short story as
a literary genre. In a review of Hawthorne's* Twice Told Tales, *Poe
insisted that a short story should aim at a single effect, everything
in the story being constructed to further the "pre-established design." His own creative writings are passionate and intense, often
dream-like. His poems are musical, sensual, and sometimes macabre.
His stories are often adventures in a world apparently grotesque and
unreal but based firmly in psychological truths. Best known of the
stories are such pieces as "The Cask of Amontillado," "The Masque
of the Red Death," "The Tell-tale Heart," and "The Fall of the
House of Usher."*

Hop-Frog

I never knew any one so keenly alive to a joke as the king was. He
seemed to live only for joking. To tell a good story of the joke kind, and to
tell it well, was the surest road to his favor. Thus it happened that his seven
ministers were all noted for their accomplishments as jokers. They all took
after the king, too, in being large, corpulent, oily men, as well as inimitable
jokers. Whether people grow fat by joking, or whether there is something
in fat itself which predisposes to a joke, I have never been quite able to
determine; but certain it is that a lean joker is a *rara avis in terris.*[1]

About the refinements, or, as he called them, the "ghosts" of wit, the
king troubled himself very little. He had an especial admiration for *breadth*
in a jest, and would often put up with *length*, for the sake of it. Overniceties wearied him. He would have preferred Rabelais's *Gargantua*, to the

---

[1] *rara avis in terris:* Rare creature on earth.

Zadig of Voltaire: and, upon the whole, practical jokes suited his taste far better than verbal ones.

At the date of my narrative, professing jesters had not altogether gone out of fashion at court. Several of the great continental "powers" still retained their "fools," who wore motley, with caps and bells, and who were expected to be always ready with sharp witticisms, at a moment's notice, in consideration of the crumbs that fell from the royal table.

Our king, as a matter of course, retained his "fool." The fact is, he *required* something in the way of folly—if only to counterbalance the heavy wisdom of the seven wise men who were his ministers—not to mention himself.

His fool, or professional jester, was not *only* a fool, however. His value was trebled in the eyes of the king, by the fact of his being also a dwarf and a cripple. Dwarfs were as common at court, in those days, as fools; and many monarchs would have found it difficult to get through their days (days are rather longer at court than elsewhere) without both a jester to laugh *with*, and a dwarf to laugh *at*. But, as I have already observed, your jesters, in ninety-nine cases out of a hundred, are fat, round and unwieldy —so that it was no small source of self-gratulation with our king that, in Hop-Frog (this was the fool's name,) he possessed a triplicate treasure in one person.

I believe the name "Hop-Frog" was *not* that given to the dwarf by his sponsors at baptism, but it was conferred upon him, by general consent of the seven ministers, on account of his inability to walk as other men do. In fact, Hop-Frog could only get along by a sort of interjectional gait—something between a leap and a wriggle—a movement that afforded illimitable amusement, and of course consolation, to the king, for (notwithstanding the protuberance of his stomach and a constitutional swelling of the head) the king, by his whole court, was accounted a capital figure.

But although Hop-Frog, through the distortion of his legs, could move only with great pain and difficulty along a road or floor, the prodigious muscular power which nature seemed to have bestowed upon his arms, by way of compensation for deficiency in the lower limbs, enabled him to perform many feats of wonderful dexterity, where trees or ropes were in question, or anything else to climb. At such exercises he certainly much more resembled a squirrel, or a small monkey, than a frog.

I am not able to say, with precision, from what country Hop-Frog originally came. It was from some barbarous region, however, that no person ever heard of—a vast distance from the court of our king. Hop-Frog, and a young girl very little less dwarfish than himself (although of exquisite proportions, and a marvellous dancer,) had been forcibly carried off from their respective homes in adjoining provinces, and sent as presents to the king, by one of his ever-victorious generals.

Under these circumstances, it is not to be wondered at that a close intimacy arose between the two little captives. Indeed, they soon became sworn friends. Hop-Frog, who, although he made a great deal of sport, was by no means popular, had it not in his power to render Trippetta many services; but *she*, on account of her grace and exquisite beauty (although a dwarf,) was universally admired and petted: so she possessed much influence; and never failed to use it, whenever she could, for the benefit of Hop-Frog.

On some grand state occasion—I forget what—the king determined to have a masquerade; and whenever a masquerade, or anything of that kind, occurred at our court, then the talents both of Hop-Frog and Trippetta were sure to be called in play. Hop-Frog, in especial, was so inventive in the way of getting up pageants, suggesting novel characters, and arranging costume, for masked balls, that nothing could be done, it seems, without his assistance.

The night appointed for the *fête* had arrived. A gorgeous hall had been fitted up, under Trippetta's eye, with every kind of device which could possibly give *éclat* to a masquerade. The whole court was in a fever of expectation. As for costumes and characters, it might well be supposed that everybody had come to a decision on such points. Many had made up their minds (as to what *rôles* they should assume) a week, or even a month, in advance; and, in fact, there was not a particle of indecision anywhere—except in the case of the king and his seven ministers. Why *they* hesitated I never could tell, unless they did it by way of a joke. More probably, they found it difficult, on account of being so fat, to make up their minds. At all events, time flew; and, as a last resource, they sent for Trippetta and Hop-Frog.

When the two little friends obeyed the summons of the king, they found him sitting at his wine with the seven members of his cabinet council; but the monarch appeared to be in a very ill humor. He knew that Hop-Frog was not fond of wine; for it excited the poor cripple almost to madness, and madness is no comfortable feeling. But the king loved his practical jokes, and took pleasure in forcing Hop-Frog to drink and (as the king called it) "to be merry."

"Come here, Hop-Frog," said he, as the jester and his friend entered the room: "swallow this bumper to the health of your absent friends (here Hop-Frog sighed,) and then let us have the benefit of your invention. We want characters—*characters*, man—something novel—out of the way. We are wearied with this everlasting sameness. Come, drink! the wine will brighten your wits."

Hop-Frog endeavored, as usual, to get up a jest in reply to these advances from the king; but the effort was too much. It happened to be the poor dwarf's birthday, and the command to drink to his "absent friends" forced the tears to his eyes. Many large, bitter drops fell into the goblet as he took it, humbly, from the hand of the tyrant.

"Ah! ha! ha! ha!" roared the latter, as the dwarf reluctantly drained the beaker. "See what a glass of good wine can do! Why, your eyes are shining already!"

Poor fellow! his large eyes *gleamed,* rather than shone; for the effect of wine on his excitable brain was not more powerful than instantaneous. He placed the goblet nervously on the table, and looked round upon the company with a half-insane stare. They all seemed highly amused at the success of the king's "*joke.*"

"And now to business," said the prime minister, a *very* fat man.

"Yes," said the king; "come, Hop-Frog, lend us your assistance. Characters, my fine fellow; we stand in need of characters—all of us—ha! ha! ha!" and as this was seriously meant for a joke, his laugh was chorused by the seven.

Hop-Frog also laughed, although feebly and somewhat vacantly.

"Come, come," said the king, impatiently, "have you nothing to suggest?"

"I am endeavoring to think of something *novel,*" replied the dwarf, abstractedly, for he was quite bewildered by the wine.

"Endeavoring!" cried the tyrant, fiercely; "what do you mean by *that?* Ah, I perceive. You are sulky, and want more wine. Here, drink this!" and he poured out another goblet full and offered it to the cripple, who merely gazed at it, gasping for breath.

"Drink, I say!" shouted the monster, "or by the fiends—"

The dwarf hesitated. The king grew purple with rage. The courtiers smirked. Trippetta, pale as a corpse, advanced to the monarch's seat, and, falling on her knees before him, implored him to spare her friend.

The tyrant regarded her, for some moments, in evident wonder at her audacity. He seemed quite at a loss what to do or say—how most becomingly to express his indignation. At last, without uttering a syllable, he pushed her violently from him, and threw the contents of the brimming goblet in her face.

The poor girl got up as best she could, and, not daring even to sigh, resumed her position at the foot of the table.

There was a dead silence for about half a minute, during which the falling of a leaf, or of a feather might have been heard. It was interrupted by a low, but harsh and protracted *grating* sound which seemed to come at once from every corner of the room.

"What—what—*what* are you making that noise for?" demanded the king, turning furiously to the dwarf.

The latter seemed to have recovered, in great measure, from his intoxication, and looking fixedly but quietly into the tyrant's face, merely ejaculated:

"I—I? How could it have been me?"

"The sound appeared to come from without," observed one of the courtiers. "I fancy it was the parrot at the window, whetting his bill upon his cage-wires."

"True," replied the monarch, as if much relieved by the suggestion; "but, on the honor of a knight, I could have sworn that it was the gritting of this vagabond's teeth."

Hereupon the dwarf laughed (the king was too confirmed a joker to object to any one's laughing), and displayed a set of large, powerful, and very repulsive teeth. Moreover, he avowed his perfect willingness to swallow as much wine as desired. The monarch was pacified; and having drained another bumper with no very perceptible ill effect, Hop-Frog entered at once, and with spirit, into the plans for the masquerade.

"I cannot tell what was the association of idea," observed he, very tranquilly, and as if he had never tasted wine in his life, "but *just after* your majesty had struck the girl and thrown the wine in her face—*just after* your majesty had done this, and while the parrot was making that odd noise outside the window, there came into my mind a capital diversion—one of my own country frolics—often enacted among us, at our masquerades: but here it will be new altogether. Unfortunately, however, it requires a company of eight persons, and—"

"Here we *are!*" cried the king, laughing at his acute discovery of the coincidence; "eight to a fraction—I and my seven ministers. Come! what is the diversion?"

"We call it," replied the cripple, "the Eight Chained Ourang-Outangs, and it really is excellent sport if well enacted."

"We will enact it," remarked the king, drawing himself up, and lowering his eyelids.

"The beauty of the game," continued Hop-Frog, "lies in the fright it occasions among the women."

"Capital!" roared in chorus the monarch and his ministry.

"I will equip you as ourang-outangs," proceeded the dwarf; "leave all that to me. The resemblance shall be so striking, that the company of masqueraders will take you for real beasts—and, of course, they will be as much terrified as astonished."

"O, this is exquisite!" exclaimed the king. "Hop-Frog! I will make a man of you."

"The chains are for the purpose of increasing the confusion by their jangling. You are supposed to have escaped, *en masse*, from your keepers. Your majesty cannot conceive the *effect* produced, at a masquerade, by eight chained ourang-outangs, imagined to be real ones by most of the company; and rushing in with savage cries, among the crowd of delicately and gorgeously habited men and women. The *contrast* is inimitable."

"It *must* be," said the king: and the council arose hurriedly (as it was growing late), to put in execution the scheme of Hop-Frog.

His mode of equipping the party as ourang-outangs was very simple, but effective enough for his purposes. The animals in question had, at the epoch of my story, very rarely been seen in any part of the civilized world; and as the imitations made by the dwarf were sufficiently beast-like and more than sufficiently hideous, their truthfulness to nature was thus thought to be secured.

The king and his ministers were first encased in tight-fitting stockinet shirts and drawers. They were then saturated with tar. At this stage of the process, some one of the party suggested feathers; but the suggestion was at once overruled by the dwarf, who soon convinced the eight, by ocular demonstration, that the hair of such a brute as the ourang-outang was much more efficiently represented by *flax*. A thick coating of the latter was accordingly plastered upon the coating of tar. A long chain was now procured. First, it was passed about the waist of the king, *and tied*; then about another of the party, and also tied; then about all successively, in the same manner. When this chaining arrangement was complete, and the party stood as far apart from each other as possible, they formed a circle; and to make all things appear natural, Hop-Frog passed the residue of the chain, in two diameters, at right angles, across the circle, after the fashion adopted, at the present day, by those who capture Chimpanzees, or other large apes, in Borneo.

The grand saloon in which the masquerade was to take place, was a circular room, very lofty, and receiving the light of the sun only through a single window at top. At night (the season for which the apartment was especially designed,) it was illuminated principally by a large chandelier, depending by a chain from the centre of the sky-light, and lowered, or elevated, by means of a counter-balance as usual; but (in order not to look unsightly) this latter passed outside the cupola and over the roof.

The arrangements of the room had been left to Trippetta's superintendence; but, in some particulars, it seems, she had been guided by the calmer judgment of her friend the dwarf. At his suggestion it was that, on this occasion, the chandelier was removed. Its waxen drippings (which, in weather so warm, it was quite impossible to prevent,) would have been seriously detrimental to the rich dresses of the guests, who, on account of the crowded state of the saloon, could not *all* be expected to keep from out its centre—that is to say, from under the chandelier. Additional sconces were set in various parts of the hall, out of the way; and a flambeau, emitting sweet odor, was placed in the right hand of each of the Caryatides that stood against the wall—some fifty or sixty altogether.

The eight ourang-outangs, taking Hop-Frog's advice, waited patiently until midnight (when the room was thoroughly filled with masqueraders) before making their appearance. No sooner had the clock ceased striking, however, than they rushed, or rather rolled in, all together—for the impediment of their chains caused most of the party to fall, and all to stumble as they entered.

The excitement among the masqueraders was prodigious, and filled the heart of the king with glee. As had been anticipated, there were not a few of the guests who supposed the ferocious-looking creatures to be beasts of *some* kind in reality, if not precisely ourang-outangs. Many of the women swooned with affright; and had not the king taken the precaution to exclude all weapons from the saloon, his party might soon have expiated their frolic in their blood. As it was, a general rush was made for the doors; but the king had ordered them to be locked immediately upon his entrance; and, at the dwarf's suggestion, the keys had been deposited with *him*.

While the tumult was at its height, and each masquerader attentive only to his own safety—(for, in fact, there was much *real* danger from the pressure of the excited crowd,)—the chain by which the chandelier ordinarily hung, and which had been drawn up on its removal, might have been seen very gradually to descend, until its hooked extremity came within three feet of the floor.

Soon after this, the king and his seven friends, having reeled about the hall in all directions, found themselves, at length, in its centre, and, of course, in immediate contact with the chain. While they were thus situated, the dwarf, who had followed closely at their heels, inciting them to keep up the commotion, took hold of their own chain at the intersection of the two portions which crossed the circle diametrically and at right angles. Here, with the rapidity of thought, he inserted the hook from which the chandelier had been wont to depend; and, in an instant, by some unseen agency, the chandelier-chain was drawn so far upward as to take the hook out of reach, and, as an inevitable consequence, to drag the ourang-outangs together in close connection, and face to face.

The masqueraders, by this time, had recovered, in some measure, from their alarm; and, beginning to regard the whole matter as a well-contrived pleasantry, set up a loud shout of laughter at the predicament of the apes.

"Leave them to *me!*" now screamed Hop-Frog, his shrill voice making itself easily heard through all the din. "Leave them to *me*. I fancy *I* know them. If I can only get a good look at them, I can soon tell who they are."

Here, scrambling over the heads of the crowd, he managed to get to the wall; when, seizing a flambeau from one of the Caryatides, he returned, as he went, to the centre of the room—leaped, with the agility of a monkey, upon the king's head—and thence clambered a few feet up the chain—holding down the torch to examine the group of ourang-outangs, and still screaming, "I shall soon find out who they are!"

And now, while the whole assembly (the apes included) were convulsed with laughter, the jester suddenly uttered a shrill whistle; when the chain flew violently up for about thirty feet—dragging with it the dismayed and struggling ourang-outangs, and leaving them suspended in mid-air between the sky-light and the floor. Hop-Frog, clinging to the chain as it rose, still maintained his relative position in respect to the eight maskers, and still (as if nothing were the matter) continued to thrust his torch down towards them, as though endeavoring to discover who they were.

So thoroughly astonished were the whole company at this ascent, that a dead silence, of about a minute's duration, ensued. It was broken by just such a low, harsh, *grating* sound, as had before attracted the attention of the king and his councillors, when the former threw the wine in the face of Trippetta. But, on the present occasion, there could be no question as to *whence* the sound issued. It came from the fang-like teeth of the dwarf, who ground them and gnashed them as he foamed at the mouth, and glared, with an expression of maniacal rage, into the upturned countenances of the king and his seven companions.

"Ah, ha!" said at length the infuriated jester. "Ah, ha! I begin to see who these people *are*, now!" Here, pretending to scrutinize the king more closely, he held the flambeau to the flaxen coat which enveloped him, and which instantly burst into a sheet of vivid flame. In less than half a minute the whole eight ourang-outangs were blazing fiercely, amid the shrieks of the multitude who gazed at them from below, horror-stricken, and without the power to render them the slightest assistance.

At length the flames, suddenly increasing in virulence, forced the jester to climb higher up the chain, to be out of their reach; and, as he made this movement, the crowd again sank, for a brief instant, into silence. The dwarf seized his opportunity, and once more spoke:

"I now see *distinctly*," he said, "what manner of people these maskers are. They are a great king and his seven privy-councillors—a king who does not scruple to strike a defenceless girl, and his seven councillors who abet him in the outrage. As for myself, I am simply Hop-Frog, the jester—and *this is my last jest.*"

Owing to the high combustibility of both the flax and the tar to which it adhered, the dwarf had scarcely made an end of his brief speech before the work of vengeance was complete. The eight corpses swung in their chains, a fetid, blackened, hideous, and indistinguishable mass. The cripple hurled his torch at them, clambered leisurely to the ceiling, and disappeared through the sky-light.

It is supposed that Trippetta, stationed on the roof of the saloon, had been the accomplice of her friend in his fiery revenge, and that, together, they effected their escape to their own country: for neither was seen again.

§ FOR COMMENT

Compare and contrast "Hop-Frog" with "The History of Krakatuk." Notice the similarities involving characters and setting and the differences in unity, tone, plot, and import. Although Hoffmann uses occasional ironies involved in specific incidents, Poe uses *irony* as the basis for the whole story, which is a terrible, grotesque joke. As in all comedy, a manifestation of incongruity results in the comic contrast. A man slips on a banana peel and is brought from his usual upright and dignified position to a lowly one by the inconsequential banana peel. If the man is dressed in an evening suit and is wearing a top hat and carrying a cane, the comic contrast between the man and the banana peel is heightened; and the observer laughs the harder. But if the man is aged and the cane that he carries helps him to walk, his condition engages our sympathies; and one does not find his slipping on the peel to be funny at all but perhaps painfully ironic. In "Hop-Frog," Poe uses the comic contrast, but involves us in the story to such an extent that the feeling of horror consequent to a reading of it is so intense as to be painful. The grotesque joke is carried through the story and provides the unity in which the parts share. Theme, characters, and structure all reinforce the joke.

The theme concerns the universal desire of men for retribution when they suffer an affront to their dignity. So it is with everyday behavior, and desires for revenge must be controlled. Who has not at some time or other wanted to take a little pistol and shoot a neat hole through the head of a practical joker? But the practical joker, debase one as he might, does not deserve to be shot in the head, and even if he did the laws of society forbid this action. But Hop-Frog defies the society, carries through his revenge, and escapes. And the reader watches, horrified and yet satisfied.

The figure of the dwarf is itself a comic contrast. Crippled and forced to walk "between a leap and a wriggle," he has prodigious strength in his arms. His intellect and cunning are juxtaposed against his position as fool in the court. This role is ambivalent, manifested in a comic contrast, for the king's prize fool makes a fool of the king.

Forced to drink wine which excites him almost to madness and seeing the king throw a glass of wine into the face of Trippetta, the dwarf is enraged and outlines to the king an artful joke which the monarch may play on the masqueraders invited to a coming ball. Ironically, the king and his ministers are to masquerade as orangutans and make excellent sport with the guests, especially frightening the women. Hop-Frog's revenge is diabolic; all goes according to his plan, and the climax is a frenzied scene where the king and his ministers, costumed as apes, face one another chained together, while the monkey-like dwarf taunts them and finally sets them afire. What has started out as the king's joke, becomes the dwarf's, as he makes his last jest.

Like the dwarf, the king and his ministers are described in comic terms. The very idea that a ruling monarch and his ministers should have practical jokes as their main preoccupation is incongruous with their positions. What are other details of characterization which reinforce this basic comic contrast? Notice, also, that Trippetta is herself a manifestation of incongruity, since the occurrence of perfectly formed dwarfs is relatively uncommon. What role does Trippetta play in the story? Ironically, her attempt to shield the dwarf from the indignity which the king forces upon him results in her own debasement and is the catalyst for Hop-Frog's revenge.

The story is told in the first person by a narrator who is aware and makes the reader aware of all the ironies in the situation. The structure of the story is characterized by a succession of double-edged statements describing the characters and giving explicit commentary on the action. Notice some of these statements and comment on their effectiveness. Does the chatty tone that the narrator assumes further the comic contrasts? What effect does this tone have on the final horror of the story?

Nathaniel Hawthorne § 1804–1864

Hawthorne was born in Salem, Massachusetts, site of many of the most brutal witchcraft trials, and was living there when he wrote The Scarlet Letter *(1850), which is usually considered not only his greatest achievement, but also one of the greatest novels in American letters. Some rate* The Scarlet Letter *second only to Melville's* Moby-Dick. *Hawthorne's major themes and techniques, especially his concern with and allegorical treatment of the ambiguous nature of good and evil, may be discovered in his short stories as well as his novels. Indeed, his position in the development of the short story is clearly established. It was in a review of his* Twice Told Tales *that Poe first set down his famous statements concerning the unity-directed tale.*

My Kinsman, Major Molineux

After the kings of Great Britain had assumed the right of appointing the colonial governors, the measures of the latter seldom met with the ready and general approbation which had been paid to those of their predecessors, under the original charters. The people looked with most jealous scrutiny to the exercise of power which did not emanate from themselves, and they usually rewarded their rulers with slender gratitude for the compliances by which, in softening their instructions from beyond the sea, they had incurred the reprehension of those who gave them. The annals of Massachusetts Bay will inform us, that of six governors in the space of about forty years from the surrender of the old charter, under James II., two were imprisoned by a popular insurrection; a third, as Hutchinson inclines to believe, was driven from the province by the whizzing of a musket-ball; a fourth, in the opinion of the same historian, was hastened to his grave by continual bickerings with the House of Representatives; and the remaining two, as well as their successors, till the Revolution, were favored with few and brief intervals of peaceful sway. The inferior members of the court party, in times of high political excitement, led scarcely a more desirable life. These remarks may serve as a preface to the following adventures, which chanced upon a summer night, not far from a hundred years ago. The reader, in order to avoid a long and dry detail of colonial affairs, is requested to dispense with an account of the train of circumstances that had caused much temporary inflammation of the popular mind.

It was near nine o'clock of a moonlight evening, when a boat crossed the ferry with a single passenger, who had obtained his conveyance at that unusual hour by the promise of an extra fare. While he stood on the landing-place, searching in either pocket for the means of fulfilling his agreement, the ferryman lifted a lantern, by the aid of which, and the newly risen moon, he took a very accurate survey of the stranger's figure. He was a youth of barely eighteen years, evidently country-bred, and now, as it should seem, upon his first visit to town. He was clad in a coarse gray coat, well worn, but in excellent repair; his under garments were durably constructed of leather, and fitted tight to a pair of serviceable and well-shaped limbs; his stockings of blue yarn were the incontrovertible work of a mother or a sister; and on his head was a three-cornered hat, which in its better days had perhaps sheltered the graver brow of the lad's father. Under his left arm was a heavy cudgel formed of an oak sapling, and retaining a part of the hardened root; and his equipment was completed by a wallet, not so abundantly stocked as to incommode the vigorous shoulders on which it hung. Brown, curly hair, well-shaped features, and bright, cheerful eyes were nature's gifts, and worth all that art could have done for his adornment.

The youth, one of whose names was Robin, finally drew from his pocket the half of a little province bill of five shillings, which, in the depreciation in that sort of currency, did but satisfy the ferryman's demand, with the surplus of a sexangular piece of parchment, valued at three pence. He then walked forward into the town, with as light a step as if his day's journey had not already exceeded thirty miles, and with as eager an eye as if he were entering London city, instead of the little metropolis of a New England colony. Before Robin had proceeded far, however, it occurred to him that he knew not whither to direct his steps; so he paused, and looked up and down the narrow street, scrutinizing the small and mean wooden buildings that were scattered on either side.

"This low hovel cannot be my kinsman's dwelling," thought he, "nor yonder old house, where the moonlight enters at the broken casement; and truly I see none hereabouts that might be worthy of him. It would have been wise to inquire my way of the ferryman, and doubtless he would have gone with me, and earned a shilling from the Major for his pains. But the next man I meet will do as well."

He resumed his walk, and was glad to perceive that the street now became wider, and the houses more respectable in their appearance. He soon discerned a figure moving on moderately in advance, and hastened his steps to overtake it. As Robin drew nigh, he saw that the passenger was a man in years, with a full periwig of gray hair, a wide-skirted coat of dark cloth, and silk stockings rolled above his knees. He carried a long and polished cane, which he struck down perpendicularly before him at every step; and at regular intervals he uttered two successive hems, of a peculiarly solemn and sepulchral intonation. Having made these observations, Robin laid hold of the skirt of the old man's coat, just when the light from the open door and windows of a barber's shop fell upon both their figures.

"Good evening to you, honored sir," said he, making a low bow, and still retaining his hold of the skirt. "I pray you tell me whereabouts is the dwelling of my kinsman, Major Molineux."

The youth's question was uttered very loudly; and one of the barbers, whose razor was descending on a well-soaped chin, and another who was dressing a Ramillies wig, left their occupations, and came to the door. The citizen, in the mean time, turned a long-favored countenance upon Robin, and answered him in a tone of excessive anger and annoyance. His two sepulchral hems, however, broke into the very centre of his rebuke, with most singular effect, like a thought of the cold grave obtruding among wrathful passions.

"Let go my garment, fellow! I tell you, I know not the man you speak of. What! I have authority, I have—hem, hem—authority; and if this be the respect you show for your betters, your feet shall be brought acquainted with the stocks by daylight, tomorrow morning!"

Robin released the old man's skirt, and hastened away, pursued by an ill-mannered roar of laughter from the barber's shop. He was at first considerably surprised by the result of his question, but, being a shrewd youth, soon thought himself able to account for the mystery.

"This is some country representative," was his conclusion, "who has never seen the inside of my kinsman's door, and lacks the breeding to answer a stranger civilly. The man is old, or verily—I might be tempted to turn back and smite him on the nose. Ah, Robin, Robin! even the barber's boys laugh at you for choosing such a guide! You will be wiser in time, friend Robin."

He now became entangled in a succession of crooked and narrow streets, which crossed each other, and meandered at no great distance from the water-side. The smell of tar was obvious to his nostrils, the masts of vessels pierced the moonlight above the tops of the buildings, and the numerous signs, which Robin paused to read, informed him that he was near the centre of business. But the streets were empty, the shops were closed, and lights were visible only in the second stories of a few dwelling-houses. At length, on the corner of a narrow lane, through which he was passing, he beheld the broad countenance of a British hero swinging before the door of an inn, whence proceeded the voice of many guests. The casement of one of the lower windows was thrown back, and a very thin curtain permitted

Robin to distinguish a party at supper, round a well-furnished table. The fragrance of the good cheer steamed forth into the outer air, and the youth could not fail to recollect that the last remnant of his traveling stock of provision had yielded to his morning appetite, and that noon had found and left him dinnerless.

"Oh, that a parchment three-penny might give me a right to sit down at yonder table!" said Robin, with a sigh. "But the Major will make me welcome to the best of his victuals; so I will even step boldly in, and inquire my way to his dwelling."

He entered the tavern, and was guided by the murmur of voices and the fumes of tobacco to the public-room. It was a long and low apartment, with oaken walls, grown dark in the continual smoke, and a floor which was thickly sanded, but of no immaculate purity. A number of persons—the larger part of whom appeared to be mariners, or in some way connected with the sea—occupied the wooden benches, or leather-bottomed chairs, conversing on various matters, and occasionally lending their attention to some topic of general interest. Three or four little groups were draining as many bowls of punch, which the West India trade had long since made a familiar drink in the colony. Others, who had the appearance of men who lived by regular and laborious handicraft, preferred the insulated bliss of an unshared potation, and became more taciturn under its influence. Nearly all, in short, evinced a predilection for the Good Creature in some of its various shapes, for this is a vice to which, as Fast Day sermons of a hundred years ago will testify, we have a long hereditary claim. The only guests to whom Robin's sympathies inclined him were two or three sheepish countrymen, who were using the inn somewhat after the fashion of a Turkish caravansary; they had gotten themselves into the darkest corner of the room, and heedless of the Nicotian atmosphere, were supping on the bread of their own ovens, and the bacon cured in their own chimney-smoke. But though Robin felt a sort of brotherhood with these strangers, his eyes were attracted from them to a person who stood near the door, holding whispered conversation with a group of ill-dressed associates. His features were separately striking almost to grotesqueness, and the whole face left a deep impression on the memory. The forehead bulged out into a double prominence, with a vale between; the nose came boldly forth in an irregular curve, and its bridge was of more than a finger's breadth; the eyebrows were deep and shaggy, and the eyes glowed beneath them like fire in a cave.

While Robin deliberated of whom to inquire respecting his kinsman's dwelling, he was accosted by the innkeeper, a little man in a stained white apron, who had come to pay his professional welcome to the stranger. Being in the second generation from a French Protestant, he seemed to have inherited the courtesy of his parent nation; but no variety of circumstances was ever known to change his voice from the one shrill note in which he now addressed Robin.

"From the country, I presume, sir?" said he, with a profound bow.

"Beg leave to congratulate you on your arrival, and trust you intend a long stay with us. Fine town here, sir, beautiful buildings, and much that may interest a stranger. May I hope for the honor of your commands in respect to supper?"

"The man sees a family likeness! the rogue has guessed that I am related to the Major!" thought Robin, who had hitherto experienced little superfluous civility.

All eyes were now turned on the country lad, standing at the door, in his worn three-cornered hat, gray coat, leather breeches, and blue yarn stockings, leaning on an oaken cudgel, and bearing a wallet on his back.

Robin replied to the courteous innkeeper, with such an assumption of confidence as befitted the Major's relative. "My honest friend," he said, "I shall make it a point to patronize your house on some occasion, when" —here he could not help lowering his voice—"when I may have more than a parchment three-pence in my pocket. My present business," continued he, speaking with lofty confidence, "is merely to inquire my way to the dwelling of my kinsman, Major Molineux."

There was a sudden and general movement in the room, which Robin interpreted as expressing the eagerness of each individual to become his guide. But the innkeeper turned his eyes to a written paper on the wall, which he read, or seemed to read, with occasional recurrences to the young man's figure.

"What have we here?" said he, breaking his speech into little dry fragments. " 'Left the house of the subscriber, bounden servant, Hezekiah Mudge,—had on, when he went away, gray coat, leather breeches, master's third-best hat. One pound currency reward to whosoever shall lodge him in any jail of the province.' Better trudge, boy; better trudge!"

Robin had begun to draw his hand towards the lighter end of the oak cudgel, but a strange hostility in every countenance induced him to relinquish his purpose of breaking the courteous innkeeper's head. As he turned to leave the room, he encountered a sneering glance from the bold-featured personage whom he had before noticed; and no sooner was he beyond the door, than he heard a general laugh, in which the innkeeper's voice might be distinguished, like the dropping of small stones into a kettle.

"Now, is it not strange," thought Robin, with his usual shrewdness,— "is it not strange that the confession of an empty pocket should outweigh the name of my kinsman, Major Molineux? Oh, if I had one of those grinning rascals in the woods, where I and my oak sapling grew up together, I would teach him that my arm is heavy though my purse be light!"

On turning the corner of the narrow lane, Robin found himself in a spacious street, with an unbroken line of lofty houses on each side, and a steepled building at the upper end, whence the ringing of a bell announced the hour of nine. The light of the moon, and the lamps from the numerous shop-windows, discovered people promenading on the pavement, and amongst them Robin hoped to recognize his hitherto inscrutable relative.

The result of his former inquires made him unwilling to hazard another, in a scene of such publicity, and he determined to walk slowly and silently up the street, thrusting his face close to that of every elderly gentleman, in search of the Major's lineaments. In his progress, Robin encountered many gay and gallant figures. Embroidered garments of showy colors, enormous periwigs, gold-laced hats, and silver-hilted swords glided past him and daz-zled his optics. Travelled youths, imitators of the European fine gentlemen of the period, trod jauntily along, half dancing to the fashionable tunes which they hummed, and making poor Robin ashamed of his quiet and natural gait. At length, after many pauses to examine the gorgeous display of goods in the shop-windows, and after suffering some rebukes for the imper-tinence of his scrutiny into people's faces, the Major's kinsman found him-self near the steepled building, still unsuccessful in his search. As yet, how-ever, he had seen only one side of the thronged street; so Robin crossed, and continued the same sort of inquisition down the opposite pavement, with stronger hopes than the philosopher seeking an honest man, but with no better fortune. He had arrived about midway towards the lower end, from which his course began, when he overheard the approach of some one who struck down a cane on the flag-stones at every step, uttering, at regular intervals, two sepulchral hems.

"Mercy on us!" quoth Robin, recognizing the sound.

Turning a corner, which chanced to be close at his right hand, he hastened to pursue his researches in some other part of the town. His pa-tience now was wearing low, and he seemed to feel more fatigue from his rambles since he crossed the ferry, than from his journey of several days on the other side. Hunger also pleaded loudly within him, and Robin began to balance the propriety of demanding, violently, and with lifted cudgel, the necessary guidance from the first solitary passenger whom he should meet. While a resolution to this effect was gaining strength, he entered a street of mean appearance, on either side of which a row of ill-built houses was straggling towards the harbor. The moonlight fell upon no passenger along the whole extent, but in the third domicile which Robin passed there was a half-opened door, and his keen glance detected a woman's garment within.

"My luck may be better here," said he to himself.

Accordingly, he approached the door, and beheld it shut closer as he did so; yet an open space remained, sufficing for the fair occupant to ob-serve the stranger, without a corresponding display on her part. All that Robin could discern was a strip of scarlet petticoat, and the occasional sparkle of an eye, as if the moonbeams were trembling on some bright thing.

"Pretty mistress," for I may call her so with a good conscience, thought the shrewd youth, since I know nothing to the contrary,—"my sweet pretty mistress, will you be kind enough to tell me whereabouts I must seek the dwelling of my kinsman, Major Molineux?"

Robin's voice was plaintive and winning, and the female, seeing nothing to be shunned in the handsome country youth, thrust open the door, and came forth into the moonlight. She was a dainty little figure, with a white neck, round arms, and a slender waist, at the extremity of which her scarlet petticoat jutted out over a hoop, as if she were standing in a balloon. Moreover, her face was oval and pretty, her hair dark beneath the little cap, and her bright eyes possessed a sly freedom, which triumphed over those of Robin.

"Major Molineux dwells here," said this fair woman.

Now, her voice was the sweetest Robin had heard that night, the airy counterpart of a stream of melted silver; yet he could not help doubting whether that sweet voice spoke Gospel truth. He looked up and down the mean street, and then surveyed the house before which they stood. It was a small, dark edifice of two stories, the second of which projected over the lower floor, and the front apartment had the aspect of a shop for petty commodities.

"Now, truly, I am in luck," replied Robin, cunningly, "and so indeed is my kinsman, the Major, in having so pretty a housekeeper. But I prithee trouble him to step to the door; I will deliver him a message from his friends in the country, and then go back to my lodgings at the inn."

"Nay, the Major has been abed this hour or more," said the lady of the scarlet petticoat; "and it would be to little purpose to disturb him to-night, seeing his evening draught was of the strongest. But he is a kind-hearted man, and it would be as much as my life's worth to let a kinsman of his turn away from the door. You are the good old gentleman's very picture, and I could swear that was his rainy-weather hat. Also he has garments very much resembling those leather small-clothes. But come in, I pray, for I bid you hearty welcome in his name."

So saying, the fair and hospitable dame took our hero by the hand; and the touch was light, and the force was gentleness, and though Robin read in her eyes what he did not hear in her words, yet the slender-waisted woman in the scarlet petticoat proved stronger than the athletic country youth. She had drawn his half-willing footsteps nearly to the threshold, when the opening of a door in the neighborhood startled the Major's housekeeper, and, leaving the Major's kinsman, she vanished speedily into her own domicile. A heavy yawn preceded the appearance of a man, who, like the Moonshine of Pyramus and Thisbe, carried a lantern, needlessly aiding his sister luminary in the heavens. As he walked sleepily up the street, he turned his broad, dull face on Robin, and displayed a long staff, spiked at the end.

"Home, vagabond, home!" said the watchman, in accents that seemed to fall asleep as soon as they were uttered. "Home, or we'll set you in the stocks by peep of day!"

"This is the second hint of the kind," thought Robin. "I wish they would end my difficulties, by setting me there to-night."

Nevertheless, the youth felt an instinctive antipathy towards the guardian of midnight order, which at first prevented him from asking his usual question. But just when the man was about to vanish behind the corner, Robin resolved not to lose the opportunity, and shouted lustily after him,—

"I say, friend! will you guide me to the house of my kinsman, Major Molineux?"

The watchman made no reply, but turned the corner and was gone; yet Robin seemed to hear the sound of drowsy laughter stealing along the solitary street. At that moment, also, a pleasant titter saluted him from the open window above his head; he looked up, and caught the sparkle of a saucy eye; a round arm beckoned to him, and next he heard light footsteps descending the staircase within. But Robin, being of the household of a New England clergyman, was a good youth, as well as a shrewd one; so he resisted temptation, and fled away.

He now roamed desperately, and at random, through the town, almost ready to believe that a spell was on him, like that by which a wizard of his country had once kept three pursuers wandering, a whole winter night, within twenty paces of the cottage which they sought. The streets lay before him, strange and desolate, and the lights were extinguished in almost every house. Twice, however, little parties of men, among whom Robin distinguished individuals in outlandish attire, came hurrying along; but, though on both occasions they paused to address him, such intercourse did not at all enlighten his perplexity. They did but utter a few words in some language of which Robin knew nothing, and perceiving his inability to answer, bestowed a curse upon him in plain English and hastened away. Finally, the lad determined to knock at the door of every mansion that might appear worthy to be occupied by his kinsman, trusting that perseverance would overcome the fatality that had hitherto thwarted him. Firm in this resolve, he was passing beneath the walls of a church, which formed the corner of two streets, when, as he turned into the shade of its steeple, he encountered a bulky stranger, muffled in a cloak. The man was proceeding with the speed of earnest business, but Robin planted himself full before him, holding the oak cudgel with both hands across his body as a bar to further passage.

"Halt, honest man, and answer me a question," said he, very resolutely. "Tell me, this instant, whereabouts is the dwelling of my kinsman, Major Molineux!"

"Keep your tongue between your teeth, fool, and let me pass!" said a deep, gruff voice, which Robin partly remembered. "Let me pass, I say, or I'll strike you to the earth!"

"No, no, neighbor!" cried Robin, flourishing his cudgel, and then thrusting its larger end close to the man's muffled face. "No, no, I'm not the fool you take me for, nor do you pass till I have an answer to my question. Whereabouts is the dwelling of my kinsman, Major Molineux?"

The stranger, instead of attempting to force his passage, stepped back into the moonlight, unmuffled his face, and stared full into that of Robin.

"Watch here an hour, and Major Molineux will pass by," said he.

Robin gazed with dismay and astonishment on the unprecedented physiognomy of the speaker. The forehead with its double prominence, the broad hooked nose, the shaggy eyebrows, and fiery eyes were those which he had noticed at the inn, but the man's complexion had undergone a singular, or, more properly, a twofold change. One side of the face blazed an intense red, while the other was black as midnight, the division line being in the broad bridge of the nose; and a mouth which seemed to extend from ear to ear was black or red, in contrast to the color of the cheek. The effect was as if two individual devils, a fiend of fire and a fiend of darkness, had united themselves to form this infernal visage. The stranger grinned in Robin's face, muffled his parti-colored features, and was out of sight in a moment.

"Strange things we travellers see!" ejaculated Robin.

He seated himself, however, upon the steps of the church-door, resolving to wait the appointed time for his kinsman. A few moments were consumed in philosophical speculations upon the species of man who had just left him; but having settled this point shrewdly, rationally, and satisfactorily, he was compelled to look elsewhere for his amusement. And first he threw his eyes along the street. It was of more respectable appearance than most of those into which he had wandered, and the moon, creating, like the imaginative power, a beautiful strangeness in familiar objects, gave something of romance to a scene that might not have possessed it in the light of day. The irregular and often quaint architecture of the houses, some of whose roofs were broken into numerous little peaks, while others ascended, steep and narrow, into a single point, and others again were square; the pure snow-white of some of their complexions, the aged darkness of others, and the thousand sparklings, reflected from bright substances in the walls of many; these matters engaged Robin's attention for a while, and then began to grow wearisome. Next he endeavored to define the forms of distant objects, starting away, with almost ghostly indistinctness, just as his eye appeared to grasp them; and finally he took a minute survey of an edifice which stood on the opposite side of the street, directly in front of the church door, where he was stationed. It was a large, square mansion, distinguished from its neighbors by a balcony, which rested on tall pillars, and by an elaborate Gothic widow, communicating therewith.

"Perhaps this is the very house I have been seeking," thought Robin.

Then he strove to speed away the time, by listening to a murmur which swept continually along the street, yet was scarcely audible, except to an unaccustomed ear like his; it was a low, dull, dreamy sound, compounded of many noises, each of which was at too great a distance to be separately heard. Robin marvelled at this snore of a sleeping town, and marvelled more whenever its continuity was broken by now and then a distant shout, apparently loud where it originated. But altogether it was a sleep-inspiring sound, and, to shake off its drowsy influence, Robin arose, and climbed a window-frame, that he might view the interior of the church. There the moonbeams came trembling in, and fell down upon the deserted pews, and extended along the quiet aisles. A fainter yet more awful radiance was hovering around the pulpit, and one solitary ray had dared to rest upon the open page of the great Bible. Had nature, in that deep hour, become a worshipper in the house which man had builded? Or was that heavenly light the visible sanctity of the place,—visible because no earthly and impure feet were within the walls? The scene made Robin's heart shiver with a sensation of loneliness stronger than he had ever felt in the remotest depths of his native woods; so he turned away and sat down again before the door. There were graves around the church, and now an uneasy thought obtruded into Robin's breast. What if the object of his search, which had been so often and so strangely thwarted, were all the time mouldering in his shroud? What if his kinsman should glide through yonder gate, and nod and smile to him in dimly passing by?

"Oh that any breathing thing were here with me!" said Robin.

Recalling his thoughts from this uncomfortable track, he sent them over forest, hill, and stream, and attempted to imagine how that evening of ambiguity and weariness had been spent by his father's household. He pictured them assembled at the door, beneath the tree, the great old tree, which had been spared for its huge twisted trunk and venerable shade, when a thousand leafy brethren fell. There, at the going down of the summer sun, it was his father's custom to perform domestic worship, that the neighbors might come and join with him like brothers of the family, and that the wayfaring man might pause to drink at that fountain, and keep his heart pure by freshening the memory of home. Robin distinguished the seat of every individual of the little audience; he saw the good man in the midst, holding the Scriptures in the golden light that fell from the western clouds; he beheld him close the book and all rise up to pray. He heard the old thanksgivings for daily mercies, the old supplications for their continuance, to which he had so often listened in weariness, but which were now among his dear remembrances. He perceived the slight inequality of his father's voice when he came to speak of the absent one; he noted how his mother turned her face to the broad and knotted trunk; how his elder brother scorned, because the beard was rough upon his upper lip, to permit his features to be moved; how the younger sister drew down a low hanging branch before her eyes; and how the little one of all, whose sports had hitherto broken the decorum of the scene, understood the prayer for her playmate, and burst into clamorous grief. Then he saw them go in at the door; and when Robin would have entered also, the latch tinkled into its place, and he was excluded from his home.

"Am I here, or there?" cried Robin, starting; for all at once, when his thoughts had become visible and audible in a dream, the long, wide, solitary street shone out before him.

He aroused himself, and endeavored to fix his attention steadily upon the large edifice which he had surveyed before. But still his mind kept vibrating between fancy and reality; by turns, the pillars of the balcony lengthened into the tall, bare stems of pines, dwindled down to human figures, settled again into their true shape and size, and then commenced a new succession of changes. For a single moment, when he deemed himself awake, he could have sworn that a visage—one which he seemed to remember, yet could not absolutely name as his kinsman's—was looking towards him from the Gothic window. A deeper sleep wrestled with and nearly overcame him, but fled at the sound of footsteps along the opposite pavement. Robin rubbed his eyes, discerned a man passing at the foot of the balcony, and addressed him in a loud, peevish, and lamentable cry.

"Hallo, friend! must I wait here all night for my kinsman, Major Molineux?"

The sleeping echoes awoke, and answered the voice; and the passenger, barely able to discern a figure sitting in the oblique shade of the steeple, traversed the street to obtain a nearer view. He was himself a gentleman in his prime, of open, intelligent, cheerful, and altogether prepossessing countenance. Perceiving a country youth, apparently homeless and without friends, he accosted him in a tone of real kindness, which had become strange to Robin's ears.

"Well, my good lad, why are you sitting here?" inquired he. "Can I be of service to you in any way?"

"I am afraid not, sir," replied Robin, despondingly; "yet I shall take it kindly, if you'll answer me a single question. I've been searching, half the night, for one Major Molineux; now, sir, is there really such a person in these parts, or am I dreaming?"

"Major Molineux! The name is not altogether strange to me," said the gentleman, smiling. "Have you any objection to telling me the nature of your business with him?"

Then Robin briefly related that his father was a clergyman, settled on a small salary, at a long distance back in the country, and that he and Major Molineux were brothers' children. The Major, having inherited riches, and acquired civil and military rank, had visited his cousin, in great pomp, a year or two before; had manifested much interest in Robin and an elder brother, and, being childless himself, had thrown out hints respecting the future establishment of one of them in life. The elder brother was destined to succeed to the farm which his father cultivated in the interval of sacred duties; it was therefore determined that Robin should profit by his kinsman's generous intentions, especially as he seemed to be rather the favorite, and was thought to possss other necessary endowments.

"For I have the name of being a shrewd youth," observed Robin, in this part of his story.

"I doubt not you deserve it," replied his new friend, good-naturedly; "but pray proceed."

"Well, sir, being nearly eighteen years old, and well grown, as you see," continued Robin, drawing himself up to his full height, "I thought it high time to begin the world. So my mother and sister put me in handsome trim, and my father gave me half the remnant of his last year's salary, and five days ago I started for this place, to pay the Major a visit. But, would you believe it, sir! I crossed the ferry a little after dark, and have yet found nobody that would show me the way to his dwelling; only, an hour or two since, I was told to wait here, and Major Molineux would pass by."

"Can you describe the man who told you this?" inquired the gentleman.

"Oh, he was a very ill-favored fellow, sir," replied Robin, "with two great bumps on his forehead, a hook nose, fiery eyes; and, what struck me as the strangest, his face was of two different colors. Do you happen to know such a man, sir?"

"Not intimately," answered the stranger, "but I chanced to meet him a little time previous to your stopping me. I believe you may trust his word, and that the Major will very shortly pass through this street. In the mean time, as I have a singular curiosity to witness your meeting, I will sit down here upon the steps and bear you company."

He seated himself accordingly, and soon engaged his companion in animated discourse. It was but of brief continuance, however, for a noise of shouting, which had long been remotely audible, drew so much nearer that Robin inquired its cause.

"What may be the meaning of this uproar?" asked he. "Truly, if your town be always as noisy, I shall find little sleep while I am an inhabitant."

"Why, indeed, friend Robin, there do appear to be three or four riotous fellows abroad to-night," replied the gentleman. "You must not expect all the stillness of your native woods here in our streets. But the watch will shortly be at the heels of these lads and"—

"Ay, and set them in the stocks by peep of day," interrupted Robin, recollecting his own encounter with the drowsy lantern-bearer. "But, dear sir, if I may trust my ears, an army of watchmen would never make head against such a multitude of rioters. There were at least a thousand voices went up to make that one shout."

"May not a man have several voices, Robin, as well as two complexions?" said his friend.

"Perhaps a man may; but Heaven forbid that a woman should!" responded the shrewd youth, thinking of the seductive tones of the Major's housekeeper.

The sounds of a trumpet in some neighboring street now became so evident and continual, that Robin's curiosity was strongly excited. In addition to the shouts, he heard frequent bursts from many instruments of discord, and a wild and confused laughter filled up the intervals. Robin rose from the steps, and looked wistfully towards a point whither people seemed to be hastening.

"Surely some prodigious merry-making is going on," exclaimed he. "I have laughed very little since I left home, sir, and should be sorry to lose an opportunity. Shall we step round the corner by that darkish house, and take our share of the fun?"

"Sit down again, sit down, good Robin," replied the gentleman, laying his hand on the skirt of the gray coat. "You forget that we must wait here for your kinsman; and there is reason to believe that he will pass by, in the course of a very few moments."

The near approach of the uproar had now disturbed the neighborhood; windows flew open on all sides; and many heads, in the attire of the pillow, and confused by sleep suddenly broken, were protruded to the gaze of whoever had leisure to observe them. Eager voices hailed each other from house to house, all demanding the explanation, which not a soul could give. Half-dressed men hurried towards the unknown commotion, stumbling as they went over the stone steps that thrust themselves into the narrow foot-walk. The shouts, the laughter, and the tuneless bray, the antipodes of music, came onwards with increasing din, till scattered individuals, and then denser bodies, began to appear round a corner at the distance of a hundred yards.

"Will you recognize your kinsman, if he passes in this crowd?" inquired the gentleman.

"Indeed, I can't warrant it, sir; but I'll take my stand here, and keep a bright lookout," answered Robin, descending to the outer edge of the pavement.

A mighty stream of people now emptied into the street, and came rolling slowly towards the church. A single horseman wheeled the corner in the midst of them, and close behind him came a band of fearful wind-instruments, sending forth a fresher discord now that no intervening buildings kept it from the ear. Then a redder light disturbed the moonbeams, and a dense multitude of torches shone along the street, concealing, by their glare, whatever object they illuminated. The single horseman, clad in a military dress, and bearing a drawn sword, rode onward as the leader, and, by his fierce and variegated countenance, appeared like war personified; the red of one cheek was an emblem of fire and sword; the blackness of the other betokened the mourning that attends them. In his train were wild figures in the Indian dress, and many fantastic shapes without a model, giving the whole march a visionary air, as if a dream had broken forth from some feverish brain, and were sweeping visibly through the midnight streets. A mass of people, inactive, except as applauding spectators, hemmed the procession in; and several women ran along the sidewalk, piercing the confusion of heavier sounds with their shrill voices of mirth or terror.

"The double-faced fellow has his eye upon me," muttered Robin, with an indefinite but an uncomfortable idea that he was himself to bear a part in the pageantry.

The leader turned himself in the saddle, and fixed his glance full upon the country youth, as the steed went slowly by. When Robin had freed his eyes from those fiery ones, the musicians were passing before him, and the torches were close at hand; but the unsteady brightness of the latter formed a veil which he could not penetrate. The rattling of wheels over the stones sometimes found its way to his ear, and confused traces of a human form appeared at intervals, and then melted into the vivid light. A moment more, and the leader thundered a command to halt: the trumpets vomited a horrid breath, and then held their peace; the shouts and laughter of the people died away, and there remained only a universal hum, allied to silence. Right before Robin's eyes was an uncovered cart. There the torches blazed the brightest, there the moon shone out like day, and there, in tar-and-feathery dignity, sat his kinsman, Major Molineux!

He was an elderly man, of large and majestic person, and strong, square features, betokening a steady soul; but steady as it was, his enemies had found means to shake it. His face was pale as death, and far more ghastly; the broad forehead was contracted in his agony, so that his eyebrows formed one grizzled line; his eyes were red and wild, and the foam hung white upon his quivering lip. His whole frame was agitated by a quick and continual tremor, which his pride strove to quell, even in those circumstances of overwhelming humiliation. But perhaps the bitterest pang of all was when his eyes met those of Robin; for he evidently knew him on the instant, as the youth stood witnessing the foul disgrace of a head grown gray in honor. They stared at each other in silence, and Robin's knees shook, and his hair bristled, with a mixture of pity and terror. Soon, however, a bewildering excitement began to seize upon his mind; the preceding adventures of the night, the unexpected appearance of the crowd, the torches, the confused din and the hush that followed, the spectre of his kinsman reviled by that great multitude,—all this, and, more than all, a perception of tremendous ridicule in the whole scene, affected him with a sort of mental inebriety. At that moment a voice of sluggish merriment saluted Robin's ears; he turned instinctively, and just behind the corner of the church stood the lantern-bearer, rubbing his eyes, and drowsily enjoying the lad's amazement. Then he heard a peal of laughter like the ringing of silvery bells; a woman twitched his arm, a saucy eye met his, and he saw the lady of the scarlet petticoat. A sharp, dry cachinnation appealed to his memory, and, standing on tiptoe in the crowd, with his white apron over his head, he beheld the courteous little innkeeper. And lastly, there sailed over the heads of the multitude a great, broad laugh, broken in the midst by two sepulchral hems; thus, "Haw, haw, haw,—hem, hem,—haw, haw, haw, haw!"

The sound proceeded from the balcony of the opposite edifice, and thither Robin turned his eyes. In front of the Gothic window stood the old citizen, wrapped in a wide gown, his gray periwig exchanged for a nightcap, which was thrust back from his forehead, and his silk stockings hanging about his legs. He supported himself on his polished cane in a fit of convulsive merriment, which manifested itself on his solemn old features like a funny inscription on a tombstone. Then Robin seemed to hear the voices of the barbers, of the guests of the inn, and of all who had made sport of him that night. The contagion was spreading among the multitude, when all at once, it seized upon Robin, and he sent forth a shout of laughter that echoed through the street—every man shook his sides, every man emptied his lungs, but Robin's shout was the loudest there. The cloud-spirits peeped from their silvery islands, as the congregated mirth went roaring up the sky! The Man in the Moon heard the far bellow. "Oho," quoth he, "the old earth is frolicsome to-night!"

When there was a momentary calm in that tempestuous sea of sound, the leader gave the sign, the procession resumed its march. On they went, like fiends that throng in mockery around some dead potentate, mighty no more, but majestic still in his agony. On they went, in counterfeited pomp, in senseless uproar, in frenzied merriment, trampling all on an old man's heart. On swept the tumult, and left a silent street behind.

"Well, Robin, are you dreaming?" inquired the gentleman, laying his hand on the youth's shoulder.

Robin started, and withdrew his arm from the stone post to which he had instinctively clung, as the living stream rolled by him. His cheek was somewhat pale, and his eye not quite as lively as in the earlier part of the evening.

"Will you be kind enough to show me the way to the ferry?" said he, after a moment's pause.

"You have, then, adopted a new subject of inquiry?" observed his companion, with a smile.

"Why, yes, sir," replied Robin, rather dryly. "Thanks to you, and to my other friends, I have at last met my kinsman, and he will scarce desire to see my face again. I begin to grow weary of a town life, sir. Will you show me the way to the ferry?"

"No, my good friend Robin,—not to-night, at least," said the gentleman. "Some few days hence, if you wish it, I will speed you on your journey. Or, if you prefer to remain with us, perhaps, as you are a shrewd youth, you may rise in the world without the help of your kinsman, Major Molineux."

§ FOR COMMENT

Published in 1832, "My Kinsman, Major Molineux" is one of the earliest examples of the short story form. An exceedingly complex story, it is remarkably modern in theme and structure. The conflict involves the problems faced by a youth, Robin, his father's second son, who is sent into town to seek the protection of his kinsman, Major Molineux. The youth comes into town on a night when the people of the town have disguised themselves in preparation for a demonstration against one of the authorities of the king, the same Major Molineux whom Robin seeks. In his search for his kinsman, the boy goes to most unlikely places and is rebuffed by every man he meets. Only a girl who is attracted by his appearance is friendly to him. Finally Robin is told that if he waits he will soon see his kinsman. He is joined by a friendly gentleman, the first man who is kind to him. The boy's kinsman finally arrives, tarred and feathered, the object of the hooting derision of the crowd of demonstrators. Unable to control himself, the boy joins in the laughter directed at his kinsman. After the procession the boy's first thought is to go back home, but he is advised by the kindly gentleman that should he remain in town for a few days he might rise in the world without the help of his kinsman.

Examine the terms of the conflict. What does Robin's background reveal about him? Is the fact that Robin is a second son important? Notice that the youth is sent to seek help from a kinsman who becomes a kind of father substitute. Robin is eighteen years old, well grown and eager, but not yet ready to assume adult responsibilities. How many indications are there in the story that reveal Robin's need to retain dependency? Does he at the same time have a corresponding need to free himself from parental authority? Is this complex of feelings usual? What is the symbolic function of the cudgel that Robin carries? The sapling is strong, but hardly full grown, and it retains part of its root. Is it possible to compare the cudgel with the long and polished cane carried by the first gentleman whom Robin meets? How about the spiked staff carried by the watchman?

An interesting and revealing structural pattern emerges from the narrative. Robin seeks directions from a man, is rebuked and turned away to the accompaniment of laughter, and consequently finds himself lost in a succession of streets. The boy begins a search for his kinsman with a light step and an eager eye, but before long he realizes that he doesn't know the way. To ask directions he overtakes an elderly gentleman, the one with the polished cane. Robin takes hold of the old man's coat and asks about his kinsman in a voice so loud that it brings barbers from their shops into the street. The elderly gentleman reacts with excessive annoyance and threatens Robin with punishment. Is this reaction credible? Certainly, in terms of the uneasiness generated by the political situation in the town, the old gentleman might have been loath to answer questions about Major Molineux. But the situation seems to be more complex. Examine Robin's childish behavior: his grabbing hold of the gentleman's coat, the sound of his voice as he asks directions, his assumption that anyone ought to be willing to help him.

After being threatened with punishment, Robin releases the old man's coat and hurries away, pursued, the author says, by the laughter of the bystanders. Soon the boy is lost in a succession of tangled and narrow streets. This symbolic action is repeated three times in the opening pages of the story. The second time, with an "assumption of confidence" that he feels befits the major's relative, Robin confronts an innkeeper; but the inn-keeper threatens the boy with jail; and again Robin flees, followed by the laughter of the people in the inn. This time he gets lost not in darkened streets but in a well lighted thoroughfare. Finally he wanders into a street of mean appearance where a girl in a doorway catches his eye. Robin really doubts the girl's statement that Major Molineux lives in this house, but the boy allows the girl to draw him half-way inside the door. Her actions, how-ever, are interrupted by a watchman who threatens Robin with the stocks; and when the watchman turns the corner Robin hears the sound of laugh-ter. Thereafter the boy roams "desperately and at random through the town."

What is the significance of this recurrent situation? Are there other situations in the story that can be related to this pattern? How about the kindly gentleman at the end of the story or the man with the red and black face who tells Robin where to wait to find his kinsman? What is the func-tion of the girl? Who is she and why does she lie to Robin? Are her scarlet petticoats significant?

The story makes use of what is known as a dream sequence. The cir-cumstances of the search and the search itself make up a typical dream pat-tern of isolation and rejection. The crossing of the river in the moonlight is suggestive of the passing from consciousness into sleep. The boy's move-ments up and down the streets of the city, the bizarre characters he meets, the inconsistencies and incongruities, the various tonal effects, all combine to create the aura of a dream. Notice particularly the sound effects: the laughter, the tinkling of bells, the tapping of the cane, the sounds of the voices.

Why would the story take this form? Remember that objects and ac-tions in a dream become symbolic to reveal motivations perhaps hidden from conscious awareness. Is it possible that everything in the story might function as a reflection of Robin's inner feelings and a revelation of their source? That is, might the whole story be considered to be a dream Robin might have had? If so, what would the man with the red and black face signify? And what is the significance of the tarring and feathering of Major Molineux? Why does Robin join in the laughter directed at his kinsman? At one time in the story Robin actually falls asleep and dreams. What is the significance of this dream? Why is the dream placed immediately be-fore the arrival of the procession and the climactic action?

Hawthorne prefaces his account of Robin's search for his kinsman with a reference to the colonists who have been denied the right to appoint their own governors. Angered and rebellious, they vent their feelings on the rep-resentative of the king, the same Major Molineux whom the youth seeks. Is the youthful Robin who has the same appointed guardian to be identi-fied with the colonists? Major Molineux is described as a man of steady soul, a majestic person with a head grown gray in honor. Why does Hawthorne set the boy's search in juxtaposition to the rebellion of the colonists, and why does he bring both actions to a climax in a scene of senseless uproar, a frenzied merriment, "in trampling on an old man's heart"? Notice that Robin's laugh is the loudest of all and that his laugh appears to be a signal to the leader to resume the march.

Compare the structure of "My Kinsman, Major Molineux" with the structure of "Hop-Frog." Notice that in Hawthorne's story meaning is revealed primarily through symbolic identifications, whereas in Poe's story meaning is revealed primarily through ironic juxtapositions. Which method appears to yield greater meaning? Why? Is the one story, therefore, better than the other? Reread the discussion on page 27 before you answer this question.

Herman Melville § 1819–1891

Melville was born in New York, and ran away to sea at eighteen. He served as a seaman on two whaling-ships, the Acushnet *and the* Lucy Ann, *and the frigate* United States, *adventures which account for his unusual knowledge of sea-going life. Toward the end of his life he was customs inspector in New York. Melville won fame with his first book,* Typee *(1846), a novel based on his South Sea experiences. His masterpiece,* Moby-Dick *(1851), is considered by many the greatest American novel. "Benito Cereno," "Bartleby, the Scrivener," and "Billy Budd" are among his justly famous short fiction, and like* Moby-Dick, *show a complex vision of the world expressed by means of an elaborate network of symbols and symbolic situations.*

Benito Cereno

In the year 1799, Captain Amasa Delano, of Duxbury, in Massachusetts, commanding a large sealer and general trader, lay at anchor with a valuable cargo, in the harbour of Santa Maria—a small, desert, uninhabited island toward the southern extremity of the long coast of Chile. There he had touched for water.

On the second day, not long after dawn, while lying in his berth, his mate came below, informing him that a strange sail was coming into the bay. Ships were then not so plenty in those waters as now. He rose, dressed, and went on deck.

The morning was one peculiar to that coast. Everything was mute and calm; everything grey. The sea, though undulated into long roods of swells, seemed fixed, and was sleeked at the surface like waved lead that has cooled and set in the smelter's mould. The sky seemed a grey surtout. Flights of troubled grey fowl, kith and kin with flights of troubled grey vapours among which they were mixed, skimmed low and fitfully over the waters, as swallows over meadows before storms. Shadows present, foreshadowing deeper shadows to come.

To Captain Delano's surprise, the stranger, viewed through the glass, showed no colours; though to do so upon entering a haven, however uninhabited in its shores, where but a single other ship might be lying, was the custom among peaceful seamen of all nations. Considering the lawlessness and loneliness of the spot, and the sort of stories, at that day, associated with those seas, Captain Delano's surprise might have deepened into some uneasiness had he not been a person of a singularly undistrustful good nature, not liable, except on extraordinary and repeated incentives, and hardly then, to indulge in personal alarms, any way involving the imputation of malign evil in man. Whether, in view of what humanity is capable, such a trait implies, along with a benevolent heart, more than ordinary quickness and accuracy of intellectual perception, may be left to the wise to determine.

But whatever misgivings might have obtruded on first seeing the stranger, would almost, in any seaman's mind, have been dissipated by observing, that the ship, in navigating into the harbour, was drawing too near the land; a sunken reef making out off her bow. This seemed to prove her a stranger, indeed, not only to the sealer, but the island; consequently, she could be no wonted freebooter on that ocean. With no small interest, Captain Delano continued to watch her—a proceeding not much facilitated by the vapours partly mantling the hull, through which the far matin light from her cabin streamed equivocally enough; much like the sun—by this time hemisphered on the rim of the horizon, and, apparently, in company with the strange ship entering the harbour—which, wimpled by the same low, creeping clouds, showed not unlike a Lima intriguante's one sinister eye peering across the Plaza from the Indian loop-hole of her dusk *saya-y-manto*.[1]

It might have been but a deception of the vapours, but, the longer the stranger was watched the more singular appeared her manœuvres. Ere long it seemed hard to decide whether she meant to come in or no—what she wanted, or what she was about. The wind, which had breezed up a little during the night, was not extremely light and baffling, which the more increased the apparent uncertainty of her movements.

Surmising, at last, that it might be a ship in distress, Captain Delano ordered his whale-boat to be dropped, and, much to the wary opposition of his mate, prepared to board her, and, at the least, pilot her in. On the night

[1] *saya-y-manto*: Tunic-and-mantle.

previous, a fishing party of the seamen had gone a long distance to some detached rocks out of sight from the sealer, and, an hour or two before daybreak, had returned, having met with no small success. Presuming that the stranger might have been long off soundings, the good captain put several baskets of the fish, for presents, into his boat, and so pulled away. From her continuing too near the sunken reef, deeming her in danger, calling to his men, he made all haste to apprise those on board of their situation. But, some time ere the boat came up, the wind, light though it was, having shifted, had headed the vessel off, as well as partly broken the vapours from about her.

Upon gaining a less remote view, the ship, when made signally visible on the verge of the leaden-hued swells, with the shreds of fog here and there raggedly furring her, appeared like a whitewashed monastery after a thunder-storm, seen perched upon some dun cliff among the Pyrenees. But it was no purely fanciful resemblance which now, for a moment, almost led Captain Delano to think that nothing less than a ship-load of monks was before him. Peering over the bulwarks were what really seemed, in the hazy distance, throngs of dark cowls; while, fitfully revealed through the open port holes, other dark moving figures were dimly descried, as of Black Friars pacing the cloisters.

Upon a still nigher approach, this appearance was modified, and the true character of the vessel was plain—a Spanish merchantman of the first class, carrying negro slaves, amongst other valuable freight, from one colonial port to another. A very large, and, in its time, a very fine vessel, such as in those days were at intervals encountered along that main; sometimes superseded Acapulco treasure-ships, or retired frigates of the Spanish king's navy, which, like superannuated Italian palaces, still, under a decline of masters, preserved signs of former state.

As the whale-boat drew more and more nigh, the cause of the peculiar pipe-clayed aspect of the stranger was seen in the slovenly neglect pervading her. The spars, ropes, and great part of the bulwarks, looked woolly, from long unacquaintance with the scraper, tar, and the brush. Her keel seemed laid, her ribs put together, and she launched, from Ezekiel's Valley of Dry Bones.

In the present business in which she was engaged, the ship's general model and rig appeared to have undergone no material change from their original warlike and Froissart pattern. However, no guns were seen.

The tops were large, and were railed about with what had once been octagonal net-work, all now in sad disrepair. These tops hung overhead like three ruinous aviaries, in one of which was seen perched, on a ratlin, a white noddy, a strange fowl, so called from its lethargic, somnambulistic character, being frequently caught by hand at sea. Battered and mouldy, the castellated forecastle seemed some ancient turret, long ago taken by assault, and then left to decay. Toward the stern, two high-raised quarter-galleries—the balustrades here and there covered with dry, tindery sea-moss

—opening out from the unoccupied state-cabin, whose dead-lights, for all the mild weather, were hermetically closed and calked—these tenantless balconies hung over the sea as if it were the grand Venetian canal. But the principal relic of faded grandeur was the ample oval of the shield-like stern-piece, intricately carved with the arms of Castile and León, medallioned about by groups of mythological or symbolical devices; uppermost and central of which was a dark satyr in a mask, holding his foot on the prostrate neck of a writhing figure, likewise masked.

Whether the ship had a figure-head, or only a plain beak, was not quite certain, owing to canvas wrapped about that part, either to protect it while undergoing a refurbishing, or else decently to hide its decay. Rudely painted or chalked, as in a sailor freak, along the forward side of a sort of pedestal below the canvas was the sentence, "*Sequid vuestro jefe,*" (follow your leader); while upon the tarnished headboards, near by, appeared, in stately capitals, once gilt, the ship's name, "SAN DOMINICK," each letter streakingly corroded with tricklings of copper-spike rust; while, like mourning weeds, dark festoons of sea-grass slimily swept to and fro over the name, with every hearse-like roll of the hull.

As, at last, the boat was hooked from the bow along toward the gangway amidship, its keel, while yet some inches separated from the hull, harshly grated as on a sunken coral reef. It proved a huge bunch of conglobated barnacles adhering below the water to the side like a wen—a token of baffling airs and long calms passed somewhere in those seas.

Climbing the side, the visitor was at once surrounded by a clamorous throng of whites and blacks, but the latter outnumbering the former more than could have been expected, negro transportation-ship as the stranger in port was. But, in one language, and as with one voice, all poured out a common tale of suffering; in which the negresses, of whom there were not a few, exceeded the others in their dolorous vehemence. The survey, together with the fever, had swept off a great part of their number, more especially the Spaniards. Off Cape Horn they had narrowly escaped shipwreck; then, for days together, they had lain tranced without wind; their provisions were low; their water next to none; their lips that moment were baked.

While Captain Delano was thus made the mark of all eager tongues, his one eager glance took in all faces, with every other object about him.

Always upon first boarding a large and populous ship at sea, especially a foreign one, with a nondescript crew such as Lascars or Manila men, the impression varies in a peculiar way from that produced by first entering a strange house with strange inmates in a strange land. Both house and ship —the one by its walls and blinds, the other by its high bulwarks like ramparts—hoard from view their interiors till the last moment; but in the case of the ship there is this addition: that the living spectacle it contains, upon its sudden and complete disclosure, has, in contrast with the blank ocean which zones it, something of the effect of enchantment. The ship seems unreal; these strange costumes, gestures, and faces, but a shadowy tableau just emerged from the deep, which directly must receive back what it gave.

Perhaps it was some such influence, as above is attempted to be described, which, in Captain Delano's mind, heightened whatever, upon a staid scrutiny, might have seemed unusual; especially the conspicuous figures of four elderly grizzled negroes, their heads like black, doddered willow tops, who, in venerable contrast to the tumult below them, were couched, sphynx-like, one on the starboard cat-head, another on the larboard, and the remaining pair face to face on the opposite bulwarks above the main-chains. They each had bits of unstranded old junk in their hands, and, with a sort of stoical self-content, were picking the junk into oakum, a small heap of which lay by their sides. They accompanied the task with a continuous, low, monotonous chant; droning and drooling away like so many grey-headed bag-pipers playing a funeral march.

The quarter-deck rose into an ample elevated poop, upon the forward verge of which, lifted, like the oakum-pickers, some eight feet above the general throng, sat along in a row, separated by regular spaces, the cross-legged figures of six other blacks; each with a rusty hatchet in his hand, which, with a bit of brick and a rag, he was engaged like a scullion in scouring; while between each two was a small stack of hatchets, their rusted edges turned forward awaiting a like operation. Though occasionally the four oakum-pickers would briefly address some person or persons in the crowd below, yet the six hatchet-polishers neither spoke to others, nor breathed a whisper among themselves, but sat intent upon their task, except at intervals, when, with the peculiar love in negroes of uniting industry with pastime, two and two they sideways clashed their hatchets together, like cymbals, with a barbarous din. All six, unlike the generality, had the raw aspect of unsophisticated Africans.

But that first comprehensive glance which took in those ten figures, with scores less conspicuous, rested but an instant upon them, as, impatient of the hubbub of voices, the visitor turned in quest of whomsoever it might be that commanded the ship.

But as if not unwilling to let nature make known her own case among his suffering charge, or else in despair of restraining it for the time, the Spanish captain, a gentlemanly, reserved-looking, and rather young man to a stranger's eye, dressed with singular richness, but bearing plain traces of recent sleepless cares and disquietudes, stood passively by, leaning against the main-mast, at one moment casting a dreary, spiritless look upon his excited people, at the next an unhappy glance toward his visitor. By his side stood a black of small stature, in whose rude face, as occasionally, like a shepherd's dog, he mutely turned it up into the Spaniard's, sorrow and affection were equally blended.

Struggling through the throng, the American advanced to the Spaniard, assuring him of his sympathies, and offering to render whatever assistance might be in his power. To which the Spaniard returned for the present but grave and ceremonious acknowledgments, his national formality ducked by the saturnine mood of ill-health.

But losing no time in mere compliments, Captain Delano, returning to the gangway, had his baskets of fish brought up; and as the wind still continued light, so that some hours at least must elapse ere the ship could be brought to the anchorage, he bade his men return to the sealer, and fetch back as much water as the whale-boat could carry, with whatever soft bread the steward might have, all the remaining pumpkins on board, with a box of sugar, and a dozen of his private bottles of cider.

Not many minutes after the boat's pushing off, to the vexation of all, the wind entirely died away, and the tide turning, began drifting back the ship helplessly seaward. But trusting this would not long last, Captain Delano sought, with good hopes, to cheer up the strangers, feeling no small satisfaction that, with persons in their condition, he could—thanks to his frequent voyages along the Spanish Main—converse with some freedom in their native tongue.

While left alone with them, he was not long in observing some things tending to heighten his first impressions; but surprise was lost in pity, both for the Spaniards and blacks, alike evidently reduced from scarcity of water and provisions; while long-continued suffering seemed to have brought out the less good-natured qualities of the negroes, besides, at the same time, impairing the Spaniard's authority over them. But, under the circumstances, precisely this condition of things was to have been anticipated. In armies, navies, cities, or families, in nature herself, nothing more relaxes good order than misery. Still, Captain Delano was not without the idea, that had Benito Cereno been a man of greater energy, misrule would hardly have come to the present pass. But the debility, constitutional or induced by hardships, bodily and mental, of the Spanish captain, was too obvious to be overlooked. A prey to settled dejection, as if long mocked with hope he would not now indulge it, even when it had ceased to be a mock, the prospect of that day, or evening at furthest, lying at anchor, with plenty of water for his people, and a brother captain to counsel and befriend, seemed in no perceptible degree to encourage him. His mind appeared unstrung, if not still more seriously affected. Shut up in these oaken walls, chained to one dull round of command, whose unconditionality cloyed him, like some hypochondriac abbot he moved slowly about, at times suddenly pausing, starting, or staring, biting his lip, biting his finger-nail, flushing, paling, twitching his beard, with other symptoms of an absent or moody mind. This distempered spirit was lodged, as before hinted, in as distempered a frame. He was rather tall, but seemed never to have been robust, and now with nervous suffering was almost worn to a skeleton. A tendency to some pulmonary complaint appeared to have been lately confirmed. His voice was like that of one with lungs half gone—hoarsely suppressed, a husky whisper. No wonder that, as in this state he tottered about, his private servant apprehensively followed him. Sometimes the negro gave his master his arm, or took his handkerchief out of his pocket for him; performing these and similar offices with that affectionate zeal which transmutes into something filial or fraternal acts in themselves but menial; and which has gained for the negro the repute of making the most pleasing body-servant in the world; one, too, whom a master need be on no stiffly superior terms with, but may treat with familiar trust; less a servant than a devoted companion.

Marking the noisy indocility of the blacks in general, as well as what seemed the sullen inefficiency of the whites, it was not without humane satisfaction that Captain Delano witnessed the steady good conduct of Babo.

But the good conduct of Babo, hardly more than the ill-behaviour of others, seemed to withdraw the half-lunatic Don Benito from his cloudy languor. Not that such precisely was the impression made by the Spaniard on the mind of his visitor. The Spaniard's individual unrest was, for the present, but noted as a conspicuous feature in the ship's general affliction. Still, Captain Delano was not a little concerned at what he could not help taking for the time to be Don Benito's unfriendly indifference towards himself. The Spaniard's manner, too, conveyed a sort of sour and gloomy disdain, which he seemed at no pains to disguise. But this the American in charity ascribed to the harassing effects of sickness, since, in former instances, he had noted that there are peculiar natures on whom prolonged physical suffering seems to cancel every social instinct of kindness; as if, forced to black bread themselves, they deemed it but equity that each person coming nigh them should, indirectly, by some slight or affront, be made to partake of their fare.

But ere long Captain Delano bethought him that, indulgent as he was at the first, in judging the Spaniard, he might not, after all, have exercised charity enough. At bottom it was Don Benito's reserve which displeased him; but the same reserve was shown towards all but his faithful personal attendant. Even the formal reports which, according to sea-usage, were, at stated times, made to him by some petty underling, either a white, mulatto or black, he hardly had patience enough to listen to, without betraying contemptuous aversion. His manner upon such occasions was, in its degree, not unlike that which might be supposed to have been his imperial countryman's, Charles V, just previous to the anchoritish retirement of that monarch from the throne.

This splenetic disrelish of his place was evinced in almost every function pertaining to it. Proud as he was moody, he condescended to no personal mandate. Whatever special orders were necessary, their delivery was delegated to his body-servant, who in turn transferred them to their ultimate destination, through runners, alert Spanish boys or slave boys, like pages or pilot-fish within easy call continually hovering round Don Benito. So that to have beheld this undemonstrative invalid gliding about, apathetic and mute, no landsman could have dreamed that in him was lodged a dictatorship beyond which, while at sea, there was no earthly appeal.

Thus, the Spaniard, regarded in his reserve, seemed the involuntary victim of mental disorder. But, in fact, his reserve might, in some degree, have proceeded from design. If so, then here was evinced the unhealthy climax of that icy though conscientious policy, more or less adopted by all commanders of large ships, which, except in signal emergencies, obliterates alike the manifestation of sway with every trace of sociality; transforming the man into a block, or rather into a loaded cannon, which, until there is call for thunder, has nothing to say.

Viewing him in this light, it seemed but a natural token of the perverse habit induced by a long course of such hard self-restraint, that, notwithstanding the present condition of his ship, the Spaniard should still persist in a demeanour, which, however harmless, or, it may be, appropriate, in a well-appointed vessel, such as the *San Dominick* might have been at the outset of the voyage, was anything but judicious now. But the Spaniard, perhaps, thought that it was with captains as with gods: reserve, under all events, must still be their cue. But probably this appearance of slumbering dominion might have been but an attempted disguise to conscious imbecility—not deep policy, but shallow device. But be all this as it might, whether Don Benito's manner was designed or not, the more Captain Delano noted its pervading reserve, the less he felt uneasiness at any particular manifestation of that reserve towards himself.

Neither were his thoughts taken up by the captain alone. Wonted to the quiet orderliness of the sealer's comfortable family of a crew, the noisy confusion of the *San Dominick*'s suffering host repeatedly challenged his eye. Some prominent breaches, not only of discipline but of decency, were observed. These Captain Delano could not but ascribe, in the main, to the absence of those subordinate deck-officers to whom, along with higher duties, is intrusted what may be styled the police department of a populous ship. True, the old oakum-pickers appeared at times to act the part of monitorial constables to their countrymen, the blacks; but though occasionally succeeding in allaying trifling outbreaks now and then between man and man, they could do little or nothing toward establishing general quiet. The *San Dominick* was in the condition of a transatlantic emigrant ship, among whose multitude of living freight are some individuals, doubtless, as little troublesome as crates and bales; but the friendly remonstrances of such with their ruder companions are of not so much avail as the unfriendly arm of the mate. What the *San Dominick* wanted was, what the emigrant ship has, stern superior officers. But on these decks not so much as a fourth-mate was to be seen.

The visitor's curiosity was roused to learn the particulars of those mishaps which had brought about such absenteeism, with its consequences; because, though deriving some inkling of the voyage from the wails which at the first moment had greeted him, yet of the details no clear understanding had been had. The best account would, doubtless, be given by the captain. Yet at first the visitor was loth to ask it, unwilling to provoke some distant rebuff. But plucking up courage, he at last accosted Don Benito, renewing the expression of his benevolent interest, adding, that did he (Captain Delano) but know the particulars of the ship's misfortunes, he would, perhaps, be better able in the end to relieve them. Would Don Benito favour him with the whole story?

Don Benito faltered; then, like some somnambulist suddenly interfered with, vacantly stared at his visitor, and ended by looking down on the deck. He maintained this posture so long, that Captain Delano, almost equally disconcerted, and involuntarily almost as rude, turned suddenly from him, walking forward to accost one of the Spanish seamen for the desired information. But he had hardly gone five paces, when, with a sort of eagerness, Don Benito invited him back, regretting his momentary absence of mind, and professing readiness to gratify him.

While most part of the story was being given, the two captains stood on the after part of the main-deck, a privileged spot, no one being near but the servant.

"It is now a hundred and ninety days," began the Spaniard, in his husky whisper, "that this ship, well officered and well-manned, with several cabin passengers—some fifty Spaniards in all—sailed from Buenos Ayres bound to Lima, with a general cargo, hardware, Paraguay tea and the like—and," pointing forward, "that parcel of negroes, now not more than a hundred and fifty, as you see, but then numbering over three hundred souls. Off Cape Horn we had heavy gales. In one moment, by night, three of my best officers, with fifteen sailors, were lost, with the main-yard; the spar snapping under them in the slings, as they sought, with heavers, to beat down the icy sail. To lighten the hull, the heavier sacks of maté were thrown into the sea, with most of the water-pipes lashed on deck at the time. And this last necessity it was, combined with the prolonged detentions afterwards experienced, which eventually brought about our chief causes of suffering. When——"

Here there was a sudden fainting attack of his cough, brought on, no doubt, by his mental distress. His servant sustained him, and drawing a cordial from his pocket placed it to his lips. He a little revived. But unwilling to leave him unsupported while yet imperfectly restored, the black with one arm still encircled his master, at the same time keeping his eye fixed on his face, as if to watch for the first sign of complete restoration, or relapse, as the event might prove.

The Spaniard proceeded, but brokenly and obscurely, as one in a dream.

—"Oh, my God! rather than pass through what I have, with joy I would have hailed the most terrible gales; but——"

His cough returned and with increased violence; this subsiding, with reddened lips and closed eyes he fell heavily against his supporter.

"His mind wanders. He was thinking of the plague that followed the gales," plaintively sighed the servant; "my poor, poor master!" wringing one hand, and with the other wiping the mouth. "But be patient, Señor," again turning to Captain Delano, "these fits do not last long; master will soon be himself."

Don Benito reviving, went on; but as this portion of the story was very brokenly delivered, the substance only will here be set down.

It appeared that after the ship had been many days tossed in storms off the Cape, the scurvy broke out, carrying off numbers of the whites and blacks. When at last they had worked round into the Pacific, their spars and sails were so damaged, and so inadequately handled by the surviving mariners, most of whom were become invalids, that, unable to lay her northerly course by the wind which was powerful, the unmanageable ship, for successive days and nights, was blown northwestward, where the breeze suddenly deserted her, in unknown waters, to sultry calms. The absence of the water-pipes now proved as fatal to life as before their presence had menaced it. Induced, or at least aggravated, by the more than scanty allowance of water, a malignant fever followed the scurvy; with the excessive heat of the lengthened calm, making such short work of it as to sweep away, as by billows, whole families of the Africans, and a yet larger number, proportionably, of the Spaniards, including, by a luckless fatality, every remaining officer on board. Consequently, in the smart west winds eventually following the calm, the already rent sails, having to be simply dropped, not furled, at need, had been gradually reduced to the beggars' rags they were now. To procure substitutes for his lost sailors, as well as supplies of water and sails, the captain, at the earliest opportunity, had made for Valdivia, the southernmost civilized port of Chile and South America; but upon nearing the coast the thick weather had prevented him from so much as sighting that harbour. Since which period, almost without a crew, and almost without canvas and almost without water, and, at intervals, giving its added dead to the sea, the *San Dominick* had been battledored about by contrary winds, inveigled by currents, or grown weedy in calms. Like a man lost in woods, more than once she had doubled upon her own track.

"But throughout these calamities," huskily continued Don Benito, painfully turning in the half embrace of his servant, "I have to thank those negroes you see, who, though to your inexperienced eyes appearing unruly, have, indeed, conducted themselves with less of restlessness than even their owner could have thought possible under such circumstances."

Here he again fell faintly back. Again his mind wandered; but he rallied, and less obscurely proceeded.

"Yes, their owner was quite right in assuring me that no fetters would be needed with his blacks; so that while, as is wont in this transportation, those negroes have always remained upon deck—not thrust below, as in the Guineamen—they have, also, from the beginning, been freely permitted to range within given bounds at their pleasure."

Once more the faintness returned—his mind roved—but, recovering, he resumed:

"But it is Babo here to whom, under God, I owe not only my own preservation, but likewise to him, chiefly, the merit is due, of pacifying his more ignorant brethren, when at intervals tempted to murmurings."

"Ah, master," sighed the black, bowing his face, "don't speak of me; Babo is nothing; what Babo has done was but duty."

"Faithful fellow!" cried Captain Delano. "Don Benito, I envy you such a friend; slave I cannot call him."

As master and man stood before him, the black upholding the white, Captain Delano could not but bethink him of the beauty of that relationship which could present such a spectacle of fidelity on the one hand and confidence on the other. The scene was heightened by the contrast in dress, denoting their relative positions. The Spaniard wore a loose Chile jacket of dark velvet, white small-clothes and stockings, with silver buckles at the knee and instep; a high-crowned sombrero, of fine grass; a slender sword, silver mounted, hung from a knot in his sash—the last being an almost invariable adjunct, more for utility than ornament, of a South American gentleman's dress to this hour. Excepting when his occasional nervous contortions brought about disarray, there was a certain precision in his attire curiously at variance with the unsightly disorder around; especially in the belittered Ghetto, forward of the main-mast, wholly occupied by the blacks.

The servant wore nothing but wide trousers, apparently, from their coarseness and patches, made out of some old topsail; they were clean, and confined at the waist by a bit of unstranded rope, which, with his composed, deprecatory air at times, made him look something like a begging friar of St. Francis.

However unsuitable for the time and place, at least in the blunt-thinking American's eyes, and however strangely surviving in the midst of all his afflictions, the toilette of Don Benito might not, in fashion at least, have gone beyond the style of the day among South Americans of his class. Though on the present voyage sailing from Buenos Ayres, he had avowed himself a native and resident of Chile, whose inhabitants had not so generally adopted the plain coat and once plebeian pantaloons; but, with a becoming modification, adhered to their provincial costume, picturesque as any in the world. Still, relatively to the pale history of the voyage, and his pale face, there seemed something so incongruous in the Spaniard's apparel, as almost to suggest the image of an invalid courtier tottering about London streets in the time of the plague.

The portion of the narrative which, perhaps, most excited interest, as well as some surprise, considering the latitudes in question, was the long calms spoken of, and more particularly the ship's so long drifting about. Without communicating the opinion, of course, the American could not but impute at least part of the detentions both to clumsy seamanship and faulty navigation. Eyeing Don Benito's small, yellow hands, he easily inferred that the young captain had not got into command at the hawse-hole, but the cabin-window; and if so, why wonder at incompetence, in youth, sickness, and gentility united?

But drowning criticism in compassion, after a fresh repetition of his sympathies, Captain Delano, having heard out his story, not only engaged, as in the first place, to see Don Benito and his people supplied in their immediate bodily needs, but, also, now further promised to assist him in procuring a large permanent supply of water, as well as some sails and rigging, and, though it would involve no small embarrassment to himself, yet he would spare three of his best seamen for temporary deck-officers; so that without delay the ship might proceed to Concepcion, there fully to refit for Lima, her destined port.

Such generosity was not without its effect, even upon the invalid. His face lighted up; eager and hectic, he met the honest glance of his visitor. With gratitude he seemed overcome.

"This excitement is bad for master," whispered the servant, taking his arm, and with soothing words gently drawing him aside.

When Don Benito returned, the American was pained to observe that his hopefulness, like the sudden kindling in his cheek, was but febrile and transient.

Ere long, with a joyless mien, looking up towards the poop, the host invited his guest to accompany him there, for the benefit of what little breath of wind might be stirring.

As during the telling of the story, Captain Delano had once or twice started at the occasional cymballing of the hatchet-polishers, wondering why such an interruption should be allowed, especially in that part of the ship, and in the ears of an invalid; and moreover, as the hatchets had anything but an attractive look, and the handlers of them still less so, it was, therefore, to tell the truth, not without some lurking reluctance, or even shrinking, it may be, that Captain Delano, with apparent complaisance, acquiesced in his host's invitation. The more so, since, with an untimely caprice of punctilio, rendered distressing by his cadaverous aspect, Don Benito, with Castilian bows, solemnly insisted upon his guest's preceding him up the ladder leading to the elevation; where, one on each side of the last step, sat for armorial supporters and sentries two of the ominous file. Gingerly enough stepped good Captain Delano between them, and in the instant of leaving them behind, like one running the gauntlet, he felt an apprehensive twitch in the calves of his legs.

But when, facing about, he saw the whole file, like so many organ grinders, still stupidly intent on their work, unmindful of everything beside, he could not but smile at his late fidgety panic.

Presently, while standing with his host, looking forward upon the decks below, he was struck by one of those instances of insubordination previously alluded to. Three black boys, with two Spanish boys, were sitting together on the hatches, scraping a rude wooden platter, in which some scanty mess had recently been cooked. Suddenly, one of the black boys, enraged at a word dropped by one of his white companions, seized a knife, and, though called to forbear by one of the oakum-pickers, struck the lad over the head, inflicting a gash from which blood flowed.

In amazement, Captain Delano inquired what this meant. To which the pale Don Benito dully muttered, that it was merely the sport of the lad.

"Pretty serious sport, truly," rejoined Captain Delano. "Had such a thing happened on board the *Bachelor's Delight,* instant punishment would have followed."

At these words the Spaniard turned upon the American one of his sudden, staring, half-lunatic looks; then, relapsing into his torpor, answered, "Doubtless, doubtless, Señor."

Is it, thought Captain Delano, that this hapless man is one of those paper captains I've known, who by policy wink at what by power they cannot put down? I know no sadder sight than a commander who has little of command but the name.

"I should think, Don Benito," he now said, glancing towards the oakum-picker who had sought to interfere with the boys, "that you would find it advantageous to keep all your blacks employed, especially the younger ones, no matter at what useless task, and no matter what happens to the ship. Why, even with my little band, I find such a course indispensable. I once kept a crew on my quarter-deck thrumming mats for my cabin, when, for three days, I had given up my ship—mats, men, and all—for a speedy loss, owing to the violence of a gale, in which we could do nothing but helplessly drive before it."

"Doubtless, doubtless," muttered Don Benito.

"But," continued Captain Delano, again glancing upon the oakum-pickers and then at the hatchet-polishers, near by, "I see you keep some, at least, of your host employed."

"Yes," was again the vacant response.

"Those old men there, shaking their pows from their pulpits," continued Captain Delano, pointing to the oakum-pickers, "seem to act the part of old dominies to the rest, little heeded as their admonitions are at times. Is this voluntary on their part, Don Benito, or have you appointed them shepherds to your flock of black sheep?"

"What posts they fill, I appointed them," rejoined the Spaniard, in an acrid tone, as if resenting some supposed satiric reflection.

"And these others, these Ashantee conjurors here," continued Captain Delano, rather uneasily eyeing the brandished steel of the hatchet-polishers, where, in spots, it had been brought to a shine, "this seems a curious business they are at, Don Benito?"

"In the gales we met," answered the Spaniard, "what of our general cargo was not thrown overboard was much damaged by the brine. Since coming into calm weather, I have had several cases of knives and hatchets daily brought up for overhauling and cleaning."

"A prudent idea, Don Benito. You are part owner of ship and cargo, I presume; but none of the slaves, perhaps?"

"I am owner of all you see," impatiently returned Don Benito, "except the main company of blacks, who belonged to my late friend, Alexandro Aranda."

As he mentioned this name, his air was heart-broken; his knees shook; his servant supported him.

Thinking he divined the cause of such unusual emotion, to confirm his surmise, Captain Delano, after a pause, said: "And may I ask, Don Benito, whether—since a while ago you spoke of some cabin passengers—the friend, whose loss so afflicts you, at the outset of the voyage accompanied his blacks?"

"Yes."

"But died of the fever?"

"Died of the fever. Oh, could I but—" Again quivering, the Spaniard paused.

"Pardon me," said Captain Delano, slowly, "but I think that, by a sympathetic experience, I conjecture, Don Benito, what it is that gives the keener edge to your grief. It was once my hard fortune to lose, at sea, a dear friend, my own brother then supercargo. Assured of the welfare of his spirit, its departure I could have borne like a man; but that honest eye, that honest hand—both of which had so often met mine—and that warm heart; all, all—like scraps to the dogs—to throw all to the sharks! It was then I vowed never to have for fellow-voyager a man I loved, unless, unbeknown to him, I had provided every requisite, in case of a fatality, for embalming his mortal part for interment on shore. Were your friend's remains now on board this ship, Don Benito, not thus strangely would the mention of his name affect you."

"On board this ship?" echoed the Spaniard. Then, with horrified gestures, as directed against some spectre, he unconsciously fell into the ready arms of his attendant, who, with a silent appeal toward Captain Delano, seemed beseeching him not again to broach a theme so unspeakably distressing to his master.

This poor fellow now, thought the pained American, is the victim of that sad superstition which associates goblins with the deserted body of man, as ghosts with an abandoned house. How unlike are we made! What to me, in like case, would have been a solemn satisfaction, the bare suggestion, even, terrifies the Spaniard into this trance. Poor Alexandro Aranda! what would you say could you here see your friend—who, on former voyages, when you, for months, were left behind, has, I dare say, often longed, and longed, for one peep at you—now transported with terror at the least thought of having you anyway nigh him.

At this moment, with a dreary grave-yard toll, betokening a flaw, the ship's forecastle bell, smote by one of the grizzled oakum-pickers, proclaimed ten o'clock, through the leaden calm; when Captain Delano's attention was caught by the moving figure of a gigantic black, emerging from the general crowd below, and slowly advancing towards the elevated poop. An iron collar was about his neck, from which depended a chain, thrice wound round his body; the terminating links padlocked together at a broad band of iron, his girdle.

"How like a mute Atufal moves," murmured the servant.

The black mounted the steps of the poop, and, like a brave prisoner, brought up to receive sentence, stood in unquailing muteness before Don Benito, now recovered from his attack.

At the first glimpse of his approach, Don Benito had started, a resentful shadow swept over his face; and, as with the sudden memory of bootless rage, his white lips glued together.

This is some mulish mutineer, thought Captain Delano, surveying, not without a mixture of admiration, the colossal form of the negro.

"See, he waits your question, master," said the servant.

Thus reminded, Don Benito, nervously averting his glance, as if shunning, by anticipation, some rebellious response, in a disconcerted voice, thus spoke:—

"Atufal, will you ask my pardon, now?"

The black was silent.

"Again, master," murmured the servant, with bitter upbraiding eyeing his countryman. "Again, master; he will bend to master yet."

"Answer," said Don Benito, still averting his glance, "say but the one word, *pardon*, and your chains shall be off."

Upon this, the black, slowly raising both arms, let them lifelessly fall, his links clanking, his head bowed; as much as to say, "No, I am content."

"Go," said Don Benito, with inkept and unknown emotion.

Deliberately as he had come, the black obeyed.

"Excuse me, Don Benito," said Captain Delano, "but this scene surprises me; what means it, pray?"

"It means that the negro alone, of all the band, has given me peculiar cause of offence. I have put him in chains; I——"

Here he paused; his hand to his head, as if there were a swimming there, or a sudden bewilderment of memory had come over him; but meeting his servant's kindly glance seemed reassured, and proceeded:—

"I could not scourge such a form. But I told him he must ask my pardon. As yet he has not. At my command, every two hours he stands before me."

"And how long has this been?"

"Some sixty days."

"And obedient in all else? And respectful?"

"Yes."

"Upon my conscience, then," exclaimed Captain Delano, impulsively, "he has a royal spirit in him, this fellow."

"He may have some right to it," bitterly returned Don Benito, "he says he was king in his own land."

"Yes," said the servant, entering a word, "those slits in Atufal's ears once held wedges of gold; but poor Babo here, in his own land, was only a poor slave; a black man's slave was Babo, who now is the white's."

Somewhat annoyed by these conversational familiarities, Captain Delano turned curiously upon the attendant, then glanced inquiringly at his master; but, as if long wonted to these little informalities, neither master nor man seemed to understand him.

"What, pray, was Atufal's offence, Don Benito?" asked Captain Delano; "if it was not something very serious, take a fool's advice, and, in view of his general docility, as well as in some natural respect for his spirit, remit him his penalty."

"No, no, master never will do that," here murmured the servant to himself, "proud Atufal must first ask master's pardon. The slave there carries the padlock, but master here carries the key."

His attention thus directed, Captain Delano now noticed for the first time that, suspended by a slender silken cord, from Don Benito's neck, hung a key. At once, from the servant's muttered syllables, divining the key's purpose, he smiled and said:—"So, Don Benito—padlock and key— significant symbols, truly."

Biting his lip, Don Benito faltered.

Though the remark of Captain Delano, a man of such native simplicity as to be incapable of satire or irony, had been dropped in playful allusion to the Spaniard's singularly evidenced lordship over the black; yet the hypochondriac seemed some way to have taken it as a malicious reflection upon his confessed inability thus far to break down, at least, on a verbal summons, the entrenched will of the slave. Deploring this supposed misconception, yet despairing of correcting it, Captain Delano shifted the subject; but finding his companion more than ever withdrawn, as if still sourly digesting the lees of the presumed affront above-mentioned, by and by Captain Delano likewise became less talkative, oppressed, against his own will, by what seemed the secret vindictiveness of the morbidly sensitive Spaniard. But the good sailor, himself of a quite contrary disposition, refrained, on his part, alike from the appearance as from the feeling of resentment, and if silent, was only so from contagion.

Presently the Spaniard, assisted by his servant, somewhat discourteously crossed over from his guest; a procedure which, sensibly enough, might have been allowed to pass from idle caprice of ill-humour, had not master and man, lingering round the corner of the elevated skylight, begun whispering together in low voices. This was unpleasing. And more: the moody air of the Spaniard, which at times had not been without a sort of valetudinarian stateliness, now seemed anything but dignified; while the menial familiarity of the servant lost its original charm of simple-hearted attachment.

In his embarrassment, the visitor turned his face to the other side of the ship. By so doing, his glance accidentally fell on a young Spanish sailor, a coil of rope in his hand, just stepped from the deck to the first round of the mizzen-rigging. Perhaps the man would not have been particularly noticed, were it not that, during his ascent to one of the yards, he, with a sort of covert intentness, kept his eye fixed on Captain Delano, from whom, presently, it passed, as if by a natural sequence, to the two whisperers.

His own attention thus redirected to that quarter, Captain Delano gave a slight start. From something in Don Benito's manner just then, it seemed as if the visitor had, at least partly, been the subject of the withdrawn consultation going on—a conjecture as little agreeable to the guest as it was little flattering to the host.

The singular alternations of courtesy and ill-breeding in the Spanish captain were unaccountable, except on one of two suppositions—innocent lunacy, or wicked imposture.

But the first idea, though it might naturally have occurred to an indifferent observer, and, in some respect, had not hitherto been wholly a stranger to Captain Delano's mind, yet, now that, in an incipient way, he began to regard the stranger's conduct something in the light of an intentional affront, of course the idea of lunacy was virtually vacated. But if not a lunatic, what then? Under the circumstances, would a gentleman, nay, any honest boor, act the part now acted by his host? The man was an imposter. Some low-born adventurer, masquerading as an oceanic grandee; yet so ignorant of the first requisites of mere gentlemanhood as to be betrayed into the present remarkable indecorum. The strange ceremoniousness, too, at other times evinced, seemed not uncharacteristic of one playing a part above his real level. Benito Cereno—Don Benito Cereno—a sounding name. One, too, at that period, not unknown, in the surname, to supercargoes and sea captains trading along the Spanish Main, as belonging to one of the most enterprising and extensive mercantile families in all those provinces; several members of it having titles; a sort of Castilian Rothschild, with a noble brother, or cousin, in every great trading town of South America. The alleged Don Benito was in early manhood, about twenty-nine or thirty. To assume a sort of roving cadetship in the maritime affairs of such a house, what more likely scheme for a young knave of talent and spirit? But the Spaniard was a pale invalid. Never mind. For even to the degree of simulating mortal disease, the craft of some tricksters had been known to attain. To think that, under the aspect of infantile weakness, the most savage energies might be couched—those velvets of the Spaniard but the silky paw to his fangs.

From no train of thought did these fancies come; not from within, but from without; suddenly, too, and in one throng, like hoar frost; yet as soon to vanish as the mild sun of Captain Delano's good nature regained its meridian.

Glancing over once more towards his host—whose sideface, revealed above the skylight, was now turned towards him—he was struck by the profile, whose clearness of cut was refined by the thinness, incident to ill-health, as well as ennobled about the chin by the beard. Away with suspicion. He was a true off-shoot of a true hidalgo Cereno.

Relieved by these and other better thoughts, the visitor, lightly humming a tune, now began indifferently pacing the poop, so as not to betray to Don Benito that he had at all mistrusted incivility, much less duplicity; for such mistrust would yet be proved illusory, and by the event; though, for the present, the circumstance which had provoked that distrust remained unexplained. But when that little mystery should have been cleared up, Captain Delano thought he might extremely regret it, did he allow Don Benito to become aware that he had indulged in ungenerous surmises. In short, to the Spaniard's black-letter text, it was best, for a while, to leave open margin.

Presently, his pale face twitching and overcast, the Spaniard, still supported by his attendant, moved over towards his guest, when, with even more than his usual embarrassment, and a strange sort of intriguing intonation in his husky whisper, the following conversation began:—

"Señor, may I ask how long you have lain at this isle?"

"Oh, but a day or two, Don Benito."

"And from what port are you last?"

"Canton."

"And there, Señor, you exchanged your sealskins for teas and silks, I think you said?"

"Yes. Silks mostly."

"And the balance you took in specie, perhaps?"

Captain Delano, fidgeting a little, answered—

"Yes; some silver; not a very great deal, though."

"Ah—well. May I ask how many men have you, Señor?"

Captain Delano slightly started, but answered—

"About five-and-twenty, all told."

"And at present, Señor, all on board, I suppose?"

"All on board, Don Benito," replied the Captain, now with satisfaction.

"And will be to-night, Señor?"

At this last question, following so many pertinacious ones, for the soul of him Captain Delano could not but look very earnestly at the questioner, who, instead of meeting the glance, with every token of craven discomposure dropped his eyes to the deck; presenting an unworthy contrast to his servant, who, just then, was kneeling at his feet, adjusting a loose shoe-buckle; his disengaged face meantime, with humble curiosity, turned openly up into his master's downcast one.

The Spaniard, still with a guilty shuffle, repeated his question:
"And—and will be to-night, Señor?"

"Yes, for aught I know," returned Captain Delano—"but nay," rallying himself into fearless truth, "some of them talked of going off on another fishing party about midnight."

"Your ships generally go—go more or less armed, I believe, Señor?"

"Oh, a six-pounder or two, in case of emergency," was the intrepidly indifferent reply, "with a small stock of muskets, sealing-spears, and cutlasses, you know."

As he thus responded, Captain Delano again glanced at Don Benito, but the latter's eyes were averted; while abruptly and awkwardly shifting the subject, he made some peevish allusion to the calm, and then, without apology, once more, with his attendant, withdrew to the opposite bulwarks, where the whispering was resumed.

At this moment, and ere Captain Delano could cast a cool thought upon what had just passed, the young Spanish sailor, before mentioned, was seen descending from the rigging. In act of stooping over to spring inboard to the deck, his voluminous, unconfined frock, or shirt, of coarse woolen, much spotted with tar, opened out far down the chest, revealing a soiled undergarment of what seemed the finest linen, edged, about the neck, with a narrow blue ribbon, sadly faded and worn. At this moment the young sailor's eye was again fixed on the whisperers, and Captain Delano thought he observed a lurking significance in it, as if silent signs, of some Freemason sort, had that instant been interchanged.

This once more impelled his own glance in the direction of Don Benito, and, as before, he could not but infer that himself formed the subject of the conference. He paused. The sound of the hatchet-polishing fell on his ears. He cast another swift side-look at the two. They had the air of conspirators. In connection with the late questionings, and the incident of the young sailor, these things now begat such return of involuntary suspicion, that the singular guilelessness of the American could not endure it. Plucking up a gay and humorous expression, he crossed over to the two rapidly, saying:—"Ha, Don Benito, your black here seems high in your trust; a sort of privy-counsellor, in fact."

Upon this, the servant looked up with a good-natured grin, but the master started as from a venomous bite. It was a moment or two before the Spaniard sufficiently recovered himself to reply; which he did, at last, with cold constraint:—"Yes, Señor, I have trust in Babo."

Here Babo, changing his previous grin of mere animal humour into an intelligent smile, not ungratefully eyed his master.

Finding that the Spaniard now stood silent and reserved, as if involuntarily, or purposely giving hint that his guest's proximity was inconvenient just then, Captian Delano, unwilling to appear uncivil even to incivility itself, made some trivial remark and moved off; again and again turning over in his mind the mysterious demeanor of Don Benito Cereno.

He had descended from the poop, and, wrapped in thought, was passing near a dark hatchway, leading down into the steerage, when, perceiving motion there, he looked to see what moved. The same instant there was a sparkle in the shadowy hatchway, and he saw one of the Spanish sailors, prowling there, hurriedly placing his hand in the bosom of his frock, as if hiding something. Before the man could have been certain who it was that was passing, he slunk below out of sight. But enough was seen of him to make it sure that he was the same young sailor before noticed in the rigging.

What was that which so sparkled? thought Captain Delano. It was no lamp—no match—no live coal. Could it have been a jewel? But how come sailors with jewels?—or with silk-trimmed under-shirts either? Has he been robbing the trunks of the dead cabin-passengers? But if so, he would hardly wear one of the stolen articles on board ship here. Ah, ah—if, now, that was, indeed, a secret sign I saw passing between this suspicious fellow and his captain awhile since; if I could only be certain that, in my uneasiness, my senses did not deceive me, then——

Here, passing from one suspicious thing to another, his mind revolved the strange questions put to him concerning his ship.

By a curious coincidence, as each point was recalled, the black wizards of Ashantee would strike up with their hatchets, as in ominous comment on the white stranger's thoughts. Pressed by such enigmas and portents, it would have been almost against nature, had not, even into the least distrustful heart, some ugly misgivings obtruded.

Observing the ship, now helplessly fallen into a current, with enchanted sails, drifting with increased rapidity seaward; and noting that, from a lately intercepted projection of the land, the sealer was hidden, the stout mariner began to quake at thoughts which he barely durst confess to himself. Above all, he began to feel a ghostly dread of Don Benito. And yet, when he roused himself, dilated his chest, felt himself strong on his legs, and coolly considered it—what did all these phantoms amount to?

Had the Spaniard any sinister scheme, it must have reference not so much to him (Captain Delano) as to his ship (the *Bachelor's Delight*). Hence the present drifting away of the one ship from the other, instead of favouring any such possible scheme, was, for the time, at least, opposed to it. Clearly any suspicion, combining such contradictions, must need be delusive. Besides, was it not absurd to think of a vessel in distress—a vessel by sickness almost dismanned of her crew—a vessel whose inmates were parched for water—was it not a thousand times absurd that such a craft should, at present, be of a piratical character; or her commander, either for himself or those under him, cherish any desire but for speedy relief and refreshment? But then, might not general distress, and thirst in particular, be affected? And might not that same undiminished Spanish crew, alleged to have perished off to a remnant, be at that very moment lurking in the hold? On heart-broken pretence of entreating a cup of cold water, fiends in human form had got into lonely dwellings, nor retired until a dark deed had been done. And among the Malay pirates, it was no unusual thing to lure ships after them into their treacherous harbours, or entice boarders from a declared enemy at sea, by the spectacle of thinly manned or vacant decks, beneath which prowled a hundred spears with yellow arms ready to upthrust them through the mats. Not that Captain Delano had entirely credited such things. He had heard of them—and now, as stories, they recurred. The present destination of the ship was the anchorage. There she would be near his own vessel. Upon gaining that vicinity, might not the *San Dominick*, like a slumbering volcano, suddenly let loose energies now hid?

He recalled the Spaniard's manner while telling his story. There was a gloomy hesitancy and subterfuge about it. It was just the manner of one making up his tale for evil purposes, as he goes. But if that story was not true, what was the truth? That the ship had unlawfully come into the Spaniard's possession? But in many of its details, especially in reference to the more calamitous parts, such as the fatalities among the seamen, the consequent prolonged beating about, the past sufferings from obstinate calms, and still continued suffering from thirst; in all these points, as well as others, Don Benito's story had corroborated not only the wailing ejaculations of the indiscriminate multitude, white and black, but likewise—what seemed impossible to be counterfeit—by the very expression and play of every human feature, which Captain Delano saw. If Don Benito's story was, throughout, an invention, then every soul on board, down to the youngest negress, was his carefully drilled recruit in the plot: an incredible inference. And yet, if there was ground for mistrusting his veracity, that inference was a legitimate one.

But those questions of the Spaniard. There, indeed, one might pause. Did they not seem put with much the same object with which the burglar or assassin, by day-time, reconnoitres the walls of a house? But, with ill purposes, to solicit such information openly of the chief person endangered, and so, in effect, setting him on his guard; how unlikely a procedure was that? Absurd, then, to suppose that those questions had been prompted by evil designs. Thus, the same conduct, which, in this instance, had raised the alarm, served to dispel it. In short, scarce any suspicion or uneasiness, however apparently reasonable at the time, which was not now, with equally apparent reason, dismissed.

At last he began to laugh at his former forebodings; and laugh at the strange ship for, in its aspect, someway siding with them, as it were; and laugh, too, at the odd-looking blacks, particularly those old scissors-grinders, the Ashantees; and those bed-ridden old knitting women, the oakumpickers; and almost at the dark Spaniard himself, the central hobgoblin of all.

For the rest, whatever in a serious way seemed enigmatical, was now good-naturedly explained away by the thought that, for the most part, the

poor invalid scarcely knew what he was about; either sulking in black vapours, or putting idle questions without sense of object. Evidently, for the
present, the man was not fit to be intrusted with the ship. On some benevolent plea withdrawing the command from him, Captain Delano would yet
have to send her to Concepcion, in charge of his second mate, a worthy
person and good navigator—a plan not more convenient for the *San Dominick* than for Don Benito; for, relieved from all anxiety, keeping wholly to
his cabin, the sick man, under the good nursing of his servant, would, probably, by the end of the passage, be in a measure restored to health, and with
that he should also be restored to authority.

Such were the American's thoughts. They were tranquilizing. There
was a difference between the idea of Don Benito's darkly pre-ordaining
Captain Delano's fate, and Captain Delano's lightly arranging Don Benito's. Nevertheless, it was not without something of relief that the good
seaman presently perceived his whale-boat in the distance. Its absence had
been prolonged by unexpected detention at the sealer's side, as well as its
returning trip lengthened by the continual recession of the goal.

The advancing speck was observed by the blacks. Their shouts attracted the attention of Don Benito, who, with a return of courtesy, approaching Captain Delano, expressed satisfaction at the coming of some
supplies, slight and temporary as they must necessarily prove.

Captain Delano responded; but while doing so, his attention was
drawn to something passing on the deck below: among the crowd climbing
the landward bulwarks, anxiously watching the coming boat, two blacks, to
all appearances accidentally incommoded by one of the sailors, violently
pushed him aside, which the sailor someway resenting, they dashed him to
the deck, despite the earnest cries of the oakum-pickers.

"Don Benito," said Captain Delano quickly, "do you see what is going
on there? Look!"

But, seized by his cough, the Spaniard staggered, with both hands to
his face, on the point of falling. Captain Delano would have supported
him, but the servant was more alert, who, with one hand sustaining his
master, with the other applied the cordial. Don Benito restored, the black
withdrew his support, slipping aside a little, but dutifully remaining within
call of a whisper. Such discretion was here evinced as quite wiped away, in
the visitor's eyes, any blemish of impropriety which might have attached to
the attendant, from the indecorous conferences before mentioned; showing, too, that if the servant were to blame, it might be more the master's
fault than his own, since, when left to himself, he could conduct thus well.

His glance called away from the spectacle of disorder to the more
pleasing one before him, Captain Delano could not avoid again congratulating his host upon possessing such a servant, who, though perhaps a little
too forward now and then, must upon the whole be invaluable to one in
the invalid's situation.

"Tell me, Don Benito," he added, with a smile—"I should like to have your man here, myself—what will you take for him? Would fifty doubloons be any object?"

"Master wouldn't part with Babo for a thousand doubloons," murmured the black, overhearing the offer, and taking it in earnest, and, with the strange vanity of a faithful slave, appreciated by his master, scorning to hear so paltry a valuation put upon him by a stranger. But Don Benito, apparently hardly yet completely restored, and again interrupted by his cough, made but some broken reply.

Soon his physical distress became so great, affecting his mind, too, apparently, that, as if to screen the sad spectacle, the servant gently conducted his master below.

Left to himself, the American, to while away the time till his boat should arrive, would have pleasantly accosted some one of the few Spanish seamen he saw; but recalling something that Don Benito had said touching their ill conduct, he refrained; as a shipmaster indisposed to countenance cowardice or unfaithfulness in seamen.

While, with these thoughts, standing with eye directed forward towards that handful of sailors, suddenly he thought that one or two of them returned the glance and with a sort of meaning. He rubbed his eyes, and looked again; but again seemed to see the same thing. Under a new form, but more obscure than any previous one, the old suspicions recurred, but, in the absence of Don Benito, with less of panic than before. Despite the bad account given of the sailors, Captain Delano resolved forthwith to accost one of them. Descending the poop, he made his way through the blacks, his movement drawing a queer cry from the oakum-pickers, prompted by whom, the negroes, twitching each other aside, divided before him; but, as if curious to see what was the object of this deliberate visit to their Ghetto, closing in behind, in tolerable order, followed the white stranger up. His progress thus proclaimed as by mounted kings-at-arms, and escorted as by a Kaffir guard of honour, Captain Delano, assuming a good-humoured, off-handed air, continued to advance; now and then saying a blithe word to the negroes, and his eye curiously surveying the white faces, here and there sparsely mixed in with the blacks, like stray white pawns venturously involved in the ranks of the chess-men opposed.

While thinking which of them to select for his purpose, he chanced to observe a sailor seated on the deck engaged in tarring the strap of a large block, a circle of blacks squatted round him inquisitively eyeing the process.

The mean employment of the man was in contrast with something superior in his figure. His hand, black with continually thrusting it into the tar-pot held for him by a negro, seemed not naturally allied to his face, a face which would have been a very fine one but for its haggardness. Whether this haggardness had aught to do with criminality, could not be determined; since, as intense heat and cold, though unlike, produce like sensations, so innocence and guilt, when, through casual association with mental pain, stamping any visible impress, use one seal—a hacked one.

Not again that this reflection occurred to Captain Delano at the time, charitable man as he was. Rather another idea. Because observing so singular a haggardness combined with a dark eye, averted as in trouble and shame, and then again recalling Don Benito's confessed ill opinion of his crew, insensibly he was operated upon by certain general notions which, while disconnecting pain and abashment from virtue, invariably link them with vice.

If, indeed, there be any wickedness on board this ship, thought Captain Delano, be sure that man there has fouled his hand in it, even as now he fouls it in the pitch. I don't like to accost him. I will speak to this other, this old Jack here on the windlass.

He advanced to an old Barcelona tar, in ragged red breeches and dirty night-cap, cheeks trenched and bronzed, whiskers dense as thorn hedges. Seated between two sleepy-looking Africans, this mariner, like his younger shipmate, was employed upon some rigging—splicing a cable—the sleepy-looking blacks performing the inferior function of holding the outer parts of the ropes for him.

Upon Captain Delano's approach, the man at once hung his head below its previous level; the one necessary for business. It appeared as if he desired to be thought absorbed, with more than common fidelity, in his task. Being addressed, he glanced up, but with what seemed a furtive, diffident air, which sat strangely enough on his weather-beaten visage, much as if a grizzly bear, instead of growling and biting, should simper and cast sheep's eyes. He was asked several questions concerning the voyage—questions purposely referring to several particulars in Don Benito's narrative, not previously corroborated by those impulsive cries greeting the visitor on the first coming on board. The questions were briefly answered, confirming all that remained to be confirmed of the story. The negroes about the windlass joined in with the old sailor; but, as they became talkative, he by degrees became mute, and at length quite glum, seemed morosely unwilling to answer more questions, and yet, all the while, this ursine air was somehow mixed with his sheepish one.

Despairing of getting into unembarrassed talk with such a centaur, Captain Delano, after glancing round for a more promising countenance, but seeing none, spoke pleasantly to the blacks to make way for him; and so, amid various grins and grimaces, returned to the poop, feeling a little strange at first, he could hardly tell why, but upon the whole with regained confidence in Benito Cereno.

How plainly, thought he, did that old whiskerando yonder betray a consciousness of ill desert. No doubt, when he saw me coming, he dreaded lest I, appraised by his captain of the crew's general misbehaviour, came with sharp words for him, and so down with his head. And yet—and yet, now that I think of it, that very fellow, if I err not, was one of those who seemed so earnestly eyeing me here awhile since. Ah, these currents spin one's head round almost as much as they do the ship. Ha, there now's a pleasant sort of sunny sight; quite sociable, too.

His attention had been drawn back to a slumbering negress, partly disclosed through the lacework of some rigging, lying, with youthful limbs carelessly disposed, under the lee of the bulwarks, like a doe in the shade of a woodland rock. Sprawling at her lapped breasts was her wide-awake fawn, stark naked, its black little body half lifted from the deck, crosswise with its dam's; its hands, like two paws, clambering upon her; its mouth and nose ineffectually rooting to get at the mark; and meantime giving a vexatious half-grunt, blending with the composed snore of the negress.

The uncommon vigour of the child at length roused the mother. She started up, at a distance facing Captain Delano. But as if not at all concerned at the attitude in which she had been caught, delightedly she caught the child up, with maternal transports, covering it with kisses.

There's naked nature, now; pure tenderness and love, thought Captain Delano, well pleased.

This incident prompted him to remark the other negresses more particularly than before. He was gratified with their manners: like most uncivilized women, they seemed at once tender of heart and tough of constitution; equally ready to die for their infants or fight for them. Unsophisticated as leopardesses; loving as doves. Ah! thought Captain Delano, these, perhaps, are some of the very women whom Ledyard saw in Africa, and gave such a noble account of.

These natural sights somehow insensibly deepened his confidence and ease. At last he looked to see how his boat was getting on; but it was still pretty remote. He turned to see if Don Benito had returned; but he had not.

To change the scene, as well as to please himself with a leisurely observation of the coming boat, stepping over into the mizzen-chains, he clambered his way into the starboard quarter-gallery one of those abandoned Venetian-looking water-balconies previously mentioned—retreats cut off from the deck. As his foot pressed the half-damp, half-dry sea-mosses matting the place, and a chance phantom cats-paw—an islet of breeze, unheralded, unfollowed—as this ghostly cats-paw came fanning his cheek; as his glance fell upon the row of small, round dead-lights—all closed like coppered eyes of the coffined—and the state-cabin door, once connecting with the gallery, even as the dead-lights had once looked out upon it, but now calked fast like a sarcophagus lid; and to a purple-black, tarred-over panel, threshold, and post; and he bethought him of the time, when that state-cabin and this state-balcony had heard the voices of the Spanish king's officers, and the forms of the Lima viceroy's daughters had perhaps leaned where he stood—as these and other images flitted through his mind, as the cats-paw through the calm, gradually he felt rising a dreamy inquietude, like that of one who alone on the prairie feels unrest from the repose of the noon.

He leaned against the carved balustrade, again looking off toward his boat; but found his eye falling upon the ribbon grass, trailing along the ship's water-line, straight as a border of green box; and parterres of sea-weed, broad ovals and crescents, floating nigh and far, with what seemed long formal alleys between, crossing the terraces of swells, and sweeping round as if leading to the grottoes below. And overhanging all was the balustrade by his arm, which, partly stained with pitch and partly embossed with moss, seemed the charred ruin of some summer-house in a grand garden long running to waste.

Trying to break one charm, he was but becharmed anew. Though upon the wide sea, he seemed in some far inland country; prisoner in some deserted château, left to stare at empty grounds, and peer out at vague roads, where never wagon or wayfarer passed.

But these enchantments were a little disenchanted as his eye fell on the corroded main-chains. Of an ancient style, massy and rusty in link, shackle and bolt, they seemed even more fit for the ship's present business than the one for which she had been built.

Presently he thought something moved nigh the chains. He rubbed his eyes, and looked hard. Groves of rigging were about the chains; and there, peering from behind a great stay, like an Indian from behind a hemlock, a Spanish sailor, a marlingspike in his hand, was seen, who made what seemed an imperfect gesture towards the balcony, but immediately, as if alarmed by some advancing step along the deck within, vanished into the recesses of the hempen forest, like a poacher.

What meant this? Something the man had sought to communicate, unbeknown to any one, even to his captain. Did the secret involve aught unfavourable to his captain? Were those previous misgivings of Captain Delano's about to be verified? Or, in his haunted mood at the moment, had some random, unintentional motion of the man, while busy with the stay, as if repairing it, been mistaken for a significant beckoning?

Not unbewildered, again he gazed off for his boat. But it was temporarily hidden by a rocky spur of the isle. As with some eagerness he bent forward, watching for the first shooting view of its beak, the balustrade gave way before him like charcoal. Had he not clutched an outreaching rope he would have fallen into the sea. The crash, though feeble, and the fall, though hollow, of the rotten fragments, must have been overheard. He glanced up. With sober curiosity peering down upon him was one of the old oakum-pickers, slipped from his perch to an outside boom; while below the old negro, and, invisible to him, reconnoitring from a port-hole like a fox from the mouth of its den, crouched the Spanish sailor again. From something suddenly suggested by the man's air, the mad idea now darted into Captain Delano's mind, that Don Benito's plea of indisposition, in withdrawing below, was but a pretence: that he was engaged there maturing his plot, of which the sailor, by some means gaining an inkling, had a mind to warn the stranger against; incited, it may be, by gratitude for a kind word on first boarding the ship. Was it from foreseeing some possible interference like this, that Don Benito had, beforehand, given such a bad character of his sailors, while praising the negroes; though, indeed, the former seemed as docile as the latter the contrary? The whites, too, by nature, were the shrewder race. A man with some evil design, would he not be likely to speak well of that stupidity which was blind to his depravity, and malign that intelligence from which it might not be hidden? Not unlikely, perhaps. But if the whites had dark secrets concerning Don Benito, could then Don Benito be any way in complicity with the blacks? But they were too stupid. Besides, who ever heard of a white so far a renegade as to apostatize from his very species almost, by leaguing in against it with negroes? These difficulties recalled former ones. Lost in their mazes, Captain Delano, who had now regained the deck, was uneasily advancing along it, when he observed a new face; an aged sailor seated cross-legged near the main hatchway. His skin was shrunk up with wrinkles like a pelican's empty pouch; his hair frosted; his countenance grave and composed. His hands were full of ropes, which he was working into a large knot. Some blacks were about him obligingly dipping the strands for him, here and there, as the exigencies of the operation demanded.

Captain Delano crossed over to him, and stood in silence surveying the knot; his mind, by a not uncongenial transition, passing from its own entanglements to those of the hemp. For intricacy, such a knot he had never seen in an American ship, nor indeed any other. The old man looked like an Egyptian priest, making Gordian knots for the temple of Ammon. The knot seemed a combination of double-bowline-knot, treble-crown-knot, back-handed-well-knot, knot-in-and-out-knot, and jamming knot.

At last, puzzled to comprehend the meaning of such a knot, Captain Delano addressed the knotter:—

"What are you knotting there, my man?"

"The knot," was the brief reply, without looking up.

"So it seems; but what is it for?"

"For some one else to undo," muttered back the old man, plying his fingers harder than ever, the knot being now nearly completed.

While Captain Delano stood watching him, suddenly the old man threw the knot towards him, saying in broken English—the first heard in the ship—something to this effect: "Undo it, cut it, quick." It was said lowly, but with such condensation of rapidity, that the long, slow words in Spanish, which had preceded and followed, almost operated as covers to the brief English between.

For a moment, knot in hand, and knot in head, Captain Delano stood mute; while, without further heeding him, the old man was now intent upon other ropes. Presently there was a slight stir behind Captain Delano.

Turning, he saw the chained negro, Atufal, standing quietly there. The next moment the old sailor rose, muttering, and, followed by his subordinate negroes, removed to the forward part of the ship, where in the crowd he disappeared.

An elderly negro, in a clout like an infant's, and with a pepper-and-salt head, and a kind of attorney air, now approached Captain Delano. In tolerable Spanish, and with a good-natured, knowing wink, he informed him that the old knotter was simple-witted, but harmless; often playing his odd tricks. The negro concluded by begging the knot, for of course the stranger would not care to be troubled with it. Unconsciously, it was handed to him. With a sort of congé, the negro received it, and, turning his back, ferreted into it like a detective custom-house officer after smuggled laces. Soon, with some African word, equivalent to pshaw, he tossed the knot overboard.

All this is very queer now, thought Captain Delano, with a qualmish sort of emotion; but, as one feeling incipient sea-sickness, he strove, by ignoring the symptoms, to get rid of the malady. Once more he looked off for his boat. To his delight, it was now again in view, leaving the rocky spur astern.

The sensation here experienced, after at first relieving his uneasiness, with unforeseen efficacy soon began to remove it. The less distant sight of that well-known boat—showing it, not as before, half blended with the haze, but with outline defined, so that its individuality, like a man's, was manifest; that boat, *Rover* by name, which, though now in strange seas, had often pressed the beach of Captain Delano's home, and, brought to its threshold for repairs, had familiarly lain there, as a Newfoundland dog; the sight of that household boat evoked a thousand trustful associations, which, contrasted with previous suspicions, filled him not only with lightsome confidence, but somehow with half-humorous self-reproaches at his former lack of it.

"What, I, Amasa Delano—Jack of the Beach, as they called me when a lad—I, Amasa; the same that, duck-satchel in hand, used to paddle along the water-side to the school-house made from the old hulk—I, little Jack of the Beach, that used to go berrying with cousin Nat and the rest; I to be murdered here at the ends of the earth, on board a haunted pirate-ship by a horrible Spaniard? Too nonsensical to think of! Who would murder Amasa Delano? His conscience is clean. There is someone above. Fie, fie, Jack of the Beach! you are a child indeed; a child of the second childhood, old boy; you are beginning to dote and drool, I'm afraid."

Light of heart and foot, he stepped aft, and there was met by Don Benito's servant, who, with a pleasing expression, responsive to his own present feelings, informed him that his master had recovered from the effects of his coughing fit, and had just ordered him to go present his compliments to his good guest, Don Amasa, and say that he (Don Benito) would soon have the happiness to rejoin him.

There now, do you mark that? again thought Captain Delano, walking the poop. What a donkey I was. This kind gentleman who here sends me his kind compliments, he, but ten minutes ago, dark-lantern in hand, was dodging round some old grindstone in the hold, sharpening a hatchet for me, I thought. Well, well; these long calms have a morbid effect on the mind, I've often heard, though I never believed it before. Ha! glancing towards the boat; there's *Rover*; good dog; a white bone in her mouth. A pretty big bone though, seems to me.—What? Yes, she has fallen afoul of the bubbling tide-rip there. It sets her the other way, too, for the time. Patience.

It was now about noon, though, from the greyness of everything, it seemed to be getting towards dusk.

The calm was confirmed. In the far distance away from the influence of land, the leaden ocean seemed laid out and leaded up, its course finished, soul gone, defunct. But the current from landward, where the ship was, increased; silently sweeping her further and further towards the tranced waters beyond.

Still, from his knowledge of those latitudes, cherishing hopes of a breeze, and a fair and fresh one, at any moment, Captain Delano, despite present prospects, buoyantly counted upon bringing the *San Dominick* safely to anchor ere night. The distance swept over was nothing; since, with a good wind, ten minutes' sailing would retrace more than sixty minutes' drifting. Meantime, one moment turning to mark *Rover* fighting the tide-rip, and the next to see Don Benito approaching, he continued walking the poop.

Gradually he felt a vexation arising from the delay of his boat; this soon merged into uneasiness; and at last—his eye falling continually, as from a stage-box into the pit, upon the strange crowd before and below him, and, by and by, recognizing there the face—now composed to indifference—of the Spanish sailor who had seemed to beckon from the main-chains—something of his old trepidations returned.

Ah, thought he—gravely enough—this is like the ague: because it went off, it follows not that it won't come back.

Though ashamed of the relapse, he could not altogether subdue it; and so, exerting his good nature to the utmost, insensibly he came to a compromise.

Yes, this is a strange craft; a strange history, too, and strange folks on board. But—nothing more.

By way of keeping his mind out of mischief till the boat should arrive, he tried to occupy it with turning over and over, in a purely speculative sort of way, some lesser peculiarities of the captain and crew. Among others, four curious points recurred:

First, the affair of the Spanish lad assailed with a knife by the slave boy; an act winked at by Don Benito. Second, the tyranny in Don Benito's treatment of Atufal, the black, as if a child should lead a bull of the Nile by the ring in his nose. Third, the trampling of the sailor by the two negroes; a piece of insolence passed over without so much as a reprimand. Fourth, the cringing submission to their master, of all the ship's underlings, mostly blacks; as if by the least inadvertence they feared to draw down his despotic displeasure.

Coupling these points, they seemed somewhat contradictory. But what then, thought Captain Delano, glancing towards his now nearing boat—what then? Why, Don Benito is a very capricious commander. But he is not the first of the sort I have seen; thought it's true he rather exceeds any other. But as a nation—continued he in his reveries—these Spaniards are all an odd set; the very word Spaniard has a curious, conspirator, Guy-Fawkish twang to it. And yet, I dare say, Spaniards in the main are as good folks as any in Duxbury, Massachusetts. Ah, good! At last *Rover* has come.

As, with its welcome freight, the boat touched the side, the oakum-pickers, with venerable gestures, sought to restrain the blacks, who, at the sight of three gurried water casks in its bottom, and a pile of wilted pumpkins in its bow, hung over the bulwarks in disorderly raptures.

Don Benito, with his servant, now appeared; his coming, perhaps, hastened by hearing the noise. Of him Captain Delano sought permission to serve out the water, so that all might share alike, and none injure themselves by unfair excess. But sensible, and, on Don Benito's account, kind as this offer was, it was received with what seemed impatience; as if aware that he lacked energy as a commander, Don Benito, with the true jealousy of weakness, resented as an affront any interference. So, at least, Captain Delano inferred.

In another moment the casks were being hoisted in, when some of the eager negroes accidently jostled Captain Delano, where he stood by the gangway; so that, unmindful of Don Benito, yielding to the impulse of the moment, with good-natured authority he bade the blacks stand back; to enforce his words making use of a half-mirthful, half-menacing gesture. Instantly the blacks paused, just where they were, each negro and negress suspended in his or her posture, exactly as the word had found them—for a few seconds continuing so—while, as between the responsive posts of a telegraph, an unknown syllable ran from man to man among the perched oakum-pickers. While the visitor's attention was fixed by this scene, suddenly the hatchet-polishers half rose, and a rapid cry came from Don Benito.

Thinking that at the signal of the Spaniard he was about to be massacred, Captain Delano would have sprung for his boat, but paused, as the oakum-pickers, dropping down into the crowd with earnest exclamations, forced every white and every negro back, at the same moment, with gestures friendly and familiar, almost jocose, bidding him, in substance, not be a fool. Simultaneously the hatchet-polishers resumed their seats, quietly as so many tailors, and at once, as if nothing had happened, the work of hoisting in the casks was resumed, whites and black singing at the tackle.

Captain Delano glanced towards Don Benito. As he saw his meagre form in the act of recovering itself from reclining in the servant's arms, into which the agitated invalid had fallen, he could not but marvel at the panic by which himself had been surprised, on the darting supposition that such a commander, who, upon a legitimate occasion, so trivial, too, as it now appeared, could lose all self-command, was, with energetic iniquity, going to bring about his murder.

The casks being on deck, Captain Delano was handed a number of jars and cups by one of the steward's aids, who, in the name of his captain, entreated him to do as he had proposed—dole out the water. He complied, with republican impartiality as to this republican element, which always seeks one level, serving the oldest white no better than the youngest black; excepting, indeed, poor Don Benito, whose condition, if not rank, demanded an extra allowance. To him, in the first place, Captain Delano presented a fair pitcher of the fluid; but, thirsting as he was for it, the Spaniard quaffed not a drop until after several grave bows and salutes. A reciprocation of courtesies which the sight-loving Africans hailed with clapping of hands.

Two of the less wilted pumpkins being reserved for the cabin table, the residue were minced up on the spot for the general regalement. But the soft bread, sugar, and bottled cider, Captain Delano would have given the whites alone, and in chief Don Benito; but the latter objected; which disinterestedness not a little pleased the American; and so mouthfuls all around were given alike to whites and blacks; excepting one bottle of cider, which Babo insisted upon setting aside for his master.

Here it may be observed that as, on the first visit of the boat, the American had not permitted his men to board the ship, neither did he now; being unwilling to add to the confusion of the decks.

Not uninfluenced by the peculiar good-humor at present prevailing, and for the time oblivious of any but benevolent thoughts, Captain Delano, who, from recent indications, counted upon a breeze within an hour or two at furthest, dispatched the boat back to the sealer, with orders for all the hands that could be spared immediately to set about rafting casks to the watering-place and filling them. Likewise he bade word be carried to his chief officer, that if, against present expectation, the ship was not brought to anchor by sunset, he need be under no concern; for as there was to be a full moon that night, he (Captain Delano) would remain on board ready to play the pilot, come the wind soon or late.

As the two captains stood together, observing the departing boat—the servant, as it happened, having just spied a spot on his master's velvet sleeve, and silently engaged rubbing it out—the American expressed his regrets that the *San Dominick* had no boats; none, at least, but the unseaworthy old hulk of the long-boat, which, warped as a camel's skeleton in the desert, and almost as bleached, lay pot-wise inverted amid-ships, one side a little tipped, furnishing a subterraneous sort of den for family groups of the blacks, mostly women and small children; who, squatting on old mats below, or perched above in the dark dome, on the elevated seats, were descried, some distance within, like a social circle of bats, sheltering in some friendly cave; at intervals, ebon flights of naked boys and girls, three or four years old, darting in and out of the den's mouth.

"Had you three or four boats now, Don Benito," said Captain Delano, "I think that, by tugging at the oars, your negroes here might help along matters some. Did you sail from port without boats, Don Benito?"

"They were stove in the gales, Señor."

"That was bad. Many men, too, you lost then. Boats and men. Those must have been hard gales, Don Benito."

"Past all speech," cringed the Spaniard.

"Tell me, Don Benito," continued his companion with increased interest, "tell me, were these gales immediately off the pitch of Cape Horn?"

"Cape Horn?—who spoke of Cape Horn?"

"Yourself did, when giving me an account of your voyage," answered Captain Delano, with almost equal astonishment at this eating of his own words, even as he ever seemed eating his own heart, on the part of the Spaniard. "You yourself, Don Benito, spoke of Cape Horn," he emphatically repeated.

The Spaniard turned, in a sort of stooping posture, pausing an instant, as one about to make a plunging exchange of elements, as from air to water.

At this moment a messenger-boy, a white, hurried by, in the regular performance of his function carrying the last expired half-hour forward to the forecastle, from the cabin time-piece, to have it struck at the ship's large bell.

"Master," said the servant, discontinuing his work on the coat sleeve, and addressing the rapt Spaniard with a sort of timid apprehensiveness, as one charged with a duty, the discharge of which, it was foreseen, would prove irksome to the very person who had imposed it, and for whose benefit it was intended, "master told me never mind where he was, or how engaged, always to remind him, to a minute, when shaving-time comes. Miguel has gone to strike the half-hour afternoon. It is *now*, master. Will master go into the cuddy?"

"Ah—yes," answered the Spaniard, starting, as from dreams into realities; then turning upon Captain Delano, he said that ere long he would resume the conversation.

"Then if master means to talk more to Don Amasa," said the servant, "why not let Don Amasa sit by master in the cuddy, and master can talk, and Don Amasa can listen, while Babo here lathers and strops."

"Yes," said Captain Delano, not unpleased with this sociable plan, "yes, Don Benito, unless you had rather not, I will go with you."

"Be it so, Señor."

As the three passed aft, the American could not but think it another strange instance of his host's capriciousness, this being shaved with such uncommon punctuality in the middle of the day. But he deemed it more than likely that the servant's anxious fidelity had something to do with the matter; inasmuch as the timely interruption served to rally his master from the mood which had evidently been coming upon him.

The place called the cuddy was a light deck-cabin formed by the poop, a sort of attic to the large cabin below. Part of it had formerly been the quarters of the officers; but since their death all the partitionings had been thrown down, and the whole interior converted into one spacious and airy marine hall; for absence of fine furniture and picturesque disarray of odd appurtenances, somewhat answering to the wide, cluttered hall of some eccentric bachelor-squire in the country, who hangs his shooting-jacket and tobacco-pouch on deer antlers, and keeps his fishing-rod, tongs, and walking-stick in the same corner.

The similitude was heightened, if not originally suggested, by glimpses of the surrounding sea; since, in one aspect, the country and the ocean seem cousins-german.

The floor of the cuddy was matted. Overhead, four or five old muskets were stuck into horizontal holes along the beams. On one side was a claw-footed old table lashed to the deck; a thumbed missal on it, and over it a small, meagre crucifix attached to the bulk-head. Under the table lay a dented cutlass or two, with a hacked harpoon, among some melancholy old rigging, like a heap of poor friars' girdles. There were also two long, sharp, ribbed settees of Malacca cane, black with age, and uncomfortable to look at as inquisitors' racks, with a large, misshapen arm-chair, which, furnished with a rude barber's crotch at the back, working with a screw, seemed some grotesque engine of torment. A flag-locker was in one corner, open, exposing various coloured bunting, some rolled up, others half unrolled, still others tumbled. Opposite was a cumbrous washstand, of black mahogany, all of one block, with a pedestal, like a font, and over it a railed shelf, containing combs, brushes, and other implements of the toilet. A torn hammock of stained grass swung near; the sheets tossed, and the pillow wrinkled up like a brow, as if whoever slept here slept but illy, with alternate visitations of sad thoughts and bad dreams.

The further extremity of the cuddy, overhanging the ship's stern, was pierced with three openings, windows or port-holes, according as men or cannon might peer, socially or unsocially, out of them. At present neither men nor cannon were seen, though huge ring-bolts and other rusty iron fixtures of the woodwork hinted of twenty-four-pounders.

Glancing towards the hammock as he entered, Captain Delano said, "You sleep here, Don Benito?"

"Yes, Señor, since we got into mild weather."

"This seems a sort of dormitory, sitting-room, sail-loft, chapel, armoury, and private closet altogether, Don Benito," added Captain Delano, looking round.

"Yes, Señor; events have not been favourable to much order in my arrangements."

Here the servant, napkin on arm, made a motion as if waiting his master's good pleasure. Don Benito signified his readiness, when, seating him in the Malacca arm-chair, and for the guest's convenience drawing opposite one of the settees, the servant commenced operations by throwing back his master's collar and loosening his cravat.

There is something in the negro which, in a peculiar way, fits him for avocations about one's person. Most negroes are natural valets and hair-dressers; taking to the comb and brush congenially as to the castanets, and flourishing them apparently with almost equal satisfaction. There is, too, a smooth tact about them in this employment, with a marvellous, noiseless, gliding briskness, not ungraceful in its way, singularly pleasing to behold, and still more so to be the manipulated subject of. And above all is the great gift of good-humour. Not the mere grin or laugh is here meant. Those were unsuitable. But a certain easy cheerfulness, harmonious in every glance and gesture; as though God had set the whole negro to some pleasant tune.

When to this is added the docility arising from the unaspiring contentment of a limited mind, and that susceptibility of blind attachment sometimes inhering in indisputable inferiors, one readily perceives why those hypochondriacs, Johnson and Byron—it may be, something like the hypochondriac Benito Cereno—took to their hearts, almost to the exclusion of the entire white race, their serving men, the negroes, Barber and Fletcher. But if there be that in the negro which exempts him from the inflicted sourness of the morbid or cynical mind, how, in his most prepossessing aspects, must he appear to a benevolent one? When at ease with respect to exterior things, Captain Delano's nature was not only benign, but familiarly and humorously so. At home, he had often taken rare satisfaction in sitting in his door, watching some free man of colour at his work or play. If on a voyage he chanced to have a black sailor, invariably he was on chatty and half-gamesome terms with him. In fact, like most men of a good, blithe heart, Captain Delano took to negroes, not philanthropically, but genially, just as other men to Newfoundland dogs.

Hitherto, the circumstances in which he found the *San Dominick* had repressed the tendency. But in the cuddy, relieved from his former uneasiness, and, for various reasons, more sociably inclined than at any previous period of the day, and seeing the coloured servant, napkin on arm, so debonair about his master, in a business so familiar as that of shaving, too, all his old weakness for negroes returned.

Among other things, he was amused with an odd instance of the African love of bright colours and fine shows, in the black's informally taking from the flag-locker a great piece of bunting of all hues, and lavishly tucking it under his master's chin for an apron.

The mode of shaving among the Spaniards is a little different from what it is with other nations. They have a basin, specifically called a barber's basin, which on one side is scooped out, so as accurately to receive the chin, against which it is closely held in lathering; which is done, not with a brush, but with soap dipped in the water of the basin and rubbed on the face.

In the present instance salt-water was used for lack of better; and the parts lathered were only the upper lip, and low down under the throat, all the rest being cultivated beard.

The preliminaries being somewhat novel to Captain Delano, he sat curiously eyeing them, so that no conversation took place, nor, for the present, did Don Benito appear disposed to renew any.

Setting down his basin, the negro searched among the razors, as for the sharpest, and having found it, gave it an additional edge by expertly stropping it on the firm, smooth, oily skin of his open palm; he then made a gesture as if to begin, but midway stood suspended for an instant, one hand elevating the razor, the other professionally dabbling among the bubbling suds on the Spaniard's lank neck. Not unaffected by the close sight of the gleaming steel, Don Benito nervously shuddered; his usual ghastliness was heightened by the lather, which lather, again, was intensified in its hue by the contrasting sootiness of the negro's body. Altogether the scene was somewhat peculiar, at least to Captain Delano, nor, as he saw the two thus postured, could he resist the vagary, that in the black he saw a headsman, and in the white a man at the block. But this was one of those antic conceits, appearing and vanishing in a breath, from which, perhaps, the best regulated mind is not always free.

Meantime the agitation of the Spaniard had a little loosened the bunting from around him, so that one broad fold swept curtain-like over the chair-arm to the floor, revealing, amid a profusion of armorial bars and ground-colours—black, blue, and yellow—a closed castle in a blood-red field diagonal with a lion rampant in a white.

"The castle and the lion," exclaimed Captain Delano—"why, Don Benito, this is the flag of Spain you use here. It's well it's only I, and not the King, that see this," he added, with a smile, "but,"—turning towards the black—"it's all one, I suppose, so the colours be gay," which playful remark did not fail somewhat to tickle the negro.

"Now, master," he said, readjusting the flag, and pressing the head gently further back into the crotch of the chair; "now, master," and the steel glanced nigh that throat.

Again Don Benito faintly shuddered.

"You must not shake so, master. See, Don Amasa, master always shakes when I shave him. And yet master knows I never yet have drawn blood, though it's true, if master will shake so, I may some of these times. Now, master," he continued. "And now, Don Amasa, please go on with your talk about the gale, and all that; master can hear, and, between times, master can answer."

"Ah yes, these gales," said Captain Delano; "but the more I think of your voyage, Don Benito, the more I wonder, not at the gales, terrible as they must have been, but at the disastrous interval following them. For here, by your account, have you been these two months and more getting from Cape Horn to Santa Maria, a distance which I myself, with a good wind, have sailed in a few days. True, you had calms, and long ones, but to be becalmed for two months, that is, at least, unusual. Why, Don Benito, had almost any other gentleman told me such a story, I should have been half disposed to a little incredulity."

Here an involuntary expression came over the Spaniard, similiar to that just before on the deck, and whether it was the start he gave, or a sudden gawky roll of the hull in the calm, or a momentary unsteadiness of the servant's hand, however it was, just then the razor drew blood, spots of which stained the creamy lather under the throat: immediately the black barber drew back his steel, and, remaining in his professional attitude, back to Captain Delano, and face to Don Benito, held up the trickling razor, saying, with a sort of half-humorous sorrow, "See, master—you shook so—here's Babo's first blood."

No sword drawn before James the First of England, no assassination in that timid King's presence, could have produced a more terrified aspect than was now presented by Don Benito.

Poor fellow, thought Captain Delano, so nervous he can't even bear the sight of barber's blood; and this unstrung, sick man, is it credible that I should have imagined he meant to spill all my blood, who can't endure the sight of one little drop of his own? Surely, Amasa Delano, you have been beside yourself this day. Tell it not when when you get home, sappy Amasa. Well, he looks like a murderer, doesn't he? More like as if himself were to be done for. Well, well, this day's experience shall be a good lesson.

Meantime, while these things were running through the honest seaman's mind, the servant had taken the napkin from under his arm, and to Don Benito had said—"But answer Don Amasa, please, master, while I wipe this ugly stuff off the razor, and strop it again."

As he said the words, his face was turned half round, so as to be alike visible to the Spaniard and the American, and seemed, by its expression, to hint, that he was desirous, by getting his master to go on with the conversation, considerately to withdraw his attention from the recent annoying accident. As if glad to snatch the offered relief, Don Benito resumed, rehearsing to Captain Delano, that not only were the calms of unusual duration, but the ship had fallen in with obstinate currents; and other things he added, some of which were but repetitions of former statements, to explain how it came to pass that the passage from Cape Horn to Santa Maria had been so exceedingly long; now and then mingling with his words, incidental praises, less qualified than before, to the blacks, for their general good conduct. These particulars were not given consecutively, the servant, at convenient times, using his razor, and so, between the intervals of shaving, the story and panegyric went on with more than usual huskiness.

To Captain Delano's imagination, now again not wholly at rest, there was something so hollow in the Spaniard's manner, with apparently some reciprocal hollowness in the servant's dusky comment of silence, that the idea flashed across him, that possibly master and man, for some unknown purpose, were acting out, both in word and deed, nay, to the very tremor of Don Benito's limbs, some juggling play before him. Neither did the suspicion of collusion lack apparent support, from the fact of those whispered conferences before mentioned. But then, what could be the object of enacting this play of the barber before him? At last, regarding the notion as a whimsy, insensibly suggested, perhaps, by the theatrical aspect of Don Benito in his harlequin ensign, Captain Delano speedily banished it.

The shaving over, the servant bestirred himself with a small bottle of scented waters, pouring a few drops on the head, and then diligently rubbing; the vehemence of the exercise causing the muscles of his face to twitch rather strangely.

His next operation was with comb, scissors, and brush; going round and round, smoothing a curl here, clipping an unruly whisker-hair there, giving a graceful sweep to the temple-lock, with other inpromptu touches evincing the hand of a master; while, like any resigned gentleman in barber's hands, Don Benito bore all, much less uneasily, at least, than he had done the razoring; indeed, he sat so pale and rigid now, that the negro seemed a Nubian sculptor finishing off a white statue-head.

All being over at last, the standard of Spain removed, tumbled up, and tossed back into the flag-locker, the negro's warm breath blowing away any stray hair which might have lodged down his master's neck; collar and cravat readjusted; a speck of lint whisked off the velvet lapel; all this being done, backing off a little space, and pausing with an expression of subdued self-complacency, the servant for a moment surveyed his master, as, in toilet at least, the creature of his own tasteful hands.

Captain Delano playfully complimented him upon his achievement; at the same time congratulating Don Benito.

But neither sweet waters, nor shampooing, nor fidelity, nor sociality, delighted the Spaniard. Seeing him relapsing into forbidding gloom, and still remaining seated, Captain Delano, thinking that his presence was undesired just then, withdrew, on pretence of seeing whether, as he had prophesied, any signs of a breeze were visible.

Walking forward to the main-mast, he stood awhile thinking over the scene, and not without some undefined misgivings, when he heard a noise near the cuddy, and turning, saw the negro, his hand to his cheek. Advancing, Captain Delano perceived that the cheek was bleeding. He was about to ask the cause, when the negro's wailing soliloquy enlightened him.

"Ah, when will master get better from his sickness; only the sour heart that sour sickness breeds made him serve Babo so; cutting Babo with the razor, because, only by accident, Babo had given master one little scratch; and for the first time in so many a day, too. Ah, ah, ah," holding his hand to his face.

It is possible, thought Captain Delano; was it to wreak in private his Spanish spite against this poor friend of his, that Don Benito, by his sullen manner, impelled me to withdraw? Ah, this slavery breeds ugly passions in man.—Poor fellow!

He was about to speak in sympathy to the negro, but with a timid reluctance he now re-entered the cuddy.

Presently master and man came forth; Don Benito leaning on his servant as if nothing had happened.

But a sort of love-quarrel, after all, thought Captain Delano.

He accosted Don Benito, and they slowly walked together. They had gone but a few paces, when the steward—a tall, rajah-looking mulatto, orientally set off with a pagoda turban formed by three or four Madras handkerchiefs wound about his head, tier on tier—approaching with a salaam, announced lunch in the cabin.

On their way thither, the two captains were preceded by the mulatto, who, turning round as he advanced, with continual smiles and bows, ushered them on, a display of elegance which quite completed the insignificance of the small bare-headed Babo, who, as if not unconscious of inferiority, eyed askance the graceful steward. But in part, Captain Delano imputed his jealous watchfulness to that peculiar feeling which the full-blooded African entertains from the adulterated one. As for the steward, his manner, if not bespeaking much dignity of self-respect, yet evidenced his extreme desire to please; which is doubly meritorious, as at once Chrisian and Chesterfieldian.

Captain Delano observed with interest that while the complexion of the mulatto was hybrid, his physiognomy was European—classically so.

"Don Benito," whispered he, "I am glad to see this usher-of-the-golden-rod of yours; the sight refutes an ugly remark once made to me by a Barbados planter; that when a mulatto has a regular European face, look out for him; he is a devil. But see, your steward here has features more regular than King George's of England; and yet there he nods, and bows, and smiles; a king, indeed—the king of kind hearts and polite fellows. What a pleasant voice he has, too."

"He has, Señor."

"But tell me, has he not, so far as you have known him, always proved a good, worthy fellow?" said Captain Delano, pausing, while with a final genuflexion the steward disappeared into the cabin; "come, for the reason just mentioned, I am curious to know."

"Francesco is a good man," sort of sluggishly responded Don Benito, like a phlegmatic appreciator, who would neither find fault nor flatter.

"Ah, I thought so. For it were strange, indeed, and not very creditable to us white-skins, if a little of our blood mixed with the African's, should, far from improving the latter's quality, have the sad effect of pouring vitriolic acid into black broth; improving the hue, perhaps, but not the wholesomeness."

"Doubtless, doubtless, Señor, but,"—glancing at Babo—"not to speak of negroes, your planter's remark I have heard applied to the Spanish and Indian intermixtures in our provinces. But I know nothing about the matter," he listlessly added.

And here they entered the cabin.

The lunch was a frugal one. Some of Captain Delano's fresh fish and pumpkins, biscuit and salt beef, the reserved bottle of cider, and the *San Dominick*'s last bottle of Canary.

As they entered, Francesco, with two or three coloured aids, was hovering over the table giving the last adjustments. Upon perceiving their master they withdrew, Francesco making a smiling congé, and the Spaniard, without condescending to notice it, fastidiously remarking to his companion that he relished not superfluous attendance.

Without companions, host and guest sat down, like a childless married couple, at opposite ends of the table, Don Benito waving Captain Delano to his place, and, weak as he was, insisting upon that gentleman being seated before himself.

The negro placed a rug under Don Benito's feet, and a cushion behind his back, and then stood behind, not his master's chair, but Captain Delano's. At first, this a little surprised the latter. But it was soon evident that, in taking his position, the black was still true to his master; since by facing him he could the more readily anticipate his slightest want.

"This is an uncommonly intelligent fellow of yours, Don Benito," whispered Captain Delano across the table.

"You say true, Señor."

During the repast, the guest again reverted to parts of Don Benito's story, begging further particulars here and there. He inquired how it was that the scurvy and fever should have committed such wholesale havoc upon the whites, while destroying less than half the blacks. As if this question reproduced the whole scenes of plague before the Spaniard's eyes, miserably reminding him of his solitude in a cabin where before he had had so many friends and officers round him, his hand shook, his face became hueless, broken words escaped; but directly the same memory of the past seemed replaced by insane terrors of the present. With starting eyes he stared before him at vacancy. For nothing was to be seen but the hand of his servant pushing the Canary over towards him. At length a few sips served partially to restore him. He made random reference to the different constitution of races, enabling one to offer more resistance to certain maladies than another. The thought was new to his companion.

Presently Captain Delano, intending to say something to his host concerning the pecuniary part of the business he had undertaken for him, especially—since he was strictly accountable to his owners—with reference to the new suite of sails, and other things of that sort; and naturally preferring to conduct such affairs in private, was desirous that the servant should withdraw; imagining that Don Benito for a few minutes could dispense with his attendance. He, however, waited awhile; thinking that, as the conversation proceeded, Don Benito, without being prompted, would perceive the propriety of the step.

But it was otherwise. At last catching his host's eye, Captain Delano, with a slight backward gesture of his thumb, whispered, "Don Benito, pardon me, but there is interference with the full expression of what I have to say to you."

Upon this the Spaniard changed countenance; which was imputed to his resenting the hint, as in some way a reflection upon his servant. After a moment's pause, he assured his guest that the black's remaining with them could be of no disservice; because since losing his officers he had made Babo (whose original office, it now appeared, had been captain of the slaves) not only his constant attendant and companion, but in all things his confidant.

After this, nothing more could be said; though, indeed, Captain Delano could hardly avoid some little tinge of irritation upon being left ungratified in so inconsiderable a wish, by one, too, for whom he intended such solid services. But it is only his querulousness, thought he; and so filling his glass he proceeded to business.

The price of the sails and other matters were fixed upon. But while this was being done, the American observed that, though his original offer of assistance had been hailed with hectic animation, yet now, when it was reduced to a business transaction, indifference and apathy were betrayed. Don Benito, in fact, appeared to submit to hearing the details more out of regard to common propriety, than from any impression that weighty benefit to himself and his voyage was involved.

Soon, his manner became still more reserved. The effort was vain to seek to draw him into social talk. Gnawed by his splenetic mood, he sat twitching his beard, while to little purpose the hand of his servant, mute as that on the wall, slowly pushed over the Canary.

Lunch being over, they sat down on the cushioned transom; the servant placing a pillow behind his master. The long continuance of the calm had now affected the atmosphere. Don Benito sighed heavily, as if for breath.

"Why not adjourn to the cuddy?" said Captain Delano. "There is more air there." But the host sat silent and motionless.

Meantime his servant knelt before him, with a large fan of feathers. And Francesco coming in on tiptoes, handed the negro a little cup of aromatic waters, with which at intervals he chafed his master's brow; smoothing the hair along the temples as a nurse does a child's. He spoke no word. He only rested his eye on his master's, as if, amid all Don Benito's distress, a little to refresh his spirit by the silent sight of fidelity.

Presently the ship's bell sounded two o'clock; and through the cabin windows a slight rippling of the sea was discerned; and from the desired direction.

"There," exclaimed Captain Delano, "I told you so, Don Benito, look!"

He had risen to his feet, speaking in a very animated tone, with a view the more to rouse his companion. But though the crimson curtain of the stern-window near him that moment fluttered against his pale cheek, Don Benito seemed to have even less welcome for the breeze than the calm.

Poor fellow, thought Captain Delano, bitter experience has taught him that one ripple does not make a wind, any more than one swallow a summer. But he is mistaken for once. I will get his ship in for him, and prove it.

Briefly alluding to his weak condition, he urged his host to remain quietly where he was, since he (Captain Delano) would with pleasure take upon himself the responsibility of making the best use of the wind.

Upon gaining the deck, Captain Delano started at the unexpected figure of Atufal, monumentally fixed at the threshold, like one of those sculptured porters of black marble guarding the porches of Egyptian tombs.

But this time the start was, perhaps, purely physical. Atufal's presence, singularly attesting docility even in sullenness, was contrasted with that of the hatchet-polishers, who in patience evinced their industry; while both spectacles showed, that lax as Don Benito's general authority might be, still, whenever he chose to exert it, no man so savage or colossal but must, more or less, bow.

Snatching a trumpet which hung from the bulwarks, with a free step Captain Delano advanced to the forward edge of the poop, issuing his orders in his best Spanish. The few sailors and many negroes, all equally pleased, obediently set about heading the ship towards the harbour.

While giving some directions about setting a lower stu'n-sail, suddenly Captain Delano heard a voice faithfully repeating his orders. Turning, he saw Babo, now for the time acting, under the pilot, his original part of the captain of the slaves. This assistance proved valuable. Tattered sails and warped yards were soon brought into some trim. And no brace or halyard was pulled but to the blithe songs of the inspirited negroes.

Good fellows, thought Captain Delano, a little training would make fine sailors of them. Why see, the very women pull and sing too. These must be some of those Ashantee negresses that make such capital soldiers, I've heard. But who's at the helm? I must have a good hand there.

He went to see.

The *San Dominick* steered with a cumbrous tiller, with large horizontal pulleys attached. At each pulley-end stood a subordinate black, and between then, at the tiller-head, the responsible post, a Spanish seaman, whose countenance evinced his due share in the general hopefulness and confidence at the oncoming of the breeze.

He proved the same man who had behaved with so shame-faced an air on the windlass.

"Ah,—it is you, my man," exclaimed Captain Delano—"well, no more sheep's eyes now;—look straight forward and keep the ship so. Good hand, I trust? And want to get into the harbour, don't you?"

The man assented with an inward chuckle, grasping the tiller-head firmly. Upon this, unperceived by the American, the two blacks eyed the sailor intently.

Finding all right at the helm, the pilot went forward to the forecastle, to see how matters stood there.

The ship now had way enough to breast the current. With the approach of evening, the breeze would be sure to freshen.

Having done all that was needed for the present, Captain Delano, giving his last orders to the sailors, turned aft to report affairs to Don Benito in the cabin; perhaps additionally incited to rejoin him by the hope of snatching a moment's private chat while the servant was engaged upon deck.

From opposite sides, there were, beneath the poop, two approaches to the cabin; one further forward than the other, and consequently communicating with a longer passage. Marking the servant still above, Captain Delano, taking the nighest entrance—the one last named, and at whose porch Atufal still stood—hurried on his way, till, arrived at the cabin threshold, he paused an instant, a little to recover from his eagerness. Then, with the words of his intended business upon his lips, he entered. As he advanced toward the seated Spaniard, he heard another footstep, keeping time with his. From the opposite door, a salver in hand, the servant was likewise advancing.

"Confound the faithful fellow," thought Captain Delano; "what a vexatious coincidence."

Possibly, the vexation might have been something different, were it not for the brisk confidence inspired by the breeze. But even as it was, he felt a slight twinge, from a sudden indefinite association in his mind of Babo with Atufal.

"Don Benito," said he, "I give you joy; the breeze will hold, and will increase. By the way, your tall man and time-piece, Atufal, stands without. By your order, of course?"

Don Benito recoiled, as if at some bland satirical touch, delivered with such adroit garnish of apparent good breeding as to present no handle for retort.

He is like one flayed alive, thought Captain Delano; where may one touch him without causing a shrink?

The servant moved before his master, adjusting a cushion; recalled to civility, the Spaniard stiffly replied: "You are right. The slave appears where you saw him, according to my command; which is, that if at the given hour I am below, he must take his stand and abide my coming."

"Ah now, pardon me, but that is treating the poor fellow like an ex-king indeed. Ah, Don Benito," smiling, "for all the licence you permit in some things, I fear lest, at bottom, you are a bitter hard master."

Again Don Benito shrank; and this time, as the good sailor thought, from a genuine twinge of his conscience.

Again conversation became constrained. In vain Captain Delano called attention to the now perceptible motion of the keel gently cleaving the sea; with lack-lustre eye, Don Benito returned words few and reserved.

By and by, the wind having steadily risen, and still blowing right into the harbour, bore the *San Dominick* swiftly on. Rounding a point of land, the sealer at a distance came into open view.

Meantime Captain Delano had again repaired to the deck, remaining there some time. Having at last altered the ship's course, so as to give the reef a wide berth, he returned for a few moments below.

I will cheer up my poor friend, this time, thought he.

"Better and better, Don Benito," he cried as he blithely re-entered: "there will soon be an end to your cares, at least for a while. For when, after a long, sad voyage, you know, the anchor drops into the haven, all its vast weight seems lifted from the captain's heart. We are getting on famously, Don Benito. My ship is in sight. Look through this side-light here; there she is; all a-taunt-o! The *Bachelor's Delight*, my good friend. Ah, how this wind braces one up. Come, you must take a cup of coffee with me this evening. My old steward will give you as fine a cup as ever any sultan tasted. What say you, Don Benito, will you?"

At first, the Spaniard glanced feverishly up, casting a longing look towards the sealer, while with mute concern his servant gazed into his face. Suddenly the old ague of coldness returned, and dropping back to his cushions he was silent.

"You do not answer. Come, all day you have been my host; would you have hospitality all on one side?"

"I cannot go," was the response.

"What? It will not fatigue you. The ships will lie together as near as they can, without swinging foul. It will be little more than stepping from deck to deck; which is but as from room to room. Come, come, you must not refuse me."

"I cannot go," decisively and repulsively repeated Don Benito.

Renouncing all but the last appearance of courtesy, with a sort of cadaverous sullenness, and biting his thin nails to the quick he glanced, almost glared, at his guest, as if impatient that a stranger's presence should interfere with the full indulgence of his morbid hour. Meantime the sound of the parted waters came more and more gurglingly and merrily in at the windows; as reproaching him for his dark spleen; as telling him that, sulk as he might, and go mad with it, nature cared not a jot; since, whose fault was it, pray?

But the foul mood was now at its depth, as the fair wind at its height.

There was something in the man so far beyond any mere unsociality or sourness previously evinced, that even the forbearing good-nature of his guest could no longer endure it. Wholly at a loss to account for such demeanour, and deeming sickness with eccentricity, however extreme, no adequate excuse, well satisfied, too, that nothing in his own conduct could justify it, Captain Delano's pride began to be roused. Himself became reserved. But all seemed one to the Spaniard. Quitting him, therefore, Captain Delano once more went to the deck.

The ship was now within less than two miles of the sealer. The whaleboat was seen darting over the interval.

To be brief, the two vessels, thanks to the pilot's skill, ere long in neighbourly style lay anchored together.

Before returning to his own vessel, Captain Delano had intended communicating to Don Benito the smaller details of the proposed services to be rendered. But, as it was, unwilling anew to subject himself to rebuffs, he resolved, now that he had seen the *San Dominick* safely moored, immediately to quit her, without further allusion to hospitality or business. Indefinitely postponing his ulterior plans, he would regulate his future actions according to future circumstances. His boat was ready to receive him; but his host still tarried below. Well, thought Captain Delano, if he has little breeding, the more need to show mine. He descended to the cabin to bid a ceremonious, and it may be, tacitly rebukeful adieu. But to his great satisfaction, Don Benito, as if he began to feel the weight of that treatment with which his slighted guest had, not indecorously, retaliated upon him, now supported by his servant, rose to his feet, and grasping Captain Delano's hand, stood tremulous; too much agitated to speak. But the good augury hence drawn was suddenly dashed, by his resuming all his previous reserve, with augmented gloom, as, with half-averted eyes, he silently reseated himself on his cushions. With a corresponding return of his own chilled feelings, Captain Delano bowed and withdrew.

He was hardly midway in the narrow corridor, dim as a tunnel, leading from the cabin to the stairs, when a sound, as of the tolling for execution in some jail-yard, fell on his ears. It was the echo of the ship's flawed bell, striking the hour, drearily reverberated in this subterranean vault. Instantly, by a fatality not to be withstood, his mind, responsive to the portent, swarmed with superstitious suspicions. He paused. In images far swifter than these sentences, the minutest details of all his former distrusts swept through him.

Hitherto, credulous good-nature had been too ready to furnish excuses for reasonable fears. Why was the Spaniard, so superfluously punctilious at times, now heedless of common propriety in not accompanying to the side his departing guest? Did indisposition forbid? Indisposition had not forbidden more irksome exertion that day. His last equivocal demeanour recurred. He had risen to his feet, grasped his guest's hand, motioned toward his hat; then, in an instant, all was eclipsed in sinister muteness and gloom. Did this imply one brief, repentant relenting at the final moment, from some iniquitous plot, followed by remorseless return to it? His last glance seemed to express a calamitous, yet acquiescent farewell to Captain Delano forever. Why decline the invitation to visit the sealer that evening? Or was the Spaniard less hardened than the Jew, who refrained not from supping at the board of him whom the same night he meant to betray? What imported all those day-long enigmas and contradictions, except they were intended to mystify, preliminary to some stealthy blow? Atufal, the pretended rebel, but punctual shadow, that moment lurked by the threshold without. He seemed a sentry, and more. Who, by his own confession, had stationed him there? Was the negro now lying in wait?

The Spaniard behind—his creature before: to rush from darkness to light was the involuntary choice.

The next moment, with clenched jaw and hand, he passed Atufal, and stood unharmed in the light. As he saw his trim ship lying peacefully at anchor, and almost within ordinary call; as he saw his household boat, with familiar faces in it, patiently rising and falling on the short waves by the *San Dominick*'s side; and then, glancing about the decks where he stood, saw the oakum-pickers still gravely plying their fingers; and heard the low, buzzing whistle and industrious hum of the hatchet-polishers, still bestirring themselves over their endless occupation; and more than all, as he saw the benign aspect of nature, taking her innocent repose in the evening; the screened sun in the quiet camp of the west shining out like the mild light from Abraham's tent; as charmed eye and ear took in all these, with the chained figure of the black, clenched jaw and hand relaxed. Once again he smiled at the phantoms which had mocked him, and felt something like a tinge of remorse, that, by harbouring them even for a moment, he should, by implication, have betrayed an atheist doubt of the ever-watchful Providence above.

There was a few minutes' delay, while, in obedience to his orders, the boat was being hooked along to the gangway. During this interval, a sort of saddened satisfaction stole over Captain Delano, at thinking of the kindly offices he had that day discharged for a stranger. Ah, thought he, after good actions one's conscience is never ungrateful, however much so the benefitted party may be.

Presently, his foot, in the first act of descent into the boat, pressed the first round of the side ladder, his face presented inward upon the deck. In the same moment, he heard his name courteously sounded; and, to his pleased surprise, saw Don Benito advancing—an unwonted energy in his air, as if, at the last moment, intent upon making amends for his recent discourtesy. With instinctive good feeling, Captain Delano, withdrawing his foot, turned and reciprocally advanced. As he did so, the Spaniard's nervous eagerness increased, but his vital energy failed; so that, the better to support him, the servant, placing his master's hand on his naked shoulder, and gently holding it there, formed himself into a sort of crutch.

When the two captains met, the Spaniard again fervently took the hand of the American, at the same time casting an earnest glance into his eyes, but, as before, too much overcome to speak.

I have done him wrong, self-reproachfully thought Captain Delano; his apparent coldness has deceived me; in no instance has he meant to offend.

Meantime, as if fearful that the continuance of the scene might too much unstring his master, the servant seemed anxious to terminate it. And so still presenting himself as a crutch, and walking between the two captains, he advanced with them towards the gangway; while still, as if full of kindly contrition, Don Benito would not let go the hand of Captain Delano, but retained it in his, across the black's body.

Soon they were standing by the side, looking over into the boat, whose crew turned up their curious eyes. Waiting a moment for the Spaniard to relinquish his hold, the now embarrassed Captain Delano lifted his foot, to overstep the threshold of the open gangway; but still Don Benito would not let go his hand. And yet, with an agitated tone, he said, "I can go no further; here I must bid you adieu. Adieu, my dear, dear Don Amasa. Go—go!" suddenly tearing his hand loose, "go, and God guard you better than me, my best friend."

Not unaffected, Captain Delano would now have lingered; but catching the meekly admonitory eye of the servant, with a hasty farewell he descended into his boat, followed by the continual adieus of Don Benito, standing rooted in the gangway.

Seating himself in the stern, Captain Delano, making a last salute, ordered the boat shoved off. The crew had their oars on end. The bowsman pushed the boat a sufficient distance for the oars to be lengthwise dropped. The instant that was done, Don Benito sprang over the bulwarks, falling at the feet of Captain Delano; at the same time calling towards his ship, but in tones so frenzied, that none in the boat could understand him. But, as if not equally obtuse, three sailors, from three different and distant parts of the ship, splashed into the sea, swimming after their captain, as if intent upon his rescue.

The dismayed officer of the boat eagerly asked what this meant. To which, Captain Delano, turning a disdainful smile upon the unaccountable Spaniard, answered that, for his part, he neither knew nor cared; but it seemed as if Don Benito had taken it into his head to produce the impression among his people that the boat wanted to kidnap him. "Or else—give way for your lives," he wildly added, starting at a clattering hubbub in the ship, above which rang the tocsin of the hatchet-polishers; and seizing Don Benito by the throat he added, "this plotting pirate means murder!" Here, in apparent verification of the words, the servant, a dagger in his hand, was seen on the rail overhead, poised, in the act of leaping, as if with desperate fidelity to befriend his master to the last; while, seemingly to aid the black, the three white sailors were trying to clamber into the hampered bow. Meantime, the whole host of negroes, as if inflamed at the sight of their jeopardized captain, impended in one sooty avalanche over the bulwarks.

All this, with what preceded, and what followed, occurred with such involutions of rapidity, that past, present, and future seemed one.

Seeing the negro coming, Captain Delano had flung the Spaniard aside, almost in the very act of clutching him, and by the unconscious recoil, shifting his place, with arms thrown up, so promptly grappled the servant in his descent, that with dagger presented at Captain Delano's heart, the black seemed of purpose to have leaped there as to his mark. But the weapon was wrenched away, and the assailant dashed down into the bottom of the boat, which now, with disentangled oars, began to speed through the sea.

At this juncture, the left hand of Captain Delano, on one side, again clutched the half-reclining Don Benito, heedless that he was in a speechless faint, while his right foot, on the other side, ground the prostrate negro; and his right arm pressed for added speed on the after oar, his eye bent forward, encouraging his men to their utmost.

But here, the officer of the boat, who had at last succeeded in beating off the towing sailors, and was now, with face turned aft, assisting the bowsman at his oar, suddenly called to Captain Delano, to see what the black was about; while a Portuguese oarsman shouted to him to give heed to what the Spaniard was saying.

Glancing down at his feet, Captain Delano saw the freed hand of the servant aiming with a second dagger—a small one, before concealed in his wool—with this he was snakishly writhing up from the boat's bottom, at the heart of his master, his countenance lividly vindictive, expressing the centered purpose of his soul; while the Spaniard, half-choked, was vainly shrinking away, with husky words, incoherent to all but the Portuguese.

That moment, across the long-benighted mind of Captain Delano, a flash of revelation swept, illuminating, in unanticipated clearness, his host's whole mysterious demeanor, with every enigmatic event of the day, as well as the entire past voyage of the *San Dominick*. He smote Babo's hand down, but his own heart smote him harder. With infinite pity he withdrew his hold from Don Benito. Not Captain Delano, but Don Benito, the black, in leaping into the boat, had intended to stab.

Both the black's hands were held, as, glancing up towards the *San Dominick*, Captain Delano, now with scales dropped from his eyes, saw the negroes, not in misrule, not in tumult, not as if frantically concerned for Don Benito, but with mask torn away, flourishing hatchets, and knives, in ferocious piratical revolt. Like delirious black dervishes, the six Ashantees danced on the poop. Prevented by their foes from springing into the water, the Spanish boys were hurrying up to the top-most spars, while such of the few Spanish sailors, not already in the sea, less alert, were descried, helplessly mixed in, on deck, with the blacks.

Meantime Captain Delano hailed his own vessel, ordering the ports up, and the guns run out. But by this time the cable of the *San Dominick* had been cut; and the fag-end, in lashing out, whipped away the canvas shroud about the beak, suddenly revealing, as the bleached hull swung round towards the open ocean, death for the figure-head, in a human skeleton; chalky comment on the chalked words below, *"Follow your leader."*

At the sight, Don Benito, covering his face, wailed out:

" 'Tis he, Aranda! my murdered, unburied friend!"

Upon reaching the sealer, calling for ropes, Captain Delano bound the negro, who made no resistance, and had him hoisted to the deck. He would then have assisted the now almost helpless Don Benito up the side; but Don Benito, wan as he was, refused to move, or be moved, until the negro should have been first put below out of view. When, presently assured that it was done, he no more shrank from the ascent.

The boat was immediately dispatched back to pick up the three swimming sailors. Meantime, the guns were in readiness, though, owing to the *San Dominick* having glided somewhat astern of the sealer, only the aftermost one could be brought to bear. With this, they fired six times; thinking to cripple the fugitive ship by bringing down her spars. But only a few inconsiderable ropes were shot away. Soon the ship was beyond the gun's range, steering broad out of the bay; the blacks thickly clustering round the bowsprit, one moment with taunting cries towards the whites, the next with upthrown gestures hailing the now dusky moors of ocean—cawing crows escaped from the hand of the fowler.

The first impulse was to slip the cables and give chase. But, upon second thoughts, to pursue with whale-boat and yawl seemed more promising.

Upon inquiring of Don Benito what fire-arms they had on board the *San Dominick*, Captain Delano was answered that they had none that could be used; because, in the earlier stages of the mutiny, a cabin-passenger, since dead, had secretly put out of order the locks of what few muskets there were. But with all his remaining strength, Don Benito entreated the American not to give chase, either with ship or boat; for the negroes had already proved themselves such desperadoes, that, in case of a present assault, nothing but a total massacre of the whites could be looked for. But, regarding this warning as coming from one whose spirit had been crushed by misery, the American did not give up his design.

The boats were got ready and armed. Captain Delano ordered his men into them. He was going himself when Don Benito grasped his arm.

"What! have you saved my life, Señor, and are you now going to throw away your own?"

The officers also, for reasons connected with their interests and those of the voyage, and a duty owing to the owners, strongly objected against their commander's going. Weighing their remonstrances a moment, Captain Delano felt bound to remain; appointing his chief mate—an athletic and resolute man, who had been a privateer's-man—to head the party. The more to encourage the sailors, they were told, that the Spanish captain considered his ship good as lost; that she and her cargo, including some gold and silver, were worth more than a thousand doubloons. Take her, and no small part should be theirs. The sailors replied with a shout.

The fugitives had now almost gained an offing. It was nearly night; but the moon was rising. After hard, prolonged pulling, the boats came up on the ship's quarters, at a suitable distance laying upon their oars to discharge their muskets. Having no bullets to return, the negroes sent their yells. But, upon the second volley, Indian-like, they hurled their hatchets. One took off a sailor's fingers. Another struck the whale-boat's bow, cutting off the rope there, and remaining stuck in the gunwale like a woodman's axe. Snatching it, quivering from its lodgment, the mate hurled it back. The returned gauntlet now stuck in the ship's broken quarter-gallery, and so remained.

The negroes giving too hot a reception, the whites kept a more respectful distance. Hovering now just out of reach of the hurtling hatchets, they, with a view to the close encounter which must soon come, sought to decoy the blacks into entirely disarming themselves of their most murderous weapons in a hand-to-hand fight, by foolishly flinging them, as missiles, short of the mark, into the sea. But, ere long, perceiving the stratagem, the negroes desisted, though not before many of them had to replace their lost hatchets with handspikes; an exchange which, as counted upon, proved, in the end, favourable to the assailants.

Meantime, with a strong wind, the ship still clove the water; the boats alternately falling behind, and pulling up, to discharge fresh volleys.

The fire was mostly directed towards the stern, since there, chiefly, the negroes, at present, were clustering. But to kill or maim the negroes was not the object. To take them, with the ship, was the object. To do it, the ship must be boarded; which could not be done by boats while she was sailing so fast.

A thought now struck the mate. Observing the Spanish boys still aloft, high as they could get, he called to them to descend to the yards, and cut adrift the sails. It was done. About this time, owing to causes hereafter to be shown, two Spaniards, in the dress of sailors, and conspicuously showing themselves, were killed; not by volleys, but by deliberate marksman's shots; while, as it afterwards appeared, by one of the general discharges, Atufal, the black, and the Spaniard at the helm likewise were killed. What now, with the loss of sails, and loss of leaders, the ship became unmanageable to the negroes.

With creaking masts, she came heavily round to the wind; the prow slowly swinging into view of the boats, its skeleton gleaming in the horizontal moonlight, and casting a gigantic ribbed shadow upon the water. One extended arm of the ghost seemed beckoning the whites to avenge it.

"Follow your leader!" cried the mate; and, one on each bow, the boats boarded. Sealing-spears and cutlasses crossed hatchets and handspikes. Huddled upon the long-boat amidships, the negresses raised a wailing chant, whose chorus was the clash of the steel.

For a time, the attack wavered; the negroes wedging themselves to beat it back; the half-repelled sailors, as yet unable to gain a footing, fighting as troopers in the saddle, one leg sideways flung over the bulwarks, and one without, plying their cutlasses like carters' whips. But in vain. They were almost overborne, when, rallying themselves into a squad as one man, with a huzza, they sprang inboard, where, entangled, they involuntarily separated again. For a few breaths' space, there was a vague, muffled, inner sound, as of submerged sword-fish rushing hither and thither through shoals of black-fish. Soon, in a reunited band, and joined by the Spanish seamen, the whites came to the surface, irresistibly driving the negroes towards the stern. But a barricade of casks and sacks, from side to side, had been thrown up by the main-mast. Here the negroes faced about, and though scorning peace or truce, yet fain would have had respite. But, without pause, overleaping the barrier, the unflagging sailors again closed. Exhausted, the blacks now fought in despair. Their red tongues lolled, wolf-like, from their black mouths. But the pale sailors' teeth were set; not a word was spoken; and in five minutes more, the ship was won.

Nearly a score of the negroes were killed. Exclusive of those by the balls, many were mangled; their wounds—mostly inflicted by the long-edged sealing-spears, resembling those shaven ones of the English at Preston Pans, made by the poled scythes of the Highlanders. On the other side, none were killed, though several were wounded; some severely, including the mate. The surviving negroes were temporarily secured, and the ship, towed back into the harbour at midnight, once more lay anchored.

Omitting the incidents and arrangements ensuing, suffice it that, after two days spent in refitting, the ships sailed in company for Concepcion, in Chile, and thence for Lima, in Peru; where, before the vice-regal courts, the whole affair, from the beginning, underwent investigation.

Though, midway on the passage, the ill-fated Spaniard, relaxed from constraint, showed some signs of regaining health with free-will; yet, agreeably to his own foreboding, shortly before arriving at Lima, he relapsed, finally becoming so reduced as to be carried ashore in arms. Hearing of his story and plight, one of the many religious institutions of the City of Kings opened an hospitable refuge to him, where both physician and priest were his nurses, and a member of the order volunteered to be his one special guardian and consoler, by night and by day.

The following extracts, translated from one of the official Spanish documents, will, it is hoped, shed light on the preceding narrative, as well as, in the first place, reveal the true port of departure and true history of the *San Dominick*'s voyage, down to the time of her touching at the island of Santa Maria.

But, ere the extracts come, it may be well to preface them with a remark.

The document selected, from among many others, for partial translation, contains the deposition of Benito Cereno; the first taken in the case. Some disclosures therein were, at the time, held dubious for both learned and natural reasons. The tribunal inclined to the opinion that the deponent, not undisturbed in his mind by recent events, raved of some things which could never have happened. But subsequent depositions of the surviving sailors, bearing out the revelations of their captain in several of the strangest particulars, gave credence to the rest. So that the tribunal, in its final decision, rested its capital sentences upon statements which, had they lacked confirmation, it would have deemed it but duty to reject.

I, DON JOSÉ DE ABOS AND PADILLA, *His Majesty's Notary for the Royal Revenue, and Register of this Province, and Notary Public of the Holy Crusade of this Bishoprick, &c.*

Do certify and declare, as much as is requisite in law, that, in the criminal cause commenced the twenty-fourth of the month of September, in the year seventeen hundred and ninety-nine, against the negroes of the ship San Dominick, *the following declaration before me was made:*

Declaration of the first Witness, DON BENITO CERENO.

The same day and month and year, His Honour, Doctor Juan Martinez de Rozas, Councillor of the Royal Audience of this Kingdom, and learned in the law of this Intendency, ordered the captain of the ship San Dominick, *Don Benito Cereno, to appear; which he did in his litter, attended by the monk Infelez; of whom he received the oath, which he took by God, our Lord, and a Sign of the Cross; under which he promised to tell the truth of whatever he should know and should be asked;—and being interrogated agreeably to the tenor of the act, commencing the process, he said, that on the twentieth of May last, he set sail with his ship from the port of Valparaiso, bound to that of Callao; loaded with the produce of the country beside thirty cases of hardware and one hundred and sixty blacks, of both sexes, mostly belonging to Don Alexandro Aranda, gentleman, of the City of Mendoza; that the crew of the ship consisted of thirty-six men, beside the persons who went as passengers; that the negroes were in part as follows:*

[Here, in the original, follows a list of some fifty names, descriptions, and ages, compiled from certain recovered documents of Aranda's and also from recollections of the deponent, from which portions only are extracted.]

—One, from about eighteen to nineteen years, named José, and this was the man that waited upon his master, Don Alexandro, and who speaks well the Spanish, having served him four or five years; * * * a mulatto, named Francesco, the cabin steward, of a good person and voice having sung in the Valparaiso churches, native of the province of Buenos Ayres, aged about thirty-five years. * * * A smart negro, named Dago, who had been for many years a grave-digger among the Spaniards, aged forty-six years. * * * Four old negroes, born in Africa, from sixty to seventy, but sound, calkers by trade, whose names are as follows:—the first was named Mure, and he was killed (as was also his son named Diamelo); the second, Nacta; the third, Yola, likewise killed; the fourth, Ghofan; and six full-grown negroes, aged from thirty to forty-five, all raw, and born among the Ashantees —Matinqui, Yau, Lecbe, Mapenda, Yambaio, Akim, four of whom were killed; * * * a powerful negro named Atufal, who being supposed to have been a chief in Africa, his owner set great store by him. * * * And a small negro of Senegal, but some years among the Spaniards, aged about thirty, which negro's name was Babo; * * * that he does not remember the names of the others, but that still expecting the residue of Don Alexandro's papers will be found, will then take due account of them all, and remit to the court; * * * and thirty-nine women and children of all ages.

[The catalogue over, the deposition goes on:]

* * * That all the negroes slept upon deck, as is customary in this navigation, and none wore fetters, because the owner, his friend Aranda, told him that they were all tractable; * * * that on the seventh day after leaving port, at three o'clock in the morning, all the Spaniards being asleep except two officers at the watch, who were the boat-swain, Juan Robles, and the carpenter, Juan Bautista Gayete, and the helmsman and his boy, the negroes revolted suddenly, wounded dangerously the boat-swain and the carpenter, and successively killed eighteen men of those who were sleeping upon deck, some with hand-spikes and hatchets, and others by throwing them alive overboard, after tying them; that of the Spaniards upon deck, they left about seven, as he thinks, alive and tied, to manœuvre the ship, and three or four more, who hid themselves, remained also alive. Although in the act of revolt the negroes made themselves masters of the hatchway, six or seven wounded went through it to the cockpit, without any hindrance on their part; that during the act of revolt, the mate and another person, whose name he does not recollect, attempted to come up through the hatchway, but being quickly wounded, were obliged to return to the cabin; that the deponent resolved at break of day to come up the companion-way, where the negro Babo was, being the ringleader, and Atufal, who assisted him, and having spoken to them, exhorted them to cease committing such atrocities asking them, at the same time, what they wanted and intended to do, offering, himself, to obey their commands; that notwithstanding this,

they threw, in his presence, three men, alive and tied, overboard; that they told the deponent to come up, and that they would not kill him; which having done, the negro Babo asked him whether there were in those seas any negro countries where they might be carried, and he answered them, No; that the negro Babo afterwards told him to carry them to Senegal, or to the neighbouring islands of St. Nicholas; and he answered, that this was impossible, on account of the great distance, the necessity involved of rounding Cape Horn, the bad condition of the vessel, the want of provisions, sails, and water; but that the negro Babo replied to him he must carry them in any way; that they would do and conform themselves to anything the deponent should require as to eating and drinking; that after a long conference, being absolutely compelled to please them, for they threatened to kill all the whites if they were not, at all events, carried to Senegal, he told them that what was most wanting for the voyage was water; that they would go near the coast to take it, and thence they would proceed on their course; that the negro Babo agreed to it; and the deponent steered towards the intermediate ports, hoping to meet some Spanish or foreign vessel that would save them; that within ten or eleven days they saw the land, and continued their course by it in the vicinity of Nasca; that the deponent observed that the negroes were now restless and mutinous, because he did not effect the taking in of water, the negro Babo having required, with threats, that it should be done, without fail, the following day; he told him he saw plainly that the coast was steep, and the rivers designated in the maps were not to be found, with other reasons suitable to the circumstances; that the best way would be to go to the island of Santa Maria, where they might water easily, it being a solitary island, as the foreigners did; that the deponent did not go to Pisco, that was near, nor make any other port of the coast, because the negro Babo had intimated to him several times, that he would kill all the whites the very moment he should perceive any city, town, or settlement of any kind on the shores to which they should be carried: that having determined to go to the island of Santa Maria, as the deponent had planned, for the purpose of trying whether, on the passage or near the island itself, they could find any vessel that should favour them, or whether he could escape from it in a boat to the neighbouring coast of Arauco, to adopt the necessary means he immediately changed his course, steering for the island; that the negroes Babo and Atufal held daily conferences, in which they discussed what was necessary for their design of returning to Senegal, whether they were to kill all the Spaniards, and particularly the deponent; that eight days after parting from the coast of Nasca, the deponent being on the watch a little after day-break, and soon after the negroes had their meeting, the negro Babo came to the place where the deponent was, and told him that he had determined to kill his master, Don Alexandro Aranda, both because he and his companions could not otherwise be sure of their liberty, and that to keep the seamen in subjection, he wanted to prepare a warning of what road they should be made to take *did they or any of them oppose him; and that, by means of the death of Don Alexandro, that warning would best be given; but, that what this last meant, the deponent did not at the time comprehend, nor could not, further than the death of Don Alexandro was intended; and moreover the negro Babo proposed to the deponent to call the mate Raneds, who was sleeping in the cabin, before the thing was done, for fear, as the deponent understood it, that the mate, who was a good navigator, should not be killed with Don Alexandro and the rest; that the deponent, who was the friend, from youth, of Don Alexandro, prayed and conjured, but all was useless; for the negro Babo answered him that the thing could not be prevented, and that all the Spaniards risked their death if they should attempt to frustrate his will in this matter, or any other; that, in this conflict, the deponent called the mate, Raneds, who was forced to go apart, and immediately the negro Babo commanded the Ashantee Matinqui and the Ashantee Lecbe to go and commit the murder; that those two went down with hatchets to the berth of Don Alexandro; that, yet half alive and mangled, they dragged him on deck; that they were going to throw him overboard in that state, but the negro Babo stopped them, bidding the murder be completed on the deck before him, which was done, when, by his orders, the body was carried below, forward; that nothing more was seen of it by the deponent for three days; * * * that Don Alonzo Sidonia, an old man, long resident at Valparaiso, and lately appointed to a civil office in Peru, whither he had taken passage, was at the time sleeping in the berth opposite Don Alexandro's; that awakening at his cries, surprised by them, and at the sight of the negroes with their bloody hatchets in their hands, he threw himself into the sea through a window which was near him, and was drowned, without it being in the power of the deponent to assist or take him up; * * * that a short time after killing Aranda, they brought upon deck his cousin-german, of middle-age, Don Francisco Masa, of Mendoza, and the young Don Joaquin, Marques de Aramboalaza, then lately from Spain, with his Spanish servant Ponce, and the three young clerks of Aranda, José Morairi, Lorenzo Bargas, and Hermenegildo Gandix, all of Cadiz; that Don Joaquin and Hermenegildo Gandix, the negro Babo, for purposes hereafter to appear, preserved alive; but Don Francisco Masa, José Morairi, and Lorenzo Bargas, with Ponce the servant, beside the boat-swain, Juan Robles, the boat-swain's mates, Manuel Viscaya and Roderigo Hurta, and four of the sailors, the negro Babo ordered to be thrown alive into the sea, although they made no resistance, nor begged for anything else but mercy; that the boat-swain Juan Robles, who knew how to swim, kept the longest above water, making acts of contrition, and, in the last words he uttered, charged this deponent to cause mass to be said for his soul to our Lady of Succour; * * * that, during the three days which followed, the deponent, uncertain what fate had befallen the remains of Don Alexandro, frequently asked the negro Babo where they were, and, if still on board, whether they were to be preserved for interment ashore, entreating him so to order it;*

that the negro Babo answered nothing till the fourth day, when at sunrise, the deponent coming on deck, the negro Babo showed him a skeleton, which had been substituted for the ship's proper figurehead—the image of Cristobal Colon, the discoverer of the New World; that the negro Babo asked him whose skeleton that was, and whether from its whiteness, he should not think it a white's; that, upon his covering his face the negro Babo, coming close, said words to this effect: "Keep faith with the blacks from here to Senegal, or you shall in spirit, as now in body, follow your leader," pointing to the prow; * * * that the same morning the negro Babo took by succession each Spaniard forward, and asked him whose skeleton that was, and whether, from its whiteness, he should not think it a white's; that each Spaniard covered his face; that then to each the negro Babo repeated the words in the first place said to the deponent; * * * that they (the Spaniards), being then assembled aft, the negro Babo harangued them, saying that he had now done all; that the deponent (as navigator for the negroes) might pursue his course, warning him and all of them that they should, soul and body, go the way of Don Alexandro, if he saw them (the Spaniards) speak or plot anything against them (the negroes), a threat which was repeated every day, that, before the events last mentioned, they had tied the cook to throw him overboard, for it is not known what thing they heard him speak, but finally the negro Babo spared his life, at the request of the deponent; that a few days after, the deponent, endeavouring not to omit any means to preserve the lives of the remaining whites, spoke to the negroes peace and tranquillity, and agreed to draw up a paper, signed by the deponent and the sailors who could write, as also by the negro Babo, for himself and all the blacks, in which the deponent obliged himself to carry them to Senegal, and they not to kill any more, and he formally to make over to them the ship, with the cargo, with which they were for that time satisfied and quieted. * * * But the next day, the more surely to guard against the sailors' escape, the negro Babo commanded all the boats to be destroyed but the long-boat, which was unseaworthy, and another, a cutter in good condition, which knowing it would yet be wanted for towing the water casks, he had it lowered down into the hold. * * *

[Various particulars of the prolonged and perplexed navigation ensuing here follow, with incidents of a calamitous calm, from which portion one passage is extracted, to wit:]

—That on the fifth day of the calm, all on board suffering much from the heat, and want of water, and five having died in fits, and mad, the negroes became irritable, and for a chance gesture, which they deemed suspicious—though it was harmless—made by the mate, Raneds, to the deponent in the act of handing a quadrant, they killed him; but that for this they afterwards were sorry, the mate being the only remaining navigator on board, except the deponent.

* * *

—That omitting other events which daily happened, and which can only serve uselessly to recall past misfortunes and conflicts, after seventy-three days' navigation, reckoned from the time they sailed from Nasca, during which they navigated under a scanty allowance of water, and were afflicted with the calms before mentioned, they at last arrived at the island of Santa Maria, on the seventeenth of the month of August, at about six o'clock in the afternoon, at which hour they cast anchor very near the American ship, Bachelor's Delight, which lay in the same bay, commanded by the generous Captain Amasa Delano; but at six o'clock in the morning, they had already described the port, and the negroes became uneasy, as soon as at distance they saw the ship, not having expected to see one there; that the negro Babo pacified them, assuring them that no fear need be had; that straightway he ordered the figure on the bow to be covered with canvas, as for repairs, and had the decks a little set in order; that for a time the negro Babo and the negro Atufal conferred; that the negro Atufal was for sailing away, but the negro Babo would not, and, by himself, cast about what to do; that at last he came to the deponent, proposing to him to say and do all that the deponent declares to have said and done to the American captain; * * * that the negro Babo warned him that if he varied in the least, or uttered any word, or gave any look that should give the least intimation of the past events or present state, he would instantly kill him, with all his companions, showing a dagger, which he carried hid, saying something which, as he understood it, meant that that dagger would be alert as his eyes; that the negro Babo then announced the plan to all his companions, which pleased them; that he then, the better to disguise the truth, devised many expedients, in some of them uniting deceit and defense; that of this sort was the device of the six Ashantees before named, who were his bravoes; that them he stationed on the break of the poop, as if to clean certain hatchets (in cases, which were part of the cargo), but in reality to use them, and distribute them at need, and at a given word he told them; that, among other devices, was the device of presenting Atufal, his right hand man, as chained, though in a moment the chains could be dropped; that in every particular he informed the deponent what part he was expected to enact in every device, and what story he was to tell on every occasion, always threatening him with instant death if he varied in the least: that, conscious that many of the negroes would be turbulent, the negro Babo appointed the four aged negroes who were calkers, to keep what domestic order they could on the decks; that again and again he harangued the Spaniards and his companions, informing them of his intent, and of his devices, and of the invented story that this deponent was to tell; charging them lest any of them varied from that story; that these arrangements were made and matured during the interval of two or three hours, between their first sighting the ship and the arrival on board of Captain

Amasa Delano; that this happened about half-past seven o'clock in the morning, Captain Amasa Delano coming in his boat, and all gladly receiving him; that the deponent, as well as he could force himself, acting then the part of principal owner, and a free captain of the ship, told Captain Amasa Delano, when called upon, that he came from Buenos Ayres, bound to Lima, with three hundred negroes; that off Cape Horn, and in a subsequent fever, many negroes had died; that also, by similar casualties, all the sea-officers and the greatest part of the crew had died.

* * *

[And so the deposition goes on, circumstantially recounting the fictitious story dictated to the deponent by Babo, and through the deponent imposed upon Captain Delano; and also recounting the friendly offers of Captain Delano, with other things, but all of which is here omitted. After the fictitious story, etc., the deposition proceeds:]

—that that generous Captain Delano remained on board all the day, till he left the ship anchored at six o'clock in the evening, deponent speaking to him always of his pretended misfortunes, under the forementioned principles, without having had it in his power to tell a single word, or give him the least hint, that he might know the truth and state of things; because the negro Babo, performing the office of an officious servant with all the appearance of submission of the humble slave, did not leave the deponent one moment; that this was in order to observe the deponent's actions and words, for the negro Babo understands well the Spanish; and besides, there were thereabouts some others who were constantly on the watch, and likewise understood the Spanish; * * * that upon one occasion, while deponent was standing on the deck conversing with Amasa Delano, by a secret sign the negro Babo drew him (the deponent) aside, the act appearing as if originating with the deponent; that then, he being drawn aside, the negro Babo proposed to him to gain from Amasa Delano full particulars about his ship, and crew, and arms; that the deponent asked "for what?" that the negro Babo answered he might conceive; that, grieved at the prospect of what might overtake the generous Captain Amasa Delano, the deponent at first refused to ask the desired questions, and used every argument to induce the negro Babo to give up this new design; that the negro Babo showed the point of his dagger; that, after the information had been obtained, the negro Babo again drew him aside, telling him that that very night he (the deponent) would be captain of two ships, instead of one, for that, great part of the American's ship's crew being to be absent fishing, the six Ashantees without any one else, would easily take it; that at this time he said other things to the same purpose; that no entreaties availed; that, before Amasa Delano's coming on board, no hint had been given touching the capture of the American ship; that to prevent this project the deponent

was powerless; * * * —that in some things his memory is confused, he cannot distinctly recall every event; * * * that as soon as they had cast anchor at six o'clock in the evening, as has before been stated, the American captain took leave, to return to his vessel; that upon a sudden impulse, which the deponent believes to have come from God and his angels, he, after the farewell had been said, followed the generous Captain Amasa Delano as far as the gunwale, where he stayed, under pretence of taking leave until Amasa Delano should have been seated in his boat; that on shoving off, the deponent sprang from the gunwale into the boat and fell into it, he knows not how, God guarding him; that—

[Here, in the original, follows the account of what further happened at the escape, and how the *San Dominick* was retaken, and of the passage to the coast; including in the recital many expressions of "eternal gratitude" to the "generous Captain Amasa Delano." The deposition then proceeds with recapitulatory remarks, and a partial renumeration of the negroes, making record of their individual part in the past events, with a view to furnishing, according to command of the court, the data whereon to found the criminal sentences to be pronounced. From this portion is the following:]

—That he believes that all the negroes, though not in the first place knowing to the design of revolt, when it was accomplished, approved it. * * * That the negro José, eighteen years old, and in the personal service of Don Alexandro, was the one who communicated the information to the negro Babo about the state of things in the cabin, before the revolt; that this is known, because, in the preceding nights, he used to come from his berth, which was under his master's, in the cabin, to the deck where the ringleader and his associates were, and had secret conversations with the negro Babo, in which he was several times seen by the mate; that one night, the mate drove him away twice; * * * that this same negro José was the one who, without being commanded to do so by the negro Babo, as Lecbe and Martinqui were, stabbed his master, Don Alexandro, after he had been dragged half lifeless to the deck; * * * that the mulatto steward, Francesco, was of the first band of revolters, that he was, in all things, the creature and tool of the negro Babo; that, to make his court, he, just before a repast in the cabin, proposed to the negro Babo, poisoning a dish for the generous Captain Amasa Delano; this is known and believed, because the negroes have said it; but that the negro Babo, having another design, forbade Francesco; * * * that the Ashantee Lecbe was one of the worst of them; for that, on the day the ship was retaken, he assisted in the defence of her, with a hatchet in each hand, with one of which he wounded in the breast, the chief mate of Amasa Delano, in the first act of boarding; this all knew; that, in sight of the deponent, Lecbe struck with a hatchet, Don Francisco Masa, when, by the negro Babo's orders, he was carrying him to throw him overboard alive, beside participating in the murder, before mentioned, of Don

Alexandro Aranda, and others of the cabin-passengers; that, owing to the fury with which the Ashantees fought in the engagement with the boats, but this Lecbe and Yau survived; that Yau was bad as Lecbe; that Yau was the man who, by Babo's command, willingly prepared the skeleton of Don Alexandro, in a way the negroes afterwards told the deponent, but which he, so long as reason is left him, can never divulge; that Yau and Lecbe were the two who, in a calm by night, riveted the skeleton to the bow; this also the negroes told him; that the negro Babo was he who traced the in-scription below it; that the negro Babo was the plotter from first to last; he ordered every murder, and was the helm and keel of the revolt; that Atufal was his lieutenant in all; but Atufal, with his own hand, committed no murder; nor did the negro Babo; * * * that Atufal was shot, being killed in the fight with the boats, ere boarding; * * * that the negresses of age, were known to the revolt, and testified themselves satisfied at the death of their master, Don Alexandro; that, had the negroes not restrained them, they would have tortured to death, instead of simply killing, the Spaniards slain by command of the negro Babo; that the negresses used their utmost influ-ence to have the deponent made away with; that, in the various acts of murder, they sang songs and danced—not gaily, but solemnly; and before the engagement with the boats, as well as during the action, they sang melancholy songs to the negroes, and that this melancholy tone was more inflaming than a different one would have been, and was so intended; that all this is believed, because the negroes have said it;—that of the thirty-six men of the crew, exclusive of the passengers (all of whom are now dead), which the deponent had knowledge of, six only remained alive, with four cabin-boys and ship-boys, not included with the crew; * * * —that the ne-groes broke an arm of one of the cabin-boys and gave him strokes with hatchets.

[Then follow various random disclosures referring to various periods of time. The following are extracted:]

—That during the presence of Captain Amasa Delano on board, some at-tempts were made by the sailors, and one by Hermenegildo Candix, to convey hints to him of the true state of affairs; but that these attempts were ineffectual, owing to fear of incurring death, and furthermore, owing to the devices which offered contradictions to the true state of affairs, as well as the owing to the generosity and piety of Amasa Delano incapable of sounding such wickedness; * * * that Luys Galgo, a sailor about sixty years of age, and formerly of the King's navy, was one of those who sought to convey tokens to Captain Amasa Delano; but his intent, though undiscovered, being suspected, he was, on a pretence, made to retire out of sight, and at last into the hold and there was made away with. This the negroes have since said; * * * that one of the ship-boys, feeling from Captain Amasa Delano's presence, some hopes of release, and not having enough prudence,

dropped some chance word respecting his expectations, which being over-heard and understood by a slave-boy with whom he was eating at the time, the latter struck him on the head with a knife, inflicting a bad wound, but of which the boy is now healing; that likewise, not long before the ship was brought to anchor, one of the seamen, steering at the time, endangered himself by letting the blacks remark some expression in his countenance, arising from a similar cause to the above; but this sailor, by his heedful after conduct, escaped; * * * that these statements are made to show the court that from the beginning to the end of the revolt, it was impossible for the deponent and his men to act otherwise than they did; * * * —that the third clerk, Hermenegildo Gandix, who before had been forced to live among the seamen, wearing a seaman's habit, and in all respects appearing to be one for the time, he, Gandix, was killed by a musket ball fired through mistake from the boats before boarding; having in his fright run up the mizzen-rigging, calling to the boats—"don't board," lest upon their boarding the negroes should kill him; that this inducing the Americans to believe he some way favoured the cause of the negroes, they fired two balls at him, so that he fell wounded from the rigging, and was drowned in the sea; * * * —that the young Don Joaquin, Marques de Aramboalaza, like Hermenegildo Gandix, the third clerk, was degraded to the office and appearance of a common seaman; that upon one occasion when Don Joaquin shrank, the negro Babo commanded the Ashantee Lecbe to take tar and heat it, and pour it upon Don Joaquin's hands; * * * —that Don Joaquin was killed owing to another mistake of the Americans, but one impossible to be avoided, as upon the approach of the boats, Don Joaquin, with a hatchet tied edge out and upright to his hand, was made by the negroes to appear on the bulwarks; whereupon, seen with arms in his hands, and in a questionable attitude, he was shot for a renegade seaman; * * * that on the person of Don Joaquin was found secreted a jewel, which, by papers that were discovered, proved to have been meant for the shrine of our Lady of Mercy in Lima; a votive offering, beforehand prepared and guarded, to attest his gratitude, when he should have landed in Peru, his last destination for the safe conclusion of his entire voyage from Spain; * * * —that the jewel, with the other effects of the late Don Joaquin, is in the custody of the Hospital de Sacerdotes, awaiting the disposition of the honourable court; * * * —that, owing to the condition of the deponent, as well as the haste in which the boats departed for the attack, the Americans were not forewarned that there were, among the apparent crew, a passenger and one of the clerks disguised by the negro Babo; * * * —that, beside the negroes killed in the action, some were killed after the capture and re-anchoring at night, when shackled to the ring-bolts on deck; that these deaths were committed by the sailors, ere they could be prevented. That so soon as informed of it, Captain Amasa Delano used all his authority, and in particular with his own hand, struck down Martinez Gola, who, *having found a razor in the pocket of an old jacket of his, which one of the shackled negroes had on, was aiming it at the negro's throat; that the noble Captain Amasa Delano also wrenched from the hand of Bartholomew Barlo a dagger, secreted at the time of the massacre of the whites, with which he was in the act of stabbing a shackled negro, who, the same day, with another negro had thrown him down and jumped upon him; * * * —that, for all the events befalling through so long a time, during which the ship was in the hands of the negro Babo, he cannot here give account; but that, what he has said is the most substantial of what occurs to him at present, and is the truth under the oath which he has taken; which declaration he affirmed and ratified, after hearing it read to him.*

He said that he is twenty-nine years of age, and broken in body and mind; that when finally dismissed by the court, he shall not return home to Chile, but betake himself to the monastery of Mount Agonia without; and signed with his honour, and crossed himself, and, for the time, departed as he came, in his litter, with the monk Infelez, to the Hospital de Sacerdotes. BENITO CERENO. DR. ROZAS.

If the Deposition have served as the key to fit into the lock of the complications which precede it, then, as a vault whose door has been flung back, the *San Dominick's* hull lies open to-day.

Hitherto the nature of this narrative, besides rendering the intricacies in the beginning unavoidable, has more or less required that many things, instead of being set down in order of occurrence, should be retrospectively, or irregularly given; this last is the case with the following passages, which will conclude the account.

During the long, mild voyage to Lima, there was, as before hinted, a period during which the sufferer a little recovered his health, or, at least in some degree, his tranquillity. Ere the decided relapse which came, the two captains had many cordial conversations—their fraternal unreserve in similar contrast with former withdrawments.

Again and again it was repeated, how hard it had been to enact the part forced on the Spaniard by Babo.

"Ah, my dear friend," Don Benito once said, "at those very times you thought me so morose and ungrateful, nay, when, as you now admit, you have thought me plotting your murder, at those very times my heart was frozen; I could not look at you, thinking of what, both on board this ship and your own, hung, from other hands, over my kind benefactor. And as God lives, Don Amasa, I know not whether desire for my own safety alone could have nerved me to that leap into your boat, had it not been for the thought that, did you, unenlightened, return to your ship, you, my best friend, with all who might be with you, stolen upon, that night, in your hammocks, would never in this world have wakened again. Do but think how you walked this deck, how you sat in this cabin, every inch of ground mined into honey-combs under you. Had I dropped the least hint, made the least advance towards an understanding between us; death, explosive death—yours and mine—would have ended the scene."

"True, true," cried Captain Delano, starting, "you have saved my life, Don Benito, more than I yours; saved it, too, against my knowledge and will."

"Nay, my friend," rejoined the Spaniard, courteous even to the point of religion, "God charmed your life, but you saved mine. To think of some things you did—those smilings and chattings, rash pointings and gesturings. For less than these, they slew my mate, Raneds; but you had the Prince of Heaven's safe-conduct through all ambuscades."

"Yes, all is owing to Providence, I know: but the temper of my mind that morning was more than commonly pleasant, while the sight of so much suffering, more apparent than real, added to my good-nature, compassion, and charity, happily interweaving the three. Had it been otherwise, doubtless, as you hint, some of my interferences might have ended unhappily enough. Besides, those feelings I spoke of enabled me to get the better of momentary distrust, at times when acuteness might have cost me my life without saving another's. Only at the end did my suspicions get the better of me, and you know how wide of the mark they then proved."

"Wide, indeed," said Don Benito, sadly; "you were with me all day; stood with me, sat with me, talked with me, looked at me, ate with me, drank with me, and yet, your last act was to clutch for a monster, not only an innocent man, but the most pitiable of all men. To such degree may malign machinations and deceptions impose. So far may even the best man err, in judging the conduct of one with the recesses of whose condition he is not acquainted. But you were forced to it; and you were in time undeceived. Would that, in both respects, it was so ever, and with all men."

"You generalize, Don Benito; and mournfully enough. But the past is passed; why moralize upon it? Forget it. See, yon bright sun has forgotten it all, and the blue sea, and the blue sky; these have turned over new leaves."

"Because they have no memory," he dejectedly replied; "because they are not human."

"But these mild trades that now fan your cheek, do they not come with a human-like healing to you? Warm friends, steadfast friends are the trades."

"With their steadfastness they but waft me to my tomb, Señor," was the foreboding response.

"You are saved," cried Captain Delano, more and more astonished and pained; "You are saved: what has cast such a shadow upon you?"

"The negro."

There was silence, while the moody man sat, slowly and unconsciously gathering his mantle about him, as if it were a pall.

There was no more conversation that day.

But if the Spaniard's melancholy sometimes ended in muteness upon topics like the above, there were others upon which he never spoke at all; on which, indeed, all his old reserves were piled. Pass over the worst, and, only to elucidate, let an item or two of these be cited. The dress, so precise and costly, worn by him on the day whose events have been narrated, had not willingly been put on. And that silver-mounted sword, apparent symbol of despot command, was not, indeed, a sword, but the ghost of one. The scabbard, artificially stiffened, was empty.

As for the black—whose brain, not body, had schemed and led the revolt, with the plot—his slight frame, inadequate to that which it held, had at once yielded to the superior muscular strength of his captor, in the boat. Seeing all was over, he uttered no sound, and could not be forced to. His aspect seemed to say, since I cannot do deeds, I will not speak words. Put in irons in the hold, with the rest, he was carried to Lima. During the passage, Don Benito did not visit him. Nor then, nor at any time after would he look at him. Before the tribunal he refused. When pressed by the judges he fainted. On the testimony of the sailors alone rested the legal identity of Babo.

Some months after, dragged to the gibbet at the tail of a mule, the black met his voiceless end. The body was burned to ashes; but for many days, the head, that hive of subtlety, fixed on a pole in the Plaza, met, unabashed, the gaze of the whites; and across the Plaza looked towards St. Bartholomew's church, in whose vaults slept then, as now, the recovered bones of Aranda: and across the Rimac bridge looked towards the monastery, on Mount Agonia without; where, three months after being dismissed by the court, Benito Cereno, borne on the bier, did, indeed, follow his leader.

§ FOR COMMENT

Hailed by many critics as one of Melville's most brilliant stories, "Benito Cereno" is also one of the most complex. It is, first, a suspense story, a mystery involving captor and captive where the primary question "who is the captor and who the captive?" raises further questions: "What is the good; what the evil?" "What is the appearance; what the reality?" The larger question: "What is the real?" is metaphysical, and its answer shapes the entire story. Is the reality the world seen by the Yankee sea captain, Amasa Delano, or is it that seen by the Spanish captain, Benito Cereno, or is it something different from both their views? In attempting to answer this question it is necessary to understand both men.

Delano is a kind of central observer, but the omniscient author places certain restrictions on him which might put his observations in some question. Is he somewhat weak-witted and remarkably naive or is he a hard-headed practical man of good common sense? Certainly his strong command of his own ship, the *Bachelor's Delight*, cannot be doubted. Is the name of the ship significant? How is it possible to get to know Don Benito? Does the deposition help? Why does Melville cease to use Delano as central observer as soon as the first mystery is solved?

What parts do the other characters play, especially Babo and Atufal? Are the Negroes the villains of the piece, the embodiment of evil, or are they the victims of a system that makes slavery a way of life? How does Don Benito feel about the system? Delano? The Negroes themselves? Remember that Babo was a slave in his own country and Atufal a member of the royalty. Remember, also, that although the behavior of the Negroes on board ship is cruel and inhuman, the treatment of the Negroes by the whites, especially Babo's punishment, is marked by the same inhumanity.

Notice the skillful use Melville makes of the device of foreshadowing. Go back over the story and see how often the metaphors, the juxtaposition of events, and the prevailing ominous mood invite the reader to consider implications. Pay attention, for example, to the stern-piece of the ship with the figure of the dark satyr, the motto, "Follow your leader," the incidents involving the padlock and the key and the knot that needs to be undone, the shaving scene with the Spanish flag used as an apron. In line with the studied contrast between appearance and reality, notice how often and where the omniscient author uses the words: "seems," "appears," "like," "as if." How does the omniscient author control the reader's response by the use of such words?

Joseph Conrad § 1857–1924

Although a Pole by birth, Conrad, at the age of seventeen, went to sea and traveled widely before settling in England in 1895. All of his fiction is written in English, a remarkable feat for someone who did not begin to learn the language until he was grown. Although many of his works are about the sea, they are not mere adventure stories but become complex probings of human personality and motivation, marked by a distinctive prose style and a particular genius in the creation of atmosphere and character. A highly moral writer, Conrad expresses over and over man's need to integrate himself into the community of mankind. The Nigger of the Narcissus *(1897),* Lord Jim *(1900), and* Nostromo *(1904) are among the best novels;* "Heart of Darkness" *(1902) has been called the greatest short story in the language.*

The Secret Sharer

I

On my right hand there were lines of fishing stakes resembling a mysterious system of half-submerged bamboo fences, incomprehensible in its division of the domain of tropical fishes, and crazy of aspect as if abandoned forever by some nomad tribe of fishermen now gone to the other end of the ocean; for there was no sign of human habitation as far as the eye could reach. To the left a group of barren islets, suggesting ruins of stone walls, towers, and block-houses, had its foundations set in a blue sea that itself looked solid, so still and stable did it lie below my feet; even the track of light from the westering sun shone smoothly, without that animated glitter which tells of an imperceptible ripple. And when I turned my head to take a parting glance at the tug which had just left us anchored outside the bar, I saw the straight line of the flat shore joined to the stable sea, edge to edge, and with a perfect and unmarked closeness, in one leveled floor half brown, half blue under the enormous dome of the sky. Corresponding in their insignificance to the islets of the sea, two small clumps of trees, one on each side of the only fault in the impeccable joint, marked the mouth of the river Meinam we had just left on the first preparatory stage of our homeward journey; and, far back on the inland level, a larger and loftier mass, the grove surrounding the great Paknam pagoda, was the only thing on which the eye could rest from the vain task of exploring the monotonous sweep of the horizon. Here and there gleams as of a few scattered pieces of silver marked the windings of the great river; and on the nearest of them, just within the bar, the tug steaming right into the land became lost to my sight, hull and funnel and masts, as though the impassive earth had swallowed her up without an effort, without a tremor. My eye followed the light cloud of her smoke, now here, now there, above the plain, according to the devious curves of the stream, but always fainter and farther away, till I lost it at last behind the miter-shaped hill of the great pagoda. And then I was left alone with my ship, anchored at the head of the Gulf of Siam.

She floated at the starting point of a long journey, very still in an immense stillness, the shadows of her spars flung far to the eastward by the setting sun. At that moment I was alone on her decks. There was not a sound in her—and around us nothing moved, nothing lived, not a canoe on the water, not a bird in the air, not a cloud in the sky. In this breathless pause at the threshold of a long passage we seemed to be measuring our fitness for a long and arduous enterprise, the appointed task of both our existences to be carried out, far from all human eyes, with only sky and sea for spectators and for judges.

There must have been some glare in the air to interfere with one's sight, because it was only just before the sun left us that my roaming eyes made out beyond the highest ridge of the principal islet of the group something which did away with the solemnity of perfect solitude. The tide of darkness flowed on swiftly; and with tropical suddenness a swarm of stars came out above the shadowy earth, while I lingered yet, my hand resting lightly on my ship's rail as if on the shoulder of a trusted friend. But, with all that multitude of celestial bodies staring down at one, the comfort of quiet communion with her was gone for good. And there were also disturbing sounds by this time—voices, footsteps forward; the steward flitted along the main deck, a busily ministering spirit; a hand bell tinkled urgently under the poop deck. . . .

I found my two officers waiting for me near the supper table, in the lighted cuddy. We sat down at once, and as I helped the chief mate, I said:

"Are you aware that there is a ship anchored inside the islands? I saw her mastheads above the ridge as the sun went down."

He raised sharply his simple face, overcharged by a terrible growth of whisker, and emitted his usual ejaculations: "Bless my soul, sir! You don't say so!"

My second mate was a round-cheeked, silent young man, grave beyond his years, I thought; but as our eyes happened to meet I detected a slight quiver on his lips. I looked down at once. It was not my part to encourage sneering on board my ship. It must be said, too, that I knew very little of my officers. In consequence of certain events of no particular significance, except to myself, I had been appointed to the command only a fortnight before. Neither did I know much of the hands forward. All these people had been together for eighteen months or so, and my position was that of the only stranger on board. I mention this because it has some bearing on what is to follow. But what I felt most was my being a stranger to the ship; and if all the truth must be told, I was somewhat of a stranger to myself. The youngest man on board (barring the second mate), and untried as yet by a position of the fullest responsibility, I was willing to take the adequacy of the others for granted. They had simply to be equal to their tasks; but I wondered how far I should turn out faithful to that ideal conception of one's own personality every man sets up for himself secretly.

Meantime the chief mate, with an almost visible effect of collaboration on the part of his round eyes and frightful whiskers, was trying to evolve a theory of the anchored ship. His dominant trait was to take all things into earnest consideration. He was of a painstaking turn of mind. As he used to say, he "liked to account to himself" for practically everything that came in his way, down to a miserable scorpion he had found in his cabin a week before. The why and the wherefore of that scorpion—how it got on board and came to select his room rather than the pantry (which was a dark place and more what a scorpion would be partial to), and how on earth it managed to drown itself in the inkwell of his writing desk—had exercised him infinitely. The ship within the islands was much more easily accounted for;

and just as we were about to rise from the table he made his pronouncement. She was, he doubted not, a ship from home lately arrived. Probably she drew too much water to cross the bar except at the top of spring tides. Therefore she went into that natural harbor to wait for a few days in preference to remaining in an open roadstead.

"That's so," confirmed the second mate, suddenly, in his slightly hoarse voice. "She draws over twenty feet. She's the Liverpool ship *Sephora* with a cargo of coal. Hundred and twenty-three days from Cardiff."

We looked at him in surprise.

"The tugboat skipper told me when he came on board for your letters, sir," explained the young man. "He expects to take her up the river the day after tomorrow."

After thus overwhelming us with the extent of his information he slipped out of the cabin. The mate observed regretfully that he "could not account for that young fellow's whims." What prevented him telling us all about it at once, he wanted to know.

I detained him as he was making a move. For the last two days the crew had had plenty of hard work, and the night before they had very little sleep. I felt painfully that I—a stranger—was doing something unusual when I directed him to let all hands turn in without setting an anchor watch. I proposed to keep on deck myself till one o'clock or thereabouts. I would get the second mate to relieve me at that hour.

"He will turn out the cook and the steward at four," I concluded, "and then give you a call. Of course at the slightest sign of any sort of wind we'll have the hands up and make a start at once."

He concealed his astonishment. "Very well, sir." Outside the cuddy he put his head in the second mate's door to inform him of my unheard-of caprice to take a five hours' anchor watch on myself. I heard the other raise his voice incredulously: "What? The captain himself?" Then a few more murmurs, a door closed, then another. A few moments later I went on deck.

My strangeness, which had made me sleepless, had prompted that unconventional arrangement, as if I had expected in those solitary hours of the night to get on terms with the ship of which I knew nothing, manned by men of whom I knew very little more. Fast alongside a wharf, littered like any ship in port with a tangle of unrelated things, invaded by unrelated shore people, I had hardly seen her yet properly. Now, as she lay cleared for sea, the stretch of her main deck seemed to me very fine under the stars. Very fine, very roomy for her size, and very inviting. I descended the poop and paced the waist, my mind picturing to myself the coming passage through the Malay Archipelago, down the Indian Ocean, and up the Atlantic. All its phases were familiar enough to me, every characteristic, all the alternatives which were likely to face me on the high seas—everything! . . . except the novel responsibility of command. But I took heart from the reasonable thought that the ship was like other ships, the men like other men, and that the sea was not likely to keep any special surprises expressly for my discomfiture.

Arrived at that comforting conclusion, I bethought myself of a cigar and went below to get it. All was still down there. Everybody at the after end of the ship was sleeping profoundly. I came out again on the quarter-deck, agreeably at ease in my sleeping suit on that warm breathless night, barefooted, a glowing cigar in my teeth, and, going forward, I was met by the profound silence of the fore end of the ship. Only as I passed the door of the forecastle I heard a deep, quiet, trustful sigh of some sleeper inside. And suddenly I rejoiced in the great security of the sea as compared with the unrest of the land, in my choice of that untempted life presenting no disquieting problems, invested with an elementary moral beauty by the absolute straightforwardness of its appeal and by the singleness of its purpose.

The riding light in the fore-rigging burned with a clear, untroubled, as if symbolic, flame, confident and bright in the mysterious shades of the night. Passing on my way aft along the other side of the ship, I observed that the rope side ladder, put over, no doubt, for the master of the tug when he came to fetch away our letters, had not been hauled in as it should have been. I became annoyed at this, for exactitude in small matters is the very soul of discipline. Then I reflected that I had myself peremptorily dismissed my officers from duty, and by my own act had prevented the anchor watch being formally set and things properly attended to. I asked myself whether it was wise ever to interfere with the established routine of duties even from the kindest of motives. My action might have made me appear eccentric. Goodness only knew how that absurdly whiskered mate would "account" for my conduct, and what the whole ship thought of that informality of their new captain. I was vexed with myself.

Not from compunction certainly, but, as it were mechanically, I proceeded to get the ladder in myself. Now a side ladder of that sort is a light affair and comes in easily, yet my vigorous tug, which should have brought it flying on board, merely recoiled upon my body in a totally unexpected jerk. What the devil! . . . I was so astounded by the immovableness of that ladder that I remained stock-still, trying to account for it to myself like that imbecile mate of mine. In the end, of course, I put my head over the rail.

The side of the ship made an opaque belt of shadow on the darkling glassy shimmer of the sea. But I saw at once something elongated and pale floating very close to the ladder. Before I could form a guess a faint flash of phosphorescent light, which seemed to issue suddenly from the naked body of a man, flickered in the sleeping water with the elusive, silent play of summer lightning in a night sky. With a gasp I saw revealed to my stare a pair of feet, the long legs, a broad livid back immersed right up to the neck in a greenish cadaverous glow. One hand, awash, clutched the bottom rung of the ladder. He was complete but for the head. A headless corpse! The cigar dropped out of my gaping mouth with a tiny plop and a short hiss quite audible in the absolute stillness of all things under heaven. At that I suppose he raised up his face, a dimly pale oval in the shadow of the ship's side. But even then I could only barely make out down there the shape of his black-haired head. However, it was enough for the horrid, frost-bound sensation which had gripped me about the chest to pass off. The moment of vain exclamations was past, too. I only climbed on the spare spar and leaned over the rail as far as I could, to bring my eyes nearer to that mystery floating alongside.

As he hung by the ladder, like a resting swimmer, the sea lightning played about his limbs at every stir; and he appeared in it ghastly, silvery, fishlike. He remained as mute as a fish, too. He made no motion to get out of the water, either. It was inconceivable that he should not attempt to come on board, and strangely troubling to suspect that perhaps he did not want to. And my first words were prompted by just that troubled incertitude.

"What's the matter?" I asked in my ordinary tone, speaking down to the face upturned exactly under mine.

"Cramp," it answered, no louder. Then slightly anxious, "I say, no need to call anyone."

"I was not going to," I said.

"Are you alone on deck?"

"Yes."

I had somehow the impression that he was on the point of letting go the ladder to swim away beyond my ken—mysterious as he came. But, for the moment, this being appearing as if he had risen from the bottom of the sea (it was certainly the nearest land to the ship) wanted only to know the time. I told him. And he, down there, tentatively:

"I suppose your captain's turned in?"

"I'm sure he isn't," I said.

He seemed to struggle with himself, for I heard something like the low, bitter murmur of doubt. "What's the good?" His next words came out with a hesitating effort.

"Look here, my man. Could you call him out quietly?"

I thought the time had come to declare myself.

"I am the captain."

I heard a "By Jove!" whispered at the level of the water. The phosphorescence flashed in the swirl of the water all about his limbs, his other hand seized the ladder.

"My name's Leggatt."

The voice was calm and resolute. A good voice. The self-possession of that man had somehow induced a corresponding state in myself. It was very quietly that I remarked:

"You must be a good swimmer."

"Yes. I've been in the water practically since nine o'clock. The question for me now is whether I am to let go this ladder and go on swimming till I sink from exhaustion, or—to come on board here."

I felt this was no mere formula of desperate speech, but a real alternative in the view of a strong soul. I should have gathered from this that he was young; indeed, it is only the young who are ever confronted by such clear issues. But at the time it was pure intuition on my part. A mysterious communication was established already between us two—in the face of that silent, darkened tropical sea. I was young, too; young enough to make no comment. The man in the water began suddenly to climb up the ladder, and I hastened away from the rail to fetch some clothes.

Before entering the cabin I stood still, listening in the lobby at the foot of the stairs. A faint snore came through the closed door of the chief mate's room. The second mate's door was on the hook, but the darkness in there was absolutely soundless. He, too, was young and could sleep like a stone. Remained the steward, but he was not likely to wake up before he was called. I got a sleeping suit out of my room and, coming back on deck, saw the naked man from the sea sitting on the main hatch, glimmering white in the darkness, his elbows on his knees and his head in his hands. In a moment he had concealed his damp body in a sleeping suit of the same gray-stripe pattern as the one I was wearing and followed me like my double on the poop. Together we moved right aft, barefooted, silent.

"What is it?" I asked in a deadened voice, taking the lighted lamp out of the binnacle, and raising it to his face.

"An ugly business."

He had rather regular features; a good mouth; light eyes under somewhat heavy, dark eyebrows; a smooth, square forehead; no growth on his cheeks; a small, brown mustache, and a well-shaped, round chin. His expression was concentrated, meditative, under the inspecting light of the lamp I held up to his face; such as a man thinking hard in solitude might wear. My sleeping suit was just right for his size. A well-knit young fellow of twenty-five at most. He caught his lower lip with the edge of white, even teeth.

"Yes," I said, replacing the lamp in the binnacle. The warm, heavy tropical night closed upon his head again.

"There's a ship over there," he murmured.

"Yes, I know. The *Sephora*. Did you know of us?"

"Hadn't the slightest idea. I am the mate of her—" He paused and corrected himself. "I should say I *was*."

"Aha! Something wrong?"

"Yes. Very wrong indeed. I've killed a man."

"What do you mean? Just now?"

"No, on the passage. Weeks ago. Thirty-nine south. When I say a man—"

"Fit of temper," I suggested, confidently.

The shadowy, dark head, like mine, seemed to nod imperceptibly above the ghostly gray of my sleeping suit. It was, in the night, as though I had been faced by my own reflection in the depths of a somber and immense mirror.

"A pretty thing to have to own up to for a Conway boy," murmured my double, distinctly.

"You're a Conway boy?"

"I am," he said, as if startled. Then, slowly . . . "Perhaps you too—"

It was so; but being a couple of years older I had left before he joined. After a quick interchange of dates a silence fell; and I thought suddenly of my absurd mate with his terrific whiskers and the "Bless my soul—you don't say so" type of intellect. My double gave me an inkling of his thoughts by saying:

"My father's a parson in Norfolk. Do you see me before a judge and jury on that charge? For myself I can't see the necessity. There are fellows that an angel from heaven—— And I am not that. He was one of those creatures that are just simmering all the time with a silly sort of wickedness. Miserable devils that have no business to live at all. He wouldn't do his duty and wouldn't let anybody else do theirs. But what's the good of talking! You know well enough the sort of ill-conditioned snarling cur—"

He appealed to me as if our experiences had been as identical as our clothes. And I knew well enough the pestiferous danger of such a character where there are no means of legal repression. And I knew well enough also that my double there was no homicidal ruffian. I did not think of asking him for details, and he told me the story roughly in brusque, disconnected sentences. I needed no more. I saw it all going on as though I were myself inside that other sleeping suit.

"It happened while we were setting a reefed foresail, at dusk. Reefed foresail! You understand the sort of weather. The only sail we had left to keep the ship running; so you may guess what it had been like for days. Anxious sort of job, that. He gave me some of his cursed insolence at the sheet. I tell you I was overdone with this terrific weather that seemed to have no end to it. Terrific, I tell you—and a deep ship. I believe the fellow himself was half crazed with funk. It was no time for gentlemanly reproof, so I turned round and felled him like an ox. He up and at me. We closed just as an awful sea made for the ship. All hands saw it coming and took to the rigging, but I had him by the throat, and went on shaking him like a rat, the men above us yelling, 'Look out! look out!' Then a crash as if the sky had fallen on my head. They say that for over ten minutes hardly anything was to be seen of the ship—just the three masts and a bit of the forecastle head and of the poop all awash driving along in a smother of foam. It was a miracle that they found us, jammed together behind the forebits. It's clear that I meant business, because I was holding him by the throat still when they picked us up. He was black in the face. It was too much for them. It seems they rushed us aft together, gripped as we were, screaming 'Murder!' like a lot of lunatics, and broke into the cuddy. And the ship running for her life, touch and go all the time, any minute her last in a sea fit to turn your hair gray only a-looking at it. I understand that the skipper, too, started raving like the rest of them. The man had been deprived of sleep for more than a week, and to have this sprung on him at the height of a furious gale nearly drove him out of his mind. I wonder they didn't fling me overboard after getting the carcass of their precious shipmate out of my fingers. They had rather a job to separate us, I've been told. A sufficiently fierce story to make an old judge and a respectable jury sit up a bit. The first thing I heard when I came to myself was the maddening howling of that endless gale, and on that the voice of the old man. He was hanging on to my bunk, staring into my face out of his sou'wester.

" 'Mr. Leggatt, you have killed a man. You can act no longer as chief mate of this ship.' "

His care to subdue his voice made it sound monotonous. He rested a hand on the end of the skylight to steady himself with, and all that time did not stir a limb, so far as I could see. "Nice little tale for a quiet tea party," he concluded in the same tone.

One of my hands, too, rested on the end of the skylight; neither did I stir a limb, so far as I knew. We stood less than a foot from each other. It occurred to me that if old "Bless my soul—you don't say so" were to put his head up the companion and catch sight of us, he would think he was seeing double, or imagine himself come upon a scene of weird witchcraft; the strange captain having a quiet confabulation by the wheel with his own gray ghost. I became very much concerned to prevent anything of the sort. I heard the other's soothing undertone.

"My father's a parson in Norfolk," it said. Evidently he had forgotten he had told me this important fact before. Truly a nice little tale.

"You had better slip down into my stateroom now," I said, moving off stealthily. My double followed my movements; our bare feet made no sound; I let him in, closed the door with care, and, after giving a call to the second mate, returned on deck for my relief.

"Not much sign of any wind yet," I remarked when he approached.

"No, sir. Not much," he assented, sleepily, in his hoarse voice, with just enough deference, no more, and barely suppressing a yawn.

"Well, that's all you have to look out for. You have got your orders."

"Yes, sir."

I paced a turn or two on the poop and saw him take up his position face forward with his elbow in the ratlines of the mizzen-rigging before I went below. The mate's faint snoring was still going on peacefully. The cuddy lamp was burning over the table on which stood a vase with flowers, a polite attention from the ship's provision merchant—the last flowers we should see for the next three months at the very least. Two bunches of bananas hung from the beam symmetrically, one on each side of the rudder casing. Everything was as before in the ship—except that two of her captain's sleeping suits were simultaneously in use, one motionless in the cuddy, the other keeping very still in the captain's stateroom.

It must be explained here that my cabin had the form of the capital letter L, the door being within the angle and opening into the short part of the letter. A couch was to the left, the bed-place to the right; my writing desk and the chronometers' table faced the door. But anyone opening it, unless he stepped right inside, had no view of what I call the long (or vertical) part of the letter. It contained some lockers surmounted by a bookcase; and a few clothes, a thick jacket or two, caps, oilskin coat, and such like, hung on hooks. There was at the bottom of that part a door opening into my bathroom, which could be entered also directly from the saloon. But that way was never used.

The mysterious arrival had discovered the advantage of this particular shape. Entering my room, lighted strongly by a big bulkhead lamp swung on gimbals above my writing desk, I did not see him anywhere till he stepped out quietly from behind the coats hung in the recessed part.

"I heard somebody moving about, and went in there at once," he whispered.

I, too, spoke under my breath.

"Nobody is likely to come in here without knocking and getting permission."

He nodded. His face was thin and the sunburn faded, as though he had been ill. And no wonder. He had been, I heard presently, kept under arrest in his cabin for nearly seven weeks. But there was nothing sickly in his eyes or in his expression. He was not a bit like me, really; yet, as we stood leaning over my bed-place, whispering side by side, with our dark heads together and our backs to the door, anybody bold enough to open it stealthily would have been treated to the uncanny sight of a double captain busy talking in whispers with his other self.

"But all this doesn't tell me how you came to hang on to our side ladder," I inquired, in the hardly audible murmurs we used, after he had told me something more of the proceedings on board the *Sephora* once the bad weather was over.

"When we sighted Java Head I had had time to think all those matters out several times over. I had six weeks of doing nothing else, and with only an hour or so every evening for a tramp on the quarter-deck."

He whispered, his arms folded on the side of my bed-place, staring through the open port. And I could imagine perfectly the manner of this thinking out—a stubborn if not a steadfast operation; something of which I should have been perfectly incapable.

"I reckoned it would be dark before we closed with the land," he continued, so low that I had to strain my hearing, near as we were to each other, shoulder touching shoulder almost. "So I asked to speak to the old man. He always seemed very sick when he came to see me—as if he could not look me in the face. You know, that foresail saved the ship. She was too deep to have run long under bare poles. And it was I that managed to set it for him. Anyway, he came. When I had him in my cabin—he stood by the door looking at me as if I had the halter around my neck already—I asked him right away to leave my cabin door unlocked at night while the ship was going through Sunda Straits. There would be the Java coast within two or three miles, off Angier Point. I wanted nothing more. I've had a prize for swimming my second year in the Conway."

"I can believe it," I breathed out.

"God only knows why they locked me in every night. To see some of their faces you'd have thought they were afraid I'd go about at night strangling people. Am I a murdering brute? Do I look it? By Jove! if I had been he wouldn't have trusted himself like that into my room. You'll say I might have chucked him aside and bolted out, there and then—it was dark already. Well, no. And for the same reason I wouldn't think of trying to smash the door. There would have been a rush to stop me at the noise, and I did not mean to get into a confounded scrimmage. Somebody else might have got killed—for I would not have broken out only to get chucked back, and I did not want any more of that work. He refused, looking more sick than ever. He was afraid of the men, and also of that old second mate of his who had been sailing with him for years—a gray-headed old humbug; and his steward, too, had been with him devil knows how long—seventeen years or more—a dogmatic sort of loafer who hated me like poison, just because I was the chief mate. No chief mate ever made more than one voyage in the *Sephora*, you know. Those two old chaps ran the ship. Devil only knows what the skipper wasn't afraid of (all his nerve went to pieces altogether in that hellish spell of bad weather we had)—of what the law would do to him—of his wife, perhaps. Oh, yes! she's on board. Though I don't think she would have meddled. She would have been only too glad to have me out of the ship in any way. The 'brand of Cain' business, don't you see. That's all right. I was ready enough to go off wandering on the face of the earth—and that was price enough to pay for an Abel of that sort. Anyhow, he wouldn't listen to me. 'This thing must take its course. I represent the law here.' He was shaking like a leaf. 'So you won't?' 'No!' 'Then I hope you will be able to sleep on that,' I said, and turned my back on him. 'I wondered that *you* can,' cries he, and locks the door.

"Well, after that, I couldn't. Not very well. That was three weeks ago. We have had a slow passage through the Java Sea; drifted about Carimata for ten days. When we anchored here they thought, I suppose, it was all right. The nearest land (and that's five miles) is the ship's destination; the consul would soon set about catching me; and there would have been no object in bolting to these islets there. I don't suppose there's a drop of water on them. I don't know how it was, but tonight that steward, after bringing me my supper, went out to let me eat it, and left the door unlocked. And I ate it—all there was, too. After I had finished I strolled out on the quarter-deck. I don't know that I meant to do anything. A breath of fresh air was all I wanted, I believe. Then a sudden temptation came over me. I kicked off my slippers and was in the water before I had made up my mind fairly. Somebody heard the splash and they raised an awful hullaba-loo. 'He's gone! Lower the boats! He's committed suicide! No, he's swim-ming.' Certainly I was swimming. It's not so easy for a swimmer like me to commit suicide by drowning. I landed on the nearest islet before the boat left the ship's side. I heard them pulling about in the dark, hailing, and so on, but after a bit they gave up. Everything quieted down and the anchor-age became as still as death. I sat down on a stone and began to think. I felt certain they would start searching for me at daylight. There was no place to hide on those stony things—and if there had been, what would have been the good? But now I was clear of that ship, I was not going back. So after a while I took off all my clothes, tied them up in a bundle with a stone inside, and dropped them in the deep water on the outer side of that islet. That was suicide enough for me. Let them think what they liked, but I didn't mean to drown myself. I meant to swim till I sank—but that's not the same thing. I struck out for another of these little islands, and it was from that one that I first saw your riding light. Something to swim for. I went on easily, and on the way I came upon a flat rock a foot or two above water. In the daytime, I dare say, you might make it out with a glass from your poop. I scrambled up on it and rested myself for a bit. Then I made another start. That last spell must have been over a mile."

His whisper was getting fainter and fainter, and all the time he stared straight out through the porthole, in which there was not even a star to be seen. I had not interrupted him. There was something that made comment impossible in his narrative, or perhaps in himself; a sort of feeling, a quality, which I can't find a name for. And when he ceased, all I found was a futile whisper: "So you swam for our light?"

"Yes—straight for it. It was something to swim for. I couldn't see any stars low down because the coast was in the way, and I couldn't see the land, either. The water was like glass. One might have been swimming in a confounded thousand-feet deep cistern with no place for scrambling out anywhere; but what I didn't like was the notion of swimming round and round like a crazed bullock before I gave out; and as I didn't mean to go back . . . No. Do you see me being hauled back, stark naked, off one of these little islands by the scruff of the neck and fighting like a wild beast? Somebody would have got killed for certain, and I did not want any of that. So I went on. Then your ladder—"

"Why didn't you hail the ship?" I asked, a little louder.

He touched my shoulder lightly. Lazy footsteps came right over our heads and stopped. The second mate had crossed from the other side of the poop and might have been hanging over the rail, for all we knew.

"He couldn't hear us talking—could he?" My double breathed into my very ear, anxiously.

His anxiety was an answer, a sufficient answer, to the question I had put to him. An answer containing all the difficulty of that situation. I closed the porthole quietly, to make sure. A louder word might have been overheard.

"Who's that?" he whispered then.

"My second mate. But I don't know much more of the fellow than you do."

And I told him a little about myself. I had been appointed to take charge while I least expected anything of the sort, not quite a fortnight ago. I didn't know either the ship or the people. Hadn't had the time in port to look about me or size anybody up. And as to the crew, all they knew was that I was appointed to take the ship home. For the rest, I was almost as much of a stranger on board as himself, I said. And at the moment I felt it most acutely. I felt that it would take very little to make me a suspect person in the eyes of the ship's company.

He had turned about meantime; and we, the two strangers in the ship, faced each other in identical attitudes.

"Your ladder—" he murmured, after a silence. "Who'd have thought of finding a ladder hanging over at night in a ship anchored out here! I felt just then a very unpleasant faintness. After the life I've been leading for nine weeks, anybody would have got out of condition. I wasn't capable of swimming round as far as your rudder chains. And, lo and behold! there was a ladder to get hold of. After I gripped it I said to myself, 'What's the good?' When I saw a man's head looking over I thought I would swim away presently and leave him shouting—in whatever language it was. I didn't mind being looked at. I—I liked it. And then you speaking to me so quietly—as if you had expected me—made me hold on a little longer. It had been a confounded lonely time—I don't mean while swimming. I was glad to talk a little to somebody that didn't belong to the *Sephora*. As to asking for the captain, that was a mere impulse. It could have been no use, with all the ship knowing about me and the other people pretty certain to be round here in the morning. I don't know—I wanted to be seen, to talk with somebody, before I went on. I don't know what I would have said. . . . 'Fine night, isn't it?' or something of the sort."

"Do you think they will be round here presently?" I asked with some incredulity.

"Quite likely," he said, faintly.

He looked extremely haggard all of a sudden. His head rolled on his shoulders.

"H'm. We shall see then. Meantime get into that bed," I whispered. "Want help? There."

It was a rather high bed-place with a set of drawers underneath. This amazing swimmer really needed the lift I gave him by seizing his leg. He tumbled in, rolled over on his back, and flung one arm across his eyes. And then, with his face nearly hidden, he must have looked exactly as I used to look in that bed. I gazed upon my other self for a while before drawing across carefully the two green serge curtains which ran on a brass rod. I thought for a moment of pinning them together for greater safety, but I sat down on the couch, and once there I felt unwilling to rise and hunt for a pin. I would do it in a moment. I was extremely tired, in a peculiarly intimate way, by the strain of stealthiness, by the effort of whispering and the general secrecy of this excitement. It was three o'clock by now and I had been on my feet since nine, but I was not sleepy; I could not have gone to sleep. I sat there, fagged out, looking at the curtains, trying to clear my mind of the confused sensation of being in two places at once, and greatly bothered by an exasperating knocking in my head. It was a relief to discover suddenly that it was not in my head at all, but on the outside of the door. Before I could collect myself the words "Come in" were out of my mouth, and the steward entered with a tray, bringing in my morning coffee. I had slept, after all, and I was so frightened that I shouted, "This way! I am here, steward," as though he had been miles away. He put down the tray on the table next the couch and only then said, very quietly, "I can see you are here, sir." I felt him give me a keen look, but I dared not meet his eyes just then. He must have wondered why I had drawn the curtains of my bed before going to sleep on the couch. He went out, hooking the door open as usual.

I heard the crew washing decks above me. I knew I would have been told at once if there had been any wind. Calm, I thought, and I was doubly vexed. Indeed, I felt dual more than ever. The steward reappeared suddenly in the doorway. I jumped up from the couch so quickly that he gave a start.

"What do you want here?"

"Close your port, sir—they are washing decks."

"It is closed," I said, reddening.

"Very well, sir." But he did not move from the doorway and returned my stare in an extraordinary, equivocal manner for a time. Then his eyes wavered, all his expression changed, and in a voice unusually gentle, almost coaxingly:

"May I come in to take the empty cup away, sir?"

"Of course!" I turned my back on him while he popped in and out. Then I unhooked and closed the door and even pushed the bolt. This sort of thing could not go on very long. The cabin was as hot as an oven, too. I took a peep at my double, and discovered that he had not moved, his arm was still over his eyes; but his chest heaved; his hair was wet; his chin glistened with perspiration. I reached over him and opened the port.

"I must show myself on deck," I reflected.

Of course, theoretically, I could do what I liked, with no one to say nay to me within the whole circle of the horizon; but to lock my cabin door and take the key away I did not dare. Directly I put my head out of the companion I saw the group of my two officers, the second mate barefooted, the chief mate in long india-rubber boots, near the break of the poop, and the steward halfway down the poop ladder talking to them eagerly. He happened to catch sight of me and dived, the second ran down on the main deck shouting some order or other, and the chief mate came to meet me, touching his cap.

There was a sort of curiosity in his eye that I did not like. I don't know whether the steward had told them that I was "queer" only, or downright drunk, but I know the man meant to have a good look at me. I watched him coming with a smile which, as he got into point-blank range, took effect and froze his very whiskers. I did not give him time to open his lips.

"Square the yards by lifts and braces before the hands go to breakfast."

It was the first particular order I had given on board that ship; and I stayed on deck to see it executed, too. I had felt the need of asserting myself without loss of time. That sneering young cub got taken down a peg or two on that occasion, and I also seized the opportunity of having a good look at the face of every foremast man as they filed past me to go to the after braces. At breakfast time, eating nothing myself, I presided with such frigid dignity that the two mates were only too glad to escape from the cabin as soon as decency permitted; and all the time the dual working of my mind distracted me almost to the point of insanity. I was constantly watching myself, my secret self, as dependent on my actions as my own personality, sleeping in that bed, behind that door which faced me as I sat at the head of the table. It was very much like being mad, only it was worse because one was aware of it.

I had to shake him for a solid minute, but when at last he opened his eyes it was in the full possession of his senses, with an inquiring look.

"All's well so far," I whispered. "Now you must vanish into the bathroom."

He did so, as noiseless as a ghost, and I then rang for the steward, and facing him boldly, directed him to tidy up my stateroom while I was having my bath—"and be quick about it." As my tone admitted of no excuses, he said, "Yes, sir," and ran off to fetch his dustpan and brushes. I took a bath and did most of my dressing, splashing, and whistling softly for the steward's edification, while the secret sharer of my life stood drawn up bolt upright in that little space, his face looking very sunken in daylight, his eyelids lowered under the stern, dark line of his eyebrows drawn together by a slight frown.

When I left him there to go back to my room the steward was finishing dusting. I sent for the mate and engaged him in some insignificant conversation. It was, as it were, trifling with the terrific character of his whiskers; but my object was to give him an opportunity for a good look at my cabin. And then I could at last shut, with a clear conscience, the door of my stateroom and get my double back into the recessed part. There was nothing else for it. He had to sit still on a small folding stool, half smothered by the heavy coats hanging there. We listened to the steward going into the bathroom out of the saloon, filling the water bottles there, scrubbing the bath, setting things to rights, whisk, bang, clatter—out again into the saloon—turn the key—click. Such was my scheme for keeping my second self invisible. Nothing better could be contrived under the circumstances. And there we sat; I at my writing desk ready to appear busy with some papers, he behind me, out of sight of the door. It would not have been prudent to talk in daytime; and I could not have stood the excitement of that queer sense of whispering to myself. Now and then, glancing over my shoulder, I saw him far back there, sitting rigidly on the low stool, his bare feet close together, his arms folded, his head hanging on his breast—and perfectly still. Anybody would have taken him for me.

I was fascinated by it myself. Every moment I had to glance over my shoulder. I was looking at him when a voice outside the door said:

"Beg pardon, sir."

"Well!" . . . I kept my eyes on him, and so, when the voice outside the door announced, "There's a ship's boat coming our way, sir," I saw him give a start—the first movement he had made for hours. But he did not raise his bowed head.

"All right. Get the ladder over."

I hesitated. Should I whisper something to him? But what? His immobility seemed to have been never disturbed. What could I tell him he did not know already? . . . Finally I went on deck.

II

The skipper of the *Sephora* had a thin red whisker all round his face, and the sort of complexion that goes with hair of that color; also the particular, rather smeary shade of blue in the eyes. He was not exactly a showy figure; his shoulders were high, his stature but middling—one leg slightly more bandy than the other. He shook hands, looking vaguely around. A spiritless tenacity was his main characteristic, I judged. I behaved with a politeness which seemed to disconcert him. Perhaps he was shy. He mumbled to me as if he were ashamed of what he was saying; gave his name (it was something like Archbold—but at this distance of years I hardly am sure), his ship's name, and a few other particulars of that sort, in the manner of a criminal making a reluctant and doleful confession. He had had terrible weather on the passage out—terrible—terrible—wife aboard, too.

By this time we were seated in the cabin and the steward brought in a tray with a bottle and glasses. "Thanks! No." Never took liquor. Would have some water, though. He drank two tumblerfuls. Terrible thirsty work. Ever since daylight had been exploring the islands round his ship.

"What was that for—fun?" I asked, with an appearance of polite interest.

"No!" He sighed. "Painful duty."

As he persisted in his mumbling and I wanted my double to hear every word, I hit upon the notion of informing him that I regretted to say I was hard of hearing.

"Such a young man, too!" he nodded, keeping his smeary blue, unintelligent eyes fastened upon me. What was the cause of it—some disease? he inquired, without the least sympathy and as if he thought that, if so, I'd got no more than I deserved.

"Yes; disease," I admitted in a cheerful tone which seemed to shock him. But my point was gained, because he had to raise his voice to give me his tale. It is not worth while to record that version. It was just over two months since all this had happened, and he had thought so much about it that he seemed completely muddled as to its bearings, but still immensely impressed.

"What would you think of such a thing happening on board your own ship? I've had the *Sephora* for these fifteen years. I am a well-known shipmaster."

He was densely distressed—and perhaps I should have sympathized with him if I had been able to detach my mental vision from the unsuspected sharer of my cabin as though he were my second self. There he was on the other side of the bulkhead, four or five feet from us, no more, as we sat in the saloon. I looked politely at Captain Archbold (if that was his name), but it was the other I saw, in a gray sleeping suit, seated on a low stool, his bare feet close together, his arms folded, and every word said between us falling into the ears of his dark head bowed on his chest.

"I have been at sea now, man and boy, for seven-and-thirty years, and I've never heard of such a thing happening in an English ship. And that it should be my ship. Wife on board, too."

I was hardly listening to him.

"Don't you think," I said, "that the heavy sea which, you told me, came aboard just then might have killed the man? I have seen the sheer weight of a sea kill a man very neatly, by simply breaking his neck."

"Good God!" he uttered, impressively, fixing his smeary blue eyes on me. "The sea! No man killed by the sea ever looked like that." He seemed positively scandalized at my suggestion. And as I gazed at him, certainly not prepared for anything original on his part, he advanced his head close to mine and thrust his tongue out at me so suddenly that I couldn't help starting back.

After scoring over my calmness in this graphic way he nodded wisely. If I had seen the sight, he assured me, I would never forget it as long as I lived. The weather was too bad to give the corpse a proper sea burial. So next day at dawn they took it up on the poop, covering its face with a bit of bunting; he read a short prayer, and then, just as it was, in its oilskins and long boots, they launched it amongst those mountainous seas that seemed ready every moment to swallow up the ship herself and the terrified lives on board of her.

"That reefed foresail saved you," I threw in.

"Under God—it did," he exclaimed fervently. "It was by a special mercy, I firmly believe, that it stood some of those hurricane squalls."

"It was the setting of that sail which—" I began.

"God's own hand in it," he interrupted me. "Nothing less could have done it. I don't mind telling you that I hardly dared give the order. It seemed impossible that we could touch anything without losing it, and then our last hope would have been gone."

The terror of that gale was on him yet. I let him go on for a bit, then said, casually—as if returning to a minor subject:

"You were very anxious to give up your mate to the shore people, I believe?"

He was. To the law. His obscure tenacity on that point had in it something incomprehensible and a little awful; something, as it were, mystical, quite apart from his anxiety that he should not be suspected of "countenancing any doings of that sort." Seven-and-thirty virtuous years at sea, of which over twenty of immaculate command, and the last fifteen in the *Sephora*, seemed to have laid him under some pitiless obligation.

"And you know," he went on, groping shamefacedly amongst his feelings, "I did not engage that young fellow. His people had some interest with my owners. I was in a way forced to take him on. He looked very smart, very gentlemanly, and all that. But do you know—I never liked him, somehow. I am a plain man. You see, he wasn't exactly the sort for the chief mate of a ship like the *Sephora*."

I had become so connected in thoughts and impressions with the secret sharer of my cabin that I felt as if I, personally, were being given to understand that I, too, was not the sort that would have done for the chief mate of a ship like the *Sephora*. I had no doubt of it in my mind.

"Not at all the style of man. You understand," he insisted, superfluously, looking hard at me.

I smiled urbanely. He seemed at a loss for a while.

"I suppose I must report a suicide."

"Beg pardon?"

"Sui-cide! That's what I'll have to write to my owners directly I get in."

"Unless you manage to recover him before tomorrow," I assented, dispassionately. . . . "I mean, alive."

He mumbled something which I really did not catch, and I turned my ear to him in a puzzled manner. He fairly bawled:

"The land—I say, the mainland is at least seven miles off my anchorage."

"About that."

My lack of excitement, of curiosity, of surprise, of any sort of pronounced interest, began to arouse his distrust. But except for the felicitous pretense of deafness I had not tried to pretend anything. I had felt utterly incapable of playing the part of ignorance properly, and therefore was afraid to try. It is also certain that he had brought some ready-made suspicions with him, and that he viewed my politeness as a strange and unnatural phenomenon. And yet how else could I have received him? Not heartily! That was impossible for psychological reasons, which I need not state here. My only object was to keep off his inquiries. Surlily? Yes, but surliness might have provoked a point-blank question. From its novelty to him and from its nature, punctilious courtesy was the manner best calculated to restrain the man. But there was the danger of his breaking through my defense bluntly. I could not, I think, have met him by a direct lie, also for psychological (not moral) reasons. If he had only known how afraid I was of his putting my feeling of identity with the other to the test! But, strangely enough—(I thought of it only afterward)—I believe that he was not a little disconcerted by the reverse side of that weird situation, by something in me that reminded him of the man he was seeking—suggested a mysterious similitude to the young fellow he had distrusted and disliked from the first.

However that might have been, the silence was not very prolonged. He took another oblique step.

"I reckon I had no more than a two-mile pull to your ship. Not a bit more."

"And quite enough, too, in this awful heat," I said.

Another pause full of mistrust followed. Necessity, they say, is mother of invention, but fear, too, is not barren of ingenious suggestions. And I was afraid he would ask me point-blank for news of my other self.

"Nice little saloon, isn't it?" I remarked, as if noticing for the first time the way his eyes roamed from one closed door to the other. "And very well fitted out, too. Here, for instance," I continued, reaching over the back of my seat negligently and flinging the door open, "is my bathroom."

He made an eager movement, but hardly gave it a glance. I got up, shut the door of the bathroom, and invited him to have a look around, as if I were very proud of my accommodation. He had to rise and be shown round, but he went through the business without any raptures whatever.

"And now we'll have a look at my stateroom," I declared, in a voice as loud as I dared to make it, crossing the cabin to the starboard side with purposely heavy steps.

He followed me in and gazed around. My intelligent double had vanished. I played my part.

"Very convenient—isn't it?"

"Very nice. Very comf . . . ." He didn't finish, and went out brusquely as if to escape from some unrighteous wiles of mine. But it was not to be. I had been too frightened not to feel vengeful; I felt I had him on the run, and I meant to keep him on the run. My polite insistence must have had something menacing in it, because he gave in suddenly. And I did not let him off a single item; mate's room, pantry, storerooms, the very sail locker which was also under the poop—he had to look into them all. When at last I showed him out on the quarter-deck he drew a long, spiritless sigh, and mumbled dismally that he must really be going back to his ship now. I desired my mate, who had joined us, to see to the captain's boat.

The man of whiskers gave a blast on the whistle which he used to wear hanging round his neck, and yelled, "*Sephoras* away!" My double down there in my cabin must have heard, and certainly could not feel more relieved than I. Four fellows came running out from somewhere forward and went over the side, while my own men, appearing on deck too, lined the rail. I escorted my visitor to the gangway ceremoniously, and nearly overdid it. He was a tenacious beast. On the very ladder he lingered, and in that unique, guiltily conscientious manner of sticking to the point:

"I say . . . you . . . you don't think that—"

I covered his voice loudly:

"Certainly not. . . . I am delighted. Good-by."

I had an idea of what he meant to say, and just saved myself by the privilege of defective hearing. He was too shaken generally to insist, but my mate, close witness of that parting, looked mystified and his face took on a thoughtful cast. As I did not want to appear as if I wished to avoid all communication with my officers, he had the opportunity to address me.

"Seems a very nice man. His boat's crew told our chaps a very extraordinary story, if what I am told by the steward is true. I suppose you had it from the captain, sir?"

"Yes. I had a story from the captain."

"A very horrible affair—isn't it, sir?"

"It is."

"Beats all these tales we hear about murders in Yankee ships."

"I don't think it beats them. I don't think it resembles them in the least."

"Bless my soul—you don't say so! But of course I've no acquaintance whatever with American ships, not I, so I couldn't go against your knowledge. It's horrible enough for me. . . . But the queerest part is that those fellows seemed to have some idea the man was hidden aboard here. They had really. Did you ever hear of such a thing?"

"Preposterous—isn't it?"

We were walking to and fro athwart the quarter-deck. No one of the crew forward could be seen (the day was Sunday), and the mate pursued:

"There was some little dispute about it. Our chaps took offense. 'As if we would harbor a thing like that,' they said. 'Wouldn't you like to look for him in our coal hole?' Quite a tiff. But they made it up in the end. I suppose he did drown himself. Don't you, sir?"

"I don't suppose anything."

"You have no doubt in the matter, sir?"

"None whatever."

I left him suddenly. I felt I was producing a bad impression, but with my double down there it was most trying to be on deck. And it was almost as trying to be below. Altogether a nerve-trying situation. But on the whole I felt less torn in two when I was with him. There was no one in the whole ship whom I dared take into my confidence. Since the hands had got to know his story, it would have been impossible to pass him off for anyone else, and an accidental discovery was to be dreaded now more than ever. . . .

The steward being engaged in laying the table for dinner, we could talk only with our eyes when I first went down. Later in the afternoon we had a cautious try at whispering. The Sunday quietness of the ship was against us; the stillness of air and water around her was against us; the elements, the men were against us—everything was against us in our secret partnership; time itself—for this could not go on forever. The very trust in Providence was, I suppose, denied to his guilt. Shall I confess that this thought cast me down very much? And as to the chapter of accidents which counts for so much in the book of success, I could only hope that it was closed. For what favorable accident could be expected?

"Did you hear everything?" were my first words as soon as we took up our position side by side, leaning over my bed-place.

He had. And the proof of it was his earnest whisper, "The man told you he hardly dared to give the order."

I understood the reference to be to that saving foresail.

"Yes. He was afraid of it being lost in the setting."

"I assure you he never gave the order. He may think he did, but he never gave it. He stood there with me on the break of the poop after the maintopsail blew away, and whimpered about our last hope—positively whimpered about it and nothing else—and the night coming on! To hear one's skipper go on like that in such weather was enough to drive any fellow out of his mind. It worked me up into a sort of desperation. I just took it into my own hands and went away from him, boiling, and—. But what's the use telling you? *You* know! . . . Do you think that if I had not been pretty fierce with them I should have got the men to do anything? Not it! The bosun perhaps? Perhaps! It wasn't a heavy sea—it was a sea gone mad! I suppose the end of the world will be something like that; and a man may have the heart to see it coming once and be done with it—but to have to face it day after day—I don't blame anybody. I was precious little better than the rest. Only—I was an officer of that old coal-wagon, anyhow—"

"I quite understand," I conveyed that sincere assurance into his ear. He was out of breath with whispering; I could hear him pant slightly. It was all very simple. The same strung-up force which had given twenty-four men a chance, at least, for their lives, had, in a sort of recoil, crushed an unworthy mutinous existence.

But I had no leisure to weigh the merits of the matter—footsteps in the saloon, a heavy knock. "There's enough wind to get under way with, sir." Here was the call of a new claim upon my thoughts and even upon my feelings.

"Turn the hands up," I cried through the door. "I'll be on deck directly."

I was going out to make the acquaintance of my ship. Before I left the cabin our eyes met—the eyes of the only two strangers on board. I pointed to the recessed part where the little campstool awaited him and laid my finger on my lips. He made a gesture—somewhat vague—a little mysterious, accompanied by a faint smile, as if of regret.

This is not the place to enlarge upon the sensations of a man who feels for the first time a ship move under his feet to his own independent word. In my case they were not unalloyed. I was not wholly alone with my command; for there was that stranger in my cabin. Or rather, I was not completely and wholly with her. Part of me was absent. That mental feeling of being in two places at once affected me physically as if the mood of secrecy had penetrated my very soul. Before an hour had elapsed since the ship had begun to move, having occasion to ask the mate (he stood by my side) to take a compass bearing of the Pagoda, I caught myself reaching up to his ear in whispers. I say I caught myself, but enough had escaped to startle the man. I can't describe it otherwise than by saying that he shied. A grave, preoccupied manner, as though he were in possession of some perplexing intelligence, did not leave him henceforth. A little later I moved away from the rail to look at the compass with such a stealthy gait that the helmsman noticed it—and I could not help noticing the unusual roundness of his eyes. These are trifling instances, though it's to no commander's advantage to be suspected of ludicrous eccentricities. But I was also more seriously affected. There are to a seaman certain words, gestures, that should in given conditions come as naturally, as instinctively as the winking of a menaced eye. A certain order should spring on to his lips without thinking; a certain sign should get itself made, so to speak, without reflection. But all unconscious alertness had abandoned me. I had to make an effort of will to recall myself back (from the cabin) to the conditions of the moment. I felt that I was appearing an irresolute commander to those people who were watching me more or less critically.

And, besides, there were the scares. On the second day out, for instance, coming off the deck in the afternoon (I had straw slippers on my bare feet) I stopped at the open pantry door and spoke to the steward. He was doing something there with his back to me. At the sound of my voice he nearly jumped out of his skin, as the saying is, and incidentally broke a cup.

"What on earth's the matter with you?" I asked, astonished.

He was extremely confused. "Beg your pardon, sir. I made sure you were in your cabin."

"You see I wasn't."

"No, sir. I could have sworn I had heard you moving in there not a moment ago. It's most extraordinary . . . very sorry, sir."

I passed on with an inward shudder. I was so identified with my secret double that I did not even mention the fact in those scanty, fearful whispers we exchanged. I suppose he had made some slight noise of some kind or other. It would have been miraculous if he hadn't at one time or another. And yet, haggard as he appeared, he looked always perfectly self-controlled, more than calm—almost invulnerable. On my suggestion he remained almost entirely in the bathroom, which, upon the whole, was the safest place. There could be really no shadow of an excuse for anyone ever wanting to go in there, once the steward had done with it. It was a very tiny place. Sometimes he reclined on the floor, his legs bent, his head sustained on one elbow. At others I would find him on the campstool, sitting in his gray sleeping suit and with his cropped dark hair like a patient, unmoved convict. At night I would smuggle him into my bed-place, and we would whisper together, with the regular footfalls of the officer of the watch passing and repassing over our heads. It was an infinitely miserable time. It was lucky that some tins of fine preserves were stowed in a locker in my stateroom; hard bread I could always get hold of; and so he lived on stewed chicken, paté de foie gras, asparagus, cooked oysters, sardines—on all sorts of abominable sham delicacies out of tins. My early morning coffee he always drank; and it was all I dared do for him in that respect.

Every day there was the horrible maneuvering to go through so that my room and then the bathroom should be done in the usual way. I came to hate the sight of the steward, to abhor the voice of that harmless man. I felt that it was he who would bring on the disaster of discovery. It hung like a sword over our heads.

The fourth day out, I think (we were then working down the east side of the Gulf of Siam, tack for tack, in light winds and smooth water)—the fourth day, I say, of this miserable juggling with the unavoidable, as we sat at our evening meal, that man, whose slightest movement I dreaded, after putting down the dishes ran up on deck busily. This could not be dangerous. Presently he came down again; and then it appeared that he had remembered a coat of mine which I had thrown over a rail to dry after having been wetted in a shower which had passed over the ship in the afternoon. Sitting stolidly at the head of the table I became terrified at the sight of the garment on his arm. Of course he made for my door. There was no time to lose.

"Steward," I thundered. My nerves were so shaken that I could not govern my voice and conceal my agitation. This was the sort of thing that made my terrifically whiskered mate tap his forehead with his forefinger. I had detected him using that gesture while talking on deck with a confidential air to the carpenter. It was too far to hear a word, but I had no doubt that this pantomime could only refer to the strange new captain.

"Yes, sir," the pale-faced steward turned resignedly to me. It was this maddening course of being shouted at, checked without rhyme or reason, arbitrarily chased out of my cabin, suddenly called into it, sent flying out of his pantry on incomprehensible errands, that accounted for the growing wretchedness of his expression.

"Where are you going with that coat?"

"To your room, sir."

"Is there another shower coming?"

"I'm sure I don't know, sir. Shall I go up again and see, sir?"

"No! never mind."

My object was attained, as of course my other self in there would have heard everything that passed. During this interlude my two officers never raised their eyes off their respective plates; but the lip of that confounded cub, the second mate, quivered visibly.

I expected the steward to hook my coat on and come out at once. He was very slow about it; but I dominated my nervousness sufficiently not to shout after him. Suddenly I became aware (it could be heard plainly enough) that the fellow for some reason or other was opening the door of the bathroom. It was the end. The place was literally not big enough to swing a cat in. My voice died in my throat and I went stony all over. I expected to hear a yell of surprise and terror, and made a movement, but had not the strength to get on my legs. Everything remained still. Had my second self taken the poor wretch by the throat? I don't know what I would have done next moment if I had not seen the steward come out of my room, close the door, and then stand quietly by the sideboard.

Saved, I thought. But, no! Lost! Gone! He was gone!

I laid my knife and fork down and leaned back in my chair. My head swam. After a while, when sufficiently recovered to speak in a steady voice, I instructed my mate to put the ship round at eight o'clock himself.

"I won't come on deck," I went on. "I think I'll turn in, and unless the wind shifts I don't want to be disturbed before midnight. I feel a bit seedy."

"You did look middling bad a little while ago," the chief mate remarked without showing any great concern.

They both went out, and I stared at the steward clearing the table. There was nothing to be read on that wretched man's face. But why did he avoid my eyes I asked myself. Then I thought I should like to hear the sound of his voice.

"Steward!"

"Sir!" Startled as usual.

"Where did you hang up that coat?"

"In the bathroom, sir." The usual anxious tone. "It's not quite dry yet, sir."

For some time longer I sat in the cuddy. Had my double vanished as he had come? But of his coming there was an explanation, whereas his disappearance would be inexplicable. . . . I went slowly into my dark room, shut the door, lighted the lamp, and for a time dared not turn round. When at last I did I saw him standing bolt upright in the narrow recessed part. It would not be true to say I had a shock, but an irresistible doubt of his bodily existence flitted through my mind. Can it be, I asked myself, that he is not visible to other eyes than mine? It was like being haunted. Motionless, with a grave face, he raised his hands slightly at me in a gesture which meant clearly, "Heavens! what a narrow escape!" Narrow indeed. I think I had come creeping quietly as near insanity as any man who has not actually gone over the border. That gesture restrained me, so to speak.

The mate with the terrific whiskers was now putting the ship on the other tack. In the moment of profound silence which follows upon the hands going to their stations I heard on the poop his raised voice: "Hard alee!" and the distant shout of the order repeated on the maindeck. The sails, in that light breeze, made but a faint fluttering noise. It ceased. The ship was coming around slowly; I held my breath in the renewed stillness of expectation; one wouldn't have thought that there was a single living soul on her decks. A sudden brisk shout, "Mainsail haul!" broke the spell, and in the noisy cries and rush overhead of the men running away with the main brace we two, down in my cabin, came together in our usual position by the bed-place.

He did not wait for my question. "I heard him fumbling here and just managed to squat myself down in the bath," he whispered to me. "The fellow only opened the door and put his arm in to hang the coat up. All the same—"

"I never thought of that," I whispered back, even more appalled than before at the closeness of the shave, and marveling at that something unyielding in his character which was carrying him through so finely. There was no agitation in his whisper. Whoever was being driven distracted, it was not he. He was sane. And the proof of his sanity was continued when he took up the whispering again.

"It would never do for me to come to life again."

It was something that a ghost might have said. But what he was alluding to was his old captain's reluctant admission of the theory of suicide. It would obviously serve his turn—if I had understood at all the view which seemed to govern the unalterable purpose of his action.

"You must maroon me as soon as ever you can get amongst these islands off the Cambodje shore," he went on.

"Maroon you! We are not living in a boy's adventure tale," I protested. His scornful whispering took me up.

"We aren't indeed! There's nothing of a boy's tale in this. But there's nothing else for it. I want no more. You don't suppose I am afraid of what can be done to me? Prison or gallows or whatever they may please. But you don't see me coming back to explain such things to an old fellow in a wig and twelve respectable tradesmen, do you? What can they know whether I am guilty or not—or of *what* I am guilty, either? That's my affair. What does the Bible say? 'Driven off the face of the earth.' Very well. I am off the face of the earth now. As I came at night so I shall go."

"Impossible!" I murmured. "You can't."

"Can't? . . . Not naked like a soul on the Day of Judgment. I shall freeze on to this sleeping suit. The Last Day is not yet—and . . . you have understood thoroughly. Didn't you?"

I felt suddenly ashamed of myself. I may say truly that I understood—and my hesitation in letting that man swim away from my ship's side had been a mere sham sentiment, a sort of cowardice.

"It can't be done now till next night," I breathed out. "The ship is on the offshore tack and the wind may fail us."

"As long as I know that you understand," he whispered. "But of course you do. It's a great satisfaction to have got somebody to understand. You seem to have been there on purpose." And in the same whisper, as if we two whenever we talked had to say things to each other which were not fit for the world to hear, he added, "It's very wonderful."

We remained side by side talking in our secret way—but sometimes silent or just exchanging a whispered word or two at long intervals. And as usual he stared through the port. A breath of wind came now and again onto our faces. The ship might have been moored in dock, so gently and on an even keel she slipped through the water, that did not murmur even at our passage, shadowy and silent like a phantom sea.

At midnight I went on deck, and to my mate's great surprise put the ship round on the other tack. His terrible whiskers flitted round me in silent criticism. I certainly should not have done it if it had been only a question of getting out of that sleepy gulf as quickly as possible. I believe he told the second mate, who relieved him, that it was a great want of judg-ment. The other only yawned. That intolerable cub shuffled about so sleep-ily and lolled against the rails in such a slack, improper fashion that I came down on him sharply.

"Aren't you properly awake yet?"

"Yes, sir! I am awake."

"Well, then, be good enough to hold yourself as if you were. And keep a lookout. If there's any current we'll be closing with some islands before daylight."

The east side of the gulf is fringed with islands, some solitary, others in groups. On the blue background of the high coast they seem to float on silvery patches of calm water, arid and gray, or dark green and rounded like clumps of evergreen bushes, with the larger ones, a mile or two long, show-ing the outlines of ridges, ribs of gray rock under the dark mantle of matted leafage. Unknown to trade, to travel, almost to geography, the manner of life they harbor is an unsolved secret. There must be villages—settlements of fishermen at least—on the largest of them, and some communication with the world is probably kept up by native craft. But all the forenoon, as we headed for them, fanned along by the faintest of breezes, I saw no sign of man or canoe in the field of the telescope I kept on pointing at the scattered group.

At noon I gave no orders for a change of course, and the mate's whiskers became much concerned and seemed to be offering themselves unduly to my notice. At last I said:

"I am going to stand right in. Quite in—as far as I can take her."

The stare of extreme surprise imparted an air of ferocity also to his eyes, and he looked truly terrific for a moment.

"We're not doing well in the middle of the gulf," I continued, casually. "I am going to look for the land breezes tonight."

"Bless my soul! Do you mean, sir, in the dark amongst the lot of all them islands and reefs and shoals?"

"Well—if there are any regular land breezes at all on this coast one must get close inshore to find them, mustn't one?"

"Bless my soul!" he exclaimed again under his breath. All that afternoon he wore a dreamy, contemplative appearance which in him was a mark of perplexity. After dinner I went into my stateroom as if I meant to take some rest. There we two bent our dark heads over a half-unrolled chart lying on my bed.

"There," I said. "It's got to be Koh-ring. I've been looking at it ever since sunrise. It has got two hills and a low point. It must be inhabited. And on the coast opposite there is what looks like the mouth of a biggish river—with some town, no doubt, not far up. It's the best chance for you that I can see."

"Anything. Koh-ring let it be."

He looked thoughtfully at the chart as if surveying chances and distances from a lofty height—and following with his eyes his own figure wandering on the blank land of Cochin-China, and then passing off that piece of paper clean out of sight into uncharted regions. And it was as if the ship had two captains to plan her course for her. I had been so worried and restless running up and down that I had not had the patience to dress that day. I had remained in my sleeping suit, with straw slippers and a soft floppy hat. The closeness of the heat in the gulf had been most oppressive, and the crew were used to see me wandering in that airy attire.

"She will clear the south point as she heads now," I whispered into his ear. "Goodness only knows when, though, but certainly after dark. I'll edge her in to half a mile, as far as I may be able to judge in the dark—"

"Be careful," he murmured, warningly—and I realized suddenly that all my future, the only future of which I was fit, would perhaps go irretrievably to pieces in any mishap to my first command.

I could not stop a moment longer in the room. I motioned him to get out of sight and made my way on the poop. That unplayful cub had the watch. I walked up and down for a while thinking things out, then beckoned him over.

"Send a couple of hands to open the two quarter-deck ports," I said, mildly.

He actually had the impudence, or else so forgot himself in his wonder at such an incomprehensible order, as to repeat:

"Open the quarter-deck ports! What for, sir?"

"The only reason you need concern yourself about is because I tell you to do so. Have them open wide and fastened properly."

He reddened and went off, but I believe made some jeering remark to the carpenter as to the sensible practice of ventilating a ship's quarter-deck. I know he popped into the mate's cabin to impart the fact to him because the whiskers came on deck, as it were by chance, and stole glances at me from below—for signs of lunacy or drunkenness, I suppose.

A little before supper, feeling more restless than ever, I rejoined, for a moment, my second self. And to find him sitting so quietly was surprising, like something against nature, inhuman.

I developed my plan in a hurried whisper.

"I shall stand in as close as I dare and then put her round. I shall presently find means to smuggle you out of here into the sail locker, which communicates with the lobby. But there is an opening, a sort of square for hauling the sails out, which gives straight on the quarter-deck and which is never closed in fine weather, so as to give air to the sails. When the ship's way is deadened in stays and all the hands are aft at the main braces you shall have a clear road to slip out and get overboard through the open quarter-deck port. I've had them both fastened up. Use a rope's end to lower yourself into the water so as to avoid a splash—you know. It could be heard and cause some beastly complication."

He kept silent for a while, then whispered, "I understand."

"I won't be there to see you go," I began with an effort. "The rest . . . I only hope I have understood, too."

"You have. From first to last," and for the first time there seemed to be a faltering, something strained in his whisper. He caught hold of my arm, but the ringing of the supper bell made me start. He didn't, though; he only released his grip.

After supper I didn't come below again till well past eight o'clock. The faint, steady breeze was loaded with dew; and the wet, darkened sails held all there was of propelling power in it. The night, clear and starry, sparkled darkly, and the opaque, lightless patches shifting slowly against the low stars were the drifting islets. On the port bow there was a big one more distant and shadowily imposing by the great space of sky it eclipsed.

On opening the door I had a back view of my very own self looking at a chart. He had come out of the recess and was standing near the table.

"Quite dark enough," I whispered.

He stepped back and leaned against my bed with a level, quiet glance. I sat on the couch. We had nothing to say to each other. Over our heads the officer of the watch moved here and there. Then I heard him move quickly. I knew what that meant. He was making for the companion; and presently his voice was outside my door.

"We are drawing in pretty fast, sir. Land looks rather close."

"Very well," I answered. "I am coming on deck directly."

I waited till he was gone out of the cuddy, then rose. My double moved too. The time had come to exchange our last whispers, for neither of us was ever to hear each other's natural voice.

"Look here!" I opened a drawer and took out three sovereigns. "Take this, anyhow. I've got six and I'd give you the lot, only I must keep a little money to buy some fruit and vegetables for the crew from native boats as we go through Sunda Straits."

He shook his head.

"Take it," I urged him, whispering desperately. "No one can tell what—"

He smiled and slapped meaningly the only pocket of the sleeping jacket. It was not safe, certainly. But I produced a large old silk handkerchief of mine, and tying the three pieces of gold in a corner, pressed it on him. He was touched, I suppose, because he took it at last and tied it quickly round his waist under the jacket, on his bare skin.

Our eyes met; several seconds elapsed, till, our glances still mingled, I extended my hand and turned the lamp out. Then I passed through the cuddy, leaving the door of my room wide open. . . . "Steward!"

He was still lingering in the pantry in the greatness of his zeal, giving a rub-up to a plated cruet stand the last thing before going to bed. Being careful not to wake up the mate, whose room was opposite, I spoke in an undertone.

He looked round anxiously. "Sir!"

"Can you get me a little hot water from the galley?"

"I am afraid, sir, the galley fire's been out for some time now."

"Go and see."

He fled up the stairs.

"Now," I whispered, loudly, into the saloon—too loudly, perhaps, but I was afraid I couldn't make a sound. He was by my side in an instant—the double captain slipped past the stairs—through the tiny dark passage . . . a sliding door. We were in the sail locker, scrambling on our knees over the sails. A sudden thought struck me. I saw myself wandering barefooted, bareheaded, the sun beating on my dark poll. I snatched off my floppy hat and tried hurriedly in the dark to ram it on my other self. He dodged and fended off silently. I wonder what he thought had come to me before he understood and suddenly desisted. Our hands met gropingly, lingered united in a steady, motionless clasp for a second. . . . No word was breathed by either of us when they separated.

I was standing quietly by the pantry door when the steward returned.

"Sorry, sir. Kettle barely warm. Shall I light the spirit lamp?"

"Never mind."

I came out on deck slowly. It was now a matter of conscience to shave the land as close as possible—for now he must go overboard whenever the ship was put in stays. Must! There could be no going back for him. After a moment I walked over to leeward and my heart flew into my mouth at the nearness of the land on the bow. Under any other circumstances I would not have held on a minute longer. The second mate had followed me anxiously.

I looked on till I felt I could command my voice.

"She will weather," I said then in a quiet tone.

"Are you going to try that, sir?" he stammered out incredulously.

I took no notice of him and raised my tone just enough to be heard by the helmsman.

"Keep her good full."

"Good full, sir."

The wind fanned my cheek, the sails slept, the world was silent. The strain of watching the dark loom of the land grow bigger and denser was too much for me. I had shut my eyes—because the ship must go closer. She must! The stillness was intolerable. Were we standing still?

When I opened my eyes the second view started my heart with a thump. The black southern hill of Koh-ring seemed to hang right over the ship like a towering fragment of the everlasting night. On that enormous mass of blackness there was not a gleam to be seen, not a sound to be heard. It was gliding irresistibly toward us and yet seemed already within reach of the hand. I saw the vague figures of the watch grouped in the waist, gazing in awed silence.

"Are you going on, sir?" inquired an unsteady voice at my elbow.

I ignored it. I had to go on.

"Keep her full. Don't check her way. That won't do now," I said warningly.

"I can't see the sails very well," the helmsman answered me, in strange, quavering tones.

Was she close enough? Already she was, I won't say in the shadow of the land, but in the very blackness of it, already swallowed up as it were, gone too close to be recalled, gone from me altogether.

"Give the mate a call," I said to the young man who stood at my elbow as still as death. "And turn all hands up."

My tone had a borrowed loudness reverberated from the height of the land. Several voices cried out together: "We are all on deck, sir."

Then stillness again, with the great shadow gliding closer, towering higher, without a light, without a sound. Such a hush had fallen on the ship that she might have been a bark of the dead floating in slowly under the very gate of Erebus.

"My God! Where are we?"

It was the mate moaning at my elbow. He was thunderstruck, and as it were deprived of the moral support of his whiskers. He clapped his hands and absolutely cried out, "Lost!"

"Be quiet," I said sternly.

He lowered his tone, but I saw the shadowy gesture of his despair. "What are we doing here?"

"Looking for the land wind."

He made as if to tear his hair, and addressed me recklessly.

"She will never get out. You have done it, sir. I knew it'd end in something like this. She will never weather, and you are too close now to stay. She'll drift ashore before she's round. O my God!"

I caught his arm as he was raising it to batter his poor devoted head, and shook it violently.

"She's ashore already," he wailed, trying to tear himself away.

"Is she? . . . Keep good full there!"

"Good full, sir," cried the helmsman in a frightened, thin childlike voice.

I hadn't let go the mate's arm and went on shaking it. "Ready about, do you hear? You go forward"—shake—"and stop there"—shake—"and hold your noise"—shake—"and see these head sheets properly overhauled" —shake, shake—shake.

And all the time I dared not look toward the land lest my heart should fail me. I released my grip at last and he ran forward as if fleeing for dear life.

I wondered what my double there in the sail locker thought of this commotion. He was able to hear everything and perhaps he was able to understand why, on my conscience, it had to be thus close—no less. My first order "Hard alee!" re-echoed ominously under the towering shadow of Koh-ring as if I had shouted in a mountain gorge. And then I watched the land intently. In that smooth water and light wind it was impossible to feel the ship coming-to. No! I could not feel her. And my second self was making now ready to slip out and lower himself overboard. Perhaps he was gone already . . . ?

The great black mass brooding over our very mastheads began to pivot away from the ship's side silently. And now I forgot the secret stranger ready to depart, and remembered only that I was a total stranger to the ship. I did not know her. Would she do it? How was she to be handled?

I swung the mainyard and waited helplessly. She was perhaps stopped, and her very fate hung in the balance, with the black mass of Koh-ring like the gate of the everlasting night towering over her taffrail. What would she do now? Had she way on her yet? I stepped to the side swiftly, and on the shadowy water I could see nothing except a faint phosphorescent flash revealing the glassy smoothness of the sleeping surface. It was impossible to tell—and I had not learned yet the feel of my ship. Was she moving? What I needed was something easily seen, a piece of paper, which I could throw overboard and watch. I had nothing on me. To run down for it I didn't dare. There was no time. All at once my strained, yearning stare distinguished a white object floating within a yard of the ship's side. White on the black water. A phosphorescent flash passed under it. What was that thing? . . . I recognized my own floppy hat. It must have fallen off his head . . . and he didn't bother. Now I had what I wanted—the saving mark for my eyes. But I hardly thought of my other self, now gone from the ship, to be hidden forever from all friendly faces, to be a fugitive and a vagabond on the earth, with no brand of the curse on his sane forehead to stay a slaying hand . . . too proud to explain.

And I watched the hat—the expression of my sudden pity for his mere flesh. It had been meant to save his homeless head from the dangers of the sun. And now—behold—it was saving the ship, by serving me for a mark to help out the ignorance of my strangeness. Ha! It was drifting forward, warning me just in time that the ship had gathered sternway.

"Shift the helm," I said in a low voice to the seaman standing still like a statue.

The man's eyes glistened wildly in the binnacle light as he jumped round to the other side and spun round the wheel.

I walked to the break of the poop. On the overshadowed deck all hands stood by the forebraces waiting for my order. The stars ahead seemed to be gliding from right to left. And all was so still in the world that I heard the quiet remark "She's round," passed in a tone of intense relief between two seamen.

"Let go and haul."

The foreyards ran round with a great noise, amidst cheery cries. And now the frightful whiskers made themselves heard giving various orders. Already the ship was drawing ahead. And I was alone with her. Nothing! no one in the world should stand now between us, throwing a shadow on the way of silent knowledge and mute affection, the perfect communion of a seaman with his first command.

Walking to the taffrail, I was in time to make out, on the very edge of a darkness thrown by a towering black mass like the very gateway of Erebus —yes, I was in time to catch an evanescent glimpse of my white hat left behind to mark the spot where the secret sharer of my cabin and of my thoughts, as though he were my second self, had lowered himself into the water to take his punishment: a free man, a proud swimmer striking out for a new destiny.

§ FOR COMMENT

"And I was alone with her [the ship]. . . ." What is the significance of this statement? Is it symbolic? Is the ship symbolic? Notice how the captain feels about his first command. "But what I felt most was my being a stranger to the ship; and if all the truth must be told, I was somewhat of a stranger to myself." The captain's feelings of strangeness and his desire to get to know his ship cause him to take the watch. As he stands watch, he suddenly feels a great rejoicing in the security of the ship. This feeling of rejoicing is juxtaposed with a feeling of vexation. Why? The captain gives a vigorous tug to the side-ladder (its being there is his fault), and his tug is answered. The man in the water is another stranger, and after talking with him for a few minutes, the captain feels that a mysterious bond is established.

What is the relationship between the captain and Leggatt? Notice that the word "double" is used some twenty times in the narrative. It would appear that Conrad is making a close identification between the two men to the extent that some critics have called Leggatt the captain's alter ego. Leggatt emerges in a sudden glow from the dark waters. If he is the captain's second self, then he needs to be significantly different in some way from the captain. Is he? Some critics think Leggatt is the psychological embodiment of the ideal of selfhood to which the captain must measure up. Can this statement be supported by reference to the story? Remember that Leggatt has killed a man.

Why does Conrad tell this story in the first person? Can this narrator be trusted? What is the significance of the L-shaped room? What roles do the crewmen and the captain of the *Sephora* play?

Thomas Mann § 1875–1955

A major figure with a worldwide reputation and winner of the 1929 Nobel Prize for literature, Mann published his first novel, Buddenbrooks, *in Germany when he was only twenty-five. A fine first novel, it incorporates many of the themes Mann later reworked and elaborated on, especially in the area of cultural and psychological problems, more especially the relationship between creativity and neurosis and between genius and disease. To recognize his real achievement, however, one must read his later novels among which are* The Magic Mountain (1924) *and* Dr. Faustus (1948) *and some of his long short stories such as the masterpiece "Death in Venice" (1913). Mann was an exile from the Nazi regime. Although he continued to write in German, he took up residence in the United States and became an American citizen in 1944. Then, in 1952, troubled by increasing political tensions in the United States, he moved to Switzerland. This translation is by H. T. Lowe-Porter.*

The Infant Prodigy

The infant prodigy entered. The hall became quiet.

It became quiet and then the audience began to clap, because somewhere at the side a leader of mobs, a born organizer, clapped first. The audience had heard nothing yet, but they applauded; for a mighty publicity organization had heralded the prodigy and people were already hypnotized, whether they knew it or not.

The prodigy came from behind a splendid screen embroidered with Empire garlands and great conventionalized flowers, and climbed nimbly up the steps to the platform, diving into the applause as into a bath; a little chilly and shivering, but yet as though into a friendly element. He advanced to the edge of the platform and smiled as though he were about to be photographed; he made a shy, charming gesture of greeting, like a little girl.

He was dressed entirely in white silk, which the audience found enchanting. The little white jacket was fancifully cut, with a sash underneath it, and even his shoes were made of white silk. But against the white socks his bare little legs stood out quite brown; for he was a Greek boy.

He was called Bibi Saccellaphylaccas. And such indeed was his name. No one knew what Bibi was the pet name for, nobody but the impresario, and he regarded it as a trade secret. Bibi had smooth black hair reaching to his shoulders; it was parted on the side and fastened back from the narrow domed forehead by a little silk bow. His was the most harmless childish countenance in the world, with an unfinished nose and guileless mouth. The area beneath his pitch-black mouselike eyes was already a little tired and visibly lined. He looked as though he were nine years old but was really eight and given out for seven. It was hard to tell whether to believe this or not. Probably everybody knew better and still believed it, as happens about so many things. The average man thinks that a little falseness goes with beauty. Where should we get any excitement out of our daily life if we were not willing to pretend a bit? And the average man is quite right, in his average brains!

The prodigy kept on bowing until the applause died down, then he went up to the grand piano, and the audience cast a last look at its programmes. First came a *Marche solennelle,*[1] then a *Rêverie,* and then *Le Hibou et les moineaux*[2]—all by Bibi Saccellaphylaccas. The whole programme was by him, they were all his compositions. He could not score them, of course, but he had them all in his extraordinary little head and they possessed real artistic significance, or so it said, seriously and objectively, in the programme. The programme sounded as though the impresario had wrested these concessions from his critical nature after a hard struggle.

[1] *Marche solennelle:* Solemn march.
[2] *Le Hibou et les moineaux:* The owl and the sparrows.

The prodigy sat down upon the revolving stool and felt with his feet for the pedals, which were raised by means of a clever device so that Bibi could reach them. It was Bibi's own piano, he took it everywhere with him. It rested upon wooden trestles and its polish was somewhat marred by the constant transportation—but all that only made things more interesting.

Bibi put his silk-shod feet on the pedals; then he made an artful little face, looked straight ahead of him, and lifted his right hand. It was a brown, childish little hand; but the wrist was strong and unlike a child's, with well-developed bones.

Bibi made his face for the audience because he was aware that he had to entertain them a little. But he had his own private enjoyment in the thing too, an enjoyment which he could never convey to anybody. It was that prickling delight, that secret shudder of bliss, which ran through him every time he sat at an open piano—it would always be with him. And here was the keyboard again, these seven black and white octaves, among which he had so often lost himself in abysmal and thrilling adventures—and yet it always looked as clean and untouched as a newly washed blackboard. This was the realm of music that lay before him. It lay spread out like an inviting ocean, where he might plunge in and blissfully swim, where he might let himself be borne and carried away, where he might go under in night and storm, yet keep the mastery: control, ordain—he held his right hand poised in the air.

A breathless stillness reigned in the room—the tense moment before the first note came. . . . How would it begin? It began so. And Bibi, with his index finger, fetched the first note out of the piano, a quite unexpectedly powerful first note in the middle register, like a trumpet blast. Others followed, an introduction developed—the audience relaxed.

The concert was held in the palatial hall of a fashionable first-class hotel. The walls were covered with mirrors framed in gilded arabesques, between frescoes of the rosy and fleshly school. Ornamental columns supported a ceiling that displayed a whole universe of electric bulbs, in clusters darting a brilliance far brighter than day and filling the whole space with thin, vibrating golden light. Not a seat was unoccupied, people were standing in the side aisles and at the back. The front seats cost twelve marks; for the impresario believed that anything worth having was worth paying for. And they were occupied by the best society, for it was in the upper classes, of course, that the greatest enthusiasm was felt. There were even some children, with their legs hanging down demurely from their chairs and their shining eyes staring at their gifted little white-clad contemporary.

Down in front on the left side sat the prodigy's mother, an extremely obese woman with a powdered double chin and a feather on her head. Beside her was the impresario, a man of oriental appearance with large gold buttons on his conspicuous cuffs. The princess was in the middle of the front row—a wrinkled, shrivelled little old princess but still a patron of the arts, especially everything full of sensibility. She sat in a deep, velvet-upholstered arm chair, and a Persian carpet was spread before her feet. She held her hands, folded over her grey striped-silk breast, put her head on one side, and presented a picture of elegant composure as she sat looking up at the performing prodigy. Next her sat her lady-in-waiting, in a green striped-silk gown. Being only a lady-in-waiting she had to sit up very straight in her chair.

Bibi ended in a grand climax. With what power this wee manikin belaboured the keyboard! The audience could scarcely trust its ears. The march theme, an infectious, swinging tune, broke out once more, fully harmonized, bold and showy; with every note Bibi flung himself back from the waist as though he were marching in a triumphal procession. He ended *fortissimo*, bent over, slipped sideways off the stool, and stood with a smile awaiting the applause.

And the applause burst forth, unanimously, enthusiastically; the child made his demure little maidenly curtsy and people in the front seat thought: "Look what slim little hips he has! Clap, clap! Hurrah, bravo, little chap, Saccophylax or whatever your name is! Wait, let me take off my gloves—what a little devil of a chap he is!"

Bibi had to come out three times from behind the screen before they would stop. Some latecomers entered the hall and moved about looking for seats. Then the concert continued. Bibi's *Rêverie* murmured its numbers, consisting almost entirely of arpeggios, above which a bar of melody rose now and then, weak-winged. Then came *Le Hibou et les moineaux*. This piece was brilliantly successful, it made a strong impression; it was an effective childhood fantasy, remarkably well envisaged. The bass represented the owl, sitting morosely rolling his filmy eyes; while in the treble the impudent, half-frightened sparrows chirped. Bibi received an ovation when he finished, he was called out four times. A hotel page with shiny buttons carried up three great laurel wreaths onto the stage and proffered them from one side while Bibi nodded and expressed his thanks. Even the princess shared in the applause, daintily and noiselessly pressing her palms together.

Ah, the knowing little creature understood how to make people clap! He stopped behind the screen, they had to wait for him; lingered a little on the steps of the platform, admired the long streamers on the wreaths—although actually such things bored him stiff by now. He bowed with the utmost charm, he gave the audience plenty of time to rave itself out, because applause is valuable and must not be cut short. "*Le Hibou* is my drawing card," he thought—this expression he had learned from the impresario. "Now I will play the fantasy, it is a lot better than *Le Hibou*, of course, especially the C-sharp passage. But you idiots dote on the *Hibou*, though it is the first and the silliest thing I wrote." He continued to bow and smile.

Next came a *Méditation* and then an *Étude*—the programme was quite comprehensive. The *Méditation* was very like the *Rêverie*—which was nothing against it—and the *Étude* displayed all of Bibi's virtuosity, which naturally fell a little short of his inventiveness. And then the *Fantaisie*. This was his favourite; he varied it a little each time, giving himself free rein and sometimes surprising even himself, on good evenings, by his own inventiveness.

He sat and played, so little, so white and shining, against the great black grand piano, elect and alone, above that confused sea of faces, above the heavy, insensitive mass soul, upon which he was labouring to work with his individual, differentiated soul. His lock of soft black hair with the white silk bow had fallen over his forehead, his trained and bony little wrists pounded away, the muscles stood out visibly on his brown childish cheeks.

Sitting there he sometimes had moments of oblivion and solitude, when the gaze of his strange little mouselike eyes with the big rings beneath them would lose itself and stare through the painted stage into space that was peopled with strange vague life. Then out of the corner of his eye he would give a quick look back into the hall and be once more with his audience.

"Joy and pain, the heights and the depths—that is my *Fantaisie*," he thought lovingly. "Listen, here is the C-sharp passage." He lingered over the approach, wondering if they would notice anything. But no, of course not, how should they? And he cast his eyes up prettily at the ceiling so that at least they might have something to look at.

All these people sat there in their regular rows, looking at the prodigy and thinking all sorts of things in their regular brains. An old gentleman with a white beard, a seal ring on his finger and a bulbous swelling on his bald spot, a growth if you like, was thinking to himself: "Really, one ought to be ashamed." He had never got any further than "Ah, thou dearest Augustin" on the piano, and here he sat now, a grey old man, looking on while this little hop-o'-my-thumb performed miracles. Yes, yes, it is a gift of God, we must remember that. God grants His gifts, or He withholds them, and there is no shame in being an ordinary man. Like with the Christ Child. —Before a child one may kneel without feeling ashamed. Strange that thoughts like these should be so satisfying—he would even say so sweet, if it was not too silly for a tough old man like him to use the word. That was how he felt, anyhow.

Art . . . the business man with the parrot-nose was thinking. "Yes, it adds something cheerful to life, a little good white silk and a little tumty-ti-ti-tum. Really he does not play so badly. Fully fifty seats, twelve marks apiece, that makes six hundred marks—and everything else besides. Take off the rent of the hall, the lighting and the programmes, you must have fully a thousand marks profit. That is worth while."

That was Chopin he was just playing, thought the piano teacher, a lady with a pointed nose; she was of an age when the understanding sharpens as the hopes decay. "But not very original—I will say that afterwards, it sounds well. And his hand position is entirely amateur. One must be able to lay a coin on the back of the hand—I would use a ruler on him."

Then there was a young girl, at that self-conscious and chlorotic time of life when the most ineffable ideas come into the mind. She was thinking to herself: "What is it he is playing? It is expressive of passion, yet he is a child. If he kissed me it would be as though my little brother kissed me— no kiss at all. Is there such a thing as passion all by itself, without any earthly object, a sort of child's-play of passion? What nonsense! If I were to say such things aloud they would just be at me with some more cod-liver oil. Such is life."

An officer was leaning against a column. He looked on at Bibi's success and thought: "Yes, you are something and I am something, each in his own way." So he clapped his heels together and paid to the prodigy the respect which he felt to be due to all the powers that be.

Then there was a critic, an elderly man in a shiny black coat and turned-up trousers splashed with mud. He sat in his free seat and thought: "Look at him, this young beggar of a Bibi. As an individual he has still to develop, but as a type he is already quite complete, the artist *par excellence*. He has in himself all the artist's exaltation and his utter worthlessness, his charlatanry and his sacred fire, his burning contempt and his secret raptures. Of course I can't write all that, it is too good. Of course, I should have been an artist myself if I had not seen through the whole business so clearly."

Then the prodigy stopped playing and a perfect storm arose in the hall. He had to come out again and again from behind his screen. The man with the shiny buttons carried up more wreaths: four laurel wreaths, a lyre made of violets, a bouquet of roses. He had not arms enough to convey all these tributes, the impresario himself mounted the stage to help him. He hung a laurel wreath round Bibi's neck, he tenderly stroked the black hair—and suddenly as though overcome he bent down and gave the prodigy a kiss, a resounding kiss, square on the mouth. And then the storm became a hurricane. That kiss ran through the room like an electric shock, it went direct to peoples' marrow and made them shiver down their backs. They were carried away by a helpless compulsion of sheer noise. Loud shouts mingled with the hysterical clapping of hands. Some of Bibi's commonplace little friends down there waved their handkerchiefs. But the critic thought: "Of course that kiss had to come—it's a good old gag. Yes, good Lord, if only one did not see through everything quite so clearly—"

And so the concert drew to a close. It began at half past seven and finished at half past eight. The platform was laden with wreaths and two little pots of flowers stood on the lamp stands of the piano. Bibi played as his last number his *Rhapsodie grecque*, which turned into the Greek national hymn at the end. His fellow-countrymen in the audience would gladly have sung it with him if the company had not been so august. They made up for it with a powerful noise and hullabaloo, a hot-blooded national demonstration. And the aging critic was thinking: "Yes, the hymn had to come too. They have to exploit every vein—publicity cannot afford to neglect any means to its end. I think I'll criticize that as inartistic. But perhaps I am wrong, perhaps that is the most artistic thing of all. What is the artist? A jack-in-the-box. Criticism is on a higher plane. But I can't say that." And away he went in his muddy trousers.

After being called out nine or ten times the prodigy did not come any more from behind the screen but went to his mother and the impresario down in the hall. The audience stood about among the chairs and applauded and pressed forward to see Bibi close at hand. Some of them wanted to see the princess too. Two dense circles formed, one round the prodigy, the other round the princess, and you could actually not tell which of them was receiving more homage. But the court lady was commanded to go over to Bibi; she smoothed down his silk jacket a bit to make it look suitable for a court function, led him by the arm to the princess, and solemnly indicated to him that he was to kiss the royal hand. "How do you do it, child?" asked the princess. "Does it come into your head of itself when you sit down?" "Oui, madame," answered Bibi. To himself he thought: "Oh, what a stupid old princess!" Then he turned round shyly and uncourtierlike and went back to his family.

Outside in the cloak room there was a crowd. People held up their numbers and received with open arms furs, shawls, and galoshes. Somewhere among her acquaintances the piano teacher stood making her critique. "He is not very original," she said audibly and looked about her.

In front of one of the great mirrors an elegant young lady was being arrayed in her evening cloak and fur shoes by her brothers, two lieutenants. She was exquisitely beautiful, with her steel-blue eyes and her clean-cut, well-bred face. A really noble dame. When she was ready she stood waiting for her brothers. "Don't stand so long in front of the glass, Adolf," she said softly to one of them, who could not tear himself away from the sight of his simple, good-looking young features. But Lieutenant Adolf thinks: What cheek! He would button his overcoat in front of the glass, just the same. Then they went out on the street where the arc lights gleamed cloudily through the white mist. Lieutenant Adolf struck up a little nigger dance on the frozen snow to keep warm, with his hands in his slanting overcoat pockets and his collar turned up.

A girl with untidy hair and swinging arms, accompanied by a gloomy-faced youth, came out just behind them. A child! she thought. A charming child. But in there he was an awe-inspiring . . . and aloud in a toneless voice she said: "We are all infant prodigies, we artists."

"Well, bless my soul!" thought the old gentleman who had never got further than Augustin on the piano, and whose boil was now concealed by a top hat. "What does all that mean? She sounds very oracular." But the gloomy youth understood. He nodded his head slowly.

Then they were silent and the untidy-haired girl gazed after the brothers and sister. She rather despised them, but she looked after them until they had turned the corner.

§ FOR COMMENT

In his writings Mann returns again and again to the subject of the artist in society and to explorations of the artist's personality, his tensions and conflicts, and his relationship to his art. In this story the artist is a child, an infant prodigy. But the term has an ironic ring to it. Indeed, the omniscient narrator makes pointed ironic commentary throughout the story. Point out several instances of this kind of commentary and discuss its function in the story. What would the story be like without any kind of commentary?

The concert is staged as a play by an impresario knowledgeable in the devices that draw audience attention and applause. Everything, the stage, the concert hall, the boy himself, seems showy, splendid, and false. But in spite of appearances, there is something about the boy that remains real. He has a vital relationship with the music, a private enjoyment, not conveyed to the audience before him. His is the only real response to the music itself; the responses of the members of the audience are not to the music but to their own individual problems and needs. Their responses thus reveal nothing about the music, but everything about themselves. Examine these responses and try to account for them. Pay particular attention to the critic's response, for he is the one who asks the question, "What is the artist?" and to the response of the untidy-haired girl whose actions end the story.

Sherwood Anderson § 1876–1941

Although he had little formal education, Sherwood Anderson became a successful businessman, but abandoned his career and his family and went to Chicago to become a writer. While there he took part in the so-called "Chicago Renaissance" with such authors as Carl Sandburg, Floyd Dell, and Ben Hecht. His first two novels were not successful, but Dark Laughter *(1925) became a best seller. Other novels followed. Not the novels, however, but the short stories provide for Anderson a secure position in American literary history. His collection,* Winesburg, Ohio, *a volume of stories rather loosely organized around the character George Willard, gave new life to the genre. After the publication of this volume, Anderson*

*wrote numerous other stories, some of the more famous being pub-
lished in* The Triumph of the Egg (1921) *and* Death in the Woods
(1933).

The Egg

My father was, I am sure, intended by nature to be a cheerful,
kindly man. Until he was thirty-four years old he worked as a farmhand for
a man named Thomas Butterworth whose place lay near the town of Bidwell, Ohio. He had then a horse of his own, and on Saturday evenings
drove into town to spend a few hours in social intercourse with other farmhands. In town he drank several glasses of beer and stood about in Ben
Head's saloon—crowded on Saturday evenings with visiting farmhands.
Songs were sung and glasses thumped on the bar. At ten o'clock father
drove home along a lonely country road, made his horse comfortable for the
night, and himself went to bed, quite happy in his position in life. He had
at that time no notion of trying to rise in the world.

It was in the spring of his thirty-fifth year that father married my
mother, then a country school-teacher, and in the following spring I came
wriggling and crying into the world. Something happened to the two people. They became ambitious. The American passion for getting up in the
world took possession of them.

It may have been that mother was responsible. Being a school-teacher
she had no doubt read books and magazines. She had, I presume, read of
how Garfield, Lincoln, and other Americans rose from poverty to fame and
greatness, and as I lay beside her—in the days of her lying-in—she may have
dreamed that I would some day rule men and cities. At any rate she induced father to give up his place as a farmhand, sell his horse, and embark
on an independent enterprise of his own. She was a tall silent woman with
a long nose and troubled gray eyes. For herself she wanted nothing. For
father and myself she was incurably ambitious.

The first venture into which the two people went turned out badly.
They rented ten acres of poor stony land on Grigg's Road, eight miles from
Bidwell, and launched into chicken-raising. I grew into boyhood on the
place and got my first impressions of life there. From the beginning they
were impressions of disaster, and if, in my turn, I am a gloomy man inclined to see the darker side of life, I attribute it to the fact that what
should have been for me the happy joyous days of childhood were spent on
a chicken farm.

One unversed in such matters can have no notion of the many and
tragic things that can happen to a chicken. It is born out of an egg, lives for
a few weeks as a tiny fluffy thing such as you will see pictured on Easter
cards, then becomes hideously naked, eats quantities of corn and meal

bought by the sweat of your father's brow, gets diseases called pip, cholera, and other names, stands looking with stupid eyes at the sun, becomes sick and dies. A few hens and now and then a rooster, intended to serve God's mysterious ends, struggle through to maturity. The hens lay eggs out of which come other chickens and the dreadful cycle is thus made complete. It is all unbelievably complex. Most philosophers must have been raised on chicken farms. One hopes for so much from a chicken and is so dreadfully disillusioned. Small chickens, just setting out on the journey of life, look so bright and alert and they are in fact so dreadfully stupid. They are so much like people they mix one up in one's judgments of life. If disease does not kill them, they wait until your expectations are thoroughly aroused and then walk under the wheels of a wagon—to go squashed and dead back to their maker. Vermin infest their youth, and fortunes must be spent for curative powders. In later life I have seen how a literature has been built up on the subject of fortunes to be made out of the raising of chickens. It is intended to be read by the gods who have just eaten of the tree of the knowledge of good and evil. It is a hopeful literature and declares that much may be done by simple ambitious people who own a few hens. Do not be led astray by it. It was not written for you. Go hunt for gold on the frozen hills of Alaska, put your faith in the honesty of a politician, believe if you will that the world is daily growing better and that good will triumph over evil, but do not read and believe the literature that is written concerning the hen. It was not written for you.

I, however, digress. My tale does not primarily concern itself with the hen. If correctly told it will center on the egg. For ten years my father and mother struggled to make our chicken farm pay and then they gave up their struggle and began another. They moved into the town of Bidwell, Ohio, and embarked in the restaurant business. After ten years of worry with incubators that did not hatch, and with tiny—and in their own way lovely —balls of fluff that passed on into semi-naked pullethood and from that into dead henhood, we threw all aside and, packing our belongings on a wagon, drove down Grigg's Road toward Bidwell, a tiny caravan of hope looking for a new place from which to start on our upward journey through life.

We must have been a sad-looking lot, not, I fancy, unlike refugees fleeing from a battlefield. Mother and I walked in the road. The wagon that contained our goods had been borrowed for the day from Mr. Albert Griggs, a neighbor. Out of its sides stuck the legs of cheap chairs, and at the back of the pile of beds, tables, and boxes filled with kitchen utensils was a crate of live chickens, and on top of that the baby carriage in which I had been wheeled about in my infancy. Why we stuck to the baby carriage I don't know. It was unlikely other children would be born and the wheels were broken. People who have few possessions cling tightly to those they have. That is one of the facts that make life so discouraging.

Father rode on top of the wagon. He was then a bald-headed man of forty-five, a little fat, and from long association with mother and the chickens he had become habitually silent and discouraged. All during our ten years on the chicken farm he had worked as a laborer on neighboring farms and most of the money he had earned had been spent for remedies to cure chicken diseases, in Wilmer's White Wonder Cholera Cure or Professor Bidlow's Egg Producer or some other preparations that mother found advertised in the poultry papers. There were two little patches of hair on father's head just above his ears. I remember that as a child I used to sit looking at him when he had gone to sleep in a chair before the stove on Sunday afternoons in the winter. I had at that time already begun to read books and have notions of my own, and the bald path that led over the top of his head was, I fancied, something like a broad road, such a road as Caesar might have made on which to lead his legions out of Rome and into the wonders of an unknown world. The tufts of hair that grew above father's ears were, I thought, like forests. I fell into a half-sleeping, half-waking state and dreamed I was a tiny thing going along the road into a far beautiful place where there were no chicken farms and where life was a happy eggless affair.

One might write a book concerning our flight from the chicken farm into town. Mother and I walked the entire eight miles—she to be sure that nothing fell from the wagon and I to see the wonders of the world. On the seat of the wagon beside father was his greatest treasure. I will tell you of that.

On a chicken farm, where hundreds and even thousands of chickens come out of eggs, surprising things sometimes happen. Grotesques are born out of eggs as out of people. The accident does not often occur—perhaps once in a thousand births. A chicken is, you see, born that has four legs, two pairs of wings, two heads, or what not. The things do not live. They go quickly back to the hand of their maker that has for a moment trembled. The fact that the poor little things could not live was one of the tragedies of life to father. He had some sort of notion that if he could but bring into henhood or roosterhood a five-legged hen or a two-headed rooster his fortune would be made. He dreamed of taking the wonder about the county fairs and of growing rich by exhibiting it to other farmhands.

At any rate, he saved all the little monstrous things that had been born on our chicken farm. They were preserved in alcohol and put each in its own glass bottle. These he had carefully put into a box, and on our journey into town it was carried on the wagon seat beside him. He drove the horses with one hand and with the other clung to the box. When we got to our destination, the box was taken down at once and the bottles removed. All during our days as keepers of a restaurant in the town of Bidwell, Ohio, the grotesques in their little glass bottles sat on a shelf back of the counter. Mother sometimes protested, but father was a rock on the subject of his treasure. The grotesques were, he declared, valuable. People, he said, liked to look at strange and wonderful things.

Did I say that we embarked in the restaurant business in the town of Bidwell, Ohio? I exaggerated a little. The town itself lay at the foot of a low hill and on the shore of a small river. The railroad did not run through the town and the station was a mile away to the north at a place called Pickleville. There had been a cider mill and pickle factory at the station, but before the time of our coming they had both gone out of business. In the morning and in the evening busses came down to the station along a road called Turner's Pike from the hotel on the main street of Bidwell. Our going to the out of-the-way place to embark in the restaurant business was mother's idea. She talked of it for a year and then one day went off and rented an empty store building opposite the railroad station. It was her idea that the restaurant would be profitable. Traveling men, she said, would be always waiting around to take trains out of town and town people would come to the station to await incoming trains. They would come to the restaurant to buy pieces of pie and drink coffee. Now that I am older I know that she had another motive in going. She was ambitious for me. She wanted me to rise in the world, to get into a town school and become a man of the towns.

At Pickleville father and mother worked hard, as they always had done. At first there was the necessity of putting our place into shape to be a restaurant. That took a month. Father built a shelf on which he put tins of vegetables. He painted a sign on which he put his name in large red letters. Below his name was the sharp command—"EAT HERE"—that was so seldom obeyed. A showcase was bought and filled with cigars and tobacco. Mother scrubbed the floors and the walls of the room. I went to school in the town and was glad to be away from the farm from the presence of the discouraged, sad looking chickens. Still I was not very joyous. In the evening I walked home from school along Turner's Pike and remembered the children I had seen playing in the town school yard. A troop of little girls had gone hopping about and singing. I tried that. Down along the frozen road I went hopping solemnly on one leg. "Hippity Hop To The Barber Shop," I sang shrilly. Then I stopped and looked doubtfully about. I was afraid of being seen in my gay mood. It must have seemed to me that I was doing a thing that should not be done by one who, like myself, had been raised on a chicken farm where death was a daily visitor.

Mother decided that our restaurant should remain open at night. At ten in the evening a passenger train went north past our door followed by a local freight. The freight crew had switching to do in Pickleville, and when the work was done they came to our restaurant for hot coffee and food. Sometimes one of them ordered a fried egg. In the morning at four they returned north-bound and again visited us. A little trade began to grow up. Mother slept at night and during the day tended the restaurant and fed our boarders while father slept. He slept in the same bed mother had occupied during the night and I went off to the town of Bidwell and to school. During the long nights, while mother and I slept, father cooked meats that were to go into sandwiches for the lunch baskets of our boarders. Then an idea in regard to getting up in the world came into his head. The American spirit took hold of him. He also became ambitious.

In the long nights when there was little to do, father had time to think. That was his undoing. He decided that he had in the past been an unsuccessful man because he had not been cheerful enough and that in the future he would adopt a cheerful outlook on life. In the early morning he came upstairs and got into bed with mother. She woke and the two talked. From my bed in the corner I listened.

It was father's idea that both he and mother should try to entertain the people who came to eat at our restaurant. I cannot now remember his words, but he gave the impression of one about to become in some obscure way a kind of public entertainer. When people, particularly young people from the town of Bidwell, came into our place, as on very rare occasions they did, bright entertaining conversation was to be made. From father's words I gathered that something of the jolly innkeeper effect was to be sought. Mother must have been doubtful from the first, but she said nothing discouraging. It was father's notion that a passion for the company of himself and mother would spring up in the breasts of the younger people of the town of Bidwell. In the evening bright happy groups would come singing down Turner's Pike. They would troop shouting with joy and laughter into our place. There would be song and festivity. I do not mean to give the impression that father spoke so elaborately of the matter. He was, as I have said, an uncommunicative man. "They want some place to go. I tell you they want some place to go," he said over and over. That was as far as he got. My own imagination has filled in the blanks.

For two or three weeks this notion of father's invaded our house. We did not talk much, but in our daily lives tried earnestly to make smiles take the place of glum looks. Mother smiled at the boarders and I, catching the infection, smiled at our cat. Father became a little feverish in his anxiety to please. There was, no doubt, lurking somewhere in him, a touch of the spirit of the showman. He did not waste much of his ammunition on the railroad men he served at night, but seemed to be waiting for a young man or woman from Bidwell to come in to show what he could do. On the counter in the restaurant there was a wire basket kept always filled with eggs, and it must have been before his eyes when the idea of being entertaining was born in his brain. There was something pre-natal about the way eggs kept themselves connected with the development of his idea. At any rate, an egg ruined his new impulse in life. Late one night I was awakened by a roar of anger coming from father's throat. Both mother and I sat upright in our beds. With trembling hands she lighted a lamp that stood on a table by her head. Downstairs the front door of our restaurant went shut with a bang and in a few minutes father tramped up the stairs. He held an egg in his hand and his hand trembled as though he were having a chill. There was a half-insane light in his eyes. As he stood glaring at us I was sure he intended throwing the egg at either mother or me. Then he laid it gently on the table beside the lamp and dropped on his knees beside mother's bed. He began to cry like a boy, and I, carried away by his grief, cried with him. The two of us filled the little upstairs room with our wailing voices. It is ridiculous, but of the picture we made I can remember only the fact that mother's hand continually stroked the bald path that ran across the top of his head. I have forgotten what mother said to him and how she induced him to tell her of what had happened downstairs. His explanation also has gone out of my mind. I remember only my own grief and fright and the shiny path over father's head glowing in the lamplight as he knelt by the bed.

As to what happened downstairs. For some unexplainable reason I know the story as well as though I had been a witness to my father's discomfiture. One in time gets to know many unexplainable things. On that evening young Joe Kane, son of a merchant of Bidwell, came to Pickleville to meet his father, who was expected on the ten-o'clock evening train from the South. The train was three hours late and Joe came into our place to loaf about and to wait for its arrival. The local freight train came in and the freight crew were fed. Joe was left alone in the restaurant with father.

From the moment he came into our place the Bidwell young man must have been puzzled by my father's actions. It was his notion that father was angry at him for hanging around. He noticed that the restaurant-keeper was apparently disturbed by his presence and he thought of going out. However, it began to rain and he did not fancy the long walk to town and back. He bought a five-cent cigar and ordered a cup of coffee. He had a newspaper in his pocket and took it out and began to read. "I'm waiting for the evening train. It's late," he said apologetically.

For a long time father, whom Joe Kane had never seen before, remained silently gazing at his visitor. He was no doubt suffering from an attack of stage fright. As so often happens in life he had thought so much and so often of the situation that now confronted him that he was somewhat nervous in its presence.

For one thing, he did not know what to do with his hands. He thrust one of them nervously over the counter and shook hands with Joe Kane. "How-de do," he said. Joe Kane put his newspaper down and stared at him. Father's eyes lighted on the basket of eggs that sat on the counter and he began to talk. "Well," he began hesitatingly, "well, you have heard of Christopher Columbus, eh?" He seemed to be angry. "That Christopher Columbus was a cheat," he declared emphatically. "He talked of making an egg stand on its end. He talked, he did, and then he went and broke the end of the egg."

My father seemed to his visitor to be beside himself at the duplicity of Christopher Columbus. He muttered and swore. He declared it was wrong to teach children that Christopher Columbus was a great man when, after all, he cheated at the critical moment. He had declared he would make an egg stand on end and then, when his bluff had been called, he had done a trick. Still grumbling at Columbus, father took an egg from the basket on the counter and began to walk up and down. He rolled the egg between the palms of his hands. He smiled genially. He began to mumble words regarding the effect to be produced on an egg by the electricity that comes out of the human body. He declared that, without breaking its shell and by virtue of rolling it back and forth in his hands, he could stand the egg on its end. He explained that the warmth of his hands and the gentle rolling movement he gave the egg created a new center of gravity, and Joe Kane was mildly interested. "I have handled thousands of eggs," father said. "No one knows more about eggs than I do."

He stood the egg on the counter and it fell on its side. He tried the trick again and again, each time rolling the egg between the palms of his hands and saying the words regarding the wonders of electricity and the laws of gravity. When after a half-hour's effort he did succeed in making the egg stand for a moment, he looked up to find that his visitor was no longer watching. By the time he had succeeded in calling Joe Kane's attention to the success of his effort, the egg had again rolled over and lay on its side.

Afire with the showman's passion and at the same time a good deal disconcerted by the failure of his first effort, father now took the bottles containing the poultry monstrosities down from their place on the shelf and began to show them to his visitor. "How would you like to have seven legs and two heads like this fellow?" he asked, exhibiting the most remarkable of his treasures. A cheerful smile played over his face. He reached over the counter and tried to slap Joe Kane on the shoulder as he had seen men do in Ben Head's saloon when he was a young farmhand and drove to town on Saturday evenings. His visitor was made a little ill by the sight of the body of the terribly deformed bird floating in the alcohol in the bottle and got up to go. Coming from behind the counter, father took hold of the young man's arm and led him back to his seat. He grew a little angry and for a moment had to turn his face away and force himself to smile. Then he put the bottles back on the shelf. In an outburst of generosity he fairly compelled Joe Kane to have a fresh cup of coffee and another cigar at his expense. Then he took a pan and filling it with vinegar, taken from a jug that sat beneath the counter, he declared himself about to do a new trick. "I will heat this egg in this pan of vinegar," he said. "Then I will put it through the neck of a bottle without breaking the shell. When the egg is inside the bottle it will resume its normal shape and the shell will become hard again. Then I will give the bottle with the egg in it to you. You can take it about with you wherever you go. People will want to know how you got the egg in the bottle. Don't tell them. Keep them guessing. That is the way to have fun with this trick."

Father grinned and winked at his visitor. Joe Kane decided that the man who confronted him was mildly insane but harmless. He drank the cup of coffee that had been given him and began to read his paper again. When the egg had been heated in vinegar, father carried it on a spoon to the counter and going into a back room got an empty bottle. He was angry because his visitor did not watch him as he began to do his trick, but nevertheless went cheerfully to work. For a long time he struggled, trying to get the egg to go through the neck of the bottle. He put the pan of vinegar back on the stove, intending to reheat the egg, then picked it up and burned his fingers. After a second bath in the hot vinegar, the shell of the egg had been softened a little, but not enough for his purpose. He worked and worked and a spirit of desperate determination took possession of him. When he thought that at last the trick was about to be consummated, the delayed train came in at the station and Joe Kane started to go nonchalantly out at the door. Father made a last desperate effort to conquer the egg and make it do the thing that would establish his reputation as one who knew how to entertain guests who came into his restaurant. He worried the egg. He attempted to be somewhat rough with it. He swore and the sweat stood out on his forehead. The egg broke under his hand. When the contents spurted over his clothes, Joe Kane, who had stopped at the door, turned and laughed.

A roar of anger rose from my father's throat. He danced and shouted a string of inarticulate words. Grabbing another egg from the basket on the counter, he threw it, just missing the head of the young man as he dodged through the door and escaped.

Father came upstairs to mother and me with an egg in his hand. I do not know what he intended to do. I imagine he had some idea of destroying it, of destroying all eggs, and that he intended to let mother and me see him begin. When, however, he got into the presence of mother, something happened to him. He laid the egg gently on the table and dropped on his knees by the bed as I have already explained. He later decided to close the restaurant for the night and to come upstairs and get into bed. When he did so, he blew out the light and after much muttered conversation both he and mother went to sleep. I suppose I went to sleep also, but my sleep was troubled. I awoke at dawn and for a long time looked at the egg that lay on the table. I wondered why eggs had to be and why from the egg came the hen who again laid the egg. The question got into my blood. It has stayed there, I imagine, because I am the son of my father. At any rate, the problem remains unsolved in my mind. And that, I conclude, is but another evidence of the complete and final triumph of the egg—at least as far as my family is concerned.

§ FOR COMMENT

The symbolic terms of this story are set forth in the fifth paragraph, where the narrator defines the world as a chicken farm, thus making the farm a *microcosm* (a little world that reflects the larger world, or macrocosm). Reread the story and note the abundant use of what we might call "chicken imagery." The family moves, for example, close to Bi[r]dwell, Ohio, where they settle at a place called Pickleville. The narrator, however, insists that this story does not concern itself with the hen. "If correctly told it will center on the egg." Remember that eggs become little chickens who must set out on the "journey of life." Is the narrator to be considered a little chicken struggling on the "upward journey through life"?

One of the more important symbolic situations involves the grotesques. "Grotesques are born out of eggs as out of people." The father keeps his grotesques in little glass bottles. What is the father's relation to the central symbolism? A grotesque chicken is physically deformed. Does Anderson mean that grotesque people should be identified in exactly these terms? What kind of people would be called grotesques? Does Anderson suggest how they became grotesques? Remember that the father when he was a bachelor was a happy fellow without ambition. What happens after he marries and has a son?

What is the relationship between the central symbolism and the climactic scene? Do you consider the narrator's account of this scene credible? He was not, after all, a witness. He comments: "As to what happened downstairs. For some unexplainable reason I know the story as well as though I had been a witness to my father's discomfiture. One in time gets to know many unexplainable things." Is this unexplainable thing related to what the narrator insists is the central question? "I wondered what eggs had to be and why from the egg came the hen who again laid the egg."

James Joyce § 1882–1941

Born in Dublin, Joyce was educated in Jesuit schools, and both his native city and his Catholic training are reflected in his works, as are feelings of alienation and isolation which were perhaps at the root of his self-imposed exile from his native country. For except for two brief visits back to Ireland, Joyce lived with his family in Trieste, Zurich, and Paris, in poverty, struggling to write, while at the same time suffering near blindness. Like Thomas Mann, Joyce has received worldwide recognition and acclaim. His reputation rests on three novels, one volume of short stories, and to a lesser extent, one play and two slim volumes of poetry—his total output. His three novels, A Portrait of the Artist as a Young Man *(1916),* Ulysses *(1922), and* Finnegans Wake *(1939), are all considered landmarks in the history of fiction; his short stories published in* Dubliners

(1914) are considered by some to be among the best in the language. Through most of his writing career, Joyce was bothered by censorship problems. The publication of Dubliners was delayed several years, and Ulysses was not allowed to be published in the United States until 1933.

Araby

North Richmond Street, being blind, was a quiet street except at the hour when the Christian Brothers' School set the boys free. An uninhabited house of two stories stood at the blind end, detached from its neighbors in a square ground. The other houses of the street, conscious of decent lives within them, gazed at one another with brown imperturbable faces.

The former tenant of our house, a priest, had died in the back drawing-room. Air, musty from having been long enclosed, hung in all the rooms, and the waste room behind the kitchen was littered with old useless papers. Among these I found a few paper-covered books, the pages of which were curled and damp: *The Abbot*, by Walter Scott, *The Devout Communicant*, and *The Memoirs of Vidocq*. I liked the last best, because its leaves were yellow. The wild garden behind the house contained a central apple tree and a few straggling bushes, under one of which I found the late tenant's rusty bicycle-pump. He had been a very charitable priest; in his will he had left all his money to institutions and the furniture of his house to his sister.

When the short days of winter came, dusk fell before we had well eaten our dinners. When we met in the street, the houses had grown sombre. The space of sky above us was the color of ever-changing violet, and towards it the lamps of the street lifted their feeble lanterns. The cold air stung us and we played till our bodies glowed. Our shouts echoed in the silent street. The career of our play brought us through the dark muddy lanes behind the houses where we ran the gauntlet of the rough tribes from the cottages, to the back doors of the dark dripping gardens where odors arose from the ashpits, to the dark odorous stables where a coachman smoothed and combed the horse or shook music from the buckled harness. When we returned to the street, if uncle was seen turning the corner, we hid in the shadow until we had seen him safely housed. Or if Mangan's sister came out on the doorstep to call her brother in to his tea, we watched her from our shadow peer up and down the street. We waited to see whether she would remain or go in, and, if she remained, we left our shadow and walked up to Mangan's steps resignedly. She was waiting for us, her figure defined by the light from the half-opened door. Her brother always teased her before he obeyed, and I stood by the railings looking at her. Her dress swung as she moved her body, and the soft rope of her hair tossed from side to side.

Every morning I lay on the floor in the front parlor watching her door. The blind was pulled down to within an inch of the sash, so that I could not be seen. When she came out on the doorstep my heart leaped. I ran to the hall, seized my books, and followed her. I kept her brown figure always in my eye, and, when we came near the point at which our ways diverged, I quickened my pace and passed her. This happened morning after morning. I had never spoken to her, except for a few casual words, and yet her name was like a summons to all my foolish blood.

Her image accompanied me even in places the most hostile to romance. On Saturday evenings, when my aunt went marketing, I had to go to carry some of the parcels. We walked through the flaring streets, jostled by drunken men and bargaining women, amid the curses of laborers, the shrill litanies of shop-boys, who stood on guard by the barrels of pigs' cheeks, the nasal chanting of street-singers, who sang a *come-all-you* about O'Donovan Rossa, or a ballad about the troubles in our native land. These noises converged in a single sensation of life for me: I imagined that I bore my chalice safely through a throng of foes. Her name sprang to my lips at moments in strange prayers and praises which I myself did not understand. My eyes were often full of tears (I could not tell why) and at times a flood from my heart seemed to pour itself out into my bosom. I thought little of the future. I did not know whether I would ever speak to her or not, or, if I spoke to her, how I could tell her of my confused adoration. But my body was like a harp, and her words and gestures were like fingers running upon the wires.

One evening I went into the back drawing-room, in which the priest had died. It was a dark rainy evening, and there was no sound in the house. Through one of the broken panes I heard the rain impinge upon the earth, the fine incessant needles of water playing in the sodden beds. Some distant lamp or lighted window gleamed below me. I was thankful that I could see so little. All my senses seemed to desire to veil themselves, and, feeling that I was about to slip from them, I pressed the palms of my hands together until they trembled, murmuring: "O love! O love!" many times.

At last she spoke to me. When she addressed the first words to me, I was so confused that I did not know what to answer. She asked me was I going to *Araby*. I forget whether I answered yes or no. It would be a splendid bazaar; she said she would love to go.

"And why can't you?" I asked.

While she spoke, she turned a silver bracelet round and round her wrist. She could not go, she said, because there would be a retreat that week in her convent. Her brother and two other boys were fighting for their caps, and I was alone at the railings. She held one of the spikes, bowing her head towards me. The light from the lamp opposite our door caught the white curve of her neck, lit up her hair that rested there, and, falling, lit up the hand upon the railing. It fell over one side of her dress and caught the white border of a petticoat, just visible as she stood at ease.

"It's well for you," she said.

"If I go," I said, "I will bring you something."

What innumerable follies laid waste my waking and sleeping thoughts after that evening! I wished to annihilate the tedious intervening days. I chafed against the work of school. At night in my bedroom and by day in the classroom her image came between me and the page I strove to read. The syllables of the word *Araby* were called to me through the silence in which my soul luxuriated and cast an Eastern enchantment over me. I asked for leave to go to the bazaar on Saturday night. My aunt was surprised and hoped it was not some Freemason affair. I answered few questions in class. I watched my master's face pass from amiability to sternness; he hoped I was not beginning to idle. I could not call my wandering thoughts together. I had hardly any patience with the serious work of life, which, now that it stood between me and my desire, seemed to me child's play, ugly monotonous child's play.

On Saturday morning I reminded my uncle that I wished to go to the bazaar in the evening. He was fussing at the hallstand looking for the hatbrush, and answered me curtly:

"Yes, boy, I know."

As he was in the hall, I could not go into the front parlor and lie at the window. I left the house in bad humor and walked slowly towards the school. The air was pitilessly raw, and already my heart misgave me.

When I came home to dinner, my uncle had not yet been home. Still, it was early. I sat staring at the clock for some time, and, when its ticking began to irritate me, I left the room. I mounted the staircase and gained the upper part of the house. The high cold empty gloomy rooms liberated me and I went from room to room singing. From the front window I saw my companions playing below in the street. Their cries reached me weakened and indistinct, and, leaning my forehead against the cool glass, I looked over at the dark house where she lived. I may have stood there for an hour, seeing nothing but the brown-clad figure cast by my imagination, touched discreetly by the lamplight at the curved neck, at the hand upon the railings, and at the border below the dress.

When I came downstairs again, I found Mrs. Mercer sitting at the fire. She was an old garrulous woman, a pawn-broker's widow, who collected used stamps for some pious purpose. I had to endure the gossip of the teatable. The meal was prolonged beyond an hour, and still my uncle did not come. Mrs. Mercer stood up to go: she was sorry she couldn't wait any longer, but it was after eight o'clock and she did not like to be out late, as the night air was bad for her. When she had gone, I began to walk up and down the room, clenching my fists. My aunt said:

"I'm afraid you may put off your bazaar for this night of Our Lord."

At nine o'clock I heard my uncle's latchkey in the hall-door. I heard him talking to himself and heard the hallstand rocking when it had received the weight of his overcoat. I could interpret these signs. When he was midway through his dinner, I asked him to give me the money to go to the bazaar. He had forgotten.

"The people are in bed and after their first sleep now," he said.

I did not smile. My aunt said to him energetically:

"Can't you give him the money and let him go? You've kept him late enough as it is."

My uncle said he was very sorry he had forgotten. He said he believed in the old saying: "All work and no play makes Jack a dull boy." He asked me where I was going, and, when I had told him a second time, he asked me did I know *The Arab's Farewell to His Steed*. When I left the kitchen, he was about to recite the opening lines of the piece to my aunt.

I held a florin tightly in my hand as I strode down Buckingham Street towards the station. The sight of the streets thronged with buyers and glaring with gas recalled to me the purpose of my journey. I took my seat in a third-class carriage of a deserted train. After an intolerable delay the train moved out of the station slowly. It crept onward among ruinous houses and over the twinkling river. At Westland Row Station a crowd of people pressed to the carriage doors; but the porters moved them back, saying that it was a special train for the bazaar. I remained alone in the bare carriage. In a few minutes the train drew up beside an improvised wooden platform. I passed out on to the road and saw by the lighted dial of a clock that it was ten minutes to ten. In front of me was a large building which displayed the magical name.

I could not find any sixpenny entrance, and, fearing that the bazaar would be closed, I passed in quickly through a turnstile, handing a shilling to a weary-looking man. I found myself in a big hall girdled at half its height by a gallery. Nearly all the stalls were closed and the greater part of the hall was in darkness. I recognized a silence like that which pervades a church after a service. I walked into the center of the bazaar timidly. A few people were gathered about the stalls which were still open. Before a curtain, over which the words *Café Chantant* were written in colored lamps, two men were counting money on a salver. I listened to the fall of the coins.

Remembering with difficulty why I had come, I went over to one of the stalls and examined porcelain vases and flowered tea-sets. At the door of the stall a young lady was talking and laughing with two young gentleman. I remarked their English accents and listened vaguely to their conversation.

"O, I never said such a thing!"

"O, but you did!"

"O, but I didn't!"

"Didn't she say that?"

"Yes. I heard her."

"O, there's a . . . fib!"

Observing me, the young lady came over and asked me did I wish to buy anything. The tone of her voice was not encouraging; she seemed to have spoken to me out of a sense of duty. I looked humbly at the great jars that stood like eastern guards at either side of the dark entrance to the stall and murmured:

"No, thank you."

The young lady changed the position of one of the vases and went back to the two young men. They began to talk of the same subject. Once or twice the young lady glanced at me over her shoulder.

I lingered before her stall, though I knew my stay was useless, to make my interest in her wares seem the more real. Then I turned away slowly and walked down the middle of the bazaar. I allowed the two pennies to fall against the sixpence in my pocket. I heard a voice call from one end of the gallery that the light was out. The upper part of the hall was now completely dark.

Gazing up into the darkness, I saw myself as a creature driven and derided by vanity; and my eyes burned with anguish and anger.

§ FOR COMMENT

"Araby" is told in the first person by an adult who recalls an experience that took place in his youth. What can we tell about the narrator from the way he tells the story? What kind of youth was he?

What is the prevailing mood of the story? Does the setting contribute to the mood or have symbolic significance?

Notice the abundance of religious allusions: The boy goes to the Christian Brothers School; he lives in a house whose former occupant was a priest; he reads the books left by the priest; he imagines he bears a chalice through a throng of foes; Mangan's sister is going on retreat in her convent school; the boy's aunt hopes that the bazaar is not some Freemason affair; at the bazaar there is silence like that which pervades a church; the boy listens to the fall of coins as two men count money on a salver. How significant is this imagery? Can you find more? The boy's relationship with Mangan's sister is also tied to religious imagery. He thinks of her as his chalice; he clasps his hands in the attitude of prayer and says, "O love! O love!" many times. Note the description of her. She is standing at a railing above him while she twists a silver bracelet around her wrist:

She held one of the spikes, bowing her head towards me. The light from the lamp opposite our door caught the white curve of the neck, lit up her hair that rested there and, falling, lit up the hand upon the railing. It fell over one side of her dress and caught the white border of a petticoat, just visible as she stood at ease.

What is the "confused adoration" of which the narrator speaks? Why, at the end, does he see himself as a creature "driven and derided by vanity"?

What is the relationship of Araby to the total story? Notice the youth's increasing depression, frustration, and disappointment beginning with his uncle's tardiness and carrying through to the conversation at the bazaar that is the climax of the story.

A common theme in literature involves the initiation of youth into the realities of the world. Does this theme appear in this story? in "The Secret Sharer"? in "My Kinsman, Major Molineux"? How are the "realities of the world" in "Araby" different from or similar to those in "The Secret Sharer"? "My Kinsman, Major Molineux"? How different or similar are the three protagonists?

Franz Kafka § 1883–1924

Born in Prague of a middle-class Jewish family, Kafka studied law and then obtained a government position. But his major interest was his writing, although none of his novels was published during his lifetime. Indeed, most of his works were published posthumously, contrary to his written request that they be destroyed. A student of Kierkegaard's writings, Kafka anticipates modern existentialist thinking. Strikingly modern in tone and subject matter, his stories portray a nightmare world in which man is a doomed and solitary figure seeking his identity through endless labyrinths and grotesque encounters. Typical are the famous "Metamorphosis" (1937) and The Trial (1924). Most of the pieces take a dream pattern whose latent content must be derived from a deceptively simple surface level. They are highly symbolic, many of them including several levels of allegorical meaning. This translation is by Willa and Edwin Muir.

A Hunger Artist

During these last decades the interest in professional fasting has markedly diminished. It used to pay very well to stage such great performances under one's own management, but today that is quite impossible. We live in a different world now. At one time the whole town took a lively interest in the hunger artist; from day to day of his fast the excitement mounted; everybody wanted to see him at least once a day; there were people who bought season tickets for the last few days and sat from morning till night in front of his small barred cage; even in the nighttime there were visiting hours, when the whole effect was heightened by torch flares; on fine days the cage was set out in the open air, and then it was the children's special treat to see the hunger artist; for their elders he was often just a joke that happened to be in fashion, but the children stood open-mouthed, holding each other's hands for greater security, marveling at him as he sat there pallid in black tights, with his ribs sticking out so prominently, not even on a seat but down among straw on the ground, sometimes giving a courteous nod, answering questions with a constrained smile, or perhaps stretching an arm through the bars so that one might feel how thin it was, and then again withdrawing deep into himself, paying no attention to anyone or anything, not even to the all-important striking of the clock that was the only piece of furniture in his cage, but merely staring into vacancy with half-shut eyes, now and then taking a sip from a tiny glass of water to moisten his lips.

Besides casual onlookers there were also relays of permanent watchers selected by the public, usually butchers, strangely enough, and it was their task to watch the hunger artist day and night, three of them at a time, in case he should have some secret recourse to nourishment. This was nothing but a formality, instituted to reassure the masses, for the initiates knew well enough that during his fast the artist would never in any circumstances, not even under forcible compulsion, swallow the smallest morsel of food; the honor of his profession forbade it. Not every watcher, of course, was capable of understanding this, there were often groups of night watchers who were very lax in carrying out their duties and deliberately huddled together in a retired corner to play cards with great absorption, obviously intending to give the hunger artist the chance of a little refreshment, which they supposed he could draw from some private hoard. Nothing annoyed the artist more than such watchers; they made him miserable; they made his fast seem unendurable; sometimes he mastered his feebleness sufficiently to sing during their watch for as long as he could keep going, to show them how unjust their suspicions were. But that was of little use; they only wondered at his cleverness in being able to fill his mouth even while singing. Much more to his taste were the watchers who sat close up to the bars, who were not content with the dim night lighting of the hall but focused him in the full glare of the electric pocket torch given them by the impresario. The harsh light did not trouble him at all. In any case he could never sleep properly, and he could always drowse a little, whatever the light, at any hour, even when the hall was thronged with noisy onlookers. He was quite happy at the prospect of spending a sleepless night with such watchers; he was ready to exchange jokes with them, to tell them stories out of his nomadic life, anything at all to keep them awake and demonstrate to them again that he had no eatables in his cage and that he was fasting as not one of them could fast. But his happiest moment was when the morning came and an enormous breakfast was brought them, at his expense, on which they flung themselves with the keen appetite of healthy men after a weary night of wakefulness. Of course there were people who argued that this breakfast was an unfair attempt to bribe the watchers, but that was going rather too far, and when they were invited to take on a night's vigil without a breakfast, merely for the sake of the cause, they made themselves scarce, although they stuck stubbornly to their suspicions.

Such suspicions, anyhow, were a necessary accompaniment to the profession of fasting. No one could possibly watch the hunger artist continuously, day and night, and so no one could produce first-hand evidence that the fast had really been rigorous and continuous; only the artist himself could know that; he was therefore bound to be the sole completely satisfied spectator of his own fast. Yet for other reasons he was never satisfied; it was not perhaps mere fasting that had brought him to such skeleton thinness that many people had regretfully to keep away from his exhibitions, because the sight of him was too much for them, perhaps it was dissatisfaction with himself that had worn him down. For he alone knew, what no other initiate knew, how easy it was to fast. It was the easiest thing in the world. He made no secret of this, yet people did not believe him; at the best they set him down as modest, most of them, however, thought he was out for publicity or else was some kind of cheat who found it easy to fast because he had discovered a way of making it easy, and then had the impudence to admit the fact, more or less. He had put up with all that, and in the course of time had got used to it, but his inner dissatisfaction always rankled, and never yet, after any term of fasting—this must be granted to his credit—had he left the cage of his own free will. The longest period of fasting was fixed by his impresario at forty days, beyond the term he was not allowed to go, not even in great cities, and there was good reason for it, too. Experience had proved that for about forty days the interest of the public could be stimulated by a steadily increasing pressure of advertisement, but after that the town began to lose interest, sympathetic support began notably to fall off; there were of course local variations as between one town and another or one country and another, but as a general rule forty days marked the limit. So on the fortieth day the flower-bedecked cage was opened, enthusiastic spectators filled the hall, a military band played, two doctors entered the cage to measure the results of the fast, which were announced through a megaphone, and finally two young ladies appeared, blissful at having been selected for the honor, to help the hunger artist down the few steps leading to a small table on which was spread a carefully chosen invalid repast. And at this very moment the artist always turned stubborn. True, he would entrust his bony arms to the outstretched helping hands of the ladies bending over him, but stand up he would not.

Why stop fasting at this particular moment, after forty days of it? He had held out for a long time, an illimitably long time; why stop now, when he was in his best fasting form, or rather, not yet quite in his best fasting form? Why should he be cheated of the fame he would get for fasting longer, for being not only the record hunger artist of all time, which presumably he was already, but for beating his own record by a performance beyond human imagination, since he felt that there were no limits to his capacity for fasting? His public pretended to admire him so much, why should it have so little patience with him; if he could endure fasting longer, why shouldn't the public endure it? Besides, he was tired, he was comfortable sitting in the straw, and now he was supposed to lift himself to his full height and go down to a meal the very thought of which gave him a nausea that only the presence of the ladies kept him from betraying, and even that with an effort. And he looked up into the eyes of the ladies who were apparently so friendly and in reality so cruel, and shook his head, which felt too heavy on its strengthless neck. But then there happened yet again what always happened. The impresario came forward, without a word—for the band made speech impossible—lifted his arms in the air above the artist, as if inviting Heaven to look down upon its creature here in the straw, this suffering martyr, which indeed he was, although in quite another sense; grasped him round the emaciated waist, with exaggerated caution, so that the frail condition he was in might be appreciated; and committed him to the care of the blenching ladies, not without secretly giving him a shaking so that his legs and body tottered and swayed. The artist now submitted completely; his head lolled on his breast as if it had landed there by chance; his body was hollowed out; his legs in a spasm of self-preservation clung close to each other at the knees, yet scraped on the ground as if it were not really solid ground, as if they were only trying to find solid ground; and the whole weight of his body, a featherweight after all, relapsed onto one of the ladies, who, looking round for help and panting a little—this post of honor was not at all what she had expected it to be—first stretched her neck as far as she could to keep her face at least free from contact with the artist, then finding this impossible, and her more fortunate companion not coming to her aid but merely holding extended on her own trembling hand the little bunch of knucklebones that was the artist's, to the great delight of the spectators burst into tears and had to be replaced by an attendant who had long been stationed in readiness. Then came the food, a little of which the impresario managed to get between the artist's lips, while he sat in a kind of half-fainting trance, to the accompaniment of cheerful patter designed to distract the public's attention from the artist's condition; after that, a toast was drunk to the public, supposedly prompted by a whisper from the artist in the impresario's ear; the band confirmed it with a mighty flourish, the spectators melted away, and no one had any cause to be dissatisfied with the proceedings, no one except the hunger artist himself, he only, as always.

So he lived for many years, with small regular intervals of recuperation, in visible glory, honored by the world, yet in spite of that troubled in spirit, and all the more troubled because no one would take his trouble seriously. What comfort could he possibly need? What more could he possibly wish for? And if some good-natured person, feeling sorry for him, tried to console him by pointing out that his melancholy was probably caused by fasting, it could happen, especially when he had been fasting for some time, that he reacted with an outburst of fury and to the general alarm began to shake the bars of his cage like a wild animal. Yet the impresario had a way of punishing these outbreaks which he rather enjoyed putting into operation. He would apologize publicly for the artist's behavior, which was only to be excused, he admitted, because of the irritability caused by fasting; a condition hardly to be understood by well-fed people; then by natural transition he went on to mention the artist's equally incomprehensible boast that he could fast for much longer than he was doing; he praised the high ambition, the good will, the great self-denial undoubtedly implicit in such a statement; and then quite simply countered it by bringing out photographs, which were also on sale to the public, showing the artist on the fortieth day of a fast laying in bed almost dead from exhaustion. This perversion of the truth, familiar to the artist though it was, always unnerved him afresh and proved too much for him. What was a consequence of the premature ending of his fast was here presented as the cause of it! To fight against this lack of understanding, against a whole world of non-understanding, was impossible. Time and again in good faith he stood by the bars listening to the impresario, but as soon as the photographs appeared he always let go and sank with a groan back on to his straw, and the reassured public could once more come close and gaze at him.

A few years later when the witnesses of such scenes called them to mind, they often failed to understand themselves at all. For meanwhile the aforementioned change in public interest had set in; it seemed to happen almost overnight; there may have been profound causes for it, but who was going to bother about that; at any rate the pampered hunger artist suddenly found himself deserted one fine day by the amusement seekers, who went streaming past him to other more favored attractions. For the last time the impresario hurried him over half Europe to discover whether the old interest might still survive here and there; all in vain; everywhere, as if by secret agreement, a positive revulsion from professional fasting was in evidence. Of course it could not really have sprung up so suddenly as all that, and many premonitory symptoms which had not been sufficiently remarked or suppressed during the rush and glitter of success now came retrospectively to mind, but it was now too late to take any countermeasures. Fasting would surely come into fashion again at some future date, yet that was no comfort for those living in the present. What, then, was the hunger artist to do? He had been applauded by thousands in his time and could hardly come down to showing himself in a street booth at village fairs, and as for adopting another profession, he was not only too old for that but too fanatically devoted to fasting. So he took leave of the impresario, his partner in an unparalleled career, and hired himself to a large circus; in order to spare his own feelings he avoided reading the conditions of his contract.

A large circus with its enormous traffic in replacing and recruiting men, animals and apparatus can always find a use for people at any time, even for a hunger artist, provided of course that he does not ask too much, and in this particular case anyhow it was not only the artist who was taken on but his famous and long-known name as well; indeed considering the peculiar nature of his performance, which was not impaired by advancing age, it could not be objected that here was an artist past his prime, no longer at the height of his professional skill, seeking a refuge in some quiet corner of a circus; on the contrary, the hunger artist averred that he could fast as well as ever, which was entirely credible; he even alleged that if he were allowed to fast as he liked, and this was at once promised him without more ado, he could astound the world by establishing a record never yet achieved, a statement which certainly provoked a smile among the other professionals, since it left out of account the change in public opinion, which the hunger artist in his zeal conveniently forgot.

He had not, however, actually lost his sense of the real situation and took it as a matter of course that he and his cage should be stationed, not in the middle of the ring as a main attraction, but outside, near the animal cages, on a site that was after all easily accessible. Large and gaily painted placards made a frame for the cage and announced what was to be seen inside it. When the public came thronging out in the intervals to see the animals, they could hardly avoid passing the hunger artist's cage and stopping there for a moment, perhaps they might even have stayed longer had not those pressing behind them in the narrow gangway, who did not understand why they should be held up on their way towards the excitements of the menagerie, made it impossible for anyone to stand gazing quietly for any length of time. And that was the reason why the hunger artist, who had of course been looking forward to these visiting hours as the main achievement of his life, began instead to shrink from them. At first he could hardly wait for the intervals; it was exhilarating to watch the crowds come streaming his way, until only too soon—not even the most obstinate self-deception, clung to almost consciously, could hold out against the fact—the conviction was borne in upon him that these people, most of them, to judge from their actions, again and again, without exception, were all on their way to the menagerie. And the first sight of them from the distance remained the best. For when they reached his cage he was at once deafened by the storm of shouting and abuse that arose from the two contending factions, which renewed themselves continuously, of those who wanted to stop and stare at him—he soon began to dislike them more than the others —not out of real interest but only out of obstinate self-assertiveness, and whose who wanted to go straight on to the animals. When the first great rush was past, the stragglers came along, and these, whom nothing could have prevented from stopping to look at him as long as they had breath, raced past with long strides, hardly even glancing at him, in their haste to get to the menagerie in time. And all too rarely did it happen that he had a stroke of luck, when some father of a family fetched up before him with his children, pointed a finger at the hunger artist and explained at length what the phenomenon meant, telling stories of earlier years when he himself had watched similar but much more thrilling performances, and the children, still rather uncomprehending, since neither inside nor outside school had they been sufficiently prepared for this lesson—what did they care about fasting?—yet showed by the brightness of their intent eyes that new and better times might be coming. Perhaps, said the hunger artist to himself many a time, things would be a little better if his cage were set not quite so near the menagerie. That made it too easy for people to make their choice, to say nothing of what he suffered from the stench of the menagerie, the animals' restlessness by night, the carrying past of raw lumps of flesh for the beasts of prey, the roaring at feeding times, which depressed him continually. But he did not dare to lodge a complaint with the management; after all, he had the animals to thank for the troops of people who passed his cage, among whom there might always be one here and there to take an interest in him, and who could tell where they might seclude him if he called attention to his existence and thereby to the fact that, strictly speaking, he was only an impediment on the way to the menagerie.

A small impediment, to be sure, one that grew steadily less. People grew familiar with the strange idea that they could be expected, in times like these, to take an interest in a hunger artist, and with this familiarity the verdict went out against him. He might fast as much as he could, and he did so; but nothing could save him now, people passed him by. Just try to explain to anyone the art of fasting! Anyone who has no feeling for it cannot be made to understand it. The fine placards grew dirty and illegible, they were torn down; the little notice board telling the number of fast days achieved, which at first was changed carefully every day, had long stayed at the same figure, for after the first few weeks even this small task seemed pointless to the staff; and so the artist simply fasted on and on, as he had once dreamed of doing, and it was no trouble to him, just as he had always foretold, but no one counted the days, no one, not even the artist himself, knew what records he was already breaking, and his heart grew heavy. And when once in a time some leisurely passer-by stopped, made merry over the old figure on the board and spoke of swindling, that was in its way the stupidest lie ever invented by indifference and inborn malice, since it was not the hunger artist who was cheating; he was working honestly, but the world was cheating him of his reward.

Many more days went by, however, and that too came to an end. An overseer's eye fell on the cage one day and he asked the attendants why this perfectly good stage should be left standing there unused with dirty straw inside it; nobody knew, until one man, helped out by the notice board, remembered about the hunger artist. They poked into the straw with sticks and found him in it. "Are you still fasting?" asked the overseer. "When on earth do you mean to stop?" "Forgive me, everybody," whispered the hunger artist; only the overseer, who had his ear to the bars, understood him. "Of course," said the overseer, and tapped his forehead with a finger to let the attendants know what state the man was in, "we forgive you." "I always wanted you to admire my fasting," said the hunger artist. "We do admire it," said the overseer, affably. "But you shouldn't admire it," said the hunger artist. "Well, then we don't admire it," said the overseer, "but why shouldn't we admire it?" "Because I have to fast, I can't help it," said the hunger artist. "What a fellow you are," said the overseer, "and why can't you help it?" "Because," said the hunger artist, lifting his head a little and speaking, with his lips pursed, as if for a kiss, right into the overseer's ear, so that no syllable might be lost, "because I couldn't find the food I liked. If I had found it, believe me, I should have made no fuss and stuffed myself like you or anyone else." These were his last words, but in his dimming eyes remained the firm though no longer proud persuasion that he was still continuing to fast.

"Well, clear this out now!" said the overseer, and they buried the hunger artist, straw and all. Into the cage they put a young panther. Even the most insensitive felt it refreshing to see this wild creature leaping around the cage that had so long been dreary. The panther was all right. The food he liked was brought him without hesitation by the attendants; he seemed not even to miss his freedom; his noble body, furnished almost to the bursting point with all that it needed, seemed to carry freedom around with it too; somewhere in his jaws it seemed to lurk; and the joy of life streamed with such ardent passion from his throat that for the onlookers it was not easy to stand the shock of it. But they braced themselves, crowded round the cage, and did not want ever to move away.

§ FOR COMMENT

Who is the hunger artist? What does he represent? One answer, perhaps the most obvious, is that he represents the artist seeking acceptance and understanding for his work from a fickle and imperceptive audience. Follow through this interpretation. According to the story, what is the role of the artist in present day society? How important to the artist is his art? Does he need an audience? If so, why? What is the significance of the artist's compelling need to fast? Remember that the necessary end to fasting is death. Comment on the clock as symbol here: What role does time play in the story? Was there a time when the artist had a more secure position in the world? What is the role of the impresario? What does the circus represent? the artist's cage?

It is also possible to interpret the hunger artist in broader terms, as a representative of mankind seeking to transcend the physical to reach a realm of the purely spiritual. What details of the story would support this interpretation?

Or do you consider that the story deals primarily with the place of a religion or a religious man in a materialistic society? Is there reason to believe that Kafka might be presenting us with an allegory of the history of Christianity? Could the hunger artist represent Christ? Support your answer with as many details from the story as possible.

It is important to remember that the hunger artist fails, dying at the end in a cage filled with putrid straw and being replaced by a sleek panther who draws large crowds of hesitant but fascinated spectators. What is the significance of the ending of the story to the three different interpretations suggested?

What is the tone of this story? How does Kafka's writing, which is completely straightforward and factual, contribute to the tone and meaning of the story?

D. H. Lawrence § 1885–1930

During his lifetime and even afterwards Lawrence was a controversial figure because of his frank treatment of sex and his outspoken insistence upon a need for a readjustment in the relationship between the sexes. His most controversial novel is Lady Chatterly's Lover *(1928), the best probably* The Rainbow *(1915). Sons and Lovers (1913), perhaps his most popular novel, is often taken to be largely biographical, its subject matter paralleling much of his early life. Born in Nottingham, the son of a coal miner, Lawrence was dominated by his mother, who insisted that he be educated. The theme of* Sons and Lovers *is usually said to concern the effect of mother-love upon the development of a son. Lawrence is often criticized for the didactic elements in his novels and the looseness in structure. The short stories are generally considered to be superior in unity of mood and artistic form.*

The Rocking-Horse Winner

There was a woman who was beautiful, who started with all the advantages, yet she had no luck. She married for love, and the love turned to dust. She had bonny children, yet she felt they had been thrust upon her, and she could not love them. They looked at her coldly, as if they were finding fault with her. And hurriedly she felt she must cover up some fault in herself. Yet what it was that she must cover up she never knew. Nevertheless, when her children were present, she always felt the centre of her heart go hard. This troubled her, and in her manner she was all the more gentle and anxious for her children, as if she loved them very much. Only she herself knew that at the centre of her heart was a hard little place that could not feel love, no, not for anybody. Everybody else said of her: "She is such a good mother. She adores her children." Only she herself, and her children themselves, knew it was not so. They read it in each other's eyes.

There were a boy and two little girls. They lived in a pleasant house, with a garden, and they had discreet servants, and felt themselves superior to anyone in the neighbourhood.

Although they lived in style, they felt always an anxiety in the house. There was never enough money. The mother had a small income, and the father had a small income, but not nearly enough for the social position which they had to keep up. The father went into town to some office. But though he had good prospects, these prospects never materialized. There was always the grinding sense of the shortage of money, though the style was always kept up.

At last the mother said: "I will see if I can't make something." But she did not know where to begin. She racked her brains, and tried this thing and the other, but could not find anything successful. The failure made deep lines come into her face. Her children were growing up, they would have to go to school. There must be more money, there must be more money. The father, who was always very handsome and expensive in his tastes, seemed as if he never would be able to do anything worth doing. And the mother, who had a great belief in herself, did not succeed any better, and her tastes were just as expensive.

And so the house came to be haunted by the unspoken phrase: there must be more money! There must be more money! The children could hear it all the time, though nobody said it aloud. They heard it at Christmas, when the expensive and splendid toys filled the nursery. Behind the shining modern rocking-horse, behind the smart doll's-house, a voice would start whispering: "There must be more money! There must be more money!" And the children would stop playing, to listen for a moment. They would look into each other's eyes, to see if they had all heard. And each one saw in the eyes of the other two that they too had heard. "There must be more money! There must be more money!"

It came whispering from the springs of the still-swaying rocking-horse, and even the horse, bending his wooden, champing head, heard it. The big doll, sitting so pink and smirking in her new pram, could hear it quite plainly, and seemed to be smirking all the more self-consciously because of it. The foolish puppy, too, that took the place of the Teddy bear, he was looking so extraordinarily foolish for no other reason but that he heard the secret whisper all over the house: "There must be more money!"

Yet nobody ever said it aloud. The whisper was everywhere, and therefore no one spoke it. Just as no one ever says: "We are breathing!" in spite of the fact that breath is coming and going all the time.

"Mother," said the boy Paul one day, "why don't we keep a car of our own? Why do we always use uncle's, or else a taxi?"

"Because we're the poor members of the family," said the mother.

"But why are we, mother?"

"Well—I suppose," she said slowly and bitterly, "it's because your father has no luck."

The boy was silent for some time.

"Is luck money, mother?" he asked, rather timidly.

"No, Paul. Not quite. It's what causes you to have money."

"Oh!" said Paul vaguely. "I thought when Uncle Oscar said filthy lucker, it meant money."

"Filthy lucre does mean money," said the mother. "But it's lucre, not luck."

"Oh!" said the boy. "Then what is luck, mother?"

"It's what causes you to have money. If you're lucky you have money. That's why it's better to be born lucky than rich. If you're rich, you may lose your money. But if you're lucky, you will always get more money."

"Oh! Will you? And is father not lucky?"

"Very unlucky, I should say," she said bitterly.

The boy watched her with unsure eyes.

"Why?" he asked.

"I don't know. Nobody ever knows why one person is lucky and another unlucky."

"Don't they? Nobody at all? Does nobody know?"

"Perhaps God. But He never tells."

"He ought to, then. And aren't you lucky either, mother?"

"I can't be, if I married an unlucky husband."

"But by yourself, aren't you?"

"I used to think I was, before I married. Now I think I am very unlucky indeed."

"Why?"

"Well—never mind! Perhaps I'm not really," she said.

The child looked at her, to see if she meant it. But he saw, by the lines of her mouth, that she was only trying to hide something from him.

"Well, anyhow," he said stoutly, "I'm a lucky person."

"Why?" said his mother, with a sudden laugh.

He stared at her. He didn't even know why he had said it.

"God told me," he asserted, brazening it out.

"I hope He did, dear!" she said, again with a laugh, but rather bitter.

"He did, mother!"

"Excellent!" said the mother, using one of her husband's exclamations.

The boy saw she did not believe him; or, rather, that she paid no attention to his assertion. This angered him somewhat, and made him want to compel her attention.

He went off by himself, vaguely, in a childish way, seeking for the clue to "luck." Absorbed, taking no heed of other people, he went about with a sort of stealth, seeking inwardly for luck. He wanted luck, he wanted it, he wanted it. When the two girls were playing dolls in the nursery, he would sit on his big rocking-horse, charging madly into space, with a frenzy that made the little girls peer at him uneasily. Wildly the horse careered, the waving dark hair of the boy tossed, his eyes had a strange glare in them. The little girls dared not speak to him.

When he had ridden to the end of his mad little journey, he climbed down and stood in front of his rocking-horse, staring fixedly into its lowered face. Its red mouth was slightly open, its big eye was wide and glassy-bright.

"Now!" he would silently command the snorting steed. "Now, take me to where there is luck! Now take me!"

And he would slash the horse on the neck with the little whip he had asked Uncle Oscar for. He knew the horse could take him to where there was luck, if only he forced it. So he would mount again, and start on his furious ride, hoping at last to get there. He knew he could get there.

"You'll break your horse, Paul!" said the nurse.

"He's always riding like that! I wish he'd leave off!" said his elder sister Joan.

But he only glared down on them in silence. Nurse gave him up. She could make nothing of him. Anyhow he was growing beyond her.

One day his mother and his Uncle Oscar came in when he was on one of his furious rides. He did not speak to them.

"Hallo, you young jockey! Riding a winner?" said his uncle.

"Aren't you growing too big for a rocking-horse? You're not a very little boy any longer, you know," said his mother.

But Paul only gave a blue glare from his big, rather close-set eyes. He would speak to nobody when he was in full tilt. His mother watched him with an anxious expression on her face.

At last he suddenly stopped forcing his horse into the mechanical gallop, and slid down.

"Well, I got there!" he announced fiercely, his blue eyes still flaring, and his sturdy long legs straddling apart.

"Where did you get to?" asked his mother.

"Where I wanted to go," he flared back at her.

"That's right, son!" said Uncle Oscar. "Don't you stop till you get there. What's the horse's name?"

"He doesn't have a name," said the boy.

"Gets on without all right?" asked the uncle.

"Well, he has different names. He was called Sansovino last week."

"Sansovino, eh? Won the Ascot. How did you know his name?"

"He always talks about horse races with Bassett," said Joan.

The uncle was delighted to find that his small nephew was posted with all the racing news. Bassett, the young gardener, who had been wounded in the left foot in the war and had got his present job through Oscar Cresswell, whose batman he had been, was a perfect blade of the "turf." He lived in the racing events, and the small boy lived with him.

Oscar Cresswell got it all from Bassett.

"Master Paul comes and asks me, so I can't do more than tell him, sir," said Bassett, his face terribly serious, as if he were speaking of religious matters.

"And does he ever put anything on a horse he fancies?"

"Well—I don't want to give him away—he's a young sport, a fine sport, sir. Would you mind asking him yourself? He sort of takes a pleasure in it, and perhaps he'd feel I was giving him away, sir, if you don't mind."

Bassett was serious as a church.

The uncle went back to his nephew, and took him off for a ride in the car.

"Say, Paul, old man, do you ever put anything on a horse?" the uncle asked.

The boy watched the handsome man closely.

"Why, do you think I oughn't to?" he parried.

"Not a bit of it! I thought perhaps you might give me a tip for the Lincoln."

The car sped on into the country, going down to Uncle Oscar's place in Hampshire.

"Honour bright?" said the nephew.

"Honour bright, son!" said the uncle.

"Well, then, Daffodil."

"Daffodil! I doubt it, sonny. What about Mirza?"

"I only know the winner," said the boy. "That's Daffodil."

"Daffodil, eh?"

There was a pause. Daffodil was an obscure horse comparatively.

"Uncle!"

"Yes, son?"

"You won't let it go any further, will you? I promised Bassett."

"Bassett be damned, old man! What's he got to do with it?"

"We're partners. We've been partners from the first. Uncle, he lent me my first five shillings, which I lost. I promised him, honour bright, it was only between me and him; only you gave me that ten-shilling note I started winning with, so I thought you were lucky. You won't let it go any further, will you?"

The boy gazed at his uncle from those big, hot, blue eyes, set rather close together. The uncle stirred and laughed uneasily.

"Right you are, son! I'll keep your tip private. Daffodil, eh? How much are you putting on him?"

"All except twenty pounds," said the boy. "I keep that in reserve."

The uncle thought it a good joke.

"You keep twenty pounds in reserve, do you, you young romancer? What are you betting, then?"

"I'm betting three hundred," said the boy gravely. "But it's between you and me, Uncle Oscar! Honour bright?"

The uncle burst into a roar of laughter.

"It's between you and me all right, you young Nat Gould," he said, laughing. "But where's your three hundred?"

"Bassett keeps it for me. We're partners."

"You are, are you! And what is Bassett putting on Daffodil?"

"He won't go quite as high as I do, I expect. Perhaps he'll go a hundred and fifty."

"What, pennies?" laughed the uncle.

"Pounds," said the child, with a surprised look at his uncle. "Bassett keeps a bigger reserve than I do."

Between wonder and amusement Uncle Oscar was silent. He pursued the matter no further, but he determined to take his nephew with him to the Lincoln races.

"Now, son," he said, "I'm putting twenty on Mirza, and I'll put five for you on any horse you fancy. What's your pick?"

"Daffodil, uncle."

"No, not the fiver on Daffodil!"

"I should if it was my own fiver," said the child.

"Good! Good! Right you are! A fiver for me and a fiver for you on Daffodil."

The child had never been to a race meeting before, and his eyes were blue fire. He pursed his mouth tight, and watched. A Frenchman just in front had put his money on Lancelot. Wild with excitement, he flayed his arms up and down, yelling "Lancelot! Lancelot!" in his French accent.

Daffodil came in first, Lancelot second, Mirza third. The child, flushed and with eyes blazing, was curiously serene. His uncle brought him four five-pound notes, four to one.

"What am I to do with these?" he cried, waving them before the boy's eyes.

"I suppose we'll talk to Bassett," said the boy. "I expect I have fifteen hundred now; and twenty in reserve; and this twenty."

His uncle studied him for some moments.

"Look here, son!" he said. "You're not serious about Bassett and that fifteen hundred, are you?"

"Yes, I am. But it's between you and me, uncle. Honour bright!"

"Honour bright all right, son! But I must talk to Bassett."

"If you'd like to be a partner, uncle, with Bassett and me, we could all be partners. Only, you'd have to promise, honour bright, uncle, not to let it go beyond us three. Bassett and I are lucky, and you must be lucky, because it was your ten shillings I started winning with. . . ."

Uncle Oscar took both Bassett and Paul into Richmond Park for an afternoon, and there they talked.

"It's like this, you see, sir," Bassett said. "Master Paul would get me talking about racing events, spinning yarns, you know, sir. And he was always keen on knowing if I'd made or if I'd lost. It's about a year since, now, that I put five shillings on Blush of Dawn for him—and we lost. Then the luck turned, with that ten shillings he had from you, that we put on Singhalese. And since that time, it's been pretty steady, all things considering. What do you say, Master Paul?"

"We're all right when we're sure," said Paul. "It's when we're not quite sure that we go down."

"Oh, but we're careful then," said Bassett.

"But when are you sure?" smiled Uncle Oscar.

"It's Master Paul, sir," said Bassett, in a secret, religious voice. "It's as if he had it from heaven. Like Daffodil, now, for the Lincoln. That was as sure as eggs."

"Did you put anything on Daffodil?" asked Oscar Cresswell.

"Yes, sir, I made my bit."

"And my nephew?"

Bassett was obstinately silent, looking at Paul.

"I made twelve hundred, didn't I, Bassett? I told uncle I was putting three hundred on Daffodil."

"That's right," said Bassett, nodding.

"But where's the money?" asked the uncle.

"I keep it safe locked up, sir. Master Paul he can have it any minute he likes to ask for it."

"What, fifteen hundred pounds?"

"And twenty! and forty, that is, with the twenty he made on the course."

"It's amazing!" said the uncle.

"If Master Paul offers you to be partners, sir, I would, if I were you; if you'll excuse me," said Bassett.

Oscar Cresswell thought about it.

"I'll see the money," he said.

They drove home again, and sure enough, Bassett came round to the garden-house with fifteen hundred pounds in notes. The twenty pounds reserve was left with Joe Glee, in the Turf Commission deposit.

"You see, it's all right, uncle, when I'm sure! Then we go strong, for all we're worth. Don't we, Bassett?"

"We do that, Master Paul."

"And when are you sure?" said the uncle, laughing.

"Oh, well, sometimes I'm absolutely sure, like about Daffodil," said the boy; "and sometimes I have an idea; and sometimes I haven't even an idea, have I, Bassett? Then we're careful, because we mostly go down."

"You do, do you! And when you're sure, like about Daffodil, what makes you sure, sonny?"

"Oh, well, I don't know," said the boy uneasily. "I'm sure, you know, uncle; that's all."

"It's as if he had it from heaven, sir," Bassett reiterated.

"I should say so!" said the uncle.

But he became a partner. And when the Leger was coming on, Paul was "sure" about Lively Spark, which was a quite inconsiderable horse. The boy insisted on putting a thousand on the horse. Bassett went for five hundred, and Oscar Cresswell two hundred. Lively Spark came in first, and the betting had been ten to one against him. Paul had made ten thousand.

"You see," he said, "I was absolutely sure of him."

Even Oscar Cresswell had cleared two thousand.

"Look here, son," he said, "this sort of thing makes me nervous."

"It needn't, uncle! Perhaps I shan't be sure again for a long time."

"But what are you going to do with your money?" asked the uncle.

"Of course," said the boy, "I started it for mother. She said she had no luck, because father is unlucky, so I thought if I was lucky, it might stop whispering."

"What might stop whispering?"

"Our house. I hate our house for whispering."

"What does it whisper?"

"Why—why"—the boy fidgeted—"why, I don't know. But it's always short of money, you know, uncle."

"I know it, son, I know it."

"You know people send mother writs, don't you, uncle?"

"I'm afraid I do," said the uncle.

"And then the house whispers, like people laughing at you behind your back. It's awful, that is! I thought if I was lucky . . ."

"You might stop it," added the uncle.

The boy watched him with big blue eyes that had an uncanny cold fire in them, and he said never a word.

"Well, then!" said the uncle. "What are we doing?"

"I shouldn't like mother to know I was lucky," said the boy.

"Why not, son?"

"She'd stop me."

"I don't think she would."

"Oh!"—and the boy writhed in an odd way—"I don't want her to know, uncle."

"All right, son! We'll manage it without her knowing."

They managed it very easily. Paul, at the other's suggestion, handed over five thousand pounds to his uncle, who deposited it with the family lawyer, who was then to inform Paul's mother that a relative had put five thousand pounds into his hands, which sum was to be paid out a thousand pounds at a time, on the mother's birthday, for the next five years.

"So she'll have a birthday present of a thousand pounds for five successive years," said Uncle Oscar. "I hope it won't make it all the harder for her later."

Paul's mother had her birthday in November. The house had been "whispering" worse than ever lately, and, even in spite of his luck, Paul could not bear up against it. He was very anxious to see the effect of the birthday letter, telling his mother about the thousand pounds.

When there were no visitors, Paul now took his meals with his parents, as he was beyond the nursery control. His mother went into town nearly every day. She had discovered that she had an odd knack of sketching furs and dress materials, so she worked secretly in the studio of a friend who was the chief "artist" for the leading drapers. She drew the figures of ladies in furs and ladies in silk and sequins for the newspaper advertisements. This young woman artist earned several thousand pounds a year, but Paul's mother only made several hundreds, and she was again dissatisfied. She so wanted to be first in something, and she did not succeed, even in making sketches for drapery advertisements.

She was down to breakfast on the morning of her birthday. Paul watched her face as she read her letters. He knew the lawyer's letter. As his mother read it, her face hardened and became more expressionless. Then a cold, determined look came on her mouth. She hid the letter under the pile of others, and said not a word about it.

"Didn't you have anything nice in the post for your birthday, mother?" said Paul.

"Quite moderately nice," she said, her voice cold and absent.

She went away to town without saying more.

But in the afternoon Uncle Oscar appeared. He said Paul's mother had had a long interview with the lawyer, asking if the whole five thousand could be advanced at once, as she was in debt.

"What do you think, uncle?" said the boy.

"I leave it to you, son."

"Oh, let her have it, then! We can get some more with the other," said the boy.

"A bird in the hand is worth two in the bush, laddie!" said Uncle Oscar.

"But I'm sure to know for the Grand National; or the Lincolnshire; or else the Derby. I'm sure to know for one of them," said Paul.

So Uncle Oscar signed the agreement, and Paul's mother touched the whole five thousand. Then something very curious happened. The voices in the house suddenly went mad, like a chorus of frogs on a spring evening. There were certain new furnishings, and Paul had a tutor. He was really going to Eton, his father's school, in the following autumn. There were flowers in the winter, and a blossoming of the luxury Paul's mother had been used to. And yet the voices in the house, behind the sprays of mimosa and almond blossom, and from under the piles of iridescent cushions, simply trilled and screamed in a sort of ecstasy: "There must be more money! Oh-h-h, there must be more money. Oh, now, now-w! Now-w-w-w—there must be more money!—more than ever! More than ever!"

It frightened Paul terribly. He studied away at his Latin and Greek with his tutors. But his intense hours were spent with Bassett. The Grand National had gone by: he had not "known," and had lost a hundred pounds. Summer was at hand. He was in agony for the Lincoln. But even for the Lincoln he didn't "know" and he lost fifty pounds. He became wild-eyed and strange, as if something were going to explode in him.

"Let it alone, son! Don't you bother about it!" urged Uncle Oscar. But it was as if the boy couldn't really hear what his uncle was saying.

"I've got to know for the Derby! I've got to know for the Derby!" the child reiterated, his big blue eyes blazing with a sort of madness.

His mother noticed how overwrought he was.

"You'd better go to the seaside. Wouldn't you like to go now to the seaside, instead of waiting? I think you'd better," she said, looking down at him anxiously, her heart curiously heavy because of him.

But the child lifted his uncanny blue eyes.

"I couldn't possibly go before the Derby, mother!" he said. "I couldn't possibly!"

"Why not?" she said, her voice becoming heavy when she was opposed. "Why not? You can still go from the seaside to see the Derby with your Uncle Oscar, if that's what you wish. No need for you to wait here. Besides, I think you care too much about those races. It's a bad sign. My family has been a gambling family, and you won't know till you grow up how much damage it has done. But it has done damage. I shall have to send Bassett away, and ask Uncle Oscar not to talk racing to you, unless you promise to be reasonable about it; go away to the seaside and forget it. You're all nerves!"

"I'll do what you like, mother, so long as you don't send me away till after the Derby," the boy said.

"Send you away from where? Just from this house?"

"Yes," he said, gazing at her.

"Why, you curious child, what makes you care about this house so much, suddenly? I never knew you loved it."

He gazed at her without speaking. He had a secret within a secret, something he had not divulged, even to Bassett or to his Uncle Oscar.

But his mother, after standing undecided and a little bit sullen for some moments, said:

"Very well, then! Don't go to the seaside till after the Derby, if you don't wish it. But promise me you won't let your nerves go to pieces. Promise you won't think so much about horse racing and events, as you call them!"

"Oh, no," said the boy casually. "I won't think much about them, mother. You needn't worry. I wouldn't worry, mother, if I were you."

"If you were me and I were you," said his mother, "I wonder what we should do!"

"But you know you needn't worry, mother, don't you?" the boy repeated.

"I should be awfully glad to know it," she said wearily.

"Oh, well, you can, you know. I mean, you ought to know you needn't worry," he insisted.

"Ought I? Then I'll see about it," she said.

Paul's secret of secrets was his wooden horse, that which had no name. Since he was emancipated from a nurse and a nursery-governess, he had had his rocking-horse removed to his own bedroom at the top of the house.

"Surely, you're too big for a rocking-horse!" his mother had remonstrated.

"Well, you see, mother, till I can have a real horse, I like to have some sort of animal about," had been his quaint answer.

"Do you feel he keeps you company?" she laughed.

"Oh, yes! He's very good, he always keeps me company, when I'm there," said Paul.

So the horse, rather shabby, stood in an arrested prance in the boy's bedroom.

The Derby was drawing near, and the boy grew more and more tense. He hardly heard what was spoken to him, he was very frail, and his eyes were really uncanny. His mother had sudden seizures of uneasiness about him. Sometimes, for half-an-hour, she would feel a sudden anxiety about him that was almost anguish. She wanted to rush to him at once, and know he was safe.

Two nights before the Derby, she was at a big party in town, when one of her rushes of anxiety about her boy, her first-born, gripped her heart till she could hardly speak. She fought with the feeling, might and main, for she believed in common sense. But it was too strong. She had to leave the dance and go downstairs to telephone to the country. The children's nursery-governess was terribly surprised and startled at being rung up in the night.

"Are the children all right, Miss Wilmot?"

"Oh, yes, they are quite all right."

"Master Paul? Is he all right?"

"He went to bed as right as a trivet. Shall I run up and look at him?"

"No," said Paul's mother reluctantly. "No! Don't trouble. It's all right. Don't sit up. We shall be home fairly soon." She did not want her son's privacy intruded upon.

"Very good," said the governess.

It was about one o'clock when Paul's mother and father drove up to their house. All was still. Paul's mother went to her room and slipped off her white fur coat. She had told her maid not to wait up for her. She heard her husband downstairs, mixing a whisky-and-soda.

And then, because of the strange anxiety at her heart, she stole upstairs to her son's room. Noiselessly she went along the upper corridor. Was there a faint noise? What was it?

She stood, with arrested muscles, outside his door, listening. There was a strange, heavy, and yet not loud noise. Her heart stood still. It was a soundless noise, yet rushing and powerful. Something huge, in violent, hushed motion. What was it? What in God's name was it? She ought to know. She felt that she knew the noise. She knew what it was.

Yet she could not place it. She couldn't say what it was. And on and on it went, like a madness.

Softly, frozen with anxiety and fear, she turned the door handle.

The room was dark. Yet in the space near the window, she heard and saw something plunging to and fro. She gazed in fear and amazement.

Then suddenly she switched on the light, and saw her son, in his green pyjamas, madly surging on the rocking-horse. The blaze of light suddenly lit him up, as he urged the wooden horse, and lit her up, as she stood, blonde, in her dress of pale green and crystal, in the doorway.

"Paul!" she cried. "Whatever are you doing?"

"It's Malabar!" he screamed, in a powerful, strange voice. "It's Malabar."

His eyes blazed at her for one strange and senseless second, as he ceased urging his wooden horse. Then he fell with a crash to the ground, and she, all her tormented motherhood flooding upon her, rushed to gather him up.

But he was unconscious, and unconscious he remained, with some brain-fever. He talked and tossed, and his mother sat stonily by his side.

"Malabar! It's Malabar! Bassett, Bassett, I know! It's Malabar!"

So the child cried, trying to get up and urge the rocking-horse that gave him his inspiration.

"What does he mean by Malabar?" asked the heart-frozen mother.

"I don't know," said the father stonily.

"What does he mean by Malabar?" she asked her brother Oscar.

"It's one of the horses running for the Derby," was the answer.

And, in spite of himself, Oscar Cresswell spoke to Bassett, and himself put a thousand on Malabar: at fourteen to one.

The third day of the illness was critical: they were waiting for a change. The boy, with his rather long, curly hair, was tossing ceaselessly on the pillow. He neither slept nor regained consciousness, and his eyes were like blue stones. His mother sat, feeling her heart had gone, turned actually into a stone.

In the evening, Oscar Cresswell did not come, but Bassett sent a message, saying could he come up for one moment, just one moment? Paul's mother was very angry at the intrusion, but on second thought she agreed. The boy was the same. Perhaps Bassett might bring him to consciousness.

The gardener, a shortish fellow with a little brown moustache, and sharp little brown eyes, tiptoed into the room, touched his imaginary cap to Paul's mother, and stole to the bedside, staring with glittering, smallish eyes, at the tossing, dying child.

"Master Paul!" he whispered. "Master Paul! Malabar come in first all right, a clean win. I did as you told me. You've made over seventy thousand pounds, you have; you've got over eighty thousand. Malabar came in all right, Master Paul."

"Malabar! Malabar! Did I say Malabar, mother? Did I say Malabar? Do you think I'm lucky, mother? I knew Malabar, didn't I? Over eighty thousand pounds! I call that lucky, don't you, mother? Over eighty thousand pounds! I knew, didn't I know I knew? Malabar came in all right. If I ride my horse till I'm sure, then I tell you, Bassett, you can go as high as you like. Did you go for all you were worth, Bassett?"

"I went a thousand on it, Master Paul."

"I never told you, mother, that if I can ride my horse, and get there, then I'm absolutely sure—oh, absolutely! Mother, did I ever tell you? I am lucky."

"No, you never did," said the mother.

But the boy died in the night.

And even as he lay dead, his mother heard her brother's voice saying to her: "My God, Hester, you're eighty-odd thousand to the good and a poor devil of a son to the bad. But, poor devil, poor devil, he's best gone out of a life where he rides his rocking-horse to find a winner."

§ FOR COMMENT

Notice the characteristic elements of the fable: the diction and sentences structure, for example, suggesting the "once upon a time" formulaic beginning, the moral stated in the form of a proverb, the mysterious elements, the situation involving a young man who mounts a horse to pursue fame and fortune. But in this story the horse is wooden and the young man dies. What is the significance of this ironic variation on the usual pattern?

The rocking-horse is the central symbol. What does Paul's mechanical but furious gallop signify? Consider the house that whispers, "There must be more money. There must be more money"; the apparent scheme of values, where luck is equated with love; the interest in the race horse; and the position of the mother and father. Does it appear that Lawrence is commenting on society?

In his characterization of the mother Lawrence presents an effective picture of the neurotic woman. How would you say she feels about her son? The father is the most elusive character in the story. His overt actions are limited. He mixes a whisky and soda and he says, "I don't know," in response to a question put by his wife. Does the sparseness of detail in his characterization contribute to Lawrence's picture of the ineffectual man?

Katherine Mansfield § 1888–1923

Born in New Zealand, precocious, headstrong Katherine Mansfield (pseudonym for Kathleen Beauchamp) set out in 1903 to study for a time in London. After her first taste of London life and her introduction to the study of literature, she was not happy again in New Zealand and finally persuaded her father to grant her a small subsidy so that she might live and write in London. In 1911, when she was twenty-three years old, she published a volume of stories, In a German Pension. *There followed* Bliss *(1920) and* The Garden Party *(1922), which established her reputation as a master craftsman of the form. Other volumes include* The Dove's Nest *(1923) and* Something Childish *(1924). Her collected stories, edited by her husband, J. Middleton Murry, appeared in 1937. Miss Mansfield expressed an indebtedness to Anton Chekhov, the great Russian short story writer. Miss Mansfield's stories, like Chekhov's, are relatively plotless, usually presenting a moment in time devised in such a way as to show the relationship between the moment expressed and all time, and for this reason are often called expanded moments.*

The Fly

"Y'are very snug in here," piped old Mr. Woodifield, and he peered out of the great green leather armchair by his friend the boss's desk as a baby peers out of its pram. His talk was over; it was time for him to be off. But he did not want to go. Since he had retired, since his . . . stroke, the wife and the girls kept him boxed up in the house every day of the week except Tuesday. On Tuesday he was dressed up and brushed and allowed to cut back to the City for the day. Though what he did there the wife and girls couldn't imagine. Made a nuisance of himself to his friends, they supposed. . . . Well, perhaps so. All the same, we cling to our last pleasures as the tree clings to its last leaves. So there sat old Woodifield, smoking a cigar and staring almost greedily at the boss, who rolled in his office chair, stout, rosy, five years older than he, and still going strong, still at the helm. It did one good to see him.

Wistfully, admiringly, the old voice added, "It's snug in here, upon my word!"

"Yes, it's comfortable enough," agreed the boss, and he flipped *The Financial Times* with a paperknife. As a matter of fact he was proud of his room; he liked to have it admired, especially by old Woodifield. It gave him a feeling of deep, solid satisfaction to be planted there in the midst of it in full view of that frail old figure in the muffler.

"I've had it done up lately," he explained, as he had explained for the past—how many?—weeks. "New carpet," and he pointed to the bright red carpet with a pattern of large white rings. "New furniture," and he nodded towards the massive bookcase and the table with legs like twisted treacle. "Electric heating!" He waved almost exultantly towards the five transparent, pearly sausages glowing so softly in the tilted copper pan.

But he did not draw old Woodifield's attention to the photograph over the table of a grave-looking boy in uniform standing in one of those spectral photographers' parks with photographers' storm clouds behind him. It was not new. It had been there for over six years.

"There was something I wanted to tell you," said old Woodifield, and his eyes grew dim remembering. "Now what was it? I had it in my mind when I started out this morning." His hands began to tremble, and patches of red showed above his beard.

Poor old chap, he's on his last pins, thought the boss. And, feeling kindly, he winked at the old man, and said jokingly, "I tell you what. I've got a little drop of something here that'll do you good before you go out into the cold again. It's beautiful stuff. It wouldn't hurt a child." He took a key off his watch chain, unlocked a cupboard below his desk, and drew forth a dark, squat bottle. "That's the medicine," said he. "And the man from whom I got it told me on the strict Q.T. it came from the cellars at Windsor Castle."

Old Woodifield's mouth fell open at the sight. He couldn't have looked more surprised if the boss had produced a rabbit.

"It's whisky, ain't it?" he piped, feebly.

The boss turned the bottle and lovingly showed him the label. Whisky it was.

"D'you know," said he, peering up at the boss wonderingly, "they won't let me touch it at home." And he looked as though he was going to cry.

"Ah, that's where we know a bit more than the ladies," cried the boss, swooping across for two tumblers that stood on the table with the water bottle, and pouring a generous finger into each. "Drink it down. It'll do you good. And don't put any water with it. It's sacrilege to tamper with stuff like this. Ah!" He tossed off his, pulled out his handkerchief, hastily wiped his moustaches, and cocked an eye at old Woodifield, who was rolling his in his chaps.

The old man swallowed, was silent a moment, and then said faintly, "It's nutty!"

But it warmed him; it crept into his chill old brain—he remembered.

"That was it," he said, heaving himself out of his chair. "I thought you'd like to know. The girls were in Belgium last week having a look at poor Reggie's grave, and they happened to come across your boy's. They're quite near each other, it seems."

Old Woodifield paused, but the boss made no reply. Only a quiver in his eyelids showed that he heard.

"The girls were delighted with the way the place is kept," piped the old voice. "Beautifully looked after. Couldn't be better if they were at home. You've not been across, have yer?"

"No, no!" For various reasons the boss had not been across.

"There's miles of it," quavered old Woodifield, "and it's all as neat as a garden. Flowers growing on all the graves. Nice broad paths." It was plain from his voice how much he liked a nice broad path.

The pause came again. Then the old man brightened wonderfully.

"D'you know what the hotel made the girls pay for a pot of jam?" he piped. "Ten francs! Robbery, I call it. It was a little pot, so Gertrude says, no bigger than a half crown. And she hadn't taken more than a spoonful when they charged her ten francs. Gertrude brought the pot away with her to teach 'em a lesson. Quite right, too; it's trading on our feelings. They think because we're over there having a look around we're ready to pay anything. That's what it is." And he turned towards the door.

"Quite right, quite right!" cried the boss, though what was quite right he hadn't the least idea. He came round by his desk, followed the shuffling footsteps to the door, and saw the old fellow out. Woodifield was gone.

For a long moment the boss stayed, staring at nothing, while the gray-haired office messenger, watching him, dodged in and out of his cubby-hole like a dog that expects to be taken for a run. Then: "I'll see nobody for half an hour, Macey," said the boss. "Understand? Nobody at all."

"Very good, sir."

The door shut, the firm heavy steps recrossed the bright carpet, the fat body plumped down in the spring chair, and leaning forward, the boss covered his face with his hands. He wanted, he intended, he had arranged to weep. . . .

It had been a terrible shock to him when old Woodifield sprang that remark upon him about the boy's grave. It was exactly as though the earth had opened and he had seen the boy lying there with Woodifield's girls staring down at him. For it was strange. Although over six years had passed away, the boss never thought of the boy except as lying unchanged, unblemished in his uniform, asleep for ever. "My son!" groaned the boss. But no tears came yet. In the past, in the first months and even years after the boy's death, he had only to say those words to be overcome by such grief that nothing short of a violent fit of weeping could relieve him. Time, he had declared then, he had told everybody, could make no difference. Other men perhaps might recover, might live their loss down, but not he. How was it possible? His boy was an only son. Ever since his birth the boss had worked at building up this business for him; it had no other meaning if it was not for the boy. Life itself had come to have no other meaning. How on earth could he have slaved, denied himself, kept going all those years without the promise forever before him of the boy's stepping into his shoes and carrying on where he left off?

And that promise had been so near being fulfilled. The boy had been in the office learning the ropes for a year before the war. Every morning they had started off together; they had come back by the same train. And what congratulations he had received as the boy's father! No wonder; he had taken to it marvellously. As to his popularity with the staff, every man jack of them down to old Macey couldn't make enough of the boy. And he wasn't in the least spoilt. No, he was just his bright, natural self, with the right word for everybody, with that boyish look and his habit of saying, "Simply splendid!"

But all that was over and done with as though it never had been. The day had come when Macey had handed him the telegram that brought the whole place crashing about his head. "Deeply regret to inform you. . . ." And he had left the office a broken man, with his life in ruins.

Six years ago, six years. . . . How quickly time passed! It might have happened yesterday. The boss took his hands from his face; he was puzzled. Something seemed to be wrong with him. He wasn't feeling as he wanted to feel. He decided to get up and have a look at the boy's photograph. But it wasn't a favorite photograph of his; the expression was unnatural. It was cold, even stern-looking. The boy had never looked like that.

At that moment the boss noticed that a fly had fallen into his broken inkpot, and was trying feebly but desperately to clamber out again. Help! help! said those struggling legs. But the sides of the inkpot were wet and slippery; it fell back again and began to swim. The boss took up a pen, picked the fly out of the ink, and shook it onto a piece of blotting paper. For a fraction of a second it lay still on the dark patch that oozed round it. Then the front legs waved, took hold, and, pulling its small sodden body up, it began the immense task of cleaning the ink from its wings. Over and under, over and under, went a leg along a wing, as the stone goes over and under the scythe. Then there was a pause, while the fly, seeming to stand on the tips of its toes, tried to expand first one wing and then the other. It succeeded at last, and, sitting down, it began, like a minute cat, to clean its face. Now one could imagine that the little front legs rubbed against each other lightly, joyfully. The horrible danger was over; it had escaped; it was ready for life again.

But just then the boss had an idea. He plunged his pen back into the ink, leaned his thick wrist on the blotting paper, and as the fly tried its wings down came a great heavy blot. What would it make of that? What indeed! The little beggar seemed absolutely cowed, stunned, and afraid to move because of what would happen next. But then, as if painfully, it dragged itself forward. The front legs waved, caught hold, and, more slowly this time, the task began from the beginning.

"He's a plucky little devil," thought the boss, and he felt a real admiration for the fly's courage. That was the way to tackle things; that was the right spirit. Never say die; it was only a question of . . . But the fly had again finished its laborious task, and the boss had just time to refill his pen, to shake fair and square on the new-cleaned body yet another dark drop. What about it this time? A painful moment of suspense followed. But behold, the front legs were again waving; the boss felt a rush of relief. He leaned over the fly and said to it tenderly, "You artful little b . . ." And he actually had the brilliant notion of breathing on it to help the drying process. All the same, there was something timid and weak about its efforts now, and the boss decided that this time should be the last, as he dipped the pen into the inkpot.

It was. The last blot fell on the soaked blotting paper, and the draggled fly lay in it and did not stir. The back legs were stuck to the body; the front legs were not to be seen.

"Come on," said the boss. "Look sharp!" And he stirred it with his pen—in vain. Nothing happened or was likely to happen. The fly was dead.

The boss lifted the corpse on the end of the paper knife and flung it into the waste-paper basket. But such a grinding feeling of wretchedness seized him that he felt positively frightened. He started forward and pressed the bell for Macey.

"Bring me some fresh blotting paper," he said, sternly, "and look sharp about it." And while the old dog padded away he fell to wondering what it was he had been thinking about before. What was it? It was . . . He took out his handkerchief and passed it inside his collar. For the life of him he could not remember.

§ FOR COMMENT

In her *Journal*, Miss Mansfield wrote:

> Oh, the times when she had walked upside down on the ceiling, run up glittering panes, floated on a lake of light, flashed through a shining beam!
> And God looked upon the fly fallen into the jug of milk and saw that it was good. And the smallest Cherubim and Seraphim of all, who delight

in misfortune, struck their silver harps and shrilled: "How is the fly fallen, fallen!" [1]

Is there some relationship between the ideas expressed in this quotation and the symbolic role of the fly in the story? Consider also Shakespeare's lines in *King Lear:* "As flies to wanton boys are we to th' gods./ They kill us for their sport."

How many people in the story can be identified as flies? All of them? If so, how is it possible to explain the symbolic role the boss plays in the climactic episode where he assumes the role of a god figure? Notice that he has played this role also in his attempt to order his son's life, in his giving of the whiskey to old Woodifield, and in his position as boss. Might the symbol be extended to suggest man's aspirations as well as his temporal existence? To fly is to escape earth-bound reality and to soar through the heavens. But, as in the Icarus legend, to fly might mean to travel too near the sun and thus to fall. Consider the biblical style and allusions of the passage quoted above and remember the lines from Isaiah: "How art thou fallen from heaven, O Lucifer, son of the morning!"

Compare the plot in this story with the plot in "The Secret Sharer" and comment upon the often repeated statement that Miss Mansfield's stories are relatively plotless. Reread the biographical headnote and comment upon the symbolism in the story which causes the moment presented to expand to encompass all time.

Is the world in "The Rocking-Horse Winner" a microcosm also? How about in "The Fly"? Support your answers with relevant details from the stories.

Does Miss Mansfield use the central symbol in "The Fly" in the same way that Lawrence uses the rocking-horse? Is each symbol defined by the context of the story? Why or why not?

James Thurber § 1894–1961

Born in Ohio, Thurber attended Ohio State University, then worked on various newspapers before he joined the staff of The New Yorker *in 1927, where he achieved fame as a writer (short stories, essays, anecdotes) and cartoonist.* Is Sex Necessary? *(1929), written with E. B. White, is a satire on books on psychoanalysis. A play written with Elliot Nugent,* The Male Animal *(1940), was successful both*

---

[1] *Journal of Katherine Mansfield,* ed. J. Middleton Murry (New York: Alfred A. Knopf, 1927), p. 103.

*on the Broadway stage and in film. The Thurber Carnival (1945),
a collection of some of his most familiar works, was successfully
dramatized a year before his death. Primarily a humorist, Thurber's
famous line drawings of dogs and people comment on the vagaries
of American life, and one of his favorite subjects (explored in all his
various media) is the domination of the American male by the
American female. "The Secret Life of Walter Mitty" is perhaps the
best known of his stories.*

The Catbird Seat

Mr. Martin brought the pack of Camels on Monday night in the most crowded cigar store on Broadway. It was theater time and seven or eight men were buying cigarettes. The clerk didn't even glance at Mr. Martin, who put the pack in his overcoat pocket and went out. If any of the staff at F & S had seen him buy the cigarettes, they would have been astonished, for it was generally known that Mr. Martin did not smoke, and never had. No one saw him.

It was just a week to the day since Mr. Martin had decided to rub out Mrs. Ulgine Barrows. The term "rub out" pleased him because it suggested nothing more than the correction of an error—in this case an error of Mr. Fitweiler. Mr. Martin had spent each night of the past week working out his plan and examining it. As he walked home now he went over it again. For the hundredth time he resented the element of imprecision, the margin of guesswork that entered into the business. The project as he had worked it out was casual and bold, the risks were considerable. Something might go wrong anywhere along the line. And therein lay the cunning of his scheme. No one would ever see in it the cautious, painstaking hand of Erwin Martin, head of the filing department at F & S, of whom Mr. Fitweiler had once said, "Man is fallible but Martin isn't." No one would see his hand, that is, unless it were caught in the act.

Sitting in his apartment, drinking a glass of milk, Mr. Martin reviewed his case against Mrs. Ulgine Barrows, as he had every night for seven nights. He began at the beginning. Her quacking voice and braying laugh had first profaned the halls of F & S on March 7, 1941 (Mr. Martin had a head for dates). Old Roberts, the personnel chief, had introduced her as the newly appointed special adviser to the president of the firm, Mr. Fitweiler. The woman had appalled Mr. Martin instantly, but he hadn't shown it. He had given her his dry hand, a look of studious concentration, and a faint smile. "Well," she had said, looking at the papers on his desk, "are you lifting the oxcart out of the ditch?" As Mr. Martin recalled that moment, over his milk, he squirmed slightly. He must keep his mind on her crimes as a special adviser, not on her peccadillos as a personality. This he found difficult to do, in spite of entering an objection and sustaining it. The faults of the woman as a woman kept chattering on in his mind like an unruly witness. She had, for almost two years now, baited him. In the halls, in the elevator, even in his own office, into which she romped now and then like a circus horse, she was constantly shouting these silly questions at him. "Are you lifting the oxcart out of the ditch? Are you tearing up the pea patch? Are you hollering down the rain barrel? Are you scraping around the bottom of the pickle barrel? Are you sitting in the catbird seat?"

It was Joey Hart, one of Mr. Martin's two assistants, who had explained what the gibberish meant. "She must be a Dodger fan," he had said. "Red Barber announces the Dodger games over the radio and he uses those expressions—picked 'em up down South." Joey had gone on to explain one or two. "Tearing up the pea patch" meant going on a rampage; "sitting in the catbird seat" meant sitting pretty, like a batter with three balls and no strikes on him. Mr. Martin dismissed all this with an effort. It had been annoying, it had driven him near to distraction, but he was too solid a man to be moved to murder by anything so childish. It was fortunate, he reflected as he passed on to the important charges against Mrs. Barrows, that he had stood up under it so well. He had maintained always an outward appearance of polite tolerance. "Why, I even believe you like the woman," Miss Paird, his other assistant, had once said to him. He had simply smiled.

A gavel rapped in Mr. Martin's mind and the case proper was resumed. Mrs. Ulgine Barrows stood charged with willful, blatant, and persistent attempts to destroy the efficiency and system of F & S. It was competent, material, and relevant to review her advent and rise to power. Mr. Martin had got the story from Miss Paird, who seemed always able to find things out. According to her, Mrs. Barrows had met Mr. Fitweiler at a party where she had rescued him from the embraces of a powerfully built drunken man who had mistaken the president of F & S for a famous retired Middle Western football coach. She had led him to a sofa and somehow worked upon him a monstrous magic. The aging gentleman had jumped to the conclusion there and then that this was a woman of singular attainments, equipped to bring out the best in him and in the firm. A week later he had introduced her into F & S as his special adviser. On that day confusion got its foot in the door. After Miss Tyson, Mr. Brundage, and Mr. Bartlett had been fired and Mr. Munson had taken his hat and stalked out, mailing in his resignation later, old Roberts had been emboldened to speak to Mr. Fitweiler. He mentioned that Mr. Munson's department had been "a little disrupted" and hadn't they perhaps better resume the old system there? Mr. Fitweiler had said certainly not. He had the greatest faith in Mrs. Barrow's ideas. "They require a little seasoning, a little seasoning, is all," he had added. Mr. Roberts had given it up. Mr. Martin reviewed in detail all the changes wrought by Mrs. Barrows. She had begun chipping at the cornices of the firm's edifice and now she was swinging at the foundation stones with a pickaxe.

Mr. Martin came now, in his summing up, to the afternoon of Monday, November 2, 1942—just one week ago. On that day, at 3 P.M., Mrs. Barrows had bounced into his office. "Boo!" she had yelled. "Are you scraping around the bottom of the pickle barrel?" Mr. Martin had looked at her from under his green eyeshade, saying nothing. She had begun to wander about the office, taking it in with her great, popping eyes. "Do you really need *all* these filing cabinets?" she had demanded suddenly. Mr. Martin's heart had jumped. "Each of these files," he had said, keeping his voice even, "plays an indispensable part in the system of F & S." She had brayed at him, "Well, don't tear up the pea patch!" and gone to the door. From there she had bawled, "But you sure have got a lot of fine scrap in here!" Mr. Martin could no longer doubt that the finger was on his beloved department. Her pickaxe was on the upswing, poised for the first blow. It had not come yet; he had received no blue memo from the enchanted Mr. Fitweiler bearing nonsensical instructions deriving from the obscene woman. But there was no doubt in Mr. Martin's mind that one would be forthcoming. He must act quickly. Already a precious week had gone by. Mr. Martin stood up in his living room, still holding his milk glass. "Gentlemen of the jury," he said to himself, "I demand the death penalty for this horrible person."

The next day Mr. Martin followed his routine, as usual. He polished his glasses more often and once sharpened an already sharp pencil, but not even Miss Paird noticed. Only once did he catch sight of his victim; she swept past him in the hall with a patronizing "Hi!" At five thirty he walked home, as usual, and had a glass of milk, as usual. He had never drunk anything stronger in his life—unless you could count ginger ale. The late Sam Schlosser, the S of F & S, had praised Mr. Martin at a staff meeting several years before for his temperate habits. "Our most efficient worker neither drinks nor smokes," he had said. "The results speak for themselves." Mr. Fitweiler had sat by, nodding approval.

Mr. Martin was still thinking about that red-letter day as he walked over to the Schrafft's on Fifth Avenue near Forty-sixth Street. He got there, as he always did, at eight o'clock. He finished his dinner and the financial page of the *Sun* at a quarter to nine, as he always did. It was his custom after dinner to take a walk. This time he walked down Fifth Avenue at a casual pace. His gloved hands felt moist and warm, his forehead cold. He transferred the Camels from his overcoat to a jacket pocket. He wondered, as he did so, if they did not represent an unnecessary note of strain. Mrs. Barrows smoked only Luckies. It was his idea to puff a few puffs on a Camel (after the rubbing-out), stub it out in the ashtray holding her lip-stick-stained Luckies, and thus drag a small red herring across the trail. Perhaps it was not a good idea. It would take time. He might even choke, too loudly.

Mr. Martin had never seen the house on West Twelfth Street where Mrs. Barrows lived, but he had a clear enough picture of it. Fortunately, she had bragged to everybody about her ducky first-floor apartment in the perfectly darling three-story red-brick. There would be no doorman or other attendants; just the tenants of the second and third floors. As he walked along, Mr. Martin realized that he would get there before nine-thirty. He had considered walking north on Fifth Avenue from Schrafft's to a point from which it would take him until ten o'clock to reach the house. At that hour people were less likely to be coming in or going out. But the procedure would have made an awkward loop in the straight thread of his casualness, and he had abandoned it. It was impossible to figure when people would be entering or leaving the house, anyway. There was a great risk at any hour. If he ran into anybody, he would simply have to place the rubbing-out of Ulgine Barrows in the inactive file forever. The same thing would hold true if there were someone in her apartment. In that case he would just say that he had been passing by, recognized her charming house and thought to drop in.

It was eighteen minutes after nine when Mr. Martin turned into Twelfth Street. A man passed him, and a man and a woman talking. There was no one within fifty paces when he came to the house, halfway down the block. He was up the steps and in the small vestibule in no time, pressing the bell under the card that said "Mrs. Ulgine Barrows." When the clicking in the lock started, he jumped forward against the door. He got inside fast, closing the door behind him. A bulb in a lantern hung from the hall ceiling on a chain seemed to give a monstrously bright light. There was nobody on the stair, which went up ahead of him along the left wall. A door opened down the hall in the wall on the right. He went toward it swiftly, on tiptoe.

"Well, for God's sake, look who's here!" bawled Mrs. Barrows, and her braying laugh rang out like the report of a shotgun. He rushed past her like a football tackle, bumping her. "Hey, quit shoving!" she said, closing the door behind them. They were in her living room, which seemed to Mr. Martin to be lighted by a hundred lamps. "What's after you?" she said. "You're as jumpy as a goat." He found he was unable to speak. His heart was wheezing in his throat. "I—yes," he finally brought out. She was jabbering and laughing as she started to help him off with his coat. "No, no," he said. "I'll put it here." He took it off and put it on a chair near the door. "Your hat and gloves, too," she said. "You're in a lady's house." He put his hat on top of the coat. Mrs. Barrows seemed larger than he had thought. He kept his gloves on. "I was passing by," he said. "I recognized—is there anyone here?" She laughed louder than ever. "No," she said, "we're all alone. You're as white as a sheet, you funny man. Whatever *has* come over you? I'll mix you a toddy." She started toward a door across the room. "Scotch-and-soda be all right? But say, you don't drink, do you?" She turned and gave him her amused look. Mr. Martin pulled himself together. "Scotch-and-soda will be all right," he heard himself say. He could hear her laughing in the kitchen.

Mr. Martin looked quickly around the living room for the weapon. He had counted on finding one there. There were andirons and a poker and something in a corner that looked like an Indian club. None of them would do. It couldn't be that way. He began to pace around. He came to a desk. On it lay a metal paper knife with an ornate handle. Would it be sharp enough? He reached for it and knocked over a small brass jar. Stamps spilled out of it and it fell to the floor with a clatter. "Hey," Mrs. Barrows yelled from the kitchen, "are you tearing up the pea patch?" Mr. Martin gave a strange laugh. Picking up the knife, he tried its point against his left wrist. It was blunt. It wouldn't do.

When Mrs. Barrows reappeared, carrying two highballs, Mr. Martin, standing there with his gloves on, became acutely conscious of the fantasy he had wrought. Cigarettes in his pocket, a drink prepared for him—it was all too grossly improbable. It was more than that; it was impossible. Somewhere in the back of his mind a vague idea stirred, sprouted. "For heaven's sake, take off those gloves," said Mrs. Barrows. "I always wear them in the house," said Mr. Martin. The idea began to bloom, strange and wonderful. She put the glasses on a coffee table in front of a sofa and sat on the sofa. "Come over here, you odd little man," she said. Mr. Martin went over and sat beside her. It was difficult getting a cigarette out of the pack of Camels, but he managed it. She held a match for him, laughing. "Well," she said, handing him his drink, "this is perfectly marvelous. You with a drink and a cigarette."

Mr. Martin puffed, not too awkwardly, and took a gulp of the highball. "I drink and smoke all the time," he said. He clinked his glass against hers. "Here's nuts to that old windbag, Fitweiler," he said, and gulped again. The stuff tasted awful, but he made no grimace. "Really, Mr. Martin," she said, her voice and posture changing, "you are insulting our employer." Mrs. Barrows was now all special adviser to the president. "I am preparing a bomb," said Mr. Martin, "which will blow the old goat higher than hell." He had only had a little of the drink, which was not strong. It couldn't be that. "Do you take dope or something?" Mrs. Barrows asked coldly. "Heroin," said Mr. Martin. "I'll be coked to the gills when I bump that old buzzard off." "Mr. Martin!" she shouted, getting to her feet. "That will be all of that. You must go at once." Mr. Martin took another swallow of his drink. He tapped his cigarette out in the ashtray and put the pack of Camels on the coffee table. Then he got up. She stood glaring at him. He walked over and put on his hat and coat. "Not a word about this," he said, and laid an index finger against his lips. All Mrs. Barrows could bring out was "Really!" Mr. Martin put his hand on the doorknob. "I'm sitting in the catbird seat," he said. He stuck his tongue out at her and left. Nobody saw him go.

Mr. Martin got to his apartment, walking, well before eleven. No one saw him go in. He had two glasses of milk after brushing his teeth, and he felt elated. It wasn't tipsiness, because he hadn't been tipsy. Anyway, the walk had worn off all effects of the whisky. He got in bed and read a magazine for a while. He was asleep before midnight.

Mr. Martin got to the office at eight-thirty the next morning, as usual. At a quarter to nine, Ulgine Barrows, who had never before arrived at work before ten, swept into his office. "I'm reporting to Mr. Fitweiler now!" she shouted. "If he turns you over to the police, it's no more than you deserve!" Mr. Martin gave her a look of shocked surprise. "I beg your pardon?" he said. Mrs. Barrows snorted and bounced out of the room, leaving Miss Paird and Joey Hart staring after her. "What's the matter with that old devil now?" asked Miss Paird. "I have no idea," said Mr. Martin, resuming his work. The other two looked at him and then at each other. Miss Paird got up and went out. She walked slowly past the closed door of Mr. Fitweiler's office. Mrs. Barrows was yelling inside, but she was not braying. Miss Paird could not hear what the woman was saying. She went back to her desk.

Forty-five minutes later, Mrs. Barrows left the president's office and went into her own, shutting the door. It wasn't until half an hour later that Mr. Fitweiler sent for Mr. Martin. The head of the filing department, neat, quiet, attentive, stood in front of the old man's desk. Mr. Fitweiler was pale and nervous. He took his glasses off and twiddled them. He made a small, bruffing sound in his throat. "Martin," he said, "you have been with us more than twenty years." "Twenty-two, sir," said Mr. Martin. "In that time," pursued the president, "your work and your—uh—manner have been exemplary." "I trust so, sir," said Mr. Martin. "I have understood, Martin," said Mr. Fitweiler, "that you have never taken a drink or smoked." "That is correct, sir," said Mr. Martin. "Ah, yes." Mr. Fitweiler polished his glasses. "You may describe what you did after leaving the office yesterday, Martin," he said. Mr. Martin allowed less than a second for his bewildered pause. "Certainly, sir," he said. "I walked home. Then I went to Schrafft's for dinner. Afterward I walked home again. I went to bed early, sir, and read a magazine for a while. I was asleep before eleven." "Ah, yes," said Mr. Fitweiler again. He was silent for a moment, searching for the proper words to say to the head of the filing department. "Mrs. Barrows," he said finally, "Mrs. Barrows has worked hard, Martin, very hard. It grieves me to report that she has suffered a severe breakdown. It has taken the form of a persecution complex accompanied by distressing hallucinations." "I am very sorry, sir," said Mr. Martin. "Mrs. Barrows is under the delusion," continued Mr. Fitweiler, "that you visited her last evening and behaved yourself in an—uh—unseemly manner." He raised his hand to silence Mr. Martin's little pained outcry. "It is the nature of these psychological diseases," Mr. Fitweiler said, "to fix upon the least likely and most innocent party as the—uh—source of persecution. These matters are not for the lay mind to grasp, Martin. I've just had my psychiatrist, Dr. Fitch, on the phone. He would not, of course, commit himself, but he made enough generalizations to substantiate my suspicions. I suggested to Mrs. Barrows when she had completed her—uh—story to me this morning, that she visit Dr. Fitch, for I suspected a condition at once. She flew, I regret to say, into a rage, and demanded—uh—requested that I call you on the carpet. You may not know, Martin, but Mrs. Barrows had planned a reorganization of your department—subject to my approval, of course, subject to my approval. This brought you, rather than anyone else, to her mind—but again that is a phenomenon for Dr. Fitch and not for us. So, Martin, I am afraid Mrs. Barrows' usefulness here is at an end." "I am dreadfully sorry, sir," said Mr. Martin.

It was at this point that the door to the office blew open with the suddenness of a gas-main explosion and Mrs. Barrows catapulted through it. "Is the little rat denying it?" she screamed. "He can't get away with that!" Mr. Martin got up and moved discreetly to a point beside Mr. Fitweiler's chair. "You drank and smoked at my apartment," she bawled at Mr. Martin, "and you know it! You called Mr. Fitweiler an old windbag and said you were going to blow him up when you got coked to the gills on your heroin!" She stopped yelling to catch her breath and a new glint came into her popping eyes. "If you weren't such a drab, ordinary little man," she said, "I'd think you'd planned it all. Sticking your tongue out, saying you were sitting in the catbird seat, because you thought no one would believe me when I told it! My God, it's really too perfect!" She brayed loudly and hysterically, and the fury was on her again. She glared at Mr. Fitweiler. "Can't you see how he has tricked us, you old fool? Can't you see his little game?" But Mr. Fitweiler had been surreptitiously pressing all the buttons under the top of his desk and employees of F & S began pouring into the room. "Stockton," said Mr. Fitweiler, "you and Fishbein will take Mrs. Barrows to her home. Mrs. Powell, you will go with them." Stockton, who had played a little football in high school, blocked Mrs. Barrows as she made for Mr. Martin. It took him and Fishbein together to force her out of the door into the hall, crowded with stenographers and office boys. She was still screaming imprecations at Mr. Martin, tangled and contradictory imprecations. The hubbub finally died out down the corridor.

"I regret that this has happened," said Mr. Fitweiler. "I shall ask you to dismiss it from your mind, Martin." "Yes, sir," said Mr. Martin, anticipating his chief's "That will be all" by moving to the door. "I will dismiss it." He went out and shut the door, and his step was light and quick in the hall. When he entered his department he had slowed down to his custom-ary gait, and he walked quietly across the room to the W20 file, wearing a look of studious concentration.

§ FOR COMMENT

This story is an ironic reversal on Thurber's usual theme: Here the "little" man triumphs over the "dominant" woman. What kind of man is Mr. Martin? What methods does Thurber use to affect characterization? What kind of woman is Mrs. Barrows? Does Thurber allow the reader to feel any sympathy for her? Why? What does Mr. Martin have against her? Why does he hold a trial against her in his mind?

Justify Thurber's use of third-person narration limited to Mr. Martin's viewpoint. Why could not the omniscient author's view be just as effective? Could a first-person narration have been used?

What is the central comic situation here? What makes it funny?

This story follows the conventional line of development: exposition, complication, climax, resolution. Identify each part and show how comic juxtaposition occurs in each part.

William Faulkner § 1897–1962

One of America's literary giants with an international reputation, Faulkner attended a university, but never took a degree, visited in New York and Europe, but spent most of his life in his native Mississippi. Considered by many critics to be the greatest American author of this century, he won the Nobel Prize in 1949 and a Pulitzer Prize for A Fable *in 1954. Most of his fiction is set in the mythical county of Yoknapatawpha and concerns itself with the people, the history, and the complexities involved in the human situation. Although the novels and short stories fit into a larger pat-tern, they are also complete and separate entities, significant in themselves. His Nobel Prize speech delivered at Stockholm in 1950 contains the following eloquent lines: "I believe that man will not merely endure: he will prevail. He is immortal, not because he alone among creatures has an inexhaustible voice, but because he has a soul, a spirit capable of compassion and sacrifice and endurance."* [1]

[1] William Faulkner, *Essays, Speeches, and Public Letters,* ed. James B. Meri-wether (New York: Random House, 1965), p. 120.

Wash

Sutpen stood above the pallet bed on which the mother and child lay. Between the shrunken planking of the wall the early sunlight fell in long pencil strokes, breaking upon his straddled legs and upon the riding whip in his hand, and lay across the still shape of the mother, who lay looking up at him from still, inscrutable, sullen eyes, the child at her side wrapped in a piece of dingy clean cloth. Behind them an old Negro woman squatted beside the rough hearth where a meager fire smoldered.

"Well, Milly," Sutpen said, "too bad you're not a mare. Then I could give you a decent stall in the stable."

Still the girl on the pallet did not move. She merely continued to look up at him without expression, with a young, sullen, inscrutable face still pale from recent travail. Sutpen moved, bringing into the splintered pencils of sunlight the face of a man of sixty. He said quietly to the squatting Negress, "Griselda foaled this morning."

"Horse or mare?" the Negress said.

"A horse. A damned fine colt. . . . What's this?" He indicated the pallet with the hand which held the whip.

"That un's a mare, I reckon."

"Hah," Sutpen said. "A damned fine colt. Going to be the spit and image of old Rob Roy when I rode him North in '61. Do you remember?"

"Yes, Marster."

"Hah." He glanced back towards the pallet. None could have said if the girl still watched him or not. Again his whip hand indicated the pallet. "Do whatever they need with whatever we've got to do it with." He went out, passing out the crazy doorway and stepping down into the rank weeds (there yet leaned rusting against the corner of the porch the scythe which Wash had borrowed from him three months ago to cut them with) where his horse waited, where Wash stood holding the reins.

When Colonel Sutpen rode away to fight the Yankees, Wash did not go. "I'm looking after the Kernel's place and niggers," he would tell all who asked him and some who had not asked—a gaunt, malaria-ridden man with pale, questioning eyes, who looked about thirty-five, though it was known that he had not only a daughter but an eight-year-old granddaughter as well. This was a lie, as most of them—the few remaining men between eighteen and fifty—to whom he told it, knew, though there were some who believed that he himself really believed it, though even these believed that he had better sense than to put it to the test with Mrs. Sutpen or the Sutpen slaves. Knew better or was just too lazy and shiftless to try it, they said, knowing that his sole connection with the Sutpen plantation lay in the fact that for years now Colonel Sutpen had allowed him to squat in a crazy shack on a slough in the river bottom on the Sutpen place, which Sutpen had built for a fishing lodge in his bachelor days and which had since fallen in dilapidation from disuse, so that now it looked like an aged or sick wild beast crawled terrifically there to drink in the act of dying.

The Sutpen slaves themselves heard of his statement. They laughed. It was not the first time they had laughed at him, calling him white trash behind his back. They began to ask him themselves, in groups, meeting him in the faint road which led up from the slough and the old fish camp, "Why ain't you at de war, white man?"

Pausing, he would look about the ring of black faces and white eyes and teeth behind which derision lurked. "Because I got a daughter and family to keep," he said. "Git out of my road, niggers."

"Niggers?" they repeated; "niggers?" laughing now. "Who him, calling us niggers?"

"Yes," he said. "I ain't got no niggers to look after my folks if I was gone."

"Nor nothing else but dat shack down yon dat Cunnel wouldn't *let* none of us live in."

Now he cursed them; sometimes he rushed at them, snatching up a stick from the ground while they scattered before him, yet seeming to surround him still with that black laughing, derisive, evasive, inescapable, leaving him panting and impotent and raging. Once it happened in the very back yard of the big house itself. This was after bitter news had come down from the Tennessee mountains and from Vicksburg, and Sherman had passed through the plantation, and most of the Negroes had followed him. Almost everything else had gone with the Federal troops, and Mrs. Sutpen had sent word to Wash that he could have the scuppernongs ripening in the arbor in the back yard. This time it was a house servant, one of the few Negroes who remained; this time the Negress had to retreat up the kitchen steps, where she turned. "Stop right dar, white man. Stop right whar you is. You ain't never crossed dese steps whilst Cunnel here, and you ain't ghy' do hit now."

This was true. But there was this of a kind of pride: he had never tried to enter the big house, even though he believed that if he had, Sutpen would have received him, permitted him. "But I ain't going to give no black nigger the chance to tell me I can't go nowhere," he said to himself. "I ain't even going to give Kernel the chance to have to cuss a nigger on my account." This, though he and Sutpen had spent more than one afternoon together on those rare Sundays when there would be no company in the house. Perhaps his mind knew that it was because Sutpen had nothing else to do, being a man who could not bear his own company. Yet the fact remained that the two of them would spend whole afternoons in the scuppernong arbor, Sutpen in the hammock and Wash squatting against a post, a pail of cistern water between them, taking drink for drink from the same demijohn. Meanwhile on weekdays he would see the fine figure of the man —they were the same age almost to a day, though neither of them (perhaps

because Wash had a grandchild while Sutpen's son was a youth in school)
ever thought of himself as being so—on the fine figure of the black stallion,
galloping about the plantation. For that moment his heart would be quiet
and proud. It would seem to him that that world in which Negroes, whom
the Bible told him had been created and cursed by God to be brute and
vassal to all men of white skin, were better found and housed and even
clothed than he and his; that world in which he sensed always about him
mocking echoes of black laughter was but a dream and an illusion, and that
the actual world was this one across which his own lonely apotheosis
seemed to gallop on the black thoroughbred, thinking how the Book said
also that all men were created in the image of God and hence all men made
the same image in God's eyes at least; so that he could say, as though
speaking of himself, "A fine proud man. If God Himself was to come down
and ride the natural earth, that's what He would aim to look like."

Sutpen returned in 1865, on the black stallion. He seemed to have
aged ten years. His son had vanished the same winter in which his wife had
died. He returned with his citation for gallantry from the hand of General
Lee to a ruined plantation, where for a year now his daughter had subsisted
partially on the meager bounty of the man to whom fifteen years ago he
had granted permission to live in that tumbledown fishing camp whose very
existence he had at the time forgotten. Wash was there to meet him, unchanged: still gaunt, still ageless, with his pale, questioning gaze, his air
diffident, a little servile, a little familiar. "Well, Kernel," Wash said, "they
kilt us but they ain't whupped us yit, air they?"

That was the tenor of their conversation for the next five years. It was
inferior whiskey which they drank now together from a stoneware jug, and
it was not in the scuppernong arbor. It was in the rear of the little store
which Sutpen managed to set up on the highroad: a frame shelved room
where, with Wash for clerk and porter, he dispensed kerosene and staple
foodstuffs and stale gaudy candy and cheap beads and ribbons to Negroes
or poor whites of Wash's own kind, who came afoot or on gaunt mules to
haggle tediously for dimes and quarters with a man who at one time could
gallop (the black stallion was still alive; the stable in which his jealous get
lived was in better repair than the house where the master himself lived)
for ten miles across his own fertile land and who had led troops gallantly in
battle; until Sutpen in fury would empty the store, close and lock the doors
from the inside. Then he and Wash would repair to the rear and the jug.
But the talk would not be quiet now, as when Sutpen lay in the hammock,
delivering an arrogant monologue while Wash squatted guffawing against
his post. They both sat now, though Sutpen had the single chair while
Wash used whatever box or keg was handy, and even this for just a little
while, because soon Sutpen would reach that stage of impotent and furious
undefeat in which he would rise, swaying and plunging, and declare again
that he would take his pistol and the black stallion and ride single-handed

into Washington and kill Lincoln, dead now, and Sherman, now a private citizen. "Kill them!" he would shout. "Shoot them down like the dogs they are—"

"Sho, Kernel; sho, Kernel," Wash would say, catching Sutpen as he fell. Then he would commandeer the first passing wagon or, lacking that, he would walk the mile to the nearest neighbor and borrow one and return and carry Sutpen home. He entered the house now. He had been doing so for a long time, taking Sutpen home in whatever borrowed wagon might be, talking him into locomotion with cajoling murmurs as though he were a horse, a stallion himself. The daughter would meet them and hold open the door without a word. He would carry his burden through the once white formal entrance, surmounted by a fanlight imported piece by piece from Europe and with a board now nailed over a missing pane, across a velvet carpet from which all nap was now gone, and up a formal stairs, now but a fading ghost of bare boards between two strips of fading paint, and into the bedroom. It would be dusk by now, and he would let his burden sprawl onto the bed and undress it and then he would sit quietly in a chair beside. After a time the daughter would come to the door. "We're all right now," he would tell her. "Don't you worry none, Miss Judith."

Then it would become dark, and after a while he would lie down on the floor beside the bed, though not to sleep, because after a time— sometimes before midnight—the man on the bed would stir and groan and then speak. "Wash?"

"Hyer I am, Kernel. You go back to sleep. We ain't whupped yit, air we? Me and you kin do hit."

Even then he had already seen the ribbon about his granddaughter's waist. She was now fifteen, already mature, after the early way of her kind. He knew where the ribbon came from; he had been seeing it and its kind daily for three years, even if she had lied about where she got it, which she did not, at once bold, sullen, and fearful.

"Sho now," he said. "Ef Kernel want to give hit to you, I hope you minded to thank him."

His heart was quiet, even when he saw the dress, watching her secret, defiant, frightened face when she told him that Miss Judith, the daughter, had helped her to make it. But he was quite grave when he approached Sutpen after they closed the store that afternoon, following the other to the rear.

"Get the jug," Sutpen directed.

"Wait," Wash said. "Not yit for a minute."

Neither did Sutpen deny the dress. "What about it?" he said.

But Wash met his arrogant stare; he spoke quietly. "I've knowed you for going on twenty years. I ain't yit denied to do what you told me to do. And I'm a man nigh sixty. And she ain't nothing but a fifteen-year-old gal."

"Meaning that I'd harm a girl? I, a man as old as you are?"

"If you was ara other man, I'd say you was as old as me. And old or no old, I wouldn't let her keep that dress nor nothing else that come from your hand. But you are different."

"How different?" But Wash merely looked at him with his pale, questioning, sober eyes. "So that's why you are afraid of me?"

Now Wash's gaze no longer questioned. It was tranquil, serene. "I ain't afraid. Because you air brave. It ain't that you were a brave man at one minute or day of your life and got a paper to show hit from General Lee. But you air brave, the same as you air alive and breathing. That's where hit's different. Hit don't need no ticket from nobody to tell me that. And I know that whatever you handle or tech, whether hit's a regiment of men or a ignorant gal or just a hound dog, that you will make it right."

Now it was Sutpen who looked away, turning suddenly, brusquely. "Get the jug," he said sharply.

"Sho, Kernel," Wash said.

So on that Sunday dawn two years later, having watched the Negro midwife, whom he had walked three miles to fetch, enter the crazy door beyond which his granddaughter lay wailing, his heart was still quiet though concerned. He knew what they had been saying—the Negroes in cabins about the land, the white men who loafed all day long about the store, watching quietly the three of them: Sutpen, himself, his granddaughter with her air of brazen and shrinking defiance as her condition become daily more and more obvious, like three actors that came and went upon a stage. "I know what they say to one another," he thought. "I can almost hyear them: *Wash Jones has fixed old Sutpen at last. Hit taken him twenty years, but he has done hit at last.*"

It would be dawn after a while, though not yet. From the house, where the lamp shone dim beyond the warped door frame, his granddaughter's voice came steadily as though run by a clock, while thinking went slowly and terrifically, fumbling, involved somehow with a sound of galloping hooves, until there broke suddenly free in mid-gallop the fine proud figure of the man on the fine proud stallion, galloping; and then that at which thinking fumbled, broke free too and quite clear, not in justification nor even explanation, but as the apotheosis, lonely, explicable, beyond all fouling by human touch: "He is bigger than all them Yankees that kilt his son and his wife and taken his niggers and ruined his land, bigger than this hyer durn country that he fit for and that has denied him into keeping a little country store; bigger than the denial which it helt to his lips like the bitter cup in the Book. And how could I have lived this nigh to him for twenty years without being teched and changed by him? Maybe I ain't as big as him and maybe I ain't done none of the galloping. But at least I done been drug along. Me and him kin do hit, if so be he will show me what he aims for me to do."

Then it was dawn. Suddenly he could see the house and the old Negress in the door looking at him. Then he realized that his granddaughter's voice had ceased. "It's a girl," the Negress said. "You can go tell him if you want to." She reëntered the house.

"A girl," he repeated; "a girl"; in astonishment, hearing the galloping hooves, seeing the proud galloping figure emerge again. He seemed to watch it pass, galloping through avatars which marked the accumulation of years, time, to the climax where it galloped beneath a brandished sabre and a shot-torn flag rushing down a sky in color like thunderous sulphur, thinking for the first time in his life that perhaps Sutpen was an old man like himself. "Gittin a gal," he thought in that astonishment; then he thought with the pleased surprise of a child: "Yes, sir. Be dawg if I ain't lived to be a great-grandpaw after all."

He entered the house. He moved clumsily, on tiptoe, as if he no longer lived there, as if the infant which had just drawn breath and cried in light had dispossessed him, be it of his own blood too though it might. But even above the pallet he could see little save the blur of his granddaughter's exhausted face. Then the Negress squatting at the hearth spoke, "You better gawn tell him if you going to. Hit's daylight now."

But this was not necessary. He had no more than turned the corner of the porch where the scythe leaned which he had borrowed three months ago to clear away the weeds through which he walked, when Sutpen himself rode up on the old stallion. He did not wonder how Sutpen had got the word. He took it for granted that this was what had brought the other out at this hour on Sunday morning, and he stood while the other dismounted, and he took the reins from Sutpen's hand, an expression on his gaunt face almost imbecile with a kind of weary triumph, saying, "Hit's a gal, Kernel. I be dawg if you ain't as old as I am—" until Sutpen passed him and entered the house. He stood there with the reins in his hand and heard Sutpen cross the floor to the pallet. He heard what Sutpen said, and something seemed to stop dead in him before going on.

The sun was now up, the swift sun of Mississippi latitudes, and it seemed to him that he stood beneath a strange sky, in a strange scene familiar only as things are familiar in dreams, like the dreams of falling to one who has never climbed. "I kain't have heard what I thought I heard," he thought quietly. "I know I kain't." Yet the voice, the familiar voice which had said the words was still speaking, talking now to the old Negress about a colt foaled that morning. "That's why he was up so early," he thought. "That was hit. Hit ain't me and mine. Hit ain't even hisn that got him outen bed."

Sutpen emerged. He descended into the weeds, moving with that heavy deliberation which would have been haste when he was younger. He had not yet looked full at Wash. He said, "Dicey will stay and tend to her. You better—" Then he seemed to see Wash facing him and paused. "What?" he said.

"You said—" To his own ears Wash's voice sounded flat and ducklike,

like a deaf man's. "You said if she was a mare, you could give her a good stall in the stable."

"Well?" Sutpen said. His eyes widened and narrowed, almost like a man's fists flexing and shutting, as Wash began to advance towards him, stooping a little. Very astonishment kept Sutpen still for the moment, watching that man whom in twenty years he had no more known to make any motion save at command than he had the horse which he rode. Again his eyes narrowed and widened; without moving he seemed to rear suddenly upright. "Stand back," he said suddenly and sharply. "Don't you touch me."

"I'm going to tech you, Kernel," Wash said in that flat, quiet, almost soft voice, advancing.

Sutpen raised the hand which held the riding whip; the old Negress peered around the crazy door with her black gargoyle face of a worn gnome. "Stand back, Wash," Sutpen said. Then he struck. The old Negress leaped down into the weeds with the agility of a goat and fled. Sutpen slashed Wash again across the face with the whip, striking him to his knees. When Wash rose and advanced once more he held in his hands the scythe which he had borrowed from Sutpen three months ago and which Sutpen would never need again.

When he reëntered the house his granddaughter stirred on the pallet bed and called his name fretfully. "What was that?" she said.

"What was what, honey?"

"That ere racket out there."

" 'Twarn't nothing," he said gently. He knelt and touched her hot forehead clumsily. "Do you want ara thing?"

"I want a sup of water," she said querulously. "I been laying here wanting a sup of water a long time, but don't nobody care enough to pay me no mind."

"Sho now," he said soothingly. He rose stiffly and fetched the dipper of water and raised her head to drink and laid her back and watched her turn to the child with an absolutely stonelike face. But a moment later he saw that she was crying quietly. "Now, now," he said, "I wouldn't do that. Old Dicey says hit's a right fine gal. Hit's all right now. Hit's all over now. Hit ain't no need to cry now."

But she continued to cry quietly, almost sullenly, and he rose again and stood uncomfortably above the pallet for a time, thinking as he had thought when his own wife lay so and then his daughter in turn: "Women. Hit's a mystry to me. They seem to want em, and yit when they git em they cry about hit. Hit's a mystry to me. To ara man." Then he moved away and drew a chair up to the window and sat down.

Through all that long, bright sunny forenoon he sat at the window, waiting. Now and then he rose and tiptoed to the pallet. But his granddaughter slept now, her face sullen and calm and weary, the child in the crook of her arm. Then he returned to the chair and sat again, waiting, wondering why it took them so long, until he remembered that it was Sunday. He was sitting there at mid-afternoon when a half-grown white boy came around the corner of the house upon the body and gave a choked cry and looked up and glared for a mesmerized instant at Wash in the window before he turned and fled. Then Wash rose and tiptoed again to the pallet.

The granddaughter was awake now, wakened perhaps by the boy's cry without hearing it. "Milly," he said, "air you hungry?" She didn't answer, turning her face away. He built up the fire on the hearth and cooked the food which he had brought home the day before: fatback it was, and cold corn pone; he poured water into the stale coffee pot and heated it. But she would not eat when he carried the plate to her, so he ate himself, quietly, alone, and left the dishes as they were and returned to the window.

Now he seemed to sense, feel, the men who would be gathering with horses and guns and dogs—the curious, and the vengeful: men of Sutpen's own kind, who had made the company about Sutpen's table in the time when Wash himself had yet to approach nearer to the house than the scuppernong arbor—men who had also shown the lesser ones how to fight in battle, who maybe also had signed papers from the generals saying that they were among the first of the brave; who had also galloped in the old days arrogant and proud on the fine horses across the fine plantations—symbols also of admiration and hope; instruments too of despair and grief.

That was who they would expect him to run from. It seemed to him that he had no more to run from than he had to run to. If he ran, he would merely be fleeing one set of bragging and evil shadows for another just like them, since they were all of a kind throughout all the earth which he knew, and he was old, too old to flee far even if he were to flee. He could never escape them, no matter how much or how far he ran: a man going on sixty could not run that far. Not far enough to escape beyond the boundaries of earth where such men lived, set the order and the rule of living. It seemed to him that he now saw for the first time, after five years, how it was that Yankees or any other living armies had managed to whip them: the gallant, the proud, the brave; the acknowledged and chosen best among them all to carry courage and honor and pride. Maybe if he had gone to the war with them he would have discovered them sooner. But if he had discovered them sooner, what would he have done with his life since? How could he have borne to remember for five years what his life had been before?

Now it was getting toward sunset. The child had been crying; when he went to the pallet he saw his granddaughter nursing it, her face still bemused, sullen, inscrutable. "Air you hungry yit?" he said.

"I don't want nothing."

"You ought to eat."

This time she did not answer at all, looking down at the child. He returned to his chair and found that the sun had set. "Hit kain't be much longer," he thought. He could feel them quite near now, the curious and the vengeful. He could even seem to hear what they were saying about him, the undercurrent of believing beyond the immediate fury: *Old Wash Jones he come a tumble at last. He thought he had Sutpen, but Sutpen fooled him. He thought he had Kernel where he would have to marry the gal or pay up. And Kernel refused.* "But I never expected that, Kernel!" he cried aloud, catching himself at the sound of his own voice, glancing quickly back to find his granddaughter watching him.

"Who you talking to now?" she said.

"Hit ain't nothing. I was just thinking and talked out before I knowed hit."

Her face was becoming indistinct again, again a sullen blur in the twilight. "I reckon so. I reckon you'll have to holler louder than that before he'll hear you, up yonder at that house. And I reckon you'll need to do more than holler before you get him down here too."

"Sho now," he said. "Don't you worry none." But already thinking was going smoothly on: "You know I never. You know how I ain't never expected or asked nothing from ara living man but what I expected from you. And I never asked that. I didn't think hit would need. I said, *I don't need to. What need has a fellow like Wash Jones to question or doubt the man that General Lee himself says in a handwrote ticket that he was brave?* Brave," he thought. "Better if nara one of them had never rid back home in '65"; thinking *Better if his kind and mine too had never drawn the breath of life on this earth. Better that all who remain of us be blasted from the face of earth than that another Wash Jones should see his whole life shredded from him and shrivel away like a dried shuck thrown onto the fire.*

He ceased, became still. He heard the horses, suddenly and plainly; presently he saw the lantern and the movement of men, the glint of gun barrels, in its moving light. Yet he did not stir. It was quite dark now, and he listened to the voices and the sounds of underbrush as they surrounded the house. The lantern itself came on; its light fell upon the quiet body in the weeds and stopped, the horses tall and shadowy. A man descended and stooped in the lantern light, above the body. He held a pistol; he rose and faced the house. "Jones," he said.

"I'm here," Wash said quietly from the window. "That you, Major?"

"Come out."

"Sho," he said quietly. "I just want to see to my granddaughter."

"We'll see to her. Come on out."

"Sho, Major. Just a minute."

"Show a light. Light your lamp."

"Sho. In just a minute." They could hear his voice retreat into the house, though they could not see him as he went swiftly to the crack in the chimney where he kept the butcher knife: the one thing in his slovenly life and house in which he took pride, since it was razor sharp. He approached the pallet, his granddaughter's voice:

"Who is it? Light the lamp, grandpaw."

"Hit won't need no light, honey. Hit won't take but a minute," he said, kneeling, fumbling toward her voice, whispering now. "Where are you?"

"Right here," she said fretfully. "Where would I be? What is. . . ." His hand touched her face. "What is. . . . Grandpaw! Grand. . . ."

"Jones!" the sheriff said. "Come out of there!"

"In just a minute, Major," he said. Now he rose and moved swiftly. He knew where in the dark the can of kerosene was, just as he knew that it was full, since it was not two days ago that he had filled it at the store and held it there until he got a ride home with it, since the five gallons were heavy. There were still coals on the hearth; besides the crazy building itself was like tinder: the coals, the hearth, the walls exploding in a single blue glare. Against it the waiting men saw him in a wild instant springing toward them with the lifted scythe before the horses reared and whirled. They checked the horses and turned them back toward the glare, yet still in wild relief against it the gaunt figure ran toward them with the lifted scythe.

"Jones!" the sheriff shouted. "Stop! Stop, or I'll shoot. Jones! *Jones!*" Yet still the gaunt, furious figure came on against the glare and roar of the flames. With the scythe lifted, it bore down upon them, upon the wild glaring eyes of the horses and the swinging glints of gun barrels, without any cry, any sound.

§ FOR COMMENT

"Wash" was published originally in the collection *Doctor Martino and Other Stories*, but it was later reworked to take a climactic place in the novel *Absalom, Absalom!* In the novel the protagonist is Thomas Sutpen, but in the short story the protagonist is Wash, who stands as a representative of the poor white man. What is his relationship to Sutpen, the plantation owner who runs the land and owns the Negroes? It would appear that the inequalities of the social system, as represented in this story, are suffered not so much by the slaves as by the poor whites. Examine Wash's relationship with the Negroes, and notice the inferior position he holds even to them. Wash is able to exist only by Sutpen's dispensation. The inequalities of a system that gives a man no place in society make the system unbearable. Is this because the society harbors the elements of its own destruction? Notice that despite his apparent submission, Wash keeps hidden a razor-sharp knife that he later uses to murder Milly and her child.

Why does Wash kill Sutpen? Is it because Sutpen has been cruel to Milly? Or is Wash's motivation more complex? Remember that the stalls in the stable are in better repair than the house where Sutpen lives, and remember Sutpen's parting comment to Dicey: "Do whatever they need with whatever we've got to do it with." Is Sutpen a completely inhuman fiend? Why did he take up with Milly in the first place, and what is the significance of the birth of a girl child? Why does Wash kill Milly and the child? Comment on the relationship of this murder to the image of Wash with the scythe at the end of the story.

Ernest Hemingway § 1899–1961

Born in Illinois, the son of a physician, Hemingway served as an ambulance driver during World War I. Later he went to France and was involved with the group of Paris expatriates who were collected around Gertrude Stein. An early novel, The Torrents of Spring *(1926), was a parody of Sherwood Anderson's writing style. This, together with an earlier collection of short stories,* In Our Time *(1924), went virtually unnoticed. But with the publication of* The Sun Also Rises *(1926) he came to be recognized as a spokesman for the so-called "lost generation." Other novels and short stories followed. Most notable are* A Farewell to Arms *(1929) and* For Whom the Bell Tolls *(1940). He received the Pulitzer Prize in 1952 for* The Old Man and the Sea *and the Nobel Prize in 1954. He is recognized not only for his achievement as a novelist, having been a legend in his own time, but also as a master of the short story, his laconic but often poetic style lending itself well to the brevity of the form.*

The Short Happy Life of Francis Macomber

It was now lunch time and they were all sitting under the double green fly of the dining tent pretending that nothing had happened.

"Will you have lime juice or lemon squash?" Macomber asked.

"I'll have a gimlet," Robert Wilson told him.

"I'll have a gimlet too. I need something," Macomber's wife said.

"I suppose it's the thing to do," Macomber agreed. "Tell him to make three gimlets."

The mess boy had started them already, lifting the bottles out of the canvas cooling bags that sweated wet in the wind that blew through the trees that shaded the tents.

"What had I ought to give them?" Macomber asked.

"A quid would be plenty," Wilson told him. "You don't want to spoil them."

"Will the headman distribute it?"

"Absolutely."

Francis Macomber had, half an hour before, been carried to his tent from the edge of the camp in triumph on the arms and shoulders of the cook, the personal boys, the skinner and the porters. The gun-bearers had taken no part in the demonstration. When the native boys put him down at the door of his tent, he had shaken all their hands, received their congratulations, and then gone into the tent and sat on the bed until his wife came in. She did not speak to him when she came in and he left the tent at once to wash his face and hands in the portable wash basin outside and go over to the dining tent to sit in a comfortable canvas chair in the breeze and the shade.

"You've got your lion," Robert Wilson said to him, "and a damned fine one too."

Mrs. Macomber looked at Wilson quickly. She was an extremely handsome and well-kept woman of the beauty and social position which had, five years before, commanded five thousand dollars as the price of endorsing, with photographs, a beauty product which she had never used. She had been married to Francis Macomber for eleven years.

"He is a good lion, isn't he?" Macomber said. His wife looked at him now. She looked at both these men as though she had never seen them before.

One, Wilson, the white hunter, she knew she had never truly seen before. He was about middle height with sandy hair, a stubby mustache, a very red face and extremely cold blue eyes with faint white wrinkles at the corners that grooved merrily when he smiled. He smiled at her now and she looked away from his face at the way his shoulders sloped in the loose tunic he wore with the four big cartridges held in loops where the left breast pocket should have been, at his big brown hands, his old slacks, his very dirty boots and back to his red face again. She noticed where the baked red of his face stopped in a white line that marked the circle left by his Stetson hat that hung now from one of the pegs of the tent pole.

"Well, here's to the lion," Robert Wilson said. He smiled at her again and, not smiling, she looked curiously at her husband.

Francis Macomber was very tall, very well built if you did not mind that length of bone, dark, his hair cropped like an oarsman, rather thin-lipped, and was considered handsome. He was dressed in the same sort of safari clothes that Wilson wore except that his were new, he was thirty-five years old, kept himself very fit, was good at court games, had a number of big-game fishing records, and had just shown himself, very publicly, to be a coward.

"Here's to the lion," he said. "I can't ever thank you for what you did."

Margaret, his wife, looked away from him and back to Wilson.

"Let's not talk about the lion," she said.

Wilson looked over at her without smiling and now she smiled at him.

"It's been a very strange day," she said. "Hadn't you ought to put your hat on even under the canvas at noon? You told me that, you know."

"Might put it on," said Wilson.

"You know you have a very red face, Mr. Wilson," she told him and smiled again.

"Drink," said Wilson.

"I don't think so," she said. "Francis drinks a great deal, but his face is never red."

"It's red today," Macomber tried a joke.

"No," said Margaret. "It's mine that's red today. But Mr. Wilson's is always red."

"Must be racial," said Wilson. "I say, you wouldn't like to drop my beauty as a topic, would you?"

"I've just started on it."

"Let's chuck it," said Wilson.

"Conversation is going to be so difficult," Margaret said.

"Don't be silly, Margot," her husband said.

"No difficulty," Wilson said. "Got a damn fine lion."

Margot looked at them both and they both saw that she was going to cry. Wilson had seen it coming for a long time and he dreaded it. Macomber was past dreading it.

"I wish it hadn't happened. Oh, I wish it hadn't happened," she said and started for her tent. She made no noise of crying but they could see that her shoulders were shaking under the rose-colored, sun-proofed shirt she wore.

"Women upset," said Wilson to the tall man. "Amounts to nothing. Strain on the nerves and one thing'n another."

"No," said Macomber. "I suppose that I rate that for the rest of my life now."

"Nonsense. Let's have a spot of the giant killer," said Wilson. "Forget the whole thing. Nothing to it anyway."

"We might try," said Macomber. "I won't forget what you did for me though."

"Nothing," said Wilson. "All nonsense."

So they sat there in the shade where the camp was pitched under some wide-topped acacia trees with a boulder-strewn cliff behind them, and a stretch of grass that ran to the bank of a boulder-filled stream in front with forest beyond it, and drank their just-cool lime drinks and avoided one another's eyes while the boys set the table for lunch. Wilson could tell that the boys all knew about it now and when he saw Macomber's personal boy looking curiously at his master while he was putting dishes on the table he snapped at him in Swahili. The boy turned away with his face blank.

"What were you telling him?" Macomber asked.

"Nothing. Told him to look alive or I'd see he got about fifteen of the best."

"What's that? Lashes?"

"It's quite illegal," Wilson said. "You're supposed to fine them."

"Do you still have them whipped?"

"Oh, yes. They could raise a row if they chose to complain. But they don't. They prefer it to the fines."

"How strange!" said Macomber.

"Not strange, really," Wilson said. "Which would you rather do? Take a good birching or lose your pay?"

Then he felt embarrassed at asking it and before Macomber could answer he went on, "We all take a beating every day, you know, one way or another."

This was no better. "Good God," he thought. "I am a diplomat, aren't I?"

"Yes, we take a beating," said Macomber, still not looking at him. "I'm awfully sorry about that lion business. It doesn't have to go any further, does it? I mean no one will hear about it, will they?"

"You mean will I tell it at the Mathaiga Club?" Wilson looked at him now coldly. He had not expected this. So he's a bloody four-letter man as well as a bloody coward, he thought. I rather liked him too until today. But how is one to know about an American?

"No," said Wilson. "I'm a professional hunter. We never talk about our clients. You can be quite easy on that. It's supposed to be bad form to ask us not to talk though."

He had decided now that to break would be much easier. He would eat, then, by himself and could read a book with his meals. They would eat by themselves. He would see them through the safari on a very formal basis—what was it the French called it? Distinguished consideration—and it would be a damn sight easier than having to go through this emotional trash. He'd insult him and make a good clean break. Then he could read a book with his meals and he'd still be drinking their whisky. That was the phrase for it when a safari went bad. You ran into another white hunter and you asked, "How is everything going?" and he answered, "Oh, I'm still drinking their whisky," and you knew everything had gone to pot.

"I'm sorry," Macomber said and looked at him with his American face that would stay adolescent until it became middle-aged, and Wilson noted his crew-cropped hair, fine eyes only faintly shifty, good nose, thin lips and handsome jaw. "I'm sorry I didn't realize that. There are lots of things I don't know."

So what could he do, Wilson thought. He was all ready to break it off quickly and neatly and here the beggar was apologizing after he had just insulted him. He made one more attempt. "Don't worry about me talking," he said. "I have a living to make. You know in Africa no woman ever misses her lion and no white man ever bolts."

"I bolted like a rabbit," Macomber said.

Now what in hell were you going to do about a man who talked like that, Wilson wondered.

Wilson looked at Macomber with his flat, blue, machine-gunner's eyes and the other smiled back at him. He had a pleasant smile if you did not notice how his eyes showed when he was hurt.

"Maybe I can fix it up on buffalo," he said. "We're after them next, aren't we?"

"In the morning if you like," Wilson told him. Perhaps he had been wrong. This was certainly the way to take it. You most certainly could not tell a damned thing about an American. He was all for Macomber again. If you could forget the morning. But, of course, you couldn't. The morning had been about as bad as they come.

"Here comes the Memsahib," he said. She was walking over from her tent refreshed and cheerful and quite lovely. She had a very perfect oval face, so perfect that you expected her to be stupid. But she wasn't stupid, Wilson thought, no, not stupid.

"How is the beautiful red-faced Mr. Wilson? Are you feeling better, Francis, my pearl?"

"Oh, much," said Macomber.

"I've dropped the whole thing," she said, sitting down at the table. "What importance is there to whether Francis is any good at killing lions? That's not his trade. That's Mr. Wilson's trade. Mr. Wilson is really very impressive killing anything. You do kill anything, don't you?"

"Oh, anything," said Wilson. "Simply anything." They are, he thought, the hardest in the world; the hardest, the cruelest, the most predatory and the most attractive and their men have softened or gone to pieces nervously as they have hardened. Or is it that they pick men they can handle? They can't know that much at the age they marry, he thought. He was grateful that he had gone through his education on American women before now because this was a very attractive one.

"We're going after buff in the morning," he told her.

"I'm coming," she said.

"No, you're not."

"Oh, yes, I am. Mayn't I, Francis?"

"Why not stay in camp?"

"Not for anything," she said. "I wouldn't miss something like today for anything."

When she left, Wilson was thinking, when she went off to cry, she seemed a hell of a fine woman. She seemed to understand, to realize, to be hurt for him and for herself and to know how things really stood. She is away for twenty minutes and now she is back, simply enamelled in that

American female cruelty. They are the damnedest women. Really the damnedest.

"We'll put on another show for you tomorrow," Francis Macomber said.

"You're not coming," Wilson said.

"You're very mistaken," she told him. "And I want *so* to see you perform again. You were lovely this morning. That is if blowing things' heads off is lovely."

"Here's the lunch," said Wilson. "You're very merry, aren't you?"

"Why not? I didn't come out here to be dull."

"Well, it hasn't been dull," Wilson said. He could see the boulders in the river and the high bank beyond with the trees and he remembered the morning.

"Oh, no," she said. "It's been charming. And tomorrow. You don't know how I look forward to tomorrow."

"That's eland he's offering you," Wilson said.

"They're the big cowy things that jump like hares, aren't they?"

"I suppose that describes them," Wilson said.

"It's very good meat," Macomber said.

"Did you shoot it, Francis?" she asked.

"Yes."

"They're not dangerous, are they?"

"Only if they fall on you," Wilson told her.

"I'm so glad."

"Why not let up on the bitchery just a little, Margot," Macomber said, cutting the eland steak and putting some mashed potato, gravy and carrot on the down-turned fork that tined through the piece of meat.

"I suppose I could," she said, "since you put it so prettily."

"Tonight we'll have champagne for the lion," Wilson said. "It's a bit too hot at noon."

"Oh, the lion," Margot said. "I'd forgotten the lion!"

So, Robert Wilson thought to himself, she *is* giving him a ride, isn't she? Or do you suppose that's her idea of putting up a good show? How should a woman act when she discovers her husband is a bloody coward? She's damn cruel but they're all cruel. They govern, of course, and to govern one has to be cruel sometimes. Still, I've seen enough of their damn terrorism.

"Have some more eland," he said to her politely.

That afternoon, late, Wilson and Macomber went out in the motor car with the native driver and the two gun-bearers. Mrs. Macomber stayed in the camp. It was too hot to go out, she said, and she was going with them in the early morning. As they drove off Wilson saw her standing under the big tree, looking pretty rather than beautiful in her faintly rosy khaki, her dark hair drawn back off her forehead and gathered in a knot low on her neck, her face as fresh, he thought, as though she were in England. She waved to them as the car went off through the swale of high grass and curved around through the trees into the small hills of orchard bush.

In the orchard bush they found a herd of impala, and leaving the car they stalked one old ram with long, wide-spread horns and Macomber killed it with a very creditable shot that knocked the buck down at a good two hundred yards and sent the herd off bounding wildly and leaping over one another's backs in long, leg-drawn-up leaps as unbelievable and as floating as those one makes sometimes in dreams.

"That was a good shot," Wilson said. "They're a small target."

"Is it a worth-while head?" Macomber asked.

"It's excellent," Wilson told him. "You shoot like that and you'll have no trouble."

"Do you think we'll find buffalo tomorrow?"

"There's a good chance of it. They feed out early in the morning and with luck we may catch them in the open."

"I'd like to clear away the lion business," Macomber said. "It's not very pleasant to have your wife see you do something like that."

I should think it would be even more unpleasant to do it, Wilson thought, wife or no wife, or to talk about having done it. But he said, "I wouldn't think about that any more. Any one could be upset by his first lion. That's all over."

But that night after dinner and a whisky and soda by the fire before going to bed, as Francis Macomber lay on his cot with the mosquito bar over him and listened to the night noises it was not all over. It was neither all over nor was it beginning. It was there exactly as it happened with some parts of it indelibly emphasized and he was miserably ashamed at it. But more than shame he felt cold, hollow fear in him. The fear was still there like a cold slimy hollow in all the emptiness where once his confidence had been and it made him feel sick. It was still there with him now.

It had started the night before when he had wakened and heard the lion roaring somewhere up along the river. It was a deep sound and at the end there were sort of coughing grunts that made him seem just outside the tent, and when Francis Macomber woke in the night to hear it he was afraid. He could hear his wife breathing quietly, asleep. There was no one to tell he was afraid, nor to be afraid with him, and, lying alone, he did not know the Somali proverb that says a brave man is always frightened three times by a lion; when he first sees his track, when he first hears him roar and when he first confronts him. Then while they were eating breakfast by lantern light out in the dining tent, before the sun was up, the lion roared again and Francis thought he was just at the edge of camp.

"Sounds like an old-timer," Robert Wilson said, looking up from his kippers and coffee. "Listen to him cough."

"Is he very close?"

"A mile or so up the stream."

"Will we see him?"

"We'll have a look."

"Does his roaring carry that far? It sounds as though he were right in camp."

"Carries a hell of a long way," said Robert Wilson. "It's strange the way it carries. Hope he's a shootable cat. The boys said there was a very big one about here."

"If I get a shot, where should I hit him," Macomber asked, "to stop him?"

"In the shoulders," Wilson said. "In the neck if you can make it. Shoot for bone. Break him down."

"I hope I can place it properly," Macomber said.

"You shoot very well," Wilson told him. "Take your time. Make sure of him. The first one in is the one that counts."

"What range will it be?"

"Can't tell. Lion has something to say about that. Won't shoot unless it's close enough so you can make sure."

"At under a hundred yards?" Macomber asked.

Wilson looked at him quickly.

"Hundred's about right. Might have to take him a bit under. Shouldn't chance a shot at much over that. A hundred's a decent range. You can hit him wherever you want at that. Here comes the Memsahib."

"Good morning," she said. "Are we going after that lion?"

"As soon as you deal with your breakfast," Wilson said. "How are you feeling?"

"Marvellous," she said. "I'm very excited."

"I'll just go and see that everything is ready," Wilson went off. As he left the lion roared again.

"Noisy beggar," Wilson said. "We'll put a stop to that."

"What's the matter, Francis?" his wife asked him.

"Nothing," Macomber said.

"Yes, there is," she said. "What are you upset about?"

"Nothing," he said.

"Tell me," she looked at him. "Don't you feel well?"

"It's that damned roaring," he said. "It's been going on all night, you know."

"Why didn't you wake me," she said. "I'd love to have heard it."

"I've got to kill the damned thing," Macomber said, miserably.

"Well, that's what you're out here for, isn't it?"

"Yes. But I'm nervous. Hearing the thing roar gets on my nerves."

"Well then, as Wilson said, kill him and stop his roaring."

"Yes, darling," said Francis Macomber. "It's sounds easy, doesn't it?"

"You're not afraid, are you?"

"Of course not. But I'm nervous from hearing him roar all night."

"You'll kill him marvellously," she said. "I know you will. I'm awfully anxious to see it."

"Finish your breakfast and we'll be starting."

"It's not light yet," she said. "This is a ridiculous hour."

Just then the lion roared in a deep-chested moaning, suddenly guttural, ascending vibration that seemed to shake the air and ended in a sigh and a heavy, deep-chested grunt.

"He sounds almost here," Macomber's wife said.

"My God," said Macomber. "I hate that damned noise."

"It's very impressive."

"Impressive. It's frightful."

Robert Wilson came up then carrying his short, ugly, shockingly big-bored .505 Gibbs and grinning.

"Come on," he said. "Your gun-bearer has your Springfield and the big gun. Everything's in the car. Have you solids?"

"Yes."

"I'm ready," Mrs. Macomber said.

"Must make him stop that racket," Wilson said. "You get in front. The Memsahib can sit back here with me."

They climbed into the motor car and, in the gray first daylight, moved off up the river through the trees. Macomber opened the breech of his rifle and saw he had metal-cased bullets, shut the bolt and put the rifle on safety. He saw his hand was trembling. He felt in his pocket for more cartridges and moved his fingers over the cartridges in the loops of his tunic front. He turned back to where Wilson sat in the rear seat of the doorless, box-bodied motor car beside his wife, them both grinning with excitement, and Wilson leaned forward and whispered,

"See the birds dropping. Means the old boy has left his kill."

On the far bank of the stream Macomber could see, above the trees, vultures circling and plummeting down.

"Chances are he'll come to drink along here," Wilson whispered. "Before he goes to lay up. Keep an eye out."

They were driving slowly along the high bank of the stream which here cut deeply to its boulder-filled bed, and they wound in and out through big trees as they drove. Macomber was watching the opposite bank when he felt Wilson take hold of his arm. The car stopped.

"There he is," he heard the whisper. "Ahead and to the right. Get out and take him. He's a marvellous lion."

Macomber saw the lion now. He was standing almost broadside, his great head up and turned toward them. The early morning breeze that blew toward them was just stirring his dark mane, and the lion looked huge, silhouetted on the rise of bank in the gray morning light, his shoulders heavy, his barrel of a body bulking smoothly.

"How far is he?" asked Macomber, raising his rifle.

"About seventy-five. Get out and take him."

"Why not shoot from where I am?"

"You don't shoot them from cars," he heard Wilson saying in his ear. "Get out. He's not going to stay there all day."

Macomber stepped out of the curved opening at the side of the front seat, onto the step and down onto the ground. The lion still stood looking majestically and coolly toward this object that his eyes only showed in silhouette, bulking like some super-rhino. There was no man smell carried toward him and he watched the object, moving his great head a little from side to side. Then watching the object, not afraid, but hesitating before going down the bank to drink with such a thing opposite him, he saw a man figure detach itself from it and he turned his heavy head and swung away toward the cover of the trees as he heard a cracking crash and felt the slam of a .30–06 220-grain solid bullet that bit his flank and ripped in sudden hot scalding nausea through his stomach. He trotted, heavy, big-footed, swinging wounded full-bellied, through the trees toward the tall grass and cover, and the crash came again to go past him ripping the air apart. Then it crashed again and he felt the blow as it hit his lower ribs and ripped on through, blood sudden hot and frothy in his mouth, and he galloped toward the high grass where he could crouch and not be seen and make them bring the crashing thing close enough so he could make a rush and get the man that held it.

Macomber had not thought how the lion felt as he got out of the car. He only knew his hands were shaking and as he walked away from the car it was almost impossible for him to make his legs move. They were stiff in the thighs, but he could feel the muscles fluttering. He raised the rifle, sighted on the junction of the lion's head and shoulders and pulled the trigger. Nothing happened though he pulled until he thought his finger would break. Then he knew he had the safety on and as he lowered the rifle to move the safety over he moved another frozen pace forward, and the lion seeing his silhouette now clear of the silhouette of the car, turned and started off at a trot, and, as Macomber fired, he heard a whunk that meant that the bullet was home; but the lion kept on going. Macomber shot again and every one saw the bullet throw a spout of dirt beyond the trotting lion. He shot again, remembering to lower his aim, and they all heard the bullet hit, and the lion went into a gallop and was in the tall grass before he had the bolt pushed forward.

Macomber stood there feeling sick at his stomach, his hands that held the Springfield still cocked, shaking, and his wife and Robert Wilson were standing by him. Beside him too were the two gun-bearers chattering in Wakamba.

"I hit him," Macomber said. "I hit him twice."

"You gut-shot him and you hit him somewhere forward," Wilson said without enthusiasm. The gun-bearers looked very grave. They were silent now.

"You may have killed him," Wilson went on. "We'll have to wait a while before we go in to find out."

"What do you mean?"

"Let him get sick before we follow him up."

"Oh," said Macomber.

"He's a hell of a fine lion," Wilson said cheerfully. "He's gotten into a bad place though."

"Why is it bad?"

"Can't see him until you're on him."

"Oh," said Macomber.

"Come on," said Wilson. "The Memsahib can stay here in the car. We'll go to have a look at the blood spoor."

"Stay here, Margot," Macomber said to his wife. His mouth was very dry and it was hard for him to talk.

"Why?" she asked.

"Wilson says to."

"We're going to have a look," Wilson said. "You stay here. You can see even better from here."

"All right."

Wilson spoke in Swahili to the driver. He nodded and said,

"Yes, Bwana."

Then they went down the steep bank and across the stream, climbing over and around the boulders and up the other bank, pulling up by some projecting roots, and along it until they found where the lion had been trotting when Macomber first shot. There was dark blood on the short grass that the gun-bearers pointed out with grass stems, and that ran away behind the river bank trees.

"What do we do?" asked Macomber.

"Not much choice," said Wilson. "We can't bring the car over. Bank's too steep. We'll let him stiffen up a bit and then you and I'll go in and have a look for him."

"Can't we set the grass on fire?" Macomber asked.

"Too green."

"Can't we send beaters?"

Wilson looked at him appraisingly. "Of course we can," he said. "But it's just a touch murderous. You see we know the lion's wounded. You can drive an unwounded lion—he'll move on ahead of a noise—but a wounded lion's going to charge. You can't see him until you're right on him. He'll make himself perfectly flat in cover you wouldn't think would hide a hare. You can't very well send boys in there to that sort of a show. Somebody bound to get mauled."

"What about the gun-bearers?"

"Oh, they'll go with us. It's their *shauri*.[1] You see, they signed on for it. They don't look too happy though, do they?"

"I don't want to go in there," said Macomber. It was out before he knew he'd said it.

"Neither do I," said Wilson very cheerily. "Really no choice though." Then, as an afterthought, he glanced at Macomber and saw suddenly how he was trembling and the pitiful look on his face.

"You don't have to go in, of course," he said. "That's what I'm hired for, you know. That's why I'm so expensive."

"You mean you'd go in by yourself? Why not leave him there?"

Robert Wilson, whose entire occupation had been with the lion and the problem he presented, and who had not been thinking about Macomber except to note that he was rather windy, suddenly felt as though he had opened the wrong door in a hotel and seen something shameful.

"What do you mean?"

"Why not just leave him?"

"You mean pretend to ourselves he hasn't been hit?"

"No. Just drop it."

"It isn't done."

"Why not?"

"For one thing, he's certain to be suffering. For another, some one else might run onto him."

"I see."

"But you don't have to have anything to do with it."

"I'd like to," Macomber said. "I'm just scared, you know."

"I'll go ahead when we go in," Wilson said, "with Kongoni tracking. You keep behind me and a little to one side. Chances are we'll hear him growl. If we see him we'll both shoot. Don't worry about anything. I'll keep you backed up. As a matter of fact, you know, perhaps you'd better not go. It might be much better. Why don't you go over and join the Memsahib while I just get it over with?"

"No, I want to go."

"All right," said Wilson. "But don't go in if you don't want to. This is my *shauri* now, you know."

"I want to go," said Macomber.

They sat under a tree and smoked.

"Want to go back and speak to the Memsahib while we're waiting?" Wilson asked.

"No."

"I'll just step back and tell her to be patient."

"Good," said Macomber. He sat there, sweating under his arms, his mouth dry, his stomach hollow feeling, wanting to find courage to tell Wilson to go on and finish off the lion without him. He could not know that

---

[1] *shauri*: Probably an attempt to approximate the actual sound of the Swahili word usually given as "safari."

Wilson was furious because he had not noticed the state he was in earlier and sent him back to his wife. While he sat there Wilson came up. "I have your big gun," he said. "Take it. We've given him time, I think. Come on."

Macomber took the big gun and Wilson said:

"Keep behind me and about five yards to the right and do exactly as I tell you." Then he spoke in Swahili to the two gun-bearers who looked the picture of gloom.

"Let's go," he said.

"Could I have a drink of water?" Macomber asked. Wilson spoke to the older gun-bearer, who wore a canteen on his belt, and the man unbuckled it, unscrewed the top and handed it to Macomber, who took it noticing how heavy it seemed and how hairy and shoddy the felt covering was in his hand. He raised it to drink and looked ahead at the high grass with the flat-topped trees behind it. A breeze was blowing toward them and the grass rippled gently in the wind. He looked at the gun-bearer and he could see the gun-bearer was suffering too with fear.

Thirty-five yards into the grass the big lion lay flattened out along the ground. His ears were back and his only movement was a slight twitching up and down of his long, black-tufted tail. He had turned at bay as soon as he had reached this cover and he was sick with the wound through his full belly, and weakening with the wound through his lungs that brought a thin foamy red to his mouth each time he breathed. His flanks were wet and hot and flies were on the little openings the solid bullets had made in his tawny hide, and his big yellow eyes, narrowed with hate, looked straight ahead, only blinking when the pain came as he breathed, and his claws dug in the soft baked earth. All of him, pain, sickness, hatred and all of his remaining strength, was tightening into an absolute concentration for a rush. He could hear the men talking and he waited, gathering all of himself into this preparation for a charge as soon as the men would come into the grass. As he heard their voices his tail stiffened to twitch up and down, and, as they came into the edge of the grass, he made a coughing grunt and charged.

Kongoni, the old gun-bearer, in the lead watching the blood spoor, Wilson watching the grass for any movement, his big gun ready, the second gun-bearer looking ahead and listening, Macomber close to Wilson, his rifle cocked, they had just moved into the grass when Macomber heard the blood-choked coughing grunt, and saw the swishing rush in the grass. The next thing he knew he was running; running wildly, in panic in the open, running toward the stream.

He heard the *ca-ra-wong!* of Wilson's big rifle, and again in a second crashing *carawong!* and turning saw the lion, horrible-looking now, with half his head seeming to be gone, crawling toward Wilson in the edge of the tall grass while the red-faced man worked the bolt on the short ugly rifle and aimed carefully as another blasting *carawong!* came from the muzzle, and the crawling, heavy, yellow bulk of the lion stiffened and the huge, mutilated head slid forward and Macomber, standing by himself in the clearing where he had run, holding a loaded rifle, while two black men and a white man looked back at him in contempt, knew the lion was dead. He came toward Wilson, his tallness all seeming a naked reproach, and Wilson looked at him and said:

"Want to take pictures?"

"No," he said.

That was all any one had said until they reached the motor car. Then Wilson had said:

"Hell of a fine lion. Boys will skin him out. We might as well stay here in the shade."

Macomber's wife had not looked at him nor he at her and he had sat by her in the back seat with Wilson sitting in the front seat. Once he had reached over and taken his wife's hand without looking at her and she had removed her hand from his. Looking across the stream to where the gun-bearers were skinning out the lion he could see that she had been able to see the whole thing. While they sat there his wife had reached forward and put her hand on Wilson's shoulder. He turned and she had leaned forward over the low seat and kissed him on the mouth.

"Oh, I say," said Wilson, going redder than his natural baked color.

"Mr. Robert Wilson," she said. "The beautiful red-faced Mr. Robert Wilson."

Then she sat down beside Macomber again and looked away across the stream to where the lion lay, with uplifted, white-muscled, tendon-marked naked forearms, and white bloating belly, as the black men fleshed away the skin. Finally the gun-bearers brought the skin over, wet and heavy, and climbed in behind with it, rolling it up before they got in, and the motor car started. No one had said anything more until they were back in camp.

That was the story of the lion. Macomber did not know how the lion had felt before he started his rush, nor during it when the unbelievable smash of the .505 with a muzzle velocity of two tons had hit him in the mouth, nor what kept him coming after that, when the second ripping crash had smashed his hind quarters and he had come crawling on toward the crashing, blasting thing that had destroyed him. Wilson knew something about it and only expressed it by saying, "Damned fine lion," but Macomber did not know how Wilson felt about things either. He did not know how his wife felt except that she was through with him.

His wife had been through with him before but it never lasted. He was very wealthy, and would be much wealthier, and he knew she would not leave him ever now. That was one of the few things that he really knew. He knew about that, about motor cycles—that was earliest—about motor cars, about duck-shooting, about fishing, trout, salmon and big-sea, about sex in books, many books, too many books, about all court games, about dogs, not much about horses, about hanging on to his money, about most of the other things his world dealt in, and about his wife not leaving him. His wife had been a great beauty and she was still a great beauty in Africa, but she was not a great enough beauty any more at home to be able to leave him and better herself and she knew it and he knew it. She had missed the chance to leave him and he knew it. If he had been better with women she would probably have started to worry about him getting another new, beautiful wife; but she knew too much about him to worry about him either. Also, he had always had a great tolerance which seemed the nicest thing about him if it were not the most sinister.

All in all they were known as a comparatively happily married couple, one of those whose disruption is often rumored but never occurs, and as the society columnist put it, they were adding more than a spice of *adventure* to their much envied and ever-enduring *Romance* by a *Safari* in what was known as *Darkest Africa* until the Martin Johnsons lighted it on so many silver screens where they were pursuing *Old Simba* the lion, the buffalo, *Tembo* the elephant and as well collecting specimens for the Museum of Natural History. This same columnist had reported them *on the verge* at least three times in the past and they had been. But they always made it up. They had a sound basis of union. Margot was too beautiful for Macomber to divorce her and Macomber had too much money for Margot ever to leave him.

It was now about three o'clock in the morning and Francis Macomber, who had been asleep a little while after he had stopped thinking about the lion, wakened and then slept again, woke suddenly, frightened in a dream of the bloody-headed lion standing over him, and listening while his heart pounded, he realized that his wife was not in the other cot in the tent. He lay awake with that knowledge for two hours.

At the end of that time his wife came into the tent, lifted her mosquito bar and crawled cozily into bed.

"Where have you been?" Macomber asked in the darkness.

"Hello," she said. "Are you awake?"

"Where have you been?"

"I just went out to get a breath of air."

"You did, like hell."

"What do you want me to say, darling?"

"Where have you been?"

"Out to get a breath of air."

"That's a new name for it. You *are* a bitch."

"Well, you're a coward."

"All right," he said. "What of it?"

"Nothing as far as I'm concerned. But please let's not talk, darling, because I'm very sleepy."

"You think that I'll take anything."

"I know you will, sweet."

"Well, I won't."

"Please, darling, let's not talk. I'm so very sleepy."

"There wasn't going to be any of that. You promised there wouldn't be."

"Well, there is now," she said sweetly.

"You said if we made this trip that there would be none of that. You promised."

"Yes, darling. That's the way I meant it to be. But the trip was spoiled yesterday. We don't have to talk about it, do we?"

"You don't wait long when you have an advantage, do you?"

"Please let's not talk. I'm so sleepy, darling."

"I'm going to talk."

"Don't mind me then, because I'm going to sleep." And she did.

At breakfast they were all three at the table before daylight and Francis Macomber found that, of all the many men that he had hated, he hated Robert Wilson the most.

"Sleep well?" Wilson asked in his throaty voice, filling a pipe.

"Did you?"

"Topping," the white hunter told him.

You bastard, thought Macomber, you insolent bastard.

So she woke him when she came in, Wilson thought, looking at them both with his flat, cold eyes. Well, why doesn't he keep his wife where she belongs? What does he think I am, a bloody plaster saint? Let him keep her where she belongs. It's his own fault.

"Do you think we'll find buffalo?" Margot asked, pushing away a dish of apricots.

"Chance of it," Wilson said and smiled at her. "Why don't you stay in camp?"

"Not for anything," she told him.

"Why not order her to stay in camp?" Wilson said to Macomber.

"You order her," said Macomber coldly.

"Let's not have any ordering, nor," turning to Macomber, "any silliness, Francis," Margot said quite pleasantly.

"Are you ready to start?" Macomber asked.

"Any time," Wilson told him. "Do you want the Memsahib to go?"

"Does it make any difference whether I do or not?"

The hell with it, thought Robert Wilson. The utter complete hell with it. So this is what it's going to be like. Well, this is what it's going to be like, then.

"Makes no difference," he said.

"You're sure you wouldn't like to stay in camp with her yourself and let me go out and hunt the buffalo?" Macomber asked.

"Can't do that," said Wilson. "Wouldn't talk rot if I were you."

"I'm not talking rot. I'm disgusted."

"Bad word, disgusted."

"Francis, will you please try to speak sensibly!" his wife said.

"I speak too damned sensibly," Macomber said. "Did you ever eat such filthy food?"

"Something wrong with the food?" asked Wilson quietly.

"No more than with everything else."

"I'd pull yourself together, laddybuck," Wilson said very quietly. "There's a boy waits at table that understands a little English."

"The hell with him."

Wilson stood up and puffing on his pipe strolled away, speaking a few words in Swahili to one of the gun-bearers who was standing waiting for him. Macomber and his wife sat on at the table. He was staring at his coffee cup.

"If you make a scene I'll leave you, darling," Margot said quietly.

"No, you won't."

"You can try it and see."

"You won't leave me."

"No," she said. "I won't leave you and you'll behave yourself."

"Behave myself? That's a way to talk. Behave myself."

"Yes. Behave yourself."

"Why don't *you* try behaving?"

"I've tried it so long. So very long."

"I hate that red-faced swine," Macomber said. "I loathe the sight of him."

"He's really *very* nice."

"Oh, *shut up*," Macomber almost shouted. Just then the car came up and stopped in front of the dining tent and the driver and the two gun-bearers got out. Wilson walked over and looked at the husband and wife sitting there at the table.

"Going shooting?" he asked.

"Yes," said Macomber, standing up. "Yes."

"Better bring a woolly. It will be cool in the car," Wilson said.

"I'll get my leather jacket," Margot said.

"The boy has it," Wilson told her. He climbed into the front with the driver and Francis Macomber and his wife sat, not speaking, in the back seat.

Hope the silly beggar doesn't take a notion to blow the back of my head off, Wilson thought to himself. Women *are* a nuisance on safari.

The car was grinding down to cross the river at a pebbly ford in the gray daylight and then climbed, angling up the steep bank, where Wilson had ordered a way shovelled out the day before so they could reach the parklike wooded rolling country on the far side.

It was a good morning, Wilson thought. There was a heavy dew and as the wheels went through the grass and low bushes he could smell the odor of the crushed fronds. It was an odor like verbena and he liked this early morning smell of the dew, the crushed bracken and the look of the tree trunks showing black through the early morning mist, as the car made its way through the untracked, parklike country. He had put the two in the back seat out of his mind now and was thinking about buffalo. The buffalo that he was after stayed in the daytime in a thick swamp where it was impossible to get a shot, but in the night they fed out into an open stretch of country and if he could come between them and their swamp with the car, Macomber would have a good chance at them in the open. He did not want to hunt buff with Macomber in thick cover. He did not want to hunt buff or anything else with Macomber at all, but he was a professional hunter and he had hunted with some rare ones in his time. If they got buff today there would only be rhino to come and the poor man would have gone through his dangerous game and things might pick up. He'd have nothing more to do with the woman and Macomber would get over that too. He must have gone through plenty of that before by the look of things. Poor begger. He must have a way of getting over it. Well, it was the poor sod's own bloody fault.

He, Robert Wilson, carried a double size cot on safari to accommodate any windfalls he might receive. He had hunted for a certain clientele, the international, fast, sporting set, where the women did not feel they were getting their money's worth unless they had shared that cot with the white hunter. He despised them when he was away from them although he liked some of them well enough at the time, but he made his living by them; and their standards were his standards as long as they were hiring him.

They were his standards in all except the shooting. He had his own standards about the killing and they could live up to them or get some one else to hunt them. He knew, too, that they all respected him for this. This Macomber was an odd one though. Damned if he wasn't. Now the wife. Well, the wife. Yes, the wife. Hm, the wife. Well he'd dropped all that. He looked around at them. Macomber sat grim and furious. Margot smiled at him. She looked younger today, more innocent and fresher and not so professionally beautiful. What's in her heart God knows, Wilson thought. She hadn't talked much last night. At that it was a pleasure to see her.

The motor car climbed up a slight rise and went on through the trees and then out into a grassy prairie-like opening and kept in the shelter of the trees along the edge, the driver going slowly and Wilson looking carefully out across the prairie and all along its far side. He stopped the car and studied the opening with his field glasses. Then he motioned to the driver to go on and the car moved slowly along, the driver avoiding wart-hog holes and driving around the mud castles ants had built. Then, looking across the opening, Wilson suddenly turned and said,

"By God, there they are!"

And looking where he pointed, while the car jumped forward and Wilson spoke in rapid Swahili to the driver, Macomber saw three huge, black animals looking almost cylindrical in their long heaviness, like big black tank cars, moving at a gallop across the far edge of the open prairie.

They moved at a stiff-necked, stiff bodied gallop and he could see the up-swept wide black horns on their heads as they galloped heads out; the heads not moving.

"They're three old bulls," Wilson said. "We'll cut them off before they get to the swamp."

The car was going a wild forty-five miles an hour across the open and as Macomber watched, the buffalo got bigger and bigger until he could see the gray, hairless, scabby look of one huge bull and how his neck was a part of his shoulders and the shiny black of his horns as he galloped a little behind the others that were strung out in that steady plunging gait; and then, the car swaying as though it had just jumped a road, they drew up close and he could see the plunging hugeness of the bull, and the dust in his sparsely haired hide, the wide boss of horn and his outstretched, wide-nostrilled muzzle, and he was raising his rifle when Wilson shouted, "Not from the car, you fool!" and he had no fear, only hatred of Wilson, while the brakes clamped on and the car skidded, plowing sideways to an almost stop and Wilson was out on one side and he on the other, stumbling as his feet hit the still speeding-by of the earth, and then he was shooting at the bull as he moved away, hearing the bullets whunk into him, emptying his rifle at him as he moved steadily away, finally remembering to get his shots forward into the shoulder, and as he fumbled to re-load, he saw the bull was down. Down on his knees, his big head tossing, and seeing the other two still galloping he shot at the leader and hit him. He shot again and missed and he heard the *carawonging* roar as Wilson shot and saw the leading bull slide forward onto his nose.

"Get that other," Wilson said. "Now you're shooting!"

But the other bull was moving steadily at the same gallop and he missed, throwing a spout of dirt, and Wilson missed and the dust rose in a cloud and Wilson shouted, "Come on. He's too far!" and grabbed his arm and they were in the car again, Macomber and Wilson hanging on the sides and rocketing swayingly over the uneven ground, drawing up on the steady, plunging, heavy-necked, straight-moving gallop of the bull.

They were behind him and Macomber was filling his rifle, dropping shells onto the ground, jamming it, clearing the jam, then they were almost up with the bull when Wilson yelled "Stop," and the car skidded so that it almost swung over and Macomber fell forward onto his feet, slammed his bolt forward and fired as far forward as he could aim into the galloping, rounded black back, aimed and shot again, then again, and the bullets, all of them hitting, had no effect on the buffalo that he could see. Then Wilson shot, the roar deafening him, and he could see the bull stagger. Macomber shot again, aiming carefully, and down he came, onto his knees.

"All right," Wilson said. "Nice work. That's the three."

Macomber felt a drunken elation.

"How many times did you shoot?" he asked.

"Just three," Wilson said. "You killed the first bull. The biggest one. I helped you finish the other two. Afraid they might have got into cover. You had them killed. I was just mopping up a little. You shot damn well."

"Let's go to the car," said Macomber. "I want a drink."

"Got to finish off that buff first," Wilson told him. The buffalo was on his knees and he jerked his head furiously and bellowed in pig-eyed, roaring rage as they came toward him.

"Watch he doesn't get up," Wilson said. Then, "Get a little broadside and take him in the neck just behind the ear."

Macomber aimed carefully at the center of the huge, jerking, rage-driven neck and shot. At the shot the head dropped forward.

"That does it," said Wilson. "Got the spine. They're a hell of a looking thing, aren't they?"

"Let's get the drink," said Macomber. In his life he had never felt so good.

In the car Macomber's wife sat very white faced. "You were marvellous, darling," she said to Macomber. "What a ride."

"Was it rough?" Wilson asked.

"It was frightful. I've never been more frightened in my life."

"Let's all have a drink," Macomber said.

"By all means," said Wilson. "Give it to the Memsahib." She drank the neat whisky from the flask and shuddered a little when she swallowed. She handed the flask to Macomber who handed it to Wilson.

"It was frightfully exciting," she said. "It's given me a dreadful headache. I didn't know you were allowed to shoot them from cars though."

"No one shot from cars," said Wilson coldly.

"I mean chase them from cars."

"Wouldn't ordinarily," Wilson said. "Seemed sporting enough to me though while we were doing it. Taking more chance driving that way across the plain full of holes and one thing and another than hunting on foot. Buffalo could have charged us each time we shot if he liked. Gave him every chance. Wouldn't mention it to any one though. It's illegal if that's what you mean."

"It seemed very unfair to me," Margot said, "chasing those big helpless things in a motor car."

"Did it?" said Wilson.

"What would happen if they heard about it in Nairobi?"

"I'd lose my licence for one thing. Other unpleasantnesses," Wilson said, taking a drink from the flask. "I'd be out of business."

"Really?"

"Yes, really."

"Well," said Macomber, and he smiled for the first time all day. "Now she has something on you."

"You have such a pretty way of putting things, Francis," Margot Macomber said. Wilson looked at them both. If a four-letter man marries a five-letter woman, he was thinking, what number of letters would their children be? What he said was, "We lost a gun-bearer. Did you notice it?"

"My God, no," Macomber said.

"Here he comes," Wilson said. "He's all right. He must have fallen off when we left the first bull."

Approaching them was the middle-aged gun-bearer, limping along in his knitted cap, khaki tunic, shorts and rubber sandals, gloomy-faced and disgusted looking. As he came up he called out to Wilson in Swahili and they all saw the change in the white hunter's face.

"What does he say?" asked Margot.

"He says the first bull got up and went into the bush," Wilson said with no expression in his voice.

"Oh," said Macomber blankly.

"Then it's going to be just like the lion," said Margot, full of anticipation.

"It's not going to be a damned bit like the lion," Wilson told her. "Did you want another drink, Macomber?"

"Thanks, yes," Macomber said. He expected the feeling he had had about the lion to come back but it did not. For the first time in his life he really felt wholly without fear. Instead of fear he had a feeling of definite elation.

"We'll go and have a look at the second bull," Wilson said. "I'll tell the driver to put the car in the shade."

"What are you going to do?" asked Margaret Macomber.

"Take a look at the buff," Wilson said.

"I'll come."

"Come along."

The three of them walked over to where the second buffalo bulked blackly in the open, head forward on the grass, the massive horns swung wide.

"He's a very good head," Wilson said. "That's close to a fifty-inch spread."

Macomber was looking at him with delight.

"He's hateful looking," said Margot. "Can't we go into the shade?"

"Of course," Wilson said. "Look," he said to Macomber, and pointed. "See that patch of bush?"

"Yes."

"That's where the first bull went in. The gun-bearer said when he fell off the bull was down. He was watching us helling along and the other two buff galloping. When he looked up there was the bull up and looking at him. Gun-bearer ran like hell and the bull went off slowly into that bush."

"Can we go in after him now?" asked Macomber eagerly.

Wilson looked at him appraisingly. Damned if this isn't a strange one, he thought. Yesterday he's scared sick and today he's a ruddy fire eater.

"No, we'll give him a while."

"Let's please go into the shade," Margot said. Her face was white and she looked ill.

They made their way to the car where it stood under a single, wide-spreading tree and all climbed in.

"Chances are he's dead in there," Wilson remarked. "After a little we'll have a look."

Macomber felt a wild unreasonable happiness that he had never known before.

"By God, that was a chase," he said. "I've never felt any such feeling. Wasn't it marvellous, Margot?"

"I hated it."

"Why?"

"I hated it," she said bitterly. "I loathed it."

"You know I don't think I'd ever be afraid of anything again," Macomber said to Wilson. "Something happened in me after we first saw the buff and started after him. Like a dam bursting. It was pure excitement."

"Cleans out your liver," said Wilson. "Damn funny things happen to people."

Macomber's face was shining. "You know something did happen to me," he said. "I feel absolutely different."

His wife said nothing and eyed him strangely. She was sitting far back in the seat and Macomber was sitting forward talking to Wilson who turned sideways talking over the back of the front seat.

"You know, I'd like to try another lion," Macomber said. "I'm really not afraid of them now. After all, what can they do to you?"

"That's it," said Wilson. "Worst one can do is kill you. How does it go? Shakespeare. Damned good. See if I can remember. Oh, damned good. Used to quote it to myself at one time. Let's see. 'By my troth, I care not; a man can die but once; we owe God a death and let it go which way it will he that dies this year is quit for the next.' Damned fine, eh?"

He was very embarrassed, having brought out this thing he had lived by, but he had seen men come of age before and it always moved him. It was not a matter of their twenty-first birthday.

It had taken a strange chance of hunting, a sudden precipitation into action without opportunity for worrying beforehand, to bring this about with Macomber, but regardless of how it had happened it had most certainly happened. Look at the beggar now, Wilson thought. It's that some of them stay little boys so long, Wilson thought. Sometimes all their lives. Their figures stay boyish when they're fifty. The great American boy-men. Damned strange people. But he liked this Macomber now. Damned strange fellow. Probably meant the end of cuckoldry too. Well, that would be a damned good thing. Damned good thing. Beggar had probably been afraid all his life. Don't know what started it. But over now. Hadn't had time to be afraid with the buff. That and being angry too. Motor car too. Motor cars made it familiar. Be a damn fire eater now. He'd seen it in the war work the same way. More of a change than any loss of virginity. Fear gone like an operation. Something else grew in its place. Main thing a man had. Made him into a man. Women knew it too. No bloody fear.

From the far corner of the seat Margaret Macomber looked at the two of them. There was no change in Wilson. She saw Wilson as she had seen him the day before when she had first realized what his great talent was. But she saw the change in Francis Macomber now.

"Do you have that feeling of happiness about what's going to happen?" Macomber asked, still exploring his new wealth.

"You're not supposed to mention it," Wilson said, looking in the other's face. "Much more fashionable to say you're scared. Mind you, you'll be scared too, plenty of times."

"But you *have* a feeling of happiness about action to come?"

"Yes," said Wilson. "There's that. Doesn't do to talk too much about all this. Talk the whole thing away. No pleasure in anything if you mouth it up too much."

"You're both talking rot," said Margot. "Just because you've chased some helpless animals in a motor car you talk like heroes."

"Sorry," said Wilson. "I have been gassing too much." She's worried about it already, he thought.

"If you don't know what we're talking about why not keep out of it?" Macomber asked his wife.

"You've gotten awfully brave, awfully suddenly," his wife said contemptuously, but her contempt was not secure. She was very afraid of something.

Macomber laughed, a very natural hearty laugh. "You know I *have*," he said. "I really have."

"Isn't it sort of late?" Margot said bitterly. Because she had done the best she could for many years back and the way they were together now was no one person's fault.

"Not for me," said Macomber.

Margot said nothing but sat back in the corner of the seat.

"Do you think we've given him time enough?" Macomber asked Wilson cheerfully.

"We might have a look," Wilson said. "Have you any solids left?"

"The gun-bearer has some."

Wilson called in Swahili and the older gun-bearer, who was skinning out one of the heads, straightened up, pulled a box of solids out of his pocket and brought them over to Macomber, who filled his magazine and put the remaining shells in his pocket.

"You might as well shoot the Springfield." Wilson said. "You're used to it. We'll leave the Mannlicher in the car with the Memsahib. Your gun-bearer can carry your heavy gun. I've this damned cannon. Now let me tell you about them." He had saved this until the last because he did not want to worry Macomber. "When a buff comes he comes with his head high and thrust straight out. The boss of the horns covers any sort of a brain shot. The only shot is straight into the nose. The only other shot is into his chest or, if you're to one side, into the neck or the shoulders. After they've been hit once they take a hell of a lot of killing. Don't try anything fancy. Take the easiest shot there is. They've finished skinning out that head now. Should we get started?"

He called to the gun-bearers, who came up wiping their hands, and the older one got into the back.

"I'll only take Kongoni," Wilson said. "The other can watch to keep the birds away."

As the car moved slowly across the open space toward the island of brushy trees that ran in a tongue of foliage along a dry water course that cut the open swale, Macomber felt his heart pounding and his mouth was dry again, but it was excitement, not fear.

"Here's where he went in," Wilson said. Then to the gun-bearer in Swahili, "Take the blood spoor."

The car was parallel to the patch of bush. Macomber, Wilson and the gun-bearer got down. Macomber, looking back, saw his wife, with the rifle by her side, looking at him. He waved to her and she did not wave back.

The brush was very thick ahead and the ground was dry. The middle-aged gun-bearer was sweating heavily and Wilson had his hat down over his eyes and his red neck showed just ahead of Macomber. Suddenly the gun-bearer said something in Swahili to Wilson and ran forward.

"He's dead in there," Wilson said. "Good work," and he turned to grip Macomber's hand and as they shook hands, grinning at each other, the gun-bearer shouted wildly and they saw him coming out of the bush sideways, fast as a crab, and the bull coming, nose out, mouth tight closed, blood dripping, massive head straight out, coming in a charge, his little pig eyes bloodshot as he looked at them. Wilson, who was ahead, was kneeling shooting, and Macomber, as he fired, unhearing his shot in the roaring of Wilson's gun, saw fragments like slate burst from the huge boss of the horns, and the head jerked, he shot again at the wide nostrils and saw the horns jolt again and fragments fly, and he did not see Wilson now and, aiming carefully, shot again with the buffalo's huge bulk almost on him and his rifle almost level with the on-coming head, nose out, and he could see the little wicked eyes and the head started to lower and he felt a sudden white-hot, blinding flash explode inside his head and that was all he ever felt.

Wilson had ducked to one side to get in a shoulder shot. Macomber had stood solid and shot for the nose, shooting a touch high each time and hitting the heavy horns, splintering and chipping them like hitting a slate roof, and Mrs. Macomber, in the car, had shot at the buffalo with the 6.5 Mannlicher as it seemed about to gore Macomber and had hit her husband about two inches up and a little to one side of the base of his skull.

Francis Macomber lay now, face down, not two yards from where the buffalo lay on his side and his wife knelt over him with Wilson beside her.

"I wouldn't turn him over," Wilson said.

The woman was crying hysterically.

"I'd get back in the car," Wilson said. "Where's the rifle?"

She shook her head, her face contorted. The gun-bearer picked up the rifle.

"Leave it as it is," said Wilson. Then, "Go get Abdulla so that he may witness the manner of the accident."

He knelt down, took a handkerchief from his pocket, and spread it over Francis Macomber's crew-cropped head where it lay. The blood sank into the dry, loose earth.

Wilson stood up and saw the buffalo on his side, his legs out, his thinly-haired belly crawling with ticks. "Hell of a good bull," his brain registered automatically. "A good fifty inches, or better. Better." He called to the driver and told him to spread a blanket over the body and stay by it. Then he walked over to the motor car where the woman sat crying in the corner.

"That was a pretty thing to do," he said in a toneless voice. "He *would* have left you too."

"Stop it," she said.

"Of course it's an accident," he said. "I know that."

"Stop it," she said.

"Don't worry," he said. "There will be a certain amount of unpleasantness but I will have some photographs taken that will be very useful at the inquest. There's the testimony of the gun-bearers and the driver too. You're perfectly all right."

"Stop it," she said.

"There's a hell of a lot to be done," he said. "And I'll have to send a truck off to the lake to wireless for a plane to take the three of us into Nairobi. Why didn't you poison him? That's what they do in England."

"Stop it. Stop it. Stop it," the woman cried.

Wilson looked at her with his flat blue eyes.

"I'm through now," he said. "I was a little angry. I'd begun to like your husband."

"Oh, please stop it," she said. "Please, please stop it."

"That's better," Wilson said. "Please is much better. Now I'll stop."

§ FOR COMMENT

In this story Hemingway departs from his usual handling of point of view. Instead of employing the detached omniscient narrator who merely reports details of the action, Hemingway here chooses to enter the minds of all of the major characters, even that of the lion. How would the story have been different had Hemingway chosen the strictly objective view, entering into the mind of none of the characters? What would have been the effect of channeling the view through the mind of a single character, for example, the white hunter or Margot? Could the story have been told from the viewpoint of Francis Macomber? Does the entry into the mind of the lion bother you?

Can you justify Hemingway's choice of point of view, relating it to the theme and structure of the story? Consider, for example, the relationship between the point of view and the climactic scene. Did Margot deliberately kill her husband? Robert thinks so. Is the reader to think so too? Is there any reason to think that she did not? Notice the words of the omniscient narrator: "Mrs. Macomber had shot at the buffalo . . . and had hit her husband." Is there any effort here to mislead the reader or does the whole situation remain ambiguous?

John Steinbeck § 1902–

Born in Salinas, California, Steinbeck studied at Stanford, but did not take a degree. Instead he had a varied career, working as a newspaperman, a chemist, and a fruit picker, among other things. Among his numerous works, Tortilla Flat *(1935) was made into a movie, as were many others;* Of Mice and Men *(1937) was a Book-of-the-Month Club selection and when made into a play, won the Drama Critics' Circle Award.* The Grapes of Wrath *(1939) won for Steinbeck a Pulitzer Prize and* The Winter of Our Discontent *(1961) was cited when he was awarded the Nobel Prize in 1962. His short stories comprise a small part of his total output, but some of them, including "The Chrysanthemums," "Flight," and "The Red Pony," are considered excellent and are often anthologized.*

Flight

About fifteen miles below Monterey, on the wild coast, the Torres family had their farm, a few sloping acres above a cliff that dropped to the brown reefs and to the hissing white waters of the ocean. Behind the farm the stone mountains stood up against the sky. The farm buildings huddled like little clinging aphids on the mountains skirts, crouched low to the ground as though the wind might blow them into the sea. The little shack, the rattling, rotting barn were gray-bitten with sea salt, beaten by the damp wind until they had taken on the color of the granite hills. Two horses, a red cow and a red calf, half a dozen pigs and a flock of lean, multicolored chickens stocked the place. A little corn was raised on the sterile slope, and it grew short and thick under the wind, and all the cobs formed on the landward side of the stalks.

Mama Torres, a lean, dry woman with ancient eyes, had ruled the farm for ten years, ever since her husband tripped over a stone in the field one day and fell full length on a rattlesnake. When one is bitten on the chest there is not much that can be done.

Mama Torres had three children, two undersized black ones of twelve and fourteen, Emilio and Rosy, whom Mama kept fishing on the rocks below the farm when the sea was kind and when the truant officer was in some distant part of Monterey County. And there was Pepé, the tall smiling son of nineteen, a gentle, affectionate boy, but very lazy. Pepé had a tall head, pointed at the top, and from its peak, coarse black hair grew down like a thatch all around. Over his smiling little eyes Mama cut a straight bang so he could see. Pepé had sharp Indian cheekbones and an eagle nose, but his mouth was as sweet and shapely as a girl's mouth, and his chin was fragile and chiseled. He was loose and gangling, all legs and feet and wrists, and he was very lazy. Mama thought him fine and brave, but she never told him so. She said, "Some lazy cow must have got into thy father's family, else how could I have a son like thee." And she said, "When I carried thee, a sneaking lazy coyote came out of the brush and looked at me one day. That must have made thee so."

Pepé smiled sheepishly and stabbed at the ground with his knife to keep the blade sharp and free from rust. It was his inheritance, that knife, his father's knife. The long heavy blade folded back into the black handle. There was a button on the handle. When Pepé pressed the button, the blade leaped out ready for use. The knife was with Pepé always, for it had been his father's knife.

One sunny morning when the sea below the cliff was glinting and blue and the white surf creamed on the reef, when even the stone mountains looked kindly, Mama Torres called out the door of the shack, "Pepé, I have a labor for thee."

There was no answer. Mama listened. From behind the barn she heard a burst of laughter. She lifted her full long skirt and walked in the direction of the noise.

Pepé was sitting on the ground with his back against a box. His white teeth glistened. On either side of him stood the two black ones, tense and expectant. Fifteen feet away a redwood post was set in the ground. Pepé's right hand lay limply in his lap, and in the palm the big black knife rested. The blade was closed back into the handle. Pepé looked smiling at the sky.

Suddenly Emilio cried, "Ya!"

Pepé's wrist flicked like the head of a snake. The blade seemed to fly open in mid-air, and with a thump the point dug into the redwood post, and the black handle quivered. The three burst into excited laughter. Rosy ran to the post and pulled out the knife and brought it back to Pepé. He closed the blade and settled the knife carefully in his listless palm again. He grinned self-consciously at the sky.

"Ya!"

The heavy knife lanced out and sunk into the post again. Mama moved forward like a ship and scattered the play.

"All day you do foolish things with the knife, like a toy-baby," she stormed. "Get up on thy huge feet that eat up shoes. Get up!" She took him by one loose shoulder and hoisted at him. Pepé grinned sheepishly and came halfheartedly to his feet. "Look!" Mama cried. "Big lazy, you must catch the horse and put on him thy father's saddle. You must ride to Monterey. The medicine bottle is empty. There is no salt. Go thou now, Peanut! Catch the horse."

A revolution took place in the relaxed figure of Pepé. "To Monterey, me? Alone? *Si*, Mama."

She scowled at him. "Do not think, big sheep, that you will buy candy. No, I will give you only enough for the medicine and the salt."

Pepé smiled. "Mama, you will put the hatband on the hat?"

She relented then. "Yes, Pepé. You may wear the hatband."

His voice grew insinuating, "And the green handkerchief, Mama?"

"Yes, if you go quickly and return with no trouble, the silk green handkerchief will go. If you make sure to take off the handkerchief when you eat so no spot may fall on it. . . ."

"*Si*, Mama. I will be careful. I am a man."

"Thou? A man? Thou art a peanut."

He went into the rickety barn and brought out a rope, and he walked agilely enough up the hill to catch the horse.

When he was ready and mounted before the door, mounted on his father's saddle that was so old that the oaken frame showed through torn leather in many places, then Mama brought out the round black hat with the tooled leather band, and she reached up and knotted the green silk handkerchief about his neck. Pepé's blue denim coat was much darker than his jeans, for it had been washed much less often.

Mama handed up the big medicine bottle and the silver coins. "That for the medicine," she said, "and that for the salt. That for a candle to burn for the papa. That for *dulces*[1] for the little ones. Our friend Mrs. Rodriguez will give you dinner and maybe a bed for the night. When you go to the church say only ten Paternosters and only twenty-five Ave Marias. Oh! I know, big coyote. You would sit there flapping your mouth over Aves all day while you looked at the candles and the holy pictures. That is not good devotion to stare at the pretty things."

The black hat, covering the high pointed head and black thatched hair

[1] *dulces*: Sweets, primarily candies.

of Pepé, gave him dignity and age. He sat the rangy horse well. Mama thought how handsome he was, dark and lean and tall. "I would not send thee now alone, thou little one, except for the medicine," she said softly. "It is not good to have no medicine, for who knows when the toothache will come, or the sadness of the stomach. These things are."

"Adios, Mama," Pepé cried. "I will come back soon. You may send me often alone. I am a man."

"Thou art a foolish chicken."

He straightened his shoulders, flipped the reins against the horse's shoulder and rode away. He turned once and saw that they still watched him, Emilio and Rosy and Mama. Pepé grinned with pride and gladness and lifted the tough buckskin horse to a trot.

When he had dropped out of sight over a little dip in the road, Mama turned to the black ones, but she spoke to herself. "He is nearly a man now," she said. "It will be a nice thing to have a man in the house again." Her eyes sharpened on the children. "Go to the rocks now. The tide is going out. There will be abalones to be found." She put the iron hooks into their hands and saw them down the steep trail to the reefs. She brought the smooth stone *metate*[2] to the doorway and sat grinding her corn to flour and looking occasionally at the road over which Pepé had gone. The noonday came and then the afternoon, when the little ones beat the abalones on a rock to make them tender and Mama patted the tortillas to make them thin. They ate their dinner as the red sun was plunging down toward the ocean. They sat on the doorsteps and watched the big white moon come over the mountain tops.

Mama said, "He is now at the house of our friend Mrs. Rodriguez. She will give him nice things to eat and maybe a present."

Emilio said, "Some day I too will ride to Monterey for medicine. Did Pepé come to be a man today?"

Mama said wisely, "A boy gets to be a man when a man is needed. Remember this thing. I have known boys forty years old because there was no need for a man."

Soon afterwards they retired, Mama in her big oak bed on one side of the room, Emilio and Rosy in their boxes full of straw and sheepskins on the other side of the room.

The moon went over the sky and the surf roared on the rocks. The roosters crowed the first call. The surf subsided to a whispering surge against the reef. The moon dropped toward the sea. The roosters crowed again.

The moon was near down to the water when Pepé rode on a winded horse to his home flat. His dog bounced out and circled the horse yelping with pleasure. Pepé slid off the saddle to the ground. The weathered little

---

2 *metate*: Stone for grinding corn.

shack was silver in the moonlight and the square shadow of it was black to the north and east. Against the east the piling mountains were misty with light; their tops melted into the sky.

Pepé walked wearily up the three steps and into the house. It was dark inside. There was a rustle in the corner.

Mama cried out from her bed. "Who comes? Pepé, is it thou?"

"Sí, Mama."

"Did you get the medicine?"

"Sí, Mama."

"Well, go to sleep, then. I thought you would be sleeping at the house of Mrs. Rodriguez." Pepé stood silently in the dark room. "Why do you stand there, Pepé? Did you drink wine?"

"Sí, Mama."

"Well, go to bed then and sleep out the wine."

His voice was tired and patient, but very firm. "Light the candle, Mama. I must go away into the mountains."

"What is this, Pepé? You are crazy." Mama struck a sulphur match and held the little blue burr until the flame spread up the stick. She set light to the candle on the floor beside her bed. "Now, Pepé, what is this you say?" She looked anxiously into his face.

He was changed. The fragile quality seemed to have gone from his chin. His mouth was less full than it had been, the lines of the lips were straighter, but in his eyes the greatest change had taken place. There was no laughter in them any more nor any bashfulness. They were sharp and bright and purposeful.

He told her in a tired monotone, told her everything just as it had happened. A few people came into the kitchen of Mrs. Rodriguez. There was wine to drink. Pepé drank wine. The little quarrel—the man started toward Pepé and then the knife—it went almost by itself. It flew, it darted before Pepé knew it. As he talked, Mama's face grew stern, and it seemed to grow more lean. Pepé finished. "I am a man now, Mama. The man said names to me I could not allow."

Mama nodded. "Yes, thou art a man, my poor little Pepé. Thou art a man. I have seen it coming on thee. I have watched you throwing the knife into the post, and I have been afraid." For a moment her face had softened, but now it grew stern again. "Come! We must get you ready. Go. Awaken Emilio and Rosy. Go quickly."

Pepé stepped over to the corner where this brother and sister slept among the sheepskins. He leaned down and shook them gently. "Come, Rosy! Come, Emilio! The mama says you must arise."

The little black ones sat up and rubbed their eyes in the candlelight. Mama was out of bed now, her long black skirt over her nightgown. "Emilio," she cried. "Go up and catch the other horse for Pepé. Quickly, now! Quickly." Emilio put his legs in his overalls and stumbled sleepily out the door.

"You heard no one behind you on the road?" Mama demanded.

"No, Mama. I listened carefully. No one was on the road."

Mama darted like a bird about the room. From a nail on the wall she took a canvas water bag and threw it on the floor. She stripped a blanket from her bed and rolled it into a tight tube and tied the ends with string. From a box beside the stove she lifted a flour sack half full of black stringy jerky. "Your father's black coat, Pepé. Here, put it on."

Pepé stood in the middle of the floor watching her activity. She reached behind the door and brought out the rifle, a long 38-56, worn shiny the whole length of the barrel. Pepé took it from her and held it in the crook of his elbow. Mama brought a little leather bag and counted the cartridges into his hand. "Only ten left," she warned. "You must not waste them."

Emilio put his head in the door. " *'Qui 'st 'l caballo,*[3] Mama."

"Put on the saddle from the other horse. Tie on the blanket. Here, tie the jerky to the saddle horn."

Still Pepé stood silently watching his mother's frantic activity. His chin looked hard, and his sweet mouth was drawn and thin. His little eyes followed Mama about the room almost suspiciously.

Rosy asked softly, "Where goes Pepé?"

Mama's eyes were fierce. "Pepé goes on a journey. Pepé is a man now. He has a man's thing to do."

Pepé straightened his shoulders. His mouth changed until he looked very much like Mama.

At last the preparation was finished. The loaded horse stood outside the door. The water bag dripped a line of moisture down the bay shoulder.

The moonlight was being thinned by the dawn and the big white moon was near down to the sea. The family stood by the shack. Mama confronted Pepé. "Look, my son! Do not stop until it is dark again. Do not sleep even though you are tired. Take care of the horse in order that he may not stop of weariness. Remember to be careful with the bullets—there are only ten. Do not fill thy stomach with jerky or it will make thee sick. Eat a little jerky and fill thy stomach with grass. When thou comest to the high mountains, if thou seest any of the dark watching men, go not near to them nor try to speak to them. And forget not thy prayers." She put her lean hands on Pepé's shoulders, stood on her toes and kissed him formally on both cheeks, and Pepé kissed her on both cheeks. Then he went to Emilio and Rosy and kissed both of their cheeks.

Pepé turned back to Mama. He seemed to look for a little softness, a little weakness in her. His eyes were searching, but Mama's face remained fierce. "Go now," she said. "Do not wait to be caught like a chicken."

Pepé pulled himself into the saddle. "I am a man," he said.

It was the first dawn when he rode up the hill toward the little canyon which let a trail into the mountains. Moonlight and daylight fought with

[3] *'Qui 'st 'l caballo:* Here is the horse.

each other, and the two warring qualities made it difficult to see. Before Pepé had gone a hundred yards, the outlines of his figure were misty; and long before he entered the canyon, he had become a gray, indefinite shadow.

Mama stood stiffly in front of her doorstep, and on either side of her stood Emilio and Rosy. They cast furtive glances at Mama now and then.

When the gray shape of Pepé melted into the hillside and disappeared, Mama relaxed. She began the high, whining keen of the death wail. "Our beautiful—our brave," she cried. "Our protector, our son is gone." Emilio and Rosy moaned beside her. "Our beautiful—our brave, he is gone." It was the formal wail. It rose to a high piercing whine and subsided to a moan. Mama raised it three times and then she turned and went into the house and shut the door.

Emilio and Rosy stood wondering in the dawn. They heard Mama whimpering in the house. They went out to sit on the cliff above the ocean. They touched shoulders. "When did Pepé come to be a man?" Emilio asked.

"Last night," said Rosy. "Last night in Monterey." The ocean clouds turned red with the sun that was behind the mountains.

"We will have no breakfast," said Emilio. "Mama will not want to cook." Rosy did not answer him. "Where is Pepé gone?" he asked.

Rosy looked around at him. She drew her knowledge from the quiet air. "He has gone on a journey. He will never come back."

"Is he dead? Do you think he is dead?"

Rosy looked back at the ocean again. A little steamer, drawing a line of smoke sat on the edge of the horizon. "He is not dead," Rosy explained. "Not yet."

Pepé rested the big rifle across the saddle in front of him. He let the horse walk up the hill and he didn't look back. The stony slope took on a coat of short brush so that Pepé found the entrance to a trail and entered it.

When he came to the canyon opening, he swung once in his saddle and looked back, but the houses were swallowed in the misty light. Pepé jerked foward again. The high shoulder of the canyon closed in on him. His horse stretched out its neck and sighed and settled to the trail.

It was a well-worn path, dark soft leaf-mold earth strewn with broken pieces of sandstone. The trail rounded the shoulder of the canyon and dropped steeply into the bed of the stream. In the shallows the water ran smoothly, glinting in the first morning sun. Small round stones on the bottom were as brown as rust with sun moss. In the sand along the edges of the stream the tall, rich wild mint grew, while in the water itself the cress, old and tough, had gone to heavy seed.

The path went into the stream and emerged on the other side. The horse sloshed into the water and stopped. Pepé dropped his bridle and let the beast drink of the running water.

Soon the canyon sides became steep and the first giant sentinel redwoods guarded the trail, great round red trunks bearing foliage as green and lacy as ferns. Once Pepé was among the trees, the sun was lost. A perfumed and purple light lay in the pale green of the underbrush. Gooseberry bushes and blackberries and tall ferns lined the stream, and overhead the branches of the redwoods met and cut off the sky.

Pepé drank from the water bag, and he reached into the flour sack and brought out a black string of jerky. His white teeth gnawed at the string until the tough meat parted. He chewed slowly and drank occasionally from the water bag. His little eyes were slumberous and tired, but the muscles of his face were hard set. The earth of the trail was black now. It gave up a hollow sound under the walking hoofbeats.

The stream fell more sharply. Little waterfalls splashed on the stones. Five-fingered ferns hung over the water and dripped spray from their fingertips. Pepé rode half over in his saddle, dangling one leg loosely. He picked a bay leaf from a tree beside the way and put it into his mouth for a moment to flavor the dry jerky. He held the gun loosely across the pommel.

Suddenly he squared in his saddle, swung the horse from the trail and kicked it hurriedly up behind a big redwood tree. He pulled up the reins tight against the bit to keep the horse from whinnying. His face was intent and his nostrils quivered a little.

A hollow pounding came down the trail, and a horseman rode by, a fat man with red cheeks and a white stubble beard. His horse put down its head and blubbered at the trail when it came to the place where Pepé had turned off. "Hold up!" said the man and he pulled up his horse's head.

When the last sound of the hoofs died away, Pepé came back into the trail again. He did not relax in the saddle any more. He lifted the big rifle and swung the lever to throw a shell into the chamber, and then he let down the hammer to half cock.

The trail grew very steep. Now the redwood trees were smaller and their tops were dead, bitten dead where the wind reached them. The horse plodded on; the sun went slowly overhead and started down toward the afternoon.

Where the stream came out of a side canyon, the trail left it. Pepé dismounted and watered his horse and filled up his water bag. As soon as the trail had parted from the stream, the trees were gone and only the thick brittle sage and manzanita and chaparral edged the trail. And the soft black earth was gone, too, leaving only the light tan broken rock for the trail bed. Lizards scampered away into the brush as the horse rattled over the little stones.

Pepé turned in his saddle and looked back. He was in the open now: he could be seen from a distance. As he ascended the trail the country grew more rough and terrible and dry. The way wound about the bases of great square rocks. Little gray rabbits skittered in the brush. A bird made a monotonous high creaking. Eastward the bare rock mountaintops were pale and powder-dry under the dropping sun. The horse plodded up and up the trail toward a little V in the ridge which was the pass.

Pepé looked suspiciously back every minute or so, and his eyes sought the tops of the ridges ahead. Once, on a white barren spur, he saw a black figure for a moment, but he looked quickly away, for it was one of the dark watchers. No one knew who the watchers were, nor where they lived, but it was better to ignore them and never to show interest in them. They did not bother one who stayed on the trail and minded his own business.

The air was parched and full of light dust blown by the breeze from the eroding mountains. Pepé drank sparingly from his bag and corked it tightly and hung it on the horn again. The trail moved up the dry shale hillside, avoiding rocks, dropping under clefts, climbing in and out of old water scars. When he arrived at the little pass he stopped and looked back for a long time. No dark watchers were to be seen now. The trail behind was empty. Only the high tops of the redwoods indicated where the stream flowed.

Pepé rode on through the pass. His little eyes were nearly closed with weariness, but his face was stern, relentless and manly. The high mountain wind coasted sighing through the pass and whistled on the edges of the big blocks of broken granite. In the air, a red-tailed hawk sailed over close to the ridge and screamed angrily. Pepé went slowly through the broken jagged pass and looked down on the other side.

The trail dropped quickly, staggering among broken rock. At the bottom of the slope there was a dark crease, thick with brush, and on the other side of the crease a little flat, in which a grove of oak trees grew. A scar of green grass cut across the flat. And behind the flat another mountain rose, desolate with dead rocks and starving little black bushes. Pepé drank from the bag again for the air was so dry that it encrusted his nostrils and burned his lips. He put the horse down the trail. The hooves slipped and struggled on the steep way, starting little stones that rolled off into the brush. The sun was gone behind the westward mountain now, but still it glowed brilliantly on the oaks and on the grassy flat. The rocks and the hillsides still sent up waves of the heat they had gathered from the day's sun.

Pepé looked up to the top of the next dry withered ridge. He saw a dark form against the sky, a man's figure standing on top of a rock, and he glanced away quickly not to appear curious. When a moment later he looked up again, the figure was gone.

Downward the trail was quickly covered. Sometimes the horse floundered for footing, sometimes set his feet and slid a little way. They came at last to the bottom where the dark chaparral was higher than Pepé's head. He held up his rifle on one side and his arm on the other to shield his face from the sharp brittle fingers of the brush.

Up and out of the crease he rode, and up a little cliff. The grassy flat was before him, and the round comfortable oaks. For a moment he studied the trail down which he had come, but there was no movement and no sound from it. Finally he rode out over the flat, to the green streak, and at the upper end of the damp he found a little spring welling out of the earth and dropping into a dug basin before it seeped out over the flat.

Pepé filled his bag first, and then he let the thirsty horse drink out of the pool. He led the horse to the clump of oaks, and in the middle of the grove, fairly protected from sight on all sides, he took off the saddle and the bridle and laid them on the ground. The horse stretched his jaws sideways and yawned. Pepé knotted the lead rope about the horse's neck and tied him to a sapling among the oaks, where he could graze in a fairly large circle.

When the horse was gnawing hungrily at the dry grass, Pepé went to the saddle and took a black string of jerky from the sack and strolled to an oak tree on the edge of the grove, from under which he could watch the trail. He sat down in the crisp dry oak leaves and automatically felt for his big black knife to cut the jerky, but he had no knife. He leaned back on his elbow and gnawed at the tough strong meat. His face was blank, but it was a man's face.

The bright evening light washed the eastern ridge, but the valley was darkening. Doves flew down from the hills to the spring, and the quail came running out of the brush and joined them, calling clearly to one another.

Out of the corner of his eye Pepé saw a shadow grow out of the bushy crease. He turned his head slowly. A big spotted wildcat was creeping toward the spring, belly to the ground, moving like thought.

Pepé cocked his rifle and edged the muzzle slowly around. Then he looked apprehensively up the trail and dropped the hammer again. From the ground beside him he picked an oak twig and threw it toward the spring. The quail flew up with a roar and the doves whistled away. The big cat stood up: for a long moment he looked at Pepé with cold yellow eyes, and then fearlessly walked back into the gulch.

The dusk gathered quickly in the deep valley. Pepé muttered his prayers, put his head down on his arm and went instantly to sleep.

The moon came up and filled the valley with cold blue light, and the wind swept rustling down from the peaks. The owls worked up and down the slopes looking for rabbits. Down in the brush of the gulch a coyote gabbled. The oak trees whispered softly in the night breeze.

Pepé started up, listening. His horse had whinnied. The moon was just slipping behind the western ridge, leaving the valley in darkness behind it. Pepé sat tensely gripping his rifle. From far up the trail he heard an answering whinny and the crash of shod hooves on the broken rock. He jumped to his feet, ran to his horse and led it under the trees. He threw on the saddle and cinched it tight for the steep trail, caught the unwilling head and forced the bit into the mouth. He felt the saddle to make sure the water bag and the sack of jerky were there. Then he mounted and turned up the hill.

It was velvet dark. The horse found the entrance to the trail where it left the flat, and started up, stumbling and slipping on the rocks. Pepé's hand rose up to his head. His hat was gone. He had left it under the oak tree.

The horse had struggled far up the trail when the first change of dawn came into the air, a steel grayness as light mixed thoroughly with dark. Gradually the sharp snaggled edge of the ridge stood out above them, rotten granite tortured and eaten by the wind of time. Pepé had dropped his reins on the horn, leaving direction to the horse. The brush grabbed at his legs in the dark until one knee of his jeans was ripped.

Gradually the light flowed down over the ridge. The starved brush and rocks stood out in the half light, strange and lonely in high perspective. Then there came warmth into the light. Pepé drew up and looked back, but he could see nothing in the darker valley below. The sky turned blue over the coming sun. In the waste of the mountainside, the poor dry brush grew only three feet high. Here and there, big outcroppings of unrotted granite stood up like moldering houses. Pepé relaxed a little. He drank from his water bag and bit off a piece of jerky. A single eagle flew over, high in the light.

Without warning Pepé's horse screamed and fell on its side. He was almost down before the rifle crash echoed up from the valley. From a hole behind the struggling shoulder, a stream of bright crimson blood pumped and stopped and pumped and stopped. The hooves threshed on the ground. Pepé lay half stunned beside the horse. He looked slowly down the hill. A piece of sage clipped off beside his head and another crash echoed up from side to side of the canyon. Pepé flung himself frantically behind a bush.

He crawled up the hill on his knees and on one hand. His right hand held the rifle up off the ground and pushed it ahead of him. He moved with the instinctive care of an animal. Rapidly he wormed his way toward one of the big outcroppings of granite on the hill above him. Where the brush was high he doubled up and ran, but where the cover was slight he wriggled forward on his stomach, pushing the rifle ahead of him. In the last little distance there was no cover at all. Pepé poised and then he darted across the space and flashed around the corner of the rock.

He leaned panting against the stone. When his breath came easier he moved along behind the big rock until he came to a narrow split that offered a thin section of vision down the hill. Pepé lay on his stomach and pushed the rifle barrel through the slit and waited.

The sun reddened the western ridges now. Already the buzzards were settling down toward the place where the horse lay. A small brown bird scratched in the dead sage leaves directly in front of the rifle muzzle. The coasting eagle flew back toward the rising sun.

Pepé saw a little movement in the brush far below. His grip tightened on the gun. A little brown doe stepped daintily out on the trail and crossed it and disappeared into the brush again. For a long time Pepé waited. Far below he could see the little flat and the oak trees and the slash of green. Suddenly his eyes flashed back at the trail again. A quarter of a mile down there had been a quick movement in the chaparral. The rifle swung over. The front sight nestled in the V of the rear sight. Pepé studied for a moment and then raised the rear sight a notch. The little movement in the brush came again. The sight settled on it. Pepé squeezed the trigger. The explosion crashed down the mountain and up the other side, and came rattling back. The whole side of the slope grew still. No more movement. And then a white streak cut into the granite of the slit and a bullet whined away and a crash sounded up from below. Pepé felt a sharp pain in his right hand. A sliver of granite was sticking out from between his first and second knuckles and the point protruded from his palm. Carefully he pulled out the sliver of stone. The wound bled evenly and gently. No vein nor artery was cut.

Pepé looked into a little dusty cave in the rock and gathered a handful of spider web, and he pressed the mass into the cut, plastering the soft web into the blood. The flow stopped almost at once.

The rifle was on the ground. Pepé picked it up, levered a new shell into the chamber. And then he slid into the brush on his stomach. Far to the right he crawled, and then up the hill, moving slowly and carefully, crawling to cover and resting and then crawling again.

In the mountains the sun is high in its arc before it penetrates the gorges. The hot face looked over the hill and brought instant heat with it. The white light beat on the rocks and reflected from them and rose up quivering from the earth again, and the rocks and bushes seemed to quiver behind the air.

Pepé crawled in the general direction of the ridge peak, zig-zagging for cover. The deep cut between his knuckles began to throb. He crawled close to a rattlesnake before he saw it, and when it raised its dry head and made a soft beginning whirr, he backed up and took another way. The quick gray lizards flashed in front of him, raising a tiny line of dust. He found another mass of spider web and pressed it against his throbbing hand.

Pepé was pushing the rifle with his left hand now. Little drops of sweat ran to the ends of his coarse black hair and rolled down his cheeks. His lips and tongue were growing thick and heavy. His lips writhed to draw saliva into his mouth. His little dark eyes were uneasy and suspicious. Once when a gray lizard paused in front of him on the parched ground and turned its head sideways he crushed it flat with a stone.

When the sun slid past noon he had not gone a mile. He crawled exhaustedly a last hundred yards to a patch of high sharp manzanita, crawled desperately, and when the patch was reached he wriggled in among the tough gnarly trunks and dropped his head on his left arm. There was little shade in the meager brush, but there was cover and safety. Pepé went to sleep as he lay and the sun beat on his back. A few little birds hopped close to him and peered and hopped away. Pepé squirmed in his sleep and he raised and dropped his wounded hand again and again.

The sun went down behind the peaks and the cool evening came, and then the dark. A coyote yelled from the hillside, Pepé started awake and looked about with misty eyes. His hand was swollen and heavy; a little thread of pain ran up the inside of his arm and settled in a pocket in his armpit. He peered about and then stood up, for the mountains were black and the moon had not yet risen. Pepé stood up in the dark. The coat of his father pressed on his arm. His tongue was swollen until it nearly filled his mouth. He wriggled out of the coat and dropped it in the brush, and then he struggled up the hill, falling over rocks and tearing his way through the brush. The rifle knocked against stones as he went. Little dry avalanches of gravel and shattered stone went whispering down the hill behind him.

After a while the old moon came up and showed the jagged ridge top ahead of him. By moonlight Pepé traveled more easily. He bent forward so that his throbbing arm hung away from his body. The journey uphill was made in dashes and rests, a frantic rush up a few yards and then a rest. The wind coasted down the slope rattling the dry stems of the bushes.

The moon was at meridian when Pepé came at last to the sharp backbone of the ridge top. On the last hundred yards of the rise no soil had clung under the wearing winds. The way was on solid rock. He clambered to the top and looked down on the other side. There was a draw like the last below him, misty with moonlight, brushed with dry struggling sage and chaparral. On the other side the hill rose up sharply and at the top the jagged rotten teeth of the mountain showed against the sky. At the bottom of the cut the brush was thick and dark.

Pepé stumbled down the hill. His throat was almost closed with thirst. At first he tried to run, but immediately he fell and rolled. After that he went more carefully. The moon was just disappearing behind the mountains when he came to the bottom. He crawled into the heavy brush feeling with his fingers for water. There was no water in the bed of the stream, only damp earth. Pepé laid his gun down and scooped up a handful of mud and put it in his mouth, and then he spluttered and scraped the earth from his tongue with his finger, for the mud drew at his mouth like a poultice. He dug a hole in the stream bed with his fingers, dug a little basin to catch water; but before it was very deep his head fell forward on the damp ground and he slept.

The dawn came and the heat of the day fell on the earth, and still Pepé slept. Late in the afternoon his head jerked up. He looked slowly around. His eyes were slits of wariness. Twenty feet away in the heavy brush a big

tawny mountain lion stood looking at him. Its long thick tail waved gracefully, its ears erect with interest, not laid back dangerously. The lion
squatted down on its stomach and watched him.

Pepé looked at the hole he had dug in the earth. A half inch of muddy
water had collected in the bottom. He tore the sleeve from his hurt arm,
with his teeth ripped out a little square, soaked it in the water and put it in
his mouth. Over and over he filled the cloth and sucked it.

Still the lion sat and watched him. The evening came down but there
was no movement on the hills. No birds visited the dry bottom of the cut.
Pepé looked occasionally at the lion. The eyes of the yellow beast drooped
as though he were about to sleep. He yawned and his long thin red tongue
curled out. Suddenly his head jerked around and his nostrils quivered. His
big tail lashed. He stood up and slunk like a tawny shadow into the thick
brush.

A moment later Pepé heard the sound, the faint far crash of horses'
hooves on gravel. And he heard something else, a high whining yelp of a
dog.

Pepé took his rifle in his left hand and he glided into the brush almost
as quietly as the lion had. In the darkening evening he crouched up the hill
toward the next ridge. Only when the dark came did he stand up. His
energy was short. Once it was dark he fell over the rocks and slipped to his
knees on the steep slope, but he moved on and on up the hill, climbing and
scrabbling over the broken hillside.

When he was far up toward the top, he lay down and slept for a little
while. The withered moon, shining on his face, awakened him. He stood up
and moved up the hill. Fifty yards away he stopped and turned back, for he
had forgotten his rifle. He walked heavily down and poked about in the
brush, but he could not find his gun. At last he lay down to rest. The
pocket of pain in his armpit had grown more sharp. His arm seemed to
swell out and fall with every heartbeat. There was no position lying down
where the heavy arm did not press against his armpit.

With the effort of a hurt beast, Pepé got up and moved again toward
the top of the ridge. He held his swollen arm away from his body with his
left hand. Up the steep hill he dragged himself, a few steps and a rest, and a
few more steps. At last he was nearing the top. The moon showed the
uneven sharp back of it against the sky.

Pepé's brain spun in a big spiral up and away from him. He slumped to
the ground and lay still. The rock ridge top was only a hundred feet above
him.

The moon moved over the sky. Pepé half turned on his back. His
tongue tried to make words, but only a thick hissing came from between his
lips.

When the dawn came, Pepé pulled himself up. His eyes were sane
again. He drew his great puffed arm in front of him and looked at the angry
wound. The black line ran up from his wrist to his armpit. Automatically

he reached in his pocket for the big black knife, but it was not there. His eyes searched the ground. He picked up a sharp blade of stone and scraped at the wound, sawed at the proud flesh and then squeezed the green juice out in big drops. Instantly he threw back his head and whined like a dog. His whole right side shuddered at the pain, but the pain cleared his head.

In the gray light he struggled up the last slope to the ridge and crawled over and lay down behind a line of rocks. Below him lay a deep canyon exactly like the last, waterless and desolate. There was no flat, no oak trees, not even heavy brush in the bottom of it. And on the other side a sharp ridge stood up, thinly brushed with starving sage, littered with broken granite. Strewn over the hill there were giant outcroppings, and on the top the granite teeth stood out against the sky.

The new day was light now. The flame of sun came over the ridge and fell on Pepé where he lay on the ground. His coarse black hair was littered with twigs and bits of spider web. His eyes had retreated back into his head. Between his lips the tip of his black tongue showed.

He sat up and dragged his great arm into his lap and nursed it, rocking his body and moaning in his throat. He threw back his head and looked up into the pale sky. A big black bird circled nearly out of sight, and far to the left another was sailing near.

He lifted his head to listen, for a familiar sound had come to him from the valley he had climbed out of; it was the crying yelp of hounds, excited and feverish, on a trail.

Pepé bowed his head quickly. He tried to speak rapid words but only a thick hiss came from his lips. He drew a shaky cross on his breast with his left hand. It was a long struggle to get to his feet. He crawled slowly and mechanically to the top of a big rock on the ridge peak. Once there, he arose slowly, swaying to his feet, and stood erect. Far below he could see the dark brush where he had slept. He braced his feet and stood there, black against the morning sky.

There came a ripping sound at his feet. A piece of stone flew up and a bullet droned off into the next gorge. The hollow crash echoed up from below. Pepé looked down for a moment and then pulled himself straight again.

His body jarred back. His left hand fluttered helplessly toward his breast. The second crash sounded from below. Pepé swung forward and toppled from the rock. His body struck and rolled over and over, starting a little avalanche. And when at last he stopped against a bush, the avalanche slid slowly down and covered up his head.

§ FOR COMMENT

The first paragraph of "Flight" is an example of the consummate skill of the short story writer whose genre dictates that every word be put to maximum use. Reread the paragraph, noting every detail that functions either to characterize or to foreshadow the theme or conclusion of the story. What tone is established in this paragraph? Is the tone consistent throughout the story? How is it achieved and maintained? Notice the sentence structure in the second paragraph, how the very pattern of the sentences helps to establish a feeling of helpless despair and futility. Find and cite other such sentences.

What is the relevance of the lines that are repeated almost as a refrain where Pepé says, "I am a man," and his mother answers, "Thou? A man? Thou art a peanut," or "Thou art a foolish chicken," until finally she appears to agree, "Yes, thou art a man, my poor little Pepé"? How does the last phrase, "my poor little Pepé," qualify the mother's statement? When does Pepé actually become a man?

Pepé's father dies from a snake bite. Is the father's death related to Pepé's actions in Monterey and to Pepé's flight and eventual death? How important in the story are the father's possessions, which Pepé appropriates and then loses one by one? What is Pepé's actual inheritance from his father? His symbolic inheritance?

The major portion of the story is taken up with a description of Pepé's flight. How does Steinbeck maintain interest and suspense and at the same time indicate that the flight itself is symbolic? What is the function of the changing terrain, the animals that appear periodically, the dark watchers? Why are the pursuers never really seen?

Examine the last three paragraphs of the story and show how Pepé's death in just this way is inevitable.

Frank O'Connor § 1903–1966

Born in Cork, Ireland, and educated there, receiving a Doctor of Literature degree from Dublin University, O'Connor took part in the Irish revolution and was also for some years a director of the famed Abbey Theatre in Dublin. A most prolific writer, he is the author of some twenty collections of short stories, most of them concerned with Irish life. The Stories of Frank O'Connor appeared in 1952, other collections following. He lived in the United States for many years, teaching at Harvard, Northwestern, and Stanford. "Frank O'Connor" is a pseudonym for Michael O'Donovan.

My Oedipus Complex

Father was in the army all through the war—the first war, I mean —so, up to the age of five, I never saw much of him, and what I saw did not worry me. Sometimes I woke and there was a big figure in khaki peering down at me in the candlelight. Sometimes in the early morning I heard the slamming of the front door and the clatter of nailed boots down the cobbles of the lane. These were Father's entrances and exits. Like Santa Claus he came and went mysteriously.

In fact, I rather liked his visits, though it was an uncomfortable squeeze between Mother and him when I got into the big bed in the early morning. He smoked, which gave him a pleasant musty smell, and shaved, an operation of astounding interest. Each time he left a trail of souvenirs —model tanks and Gurkha knives with handles made of bullet cases, and German helmets and cap badges and button-sticks, and all sorts of military equipment—carefully stowed away in a long box on top of the wardrobe, in case they ever came in handy. There was a bit of the magpie about Father; he expected everything to come in handy. When his back was turned, Mother let me get a chair and rummage through his treasures. She didn't seem to think so highly of them as he did.

The war was the most peaceful period of my life. The window of my attic faced southeast. My mother had curtained it, but that had small effect. I always woke with the first light and, with all the responsibilities of the previous day melted, feeling myself rather like the sun, ready to illumine and rejoice. Life never seemed so simple and clear and full of possibilities as then. I put my feet out from under the clothes—I called them Mrs. Left and Mrs. Right—and invented dramatic situations for them in which they discussed the problems of the day. At least Mrs. Right did; she was very demonstrative, but I hadn't the same control of Mrs. Left, so she mostly contented herself with nodding agreement.

They discussed what Mother and I should do during the day, what Santa Claus should give a fellow for Christmas, and what steps should be taken to brighten the home. There was that little matter of the baby, for instance. Mother and I could never agree about that. Ours was the only house in the terrace without a new baby, and Mother said we couldn't afford one till Father came back from the war because they cost seventeen and six. That showed how simple she was. The Geneys up the road had a baby, and everyone knew they couldn't afford seventeen and six. It was probably a cheap baby, and Mother wanted something really good, but I felt she was too exclusive. The Geneys' baby would have done us fine.

Having settled my plans for the day, I got up, put a chair under the attic window, and lifted the frame high enough to stick out my head. The window overlooked the front gardens of the terrace behind ours, and beyond these it looked over a deep valley to the tall, red-brick houses terraced up the opposite hillside, which were all still in shadow, while those at our side of the valley were all lit up, though with long strange shadows that made them seem unfamiliar; rigid and painted.

After that I went into Mother's room and climbed into the big bed. She woke and I began to tell her of my schemes. By this time, though I never seem to have noticed it, I was petrified in my night-shirt, and I thawed as I talked until, the last frost melted, I fell asleep beside her and woke again only when I heard her below in the kitchen, making the breakfast.

After breakfast we went into town; heard Mass at St. Augustine's and said a prayer for Father, and did the shopping. If the afternoon was fine we either went for a walk in the country or a visit to Mother's great friend in the convent, Mother St. Dominic. Mother had them all praying for Father, and every night, going to bed, I asked God to send him back safe from the war to us. Little, indeed, did I know what I was praying for!

One morning, I got into the big bed, and there, sure enough, was Father in his usual Santa Claus manner, but later, instead of uniform, he put on his best blue suit, and Mother was as pleased as anything. I saw nothing to be pleased about, because, out of uniform, Father was altogether less interesting, but she only beamed, and explained that our prayers had been answered, and off we went to Mass to thank God for having brought Father safely home.

The irony of it! That very day when he came in to dinner he took off his boots and put on his slippers, donned the dirty old cap he wore about the house to save him from colds, crossed his legs, and began to talk gravely to Mother, who looked anxious. Naturally, I disliked her looking anxious, because it destroyed her good looks, so I interrupted him.

"Just a moment, Larry!" she said gently.

This was only what she said when we had boring visitors, so I attached no importance to it and went on talking.

"Do be quiet, Larry!" she said impatiently. "Don't you hear me talking to Daddy?"

This was the first time I had heard those ominous words, "talking to Daddy," and I couldn't help feeling that if this was how God answered prayers, he couldn't listen to them very attentively.

"Why are you talking to Daddy?" I asked with as great a show of indifference as I could muster.

"Because Daddy and I have business to discuss. Now, don't interrupt again!"

In the afternoon, at Mother's request, Father took me for a walk. This time we went into town instead of out to the country, and I thought at first, in my usual optimistic way, that it might be an improvement. It was nothing of the sort. Father and I had quite different notions of a walk in town. He had no proper interest in trams, ships, and horses, and the only thing that seemed to divert him was talking to fellows as old as himself. When I wanted to stop he simply went on, dragging me behind him by the hand; when he wanted to stop I had no alternative but to do the same. I noticed that it seemed to be a sign that he wanted to stop for a long time whenever he leaned against a wall. The second time I saw him do it I got wild. He seemed to be settling himself forever. I pulled him by the coat and trousers, but, unlike Mother who, if you were too persistent, got into a wax and said: "Larry, if you don't behave yourself, I'll give you a good slap," Father had an extraordinary capacity for amiable inattention. I sized him up and wondered would I cry, but he seemed to be too remote to be annoyed even by that. Really, it was like going for a walk with a mountain! He either ignored the wrenching and pummeling entirely, or else glanced down with a grin of amusement from his peak. I had never met anyone so absorbed in himself as he seemed.

At teatime, "talking to Daddy" began again, complicated this time by the fact that he had an evening paper, and every few minutes he put it down and told Mother something new out of it. I felt this was foul play. Man for man, I was prepared to compete with him any time for Mother's attention, but when he had it all made up for him by other people it left me no chance. Several times I tried to change the subject without success.

"You must be quiet while Daddy is reading, Larry," Mother said impatiently.

It was clear that she either genuinely liked talking to Father better than talking to me, or else that he had some terrible hold on her which made her afraid to admit the truth.

"Mummy," I said that night when she was tucking me up, "do you think if I prayed hard God would send Daddy back to the war?"

She seemed to think about that for a moment.

"No, dear," she said with a smile. "I don't think he would."

"Why wouldn't he, Mummy?"

"Because there isn't a war any longer, dear."

"But, Mummy, couldn't God make another war, if he liked?"

"He wouldn't like to, dear. It's not God who makes wars, but bad people."

"Oh!" I said.

I was disappointed about that. I began to think that God wasn't quite what he was cracked up to be.

Next morning I woke at my usual hour, feeling like a bottle of champagne. I put out my feet and invented a long conversation in which Mrs. Right talked of the trouble she had with her own father till she put him in the Home. I didn't quite know what the Home was but it sounded the right place for Father. Then I got my chair and stuck my head out of the attic window. Dawn was just breaking, with a guilty air that made me feel I had caught it in the act. My head bursting with stories and schemes, I stumbled in next door, and in the half-darkness scrambled into the big bed. There was no room at Mother's side so I had to get between her and Father. For the time being I had forgotten about him, and for several minutes

I sat bolt upright, racking my brains to know what I could do with him. He was taking up more than his fair share of the bed, and I couldn't get comfortable, so I gave him several kicks that made him grunt and stretch. He made room all right, though. Mother waked and felt for me. I settled back comfortably in the warmth of the bed with my thumb in my mouth.

"Mummy!" I hummed, loudly and contentedly.

"Sssh! dear," she whispered. "Don't wake Daddy!"

This was a new development, which threatened to be even more serious than "talking to Daddy." Life without my early-morning conferences was unthinkable.

"Why?" I asked severely.

"Because poor Daddy is tired."

This seemed to me a quite inadequate reason, and I was sickened by the sentimentality of her "poor Daddy." I never liked that sort of gush; it always struck me as insincere.

"Oh!" I said lightly. Then in my most winning tone: "Do you know where I want to go with you today, Mummy?"

"No, dear," she sighed.

"I want to go down the Glen and fish for thornybacks with my new net, and then I want to go out to the Fox and Hounds, and—"

"Don't-wake-Daddy!" she hissed angrily, clapping her hand across my mouth.

But it was too late. He was awake, or nearly so. He grunted and reached for the matches. Then he stared incredulously at his watch.

"Like a cup of tea, dear?" asked Mother in a meek, hushed voice I had never heard her use before. It sounded almost as though she were afraid.

"Tea?" he exclaimed indignantly. "Do you know what the time is?"

"And after that I want to go up the Rathcooney Road," I said loudly, afraid I'd forget something in all those interruptions.

"Go to sleep at once, Larry!" she said sharply.

I began to snivel. I couldn't concentrate, the way that pair went on, and smothering my early-morning schemes was like burying a family from the cradle.

Father said nothing, but lit his pipe and sucked it, looking out into the shadows without minding Mother or me. I knew he was mad. Every time I made a remark Mother hushed me irritably. I was mortified. I felt it wasn't fair; there was even something sinister in it. Every time I had pointed out to her the waste of making two beds when we could both sleep in one, she had told me it was healthier like that, and now here was this man, this stranger, sleeping with her without the least regard for her health!

He got up early and made tea, but though he brought Mother a cup he brought none for me.

"Mummy," I shouted, "I want a cup of tea, too."

"Yes, dear," she said patiently. "You can drink from Mummy's saucer."

That settled it. Either Father or I would have to leave the house. I didn't want to drink from Mother's saucer; I wanted to be treated as an equal in my own home, so, just to spite her, I drank it all and left none for her. She took that quietly, too.

But that night when she was putting me to bed she said gently:

"Larry, I want you to promise me something."

"What is it?" I asked.

"Not to come in and disturb poor Daddy in the morning. Promise?"

"Poor Daddy" again! I was becoming suspicious of everything involving that quite impossible man.

"Why?" I asked.

"Because poor Daddy is worried and tired and he doesn't sleep well."

"Why doesn't he, Mummy?"

"Well, you know, don't you, that while he was at the war Mummy got the pennies from the Post Office?"

"From Miss MacCarthy?"

"That's right. But now, you see, Miss MacCarthy hasn't any more pennies, so Daddy must go out and find us some. You know what would happen if he couldn't?"

"No," I said, "tell us."

"Well, I think we might have to go out and beg for them like the poor old woman on Fridays. We wouldn't like that, would we?"

"No," I agreed. "We wouldn't."

"So you'll promise not to come in and wake him?"

"Promise."

Mind you, I meant that. I knew pennies were a serious matter, and I was all against having to go out and beg like the old woman on Fridays. Mother laid out all my toys in a complete ring round the bed so that, whatever way I got out, I was bound to fall over one of them.

When I woke I remembered my promise all right. I got up and sat on the floor and played—for hours, it seemed to me. Then I got my chair and looked out the attic window for more hours. I wished it was time for Father to wake; I wished someone would make me a cup of tea. I didn't feel in the least like the sun; instead, I was bored and so very, very cold! I simply longed for the warmth and depth of the big featherbed.

At last I could stand it no longer. I went into the next room. As there was still no room at Mother's side I climbed over her and she woke with a start.

"Larry," she whispered, gripping my arm very tightly, "what did you promise?"

"But I did, Mummy," I wailed, caught in the very act. "I was quiet for ever so long."

"Oh, dear, and you're perished!" she said sadly, feeling me all over. "Now, if I let you stay will you promise not to talk?"

"But I want to talk, Mummy," I wailed.

"That has nothing to do with it," she said with a firmness that was new to me. "Daddy wants to sleep. Now, do you understand that?"

I understood it only too well. I wanted to talk, he wanted to sleep—whose house was it, anyway?

"Mummy," I said with equal firmness, "I think it would be healthier for Daddy to sleep in his own bed."

That seemed to stagger her, because she said nothing for a while.

"Now, once for all," she went on, "you're to be perfectly quiet or go back to your own bed. Which is it to be?"

The injustice of it got me down. I had convicted her out of her own mouth of inconsistency and unreasonableness, and she hadn't even attempted to reply. Full of spite, I gave Father a kick, which she didn't notice but which made him grunt and open his eyes in alarm.

"What time is it?" he asked in a panic-stricken voice, not looking at Mother but the door, as if he saw someone there.

"It's early yet," she replied soothingly. "It's only the child. Go to sleep again. . . . Now, Larry," she added, getting out of bed, "you've wakened Daddy and you must go back."

This time, for all her quiet air, I knew she meant it, and knew that my principal rights and privileges were as good as lost unless I asserted them at once. As she lifted me, I gave a screech, enough to wake the dead, not to mind Father. He groaned.

"That damn child! Doesn't he ever sleep?"

"It's only a habit, dear," she said quietly, though I could see she was vexed.

"Well, it's time he got out of it," shouted Father, beginning to heave in the bed. He suddenly gathered all the bedclothes about him, turned to the wall, and then looked back over his shoulder with nothing showing only two small, spiteful, dark eyes. The man looked very wicked.

To open the bedroom door, Mother had to let me down, and I broke free and dashed for the farthest corner, screeching. Father sat bolt upright in bed.

"Shut up, you little puppy!" he said in a choking voice.

I was so astonished that I stopped screeching. Never, never had anyone spoken to me in that tone before. I looked at him incredulously and saw his face convulsed with rage. It was only then that I fully realized how God had codded me, listening to my prayers for the safe return of this monster.

"Shut up, you!" I bawled, beside myself.

"What's that you said?" shouted Father, making a wild leap out of bed.

"Mick, Mick!" cried Mother. "Don't you see the child isn't used to you?"

"I see he's better fed than taught," snarled Father, waving his arms wildly. "He wants his bottom smacked."

All his previous shouting was as nothing to these obscene words referring to my person. They really made my blood boil.

"Smack your own!" I screamed hysterically. "Smack your own! Shut up! Shut up!"

At this he lost his patience and let fly at me. He did it with the lack of conviction you'd expect of a man under Mother's horrified eyes, and it ended up as a mere tap, but the sheer indignity of being struck at all by a stranger, a total stranger who had cajoled his way back from the war into our big bed as a result of my innocent intercession, made me completely dotty. I shrieked and shrieked, and danced in my bare feet, and Father, looking awkward and hairy in nothing but a short grey army shirt, glared down at me like a mountain out for murder. I think it must have been then that I realized he was jealous too. And there stood Mother in her night-dress, looking as if her heart was broken between us. I hoped she felt as she looked. It seemed to me that she deserved it all.

From that morning out my life was a hell. Father and I were enemies, open and avowed. We conducted a series of skirmishes against one another, he trying to steal my time with Mother and I his. When she was sitting on my bed, telling me a story, he took to looking for some pair of old boots which he alleged he had left behind him at the beginning of the war. While he talked to Mother I played loudly with my toys to show my total lack of concern. He created a terrible scene one evening when he came in from work and found me at his box, playing with his regimental badges, Gurkha knives and button-sticks. Mother got up and took the box from me.

"You mustn't play with Daddy's toys unless he lets you, Larry," she said severely. "Daddy doesn't play with yours."

For some reason Father looked at her as if she had struck him and then turned away with a scowl.

"Those are not toys," he growled, taking down the box again to see had I lifted anything. "Some of those curios are very rare and valuable."

But as time went on I saw more and more how he managed to alienate Mother and me. What made it worse was that I couldn't grasp his method or see what attraction he had for Mother. In every possible way he was less winning than I. He had a common accent and made noises at his tea. I thought for a while that it might be the newspapers she was interested in, so I made up bits of news of my own to read to her. Then I thought it might be the smoking, which I personally thought attractive, and took his pipes and went round the house dribbling into them till he caught me. I even made noises at my tea, but Mother only told me I was disgusting. It all seemed to hinge round that unhealthy habit of sleeping together, so I made a point of dropping into their bedroom and nosing round, talking to myself, so that they wouldn't know I was watching them, but they were never up to anything that I could see. In the end it beat me. It seemed to depend on being grown-up and giving people rings, and I realized I'd have to wait.

But at the same time I wanted him to see that I was only waiting, not giving up the fight. One evening when he was being particularly obnoxious, chattering away well above my head, I let him have it.

"Mummy," I said, "do you know what I'm going to do when I grow up?"

"No, dear," she replied. "What?"

"I'm going to marry you," I said quietly.

Father gave a great guffaw out of him, but he didn't take me in. I knew it must only be pretense. And Mother, in spite of everything, was pleased. I felt she was probably relieved to know that one day Father's hold on her would be broken.

"Won't that be nice?" she said with a smile.

"It'll be very nice," I said confidently. "Because we're going to have lots and lots of babies."

"That's right, dear," she said placidly. "I think we'll have one soon, and then you'll have plenty of company."

I was no end pleased about that because it showed that in spite of the way she gave in to Father she still considered my wishes. Besides, it would put the Geneys in their place.

It didn't turn out like that, though. To begin with, she was very preoccupied—I supposed about where she would get the seventeen and six—and though Father took to staying out late in the evenings it did me no particular good. She stopped taking me for walks, became as touchy as blazes, and smacked me for nothing at all. Sometimes I wished I'd never mentioned the confounded baby—I seemed to have a genius for bringing calamity on myself.

And calamity it was! Sonny arrived in the most appalling hullabaloo—even that much he couldn't do without a fuss—and from the first moment I disliked him. He was a difficult child—so far as I was concerned he was always difficult—and demanded far too much attention. Mother was simply silly about him, and couldn't see when he was only showing off. As company he was worse than useless. He slept all day, and I had to go round the house on tiptoe to avoid waking him. It wasn't any longer a question of not waking Father. The slogan now was "Don't-wake-Sonny!" I couldn't understand why the child wouldn't sleep at the proper time, so whenever Mother's back was turned I woke him. Sometimes to keep him awake I pinched him as well. Mother caught me at it one day and gave me a most unmerciful flaking.

One evening, when Father was coming in from work, I was playing trains in the front garden. I let on not to notice him; instead, I pretended to be talking to myself, and said in a loud voice: "If another bloody baby comes into this house, I'm going out."

Father stopped dead and looked at me over his shoulder.

"What's that you said?" he asked sternly.

"I was only talking to myself," I replied, trying to conceal my panic. "It's private."

He turned and went in without a word. Mind you, I intended it as a solemn warning, but its effect was quite different. Father started being quite nice to me. I could understand that, of course. Mother was quite sickening about Sonny. Even at mealtimes she'd get up and gawk at him in the cradle with an idiotic smile, and tell Father to do the same. He was always polite about it, but he looked so puzzled you could see he didn't know what she was talking about. He complained of the way Sonny cried at night, but she only got cross and said that Sonny never cried except when there was something up with him—which was a flaming lie, because Sonny never had anything up with him, and only cried for attention. It was really painful to see how simple-minded she was. Father wasn't attractive, but he had a fine intelligence. He saw through Sonny, and now he knew that I saw through him as well.

One night I woke with a start. There was someone beside me in the bed. For one wild moment I felt sure it must be Mother, having come to her senses and left Father for good, but then I heard Sonny in convulsions in the next room, and Mother saying: "There! There! There!" and I knew it wasn't she. It was Father. He was lying beside me, wide awake, breathing hard and apparently as mad as hell.

After a while it came to me what he was mad about. It was his turn now. After turning me out of the big bed, he had been turned out himself. Mother had no consideration now for anyone but that poisonous pup, Sonny. I couldn't help feeling sorry for Father. I had been through it all myself, and even at that age I was magnanimous. I began to stroke him down and say: "There! There!" He wasn't exactly responsive.

"Aren't you asleep either?" he snarled.

"Ah, come on and put your arm around us, can't you?" I said, and he did, in a sort of way. Gingerly, I suppose, is how you'd describe it. He was very bony but better than nothing.

At Christmas he went out of his way to buy me a really nice model railway.

§ FOR COMMENT

What does the author accomplish by telling his story in the first person? How much distance does the narrator have on his five-year-old self? How does this distance affect the telling of the story and the tone which it takes? What is that tone? Is it functional?

The significance of the title is obvious, as is the working out of the Oedipal pattern in the story. Does this obviousness detract from the story or add to it, or is it possible that the very obviousness of it adds to the humor of the piece? What are some of the comic situations? Would you say they are universal in character?

If you were not familiar with the Oedipus complex, would the story still make sense? Suppose the story were called something else, would the Oedipal situation still be clear?

Did you notice an Oedipal pattern in some of the other stories you read? Compare "The Rocking-Horse Winner," for example, and "My Kinsman, Major Molineux." If you can locate an Oedipal pattern in either or both of these stories, how does it function with relation to the themes of the stories?

Eudora Welty § 1909–

Miss Welty was born in Jackson, Mississippi, and has spent most of her life there. Although she has published novels, among them Delta Wedding *(1946) and* The Ponder Heart *(1954), her real achievement is in the short story. Recognized as one of the master craftsmen of this form, she is one of a group of Southern writers to receive wide critical acclaim. Her first published volume of short stories,* A Curtain of Green *(1941), showed her ability to render surface detail with remarkable verisimilitude and yet to give that detail an element of the fantastic, the unreal. She is at home with a variety of subjects, moods, and points of view, and her style is at once sensitive and evocative. Her use of symbols and depth psychology makes her stories complex and difficult, but they are among the best in our language.*

Petrified Man

"Reach in my purse and git me a cigarette without no powder in it if you kin, Mrs. Fletcher, honey," said Leota to her ten-o'clock shampoo-and-set customer. "I don't like no perfumed cigarettes."

Mrs. Fletcher gladly reached over to the lavender shelf under the lavender-framed mirror, shook a hair net loose from the clasp of the patent-leather bag, and slapped her hand down quickly on a powder puff which burst out when the purse was opened.

"Why, look at the peanuts, Leota!" said Mrs. Fletcher in her marveling voice.

"Honey, them goobers has been in my purse a week if they's been in it a day. Mrs. Pike bought them peanuts."

"Who's Mrs. Pike?" asked Mrs. Fletcher, settling back. Hidden in this den of curling fluid and henna packs, separated by a lavender swing door from the other customers, who were being gratified in other booths, she could give her curiosity its freedom. She looked expectantly at the black part in Leota's yellow curls as she bent to light the cigarette.

"Mrs. Pike is this lady from New Orleans," said Leota, puffing, and pressing into Mrs. Fletcher's scalp with strong red-nailed fingers. "A friend, not a customer. You see, like maybe I told you last time, me and Fred and Sal and Joe all had us a fuss, so Sal and Joe up and moved out, so we didn't do a thing but rent out their room. So we rented it to Mrs. Pike. And Mr. Pike." She flicked an ash into the basket of dirty towels. "Mrs. Pike is a very decided blonde. *She* bought me the peanuts."

"She must be cute," said Mrs. Fletcher.

"Honey, 'cute' ain't the word for what she is. I'm tellin' you, Mrs. Pike is attractive. She has her a good time. She's got a sharp eye out, Mrs. Pike has."

She dashed the comb through the air, and paused dramatically as a cloud of Mrs. Fletcher's hennaed hair floated out of the lavender teeth like a small storm cloud.

"Hair fallin'."

"Aw, Leota."

"Uh-huh, commencin' to fall out," said Leota, combing again, and letting fall another cloud.

"Is it any dandruff in it?" Mrs. Fletcher was frowning, her hair-line eyebrows diving down toward her nose, and her wrinkled, beady-lashed eyelids batting with concentration.

"Nope." She combed again. "Just fallin' out."

"Bet it was that last perm'nent you gave me that did it," Mrs. Fletcher said cruelly. "Remember you cooked me fourteen minutes."

"You had fourteen minutes comin' to you," said Leota with finality.

"Bound to be somethin'," persisted Mrs. Fletcher. "Dandruff, dandruff. I couldn't of caught a thing like that from Mr. Fletcher, could I?"

"Well," Leota answered at last, "you know what I heard in here yestiddy, one of Thelma's ladies was settin' over yonder in Thelma's booth gittin' a machineless, and I don't mean to insist or insinuate or anything, Mrs. Fletcher, but Thelma's lady just happ'med to throw out —I forgotten what she was talkin' about at the time—that you was p-r-e-g., and lots of times that'll make your hair do awful funny, fall out and God knows what all. It just ain't our fault is the way I look at it."

There was a pause. The women stared at each other in the mirror.

"Who was it?" demanded Mrs. Fletcher.

"Honey, I really couldn't say," said Leota. "Not that you look it."

"Where's Thelma? I'll get it out of her," said Mrs. Fletcher.

"Now, honey I wouldn't go and git mad over a little thing like that," Leota said, combing hastily, as though to hold Mrs. Fletcher down by the hair. "I'm sure it was somebody didn't mean no harm in the world. How far gone are you?"

"Just wait," said Mrs. Fletcher, and shrieked for Thelma, who came in and took a drag from Leota's cigarette.

"Thelma, honey, throw your mind back to yestiddy if you kin," said Leota, drenching Mrs. Fletcher's hair with a thick fluid and catching the overflow in a cold wet towel at her neck.

"Well, I got my lady half wound for a spiral," said Thelma doubtfully.

"This won't take but a minute," said Leota. "Who is it you got in there, old Horse Face? Just cast your mind back and try to remember who your lady was yestiddy who happ'm to mention that my customer was pregnant, that's all. She's dead to know."

Thelma drooped her blood-red lips and looked over Mrs. Fletcher's head into the mirror. "Why, honey, I ain't got the faintest," she breathed. "I really don't recollect the faintest. But I'm sure she meant no harm. I declare, I forgot my hair finally got combed and thought it was a stranger behind me."

"Was it that Mrs. Hutchinson?" Mrs. Fletcher was tensely polite.

"Mrs. Hutchinson? Oh, Mrs. Hutchinson." Thelma batted her eyes. "Naw, precious, she come on Thursday and didn't ev'm mention your name. I doubt if she ev'm knows you're on the way."

"Thelma!" cried Leota staunchly.

"All I know is, whoever it is'll be sorry someday. Why, I just barely knew it myself!" cried Mrs. Fletcher. "Just let her wait!"

"Why? What're you gonna do to her?"

It was a child's voice, and the women looked down. A little boy was making tents with aluminum wave pinchers on the floor under the sink.

"Billy Boy, hon, mustn't bother nice ladies," Leota smiled. She slapped him brightly and behind her back waved Thelma out of the booth. "Ain't Billy Boy a sight? Only three years old and already just nuts about the beauty-parlor business."

"I never saw him here before," said Mrs. Fletcher, still unmollified.

"He ain't been here before, that's how come," said Leota. "He belongs to Mrs. Pike. She got her a job but it was Fay's Millinery. He oughtn't to try on those ladies' hats, they come down over his eyes like I don't know what. They just git to look ridiculous, that's what, an' of course he's gonna put 'em on: hats. They tole Mrs. Pike they didn't appreciate him hangin' around there. Here, he couldn't hurt a thing."

"Well! I don't like children that much," said Mrs. Fletcher.

"Well!" said Leota moodily.

"Well! I'm almost tempted not to have this one," said Mrs. Fletcher. "That Mrs. Hutchinson! Just looks straight through you when she sees you on the street and then spits at you behind your back."

"Mr. Fletcher would beat you on the head if you didn't have it now," said Leota reasonably. "After going this far."

Mrs. Fletcher sat up straight. "Mr. Fletcher can't do a thing with me."

"He can't!" Leota winked at herself in the mirror.

"No siree, he can't. If he so much as raises his voice against me, he knows good and well I'll have one of my sick headaches, and then I'm just not fit to live with. And if I really look that pregnant already——"

"Well, now, honey, I just want you to know—I habm't told any of my ladies and I ain't goin' to tell 'em—even that you're losin' your hair. You just get you one of those Stork-a-Lure dresses and stop worryin'. What people don't know don't hurt anybody, as Mrs. Pike says."

"Did you tell Mrs. Pike?" asked Mrs. Fletcher sulkily.

"Well, Mrs. Fletcher, look, you ain't ever goin' to lay eyes on Mrs. Pike or her lay eyes on you, so what diffunce does it make in the long run?"

"I knew it!" Mrs. Fletcher deliberately nodded her head so as to destroy a ringlet Leota was working on behind her ear. "Mrs. Pike!"

Leota sighed. "I reckon I might as well tell you. It wasn't any more Thelma's lady tole me you was pregnant than a bat."

"Not Mrs. Hutchinson?"

"Naw, Lord! It was Mrs. Pike."

"Mrs. Pike!" Mrs Fletcher could only sputter and let curling fluid roll into the ear. "How could Mrs. Pike possibly know I was pregnant or otherwise, when she doesn't even know me? The nerve of some people!"

"Well, here's how it was. Remember Sunday?"

"Yes," said Mrs. Fletcher.

"Sunday, Mrs. Pike an' me was all by ourself. Mr. Pike and Fred had gone over to Eagle Lake, sayin' they was goin' to catch 'em some fish, but they didn't, a course. So we was settin' in Mrs. Pike's car, is a 1939 Dodge—"

"1939, eh," said Mrs. Fletcher.

"—An' we was gettin' us a Jax beer apiece—that's the beer that Mrs. Pike says is made right in N.O., so she won't drink no other kind. So I seen you drive up to the drugstore an' run in for just a secont, leavin' I reckon Mr. Fletcher in the car, an' come runnin' out with looked like a perscription. So I says to Mrs. Pike, just to be makin' talk, 'Right yonder's Mrs. Fletcher, and I reckon that's Mr. Fletcher—she's one of my regular customers,' I says."

"I had on a figured print," said Mrs. Fletcher tentatively.

"You sure did," agreed Leota. "So Mrs. Pike, she give you a good look—she's very observant, a good judge of character, cute as a minute, you know—and she says, 'I bet you another Jax that lady's three months on the way.'"

"What gall!" said Mrs. Fletcher. "Mrs. Pike!"

"Mrs. Pike ain't goin' to bite you," said Leota. "Mrs. Pike is a lovely girl, you'd be crazy about her, Mrs. Fletcher. But she can't sit still a minute. We went to the travelin' freak show yestiddy after work. I got through early—nine o'clock. In the vacant store next door? What, you ain't been?"

"No, I despise freaks," declared Mrs. Fletcher.

"Aw. Well, honey, talkin' about bein' pregnant an' all, you ought to see those twins in a bottle, you really owe it to yourself."

"What twins?" asked Mrs. Fletcher out of the side of her mouth.

"Well, honey, they got these two twins in a bottle, see? Born joined plumb together—dead a course." Leota dropped her voice into a soft lyrical hum. "They was about this long—pardon—must of been full time, all right, wouldn't you say?—an' they had these two heads an' two faces an' four arms an' four legs, all kind of joined *here.* See, this face looked this-a-way, and the other face looked that-a-way, over their shoulder, see. Kinda pathetic."

"Glah!" said Mrs. Fletcher disapprovingly.

"Well, ugly? Honey, I mean to tell you—their parents was first cousins and all like that. Billy Boy, git me a fresh towel from off Teeny's stack—this 'n's wringin' wet—an' quit ticklin' my ankles with that curler. I declare! He don't miss nothin'."

"Me and Mr. Fletcher aren't one speck of kin, or he could never of had me," said Mrs. Fletcher placidly.

"Of course not!" protested Leota. "Neither is me an' Fred, not that we know of. Well, honey, what Mrs. Pike liked was the pygmies. They've got these pygmies down there, too, an' Mrs. Pike was just wild about 'em. You know, the tee-niest men in the universe? Well honey, they can rest back on their little bohunkus an' roll around an' you can't hardly tell if they're sittin' or standin'. That'll give you some idea. They're about forty-two years old. Just suppose it was your husband!"

"Well, Mr. Fletcher is five foot nine and one half," said Mrs. Fletcher quickly.

"Fred's five foot ten," said Leota, "but I tell him he's still a shrimp, account of I'm so tall." She made a deep wave over Mrs. Fletcher's other temple with the comb. "Well, these pygmies are a kind of dark brown, Mrs. Fletcher. Not bad-lookin' for what they are, you know."

"I wouldn't care for them," said Mrs. Fletcher. "What does that Mrs. Pike see in them?"

"Aw, I don't know," said Leota. "She's just cute, that's all. But they got this man, this petrified man, that ever'-thing ever since he was nine years old, when it goes through his digestion, see, somehow Mrs. Pike says it goes to his joints and has been turning to stone."

"How awful!" said Mrs. Fletcher.

"He's forty-two too. That looks like a bad age."

"Who said so, that Mrs. Pike? I bet she's forty-two," said Mrs. Fletcher.

"Naw," said Leota, "Mrs. Pike's thirty-three, born in January, and

Aquarian. He could move his head—like this. A course his head and mind ain't a joint, so to speak, and I guess his stomach ain't either—not anyways. But see—his food, he eats it, and goes down, see, and then he digests it"— Leota rose on her toes for an instant—"and it goes out to his joints and before you can say 'Jack Robinson,' it's stone—pure stone. He's turning to stone. How'd you like to be married to a guy like that? All he can do, he can move his head just a quarter of an inch. A course he *looks* just *terrible*."

"I should think he would," said Mrs. Fletcher frostily. "Mr. Fletcher takes bending exercises every night of the world. I make him."

"All Fred does is lay around the house like a rug. I wouldn't be surprised if he woke up someday and couldn't move. The petrified man just sat there moving his quarter of an inch though," said Leota reminiscently.

"Did Mrs. Pike like the petrified man?" asked Mrs. Fletcher.

"Not as much as she did the others," said Leota deprecatingly. "And then she likes a man to be a good dresser, and all that."

"Is Mr. Pike a good dresser?" asked Mrs. Fletcher skeptically.

"Oh, well, yeah," said Leota, "but he's twelve-fourteen years older 'n her. She ast Lady Evangeline about him."

"Who's Lady Evangeline?" asked Mrs. Fletcher.

"Well, it's this mind reader they got in the freak show," said Leota. "Was real good. Lady Evangeline is her name, and if I had another dollar I wouldn't do a thing but have my other palm read. She had what Mrs. Pike said was 'sixth mind' but she had the worst manicure I ever saw on a living person."

"What did she tell Mrs. Pike?" asked Mrs. Fletcher.

"She told her Mr. Pike was as true to her as he could be and, besides, would come into some money."

"Humph!" said Mrs. Fletcher. "What does he do?"

"I can't tell," said Leota, "because he don't work. Lady Evangeline didn't tell me near enough about my nature or anything. And I would like to go back and find out some more about this boy. Used to go with this boy got married to this girl. Oh, shoot, that was about three and a half years ago, when you was still goin' to the Robert E. Lee Beauty Shop in Jackson. He married her for her money. Another fortuneteller tole me that at the time. So I'm not in love with him any more, anyway, besides being married to Fred, but Mrs. Pike thought, just for the hell of it, see, to ask Lady Evangeline was he happy."

"Does Mrs. Pike know everything about you already?" asked Mrs. Fletcher unbelievingly. "Mercy!"

"Oh yeah, I tole her ever'thing about ever'thing, from now on back to I don't know when—to when I first started goin' out," said Leota. "So I ast Lady Evangeline for one of my questions, was he happily married, and she says, just like she was glad I ask her, 'Honey,' she says, 'naw, he isn't. You write down this day, March 8, 1941,' she says, 'and mock it down three years from today him and her won't be occupyin' the same bed.' There it is, up on the wall with them other dates—see, Mrs. Fletcher? And she says, 'Child, you ought to be glad you didn't git him, because he's so mercenary.' So I'm glad I married Fred. He sure ain't mercenary, money don't mean a thing to him. But I sure would like to go back and have my other palm read."

"Did Mrs. Pike believe in what the fortuneteller said?" asked Mrs. Fletcher in a superior tone of voice.

"Lord, yes, she's from New Orleans. Ever'body in New Orleans believes ever'thing spooky. One of 'em in New Orleans before it was raided says to Mrs. Pike one summer she was goin' to go from state to state and meet some gray-headed men, and, sure enough, she says she went on a beautician convention up to Chicago. . . ."

"Oh!" said Mrs. Fletcher. "Oh, is Mrs. Pike a beautician too?"

"Sure she is," protested Leota. "She's a beautician. I'm goin' to git her in here if I can. Before she married. But it don't leave you. She says sure enough, there was three men who was a very large part of making her trip what it was, and they all three had gray in their hair and they went in six states. Got Christmas cards from 'em. Billy Boy, go see if Thelma's got any dry cotton. Look how Mrs. Fletcher's a-drippin'."

"Where did Mrs. Pike meet Mr. Pike?" asked Mrs. Fletcher primly.

"On another train," said Leota.

"I met Mr. Fletcher, or rather he met me, in a rental library," said Mrs. Fletcher with dignity, as she watched the net come down over her head.

"Honey, me an' Fred, we met in a rumble seat eight months ago and we was practically on what you might call the way to the altar inside of half an hour," said Leota in a guttural voice, and bit a bobby pin open. "Course it don't last. Mrs. Pike says nothin' like that ever lasts."

"Mr. Fletcher and myself are as much in love as the day we married," said Mrs. Fletcher belligerently as Leota stuffed cotton into her ears.

"Mrs. Pike says it don't last," repeated Leota in a louder voice. "Now go git under the dryer. You can turn yourself on can't you? I'll be back to comb you out. Durin' lunch I promised to give Mrs. Pike a facial. You know—free. Her bein' in the business, so to speak."

"I bet she needs one," said Mrs. Fletcher, letting the swing door fly back against Leota. "Oh, pardon me."

A week later, on time for her appointment, Mrs. Fletcher sank heavily into Leota's chair after first removing a drugstore rental book, called *Life is Like That,* from the seat. She stared in a discouraged way into the mirror.

"You can tell it when I'm sitting down, all right," she said.

Leota seemed preoccupied and stood shaking out a lavender cloth. She began to pin it around Mrs. Fletcher's neck in silence.

"I said you sure can tell it when I'm sitting straight on and coming at you this way," Mrs. Fletcher said.

"Why, honey, now you can't," said Leota gloomily. "Why, I'd never know. If somebody was to come up to me on the street and say, 'Mrs. Fletcher is pregnant!' I'd say, 'Heck, she don't look it to me.'"

"If a certain party hadn't found it out and spread it around, it wouldn't be too late even now," said Mrs. Fletcher frostily, but Leota was almost choking her with the cloth, pinning it so tight, and she couldn't speak clearly. She paddled her hands in the air until Leota wearily loosened her.

"Listen, honey, you're just a virgin compared to Mrs. Montjoy," Leota was going on, still absent-minded. She bent Mrs. Fletcher back in the chair and, sighing, tossed liquid from a teacup onto her head and dug both hands into her scalp. 'You know Mrs. Montjoy—her husband's that premature-gray-headed fella?"

"She's in the Trojan Garden Club is all I know," said Mrs. Fletcher.

"Well, honey," said Leota, but in a weary voice, "she come in here not the week before and not the day before she had her baby—she come in here the very selfsame day, I mean to tell. Child, we was all plumb scared to death. There she was! Come for her shampoo an' set. Why, Mrs. Fletcher, in a hour an' twenty minutes she was layin' up there in the Babtist Hospital with a seb'm-pound son. It was that close a shave. I declare, if I hadn't been so tired I would of drank up a bottle of gin that night."

"What gall," said Mrs. Fletcher. "I never knew her at all well."

"See, her husband was waitin' outside in the car, and her bags was all packed an' in the back seat, an' she was all ready, 'cept she wanted her shampoo an' set. An' havin' one pain right after another. Her husband kep' comin' in here, scared-like, but couldn't do nothin' with her a course. She yelled bloody murder, too, but she always yelled her head off when I give her a perm'nent."

"She must of been crazy," said Mrs. Fletcher. "How did she look?"

"Shoot!" said Leota.

"Well, I can guess," said Mrs. Fletcher. "Awful."

"Just wanted to look pretty while she was havin' her baby is all," said Leota airily. "Course, we was glad to give the lady what she was after— that's our motto—but I bet a hour later she wasn't payin' no mind to them little end curls. I bet she wasn't thinkin' about she ought to have on a net. It wouldn't of done her no good if she had."

"No, I don't suppose it would," said Mrs. Fletcher.

"Yeah man! She was a-yellin'. Just like when I give her a perm'nent."

"Her husband ought to could make her behave. Don't it seem that way to you?" asked Mrs. Fletcher. "He ought to put his foot down."

"Ha," said Leota. "A lot he could do. Maybe some women is soft."

"Oh, you mistake me, I don't mean for her to get soft—far from it! Women have to stand up for themselves, or there's just no telling. But now you take me—I ask Mr. Fletcher's advice now and then, and he appreciates it, especially on something important, like is it time for a permanent—not that I've told him about the baby. He says, 'Why, dear, go ahead!' Just ask their *advice*."

"Huh! If I ever ast Fred's advice we'd be floatin' down the Yazoo River on a houseboat or somethin' by this time," said Leota. "I'm sick of Fred. I tole him to go over to Vicksburg."

"Is he going?" demanded Mrs. Fletcher.

"Sure. See, the fortuneteller. I went back and had my other palm read, since we've got to rent the room again—said my lover was goin' to work in Vicksburg, so I don't know who she could mean, unless she meant Fred. And Fred ain't workin' here—that much is so."

"Is he going to work in Vicksburg?" asked Mrs. Fletcher. "And——"

"Sure, Lady Evangeline said so. Said the future is going to be brighter than the present. He don't want to go, but I ain't gonna put up with nothin' like that. Lays around the house an' bulls—did bull—with that good-for-nothin' Mr. Pike. He says if he goes who'll cook, but I says I never get to eat anyway—not meals. Billy Boy, take Mrs. Grover that *Screen Secrets* and leg it."

Mrs. Fletcher heard stamping feet go out the door.

"Is that that Mrs. Pike's little boy here again?" she asked, sitting up gingerly.

"Yeah, that's still him." Leota stuck out her tongue.

Mrs. Fletcher could hardly believe her eyes. "Well! How's Mrs. Pike, your attractive new friend with the sharp eyes who spreads it around town that perfect strangers are pregnant?" she asked in a sweetened tone.

"Oh, Mizziz Pike." Leota combed Mrs. Fletcher's hair with heavy strokes.

"You act like you're tired," said Mrs. Fletcher.

"Tired? Feel like it's four o'clock in the afternoon already," said Leota. "I ain't told you the awful luck we had, me and Fred? It's the worst thing you ever heard of. Maybe *you* think Mrs. Pike's got sharp eyes. Shoot, there's a limit! Well, you know, we rented out our room to this Mr. and Mrs. Pike from New Orleans when Sal an' Joe Fentress got mad at us 'cause they drank up some homebrew we had in the closet—Sal an' Joe did. So, a week ago Sat'day Mr. and Mrs. Pike moved in. Well, I kinda fixed up the room, you know—put a sofa pillow on the couch and picked some ragged robins and put in a vase, but they never did say they appreciated it. Anyway, then I put some old magazines on the table."

"I think that was lovely," said Mrs. Fletcher.

"Wait. So, come night 'fore last, Fred and this Mr. Pike, who Fred just took up with, was back from they said they was fishin', bein' as neither one of 'em has got a job to his name, and we was all settin' around in their room. So Mrs. Pike was settin' there, readin' a old *Startling G-Man Tales* that was mine, mind you, I'd bought it myself, and all of a sudden she jumps!—into the air—you'd 'a' thought she'd set on a spider—an' says, 'Canfield'—ain't that silly, that's Mr. Pike—'Canfield, my God A'mighty,' she says, 'honey,' she says, 'we're rich, and you won't have to work.' Not that he turned one hand anyway. Well, me and Fred rushes over to her, and Mr. Pike, too, and there she sets, pointin' her finger at a photo in my copy of *Startling G-Man*. 'See that man?' yells Mrs. Pike. 'Remember him, Canfield?' 'Never forget a face,' says Mr. Pike. 'It's Mr. Petrie, that we stayed with him in the apartment next to ours in Toulouse Street in N.O. for six weeks. Mr. Petrie.' 'Well,' says Mrs. Pike, like she can't hold out one secont longer, 'Mr. Petrie is wanted for five hundred dollars cash, for rapin' four women in California, and I know where he is.' "

"Mercy!" said Mrs. Fletcher. "Where was he?"

At some time Leota had washed her hair and now she yanked her up by the back locks and sat her up.

"Know where he was?"

"I certainly don't," Mrs. Fletcher said. Her scalp hurt all over.

Leota flung her a towel around the top of her customer's head. "Nowhere else but in that freak show! I saw him just as plain as Mrs. Pike. *He* was the petrified man!"

"Who would ever have thought that!" cried Mrs. Fletcher sympathetically.

"So Mr. Pike says, 'Well, whatta you know about that,' an' he looks real hard at the photo and whistles. And she starts dancin' and singin' about their good luck. She meant our bad luck! I made a point of telling that fortuneteller the next time I saw her. I said, 'Listen, that magazine was layin' around the house for a month, and there was five hundred dollars in it for somebody. An' there was the freak show runnin' night an' day, not two steps away from my own beauty parlor, with Mr. Petrie just settin' there waitin'. An' it had to be Mr. and Mrs. Pike, almost perfect strangers.' "

"What gall," said Mrs. Fletcher. She was only sitting there, wrapped in a turban, but she did not mind.

"Fortunetellers don't care. And Mrs. Pike, she goes around actin' like she thinks she was Mrs. God," said Leota. "So they're goin' to leave tomorrow, Mr. and Mrs. Pike. And in the meantime I got to keep that mean, bad little ole kid here, gettin' under my feet ever' minute of the day an' talkin' back too."

"Have they gotten the five hundred dollars' reward already?" asked Mrs. Fletcher.

"Well," said Leota, "at first Mr. Pike didn't want to do anything about it. Can you feature that? Said he kinda liked that ole bird and said he was real nice to 'em, lent 'em money or somethin'. But Mrs. Pike simply tole him he could just go to hell, and I can see her point. She says, 'You ain't worked a lick in six months, and here I made five hundred dollars in two seconts, and what thanks do I get for it? You go to hell, Canfield,' she says. So," Leota went on in a despondent voice, "they called up the cops and they caught the ole bird, all right, right there in the freak show where I saw him with my own eyes, thinkin' he was petrified. He's the one. Did it under his real name—Mr. Petrie. Four women in California, all in the month of August. So Mrs. Pike gits five hundred dollars. And my magazine, and right next door to my beauty parlor. I cried all night, but Fred said it wasn't a bit of use and to go to sleep, because the whole thing was just sort of coincidence—you know: can't do nothin' about it. He says it put him clean out of the notion of goin' to Vicksburg for a few days till we rent out the room agin —no tellin' who we'll git this time."

"But can you imagine anybody knowing this old man, that's raped four women?" persisted Mrs. Fletcher, and she shuddered audibly. "Did Mrs. Pike *speak* to him when she met him in the freak show?"

Leota had begun to comb Mrs. Fletcher's hair. "I says to her, I says, 'I didn't notice you fallin' on his neck when he was the petrified man—don't tell me you didn't recognize your fine friend?' And she says, 'I didn't recognize him with that white powder all over his face. He just looked familiar,' Mrs. Pike says, 'and lots of people look familiar.' But she says that ole petrified man did put her in mind of somebody. She wondered who it was! Kep' her awake, which man she'd ever knew it reminded her of. So when she seen the photo, it all come to her. Like a flash. Mr. Petrie. The way he'd turn his head and look at her when she took him in his breakfast."

"Took him in his breakfast!" shrieked Mrs. Fletcher. "Listen—don't tell me. I'd 'a' felt something."

"Four women. I guess those women didn't have the faintest notion at the time they'd be worth a hundred an' twenty-five bucks apiece someday to Mrs. Pike. We ast her how old the fella was then, an' she says he musta had one foot in the grave, at least. Can you beat it?"

"Not really petrified at all, of course," said Mrs. Fletcher meditatively. She drew herself up. "I'd 'a' felt something," she said proudly.

"Shoot! I did feel somethin'," said Leota. "I tole Fred when I got home I felt so funny. I said, 'Fred, that ole petrified man sure did leave me with a funny feelin'.' He says, 'Funny-haha or funny-peculiar?' and I says, 'Funny-peculiar.'" She pointed her comb into the air emphatically.

"I'll bet you did," said Mrs. Fletcher.

They both heard a crackling noise.

Leota screamed, "Billy Boy! What you doin' in my purse?"

"Aw, I'm just eatin' these ole stale peanuts up," said Billy Boy.

"You come here to me!" screamed Leota, recklessly flinging down the comb, which scattered a whole ash tray full of bobby pins and knocked down a row of Coca-Cola bottles. "This is the last straw!"

"I caught him! I caught him!" giggled Mrs. Fletcher. "I'll hold him on my lap. You bad, bad boy, you! I guess I better learn how to spank little old bad boys," she said.

Leota's eleven-o'clock customer pushed open the swing door upon Leota paddling him heartily with the brush, while he gave angry but belittling screams which penetrated beyond the booth and filled the whole curious beauty parlor. From everywhere ladies began to gather round to watch the paddling. Billy Boy kicked both Leota and Mrs. Fletcher as hard as he could, Mrs. Fletcher with her new fixed smile.

"There, my little man!" gasped Leota. "You won't be able to set down for a week if I knew what I was doin'."

Billy Boy stomped through the group of wild-haired ladies and went out the door, but flung back the words, "If you're so smart, why ain't you rich?"

§ FOR COMMENT

Katherine Anne Porter has described "Petrified Man" as "a fine clinical study of vulgarity, vulgarity absolute, chemically pure, exposed mercilessly to its final subhuman depths." [1] Would you agree with this description? What kind of women are portrayed? What are their main concerns? How do they feel about the qualities generally considered to be essentially feminine? What are their husbands like? Notice that the women are the breadwinners, the men dependent on them. How is the title of the story pertinent here? What does the petrified man represent? Why is his home a freak show?

The beauty parlor represents the women's world. Is the setting appropriately chosen? Why? Point out characteristics of the beauty parlor that serve also to describe the women in it. Is the women's world supposed to represent a microcosm of the larger society? Support your view.

What is the function of the child, Billy? Remember that his mother, Mrs. Pike, has tried bringing him to work with her in a millinery shop where he spends his days trying on the women's hats; but the employer objects, so Leota brings him to the beauty parlor instead, where he spends his days playing on the floor beneath the feet of the women. His playthings are hair clips, and he does small errands like getting fresh towels when Leota needs them. It is on Billy that the women vent their not too deeply submerged hostility toward each other and toward their men. Billy symbolically attempts to assert his own male role by invading Leota's purse and by carrying away and eating the stale peanuts and is caught, and the women act immediately to squelch his assertion. How does this action bear on the whole story? What is the significance of Billy's final question, flung at the group of wild-haired ladies, "If you're so smart, why ain't you rich?"

[1] Eudora Welty, *A Curtain of Green and Other Stories* (New York: Harcourt, Brace & World, 1941), pp. xx–xxi.

Flannery O'Connor § 1925–1964

Another of the Southern writers whose works have been widely hailed, Miss O'Connor published two novels and numerous short stories, some of which appeared in her collections A Good Man Is Hard to Find (1955) *and* Everything That Rises Must Converge (1965). *Like Miss Welty's stories, Miss O'Connor's are characterized by finely detailed surface levels which move rapidly to the realm of the symbolic, often through grotesquerie. Born in Savannah, Miss O'Connor received a Bachelor of Arts degree from The Woman's College of Georgia and a Master of Fine Arts degree from the State University of Iowa. She lived in Georgia most of her life and died there at the height of her writing power.*

A Good Man Is Hard to Find

The grandmother didn't want to go to Florida. She wanted to visit some of her connections in east Tennessee and she was seizing at every chance to change Bailey's mind. Bailey was the son she lived with, her only boy. He was sitting on the edge of his chair at the table, bent over the orange sports section of the *Journal*. "Now look here, Bailey," she said, "see here, read this," and she stood with one hand on her thin hip and the other rattling the newspaper at his bald head. "Here this fellow that calls himself The Misfit is aloose from the Federal Pen and headed toward Florida and you read here what it says he did to these people. Just you read it. I wouldn't take my children in any direction with a criminal like that aloose in it. I couldn't answer to my conscience if I did."

Bailey didn't look up from his reading so she wheeled around then and faced the children's mother, a young woman in slacks, whose face was broad and innocent as a cabbage and was tied around with a green headkerchief that had two points on the top like rabbit's ears. She was sitting on the sofa, feeding the baby his apricots out of a jar. "The children have been to Florida before," the old lady said. "You all ought to take them somewhere else for a change so they would see different parts of the world and be broad. They never have been to east Tennessee."

The children's mother didn't seem to hear her but the eight-year-old boy, John Wesley, a stocky child with glasses, said, "If you don't want to go to Florida, why dontcha stay at home?" He and the little girl, June Star, were reading the funny papers on the floor.

"She wouldn't stay at home to be queen for a day," June Star said without raising her yellow head.

"Yes and what would you do if this fellow, The Misfit, caught you?" the grandmother asked.

"I'd smack his face," John Wesley said.

"She wouldn't stay at home for a million bucks," June Star said. "Afraid she'd miss something. She has to go everywhere we go."

"All right, Miss," the grandmother said. "Just remember that the next time you want me to curl your hair."

June Star said her hair was naturally curly.

The next morning the grandmother was the first one in the car, ready to go. She had her big black valise that looked like the head of a hippopotamus in one corner, and underneath it she was hiding a basket with Pitty Sing, the cat, in it. She didn't intend for the cat to be left alone in the house for three days because he would miss her too much and she was afraid he might brush against one of the gas burners and accidentally asphyxiate himself. Her son, Bailey, didn't like to arrive at a motel with a cat.

She sat in the middle of the back seat with John Wesley and June Star on either side of her. Bailey and the children's mother and the baby sat in front and they left Atlanta at eight forty-five with the mileage on the car at 55890. The grandmother wrote this down because she thought it would be interesting to say how many miles they had been when they got back. It took them twenty minutes to reach the outskirts of the city.

The old lady settled herself comfortably, removing her white cotton gloves and putting them up with her purse on the shelf in front of the back window. The children's mother still had on slacks and still had her head tied up in a green kerchief, but the grandmother had on a navy blue straw sailor hat with a bunch of white violets on the brim and a navy blue dress with a small white dot in the print. Her collars and cuffs were white organdy trimmed with lace and at her neckline she had pinned a purple spray of cloth violets containing a sachet. In case of an accident, anyone seeing her dead on the highway would know at once that she was a lady.

She said she thought it was going to be a good day for driving, neither too hot nor too cold, and she cautioned Bailey that the speed limit was fifty-five miles an hour and that the patrolmen hid themselves behind billboards and small clumps of trees and sped out after you before you had a chance to slow down. She pointed out interesting details of the scenery: Stone Mountain; the blue granite that in some places came up to both sides of the highway; the brilliant red clay banks slightly streaked with purple; and the various crops that made rows of green lace-work on the ground. The trees were full of silver-white sunlight and the meanest of them sparkled. The children were reading comic magazines and their mother had gone back to sleep.

"Let's go through Georgia fast so we won't have to look at it much," John Wesley said.

"If I were a little boy," said the grandmother, "I wouldn't talk about my native state that way. Tennessee has the mountains and Georgia has the hills."

"Tennessee is just a hillbilly dumping ground," John Wesley said, "and Georgia is a lousy state too."

"You said it," June Star said.

"In my time," said the grandmother, folding her thin veined fingers, "children were more respectful of their native states and their parents and everything else. People did right then. Oh look at the cute little pickaninny!" she said and pointed to a Negro child standing in the door of a shack. "Wouldn't that make a picture, now?" she asked and they all turned and looked at the little Negro out of the back window. He waved.

"He didn't have any britches on," June Star said.

"He probably didn't have any," the grandmother explained. "Little niggers in the country don't have things like we do. If I could paint, I'd paint that picture," she said.

The children exchanged comic books.

The grandmother offered to hold the baby and the children's mother passed him over the front seat to her. She set him on her knee and bounced him and told him about the things they were passing. She rolled her eyes and screwed up her mouth and stuck her leathery thin face into his smooth bland one. Occasionally he gave her a faraway smile. They passed a large cotton field with five or six graves fenced in the middle of it, like a small island. "Look at the graveyard!" the grandmother said, pointing it out. "That was the old family burying ground. That belonged to the plantation."

"Where's the plantation?" John Wesley asked.

"Gone With the Wind," said the grandmother. "Ha. Ha."

When the children finished all the comic books they had brought, they opened the lunch and ate it. The grandmother ate a peanut butter sandwich and an olive and would not let the children throw the box and the paper napkins out the window. When there was nothing else to do they played a game by choosing a cloud and making the other two guess what shape it suggested. John Wesley took one the shape of a cow and June Star guessed a cow and John Wesley said, no, an automobile, and June Star said he didn't play fair, and they began to slap each other over the grandmother.

The grandmother said she would tell them a story if they would keep quiet. When she told a story, she rolled her eyes and waved her head and was very dramatic. She said once when she was a maiden lady she had been courted by a Mr. Edgar Atkins Teagarden from Jasper, Georgia. She said he was a very good-looking man and a gentleman and that he brought her a watermelon every Saturday afternoon with his initials cut in it, E. A. T. Well, one Saturday, she said, Mr. Teagarden brought the watermelon and there was nobody at home and he left it on the front porch and returned in his buggy to Jasper, but she never got the watermelon, she said, because a nigger boy ate it when he saw the initials, E. A. T.! This story tickled John Wesley's funny bone and he giggled and giggled but June Star didn't think it was any good. She said she wouldn't marry a man that just brought her a watermelon on Saturday. The grandmother said she would have done well to marry Mr. Teagarden because he was a gentleman and had bought Coca-Cola stock when it first came out and that he had died only a few years ago, a very wealthy man.

They stopped at The Tower for barbecued sandwiches. The Tower was a part stucco and part wood filling station and dance hall set in a clearing outside of Timothy. A fat man named Red Sammy Butts ran it and there were signs stuck here and there on the building and for miles up and down the highway saying, TRY RED SAMMY'S FAMOUS BARBE-CUE. NONE LIKE FAMOUS RED SAMMY'S! RED SAM! THE FAT BOY WITH THE HAPPY LAUGH. A VETERAN! RED SAMMY'S YOUR MAN!

Red Sammy was lying on the bare ground outside The Tower with his head under a truck while a gray monkey about a foot high, chained to a small chinaberry tree, chattered nearby. The monkey sprang back into the tree and got on the highest limb as soon as he saw the children jump out of the car and run toward him.

Inside, The Tower was a long dark room with a counter at one end and tables at the other and dancing space in the middle. They all sat down at a board table next to the nickelodeon and Red Sam's wife, a tall burnt-brown woman with hair and eyes lighter than her skin, came and took their order. The children's mother put a dime in the machine and played "The Tennessee Waltz," and the grandmother said that tune always made her want to dance. She asked Bailey if he would like to dance but he only glared at her. He didn't have a naturally sunny disposition like she did and trips made him nervous. The grandmother's brown eyes were very bright. She swayed her head from side to side and pretended she was dancing in her chair. June Star said play something she could tap to so the children's mother put in another dime and played a fast number and June Star stepped out onto the dance floor and did her tap routine.

"Ain't she cute?" Red Sam's wife said, leaning over the counter. "Would you like to come be my little girl?"

"No I certainly wouldn't," June Star said. "I wouldn't live in a broken-down place like this for a million bucks!" and she ran back to the table.

"Ain't she cute?" the woman repeated, stretching her mouth politely.

"Aren't you ashamed?" hissed the grandmother.

Red Sam came in and told his wife to quit lounging on the counter and hurry up with these people's order. His khaki trousers reached just to his hip bones and his stomach hung over them like a sack of meal swaying under his shirt. He came over and sat down at a table nearby and let out a combination sigh and yodel. "You can't win," he said. "You can't win," and he wiped his sweating red face off with a gray handkerchief. "These days you don't know who to trust," he said. "Ain't that the truth?"

"People are certainly not nice like they used to be," said the grandmother.

"Two fellers come in here last week," Red Sammy said, "driving a Chrysler. It was a old beat-up car but it was a good one and these boys looked all right to me. Said they worked at the mill and you know I let them fellers charge the gas they bought? Now why did I do that?"

"Because you're a good man!" the grandmother said at once.

"Yes'm, I suppose so," Red Sam said as if he were struck with this answer.

His wife brought the orders, carrying the five plates all at once without a tray, two in each hand and one balanced on her arm. "It isn't a soul in this green world of God's that you can trust," she said. "And I don't count nobody out of that, not nobody," she repeated, looking at Red Sammy.

"Did you read about that criminal, The Misfit, that's escaped?" asked the grandmother.

"I wouldn't be a bit surprised if he didn't attact this place right here," said the woman. "If he hears about it being here, I wouldn't be none surprised to see him. If he hears it's two cent in the cash register, I wouldn't be a tall surprised if he . . ."

"That'll do," Red Sam said. "Go bring these people their Co'-Colas," and the woman went off to get the rest of the order.

"A good man is hard to find," Red Sammy said. "Everything is getting terrible. I remember the day you could go off and leave your screen door unlatched. Not no more."

He and the grandmother discussed better times. The old lady said that in her opinion Europe was entirely to blame for the way things were now. She said the way Europe acted you would think we were made of money and Red Sam said it was no use talking about it, she was exactly right. The children ran outside into the white sunlight and looked at the monkey in the lacy chinaberry tree. He was busy catching fleas on himself and biting each one carefully between his teeth as if it were a delicacy.

They drove off again into the hot afternoon. The grandmother took cat naps and woke up every few minutes with her own snoring. Outside of Toombsboro she woke up and recalled an old plantation that she had visited in this neighborhood once when she was a young lady. She said the house had six white columns across the front and that there was an avenue of oaks leading up to it and two little wooden trellis arbors on either side in front where you sat down with your suitor after a stroll in the garden. She recalled exactly which road to turn off to get to it. She knew that Bailey would not be willing to lose any time looking at an old house, but the more she talked about it, the more she wanted to see it once again and find out if the little twin arbors were still standing. "There was a secret panel in this house," she said craftily, not telling the truth but wishing that she were, "and the story went that all the family silver was hidden in it when Sherman came through but it was never found . . ."

"Hey!" John Wesley said. "Let's go see it! We'll find it! We'll poke all the woodwork and find it! Who lives there? Where do you turn off at? Hey Pop, can't we turn off there?"

"We never have seen a house with a secret panel!" June Star shrieked. "Let's go to the house with the secret panel! Hey Pop, can't we go see the house with the secret panel!"

"It's not far from here, I know," the grandmother said. "It wouldn't take over twenty minutes."

Bailey was looking straight ahead. His jaw was as rigid as a horseshoe. "No," he said.

The children began to yell and scream that they wanted to see the house with the secret panel. John Wesley kicked the back of the front seat and June Star hung over her mother's shoulder and whined desperately into her ear that they never had any fun even on their vacation, that they could never do what THEY wanted to do. The baby began to scream and John Wesley kicked the back of the seat so hard that his father could feel the blows in his kidney.

"All right!" he shouted and drew the car to a stop at the side of the road. "Will you all shut up? Will you all just shut up for one second? If you don't shut up, we won't go anywhere."

"It would be very educational for them," the grandmother murmured.

"All right," Bailey said, "but get this: this is the only time we're going to stop for anything like this. This is the one and only time."

"The dirt road that you have to turn down is about a mile back," the grandmother directed. "I marked it when we passed."

"A dirt road," Bailey groaned.

After they had turned around and were headed toward the dirt road, the grandmother recalled other points about the house, the beautiful glass over the front doorway and the candle-lamp in the hall. John Wesley said that the secret panel was probably in the fireplace.

"You can't go inside this house," Bailey said. "You don't know who lives there."

"While you all talk to the people in front, I'll run around behind and get in a window," John Wesley suggested.

"We'll all stay in the car," his mother said.

They turned onto the dirt road and the car raced roughly along in a swirl of pink dust. The grandmother recalled the times when there were no paved roads and thirty miles was a day's journey. The dirt road was hilly and there were sudden washes in it and sharp curves on dangerous embankments. All at once they would be on a hill, looking down over the blue tops of trees for miles around, then the next minute, they would be in a red depression with the dust-coated trees looking down on them.

"This place had better turn up in a minute," Bailey said, "or I'm going to turn around."

The road looked as if no one had traveled on it in months.

"It's not much farther," the grandmother said and just as she said it, a horrible thought came to her. The thought was so embarrassing that she turned red in the face and her eyes dilated and her feet jumped up, upsetting her valise in the corner. The instant the valise moved, the newspaper top she had over the basket under it rose with a snarl and Pitty Sing, the cat, sprang onto Bailey's shoulder.

The children were thrown to the floor and their mother, clutching the baby, was thrown out the door onto the ground; the old lady was thrown into the front seat. The car turned over once and landed right-side-up in a gulch off the side of the road. Bailey remained in the driver's seat with the cat—gray-striped with a broad white face and an orange nose—clinging to his neck like a caterpillar.

As soon as the children saw they could move their arms and legs, they scrambled out of the car, shouting, "We've had an ACCIDENT!" The grandmother was curled up under the dashboard, hoping she was injured so that Bailey's wrath would not come down on her all at once. The horrible thought she had had before the accident was that the house she had remembered so vividly was not in Georgia but in Tennessee.

Bailey removed the cat from his neck with both hands and flung it out the window against the side of a pine tree. Then he got out of the car and started looking for the children's mother. She was sitting against the side of the red gutted ditch, holding the screaming baby, but she only had a cut down her face and a broken shoulder. "We've had an ACCIDENT!" the children screamed in a frenzy of delight.

"But nobody's killed," June Star said with disappointment as the grandmother limped out of the car, her hat still pinned to her head but the broken front brim standing up at a jaunty angle and the violet spray hanging off the side. They all sat down in the ditch, except the children, to recover from the shock. They were all shaking.

"Maybe a car will come along," said the children's mother hoarsely.

"I believe I have injured an organ," said the grandmother, pressing her side, but no one answered her. Bailey's teeth were clattering. He had on a yellow sport shirt with bright blue parrots designed in it and his face was as yellow as the shirt. The grandmother decided that she would not mention that the house was in Tennessee.

The road was about ten feet above and they could see only the tops of the trees on the other side of it. Behind the ditch they were sitting in there were more woods, tall and dark and deep. In a few minutes they saw a car some distance away on top of a hill, coming slowly as if the occupants were watching them. The grandmother stood up and waved both arms dramatically to attract their attention. The car continued to come on slowly, disappeared around a bend and appeared again, moving even slower, on top of the hill they had gone over. It was a big black battered hearse-like automobile. There were three men in it.

It came to a stop just over them and for some minutes, the driver looked down with a steady expressionless gaze to where they were sitting, and didn't speak. Then he turned his head and muttered something to the other two and they got out. One was a fat boy in black trousers and a red sweat shirt with a silver stallion embossed on the front of it. He moved around on the right side of them and stood staring, his mouth partly open in a kind of loose grin. The other had on khaki pants and a blue striped coat and a gray hat pulled down very low, hiding most of his face. He came around slowly on the left side. Neither spoke.

The driver got out of the car and stood by the side of it, looking down at them. He was an older man than the other two. His hair was just beginning to gray and he wore silver-rimmed spectacles that gave him a scholarly look. He had a long creased face and didn't have on any shirt or undershirt. He had on blue jeans that were too tight for him and was holding a black hat and a gun. The two boys also had guns.

"We've had an ACCIDENT!" the children screamed.

The grandmother had the peculiar feeling that the bespectacled man was someone she knew. His face was as familiar to her as if she had known him all her life but she could not recall who he was. He moved away from the car and began to come down the embankment, placing his feet carefully so that he wouldn't slip. He had on tan and white shoes and no socks, and his ankles were red and thin. "Good afternoon," he said. "I see you all had you a little spill."

"We turned over twice!" said the grandmother.

"Oncet," he corrected. "We seen it happen. Try their car and see will it run, Hiram," he said quietly to the boy with the gray hat.

"What you got that gun for?" John Wesley asked. "Whatcha gonna do with that gun?"

"Lady," the man said to the children's mother, "would you mind calling them children to sit down by you? Children make me nervous. I want all you all to sit down right together there where you're at."

"What are you telling US what to do for?" June Star asked.

Behind them the line of woods gaped like a dark open mouth. "Come here," said their mother.

"Look here now," Bailey began suddenly, "we're in a predicament! We're in . . ."

The grandmother shrieked. She scrambled to her feet and stood staring. "You're The Misfit!" she said. "I recognized you at once!"

"Yes'm," the man said, smiling slightly as if he were pleased in spite of himself to be known, "but it would have been better for all of you, lady, if you hadn't of reckernized me."

Bailey turned his head sharply and said something to his mother that shocked even the children. The old lady began to cry and The Misfit reddened.

"Lady," he said, "don't you get upset. Sometimes a man says things he don't mean. I don't reckon he meant to talk to you thataway."

"You wouldn't shoot a lady, would you?" the grandmother said and removed a clean handkerchief from her cuff and began to slap at her eyes with it.

The Misfit pointed the toe of his shoe into the ground and made a little hole and then covered it up again. "I would hate to have to," he said.

"Listen," the grandmother almost screamed, "I know you're a good man. You don't look a bit like you have common blood. I know you must come from nice people!"

"Yes mam," he said, "finest people in the world." When he smiled he showed a row of strong white teeth. "God never made a finer woman than my mother and my daddy's heart was pure gold," he said. The boy with the red sweat shirt had come around behind them and was standing with his gun at his hip. The Misfit squatted down on the ground. "Watch them children, Bobby Lee," he said. "You know they make me nervous." He looked at the six of them huddled together in front of him and he seemed to be embarrassed as if he couldn't think of anything to say. "Ain't a cloud in the sky," he remarked, looking up at it. "Don't see no sun but don't see no cloud neither."

"Yes, it's a beautiful day," said the grandmother. "Listen," she said, "you shouldn't call yourself The Misfit because I know you're a good man at heart. I can just look at you and tell."

"Hush!" Bailey yelled. "Hush! Everybody shut up and let me handle this!" He was squatting in the position of a runner about to sprint forward but he didn't move.

"I pre-chate that, lady," The Misfit said and drew a little circle in the ground with the butt of his gun.

"It'll take a half a hour to fix this here car," Hiram called, looking over the raised hood of it.

"Well, first you and Bobby Lee get him and that little boy to step over yonder with you," The Misfit said, pointing to Bailey and John Wesley. "The boys want to ast you something," he said to Bailey. "Would you mind stepping back in them woods there with them?"

"Listen," Bailey began, "we're in a terrible predicament! Nobody realizes what this is," and his voice cracked. His eyes were as blue and intense as the parrots in his shirt and he remained perfectly still.

The grandmother reached up to adjust her hat brim as if she were going to the woods with him but it came off in her hand. She stood staring at it and after a second she let it fall on the ground. Hiram pulled Bailey up by the arm as if he were assisting an old man. John Wesley caught hold of his father's hand and Bobby Lee followed. They went off toward the woods and just as they reached the dark edge, Bailey turned and supporting himself against a gray naked pine trunk, he shouted, "I'll be back in a minute, Mamma, wait on me!"

"Come back this instant!" his mother shrilled but they all disappeared into the woods.

"Bailey Boy!" the grandmother called in a tragic voice but she found she was looking at The Misfit squatting on the ground in front of her. "I just know you're a good man," she said desperately. "You're not a bit common!"

"Nome, I ain't a good man," The Misfit said after a second as if he had considered her statement carefully, "but I ain't the worst in the world neither. My daddy said I was a different breed of dog from my brothers and sisters. 'You know,' Daddy said, 'it's some that can live their whole life out without asking about it and it's others has to know why it is, and this boy is one of the latters. He's going to be into everything!'" He put on his black hat and looked up suddenly and then away deep into the woods as if he were embarrassed again. "I'm sorry I don't have on a shirt before you ladies," he said, hunching his shoulders slightly. "We buried our clothes that we had on when we escaped and we're just making do until we can get better. We borrowed these from some folks we met," he explained.

"That's perfectly all right," the grandmother said. "Maybe Bailey has an extra shirt in his suitcase."

"I'll look and see terrectly," The Misfit said.

"Where are they taking him?" the children's mother screamed.

"Daddy was a card himself," The Misfit said. "You couldn't put anything over on him. He never got in trouble with the Authorities though. Just had the knack of handling them."

"You could be honest too if you'd only try," said the grandmother. "Think how wonderful it would be to settle down and live a comfortable life and not have to think about somebody chasing you all the time."

The Misfit kept scratching in the ground with the butt of his gun as if he were thinking about it. "Yes'm, somebody is always after you," he murmured.

The grandmother noticed how thin his shoulder blades were just behind his hat because she was standing up looking down on him. "Do you ever pray?" she asked.

He shook his head. All she saw was the black hat wiggle between his shoulder blades. "Nome," he said.

There was a pistol shot from the woods, followed closely by another. Then silence. The old lady's head jerked around. She could hear the wind move through the tree tops like a long satisfied insuck of breath. "Bailey Boy!" she called.

"I was a gospel singer for a while," The Misfit said. "I been most everything. Been in the arm service, both land and sea, at home and abroad, been twict married, been an undertaker, been with the railroads, plowed Mother Earth, been in a tornado, seen a man burnt alive oncet," and he looked up at the children's mother and the little girl who were sitting close together, their faces white and their eyes glassy; "I even seen a woman flogged," he said.

"Pray, pray," the grandmother began, "pray, pray . . ."

"I never was a bad boy that I remember of," The Misfit said in an almost dreamy voice, "but somewheres along the line I done something wrong and got sent to the penitentiary. I was buried alive," and he looked up and held her attention to him by a steady stare.

"That's when you should have started to pray," she said. "What did you do to get sent to the penitentiary that first time?"

"Turn to the right, it was a wall," The Misfit said, looking up again at the cloudless sky. "Turn to the left, it was a wall. Look up it was a ceiling, look down it was floor. I forget what I done, lady. I set there and set there, trying to remember what it was I done and I ain't recalled it to this day. Oncet in a while, I would think it was coming to me, but it never come."

"Maybe they put you in by mistake," the old lady said vaguely.

"Nome," he said. "It wasn't no mistake. They had the papers on me."

"You must have stolen something," she said.

The Misfit sneered slightly. "Nobody had nothing I wanted," he said. "It was a head-doctor at the penitentiary said what I had done was kill my daddy but I known that for a lie. My daddy died in nineteen ought nineteen of the epidemic flu and I never had a thing to do with it. He was buried in the Mount Hopewell Baptist churchyard and you can go there and see for yourself."

"If you would pray," the old lady said, "Jesus would help you."

"That's right," The Misfit said.

"Well then, why don't you pray?" she asked trembling with delight suddenly.

"I don't want no hep," he said. "I'm doing all right by myself."

Bobby Lee and Hiram came ambling back from the woods. Bobby Lee was dragging a yellow shirt with bright blue parrots in it.

"Throw me that shirt, Bobby Lee," The Misfit said. The shirt came flying at him and landed on his shoulder and he put it on. The grandmother couldn't name what the shirt reminded her of. "No lady," The Misfit said while he was buttoning it up, "I found out the crime don't matter. You can do one thing or you can do another, kill a man or take a tire off his car, because sooner or later you're going to forget what it was you done and just be punished for it."

The children's mother had begun to make heaving noises as if she couldn't get her breath. "Lady," he asked, "would you and that little girl like to step off yonder with Bobby Lee and Hiram and join your husband?"

"Yes, thank you," the mother said faintly. Her left arm dangled helplessly and she was holding the baby, who had gone to sleep, in the other. "Hep that lady up, Hiram," The Misfit said as she struggled to climb out of the ditch, "and Bobby Lee, you hold onto that little girl's hand."

"I don't want to hold hands with him," June Star said. "He reminds me of a pig."

The fat boy blushed and laughed and caught her by the arm and pulled her off into the woods after Hiram and her mother.

Alone with The Misfit, the grandmother found that she had lost her voice. There was not a cloud in the sky nor any sun. There was nothing around her but woods. She wanted to tell him that he must pray. She opened and closed her mouth several times before anything came out. Finally she found herself saying, "Jesus. Jesus," meaning, Jesus will help you, but the way she was saying it, it sounded as if she might be cursing.

"Yes'm," The Misfit said as if he agreed. "Jesus thown everything off balance. It was the same case with Him as with me except He hadn't committed any crime and they could prove I had committed one because they had the papers on me. Of course," he said, "they never shown me my papers. That's why I sign myself now. I said long ago, you get you a signature and sign everything you do and keep a copy of it. Then you'll know what you done and you can hold up the crime to the punishment and see do they match and in the end you'll have something to prove you ain't been treated right. I call myself The Misfit," he said, "because I can't make what all I done wrong fit what all I gone through in punishment."

There was a piercing scream from the woods followed closely by a pistol report. "Does it seem right to you, lady, that one is punished a heap and another ain't punished at all?"

"Jesus!" the old lady cried. "You've got good blood! I know you wouldn't shoot a lady! I know you come from nice people! Pray! Jesus, you ought not to shoot a lady. I'll give you all the money I've got!"

"Lady," The Misfit said, looking beyond her far into the woods, "there never was a body that give the undertaker a tip." There were two more pistol reports and the grandmother raised her head like a parched old turkey hen crying for water and called, "Bailey Boy, Bailey Boy!" as if her heart would break.

"Jesus was the only One that ever raised the dead," The Misfit continued, "and He shouldn't have done it. He thown everything off balance. If He did what He said, then it's nothing for you to do but thow away everything and follow Him, and if He didn't, then it's nothing for you to do but enjoy the few minutes you got left the best way you can—by killing somebody or burning down his house or doing some other meanness to him. No pleasure but meanness," he said and his voice had become almost a snarl.

"Maybe He didn't raise the dead," the old lady mumbled, not knowing what she was saying and feeling so dizzy that she sank down in the ditch with her legs twisted under her.

"I wasn't there so I can't say He didn't," The Misfit said. "I wisht I had of been there," he said, hitting the ground with his fist. "It ain't right I wasn't there because if I had of been there I would of known. Listen lady," he said in a high voice, "if I had of been there I would of known and I wouldn't be like I am now." His voice seemed about to crack and the grandmother's head cleared for an instant. She saw the man's face twisted close to her own as if he were going to cry and she murmured, "Why you're one of my babies. You're one of my own children!" She reached out and touched him on the shoulder. The Misfit sprang back as if a snake had bitten him and shot her three times through the chest. Then he put his gun down on the ground and took off his glasses and began to clean them.

Hiram and Bobby Lee returned from the woods and stood over the ditch, looking down at the grandmother who half sat and half lay in a puddle of blood with her legs crossed under her like a child's and her face smiling up at the cloudless sky.

Without his glasses, The Misfit's eyes were red-rimmed and pale and defenseless-looking. "Take her off and thow her where you thown the others," he said, picking up the cat that was rubbing itself against his leg.

"She was a talker, wasn't she?" Bobby Lee said, sliding down the ditch with a yodel.

"She would of been a good woman," The Misfit said, "if it had been somebody there to shoot her every minute of her life."

"Some fun!" Bobby Lee said.

"Shut up, Bobby Lee," The Misfit said. "It's no real pleasure in life."

§ FOR COMMENT

Explain why the opening episodes of "A Good Man Is Hard to Find" focus on the grandmother. What kind of person is she? What are the other members of the family like? Is there some kind of justice in the fact that these people meet The Misfit and die at his command?

What is the purpose of the various details of the trip, the sights the travelers see, for example? How does the scene in the cafe function? Describe how the grandmother contrives to force Bailey to take a detour. Would it be possible to say that the grandmother is responsible for the disaster that befalls the family? In considering this question take particular notice of the following lines:

> She saw the man's face twisted close to her own as if he were going to cry and she murmured, "Why you're one of my babies. You're one of my own children!" She reached out and touched him on the shoulder. The Misfit

sprang back as if a snake had bitten him and shot her three times through the chest.

Is the reference to the snake functional? Consider the religious questions raised in the conversation between the grandmother and The Misfit and how they bear on the theme of the story.

The Misfit is a homocidal maniac, but is he more than this? Can you find the motivation for his behavior in the story? Whose is the final responsibility?

Shirley Ann Grau § 1930–

A younger member of the so-called Southern group, Miss Grau was born in New Orleans and lives there still. She published her first volume, The Black Prince and Other Stories, *when she was twenty-five. Hailed then as a "born writer," she has maintained a level of excellence in the novels that followed. In* The Hard Blue Sky (1958) *and* The House on Coliseum Street (1961) *she exhibits an extraordinary ability to capture moods by means of a sensitive, rhythmic prose style.* The Keepers of the House (1965) *won a Pulitzer Prize. She has since published numerous short stories in a variety of magazines, but these have not as yet been collected.*

The Black Prince

> "How art thou fallen from heaven,
> O Lucifer, son of the morning!"

Winters are short and very cold; sometimes there is even a snow like heavy frost on the ground. Summers are powdery hot; the white ball sun goes rolling around and around in a sky behind the smoke from the summer fires. There is always a burning somewhere in summer; the pines are dry and waiting; the sun itself starts the smoldering. A pine fire is quiet; there is only a kind of rustle from the flames inside the trunks until the branches and needles go up with a whistling. A whole hill often burns that way, its smoke rising straight up to the white sun, and quiet.

In the plowed patches, green things grow quickly: the ground is rich and there are underground rivers. But there are no big farms: only patches of corn, green beans, and a field or two of cotton (grown for a little cash to spend on Saturdays at Luther's General Store or Willie's Café; these are the only two places for forty miles in any direction). There is good pasture: the green places along the hillsides with pines for shade and sure water in the streams that come down from the Smokies to the north; even in the burnt-out land of five seasons back, shrubs are high. But in the whole county there are only fifty cows, gone wild most of them and dry because they were never milked. They are afraid of men and feed in the farthest ridges and the swamps that are the bottoms of some littlest of the valleys. Their numbers are slowly increasing because no one bothers them. Only once in a while some man with a hankering for cow meat takes his rifle and goes after them. But that is not often; the people prefer pork. Each family keeps enough razorbacks in a run of bark palings.

It is all colored people here, and it is the poorest part of the smallest and worst county in the state. The place at the end of the dirt road leading from the state highway, the place where Luther's Store and Willie's Café stand, does not even have a name in the county records.

The only cool time of the summer day is very early, before the mists have shriveled away. There is a breeze then, a good stiff one out of the Smokies. During the day there is no sound: it is dead hot. But in the early mornings, when the breeze from the north is blowing, it is not so lonesomely quiet: crickets and locusts and the birds that flutter about hunting them, calling frantically as if they had something of importance to settle quick before the heat sets in. (By seven they are quiet again, in the invisible places they have chosen to wait out the day.)

A pine cone rattled down on Alberta's head and bounced from her shoulder. She scooped it from the ground and threw it upward through the branches. "You just keep your cone, mister birds, I got no cause to want it." With a pumping of wings the birds were gone, their cries sliding after them, back down the air. "You just yell your head off. I can hit you any time I want. Any time I want." There was a small round piece of granite at her feet and she tossed it, without particular aim, into the biggest of the bay trees: a gray squirrel with a thin rattail tumbled from the branches and peeped at her from behind the trunk with a pointed little rat face. She jammed her hands in the pockets of her dress and went on, swaggering slightly, cool and feeling good.

She was a handsome girl, taller than most people in her part of the county, and light brown—there had been a lot of white blood in her family, back somewhere, they'd forgot where exactly. She was not graceful —not as a woman is—but light on her feet and supple as a man. Her dress, which the sun had bleached to a whitish color, leaving only a trace of pink along the seams, had shrunk out of size for her: it pulled tight across her broad, slightly hunched, muscled back, even though she had left all the front buttons open down to the waist.

As she walked along, the birds were making even more of a row, knock-ing loose cones and dry pine needles and old broad bay leaves, and twice she stopped, threw back her head, and called up to them: "Crazy fool birds. Can't do nothing to me. Fool jackass birds." Up ahead, a couple of minutes' walk, was the field and the cotton, bursting white out of the brown cups and waiting to be picked. And she did not feel like working. She leaned against a tree, stretching so that the bark crumbled in her fingers, listening to the birds.

Something different was in their calling. She listened, her head bent forward, her eyes closed, as she sorted the sounds. One jay was wrong: its long sustained note ended with the cluck of a quail. No bird did that. Alberta opened her eyes and looked slowly around. But the pines were thick and close and full of blue night shadow and wrapped with fog that moved like bits of cloth in the wind. Leaving the other birdcalls, the whistle became distinct, high, soaring, mocking, like some rare bird, proudly, insolently.

Alberta moved a few steps out from the tree and turned slowly on her heels. The whistle was going around her now, in slow circles, and she turned with it, keeping her eye on the sound, seeing nothing. The birds were still calling and fluttering in the branches, sending bits of twig and bark tumbling down.

Alberta said: "A fool thing you doing. A crazy fool jackass thing." She sat down on a tumbled pile of bricks that had been the chimney of a sugarhouse burned during the Civil War. She spoke in her best tone, while the whistling went round and round her faster. "I reckon you got nothing better to do than go around messing up folks. You got me so riled up I don't reckon I know what way I'm heading in." The sound went around her and around her, but she held her head steady, talking to the pine directly in front of her. "I don't reckon there's nothing for me but set here till you tires out and goes away." The whistle circled her twice and then abruptly stopped, the last high clear note running off down the breeze. Alberta stood up, pulling down her faded dress. "I am mighty glad you come to stopping. I reckon now I can tell what direction I got to go in."

He was right there, leaning on the same pine she had been staring at, cleaning his front teeth with a little green twig and studying her, and she told him to his face: "That was a crazy mean thing, and you ain't got nothing better to do."

"Reckon not," he said, moving the little green twig in and out of the hole between his lower front teeth.

She pushed her hands in the pockets of her dress and looked him over. "Where you come from?"

"Me?" The little green twig went in and out of his teeth with each breath. "I just come straight out the morning."

She turned and walked away. "I be glad to see you go."

He stood in front of her: he had a way of moving without a sound, of popping up in places. "I be sorry to see you go, Alberta Lacy."

She studied him before she answered: tall, not too big or heavy, and black (no other blood but his own in him, she thought). He was dressed nice—a leather jacket with fringe on the sleeves, a red plaid shirt, and new blue denim pants. "How you know what I'm called?"she asked him politely.

He grinned, and his teeth were white and perfect. "I done seen it in the fire," he said. "I done seen it in the fire and I read it clear: Alberta Lacy."

She frowned. "I don't see as how I understand."

He blew the little green twig out of his mouth. "I might could be seeing you again real soon, Alberta Lacy." Then he slipped around the tree like the last trail of night shadow and disappeared.

Alberta stood listening: only the birds and the insects and the wind. Then everything got quiet, and the sun was shining white all around, and she climbed down the slope to the field.

A little field—just a strip of cotton tucked in between two ridges. Her father and her two biggest brothers had planted it with half a morning's work, and they hadn't gone back to tend it once. They didn't even seem to remember it: whatever work they did was in the older fields closer to home. So Alberta had taken it over. Sometimes she brought along the twins: Sidney and Silvia; they were seven: young enough for her to order around and big enough to be a help. But usually she couldn't find them; they were strange ones, gone out of the house for a couple of days at a time in summer, sleeping out somewhere, always sticking together. They were strange little ones and not worth trouble looking for. So most times Alberta worked with Maggie Mary Evans, who was Josh Evans's daughter and just about the only girl her age she was friendly with. From the field there'd be maybe three bales of real early stuff; and they'd split the profit. They worked all morning, pulling off the bolls and dropping them in the sacks they slung crosswise across their shoulders. They worked very slowly, so slowly that at times their hands seemed hardly to move, dozing in the heat. When it got to be noon, when they had no shadow any more, they slipped off the sacks, leaving them between the furrows, and turned to the shade to eat their lunch.

He was waiting for them there, stretched out along the ground with his head propped up on the slender trunk of a little bay tree. He winked lazily at Alberta; his eyes were big and shiny black as oil. "How you, Miss Alberta Lacy?"

Alberta looked down at him, crooking her lips. "You got nothing to do but pester me?"

"Sure I got something to do, but ain't nothing nice like this."

Alberta looked at him through half-closed lids, then sat down to the lunch.

"You hungry, mister?" Maggie Mary asked. She had stood watching, both hands jammed into the belt of her dress, and her eyes moving from one to the other with the quickness and the color of a sparrow.

The man rolled over and looked up at her.

"Reckon I am."

"You can have some of our lunch," Maggie Mary said.

Crazy fool, Alberta thought, standing so close with him on the ground like that. He must can see all the way up her. And from the way he lay there, grinning, he must be enjoying it.

"That real nice," he said to Maggie Mary, and crawled over on his stomach to where the lunch bucket was.

Alberta watched his smooth, black hand reaching into the bucket and suddenly she remembered. "How you called?"

He put a piece of corn bread in his mouth, chewed it briefly, and swallowed it with a gulp. "I got three names."

"No fooling," Maggie Mary said, and giggled in her hand. "I got three names, too."

"Stanley Albert Thompson."

"That a good-sounding name," Alberta said. She began to eat her lunch quickly, her mouth too full to talk. Stanley Albert was staring at her, but she didn't raise her eyes. Then he began to sing, low, pounding time with the flat of his hand against the ground.

> "Alberta, let you hair hang low,
> Alberta, let you hair hang low,
> I'll give you more gold than you apron can hold
> If you just let you hair hang low."

Alberta got up slowly, not looking at him. "We got work to finish."

Stanley Albert turned over so that his face was pressed in the grass and pine needles. "All you get's the muscles in you arm."

"That right." Maggie Mary nodded quickly. "That right."

"Maggie Mary," Alberta said, "iffen you don't come with me I gonna bop you so hard you land in the middle of tomorrow."

"Goodby, Mr. Stanley Albert Thompson," Maggie Mary said, but he had fallen asleep.

By the time they finished work he was gone; there wasn't even a spot in the pine needles and short grass to show where he had been.

"Ain't that the strangest thing?" Maggie Mary said.

Alberta picked up the small bucket they carried their lunch in. "I reckon not."

"Seemed like he was fixing to wait for us."

"He ain't fixing to wait for nobody, that kind." Alberta rubbed one hand across her shoulders sighing slightly. "I got a pain fit to kill."

Maggie Mary leaned one arm against a tree and looked off across the little field where they had spent the day. "You reckon he was in here most all morning watching us?"

"Maybe." Alberta began to walk home. Maggie Mary followed slowly, her head still turned, watching the field.

"He musta spent all morning just watching."

"Nothing hard about doing that, watching us break our back out in the sun."

Maggie Mary took one long, loping step and came up with Alberta. "You reckon he coming back?"

Alberta stared full at her, head bent, chewing on her lower lip. "Maggie Mary Evans," she said, "you might could get a thought that he might be wanting you and you might could get a thought that you be wanting him—"

Maggie Mary bent down and brushed the dust off her bare feet carefully, not answering.

"You a plain crazy fool." Alberta planted both hands on her hips and bent her body forward slightly. "A plain crazy fool. You wouldn't be forgetting Jay Mastern?" Jay Mastern had gone off to Ramsey to work at the mill and never come back, but left Maggie Mary to have his baby. So one day Maggie Mary took her pa's best mule and put a blanket on it for a saddle and rode over to Blue Goose Lake, where the old woman lived who could tell her what to do. The old woman gave her medicine in a beer can: whisky and calomel and other things that were a secret. Maggie Mary took the medicine in one gulp, because it tasted so bad, waded way out into Blue Goose Lake so that the water came up to her neck, then dripping wet got up on the mule and whipped him up to a good fast pace all the way home. The baby had come off all right: there wasn't one. And Maggie Mary nearly died. It was something on to three months before she was able to do more than walk around, her arms hanging straight down and stiff and her black skin overtinged with gray.

"You wouldn't be forgetting Jay Mastern?"

"Sure," Maggie Mary said, brushing the dust off her bare feet lightly. "I clean forgot about him."

"Don't you be having nothing to do with this here Stanley Albert Thompson."

Maggie Mary began to walk again, slowly, smiling just a little bit with one corner of her mouth. "Sounds like you been thinking about him for yourself."

Alberta jammed both hands down in the pockets of her dress. "I been thinking nothing of the sort."

"Willie'll kill him."

Alberta chewed on one finger. "I reckon he could care for himself."

Maggie Mary smiled to herself softly, remembering. "I reckon he could; he's real fine-appearing man."

"He was dressed good."

"Where you reckon he come from?" Maggie Mary asked.

Alberta shrugged. "He just come walking out of the morning fog."

That was how he came into this country: he appeared one day whistling a birdcall in the woods in high summer. And he stayed on. The very first Saturday night he went down to Willie's and had four fights and won them all.

Willie's was an ordinary house made of pine slabs, older than most of the other houses, but more solid. There were two rooms: a little one where Willie lived (a heavy scrolled ironwork bed, a square oak dresser, a chest, a three-footed table, and on its cracked marble top a blue-painted mandolin without strings). And a big room: the café. Since anybody could remember, the café had been there with Willie's father or his grandfather, as long as there had been people in these parts. And that had been a long while: long before the Civil War even, runaways were settling here, knowing they'd be safe and hidden in the rough, uneven hills and the pines.

Willie had made some changes in the five or six years since his father died. He painted the counter that was the bar with varnish; that had not been a good idea: the whisky took the varnish off in a few weeks. And he painted the walls: bright blue. Then he went over them again, shaking his brush so that the walls were flecked like a mocking bird's eggs. But Willie used red to fleck—red against blue. And the mirror, gilt-edged, and hanging from a thick gold cord: that had been Willie's idea, too. He'd found it one day, lying on the shoulder alongside the state highway; it must have fallen from a truck somehow. So he took it home. It was cracked in maybe two dozen pieces. Anyone who looked into it would see his face split up into a dozen different parts, all separate. But Willie hung it right over the shelves where he kept his whisky and set one of the kerosene lamps in front of it so that the light should reflect yellow-bright from all the pieces. One of them fell out (so that Willie had to glue it back with flour and water) the night Stanley Albert had his fourth fight, which he won like the other three. Not a man in the country would stand up like that, because fighting at Willie's on Saturday night is a rough affair with razors, or knives, or bottles.

Not a man in the country could have matched the way Stanley Albert fought that night, his shirt off, and his black body shining with sweat, the muscles along his neck and shoulders twisting like grass snakes. There wasn't a finer-looking man and there wasn't a better: he proved that.

The first three fights were real orderly affairs. Everybody could see what was coming minutes ahead, and Willie got the two of them out in the yard before they got at each other. And everybody who was sober enough to walk went out on the porch and watched Stanley Albert pound first Ran Carey's and then Henry Johnson's head up and down in the dust. Alberta sat on the porch (Willie had brought her a chair from inside) and watched Stanley Albert roll around the dust of the yard and didn't even blink an eye, not even during the third fight when Tim Evans, who was Maggie Mary's brother, pull a razor. The razor got Stanley Albert all down one cheek, but Tim didn't have any teeth left and one side of his face got punched in so that it looked peculiar always afterward. Maggie Mary went running down into the yard, not bothering with her brother, to press her finger up against the little cut across Stanley Albert's cheek.

The fourth fight came up so suddenly nobody had time hardly to get out of the way: Joe Turner got one arm hooked around Stanley Albert's neck from behind. There wasn't any reason for it, except maybe that Joe was so drunk he didn't see who he had and that once there's been a couple of fights there's always more. Stanley Albert swung a bottle over his shoulder to break the hold and then nobody could see exactly what was happening: they were trying so hard to get clear. Willie pulled Alberta over the bar and pushed her down behind it and crouched alongside her, grinning. "That some fighter." And when it was all over they stood up again; first thing they saw was Joe Turner down on the floor and Stanley Albert leaning on a chair with Maggie dabbing at a cut on his hand with the edge of her petticoat.

He got a reputation from that Saturday night, and everybody was polite to him, and he could have had just about any of the girls he wanted. But he didn't seem to want them; at least he never took to coming to the houses to see them or to taking them home from Willie's. Maggie Mary Evans swore up and down that he had got her one day when she was fishing in Scanos River, but nobody paid her much attention. She liked to make up stories that way.

He had a little house in a valley to the east. Some boys who had gone out to shoot a cow for Christmas meat said they saw it. But they didn't go close even if there was three of them with a shotgun while Stanley Albert only carried a razor. Usually people only saw him on Saturday nights, and after a while they got used to him, though none of the men ever got to be friendly with him. There wasn't any mistaking the way the girls watched him. But after four or five Saturdays, by the time the summer was over, everybody expected him and waited for him, the way you'd wait for a storm to come or a freeze; not liking it, but not being able to do anything either. That's the way it went along: he'd buy his food for the coming week at Luther's Store, and then he'd come next door to Willie's.

He never stood up at the counter that was the bar. He'd take his glass and walk over to a table and sit down, and pull out a little bottle from his pocket, and add white lightning to the whisky. There wasn't anything could insult Willie more. He made the whisky and it was the best stuff in the county. He even had some customers drive clear out from Montgomery to buy some of his corn, and, being good stuff, there wasn't any call to add anything: it had enough kick of its own, raw and stinging to the throat. It was good stuff; nobody added anything to it—except Stanley Albert Thompson, while Willie looked at him and said things under his breath.

But nothing ever came of it, because everybody remembered how good a job Stanley Albert had done the first night he came.

Stanley Albert always had money, enough of it to pay for the groceries and all the whisky he wanted. There was always the sound of silver jingling in his trouser pocket. Everybody could hear that. Once when Willie was standing behind the bar, shuffling a pack of cards with a wide fancy twirl—just for amusement—Stanley Albert, who had had a couple of drinks and was feeling especially good, got up and pulled a handful of coins out of his pocket. He began to shuffle them through the air, the way Willie had done with the cards. Stanley Albert's black hands flipped the coins back and forth, faster and faster, until there was a solid silver ring hanging and shining in the air. Then Stanley Albert let one of his hands drop to his side and the silver ring poured back into the other hand and disappeared with a little clinking sound. And he dropped the money into his pocket with a short quick laugh.

That was the way Stanley Albert used his money: he had fun with it. Only thing, one night when Stanley Albert had had maybe a bit too much and sat dozing at his table, Morris Henry slipped a hand into the pocket. He wouldn't have ever dared to do that if Stanley Albert hadn't been dozing, leaning back in his chair, the bottle of white lightning empty in one hand. And Morris Henry slipped his little hand in the pocket and felt all around carefully. Then he turned his head slowly in a circle, looking at everybody in the room. He was a little black monkey Negro and his eyes were shiny and flat as mirrors. He slipped his hand back and scurried out into the yard and hid in the blackberry bushes. He wouldn't move until morning came; he just sat there, chewing on his little black fingers with his wide flaring yellow teeth. Anybody who wanted to know what was happening had to go out there and ask him. And ever afterwards Morris Henry swore that there hadn't been anything at all in Stanley Albert Thompson's pocket. But then everybody knew Morris Henry was crazy because just a few minutes later when Stanley Albert woke up and walked across to the bar, the change jingled in the pocket and he laid five quarters on the counter. And the money was good enough because Willie bounced it on the counter and it gave the clear ring of new silver.

Stanley Albert had money all right and he spent it; there wasn't anything short about him. He'd buy drinks for anybody who'd come over to his table; the only ones who came were the girls. And he didn't seem to care how much they drank. He'd just sit there, leaning way back in his chair, grinning, his teeth white and big behind his black lips, and matching them drink for drink, and every now and then running his eye up and down their length just to let them know he was appreciating their figures. Most often it was Maggie Mary who would be sitting there, warning all the other girls away with a little slanting of her eyes when they got near. And sometimes he'd sing a song: a song about whisky that would make everyone forget they didn't like him and laugh; or a song about poor boys who were going to be hanged in the morning. He had a good voice, strong and clear, and he pounded time with the flat of his hand on the table. And he'd always be looking at Alberta when he was singing until she'd get up, holding her head high and stiff, and march over to where Willie was and take hold of his arm real sweet and smile at him. And Willie would give Stanley Albert a quick mean look and then pour her a drink of his best whisky.

Stanley Albert had a watch, a big heavy gold one, round almost as a tomato, that would strike the hours. (That was how you could tell he was around sometimes—hearing his watch strike.) It was attached to a broad black ribbon and sometimes he held it up, let it swing before the eyes of whatever girl it happened to be at the time, let it swing slowly back and forth, up and down, so that her head moved with it. He had a ring too, on his right little finger: a white-colored band with a stone big as a chip of second coal and dark green. And when he fought, the first time he came into Willie's, the ring cut the same as a razor in his hand; it was maybe a little more messy, because its edges were jagged.

Those were two things—the watch and the ring—that must have cost more than all the money around here in a year. That was why all the women liked him so; they kept thinking of the nice things he could give them if he got interested. And that was why the men hated him. Things can go as smooth as glass if everybody's got about the same things and the same amount of money knocking around in a jean pocket on Saturday night. But when they don't, things begin happening. It would have been simpler maybe if they could have fought Stanley Albert Thompson, but there wasn't any man keen to fight him. That was how they started fighting each other. A feud that nobody'd paid any mind to for eight or ten years started up again.

It began one Sunday morning along toward dawn when everyone was feeling tired and leaving Willie's. Stanley Albert had gone out first and was sitting aside the porch railing. Jim Mastern was standing on the lowest step not moving, just staring across the fields, not being able to see anything in the dark, except maybe the bright-colored patterns the whisky set shooting starwise before his eyes. And Randall Stevens was standing in the doorway, looking down at his own foot, which he kept moving in a little circle around and around on the floor boards. And Stanley Albert was looking hard at him. Randall Stevens didn't lift his head; he just had his razor out and was across the porch in one minute, bringing down his arm in a sweeping motion to get at Jim Mastern's neck. But he was too drunk to aim very straight and he missed; but he did cut the ear away so that it fell on the steps. Jim Mastern was off like a bat in the daylight, running fast, crashing into things, holding one hand to the side of his head. And Randall Stevens folded up the razor and slipped it back in his pocket and walked off slowly, his head bent over, as if he was sleepy. There wasn't any more sense to it than that; but it started the feud again.

Stanley Albert swung his legs over the railing and stretched himself and yawned. Nobody noticed except Alberta, they were so busy listening to the way Jim Mastern was screaming and running across the fields, and watching Randall Stevens march off, solemnly, like a priest.

And the next night Randall Stevens tumbled down the steps of his cabin with his head full of scatter shot. It was a Monday night in November. His mother came out to see and stepped square on him, and his blood spattered on the hoarfrost. Randall Stevens had six brothers, and the next night they rode their lanky burred horses five miles south and tried to set fire to the Mastern house. That was the beginning; the fighting kept up, off and on, all through the winter. The sheriff from Gloverston came down to investigate. He came driving down the road in the new shiny white state police patrol car—the only one in the county—stopped in Willie's Café for a drink and went back taking two gallons of home brew with him. That wasn't exactly right, maybe, seeing that he had taken an oath to uphold the law; but he couldn't have done much, except get killed. And that was certain.

The Stevenses and their friends took to coming to Willie's on Friday nights; the Masterns kept on coming on Saturday. That just made two nights Willie had to keep the place open and the lamps filled with kerosene; the crowd was smaller; shotguns were leaning against the wall.

That's the way it went all winter. Everybody got on one side or the other—everybody except Stanley Albert Thompson. They both wanted him: they had seen what he could do in a fight. But Stanley Albert took to coming a night all by himself: Sunday night, and Willie had to light all the lamps for just him and stand behind the counter and watch him sit at the table adding lightning to the whisky.

Once along toward the end of February when Cy Mastern was killed and the roof of his house started burning with pine knots tossed from the ground, Stanley Albert was standing just on the rim of the light, watching. He helped the Masterns carry water, but Ed Stevens, who was hiding up in top of a pine to watch, swore that the water was like kerosene in his hands. Wherever he'd toss a bucketful, the fire would shoot up, brighter and hotter than before.

By March the frosts stopped, and there weren't any more cold winds. The farmers came out every noon, solemnly, and laid their hands on the bare ground to see if it was time to put in their earliest corn and potatoes. But the ground stayed cold a long time that year so that there wasn't any plowing until near May. All during that time from March till May there wasn't anything doing; that was the worst time for the fighting. In the winter your hand shakes so with the cold that you aren't much good with a gun or knife. But by March the air is warmer and you don't have any work to get you tired, so you spend all the time thinking.

That spring things got bad. There wasn't a crowd any more at Willie's though he kept the place open and the lights on for the three nights of the weekend. Neither the Stevenses nor the Masterns would come; they were too easy targets in a house with wall lamps burning. And on Sunday night the only person who ever came was Stanley Albert Thompson. He'd sit and drink his whisky and lightning and maybe sing a song or two for the girls who came over to see him. By the end of April that was changed too. He finally got himself the girl he wanted; the one he'd been waiting around nearly all winter for. And his courting was like this:

Thomas Henry Lacy and his sons, Luke and Tom, had gone for a walk, spoiling for a fight. They hadn't seen anything all evening, just some of the cows that had gone wild and went crashing away through the blueberry bushes. Alberta had taken herself along with them, since she was nearly as good as a man in a fight. They had been on the move all night but keeping in the range of a couple of miles and on the one side of the Scanos River. They were for Stevens and there was no telling what sort of affair the Masterns had rigged up on their ground. They rested for a while on the bluff of the river. Tom had some bread in his pocket and they ate it there, wondering if there was anybody in the laurels across the river just waiting for them to show themselves. Then they walked on again, not saying very much, seeing nothing but the moon flat against the sky and its light shiny on the heavy dew.

Alberta didn't particularly care when they left her behind. She turned her head to listen to the plaintive gargling call of a night quail, and when she looked again her father and the boys were gone. She knew where she was: on the second ridge away from home. There was just the big high ridge there to the left. The house was maybe twenty minutes away, but a hard walk, and Alberta was tired. She'd been washing all day, trying to make the clear brook water carry off the dirt and grease from the clothes, her mother standing behind her, yelling at each spot that remained, her light face black almost as her husband's with temper, and her gray fuzzy hair tied into knots like a pickaninny's. The boys had spent the whole day dozing in the shed while they put a new shoe on the mule.

Alberta listened carefully; there was nothing but night noises; her father and the boys would be halfway home by now, scrambling down the rain-washed sides of the ridge. For a moment she considered following them. "Ain't no raving rush, girl," she told herself aloud. The night was cool, but there wasn't any wind. With her bare feet she felt the dry pine needles, then sat down on them, propping her back against a tree. She slipped the razor from the cord around her neck and held it open loosely in the palm of her hand; then she fell asleep.

She woke when the singing started, opening her eyes but not moving. The moon was right overhead, shining down so that the trunks of the pines stuck straight up out of the white shiny ground. There wasn't a man could hide behind a pine, yet she didn't see him. Only the singing going round and round her.

> "Alberta, what's on you mind,
> Alberta, why you treat me so unkind?
> You keep me worried; you keep me blue
> All the time,
> Alberta, why you treat me so unkind?"

She pushed herself up to a sitting position, still looking straight ahead, not following the song around and around. She let the hand that held the razor fall in her lap, so that the moon struck on the blade.

> "Alberta, why you treat me so unkind?"

Nothing grows under pines, not much grass even, not any bushes big enough to hide a man. Only pine trees, like black matches stuck in the moonlight. Black like matches, and thin like matches. There wasn't a man could hide behind a pine under a bright moon. There wasn't a man could pass a bright open space and not be seen.

> "Alberta, let you hair hang low,
> Alberta, let you hair hang low.
> I'll give you more gold
> Than you apron can hold."

"That ain't a very nice song," she said.

> "I'll give you more gold
> Than you apron can hold."

She lifted her right hand and turned the razor's edge slowly in the light. "I got silver of my own right here," she said. "That enough for me."

The song went round in a circle, round and round, weaving in and out of the pines, passing invisible across the open moon filled spaces.

> "Alberta, let you hair hang low,
> I'll give you more gold
> Than you apron can hold
> If you just let you hair hang low."

There wasn't a man alive could do that. Go round and round.

> "Alberta, why you treat me so unkind?"

Round and round, in and out the thin black trees. Alberta stood up, following the sound, turning on her heel.

> "You keep me worried, you keep me blue
> All the time."

"I plain confused," she said. "I don't reckon I understand."

> "I'll give you more gold
> Than you apron can hold."

"I ain't got no apron," she said.

> "Alberta, let you hair hang low,
> Just let you hair hang low."

The song stopped and Stanley Albert Thompson came right out of a patch of bright moon ground, where there were only brown pine needles.

Alberta forgot she was tired; the moon-spotted ground rolled past her feet like the moon in the sky—effortless. She recognized the country they passed through: Blue Goose Lake, Scanos River, and the steeper rough ground of the north part of the country, toward the Tennessee border. It was a far piece to walk and she wondered at the lightness of her feet. By moonset they had got there—the cabin that the boys had seen one day while they were hunting cows. She hesitated a little then, not afraid, not reluctant, but just not sure how to go on. Stanley Albert Thompson had been holding her hand all evening; he still held it. Right at the beginning when he had first taken her along with him, she'd shook her head, no, she could walk; no man needed to lead her. But he'd grinned at her, and shook his head, imitating her gesture, so that the moon sparkled on his back curly hair, and his black broad forehead, and he took her hand and led her so that the miles seemed nothing and the hours like smooth water.

He showed her the cabin, from the outside first: mustard color, trimmed with white, like the cabins the railroad company builds. One room with high peaked roof.

"A real fine house," she said. "A real fine house. You work for the railroad?"

"No."

He took her inside. "You light with candles," she said.

"I ain't ever been able to stand the smell of lamps," he said.

"But it's a real nice house. I might could learn to like it."

"No might could about it." He smoothed the cloth on the table with his fingers. "You going to like it."

She bent her head and looked at him through her eyelashes. "Now I don't rightly know. Seems as how I don't know you."

"Sure you do," he said. "I'm standing right here."

"Seems as how I don't know nothing. You might could have a dozen girls all over this here state."

"I reckon there's a dozen," he said.

She glared at him, hands on hips. "You old fool jackass," she said. "I reckon you can just keep everything."

He jammed his hands into the back pockets of his denim pants and bent backward staring at the ceiling.

"Ain't you gonna try to stop me?"

"Nuh-uh."

She leaned against the doorjamb and twisted her neck to look at him. "Ain't you sorry I going?"

"Sure." He was still staring upward at the ceiling with its four crossed beams. "Sure, I real sorry."

"I don't see as how I could stay though."

"Sure you could." He did not look at her.

"I don't see as how. You ain't give me none of the things you said."

"You a driving woman," he said, and grinned, his mouth wide and white in the dark of his face.

Then he sat down at the table. There were five candles there, stuck in bottles, but only one was lighted, the one in the center. Wax had run all down the side of the candle and down the bottle in little round blobs, nubby like gravel. He picked one off, dirty white between his black fingers. He rolled it slowly between his flat palms, back and forth. Then he flipped it toward Alberta. It flashed silvery through the circle of lamplight and thudded against her skirt. She bent forward to pick it up: a coin, new silver. As she bent there, another one struck her shoulder, and another. Stanley Albert Thompson sat at the table, grinning and tossing the coins to her, until she had filled both pockets of her dress.

He pushed the candle away from him. "You all right, I reckon, now."

She held one coin in her hands, turning it over and over.

"That ain't what you promised. I remember how you came and sang:

> 'I give you more gold
> Than you apron can hold.' "

"Sure," he said and lifted a single eyebrow, very high. "I can do that all right, iffen you want it. I reckon I can do that."

She stood for a moment studying him. And Stanley Albert Thompson, from where he still sat at the table, curled up one corner of his mouth.

And very slowly Alberta began to smile. "I might could like it here," she said. "If you was real nice."

He got up then and rubbed her cheek very gently with his first finger. "I might could do that," he said. "I don't reckon it would be too heavy a thing to do."

The candle was on the table to one side. It caught the brightness of Alberta's eyes as she stood smiling at Stanley Albert Thompson. The steady yellow light threw her shadow over his body, a dark shadow that reached to his chin. His own shadow was on the wall behind. She glanced at it over his shoulder and giggled. "You better do something about your shadow there, Mr. Thompson. That there is a ugly shadow, sure."

He turned his head and glanced at it briefly. "Reckon so," he said.

It was an ugly shadow, sure. Alberta looked at Stanley Albert Thompson and shook her head. "I can't hardly believe it," she said. "You a right pretty man."

He grinned at her and shook himself so that the shadow on the wall spun around in a wild turn.

"I don't reckon you can do anything about it."

"No," he said briefly. "I can't go changing my shadow." He hunched his back so that the figure on the wall seemed to jump up and down in anger.

She stepped over to him, putting her hands behind her, leaning backward to see his face. "If he don't do any more than dance on a wall, I ain't complaining."

Stanley Albert stood looking down at her, looking down the length of his face at her, and rocking slowly back and forth on his heels. "No," he said. "He ain't gonna do more than wiggle around the wall sometimes. But you can bet I am."

The coins weighed down the pockets of her dress, and his hands were warm against her skin. "I reckon I'm satisfied," she said.

That was the way it began. That was the courting. The woman was young and attractive and strong. The man could give her whatever she wanted. There were other courtings like that in this country. Every season there were courtings like that.

People would see them around sometimes; or sometimes they'd only hear them when they were still far off. Sometimes it would be Stanley Albert Thompson singing:

> "Alberta, let you hair hang low,
>   Alberta, let you hair hang low.
>   I'll give you more gold
>   Than you apron can hold
>   If you just let you hair hang low."

He had a strong voice. It could carry far in a quiet day or night. And if any of the people heard it, they'd turn and look at each other and nod their heads toward it, not saying anything, but just being sure that everyone was listening. And whenever Willie heard it, he'd close his eyes for a minute, seeing Alberta; and then he'd rub his hands all over his little black kinky head and whistle: "Euuuu," which meant that he was very, very sorry she had left him.

And sometimes all you could hear of them would be the chiming of Stanley Albert's watch every quarter-hour. One night that August, when the moon was heavy and hot and low, Maggie Mary was out walking with Jack Belden. She heard the clear high chime and remembered the nights at Willie's and the dangling gold watch. And she turned to Jack Belden, who had just got her comfortable in one arm, and jammed her fingers in his eyes and ran off after the sound. She didn't find them; and it wouldn't have much mattered if she had. Stanley Albert was much too gone on Alberta to notice any other woman in more than a passing appraising way.

And sometimes people would come on them walking alone, arms around each other's waist; or sitting in a shady spot during the day's heat, his head on her lap and both of them dozing and smiling a little. And everybody who saw them would turn around and get out of there fast; but neither of them turned a head or looked up: there might not have been anyone there.

And then every night they'd go down to Willie's. The first night they came—it was on a Thursday—the place was closed up tight. There wasn't ever anybody came on Thursday. Stanley Albert went around back to where Willie lived and pounded on the door, and when Willie didn't answer he went around to the front again where Alberta was waiting on the steps and kicked in the front panel of the wood door. Willie came scuttling out, his eyes round and bewildered like a suckling's and saw them sitting at one of the tables drinking his home brew, only first putting lightning into it. After that they came every night, just them. It was all most people could do to afford a drink on Saturday or the weekend, but some of them would walk over to Willie's just to look at Stanley Albert and Alberta sitting there. They'd stand at the windows and look in, sweating in the hot summer nights and looking. Maybe a few of them would still be there waiting when Stanley and Alberta got ready to go, along toward morning.

That's what they did every single night of the year or so they were together. If they fell asleep, Willie would just have to stand waiting. They'd go out with their arms around each other's waist, staggering some, but not falling. And an hour or so later, people who were going out before dawn to get a little work done in the cool would see them clear over on the other side of the county, at Goose Lake, maybe, a good three hours' walk for a man cold sober. Willie had his own version of how they got around. They just picked up their feet, he said, and went sliding off down the winds. Once, he said, when they were sitting over on the bench against the wall, Stanley Albert flat on it with his head on her lap, when the whisky made the man in him come up sudden, so he couldn't wait, they went straight out the window, up the air, like a whistle sound. Willie had the broken glass to show the next morning, if you wanted to believe him.

Willie hated them, the two of them, maybe because they broke his glass, maybe because they made him stay up late every single night of the week, so that he had to hold his eyes open with his fingers, and watch them pour lightning into his very best whisky, maybe because he had wanted Alberta mighty bad himself. He'd been giving her presents—bottles of his best stuff—but he just couldn't match Stanley Albert. Those are three reasons; maybe he had others. And Maggie Mary hated them; and she had only one reason.

Once Pete Stokes shot at Stanley Albert Thompson. He hadn't wanted to: he was scared like everybody else. But Maggie Mary Evans talked him into it. She was a fine-looking girl: she could do things like that. He hid behind the privy and got a perfect bead on Stanley Albert as he came out the door. The bullet just knocked off a piece of Willie's doorframe. When Pete saw what happened he dropped the gun and began to run, jumping the rail fence and crashing face-first through the thick heavy berry bushes. Stanley Albert pursed his lips together and rubbed his hands on his chin, slow, like he was deciding what to do. Then he jumped down from the porch and went after Pete. He ran through the hackberries too; only with him it did not seem difficult: none of the crackling and crashing and waving arms. Stanley Albert just put his head down and moved his legs, and the sprays of the bushes, some of them thick as a rooster's spur, seemed to pull back and make way. Nobody saw the fight: the brave ones were too drunk to travel fast; and the sober ones didn't want to mix with a man like Stanley Albert, drunk and mad. Alberta, she just ran her hand across her mouth and then wiped it along the side of her green satin dress, yawning like she was tired. She stood listening for a while, her head cocked a little, though there wasn't anything to hear, then walked off, pulling down the dress across her hips. And the next night she and Stanley Albert were back at Willie's, and Pete never did turn up again. Willie used to swear that he ended up in the Scanos River and that if the water wasn't so yellow muddy, that if you could see to the bottom, you would see Pete lying there, along with all the others Stanley Albert had killed.

At the last it was Willie who got the idea. For a week, carefully, he put aside the coins Stanley Albert gave him. There were a lot of them, all new silver, because Stanley Albert always paid in silver. Then one morning very early, just after Stanley Albert and Alberta left, Willie melted the coins down, and using the molds he kept for his old outsized pistol, he cast four bullets.

He made a special little shelf for the pistol under the counter so that it would be near at hand. And he waited all evening, sometimes touching the heavy black handle with the tips of his fingers; and he waited, hoping that Stanley Albert would drink enough to pass out. But of course nothing like that happened. So Willie poured himself three or four fingers of his best stuff and swallowed it fast as his throat would stand, then he blinked his little eyes fast for a second or so to clear his vision, and he reached for the gun. He got two shots over the bar, two good ones: the whole front of Stanley Albert's plaid shirt folded together and sank in, after the silver bullets went through. He got up, holding the table edge, unsteady, bending over, looking much smaller, his black skin gray-filmed and dull. His eyes were larger: they reached almost across his face—and they weren't dark any more; they were silver, two polished pieces of silver. Willie was afraid to fire again; the pistol shook where he held it in his two hands.

Then Stanley Albert walked out, not unsteady any more, but bent over the hole in his chest, walked out slowly with his eyes shining like flat metal, Alberta a few steps behind. They passed right in front of Willie, who still hadn't moved; his face was stiff with fear. Quietly, smoothly, in a single motion, almost without interrupting her step, Alberta picked up a bottle (the same one from which he had poured his drink moments before) and swung it against Willie's head. He slipped down in a quiet little heap, his legs folded under him, his black kinky head on top. But his idea had worked: over by Stanley Albert's chair there was a black pool of blood.

All that was maybe eight or ten years ago. People don't see them any more—Stanley and Alberta. They don't think much about them, except when something goes wrong—like weevils getting in the cotton, or Willie's burning down and Willie inside it—then they begin to think that those two had a hand in it. Brad Tedrow swore that he had seen Stanley Albert that night, just for a second, standing on the edge of the circle of light, with a burning faggot in his hand. And the next morning Brad went back to look, knowing that your eyes play tricks at night in firelight; he went back to look for footprints or some sign. All he found was a burnt-out stick of pine wood that anybody could have dropped.

And kids sometimes think they hear the jingle of silver in Stanley Albert's pocket, or the sound of his watch. And when women talk—when there's been a miscarriage or a stillbirth—they remember and whisper together.

And they all wonder if that's not the sort of work they do, the two of them. Maybe so; maybe not. The people themselves are not too sure. They don't see them around any more.

§ FOR COMMENT

Read the following notes on "The Black Prince" prepared by the author of the story. What distinction does she make between "reasonable realistic paths" and "myth-making"? Is "The Black Prince" basically realistic as she suggests that all fiction is? How? Cite examples of "verbal dexterity" and "technical tricks" she employs in "The Black Prince." How does the writing style, for example, contribute to the mood, and what has the establishing of mood to do with the theme of the story? Do you agree that the theme of the story has to do with "the infinite ramifications of evil"? Support your answers with specific details from the story.

NOTES ON "THE BLACK PRINCE"[1]

There is only one problem for a writer—the communication of meaning. All the verbal dexterity, all the technical tricks of a fiction writer are designed to minimize the forces that oppose communication: the recalcitrance of the language itself, the limits of individual understanding, the basic paucity of human experience.

Fiction, as I see it, is basically and always realistic. What else can it be? I know nothing beyond my experience and the experiences of people like me. If my expression becomes too personal, my symbols too intimate, my readers no longer understand. The demands of communication force me—

[1] The editors wish to thank Miss Grau for her response to our request that she provide notes on "The Black Prince" for this book.

partially at least—into the common mold of thought. I find myself dancing around the edges of meaning, trying to cut off a bit of the truth here, a bit there, trying to express, to shake the limitations of experience, above all to communicate my vision of the world. And, like most writers, I sometimes lose patience and abandon the reasonable realistic paths for the simple direct truths of myth-making. This is what happened in "The Black Prince." It is a fairy story, a legend. It has a legend's logic and a legend's meaning. I wrote it when I was still in college, and it is an attempt to say directly what I have been saying obliquely ever since.

Probably as a result of my fundamentalist upbringing, this story, like my subsequent fiction, has as theme the infinite ramifications of evil. Sometimes it is called "guilt" or "sin" or "social injustice"—the names change, but the presence remains.

The Novel

Origins and Development

The novel has been the most popular literary genre since the time of its emergence in England in the early eighteenth century. Indeed, it is hard to determine whether the novel created the audience or arose because there was a ready and waiting audience. In any case, there was an enormous increase in population and in the members of the middle class and at the same time an increase in literacy.[1] In the late seventeenth century Parliament had allowed censorship of the press to lapse, and pamphlets and newspapers multiplied. Reliance on the patronage system had diminished, and authors had to begin looking to the public for support. Periodicals and books, especially prose designed for the middle classes—travel literature, diaries, manuals of piety and instruction, criminal biographies—began to be published in increasing numbers. Book clubs and circulating libraries came into existence. But, most important, there had evolved a new way of looking at the world. The emergence of the novel must be linked with the new scientific rationalism. In the past reality had been defined as a system of universal truths; it was something large and it transcended the individual. But now reality was being defined in terms of the individual and his sense impressions. The individual in interaction with the society took on greater and greater importance, and the novel arose as that form of fiction best suited to, and indeed charged with, the task of dealing with particular men in specific places at specified times. A primary assumption of the novel was that it would report the actions of individual characters with details sufficient and abundant to create the illusion of authenticity to the material facts of the everyday world. This is why the one word most often used to describe the novel is the word "realistic."

To Daniel Defoe is given credit for introducing the wealth of circumstantial details that established scene and character in such a convincing way that his readers accepted as literally true the narrative ascribed to the character Robinson Crusoe (1719). But perhaps more important than this particular convincingness of scene and character in *Robinson Crusoe* was Defoe's invention of a developing character in a plot governed by causality

[1] See Walter Allen, *The English Novel* (New York: E. P. Dutton, 1954), for a fuller discussion.

and thus the achievement of a dramatic coherence and an integration of character, theme, and structure, such as is found in his *Moll Flanders* (1722), the self-portrait of a woman, told in the first person, setting forth details of her childhood and life.

Samuel Richardson introduced the epistolary method to the novel form, a method that allowed him in such novels as *Pamela* (1740) and *Clarissa* (1747–1748) to make extensive analyses of characters as they think and feel. Richardson discovered a titillating plot formula, what has been called "the principle of procrastinated rape." *Pamela,* for example, is the story of a virtuous young housemaid whose honor is every day threatened by the son of her mistress. But her virtue triumphs, and he finally marries her.

Following Richardson, Henry Fielding, Laurence Sterne, and Tobias Smollett assured the popularity of the novel. Fielding became the first theorist of the novel with his definition of the comic epic in prose, which appears as a preface to *Joseph Andrews* (1742). He is also credited with the creation of some of the most well-rounded characters in literature—including Parson Abraham Adams, an English Don Quixote and one of the central figures in *Joseph Andrews*, and Squire Western of *Tom Jones* (1749), a coarse and lascivious but always vital figure—and with the devising of the so-called architectonic plot, a compact, tightly woven arrangement of events. As a playwright in the theater, he had learned to set scenes rapidly and to use fresh, life-like dialogue, and this together with a fundamental human sympathy and a keen perception of the ridiculous in human affairs make him perhaps the first great English novelist.

With Laurence Sterne the novel was almost literally turned upside down. *Tristram Shandy* (1760–1767) is an attempt to render life at the moment that it is being lived. Sterne knew the philosopher John Locke's theory that the association of ideas in the mind is an illogical process and used this theory as the basis for the structure of his novel, thus anticipating the modern stream-of-consciousness technique. But chaotic as the novel seems to be, it is apparent chaos and not real. Once the order of the novel is understood, its structure can be seen to be both purposeful and intriguing. Surely, also, the characters themselves, Tristram and his father, Uncle Toby, Corporal Trim, the Widow Wadman, Yorick the parson—all creatures of fixed ideas but as completely convincing as real people—helped to make the novel the popular success that it was.

Popular, too, and readable were the novels of Tobias Smollett, who used exaggerated and distorted traits of human behavior to expose a crude and brutal society. *Humphrey Clinker* (1771), perhaps his best novel and according to some critics the greatest epistolary novel in the English language, presents a picture of English life in the 1760's. Five people make a tour of Scotland and England and write letters describing the same events from different and usually conflicting points of view.

The eighteenth-century novel, then, though written with a variety of techniques, kept its primary focus on the presentation of a real world and on the delineation of individualized characters acting at a given moment in a recognizable place.

The nineteenth century is marked by the major figures Jane Austen and Sir Walter Scott. Austen is sometimes said to represent a feminization of Fielding's variety of techniques and enormous world view. Her vision is smaller, but, many think, more intense. Hers is a world of minutiae, of parlor manners, which she presents as morals in microcosmic form. *Pride and Prejudice* (1813), her most popular novel, presents as detailed a world as has been created in fiction. There is a larger world outside her book which she never touches on, but her world is none the less valid and self-contained.

If Austen's world is small, the world of Sir Walter Scott's historical romances is large and varied. The creator of a diversified gallery of characters and multifold situations, Scott is considered to be the first successful writer of historical novels. *The Heart of Midlothian* (1818) is perhaps the finest, but *The Bride of Lammermoor* (1819) and *Ivanhoe* (1820), among some half dozen others, remain popular even today.

The names of William Makepeace Thackeray, Charles Dickens, Anthony Trollope, and Charlotte and Emily Brontë come to mind as typical Victorian novelists. Their works do not form a coherent body, but these novelists seem to have more in common with each other than they have with the later Victorian novelists, George Eliot, George Meredith, Thomas Hardy. As Walter Allen says, the early Victorians shared a special set of assumptions, ideas, feelings. They were at one with the public and willingly conditioned by it. Although aware of the evils of it and voicing both doubts and fears, they took these evils to be temporary, accepting wholeheartedly the idea of progress based on respectability and on the cultivation of the virtues of industry, thrift, and self-control. Representative of this group of novelists are *Vanity Fair* (1847–1848), *Great Expectations* (1860), *Barchester Towers* (1857), *Jane Eyre* (1847), and *Wuthering Heights* (1847). On the other hand, the later Victorians questioned the fundamental assumptions, set themselves apart from their age, and were critical of it, sometimes even hostile to it. They were influenced by the great continental novelists, who had voiced the notion that the novel should be an art form, serious in intent and perfectly controlled. This period in England saw the publication of Eliot's *Adam Bede* (1859), Meredith's *The Ordeal of Richard Feverel* (1859), and Hardy's great *Tess of the d'Urbervilles* (1891) and *Jude the Obscure* (1895).

The second half of the nineteenth century was also marked by the publication of Gustave Flaubert's *Madame Bovary* (1856–1857) in France, Leo Tolstoy's *War and Peace* (1865–1869) in Russia, and Nathaniel Hawthorne's *The Scarlet Letter* (1850), Herman Melville's *Moby-Dick* (1851), Mark Twain's *Huckleberry Finn* (1885), and Stephen Crane's *The Red Badge of Courage* (1895) in America—all great world novels that set the standard for the full flowering of the novel form in this century. A list of the names of the twentieth-century novelists who have achieved world stature is long indeed and must include Thomas Mann and Franz Kafka in Germany; Marcel Proust, Albert Camus, and André Gide in France; Joseph Conrad, Virginia Woolf, James Joyce, and D. H. Lawrence in England; Henry James, William Faulkner, and Ernest Hemingway in the United States.

The achievement of the novel in the twentieth century is marked by a refinement of technique achieved by authors fully conscious of the esthetics of the novel and deliberately explorative and experimental. In his book A *Guide to the Novel*, Richard M. Eastman says, "Modern fictional technique is mainly the efflorescence of one conviction: that the novel should be a dramatic rather than assertive art. In the now-hackneyed formula, its rule is: 'Show, don't tell.' " [2] As Eastman indicates, this conviction led to the disappearance of the conspicuous and commenting author and the establishment of such indirect devices as the limited point of view, the stream-of-consciousness technique, the manipulation of various time orders, and the increasing use of images and symbols to direct meaning. The twentieth-century novel is denser than its predecessors; it is more poetic, evocative, suggestive, metaphoric, and more difficult. It exhibits the same unity and direction as the modern short story, and except for length is remarkably similar in structure. Its greater length, however, allows for the use of more characters and more situations and for more reader participation in the duration of time, all devices which aid in the creation of the illusion of reality.

Thomas Hardy § 1840–1928
Tess of the d'Urbervilles

A famed English novelist, short story writer, and poet, Hardy was trained as an architect, but turned to the writing of fiction before he was thirty and published four novels anonymously. The success of Far from the Madding Crowd (1874) *caused Hardy to put aside his work as an architect, to sign his novels with his name, and to launch his career as a novelist. The best of his novels are those which he classified under the heading of "Novels of Character and Environment." In this group are* The Return of the Native (1878), Tess of the d'Urbervilles (1891), *and* Jude the Obscure (1895). *After the*

---

[2] Richard Eastman, *A Guide to the Novel* (San Francisco: Chandler, 1965), p. 135.

publication of The Well Beloved *in 1897, Hardy wrote no more novels but turned to the great epic-drama of the Napoleonic Wars,* The Dynasts *(1904–1906–1908).*

The publication of Tess *brought Hardy great notoriety. It might be hard for the present day student to believe, but it is none the less true, that Hardy was forced to delete or alter several episodes in the novel before any magazine would publish it serially. He restored these passages before the novel was published in book form, and its publication brought outcries from many critics and reviewers. Even Henry James, in a letter to Robert Louis Stevenson dated February 17, 1893, wrote, "The pretense of 'sexuality' is only equalled by the absence of it, and the abomination of the language by the author's reputation for style." Nevertheless, in his preface to the Modern Library Edition of* Tess, *Carl J. Weber writes that today there is "general critical agreement that Hardy's* Tess *deserves to be ranked among the greatest of English works of fiction, and of all his novels it has certainly enjoyed the greatest popularity throughout the sixty years of its history."*

The analysis of Hardy's fiction that follows is an example of historical criticism at its best, and, although little specific mention is made of Tess, *most of what is said is relevant to it.*

Hardy's Cosmic Vision[1]

WALTER ALLEN

Thomas Hardy's first novel, *Desperate Remedies*, was published in 1871. He was then thirty-one. His career as a novelist ended twenty-five years later, with *Jude the Obscure*. Thereafter his life, right up to his death in 1928, was devoted to poetry, which had been his first love. He turned to the novel primarily because it was the dominant literary form of the time; writing novels was a way of earning a living. It is often said that he had little interest in the novel as an art form, but the statement needs constant qualification. His outspokenness where sex was concerned, in *Tess* and *Jude*, made him, in the eyes of his contemporaries, the English counterpart of the great European novelists, Flaubert, Tolstoi, Zola. But his was an older art of storytelling than theirs, and perhaps it is on the word storytelling that the emphasis should fall. Of current theories of realism he was highly critical. He turned naturally for his standard of reference to the primitive oral tale: "We story-tellers," he said, "are all Ancient Mariners," and just as so much of his lyric poetry is based on the rhythms of country dances, country

[1] Originally published in *The English Novel*, paperback edition (New York: E. P. Dutton, 1954), pp. 285–304. The title has been supplied by the editors.

airs, and folk songs, is a new expression of an ancient music, so behind his novels we feel the shaping presence of the ballads of love, passion, and betrayal he knew as a boy when he was a notable fiddler at dances.

Hardy was a provincial, a countryman; indeed, despite his training as an architect and his wide knowledge of literature and of the science and philosophy of his age, almost a naif, a primitive. This differentiates him from contemporaries like George Eliot and Henry James. Their work represents "the tone of the center," to use Arnold's phrase. Hardy is strictly an eccentric. It is in his provincialism and naivety, one could almost say his uncouthness, that his strength lies. When he leaves the intensely local world he knew to ape the tone of the center and try to render fashionable life, as in *The Hand of Ethelberta* (1876), he fails as badly as any novelist. But on his own ground he is practically unassailable.

In some respects he is like Scott. When he revived the word Wessex to denote a region of England, he did so in full consciousness of the historical weight of the name. Apart from *The Trumpet-Major* (1880), he wrote nothing that can be called an historical novel, yet his characters, like Scott's, live in the additional dimension of history; peasants for the most part, they are close to an earth that has changed little over centuries. Most of them as they live in our memory, the principal characters in *Jude* being the great exception, seem to live in a timeless era in which actual historical events and persons have assumed the vagueness and largeness of myth. Like Scott, Hardy was fortunate for his art in being born just as an age was ending. Acutely, painfully conscious of the modern world as he was, he looked back to the past and summed up in his fiction a life that was dying when he was a child, a life cut off from the main stream of national life, more primitive, more pagan. Set George Eliot's renderings of rural life beside Hardy's: hers are generally slightly earlier in time, yet however sequestered the scenes described may be, they strike one as much more modern. The industrial revolution is not far away, nor is the religion that came out of it, nor is eighteenth-century rationalism. The scenes of witchcraft in *The Return of the Native* would be incredible in any Midland village, however remote, in which a Dolly Winthrop lived.

Hardy was attempting something very different from the aims of most novelists. The art of the novelist who sets out to display human beings in the context of social life must be one of constant differentiation and discrimination between characters. But social life as we find it depicted variously in Jane Austen, Thackeray, Trollope, George Eliot, and James, scarcely exists in Hardy. His characters stand in relation to other things, the weather, the seasons, a traditional craft. He sees his characters much as Scott does his, first in their generic aspects; thus, before he is anything else, Giles Winterbourne is the peasant good with trees, Gabriel Oak the good shepherd, Tess the dairymaid. Individuality, as such, is not at all what he is after; what concerns him most in human beings is their response to the deep-rooted passions, above all sexual love.

Intellectually, Hardy was very much an advanced man of his time. That he was a pessimist seems to me to need no proof. But reading his work one can scarcely fail to see him as a soul naturally Christian. This involves no contradiction; as David Cecil has written in *Hardy the Novelist:* "Christian teachers have always said that there was no alternative to Christianity but pessimism, that if Christian doctrine was not true, life was a tragedy. Hardy agreed with them."

He did so because he lived at a time when the intellectual assent to Christianity was probably more difficult than it has ever been, and however much he hoped, in the words of his famous poem, that "it might be so," he could never give Christianity his intellectual assent. Yet while intellectually he was "advanced," emotionally he was a traditionalist. He wrote in a letter in 1915: "You must not think me a hard-headed rationalist for all this. Half my time—particularly when writing verse—I 'believe' (in the modern sense of the word) . . . in spectres, mysterious voices, intuitions, omens, dreams, haunted places, etc. But I do not believe in them in the old sense any more for that." He did not believe because, as G. M. Young says in *Last Essays*, the total effect of Darwin, Mill, Huxley, and Herbert Spencer on their age was to make it "almost impossible for their younger contemporaries to retain the notion of a transcendent, governing Providence." Hardy was the quintessential younger, as George Eliot had been the quintessential strict, contemporary of these scientists and philosophers, and therein lies a considerable part of the difference in their attitudes of life and to their fictional characters. Loss of faith compelled George Elliot to stress, far beyond orthodox Christianity, the individual's responsibility for his actions. For her, the choice between right and wrong was open for every human being to make; the basis of her ethics is the belief in the freedom of the will. But Hardy was scarcely a moralist at all, because in his universe morals were beside the point; between the forces of nature, including therein the forces of his own nature, and man's aspirations there could be no reconciliation; they were eternally opposed, and from the human view the workings of nature must appear hostile and malign.

What Hardy found in the science and philosophy of his day reinforced the findings of his temperament and of his observations of a largely traditional way of life and his greatness is due to this marriage between his philosophic pessimism and his habit of seeing human behavior in its more abiding aspects. It was not an easy or harmonious marriage, but its tensions were part of its strength. Without the philosophical interpretation of what he saw and felt his work might have approximated in scope to the traditional ballad; but if he had not seen human beings in depth, in their relation to traditional skills, the work and rhythm of the seasons and the force of the great non-rational, instinctual urgencies, he would probably not have been the superior of other novelists of much the same time, Gissing in England and Dreiser in America, who interpreted man according to the deterministic philosophy of the day. They, for all their pity for mankind, do not achieve more than the pathetic; Hardy rises to tragedy, and his tragedy is an arraignment of the nature of the universe as he saw it.

Believing that where man was concerned the very nature of things was malign, he believed also that it was the more malign the more sensitive, the more intelligent, the more finely organized the human being. The only characters in Hardy who need fear no fall are those already down, those who live close to earth without aspirations to rise, the wonderful gallery of peasants whose attitude to existence is unillusioned, accepting, and humorous. These Hardy portrays and records through their speech with a warmth and sympathy equivalent to love. His second novel, the delightful pastoral *Under the Greenwood Tree* (1872), he devoted to them entirely; elsewhere, they act as the chorus to the tragedy.

If any single novel may be taken as the key to Hardy's mind and art it is probably *The Return of the Native*, his sixth book, published in 1878. A tragic love story, like almost all his fiction, it is extremely simple in plot. Clym Yeobright, who has been a diamond merchant in Paris, comes home to serve his fellow men as teacher and preacher. He falls in love with and marries Eustacia Vye, who has had a secret love affair with Damon Wildeve, the husband of Clym's cousin, Thomasin. Eustacia and Wildeve resume their affair and, after their death by drowning, Thomasin marries Diggory Venn, the traveling raddleman, who has throughout brooded over the action of the novel like a guardian but not always effectual angel. The significant characters are Clym and Eustacia. Clym is the first of Hardy's idealists, the first of what have been called his "prig heroes," a man conscious all the time of what Hardy himself called "the ache of modernism." In a sense, he represents Hardy's own values:

> In Clym Yeobright's face could be dimly seen the typical countenance of the future. Should there be a classic period to art hereafter, its Pheidias may produce such faces. The view of life as a thing to be put up with, replacing that zest for existence which was so intense in early civilizations, must enter so thoroughly into the constitution of the advanced races that its facial expression will become accepted as a new artistic departure. People already feel that a man who lives without disturbing a curve of feature, or setting a mark of mental concern anywhere upon himself, is too far removed from modern perceptiveness to be a modern type. Physically beautiful men— the glory of the race when it was young—are almost an anachronism now; and we may wonder whether, at some time or other, physically beautiful women may not be an anachronism likewise.

Clym, then, is Hardy's modern man. Eustacia, however, is not his modern woman; she is woman as he most characteristically sees her. She has her affinities with Flaubert's Emma Bovary. She is a born romantic, at odds with her environment:

> To be loved to madness—such was her great desire. Love was to her the one cordial which could drive away the eating loneliness of her days. And

she seemed to long for the abstraction called passionate love more than for any particular lover.

But Hardy's depiction of her is very different from Flaubert's of Emma. Emma is revealed with cruel exactitude, exposed with the clinical remorselessness of a case history. Eustacia is magnified into a splendid romantic figure. E. M. Forster says in *Aspects of the Novel* that Hardy "conceives his novels from an enormous height." He conceives his great characters from the same height, in the case of Clym by making him a representative of what he considered modern man—and the man of the future—in his most essential qualities, in the case of Eustacia by a richly romantic view of her. There is no implied criticism of her attitudes, such as is felt throughout in Flaubert's rendering of Emma. She is too big for that, and all Hardy's powers of evocation are showered upon her:

> Eustacia Vye was the raw material of a divinity. On Olympus she would have done well with a little preparation. She had the passions and instincts which make a model goddess, that is, those which make not quite a model woman. Had it been possible for the earth and mankind to be entirely in her grasp for a while, had she handled the distaff, the spindle, and the shears at her own free will, few in the world would have noticed the change of government. There would have been the same inequality of lot, the same heaping up of favours here, of contumely there, the same generosity before justice, the same perpetual dilemmas, the same captious alternation of caresses and blows that we endure now. . . .
>
> She had Pagan eyes, full of nocturnal mysteries, and their light, as it came and went, and came again, was partially hampered by their oppressive lids and lashes; and of these the under lid was much fuller than it usually is with English women. This enabled her to indulge in reverie without seeming to do so: she might have been believed capable of sleeping without closing them up. Assuming that the souls of men and women were visible essences, you could fancy the colour of Eustacia's soul to be flame-like. The sparks from it that rose into her dark pupils gave the same impression. . . .
>
> Her presence brought memories of such things as Bourbon roses, rubies, and tropical midnights; her moods recalled lotus-eaters and the march in *Athalie*; her motions, the ebb and flow of the sea; her voice, the viola . . .

The passage reminds us that Pater had published *The Renaissance* five years before. The wonder is that so highly romantic and mannered a piece of writing could have been successfully woven into the texture of the novel. Yet it is, and one can think of no other English novelist who could have got away with it. One thing, however, is clear: the woman so described could not possibly be a fit wife for the single-minded idealist who "had a conviction that the want of most men was knowledge of a sort which brings wisdom rather than affluence," and who, wishing "to raise the class at the expense of the individuals rather than the individuals at the expense of the class," "was ready at once to be the first unit sacrificed." And indeed Eustacia marries Clym because she cannot *not* believe that he will return to Paris, taking her with him; when his eyesight fails as a result of his studies and he takes up furze cutting rather than endure idleness, she again becomes Wildeve's mistress, as she was before her marriage.

But, as *The Return of the Native* further shows, there is another way in which Hardy conceives his novels and their tragic characters from an enormous height. The anthologists of English prose have done him no service by snipping off from the book the description of Egdon Heath with which it opens and isolating it as a purple passage. The heath is not just so much scenic backcloth to the action, it is all-pervasive; without it, the novel would be unimaginable, for the heath provides it with the especial dimension in which it has its being. The heath holds the action of the novel and its characters as though in the hollow of the hand. It does not matter in the least that, living on Egdon, Eustacia dreams of Paris; that is part of her tragic destiny. The function of the heath in the novel is to describe, as carefully and thoroughly as Hardy can, the real circumstances in which man lives. What the individual man may feel about those circumstances is irrelevant, for he does not thereby escape them. The heath, one might say, is an extended image of the nature of which man is part, in which he is caught, which conditions his very being, and which cares nothing for him. His life in relation to it is as ephemeral as the bonfires the peasants make of the heath furze.

This ephemerality of man, the insignificance of his being, is brought out time and again in *The Return of the Native*, generally by reference to the brooding permanence of the vast heath. "This obscure, obsolete, superseded country" is the world of nature under the aspect of time, time geological and historical alike. Man has scarcely scratched its surface. It has its own life, which is man's only when he is content to be lowly and unassuming like the furze cutters who live off it. Hardy shows us the heath through all the seasons of the year and over immeasurably greater stretches of time. At times it "seemed to belong to the ancient world of the carboniferous period, when the forms of plants were few, and of the fern kind; when there was neither bud nor blossom, nothing but a monotonous extent of leafage, amid which no bird sang."

Such is the heath in what may be called its geological aspect. But it has another:

The month of March arrived, and the heath showed its first faint signs of awakening from winter trance. The awakening was almost feline in its stealthiness. The pool outside the bank by Eustacia's dwelling, which seemed as dead and desolate as ever to an observer who moved and made noises in his observation, would gradually disclose a state of great animation when silently watched awhile. A timid animal world had come to life for the season. Little tadpoles and efts began to bubble up through the water, and to race along beneath it; toads made noises like very young ducks, and advanced to the margin in twos and threes; overhead, bumble-bees flew hither and thither in the thickening light, their drone coming and going like the sound of a gong.

The secret life of the heath Hardy describes again and again, with all the powers of eye and ear for nature in which he is unrivaled among our novelists. The human inhabitants of the heath he sees almost from an anthropologist's point of view, or the specialist's in comparative religion. When the peasants dance in August, time, as it were, is telescoped; the centuries slip by; they behave as their ancient ancestors did. "For the time Paganism was revived in their hearts, the pride of life was all in all, and they adored none other than themselves." Christian Cantle, Granfer Cantle, Timothy Fairway, Sam the turf cutter, and the rest are as much a part of nature, of the life of the heath, as the toads in March that make noises like very young ducks. Not so Clym, Eustacia, Thomasin, and Wildeve; these are cut off from nature, and that they are cut off means that they are undone, though in the case of Thomasin, Hardy altered his original conclusion of the novel to provide her with a happy ending.

Hardy's view of life, then, was cosmic. This means that his tragic novels exist always on two planes, the plane of design and the plane of plot. As a plotter he was often defective. Sometimes—and then it seems the result of incompetence—he stumbles because the course of the action suddenly becomes implausible, as when Tess kills Alec d'Urberville with the bread knife, an implausibility underlined by the failure in tact which allows him to describe the blood seeping through the floor to the ceiling below in the likeness of "a gigantic ace of hearts." His incursions into melodrama are similar signs of a failure in tact; the final arrest of Tess at Stonehenge is an instance. It just fails to come off; the grandiose conception is somehow blurred.

But Hardy's chief weakness in plot arises from his view of causality. He is intent to show that the stars in their courses fight against the aspiring, the man or woman who would rise above the common lot through greatness of spirit, of ambition, or passion. Here his problem was difficult indeed, and it is not surprising he never solved it. For the universe itself to become suddenly hostile to man could only be shown through the working of what may be called the freak coincidence. It is silly to blame Hardy for the emphasis he places on coincidence; simply, he believed in coincidence. To take an example from *The Return of the Native*, it is part of the conspiracy of things against the exceptional man that Clym's mother should visit Eustacia, in order to make the peace between them, at the very time that Eustacia is entertaining Wildeve; it is part of nature's enmity that she should be bitten by the snake on her way home. But Hardy, as though not wholly convinced himself, does not know where to stop. He spoils his case by overstatement; when we learn later that Eustacia's letter to Clym has not been delivered because the messenger forgot to post it, we begin to protest. We begin to feel that the author has aligned himself with the nature of things against his characters, that he is manipulating fate against them.

Hardy's worst failure here is certainly "Father Time's" killing of Sue's children in *Jude*, and his suicide: "Done because we are too menny." When we first meet "Father Time" in the train he is a memorable and poetic conception, but increasingly he becomes the author's mouthpiece; and then we realize he is the good little child of sentimental Victorian fiction, who speaks wisdom in his innocence, turned upside down. He too is a sentimental creation, and made the less convincing because, according to the doctor, he is a boy "of a sort unknown in the last generation . . . the beginning of the coming universal wish not to live." The philosophical explanation high-lights the sentimentality; and when four pages on Jude quotes Aeschylus: "Things are as they are, and will be brought to their destined issue," we feel that, in this instance, the issue is being brought about not because it is in the nature of things but because Hardy wishes it to be so. It is the one turn of the screw too many.

But these failures in the management of his plots matter less in Hardy than they would in any other novelist; they are botches, but they do not ruin the work, because though large enough when measured in terms of plot they are small when seen against the vastness and the strength of the design behind the plot. Plot in Hardy is his attempt to express the significance of the great design in purely human terms. Failure was almost inescapable, for Hardy, as a man of his time and place, had no completely adequate myth through which his view of the nature of things could be bodied forth.

But the greatness of conception, the sense of cosmic scope behind the action, put Hardy's novels apart from any other fiction written in England in the nineteenth century and send us naturally for our comparisons to works of great poetry. *The Return of the Native* was the first novel in which he achieved the tragic level, and it could be argued that it is his finest. In no other does the setting of the natural world so dominate the characters. Perhaps the dichotomy between the human being and the nature in which he lives is too acute in this novel; in the tragic works that follow, *The Mayor of Casterbridge* (1886), *Tess of the d'Urbervilles* (1891), and *Jude the Obscure* (1895), one has the feeling that the tragic heroes and heroines more and more take nature into themselves, and to this extent the importance of the natural setting as something apart from man diminishes.

As a creator of character Hardy worked in a way diametrically opposite to George Eliot's. If she is a psychological novelist, then Hardy is the reverse. When he attempts analysis he generally succeeds only in diminishing the stature of his tragic figures, as with Clym and "Father Time," for as a rule his analysis is inadequate. Sometimes, as with Sue in *Jude the Obscure*, he cannot himself adequately "explain" his character's motives. In other words, subtle and complex though she is, she has been instantly apprehended; she has, like all Hardy's great tragic characters, the authority, only dimly and half apprehended, of a force of nature.

Hardy's characters, then, tend to be differentiated only in the great emotional situation, and then their triumphant life comes from the poetry that invests them. The most obvious instance of this is Bathsheba Everdene's realization in the fir plantation at night of the presence of Sergeant Troy, in *Far from the Madding Crowd* (1874), and the miraculous description of Troy's swordplay which follows a little later:

> He flourished the sword by way of introduction number two, and the next thing of which she was conscious was that the point and blade of the sword were darting with a gleam towards her left side, just above her hip; then of their reappearance on her right side, emerging as it were from between her ribs, having apparently passed through her body. The third item of consciousness was that of seeing the same sword, perfectly clean and free from blood held vertically in Troy's hand (in the position technically called "recover swords"). All was as quick as electricity . . .
>
> In an instant the atmosphere was transformed to Bathsheba's eyes. Beams of light caught from the low sun's rays, above, around, in front of her, well-nigh shut out earth and heaven—all emitted in the marvellous evolutions of Troy's reflecting blade, which seemed everywhere at once, and yet nowhere specially. These circling gleams were accompanied by a keen rush that was almost a whistling—also springing from all sides of her at once. In short, she was enclosed in a firmament of light, and of sharp hisses, resembling a sky-full of meteors close at hand.
>
> Never since the broadsword became the national weapon had there been more dexterity shown in its management than by the hands of Sergeant Troy, and never had he been in such splendid temper for the performance as now in the evening sunshine among the ferns with Bathsheba. It may safely be asserted with regard to the closeness of his cuts, that had it been possible for the edge of the sword to leave in the air a permanent substance wherever it flew past, the space left untouched would have been almost a mould of Bathsheba's figure.

After that, there is no necessity for analysis; Bathsheba's sudden subjugation to Troy, her complete possession by him, is shown in the most striking way possible; she is as much his victim, as helpless before him, as if she had really met him in the field of battle.

Poetry is the constant attendant of Hardy's tragic characters. It is not an intellectual poetry, like Meredith's; it is much more primitive and magical, and always it heightens the significance of the characters and the reader's consciousness of their tragic stature. And, as Hardy moves away, as it were, from the norm of prose intention as traditionally conceived, so he moves his novels more and more out of the realm in which they may be criticized from the prose point of view. In some respects, his simplest and most successful tragic novel is *The Mayor of Casterbridge*. Henchard is his grandest hero, as Tess is his most moving heroine, and much of Henchard's tragic greatness comes from his impercipience. He contains all nature within himself, as a truly great bull might be described as doing. This almost animal impercipience removes him far away from the tragic heroes of Shakespeare, and yet, in one respect at any rate, it is Macbeth with whom we have to compare him. External nature fights against Henchard, but it is nature interpreted by superstition, and it is the poetic quality of the whole that makes the superstition credible. The poetry heightens and deepens our sense of Henchard's tragic fate. Two instances of this poetry may be quoted: the moment when his wedding present to Elizabeth Jane is discovered, "a new bird-cage, shrouded in newspaper, and at the bottom of the cage a little ball of feathers—the dead body of a goldfinch"; and the scene in which Henchard sees the dead body, "lying stiff and stark upon the surface of the stream":

> In the circular current imparted by the central flow the form was brought forward, till it passed under his eyes; and then he perceived with a sense of horror that it was *himself*. Not a man somewhat resembling him, but one in all respects his counterpart, his actual double, was floating as if dead in Ten Hatches Hole.

To match the first for pathos and the second for the twitch of horror felt along the nerve one has to go back to Webster.

Sometimes the poetry is the poetry of attendant and pervasive circumstances. An example of this is the description—but it is more than description, it is setting—of the Valley of the Great Dairies in *Tess of the d'Urbervilles*, the setting to Tess's meeting and falling in love with Angel Clare. Yet whatever the kind may be, the poetry and the imagery through which it is rendered are always precise, not merely with the scrupulous accuracy of a poet like Clare but with the insight, the regard for minute particulars and for the pattern which contains them, of Gerard Manley Hopkins. So, reading Hardy, one is often struck with the strangeness that characterizes something seen and rendered as it were for the first time, with the innocent eye; a small instance is the road that is seen as bisecting Egdon Heath "like the parting-line on a head of black hair." But the accuracy is no less when the object rendered is of much greater moment. Thus Hardy describes Tess as having been "caught during her days of immaturity like a bird in a springe." In another novelist this could be a sentimental cliché. It is not in Hardy. As John Holloway says in his book *The Victorian Sage*, it is "an exact and insistent image to remind us that when Tess was seduced at night in the wood, her experience really was like that of an animal caught in a trap—as might have happened in the very same place." The image goes to the heart of Tess's situation. She is caught in tragedy because she is animal, but if she had been merely animal, or if she had been Retty Priddle or Izz Huett, there would have been no tragedy.

Jude the Obscure stands somewhat apart from the rest of Hardy's fiction. It is his one attempt to write a novel strictly of his own time; we remember, reading it, that he was twelve years younger than Ibsen and nine years older than Strindberg. Jude, we are to understand, is a sensualist and a man who, at crucial times in his life, seeks escape in drink. But as we see him under these aspects in the novel he is certainly not more than *l'homme moyen sensuel*; neither his sexual nor his drinking exploits are anything out of the ordinary, and they could have had little effect on the course of his life if he had been in fact *l'homme moyen sensuel*. His tragedy lies in that he is not. What brings him down are the intellectual ambitions beyond his station, his dream of the student's life at Christminster. The common-sense advice to a man in his station, with his aspirations, is the Master of Bibli-oll's: ". . . judging from your description of yourself as a working man, I venture to think that you will have a much better chance of success in life by remaining in your own sphere and sticking to your trade than by adopting any other course." Had he taken the Master's advice, he might have indulged in drink and fornication far beyond anything suggested in the novel with relative impunity. The central tragedy of Jude is one of unfulfilled aims, aims moreover, almost impossible of fulfillment at the time in which he lived, even though he had had the purity and self-control of a saint. His tragedy may be paralleled by that of the cockney workman Gilbert Grail in Gissing's *Thyrza*, which had appeared eight years before. Indeed, *Jude* should probably be considered in relation to Gissing's novels; as in them, we are conscious—admittedly for the first time in Hardy—of a strong undercurrent of what can only be called class consciousness.

It does not appear in the earlier novels because there there was no need for it; Hardy was describing events in a world still traditional. But in *Jude*, by making his tragic hero a working-class intellectual, he removed his action out of the values of Wessex altogether. He could do no other, for he had taken his theme and his hero from a strictly contemporary world, and *Jude* is a man who must be defeated by the contemporary world; his morbid sensibility is "planted" for us in the second chapter of the novel. Everyone has noticed the way in which the rich rustic chorus has disappeared in *Jude* (with the exceptions of Jude's aunt and the widow Edlin) and how thin, by comparison with *The Return of the Native* and *Tess*, the whole texture of the writing, of the world described, and the links that bind men to nature and the nature of things, has become. There is no place in *Jude* for the great heroic or poetic scenes such as Troy's swordplay and Gabriel Oak's fight to cover the ricks during the great storm in *Far from the Madding Crowd*, the remarkable episode of Wildeve and the raddleman gambling on the heath at night by the light of glowworms in *The Return of the Native*, or the wonderful opening of *The Mayor of Casterbridge*. All this represents an enormous loss, precisely where Hardy was strongest; but they had to go, for they stand for that way of life from which Jude and Sue Bridehead, by virtue of being working-class intellectuals, are totally uprooted.

These great poetic and heroic scenes are exactly what compose the design that lies behind Hardy's other novels and gives them their sense of timelessness. One can't say that design, as opposed to plot, is absent from *Jude*, but it is much shrunken; it has become an ironical symbolism: Arabella captures Jude first by throwing the boar's pizzle at him; when she marries him a second time, at the end of the novel, they are living above her father's pork shop. Again, as Jude passes from belief to unbelief, Sue progresses in the opposite direction. The effect of this shrinkage in design is to throw the emphasis precisely where Hardy is always weakest, his manipulation of the plot. Simply because Hardy is working much more nearly at the level of realism in *Jude*, one might say at Gissing's level, improbabilities become increasingly serious. The most explicit statement of Hardy's view of the tragic situation of man, *Jude* suffers artistically from its explicitness.

Nevertheless, *Jude* is a most powerful and impressive novel, and part of its power and impressiveness certainly derives from Hardy's very refusal to employ his great poetic qualities in it. These may, at times, mitigate or at least make more acceptable the tragic horror, but in *Jude* everything is subordinated to the depiction of the increasingly tragic situation of Jude and Sue. They are described from a much closer range than is usual with Hardy. Jude is the characteristic Hardy hero—hypersensitive, high-principled, essentially "soft-minded," to use William James's term—made actual in a Victorian working man; we know him in much more detail than we do Clym Yeobright or Angel Clare. But Sue Bridehead is a departure for Hardy. She is the opposite of Eustacia Vye, Bathsheba Everdene, and Tess not merely in the fact that she is an intellectual. But she is much more than Hardy's version of the "New Woman," and she utterly transcends Gissing's versions of that creature. His Rhoda Nunn in *The Odd Woman* is now an oddity of history. But Sue survives because of her ambiguity, her sexual ambivalence, which she is aware of all the time and cannot quite understand:

> "At first I did not love you, Jude; that I own. When I first knew you I merely wanted you to love me. I did not exactly flirt with you; but that inborn craving which undermines some women's morals almost more than unbridled passion—the craving to attract and captivate, regardless of the injury it may do the man—was in me; and when I found I had caught you, I was frightened."

Perhaps the key to her is in Hardy's word "intellectualized." The passage, during the account of her leaving her husband Phillotson, where, ever reasonable, she quotes J. S. Mill and he replies, "What do I care about J. S. Mill! I only want to lead a quiet life!" has amused many critics, but it is absolutely right in character and tone. The reference to Mill at that particular juncture—and allowance having been made for the date of the action, it could just as well have been Freud or Lawrence—exposes her completely. Sue is a most subtle delineation of a not uncommon type of woman in the modern world, and it is significant that the only writer on Hardy who has fully understood his achievement in creating her is D. H. Lawrence.

There will probably always be those for whom Hardy is, in Henry James's phrase, "the good little Thomas Hardy." His faults are glaring enough. His plots creak. His villains have stepped off the boards of a barn-storming company peddling melodrama. His prose is often clumsy to the point of uncouthness. Yet the true index of Hardy's stature is that he is almost the only tragic novelist in our literature and that when we consider him we have ultimately to do so in relation to Shakespeare and Webster and to the Greek dramatists. His influence has been at once enormous and slight. After his discovery of Wessex a host of minor novelists opened up regions throughout the length and breadth of England and showed us man against an ancient soil; of them all the only one who has any interest for us today is perhaps Eden Phillpotts. In many ways the later novelist most akin to Hardy is D. H. Lawrence.

§ FOR COMMENT

In the first chapter of the novel an elderly parson reveals to Tess's father that he is a lineal descendant of the ancient and knightly family of the d'Urbervilles, introducing one of the major themes of the novel. Show how this theme, together with its ironic ramifications, pervades the whole book, helping to account for what Tess is and what happens to her through the course of the action to her death on the sacrificial stone at Stonehenge.

The introduction of Tess to the reader is accomplished in an episode set in a fertile vale where she is participating in "Club-walking," a remnant of the old May Day celebration. The maidens are dressed in white and each carries in her right hand a peeled willow wand and in her left a bunch of white flowers. What is the significance of the May Day dance in history? How does this scene function in the novel? Tess's identification with the fertile valley introduces a second major theme, one which an early reviewer noted with distaste, saying that the shadow of the Goddess Aselgeia (the Greek word for "licentiousness") broods over the whole book and darkens it. But the critic here is applying a moral standard specifically denied as relevant by the omniscient author. At the end of Chapter XIII, he states:

> Walking among the sleeping birds in the hedges, watching the skipping rabbits on a moonlit warren, or standing under a pheasant-laden bough, she looked upon herself as a figure of Guilt intruding into the haunts of Innocence. But all the while she was making a distinction where there was no difference. Feeling herself in antagonism, she was quite in accord. She

had been made to break an accepted social law, but no law known to the environment in which she fancied herself such an anomaly.

What is the distinction made here between the laws of society and the laws of nature? How does this distinction bear on the total meaning of the novel?

The symbolic function of the various places in the novel has often been noted. Tess moves from the fertile valley at Marlott to the primeval forests at Cranborne Chase where her seduction takes place to her death at Stonehenge. Locate the other settings in the novel and discuss their significance. What, for example, is the function of the milking scene in Chapter XXIV, which leads to Angel's declaration of love? What motivates that declaration?

Discuss the idea that Angel and Alec are counterparts. How does each participate in Tess's destruction? Are Angel and Alec convincing as characters? What are the ironies in their characters, Angel, for example, being anything but what his name indicates?

James Joyce § 1882–1941
A Portrait of the Artist as a Young Man

Although Joyce only published three novels, A Portrait of the Artist as a Young Man *(1916),* Ulysses *(1922),* and Finnegans Wake *(1939), his work has been as influential as any other single novelist's on twentieth-century prose fiction.*

For further biographical information see pages 176–177.

Style and Point of View in A Portrait of the Artist as a Young Man
SAMUEL H. WOODS, JR.

A *Portrait of the Artist as a Young Man* is a novel of a boy growing up and finding his place in the adult world. But this boy is a particular kind, an artist. Joyce drew heavily upon the facts of his own life for the novel, and for those who wish to see how these facts are used in the novel, Richard Ellmann's biography, *James Joyce* (New York: Oxford University Press, 1959), is the indispensable guide. A further element to be considered in seeing how the novel attained its present form is *Stephen Hero*, which Joyce wrote about 1904 and which uses much the same material that appears here in a thoroughly reworked form. The manuscript of *Stephen Hero* is deposited in the Harvard College Library, but it has been edited by Theodore Spencer and published, so that those interested may make comparisons. In both versions, we see Stephen's childhood, his schooldays, adolescence and early manhood, his first experiences with the opposite sex, his awakening interest in art and philosophy, his realization that his destiny is to be an artist, and his rebellion against his background and family, against Irish politics and his Irish Roman Catholicism.

Joyce's earlier version, or at least the name he gave to the central character in that version, provides us some help with the meaning of the name he finally settled on for his protagonist: Stephen Dedalus. Clearly the earlier name, Stephen Hero, suggests that at first he regarded Stephen as heroic, but later rejected the obviousness of the earlier name for the still curious but less obvious "Dedalus." In classical mythology, Dedalus is the personification of skill in the mechanical arts. Literally, the word means "the cunning workman," and in the stories that center on Dedalus, he originated such tools as axes, awls, bevels, and the like, and also built the labyrinth for King Minos of Crete.

Minos did not wish for anyone else to have so cunningly contrived a thing, and so he imprisoned Dedalus in his own invention. Dedalus' plan for escape is probably the best known story for most of us: He devised wings for himself and for his son Icarus, who was overcome by pride and the joy of flight and soared too near the sun, causing the wax that was holding his wings together to melt, after which he plummeted to the sea and to his death. His more prudent father escaped. From all this, one may conclude that Joyce wished to suggest that Stephen is the artist personified, particularly the artist as a serious craftsman, as opposed to the artist as an inspired genius. Apparently, too, Joyce wished to suggest something with Stephen's first name. In the New Testament, Stephen is the first Christian martyr, the man stoned to death, the man at whose martyrdom Saul, or Paul, of Tarsus was present. The general view seems to be that Stephen Dedalus is to be regarded as the artist so completely committed to his craftlike art that he will endure even martyrdom, death, which in a figurative sense Stephen does, when toward the end of the book, he cuts himself off from friends, family, country, and religion, to devote himself to his art, which forms for him a kind of religion, to the practice of which he will devote his life.

The actual subject matter of Joyce's novel is ordinary enough, although it is observed with great care and rendered for us with great precision. We shall be quite as interested here in the way Joyce presents his material as in the material itself, for the method of presentation forms part of the material of the book. Everything we perceive in the novel, we perceive through Stephen's sensibility and intelligence in the third person limited point of view. This accounts for the somewhat bizarre opening, in which the child

Stephen experiences a story his father tells him. With extreme skill Joyce has here described, apparently with objectivity, but actually as these events and words registered themselves in Stephen's mind, a scene, dramatic in both the technical and the common, ordinary sense of the word. We do not know what all this means for Stephen, the ruining of a Christmas dinner—his first—and the split in the family, the bitterness over issues he cannot understand. We do know, of course, that the scene is vividly rendered, and once we begin to think about it a bit, we can infer something of the effect all this must have had upon a sensitive child. One may ask how we know Stephen is sensitive, but the presentation of his life at school, his homesickness, his uneasiness in relation to his schoolmates—all these elements establish this trait. Something of the difficulties Stephen has in school we can see in the long scene which follows that of the Christmas dinner—one which Stephen finds himself "pandied" for willfully shirking. Out of his feelings of outraged justice, he determines to go to see the rector. Stephen quakes with fear, but is egged on by his schoolmates. He does seek justice from the rector, receives it, followed by acclaim from the other boys. Thus Joyce establishes Stephen's boyish courage, though not minimizing his hesitations and doubts. The way is clear for Stephen to emerge, as he does in the section immediately following, as a school leader, despite his ineptness at athletics.

Chapter II marks another shift in style, largely because of changes in Stephen's reading—in this case *The Count of Monte Cristo*. We will see something of Stephen's fantasy-making, strongly reminiscent of Joyce's earlier short story "Araby." The section dealing with Stephen's adolescent fantasies about Mercedes are of great interest when they are contrasted with Stephen's own behavior with a real girl whom he meets at a party and with whom he rides home on the trolley. The great difference between Stephen's fantasy of himself as a masterful romantic lover and his actual ineptness in making any kind of real contact with a real girl suggests Joyce's ironic attitude. To what end does Joyce present his protagonist ironically? Stephen prefers Byron's poetry to Tennyson's, and he maintains his preference, even though he is threatened with physical violence from his schoolmates who prefer Tennyson. He also models his first attempt to write poetry on what he has seen in a collection of Byron's poems. Is his preference for Byron significant, and if so, of what? By the end of this second chapter, Stephen is more directly involved with the opposite sex. Is this experience related to his fantasies about Mercedes and his actual experience with the girl on the trolley? How?

In Chapter III, we see Stephen continuing his illicit sexual life. How does he reconcile his behavior with his being prefect of the Sodality of the Blessed Virgin Mary at school? Is he aware of any conflict? Does the rector's announcement of the retreat bear on this problem? If so, how? You will notice that in presenting the retreat, Joyce does not summarize the sermons, but includes them wholly. Is this inclusion more or less effective than some kind of summary would have been? Notice that the subject of the series is the Last Four Things: Death, Judgment, Hell, and Heaven. Are all four subjects treated? If any omission is made, explain how that omission is significant. Joyce shows the individual and cumulative effect of the sermons on Stephen. How would you explain his motivation to repent his sinful life?

Chapter IV opens with the presentation of Stephen after his repentance. Describe the quality of his religious life. What defects, if any, do you notice in his goodness? The second section of this chapter shows Stephen's conversation with the Director of Studies, who asks Stephen to consider if he has a vocation to the priesthood. Notice how Joyce shows Stephen thinking the matter over: He imagines himself a priest, but his fantasy concentrates not on himself as a minister helping those in spiritual need, but upon his desire for power and for strange, abstruse knowledge. He does, however, decide his vocation is not a religious one. Following his decision not to study for the priesthood, Stephen goes on to the university and experiences his vision of himself as an artist. Immediately following this revelation, Stephen sees a girl wading on the seashore and is overwhelmed by her beauty. Is this experience to be considered part of his realization of his destiny? How?

Chapter V shows Stephen in the university, interested in some of his courses, but less interested in others. Most of his liveliest attention he devotes not to his studies, but to his bull sessions with his friends. Notice that in his long discussion on esthetics, Stephen sets up three main categories for art. Does *A Portrait* fit into any one of these? Is Stephen's description of the relation of the artist to his work important? The last section of the book is written in a kind of staccato journal prose. It records Stephen's growing separation from his family, and his increasing desire for independence. Is the language and style here appropriate to the content?

Throughout the book, Joyce has focussed his spotlight on Stephen and shown us how he deals with his problems. How fully are other characters in the book presented? Is this a strength or weakness? The title summarizes something of Joyce's intention; does Joyce show Stephen having achieved any significant artistic creation or only ready to begin? To what extent is Joyce's presentation of Stephen sympathetic? Does Joyce's sometimes ironic view undermine sympathy or work to make Stephen seem more human?

In finally considering Stephen's rejection of family, politics, and religion, do you think he rejects these things as subject matter for the artist or as loyalties which might interfere with the artist's realization of his artistic aims? Is the writer to subordinate his art to religion or to politics or to family considerations?

❈ Franz Kafka § 1883–1924
The Trial

*Kafka's work, strikingly modern in its symbolic method, owes much
to the philosophic writings of Soren Kierkegaard. This existential
background and Kafka's remarkable skill probably account for his international reputation as a major literary figure.*
For further biographical information see page 182.

Multivalence in The Trial[1]

MARY ROHRBERGER

In his book *Franz Kafka: Parable and Paradox*, Heinz Politzer
begins with the slightest of narratives by Franz Kafka, a short story told in a
paragraph, four sentences in the German, called "Give It Up!" It is short
enough to quote in full, and we quote it, as Politzer did.

> It was very early in the morning, the streets clean and deserted, I was on
> my way to the railroad station. As I compared the tower clock with my
> watch I realized it was already much later than I had thought, I had to
> hurry, the shock of this discovery made me feel uncertain of the way, I was
> not very well acquainted with the town as yet, fortunately there was a
> policeman nearby, I ran to him and breathlessly asked him the way. He
> smiled and said: "From me you want to learn the way?" "Yes," I said,
> "since I cannot find it myself." "Give it up, give it up," said he and turned
> away with a great sweep, like someone who wants to be alone with his
> laughter.[2]

Simple? Yes, but deceptively so, for in this short story setting, characters,
and plot operate as symbols, which provide meaning on many levels. In his
book, Politzer goes on for twenty-two pages to determine the story's multivalence. He suggests a biographical reading in which the narrator would

---

[1] This analysis appears with some changes in Mary Rohrberger, *Hawthorne and
the Modern Short Story* (The Hague: Mouton, 1966), pp. 133–139.
[2] Franz Kafka, *Description of a Struggle*, trans., Tania and James Stern (New
York: Schocken Books, 1958), p. 201.

be seen as the alienated Kafka, an Austrian Jew in Czech Prague; a sociological one in which the policeman would stand as the representative of an administration "feared as well as despised," as the symbol of an "old order [which] still survives," [3] functioning, but ineffective; the psychological, in which the narrative and the narrator become a case study. "Age-old anxieties expose him [the narrator] to situations which he does not even try to master—the fear of arriving too late, . . . of losing one's life before one has come to its end. . . ." [4] Or, Politzer goes on, we might find an allegory of Kafka's childhood experiences and conflict with the father, particularly the role his father played in his upbringing, and, by extension, every man's childhood experiences and conflict with the father. A religious interpretation would find the policeman to be a "messenger from a spiritual realm," [5] having nothing to communicate to the human sphere but the command to give it up. And it would be possible to claim the figure in the narrative to be an existential hero. Then the policeman would function as "the spokesman of a universe totally unconcerned with the information seeker's personal destiny and radically hostile to him. This universe answers man's claim for direction with an icy silence." [6]

We cannot attempt here such a complex interpretation of Kafka's much longer narrative *The Trial*, since anything like a complete interpretation of the symbols within the narrative would result in a book-length study. But we can suggest meaning on personal, social, and religious grounds and in so doing show the relationship between the short story quoted above and the novel.

In *The Trial*, the events of the plot constitute an externalization of man's passage through life, a symbolic portrayal from birth to death expressed in a single year. The story opens in the morning on K's thirtieth birthday. He is at once arrested and accused, and he spends the rest of the year trying to find out what he is accused of and how the laws and the court operate, indeed, what are the laws and who the members of the court. The story ends on the evening before K's thirty-first birthday when he is put to death.

There has been a great deal of speculation concerning the nature of K's guilt. Various critics have made whole catalogues of K's sins. He has been blamed for his inability to love, for his lack of clear purpose, for his mediocrity. But in the narrative there seems to be no evidence of a positive source of guilt. Nevertheless, it is clear that K *feels* guilty from the moment of his arrest. The first chapter of *The Trial* is filled with indications that K himself actually wills the proceedings. We notice that the warders do not appear until K rings a bell, and that as soon as he admits their presence and their relationship to him, he has "in a way admitted the stranger's right to

[3] Heinz Politzer, *Franz Kafka: Parable and Paradox* (Ithaca: Cornell University Press, 1962), p. 9.
[4] Politzer, p. 10.
[5] Politzer, p. 11.
[6] Politzer, p. 13.

superintend his actions. . . ." [7] We notice, too, that he seems subconsciously to assent in the arrest, and even though the warders are standing quite a distance from him, he makes as if to wrench himself away from them. While considering possible reasons for his arrest, he thinks that the arrest might be a joke, and the thought enters his head that "perhaps he had only to laugh knowingly in these men's faces and they would laugh with him. . . ." (p. 7) And perhaps, if he had, the warders would have disappeared. But he doesn't. Instead he goes to look for his birth certificate, for visible proof of his existence. The warders, however, reject the evidence, declaring that they are only subordinates and that there are high authorities that they serve. It is interesting and revealing that these high officials " 'never go hunting for crime in the populace, but, as the Law decrees, are drawn toward the guilty. . . .' " (p. 10) The suggestion seems clear that the guilty initiate their own arrests, and, perhaps, even will their own executions. Back in his room, K is surprised that the warders have left him alone "where he had abundant opportunities to take his own life." (p. 12)

When an inspector arrives, K is brought to him for questioning. The inspector asks if K is surprised at his arrest. K answers, " 'Certainly, I am surprised, but I am by no means very much surprised.' " (p. 15) Later, in an attempt to explain to Fräulein Bürstner, K assumes the role of the inspector, becoming the tangible manifestation of his own conscience, accusing himself of crime.

Events multiply to make the same point: The court is chiefly a state of mind. K says, " '. . . it is only a trial if I recognize it as such.' " (p. 51) But why does K will the trial? What is the guilt that drives him to it? In its broadest implications, it appears that it is guilt attached to existence itself. Once born, man is not content just to exist. He questions, and as he questions, he is questioned. In effect, he tries to justify his existence. He is constantly on trial to prove his worth, to prove his right to live. But only death can justify life, and, difficult as it may be, he must accept death as a condition of life. Nothing but death finally suffices—not sexuality, not family, not art, not religion.

Not sexuality. Consider the women in the narrative, notably Fräulein Bürstner, Leni, and the washerwoman. K's feelings about Fräulein Bürstner are suggested first in his conversation with the landlady. K observes that Fräulein Bürstner often comes in late and then agrees with the landlady, " 'Young people are like that.' " But, he adds, " '. . . it can go too far.' " (p. 28) Taking her cue from him, the landlady accuses Fräulein Bürstner of loose behavior and the comment puts K into a sudden fury. " '. . . You have obviously misunderstood my remark. . . .' " (p. 29) He tries to convince himself that her appearance can be misleading and that she may be

[7] References are to *The Trial* (New York: The Modern Library, 1937), pp. 4–5. Subsequent page references are given parenthetically.

just as promiscuous as Leni or the washerwoman. At first glance Leni seems to be very affectionate, but her promiscuity is later clearly revealed and she is obviously in the pay of the lawyer. The washerwoman, too, is promiscuous and can offer K no real solace. The women seem to operate, as Politzer comments, "on the periphery of the Law." [8] All are in some way connected with the court. There is a suggestion of some kind of secret agreement between the women and the law. Indeed, it appears that the women carry on their own trial against K.

Not family, not the law, not art will suffice. K's Uncle Karl comes to visit him and tells him that he cannot become a family disgrace. It is the uncle who takes K to the lawyer, Huld. The lawyer is without human feelings and himself ill, and although he promises help, he is never able to deliver it. The painter, too, is an ambiguous figure. He is the court painter. He says, " 'I inherited the connection. My father was the Court painter before me.' " (p. 190) The door behind the bed of the artist leads straight into the offices of the court. And although he says that he might be able to help, it is clear that he cannot. His paintings are covered with dust under his bed.

Nor can religion help. In the cathedral, the priest tells K that he seeks too much for outside help. The church is always there but only for him who enters of his own volition. Its doors are open for those who come and those who go. It wants nothing of him. It contributes nothing to his defense. The priest, too, belongs to the court.

The short and graphic last chapter describes the ritual of K's death. Two men come for him. At first he recognizes the inevitable. " 'So you are meant for me?' " he asks. As the company goes down the stairs, the two men try to take K's arms. K says, " 'Wait till we're in the street, I'm not an invalid.' " (p. 280) In the street they take hold of both his arms, and he walks stiffly with one on either side. Once he tests their determination. " 'I won't go any farther,' " he says "experimentally." (p. 281) But the two men do not loosen their grip. Then suddenly before them appears a figure resembling Fräulein Bürstner. K is not sure that it is she, but the appearance causes him to realize that it is futile to resist, and he begins to walk ahead, his companions allowing him to take the lead. In complete harmony they move along until they come to a stone quarry, deserted and desolate. They help him remove his coat, his waistcoat, and his shirt, and finally they settle him on the ground, propping his head against a boulder. But in spite of all their care, K remains uncomfortable, his position contorted. There follows a ritual whereby they pass over his head a double-edged butcher's knife. In time, K realizes that he is supposed to take the knife and stab it into his own breast. But he cannot do it. He does not have the necessary strength. He looks around and thinks he sees the figure of a person, in the distance shadowy and faint. At once he begins to hope:

[8] Politzer, p. 200.

Who was it? A friend? A good man? Someone who sympathized? Someone who wanted to help? Was it one person only? Or was it mankind? Was help at hand? Were there arguments in his favor that had been overlooked? Of course there must be. Logic is doubtless unshakable, but it cannot withstand a man who wants to go on living. Where was the Judge whom he had never seen? Where was the High Court, to which he had never penetrated? (p. 286)

But the hope ends in despair. They thrust the knife into his heart and turn it twice. And he dies, aware that it is like a dog, "as if the shame of it must outlive him." (p. 286)

§ FOR COMMENT

Even a brief analysis such as we make here indicates the similarities in theme and structure between the very short "Give It Up!" and the longer *The Trial*. In each there is a single protagonist seeking to locate the nature of the real and his place in it. In each, characters, plot, and setting function symbolically to yield meaning at various levels. Both are unified, coherent, closely worked forms. But what are the essential differences between the two pieces?

Kafka's world has its own dimensions. It is different from but just as recognizable as the worlds of Hawthorne, Faulkner, or Fitzgerald. Somebody has said that Kafka stood realism on its head. It is true. He does start with the realistic, with concrete details and a matter of fact style, but the details describe a world that has little correspondence with the world of our daily experience. It is, rather, a dream world. There is a logic in operation, but it is a dream logic that we all recognize as being valid, if different. We have had dreams like this. In Kafka, though, this dreamscape is applied to the universe itself. The world, he seems to suggest, is like this. Analyze the novel in terms of its dream context. What details in the first chapter, for example, support the thesis that a dream logic controls the book? What is the artistic purpose of this kind of structure? How does it bear on the theme of the novel?

Consider some of the details and actions in the novel not touched on in the analysis above. Try to relate them to the major theme. What, for example, is the relevance of the fact that the protagonist is known only by an initial? What role does the landlady play? the manufacturer? the tradesman? Is there some relevance to the fact that K works at a bank? What is the symbolic significance of the fact that death comes to K at a stone quarry where his head is propped against a boulder?

The Trial, like most of Kafka's work, was published after his death by his literary executor, Max Brod, who insisted that Kafka regarded the novel as unfinished. Brod, in addition, was responsible for the final arrangements of the chapters. Some critics have asserted that several chapters in the novel are interchangeable, like building blocks. Can you see any possibilities for a different arrangement of chapters?

William Faulkner § 1897–1962

Absalom, Absalom!

An unresolved conflict, in almost all of Faulkner's work, exists be-tween nostalgic recollections of the days of peaceful slavery in the South and his recognition of the horrors and inequities that system has produced. His achievement is remarkable in both the novel and short story; and his highly original, experimental prose has con-tributed enormously toward "liberating" contemporary fictions from traditional notions of composition.

For further biographical information see page 216.

For further biographical information see page 216.

Theme and Structure in
Absalom, Absalom!
MARY ROHRBERGER

In *Absalom, Absalom!* (1936), his ninth published novel, William Faulkner infused the whole Yoknapatawpha region with cosmic scope, constructing plot and characters as symbols operating in a gigantic and complex myth of the South. The novel concerns the tragic downfall of proud, courageous Thomas Sutpen, originally a poor white man, who determined to create a kingdom of his own, to establish a home on his land, to people it with his Negroes, and in time with a wife and sons. Ruthlessly he stole land from the Indians, considering only himself in the frantic struggle for power and position, a struggle shadowed by incest, miscegenation, and towering passion. Slowly, doom is fitted to his measure and Thomas Sutpen falls from the peak to which he has climbed. First he loses his son, next his wife, then his Negroes, and finally his own life. The story of Sutpen, however, does not end here. Through the narrator and raisonneur, Quentin Compson (of *The Sound and the Fury*, 1929), Faulkner intimates that this is the story not only of Thomas Sutpen, but also of the whole South, the deep South, a land whose people follow the fate of Thomas Sutpen. The story of Sutpen symbolizes the past history of the South; Quentin's interest in Sutpen's story illustrates the contemporaneity of the story and dramatizes its

meaning. The method of telling the story through Quentin and so identifying it with Quentin himself fuses the past with the present and foreshadows the future. Ironically, in *The Sound and the Fury* Quentin commits
suicide.

Shreve, a Canadian and Quentin's roommate at Harvard, asks, *"Tell
about the South. What's it like there. What do they do there. Why do
they live there. Why do they live at all. . . ."* [1] [Faulkner's italics] The
story that Quentin tells is constructed from bits and fragments of conversations and memories. Parts of the story come to Quentin from Miss Rosa
Coldfield, who has first-hand knowledge of the life and death of Thomas
Sutpen; parts come from Quentin's father, who has heard much of the
story from General Compson, Quentin's grandfather, who had been Sutpen's only close friend; and parts come from Quentin's own lively imagination, for after putting together the pieces of the narration like pieces of a jig
saw puzzle, he finds that some parts are missing, and he supplies the missing pieces by conjecture.

The style in *Absalom, Absalom!*, which may be regarded as the epitome
of the Faulknerian idiom (described in Devices of Fiction, p. 26), is technically perfect, and is completely suited to the theme. In the first paragraph
Faulkner sets the mood for the entire novel:

> From a little after two oclock until almost sundown of the long still hot
> weary dead September afternoon they sat in what Miss Coldfield still called
> the office because her father had called it that—a dim hot airless room with
> the blinds all closed and fastened for forty-three summers because when
> she was a girl someone had believed that light and moving air carried heat
> and that dark was always cooler, and which (as the sun shone fuller and
> fuller on that side of the house) became latticed with yellow slashes full of
> dust motes which Quentin thought of as being flecks of the dead old dried
> paint itself blown inward from the scaling blinds as wind might have blown
> them. There was a wistaria vine blooming for the second time that summer
> on a wooden trellis before one window, into which sparrows came now and
> then in random gusts, making a dry vivid dusty sound before going away:
> and opposite Quentin, Miss Coldfield in the eternal black which she had
> worn for forty-three years now, whether for sister, father, or nothusband
> none knew, sitting so bolt upright in the straight hard chair that was so
> tall for her that her legs hung straight and rigid as if she had iron shin-
> bones and ankles, clear of the floor with that air of impotent and static rage
> like children's feet, and talking in that grim haggard amazed voice until at
> last listening would renege and hearing-sense self-confound and the long-
> dead object of her impotent yet indomitable frustration would appear, as
> though by outraged recapitulation evoked, quiet inattentive and harmless,
> out of the biding and dreamy and victorious dust. (pp. 7–8)

[1] William Faulkner, *Absalom, Absalom!* (New York: The Modern Library, 1951),
p. 174. Subsequent page references are given parenthetically.

This entire passage is composed of two sentences, the first twelve lines long and the second seventeen lines long. Six adjectives drawn together in a series of words describe the afternoon. It is a "long still hot weary dead September afternoon," an afternoon particularly suited to narrating a long tale. The room in which Miss Rosa Coldfield and Quentin sit is a "dim hot airless room," certainly very much like the afternoon. The reference to Miss Coldfield's father is a reference to the past just as the room which has been closed for forty-three years is a reference to the thought of a past time. The present-day sun which shines full on the house and enters the room through slits in the blinds is thought of by Quentin as being "dead old dried paint." The arrangement of ideas presents the merger of past and present time.

Hot weary day	*Given to past narration*
Miss Coldfield's father	*Reference to the past*
Office closed for forty-three years	*Thoughts of past*
Flashes of sun	*Remind Quentin of dead paint and consequently of past time*
The blind through which the sun passes	*Suggestion that present can throw some light on past.*

The next sentence proceeds in much the same way. The sparrows come "now and then in random gusts," making a "dry vivid dusty sound." Miss Coldfield wears eternal black, the symbol of mourning for past things. She sits straight and rigid in a static and impotent rage. Her speech is "grim haggard amazed." She talks until "listening would renege and hearing-sense self-confound," her words creating a mood that pervades the whole narrative.

The great number of clauses and phrases combined with the frequent repetition of words create a total effect not unlike the poetic. In fact the tendency to free verse is particularly outstanding in the narrative and serves to intensify the mood. The prose sentences can even be set down as free verse:

> *It seems that this demon—*
> *his name was Sutpen—*
> *(Colonel Sutpen)—*
> *Colonel Sutpen.*
> *Who came out of nowhere*
> *and without warning*
> *upon the land*
> *with a band of strange niggers*
> *and built a plantation—*

> *(Tore violently a plantation,*
> *Miss Rosa Coldfield says)—*
> *tore violently.*
> *And married her sister Ellen*
> *and begot a son and a daughter*
> *which—*
> *(Without gentleness begot,*
> *Miss Rosa Coldfield says)—*
> *without gentleness. . . .* (p. 9, Faulkner's italics)

Comprehension of Faulkner's sentences does not proceed logically as the reader reads each word, but comes only at the completion of a sentence in a single moment of time. The clustering of clauses and phrases about the subject and predicate parts of the sentence serves to prolong the conclusion of the sentence, the length of the sentence being dictated by the complexity of the idea and the number of details relevant to it.

The method of the sentences is repeated in the narrative structure of the novel. The essential details are repeated and repeated; new details are suggested and then actually told, and then repeated. The pieces are placed together in juxtaposition, but not fitted together until finally a detail is introduced which causes the other pieces to fall together in a moment of time and thus what has been merely a succession of events of a group of seeming disparate details, becomes a whole, fitting together neatly. This method is repeated until the end of the novel when all the details have been revealed and the action is stopped. It is possible to show how this method works by examining the first few pages of the Sutpen story. Here is the first statement presented almost in outline:

> *It seems that this demon—his name was Sutpen—(Colonel Sutpen)—*
> *Colonel Sutpen. Who came out of nowhere and without warning upon the*
> *land with a band of strange niggers and built a plantation—(Tore violently*
> *a plantation, Miss Rosa Coldfield says)—tore violently. And married her*
> *sister Ellen and begot a son and a daughter which—(Without gentleness*
> *begot, Miss Rosa Coldfield says)—without gentleness. Which should have*
> *been the jewels of his pride and the shield and comfort of his old age, only*
> *—(Only they destroyed him or something or he destroyed them or some-*
> *thing. And died)—and died. Without regret, Miss Rosa Coldfield says—*
> *(Save by her) Yes, save by her. (And by Quentin Compson) Yes. And by*
> *Quentin Compson.* (p. 9)

Here is the reworking of the outline of the story which occurs two pages later:

> [Sutpen] first rode into town out of no discernible past and acquired his land no one knew how and built his house, his mansion, apparently out of nothing and married Ellen Coldfield and begot his two children—the son

who widowed the daughter who had not yet been a bride—and so accomplished his allotted course to its violent (Miss Coldfield at least would have said, just) end. (p. 11)

We notice here that one detail is added. Somehow the son stopped the daughter from being a bride. Since the term Faulkner uses is "widowed," the suggestion is that the son killed the sister's fiancé. But no more is made of it here.

The next reworking occurs two pages later. More details are added, not in full, but only mentioned. Sutpen appeared in the town of Jefferson with a horse and two pistols and nothing else; he left the town and appeared again with the wild Negroes and the French architect and built a house. Because he needed the shield of respectability, he married a virtuous woman, Ellen. The son repudiated the father and the home; the wife died, leaving the daughter to the protection of her aunt, Rosa. Sutpen fought in the Civil War.

In the fourth reworking which follows immediately, we find out about the part Rosa actually played: After Sutpen came back from the war he asked Rosa to marry him. But this is all we learn here. Faulkner does no more explaining at this point, but waits for other reworkings that continue to build and build.

Details withheld add to the aura of mystery and unreality; details repeated evoke a feeling of immediacy. The action becomes real and gradually emerges from the past to the dramatic present and then proceeds back again to the past, being filtered the whole time (as the sun through the latticed blinds) through Quentin's consciousness. This constant movement causes the reader to involve himself in the action and the mood, to feel the same interest in the narrative and the same urgency that Quentin feels. Thus Quentin and the reader go through the same processes in an attempt to understand the meaning of the Sutpen story, and the reader goes one step further to understand Quentin's role in it.

§ FOR COMMENT

The title *Absalom, Absalom!* refers to the biblical cry of King David to his second son, Absalom. The events in Faulkner's story are not parallel to the story of King David and his sons, but the ancient themes of repudiation of the father by the son, love between brothers, and the incestuous love of a sister for the father's son, give added meaning to Faulkner's tale. Actually the motivation in the novel rests on the delicate relationship between Sutpen and his two sons. Discuss this motivation and Sutpen's refusal to say, "My son," to Charles, to admit, in other words, the relationship. How does Sutpen's refusal cause the outcome of the action?

What is the relationship between Sutpen's death at the hands of Wash and the whole allegory presented? In this regard comment on Sutpen's statement to General Compson:

" 'You see, I had a design in my mind. Whether it was a good or a bad design is beside the point; the question is, Where did I make the mistake in it, what did I do or misdo in it, whom or what injure by it to the extent which this [the impending doom] would indicate.' " (p. 263)

Notice that Sutpen refuses to admit that there may have been something wrong in the planning of the design, a vanity and a pride which constitutes a form of *hubris*, the Greek equivalent of unforgivable sin. How do Sutpen's actions constitute sins deserving punishment by an avenging god? What is the precise nature of that punishment?

What is Shreve's role in the narrative? Is there some suggestion that the allegory is to be extended to include Shreve?

F. Scott Fitzgerald § 1896–1940

The Great Gatsby

Born in Minnesota, Fitzgerald was educated at private schools and at Princeton, where he contributed stories and poems to the college magazines. Leaving Princeton without a degree he joined the army. After World War I, he and other expatriates of the 1920's lived in Paris and other places on the Continent. Often said to be a spokesman of "The Jazz Age," Fitzgerald achieved fame early in his career. This Side of Paradise (1920) and The Beautiful and the Damned (1922) were best-sellers; The Great Gatsby (1925) and Tender is the Night (1934) sold fairly well; and his short stories were published consistently in the popular magazines. But, with some few exceptions, critics at the time were not impressed. Indeed, some reactions were hostile, even violent. In an essay published in 1925, Paul Rosenfeld charged that Fitzgerald's good material eluded him and that his novels and the majority of his tales were on a plane inferior to his material. It was not until after his death that Fitzgerald's literary reputation came to be firmly established, on the basis of some few short stories and The Great Gatsby, the latter now having taken its place as one of the great American novels. The articles that follow illustrates two approaches by contemporary critics to The Great Gatsby.

The Theme and the Narrator of The Great Gatsby*

THOMAS HANZO

Of the two most prominent careers which figure in F. Scott Fitzgerald's The Great Gatsby, Jay Gatsby's is a variation of the American success story, and Nick Carraway's is an example, differing from others in locale and therefore also in implication, of the provincial American's career in a society more sophisticated than his own.[1] Fitzgerald was able to combine the types through the convention of the first person narration, but Nick's fate has been generally ignored in detailed criticisms of the book. Gatsby and his dream, in these interpretations, are Fitzgerald's subjects, and through them is seen his ultimate subject, "fundamentally, the heterogeneous nature of American culture," as a recent article has it.[2] Lionel Trilling has suggested a use of this conception by Fitzgerald which, by a slight distortion, I should like to develop for my own purposes: "He [Fitzgerald] exaggerated the idea of society and his dependence upon it in order, we may say, to provide a field for the activity of his conscience, for the trial of his self."[3] Gatsby surely represents one of Fitzgerald's trials of self, an incomplete one, however, in contrast with the less dramatic experience of Nick Carraway. Fitzgerald's intention cannot be clarified, nor the significance of his achievement grasped, without our sharing with Nick the trial of his self and the activity of his conscience in that society of which Gatsby is only the most notable part.

When Carraway's voice introduces and concludes the action, Fitzgerald makes us conscious of the narrator, whose role may first be outlined by a comparison in which he acts the foil to Gatsby. We may begin with a difference which Fitzgerald would rightly have approved: Gatsby is rich, Nick relatively poor. Gatsby is alone, mysterious, obsessed; Nick makes friends easily, his life is ordinary, and he is quite sane. Gatsby is without conscience except perhaps where Daisy is concerned, and Nick subjects every act and motive to the scrutiny of a lively moral sense. Gatsby learns nothing in the course of the novel, or at least until his doom has been secured, for he decided too early what he wanted and strove for it with a determination which subordinated all other demands. Although Nick is thirty years old in the summer of 1922, the time of the novel, he is still an adolescent when he settles on Long Island, with an adolescent's memory of

---

* The footnotes to this essay are those of the author, Thomas Hanzo, from his original article in Modern Fiction Studies, II (Winter, 1956–1957), 183–190.

[1] The Americans of Henry James' novels are examples of the type; James dealt, according to Yvor Winters, "with the American, uprooted from his native usages, and confronted with the alien usages of a subtle and ancient society." "Maule's Well, or Henry James and the Relation of Morals to Manners," In Defense of Reason (New York, 1947), p. 312.

[2] W. M. Frohock, "Morals, Manners and Scott Fitzgerald," Southwest Review, XL (Summer, 1955), 224.

[3] "Fitzgerald Plain," The New Yorker, 26:4 (February 3, 1951), 80.

the war, and he comes to New York to enter the bondselling business chiefly because other restless young men are doing the same thing. Nick has no purposes, he thinks of no powers to realize, and only very gradually, not until sometime in 1924, does he come to understand what his New York interlude has meant.

I cannot presume that this view of Carraway's part in the novel constitutes a revolutionary interpretation of *The Great Gatsby*. Arthur Mizener, whose analysis of *The Great Gatsby* has appeared in several forms and is undoubtedly the most widely distributed, approves Fitzgerald's choice of form and recognizes the structural importance of the first-person convention: "By means of this narrator he [Fitzgerald] was able to focus his story." [4] But the novel is the story of Gatsby, "a poor boy from the Middle West," and when Mr. Mizener classified *The Great Gatsby* as a "tragic pastoral," it is Gatsby who illustrates the difference between the "simple virtue" of the West, and the "sophistication" and "corruption" of the East.[5] The moral distance between the two localities may be measured in more profound ways if we take Nick Carraway as our example and his sensibility and intelligence as the recognizable determinants which inform the story with its meaning. Such a reading of *The Great Gatsby* must also be compared, and at several points, with the interpretation of R. W. Stallman, who, in "Gatsby and the Hole in Time," characterizes Nick as a "defunct arch-priest" and regards the notion that Nick is to be seen as the "moral center of the book" as possible only to the "duped reader." [6] Fitzgerald's intention that we understand clearly what happens to Carraway may be appreciated in the first part of the first chapter. The novel's extraordinary economy requires, at least in its best parts, an attentive reading of detail, and since there are barely two pages in the first section, a close following of the text will not be intolerable.

Nick Carraway begins his story with the recollection that his father advised him to reserve his judgment of others because they may not have had the same "advantages." Nick's tolerance has made him the confidant of some and the victim of others, but to preserve his caution he has always reminded himself that "a sense of the fundamental decencies is parcelled out unequally at birth." Carraway's father has warned him about the difficulties of moral judgment, a difficulty originating in circumstances of origin and inheritance. But conduct, Nick observes, must be principled in some fashion. There is a "limit" to toleration. "Conduct may be founded on the hard rock or on the wet marshes, but after a certain point I don't care what it's founded on." That is, while it may be impossible to fix moral responsibility or to determine derelictions of that responsibility, Nick insists that

[4] "F. Scott Fitzgerald: The Poet of Borrowed Time," *Critiques and Essays on Modern Fiction*, p. 295. Mr. Mizener, an acute reader of Fitzgerald, is well aware of Nick's moral involvement in the action of *The Great Gatsby*. I can hope to complement his analysis by a fullness of treatment he did not judge necessary.

[5] *Ibid.*, p. 296.

[6] *Modern Fiction Studies*, I (November, 1955), 7.

action reveal some principle and that toleration does not permit indifference. His criticism of the standards and conduct of his Long Island friends
has tired him, he concludes; he can wish the world "to stand at a sort of
moral attention forever"; he wants no more "riotous" glimpses into the
human heart. We should be too hasty if we condemned Nick for an unhealthy curiosity or for pompous self-righteousness. The tone of his narrative is never offensively positive, and we shall see that what may appear to
be a peculiar form of pride is actually a serious kind of candor. Nick considers not only his friends, but himself as well. He tells us plainly what should
interest us in his tale, and he introduces us to a period of his own life in
which he is not entirely blameless and neutral. The quality of plainness,
the device of direct revelation, has appeared to R. W. Stallman as the mask
of the hypocrite, who is betrayed, symbolically, by his "irregular lawn." [7]
To the contrary, Nick's irregularities of behavior, his carelessness, do not
escape his judgment; he does not grow more confused but learns to see
more clearly what Eastern society and morality are and how he has been
corrupted by them.

Nick prepares us for his personal involvement in the action by his next
words, when he reveals his own origins, or his reasons for thinking that he
had "advantages." He came from a family of "prominent, well-to-do
people" who have lived in "this Middle Western city for three generations."
They have enjoyed commercial success, act together as a family, and regard
the decisions and conduct of their relatives with grave concern. They have
inherited the moral seriousness of their Scottish ancestors, sustain their
business and social position as a manifestation of their moral superiority, and
have passed down to their heirs a strong "sense of the fundamental decencies."

The narrator's part complicates the action. We are expected to realize
that what we are told comes to us through his peculiar agency, and therefore—to complete an obvious matter—our knowledge of the narrator will
establish the limits of our knowledge of the whole action. Fitzgerald understood these limitations and in the direct, economical way of *The Great
Gatsby* engages the reader at once in the particular interests which the
novel should arouse. Immediately after his introductory remarks, Carraway
narrates his first visit to the Buchanan household, where he delivers an
exact description of a moneyed and corrupt Eastern society in Daisy's despair and in Tom's adulteries.

Here Nick meets Jordan Baker, a professional golf player who has suc-
cumbed to the ennui of the frantic search for novelty and excitement to
which she and others of her post-war generation had devoted themselves.
She is also a persistent and obvious liar, and Nick soon perceives this fault.
Yet he is interested in her, though exactly how intimate they become is
only suggested by a scene in which Jordan easily accepts Nick's first attentions. Her unconcern for any standards beyond those of a frank self-

[7] *Ibid.*

indulgence is evidence enough that the two have become lovers. This relationship is Nick's most personal involvement in the dissolution which Jordan represents, and the perception of his share in a common guilt comes with his initial revulsion to his summer's experience, directly after Myrtle Wilson's death. He is suddenly disgusted by the vicious and now violent life about him, but even in his new wisdom, his passion for Jordan has not been completely destroyed. In his last conversation with her, he can feel that he might be "making a mistake" by ending their affair and finally that he is "half in love with her." We learn most about them at this point in Jordan's accusation that Nick is a "bad driver." He is not the person she thought—not what he pretended to be—and she says, "It was careless of me to make such a wrong guess. I thought you were rather an honest, straightforward person. I thought it was your secret pride." Nick answers: "I'm thirty. I'm five years too old to lie to myself and call it honor." It was Nick's pride to feel that he could accept Jordan on her own terms, with her cynicism and her irresponsibility, and yet that he could escape the consequences of that acceptance. But what was subdued or ignored has now erupted, with Gatsby murdered and with Daisy and Tom exposed in their terrible selfishness. It can no longer be honorable for Nick to maintain the pretense that nothing serious is involved in his affair with Jordan. Nick was dishonest because he acted as though he brought no other standards of conduct to judge their liaison with than those which Jordan's hedonism impose; and it is now plain, in his disgust and self-recrimination, that Nick has in fact deceived Jordan. She accuses him of having thought of her all along as he does now, when he has given her up. She is right, of course, and Nick, who is (he tells us) the most honest man he knows, admits his twice-compounded duplicity, a duplicity analyzed in a similar way by R. W. Stallman. But he does not accept Nick's understanding of his personal responsibility. When Jordan "calls his bluff," as Stallman puts it, the effect is to make public Nick's own shame, so that, far from being "identified" with Jordan,[8] Nick is separated from her and from her society. He can no longer lie, and he leaves the East, without honor perhaps, but with a new-found vision of his own guilt.

There is another complication in Nick's discovery of his error. Even Jordan Baker, he says, came from the West. All the Westerners—Tom, Daisy, Gatsby, Jordan, and Nick—"possessed some deficiency in common which made us subtly unadaptable to Eastern life." Though the rest may have become more acclimated to the atmosphere of Eastern society than Nick, none is entirely at ease. None can rid himself of that "sense of the fundamental decencies," however attenuated it may have become, which their origins have given them. None can finally be comfortable in the hedonism cultivated by the Eastern representatives of his generation, or at least by those with money and enough intelligence to be disillusioned by the war. After his revulsion, Nick returns to the comparatively rigid moral-

[8] *Ibid.*, p. 8.

ity of his ancestral West and to its embodiment in the manners of Western society. He alone of all the Westerners can return, since the others have suffered, apparently beyond any conceivable redemption, a moral degeneration brought on by their meeting with that form of Eastern society which developed during the twenties.

Nick makes another commitment to the life he at last rejects, a commitment that includes what we should ordinarily take to be his humiliating part in the affair between Gatsby and Daisy. Nick is used and knows it, but his attachment to Gatsby leads him to make another important discovery, however vague it may remain in some respects, about the nature of morality itself. We should ask: What does Nick think of Gatsby? And why? And again a passage at the beginning of the novel will reveal the essential information.

After Nick has explained that there must be limits to his toleration, he excepts Gatsby from his general reaction, "Gatsby, who represented everything for which I have an unaffected scorn." "There was something gorgeous about him, some heightened sensitivity to the promises of life. . . ." Gatsby had "an extraordinary gift for hope, a romantic readiness." Gatsby, Nick says, "turned out all right at the end," and it was not he who drew Nick's scorn, but the "foul dust" which "floated in the wake of his dreams." We learn gradually about Gatsby's dream: about the events of his early life and his peculiar training, about his obsession, about his impersonal—indeed, royal—view of his own personality, about the reality which his vision of the perfect life must have seemed to him. Now, the capacities which Nick admires are the capacities of will: a tremendous energy to accomplish certain purposes, and a self-imposed delusion which makes those purposes meaningful. The delusion is the vision of Gatsby's life with Daisy, and the purposes are his need for money and social position to make himself worthy of her. Gatsby differs from the others of his time by virtue of these capacities. Whereas the behavior of the Eastern rich, the racketeers, and the Westerners who adopt Eastern ways is restricted and debased by the selfish motives of personal and sensual gratification, Gatsby acts for a good which he conceives, almost absurdly, as being beyond personal interest. Gatsby's last heroism in protection of the mistress of his dream confirms Nick's judgment. Gatsby does turn out all right, while Tom and Daisy sit comfortably at their family table, bound in their private safety. If Gatsby, as Nick says at the end, "felt that he had lost the old warm world, paid a high price for living too long with a single dream," his sacrifice has already been made and his life consummated. He had found a way to live as men had once lived, with a purpose and a meaning which transcended personal fate.

Nick accepts the probability that Gatsby himself realized the insufficiency of his dream. The vision was only Gatsby's and his goal only a personal one, if somehow ennobled, as Nick sees it, by Gatsby's strength of will. Further, Gatsby is a fraud. The structure of appearance erected to impress Daisy is founded on some kind of illegal traffic which only repels her, so that she is lost to Gatsby even before the accident of Myrtle's death. Nor is Nick ever in any doubt that Gatsby has valued only the tawdry and the vain. He is left at last with Gatsby's morality, or rather Gatsby's capacity to live according to a morality, his "romantic readiness." It is this ability which Nick feels that he and the others lack, presumably because of historical circumstance.

That, at least, is what I take to be the meaning of the last words of the novel, on the night when Nick left West Egg forever, and the "inessential houses began to melt away until gradually I became aware of the old island here that flowered once for Dutch sailors' eyes—a fresh green breast of the new world. Its vanished trees, the trees that had made way for Gatsby's house, had once pandered in whispers to the last and greatest of all human dreams. . . ." In Nick's day, I conclude, such dreams no longer correspond to any reality.[9] They present no real challenges, and only disillusion, even for a man like Gatsby, can ensue, if a lesser dream like Gatsby's is accepted. When Gatsby "picked out the green light at the end of Daisy's dock," Nick continues, "he did not know that it [his dream] was already behind him." A last contrast may now be made clear between Gatsby and Nick, Gatsby who thought he could remake the past and Nick who knew that it was irretrievably lost and that more than Gatsby's dream had gone with it.

Nick's discovery is that the power of will without the direction of intelligence is a destructive power, that there must be some real end beyond the satisfaction of private desire—however desire may be exalted—to justify the expenditure of life. But he believes too that, except for the anachronistic and fatal instance of Gatsby, the time when such ends could have existed is now done. We can only "beat on, boats against the current, borne back ceaselessly into the past."

Fitzgerald represents the past both as a loss and as a source of strength. It is the record of such deeds springing from such dedication as cannot now be expected, and in the Carraway family tradition, it confers a discipline and standards which, even as survivals of an old morality, may still produce better conduct than Nick witnesses on Long Island. Nick's honesty and his conception of a good existing beyond selfish ends may be only heirlooms, he realizes, honored for sentimental reasons, but they have been given a contemporary, limited reality in his own life. Nick includes his morality in his description of a graceless modern age and reduces his claims on it to the satisfaction of individual conscience. He has no real alternative—in the sense that it may be said to be available to other men—to the selfishness

9 Edwin S. Fussell suggests that the dream of the Dutch sailors was also "unreal" and relies on the associations of the word *pandered* to develop this theme of the failure of romantic wonder, the quest for youth and success. "Fitzgerald's Brave New World," *ELH*, XIX (1952), 298. The interpretation may be allowed, but only, I think, if the old dream be regarded as the "last and greatest." Gatsby's dream was, to repeat, an illusion.

he condemns in Tom or Jordan. He does not speak authoritatively. But while his voice is subdued, it is never unsure. Nick's judgments are firm because he assumes that evil may be clearly enough determined. His hopes are modest because he regards the good only as a private, incommunicable possession. He can assert his criticism and judgment of Eastern society, including the revelation of his own guilt, but he affirms no morality of his own, accepting the circumstances of his birthright rather than affirming its permanent values. That Nick proposes to "save the world by regimenting it," [10] as R. W. Stallman has it, because he wants the world to be at a "sort of moral attention forever" is a reading which attributes this understandable reaction, this moral inertia, to a rigidity which Nick's private convictions could not support. Fitzgerald—so far as we can discern from the tenor of his narration—expects to meet no disagreement with his perception of evil, but assumes that he and his readers will all be perplexed to find a common good. This combination of conviction and diffidence produces the extraordinary contrast between the effects of cryptic description (as in Gatsby's youthful regimen) and of ideographic device (as in Dr. Eckleburg's eyes) and the quiet and deprecated role of the narrator.

Such an interpretation credits Fitzgerald with a moral seriousness which has, with reason, been challenged. With R. W. Stallman, W. M. Frohock finds Nick "short on moral perspective" [11] and Fitzgerald's style catching the "feeling of things" but combined with a "romantic inability to interpret them." [12] Edwin S. Fussell, on the other hand, defines the story of *The Great Gatsby* and other works as "the work of the imagination in the New World";[13] its failure to discover an objective for the romantic capacity is an American tragedy.[14] Failure, of course, attends Gatsby's career as inexorably as the current which sweeps the boats back into the past, but the failure must be experienced through Nick's moral sense, and his difficulties must be judged not as a lack of moral perspective but as the occasion for moral action of a peculiarly limited sort. Such a reading of Nick's role restores the emphasis which Fitzgerald gave to that moral judgment (developing awkwardly, it is true) which gives the novel its very form. And it may cast some light on the question of what Fitzgerald's early Catholic training may have meant to him:[15] a training which left him with the means to analyze and judge post-war American society even while he had lost the convictions which might have produced something more positive than Nick's retreat to the West.

The Great Gatsby is not a melodrama about Jay Gatsby, but a definition of the senses in which Nick understands the word "great." Its subject

[10] "Gatsby and the Hole in Time," p. 7.
[11] "Morals, Manners, and Scott Fitzgerald," p. 227.
[12] *Ibid.*, p. 228.
[13] "Fitzgerald's Brave New World," p. 291.
[14] *Ibid.*, p. 297.
[15] See the query by Professor H. W. Hausermann in *Modern Fiction Studies*, II, 2 (May, 1956), 81–82.

is an American morality. It is explored historically through the conflict between the surviving Puritan morality of the West and the post-war hedonism of the East; topically, through characteristic manifestations of American money values; formally and most significantly, through the personal history of a young American provincial whose moral intelligence is the proper source of our understanding and whose career, in the passage from innocence to revaluation, dramatizes the possibility and mode of a moral sanction in comtemporary America.

The Eyes of Dr. Eckleburg: A Re-examination of The Great Gatsby*

TOM BURNAM

F. Scott Fitzgerald's *The Great Gatsby* seems, deceptively, to be a simple work, and the plot can be summarized in a paragraph or two. In the spring of 1922 Nick Carraway rents a house on Long Island Sound. Near by live Nick's cousin Daisy Buchanan and her rich, burly, racist, congenitally unfaithful husband Tom, whose current mistress is Myrtle Wilson. Next door to Nick in an enormous mansion is Jay Gatsby, rich too but rootless as air, mysterious as his rare smile "with a quality of eternal reassurance in it." While visiting the Buchanans, Nick meets Jordan Baker, a petulant charming girl flawed by an incurable dishonesty; from her he learns (truthfully) that Gatsby, as a young officer about to go overseas, had been in love with Daisy in 1917 before her marriage to Buchanan.

At Gatsby's request, Nick arranges a meeting between Gatsby and Daisy, the first of several. But Daisy cannot break away from Tom, particularly after she learns that Gatsby's wealth comes from racketeering. As Daisy and Gatsby are driving back to Long Island from a party in New York, they run down Myrtle Wilson and do not stop. Though Gatsby unintentionally reveals to Nick that it was Daisy at the wheel, Daisy allows Tom to tell Myrtle Wilson's husband George (who already thinks that Gatsby was his wife's lover) that Gatsby is responsible for Myrtle's death. George Wilson shoots Gatsby and then himself, and that is that.

It is even possible to read *The Great Gatsby* and remain content with a single symbol: the green light (which, as a student once informed me, ought legally to be red) at the end of Daisy's dock. To those who do not feel a need to inquire further, the light obviously stands for what Nick Carraway says it stands for: "the orgiastic future that year by year recedes before us." True, even the most pragmatic reader may wish to add that the green light might also represent to Gatsby a projection of his wishes: a

---

* The footnotes to this essay are those of the author, Tom Burnam, from his original article in *College English*, XIV (October, 1952), 7–12.

signal to go ahead, to "beat on . . . against the current," to attempt so desperately with his "unbroken series of successful gestures" the recapturing of that past which he can never attain.

But there is still more in *The Great Gatsby* than a protagonist, a plot, and a green light. Many elements in the story, perhaps, will puzzle the practical-minded, for on the level of simple narrative they cannot be accounted for. What does one make, for example, of the faded blue eyes of Dr. T. J. Eckleburg, those staring, vacant, yet somewhat terrible eyes so much more than an abandoned signboard; of the ash heap and its "ash-gray men, who move dimly and already crumbling through the powdery air" over which the eyes brood changelessly; of George Wilson's despairing mutter as he gazes at the eyes, "You may fool me, but you can't fool God!"[1]

And there is the matter, too, of the odd scene in which Nick and Jordan Baker discuss Jordan's carelessness with automobiles. One could easily find structural reasons for such a conversation between Nick and Daisy, or Gatsby and Daisy, for it is Daisy who runs down Myrtle Wilson. But why emphasize *Jordan's* inability to handle an automobile safely?[2] I believe the answers to this question and the others I have posed are concerned with a more complex organization than is commonly assumed, an organization of symbols the whole meaning of which was not entirely clear to Fitzgerald himself. For Fitzgerald-as-Fitzgerald and Fitzgerald-as-Carraway, the gleeman of the Gatsby saga, are not the same, though both appear alternately throughout the novel, intertwining like the threads in a fabric whose sheen depends not only on the materials out of which it is made but on the light in which it is viewed.

It seems to me a very interesting fact that the overt theme of *The Great Gatsby* has little to do, actually, with the novel's use of symbol. It is indeed likely, as a matter of fact, that the subdominant motif—which I hope soon to expose—very often overshadows what Fitzgerald apparently intended to be his principal theme. Of course, it is true that in making its point about the paradoxical futility of an attempt to recapture the past, *The Great Gatsby* obviously also says much more; one measure of its greatness is the complex and ironic quality of Gatsby's attempt to beat against the current. For he—and he alone, barring Carraway—survives sound and whole in character, uncorrupted by the corruption which surrounded him, which was indeed responsible for him; from his attempt at the childishly impossible he emerges with dignity and maturity. Yet no major work of fiction with which I am acquainted reserves its symbols for the subtheme;

[1] It is interesting, though not so relevant as might at first glance be supposed, that the eyes were written into the book after Fitzgerald saw what Arthur Mizener accurately calls a "very bad picture" on the dust jacket, a picture originally intended to represent Daisy's face.

[2] The scene does serve partly to foreshadow Nick's final breaking-off with Jordan; but only partly.

the more one thinks about *The Great Gatsby*, the more one comes to believe that F. Scott Fitzgerald may not have entirely realized what he was doing.

I think it is evident that not even the most skillful novelist could make us quite accept a young bond salesman of Nick Carraway's background and experience (even one who was "rather literary in college") as capable of composing the wonderful description in Chapter III of Gatsby's parties, or the passage later on in the same chapter beginning "I began to like New York," or managing to contrive that unique and poignant apostrophe to the "hundred pairs of golden and silver slippers" which "shuffled the shining dust . . . while fresh faces drifted here and there like rose petals blown by the sad horns around the floor." In other words, Nick as Nick is one thing and Fitzgerald as himself is another—something, incidentally, which Fitzgerald tacitly admits in a letter presently to be quoted. Thus the novel may very well involve not merely the theme which Nick presents in his own character, but also another which may be called, for lack of a better name, the "Fitzgerald theme." And it is toward the latter, I believe, that almost all the symbolism in *The Great Gatsby* is directed.

Nick Carraway, as Nick, could very well point everything he said toward the magnificent and at the same time sordid spectacle, Gatsby; could praise in Gatsby "something gorgeous . . . some heightened sensitivity to the promises of life" and rub out the obscene word some prowling urchin has scrawled on the white steps of the dead Gatsby's deserted mansion. But F. Scott Fitzgerald is the one who introduces, I think unconsciously, a fascinating examination of certain values only peripherally related to Gatsby's rise, his dream, and his physical downfall. And, if we turn to this other area, this non-Carraway thematic possibility, we see at once that *The Great Gatsby* is not, like *Lord Jim*, a study of illusion and integrity, but of carelessness. Our "second" theme—perhaps the more important regardless of Fitzgerald's original intention—becomes a commentary on the nature and values, or lack of them, of the reckless ones.

We know that the critics were not alone in sensing a certain lack in *The Great Gatsby*. Fitzgerald himself felt it, was uncomfortable about it, tried to explain it away even though there is evidence that he always regarded *Gatsby* as his greatest piece of work.[3] No one agreed, however, about what the lack was. Fitzgerald could not define it consistently; in a letter to John Peale Bishop postmarked August 9, 1925, he calls *The Great Gatsby* "blurred and patchy" and adds: "I never at any one time saw him clear myself—for he started out as one man I knew and then changed into

[3] See, for example, the letter to his daughter dated June 12, 1940, in which he says: ". . . I wish now I'd *never* relaxed or looked back—but said at the end of *The Great Gatsby*: 'I've found my line—from now on this comes first. This is my immediate duty—without this I am nothing' " (*The Crack-Up*, p. 294).

myself [n.b.!]—the amalgam was never complete in my mind." [4] In a letter written the same year to Edmund Wilson, however, he shifts his ground: "The worst fault in [*The Great Gatsby*] I think is a BIG FAULT: I gave no account (and had no feeling about or knowledge of) the emotional relations between Gatsby and Daisy from the time of their reunion to the catastrophe." And then he goes on to make a particularly significant remark if we keep in mind the distinction between Nick Carraway and Scott Fitzgerald: "However the lack is so astutely concealed by the retrospect of Gatsby's past *and by blankets of excellent prose* [my italics] that no one has noticed it—though everyone has felt the lack and called it by another name." Later in the same letter Fitzgerald calls this "BIG FAULT" by a still different, though cognate, term: ". . . the lack of any emotional backbone at the very height of it [i.e., the Gatsby story]." [5]

Now, all of this self-analysis, it seems to me, misses the point. The "lack" is there, all right, and Fitzgerald strikes at least a glancing blow when he speaks of the "blankets of excellent prose"—Fitzgerald prose, please note, not Nick Carraway prose; for in the letter to Wilson, Fitzgerald is clearly speaking as author and craftsman. But, still, he misses; for it is doubtful that the "emotional relations" between Gatsby and Daisy *need* any more explaining than they get in the novel. In spite of Peter Quennel's description of Daisy as "delightful," [6] one feels that neither her character nor the quality of her emotional resources justifies any very exhaustive analysis. Certainly one must assume that, if the novel means anything, it cannot concern itself with the love of Jay Gatsby, boy financier, for the pretty wife of Tom Buchanan, football hero. In other words, the point of the Carraway theme, at least, has everything to do with precisely the emptiness of the Gatsby-Daisy "emotional relations"—those same emotional relations which Fitzgerald seemed to feel, I think quite wrongly, it was a "BIG FAULT" not to elaborate upon. That Daisy exists both in, and as, an emotional vacuum into which Gatsby, being Gatsby, could attempt to pour only the most obvious and contrived cheap-novel sentimentalism has everything to do with the ironic quality of his final defeat at her hands. And the novel would be the worse, I believe, for the very thing the author says it needs: an exegesis of this vacuum and Gatsby's response to it. Fitzgerald's instinct for craftsmanship, we may be thankful, operated before his analysis as critic.

No, it is not the details of Gatsby's later love for Daisy; nor is it that Gatsby turns into Fitzgerald, though this is closer; nor yet is it (as, says Fitzgerald,[7] Mencken thought) that the central story is "a sort of anecdote"—none of these things is responsible for that feeling of some-

---

[4] *Ibid.*, p. 271.

[5] *Ibid.*, p. 270.

[6] *New Statesman and Nation*, XXI, No. 519 (February 1, 1941), 112. Apparently no irony is intended. It might be added that Quennel transforms Gatsby into "the son of a poverty-stricken Long Island farmer."

[7] In the letter to Edmund Wilson (*The Crack-Up*, p. 270).

thing missing which many readers have experienced but that none seems able to account for. As a matter of fact, what is really "missing" in *The Great Gatsby* is not so much a specific element in plot or even theme; the *sense* of something missing comes, rather, from the inherent confusion of themes, the duality of symbol-structure of which Fitzgerald seems to have been unaware. The book, great as it is, still falls short of its possibilities because its energies are spent in two directions. If *The Great Gatsby* revealed to us only its protagonist, it would be incomparable. Revealing, as it does, perhaps a little too much of the person who created it, it becomes somewhat less sharp, less pointed, more diffused in its effect.

In the last chapter of the novel, you may recall, Carraway describes the "schedule" which Gatsby, as a boy, had written in the flyleaf of a cheap western novel.[8] The "schedule" starts, "Rise from bed . . . 6.00 A.M.," and ends, "Study needed inventions . . . 7.00–9.00 P.M.," with all the hours and half-hours between thoroughly accounted for. Carraway finds the reaction of Gatsby's father to the schedule somewhat amusing: "He was reluctant to close the book, reading each item aloud and then looking eagerly at me. I think he rather expected me to copy down the list for my own use." It is, however, important to recognize that not the dream of progress, but rather the fact of such scheduling of one's resources to the quarter of an hour, is exactly the sort of thing by which F. Scott Fitzgerald was both repelled and fascinated. As Arthur Mizener makes plain in his excellent biography,[9] Fitzerald was always haunted by the theory that one's physical and emotional "capital" was a fixed and ordered quantity, to be carefully parceled out along the years of one's life and overdrawn only at one's peril. The Nick Carraway who earlier in the novel had wanted the world to be "at a sort of moral attention forever" is closer to Fitzgerald's heart, we may be sure, than the Nick Carraway who, back in his own fictional character, stands ironically detached from a young boy's effort to reduce his small world to a pattern.

It is commonplace to cite chapter, verse, and semicolon to support the view that Fitzgerald's tragedy was that he had not been born to wealth. His famous remark to Hemingway, and Hemingway's wisecracking reply;[10] the story of his extravagances and debts (towards the latter of which, however,

[8] *Hopalong Cassidy*, for the benefit of those who might wish to speculate on the coincidence of a revival of literary interest in more than one direction.

[9] *The Far Side of Paradise* (Boston, 1951).

[10] Fitzgerald is supposed to have said that the rich are different from the rest of us (a remark expanded by Fitzgerald in "The Rich Boy" and referred to by Hemingway in "The Snows of Kilimanjaro"), to which Hemingway is supposed to have answered, "Yes, they have more money." Mizener seems to treat the exchange with a rather heavy hand when he remarks that Hemingway's reply is "clever enough" as a "casual joke" but that as a reply to a serious observation it is "remarkably stupid." Mizener's comment is on p. 86 of "Scott Fitzgerald and the Imaginative Possession of American Life," *Sewanee Review*, LIV, No. 1 (January–March, 1946), 66; I do not find it repeated, however, in *The Far Side of Paradise*. The anecdote itself, as a matter of fact, is referred to only obliquely in the book (on pp. 270–71).

he was never careless)[11] and his seeking for whatever he thought he saw in the possession of money; his marriage to the belle of Montgomery, Zelda Sayre—all these are to buttress a critical edifice which seems to go no higher than an assumption that Fitzgerald might have been happier if richer. True, anyone who can define happiness as "a slowly rising scale of gratification of the normal appetites" [12] does lay himself open to certain accusations. Yet to say that Fitzgerald wanted money, and to stop there, seems to me to say nothing. What did he seek that money could, he thought, provide? Or, perhaps more accurately, what did he think the rich possessed, because of their money, that he wanted so badly?

The answer, I believe, is that he wanted order. Fitzgerald, like Mark Twain, saw around him only chaos. And, again like Mark Twain, he tried to find an ordered cosmos in his own terms. Twain plunged himself into a machine-world where B always follows A, as a lever on a typesetter always responds to the cam which actuates it. Fitzgerald seemed to think he could discover in that magic world of the rich "safe and proud above the hot struggles of the poor" the sanctuary he seems always to have sought. Like "Manley Halliday" in Budd Schulberg's *The Disenchanted*, Fitzgerald had "a strong sense of pattern." The list which Gatsby's father shows to Nick Carraway is not so important for what the old man thinks it represents, that his son "was bound to get ahead," though this is a part of the Carraway theme. Rather, in its boyish effort to reduce the world to terms in the Chaucerian sense of "boundaries," the "schedule" imposes on the haphazard circumstances of life a purpose and a discipline, just as Fitzgerald the man attempts in his novel the same sort of thing.

Many elements now seem to fall into place. The conversation about carelessness between Jordan Baker and Nick assumes a different stature, and in the thin red circle which Gatsby's blood traces in his swimming pool "like the leg of transit" we can see a meaning: the end-and-beginning within which lies, at least, something else than *khaos*, the mother of all disaster. "It is not what Gatsby was," a student of mine once wrote, "but what had hold of him that was his downfall." "What had hold of him"—and of F. Scott Fitzgerald himself—was the dream that all share who seek to impose some kind of order on a cluttered universe. The meaning Gatsby sought—the "order," if you will—was Daisy; when the betrayal came, his dream disintegrated, and Fitzgerald interposes the most remarkable and terrible "blanket of prose" of all:

> . . . he must have felt that he had lost the old warm world, paid a high price for living too long with a single dream. He must have looked up at an unfamiliar sky through frightening leaves and shivered as he found what a grotesque thing a rose is and how raw the sunlight was upon the scarcely

[11] On this point, see Mizener's comment on p. 23 of his article, "Fitzgerald in the Twenties," *Partisan Review*, XVII, No. 1 (January, 1950), 7; also see *The Far Side of Paradise*, pp. 90, 131, 144, 180, 253, 272.

[12] As Fitzgerald did in a story called "Dalyrimple Goes Wrong."

created grass. A new world, material without being real, where poor ghosts, breathing dreams like air, drifted fortuitously about . . . like that ashen, fantastic figure gliding toward him through the amorphous trees.

That "old, warm world," we feel, was not Gatsby's vision alone. Certainly by 1925, when *The Great Gatsby* appeared, Fitzgerald must have long since begun to suspect that not even the wealth of Croesus could really keep one "safe," though that might be a dream as hard of dying as Gatsby's.

Lionel Trilling thinks that Jay Gatsby "is to be thought of as standing for America itself." [13] Perhaps; everyone is Everyman, in a sense, and Gatsby can stand for America as conveniently as he can stand for himself. But it seems to me that the true significance of *The Great Gatsby* is both more personal and more specific. The "spiritual horror" which Mr. Trilling finds in the novel he ascribes to "the evocation of New York in the heat of summer, the party in the Washington Heights flat, the terrible 'valley of ashes' seen like a corner of the Inferno from the Long Island Railroad . . . Gatsby's tremendous, incoherent parties . . . the huge, sordid and ever-observant eyes of the oculist's advertising sign." [14] This we may accept; but summer heat and ashes and oculists' signs are horrible not per se but *per causam*. The cause of the horror is, in *The Great Gatsby*, the terrifying contrast between the Buchanans, Jordan Baker, the obscene barflies who descend in formless swarms on Gatsby's house, all symbolized by the gritty disorganized ash heaps with their crumbling men, and the solid ordered structure so paradoxically built on sand (or ashes) which Gatsby's great dream lends to his life. And over it all brood the eyes of Dr. Eckleburg, symbols—of what? Of the eyes of God, as Wilson, whose own world disintegrates with the death of Myrtle, calls them? As a symbol of Gatsby's dream, which like the eyes is pretty shabby after all and scarcely founded on the "hard rocks" Carraway admires? Or—and I think this most likely—do not the eyes in spite of everything they survey, perhaps even because of it, serve both as a focus and an undeviating base, a single point of reference in the midst of monstrous disorder?

It was all very careless and confused [says Nick]. They were careless people, Tom and Daisy—they smashed up things and creatures and then retreated back into their money or their vast carelessness, or whatever it was that kept them together, and let other people clean up the mess they had made.

Here Fitzgerald nearly calls his turn—yet he misses again. For Tom and Daisy retreat "back into their money *or* their vast carelessness." And in the implication of the phrase we see that Fitzgerald was himself unready to give up his old, warm world; that Jay Gatsby was not the only one to pay a high price for living too long with a single dream.

[13] P. viii, Introduction to undated "New Classics" edition of *Gatsby*.
[14] *Ibid.*, p. xii.

§ FOR COMMENT

Do you agree with Hanzo's statement of Nick's importance in the narrative? Might Nick be considered the protagonist?

Do you agree with Burnam that Gatsby survives uncorrupted and that he emerges a dignified and mature figure? Is it relevant that Fitzgerald might have identified himself with Gatsby as Burnam suggests?

The first two chapters of *The Great Gatsby* introduce most of the major characters in the novel—Nick, Tom, Daisy, Jordan, Myrtle—and what are perhaps the major symbols—the valley of ashes and the eyes of Dr. T. J. Eckleburg. There have been numerous references to Gatsby and much attention to various rumors concerning his origins, wealth, and position. When Gatsby finally is introduced in Chapter III, he slips in quietly, unobtrusively. Is this kind of entrance expected? What kind of man had you expected Gatsby to be? How does this scene function dramatically in the narrative? As soon as Gatsby introduces himself, the butler appears to inform him of a telephone call. This detail introduces a repetitive pattern in the narrative. An insistent ring from the telephone accompanies Gatsby's many appearances in the novel. What is the function of the frequent telephone calls?

Throughout the novel there are juxtaposed varying accounts of Gatsby's background. There are first the rumors, then Gatsby's story to Nick, then Jordan's account, until finally in Chapter VI Nick breaks the narrative line to introduce the true facts that he could have learned only after the tragedy. Justify the introduction of this exposition at this time and place in the novel.

What is the reason for the emphasis on the heat of the day in Chapter VII? Is this heat in any way connected with the ash heaps in the valley of ashes? Remember that after the accident which kills Myrtle, Nick notices in Gatsby's house an inexplicable amount of dust everywhere.

What is the function of Wolfshcim? Wilson? Mr. Klipspringer? The owl-eyed man, who appears periodically throughout the novel and in effect pronounces the benediction over Gatsby's body? Do you see any connection between the owl-eyed man and the eyes of Dr. Eckleburg?

Poetry

✤ *Origins and Forms*

To most people the word "poetry" is likely to bring to mind rhymes like "June"–"moon," a dreamy state of mind, vagueness and muddiness of thought, or the like. To others it may suggest wildness or freedom from the ordinary practices of language, what is sometimes called "poetic license." You will probably find at least some basis for all these reactions among the poems in this book, but all these are mostly side issues, not central ones.

Poetry is both the oldest of the literary forms and the one that the individual is likely to encounter first. In virtually every culture first songs and then poetry without musical accompaniment have been the first literature to appear. Much folk poetry does use meter, apparently because such regularly recurring rhythm is a useful aid to the memory in a preliterate culture. Thus, poems seem to appear in nearly all cultures before drama and prose narratives with fixed wording. Not only in the history of mankind generally, but in the life of each individual, poetry plays an important part in early life. Nursery rhymes are obvious examples, but so are songs, either lullabies sung to the child or those songs he learns and sings himself.

Primarily, poetry is language used in its fullest, most complete way to express both ideas and feelings. Essentially, what poetry expresses is not different from what either fiction or the drama expresses, but the methods it uses are somewhat special. If plot, characterization, and theme are the absolute essentials of the other two forms, we shall find that poetry may use all three of these—as in, for example, such ballads as "Edward" or "Sir Patrick Spens," or characterization and theme, as in Lord Tennyson's "Ulysses" or T. S. Eliot's "The Love Song of J. Alfred Prufrock," or theme alone, as in William Butler Yeats' "The Second Coming." And so while there are narrative poems, to which can be applied many of the criteria used to judge fiction, and dramatic poems, which can be judged like little plays, poetry is not restricted to these alone. There are many, indeed most, poems that are plotless or characterless, but never themeless. Poems always "say something," and you may be surprised to find that more often than not, you will find general agreement about the main meaning of a poem.

It is sometimes wrongly said that a reader can use his imagination to interpret a poem any way he wishes or "make it mean whatever I want." A very brief example will show why such statements are themselves very careless and imprecise. Carl Sandburg's line "The fog comes in on little cat feet" will serve. Sandburg's comparison of the swift, silent, perhaps curling motion of the fog to similar features in the movements of a cat is extremely apt and perceptive. But if a reader says that Sandburg's comparison really is about baseball or automobile racing, he is obviously talking nonsense. So to begin with, words in poetry do not suddenly lose all their ordinary meanings and become counters for any kind of interpretation the reader wants to place on them. They are much more likely to take on extra meanings than they are to lose their ordinary meanings. Such ordinary meanings can be discovered in a good dictionary, and these meanings are called *denotative meanings* or *denotations*. The additional meanings that words in a poem may suggest are called *connotative meanings* or *connotations*. To illustrate, the word "home" may mean, denotatively, the building where one lives, but connotatively, the word will suggest such things as parents, security, warmth, and the like. Such connotative meanings are just as much a part of the meaning of a word as are the denotations. It is part of the task of a poet to make his reader aware of the particular suggested meanings he is supposed to recall from his experience. One can see Herman Melville doing this in his discussion of whiteness in Chapter 42 of *Moby-Dick:*

> Though in many natural objects, whiteness refiningly enhances beauty, as if imparting some special virtue of its own . . . and though directly from the Latin word for white, all Christian priests derive the name of one part of their sacred vesture, the alb or tunic, worn beneath the cassock; and though among the holy pomps of the Romish faith, white is specially employed in the celebration of the passion of our lord; though in the Vision of St. John, white robes are given to the redeemed, and the four-and-twenty elders stand clothed in white before the great white throne, and the Holy One that sitteth there white like wool; yet for all these accumulated associations, with whatever is sweet, and honorable and sublime, there yet lurks an elusive something in the innermost idea of this hue, which strikes more of panic to the soul than that redness which affrights in blood.
>
> This elusive quality it is, which causes the thought of whiteness, when divorced from more kindly associations, and coupled with any object terrible in itself to heighten that terror to the furthest bounds. Witness the white bear of the poles, and the white shark of the tropics; what but their smooth, flaky whiteness makes them the transcendent horrors they are: That ghastly whiteness it is which imparts such an abhorrent mildness, even more loathsome than terrific, to the dumb gloating of their aspect. So that not the fierce-fanged tiger in his heraldic coat can so stagger courages as the white-shrouded bear or shark.

Thus Melville is able to direct his readers' responses in the directions that he wants, particularly with his images of the polar bear and the shark, so that the reader becomes aware that the very color of Moby-Dick will suggest qualities other than those of purity or innocence, two common connotations for white. We see Robert Frost working along similar lines in his sonnet "Design."

This direction by the poet of his readers' responses is immensely important. Because poems are so much shorter than the other examples of literature here, the very fact of such shortness becomes significant. Since poetry is a much more highly condensed, compressed form of language than prose, the words which are used have to bear much more meaning than those in more diffuse prose would do. As a result, the poet's process of selection must be far more rigorous than the fiction writer's. Very frequently, the mere fact that a poet uses a detail should serve as an announcement to us that that detail is significant. Just as James Joyce in "Araby" makes the details of his setting also serve purposes of characterization as well as point toward his theme, so the appearance of a particular fact in a good poem is hardly ever the result of sheer chance but is almost always the result of deliberate design on the part of the poet. In fact, one may generalize that poets almost never work by chance, any more than the great painter includes irrelevant materials or paints at random. Although even the poet himself may not at the time of writing have been consciously aware of implications within his poem, W. H. Auden's "Musée des Beaux Arts" well illustrates how even the detail of the placement of the horse to the tree reveals something of the point Pieter Brueghel wanted to make. Thus by a rigorous and careful selection of materials to serve his purpose, the poet is able to achieve a condensation and concentration of meaning that is impossible in other forms of writing.

One is likely to think of the form of poetry, its use of such devices as meter and rhyme, as its chief characteristics, perhaps those features which distinguish it from prose. These technical features of verse are indeed important (and are discussed later on in some detail), but most literary critics since the time of Aristotle have agreed that they are not the absolutely essential features of poetry. The ability to use metaphors, to see relationships between things most people would consider unlikely, to see unexpected and previously unnoticed similarities, these are the things Aristotle says are the innate gift of the poet, the one that cannot be learned.

Metaphors, in the broadest sense, are all figurative language and the poet's chief tools. Indeed they are one of the chief ways the poet can achieve his necessary concentration and condensation. It is obvious that to call a man "a lion in battle" is a highly condensed way of saying he is brave, perhaps kingly, dominating the battle. The poet calls up connotations of "lion," but his statement says that the man and the lion, members of two apparently unlike species, share some degrees of likeness, particularly bravery and leadership. This kind of statement of equivalence is called, strictly speaking, a *metaphor*. *Simile*, a somewhat less condensed statement, does not state an identity between the two things being related but merely compares them, usually with the word "like" or the word "as." Simile is also usually considered a less intense form of figurative language, and we can see that "he is as brave as a lion" is less condensed and less suggestive than "he is a lion." However, the ultimate test of whether metaphor or simile is better suited to a poet's particular needs in a particular poem will be dictated by that poem, not by any idea that per se the metaphor is superior to the simile as a device of figurative language. There are many other kinds of figurative language, but the metaphor and the simile are the most important ones, and the principal tendency in modern thinking about figurative language has not been to classify it or name the devices so much as it has been to recognize the figure and see its particular function in a particular poetic context.

For most poetry, the chief matter is what is called *imagery*, that is, language that appeals to one of our five senses: sight, hearing, touch, taste, or smell. Most imagery is likely to be visual, for the quite natural reason that most humans have developed their sense of sight more fully than their other senses. People learn chiefly through seeing things, either the actual, physical objects or the words that symbolize them. When a poet is successfully creating images, he is literally giving mental pictures, as when William Blake makes one see imaginatively the unearthly tiger "burning bright" with a kind of eerie flame "in the forest of the night." The reader may not know if the trees are oaks or elms, but unless he actively visualizes the dark shadowy trunks in the unearthly light, he is not doing his part in experiencing the poem properly. If he sees less, he sees only words. Chiefly through these verbal pictures and other appeals to the senses, rather than through abstract, logical statements, poets tell their readers what they have to say. The beginning reader of poetry should again be warned that poetry is not illogical, but that it has its own kind of logic, usually one which rises out of the connection between the images in a poem, which are often so closely and systematically related to each other that a consistent pattern may be seen among these verbal pictures.

Two final elements require some discussion here, although detailed consideration of both will come later. One is the role of sound in verse, both of individual words and of words grouped together into lines and groups of lines. Sound is such an essential element in verse that, as we have noticed already, many highly respected writers about literature have thought that rhyme or meter, both basically devices of sound, are the chief things that distinguish verse from prose. The sounds of words are certainly one of the many ways that language does convey and suggest feelings and attitudes. One can easily recognize when something about the sound of verse does not fit the meaning of the words, as in

> Death is here, death is there;
> Death is round us everywhere.

Or the following address to Sir Robert Walpole, the eighteenth-century English statesman:

> Wise disposer of affairs,
> View the end of all thy cares!
> Forward cast thy ravish'd eyes,
> See the gladning Harvest rise:
> Lo, thy people reap thy pain!
> Thine the labor, theirs the gain.

The author of these last lines, Ambrose Philips, wrote so many poems in this meter he finally came to be known by the nickname "Namby-Pamby." In both pieces, the jingling rhythm and the quick movement have little connection with the generally serious idea, and one important reason that both are bad poetry is the unsuccessful combination of serious thoughts with frivolous meter.

The second element is the physical appearance of verse as it is printed on the page. When verse was mostly recited or read aloud, this element was not a factor. However, particularly during the last fifty years, poets have experimented considerably and have used lines of various length and lines arranged in many ways to convey some part of what they wish to tell us. The American poet E. E. Cummings wrote many poems in which this kind of physical form is important. It is hard to tell whether or not other poets will follow his lead, but the many recordings of poets reading their own works and the increased popularity of public poetry readings may indicate that the sound of poetry will resume its greater importance and the picture aspect of poetry will decline.

The Devices of Poetry

Originally, poetry was a spoken art. As a result, the way it sounds remains a distinctive part of its technique and its appeal. Of all the special poetic devices, the chief is probably *meter*, the patterned rhythm that we find in all the range of verse from mnemonic rhymes like "Thirty days hath September, April, June, and November," to such highly elaborate structures in verse as Yeats' "Sailing to Byzantium." Even so-called "free verse," verse with no regular pattern of rhythm, actually presupposes that the reader has in the back of his mind the idea that poetry has rhythmical pattern.

As a device of poetry, meter probably originated and developed as an aid to the poet in remembering his lines before the invention of written language. Despite the theories of such recent poets as William Carlos Williams and other proponents of free verse, meter remains the distinctive device of poetry and is the norm rather than the deviation.

Modern English actually has a combination of two metrical systems, one in which the number of stresses determines the name given to the poetic line, and a second, the syllabic, in which the number of syllables determines the name. One reason for this unsatisfactory state of affairs is that during the Renaissance, when the true nature of the English language was poorly understood, theoreticians rather than actual poets took over, from Latin and Greek, the names used in that prosody. This borrowing would have been well enough, except that in classical prosody the base is the longness and shortness of vowels (quantity), not the stress they are given in speaking. For example, the first line of Virgil's *Aeneid* would be marked in this way:

$$\text{Arma virumque cano, Troiae qui primus ab oris.}$$

As a result, the present system of English metrics is an adaptation of a system that works well for Latin and Greek but works only fairly well in English. This does not mean that it does not work at all—it does, but not perfectly and not without some adjustments.

For most purposes, the first term it is important to know is *foot*: a poetic foot is a rhythmical unit that contains at least one stressed syllable, and at least one other syllable, which may be either stressed or unstressed. Stressed syllables are marked ´ and unstressed ones are marked ˘. Most prosodists consider the important poetic feet are the five below:

The iamb: ˘ ´, the basic foot of English and American speech, as

in hŏtél, pŏlíce

The anapest: ˘ ˘ ´, as in ĭntĕrcéde, dĭsăppéar

The trochee: ´ ˘, as in éasў, crádlĕ

The dactyl: ´ ˘ ˘, as in háppĭlў, héavĭlў

The spondee: ´ ´, as in húmdrúm

Samuel Taylor Coleridge ingeniously illustrated these feet in the poem below:

> Tróchĕe tríps frŏm lóng tŏ shórt;
> Frŏm lóng tŏ lóng ĭn sólĕmn sórt
> Slŏw Spóndĕe stálks; stróng fóot! yét íll áblĕ

Ever to come up with Dactyl trisyllable.

Iambics march from short to long;—

With a leap and a bound the swift Anapests throng.

When these feet are arranged in various combinations of one or more types, they make up a *line* of poetry. The types of lines take their names from the number of feet or stresses and the kind of poetic feet which predominate in the line. Thus, *iambic pentameter* means a five-foot line in which iambic feet predominate. It can also be called a five-stress iambic line, meaning that there are five stressed syllables and that most of the feet are iambic. Similarly, *anapestic pentameter* means a five-foot line in which anapests predominate, or a five-stress line dominated by anapests. In English the various lines are called

monometer: one foot or one stress
dimeter: two feet or two stresses
trimeter: three feet or three stresses
tetrameter: four feet or four stresses
pentameter: five feet or five stresses
hexameter: six feet or six stresses, also called an Alexandrine

Lines longer than five-stress are rare in English, although the six-stress line is not too uncommon. Unless handled with unusual skill, these longer lines have a tendency to break into two shorter lines, as in the eight-stress line of Edgar Allan Poe's "The Raven," which tends to break after the internal rhyme into two shorter units of four and four: "Once upon a midnight dreary, / while I pondered, weak and weary."

Greek and Latin meter is largely regular, that is, it follows the predetermined pattern fairly rigorously, and deviations from the preestablished pattern are usually considered flaws. In English verse, such deviations provide the combination of regularity and variety that is considered desirable. In learning to mark stress, the reader of verse will do best to begin by marking as accented those words which normally receive emphasis in ordinary speech. In a vast majority of cases, these will be, first, the verbs and nouns. Thus syllables and stresses should be marked according to actual speech, not by a preconceived pattern or by the way the words look in print. For example, "ev-er-y" appears to be a three-syllable word in print, but in speech, it really is two syllables, "ev-ry," and should be so marked because it is actually spoken that way. Thus, this prose passage from William Faulkner's *Absalom, Absalom!* would be marked as follows:

It seems that this demon—his name was Sutpen—(Colonel Sutpen)—

Colonel Sutpen. Who came out of nowhere and without warning upon the

land with a band of strange niggers and built a plantation—(Tore violently

a plantation, Miss Rosa Coldfield says)—tore violently. And married her
sister Ellen and begot a son and a daughter which—(Without gentleness
begot, Miss Rosa Coldfield says)—without gentleness.[1]

There will be exceptions to the foregoing, but as Paul Fussell says, "It is safe to say that only very infrequently will a metrical pattern predominate so powerfully over the actual rhythm of the language that it will force the pronunciation to bend to its will. If we must give a preference to the metrical or the actual, it is probably safest to err in scansion on behalf of the actual rhythm." [2] The reader should always remember that the purpose of scansion is to lead him to where he can see what the meter contributes by its rhythm to the meaning of the poem. Meter is *one* element in the total meaning of the poem, but not the only one. Absolute adherence to a rigid metrical pattern is not a sign of poetic merit at all but is much more likely to be a sign of weakness. Simply making such statements as "This poem is written in trochaic tetrameter" is not saying very much. But when one notices that in Robert Burns' "Flow Gently, Sweet Afton," each line begins with an iamb and then anapests follow, one also sees that the quiet, controlled movement of the lines suggests the movement of the river, flowing slowly and gently to the sea. Here, the meter of the poem definitely contributes to the larger meaning of the poem.

For much poetry, particularly five-stress lines, the natural rhythm of speech seems to dictate a pause within the line, even though the meter itself does not require it. This device is called a *caesura* (marked with /, or // for a very strong caesura), and the way in which a poet uses it is some index of his skill. John Milton in particular achieves great variety within the blank verse of "Paradise Lost" through changing the position of the caesura. Less widely known is Alexander Pope's skillful modulation through such variation, as the opening lines of *The Rape of the Lock* show:

> What dire offense / from amorous causes springs,
> What mighty contests / rise from trivial things,
> I sing // —This verse to CARYL, Muse! is due:
> This, / even Belinda may vouchsafe to view:
> Slight is the subject, / but not so the praise,
> If She inspire, / and He approve my lays.

This example will also show how Pope carries his idea through the two lines of each couplet, but not beyond. Such couplets are called *closed* or *end-stopped couplets*. The opposite extreme, in which the sense carries over

[1] William Faulkner, *Absalom, Absalom!* (New York: The Modern Library, 1951), p. 9.
[2] Paul Fussell, Jr., *Poetic Meter and Poetic Form* (New York, Random House, 1965), p. 34.

through several lines, is called *enjambement*, and the lines are described as *run-on* or *enjambed*. Tennyson's "Ulysses" affords a fine example:

> I cannot rest from travel: I will drink
> Life to the lees: all times I have enjoy'd
> Greatly, have suffer'd greatly, both with those
> That loved me, and alone; on shore, and when
> Thro' scudding drifts the rainy Hyades
> Vext the dim sea: I am become a name.

To the untrained reader, *rhyme* often seems the most characteristic device of poetry, although the existence of large amounts of unrhymed poetry in English argues it is not *the* poetic device. Nevertheless, it is a very important one. Rhyme is the repetition of the terminal sound of words, as in "light"–"right." When these sounds fall in a stressed position, as in the example just given, they are called *masculine rhyme*. When unstressed syllables are rhymed they are called *feminine rhyme*, as in "able"–"table." Exact repetition of sound is *true rhyme*. Less than exact repetition is *imperfect rhyme* or *half rhyme*. Some of the kinds of imperfect rhyme are *eye rhyme*, as in "move"–"love," in which modern pronunciation has changed and what was once a true rhyme is no longer, although the eyes see the original likeness; and *slant rhyme* occurs in "food"–"good," in which one element in the two sounds differs.

A convenient kind of short hand is almost universally used to describe the rhyme scheme of poems. In this system each separate sound is designated by a letter, the first sound by *a*, the second by *b*, the third by *c*, and so on throughout all the lines of a *stanza*. Thus in "Sir Patrick Spens," the first stanza's rhyme scheme would be marked:

> The king sits in Dumferling toune,   *a*
> Drinking the blude-reid wine: *b*
> "O whar will I get guid sailor,   *c*
> To sail this schip of mine?"   *b*

This same pattern of sound relationships, *abcb*, are found to exist in the second stanza, although of course the sounds are not the same. Sometimes the reader needs to study more than one stanza to arrive at an accurate description of the poem's rhyme scheme. In Emily Dickenson's "I heard a fly buzz" for example, one is never completely sure about the rhyme scheme until the final stanza, when a true rhyme in the last line of the poem finally confirms what one has suspected about the rhyme scheme but until then had never known for certain, because until then the rhymes are imperfect. Rhyme, like meter, may contribute significantly to the meaning of a poem. In the hands of the finest poets it is not mere jingling, but a significant element by which the poet conveys meaning.

Besides rhyme, other devices of sound are used. The most common of these are *alliteration*, *assonance*, and *consonance*. In *alliteration*, the initial sound is repeated, as in "apt *a*lliteration's *a*rtful *a*id." In *assonance*, vowel sounds are repeated, as in "*h*eave–*t*eam–*s*ee"; and in *consonance* consonant patterns are repeated, although the vowels are different, as in "*live–love–lave*." A more complex kind of sound device is what is called *onomatopoeia*, in which the sound of the words imitates the meaning, as in "hiss," "fizzle," and "buzz." Related to this device are onomatopoeic effects, in which the words may not directly imitate through their sound, but which strongly suggest the ideas which the words convey. The beginning reader of poetry should, however, view the relation of sound to meaning with considerable caution. It is sometimes said that certain sounds have a particular meaning ("s" has a sinister sound, as in "serpent"), but actually sounds in and of themselves have no more meaning than do musical notes in isolation. They nearly always derive whatever connotations and suggestions they have for us from the meanings of the words themselves. If "s" always had a suggestion of danger to it, then the word "safety" would not have the kind of connotations that it does.

COMBINATION OF LINES

Any two lines of verse can be spoken of as a *couplet*, but nearly always this term refers to two lines rhyming consecutively. When the couplet is made up of two five-stress iambic lines, it is usually called an heroic couplet, because John Dryden's translation of Virgil and Pope's translation of Homer's heroic poems were done in this meter.

A three-line stanza is usually called a *tercet* or a *triplet*, though the term *triplet* nearly always means three lines rhyming together. Often in heroic couplet poems, the triplet is used to mark points of importance. Three-line stanza forms are relatively uncommon in English.

A four-line stanza is commonly called a *quatrain*. Many nursery rhymes, most ballads, most hymns, and many other poems are written in quatrains.

Five- and six-line stanzas are not uncommon in English, but do not have standardized names applied to them. Something of the variety possible in these forms may be seen in the following examples: "Go, Lovely Rose," a five-line stanza; or in "Oh Mistress mine, where are you roaming," a six-line stanza.

As with the five- and six-line stanzas, numerous combinations are possible in the seven-line stanza, though one particular combination does have a standardized name, *rhyme royal*, which describes the *ababbcc* rhyme scheme. It gained its name from its use by James I of Scotland, though probably the best-known poems in this meter are by Geoffrey Chaucer, especially "Troilus and Criseyde."

Most eight-line stanzas are really two quatrains put together, although the form known as *ottava rima* is a genuine eight-line form, with an *abababcc* rhyme scheme. It is admirably adapted for long narrative poems, like Lord Byron's *Don Juan,* but Yeats also used it to masterful purpose in "Sailing to Byzantium."

The only nine-line stanza to which a regular name has been given is the *Spenserian* stanza, so-called in honor of Edmund Spenser, who used it in his masterpiece, *The Faerie Queen.* The first stanza of this poem will illustrate the *ababbcbcc* rhyme scheme. Notice that the last line is an Alexandrine.

A Gentle Knight was pricking on the plaine,	*a*
Y-cladd in mightie armes and silver shielde,	*b*
Wherein old dints of deepe wounds did remaine,	*a*
The cruell markes of many a bloudy fielde;	*b*
Yet armes till that time did he never wield:	*b*
His angry steede did chide his foming bitt,	*c*
As much disdayning to the curbe to yield:	*b*
Full jolly knight he seemd, and faire did sitt,	*c*
As one for knightly giusts and fierce encounters fitt.	*c*

Longer stanza forms are possible, but are nearly always made of combinations of these shorter units. The exception to this is, of course, the *sonnet.* The word originally meant "little song" and originally was applied to any shorter poem. Very soon it became restricted to a fourteen-line poem written in five-stress iambic lines, rhymed in a variety of ways. The two principal variations in rhyme schemes are usually named after the poet who originated or perfected that particular form.

The *Petrarchan* sonnet, also called the *Italian* sonnet, is divided into two parts: the first eight lines, called the *octave,* with a set rhyme scheme, *abbaabba,* presenting a continuously developed idea; and the six line conclusion, called the *sestet,* with two or three new rhymes arranged in a great variety of ways, such as *cdcdcd, ccddcd,* or *cdecde.* John Keats' "On First Looking into Chapman's Homer" is a fine Petrarchan sonnet:

Much have I travell'd in the realms of gold,	*a*
And many goodly states and kingdoms seen;	*b*
Round many western islands have I been	*b*
Which bards in fealty to Apollo hold.	*a*
Oft of one wide expanse had I been told	*a*
That deep-brow'd Homer ruled as his demesne;	*b*
Yet did I never breathe its pure serene	*b*
Till I heard Chapman speak out loud and bold:	*a*
Then felt I like some watcher of the skies	*c*
When a new planet swims into his ken;	*d*
Or like stout Cortez when with eagle eyes	*c*
He star'd at the Pacific—and all his men	*d*
Look'd at each other with a wild surmise—	*c*
Silent, upon a peak in Darien.	*d*

Some critics consider the *Miltonic* sonnet, which uses the Petrarchan rhyme scheme but has a continuous train of thought, a separate kind.

The other main kind of sonnet is that perfected by William Shakespeare and called *Shakespearean*, consisting of three quatrains, followed by a summarizing couplet. His Sonnet No. 130 illustrates these features:

My mistress' eyes are nothing like the sun;	*a*
Coral is far more red than her lips' red:	*b*
If snow be white, why then her breasts are dun;	*a*
If hairs be wires, black wires grow on her head.	*b*
I have seen roses damasked, red and white,	*c*
But no such roses see I in her cheeks;	*d*
And in some perfumes is there more delight	*c*
Than in the breath that from my mistress reeks.	*d*
I love to hear her speak, yet well I know	*e*
That music hath a far more pleasing sound:	*f*
I grant I never saw a goddess go,—	*e*
My mistress, when she walks, treads on the ground:	*f*
And yet, by heaven, I think my love as rare	*g*
As any she belied with false compare.	*g*

❈ Medieval Ballads and Lyrics

In the following section will be found nine anonymous poems from the Middle Ages. We do not know the authors, although most experts now incline to the theory of a single author for individual poems rather than the view once held that such poems were the compositions of groups of people. However, since the poems were sung by large numbers of people, they were undoubtedly modified in the process just as jokes and stories are changed slightly as they are handed down from one teller to another.

At first glance, the dialect in which several of the poems are written may seem to offer real difficulties. Most of these obscurities will disappear if the poems are read aloud, and unfamiliar spelling such as "mair" or "mither" become clear as "more" or "mother." The best versions we have, often in Scottish or Middle English forms, were first written down before English spelling became standardized. In addition, since these poems were often more sung than read, a certain amount of change occurred in the natural course of events since each singer's pronunciation was slightly different. Most of the ballads exist in several different forms, called variants, of which the master collection is by Francis James Child: *English and Scottish Popular Ballads* (Boston: 1882–1898, 5 vols.), from which these versions are reprinted.

Edward

'Why dois your brand sae drap wi bluid,
    Edward, Edward,
Why dois your brand sae drap wi bluid,
    And why sae sad gang yee O?'
'O I hae killed my hauke sae guid,
    Mither, mither,
O I hae killed my hauke sae guid,
    And I had nae mair bot hee O.'

'Your haukis bluid was nevir sae reid,
        Edward, Edward,   10
Your haukis bluid was nevir sae reid,
  My deir son I tell thee O.'
'O I hae killed my reid-roan steid,
        Mither, mither,
O I hae killed my reid-roan steid,
  That erst was sae fair and frie O.'

'Your steid was auld, and ye hae gat mair,
        Edward, Edward,
Your steid was auld, and ye hae gat mair,
  Sum other dule ye drie O.'   20
'O I hae killed my fadir deir,
        Mither, mither,
O I hae killed my fadir deir,
  Alas, and wae is mee O!'

'And whatten penance wul ye drie for that,
        Edward, Edward?
And whatten penance will ye drie for that?
  My deir son, now tell me O.'
'Ile set my feit in yonder boat,
        Mither, mither,   30
Ile set my feit in yonder boat,
  And Ile fare ovir the sea O.'

'And what wul ye doe wi your towirs and your ha,
        Edward, Edward?
And what wul ye doe wi your towirs and your ha,
  That were sae fair to see O?'
'Ile let thame stand tul they doun fa,
        Mither, mither,
Ile let thame stand tul they doun fa,
  For here nevir mair maun I bee O.'   40

'And what wul ye leive to your bairns and your wife,
        Edward, Edward?
And what wul ye leive to your bairns and your wife,
  Whan ye gang ovir the sea O?'
'The warldis room, late them beg thrae life,
        Mither, mither,
The warldis room, late them beg thrae life,
  For thame nevir mair wul I see O.'

l. 20. *dule ye drie:* Grief you suffer.

> 'And what wul ye leive to your ain mither deir,
> > Edward, Edward?   50
> And what wul ye leive to your ain mither deir?
> > My deir son, now tell me O.'
> 'The curse of hell frae me sall ye beir,
> > Mither, mither,
> The curse of hell frae me sall ye beir,
> > Sic counseils ye gave to me O.'

§ FOR COMMENT

The reader will discover a tale of horror unfolds in the dialogue between mother and son. From the mother's questions and from her son's answers, we see the tale of son killing father. At first, we notice the son's attempts to evade his mother's questions and his efforts to put her off—the blood on his sword comes from killing his hawk or his horse—though the strangeness of these actions might arouse suspicions that he is not telling the whole truth. What hunter kills those favorite animals he uses to hunt with? We might wonder what further climactic horror can arise from the poem once we know the son has killed his father. Surely hardly any crime is more horrifying than the one Edward admits. Whether his flight across the sea is to be a self-imposed exile or flight from the law, we do not know; from his lack of concern about his towers and hall, his wife and children, we may infer something of his lack of concern except with his own deep self-disgust and self-hatred at what he has done. At the end of the poem, we see the final tragic climax and horror to which the poem rises: the son cursing his mother for, in some way, leading him to kill his father.

There are several reasons why "Edward" has always been among the most widely admired of the popular ballads. First, the poem is dramatic in both the general and the technical literary senses of the word. Its substance is the same as that of the murder that gets front-page headlines: "SON SLAYS FATHER AT MOTHER'S URGING"—except, of course, through skillful handling of the suspense, the ultimate horror of the poem is concealed until its final moment.

For our purposes it is perhaps more important to discuss the technical sense of the word "dramatic." Briefly, it means that the characters speak for themselves and from what they say the reader draws his own conclusions about their actions, feelings, states of mind, motives, and so forth. He is not told about these things by someone else, but just as in a play, he makes his judgments from what the characters themselves say. In general, poems that use this dramatic technique are usually more effective than those that do not because the reader is more intensely involved in the experiences such poems present. Thus, a poem gains a great deal of vividness and intensity from this dramatic method.

Another source of this poem's vividness and interest arises from its use of concrete, particular details. Notice how the poem dwells on the redness of the blood that drips from Edward's sword. Notice too that the hawk and the red-roan horse are presented in particular terms—not just any bird, but the bird used for hunting; not just any horse, but the special red-roan one, so that they can be seen in the mind's eye. Through the use of such details, the poet makes it easier to see those things he wants seen. For one thing, it is obviously easier to imagine a horse of some particular color than just a horse in general.

What other examples of striking particularity and concreteness do you find in this poem? What details are vivid enough that they actually create pictures in your mind's eye?

Earlier we noted in passing the skillful management of suspense and the avoiding of anticlimax, which in this poem was a real danger. Let us consider in some detail how these effects are achieved, by tracing the way in which the poem reveals the story. What is the situation as the poem opens? A mother confronts her son, standing there with his sword dripping with blood. In turn, he tells her first that he has killed his hawk, then his red-roan horse, before he finally admits he has killed his own father. One might well think this admission would be the real climax of tension in the poem, but the mother asks relentlessly what penance Edward will do for his crime. He answers that he will sail beyond the sea, leaving his castle to rack and ruin, his wife and children to beg their way through life. Only with her final, greedy inquiry about her own legacy does he damn her with hell's curse. With consummate skill the poem has taken the reader through Edward's evasions to his admission of guilt, but beyond that to show his disgust and hatred for himself and his final curse on his mother as the evil genius of the murder.

Thus, one can see that "Edward" stands out as one of the finest of the popular ballads. Like the great tragic plays, it finds its conflict within a family. It is vividly dramatic and skillful in its use of concrete, particular detail—and the economy with which these are used is also striking. Finally, the suspense is masterful.

Sir Patrick Spens

The king sits in Dumferling toune,
    Drinking the blude-reid wine:
'O whar will I get guid sailor,
    To sail this schip of mine?'

Up and spak an eldern knicht,
    Sat at the kings richt kne:

'Sir Patrick Spence is the best sailor
  That sails upon the se.'

The king has written a braid letter,
  And signd it wi his hand,   10
And sent it to Sir Patrick Spence,
  Was walking on the sand.

The first line that Sir Patrick red,
  A loud lauch lauched he;
The next line that Sir Patrick red,
  The teir blinded his ee.

'O wha is this has don this deid,
  This ill deid don to me,
To send me out this time o' the yeir,
  To sail upon the se!   20

'Mak hast, mak haste, my mirry men all,
  Our guid schip sails the morne:'
'O say na sae, my master deir,
  For I feir a deadlic storme.

'Late late yestreen I saw the new moone,
  Wi the auld moone in hir arme,
And I feir, I feir, my deir master
  That we will cum to harme.'

O our Scots nobles wer richt laith
  To weet their cork-heild schoone;   30
But lang owre a' the play wer playd,
  Thair hats they swam aboone.

O lang, lang may their ladies sit,
  Wi thair fans into their hand,
Or eir they se Sir Patrick Spence
  Cum sailing to the land.

O lang, lang may the ladies stand,
  Wi thair gold kems in their hair,
Waiting for thair ain deir lords,
  For they'll se thame na mair.   40

l. 29. *laith*: Loathe.
l. 32. *aboone*: Above.

Haf-owre, haf-owre to Aberdour,
 It's fiftie fadom deip,
And thair lies guid Sir Patrick Spence,
 Wi the Scots lords at his feit.

The Twa Corbies

As I was walking all alane,
I heard twa corbies making a mane:
The tane unto the tither did say,
"Whar sall we gang and dine the day?"

"In behint yon auld fail dyke
I wot there lies a new-slain knight;
And naebody kens that he lies there
But his hawk, his hound, and his lady fair.

"His hound is to the hunting gane,
His hawk to fetch the wild-fowl hame,   10
His lady's ta'en anither mate,
So we may mak our dinner sweet.

"Ye'll sit on his white hause bane,
And I'll pike out his bonny blue e'en:
Wi' ae lock o' his gowden hair
We'll theek our nest when it grows bare.

"Mony a one for him maks mane,
But nane sall ken whar he is gane:
O'er his white banes, when they are bare,
The wind sall blaw for evermair."   20

l. 2. *corbies:* Ravens.
l. 5. *fail:* Turf.
l. 7. *kens:* Knows.
l. 13. *hause:* Neck.
l. 16. *theek:* Thatch.

The Unquiet Grave

'The wind doth blow today, my love,
 And a few small drops of rain;
I never had but one true-love,
 In cold grave she was lain.

'I'll do as much for my true-love
 As any young man may;
I'll sit and mourn all at her grave
 For a twelvemonth and a day.'

The twelvemonth and a day being up,
 The dead began to speak: 10
'Oh who sits weeping on my grave,
 And will not let me sleep?'

' 'T is I, my love, sits on your grave,
 And will not let you sleep;
For I crave one kiss of your clay-cold lips,
 And that is all I seek.'

'You crave one kiss of my clay-cold lips;
 But my breath smells earthy strong;
If you have one kiss of my clay-cold lips,
 Your time will not be long.   20

' 'Tis down in yonder garden green,
 Love, where we used to walk,
The finest flower that ere was seen
 Is withered to a stalk.

'The stalk is withered dry, my love,
 So will our hearts decay;
So make yourself content, my love,
 Till God calls you away.'

Sumer Is Icumen In

Sing cuccu nu! Sing cuccu!
Sing cuccu! Sing cuccu nu!

Sumer is icumen in,
 Lhude sing cuccu;
Groweth sed and bloweth med
 And springth the wde nu.
  Sing cuccu!

l. 1. *nu:* Now.
l. 5. *bloweth med:* Blooms (the) meadow.
l. 6. *wde:* Wood.

> Awe bleteth after lomb,
>   Lhouth after calve cu;
> Bulluc sterteth, bucke verteth;   10
>   Murie sing cuccu.
>   Cuccu, cuccu,
> Wel singes thu, cuccu,
>   Ne swik thu naver nu.

l. 8. *awe:* Ewe.
l. 10. *sterteth:* Leaps.
l. 10. *verteth:* Breaks wind.
l. 11. *murie:* Merry, merrily.
l. 14. *swik:* Cease.

I Sing of a Maiden

> I sing of a maiden
>   That is makeles;
> King of all kings
>   To her son she ches.
>
> He came al so still
>   Where his mother was,
> As dew in April
>   That falleth on the grass.
>
> He came al so still
>   To his mother's bower,   10
> As dew in April
>   That falleth on the flower.
>
> He came al so still
>   Where his mother lay,
> As dew in April
>   That falleth on the spray.
>
> Mother and maiden
>   Was never none but she;
> Well may such a lady
>   Goddes mother be.   20

l. 2. *makeles:* Matchless.
l. 4. *ches:* Choose.

Lully, Lulley, Lully, Lulley

Lully, lulley! lully, lulley!
The faucon hath borne my make away!

He bare him up, he bare him down,
He bare him into an orchard brown.

In that orchard there was an halle,
That was hanged with purple and pall

And in that hall there was a bed,
It was hanged with gold sa red.

And in that bed there lith a knight,
His woundes bleeding day and night.   10

At that bed's foot there lith a hound,
Licking the blood as it runs down.

By that bed-side kneeleth a may,
And she weepeth both night and day.

And at that bed's head standeth a stone,
Corpus Christi written thereon.

Lully, lulley! lully, lulley!
The faucon hath borne my make away.

l. 2. *make:* Mate.
l. 13. *may:* Maid.

O Western Wind

O Western wind, when wilt thou blow
　　That the small rain down can rain?
Christ, that my love were in my arms,
　　And I in my bed again!

By-Low, My Babe

By-low, my babe, lie still and sleep;
It grieves me sore to see thee weep.
If thou wert quiet I'd be glad;

Thy mourning makes my sorrow sad.
By-low, my boy, thy mother's joy,
Thy father breeds me great annoy—
    By-low, lie low.

When he began to court my love,
And me with sugared words to move,
His feignings false and flattering cheer   10
To me that time did not appear.
But now I see most cruelly
He cares not for my babe nor me—
    By-low, lie low.

Lie still, my darling, sleep awhile,
And when thou wak'st thou'llt sweetly smile;
But smile not as thy father did,
To cozen maids—nay, God forbid!
But yet I fear thou wilt grow near
Thy father's heart and face to bear—   20
    By-low, lie low.

I cannot choose, but ever will
Be loving to thy father still;
Where'er he stay, where'er he ride
My love with him doth still abide.
In weal or woe, where'er he go,
My heart shall not forsake him; so
    By-low, lie low.

❈ *The Renaissance*

For English poetry, the Renaissance can be considered as lasting from about 1500 until around 1660, when the last representatives of the period, John Milton and Andrew Marvell, wrote their best work. Besides the staggering outpouring of drama, it was a very fertile time for non-dramatic poetry, especially lyrics. Many graceful examples survive, ranging from those by Marlowe, Ralegh, and Donne that make skillful use of *pastoral* motifs, to the more complex poems like Wyatt's "They fle from me." In the later Renaissance, particularly after about 1590, the style that is usually called "metaphysical" developed, particularly in the hands of Donne. His "Valediction: Forbidding Mourning" offers a striking example of the *conceit*, an extended comparison between two widely different things. Some of the later Renaissance lyricists like Sir John Suckling and Richard Lovelace are sometimes thought of as being unlike Donne in the smoothness of their verse, but careful attention to the metrics of these poets will show them much given to the abrupt, dramatic beginnings so common in Donne's poetry, and their frequent use of the *carpe diem* (literally, seize the day; well illustrated in Herrick's "To the Virgins, to make much of Time") shows their close kinship to this masterful poet.

Renaissance sonnets require a brief note, since we often think of sonnets as if they were intense expressions of personal feelings, but most Renaissance sonnets were written in series with a story framework. Since the best sonnets deal with universal situations, like the pleasures and pains of love, it is possible to read them separated from their original context. Readers should be extremely wary, though, of believing the sonnets describe experiences that actually happened to their authors. With Shakespeare, we know so little about his life, we can say very little indeed with any certainty.

Sir Thomas Wyatt § 1503?–1542

A Renaissance courtier and diplomat, Wyatt introduced the Petrarchan sonnet to English literature. "They fle from me" strikes a very modern note.

They fle from me

They fle from me that sometyme did me seke
   With naked fote stalking in my chambre.
I have sene theim gentill tame and meke
    That nowe are wyld and do not remember
    That sometyme they put theimself in daunger
To take bred at my hand; and nowe they raunge
Besely seking with a continuell chaunge.

Thancked be fortune, it hath ben othrewise
   Twenty tymes better; but ons in speciall,
In thyn arraye after a pleasaunt gyse,   **10**
    When her lose gowne from her shoulders did fall,
    And she me caught in her armes long and small;

Therewithall swetely did me kysse,
And softely saide, *dere hert, howe like you this?*

It was no dreme: I lay brode waking.
　But all is torned thorough my gentilnes
Into a straunge fasshion of forsaking;
　And I have leve to goo of her goodenes,
　And she also to vse new fangilnes.
But syns that I so kyndely ame serued,　　　　20
I would fain knowe what she hath deserued.

Christopher Marlowe § 1564–1593

Marlowe was the most important playwright before Shakespeare and also a fine non-dramatic poet, as this graceful pastoral lyric shows.

The passionate Sheepheard to his love

Come live with mee, and be my love,
And we will all the pleasures prove,
That Vallies, groves, hills and fieldes,
Woods, or steepie mountaine yeeldes.

And wee will sit upon the Rocks,
Seeing the Sheepheards feede theyr flocks,
By shallow Rivers, to whose falls,
Melodious byrds sing Madrigalls.

And I will make thee beds of Roses,
And a thousand fragrant poesies,　　　　10
A cap of flowers, and a kirtle,
Imbroydred all with leaves of Mirtle.

A gowne made of the finest wooll,
Which from our pretty Lambes we pull,
Fayre lined slippers for the cold:
With buckles of the purest gold.

A belt of straw, and Ivie buds,
With Corall clasps and Amber studs,

And if these pleasures may thee move,
Come live with mee, and be my love.   20

The Sheepheards Swaines shall daunce & sing,
For thy delight each May-morning,
If these delights thy minde may move;
Then live with mee, and be my love.

Sir Walter Ralegh § 1552?–1618

*A courtier and adventurer, his career ranged from being a favorite
of Queen Elizabeth to his disgrace and execution by James I. Something of his realistic, half-cynical approach to life can be seen in
his poem in answer to Marlowe's fanciful idyll.*

The Nimphs reply to the Sheepheard

If all the world and love were young,
And truth in every Sheepheards tongue,
These pretty pleasures might me move,
To live with thee, and be thy love.

Time drives the flocks from field to fold,
When Rivers rage, and Rocks grow cold,
And *Philomell* becommeth dombe,
The rest complaines of cares to come.

The flowers doe fade, & wanton fieldes,
To wayward winter reckoning yeeldes,   10
A honny tongue, a hart of gall,
Is fancies spring, but sorrowes fall.

Thy gownes, thy shooes, thy beds of Roses,
Thy cap, thy kirtle, and thy poesies,
Soone breake, soone wither, soone forgotten:
In follie ripe, in reason rotten.

Thy belt of straw and Ivie buddes,
Thy Corall claspes and Amber studdes,
All these in mee no meanes can move,
To come to thee, and be thy love.   20

But could youth last, and love still breede,
Had joyes no date, nor age no neede,
Then these delights my minde might move,
To live with thee, and be thy love.

William Shakespeare § 1564–1616

The greatest literary genius of English literature and perhaps of any other literature, Shakespeare won fame for his plays, but was also an excellent non-dramatic poet. His sequence of 154 sonnets is the best and best known of all the Renaissance series.

Sonnet 18: *Shall I compare thee to a summer's day*

Shall I compare thee to a summer's day?
Thou art more lovely and more temperate:
Rough winds do shake the darling buds of May,
And summer's lease hath all too short a date;
Sometime too hot the eye of heaven shines,
And often is his gold complexion dimm'd;
And every fair from fair sometime declines,
By chance or nature's changing course untrimm'd:
But thy eternal summer shall not fade
Nor lose possession of that fair thou ow'st;   10
Nor shall Death brag thou wand'rest in his shade,
When in eternal lines to time thou grow'st;
   So long as men can breathe or eyes can see,
   So long lives this, and this gives life to thee.

Sonnet 55: *Not marble nor the gilded monuments*

Not marble nor the gilded monuments
Of princes shall outlive this pow'rful rhyme;
But you shall shine more bright in these contents
Than unswept stone besmear'd with sluttish time.
When wasteful war shall statues overturn,
And broils root out the work of masonry,
Nor Mars his sword nor war's quick fire shall burn
The living record of your memory.

'Gainst death and all-oblivious enmity
Shall you pace forth; your praise shall still find room   10
Even in the eyes of all posterity
That wear this world out to the ending doom.
   So, till the Judgement that yourself arise,
   You live in this, and dwell in lovers' eyes.

Sonnet 73: *That time of year thou mayst in me behold*

That time of year thou mayst in me behold
When yellow leaves, or none, or few, do hang
Upon those boughs which shake against the cold,
Bare [ruin'd] choirs where late the sweet birds sang.
In me thou see'st the twilight of such day
As after sunset fadeth in the west,
Which by and by black night doth take away,
Death's second self, that seals up all in rest.
In me thou see'st the glowing of such fire
That on the ashes of his youth doth lie,   10
As the death-bed whereon it must expire,
Consum'd with that which it was nourish'd by.
   This thou perceiv'st, which makes thy love more strong,
   To love that well which thou must leave ere long.

l. 10. *his:* Its.

Sonnet 116: *Let me not to the marriage of true minds*

Let me not to the marriage of true minds
Admit impediments. Love is not love
Which alters when it alteration finds,
Or bends with the remover to remove.
O, no! it is an ever-fixed mark
That looks on tempests and is never shaken;
It is the star to every wand'ring bark,
Whose worth's unknown, although his height be taken.
Love's not Time's fool, though rosy lips and cheeks
Within his bending sickle's compass come;   10
Love alters not with his brief hours and weeks,
But bears it out even to the edge of doom.
   If this be error and upon me proved,
   I never writ, nor no man ever loved.

l. 5. *mark:* Star.

Michael Drayton § 1563–1631

Throughout his long career Drayton showed that a good poet can become better with constant practice. He wrote most of the kinds of poetry that were popular throughout his life. His best known single poem is the sonnet below, from his series Idea's Mirrour, *written during the height of popularity of the sonnet sequences.*

Sonnet: Since ther's no helpe

Since ther's no helpe, come let us kisse and part,
Nay, I have done: you get no more of me,
And I am glad, yea glad with all my heart,
That thus so cleanly, I my selfe can free,
Shake hands for ever, cancell all our vowes,
And when we meet at any time againe,
Be it not seene in either of our browes,
That we one jot of former love reteyne;
Now at the last gaspe, of loves latest breath,
When his pulse fayling, passion speechlesse lies,   10
When faith is kneeling by his bed of death,
And innocence is closing up his eyes,
   Now if thou would'st, when all have given him over,
   From death to life, thou might'st him yet recover.

§ FOR COMMENT

Notice that in Drayton's time, the word "mistress" meant simply "beloved" or "sweetheart." To what extent does the poem use images in the first eight lines? Do the last six lines follow the same technique or some other? Does the speaker contradict what he has said in the first part of the poem? Which of the two positions he takes is acceptable as representing the final position of the poem? Are you finally convinced of the speaker's strong love for his beloved or of his fickleness? Does the amount of imagery used affect your judgment of the speaker's real attitude toward his beloved?

John Donne § 1572?–1631

A courtier, soldier, scapegrace, he was finally the Dean of St. Paul's Cathedral. Donne's work ranges from the cynical lyric "Goe, and catche a falling starre" to the somber "Death be not proud." Perhaps because of the great variety and intensity of his poetry, Donne has been among the most popular and influential poets in the twentieth century.

Song

Goe, and catche a falling starre,
   Get with child a mandrake roote,
Tell me, where all past yeares are,
   Or who cleft the Divels foot,
Teach me to heare Mermaides singing,
   Or to keep off envies stinging,
         And finde
         What winde
Serves to advance an honest minde.

If thou beest borne to strange sights,   10
   Things invisible to see,
Ride ten thousand daies and nights,
   Till age snow white haires on thee,
Thou, when thou retorn'st, wilt tell mee
All strange wonders that befell thee,
         And sweare
         No where
Lives a woman true, and faire.

If thou findst one, let mee know,
   Such a Pilgrimage were sweet;   20
Yet doe not, I would not goe,
   Though at next doore wee might meet,
Though shee were true, when you met her,
And last, till you write your letter,
         Yet shee
         Will bee
False, ere I come, to two, or three.

The Baite

Come live with mee, and bee my love,
And wee will some new pleasures prove
Of golden sands, and christall brookes,
With silken lines, and silver hookes.

There will the river whispering runne
Warm'd by thy eyes, more than the Sunne.
And there the'inamor'd fish will stay,
Begging themselves they may betray.

When thou wilt swimme in that live bath,
Each fish, which every channell hath,   10
Will amorously to thee swimme,
Gladder to catch thee, than thou him.

If thou, to be so seene, beest loath,
By Sunne, or Moone, thou darknest both,
And if my selfe have leave to see,
I need not their light, having thee.

Let others freeze with angling reeds,
And cut their legges, with shells and weeds,
Or treacherously poore fish beset,
With strangling snare, or windowie net: 20

Let coarse bold hands, from slimy nest
The bedded fish in banks out-wrest,
Or curious traitors, sleavesilke flies
Bewitch poore fishes wandring eyes.

For thee, thou needst no such deceit,
For thou thy selfe art thine owne bait;
That fish, that is not catch'd thereby,
Alas, is wiser farre than I.

The Flea

Marke but this flea, and marke in this,
How little that which thou deny'st me is;
It suck'd me first, and now sucks thee,
And in this flea, our two bloods mingled bee;
Thou know'st that this cannot be said

A sinne, nor shame, nor losse of maidenhead,
   Yet this enjoyes before it wooe,
   And pamper'd swells with one blood made of two,
   And this, alas, is more than wee would doe.

Oh stay, three lives in one flea spare,   10
Where wee almost, yea more than maryed are.
This flea is you and I, and this
Our mariage bed, and mariage temple is;
Though parents grudge, and you, w'arc met,
And cloysterd in these living walls of Jet.
   Though use make you apt to kill mee,
   Let not to that, selfe murder added bee,
   And sacrilege, three sinnes in killing three.

Cruell and sodaine, hast thou since
Purpled thy naile, in blood of innocence?   20
Whcrcin could this flea guilty bee,
Except in that drop which it suckt from thee?
Yet thou triumph'st, and saist that thou
Find'st not thy sclfe, nor mee the weaker now;
   'Tis true, then learne how false, feares bee;
   Just so much honor, when thou yeeld'st to mee,
   Will wast, as this flca's death tooke life from thee.

A Valediction: Forbidding Mourning

As virtuous men passe mildly away,
   And whisper to their soules, to goe,
Whilst some of their sad friends doe say,
   The breath gocs now, and some say, no;

So let us melt, and make no noise,
   No teare-floods, nor sigh-tempests move,
T'were prophanation of our joyes
   To tell the layetie our love.

Moving of th'earth brings harmes and feares,
   Men reckon what it did and meant,   10
But trepidation of the spheares,
   Though greater farre, is innocent.

Dull sublunary lovers love
   (Whose soule is sense) cannot admit

Absence, because it doth remove
Those things which elemented it.

But we by a love, so much refin'd,
That our selves know not what it is,
Inter-assured of the mind,
Care lesse, eyes, lips, and hands to misse.   20

Our two soules therefore, which are one,
Though I must goe, endure not yet
A breach, but an expansion,
Like gold to ayery thinnesse beate.

If they be two, they are two so
As stiffe twin compasses are two,
Thy soule the fixt foot, makes no show
To move, but doth, if th'other doe.

And though it in the center sit,
Yet when the other far doth rome,   30
It leanes, and hearkens after it,
And growes erect, as that comes home.

Such wilt thou be to mee, who must
Like th'other foot, obliquely runne;
Thy firmnes drawes my circle just,
And makes me end, where I begunne.

Sonnet: Death be not proud

Death be not proud, though some have called thee
Mighty and dreadfull, for, thou art not soe,
For, those, whom thou think'st, thou dost overthrow,
Die not, poore death, nor yet canst thou kill mee.
From rest and sleepe, which but thy pictures bee,
Much pleasure, then from thee, much more must flow,
And soonest our best men with thee doe goe,
Rest of their bones, and soules deliverie.
Thou art slave to Fate, Chance, kings, and desperate men
And dost with poyson, warre, and sicknesse dwell,   10
And poppie, or charmes can make us sleepe as well,
And better than thy stroake; why swell'st thou then?

One short sleepe past, wee wake eternally,
And death shall be no more; death, thou shalt die.

Sonnet: At the round earths imagin'd corners

At the round earths imagin'd corners, blow
Your trumpets, Angells, and arise, arise
From death, you numberlesse infinities
Of soules, and to your scattred bodies goe,
All whom the flood did, and fire shall o'erthrow,
All whom warre, dearth, age, agues, tyrannies,
Despaire, law, chance, hath slaine, and you whose eyes,
Shall behold God, and never tast deaths woe.
But let them sleepe, Lord, and mee mourne a space,
For, if above all these, my sinnes abound,   10
'Tis late to aske abundance of thy grace,
When wee are there; here on this lowly ground,
Teach mee how to repent; for that's as good
As if thou'hadst seal'd my pardon, with thy blood.

George Herbert § 1593–1631

*Herbert made the religious lyric poem particularly his own. His
poetry is less tumultuous than Donne's but no less fine for being
quiet.*

Easter-wings

Lord, who createdst man in wealth and store,
   Though foolishly he lost the same,
      Decaying more and more,
         Till he became
           Most poore:
           With   thee
          O let me rise
        As larks, harmoniously,
      And sing this day thy victories:
Then shall the fall further the flight in me.   10

My tender age in sorrow did beginne:
And still with sicknesses and shame
Thou didst so punish sinne,
That I became
Most thinne.
With thee
Let me combine
And feel this day thy victorie:
For, if I imp my wing on thine,
Affliction shall advance the flight in me.   20

l. 19. *imp:* Repair with feathers.

The Collar

I struck the board, and cry'd, No more.
I will abroad.
What? shall I ever sigh and pine?
My lines and life are free; free as the rode,
Loose as the winde, as large as store.
Shall I be still in suit?
Have I no harvest but a thorn
To let me bloud, and not restore
What I have lost with cordiall fruit?
Sure there was wine   10
Before my sighs did drie it: there was corn
Before my tears did drown it.
Is the yeare onely lost to me?
Have I no bayes to crown it?
No flowers, no garlands gay? all blasted?
All wasted?
Not so, my heart: but there is fruit,
And thou hast hands.
Recover all thy sigh-blown age
On double pleasures: leave thy cold dispute   20
Of what is fit, and not. Forsake thy cage,
Thy rope of sands,
Which pettie thoughts have made, and made to thee
Good cable, to enforce and draw,
And be thy law,
While thou didst wink and wouldst not see.
Away; take heed:
I will abroad.
Call in thy deaths head there: tie up thy fears.
He that forbears   30

To suit and serve his need,
          Deserves his load.
But as I rav'd and grew more fierce and wilde
          At every word,
Me thoughts I heard one calling, *Child!*
          And I reply'd, *My Lord.*

The Altar

A broken ALTAR, Lord, thy servant reares,
Made of a heart, and ccmented with teares:
   Whose parts are as thy hand did frame;
   No workmans tool hath touch'd the same.
          A HEART alone
          Is such a stone,
          As nothing but
          Thy pow'r doth cut
          Wherefore each part
          Of my hard heart   10
          Meets in this frame,
          To praise thy Name:
   That, if I chance to hold my peace,
   These stones to praise thee may not cease.
O let thy blessed SACRIFICE be mine,
And sanctifie this ALTAR to be thine.

Vertue

   Sweet day, so cool, so calm, so bright,
   The bridall of the earth and skie:
   The dew shall weep thy fall to night;
          For thou must die.

   Sweet rose, whose hue angrie and brave
   Bids the rash gazer wipe his eye:
   Thy root is ever in its grave,
          And thou must die.

   Sweet spring, full of sweet dayes and roses,
   A box where sweets compacted lie;   10
   My musick shows ye have your closes,
          And all must die.

Onely a sweet and vertuous soul,
Like season'd timber, never gives;
But though the whole world turn to coal,
Then chiefly lives.

Love

Love bade me welcome: yet my soul drew back,
Guiltie of dust and sinne.
But quick-ey'd Love, observing me grow slack
From my first entrance in,
Drew nearer to me, sweetly questioning,
If I lack'd any thing.

A guest, I answer'd, worthy to be here:
Love said, You shall be he.
I the unkinde, ungrateful? Ah my deare,
I cannot look on thee.   10
Love took my hand, and smiling did reply,
Who made the eyes but I?

Truth Lord, but I have marr'd them: let my shame
Go where it doth deserve.
And know you not, sayes Love, who bore the blame?
My deare, then I will serve.
You must sit down, sayes Love, and taste my meat:
So I did sit and eat.

Robert Herrick § 1591–1674

Cherrie-Ripe

Cherrie-Ripe, Ripe, Ripe, I cry,
Full and faire ones; come and buy:
If so be, you ask me where
They doe grow? I answer, There,
Where my *Julia*'s lips doe smile;
There's the Land, or Cherry-Ile:
Whose Plantations fully show
All the yeere, where Cherries grow.

Delight in Disorder

A sweet disorder in the dresse
Kindles in cloathes a wantonnesse:
A Lawne about the shoulders thrown
Into a fine distraction:
An erring Lace, which here and there
Enthralls the Crimson Stomacher:
A Cuffe neglectfull, and thereby
Ribbands to flow confusedly:
A winning wave (deserving Note)
In the tempestuous petticote: 10
A carelesse shooe-string, in whose tye
I see a wilde civility:
Doe more bewitch me, then when Art
Is too precise in every part.

Upon Julia's Clothes

When as in silks my *Julia* goes,
Then, then (me thinks) how sweetly flowes
That liquefaction of her clothes.

Next, when I cast mine eyes and see
That brave Vibration each way free;
O how that glittering taketh me!

To the Virgins, to make much of Time

1. Gather ye Rose-buds while ye may,
      Old Time is still a flying:
   And this same flower that smiles to day,
      To morrow will be dying.

2. The glorious Lamp of Heaven, the Sun,
      The higher he's a getting;
   The sooner will his Race be run,
      And neerer he's to Setting.

3. That Age is best, which is the first,
      When Youth and Blood are warmer;   30
   But being spent, the worse, and worst
      Times, still succeed the former.

4. Then be not coy, but use your time;
   And while ye may, goe marry:
   For having lost but once your prime,
   You may for ever tarry.

To the Rose. Song

1. Goe happy Rose, and enterwove
   With other Flowers, bind my Love.
      Tell her too, she must not be,
      Longer flowing, longer free,
      That so oft has fetter'd me.

2. Say (if she's fretfull) I have bands
   Of Pearle, and Gold, to bind her hands:
      Tell her, if she struggle still,
      I have Mirtle rods, (at will)
      For to tame, though not to kill.   10

3. Take thou my blessing, thus, and goe,
   And tell her this, but doe not so,
      Lest a handsome anger flye,
      Like a Lightning, from her eye,
      And burn thee'up, as well as I.

Thomas Carew § 1595?–1639?

Song: Aske me no more where Iove bestowes

Aske me no more where Iove bestowes,
When *Iune* is past, the fading rose:
For in your beauties orient deepe,
These flowers as in their causes, sleepe.

Aske me no more whether doth stray,
The golden Atomes of the day:
For in pure love heaven did prepare
Those powders to inrich your haire.

Aske me no more whether doth hast,
The Nightingale when May is past: 10

For in your sweet dividing throat,
She winters and keepes warme her note.

Aske me no more where those starres light,
That downewards fall in dead of night:
For in your eyes they sit, and there,
Fixed become as in their sphere.

Aske me no more if East or West,
The Phenix builds her spicy nest:
For unto you at last shee flies,
And in your fragrant bosome dyes.   20

Edmund Waller § 1606–1687

On a Girdle

That which her slender waist confined
Shall now my joyful temples bind;
No monarch but would give his crown,
His arms might do what this has done.

It was my heaven's extremest sphere,
The pale which held that lovely deer;
My joy, my grief, my hope, my love,
Did all within this circle move.

A narrow compass, and yet there
Dwelt all that's good and all that's fair;   10
Give me but what this ribband bound,
Take all the rest the sun goes round!

Go, lovely rose

Go, lovely rose!
Tell her that wastes her time and me,
That now she knows,
When I resemble her to thee,
How sweet and fair she seems to be.

Tell her that's young,
And shuns to have her graces spied,

That hadst thou sprung
In deserts, where no men abide,
Thou must have uncommended died.   10

Small is the worth
Of beauty from the light retired;
Bid her come forth,
Suffer herself to be desired,
And not blush so to be admired.

Then die! that she
The common fate of all things rare
May read in thee;
How small a part of time they share
That are so wondrous sweet and fair!   20

§ FOR COMMENT

Describe the rhyme and meter of the poem. What contribution do the
shorter first and third lines make in each stanza? Waller makes a basic
comparison here between his sweetheart and a beautiful flower. How has
he kept his poem from being trite and commonplace?

Sir John Suckling § 1609–1642

Why so pale and wan, fond lover

Why so pale and wan, fond lover?
  Prithee, why so pale?
Will, when looking well can't move her,
  Looking ill prevail?
  Prithee, why so pale?

Why so dull and mute, young sinner?
  Prithee, why so mute?
Will, when speaking well can't win her,
  Saying nothing do't?
  Prithee, why so mute?   10

Quit, quit for shame! This will not move,
  This cannot take her.

If of herself she will not love,
　　Nothing can make her:
　　The devil take her!

Constancy

Out upon it, I have loved
　　Three whole days together!
And am like to love three more,
　　If it prove fair weather.

Time shall molt away his wings
　　Ere he shall discover
In the whole wide world again
　　Such a constant lover.

But the spite on 't is, no praise
　　Is due at all to me:　　　　　　　　　10
Love with me had made no stays,
　　Had it any been but she.

Had it any been but she,
　　And that very face,
There had been at least ere this
　　A dozen dozen in her place.

Richard Lovelace § 1618 1657

The Grass-Hopper

To My Noble Friend, Mr. Charles Cotton

Oh thou that swings't upon the waving haire
　　Of some well-filled Oaten Beard,
Drunke ev'ry night a Delicious teare
　　Dropt from Heav'n, where now th'art reard.

The Joyes of Earth and Ayre are thine intire,
　　That with thy feet and wings dost hop and flye.
And when thy Poppy workes thou dost retire
　　To thy Carv'd Acron-bed to lye.

Up with the Day, the Sun thou welcomst then,
    Sportst in the guilt-plats of his Beames,   10
And all these merry dayes mak'st merry men,
    Thy selfe, and Melancholy streames.

But ah the Sickle! Golden Eares are Cropt:
    Ceres and *Bacchus* bid good night;
Sharpe frosty fingers all your Flowr's have topt,
    And what sithes spar'd, Winds shave off quite.

Poore verdant foole! and now green Ice, thy Joys
    Large and as lasting, as thy Peirch of Grasse,
Bid us lay in 'gainst Winter, Raine, and poize,
    Their flouds, with an o'reflowing glasse.   20

Thou best of *Men* and *Friends!* We will create
    A Genuine Summer in each others breast,
And spite of this cold Time and frosen Fate
    Thaw us a warme seate to our rest.

Our sacred harthes shall burne eternally
    As Vestall Flames the North-wind he
Shall strike his frost-stretch'd Winges, dissolve and flye
    This *Ætna* in Epitome.

Dropping December shall come weeping in,
    Bewayle th'usurping of his Raigne;   30
But when in show'rs of old Greeke we beginne
    Shall crie, he hath his Crowne againe!

Night as cleare *Hesper* shall our Tapers whip,
    From the light Casements where we play,
And the darke Hagge from her black mantle strip,
    And sticke there everlasting Day.

Thus richer then untempted Kings are we,
    That asking nothing, nothing need:
Though Lord of all what Seas imbrace; yet he
    That wants himselfe, is poore indeed.   40

l. 10. *guilt-plats*: Plots (of ground) gilded by the sun.

To Lucasta: The Rose

Sweet serene skye-like Flower,
Haste to adorn her Bower:
    From thy long clowdy bed,
    Shoot forth thy damaske head.

New-startled blush of *Flora!*
The griefe of pale *Aurora*,
    Who will contest no more;
    Haste, haste, to strowe her floore.

Vermilion Ball that's given
From lip to lip in Heaven;   10
    Loves Couches cover-led;
    Haste, haste, to make her bed.

Deare Offpring of pleas'd *Venus*,
And Jollie, plumpe *Silenus*;
    Haste, haste, to decke the Haire
    Of th' only, sweetly Faire.

See! Rosie is her Bower,
Her floore is all this Flower;
    Her Bed a Rosie nest
    By a Bed of Roses prest.   20

But early as she dresses,
Why fly you her bright Tresses?
    Ah! I have found I feare;
    Because her Checkes are neere.

John Milton § 1608–1674

The traditional third (Shakespeare first and Chaucer second) of the great English poets, Milton is seen at his best in Paradise Lost, *his epic poem "of man's first disobedience," but the typical Miltonic quality can also be seen in "Lycidas" and his sonnets.*

Lycidas

In this Monody the Author bewails a learned Friend, unfortunately drown'd in his Passage from Chester on the Irish Seas, 1637. And by occasion foretells the ruin of our corrupted Clergy then in their height.

Yet once more, O ye Laurels, and once more
Ye Myrtles brown, with Ivy never sere,
I come to pluck your Berries harsh and crude,
And with forc'd fingers rude,
Shatter your leaves before the mellowing year.
Bitter constraint, and sad occasion dear,
Compels me to disturb your season due:
For *Lycidas* is dead, dead ere his prime,
Young *Lycidas*, and hath not left his peer:
Who would not sing for *Lycidas*? he knew   10
Himself to sing, and build the lofty rhyme.
He must not float upon his wat'ry bier
Unwept, and welter to the parching wind,
Without the meed of some melodious tear.
    Begin then, Sisters of the sacred well,
That from beneath the seat of *Jove* doth spring,
Begin, and somewhat loudly sweep the string.
Hence with denial vain, and coy excuse,
So may some gentle Muse
With lucky words favor my destin'd Urn,   20
And as he passes turn,
And bid fair peace be to my sable shroud.
For we were nurst upon the self-same hill,
Fed the same flock, by fountain, shade, and rill.
    Together both, ere the high Lawns appear'd
Under the opening eyelids of the morn,
We drove afield, and both together heard
What time the Gray-fly winds her sultry horn,
Batt'ning our flocks with the fresh dews of night,
Oft till the Star that rose, at Ev'ning, bright   30
Toward Heav'n's descent had slop'd his westering wheel.
Meanwhile the Rural ditties were not mute,
Temper'd to th'Oaten Flute;
Rough *Satyrs* danc'd, and *Fauns* with clov'n heel
From the glad sound would not be absent long,
And old *Damaetas* lov'd to hear our song.
    But O the heavy change, now thou art gone,

---

l. 8. *Lycidas*: One of the traditional pastoral names for a shepherd, as is Damaetas
(l. 46). Amaryllis and Neaera (ll. 68–69) are traditional names for shepherdesses.

Now thou art gone, and never must return!
Thee Shepherd, thee the Woods, and desert Caves,
With wild Thyme and the gadding Vine o'ergrown,   40
And all their echoes mourn.
The Willows and the Hazel Copses green
Shall now no more be seen,
Fanning their joyous Leaves to thy soft lays.
As killing as the Canker to the Rose,
Or Taint-worm to the weanling Herds that graze,
Or Frost to Flowers, that their gay wardrobe wear,
When first the White-thorn blows;
Such, *Lycidas*, thy loss to Shepherd's ear.
 Where were ye Nymphs when the remorseless deep   50
Clos'd o'er the head of your lov'd *Lycidas*?
For neither were ye playing on the steep,
Where your old *Bards*, the famous *Druids*, lie,
Nor on the shaggy top of *Mona* high,
Nor yet where *Deva* spreads her wizard stream:
Ay me, I fondly dream!
Had ye been there—for what could that have done?
What could the Muse herself that *Orpheus* bore,
The Muse herself, for her enchanting son
Whom Universal nature did lament,   60
When by the rout that made the hideous roar,
His gory visage down the stream was sent,
Down the swift *Hebrus* to the *Lesbian* shore?
 Alas! What boots it with uncessant care
To tend the homely slighted Shepherd's trade,
And strictly meditate the thankless Muse?
Were it not better done as others use,
To sport with *Amaryllis* in the shade,
Or with the tangles of *Neaera's* hair?
Fame is the spur that the clear spirit doth raise   70
(That last infirmity of Noble mind)
To scorn delights, and live laborious days;
But the fair Guerdon when we hope to find,
And think to burst out into sudden blaze,
Comes the blind *Fury* with th'abhorred shears,
And slits the thin-spun life. "But not the praise,"
Phoebus repli'd, and touch'd my trembling ears;
"*Fame* is no plant that grows on mortal soil,

   l. 54. *Mona:* The Latin name for the island of Anglesley, off the Welsh coast, a
Druidic center.
   l. 55. *Deva:* The Latin name for the river Dee, which flows between England
and Wales.
   l. 63. *Hebrus:* A river on the island of Lesbos.

Nor in the glistering foil
Set off to th'world, nor in broad rumor lies,   80
But lives and spreads aloft by those pure eyes
And perfect witness of all-judging *Jove*;
As he pronounces lastly on each deed,
Of so much fame in Heav'n expect thy meed."
    O Fountain *Arethuse*, and thou honor'd flood,
Smooth-sliding *Mincius*; crown'd with vocal reeds,
That strain I heard was of a higher mood:
But now my Oat proceeds,
And listens to the Herald of the Sea
That came in *Neptune's* plea.   90
He ask'd the Waves, and ask'd the Felon winds,
What hard mishap hath doom'd this gentle swain?
And question'd every gust of rugged wings
That blows from off each beaked Promontory.
They knew not of his story,
And sage *Hippotades* their answer brings,
That not a blast was from his dungeon stray'd,
The Air was calm, and on the level brine,
Sleek *Panope* with all her sisters play'd.
It was that fatal and perfidious Bark   100
Built in th'eclipse, and rigg'd with curses dark,
That sunk so low that sacred head of thine.
    Next *Camus*, reverend Sire, went footing slow,
His Mantle hairy, and his Bonnet sedge,
Inwrought with figures dim, and on the edge
Like to that sanguine flower inscrib'd with woe.
"Ah! Who hath reft" (quoth he) "my dearest pledge?"
Last came, and last did go,
The Pilot of the *Galilean* lake.
Two massy Keys he bore of metals twain   110
(The Golden opes, the Iron shuts amain).
He shook his Mitred locks, and stern bespake:
"How well could I have spar'd for thee, young swain,
Enough of such as for their bellies' sake,
Creep and intrude and climb into the fold?
Of other care they little reck'ning make,

1. 85. *Arethuse:* A spring in Sicily, associated with Theocritus and the Greek pastoral tradition.
1. 86. *Mincius:* The river near which Virgil was born, representing the Latin pastoral tradition.
1. 96. *Hippotades:* Æolus, god of the winds and son of Hippotes.
1. 99. *Panope:* A sea nymph.
1. 103. *Camus:* The Latin name for the river Cam, which flows through Cambridge, where Milton and King were both students.

Than how to scramble at the shearers' feast,
And shove away the worthy bidden guest;
Blind mouths! that scarce themselves know how to hold
A Sheep-hook, or have learn'd aught else the least   120
That to the faithful Herdman's art belongs!
What recks it them? What need they? They are sped;
And when they list, their lean and flashy songs
Grate on their scrannel Pipes of wretched straw.
The hungry Sheep look up, and are not fed,
But swoln with wind, and the rank mist they draw,
Rot inwardly, and foul contagion spread:
Besides what the grim Wolf with privy paw
Daily devours apace, and nothing said;
But that two-handed engine at the door   130
Stands ready to smite once, and smite no more."
      Return *Alpheus*, the dread voice is past
That shrunk thy streams; Return *Sicilian* Muse,
And call the Vales, and bid them hither cast
Their Bells and Flowrets of a thousand hues.
Ye valleys low where the mild whispers use
Of shades and wanton winds and gushing brooks,
On whose fresh lap the swart Star sparely looks,
'Throw hither all your quaint enamell'd eyes,
That on the green turf suck the honied showers,   140
And purple all the ground with vernal flowers.
Bring the rathe Primrose that forsaken dies,
The tufted Crow-toe, and pale Jessamine,
The white Pink, and the Pansy freakt with jet,
The glowing Violet,
The Musk-rose, and the well-attir'd Woodbine,
With Cowslips wan that hang the pensive head,
And every flower that sad embroidery wears:
Bid *Amaranthus* all his beauty shed,
And Daffadillies fill their cups with tears,   150
To strew the Laureate Hearse where *Lycid* lies.
For so to interpose a little ease,
Let our frail thoughts dally with false surmise.
Ay me! Whilst thee the shores and sounding Seas
Wash far away, where'er thy bones are hurl'd,
Whether beyond the stormy *Hebrides*,
Where thou perhaps under the whelming tide
Visit'st the bottom of the monstrous world;

    l. 132. *Alpheus:* A river whose god loved Arethusa, the nymph of the fountain
in l. 85.
    l. 149. *Amaranthus:* A flower that never fades.

Or whether thou to our moist vows denied,
Sleep'st by the fable of *Bellerus* old,   160
Where the great vision of the guarded Mount
Looks toward *Namancos* and *Bayona's* hold;
Look homeward Angel now, and melt with ruth:
And, O ye *Dolphins*, waft the hapless youth.
　　Weep no more, woeful Shepherds weep no more,
For *Lycidas* your sorrow is not dead,
Sunk though he be beneath the wat'ry floor,
So sinks the day-star in the Ocean bed,
And yet anon repairs his drooping head,
And tricks his beams, and with new-spangled Ore,   170
Flames in the forehead of the morning sky:
So *Lycidas*, sunk low, but mounted high,
Through the dear might of him that walk'd the waves,
Where other groves, and other streams along,
With *Nectar* pure his oozy Locks he laves,
And hears the unexpressive nuptial Song,
In the blest Kingdoms meek of joy and love.
There entertain him all the Saints above,
In solemn troops, and sweet Societies
That sing, and singing in their glory move,   180
And wipe the tears for ever from his eyes.
Now *Lycidas*, the Shepherds weep no more;
Henceforth thou art the Genius of the shore,
In thy large recompense, and shalt be good
To all that wander in that perilous flood.
　　Thus sang the uncouth Swain to th'Oaks and rills,
While the still morn went out with Sandals gray;
He touch't the tender stops of various Quills,
With eager thought warbling his *Doric* lay:
And now the Sun had stretch't out all the hills,   190
And now was dropt into the Western bay;
At last he rose, and twitch't his Mantle blue:
Tomorrow to fresh Woods, and Pastures new.

§ FOR COMMENT

"Lycidas" was occasioned by the death of Milton's college friend, Edward
King, who was drowned at sea in 1637. The poem was published in a volume memorializing King's death. King and Milton had not been bosom

l. 160. *Bellerus*: A mythical giant of Cornwall.
l. 162. *Namancos and Bayona*: Places in Spain.

friends, and those who expect to find in the poem an expression of profound personal grief will be disappointed.

Milton's poem does, of course, mourn King's death, but within the traditional framework of the pastoral elegy—a literary convention dating back to the Greeks Theocritus, Bion, and Moschus, but more especially indebted to Virgil's *Eclogues* ("Eclogue 10" in particular), in which Virgil laments the death of the Roman poet Gallus. Nearly all the Renaissance poets wrote in this pastorial tradition: French, Italian, and such Englishmen as Edmund Spenser in *The Shepheardes Calendar*. One should not think of Milton as slavishly imitating his predecessors, but instead as adapting with great ingenuity the conventions of the pastoral mode to seventeenth-century English conditions.

The essence of the pastoral convention in literature is that it uses the relatively restricted world of shepherds to comment on the larger, more complex world in which everyone lives. Much of the pleasure in this kind of poetry comes from seeing the skill with which the poet can reflect the real world in the mirror of the shepherd's life. Under no circumstances should the poem be considered a "realistic" picture of life. When Milton refers to King and himself "being nursed by fountain, shade, and rill," he does not mean that they actually had this kind of life but uses the pastoral metaphor to say that he and King were at Cambridge together as undergraduates. Pastoral poetry is not about herding sheep.

Thus Milton was working within a conventional framework as definitely established as the Western story is in twentieth-century American culture.

There were several particular kinds of pastoral poems: the singing contest, in which two shepherds competed at extemporaneous verse-making; the celebration of a sweetheart's beauty; the shepherd's complaint about his sweetheart's cold heartedness; the invitation, of which Christopher Marlowe's "Come Live with Me and Be My Love" is a graceful example; and the shepherd's lament at the loss of his lands. The elegy mourning a dead companion was among the most popular and, at least since Virgil's elegy for Gallus, had allowed the poet to comment on the significance of the departed friend's life. One of the traditional conventional elements that Milton uses is that all nature mourns the death of the shepherd (lines 50, 91, 103, 109, 132), though he draws in various water spirits, such as Camus, the god of the river flowing through Cambridge and Triton, the minor sea god. St. Peter appears since King was a young clergyman, and then finally in line 132 Milton returns to the pastoral strain with the invocation of Alpheus and the Sicilian Muse of pastoral poetry. Notice that the lines following the introduction of St. Peter allow Milton to attack seventeenth-century corruptions in the Church of England. Such social commentary was a well established part of the pastoral convention, dating back to Virgil's first and ninth "Eclogues," and Spenser had also criticized social evils in *The Shep-*

heardes Calendar. Traditionally, the pastoral offered a contrast between the simple, uncomplicated life of the shepherds and the complex, corrupt life of the city.

The introduction of Christian material into pastoral was not looked upon in the Renaissance as inconsistent, because of the large amount of pastoral imagery in the Bible, such as in the Twenty-Third Psalm and the parables of the New Testament. Do these Christian references help prepare for the assertion that Lycidas has achieved immortality? What does the poet gain by his shift from the third-person description in the opening lines of the poem to the direct address of Lycidas in line 38? Notice that the conclusion of the poem shifts back to the third person. What effect does this shift have? Does it help keep the feeling of the poem under better control? How? Milton is usually considered extraordinarily sensitive to the sound of words. Cite examples of his use of onomatopoeia, assonance, and alliteration. How do these devices contribute to the total effect of the poem?

Sonnet: When I consider how my light is spent

When I consider how my light is spent,
    Ere half my days, in this dark world and wide,
    And that one Talent which is death to hide,
    Lodg'd with me useless, though my Soul more bent
To serve therewith my Maker, and present
    My true account, lest he returning chide;
    "Doth God exact day-labor, light denied,"
I fondly ask; But patience to prevent
That murmur, soon replies, "God doth not need
    Either man's work or his own gifts; who best   10
    Bear his mild yoke, they serve him best; his state
Is Kingly. Thousands at his bidding speed
    And post o'er Land and Ocean without rest:
    They also serve who only stand and wait."

Sonnet: Methought I saw my late espoused Saint

Methought I saw my late espoused Saint
    Brought to me like *Alcestis* from the grave,
    Whom *Jove's* great Son to her glad Husband gave,
    Rescu'd from death by force though pale and faint.
Mine as whom washt from spot of child-bed taint,
    Purification in the old Law did save,

And such, as yet once more I trust to have
Full sight of her in Heaven without restraint,
Came vested all in white, pure as her mind:
Her face was veil'd, yet to my fancied sight,
Love, sweetness, goodness, in her person shin'd
So clear, as in no face with more delight.
But O, as to embrace me she inclin'd,
I wak'd, she fled, and day brought back my night.

10

Andrew Marvell § 1621–1678

*Like Donne, Marvell has been a poet whose popularity has revived
in the twentieth century. His work combines much of the smoothness of poets like Suckling and Herrick with the witty vigor of
Donne. Both the poems below illustrate Marvell's ability to imply
serious overtones in a light and clever treatment.*

The Definition of Love

I

My Love is of a birth as rare
As 'tis for object strange and high:
It was begotten by despair
Upon Impossibility.

II

Magnanimous Despair alone
Could show me so divine a thing,
Where feeble Hope could ne'r have flown
But vainly flapt its Tinsel Wing,

III

And yet I quickly might arrive
Where my extended Soul is fixt,
But Fate does Iron wedges drive,
And alwaies crouds it self betwixt.

10

IV

For Fate with jealous Eye does see
Two perfect Loves; nor lets them close:

Their union would her ruine be,
And her Tyrannick pow'r depose.

V

And therefore her Decrees of Steel
Us as the distant Poles have plac'd,
(Though Loves whole World on us doth wheel)
Not by themselves to be embrac'd.   20

VI

Unless the giddy Heaven fall,
And Earth some new Convulsion tear;
And, us to joyn, the World should all
Be cramp'd into a *Planisphere*.

VII

As Lines so Loves *oblique* may well
Themselves in every Angle greet:
But ours so truly *Paralel*,
Though infinite can never meet.

VIII

Therefore the Love which us doth bind.
But Fate so enviously debarrs,   30
Is the Conjunction of the Mind,
And Opposition of the Stars.

To His Coy Mistress

Had we but World enough, and Time,
This coyness Lady were no crime.
We would sit down, and think which way
To walk, and pass our long Loves Day.
Thou by the *Indian Ganges* side
Should'st Rubies find: I by the Tide
Of *Humber* would complain. I would
Love you ten years before the Flood:
And you should if you please refuse
Till the Conversion of the *Jews*.   10
My vegetable Love should grow
Vaster then Empires, and more slow.
An hundred years should go to praise
Thine Eyes, and on thy Forehead Gaze.
Two hundred to adore each Breast:

But thirty thousand to the rest.
An Age at least to every part,
And the last Age should show your Heart.
For Lady you deserve this State;
Nor would I love at lower rate.   20
    But at my back I alwaies hear
Times winged Charriot hurrying near:
And yonder all before us lye
Desarts of vast Eternity.
Thy Beauty shall no more be found;
Nor, in thy marble Vault, shall sound
My ecchoing Song: then Worms shall try
That long preserv'd Virginity:
And your quaint Honour turn to dust;
And into ashes all my Lust.   30
The Grave's a fine and private place,
But none I think do there embrace.
    Now therefore, while the youthful hew
Sits on thy skin like morning dew,
And while thy willing Soul transpires
At every pore with instant Fires,
Now let us sport us while we may;
And now, like am'rous birds of prey,
Rather at once our Time devour,
Than languish in his slow-chapt pow'r.   40
Let us roll all our Strength, and all
Our sweetness, up into one Ball:
And tear our Pleasures with rough strife,
Thorough the Iron gates of Life.
Thus, though we cannot make our Sun
Stand still, yet we will make him run.

§ FOR COMMENT

What are the main parts of the poem, and what is the principal subject of
each? Do you consider this poem *primarily* a witty invitation to love or a
philosophical discussion of life, death, and time? What specific lines in the
poem support your answer?

❧ Neo-Classical Poetry

After the Restoration of King Charles to the throne in 1660, England relaxed from the rigors of Puritanism and from the idealism of the Renaissance. In the easing of moral standards which occurred, English satire came into its own. In the early seventeenth century some poets, like Donne, had tried their hands at ridiculing vice and folly, but had devoted their main talents to other kinds of poetry. Dryden and Pope are the finest English satirists and are capable of both comic thrusts as well as serious criticism of major faults. Whether they are attacking bad writers who try to pass themselves off as geniuses, as Dryden does in *Mac Flecknoe*, or the absurdity of two families fighting over a lock of hair, as Pope does in *The Rape of the Lock*, each poet manages to make us see both the ridiculous side of what he is poking fun at and the serious values of life that all sensible people take to heart.

After Pope, satire became less of a preoccupation for writers as English society reflected the social dislocations that urbanization and the growth of England's empire brought. Goldsmith's *Deserted Village* strikes a number of modern notes as it comments on colonialism, the accumulation of great fortunes, and rural depopulation, though in a poetic style that stems from Dryden and Pope and reveals the author's basically conservative attitude toward social problems.

John Dryden § 1631–1700

The dominant literary figure of the Restoration period, Dryden was also among the most versatile writers English literature has ever produced. His heroic dramas dominated the theater, his essays marked the beginnings of English literary criticism, and his verse satires reach a mark equalled only by Pope. Here he is ridiculing Thomas Shadwell.

Mac Flecknoe

All humane things are subject to decay,
And, when Fate summons, Monarchs must obey:
This *Fleckno* found, who, like *Augustus*, young
Was call'd to Empire, and had govern'd long:
In Prose and Verse, was own'd, without dispute
Through all the Realms of *Non-sense*, absolute.
This aged Prince now flourishing in Peace,
And blest with issue of a large increase,
Worn out with business, did at length debate
To settle the succession of the State: 10
And pond'ring which of all his Sons was fit
To Reign, and wage immortal War with Wit;
Cry'd, 'tis resolv'd; for Nature pleads that He
Should onely rule, who most resembles me:
Sh—— alone my perfect image bears,
Mature in dullness from his tender years.
Sh—— alone, of all my Sons, is he
Who stands confirm'd in full stupidity.
The rest to some faint meaning make pretence,
But *Sh*—— never deviates into sense.   20
Some Beams of Wit on other souls may fall,
Strike through and make a lucid intervall;
But *Sh*——'s genuine night admits no ray,
His rising Fogs prevail upon the Day:
Besides his goodly Fabrick fills the eye,
And seems design'd for thoughtless Majesty:
Thoughtless as Monarch Oakes, that shade the plain,
And, spread in solemn state, supinely reign.
Heywood and *Shirley* were but Types of thee,
Thou last great Prophet of Tautology: 30
Even I, a dunce of more renown than they,
Was sent before but to prepare thy way;
And coursly clad in *Norwich* Drugget came
To teach the Nations in thy greater name.
My warbling Lute, the Lute I whilom strung
When to King *John* of *Portugal* I sung,
Was but the prelude to that glorious day,
When thou on silver *Thames* did'st cut thy way,
With well tim'd Oars before the Royal Barge,
Swell'd with the Pride of thy Celestial charge;   40
And big with Hymn, Commander of an Host,
The like was ne'er in *Epsom* Blankets tost.
Methinks I see the new *Arion* Sail,

The Lute still trembling underneath thy nail.
At thy well sharpned thumb from Shore to Shore
The Treble squeaks for fear, the Bases roar:
Echoes from *Pissing-Ally*, *Sh*—— call,
And *Sh*—— they resound from A—— *Hall*.
About thy boat the little Fishes throng,
As at the Morning Toast, that Floats along.   50
Sometimes as Prince of thy Harmonious band
Thou weild'st thy Papers in thy threshing hand.
St. *Andre*'s feet ne'er kept more equal time,
Not ev'n the feet of thy own *Psyche*'s rhime:
Though they in number as in sense excell;
So just, so like tautology they fell,
That, pale with envy, *Singleton* forswore
The Lute and Sword which he in Triumph bore,
And vow'd he ne'er would act *Villerius* more.
Here stopt the good old *Syre*; and wept for joy   60
In silent raptures of the hopefull boy.
All arguments, but most his Plays, perswade,
That for anointed dullness he was made.
  Close to the Walls which fair *Augusta* bind,
(The fair *Augusta* much to fears inclin'd)
An ancient fabrick, rais'd t'inform the sight,
There stood of yore, and *Barbican* it hight:
A watch Tower once; but now, so Fate ordains,
Of all the Pile an empty name remains.
From its old Ruins Brothel-houses rise,   70
Scenes of lewd loves, and of polluted joys.
Where their vast Courts the Mother-Strumpets keep,
And, undisturb'd by Watch, in silence sleep.
Near these a Nursery erects its head,
Where Queens are form'd, and future Hero's bred;
Where unfledg'd Actors learn to laugh and cry,
Where infant Punks their tender Voices try,
And little *Maximins* the Gods defy.
Great *Fletcher* never treads in Buskins here,
Nor greater *Johnson* dares in Socks appear.   80
But gentle *Simkin* just reception finds
Amidst this Monument of vanisht minds:
Pure Clinches, the suburbian Muse affords;
And *Panton* waging harmless War with words.
Here *Fleckno*, as a place to Fame well known,
Ambitiously design'd his *Sh*——'s Throne.
For ancient *Decker* prophesi'd long since,
That in this Pile should Reign a mighty Prince,

Born for a scourge of Wit, and flayle of Sense:
To whom true dulness should some *Psyches* owe,   90
But Worlds of *Misers* from his pen should flow;
Humorists and *Hypocrites* it should produce,
Whole *Raymond* families, and Tribes of *Bruce.*
  Now Empress *Fame* had publisht the Renown
Of *Sh*——'s Coronation through the Town.
Rows'd by report of Fame, the Nations meet,
From near *Bun-Hill*, and distant *Watling-street.*
No *Persian* Carpets spread th' Imperial way,
But scatter'd Limbs of mangled Poets lay:
From dusty shops neglected Authors come,   100
Martyrs of Pies, and Reliques of the Bum.
Much *Heywood, Shirly, Ogleby* there lay,
But loads of *Sh*—— almost choakt the way.
Bilk't *Stationers* for Yeomen stood prepar'd,
And *H*—— was Captain of the Guard.
The hoary Prince in Majesty appear'd,
High on a Throne of his own Labours rear'd.
At his right hand our young *Ascanius* sate
Rome's other hope, and pillar of the State.
His Brows thick fogs, instead of glories, grace,   110
And lambent dullness plaid arround his face.
As *Hannibal* did to the Altars come,
Sworn by his *Syre* a mortal Foe to *Rome;*
So *Sh* —— swore, nor should his Vow bee vain,
That he till Death true dullness would maintain;
And in his father's Right, and Realms defence,
Ne'er to have peace with Wit, nor truce with Sense.
The King himself the sacred Unction made,
As King by Office, and as Priest by Trade:
In his sinister hand, instead of Ball,   120
He plac'd a mighty Mug of potent Ale;
Love's Kingdom to his right he did convey,
At once his Sceptre and his rule of Sway;
Whose righteous Lore the Prince had practis'd young,
And from whose Loyns recorded *Psyche* sprung.
His Temples last with Poppies were o'erspread,
That nodding seem'd to consecrate his head:
Just at that point of time, if Fame not lye,
On his left hand twelve reverend *Owls* did fly.
So *Romulus*, 'tis sung, by *Tyber's Brook,*   130
Presage of Sway from twice six Vultures took.
Th' admiring throng loud acclamations make,
And Omens of his future Empire take.

The *Syre* then shook the honours of his head,
And from his brows damps of oblivion shed
Full on the filial dullness: long he stood,
Repelling from his Breast the raging God;
At length burst out in this prophetick mood:
   Heaven bless my Son, from *Ireland* let him reign
To farr *Barbadoes* on the Western main;   140
Of his Dominion may no end be known,
And greater than his Father's be his Throne.
Beyond loves Kingdom let him stretch his Pen;
He paus'd, and all the people cry'd *Amen.*
Then thus, continu'd he, my Son advance
Still in new Impudence, new Ignorance.
Success let others teach, learn thou from me
Pangs without birth, and fruitless Industry.
Let *Virtuoso*'s in five years be Writ;
Yet not one thought accuse thy toyl of wit.   150
Let gentle *George* in triumph tread the Stage,
Make *Dorimant* betray, and *Loveit* rage;
Let *Cully, Cockwood, Fopling,* charm the Pit,
And in their folly shew the Writers wit.
Yet still thy fools shall stand in thy defence,
And justifie their Author's want of sense.
Let 'em be all by thy own model made
Of dullness, and desire no foreign aid:
That they to future ages may be known,
Not Copies drawn, but Issue of thy own.   160
Nay let thy men of wit too be the same,
All full of thee, and differing but in name;
But let no alien *S—dl—y* interpose
To lard with wit thy hungry *Epsom* prose.
And when false flowers of *Rhetorick* thou would'st cull,
Trust Nature, do not labour to be dull;
But write thy best, and top; and in each line,
Sir *Formal*'s oratory will be thine.
Sir *Formal*, though unsought, attends thy quill,
And does thy *Northern Dedications* fill.   170
Nor let false friends seduce thy mind to fame,
By arrogating *Johnson*'s Hostile name.
Let Father *Fleckno* fire thy mind with praise,
And Uncle *Ogleby* thy envy raise.
Thou art my blood, where *Johnson* has no part;
What share have we in Nature or in Art?
Where did his wit on learning fix a brand,
And rail at Arts he did not understand?

Where made he love in Prince *Nicander*'s vein,
Or swept the dust in *Psyche*'s humble strain? 180
Where sold he Bargains, Whip-stitch, kiss my Arse,
Promis'd a Play and dwindled to a Farce?
When did his Muse from *Fletcher* scenes purloin,
As thou whole *Eth'ridg* dost transfuse to thine?
But so transfus'd as Oyl on Waters flow,
His always floats above, thine sinks below.
This is thy Province, this thy wondrous way,
New Humours to invent for each new Play:
This is that boasted Byas of thy mind,
By which one way, to dullness, 'tis inclin'd. 190
Which makes thy writings lean on one side still,
And in all changes that way bends thy will.
Nor let thy mountain belly make pretence
Of likeness; thine's a tympany of sense.
A Tun of Man in thy Large bulk is writ,
But sure thou'rt but a Kilderkin of wit.
Like mine thy gentle numbers feebly creep,
Thy Tragick Muse gives smiles, thy Comick sleep.
With whate'er gall thou sett'st thy self to write,
Thy inoffensive Satyrs never bite. 200
In thy fellonious heart, though Venom lies,
It does but touch thy *Irish* pen, and dyes.
Thy Genius calls thee not to purchase fame
In keen Iambicks, but mild Anagram:
Leave writing Plays, and chuse for thy command
Some peacefull Province at Acrostick Land.
There thou maist wings display and Altars raise,
And torture one poor word Ten thousand ways.
Or if thou would'st thy diff'rent talents suit,
Set thy own Songs, and sing them to thy lute. 210
He said, but his last words were scarcely heard,
For *Bruce* and *Longvil* had a Trap prepar'd,
And down they sent the yet declaiming Bard.
Sinking he left his Drugget robe behind,
Born upwards by a subterranean wind.
The Mantle fell to the young Prophet's part,
With double portion of his Father's Art.

Alexander Pope § 1688–1744

Pope perfected the formal heroic-couplet style begun by Denham, Waller, and Dryden. Much of his satire is directed against more serious vices (especially in his masterpiece, The Dunciad) than he attacked in The Rape of the Lock, his most popular poem.

The Rape of the Lock

> Nolueram, Belinda, tuos violare capillos,
> Sed juvat hoc precibus me tribuisse tuis.
>
> MARTIAL

CANTO I

What dire Offence from am'rous Causes springs,
What mighty Contests rise from trivial Things,
I sing—This Verse to *Caryll*, Muse! is due;
This, ev'n *Belinda* may vouchsafe to view:
Slight is the Subject, but not so the Praise,
If She inspire, and He approve my Lays.
  Say what strange Motive, Goddess! cou'd compel
A well-bred *Lord* t'assault a gentle *Belle?*
Oh say what stranger Cause, yet unexplor'd,
Cou'd make a gentle *Belle* reject a *Lord?*   10
In Tasks so bold, can Little Men engage,
And in soft Bosoms dwells such mighty Rage?
  Sol thro' white Curtains shot a tim'rous Ray,
And op'd those Eyes that must eclipse the Day;
Now Lapdogs give themselves the rowzing Shake,
And sleepless Lovers, just at Twelve, awake:
Thrice rung the Bell, the Slipper knock'd the Ground,
And the press'd Watch return'd a silver Sound.
Belinda still her downy Pillow prest,
Her Guardian *Sylph* prolong'd the balmy Rest.   20
'Twas he had summon'd to her silent Bed
The Morning-Dream that hover'd o'er her Head.
A Youth more glitt'ring than a *Birth-night Beau,*
(That ev'n in Slumber caus'd her Cheek to glow)
Seem'd to her Ear his winning Lips to lay,
And thus in Whispers said, or seem'd to say.
  Fairest of Mortals, thou distinguish'd Care

Epigraph. *Nolueram . . . tuis:* I did not wish, Belinda, to profane your locks; but I am glad to have this much granted to your prayers.

Of thousand bright Inhabitants of Air!
If e'er one Vision touch'd thy infant Thought,
Of all the Nurse and all the Priest have taught,   30
Of airy Elves by Moonlight Shadows seen,
The silver Token, and the circled Green,
Or Virgins visited by Angel-Pow'rs,
With Golden Crowns and Wreaths of heavn'ly Flow'rs,
Hear and believe! thy own Importance know,
Nor bound thy narrow Views to Things below.
Some secret Truths from Learned Pride conceal'd,
To Maids alone and Children are reveal'd:
What tho' no Credit doubting Wits may give?
The Fair and Innocent shall still believe.   40
Know then, unnumber'd Spirits round thee fly,
The light *Militia* of the lower Sky;
These, tho' unseen, are ever on the Wing,
Hang o'er the *Box*, and hover round the *Ring*.
Think what an Equipage thou hast in Air,
And view with scorn *Two Pages* and a *Chair*.
As now your own, our Beings were of old,
And once inclos'd in Woman's beauteous Mold;
Thence, by a soft Transition, we repair
From earthly Vehicles to these of Air.   50
Think not, when Woman's transient Breath is fled,
That all her Vanities at once are dead:
Succeeding Vanities she still regards,
And tho' she plays no more, o'erlooks the Cards.
Her Joy in gilded Chariots, when alive,
And Love of *Ombre*, after Death survive.
For when the Fair in all their Pride expire,
To their first Elements their Souls retire:
The Sprights of fiery Termagants in Flame
Mount up, and take a *Salamander's* Name.   60
Soft yielding Minds to Water glide away,
And sip with *Nymphs*, their Elemental Tea.
The graver Prude sinks downward to a *Gnome*,
In search of Mischief still on Earth to roam.
The light Coquettes in *Sylphs* aloft repair,
And sport and flutter in the Fields of Air.
   Know farther yet; Whoever fair and chaste
Rejects Mankind, is by some *Sylph* embrac'd:
For Spirits, freed from mortal Laws, with ease
Assume what Sexes and what Shapes they please.   70
What guards the Purity of melting Maids,
In Courtly Balls, and Midnight Masquerades,

Safe from the treach'rous Friend, the daring Spark,
The Glance by Day, the Whisper in the Dark;
When kind Occasion prompts their warm Desires,
When Musick soften, and when Dancing fires?
'Tis but their *Sylph*, the wise Celestials know,
Tho' *Honour* is the Word with Men below.
    Some Nymphs there are, too conscious of their Face,
For Life predestin'd to the *Gnomes*' Embrace.   80
These swell their Prospects and exalt their Pride,
When Offers are disdain'd, and Love deny'd.
Then gay Ideas crowd the vacant Brain;
While Peers and Dukes, and all their sweeping Train,
And Garters, Stars and Coronets appear,
And in soft Sounds, *Your Grace* salutes their Ear.
'Tis these that early taint the Female Soul,
Instruct the Eyes of young *Coquettes* to roll,
Teach Infant-Cheeks a bidden Blush to know,
And little Hearts to flutter at a *Beau*.   90
    Oft when the World imagine Women stray,
The *Sylphs* thro' mystick Mazes guide their Way,
Thro' all the giddy Circle they pursue,
And old Impertinence expel by new.
What tender Maid but must a Victim fall
To one Man's Treat, but for another's Ball?
When *Florio* speaks, what Virgin could withstand,
If gentle *Damon* did not squeeze her Hand?
With varying Vanities, from ev'ry Part,
They shift the moving Toyshop of their Heart;   100
Where Wigs with Wigs, with Sword-knots Sword-knots strive,
Beaus banish Beaus, and Coaches Coaches drive.
This erring Mortals Levity may call,
Oh blind to Truth! the *Sylphs* contrive it all,
    Of these am I, who thy Protection claim,
A watchful Sprite, and *Ariel* is my Name.
Late, as I rang'd the Crystal Wilds of Air,
In the clear Mirror of thy ruling *Star*
I saw, alas! some dread Event impend,
Ere to the Main this Morning Sun descend.   110
But Heav'n reveals not what, or how, or where:
Warn'd by thy *Sylph*, oh Pious Maid beware!
This to disclose is all thy Guardian can.
Beware of all, but most beware of man!
    He said; when *Shock*, who thought she slept too long,
Leapt up, and wak'd his Mistress with his Tongue.
'Twas then *Belinda!* if Report say true,

Thy Eyes first open'd on a *Billet-doux*;
Wounds, *Charms*, and *Ardors*, were no sooner read,
But all the Vision vanish'd from thy Head.   120
  And now, unveil'd, the *Toilet* stands display'd,
Each Silver Vase in mystic Order laid.
First, rob'd in White, the Nymph intent adores
With Head uncover'd, the *Cosmetic* Pow'rs.
A heav'nly Image in the Glass appears,
To that she bends, to that her Eyes she rears;
Th'inferior Priestess, at her Altar's side,
Trembling, begins the sacred Rites of Pride.
Unnumber'd Treasures ope at once, and here
The various Off'rings of the World appear;   130
From each she nicely culls with curious Toil,
And decks the Goddess with the glitt'ring Spoil.
This Casket *India*'s glowing Gems unlocks,
And all *Arabia* breathes from yonder Box.
The Tortoise here and Elephant unite,
Transform'd to *Combs*, the speckled and the white.
Here Files of Pins extend their shining Rows,
Puffs, Powders, Patches, Bibles, Billet-doux.
Now awful Beauty puts on all its Arms;
The Fair each moment rises in her Charms,   140
Repairs her Smiles, awakens ev'ry Grace,
And calls forth all the Wonders of her Face;
Sees by Degrees a purer Blush arise,
And keener Lightnings quicken in her Eyes.
The busy *Sylphs* surround their darling Care;
These set the Head, and those divide the Hair,
Some fold the Sleeve, whilst others plait the Gown;
And *Betty*'s prais'd for Labours not her own.

CANTO II

Not with more Glories, in th' Etherial Plain,
The Sun first rises o'er the purpled Main,
Than issuing forth, the Rival of his Beams
Lanch'd on the Bosom of the Silver *Thames*.
Fair Nymphs, and well-drest Youths around her shone,
But ev'ry Eye was fix'd on her alone.
On her white Breast a sparkling *Cross* she wore,
Which *Jews* might kiss, and Infidels adore.
Her lively Looks a sprightly Mind disclose,
Quick as her Eyes, and as unfix'd as those: 10
Favours to none, to all she Smiles extends,
Oft she rejects, but never once offends.

Bright as the Sun, her Eyes the Gazers strike,
And, like the Sun, they shine on all alike.
Yet graceful Ease, and Sweetness void of Pride,
Might hide her Faults, if *Belles* had Faults to hide:
If to her share some Female Errors fall,
Look on her Face, and you'll forget 'em all.

   This Nymph, to the Destruction of Mankind,
Nourish'd two Locks, which graceful hung behind   20
In equal Curls, and well conspir'd to deck
With shining Ringlets the smooth Iv'ry Neck.
Love in these Labyrinths his Slaves detains,
And mighty Hearts are held in slender Chains.
With hairy Sprindges we the Birds betray,
Slight Lines of Hair surprize the Finny Prey,
Fair Tresses Man's Imperial Race insnare,
And Beauty draws us with a single Hair.

   Th' Adventrous *Baron* the bright Locks admir'd,
He saw, he wish'd, and to the Prize aspir'd: 30
Resolv'd to win, he meditates the way,
By Force to ravish, or by Fraud betray;
For when Success a Lover's Toil attends,
Few ask, if Fraud or Force attain'd his Ends.

   For this, ere *Phœbus* rose, he had implor'd
Propitious Heav'n, and ev'ry Pow'r ador'd,
But chiefly *Love*—to *Love* an Altar built,
Of twelve vast *French* Romances, neatly gilt.
There lay three Garters, half a Pair of Gloves;
And all the Trophies of his former Loves.   40
With tender *Billet-doux* he lights the Pyre,
And breathes three am'rous Sighs to raise the Fire.
Then prostrate falls, and begs with ardent Eyes
Soon to obtain, and long possess the Prize:
The Pow'rs gave Ear, and granted half his Pray'r,
The rest, the Winds dispers'd in empty Air.

   But now secure the painted Vessel glides,
The Sun-beams trembling on the floating Tydes,
While melting Musick steals upon the Sky,
And soften'd Sounds along the Waters die.   50
Smooth flow the Waves, the Zephyrs gently play,
Belinda smil'd, and all the World was gay.
All but the *Sylph*—With careful Thoughts opprest,
Th'impending Woe sate heavy on his Breast.
He summons straight his Denizens of Air;
The lucid Squadrons round the Sails repair:
Soft o'er the Shrouds Aerial Whispers breathe,

That seem'd but *Zephyrs* to the Train beneath.
Some to the Sun their Insect-Wings unfold,
Waft on the Breeze, or sink in Clouds of Gold. 60
Transparent Forms, too fine for mortal Sight,
Their fluid Bodies half dissolv'd in Light.
Loose to the Wind their airy Garments flew,
Thin glitt'ring Textures of the filmy Dew;
Dipt in the richest Tincture of the Skies,
Where Light disports in ever-mingling Dies,
While ev'ry Beam now transient Colours flings,
Colours that change whene'er they wave their Wings.
Amid the Circle, on the gilded Mast,
Superior by the Head, was *Ariel* plac'd; 70
His Purple Pinions opening to the Sun,
He rais'd his Azure Wand, and thus begun.

Ye *Sylphs* and *Sylphids*, to your Chief give Ear,
Fays, Fairies, Genii, Elves, and *Dæmons* hear!
Ye know the Spheres and various Tasks assign'd,
By Laws Eternal, to th' Aerial Kind.
Some in the Fields of purest *Æther* play,
And bask and whiten in the Blaze of Day.
Some guide the Course of wandring Orbs on high,
Or roll the Planets thro' the boundless Sky. 80
Some less refin'd, beneath the Moon's pale Light
Pursue the Stars that shoot athwart the Night,
Or suck the Mists in grosser Air below,
Or dip their Pinions in the painted Bow,
Or brew fierce Tempests on the wintry Main,
Or o'er the Glebe distill the kindly Rain.
Others on Earth o'er human Race preside,
Watch all their Ways, and all their Actions guide:
Of these the Chief the Care of Nations own,
And guard with Arms Divine the *British Throne.* 90

Our humbler Province is to tend the Fair,
Not a less pleasing, tho' less glorious Care.
To save the Powder from too rude a Gale,
Nor let th' imprison'd Essences exhale,
To draw fresh Colours from the vernal Flow'rs,
To steal from Rainbows ere they drop in Show'rs
A brighter Wash; to curl their waving Hairs,
Assist their Blushes, and inspire their Airs;
Nay oft, in Dreams, Invention we bestow,
To change a *Flounce,* or add a *Furbelo.* 100

This Day, black Omens threat the brightest Fair
That e'er deserv'd a watchful Spirit's Care;

Some dire Disaster, or by Force, or Slight,
But what, or where, the Fates have wrapt in Night.
Whether the Nymph shall break *Diana*'s Law,
Or some frail *China* Jar receive a Flaw,
Or stain her Honour, or her new Brocade,
Forget her Pray'rs, or miss a Masquerade,
Or lose her Heart, or Necklace, at a Ball;
Or whether Heav'n has doom'd that *Shock* must fall.   110
Haste then ye Spirits! to your Charge repair;
The flutt'ring Fan be *Zephyretta*'s Care;
The Drops to thee, *Brillante*, we consign;
And, *Momentilla*, let the Watch be thine;
Do thou, *Crispissa*, tend her fav'rite Lock;
Ariel himself shall be the Guard of *Shock*.

  To Fifty chosen *Sylphs*, of special Note,
We trust th' important Charge, the *Petticoat*:
Oft have we known that sev'nfold Fence to fail,
Tho' stiff with Hoops, and arm'd with Ribs of Whale.   120
Form a strong Line about the Silver Bound,
And guard the wide Circumference around.

  Whatever Spirit, careless of his Charge,
His Post neglects, or leaves the Fair at large,
Shall feel sharp Vengeance soon o'ertake his Sins,
Be stopt in *Vials*, or transfixt with *Pins*;
Or plung'd in Lakes of bitter *Washes* lie,
Or wedg'd whole Ages in a *Bodkin*'s Eye:
Gums and *Pomatums* shall his Flight restrain,
While clog'd he beats his silken Wings in vain;   130
Or Alom-*Stypticks* with contracting Power
Shrink his thin Essence like a rivell'd Flower.
Or as *Ixion* fix'd, the Wretch shall feel
The giddy Motion of the whirling Mill,
In Fumes of burning Chocolate shall glow,
And tremble at the Sea that froaths below!

  He spoke; the Spirits from the Sails descend;
Some, Orb in Orb, around the Nymph extend,
Some thrid the mazy Ringlets of her Hair,
Some hang upon the Pendants of her Ear;   140
With beating Hearts the dire Event they wait,
Anxious, and trembling for the Birth of Fate.

CANTO III

Close by those Meads for ever crown'd with Flow'rs,
Where *Thames* with Pride surveys his rising Tow'rs,
There stands a Structure of Majestick Frame,

Which from the neighb'ring *Hampton* takes its Name.
Here *Britain*'s Statesmen oft the Fall foredoom
Of Foreign Tyrants, and of Nymphs at home;
Here Thou, Great *Anna!* whom three Realms obey,
Dost sometimes Counsel take—and sometimes *Tea.*
 Hither the Heroes and the Nymphs resort,
To taste awhile the Pleasures of a Court;   10
In various Talk th' instructive hours they past,
Who gave the *Ball*, or paid the *Visit* last:
One speaks the Glory of the *British Queen*,
And one describes a charming *Indian Screen*;
A third interprets Motions, Looks, and Eyes;
At ev'ry Word a Reputation dies.
Snuff, or the *Fan*, supply each Pause of Chat,
With singing, laughing, ogling, and all that.
 Mean while declining from the Noon of Day,
The Sun obliquely shoots his burning Ray;   20
The hungry Judges soon the Sentence sign,
And Wretches hang that Jury-men may Dine;
The Merchant from th' *Exchange* returns in Peace,
And the long Labours of the *Toilette* cease—
Belinda now, whom Thirst of Fame invites,
Burns to encounter two adventrous Knights,
At *Ombre* singly to decide their Doom;
And swells her Breast with Conquests yet to come.
Strait the three Bands prepare in Arms to join,
Each Band the number of the Sacred Nine.   30
Soon as she spreads her Hand, th' Aerial Guard
Descend, and sit on each important Card:
First *Ariel* perch'd upon a *Matadore*,
Then each, according to the Rank they bore;
For *Sylphs*, yet mindful of their ancient Race,
Are, as when Women, wondrous fond of Place.
 Behold, four *Kings* in Majesty rever'd,
With hoary Whiskers and a forky Beard;
And four fair *Queens* whose hands sustain a Flow'r,
Th' expressive Emblem of their softer Pow'r;   40
Four *Knaves* in Garbs succinct, a trusty Band,
Caps on their heads, and Halberds in their hand;
And Particolour'd Troops, a shining Train,
Draw forth to Combat on the Velvet Plain.

1. 27. *Ombre*: A popular card game. For a detailed discussion of the game of ombre in the poem, see Geoffrey Tillotson, ed., *The Rape of the Lock*, The Twickenham Edition of the Poems of Alexander Pope, second edition revised (London, 1954), Vol. II, Appendix C, pp. 361–368.

The skilful Nymph reviews her Force with Care;
Let Spades be Trumps! she said, and Trumps they were.
Now move to War her Sable *Matadores,*
In Show like Leaders of the swarthy *Moors.*
Spadillio first, unconquerable Lord!
Led off two captive Trumps, and swept the Board.   50
As many more *Manillio* forc'd to yield,
And march'd a Victor from the verdant Field.
Him *Basto* follow'd, but his Fate more hard
Gain'd but one Trump and one *Plebeian* Card.
With his broad Sabre next, a Chief in Years,
The hoary Majesty of *Spades* appears;
Puts forth one manly Leg, to sight reveal'd;
The rest his many-colour'd Robe conceal'd.
The Rebel-*Knave,* who dares his Prince engage,
Proves the just Victim of his Royal Rage.   60
Ev'n mighty *Pam* that Kings and Queens o'erthrew,
And mow'd down Armies in the Fights of *Lu,*
Sad Chance of War! now, destitute of Aid,
Falls undistinguish'd by the Victor *Spade!*
    Thus far both Armies to *Belinda* yield;
Now to the *Baron* Fate inclines the Field.
His warlike *Amazon* her Host invades,
Th' Imperial Consort of the Crown of *Spades.*
The *Club's* black Tyrant first her Victim dy'd,
Spite of his haughty Mien, and barb'rous Pride: 70
What boots the Regal Circle on his Head,
His Giant Limbs in State unwieldy spread?
That long behind he trails his pompous Robe,
And of all Monarchs only grasps the Globe?
    The *Baron* now his *Diamonds* pours apace;
Th' embroider'd *King* who shows but half his Face,
And his refulgent *Queen,* with Pow'rs combin'd,
Of broken Troops an easie Conquest find.
Clubs, Diamonds, Hearts, in wild Disorder seen,
With Throngs promiscuous strow the level Green.   80
Thus when dispers'd a routed Army runs,
Of *Asia's* Troops, and *Africk's* Sable Sons,
With like Confusion different Nations fly,
Of various Habit and of various Dye,
The pierc'd Battalions dis-united fall,
In Heaps on Heaps; one Fate o'erwhelms them all.
    The *Knave of Diamonds* tries his wily Arts,
And wins (oh shameful Chance!) the *Queen of Hearts.*
At this, the Blood the Virgin's Cheek forsook,

A livid Paleness spreads o'er all her Look;   90
She sees, and trembles at th' approaching Ill,
Just in the Jaws of Ruin, and *Codille*.
And now, (as oft in some distemper'd State)
On one nice *Trick* depends the gen'ral Fate.
An *Ace* of Hearts steps forth: The *King* unseen
Lurk'd in her Hand, and mourn'd his captive *Queen*.
He springs to Vengeance with an eager pace,
And falls like Thunder on the prostrate *Ace*.
The Nymph exulting fills with Shouts the Sky,
The Walls, the Woods, and long Canals reply.   100
    Oh thoughtless Mortals! ever blind to Fate,
Too soon dejected, and too soon elate!
Sudden these Honours shall be snatch'd away,
And curs'd for ever this Victorious Day.
    For lo! the Board with Cups and Spoons is crown'd,
The Berries crackle, and the Mill turns round.
On shining Altars of *Japan* they raise
The silver Lamp; the fiery Spirits blaze.
From silver Spouts the grateful Liquors glide,
While *China*'s Earth receives the smoking Tyde.   110
At once they gratify their Scent and Taste,
And frequent Cups prolong the rich Repast.
Strait hover round the Fair her Airy Band;
Some, as she sip'd, the fuming Liquor fann'd,
Some o'er her Lap their careful Plumes display'd,
Trembling, and conscious of the rich Brocade.
Coffee, (which makes the Politician wise,
And see thro' all things with his half-shut Eyes)
Sent up in Vapours to the *Baron*'s Brain
New Stratagems, the radiant Lock to gain.   120
Ah cease rash Youth! desist ere 'tis too late,
Fear the just Gods, and think of *Scylla*'s Fate!
Chang'd to a Bird, and sent to flit in Air,
She dearly pays for *Nisus*' injur'd Hair!
    But when to Mischief Mortals bend their Will,
How soon they find fit Instruments of Ill!
Just then, *Clarissa* drew with tempting Grace
A two-edg'd Weapon from her shining Case;
So Ladies in Romance assist their Knight,
Present the Spear, and arm him for the Fight.   130
He takes the Gift with rev'rence, and extends
The little Engine on his Fingers' Ends,
This just behind *Belinda*'s Neck he spread,
As o'er the fragrant Steams she bends her Head:

Swift to the Lock a thousand Sprights repair,
A thousand Wings, by turns, blow back the Hair,
And thrice they twitch'd the Diamond in her Ear,
Thrice she look'd back, and thrice the Foe drew near.
Just in that instant, anxious *Ariel* sought
The close Recesses of the Virgin's Thought;   140
As on the Nosegay in her Breast reclin'd,
He watch'd th' Ideas rising in her Mind,
Sudden he view'd, in spite of all her Art,
An Earthly Lover lurking at her Heart.
Amaz'd, confus'd, he found his Pow'r expir'd,
Resign'd to Fate, and with a Sigh retir'd.
   The Peer now spreads the glitt'ring *Forfex* wide,
T'inclose the Lock; now joins it, to divide.
Ev'n then, before the fatal Engine clos'd,
A wretched *Sylph* too fondly interpos'd;   150
Fate urg'd the Sheers, and cut the *Sylph* in twain,
(But Airy Substance soon unites again)
The meeting Points the sacred Hair dissever
From the fair Head, for ever and for ever!
   Then flash'd the living Lightning from her Eyes,
And Screams of Horror rend th' affrighted Skies.
Not louder Shrieks to pitying Heav'n are cast,
When Husbands or when Lap-dogs breathe their last,
Or when rich *China* Vessels, fal'n from high,
In glittring Dust and painted Fragments lie!   160
   Let Wreaths of Triumph now my Temples twine,
(The Victor cry'd) the glorious Prize is mine!
While Fish in Streams, or Birds delight in Air,
Or in a Coach and Six the *British* Fair,
As long as *Atalantis* shall be read,
Or the small Pillow grace a Lady's Bed,
While *Visits* shall be paid on solemn Days,
When numerous Wax-lights in bright Order blaze,
While Nymphs take Treats, or Assignations give,
So long my Honour, Name, and Praise shall live!   170
   What Time wou'd spare, from Steel receives its date,
And Monuments, like Men, submit to Fate!
Steel cou'd the Labour of the Gods destroy,
And strike to Dust th' Imperial Tow'rs of *Troy*;
Steel cou'd the Works of mortal Pride confound,
And hew Triumphal Arches to the Ground.
What Wonder then, fair Nymph! thy Hairs shou'd feel
The conqu'ring Force of unresisted Steel?

CANTO IV

But anxious Cares the pensive Nymph opprest,
And secret Passions labour'd in her Breast.
Not youthful Kings in Battel seiz'd alive,
Not scornful Virgins who their Charms survive,
Not ardent Lovers robb'd of all their Bliss,
Not ancient Ladies when refus'd a Kiss,
Not Tyrants fierce that unrepenting die,
Not *Cynthia* when her *Manteau's* pinn'd awry,
E'er felt such Rage, Resentment and Despair,
As Thou, sad Virgin! for thy ravish'd Hair.   10

    For, that sad moment, when the *Sylphs* withdrew,
And *Ariel* weeping from *Belinda* flew,
Umbriel, a dusky melancholy Spright,
As ever sully'd the fair face of Light,
Down to the Central Earth, his proper Scene,
Repair'd to search the gloomy Cave of *Spleen*.

    Swift on his sooty Pinions flitts the *Gnome*,
And in a Vapour reach'd the dismal Dome.
No cheerful Breeze this sullen Region knows,
The dreaded *East* is all the Wind that blows.   20
Here, in a Grotto, sheltred close from Air,
And screen'd in Shades from Day's detested Glare,
She sighs for ever on her pensive Bed,
Pain at her Side, and *Megrim* at her Head.

    Two Handmaids wait the Throne: Alike in Place,
But diff'ring far in Figure and in Face.
Here stood *Ill-nature* like an *ancient Maid*,
Her wrinkled Form in *Black* and *White* array'd;
With store of Pray'rs, for Mornings, Nights, and Noons,
Her Hand is fill'd; her Bosom with Lampoons.   30

    There *Affectation* with a sickly Mien
Shows in her Cheek the Roses of Eighteen,
Practis'd to Lisp, and hang the Head aside,
Faints into Airs, and languishes with Pride;
On the rich Quilt sinks with becoming Woe,
Wrapt in a Gown, for Sickness, and for Show.
The Fair-ones feel such Maladies as these,
When each new Night-Dress gives a new Disease.

    A constant *Vapour* o'er the Palace flies;
Strange Phantoms rising as the Mists arise;   40
Dreadful, as Hermit's Dreams in haunted Shades,
Or bright as Visions of expiring Maids.
Now glaring Fiends, and Snakes on rolling Spires,

Pale Spectres, gaping Tombs, and Purple Fires:
Now Lakes of liquid Gold, *Elysian* Scenes,
And Crystal Domes, and Angels in Machines.
　Unnumber'd Throngs on ev'ry side are seen
Of Bodies chang'd to various Forms by *Spleen*.
Here living *Teapots* stand, one Arm held out,
One bent; the Handle this, and that the Spout:　　　　50
A Pipkin there like *Homer's Tripod* walks;
Here sighs a Jar, and there a Goose-pye talks;
Men prove with Child, as pow'rful Fancy works,
And Maids turn'd Bottels, call aloud for Corks.
　Safe past the *Gnome* thro' this fantastick Band,
A Branch of healing *Spleenwort* in his hand.
Then thus addrest the Pow'r—Hail wayward Queen!
Who rule the Sex to Fifty from Fifteen,
Parent of Vapours and of Female Wit,
Who give th' *Hysteric* or *Poetic* Fit,　　　　60
On various Tempers act by various ways,
Make some take Physick, others scribble Plays;
Who cause the Proud their Visits to delay,
And send the Godly in a Pett, to pray.
A Nymph there is, that all thy Pow'r disdains,
And thousands more in equal Mirth maintains.
But oh! if e'er thy *Gnome* could spoil a Grace,
Or raise a Pimple on a beauteous Face,
Like Citron-Waters Matrons' Cheeks inflame,
Or change Complexions at a losing Game;　　　　70
If e'er with airy Horns I planted Heads,
Or rumpled Petticoats, or tumbled Beds,
Or caus'd Suspicion when no Soul was rude,
Or discompos'd the Head-dress of a Prude,
Or e'er to costive Lap-Dog gave Disease,
Which not the Tears of brightest Eyes could ease:
Hear me, and touch *Belinda* with Chagrin;
That single Act gives half the World the Spleen.
　The Goddess with a discontented Air
Seems to reject him, tho' she grants his Pray'r.　　　　80
A wondrous Bag with both her Hands she binds,
Like that where once *Ulysses* held the Winds;
There she collects the Force of Female Lungs,
Sighs, Sobs, and Passions, and the War of Tongues.
A Vial next she fills with fainting Fears,
Soft Sorrows, melting Griefs, and flowing Tears.
The *Gnome* rejoicing bears her Gifts away,
Spreads his black Wings, and slowly mounts to Day.

Sunk in *Thalestris'* Arms the Nymph he found,
Her Eyes dejected and her Hair unbound.   90
Full o'er their Heads the swelling Bag he rent,
And all the Furies issued at the Vent.
Belinda burns with more than mortal Ire,
And fierce *Thalestris* fans the rising Fire.
O wretched Maid! she spread her Hands, and cry'd,
(While *Hampton's* Ecchos, wretched Maid! reply'd)
Was it for this you took such constant Care
The *Bodkin*, *Comb*, and *Essence* to prepare;
For this your Locks in Paper-Durance bound,
For this with tort'ring Irons wreath'd around?   100
For this with Fillets strain'd your tender Head,
And bravely bore the double Loads of Lead?
Gods! shall the Ravisher display your Hair,
While the Fops envy, and the Ladies stare!
Honour forbid! at whose unrival'd Shrine
Ease, Pleasure, Virtue, All, our Sex resign.
Methinks already I your Tears survey,
Already hear the horrid things they say,
Already see you a degraded Toast,
And all your Honour in a whisper lost!   110
How shall I, then, your helpless Fame defend?
'Twill then be Infamy to seem your Friend!
And shall this Prize, th' inestimable Prize,
Expos'd thro' Crystal to the gazing Eyes,
And heighten'd by the Diamond's circling Rays,
On that Rapacious Hand for ever blaze?
Sooner shall Grass in *Hide*-Park *Circus* grow,
And Wits take Lodgings in the Sound of *Bow*;
Sooner let Earth, Air, Sea, to *Chaos* fall,
Men, Monkies, Lap-dogs, Parrots, perish all!   120
    She said; then raging to *Sir Plume* repairs,
And bids her *Beau* demand the precious Hairs:
(*Sir Plume*, of *Amber Snuff-box* justly vain,
And the nice Conduct of a *clouded Cane*)
With earnest Eyes, and round unthinking Face,
He first the Snuff-box open'd, then the Case,
And thus broke out—"My Lord, why, what the Devil?
Z—ds! damn the Lock! 'fore Gad, you must be civil!
Plague on't! 'tis past a Jest—nay prithee, Pox!
Give her the Hair"—he spoke, and rapp'd his Box.   130
    It grieves me much (reply'd the Peer again)
Who speaks so well shou'd ever speak in vain.
But by this Lock, this sacred Lock I swear,

(Which never more shall join its parted Hair,
Which never more its Honours shall renew,
Clipt from the lovely Head where late it grew)
That while my Nostrils draw the vital Air,
This Hand, which won it, shall for ever wear.
He spoke, and speaking, in proud Triumph spread
The long-contended Honours of her Head.   140
    But *Umbriel*, hateful *Gnome!* forbears not so;
He breaks the Vial whence the Sorrows flow.
Then see! the *Nymph* in beauteous Grief appears,
Her Eyes half-languishing, half-drown'd in Tears;
On her heav'd Bosom hung her drooping Head,
Which, with a Sigh, she rais'd; and thus she said.
    For ever curs'd be this detested Day,
Which snatch'd my best, my fav'rite Curl away!
Happy, ah ten times happy, had I been,
If *Hampton-Court* these Eyes had never seen!   150
Yet am not I the first mistaken Maid,
By Love of *Courts* to num'rous Ills betray'd.
Oh had I rather un-admir'd remain'd
In some lone Isle, or distant *Northern* Land;
Where the gilt *Chariot* never marks the Way,
Where none learn *Ombre*, none e'er taste *Bohea!*
There kept my Charms conceal'd from mortal Eye,
Like Roses that in Desarts bloom and die.
What mov'd my Mind with youthful Lords to rome?
O had I stay'd, and said my Pray'rs at home!   160
'Twas this, the Morning *Omens* seem'd to tell;
Thrice from my trembling hand the *Patch-box* fell;
The tott'ring *China* shook without a Wind,
Nay, *Poll* sate mute, and *Shock* was most Unkind!
A *Sylph* too warn'd me of the Threats of Fate,
In mystic Visions, now believ'd too late!
See the poor Remnants of these slighted Hairs!
My hands shall rend what ev'n thy Rapine spares:
These, in two sable Ringlets taught to break,
Once gave new Beauties to the snowie Neck.   170
The Sister-Lock now sits uncouth, alone,
And in its Fellow's Fate foresees its own;
Uncurl'd it hangs, the fatal Sheers demands;
And tempts once more thy sacrilegious Hands.
Oh hadst thou, Cruel! been content to seize
Hairs less in sight, or any Hairs but these!

CANTO V

She said: the pitying Audience melt in Tears,
But *Fate* and *Jove* had stopp'd the *Baron*'s Ears.
In vain *Thalestris* with Reproach assails,
For who can move when fair *Belinda* fails?
Not half so fixt the *Trojan* cou'd remain,
While *Anna* begg'd and *Dido* rag'd in vain.
Then grave *Clarissa* graceful wav'd her Fan;
Silence ensu'd, and thus the Nymph began.

   Say, why are Beauties prais'd and honour'd most,
The wise Man's Passion, and the vain Man's Toast?   10
Why deck'd with all that Land and Sea Afford,
Why Angels call'd, and Angel-like ador'd?
Why round our Coaches crowd the white-glov'd Beaus,
Why bows the Side-box from its inmost Rows?
How vain are all these Glories, all our Pains,
Unless good Sense preserve what Beauty gains:
That Men may say, when we the Front-box grace,
Behold the first in Virtue, as in Face!
Oh! if to dance all Night, and dress all Day,
Charm'd the Small-pox, or chas'd old Age away;   20
Who would not scorn what Huswife's Cares produce,
Or who would learn one earthly Thing of Use?
To patch, nay ogle, might become a Saint,
Nor could it sure be such a Sin to paint.
But since, alas! frail Beauty must decay,
Curl'd or uncurl'd, since Locks will turn to grey,
Since painted, or not painted, all shall fade,
And she who scorns a Man, must die a Maid;
What then remains, but well our Pow'r to use,
And keep good Humour still whate'er we lose?   30
And trust me, Dear! good Humour can prevail,
When Airs, and Flights, and Screams, and Scolding fail.
Beauties in vain their pretty Eyes may roll;
Charms strike the Sight, but Merit wins the Soul.

   So spoke the Dame, but no Applause ensu'd;
Belinda frown'd, *Thalestris* call'd her Prude.
To Arms, to Arms! the fierce Virago cries,
And swift as Lightning to the Combate flies.
All side in Parties, and begin th' Attack;
Fans clap, Silks russle, and tough Whalebones crack;   40
Heroes' and Heroins' Shouts confus'dly rise,
And base, and treble Voices strike the Skies.
No common Weapons in their Hands are found,

Like Gods they fight, nor dread a mortal Wound.
    So when bold *Homer* makes the Gods engage,
And heav'nly Breasts with human Passions rage;
'Gainst *Pallas, Mars; Latona, Hermes* arms;
And all *Olympus* rings with loud Alarms.
Jove's Thunder roars, Heav'n trembles all around;
Blue *Neptune* storms, the bellowing Deeps resound;   50
Earth shakes her nodding Tow'rs, the Ground gives way;
And the pale Ghosts start at the Flash of Day!
    Triumphant *Umbriel* on a Sconce's Height
Clapt his glad Wings, and sate to view the Fight:
Propt on their Bodkin Spears, the Sprights survey
The growing Combat, or assist the Fray,
    While thro' the Press enrag'd *Thalestris* flies,
And scatters Deaths around from both her Eyes,
A *Beau* and *Witling* perish'd in the Throng,
One dy'd in *Metaphor,* and one in *Song.*   60
O cruel Nymph! a living Death I bear,
Cry'd *Dapperwit,* and sunk beside his Chair.
A mournful Glance Sir *Fopling* upwards cast,
Those Eyes are made so killing—was his last:
Thus on *Meander*'s flow'ry Margin lies
Th' expiring Swan, and as he sings he dies.
    When bold Sir *Plume* had drawn *Clarissa* down,
Chloe stept in, and kill'd him with a Frown;
She smil'd to see the doughty Hero slain,
But at her Smile, the Beau reviv'd again.   70
    Now *Jove* suspends his golden Scales in Air,
Weighs the Men's Wits against the Lady's Hair;
The doubtful Beam long nods from side to side;
At length the Wits mount up, the Hairs subside.
    See fierce *Belinda* on the *Baron* flies,
With more than usual Lightning in her Eyes;
Nor fear'd the Chief th' unequal Fight to try,
Who sought no more than on his Foe to die.
But this bold Lord, with manly Strength indu'd,
She with one Finger and a Thumb subdu'd: 80
Just where the Breath of Life his Nostrils drew,
A Charge of *Snuff* the wily Virgin threw;
The *Gnomes* direct, to ev'ry Atome just,
The pungent Grains of titillating Dust.
Sudden, with starting Tears each Eye o'erflows,
And the high Dome re-ecchoes to his Nose.
    Now meet thy Fate, incens'd *Belinda* cry'd,
And drew a deadly *Bodkin* from her Side.

(The same, his ancient Personage to deck,
Her great great Grandsire wore about his Neck   90
In three *Seal-Rings*; which after, melted down,
Form'd a vast *Buckle* for his Widow's Gown:
Her infant Grandame's *Whistle* next it grew,
The *Bells* she gingled, and the *Whistle* blew;
Then in a *Bodkin* grac'd her Mother's Hairs,
Which long she wore, and now *Belinda* wears.)
    Boast not my Fall (he cry'd) insulting Foe!
Thou by some other shalt be laid as low.
Nor think, to die dejects my lofty Mind;
All that I dread, is leaving you behind!   100
Rather than so, ah let me still survive,
And burn in *Cupid*'s Flames,—but burn alive.
    Restore the Lock! she cries; and all around
Restore the Lock! the vaulted Roofs rebound.
Not fierce *Othello* in so loud a Strain
Roar'd for the Handkerchief that caus'd his Pain.
But see how oft Ambitious Aims are cross'd,
And Chiefs contend 'till all the Prize is lost!
The Lock, obtain'd with Guilt, and kept with Pain,
In ev'ry place is sought, but sought in vain: 110
With such a Prize no Mortal must be blest,
So Heav'n decrees! with Heav'n who can contest?
    Some thought it mounted to the Lunar Sphere,
Since all things lost on Earth, are treasur'd there.
The Heroes' Wits are kept in pond'rous Vases,
And Beaus' in *Snuff boxes* and *Tweezer-Cases*.
There broken Vows, and Death-bed Alms are found,
And Lovers' Hearts with Ends of Riband bound;
The Courtier's Promises, and Sick Man's Pray'rs,
The Smiles of Harlots, and the Tears of Heirs,   120
Cages for Gnats, and Chains to Yoak a Flea;
Dry'd Butterflies, and Tomes of Casuistry.
    But trust the Muse—she saw it upward rise,
Tho' mark'd by none but quick Poetic Eyes:
(So *Rome*'s great Founder to the Heav'ns withdrew,
To *Proculus* alone confess'd in view.)
A sudden Star, it shot thro' liquid Air,
And drew behind a radiant *Trail of Hair*.
Not *Berenice*'s Locks first rose so bright,
The Heav'ns bespangling with dishevel'd Light.   130
The *Sylphs* behold it kindling as it flies,
And pleas'd pursue its Progress thro' the Skies.
    This the *Beau-monde* shall from the *Mall* survey,

And hail with Musick its propitious Ray.
This, the blest Lover shall for *Venus* take,
And send up Vows from *Rosamonda*'s Lake.
This *Partridge* soon shall view in cloudless Skies,
When next he looks thro' *Galilæo*'s Eyes;
And hence th' Egregious Wizard shall foredoom
The Fate of *Louis*, and the Fall of *Rome*.   140
    Then cease, bright Nymph! to mourn thy ravish'd Hair
Which adds new Glory to the shining Sphere!
Not all the Tresses that fair Head can boast
Shall draw such Envy as the Lock you lost.
For, after all the Murders of your Eye,
When, after Millions slain, your self shall die;
When those fair Suns shall sett, as sett they must,
And all those Tresses shall be laid in Dust;
This Lock, the Muse shall consecrate to Fame,
And mid'st the Stars inscribe *Belinda*'s Name!   150

Oliver Goldsmith § 1730?–1774

*Goldsmith was trained for medicine but fortunately became an
author. He was one of the most versatile of authors and made
distinguished contributions in several literary forms: The Vicar of
Wakefield, a novel; She Stoops to Conquer, a rollicking comedy;
The Citizen of the World, a series of essays; and two fine poems,
The Traveller and The Deserted Village. All his writing is
pervaded by a gentle irony and genuine feeling that avoids sentimentality with consummate skill.*

The Deserted Village

Sweet Auburn, loveliest village of the plain,
Where health and plenty cheared the labouring swain,
Where smiling spring its earliest visit paid,
And parting summer's lingering blooms delayed,
Dear lovely bowers of innocence and ease,
Seats of my youth, when every sport could please,
How often have I loitered o'er thy green,
Where humble happiness endeared each scene;
How often have I paused on every charm,
The sheltered cot, the cultivated farm,   10

The never failing brook, the busy mill,
The decent church that topt the neighbouring hill,
The hawthorn bush, with seats beneath the shade,
For talking age and whispering lovers made;
How often have I blest the coming day,
When toil remitting lent its turn to play,
And all the village train from labour free
Led up their sports beneath the spreading tree;
While many a pastime circled in the shade,
The young contending as the old surveyed;　　　　　　　　20
And many a gambol frolicked o'er the ground,
And slights of art and feats of strength went round;
And still as each repeated pleasure tired,
Succeeding sports the mirthful band inspired;
The dancing pair that simply sought renown
By holding out to tire each other down;
The swain mistrustless of his smutted face,
While secret laughter tittered round the place;
The bashful virgin's side-long looks of love,
The matron's glance that would those looks reprove:　　　　30
These were thy charms, sweet village; sports like these,
With sweet succession, taught even toil to please;
These round thy bowers their chearful influence shed,
These were thy charms—But all these charms are fled.
　　Sweet smiling village, loveliest of the lawn,
Thy sports are fled, and all thy charms withdrawn;
Amidst thy bowers the tyrant's hand is seen,
And desolation saddens all thy green:
One only master grasps the whole domain,
And half a tillage stints thy smiling plain;　　　　　　40
No more thy glassy brook reflects the day,
But choaked with sedges, works its weedy way.
Along thy glades, a solitary guest,
The hollow sounding bittern guards its nest;
Amidst thy desert walks the lapwing flies,
And tires their ecchoes with unvaried cries.
Sunk are thy bowers, in shapeless ruin all,
And the long grass o'ertops the mouldering wall,
And trembling, shrinking from the spoiler's hand,
Far, far away thy children leave the land.　　　　　　50
　　Ill fares the land, to hastening ills a prey,
Where wealth accumulates, and men decay:
Princes and lords may flourish, or may fade;
A breath can make them, as a breath has made;
But a bold peasantry, their country's pride,

When once destroyed, can never be supplied.
 A time there was, ere England's griefs began,
When every rood of ground maintained its man;
For him light labour spread her wholesome store,
Just gave what life required, but gave no more: 60
His best companions, innocence and health;
And his best riches, ignorance of wealth.
 But times are altered; trade's unfeeling train
Usurp the land and disposses the swain;
Along the lawn, where scattered hamlets rose,
Unwieldly wealth, and cumbrous pomp repose;
And every want to luxury allied,
And every pang that folly pays to pride.
These gentle hours that plenty bade to bloom,
Those calm desires that asked but little room,   70
Those healthful sports that graced the peaceful scene,
Lived in each look, and brightened all the green;
These far departing seek a kinder shore,
And rural mirth and manners are no more.
 Sweet Auburn! parent of the blissful hour,
Thy glades forlorn confess the tyrant's power.
Here as I take my solitary rounds,
Amidst thy tangling walks, and ruined grounds,
And, many a year elapsed, return to view
Where once the cottage stood, the hawthorn grew,   80
Here, as with doubtful, pensive steps I range,
Trace every scene, and wonder at the change,
Remembrance wakes with all her busy train,
Swells at my breast, and turns the past to pain.
 In all my wanderings round this world of care,
In all my griefs—and God has given my share—
I still had hopes my latest hours to crown,
Amidst these humble bowers to lay me down;
My anxious day to husband near the close,
And keep life's flame from wasting by repose.   90
I still had hopes, for pride attends us still,
Amidst the swains to shew my book-learned skill,
Around my fire an evening groupe to draw,
And tell of all I felt, and all I saw;
And, as an hare whom hounds and horns pursue,
Pants to the place from whence at first she flew,
I still had hopes, my long vexations past,
Here to return—and die at home at last.
 O blest retirement, friend to life's decline,
Retreats from care that never must be mine,   100

How blest is he who crowns in shades like these,
A youth of labour with an age of ease;
Who quits a world where strong temptations try,
And, since 'tis hard to combat, learns to fly.
For him no wretches, born to work and weep,
Explore the mine, or tempt the dangerous deep;
No surly porter stands in guilty state
To spurn imploring famine from his gate,
But on he moves to meet his latter end,
Angels around befriending virtue's friend;   110
Sinks to the grave with unperceived decay,
While resignation gently slopes the way;
And all his prospects brightening to the last,
His Heaven commences ere the world be past!
    Sweet was the sound when oft at evening's close,
Up yonder hill the village murmur rose;
There as I past with careless steps and slow,
The mingling notes came softened from below;
The swain responsive as the milk-maid sung,
The sober herd that lowed to meet their young,   120
The noisy geese that gabbled o'er the pool,
The playful children just let loose from school,
The watch-dog's voice that bayed the whispering wind,
And the loud laugh that spoke the vacant mind,
These all in soft confusion sought the shade,
And filled each pause the nightingale had made.
But now the sounds of population fail,
No chearful murmurs fluctuate in the gale,
No busy steps the grass-grown foot-way tread,
But all the bloomy flush of life is fled.   130
All but yon widowed, solitary thing
That feebly bends beside the plashy spring;
She, wretched matron, forced, in age, for bread,
To strip the brook with mantling cresses spread,
To pick her wintry faggot from the thorn,
To seek her nightly shed, and weep till morn;
She only left of all the harmless train,
The sad historian of the pensive plain.
    Near yonder copse, where once the garden smil'd,
And still where many a garden flower grows wild;   140
There, where a few torn shrubs the place disclose,
The village preacher's modest mansion rose.
A man he was, to all the country dear,
And passing rich with forty pounds a year;
Remote from towns he ran his godly race,

Nor e'er had changed, nor wish'd to change his place;
Unskilful he to fawn, or seek for power,
By doctrines fashioned to the varying hour;
Far other aims his heart had learned to prize,
More bent to raise the wretched than to rise.   150
His house was known to all the vagrant train,
He chid their wanderings, but relieved their pain;
The long remembered beggar was his guest,
Whose beard descending swept his aged breast;
The ruined spendthrift, now no longer proud,
Claimed kindred there, and had his claims allowed;
The broken soldier, kindly bade to stay,
Sate by his fire, and talked the night away;
Wept o'er his wounds, or tales of sorrow done,
Shouldered his crutch, and shewed how fields were won.   160
Pleased with his guests, the good man learned to glow,
And quite forgot their vices in their woe;
Careless their merits, or their faults to scan,
His pity gave ere charity began.
    Thus to relieve the wretched was his pride,
And even his failings leaned to Virtue's side;
But in his duty prompt at every call,
He watched and wept, he prayed and felt, for all.
And, as a bird each fond endearment tries,
To tempt its new fledged offspring to the skies;   170
He tried each art, reproved each dull delay,
Allured to brighter worlds, and led the way.
    Beside the bed where parting life was layed,
And sorrow, guilt, and pain, by turns dismayed,
The reverend champion stood. At his control,
Despair and anguish fled the struggling soul;
Comfort came down the trembling wretch to raise,
And his last faultering accents whispered praise.
    At church, with meek and unaffected grace,
His looks adorned the venerable place;   180
Truth from his lips prevailed with double sway,
And fools, who came to scoff, remained to pray.
The service past, around the pious man,
With ready zeal each honest rustic ran;
Even children followed with endearing wile,
And plucked his gown, to share the good man's smile.
His ready smile a parent's warmth exprest,
Their welfare pleased him, and their cares distrest;
To them his heart, his love, his griefs were given,
But all his serious thoughts had rest in Heaven.   190

As some tall cliff that lifts its awful form,
Swells from the vale, and midway leaves the storm,
Tho' round its breast the rolling clouds are spread,
Eternal sunshine settles on its head.

    Beside yon straggling fence that skirts the way,
With blossomed furze unprofitably gay,
There, in his noisy mansion, skill'd to rule,
The village master taught his little school;
A man severe he was, and stern to view,
I knew him well, and every truant knew;   200
Well had the boding tremblers learned to trace
The day's disasters in his morning face;
Full well they laugh'd with counterfeited glee,
At all his jokes, for many a joke had he;
Full well the busy whisper circling round,
Conveyed the dismal tidings when he frowned;
Yet he was kind, or if severe in aught,
The love he bore to learning was in fault;
The village all declared how much he knew;
'Twas certain he could write, and cypher too;   210
Lands he could measure, terms and tides presage,
And even the story ran that he could gauge.
In arguing too, the parson owned his skill,
For e'en tho' vanquished, he could argue still;
While words of learned length, and thundering sound,
Amazed the gazing rustics ranged around;
And still they gazed, and still the wonder grew,
That one small head could carry all he knew.

    But past is all his fame. The very spot
Where many a time he triumphed, is forgot.   220
Near yonder thorn, that lifts its head on high,
Where once the sign-post caught the passing eye,
Low lies that house where nut-brown draughts inspired,
Where grey-beard mirth and smiling toil retired,
Where village statesmen talked with looks profound,
And news much older than their ale went round.
Imagination fondly stoops to trace
The parlour splendours of that festive place;
The white-washed wall, the nicely sanded floor,
The varnished clock that clicked behind the door;   230
The chest contrived a double debt to pay,
A bed by night, a chest of drawers by day;
The pictures placed for ornament and use,
The twelve good rules, the royal game of goose;
The hearth, except when winter chill'd the day,

With aspen boughs, and flowers, and fennel gay,
While broken tea-cups, wisely kept for shew,
Ranged o'er the chimney, glistened in a row.
　　Vain transitory splendours! Could not all
Reprieve the tottering mansion from its fall!　　　　240
Obscure it sinks, nor shall it more impart
An hour's importance to the poor man's heart;
Thither no more the peasant shall repair
To sweet oblivion of his daily care;
No more the farmer's news, the barber's tale,
No more the wood-man's ballad shall prevail;
No more the smith his dusky brow shall clear,
Relax his ponderous strength, and lean to hear;
The host himself no longer shall be found
Careful to see the mantling bliss go round;　　　　250
Nor the coy maid, half willing to be prest,
Shall kiss the cup to pass it to the rest.
　　Yes! let the rich deride, the proud disdain,
These simple blessings of the lowly train;
To me more dear, congenial to my heart,
One native charm, than all the gloss of art;
Spontaneous joys, where Nature has its play,
The soul adopts, and owns their first born sway;
Lightly they frolic o'er the vacant mind,
Unenvied, unmolested, unconfined.　　　　260
But the long pomp, the midnight masquerade,
With all the freaks of wanton wealth arrayed,
In these, ere triflers half their wish obtain,
The toiling pleasure sickens into pain;
And, even while fashion's brightest arts decoy,
The heart distrusting asks, if this be joy.
　　Ye friends to truth, ye statesmen, who survey
The rich man's joys encrease, the poor's decay,
'Tis yours to judge, how wide the limits stand
Between a splendid and an happy land.　　　　270
Proud swells the tide with loads of freighted ore,
And shouting Folly hails them from her shore;
Hoards, even beyond the miser's wish abound,
And rich men flock from all the world around.
Yet count our gains. This wealth is but a name
That leaves our useful products still the same.
Not so the loss. The man of wealth and pride,
Takes up a space that many poor supplied;
Space for his lake, his park's extended bounds,
Space for his horses, equipage, and hounds;　　　　280

The robe that wraps his limbs in silken sloth,
Has robbed the neighbouring fields of half their growth;
His seat, where solitary sports are seen,
Indignant spurns the cottage from the green;
Around the world each needful product flies,
For all the luxuries the world supplies.
While thus the land adorned for pleasure, all
In barren splendour feebly waits the fall.
    As some fair female unadorned and plain,
Secure to please while youth confirms her reign,   290
Slights every borrowed charm that dress supplies,
Nor shares with art the triumph of her eyes;
But when those charms are past, for charms are frail,
When time advances, and when lovers fail,
She then shines forth, sollicitous to bless,
In all the glaring impotence of dress;
Thus fares the land, by luxury betrayed;
In nature's simplest charms at first arrayed;
But verging to decline, its splendours rise,
Its vistas strike, its palaces surprize;   300
While scourged by famine from the smiling land,
The mournful peasant leads his humble band;
And while he sinks without one arm to save,
The country blooms—a garden, and a grave.
    Where then, ah where, shall poverty reside,
To scape the pressure of contiguous pride?
If to some common's fenceless limits strayed,
He drives his flock to pick the scanty blade,
Those fenceless fields the sons of wealth divide,
And even the bare-worn common is denied.   310
    If to the city sped—What waits him there?
To see profusion that he must not share;
To see ten thousand baneful arts combined
To pamper luxury, and thin mankind;
To see each joy the sons of pleasure know,
Extorted from his fellow-creature's woe.
Here, while the courtier glitters in brocade,
There the pale artist plies the sickly trade;
Here, while the proud their long drawn pomps display,
There the black gibbet glooms beside the way.   320
The dome where pleasure holds her midnight reign,
Here, richly deckt, admits the gorgeous train;
Tumultuous grandeur crowds the blazing square,
The rattling chariots clash, the torches glare.
Sure scenes like these no troubles e'er annoy!

Sure these denote one universal joy!
Are these thy serious thoughts?—Ah, turn thine eyes
Where the poor houseless shivering female lies.
She once, perhaps, in village plenty blest,
Has wept at tales of innocence distrest;   330
Her modest looks the cottage might adorn,
Sweet as the primrose peeps beneath the thorn;
Now lost to all; her friends, her virtue fled,
Near her betrayer's door she lays her head,
And pinch'd with cold, and shrinking from the shower,
With heavy heart deplores that luckless hour
When idly first, ambitious of the town,
She left her wheel and robes of country brown.
     Do thine, sweet AUBURN, thine, the loveliest train,
Do thy fair tribes participate her pain?   340
Even now, perhaps, by cold and hunger led,
At proud men's doors they ask a little bread!
     Ah, no. To distant climes, a dreary scene,
Where half the convex world intrudes between,
To torrid tracts with fainting steps they go,
Where wild Altama murmurs to their woe.
Far different there from all that charm'd before,
The various terrors of that horrid shore;
Those blazing suns that dart a downward ray,
And fiercely shed intolerable day;   350
Those matted woods where birds forget to sing,
But silent bats in drowsy clusters cling,
Those poisonous fields with rank luxuriance crowned,
Where the dark scorpion gathers death around;
Where at each step the stranger fears to wake
The rattling terrors of the vengeful snake;
Where crouching tigers wait their hapless prey,
And savage men, more murderous still than they;
While oft in whirls the mad tornado flies,
Mingling the ravaged landshape with the skies.   360
Far different these from every former scene,
The cooling brook, the grassy vested green,
The breezy covert of the warbling grove,
That only sheltered thefts of harmless love.
     Good Heaven! what sorrows gloom'd that parting day,
That called them from their native walks away;
When the poor exiles, every pleasure past,
Hung round their bowers, and fondly looked their last,
And took a long farewell, and wished in vain
For seats like these beyond the western main;   370

And shuddering still to face the distant deep,
Returned and wept, and still returned to weep.
The good old sire, the first prepared to go
To new found worlds, and wept for others woe.
But for himself, in conscious virtue brave,
He only wished for worlds beyond the grave.
His lovely daughter, lovelier in her tears,
The fond companion of his helpless years,
Silent went next, neglectful of her charms,
And left a lover's for a father's arms.   380
With louder plaints the mother spoke her woes,
And blest the cot where every pleasure rose;
And kist her thoughtless babes with many a tear,
And claspt them close in sorrow doubly dear;
Whilst her fond husband strove to lend relief
In all the decent manliness of grief.

     O luxury! Thou curst by Heaven's decree,
How ill exchanged are things like these for thee!
How do thy potions, with insidious joy,
Diffuse their pleasures only to destroy!   390
Kingdoms, by thee, to sickly greatness grown,
Boast of a florid vigour not their own;
At every draught more large and large they grow,
A bloated mass of rank unwieldly woe;
Till sapped their strength, and every part unsound,
Down, down they sink, and spread a ruin round.

     Even now the devastation is begun,
And half the business of destruction done;
Even now, methinks, as pondering here I stand,
I see the rural virtues leave the land: 400
Down where yon anchoring vessel spreads the sail,
That idly waiting flaps with every gale,
Downward they move, a melancholy band,
Pass from the shore, and darken all the strand.
Contented toil, and hospitable care,
And kind connubial tenderness, are there;
And piety, with wishes placed above,
And steady loyalty, and faithful love:
And thou, sweet Poetry, thou loveliest maid,
Still first to fly where sensual joys invade;   410
Unfit in these degenerate times of shame,
To catch the heart, or strike for honest fame;
Dear charming nymph, neglected and decried,
My shame in crowds, my solitary pride;
Thou source of all my bliss, and all my woe,

That found'st me poor at first, and keep'st me so;
Thou guide by which the nobler arts excell,
Thou nurse of every virtue, fare thee well.
Farewell, and O where'er thy voice be tried,
On Torno's cliffs, or Pambamarca's side,   420
Whether where equinoctial fervours glow,
Or winter wraps the polar world in snow,
Still let thy voice prevailing over time,
Redress the rigours of the inclement clime;
Aid slighted truth, with thy persuasive strain,
Teach erring man to spurn the rage of gain;
Teach him that states of native strength possest,
Tho' very poor, may still be very blest;
That trade's proud empire hastes to swift decay,
As ocean sweeps the labour'd mole away;   430
While self dependent power can time defy,
As rocks resist the billows and the sky.

§ FOR COMMENT

The Deserted Village is best seen in terms of its social and literary backgrounds. First of all, notice that the poet is not preaching a "back to nature" sermon, as the lines near the end of the poem describing the horrors
of life in the colonies make clear. The horrors of life in the corrupted city
are paralleled with the terrors of life in the colonies, and the villain of the
piece is the city merchant who uses his wealth to buy up lands in the country and turn them into an estate for his solitary enjoyment.

The contrast in the poem is between the virtuous life of the country
and the corrupt vices of the city or the barbaric savagery of the colonies.
Thus the poem is an adaptation of the pastoral convention to native English circumstances and to contemporary conditions. Goldsmith does not,
like Milton, use the Latin names from Virgil like "Lycidas" and "Amaryllis," but he does use many elements of the pastoral convention, especially
the contrast between the country virtue and the city vice, and the criticism
of social conditions is strongly reminiscent of Milton's attack on religious
corruption. In lines 10–14, where some of the pleasures of Auburn are enu-
merated, what is the common element? For example, how are the mill and
the hawthorn bush alike?

You will notice that there is a narrator who relates the poem. What
does Goldsmith gain by this device? In particular, what is gained by having
Auburn an already deserted village rather than one which faces destruction?
Does the narrator regret that he can no longer enter into the village life of
Auburn? How is his feeling about the villagers different from that of the
city merchant? The long descriptions of some of the inhabitants of Auburn

have been much admired. Do they make a contribution to the over-all meaning of the poem? How?

One of the problems a poet faces in writing a long poem in couplets is avoiding monotony. What technical devices has Goldsmith used to achieve variety? Are his rhymes predominantly true rhymes? Do you find any examples of half rhyme? Are the rhymes chiefly masculine or feminine? Consider lines 217–237. Does the use of the caesura here keep the lines from becoming singsong?

✵ Romantic and Victorian Poetry

In the later eighteenth century the poetic style established by Dryden, brought to perfection by Pope, and continued by Goldsmith, began to wane. Poets began to show a newfound interest in landscape nature, which they thought of as symbolizing the lasting and eternal truths; in the workings of the human mind; in the literature of the past, particularly in folk literature and medieval literature; and in strange, exotic countries. These new concerns do not, of course, exhaust the characteristics of Romanticism, but they do suggest some of the main tendencies and themes of this new kind of poetry.

Traditionally, literary historians mark the beginning of English Romanticism in the year 1798, the year in which William Wordsworth and Samuel Taylor Coleridge published their collaborative volume, *Lyrical Ballads*. This book was, indeed, a new milestone, but English Romanticism had been under way for some time, even though it did not become the established, dominant style until about 1820. Poets like Burns and Blake both show some of the features we classify as Romantic, especially the interest in the landscape and a somewhat more particularized interest in individualized things, in contrast to the emphasis on general qualities that characterizes Neo-Classical poetry. An example from Goldsmith's *The Deserted Village* will easily show why he is a Neo-Classical poet rather than a "Pre-Romantic." Goldsmith is describing the charming life of Auburn (ll. 115–126):

> Sweet was the sound, when oft at evening's close,
> Up yonder hill the village murmur rose.
> There, as I passed with careless steps and slow,
> The mingled notes came softened from below;
> The swain responsive as the milk-maid sung,
> The sober herd that lowed to meet their young;
> The noisy geese that gabbled o'er the pool,
> The playful children just let loose from school;
> The watch-dog's voice that bayed the whispering wind,

And the loud laugh that spoke the vacant mind;—
These all in sweet confusion sought the shade,
And filled each pause the nightingale had made.

Goldsmith has included quite a few details from nature, and that fact has made some literary critics, over-eager to find early examples of Romanticism, call him a "Pre-Romantic." But a more careful examination of the passage shows that it is "man-centered," not "nature-centered." All the pleasant noises the narrator remembers are either made by human beings— the milkmaid's song, the swain's reply, the playful children—or, if they are made by animals, they are all domesticated animals—cows, sheep, the watch-dog—whose lives are subordinated to man's needs. Even the sole wild sound here, the song of the nightingale, occupies a place subordinated to man, for the human sounds all fill up the pauses left by the bird's song. Thus, we see that the poet considered the nightingale's song, traditionally the most beautiful of bird songs, less *really* beautiful than the humble, ordinary sounds of man.

The shift away from a poetry centered on man to a poetry centered on landscape nature was characteristic of Romanticism. Poets began to find concrete objects in landscape nature more important to them than any number of human beings. When they were interested in human beings, the poets tended to be most interested in people whose lives were close to nature. The English poets' interest in other cultures, remote in either time or space, probably occurred because of their dislike for the growth of industrialism in early nineteenth-century England. We may notice that these Romantic characteristics are more a group of allied, connected tendencies, not a systematic "philosophy," and that this same group of tendencies dominated both English and American poetry throughout the nineteenth century. Poets like Tennyson used materials drawn from classical sources like "Ulysses" or from Arthurian legend like "The Lady of Shalott." Tennyson, Longfellow, and Arnold reveal the serious preoccupation with religious and moral themes we usually consider typically "Victorian," while Edgar Allan Poe continues the Romantic interest in the mysterious and dreamlike. But even while the Romantic-Victorian style was at its height, such poets as Whitman, Emily Dickinson, and Gerard Manley Hopkins, the last two virtually unknown to the poetry-reading public during their lifetimes, were experimenting in verse forms that twentieth-century poets would consider forerunners of modern style.

William Blake § 1757–1827

Blake was both an engraver and a poet and achieved first rank in both fields. A visionary and a mystic, Blake is most accessible to the ordinary reader through his songs.

Introduction

Piping down the valleys wild,
Piping songs of pleasant glee,
On a cloud I saw a child,
And he laughing said to me:

"Pipe a song about a Lamb!"
So I piped with merry chear.
"Piper, pipe that song again;"
So I piped: he wept to hear.

"Drop thy pipe, thy happy pipe;
Sing thy songs of happy chear:"   10
So I sung the same again,
While he wept with joy to hear.

"Piper, sit thee down and write
In a book, that all may read."
So he vanish'd from my sight,
And I pluck'd a hollow reed,

And I made a rural pen,
And I stain'd the water clear,
And I wrote my happy songs
Every child may joy to hear.   20

The Lamb

Little Lamb, who made thee?
Dost thou know who made thee?
Gave thee life, & bid thee feed
By the stream & o'er the mead;
Gave thee clothing of delight,
Softest clothing, wooly, bright;
Gave thee such a tender voice,

Making all the vales rejoice?
  Little Lamb, who made thee?
  Dost thou know who made thee?   10

  Little Lamb, I'll tell thee,
  Little Lamb, I'll tell thee:
He is called by thy name,
For he calls himself a Lamb.
He is meek, & he is mild;
He became a little child.
I a child, & thou a lamb,
We are called by his name.
  Little Lamb, God bless thee!
  Little Lamb, God bless thee!   20

The Tiger

Tiger! Tiger! burning bright
In the forests of the night,
What immortal hand or eye
Could frame thy fearful symmetry?

In what distant deeps or skies
Burnt the fire of thine eyes?
On what wings dare he aspire?
What the hand dare seize the fire?

And what shoulder, and what art,
Could twist the sinews of thy heart?   10
And when thy heart began to beat,
What dread hand? and what dread feet?

What the hammer? what the chain?
In what furnace was thy brain?
What the anvil? what dread grasp
Dare its deadly terrors clasp?

When the stars threw down their spears,
And water'd heaven with their tears,
Did he smile his work to see?
Did he who made the Lamb make thee?   20

Tiger! Tiger! burning bright
In the forests of the night,

What immortal hand or eye,
Dare frame thy fearful symmetry?

Never seek to tell thy love

Never seek to tell thy love,
Love that never told can be;
For the gentle wind does move
Silently, invisibly.

I told my love, I told my love,
I told her all my heart;
Trembling, cold, in ghastly fears,
Ah! she doth depart.

Soon as she was gone from me,
A traveller came by,   10
Silently, invisibly:
He took her with a sigh.

I saw a chapel

I saw a chapel all of gold
That none did dare to enter in,
And many weeping stood without,
Weeping, mourning, worshipping.

I saw a serpent rise between
The white pillars of the door,
And he forc'd & forc'd & forc'd,
Down the golden hinges tore.

And along the pavement sweet,
Set with pearls & rubies bright,   10
All his slimy length he drew,
Till upon the altar white

Vomiting his poison out
On the bread & on the wine.
So I turn'd into a sty
And laid me down among the swine.

I asked a thief

I asked a thief to steal me a peach:
He turned up his eyes.
I ask'd a lithe lady to lie her down:
Holy & meek she cries.

As soon as I went an angel came:
He wink'd at the thief
And smil'd at the dame,
And without one word spoke
Had a peach from the tree,
And 'twixt earnest & joke   10
Enjoy'd the Lady.

London

I wander thro' each charter'd street,
Near where the charter'd Thames does flow,
And mark in every face I meet
Marks of weakness, marks of woe.

In every cry of every Man,
In every Infant's cry of fear,
In every voice, in every ban,
The mind-forg'd manacles I hear.

How the Chimney-sweeper's cry
Every black'ning Church appalls;   10
And the hapless Soldier's sigh
Runs in blood down Palace walls.

But most thro' midnight streets I hear
How the youthful Harlot's curse
Blasts the new born Infant's tear,
And blights with plagues the Marriage hearse.

Robert Burns § 1759–1796

*Often thought of by his contemporaries as a peasant poet, Burns
actually was well educated, though no scholar. The songs, for which*

*he is world famous, are his own inspired reworkings of traditional
materials from Scottish folk tradition.*

Afton Water

Flow gently, sweet Afton, among thy green braes,
Flow gently, I'll sing thee a song in thy praise;
My Mary's asleep by thy murmuring stream,
Flow gently, sweet Afton, disturb not her dream.

Thou stock-dove whose echo resounds thro' the glen,
Ye wild whistling blackbirds in yon thorny den,
Thou green-crested lapwing, thy screaming forbear,
I charge you disturb not my slumbering fair.

How lofty, sweet Afton, thy neighbouring hills,
Far mark'd with the courses of clear winding rills;   10
There daily I wander as noon rises high,
My flocks and my Mary's sweet cot in my eye.

How pleasant thy banks and green valleys below,
Where wild in the woodlands the primroses blow;
There oft as mild ev'ning weeps over the lea,
The sweet-scented birk shades my Mary and me.

Thy crystal stream, Afton, how lovely it glides,
And winds by the cot where my Mary resides;
How wanton thy waters her snowy feet lave,
As gathering sweet flow'rets she stems thy clear wave.   20

Flow gently, sweet Afton, among thy green braes,
Flow gently, sweet river, the theme of my lays;
My Mary's asleep by thy murmuring stream,
Flow gently, sweet Afton, disturb not her dream.

Highland Mary

Ye banks, and braes, and streams around
   The castle o' Montgomery,
Green be your woods, and fair your flowers,
   Your waters never drumlie!
There simmer first unfauld her robes,
   And there the langest tarry;

For there I took the last fareweel
　　O' my sweet Highland Mary.

How sweetly bloom'd the gay green birk,
　　How rich the hawthorn's blossom,　　　　　　10
As underneath their fragrant shade
　　I clasp'd her to my bosom!
The golden hours on angel wings
　　Flew o'er me and my dearie;
For dear to me as light and life
　　Was my sweet Highland Mary.

Wi' mony a vow, and lock'd embrace,
　　Our parting was fu' tender;
And, pledging aft to meet again,
　　We tore oursels asunder;　　　　　　　　　20
But oh! fell death's untimely frost,
　　That nipt my flower sae early!
Now green's the sod, and cauld's the clay,
　　That wraps my Highland Mary!

O pale, pale now, those rosy lips,
　　I aft have kiss'd sae fondly!
And closed for aye the sparkling glance,
　　That dwelt on me sae kindly!
And mould'ring now in silent dust,
　　That heart that lo'ed me dearly!　　　　　30
But still within my bosom's core
　　Shall live my Highland Mary.

My love is like a red red rose

My love is like a red red rose
　　That's newly sprung in June:
My love is like the melodie
　　That's sweetly play'd in tune.

So fair art thou, my bonnie lass,
　　So deep in love am I:
And I will love thee still, my dear,
　　Till a' the seas gang dry.

Till a' the seas gang dry, my dear,
　　And the rocks melt wi' the sun:　　　　　10

And I will love thee still, my dear,
    While the sands o' life shall run.

And fare thee weel, my only love,
    And fare thee weel awhile!
And I will come again, my love,
    Tho' it were ten thousand mile.

William Wordsworth § 1770–1850

Wordsworth reveals in his lyrics and sonnets the interest in land-
scape, in psychology, and the literature of the past that mark
English Romanticism in its first generation. His plain and noble
diction marks him as one of the finest English poets.

I wandered lonely as a cloud

I wandered lonely as a cloud
That floats on high o'er vales and hills,
When all at once I saw a crowd,
A host, of golden daffodils;
Beside the lake, beneath the trees,
Fluttering and dancing in the breeze.

Continuous as the stars that shine
And twinkle on the milky way,
They stretched in never-ending line
Along the margin of a bay: 10
Ten thousand saw I at a glance,
Tossing their heads in sprightly dance.

The waves beside them danced; but they
Out-did the sparkling waves in glee:
A poet could not but be gay,
In such a jocund company:
I gazed—and gazed—but little thought
What wealth the show to me had brought:

For oft, when on my couch I lie
In vacant or in pensive mood,   20
They flash upon that inward eye

Which is the bliss of solitude;
And then my heart with pleasure fills,
And dances with the daffodils.

§ FOR COMMENT

"I wandered lonely as a cloud" beautifully shows the quality of Wordsworth's interest in nature. Notice that the first three stanzas are largely description of a particular scene, daffodils growing beside a lake under the blue sky, as seen by a solitary poet. Whatever is significant that happens will involve the individual's interaction with the landscape. Notice the terms in which the daffodils are presented to us. What is important about the poet's choice of such words as "crowd," "host," "dancing," "heads," and "company" to describe them? Is the poet chiefly interested in objective, careful description of the flowers such as a botanist would make?

If the first three stanzas describe the immediate effect of the flowers on the poet, what does the last stanza tell the reader? What is "that inward eye/ Which is the bliss of solitude"? In what sense can this poem be called "psychological"?

Describe the prevailing meter and rhyme scheme of the poem. Are they appropriate to the subject? Why? Why not?

Composed upon Westminster Bridge, September 3, 1802

Earth has not anything to show more fair:
Dull would he be of soul who could pass by
A sight so touching in its majesty:
This City now doth, like a garment, wear
The beauty of the morning; silent, bare,
Ships, towers, domes, theatres, and temples lie
Open unto the fields, and to the sky;
All bright and glittering in the smokeless air.
Never did sun more beautifully steep
In his first splendour, valley, rock, or hill;   10
Ne'er saw I, never felt, a calm so deep!
The river glideth at his own sweet will:
Dear God! the very houses seem asleep;
And all that mighty heart is lying still!

It is a beauteous evening

It is a beauteous evening, calm and free,
The holy time is quiet as a Nun
Breathless with adoration; the broad sun
Is sinking down in its tranquillity;
The gentleness of heaven broods o'er the Sea:
Listen! the mighty Being is awake,
And doth with his eternal motion make
A sound like thunder—everlastingly.
Dear Child! dear Girl! that walkest with me here,
If thou appear untouched by solemn thought,   10
Thy nature is not therefore less divine:
Thou liest in Abraham's bosom all the year;
And worshipp'st at the Temple's inner shrine,
God being with thee when we know it not.

London, 1802

Milton! thou shouldst be living at this hour:
England hath need of thee: she is a fen
Of stagnant waters: altar, sword, and pen,
Fireside, the heroic wealth of hall and bower,
Have forfeited their ancient English dower
Of inward happiness. We are selfish men;
Oh! raise us up, return to us again;
And give us manners, virtue, freedom, power.
Thy soul was like a Star, and dwelt apart;
Thou hadst a voice whose sound was like the sea: 10
Pure as the naked heavens, majestic, free,
So didst thou travel on life's common way,
In cheerful godliness; and yet thy heart
The lowliest duties on herself did lay.

The world is too much with us

The world is too much with us; late and soon,
Getting and spending, we lay waste our powers:
Little we see in Nature that is ours;
We have given our hearts away, a sordid boon!
This Sea that bares her bosom to the moon;
The winds that will be howling at all hours,
And are up-gathered now like sleeping flowers;

For this, for everything, we are out of tune;
It moves us not.—Great God! I'd rather be
A Pagan suckled in a creed outworn;   10
So might I, standing on this pleasant lea,
Have glimpses that would make me less forlorn;
Have sight of Proteus rising from the sea;
Or hear old Triton blow his wreathéd horn.

Robert Southey § 1774–1843

Southey was a diligent writer who is probably best seen in what he considered his minor works, like "The Old Man's Comforts and How He Gained Them" and "The Three Bears."

The Old Man's Comforts, and How He Gained Them

"You are old, Father William," the young man cried;
    "The few locks which are left you are gray;
You are hale, Father William,—a hearty old man:
    Now tell me the reason, I pray."

"In the days of my youth," Father William replied,
    "I remembered that youth would fly fast,
And abused not my health and my vigor at first,
    That I never might need them at last."

"You are old, Father William," the young man cried,
    "And pleasures with youth pass away;   10
And yet you lament not the days that are gone:
    Now tell me the reason, I pray."

"In the days of my youth," Father William replied,
    "I remembered that youth could not last;
I thought of the future, whatever I did,
    That I never might grieve for the past."

"You are old, Father William," the young man cried,
    "And life must be hastening away;
And are cheerful, and love to converse upon death:
    Now tell me the reason, I pray."   20

"I am cheerful, young man," Father William replied;
  "Let the cause thy attention engage:
In the days of my youth, I remembered my God;
  And he hath not forgotten my age."

John Keats § 1795–1821

Keats studied to be a surgeon but poetry was the real profession
of his far too brief life. Easily the finest poet of the second wave
of English Romanticism, he is best known for his odes and his
sonnets, though "La Belle Dame sans Merci" shows his interest
in the ballad. Virtually all his poetry shows his preoccupation with
beauty.

When I have fears that I may cease to be

When I have fears that I may cease to be
  Before my pen has glean'd my teeming brain,
Before high-piled books, in charactery,
  Hold like rich garners the full ripen'd grain;
When I behold, upon the night's starr'd face,
  Huge cloudy symbols of a high romance,
And think that I may never live to trace
  Their shadows, with the magic hand of chance;
And when I feel, fair creature of an hour,
  That I shall never look upon thee more,   10
Never have relish in the faery power
  Of unreflecting love;—then on the shore
Of the wide world I stand alone, and think
Till love and fame to nothingness do sink.

Sonnet: Bright star, would I were stedfast

Written on a Blank Page in Shakespeare's Poems, facing
'A Lover's Complaint.'

Bright star, would I were stedfast as thou art—
  Not in lone splendour hung aloft the night
And watching, with eternal lids apart,
  Like nature's patient, sleepless Eremite,
The moving waters at their priestlike task

Of pure ablution round earth's human shores,
Or gazing on the new soft-fallen mask
   Of snow upon the mountains and the moors—
No—yet still stedfast, still unchangeable,
   Pillow'd upon my fair love's ripening breast,   10
To feel for ever its soft fall and swell,
   Awake for ever in a sweet unrest,
Still, still to hear her tender-taken breath,
And so live ever—or else swoon to death.

La Belle Dame sans Merci

O what can ail thee, knight-at-arms,
   Alone and palely loitering?
The sedge has withered from the lake,
   And no birds sing.

O what can ail thee, knight-at-arms,
   So haggard and so woe-begone?
The squirrel's granary is full,
   And the harvest's done.

I see a lilly on thy brow
   With anguish moist and fever dew;   10
And on thy cheeks a fading rose
   Fast withereth too.

I met a lady in the meads,
   Full beautiful—a faery's child,
Her hair was long, her foot was light,
   And her eyes were wild.

I made a garland for her head,
   And bracelets too, and fragrant zone;
She look'd at me as she did love,
   And made sweet moan.   20

I set her on my pacing steed,
   And nothing else saw all day long,
For sidelong would she bend, and sing
   A faery's song.

She found me roots of relish sweet,
   And honey wild, and manna dew,

And sure in language strange she said,
  'I love thee true!'

She took me to her elfin grot,
  And there she wept and sigh'd full sore,   30
And there I shut her wild, wild eyes
  With kisses four.

And there she lulléd me asleep
  And there I dream'd, ah woe betide!
The latest dream I ever dream'd
  On the cold hill side.

I saw pale kings, and princes too,
  Pale warriors, death-pale were they all;
They cried—'La belle Dame sans Merci
  Hath thee in thrall!'   40

I saw their starved lips in the gloam
  With horrid warning gapéd wide,
And I awoke and found me here
  On the cold hill's side.

And this is why I sojourn here
  Alone and palely loitering,
Though the sedge is wither'd from the lake,
  And no birds sing.

Ode on a Grecian Urn

1

Thou still unravish'd bride of quietness,
  Thou foster-child of silence and slow time,
Sylvan historian, who canst thus express
  A flowery tale more sweetly than our rhyme:
What leaf-fring'd legend haunts about thy shape
  Of deities or mortals, or of both,
    In Tempe or the dales of Arcady?
  What men or gods are these? What maidens loth?
What mad pursuit? What struggle to escape?
    What pipes and timbrels? What wild ecstasy?   10

2

Heard melodies are sweet, but those unheard
  Are sweeter; therefore, ye soft pipes, play on;
Not to the sensual ear, but, more endear'd,
  Pipe to the spirit ditties of no tone:
Fair youth, beneath the trees, thou canst not leave
  Thy song, nor ever can those trees be bare;
    Bold Lover, never, never canst thou kiss,
Though winning near the goal—yet, do not grieve;
  She cannot fade, though thou hast not thy bliss,
    For ever wilt thou love, and she be fair!　　　　20

3

Ah, happy, happy boughs! that cannot shed
  Your leaves, nor ever bid the Spring adieu;
And, happy melodist, unwearied,
  For ever piping songs for ever new;
More happy love! more happy, happy love!
  For ever warm and still to be enjoy'd,
    For ever panting, and for ever young;
All breathing human passion far above,
  That leaves a heart high-sorrowful and cloy'd,
    A burning forehead, and a parching tongue.　　　　30

4

Who are these coming to the sacrifice?
  To what green altar, O mysterious priest,
Lead'st thou that heifer lowing at the skies,
  And all her silken flanks with garlands drest?
What little town by river or sea shore,
  Or mountain-built with peaceful citadel,
    Is emptied of this folk, this pious morn?
And, little town, thy streets for evermore
  Will silent be; and not a soul to tell
    Why thou art desolate, can e'er return.　　　　40

5

O Attic shape! Fair attitude! with brede
  Of marble men and maidens overwrought,
With forest branches and the trodden weed;
  Thou, silent form, dost tease us out of thought
As doth eternity: Cold Pastoral!
  When old age shall this generation waste,
    Thou shalt remain, in midst of other woe

Than ours, a friend to man, to whom thou say'st,
"Beauty is truth, truth beauty,"—that is all
   Ye know on earth, and all ye need to know.   50

Thomas Hood § 1799–1845

Hood was a full-time journalist and writer most of his adult life. Probably his most famous poem is "The Song of the Shirt," a poetic protest against industrial inhumanity, but "The Bridge of Sighs" is almost equally well known.

The Bridge of Sighs

'Drown'd! drown'd!'—Hamlet.

One more Unfortunate,
Weary of breath,
Rashly importunate,
Gone to her death!

Take her up tenderly,
Lift her with care;
Fashion'd so slenderly,
Young, and so fair!

Look at her garments
Clinging like cerements;   10
Whilst the wave constantly
Drips from her clothing;
Take her up instantly,
Loving, not loathing.—

Touch her not scornfully;
Think of her mournfully,
Gently and humanly;
Not of the stains of her,
All that remains of her
Now is pure womanly.   20

Make no deep scrutiny
Into her mutiny
Rash and undutiful:

Past all dishonour
Death has left on her
Only the beautiful.

Still, for all slips of hers,
One of Eve's family—
Wipe those poor lips of hers
Oozing so clammily.   30

Loop up her tresses
Escaped from the comb,
Her fair auburn tresses;
Whilst wonderment guesses
Where was her home?

Who was her father?
Who was her mother?
Had she a sister?
Had she a brother?
Or was there a dearer one   40
Still, and a nearer one
Yet, than all other?

Alas! for the rarity
Of Christian charity
Under the sun!
Oh! it was pitiful!
Near a whole city full,
Home she had none!

Sisterly, brotherly,
Fatherly, motherly,   50
Feelings had changed:
Love, by harsh evidence,
Thrown from its eminence;
Even God's providence
Seeming estranged.

Where the lamps quiver
So far in the river,
With many a light
From window and casement,
From garret to basement,   60
She stood, with amazement,
Houseless by night.

The bleak wind of March
Made her tremble and shiver;
But not the dark arch,
Or the black flowing river:
Mad from life's history,
Glad to death's mystery,
Swift to be hurl'd—
Anywhere, anywhere,   70
Out of the world!

In she plunged boldly,
No matter how coldly
The rough river ran,—
Over the brink of it,
Picture it—think of it,
Dissolute man!
Lave in it, drink of it,
Then, if you can!

Take her up tenderly,   80
Lift her with care;
Fashion'd so slenderly,
Young, and so fair!

Ere her limbs frigidly
Stiffen too rigidly,
Decently,—kindly,—
Smoothe and compose them:
And her eyes, close them,
Staring so blindly!

Dreadfully staring   90
Thro' muddy impurity,
As when with the daring
Last look of despairing,
Fix'd on futurity.

Perishing gloomily,
Spurr'd by contumely,
Cold inhumanity,
Burning insanity,
Into her rest.—
Cross her hands humbly,   100
As if praying dumbly,
Over her breast!

Owning her weakness,
Her evil behaviour,
And leaving, with meekness,
Her sins to her Saviour!

Henry Wadsworth Longfellow § 1807–1882

Longfellow is probably best known for such narrative poems as "Paul Revere's Ride," but his belief that Truth is the main purpose of poetry can be seen in "A Psalm of Life."

A Psalm of Life

What the Heart of the Young Man Said to the Psalmist

Tell me not, in mournful numbers,
    Life is but an empty dream!—
For the soul is dead that slumbers,
    And things are not what they seem.

Life is real! Life is earnest!
    And the grave is not its goal;
Dust thou art, to dust returnest,
    Was not spoken of the soul.

Not enjoyment, and not sorrow,
    Is our destined end or way;   10
But to act, that each to-morrow
    Find us farther than to-day.

Art is long, and Time is fleeting,
    And our hearts, though stout and brave,
Still, like muffled drums, are beating
    Funeral marches to the grave.

In the world's broad field of battle,
    In the bivouac of Life,
Be not like dumb, driven cattle!
    Be a hero in the strife!   20

Trust no Future, howe'er pleasant!
    Let the dead Past bury its dead!

Act,—act in the living Present!
   Heart within, and God o'erhead!

Lives of great men all remind us
   We can make our lives sublime,
And, departing, leave behind us
   Footprints on the sands of time;

Footprints, that perhaps another,
   Sailing o'er life's solemn main,   30
A forlorn and shipwrecked brother,
   Seeing, shall take heart again.

Let us, then, be up and doing,
   With a heart for any fate;
Still achieving, still pursuing,
   Learn to labor and to wait.

Edgar Allan Poe § 1809–1849

*Poe contributed significantly to poetry, short stories, and literary
criticism. Poe's poetry shares many of the same unusual qualities
with his short stories. While he was concerned with the formal
aspects of both genres, he was equally involved with creating suspense in the actual narrative, such as he accomplished in "The
Raven" by means of regular meter and repetition.*
   For further biographical information see p. 39.

The Raven

Once upon a midnight dreary, while I pondered, weak and weary,
Over many a quaint and curious volume of forgotten lore—
While I nodded, nearly napping, suddenly there came a tapping,
As of some one gently rapping, rapping at my chamber door.
' 'Tis some visitor,' I muttered, 'tapping at my chamber door—
   Only this and nothing more.'

Ah, distinctly I remember it was in the bleak December;
And each separate dying ember wrought its ghost upon the floor.
Eagerly I wished the morrow;—vainly I had sought to borrow
From my books surcease of sorrow—sorrow for the lost Lenore—   10

For the rare and radiant maiden whom the angels name Lenore—
    Nameless *here* for evermore.

And the silken, sad, uncertain rustling of each purple curtain
Thrilled me—filled me with fantastic terrors never felt before;
So that now, to still the beating of my heart, I stood repeating
' 'Tis some visitor entreating entrance at my chamber door—
Some late visitor entreating entrance at my chamber door:—
    This it is and nothing more.'

Presently my soul grew stronger; hesitating then no longer,
'Sir,' said I, 'or Madam, truly your forgiveness I implore;   20
But the fact is I was napping, and so gently you came rapping,
And so faintly you came tapping, tapping at my chamber door,
That I scarce was sure I heard you'—here I opened wide the
        door;—
    Darkness there and nothing more.

Deep into that darkness peering, long I stood there wondering,
        fearing,
Doubting, dreaming dreams no mortal ever dared to dream before;
But the silence was unbroken, and the stillness gave no token,
And the only word there spoken was the whispered word, 'Lenore?'
This I whispered, and an echo murmured back the word, 'Lenore!'
    Merely this and nothing more.   30

Back into the chamber turning, all my soul within me burning,
Soon again I heard a tapping somewhat louder than before.
'Surely,' said I, 'surely that is something at my window lattice;
Let me see, then, what thereat is, and this mystery explore—
Let my heart be still a moment and this mystery explore;—
    'Tis the wind and nothing more!'

Open here I flung the shutter, when, with many a flirt and flutter,
In there stepped a stately Raven of the saintly days of yore;
Not the least obeisance made he; not a minute stopped or stayed
        he;
But, with mien of lord or lady, perched above my chamber door—   40
Perched upon a bust of Pallas just above my chamber door—
    Perched, and sat, and nothing more.

Then this ebony bird beguiling my sad fancy into smiling,
By the grave and stern decorum of the countenance it wore,
'Though thy crest be shorn and shaven, thou,' I said, 'art sure no
        craven,

Ghastly grim and ancient Raven wandering from the Nightly
    shore—
Tell me what thy lordly name is on the Night's Plutonian shore!'
    Quoth the Raven, 'Nevermore.'

Much I marvelled this ungainly fowl to hear discourse so plainly,
Though its answer little meaning—little relevancy bore;   50
For we cannot help agreeing that no living human being
Ever yet was blessed with seeing bird above his chamber door—
Bird or beast upon the sculptured bust above his chamber door,
    With such name as 'Nevermore.'

But the Raven, sitting lonely on the placid bust, spoke only
That one word, as if his soul in that one word he did outpour.
Nothing farther then he uttered—not a feather then he fluttered—
Till I scarcely more than muttered 'Other friends have flown
    before—
On the morrow *he* will leave me, as my Hopes have flown before.'
    Then the bird said 'Nevermore.'   60

Startled at the stillness broken by reply so aptly spoken,
'Doubtless,' said I, 'what it utters is its only stock and store
Caught from some unhappy master whom unmerciful Disaster
Followed fast and followed faster till his songs one burden bore—
Till the dirges of his Hope that melancholy burden bore
    Of "Never—nevermore." '

But the Raven still beguiling my sad fancy into smiling,
Straight I wheeled a cushioned seat in front of bird, and bust and
    door;
Then, upon the velvet sinking, I betook myself to linking
Fancy unto fancy, thinking what this ominous bird of yore—   70
What this grim, ungainly, ghastly, gaunt, and ominous bird of yore
    Meant in croaking 'Nevermore.'

This I sat engaged in guessing, but no syllable expressing
To the fowl whose fiery eyes now burned into my bosom's core;
This and more I sat divining, with my head at ease reclining
On the cushion's velvet lining that the lamp-light gloated o'er,
But whose velvet-violet lining with the lamp-light gloating o'er,
    She shall press, ah, nevermore!

Then, methought, the air grew denser, perfumed from an unseen
    censer
Swung by seraphim whose foot-falls tinkled on the tufted floor.   80

'Wretch,' I cried, 'thy God hath lent thee—by these angels he
    hath sent thee
Respite—respite and nepenthe from thy memories of Lenore;
Quaff, oh quaff this kind nepenthe and forget this lost Lenore!'
    Quoth the Raven 'Nevermore.'

'Prophet!' said I, 'thing of evil!—prophet still, if bird or devil!—
Whether Tempter sent, or whether tempest tossed thee here
    ashore,
Desolate yet all undaunted, on this desert land enchanted—
On this home by Horror haunted—tell me truly, I implore—
Is there—*is* there balm in Gilead?—tell me—tell me, I implore!'
    Quoth the Raven 'Nevermore.'   90

'Prophet!' said I, 'thing of evil!—prophet still, if bird or devil!
By that Heaven that bends above us—by that God we both
    adore—
Tell this soul with sorrow laden if, within the distant Aidenn,
It shall clasp a sainted maiden whom the angels name Lenore—
Clasp a rare and radiant maiden whom the angels name Lenore.'
    Quoth the Raven 'Nevermore.'

'Be that word our sign of parting, bird or fiend!' I shrieked,
    upstarting—
'Get thee back into the tempest and the Night's Plutonian shore!
Leave no black plume as a token of that lie thy soul hath spoken!
Leave my loneliness unbroken!—quit the bust above my door!   100
Take thy beak from out my heart, and take thy form from off my
    door!'
    Quoth the Raven 'Nevermore.'

And the Raven, never flitting, still is sitting, *still* is sitting
On the pallid bust of Pallas just above my chamber door;
And his eyes have all the seeming of a demon's that is dreaming,
And the lamp-light o'er him streaming throws his shadow on the
    floor;
And my soul from out that shadow that lies floating on the floor
Shall be lifted—nevermore!

Ulalume—A Ballad

The skies they were ashen and sober;
    The leaves they were crispèd and sere—
    The leaves they were withering and sere:

It was night, in the lonesome October
    Of my most immemorial year:
It was hard by the dim lake of Auber,
    In the misty mid region of Weir—
It was down by the dank tarn of Auber,
    In the ghoul-haunted woodland of Weir.

Here once, through an alley Titanic,   10
    Of cypress, I roamed with my Soul—
    Of cypress, with Psyche, my Soul.
These were days when my heart was volcanic
    As the scoriac rivers that roll—
    As the lavas that restlessly roll
Their sulphurous currents down Yaanek
    In the ultimate climes of the Pole—
That groan as they roll down Mount Yaanek
    In the realms of the Boreal Pole.

Our talk had been serious and sober,   20
    But our thoughts they were palsied and sere—
    Our memories were treacherous and sere;
For we knew not the month was October,
    And we marked not the night of the year
    (Ah, night of all nights in the year!)—
We noted not the dim lake of Auber
    (Though once we had journeyed down here)—
We remembered not the dank tarn of Auber,
    Nor the ghoul-haunted woodland of Weir.

And now, as the night was senescent   30
    And star-dials pointed to morn—
    As the star-dials hinted of morn—
At the end of our path a liquescent
    And nebulous lustre was born,
Out of which a miraculous crescent
    Arose with a duplicate horn—
Astarte's bediamonded crescent
    Distinct with its duplicate horn.

And I said: 'She is warmer than Dian;
    She rolls through an ether of sighs—   40
    She revels in a region of sighs.
She has seen that the tears are not dry on
    These cheeks, where the worm never dies,
And has come past the stars of the Lion,

To point us the path to the skies—
   To the Lethean peace of the skies—
Come up, in despite of the Lion,
   To shine on us with her bright eyes—
Come up through the lair of the Lion,
   With love in her luminous eyes.'   50

But Psyche, uplifting her finger,
   Said: 'Sadly this star I mistrust—
   Her pallor I strangely mistrust:
Ah, hasten!—ah, let us not linger!
   Ah, fly!—let us fly!—for we must.'
In terror she spoke, letting sink her
   Wings till they trailed in the dust—
In agony sobbed, letting sink her
   Plumes till they trailed in the dust—
   Till they sorrowfully trailed in the dust.   60

I replied: "This is nothing but dreaming:
   Let us on by this tremulous light!
   Let us bathe in this crystalline light!
Its Sibyllic splendor is beaming
   With Hope and in Beauty to-night:—
   See!—it flickers up the sky through the night!
Ah, we safely may trust to its gleaming,
   And be sure it will lead us aright—
We surely may trust to a gleaming,
   That cannot but guide us aright,   70
   Since it flickers up to Heaven through the night.'

Thus I pacified Psyche and kissed her,
   And tempted her out of her gloom—
   And conquered her scruples and gloom;
And we passed to the end of the vista,
   But were stopped by the door of a tomb—
   By the door of a legended tomb;
And I said: 'What is written, sweet sister,
   On the door of this legended tomb?'
   She replied: 'Ulalume—Ulalume!—   80
   'T is the vault of thy lost Ulalume!'

Then my heart it grew ashen and sober
   As the leaves that were crispèd and sere—
   As the leaves that were withering and sere;
And I cried: 'It was surely October

On *this* very night of last year
That I journeyed—I journeyed down here!—
That I brought a dread burden down here—
On this night of all nights in the year,
Ah, what demon hath tempted me here?   90
Well I know, now, this dim lake of Auber—
This misty mid region of Weir—
Well I know, now, this dank tarn of Auber,
This ghoul-haunted woodland of Weir.'

Said we, then—the two, then: 'Ah, can it
Have been that the woodlandish ghouls—
The pitiful, the merciful ghouls—
To bar up our way and to ban it
From the secret that lies in these wolds—
From the thing that lies hidden in these wolds—   100
Have drawn up the spectre of a planet
From the limbo of lunary souls—
This sinfully scintillant planet
From the Hell of the planetary souls?'

The Bells

1

Hear the sledges with the bells—
    Silver bells!
What a world of merriment their melody foretells!
    How they tinkle, tinkle, tinkle,
        In the icy air of night!
    While the stars that oversprinkle
    All the heavens, seem to twinkle
        With a crystalline delight;
    Keeping time, time, time,
    In a sort of Runic rhyme,   10
To the tintinnabulation that so musically wells
    From the bells, bells, bells, bells,
        Bells, bells, bells—
From the jingling and the tinkling of the bells.

2

Hear the mellow wedding bells—
    Golden bells!
What a world of happiness their harmony foretells!
    Through the balmy air of night

How they ring out their delight!—
   From the molten-golden notes,   20
      And all in tune,
   What a liquid ditty floats
To the turtle-dove that listens, while she gloats
       On the moon!
   Oh, from out the sounding cells,
What a gush of euphony voluminously wells!
       How it swells!
       How it dwells
    On the Future!—how it tells
    Of the rapture that impels   30
   To the swinging and the ringing
     Of the bells, bells, bells—
     Of the bells, bells, bells, bells,
       Bells, bells, bells—
To the rhyming and the chiming of the bells!

3

Hear the loud alarum bells—
    Brazen bells!
What a tale of terror, now, their turbulency tells!
   In the startled ear of night
   How they scream out their affright!   40
    Too much horrified to speak,
   They can only shriek, shriek,
     Out of tune,
In a clamorous appealing to the mercy of the fire,
In a mad expostulation with the deaf and frantic fire,
    Leaping higher, higher, higher,
    With a desperate desire,
   And a resolute endeavor
   Now—now to sit, or never,
By the side of the pale-faced moon.   50
   Oh, the bells, bells, bells!
   What a tale their terror tells
     Of Despair!
How they clang, and clash, and roar!
What a horror they outpour
On the bosom of the palpitating air!
   Yet the ear, it fully knows,
    By the twanging
    And the clanging,
   How the danger ebbs and flows;   60
  Yet the ear distinctly tells,

In the jangling
And wrangling,
How the danger sinks and swells,
By the sinking or the swelling in the anger of the bells—
Of the bells,—
Of the bells, bells, bells, bells,
Bells, bells, bells—
In the clamor and the clangor of the bells!

4

Hear the tolling of the bells— 70
Iron bells!
What a world of solemn thought their monody compels!
In the silence of the night,
How we shiver with affright
At the melancholy menace of their tone!
For every sound that floats
From the rust within their throats
Is a groan.
And the people—ah, the people—
They that dwell up in the steeple, 80
All alone,
And who tolling, tolling, tolling,
In that muffled monotone,
Feel a glory in so rolling
On the human heart a stone—
They are neither man nor woman—
They are neither brute nor human—
They are Ghouls:—
And their king it is who tolls:—
And he rolls, rolls, rolls, 90
Rolls
A pæan from the bells!
And his merry bosom swells
With the pæan of the bells!
And he dances, and he yells;
Keeping time, time, time,
In a sort of Runic rhyme,
To the pæan of the bells—
Of the bells:—
Keeping time, time, time, 100
In a sort of Runic rhyme,
To the throbbing of the bells—
Of the bells, bells, bells—
To the sobbing of the bells;

Keeping time, time, time,
    As he knells, knells, knells,
In a happy Runic rhyme,
    To the rolling of the bells—
    Of the bells, bells, bells:—
    To the tolling of the bells—   110
Of the bells, bells, bells, bells,
    Bells, bells, bells—
To the the moaning and the groaning of the bells.

Annabel Lee

It was many and many a year ago,
    In a kingdom by the sea,
That a maiden there lived whom you may know
    By the name of Annabel Lee;—
And this maiden she lived with no other thought
    Than to love and be loved by me.

She was a child and I was a child,
    In this kingdom by the sea,
But we loved with a love that was more than love—
    I and my Annabel Lee—   10
With a love that the wingèd seraphs of Heaven
    Coveted her and me.

And this was the reason that, long ago,
    In this kingdom by the sea,
A wind blew out of a cloud by night
    Chilling my Annabel Lee;
So that her highborn kinsmen came
    And bore her away from me,
To shut her up in a sepulchre
    In this kingdom by the sea.   20

The angels, not half so happy in Heaven,
    Went envying her and me:—
Yes! that was the reason (as all men know,
    In this kingdom by the sea)
That the wind came out of the cloud, chilling
    And killing my Annabel Lee.

But our love it was stronger by far than the love
    Of those who were older than we—

Of many far wiser than we—
And neither the angels in Heaven above   30
    Nor the demons down under the sea,
Can ever dissever my soul from the soul
    Of the beautiful Annabel Lee:—

For the moon never beams without bringing me dreams
    Of the beautiful Annabel Lee;
And the stars never rise but I see the bright eyes
    Of the beautiful Annabel Lee;
And so, all the night-tide, I lie down by the side
Of my darling, my darling, my life and my bride,
    In her sepulchre there by the sea—   40
    In her tomb by the side of the sea.

Alfred, Lord Tennyson § 1809–1892

Tennyson composed graceful lyrics in the Romantic tradition, but also shows us a Ulysses more Faustian than classical. "The Lady of Shalott" and "Ulysses" both show Tennyson's interest in subject matter drawn from the distant past.

The Lady of Shalott

PART I

On either side the river lie
Long fields of barley and of rye,
That clothe the wold and meet the sky;
And thro' the field the road runs by
    To many-towered Camelot;
And up and down the people go,
Gazing where the lilies blow
Round an island there below,
    The island of Shalott.

Willows whiten, aspens quiver,   10
Little breezes dusk and shiver
Thro' the wave that runs for ever
By the island in the river
    Flowing down to Camelot.
Four gray walls, and four gray towers,

Overlook a space of flowers,
And the silent isle imbowers
  The Lady of Shalott.

By the margin, willow-veil'd,
Slide the heavy barges trail'd   20
By slow horses; and unhail'd
The shallop flitteth silken-sail'd
  Skimming down to Camelot:
But who hath seen her wave her hand?
Or at the casement seen her stand?
Or is she known in all the land,
  The Lady of Shalott?

Only reapers, reaping early
In among the bearded barley,
Hear a song that echoes cheerly   30
From the river winding clearly,
  Down to tower'd Camelot:
And by the moon the reaper weary,
Piling sheaves in uplands airy,
Listening, whispers ' 'Tis the fairy
  Lady of Shalott.'

PART II

There she weaves by night and day
A magic web with colours gay.
She has heard a whisper say,
A curse is on her if she stay   40
  To look down to Camelot.
She knows not what the curse may be,
And so she weaveth steadily,
And little other care hath she,
  The Lady of Shalott.

And moving thro' a mirror clear
That hangs before her all the year,
Shadows of the world appear.
There she sees the highway near
  Winding down to Camelot: 50
There the river eddy whirls,
And there the surly village-churls,
And the red cloaks of market girls,
  Pass onward from Shalott.

Sometimes a troop of damsels glad,
An abbot on an ambling pad,
Sometimes a curly shepherd-lad,
Or long-hair'd page in crimson clad,
        Goes by to tower'd Camelot;
And sometimes thro' the mirror blue   60
The knights come riding two and two:
She hath no loyal knight and true,
        The Lady of Shalott.

But in her web she still delights
To weave the mirror's magic sights,
For often thro' the silent nights
A funeral, with plumes and lights
        And music, went to Camelot:
Or when the moon was overhead,
Came two young lovers lately wed;   70
'I am half sick of shadows,' said
        The Lady of Shalott.

PART III

A bow-shot from her bower-eaves,
He rode between the barley-sheaves,
The sun came dazzling thro' the leaves,
And flamed upon the brazen greaves
        Of bold Sir Lancelot.
A red-cross knight for ever kneel'd
To a lady in his shield,
That sparkled on the yellow field,   80
        Beside remote Shalott.

The gemmy bridle glitter'd free,
Like to some branch of stars we see
Hung in the golden Galaxy.
The bridle bells rang merrily
        As he rode down to Camelot:
And from his blazon'd baldric slung
A mighty silver bugle hung,
And as he rode his armour rung,
        Beside remote Shalott.   90

All in the blue unclouded weather
Thick-jewell'd shone the saddle-leather,
The helmet and the helmet-feather

Burn'd like one burning flame together,
    As he rode down to Camelot.
As often thro' the purple night,
Below the starry clusters bright,
Some bearded meteor, trailing light,
    Moves over still Shalott.

His broad clear brow in sunlight glow'd;   100
On burnish'd hooves his war-horse trode;
From underneath his helmet flow'd
His coal-black curls as on he rode,
    As he rode down to Camelot.
From the bank and from the river
He flash'd into the crystal mirror,
'Tirra lirra,' by the river
    Sang Sir Lancelot.

She left the web, she left the loom,
She made three paces thro' the room,   110
She saw the water-lily bloom,
She saw the helmet and the plume,
    She look'd down to Camelot.
Out flew the web and floated wide;
The mirror crack'd from side to side;
'The curse is come upon me,' cried
    The Lady of Shalott.

PART IV

In the stormy east-wind straining,
The pale yellow woods were waning,
The broad stream in his banks complaining,   120
Heavily the low sky raining
    Over tower'd Camelot;
Down she came and found a boat
Beneath a willow left afloat,
And round about the prow she wrote
    The Lady of Shalott.

And down the river's dim expanse
Like some bold seër in a trance,
Seeing all his own mischance—
With a glassy countenance   130
    Did she look to Camelot.
And at the closing of the day
She loosed the chain, and down she lay;

The broad stream bore her far away,
  The Lady of Shalott.

Lying, robed in snowy white
That loosely flew to left and right—
The leaves upon her falling light—
Thro' the noises of the night
  She floated down to Camelot: 140
And as the boat-head wound along
The willowy hills and fields among,
They heard her singing her last song,
  The Lady of Shalott.

Heard a carol, mournful, holy,
Chanted loudly, chanted lowly,
Till her blood was frozen slowly,
And her eyes were darken'd wholly,
  Turn'd to tower'd Camelot.
For ere she reach'd upon the tide   150
The first house by the water-side,
Singing in her song she died,
  The Lady of Shalott.

Under tower and balcony,
By garden-wall and gallery,
A gleaming shape she floated by,
Dead-pale between the houses high,
  Silent into Camelot.
Out upon the wharfs they came,
Knight and burgher, lord and dame,   160
And round the prow they read her name,
  The Lady of Shalott.

Who is this? and what is here?
And in the lighted palace near
Died the sound of royal cheer;
And they cross'd themselves for fear,
  All the knights at Camelot:
But Lancelot mused a little space;
He said, 'She has a lovely face;
God in his mercy lend her grace,   170
  The Lady of Shalott.'

Ulysses

It little profits that an idle king,
By this still hearth, among these barren crags,
Match'd with an aged wife, I mete and dole
Unequal laws unto a savage race,
That hoard, and sleep, and feed, and know not me.
I cannot rest from travel: I will drink
Life to the lees: all times I have enjoy'd
Greatly, have suffer'd greatly, both with those
That loved me, and alone; on shore, and when
Thro' scudding drifts the rainy Hyades   10
Vext the dim sea: I am become a name;
For always roaming with a hungry heart
Much have I seen and known; cities of men
And manners, climates, councils, governments,
Myself not least, but honour'd of them all;
And drunk delight of battle with my peers,
Far on the ringing plains of windy Troy.
I am a part of all that I have met;
Yet all experience is an arch wherethro'
Gleams that untravell'd world, whose margin fades   20
For ever and for ever when I move.
How dull it is to pause, to make an end,
To rust unburnish'd, not to shine in use!
As tho' to breathe were life. Life piled on life
Were all too little, and of one to me
Little remains: but every hour is saved
From that eternal silence, something more,
A bringer of new things; and vile it were
For some three suns to store and hoard myself,
And this gray spirit yearning in desire   30
To follow knowledge like a sinking star,
Beyond the utmost bound of human thought.
    This is my son, mine own Telemachus,
To whom I leave the sceptre and the isle—
Well-loved of me, discerning to fulfil
This labour, by slow prudence to make mild
A rugged people, and thro' soft degrees
Subdue them to the useful and the good.
Most blameless is he, centred in the sphere
Or common duties, decent not to fail   40
In offices of tenderness, and pay
Meet adoration to my household gods,

When I am gone. He works his work, I mine.
   There lies the port; the vessel puffs her sail:
There gloom the dark broad seas. My mariners,
Souls that have toil'd, and wrought, and thought with me—
That ever with a frolic welcome took
The thunder and the sunshine, and opposed
Free hearts, free foreheads—you and I are old;
Old age hath yet his honour and his toil;   50
Death closes all: but something ere the end,
Some work of noble note, may yet be done,
Not unbecoming men that strove with Gods.
The lights begin to twinkle from the rocks:
The long day wanes: the slow moon climbs: the deep
Moans round with many voices. Come, my friends,
'Tis not too late to seek a newer world.
Push off, and sitting well in order smite
The sounding furrows; for my purpose holds
To sail beyond the sunset, and the baths   60
Of all the western stars, until I die.
It may be that the gulfs will wash us down:
It may be we shall touch the Happy Isles,
And see the great Achilles, whom we knew.
Tho' much is taken, much abides; and tho'
We are not now that strength which in old days
Moved earth and heaven; that which we are, we are;
One equal temper of heroic hearts,
Made weak by time and fate, but strong in will
To strive, to seek, to find, and not to yield.   70

Sweet and low

    Sweet and low, sweet and low,
      Wind of the western sea,
    Low, low, breathe and blow,
      Wind of the western sea!
    Over the rolling waters go,
    Come from the dying moon, and blow,
      Blow him again to me;
While my little one, while my pretty one sleeps.

    Sleep and rest, sleep and rest,
      Father will come to thee soon;   10
    Rest, rest, on mother's breast,
      Father will come to thee soon;

Father will come to his babe in the nest,
Silver sails all out of the west
Under the silver moon;
Sleep, my little one, sleep, my pretty one, sleep.

The splendour falls on castle walls

The splendour falls on castle walls
And snowy summits old in story:
The long light shakes across the lakes,
And the wild cataract leaps in glory.
Blow, bugle, blow, set the wild echoes flying,
Blow, bugle; answer, echoes, dying, dying, dying.

O hark, O hear; how thin and clear,
And thinner, clearer, farther going!
O sweet and far from cliff and scar
The horns of Elfland faintly blowing!   10
Blow, let us hear the purple glens replying:
Blow, bugle; answer, echoes, dying, dying, dying.

O love, they die in yon rich sky,
They faint on hill or field or river:
Our echoes roll from soul to soul,
And grow for ever and for ever.
Blow, bugle, blow, set the wild echoes flying,
And answer, echoes, answer, dying, dying, dying.

Now sleeps the crimson petal

Now sleeps the crimson petal, now the white;
Nor waves the cypress in the palace walk;
Nor winks the gold fin in the porphyry font.
The fire-fly wakens; waken thou with me.

Now droops the milk-white peacock like a ghost,
And like a ghost she glimmers on to me.

Now lies the Earth all Danaë to the stars,
And all thy heart lies open unto me.

Now slides the silent meteor on, and leaves
A shining furrow, as thy thoughts in me.   10

Now folds the lily all her sweetness up,
And slips into the bosom of the lake.
So fold thyself, my dearest, thou, and slip
Into my bosom and be lost in me.

Crossing the Bar

Sunset and evening star,
  And one clear call for me!
And may there be no moaning of the bar,
  When I put out to sea,

But such a tide as moving seems asleep,
  Too full for sound and foam,
When that which drew from out the boundless deep
  Turns again home.

Twilight and evening bell,
  And after that the dark!   10
And may there be no sadness of farewell,
  When I embark;

For tho' from out our bourne of Time and Place
  The flood may bear me far,
I hope to see my Pilot face to face
  When I have crost the bar.

Walt Whitman § 1819–1892

Whitman, an American, was an innovator in poetry whose mark is still felt. His contemporaries found his poetry shocking and "unpoetic," but his work is now universally accepted as a landmark of world literature.

Out of the cradle endlessly rocking

Out of the cradle endlessly rocking,
Out of the mocking-bird's throat, the musical shuttle,
Out of the Ninth-month midnight,

Over the sterile sands and the fields beyond, where the child leaving his
    bed wander'd alone, bareheaded, barefoot,
Down from the shower'd halo,
Up from the mystic play of shadows twining and twisting as if they
    were alive,
Out from the patches of briers and blackberries,
From the memories of the bird that chanted to me,
From your memories sad brother, from the fitful risings and
    fallings I heard,
From under that yellow half-moon late-risen and swollen as if with
    tears,   10
From those beginning notes of yearning and love there in the mist,
From the thousand responses of my heart never to cease,
From the myriad thence-arous'd words,
From the word stronger and more delicious than any,
From such as now they start the scene revisiting,
As a flock, twittering, rising, or overhead passing,
Borne hither, ere all eludes me, hurriedly,
A man, yet by these tears a little boy again,
Throwing myself on the sand, confronting the waves,
I, chanter of pains and joys, uniter of here and hereafter,   20
Taking all hints to use them, but swiftly leaping beyond them,
A reminiscence sing.

Once Paumanok,
When the lilac-scent was in the air and Fifth-month grass was growing,
Up this seashore in some briers,
Two feather'd guests from Alabama, two together,
And their nest, and four light-green eggs spotted with brown,
And every day the he-bird to and fro near at hand,
And every day she-bird crouch'd on her nest, silent, with bright
    eyes,
And every day I, a curious boy, never too close, never disturbing them,   30
Cautiously peering, absorbing, translating.

Shine! shine! shine!
Pour down your warmth, great sun!
While we bask, we two together.

Two together!
Winds blow south, or winds blow north,
Day come white, or night come black,
Home, or rivers and mountains from home,
Singing all time, minding no time,
While we two keep together.   40

Till of a sudden,
May-be kill'd, unknown to her mate,
One forenoon the she-bird crouch'd not on the nest,
Nor return'd that afternoon, nor the next,
Nor ever appear'd again.

And thenceforward all summer in the sound of the sea,
And at night under the full of the moon in calmer weather,
Over the hoarse surging of the sea,
Or flitting from brier to brier by day,
I saw, I heard at intervals the remaining one, the he-bird,   50
The solitary guest from Alabama.

Blow! blow! blow!
Blow up sea-winds along Paumanok's shore;
I wait and I wait till you blow my mate to me.

Yes, when the stars glisten'd,
All night long on the prong of a moss-scallop'd stake,
Down almost amid the slapping waves,
Sat the lone singer wonderful causing tears.

He call'd on his mate,
He pour'd forth the meanings which I of all men know.   60

Yes my brother I know,
The rest might not, but I have treasur'd every note,
For more than once dimly down to the beach gliding,
Silent, avoiding the moonbeams, blending myself with the shadows,
Recalling now the obscure shapes, the echoes, the sounds and sights
        after their sorts,
The white arms out in the breakers tirelessly tossing,
I, with bare feet, a child, the wind wafting my hair,
Listen'd long and long.

Listen'd to keep, to sing, now translating the notes,
Following you my brother.   70

Soothe! soothe! soothe!
Close on its wave soothes the wave behind,
And again another behind embracing and lapping, every one close,
But my love soothes not me, not me.

Low hangs the moon, it rose late,
It is lagging—O I think it is heavy with love, with love.

O madly the sea pushes upon the land,
With love, with love.

O night! do I not see my love fluttering out among the breakers?
What is that little black thing I see there in the white?   80

Loud! loud! loud!
Loud I call to you, my love!
High and clear I shoot my voice over the waves,
Surely you must know who is here, is here,
You must know who I am, my love.

Low-hanging moon!
What is that dusky spot in your brown yellow?
O it is the shape, the shape of my mate!
O moon do not keep her from me any longer.

Land! land! O land!   90
Whichever way I turn, O I think you could give me my mate back
    again if you only would,
For I am almost sure I see her dimly whichever way I look.

O rising stars!
Perhaps the one I want so much will rise, will rise with some of you.

O throat! O trembling throat!
Sound clearer through the atmosphere!
Pierce the woods, the earth,
Somewhere listening to catch you must be the one I want.

Shake out carols!
Solitary here, the night's carols!   100
Carols of lonesome love! death's carols!
Carols under that lagging, yellow, waning moon!
O under that moon where she droops almost down into the sea!
O reckless despairing carols.

But soft! sink low!
Soft! let me just murmur,

And do you wait a moment you husky-nois'd sea,
For somewhere I believe I heard my mate responding to me,
So faint, I must be still, be still to listen,
But not altogether still, for then she might not come
    immediately to me.   110

Hither my love!
Here I am! here!
With this just-sustain'd note I announce myself to you,
This gentle call is for you my love, for you.

Do not be decoy'd elsewhere,
That is the whistle of the wind, it is not my voice,
That is the fluttering, the fluttering of the spray,
Those are the shadows of leaves.

O darkness! O in vain!
O I am very sick and sorrowful.   120

O brown halo in the sky near the moon, drooping upon the sea!
O troubled reflection in the sea!
O throat! O throbbing heart!
And I singing uselessly, uselessly all the night.

O past! O happy life! O songs of joy!
In the air, in the woods, over fields,
Loved! loved! loved! loved! loved!
But my mate no more, no more with me!
We two together no more.

The aria sinking,   130
All else continuing, the stars shining,
The winds blowing, the notes of the bird continuous echoing,
With angry moans the fierce old mother incessantly moaning,
On the sands of Paumanok's shore gray and rustling,
The yellow half-moon enlarged, sagging down, drooping, the face
        of the sea almost touching,
The boy ecstatic, with his bare feet the waves, with his hair the
        atmosphere dallying,
The love in the heart long pent, now loose, now at last
        tumultuously bursting,
The aria's meaning, the ears, the soul, swiftly depositing,
The strange tears down the cheeks coursing,
The colloquy there, the trio, each uttering,   140
The undertone, the savage old mother incessantly crying,
To the boy's soul's questions sullenly timing, some drown'd secret
        hissing,
To the outsetting bard.

Demon or bird! (said the boy's soul,)
Is it indeed toward your mate you sing? or is it really to me?

For I, that was a child, my tongue's use sleeping, now I have heard you,
Now in a moment I know what I am for, I awake,
And already a thousand singers, a thousand songs, clearer, louder and
    more sorrowful than yours,
A thousand warbling echoes have started to life within me, never to
    die.

O you singer solitary, singing by yourself, projecting me,   150
O solitary me listening, never more shall I cease perpetuating you,
Never more shall I escape, never more the reverberations,
Never more the cries of unsatisfied love be absent from me,
Never again leave me to be the peaceful child I was before what
    there in the night,
By the sea under the yellow and sagging moon,
The messenger there arous'd, the fire, the sweet hell within,
The unknown want, the destiny of me.

O give me the clew! (it lurks in the night here somewhere,)
O if I am to have so much, let me have more!

A word then, (for I will conquer it,)   160
The word final, superior to all,
Subtle, sent up—what is it?—I listen;
Are you whispering it, and have been all the time, you sea waves?
Is that it from your liquid rims and wet sands?

Whereto answering, the sea,
Delaying not, hurrying not,
Whisper'd me through the night, and very plainly before daybreak,
Lisp'd to me the low and delicious word death,
And again death, death, death, death,
Hissing melodious, neither like the bird nor like my arous'd
    child's heart,   170
But edging near as privately for me rustling at my feet,
Creeping thence steadily up to my ears and laving me softly all over,
Death, death, death, death, death.

Which I do not forget,
But fuse the song of my dusky demon and brother,
That he sang to me in the moonlight on Paumanok's gray beach,
With the thousand responsive songs at random,
My own songs awaked from that hour,
And with them the key, the word up from the waves,
The word of the sweetest song and all songs,   180
That strong and delicious word which, creeping to my feet,

(Or like some old crone rocking the cradle, swathed in sweet
    garments, bending aside,)
The sea whisper'd me.

Come up from the fields father

Come up from the fields father, here's a letter from our Pete,
And come to the front door mother, here's a letter from thy dear son.

Lo, 'tis autumn,
Lo, where the trees, deeper green, yellower and redder,
Cool and sweeten Ohio's villages with leaves fluttering in the
    moderate wind,
Where apples ripe in the orchards hang and grapes on the trellis'd vines,
(Smell you the smell of the grapes on the vines?
Smell you the buckwheat where the bees were lately buzzing?)

Above all, lo, the sky so calm, so transparent after the rain, and
    with wondrous clouds,
Below too, all calm, all vital and beautiful, and the farm prospers well.   10

Down in the fields all prospers well,
But now from the fields come father, come at the daughter's call,
And come to the entry mother, to the front door come right away.

Fast as she can she hurries, something ominous, her steps trembling,
She does not tarry to smooth her hair nor adjust her cap.

Open the envelope quickly,
O this is not our son's writing, yet his name is sign'd,
O a strange hand writes for our dear son, O stricken mother's soul!
All swims before her eyes, flashes with black, she catches the main
    words only,
Sentences broken, *gunshot wound in the breast, cavalry skirmish,*
    taken to hospital,   20
At present low, but will soon be better.

Ah now the single figure to me,
Amid all teeming and wealthy Ohio with all its cities and farms,
Sickly white in the face and dull in the head, very faint,
By the jamb of a door leans.

Grieve not so, dear mother, (the just-grown daughter speaks
    through her sobs,

The little sisters huddle around speechless and dismay'd,)
See, dearest mother, the letter says Pete will soon be better.

Alas poor boy, he will never be better, (nor may-be needs to be
   better, that brave and simple soul,)
While they stand at home at the door he is dead already,   **30**
The only son is dead.

But the mother needs to be better,
She with thin form presently drest in black,
By day her meals untouch'd, then at night fitfully sleeping, often
   waking,
In the midnight waking, weeping, longing with one deep longing,
O that she might withdraw unnoticed, silent from life escape and with-
   draw,
To follow, to seek, to be with her dear dead son.

Matthew Arnold § 1822–1888

*Arnold was first a poet and then a distinguished critic of literature
and society. "Dover Beach" dramatizes conflicts he found present
in his own society.*

Dover Beach

The sea is calm to-night,
The tide is full, the moon lies fair
Upon the straits;—on the French coast, the light
Gleams, and is gone; the cliffs of England stand,
Glimmering and vast, out in the tranquil bay.
Come to the window, sweet is the night-air!
Only, from the long line of spray
Where the sea meets the moon-blanch'd land,
Listen! you hear the grating roar
Of pebbles which the waves draw back, and fling,   **10**
At their return, up the high strand,
Begin, and cease, and then again begin,
With tremulous cadence slow, and bring
The eternal note of sadness in.

Sophocles long ago
Heard it on the Aegean, and it brought

Into his mind the turbid ebb and flow
Of human misery; we
Find also in the sound a thought,
Hearing it by this distant northern sea.   20

The Sea of Faith
Was once, too, at the full, and round earth's shore
Lay like the folds of a bright girdle furled.
But now I only hear
Its melancholy, long, withdrawing roar,
Retreating, to the breath
Of the night-wind, down the vast edges drear
And naked shingles of the world.

Ah, love, let us be true
To one another! for the world, which seems   30
To lie before us like a land of dreams,
So various, so beautiful, so new,
Hath really neither joy, nor love, nor light,
Nor certitude, nor peace, nor help for pain;
And we are here as on a darkling plain
Swept with confused alarms of struggle and flight,
Where ignorant armies clash by night.

§ FOR COMMENT

What is the dramatic situation here: Who is speaking, to whom, and under
what circumstances? Throughout most of the poem, Arnold works with sea
imagery, but at the last of the poem, he shifts to an image of a battlefield. Is
this shift a blemish or a strength in the poem? What examples of onomatopoeia or onomatopoeic effects do you find in the poem?

Emily Dickinson § 1830–1886

*Although she had only two of her poems published in her lifetime,
Emily Dickinson gained posthumous recognition during the twentieth century. She was the daughter of a clergyman in Amherst,
Massachusetts, and her poems show strikingly original adaptations
of the rhythms of church hymns.*

I taste a liquor never brewed

I taste a liquor never brewed—
From Tankards scooped in Pearl—
Not all the Frankfort Berries
Yield such an Alcohol!

Inebriate of Air—am I—
And Debauchee of Dew—
Reeling—thro endless summer days—
From inns of Molten Blue—

When "Landlords" turn the drunken Bee
Out of the Foxglove's door—   10
When Butterflies—renounce their "drams"—
I shall but drink the more!

Till Seraphs swing their snowy Hats—
And Saints—to windows run—
To see the little Tippler
From Manzanilla come!

I felt a Funeral, in my Brain

I felt a Funeral, in my Brain,
And Mourners to and fro
Kept treading—treading—till it seemed
That Sense was breaking through—

And when they all were seated,
A Service, like a Drum—
Kept beating—beating—till I thought
My Mind was going numb—

And then I heard them lift a Box
And creak across my Soul   10
With those same Boots of Lead, again,
Then Space—began to toll,

As all the Heavens were a Bell,
And Being, but an Ear,
And I, and Silence, some strange Race
Wrecked, solitary, here—

And then a Plank in Reason, broke,
And I dropped down, and down—
And hit a World, at every plunge,
And Finished knowing—then—   20

A Bird came down the Walk

A Bird came down the Walk—
He did not know I saw—
He bit an Angleworm in halves
And ate the fellow, raw,

And then he drank a Dew
From a convenient Grass—
And then hopped sidewise to the Wall
To let a Beetle pass—

He glanced with rapid eyes
That hurried all around—   10
They looked like frightened Beads, I thought—
He stirred his Velvet Head

Like one in danger, Cautious,
I offered him a Crumb
And he unrolled his feathers
And rowed him softer home—

Than Oars divide the Ocean,
Too silver for a seam—
Or Butterflies, off Banks of Noon
Leap, plashless as they swim.   20

I heard a Fly buzz—when I died

I heard a Fly buzz—when I died—
The Stillness in the Room
Was like the Stillness in the Air—
Between the Heaves of Storm—

The Eyes around—had wrung them dry—
And Breaths were gathering firm
For that last Onset—when the King
Be witnessed—in the Room—

I willed my Keepsakes—Signed away
What portion of me be   10
Assignable—and then it was
There interposed a Fly—

With Blue—uncertain stumbling Buzz—
Between the light—and me—
And then the Windows failed—and then
I could not see to see—

§ FOR COMMENT

What paradox or incongruity is involved in the situation of the poem's speaker? What is gained by describing the mourning family as "Eyes" and "Breaths"? Who is the King of line 7? Why is "interposed" better than "entered" or "intervened" to describe the action of the fly? The only true rhyme in the poem is in the last stanza ("me"–"see"). Is the use of imperfect rhyme ("Room"–"Storm," "firm"–"Room," "be"–"Fly") elsewhere a blemish or a virtue? If a virtue, what does such imperfect rhyme contribute? Does the use of unconventional punctuation and sharp interruption in the lines serve any structural purpose?

Because I could not stop for Death

Because I could not stop for Death—
He kindly stopped for me—
The Carriage held but just Ourselves—
And Immortality.

We slowly drove—He knew no haste
And I had put away
My labor and my leisure too,
For His Civility—

We passed the School, where Children strove
At Recess—in the Ring—   10
We passed the Fields of Gazing Grain—
We passed the Setting Sun—

Or rather—He passed Us—
The Dews drew quivering and chill—

For only Gossamer, my Gown—
My Tippet—only Tulle—

We paused before a House that seemed
A Swelling of the Ground—
The Roof was scarcely visible—
The Cornice—in the Ground—   20

Since then—'tis Centuries—and yet
Feels shorter than the Day
I first surmised the Horses Heads
Were toward Eternity—

Lewis Carroll § 1832–1898

*Lewis Carroll was the pen-name of Charles Lutwidge Dodgson, a
shy English mathematician. His fantasies,* Alice in Wonderland
and Through the Looking Glass, *both contain many poems, most
of which take a sly dig at the work of other poets.*

Jabberwocky

'Twas brillig, and the slithy toves
    Did gyre and gimble in the wabe:
All mimsy were the borogoves,
    And the mome raths outgrabe.

"Beware the Jabberwock, my son!
    The jaws that bite, the claws that catch!
Beware the Jubjub bird, and shun
    The frumious Bandersnatch!"

He took his vorpal sword in hand;
    Long time the manxome foe he sought—   10
So rested he by the Tumtum tree,
    And stood awhile in thought.

And, as in uffish thought he stood,
    The Jabberwock, with eyes of flame,
Came whiffling through the tulgey wood,
    And burbled as it came!

One, two! One, two! And through and through
　　The vorpal blade went snicker-snack!
He left it dead, and with its head
　　He went galumphing back.　　　　　　　　　　　20

"And hast thou slain the Jabberwock?
　　Come to my arms, my beamish boy!
O frabjous day! Callooh, Callay!"
　　He chortled in his joy.

'Twas brillig, and the slithy toves
　　Did gyre and gimble in the wabe:
All mimsy were the borogoves,
　　And the mome raths outgrabe.

"You are old, father William"

"You are old, father William," the young man said,
　　"And your hair has become very white;
And yet you incessantly stand on your head—
　　Do you think, at your age, it is right?"

"In my youth," father William replied to his son,
　　"I feared it might injure the brain;
But now that I'm perfectly sure I have none,
　　Why, I do it again and again."

"You are old," said the youth, "as I mentioned before,
　　And have grown most uncommonly fat;　　　　　　10
Yet you turned a back-somersault in at the door—
　　Pray, what is the reason of that?"

"In my youth," said the sage, as he shook his grey locks,
　　"I kept all my limbs very supple
By the use of this ointment—one shilling the box—
　　Allow me to sell you a couple."

"You are old," said the youth, "and your jaws are too weak
　　For anything tougher than suet;
Yet you finished the goose, with the bones and the beak—
　　Pray, how did you manage to do it?"　　　　　　　20

"In my youth," said his father, "I took to the law,
　　And argued each case with my wife;

And the muscular strength, which it gave to my jaw,
   Has lasted the rest of my life."

"You are old," said the youth; "one would hardly suppose
   That your eye was as steady as ever;
Yet you balanced an eel on the end of your nose—
   What made you so awfully clever?"

"I have answered three questions, and that is enough,"
   Said his father; "don't give yourself airs!   30
Do you think I can listen all day to such stuff?
   Be off, or I'll kick you downstairs!"

Gerard Manley Hopkins § 1844–1889

*A convert from the Church of England to Roman Catholicism,
Hopkins became a Jesuit priest. His poems were known to a few
friends during his lifetime, but finally were published in 1918.
Because his poetry is so innovative rhythmically and linguistically,
he is often considered a forerunner of modern poetry.*

God's Grandeur

The world is charged with the grandeur of God.
It will flame out, like shining from shook foil;
It gathers to a greatness, like the ooze of oil
Crushed. Why do men then now not reck his rod?
Generations have trod, have trod, have trod;
And all is seared with trade; bleared, smeared with toil;
And wears man's smudge and shares man's smell: the soil
Is bare now, nor can foot feel, being shod.
And for all this, nature is never spent;
There lives the dearest freshness deep down things;   10
And though the last lights off the black West went
Oh, morning, at the brown brink eastward, springs—
Because the Holy Ghost over the bent
World broods with warm breast and with ah! bright wings.

§ FOR COMMENT

Hopkins begins the poem with a general statement. Do the details which follow illustrate the statement or limit it? Hopkins was very precise in choosing the particular word he wanted. Why is "shod" in line 8 a strikingly good word to modify "foot"? Why is "bent" in line 13 a good adjective to modify "world"? Hopkins is very daring in his use of alliteration and assonance. Cite examples of his use of these devices in this poem that contribute to its success.

Spring

Nothing is so beautiful as spring—
When weeds, in wheels, shoot long and lovely and lush;
Thrush's eggs look little low heavens, and thrush
Through the echoing timber does so rinse and wring
The ear, it strikes like lightnings to hear him sing;
The glassy peartree leaves and blooms, they brush
The descending blue; that blue is all in a rush
With richness; the racing lambs too have fair their fling.
What is all this juice and all this joy?
A strain of the earth's sweet being in the beginning   10
In Eden garden.—Have, get, before it cloy,
Before it cloud, Christ, lord, and sour with sinning,
Innocent mind and Mayday in girl and boy,
Most, O maid's child, thy choice and worthy the winning.

Pied Beauty

Glory be to God for dappled things—
　For skies of couple-colour as a brinded cow;
　　For rose-moles all in stipple upon trout that swim;
Fresh-firecoal chestnut-falls; finches' wings;
　Landscape plotted and pieced—fold, fallow, and plough;
　　And áll trádes, their gear and tackle and trim.

All things counter, original, spare, strange;
　Whatever is fickle, freckled (who knows how?)
　　With swift, slow; sweet, sour; adazzle, dim;
He fathers-forth whose beauty is past change: 10
　　　　Praise him.

1. 2. *brinded:* Brindled.

Spring and Fall: to a young child

Márgarét, are you gríeving
Over Goldengrove unleaving?
Leáves, líke the things of man, you
With your fresh thoughts care for, can you?
Áh! ás the heart grows older
It will come to such sights colder
By and by, nor spare a sigh
Though worlds of wanwood leafmeal lie;
And yet you wíll weep and know why.
Now no matter, child, the name: 10
Sórrow's spríngs áre the same.
Nor mouth had, no nor mind, expressed
What heart heard of, ghost guessed:
It ís the blight man was born for,
It is Margaret you mourn for.

A. E. Housman § 1859–1936

*A professor of Latin at London and then Cambridge, Housman
also produced and reluctantly published a small quantity of lyric
verse. His poetry is remarkably consistent in its tone and quality.*

When I was one-and-twenty

When I was one-and-twenty
  I heard a wise man say,
'Give crowns and pounds and guineas
  But not your heart away;
Give pearls away and rubies
  But keep your fancy free.'
But I was one-and-twenty,
  No use to talk to me.

When I was one-and-twenty
  I heard him say again,   10
'The heart out of the bosom
  Was never given in vain;

l. 8. *wanwood*: Pale wood. *leafmeal*: Leaf by leaf.
l. 13. *ghost*: Spirit.

'Tis paid with sighs a plenty
    And sold for endless rue.'
And I am two-and-twenty,
    And oh, 'tis true, 'tis true.

"Terence, this is stupid stuff"

"Terence, this is stupid stuff:
You eat your victuals fast enough;
There can't be much amiss, 'tis clear,
To see the rate you drink your beer.
But oh, good Lord, the verse you make,
It gives a chap the belly-ache.
The cow, the old cow, she is dead;
It sleeps well, the horned head:
We poor lads, 'tis our turn now
To hear such tunes as killed the cow.   10
Pretty friendship 'tis to rhyme
Your friends to death before their time
Moping melancholy mad:
Come, pipe a tune to dance to, lad."

Why, if 'tis dancing you would be,
There's brisker pipes than poetry.
Say, for what were hop-yards meant,
Or why was Burton built on Trent?
Oh many a peer of England brews
Livelier liquor than the Muse,   20
And malt does more than Milton can
To justify God's ways to man.
Ale, man, ale's the stuff to drink
For fellows whom it hurts to think:
Look into the pewter pot
To see the world as the world's not.
And faith, 'tis pleasant till 'tis past:
The mischief is that 'twill not last.
Oh I have been to Ludlow fair
And left my necktie God knows where,   30
And carried half-way home, or near,
Pints and quarts of Ludlow beer:
Then the world seemed none so bad,
And I myself a sterling lad;
And down in lovely muck I've lain,
Happy till I woke again.

Then I saw the morning sky:
Heigho, the tale was all a lie;
The world, it was the old world yet,
I was I, my things were wet,   40
And nothing now remained to do
But begin the game anew.

    Therefore, since the world has still
Much good, but much less good than ill,
And while the sun and moon endure
Luck's a chance, but trouble's sure,
I'd face it as a wise man would,
And train for ill and not for good.
'Tis true the stuff I bring for sale
Is not so brisk a brew as ale: 50
Out of a stem that scored the hand
I wrung it in a weary land.
But take it: if the smack is sour,
The better for the embittered hour;
It should do good to heart and head
When your soul is in my soul's stead;
And I will friend you, if I may,
In the dark and cloudy day.

    There was a king reigned in the East:
There, when kings will sit to feast,   60
They get their fill before they think
With poisoned meat and poisoned drink.
He gathered all that springs to birth
From the many-venomed earth;
First a little, thence to more,
He sampled all her killing store;
And easy, smiling, seasoned sound,
Sate the king when healths went round.
They put arsenic in his meat
And stared aghast to watch him eat;   70
They poured strychnine in his cup
And shook to see him drink it up:
They shook, they stared as white's their shirt:
Them it was their poison hurt.
—I tell the tale that I heard told.
Mithridates, he died old.

Epitaph on an Army of Mercenaries

These, in the day when heaven was falling,
　The hour when earth's foundations fled,
Followed their mercenary calling
　And took their wages and are dead.

Their shoulders held the sky suspended;
　They stood, and earth's foundations stay;
What God abandoned, these defended,
　And saved the sum of things for pay.

✿ Modern Poetry

About 1914, along with the new movements in painting, sculpture, and music, a new style in poetry began to emerge. The pioneers in the first phase of this new poetry were Ezra Pound, T. S. Eliot, and William Butler Yeats, and, though he had written much earlier, Gerard Manley Hopkins, whose poems were first generally published in 1918. Just as Wordsworth and Coleridge reacted against the tradition represented by Dryden, Pope, and Goldsmith, so these poets wrote in a manner unlike Wordsworth, Keats, and Tennyson, and attempted to establish a new style, sometimes called "Modernist" or "Post-Romantic."

Perhaps the most important thing to remember about this poetry is that it reacts against Romanticism. Instead of being greatly interested in landscape nature, writers like Eliot have chosen the modern city as their setting. Rather than concentrating primarily on the Beautiful, as did Keats, they have sought to deal with all areas of life, both beautiful and ugly. To readers used to the Romantic idea that poems are only about beautiful things, it will often seem that modern poets write only about ugly things, but a careful examination will show this charge is unfounded. They have sought, too, to avoid the pretentious and the fancy and keep their language close to what people speak in the twentieth century. Instead of being fascinated with the ordinary man living close to nature, the modern poet has been more interested in the unusual man, whether the heroic man as Yeats is or the neurotic man as Eliot is in "The Love Song of J. Alfred Prufrock."

This new poetic style, employed by Eliot, Pound, and Yeats, did not gain immediate acceptance, but by the mid-1930s had clearly displaced the older, moribund Romantic-Victorian idiom. It is, of course, far too soon to predict with any accuracy what will be the dominant style of English and American poetry during the remainder of the twentieth century, but two main tendencies have emerged: the highly formal, finished verse like Robert Lowell's early work and the verse of Theodore Spencer and Richard Wilbur; and the more experimental work of poets like Ferlinghetti and Brother Antoninus.

William Butler Yeats § 1865–1939

Poet and playwright and the leader of the Irish Renaissance, Yeats was called "the greatest poet of the twentieth century" by T. S. Eliot. It is hard to dispute Eliot's judgment; Yeats was not only a fine lyricist, but he successfully dramatized the great subjects of poetry—birth, love, war, death.

No Second Troy

Why should I blame her that she filled my days
With misery, or that she would of late
Have taught to ignorant men most violent ways,
Or hurled the little streets upon the great,
Had they but courage equal to desire?
What could have made her peaceful with a mind
That nobleness made simple as a fire,
With beauty like a tightened bow, a kind
That is not natural in an age like this,
Being high and solitary and most stern?   10
Why, what could she have done, being what she is?
Was there another Troy for her to burn?

The Mask

'Put off that mask of burning gold
With emerald eyes '
'O no, my dear, you make so bold
To find if hearts be wild and wise,
And yet not cold.'

'I would but find what's there to find,
Love or deceit.'
'It was the mask engaged your mind,
And after set your heart to beat,
Not what's behind.'   10

'But lest you are my enemy,
I must enquire.'
'O no, my dear, let all that be;
What matter, so there is but fire
In you, in me?'

The Magi

Now as at all times I can see in the mind's eye,
In their stiff, painted clothes, the pale unsatisfied ones
Appear and disappear in the blue depth of the sky
With all their ancient faces like rain-beaten stones,
And all their helms of silver hovering side by side,
And all their eyes still fixed, hoping to find once more,
Being by Calvary's turbulence unsatisfied,
The uncontrollable mystery on the bestial floor.

The Wild Swans at Coole

The trees are in their autumn beauty,
The woodland paths are dry,
Under the October twilight the water
Mirrors a still sky;
Upon the brimming water among the stones
Are nine-and-fifty swans.

The nineteenth autumn has come upon me
Since I first made my count;
I saw, before I had well finished,
All suddenly mount   10
And scatter wheeling in great broken rings
Upon their clamorous wings.

I have looked upon those brilliant creatures,
And now my heart is sore.
All's changed since I, hearing at twilight,
The first time on this shore,
The bell-beat of their wings above my head,
Trod with a lighter tread.

Unwearied still, lover by lover,
They paddle in the cold   20
Companionable streams or climb the air;
Their hearts have not grown old;
Passion or conquest, wander where they will,
Attend upon them still.

But now they drift on the still water,
Mysterious, beautiful;
Among what rushes will they build,

By what lake's edge or pool
Delight men's eyes when I awake some day
To find they have flown away?   30

The Second Coming

Turning and turning in the widening gyre
The falcon cannot hear the falconer;
Things fall apart; the centre cannot hold;
Mere anarchy is loosed upon the world,
The blood-dimmed tide is loosed, and everywhere
The ceremony of innocence is drowned;
The best lack all conviction, while the worst
Are full of passionate intensity.

Surely some revelation is at hand;
Surely the Second Coming is at hand.   10
The Second Coming! Hardly are those words out
When a vast image out of *Spiritus Mundi*
Troubles my sight: somewhere in sands of the desert
A shape with lion body and the head of a man,
A gaze blank and pitiless as the sun,
Is moving its slow thighs, while all about it
Reel shadows of the indignant desert birds.
The darkness drops again; but now I know
That twenty centuries of stony sleep
Were vexed to nightmare by a rocking cradle,   20
And what rough beast, its hour come round at last,
Slouches towards Bethlehem to be born?

§ FOR COMMENT

Though Yeats believed in a cyclical theory of history and worked out most
of the details of his theory in *A Vision*, his best poems can be understood
on their own terms and without reference to his own esoteric ideas. What
is the precise image of the first two lines? Why is Yeats' choice of "mere"
vastly better than "sheer"? Is the remainder of the first section a general
statement illustrating or interpreting this image? The "Second Coming" of
line 10 would seem to be a reference to the return of Christ to earth. Is it?
Spiritus Mundi means "spirit of the universe," a kind of reservoir of ar-
chetypal forms in which Yeats believed as the source of images which appear to man in dreams. The "shape with lion body and the head of a man"
strongly suggests the sphinx. Why is such an embodiment appropriate for

the conditions described in the first section? What is the connection between the image of the desert birds (line 17) and the falcon (lines 1–2)?
Will the second coming be of Christ or of the "rough Beast"? Does Yeats'
use of Christian material in this poem make it an exposition or dramatization of Christian concepts?

Sailing to Byzantium

That is no country for old men. The young
In one another's arms, birds in the trees
—Those dying generations—at their song,
The salmon-falls, the mackerel-crowded seas,
Fish, flesh, or fowl, commend all summer long
Whatever is begotten, born, and dies.
Caught in that sensual music all neglect
Monuments of unaging intellect.

An aged man is but a paltry thing,
A tattered coat upon a stick, unless   10
Soul clap its hands and sing, and louder sing
For every tatter in its mortal dress,
Nor is there singing school but studying
Monuments of its own magnificence;
And therefore I have sailed the seas and come
To the holy city of Byzantium.

O sages standing in God's holy fire
As in the gold mosaic of a wall,
Come from the holy fire, perne in a gyre,
And be the singing-masters of my soul.   20
Consume my heart away; sick with desire
And fastened to a dying animal
It knows not what it is; and gather me
Into the artifice of eternity.

Once out of nature I shall never take
My bodily form from any natural thing,
But such a form as Grecian goldsmiths make
Of hammered gold and gold enamelling
To keep a drowsy Emperor awake;
Or set upon a golden bough to sing   30
To lords and ladies of Byzantium
Of what is past, or passing, or to come.

Leda and the Swan

A sudden blow: the great wings beating still
Above the staggering girl, her thighs caressed
By the dark webs, her nape caught in his bill,
He holds her helpless breast upon his breast.

How can those terrified vague fingers push
The feathered glory from her loosening thighs?
And how can body, laid in that white rush,
But feel the strange heart beating where it lies?

A shudder in the loins engenders there
The broken wall, the burning roof and tower   10
And Agamemnon dead.
                    Being so caught up,
So mastered by the brute blood of the air,
Did she put on his knowledge with his power
Before the indifferent beak could let her drop?

Wallace Stevens § 1870–1955

Stevens was a lawyer and insurance-company executive, although poetry was as important a vocation to him, to which his many volumes of verse testify.

Peter Quince at the Clavier

I

Just as my fingers on these keys
Make music, so the self-same sounds
On my spirit make a music too.

Music is feeling, then, not sound;
And thus it is that what I feel,
Here in this room, desiring you,

Thinking of your blue-shadowed silk,
Is music. It is like the strain
Waked in the elders by Susanna:

Of a green evening, clear and warm,   10
She bathed in her still garden, while
The red-eyed elders, watching, felt

The basses of their being throb
In witching chords, and their thin blood
Pulse pizzicati of Hosanna.

II

In the green water, clear and warm,
Susanna lay.
She searched
The touch of springs,
And found   20
Concealed imaginings.
She sighed
For so much melody.

Upon the bank she stood
In the cool
Of spent emotions.
She felt, among the leaves,
The dew
Of old devotions.

She walked upon the grass,   30
Still quavering.
The winds were like her maids,
On timid feet,
Fetching her woven scarves,
Yet wavering.

A breath upon her hand
Muted the night.
She turned—
A cymbal crashed,
And roaring horns.   40

III

Soon, with a noise like tambourines,
Came her attendant Byzantines.

They wondered why Susanna cried
Against the elders by her side:

And as they whispered, the refrain
Was like a willow swept by rain.

Anon their lamps' uplifted flame
Revealed Susanna and her shame.

And then the simpering Byzantines
Fled, with a noise like tambourines.   50

IV

Beauty is momentary in the mind—
The fitful tracing of a portal;
But in the flesh it is immortal.
The body dies; the body's beauty lives.
So evenings die, in their green going,
A wave, interminably flowing.

So gardens die, their meek breath scenting
The cowl of Winter, done repenting.
So maidens die to the auroral
Celebration of a maiden's choral.   60

Susanna's music touched the bawdy strings
Of those white elders; but, escaping,
Left only Death's ironic scraping.
Now, in its immortality, it plays
On the clear viol of her memory,
And makes a constant sacrament of praise.

The Emperor of Ice-Cream

Call the roller of big cigars,
The muscular one, and bid him whip
In kitchen cups concupiscent curds.
Let the wenches dawdle in such dress
As they are used to wear, and let the boys
Bring flowers in last month's newspapers.
Let be be finale of seem.
The only emperor is the emperor of ice-cream.

Take from the dresser of deal,
Lacking the three glass knobs, that sheet   10
On which she embroidered fantails once

And spread it so as to cover her face.
If her horny feet protrude, they come
To show how cold she is, and dumb.
Let the lamp affix its beam.
The only emperor is the emperor of ice-cream.

Anecdote of the Jar

I placed a jar in Tennessee,
And round it was, upon a hill.
It made the slovenly wilderness
Surround that hill.

The wilderness rose up to it,
And sprawled around, no longer wild.
The jar was round upon the ground
And tall and of a port in air.

It took dominion everywhere.
The jar was gray and bare.   10
It did not give of bird or bush,
Like nothing else in Tennessee.

Bantams in Pine-Woods

Chieftain Iffucan of Azcan in caftan
Of tan with henna hackles, halt!

Damned universal cock, as if the sun
Was blackamoor to bear your blazing tail.

Fat! Fat! Fat! Fat! I am the personal.
Your world is you. I am my world.

You ten-foot poet among inchlings. Fat!
Begone! An inchling bristles in these pines,

Bristles, and points their Appalachian tangs,
And fears not portly Azcan nor his hoos.   10

Robert Frost § 1874–1963

*Frost was born in California, though he lived most of his life in
New England and wrote most of his poems about that region. He
is considered by many the finest American poet of the twentieth
century.*

After Apple-Picking

My long two-pointed ladder's sticking through a tree
Toward heaven still,
And there's a barrel that I didn't fill
Beside it, and there may be two or three
Apples I didn't pick upon some bough.
But I am done with apple-picking now.
Essence of winter sleep is on the night,
The scent of apples: I am drowsing off.
I cannot rub the strangeness from my sight
I got from looking through a pane of glass   10
I skimmed this morning from the drinking trough
And held against the world of hoary grass.
It melted, and I let it fall and break.
But I was well
Upon my way to sleep before it fell,
And I could tell
What form my dreaming was about to take.
Magnified apples appear and disappear
Stem end and blossom end,
And every fleck of russet showing clear.   20
My instep arch not only keeps the ache,
It keeps the pressure of a ladder-round.
I feel the ladder sway as the boughs bend.
And I keep hearing from the cellar bin
The rumbling sound
Of load on load of apples coming in.
For I have had too much
Of apple-picking: I am overtired
Of the great harvest I myself desired.
There were ten thousand thousand fruit to touch,   30
Cherish in hand, lift down, and not let fall.
For all
That struck the earth,

No matter if not bruised or spiked with stubble,
Went surely to the cider-apple heap
As of no worth.
One can see what will trouble
This sleep of mine, whatever sleep it is.
Were he not gone,
The woodchuck could say whether it's like his   40
Long sleep, as I describe its coming on,
Or just some human sleep.

The Road Not Taken

Two roads diverged in a yellow wood,
And sorry I could not travel both
And be one traveler, long I stood
And looked down one as far as I could
To where it bent in the undergrowth;

Then took the other, as just as fair,
And having perhaps the better claim,
Because it was grassy and wanted wear;
Though as for that the passing there
Had worn them really about the same,   10

And both that morning equally lay
In leaves no step had trodden black.
Oh, I kept the first for another day!
Yet knowing how way leads on to way,
I doubted if I should ever come back.

I shall be telling this with a sigh
Somewhere ages and ages hence:
Two roads diverged in a wood, and I—
I took the one less traveled by,
And that has made all the difference.   20

Stopping by Woods on a Snowy Evening

Whose woods these are I think I know
His house is in the village though;
He will not see me stopping here
To watch his woods fill up with snow.

My little horse must think it queer
To stop without a farmhouse near
Between the woods and frozen lake
The darkest evening of the year.

He gives his harness bells a shake
To ask if there is some mistake.   10
The only other sound's the sweep
Of easy wind and downy flake.

The woods are lovely, dark and deep
But I have promises to keep,
And miles to go before I sleep,
And miles to go before I sleep.

Departmental

An ant on the table cloth
Ran into a dormant moth
Of many times his size.
He showed not the least surprise,
His business wasn't with such.
He gave it scarcely a touch,
And was off on his duty run.
Yet if he encountered one
Of the hive's enquiry squad
Whose work is to find out God   10
And the nature of time and space,
He would put him onto the case.
Ants are a curious race;
One crossing with hurried tread
The body of one of their dead
Isn't given a moment's arrest—
Seems not even impressed.
But he no doubt reports to any
With whom he crosses antennae,
And they no doubt report   20
To the higher up at court.
Then word goes forth in Formic:
'Death's come to Jerry McCormic,
Our selfless forager Jerry.
Will the special Janizary
Whose office it is to bury

The dead of the commissary
Go bring him home to his people.
Lay him in state on a sepal.
Wrap him for shroud in a petal.   30
Embalm him with ichor of nettle.
This is the word of your Queen.'
And presently on the scene
Appears a solemn mortician;
And taking formal position
With feelers calmly atwiddle,
Seizes the dead by the middle,
And heaving him high in air,
Carries him out of there.
No one stands round to stare.   40
It is nobody else's affair.

It couldn't be called ungentle.
But how thoroughly departmental.

Design

I found a dimpled spider, fat and white,
On a white heal-all, holding up a moth
Like a white piece of rigid satin cloth—
Assorted characters of death and blight
Mixed ready to begin the morning right,
Like the ingredients of a witches' broth—
A snow-drop spider, a flower like froth,
And dead wings carried like a paper kite.

What had that flower to do with being white,
The wayside blue and innocent heal-all?   10
What brought the kindred spider to that height,
Then steered the white moth thither in the night?
What but design of darkness to appall?—
If design govern in a thing so small.

The Most of It

He thought he kept the universe alone;
For all the voice in answer he could wake
Was but the mocking echo of his own
From some tree-hidden cliff across the lake.

Some morning from the boulder-broken beach
He would cry out on life, that what it wants
Is not its own love back in copy speech,
But counter-love, original response.
And nothing ever came of what he cried
Unless it was the embodiment that crashed   10
In the cliff's talus on the other side,
And then in the far distant water splashed,
But after a time allowed for it to swim,
Instead of proving human when it neared
And someone else additional to him,
As a great buck it powerfully appeared,
Pushing the crumpled water up ahead,
And landed pouring like a waterfall,
And stumbled through the rocks with horny tread,
And forced the underbrush—and that was all.   20

Ezra Pound § 1885–

*Pound has achieved fame as a poet, literary critic, and editor. He
has been one of the most influential of modern literary men, but
has also been interested in older literatures, too, as his "Ballad of
the Goodly Fere" and "Ancient Music" both show.*

Ancient Music

Winter is icummen in,
Lhude sing Goddamm,
Raineth drop and staineth slop,
And how the wind doth ramm!
        Sing: Goddamm.
Skiddeth bus and sloppeth us,
An ague hath my ham.
Freezeth river, turneth liver,
        Damn you, sing: Goddamm.
Goddamm, Goddamm, 'tis why I am, Goddamm,   10
        So 'gainst the winter's balm.
Sing goddamm, damm, sing Goddamm,
Sing goddamm, sing goddamm, DAMM.

Ballad of the Goodly Fere

Simon Zelotes Speaketh It Somewhile after the Crucifixion

Ha' we lost the goodliest fere o' all
For the priests and the gallows tree?
Aye lover he was of brawny men,
O' ships and the open sea.

When they came wi' a host to take Our Man
His smile was good to see,
'First let these go!' qou' our Goodly Fere,
'Or I'll see ye damned,' says he.

Aye he sent us out through the crossed high spears
And the scorn of his laugh rang free,   10
'Why took ye not me when I walked about
Alone in the town?' says he.

Oh we drunk his 'Hale' in the good red wine
When we last made company,
No capon priest was the Goodly Fere
But a man o' men was he.

I ha' seen him drive a hundred men
Wi' a bundle o' cords swung free,
That they took the high and holy house
For their pawn and treasury.   20

They'll no' get him a' in a book I think
Though they write it cunningly;
No mouse of the scrolls was the Goodly Fere
But aye loved the open sea.

If they think they ha' snared our Goodly Fere
They are fools to the last degree.
'I'll go to the feast,' quo' our Goodly Fere,
'Though I go to the gallows tree.'

'Ye ha' seen me heal the lame and blind,
And wake the dead,' says he,   30
'Ye shall see one thing to master all:
'Tis how a brave man dies on the tree.'

A son of God was the Goodly Fere
That bade us his brothers be.

I ha' seen him cow a thousand men.
I have seen him upon the tree.

He cried no cry when they drave the nails
And the blood gushed hot and free,
The hounds of the crimson sky gave tongue
But never a cry cried he.   40

I ha' seen him cow a thousand men
On the hills o' Galilee,
They whined as he walked out calm between,
Wi' his eyes like the grey o' the sea,

Like the sea that brooks no voyaging
With the winds unleashed and free,
Like the sea that he cowed at Genseret
Wi' twey words spoke' suddently.

A master of men was the Goodly Fere,
A mate of the wind and sea,   50
If they think they ha' slain our Goodly Fere
They are fools eternally.

I ha' seen him cat o' the honey-comb
Sin' they nailed him to the tree.

John Crowe Ransom § 1888

*Poet, teacher, and literary critic, Ransom was a leader in the
"Fugitive" group at Vanderbilt University in the 1920's. Ransom's
poetic production has been relatively small, but the quality of it
is consistently high.*

Here Lies a Lady

Here lies a lady of beauty and high degree.
Of chills and fever she died, of fever and chills,
The delight of her husband, her aunt, an infant of three,
And of medicos marveling sweetly on her ills.

For either she burned, and her confident eyes would blaze,
And her fingers fly in a manner to puzzle their heads

What was she making? Why, nothing; she sat in a maze
Of old scraps of laces, snipped into curious shreds—

Or this would pass, and the light of her fire decline
Till she lay discouraged and cold, like a thin stalk white and
    blown,   10
And would not open her eyes, to kisses, to wine;
The sixth of these states was her last; the cold settled down.

Sweet ladies, long may ye bloom, and toughly I hope ye may
    thole,
But was she not lucky? In flowers and lace and mourning,
In love and great honor we bade God rest her soul
After six little spaces of chill, and six of burning.

Philomela

Procne, Philomela, and Itylus,
Your names are liquid, your improbable tale
Is recited in the classic numbers of the nightingale.
Ah, but our numbers are not felicitous,
It goes not liquidly for us.

Perched on a Roman ilex, and duly apostrophized,
The nightingale descanted unto Ovid;
She has even appeared to the Teutons, the swilled and gravid;
At Fontainebleau it may be the bird was gallicized;
Never was she baptized.   10

To England came Philomela with her pain,
Fleeing the hawk her husband; querulous ghost,
She wanders when he sits heavy on his roost,
Utters herself in the original again,
The untranslatable refrain.

Not to these shores she came! this other Thrace,
Environ barbarous to the royal Attic;
How could her delicate dirge run democratic,
Delivered in a cloudless boundless public place
To an inordinate race?   20

I pernoctated with the Oxford students once,
And in the quadrangles, in the cloisters, on the Cher,
Precociously knocked at antique doors ajar,

Fatuously touched the hems of the hierophants,
Sick of my dissonance.

I went out to Bagley Wood, I climbed the hill;
Even the moon had slanted off in a twinkling,
I heard the sepulchral owl and a few bells tinkling,
There was no more villainous day to unfulfil,
The diuturnity was still.   30

Up from the darkest wood where Philomela sat,
Her fairy numbers issued. What then ailed me?
My ears are called capacious but they failed me,
Her classics registered a little flat!
I rose, and venomously spat.

Philomela, Philomela, lover of song,
I am in despair if we may make us worthy,
A bantering breed sophistical and swarthy;
Unto more beautiful, persistently more young,
Thy fabulous provinces belong.   40

§ FOR COMMENT[1]

The best approach to this somewhat unusual poem is to begin with the classical myth of Philomela. Philomela, going to visit her sister Procne, was raped by her sister's husband, Tereus, who then silenced her by cutting out her tongue and imprisoning her in a lonely place. She, however, wove into a piece of tapestry the story of her sufferings and thus communicated them to her sister, who found her prison and released her. Together they took revenge on Tereus by serving him his son Itylus as a feast and then revealing to him what they had done. As he was about to stab them both, he was changed into a hawk, Procne into a swallow, and Philomela into a nightingale. Thus the nightingale, the bird with the beautiful song, has come to be called Philomela, and many poets, like John Keats in his "Ode to the Nightingale," and T. S. Eliot in *The Waste Land*, have drawn upon the story.

In turning to Ransom's poem, one finds that it may be separated into two parts of four stanzas each, the first of which can be called "The Progress of Poetry" and the second, "The Progress of the Poet." The first stanza states the situation of Philomela, but also contrasts the "classical numbers of the nightingale" with the not so felicitous, rough numbers—an old word for "meter"—of the speaker. In addition, in the first stanza, despite the speak-

[1] This analysis appeared in a longer form in Samuel H. Woods, Jr., " 'Philomela': John Crowe Ransom's *Ars Poetica*," *College English*, XXVII (February, 1966), 408–413.

er's invocation of the Greek story of Philomela in his first line ("Procne, Philomela, Itylus") he does not except perhaps obliquely use the myth—as in the first two lines of stanza 3—but deliberately rejects it as "an improbable tale." Instead of using this traditional story, he improvises one of his own in which Philomela, in these stanzas the actual bird, sings, "descants," to use Ransom's deliberately affected word, to Ovid, the great Latin poet; the bird has also appeared to "Teutons, the swilled and gravid" and was perhaps "gallicized" at Fontainebleau, although "Never was she baptized." Fleeing the hawk, she came to England where she wanders, uttering her untranslatable refrain, while her husband the hawk perches asleep on the roost. Beyond England her westward course has not continued. The impossibility of her finding a home in "this other Thrace, environ barbaric" is merely stated, but stated in words that strongly recall "Home on the Range": "Where never is heard a discouraging word, And the skies are not cloudy all day," a place perhaps congenial to the graceful white swan, but not to Philomela and her "delicate dirge."

As our name for this part of the poem, "The Progress of Poetry," suggests, these four stanzas show the bird and stress her song; and Philomela appears to be a symbol for poetry and the gradual movement of poetry in both space and time from Greece to England. With this interpretation or "key" in mind, we may see that line 8 alludes in a very condensed way to the existence of lyric poetry like Johann Wolfgang von Goethe's or Heinrich Heine's amid the generally unpoetic Germans, filled with their beer and sausages; and that lines 9–10 suggest, particularly by the conditional "may be," that poetry never fully submitted to the rigor of French neoclassical rules of the age of Louis XIV and that even the Most Christian Kings of France were not able to convert poetry to serve wholly Christian ends. Stanza 3 records the movement of poetry to England, where, like a ghost, she wanders amid a "nation of shopkeepers," Napoleon's phrase to summarize the English, while her husband sleeps at home. There she sings her original bird's song, which, of course, is literally untranslatable into any human language. Others, of course, have argued that poetry cannot be translated from one human language into another, but Ransom suggests an even greater barrier, translation to language from the lyric song of the bird.

Stanza 4 argues that Philomela, both literal nightingale and symbol of poetry, did not migrate to America, "a cloudless boundless public place." The fact that there are no nightingales in North America would appear to offer scientific proof for Ransom's poetic argument. This part of the poem provides a transition from the first to the second section of the poem, which otherwise may seem rather loosely connected with the first part. The implied connection is this: Since the inspiring spirit of poetry (Philomela) is not to be found in the United States, the poet-speaker—in this poem the speaker shares a good many characteristics with the real John Crowe Ransom, both, for instance, having been Oxford students—will himself go where the bird-poetry can be found.

Thus, in "The Progress of the Poet," we find the American, a member of "an inordinate race" but critically aware of his own weaknesses—his dissonance, his disharmony—seeking to improve himself in the best traditions of the culturally deprived. In this part of the poem, of course, the tone and the attitude are both heavily ironic, even sarcastic, at the expense of the poet's youthful earnestness. The speaker appears to be a pedant who delights in long words and who cannot say a simple thing in simple language but who once upon a time was a sincere seeker after poetry. Ransom makes his speaker into a cartoon stereotype of a pedant describing his experiences as a young poetic seeker. Both the pedant and the youth are presented ironically.

The young poet, filled with zeal and disenchanted with his now "barbaric" country, goes on pilgrimage to Oxford. There he becomes an England-worshipper and seeks to learn the mysteries of poetry from the masters of the art. Notice that the word he uses, "hierophants," is heavy with religious connotations, suggesting that the young man's attitude toward poetry is as serious as some people's belief is in their religion. He goes out to Bagley Wood (notice how the flat *a* sound suggests an extremely unpoetic place), where he seeks Philomela herself—both literal bird and spirit of poetry. Here he finds her enchanting song a bit flat, too, although he concedes with mock modesty that his ordinarily good ear may have failed him. Thus, in this part of the poem, he discovers that although he found a nightingale, she was hardly Philomela, or at any rate did not fully live up to his high expectations of her—that though the would-be poet may seek out an environment that has produced poetry in the past, he will not necessarily find that environment serves his purposes. The last stanza of the poem states two problems, both of which are implied in the opening lines: the poet's despair and his own nation's unworthiness, a nation further described as "bantering," "sophistical," and "swarthy." No solution is stated for these two dilemmas, only that Philomela's song is to remain in the more persistently young provinces, perhaps such perennially creative areas as Western Europe, but note that these provinces are described as "fabulous," that is, unreal or visionary.

Even though the poem does not explicitly answer the questions it raises, it can be argued that the poem is its own answer. In essence, Ransom has asked, how in the world is the poet to write poetry in an uncongenial place which has no traditions and where the people don't care about poetry? He has, of course, written a poem about the difficulties of writing poetry under just such circumstances. Is the style of the poem, particularly the many unusual words, appropriate here? To what extent is the poem a kind of joke on the reader? Why does Ransom seem to use classical mythology, the background knowledge most readers will think they need to understand the poem? Is a knowledge of the Philomela myth relevant at all to what the poem is really about?

Captain Carpenter

Captain Carpenter rose up in his prime
Put on his pistols and went riding out
But had got wellnigh nowhere at that time
Till he fell in with ladies in a rout.

It was a pretty lady and all her train
That played with him so sweetly but before
An hour she'd taken a sword with all her main
And twined him of his nose for evermore.

Captain Carpenter mounted up one day
And rode straightway into a stranger rogue   10
That looked unchristian but be that as may
The Captain did not wait upon prologue.

But drew upon him out of his great heart
The other swung against him with a club
And cracked his two legs at the shinny part
And let him roll and stick like any tub.

Captain Carpenter rode many a time
From male and female took he sundry harms
He met the wife of Satan crying "I'm
The she-wolf bids you shall bear no more arms."   20

Their strokes and counters whistled in the wind
I wish he had delivered half his blows
But where she should have made off like a hind
The bitch bit off his arms at the elbows.

And Captain Carpenter parted with his ears
To a black devil that used him in this wise
O jesus ere his threescore and ten years
Another had plucked out his sweet blue eyes.

Captain Carpenter got up on his roan
And sallied from the gate in hell's despite   30
I heard him asking in the grimmest tone
If any enemy yet there was to fight?

"To any adversary it is fame
If he risk to be wounded by my tongue

Or burnt in two beneath my red heart's flame
Such are the perils he is cast among.

"But if he can he has a pretty choice
From an anatomy with little to lose
Whether he cut my tongue and take my voice
Or whether it be my round red heart he choose."   40

It was the neatest knave that ever was seen
Stepping in perfume from his lady's bower
Who at this word put in his merry mien
And fell on Captain Carpenter like a tower.

I would not knock old fellows in the dust
But there lay Captain Carpenter on his back
His weapons were the old heart in his bust
And a blade shook between rotten teeth alack.

The rogue in scarlet and grey soon knew his mind
He wished to get his trophy and depart;   50
With gentle apology and touch refined
He pierced him and produced the Captain's heart.

God's mercy rest on Captain Carpenter now
I thought him Sirs an honest gentleman
Citizen husband soldier and scholar enow
Let jangling kites eat of him if they can.

But God's deep curses follow after those
That shore him of his goodly nose and ears
His legs and strong arms at the two elbows
And eyes that had not watered seventy years   60

The curse of hell upon the sleek upstart
That got the Captain finally on his back
And took the red red vitals of his heart
And made the kites to whet their beaks clack clack.

Piazza Piece

—I am a gentleman in a dustcoat trying
To make you hear. Your ears are soft and small
And listen to an old man not at all,

They want the young men's whispering and sighing.
But see the roses on your trellis dying
And hear the spectral singing of the moon;
For I must have my lovely lady soon,
I am a gentleman in a dustcoat trying.

—I am a lady young in beauty waiting
Until my truelove comes, and then we kiss.   10
But what grey man among the vines is this
Whose words are dry and faint as in a dream?
Back from my trellis, Sir, before I scream!
I am a lady young in beauty waiting.

Janet Waking

Beautifully Janet slept
Till it was deeply morning. She woke then
And thought about her dainty-feathered hen,
To see how it had kept.

One kiss she gave her mother.
Only a small one gave she to her daddy
Who would have kissed each curl of his shining baby;
No kiss at all for her brother.

"Old Chucky, old Chucky!" she cried,
Running across the world upon the grass   10
To Chucky's house, and listening. But alas,
Her Chucky had died.

It was a transmogrifying bee
Came droning down on Chucky's old bald head
And sat and put the poison. It scarcely bled,
But how exceedingly.

And purply did the knot
Swell with the venom and communicate
Its rigor! Now the poor comb stood up straight
But Chucky did not.   20

So there was Janet
Kneeling on the wet grass, crying her brown hen
(Translated far beyond the daughters of men)
To rise and walk upon it.

And weeping fast as she had breath
Janet implored us, "Wake her from her sleep!"
And would not be instructed in how deep
Was the forgetful kingdom of death.

Survey of Literature

In all the good Greek of Plato
I lack my roastbeef and potato.

A better man was Aristotle,
Pulling steady on the bottle.

I dip my hat to Chaucer,
Swilling soup from his saucer,

And to Master Shakespeare
Who wrote big on small beer.

The abstemious Wordsworth
Subsisted on a curd's-worth,   10

But a slick one was Tennyson,
Putting gravy on his venison.

What these men had to eat and drink
Is what we say and what we think.

The influence of Milton
Came wry out of Stilton.

Sing a song for Percy Shelley,
Drowned in pale lemon jelly,

And for precious John Keats,
Dripping blood of pickled beets.   20

Then there was poor Willie Blake,
He foundered on sweet cake.

God have mercy on the sinner
Who must write with no dinner,

No gravy and no grub,
No pewter and no pub,

No belly and no bowels,
Only consonants and vowels.

Of Margaret

With the fall of the first leaf that winds rend
She and the boughs trembled, and she would mourn
The wafer body as an own first born,
But with louder destruction sang the wind.

So must the others drop, there where they hung
Quaking and cold, and the blind land be filled
With dead, till one least and last wind unchild
Her of the sons of all her mothering.

No mother sorrow is but follows birth
And, beyond that, conception; hers was large,   10
And so immoderate love must be a scourge,
Needing the whole ecstasy of substant earth.

But no evil shall spot this, Margaret's page,
For her generations were of the head,
The eyes, the tender fingers, not the blood,
And the issue was all flowers and foliage.

Virgin, whose image bent to the small grass
I keep against this tide of wayfaring,
O hear the maiden pageant ever sing
Of that far away time of gentleness.   20

§ FOR COMMENT

John Crowe Ransom's "Of Margaret" seems to have been written as a comment on Gerard Manley Hopkins' "Spring and Fall." In considering the two poets' different handling of the same theme, consider the following points: Hopkins' poem is subtitled "to a young child," and apparently has a dramatic speaker talking to the young child. Characterize the speaker and the situation implied by his words to Margaret. Does he offer consolation for Margaret's sorrow?

Does Ransom's poem have any particular speaker or audience? If so, describe each one. Is Ransom's method more or less effective than Hopkins' dramatic one?

Both poems employ somewhat unusual words—"gelid," "unchild"—

and—"leafmeal," "wanwood." Are such unusual words a blemish or do they contribute something to the total effect of the poem? Examine the diction of each poem separately. The syntax in both poems is at least occasionally somewhat out of the ordinary. Is this unusual word order a distraction or an advantage?

T. S. Eliot § 1888–1965

Eliot was a poet, playwright, and as a literary critic helped formulate the dominant literary taste of his times. Born in St. Louis, educated at Harvard, Oxford, and the Sorbonne, Eliot became a British citizen, though he made frequent visits to the United States. He was one of the first modern poets to write about life in the modern city. "The Journey of the Magi" reveals his profound interest in religion.

The Love Song of J. Alfred Prufrock

> S'io credesse che mia risposta fosse
> A persona che mai tornasse al mondo,
> Questa fiamma staria senza piu scosse.
> Ma perciocche giammai di questo fondo
> Non torno vivo alcun, s'i'odo il vero,
> Senza tema d'infamia ti rispondo.

Let us go then, you and I,
When the evening is spread out against the sky
Like a patient etherised upon a table;
Let us go, through certain half-deserted streets,
The muttering retreats
Of restless nights in one-night cheap hotels
And sawdust restaurants with oyster-shells:
Streets that follow like a tedious argument
Of insidious intent
To lead you to an overwhelming question . . .   10
Oh, do not ask, 'What is it?'
Let us go and make our visit.

Epigraph. *S'io . . . rispondo:* "If I believed my answer were being made to one who could ever return to the world, this flame would gleam no more; but since, if what I hear is true, never from this abyss did living man return, I answer thee without fear of infamy." (Dante, *Inferno,* xxvi, 61–66). Guido da Montefeltro, an unrepentant sinner, speaks to Dante.

In the room the women come and go
Talking of Michelangelo.

The yellow fog that rubs its back upon the window-panes,
The yellow smoke that rubs its muzzle on the window-panes
Licked its tongue into the corners of the evening,
Lingered upon the pools that stand in drains,
Let fall upon its back the soot that falls from chimneys,
Slipped by the terrace, made a sudden leap,   20
And seeing that it was a soft October night,
Curled once about the house, and fell asleep.

And indeed there will be time
For the yellow smoke that slides along the street,
Rubbing its back upon the window-panes;
There will be time, there will be time
To prepare a face to meet the faces that you meet;
There will be time to murder and create,
And time for all the works and days of hands
That lift and drop a question on your plate;   30
Time for you and time for me,
And time yet for a hundred indecisions,
And for a hundred visions and revisions,
Before the taking of a toast and tea.

In the room the women come and go
Talking of Michelangelo.

And indeed there will be time
To wonder, 'Do I dare?' and, 'Do I dare?'
Time to turn back and descend the stair,
With a bald spot in the middle of my hair—   40
[They will say: 'How his hair is growing thin!']
My morning coat, my collar mounting firmly to the chin,
My necktie rich and modest, but asserted by a simple pin—
[They will say: 'But how his arms and legs are thin!']

Do I dare
Disturb the universe?
In a minute there is time
For decisions and revisions which a minute will reverse.

For I have known them all already, known them all:—
Have know the evenings, mornings, afternoons,   50
I have measured out my life with coffee spoons;

I know the voices dying with a dying fall
Beneath the music from a farther room.
   So how should I presume?

   And I have known the eyes already, known them all—
The eyes that fix you in a formulated phrase,
And when I am formulated, sprawling on a pin,
When I am pinned and wriggling on the wall,
Then how should I begin
To spit out all the butt-ends of my days and ways?   60
   And how should I presume?

   And I have known the arms already, known them all—
Arms that are braceleted and white and bare
[But in the lamplight, downed with light brown hair!]
Is it perfume from a dress
That makes me so digress?
Arms that lie along a table, or wrap about a shawl.
   And should I then presume?
   And how should I begin?

Shall I say, I have gone at dusk through narrow streets   70
And watched the smoke that rises from the pipes
Of lonely men in shirt sleeves, leaning out of windows? . . .

   I should have been a pair of ragged claws
Scuttling across the floors of silent seas.

     *   *   *

And the afternoon, the evening, sleeps so peacefully!
Smoothed by long fingers,
Asleep   tired . . . or it malingers,
Stretched on the floor, here beside you and me.
Should I, after tea and cakes and ices,
Have the strength to force the moment to its crisis?   80
But though I have wept and fasted, wept and prayed,
Though I have seen my head [grown slightly bald] brought in
    upon a platter,
I am no prophet—and here's no great matter;
I have seen the moment of my greatness flicker,
And I have seen the eternal Footman hold my coat, and snicker,
And in short, I was afraid.

   And would it have been worth it, after all,
After the cups, the marmalade, the tea,
Among the porcelain, among some talk of you and me,

Would it have been worth while,   90
To have bitten off the matter with a smile,
To have squeezed the universe into a ball
To roll it toward some overwhelming question,
To say: 'I am Lazarus, come from the dead,
Come back to tell you all, I shall tell you all'—
If one, settling a pillow by her head,
    Should say: 'That is not what I meant at all.
    That is not it, at all.'

    And would it have been worth it, after all,
Would it have been worth while,   100
After the sunsets and the dooryards and the sprinkled streets,
After the novels, after the teacups, after the skirts that trail along
        the floor—
And this, and so much more?—
It is impossible to say just what I mean!
But as if a magic lantern threw the nerves in patterns on a screen:
Would it have been worth while
If one, settling a pillow or throwing off a shawl,
And turning toward the window, should say:
    'That is not it at all,
    That is not what I meant, at all.'   110

No! I am not Prince Hamlet, nor was meant to be;
Am an attendant lord, one that will do
To swell a progress, start a scene or two,
Advise the prince; no doubt, an easy tool,
Deferential, glad to be of use,
Politic, cautious, and meticulous;
Full of high sentence, but a bit obtuse;
At times, indeed, almost ridiculous—
Almost, at times, the Fool.

    I grow old . . . I grow old . . .   120
I shall wear the bottoms of my trousers rolled.
    Shall I part my hair behind? Do I dare to eat a peach?
I shall wear white flannel trousers, and walk upon the beach.
I have heard the mermaids singing, each to each.

    I do not think that they will sing to me.

    I have seen them riding seaward on the waves
Combing the white hair of the waves blown back
When the wind blows the water white and black.

We have lingered in the chambers of the sea
By sea-girls wreathed with seaweed red and brown   130
Till human voices wake us, and we drown.

Preludes

I

The winter evening settles down
With smell of steaks in passageways.
Six o'clock.
The burnt-out ends of smoky days.
And now a gusty shower wraps
The grimy scraps
Of withered leaves about your feet
And newspapers from vacant lots;
The showers beat
On broken blinds and chimney-pots,   10
And at the corner of the street
A lonely cab-horse steams and stamps.
And then the lighting of the lamps.

II

The morning comes to consciousness
Of faint stale smells of beer
From the sawdust-trampled street
With all its muddy feet that press
To early coffee-stands.
With the other masquerades
That time resumes,   20
One thinks of all the hands
That are raising dingy shades
In a thousand furnished rooms.

III

You tossed a blanket from the bed,
You lay upon your back, and waited;
You dozed, and watched the night revealing
The thousand sordid images
Of which your soul was constituted;
They flickered against the ceiling.
And when all the world came back   30
And the light crept up between the shutters
And you heard the sparrows in the gutters,
You had such a vision of the street

As the street hardly understands;
Sitting along the bed's edge, where
You curled the papers from your hair,
Or clasped the yellow soles of feet
In the palms of both soiled hands.

IV

His soul stretched tight across the skies
That fade behind a city block,   40
Or trampled by insistent feet
At four and five and six o'clock;
And short square fingers stuffing pipes,
And evening newspapers, and eyes
Assured of certain certainties,
The conscience of a blackened street
Impatient to assume the world.

I am moved by fancies that are curled
Around these images, and cling:
The notion of some infinitely gentle   50
Infinitely suffering thing.

Wipe your hand across your mouth, and laugh;
The worlds revolve like ancient women
Gathering fuel in vacant lots.

The Hollow Men

A penny for the Old Guy

I

We are the hollow men
We are the stuffed men
Leaning together
Headpiece filled with straw. Alas!
Our dried voices, when
We whisper together
Are quiet and meaningless
As wind in dry grass
Or rats' feet over broken glass
In our dry cellar   10

Shape without form, shade without colour,
Paralysed force, gesture without motion;

Those who have crossed
With direct eyes, to death's other Kingdom
Remember us—if at all—not as lost
Violent souls, but only
As the hollow men
The stuffed men.

II

Eyes I dare not meet in dreams
In death's dream kingdom   20
These do not appear:
There, the eyes are
Sunlight on a broken column
There, is a tree swinging
And voices are
In the wind's singing
More distant and more solemn
Than a fading star.

Let me be no nearer
In death's dream kingdom   30
Let me also wear
Such deliberate disguises,
Rat's skin, crowskin, crossed staves
In a field
Behaving as the wind behaves
No nearer—

Not that final meeting
In the twilight kingdom

III

This is the dead land
This is cactus land   40
Here the stone images
Are raised, here they receive
The supplication of a dead man's hand
Under the twinkle of a fading star.

Is it like this
In death's other kingdom
Waking alone
At the hour when we are
Trembling with tenderness

Lips that would kiss   50
From prayers to broken stone.

IV

The eyes are not here
There are no eyes here
In this valley of dying stars
In this hollow valley
This broken jaw of our lost kingdoms

In this last of meeting places
We grope together
And avoid speech
Gathered on this beach of the tumid river   60

Sightless, unless
The eyes reappear
As the perpetual star
Multifoliate rose
Of death's twilight kingdom
The hope only
Of empty men.

V

Here we go round the prickly pear
Prickly pear prickly pear
Here we go round the prickly pear   70
At five o'clock in the morning.

Between the idea
And the reality
Between the motion
And the act
Falls the Shadow
                          For Thine is the Kingdom

Between the conception
And the creation
Between the emotion   80
And the response
Falls the Shadow
                          Life is very long

Between the desire
And the spasm

Between the potency
And the existence
Between the essence
And the descent
Falls the Shadow   90
            For Thine is the Kingdom

For Thine is
Life is
For Thine is the

This is the way the world ends
This is the way the world ends
This is the way the world ends
Not with a bang but a whimper.

Journey of the Magi

"A cold coming we had of it,
Just the worst time of the year
For a journey, and such a long journey:
The ways deep and the weather sharp,
The very dead of winter."
And the camels galled, sore-footed, refractory,
Lying down in the melting snow.
There were times we regretted
The summer palaces on slopes, the terraces,
And the silken girls bringing sherbet.   10
Then the camel men cursing and grumbling
And running away, and wanting their liquor and women,
And the night-fires going out, and the lack of shelters,
And the cities hostile and the towns unfriendly
And the villages dirty and charging high prices:
A hard time we had of it.
At the end we preferred to travel all night,
Sleeping in snatches,
With the voices singing in our ears, saying
That this was all folly.   20

Then at dawn we came down to a temperate valley,
Wet, below the snow line, smelling of vegetation;
With a running stream and a water-mill beating the darkness,
And three trees on the low sky,
And an old white horse galloped away in the meadow.

Then we came to a tavern with vine-leaves over the lintel,
Six hands at an open door dicing for pieces of silver,
And feet kicking the empty wine-skins.
But there was no information, and so we continued
And arrived at evening, not a moment too soon   30
Finding the place; it was (you may say) satisfactory.

All this was a long time ago, I remember,
And I would do it again, but set down
This set down
This: were we led all that way for
Birth or Death? There was a Birth, certainly,
We had evidence and no doubt. I had seen birth and death,
But had thought they were different; this Birth was
Hard and bitter agony for us, like Death, our death.
We returned to our places, these Kingdoms,   40
But no longer at ease here, in the old dispensation,
With an alien people clutching their gods.
I should be glad of another death.

§ FOR COMMENT

"Journey of the Magi" is a *dramatic monologue*, a kind of poem in which the speaker is identified usually by the title; and from his words the reader infers the dramatic situation, usually a moment of crisis in his life. This speaker, is of course, one of the Magi—the three wise men from the East who followed the star of Bethlehem to see the infant Jesus. At what time in the wise man's life is he speaking? What particular lines support your interpretation?

The poem contains much precise detail: the behavior of the camels and the camel-men, the various kinds of places where the travellers stayed on their long journey, the old white horse galloping away in the meadow. What purpose do these details serve? Are they included to help us recreate the narrator's experiences? to help characterize him? The last line of the second stanza would appear to be a vast understatement. Explain why the speaker describes his first view of Jesus in this way.

Throughout the last section of the poem, the speaker does not seem to understand fully what he experienced. Why should he have this feeling? You may need to recall that the Magi returned to the East and did not know of the later life of Jesus. Presumably, this wise man is back home now. If so, why does he describe his fellow human beings as "alien"? The last section contains a great many references to both birth and death. Why does the speaker say that "this Birth was/Hard and bitter agony for us, like Death, our death?" Does he refer only to the trials of the journey? If he

means something more, what is it? How do you interpret the last line?
Describe the tone of the poem. Is it appropriate to the speaker?

Would you describe the language in which the poem is written as
formal, informal, colloquial, or slangy? Is this kind of language appropriate
in a serious religious poem or should Eliot have adopted some other style?

John Peale Bishop § 1891–1944

*Bishop was both a novelist and a poet, and a contemporary and
friend of F. Scott Fitzgerald and Edmund Wilson, the literary
critic.*

Experience in the West

I. THE BURNING WHEEL

They followed the course of heaven as before
Trojan in smoky armor westward fled
Disastrous walls and on his shoulders bore
A dotard recollection had made mad,

Depraved by years, Anchises: on the strong
Tall bronze upborne, small sack of impotence;
Yet still he wore the look of one who young
Had closed with Love in cloudy radiance.

So the discoverers when they wading came
From shallow ships and climbed the wooded shores: 10
They saw the west, a sky of falling flame,
And by the streams savage ambassadors.

O happy, brave and vast adventure! Where
Each day the sun beat rivers of new gold;
The wild grape ripened, springs reflected fear;
The wild deer fled; the bright snake danger coiled.

They, too, the stalwart conquerors of space,
Each on his shoulders wore a wise delirium
Of memory and age: ghostly embrace
Of fathers slanted toward a western tomb.   20

A hundred and a hundred years they stayed
Aloft, until they were as light as autumn
Shells of locusts. Where then were they laid?
And in what wilderness oblivion?

Archibald MacLeish § 1892–

MacLeish has been an editor of Fortune, *the Librarian of Congress,
and Assistant Secretary of State, and until his retirement in 1962,
taught English at Harvard.*

Ars Poetica

A poem should be palpable and mute
As a globed fruit,

Dumb
As old medallions to the thumb,

Silent as the sleeve-worn stone
Of casement ledges where the moss has grown—

A poem should be wordless
As the flight of birds.

A poem should be motionless in time
As the moon climbs,   10

Leaving, as the moon releases
Twig by twig the night-entangled trees,

Leaving, as the moon behind the winter leaves,
Memory by memory the mind—

A poem should be motionless in time
As the moon climbs.

A poem should be equal to:
Not true.

For all the history of grief
An empty doorway and a maple leaf.   20

For love
The leaning grasses and two lights above the sea—

A poem should not mean
But be.

"Not Marble nor the Gilded Monuments"

for Adele

The praisers of women in their proud and beautiful poems,
Naming the grave mouth and the hair and the eyes,
Boasted those they loved should be forever remembered:
These were lies.

The words sound but the face in the Istrian sun is forgotten.
The poet speaks but to her dead ears no more.
The sleek throat is gone—and the breast that was troubled to
    listen:
Shadow from door.

Therefore I will not praise your knees nor your fine walking
Telling you men shall remember your name as long   10
As lips move or breath is spent or the iron of English
Rings from a tongue.

I shall say you were young, and your arms straight, and your
    mouth scarlet:
I shall say you will die and none will remember you:
Your arms change, and none remember the swish of your
    garments,
Nor the click of your shoe.

Not with my hand's strength, not with difficult labor
Springing the obstinate words to the bones of your breast
And the stubborn line to your young stride and the breath to your
    breathing
And the beat to your haste   20
Shall I prevail on the hearts of unborn men to remember.

(What is a dead girl but a shadowy ghost

Or a dead man's voice but a distant and vain affirmation
Like dream words most)

Therefore I will not speak of the undying glory of women.
I will say you were young and straight and your skin fair
And you stood in the door and the sun was a shadow of leaves
    on your shoulders
And a leaf on your hair—

I will not speak of the famous beauty of dead women:
I will say the shape of a leaf lay once on your hair.   30
Till the world ends and the eyes are out and the mouths broken
Look! It is there!

§ FOR COMMENT

MacLeish takes his title from the first line of Shakespeare's Sonnet 155. Is he treating the same theme as Shakespeare? If not, what is his theme? Is MacLeish's poem understandable without knowing Shakespeare's? If it is not, does its dependence make it less good than a poem that stands on its own? What is the form of MacLeish's poem? Would the meaning of his poem have been different if he had chosen to present it within the relatively rigid form of the sonnet?

You, Andrew Marvell

And here face down beneath the sun
And here upon earth's noonward height
To feel the always coming on
The always rising of the night:

To feel creep up the curving east
The earthy chill of dusk and slow
Upon those under lands the vast
And ever climbing shadow grow

And strange at Ecbatan the trees
Take leaf by leaf the evening strange   10
The flooding dark about their knees
The mountains over Persia change

And now at Kermanshah the gate
Dark empty and the withered grass
And through the twilight now the late
Few travelers in the westward pass

And Baghdad darken and the bridge
Across the silent river gone
And through Arabia the edge
Of evening widen and steal on   20

And deepen on Palmyra's street
The wheel rut in the ruined stone
And Lebanon fade out and Crete
High through the clouds and overblown

And over Sicily the air
Still flashing with the landward gulls
And loom and slowly disappear
The sails above the shadowy hulls

And Spain go under and the shore
Of Africa the gilded sand   30
And evening vanish and no more
The low pale light across that land

Nor now the long light on the sea:

And here face downward in the sun
To feel how swift how secretly
The shadow of the night comes on . . .

"Dover Beach"—A Note to That Poem

The wave withdrawing
Withers with seaward rustle of flimsy water
Sucking the sand down, dragging at empty shells.
The roil after it settling, too smooth, smothered . . .

After forty a man's a fool to wait in the
Sea's face for the full force and the roaring of
Surf to come over him: droves of careening water.
After forty the tug's out and the salt and the
Sea follow it: less sound and violence.

Nevertheless the ebb has its own beauty—   10
Shells sand and all and the whispering rustle.
There's earth in it then and the bubbles of foam gone.

Moreover—and this too has its lovely uses—
It's the outward wave that spills the inward forward
Tripping the proud piled mute virginal
Mountain of water in wallowing welter of light and
Sound enough—thunder for miles back. It's a fine and a
Wild smother to vanish in: pulling down—
Tripping with outward ebb the urgent inward.

Speaking alone for myself it's the steep hill and the   20
Toppling lift of the young men I am toward now,
Waiting for that as the wave for the next wave.
Let them go over us all I say with the thunder of
What's to be next in the world. It's we will be under it!

§ FOR COMMENT

What similarities or differences in form, imagery, and theme do you see
between MacLeish's poem and Arnold's "Dover Beach"? Does this poem
satisfy MacLeish's definition of a poem in "Ars Poetica"?

E. E. Cummings § 1894–1962

*Cummings experimented with both the typography and the punc-
tuation of his poetry. A fine lyric poet, Cummings also had a
notable gift for poetic sarcasm and satire.*

next to of course god america i

"next to of course god america i
love you land of the pilgrims' and so forth oh
say can you see by the dawn's early my
country 'tis of centuries come and go
and are no more what of it we should worry
in every language even deafanddumb
thy sons acclaim your glorious name by gorry
by jingo by gee by gosh by gum

why talk of beauty what could be more beautiful than these heroic happy dead
who rushed like lions to the roaring slaughter
they did not stop to think they died instead
then shall the voices of liberty be mute?"

He spoke. And drank rapidly a glass of water

r-p-o-p-h-e-s-s-a-g-r

       who

a)s w(e loo)k
upnowgath
      PPEGORHRASS
                eringint(o-
aThe):l
     eA
     !p:
S   a
         (r
rIvInG   .gRrEaPsPh()s)
                       to
rea(be)rran(com)gi(e)ngly
,grasshopper;

my father moved through dooms of love

my father moved through dooms of love
through sames of am through haves of give,
singing each morning out of each night
my father moved through depths of height

this motionless forgetful where
turned at his glance to shining here;
that if(so timid air is firm)
under his eyes would stir and squirm

newly as from unburied which
floats the first who,his april touch
drove sleeping selves to swarm their fates
woke dreamers to their ghostly roots

and should some why completely weep
my father's fingers brought her sleep:

vainly no smallest voice might cry
for he could feel the mountains grow.

Lifting the valleys of the sea
my father moved through griefs of joy;
praising a forehead called the moon
singing desire into begin   20

joy was his song and joy so pure
a heart of star by him could steer
and pure so now and now so yes
the wrists of twilight would rejoice

keen as midsummer's keen beyond
conceiving mind of sun will stand,
so strictly(over utmost him
so hugely)stood my father's dream

his flesh was flesh his blood was blood:
no hungry man but wished him food;   30
no cripple wouldn't creep one mile
uphill to only see him smile.

Scorning the pomp of must and shall
my father moved through dooms of feel;
his anger was as right as rain
his pity was as green as grain

septembering arms of year extend
less humbly wealth to foe and friend
than he to foolish and to wise
offered immeasurable is   40

proudly and(by octobering flame
beckoned)as earth will downward climb,
so naked for immortal work
his shoulders marched against the dark

his sorrow was as true as bread:
no liar looked him in the head;
if every friend became his foe
he'd laugh and build a world with snow.

My father moved through theys of we,
singing each new leaf out of each tree   50

(and every child was sure that spring
danced when she heard my father sing)

then let men kill which cannot share,
let blood and flesh be mud and mire,
scheming imagine,passion willed,
freedom a drug that's bought and sold

giving to steal and cruel kind,
a heart to fear,to doubt a mind,
to differ a disease of same,
conform the pinnacle of am   60

though dull were all we taste as bright,
bitter all utterly things sweet,
maggoty minus and dumb death
all we inherit,all bequeath

and nothing quite so least as truth
—i say though hate were why men breathe—
because my father lived his soul
love is the whole and more than all

if everything happens that can't be done

if everything happens that can't be done
(and anything's righter
than books
could plan)
the stupidest teacher will almost guess
(with a run
skip
around we go yes)
there's nothing as something as one

one hasn't a why or because or although   10
(and buds know better
than books
don't grow)
one's anything old being everything new
(with a what
which
around we come who)
one's everyanything so

so world is a leaf so tree is a bough
  (and birds sing sweeter
than books
tell how)
so here is away and so your is a my
(with a down
up
around again fly)
forever was never till now

now i love you and you love me
(and books are shuter
than books
can be)
and deep in the high that does nothing but fall
(with a shout
each
around we go all)
there's somebody calling who's we

we're anything brighter than even the sun
(we're everything greater
than books
might mean)
we're everyanything more than believe
(with a spin
leap
alive we're alive)
we're wonderful one times one

20

30

40

Allen Tate § 1899–

Poet, novelist, and literary critic, Tate was a student of Ransom at Vanderbilt and a member of the "Fugitives." Tate has greatly interested in the relation of history and traditional values to contemporary life.

Mr. Pope

When Alexander Pope strolled in the city
Strict was the glint of pearl and gold sedans.

Ladies leaned out more out of fear than pity
For Pope's tight back was rather a goat's than man's.

Often one thinks the urn should have more bones
Than skeletons provide for speedy dust,
The urn gets hollow, cobwebs brittle as stones
Weave to the funeral shell a frivolous rust.

And he who dribbled couplets like a snake
Coiled to a lithe precision in the sun   10
Is missing. The jar is empty; you may break
It only to find that Mr. Pope is gone.

What requisitions of a verity
Prompted the wit and rage between his teeth
One cannot say. Around a crooked tree
A moral climbs whose name should be a wreath.

Winter Mask: To the memory of W. B. Yeats

I

Towards nightfall when the wind
Tries the eaves and casements
(A winter wind of the mind
Long gathering its will)
I lay the mind's contents
Bare, as upon a table,
And ask, in a time of war,
Whether there is still
To a mind frivolously dull
Anything worth living for.   10

II

If I am meek and dull
And a poor sacrifice
Of perverse will to cull
The act from the attempt,
Just look into damned eyes
And give the returning glare;
For the damned like it, the more
Damnation is exempt
From what would save its heir
With a thing worth living for.   20

III

The poisoned rat in the wall
Cuts through the wall like a knife,
Then blind, drying, and small
And driven to cold water,
Dies of the water of life:
Both damned in eternal ice,
The traitor become the boor
Who had led his friend to slaughter,
Now bites his head—not nice,
The food that he lives for.   30

IV

I supposed two scenes of hell,
Two human bestiaries,
Might uncommonly well
Convey the doom I thought;
But lest the horror freeze
The gentler estimation
I go to the sylvan door
Where nature has been bought
In rational proration
As a thing worth living for.   40

V

Should the buyer have been beware?
It is an uneven trade
For man has wet his hair
Under the winter weather
With only fog for shade:
His mouth a bracketed hole
Picked by the crows that bore
Nature to their hanged brother,
Who rattles against the bole
The thing that he lived for.   50

VI

I asked the master Yeats
Whose great style could not tell
Why it is man hates
His own salvatiòn,
Prefers the way to hell,
And finds his last safety
In the self-made curse that bore

Him towards damnatiòn:
The drowned undrowned by the sea,
The sea worth living for.   60

The Cross

There is a place that some men know,
I cannot see the whole of it
Nor how I came there. Long ago
Flame burst out of a secret pit
Crushing the world with such a light
The day-sky fell to moonless black,
The kingly sun to hateful night
For those, once seeing, turning back:
For love so hates mortality
Which is the providence of life   10
She will not let it blessèd be
But curses it with mortal strife,
Until beside the blinding rood
Within that world-destroying pit
—Like young wolves that have tasted blood,
Of death, men taste no more of it.
So blind, in so severe a place
(All life before in the black grave)
The last alternatives they face
Of life, without the life to save,   20
Being from all salvation weaned—
A stag charged both at heel and head:
Who would come back is turned a fiend
Instructed by the fiery dead.

Melvin B. Tolson § 1900–1966

Poet and teacher, Tolson was educated at Fisk, Lincoln, and Co-
lumbia Universities, and recently was Avalon Visiting Professor
of Humanities at the Tuskeegee Institute.

The Ballad of the Rattlesnake

The sharecroppers sat
In the Delta night;
Many were black,
And many were white.

And this is the tale
From the bearded mouth
Of the dreamer who saw
Green lands in the South:

The Apaches stake
On the desert sands   10
The blond man's feet
And the blond man's hands.

He curses and prays
And tugs apace.
The Apaches laugh
And spit in his face.

The blond man looks
With gibbering breath
At the diamond coils
And the fangs of death.   20

The chief ties a rock
To the rattler's tail.
The blond man's blood
Congeals like hail.

The diamond head
Hisses and pries.
The horny tail
The rock defies.

As custom wills,
Bent like a bow,   30
The red chief stoops
And taunts his foe.

A madness crawls
In the rattler's brain:

The naked white thing
Is the cause of its pain.

At every lurch,
The blond man dies.
Eternity ticks
Behind the eyes.   40

In the desert world
A scream tears space,
As the rattler strikes
The blond man's face.

Five miles away
The Apaches laugh
Like a frozen wind
In a crib of chaff.

The blond man lies
Like a bar of lead.   50
No hiss or laugh
Can vex the dead.

The desert holds
In its frying-pan
The bones of a snake
And the bones of a man.

And many a thing
With a rock on its tail
Kills the nearest thing
And dies by the trail.   60

The sharecroppers sat
In the Delta night;
Many were black,
And many were white.

And this is the tale
From the bearded mouth
Of the dreamer who saw
Green lands in the South.

Robert Penn Warren § 1905–

Warren is among the most talented and versatile of American writers. He is a novelist (All the King's Men, among others), playwright, literary critic, and poet; he has won Pulitzer Prizes for both fiction and poetry. As a student of Ransom at Vanderbilt, he was the youngest member of the "Fugitives."

Infant Boy at Midcentury:

2. MODIFICATION OF LANDSCAPE

There will, indeed, be modification of landscape,
And in margin of natural disaster, substantial reduction.
There will be refinement of principle, and purified action,
And expansion, we trust, of the human heart-hope, and hand-
    scope.

But is it a meanness of spirit and indulgence of spite
To suggest that your fair time, and friends, will mirror our own,
And ourselves, for the flesh will yet grieve on the bone,
And the heart need compensation for its failure to study delight?

Some will take up religion, some discover the virtue of money.
Some will find liberal causes the mask for psychic disturbance.   10
Some will expiate ego with excessive kindness to servants,
And some make a cult of honor, though having quite little, if any.

Some, hating all humans, will cultivate love for cats,
And some from self-hate will give children a morbid devotion.
Some will glorify friendship, but watch for the slightest motion
Of eyelid, or lip-twitch, and the longed-for betrayal it indicates.

Success for the great will be heart-bread, and the soul's only ease.
For some it will stink, like mackerel shining in moonlight.
At the mere thought of failure some will wet their sheets in the
    night,
Though some wear it proud as a medal, or manhood's first social
    disease.   20

The new age will need the old lies, as our own more than once
    did;
For death is ten thousand nights—yes, it's only the process
Of accommodating flesh to idea, but there's natural distress

In learning to face Truth's glare-glory, from which our eyes are
    long hid.

Dragon Country: To Jacob Boehme

This is the dragon's country, and these his own streams.
The slime on the railroad rails is where he has crossed the track.
On a frosty morning, that field mist is where his great turd steams,
And there are those who have gone forth and not come back.

I was only a boy when Jack Simms reported the first depredation,
What something had done to his hog pen. They called him a
    God-damn liar.
Then said it must be a bear, after some had viewed the location,
With fence rails, like matchwood, splintered, and earth a bloody
    mire.

But no bear had been seen in the county in fifty years, they knew.
It was something to say, merely that, for people compelled to
    explain   10
What, standing in natural daylight, they agreed couldn't be true;
And saying the words, a man felt in the chest a constrictive pain.

At least, some admitted this later, when things had got to the
    worst—
When, for instance, they found in the woods the wagon turned
    on its side,
Mules torn from trace chains, and you saw how the harness had
    burst.
Speculators averted the face from the spot where the teamster had
    died.

But that was long back, in my youth, just the first of case after
    case.
The great hunts fizzled. You followed the track of disrepair,
Ruined fence, blood-smear, brush broken, but came in the end to
    a place
With weed unbent and leaf calm—and nothing, nothing, was
    there.   20

So what, in God's name, could men think when they couldn't
    bring to bay
That belly-dragging earth-evil, but found that it took to air?

Thirty-thirty or buckshot might fail, but then at least you could say
You had faced it—assuming, of course, that you had survived the affair.

We were promised troops, the Guard, but the Governor's skin got thin
When up in New York the papers called him Saint George of Kentucky.
Yes, even the Louisville reporters who came to Todd County would grin.
Reporters, though rarely, still come. No one talks. They think it unlucky.

If a man disappears—well, the fact is something to hide.
The family says, gone to Akron, or up to Ford, in Detroit.   30
When we found Jebb Johnson's boot, with the leg, what was left, inside,
His mother said, no, it's not his. So we took it out to destroy it.

Land values are falling, no longer do lovers in moonlight go.
The rabbit, thoughtless of air gun, in the nearest pasture cavorts.
Now certain fields go untended, the local birth rate goes low.
The coon dips his little black paw in the riffle where he nightly resorts.

Yes, other sections have problems somewhat different from ours.
Their crops may fail, bank rates rise, loans at rumor of war be called,
But we feel removed from maneuvers of Russia, or other great powers,
And from much ordinary hope we are now disenthralled.   40

The Catholics have sent in a mission, Baptists report new attendance.
All that's off the point! We are human, and the human heart
Demands language for reality that has not the slightest dependence
On desire, or need—and in church fools pray only that the Beast depart.

But if the Beast were withdrawn now, life might dwindle again
To the ennui, the pleasure, and the night sweat, known in the time before

Necessity of truth had trodden the land, and our hearts, to pain,
And left, in darkness, the fearful glimmer of joy, like a spoor.

§ FOR COMMENT

Jacob Boehme was a seventeenth-century German shoemaker and religious mystic who believed in the will of God as a basic universal force and in the existence of powerful spiritual forces that defied material explanation. His writings strongly influenced the English Quakers.

The dramatic speaker in the poem is a Kentuckian from Todd County. He tells how after a number of strange events—some horrible, some almost unexplainable—he and his neighbors have come to believe their county is inhabited by a dragon. When do the events described in the poem seem to be happening? Have any of the people actually seen the dragon, or do they assume its existence as a way of explaining the happenings? Describe the tone of the poem and the speaker's feeling toward the events he describes. How do the people of Todd County finally feel about the dragon? Can the attitude shown by Jebb Johnson's mother, for instance, be reconciled with the final stanza? Is Warren's basic assumption, that a dragon could appear in rural Kentucky, so far-fetched as to be ridiculous? Why? Why not?

Warren uses quite a long line in this poem. Is it effective or clumsy? Is the effect smooth or rough? Explain why you think he has chosen this unusual form here.

Original Sin: A Short Story

Nodding, its great head rattling like a gourd,
And locks like seaweed strung on the stinking stone,
The nightmare stumbles past, and you have heard
It fumble your door before it whimpers and is gone:
It acts like the old hound that used to snuffle your door and
    moan.

You thought you had lost it when you left Omaha,
For it seemed connected then with your grandpa, who
Had a wen on his forehead and sat on the veranda
To finger the precious protuberance, as was his habit to do,
Which glinted in sun like rough garnet or the rich old brain
    bulging through.   10

But you met it in Harvard Yard as the historic steeple
Was confirming the midnight with its hideous racket,

And you wondered how it had come, for it stood so imbecile,
With empty hands, humble, and surely nothing in pocket:
Riding the rods, perhaps—or Grandpa's will paid the ticket.

You were almost kindly then, in your first homesickness,
As it tortured its stiff face to speak, but scarcely mewed.
Since then you have outlived all your homesickness,
But have met it in many another distempered latitude:
Oh, nothing is lost, ever lost! at last you understood.   20

It never came in the quantum glare of sun
To shame you before your friends, and had nothing to do
With your public experience or private reformation:
But it thought no bed too narrow—it stood with lips askew
And shook its great head sadly like the abstract Jew.

Never met you in the lyric arsenical meadows
When children call and your heart goes stone in the bosom—
At the orchard anguish never, nor ovoid horror,
Which is furred like a peach or avid like the delicious plum.
It takes no part in your classic prudence or fondled axiom.   30

Not there when you exclaimed: "Hope is betrayed by
Disastrous glory of sea-capes, sun-torment of whitecaps
—There must be a new innocence for us to be stayed by."
But there it stood, after all the timetables, all the maps,
In the crepuscular clutter of *always, always,* or *perhaps.*

You have moved often and rarely left an address,
And hear of the deaths of friends with a sly pleasure,
A sense of cleansing and hope which blooms from distress;
But it has not died, it comes, its hand childish, unsure,
Clutching the bribe of chocolate or a toy you used to treasure.   40

It tries the lock. You hear, but simply drowse:
There is nothing remarkable in that sound at the door.
Later you may hear it wander the dark house
Like a mother who rises at night to seek a childhood picture;
Or it goes to the backyard and stands like an old horse cold in
    the pasture.

Theodore Spencer § 1902–1949

*Educated at Princeton and Harvard, he was, in 1939, the first
American ever appointed Lecturer in English at Cambridge Uni-
versity, but the outbreak of World War II prevented his going.
He remained at Harvard and taught until his untimely death.*

Epitaph

She was a high-class bitch and a dandy
Prancing man was he and a dandy
Man he was with that tall lady.

I should have known that a bitch and a dandy
Dancing man—and Oh, what a dandy!—
Would with a prance of a dapper dandy
Dance into grass; and to grass that lady.

Bitch as she was—and he was a dandy
Prancing man—it makes me angry
That those dance people should stagger and bend.   10
I think of that dandy and bitch and am angry
That over that bitch and over that dandy
Dancing man—and Oh, what a dandy
Man he was with that tall lady!—
Only crass grass should dance in the end.

Contemporary Song

When the weather is rough, said the anxious child,
Is the wise man out or in?
Which does the wise man love, said the child,
His own, or another's skin?
What does the wise man do, said the child,
Does he watch the thread, or spin?
The heavens sagged; there was nothing to say.

When the guns are out, said the anxious child,
Does the wise man grasp a gun?
Which does the wise man hate, said the child,   10
Himself or everyone?

What does the wise man do, said the child,
When the battle's never won?
The heavens sagged; there was nothing to say.

W. H. Auden § 1907–

*Auden was educated at Oxford, and has taught and lectured widely
in the United States. Since World War II, his poetry has been concerned with questions of philosophy and religion.*

Musée des Beaux Arts

About suffering they were never wrong,
The Old Masters: how well they understood
Its human position; how it takes place

While someone else is eating or opening a window or just walking
    dully along;
How, when the aged are reverently, passionately waiting
For the miraculous birth, there always must be
Children who did not specially want it to happen, skating
On a pond at the edge of the wood:
They never forgot
That even the dreadful martyrdom must run its course   10
Anyhow in a corner, some untidy spot
Where the dogs go on with their doggy life and the torturer's
    horse
Scratches its innocent behind on a tree.

In Brueghel's *Icarus*, for instance: how everything turns away
Quite leisurely from the disaster; the ploughman may
Have heard the splash, the foresaken cry,
But for him it was not an important failure; the sun shone
As it had to on the white legs disappearing into the green
Water; and the expensive delicate ship that must have seen
Something amazing, a boy falling out of the sky,   20
Had somewhere to get to and sailed calmly on.

The Labyrinth

Anthropos apteros for days
Walked whistling round and round the Maze,
Relying happily upon
His temperament for getting on.

The hundredth time he sighted, though,
A bush he left an hour ago,
He halted where four alleys crossed,
And recognized that he was lost.

"Where am I? Metaphysics says
No question can be asked unless   10
It has an answer, so I can
Assume this maze has got a plan.

If theologians are correct,
A Plan implies an Architect:
A God-built maze would be, I'm sure,
The Universe in miniature.

Are data from the world of Sense,
In that case, valid evidence?
What in the universe I know
Can give directions how to go?   20

All Mathematics would suggest
A steady straight line as the best,
But left and right alternately
Is consonant with History.

Aesthetics, though, believes all Art
Intends to gratify the Heart:
Rejecting disciplines like these,
Must I, then, go which way I please?

Such reasoning is only true
If we accept the classic view,   30
Which we have no right to assert,
According to the Introvert.

His absolute pre-supposition
Is—Man creates his own condition:

l. 1. *Anthropos apteros*: Wingless man.

This maze was not divinely built,
But is secreted by my guilt.

The centre that I cannot find
Is known to my Unconscious Mind;
I have no reason to despair
Because I am already there.   40

My problem is how *not* to will;
They move most quickly who stand still;
I'm only lost until I see
I'm lost because I want to be.

If this should fail, perhaps I should,
As certain educators would,
Content myself with the conclusion;
In theory there is no solution.

All statements about what I feel,
Like I-am-lost, are quite unreal: 50
My knowledge ends where it began;
A hedge is taller than a man."

Anthropos apteros, perplexed
To know which turning to take next,
Looked up and wished he were the bird
To whom such doubts must seem absurd.

In Memory of W. B. Yeats

(d. Jan. 1939)

I

He disappeared in the dead of winter:
The brooks were frozen, the airports almost deserted,
And snow disfigured the public statues;
The mercury sank in the mouth of the dying day.
O all the instruments agree
The day of his death was a dark cold day.

Far from his illness
The wolves ran on through the evergreen forests,
The peasant river was untempted by the fashionable quays;

By mourning tongues   10
The death of the poet was kept from his poems.

But for him it was his last afternoon as himself,
An afternoon of nurses and rumours;
The provinces of his body revolted,
The squares of his mind were empty,
Silence invaded the suburbs,
The current of his feeling failed: he became his admirers.

Now he is scattered among a hundred cities
And wholly given over to unfamiliar affections;
To find his happiness in another kind of wood   20
And be punished under a foreign code of conscience.
The words of a dead man
Are modified in the guts of the living.

But in the importance and noise of tomorrow
When the brokers are roaring like beasts on the floor of the
    Bourse,
And the poor have the sufferings to which they are fairly accus-
    tomed,
And each in the cell of himself is almost convinced of his freedom;
A few thousand will think of this day
As one thinks of a day when one did something slightly unusual.

O all the instruments agree   30
The day of his death was a dark cold day.

II

You were silly like us: your gift survived it all;
The parish of rich women, physical decay,
Yourself; mad Ireland hurt you into poetry.
Now Ireland has her madness and her weather still,
For poetry makes nothing happen: it survives
In the valley of its saying where executives
Would never want to tamper; it flows south
From ranches of isolation and the busy griefs,
Raw towns that we believe and die in; it survives,   40
A way of happening, a mouth.

III

Earth, receive an honoured guest;
William Yeats is laid to rest:

Let the Irish vessel lie
Emptied of its poetry.

Time that is intolerant
Of the brave and innocent,
And indifferent in a week
To a beautiful physique,

Worships language and forgives   50
Everyone by whom it lives;
Pardons cowardice, conceit,
Lays its honours at their feet.

Time that with this strange excuse
Pardoned Kipling and his views,
And will pardon Paul Claudel,
Pardons him for writing well.

In the nightmare of the dark
All the dogs of Europe bark,
And the living nations wait,   60
Each sequestered in its hate;

Intellectual disgrace
Stares from every human face,
And the seas of pity lie
Locked and frozen in each eye.

Follow, poet, follow right
To the bottom of the night,
With your unconstraining voice
Still persuade us to rejoice;

With the farming of a verse   70
Make a vineyard of the curse,
Sing of human unsuccess
In a rapture of distress;

In the deserts of the heart,
Let the healing fountain start,
In the prison of his days
Teach the free man how to praise.

Edward Lear

Left by his friend to breakfast alone on the white
Italian shore, his Terrible Demon arose
Over his shoulder; he wept to himself in the night,
A dirty landscape-painter who hated his nose.

The legions of cruel inquisitive They
Were so many and big like dogs: he was upset
By Germans and boats; affection was miles away:
But guided by tears he successfully reached his Regret.

How prodigious the welcome was. Flowers took his hat
And bore him off to introduce him to the tongs;   10
The demon's false nose made the table laugh; a cat
Soon had him waltzing madly, let him squeeze her hand;
Words pushed him to the piano to sing comic songs;

And children swarmed to him like settlers. He became a land.

§ FOR COMMENT

Edward Lear (1812–1888) was a shy bachelor, best known during his lifetime for his paintings of landscapes and birds. Today he is famous for his
nonsense poems like "The Owl and the Pussycat" and his many improbable limericks. Could the form Auden has chosen for this poem be called
an elegy? How do you interpret the last line of the poem? Are the comments
Auden makes about Lear equally applicable to the poems of Lewis Carroll?

Herman Melville

(For Lincoln Kirstein)

Towards the end he sailed into an extraordinary mildness,
And anchored in his home and reached his wife
And rode within the harbour of her hand,
And went across each morning to an office
As though his occupation were another island.

Goodness existed: that was the new knowledge
His terror had to blow itself quite out
To let him see it; but it was the gale had blown him

Past the Cape Horn of sensible success
Which cries: "This rock is Eden. Shipwreck here." 10

But deafened him with thunder and confused with lightning:
—The maniac hero hunting like a jewel
The rare ambiguous monster that had maimed his sex,
Hatred for hatred ending in a scream,
The unexplained survivor breaking off the nightmare—
All that was intricate and false; the truth was simple.

Evil is unspectacular and always human,
And shares our bed and eats at our own table,
And we are introduced to Goodness every day,
Even in drawing-rooms among a crowd of faults; 20
He has a name like Billy and is almost perfect
But wears a stammer like a decoration:
And every time they meet the same thing has to happen;
It is the Evil that is helpless like a lover
And has to pick a quarrel and succeeds,
And both are openly destroyed before our eyes.

For now he was awake and knew
No one is ever spared except in dreams;
But there was something else the nightmare had distorted—
Even the punishment was human and a form of love: 30
The howling storm had been his father's presence
And all the time he had been carried on his father's breast.

Who now had set him gently down and left him.
He stood upon the narrow balcony and listened:
And all the stars above him sang as in his childhood
"All, all is vanity," but it was not the same;
For now the words descended like the calm of mountains—
—Nathaniel had been shy because his love was selfish—
But now he cried in exultation and surrender
"The Godhead is broken like bread. We are the pieces." 40

And sat down at his desk and wrote a story.

O what is that sound which so thrills the ear

O what is that sound which so thrills the ear
    Down in the valley drumming, drumming?

Only the scarlet soldiers, dear,
    The soldiers coming.

O what is that light I see flashing so clear
    Over the distance brightly, brightly?
Only the sun on their weapons, dear,
    As they step lightly.

O what are they doing with all that gear,
    What are they doing this morning, this morning?   10
Only their usual manoeuvres, dear,
    Or perhaps a warning.

O why have they left the road down there,
    Why are they suddenly wheeling, wheeling?
Perhaps a change in their orders, dear.
    Why are you kneeling?

O haven't they stopped for the doctor's care,
    Haven't they reined their horses, their horses?
Why, they are none of them wounded, dear,
    None of these forces   20

O is it the parson they want, with white hair,
    Is it the parson, is it, is it?
No, they are passing his gateway, dear,
    Without a visit.

O it must be the farmer who lives so near.
    It must be the farmer so cunning, so cunning?
They have passed the farmyard already, dear,
    And now they are running.

O where are you going? Stay with me here!
    Were the vows you swore deceiving, deceiving?   30
No, I promised to love you, dear,
    But I must be leaving.

O it's broken the lock and splintered the door,
    O it's the gate where they're turning, turning;
Their boots are heavy on the floor
    And their eyes are burning.

Theodore Roethke § 1908–1963

Roethke was born in Michigan, though from 1947 on he lived in Seattle, where he taught at the University of Washington until his premature death in 1963. His work is marked by widely varied styles.

Dolor

I have known the inexorable sadness of pencils,
Neat in their boxes, dolor of pad and paper-weight,
All the misery of manila folders and mucilage,
Desolation in immaculate public places,
Lonely reception room, lavatory, switchboard,
The unalterable pathos of basin and pitcher,
Ritual of multigraph, paper-clip, comma,
Endless duplication of lives and objects.
And I have seen dust from the walls of institutions,
Finer than flour, alive, more dangerous than silica,   10
Sift, almost invisible, through long afternoons of tedium,
Dripping a fine film on nails and delicate eyebrows,
Glazing the pale hair, the duplicate gray standard faces.

My Papa's Waltz

The whiskey on your breath
Could make a small boy dizzy;
But I held on like death:
Such waltzing was not easy.

We romped until the pans
Slid from the kitchen shelf;
My mother's countenance
Could not unfrown itself.

The hand that held my wrist
Was battered on one knuckle;   10
At every step I missed
My right ear scraped a buckle.

You beat time on my head
With a palm caked hard by dirt,

Then waltzed me off to bed
Still clinging to your shirt.

I Knew a Woman

I knew a woman, lovely in her bones,
When small birds sighed, she would sigh back at them;
Ah, when she moved, she moved more ways than one:
The shapes a bright container can contain!
Of her choice virtues only gods should speak,
Or English poets who grew up on Greek
(I'd have them sing in chorus, cheek to cheek).

How well her wishes went! She stroked my chin,
She taught me Turn, and Counter-turn, and Stand;
She taught me Touch, that undulant white skin;   10
I nibbled meekly from her proffered hand;
She was the sickle, I, poor I, the rake,
Coming behind her for her pretty sake
(But what prodigious mowing we did make).

Love likes a gander, and adores a goose:
Her full lips pursed, the errant note to seize;
She played it quick, she played it light and loose;
My eyes, they dazzled at her flowing knees;
Her several parts could keep a pure repose,
Or one hip quiver with a mobile nose   20
(She moved in circles, and those circles moved).

Let seed be grass, and grass turn into hay:
I'm martyr to a motion not my own;
What's freedom for? To know eternity.
I swear she cast a shadow white as stone.
But who would count eternity in days?
These old bones live to learn her wanton ways:
(I measure time by how a body sways).

Brother Antoninus § 1912–

*As William Everson, Brother Antoninus began writing poetry after
World War II, during which he had been a consciencious objector.*

He was active in the poetic revival around San Francisco in the late 1940's. He was converted to Roman Catholicism in 1949 and entered the Dominican Order as a lay brother in 1951.

August

Smoke color:
Haze thinly over the hills, low hanging,
But the sky steel, the sky shiny as steel, and the sun shouting.
The vineyard: in August the green-deep and heat-loving vines
Without motion grow heavy with grapes.
And he in the shining, on the turned earth, loose-lying,
The muscles clean and the limbs golden, turns to the sun the lips
    and the eyes;
As the virgin yields, impersonally passionate,
From the bone core and the aching flesh, the offering.

He has found the power and come to the glory.   10
He has turned clean-hearted to the last god, the symbolic sun.
With earth on his hands, bearing shoulder and arm the light's
    touch, he has come.
And having seen, the mind loosens, the nerve lengthens,
All the haunting abstractions slip free and are gone;
And the peace is enormous.

The Stranger

Pity this girl.
At callow sixteen,
Glib in the press of rapt companions,
She bruits her smatter,
Her bed-lore brag.
She prattles the lip-learned, light-love list.
In the new itch and squirm of sex,
How can she foresee?

How can she foresee the thick stranger,
Over the hills from Omaha,   10
Who will break her across a hired bed,
Open the loins,
Rive the breach,
And set the foetus wailing within the womb,

To hunch toward the knowledge of its disease,
And shamble down time to doomsday?

Karl Shapiro § 1913–

*Shapiro was educated at the University of Virginia and Johns
Hopkins University, where he also taught from 1947–1950. He was
editor of* Poetry *for six years, and since 1956 has been Professor
of English at the University of Nebraska and editor of the* Prairie
Schooner.

University

To hurt the Negro and avoid the Jew
Is the curriculum. In mid-September
The entering boys, identified by hats,
Wander in a maze of mannered brick
    Where boxwood and magnolia brood
    And columns with imperious stance
    Like rows of ante-bellum girls
        Eye them, outlanders.

In whited cells, on lawns equipped for peace,
Under the arch, and lofty banister,   10
Equals shake hands, unequals blankly pass;
The exemplary weather whispers, "Quiet, quiet"
    And visitors on tiptoe leave
    For the raw North, the unfinished West,
    As the young, detecting an advantage,
        Practice a face.

Where, on their separate hill, the colleges,
Like manor houses of an older law,
Gaze down embankments on a land in fee,
The Deans, dry spinsters over family plate,   20
    Ring out the English name like coin,
    Humor the snob and lure the lout.
    Within the precincts of this world
        Poise is a club.

But on the neighboring range, misty and high,
The past is absolute: some luckless race
Dull with inbreeding and conformity
Wears out its heart, and comes barefoot and bad
   For charity or jail. The scholar
   Sanctions their obsolete disease;   30
   The gentleman revolts with shame
      At his ancestor.

And the true nobleman, once a democrat,
Sleeps on his private mountain. He was one
Whose thought was shapely and whose dream was broad;
This school he held his art and epitaph.
   But now it takes from him his name,
   Falls open like a dishonest look,
   And shows us, rotted and endowed,
      Its senile pleasure.   40

Jew

The name is immortal but only the name, for the rest
Is a nose that can change in the weathers of time or persist
Or die out in confusion or model itself on the best.

But the name is a language itself that is whispered and hissed
Through the houses of ages, and ever a language the same,
And ever and ever a blow on our heart like a fist.

And this last of our dream in the desert, O curse of our name,
Is immortal as Abraham's voice in our fragment of prayer
Adonai, Adonai, for our bondage of murder and shame!

And the word for the murder of God will cry out on the air   10
Though the race is no more and the temples are closed of our will
And the peace is made fast on the earth and the earth is made fair;

Our name is impaled in the heart of the world on a hill
Where we suffer to die by the hands of ourselves, and to kill.

Dylan Thomas § 1914–1953

*Thomas, an English poet, was born in Wales. His vivid and unusual
style has made him one of the most widely read of the recent poets,
and his intense feeling for landscape nature can be seen in both
"The force that through the green fuse" and "Fern Hill."*

The force that through the green fuse

The force that through the green fuse drives the flower
Drives my green age; that blasts the roots of trees
Is my destroyer.
And I am dumb to tell the crooked rose
My youth is bent by the same wintry fever.

The force that drives the water through the rocks
Drives my red blood; that dries the mouthing streams
Turns mine to wax.
And I am dumb to mouth unto my veins
How at the mountain spring the same mouth sucks.   10

The hand that whirls the water in the pool
Stirs the quicksand; that ropes the blowing wind
Hauls my shroud sail.
And I am dumb to tell the hanging man
How of my clay is made the hangman's lime.

The lips of time leech to the fountain head;
Love drips and gathers, but the fallen blood
Shall calm her sores.
And I am dumb to tell a weather's wind
How time has ticked a heaven round the stars.   20

And I am dumb to tell the lover's tomb
How at my sheet goes the same crooked worm.

And death shall have no dominion

And death shall have no dominion.
Dead men naked they shall be one
With the man in the wind and the west moon;
When their bones are picked clean and the clean bones gone,

They shall have stars at elbow and foot;
Though they go mad they shall be sane,
Though they sink through the sea they shall rise again;
Though lovers be lost love shall not;
And death shall have no dominion.

And death shall have no dominion.　　　　　　　　　　10
Under the windings of the sea
They lying long shall not die windily;
Twisting on racks when sinews give way,
Strapped to a wheel, yet they shall not break;
Faith in their hands shall snap in two,
And the unicorn evils run them through;
Split all ends up they shan't crack;
And death shall have no dominion.

And death shall have no dominion.
No more may gulls cry at their ears　　　　　　　　　　20
Or waves break loud on the seashores;
Where blew a flower may a flower no more
Lift its head to the blows of the rain;
Though they be mad and dead as nails,
Heads of the characters hammer through daisies;
Break in the sun till the sun breaks down,
And death shall have no dominion.

A Refusal to Mourn the Death, by Fire, of a Child in London

Never until the mankind making
Bird beast and flower
Fathering and all humbling darkness
Tells with silence the last light breaking
And the still hour
Is come of the sea tumbling in harness

And I must enter again the round
Zion of the water bead
And the synagogue of the ear of corn
Shall I let pray the shadow of a sound　　　　　　　　10
Or sow my salt seed
In the least valley of sackcloth to mourn

The majesty and burning of the child's death.
I shall not murder
The mankind of her going with a grave truth
Nor blaspheme down the stations of the breath
With any further
Elegy of innocence and youth

Deep with the first dead lies London's daughter,   20
Robed in the long friends,
The grains beyond age, the dark veins of her mother
Secret by the unmourning water
Of the riding Thames
After the first death, there is no other.

Fern Hill

Now as I was young and easy under the apple boughs
About the lilting house and happy as the grass was green,
    The night above the dingle starry,
      Time let me hail and climb
    Golden in the heydays of his eyes,
And honoured among wagons I was prince of the apple towns
And once below a time I lordly had the trees and leaves
      Trail with daisies and barley
    Down the rivers of the windfall light.

And as I was green and carefree, famous among the barns   10
About the happy yard and singing as the farm was home,
    In the sun that is young once only,
      Time let me play and be
    Golden in the mercy of his means,
And green and golden I was huntsman and herdsman, the calves
Sang to my horn, the foxes on the hills barked clear and cold,
      And the sabbath rang slowly
    In the pebbles of the holy streams.

All the sun long it was running, it was lovely, the hay-
Fields high as the house, the tunes from the chimneys, it was air   20
    And playing, lovely and watery
      And fire green as grass.
    And nightly under the simple stars
As I rode to sleep the owls were bearing the farm away,

All the moon long I heard, blessed among stables, the nightjars
    Flying with the ricks, and the horses
        Flashing into the dark.

And then to awake, the farm, like a wanderer white
With the dew, come back, the cock on his shoulder: it was all
    Shining, it was Adam and maiden,   30
        The sky gathered again
And the sun grew round that very day.
So it must have been after the birth of the simple light
In the first, spinning place, the spellbound horses walking warm
    Out of the whinnying green stable
        On to the fields of praise.

And honoured among foxes and pheasants by the gay house
Under the new-made clouds and happy as the heart was long
    In the sun born over and over,
        I ran my heedless ways,   40
    My wishes raced through the house-high hay
And nothing I cared, at my sky blue trades, that time allows
In all his tuneful turning so few and such morning songs
    Before the children green and golden
        Follow him out of grace.

Nothing I cared, in the lamb white days, that time would take me
Up to the swallow-thronged loft by the shadow of my hand,
    In the moon that is always rising,
        Nor that riding to sleep
    I should hear him fly with the high fields   50
And wake to the farm forever fled from the childless land.
Oh as I was young and easy in the mercy of his means,
        Time held me green and dying
    Though I sang in my chains like the sea.

John Ciardi § 1916–

Ciardi has taught at Harvard and Rutgers. He is director of the Bread Loaf Writers Conference and poetry editor of the Saturday Review. *Since 1950, he has been translating Dante.*

After Sunday Dinner We Uncles Snooze

Banana-stuffed, the ape behind the brain
scratches his crotch in nature and lies back,
one arm across his eyes, one on his belly.
Thanksgiving afternoon in Africa,
the jungle couches heaped with hairy uncles
between a belch and a snore. All's well that yawns.

Seas in the belly lap a high tide home.
A kind of breathing flip-flop, all arrival,
souses the world full in the sog of time,
lifting slopped apes and uncles from their couches   10
for the long drift of self to self. Goodbye:
I'm off to idiot heaven in a drowse.

This is a man. This blubbermouth at air
sucking its flaps of breath, grimacing, blowing,
rasping, whistling. Walked through by a zoo
of his own reveries, he changes to it.
His palm's huge dabble over his broken face
rubs out the carnivores. His pixie pout

diddles a butterfly across his lip.
His yeasty smile drools Edens at a spring   20
where girls from Bali, kneeling to their bath,
cup palms of golden water to their breasts.
His lower lip thrusts back the angry chiefs:
he snarls and clicks his teeth: "Stand back, by God!"

And so, by God, they do, while he descends
to rape those knobs of glory with a sigh,
then clouds, surceased, and drifts away or melts
into another weather of himself
where only a drowned mumble far away
sounds in his throat the frog-pond under time.   30

O apes and hairy uncles of us all,
I hear the gibberish of a mother tongue
inside this throat. (A prattle from the sea.
A hum in the locked egg. A blather of bloods.)
O angels and attendants past the world,
what shall the sleeps of heaven dream but time?

Vodka

Vodka, I hope you will note, is
upwind from all other essences.
Drink it all night and all day
and your aunt's minister could
not track you to perdition, not
even with his nose for it. Vodka
has no breath. Call it the dead-
man's drink. But praise it. As
long as he can stand, a vodka-
drinker is sober, and when he   10
falls down he is merely sleepy.
Like poetry, vodka informs anything with which it is diluted,
and like poetry, alas, it must be
diluted. Only a Russian can take
it straight, and only after long
conditioning, and just see what
seems to be coming of that!

English A

No paraphrase does
between understanding
and understanding.

You are either
that noun beyond
qualification into

whose round fact
I pass unparsed
and into whose eyes

I speak idioms   10
beyond construction;
or else get up,

fasten your suffixes
and your hyphenations,
buckle your articles,

spray modifiers
and moods
behind your ears

and take the whole
developed discourse   20
of your thighs to

any damned grammarian
you whatsoever
wish. Period.

Suburban Homecoming

As far as most of what you call people, my darling, are
concerned, I don't care who or what gets into the phone. I
am not home and not expected and I even, considerably, doubt I live here.

I mean this town and its everlasting katzenjammer whenever whoever dials again, is going to hell, or to some other
perpetual buffet, in a wheelbarrowful of bad martinis: and you, my

legal sweet, forever in the act of putting your hat on
as I come in the door to be told I have exactly five—
or, on good days, ten—minutes to change in because here we go

again to some collection of never quite-the-same-but-   10
always-no-different faces; you, my moth-brained flutter
from bright cup to cup, no matter what nothing is in them; you, my own

brand-named, laboratory-tested, fair-trade priced, wedded
(as advertised in *Life*) feather-duster, may go jump into
twenty fathoms of Advice to the Lovelorn and pull it in after you—

but I have not arrived, am not it, the phone did not ring
and was not answered, we have not really, I believe, met, and
if we do and if I stay to be (I doubt it) introduced, I'm still not going.

Robert Lowell § 1917–

Lowell was educated at Harvard and then studied under John Crowe Ransom at Kenyon College. A member of the famous Lowell family of Boston, he now lives in New York, where he has also written plays, notably adapting "Benito Cereno" and "My Kins-man, Major Molineux" for the stage. He is generally recognized as the major American poet of his generation.

Children of Light

Our fathers wrung their bread from stocks and stones
And fenced their gardens with the Redman's bones;
Embarking from the Nether Land of Holland,
Pilgrims unhouseled by Geneva's night,
They planted here the Serpent's seeds of light;
And here the pivoting searchlights probe to shock
The riotous glass houses built on rock,
And candles gutter by an empty altar,
And light is where the landless blood of Cain
Is burning, burning the unburied grain.   10

Mr. Edwards and the Spider

I saw the spiders marching through the air,
Swimming from tree to tree that mildewed day
    In latter August when the hay
    Came creaking to the barn. But where
        The wind is westerly,
Where gnarled November makes the spiders fly
Into the apparitions of the sky,
They purpose nothing but their ease and die
Urgently beating east to sunrise and the sea;

What are we in the hands of the great God?   10
It was in vain you set up thorn and briar
    In battle array against the fire
    And treason crackling in your blood;
        For the wild thorns grow tame
And will do nothing to oppose the flame;
Your lacerations tell the losing game

You play against a sickness past your cure.
How will the hands be strong? How will the heart endure?

A very little thing, a little worm,
Or hourglass-blazoned spider, it is said,   20
   Can kill a tiger. Will the dead
   Hold up his mirror and affirm
     To the four winds the smell
And flash of his authority? It's well
If God who holds you to the pit of hell,
   Much as one holds a spider, will destroy,
Baffle and dissipate your soul. As a small boy

On Windsor Marsh, I saw the spider die
When thrown into the bowels of fierce fire:
   There's no long struggle, no desire   30
   To get up on its feet and fly—
     It stretches out its feet
And dies. This is the sinner's last retreat;
Yes, and no strength exerted on the heat
   Then sinews the abolished will, when sick
And full of burning, it will whistle on a brick.

But who can plumb the sinking of that soul?
Josiah Hawley, picture yourself cast
   Into a brick kiln where the blast
   Fans your quick vitals to a coal—   40
     If measured by a glass,
How long would it seem burning! Let there pass
A minute, ten, ten trillion; but the blaze
   Is infinite, eternal: this is death,
To die and know it. This is the Black Widow, death.

Lawrence Ferlinghetti § 1919–

Ferlinghetti was born in New York and educated at the University of North Carolina, Columbia, and the Sorbonne. His name is inescapably connected with San Francisco, where he not only wrote but published some of the first Beat poetry to see print. He has read his poetry widely on college campuses throughout the United States.

A Coney Island of the Mind

15

Constantly risking absurdity
                and death
      whenever he performs
          above the heads
              of his audience
   the poet like an acrobat
        climbs on rime
          to a high wire of his own making
and balancing on eyebeams
         above a sea of faces   10
     paces his way
        to the other side of day
    performing entrechats
        and sleight-of-foot tricks
and other high theatrics
        and all without mistaking
     any thing
       for what it may not be

    For he's the super realist
        who must perforce perceive   20
    taut truth
      before the taking of each stance or step
in his supposed advance
       toward that still higher perch
where Beauty stands and waits
       with gravity
         to start her death-defying leap
  And he
     a little charleychaplin man
       who may or may not catch   30
her fair eternal form
     spreadeagled in the empty air
  of existence

28

Dove sta amore
Where lies love
Dove sta amore
Here lies love
The ring dove love
In lyrical delight
Hear love's hillsong

Love's true willsong
Love's low plainsong
 Too sweet painsong   10
In passages of night
 Dove sta amore
 Here lies love
The ring dove love
 Dove sta amore
 Here lies love

Richard Wilbur § 1921–

Wilbur has, like Lowell, adapted plays, especially Molière's Misanthrope *and* Tartuffe, *in addition to writing poems. From the publication of his first book of poems in 1947, he has been praised for his versatility and technical skill.*

The Death of a Toad

A toad the power mower caught,
Chewed and clipped of a leg, with a hobbling hop has got
 To the garden verge, and sanctuaried him
Under the cineraria leaves, in the shade
 Of the ashen heart-shaped leaves, in a dim,
  Low, and a final glade.

The rare original heartsblood goes,
Spends on the earthen hide, in the folds and wizenings, flows
 In the gutters of the banked and staring eyes. He lies
As still as if he would return to stone,   10
 And soundlessly attending, dies
  Toward some deep monotone,

Toward misted and ebullient seas
And cooling shores, toward lost Amphibia's emperies
 Day dwindles, drowning, and at length is gone
In the wide and antique eyes, which still appear
 To watch, across the castrate lawn,
  The haggard daylight steer.

Edgar Bowers § 1921–

Born in Georgia, Bowers was educated at the University of North Carolina and Stanford. He has taught at Duke and the University of California at Santa Barbara.

For W. A. Mozart

Against each perfect note I bear all thought.
Before the passion of thy complex grace
Flesh melts from bone that lies across the face,
And thought lies bare to what thy genius wrought.

But thought to most with faint acceptance blames,
Who find no human feeling in such form;
And the desire that rhetoric perform
Its unique cries I counter with no claims

But say that in Saalfelden once I played
Upon thine own clavier, now black with age,   10
Some remnant of thy sweet and decorous rage
Until such condescending minds, afraid
To cant against such naked elegance,
Could speak no more of spectacular innocence.

The Wise Men

Far to the east I see them in my mind
Coming in every year to that one place.
They carry in their hands what they must find,
In their own faces bare what they shall face.

They move in silence, permanent and sure,
Like figurines of porcelain set with gold,
The colors of their garments bright and pure,
Their graceful features elegant and old.

They do not change: nor war nor peace define
Nor end the journey that each year the same   10
Renders them thus. They wait upon a sign
That promises no future but their name.

§ FOR COMMENT

Bowers' "The Wise Men" was written after W. B. Yeats' "The Magi," and
its first lines strongly recall the phrasing of Yeats' poem. Comment on how
certain characteristics of the Wise Men are stressed in both poems. In what
ways are Bowers' and Yeats' descriptions similar? different?

Why does Yeats use the words "unsatisfied" or "dissatisfied" to describe the Magi? Of what human tendencies or types of human beings do
his Magi become symbolic? Tell which of the two poems you prefer and
why.

In the Yeats poem, be sure you paraphrase "Calvary's turbulence" and
"The uncontrollable mystery on the bestial floor."

Bink Noll § 1927–

*A graduate of Princeton, Johns Hopkins, and the University of
Colorado, Noll has taught at Dartmouth and since 1961 has been
at Beloit College, where he is one of the editors of the* Beloit
Poetry Journal.

Abraham's Madness

When Isaac watched his father strain back
the ram's head, its throat separate and bleed,
evisceration, and fat turn to smoke,

not *he* had heard any angel speak
but felt sharply where the rope still cut,
how his own neck cracked, his own flesh burned.

I likewise learned to distrust my sire
whose god in our house was powerful
as revenge shuddering through a plot.

Mornings, his story would begin,   10
"My dear boy, God will provide the lamb,"
when I knew I went the only lamb,

knew the god had repeated his demand
and violence on this man who adored
both of us past any hope of reason.

I was proving tall, bright, soft of voice.
Then he—his love wild to get me grown—
would change and cheat the law, then reach out

to slay some cheap and easy innocent,
then stop the silence raging in his ear   20
by reports of angels I never heard.

How we sons lay awake to ponder
The misery of such divided men
to whom patriarchal lies come true.

My son shall not watch me in a fury
of faith take fire to the altar where
I sacrifice nothing I cherish.

He may feel my hands grab like priest hands,
his eyes may die in the brightness
that I have meant obedience entire.   30

So much I walked with my mad Abraham.

Afternoon for a Small Boy

In that rest made green by window shades
Drawn two thirds against the open blaze
(The blinds slipping in the lilac breeze)
Christopher floats, bones gently askew
But wake as the eyes of a statue—
Floats inside the hushing of the bees
That sweetly sift the upstairs air.
The mower in the distance of his ear
Makes buzz; his sister whirs on tricycle
But he cribs a peace beyond words still   10
While down the sun flings parallelograms
Upon the rug and waits for him like games.

The Drama

The Drama

✿ *Origins and Development*

The chief difficulty in discussing the origins of the drama is that no one knows how the drama originated. Traditionalists maintain that ancient Greek drama, the oldest that has come down to us in a developed form, evolved slowly. The beginnings, they claim, were celebrations in honor of Dionysos, god of wine and fertility, identified with the crops and the seasonal pattern of winter and spring, the symbolic pattern of death and resurrection. At first choruses of revelers ecstatically worshiped him in song and dance. Eventually audiences and performers were separated, with a chorus made up of the latter chanting *dithyrambs*, poetic songs about incidents in the life of Dionysos. At a later date, a leader of the chorus sang *solus*, and the remaining members of the chorus—sometimes joined by their leader—chanted and danced in unison. Later, choruses sang dithyrambs about other gods and then of heroes.

In approximately 534 B.C., an actor-playwright introduced into the performance a single character who embodied the god or hero about whom the chorus sang. This innovator, the first actor, was named Thespis, and to this day actors are called "thespians," after him. Aeschylus added a second actor, thereby diminishing the importance of the chorus and placing greater emphasis upon the dialogue. Sophocles added a third actor, and there it stopped. The plays of these dramatists were presented in competition at a major civic and religious event, the Great Dionysia, or City Dionysia, held annually at the end of March. The works of three playwrights were selected for production: each contributed a tetralogy composed of three tragedies and a satyr play, a burlesque with a chorus of satyrs, which provided comic relief after the tragedies.

Although the maximum number of actors was three, this meant not that only three characters were in the play but that only three speaking actors were on stage at one time. Nonspeaking actors could also be present, and the speaking actors could double and even triple their roles. Plays were performed before a single-story scene building (*skene*) and then a larger, two-story building with enormous side wings. In front of the *skene* the chorus sang and danced in a large, circular *orchestra*. The seating capacity of the open-air Theater of Dionysos in Athens in the fifth century B.C. was approximately 14,000 persons. The size of the auditorium may partially explain some of the particular conventions of Greek tragedy: masks, large headdresses, thick soles on the shoes, and built up shoulders helped the audience see the actors. The masks had features larger than life and also helped to amplify the actors' voices; costumes were bigger than those in real life and movements more stylized than those in life—these exaggerative elements carried to the spectators sitting far from the stage more clearly than would normal features, clothes, and movements. Other conventions of Greek tragedy were off-stage deaths (it is difficult to remove corpses in an open-air theater with no front curtain), the use of a messenger to report off-stage violence, and a chorus that danced while singing.

Much of the traditional view of the gradual development of Greek *tragedy* has been questioned on the basis that there is little factual evidence of tragedy gradually evolving from Dionysiac celebrations. According to a new interpretation, Thespis did not revise or adapt an existing dramatic form but created that form. Taking the dithyrambs sung by the epic poets, Thespis invented embodiment and enactment. The epic hero was impersonated rather than described, and the chorus, composed not of great heroes but of ordinary mortals like the audience, was a foil to him. Aeschylus' addition of a second actor made possible dramatic scenes of conflict.[1]

Chapter 6 of Aristotle's *Poetics* (as translated by S. H. Butcher) defines *tragedy* as

> an imitation of an action that is serious, complete, and of a certain magnitude; in language embellished with each kind of artistic ornament, the several kinds being found in separate parts of the play; in the form of action, not of narrative; through pity and fear effecting the proper purgation of these emotions.

Tragedy, according to Aristotle, is primarily an imitation not of life, not of characters, not of events, not of plot, but of an action: that is, a subtextual motive or movement underlying the events involving the characters. The action, embedded in a serious plot and performed by characters who are neither frivolous nor comic, is completed at the end of the play. The story is not narrated but is presented by characters enacting the events as they occur. (The word "drama," it may be noted at this point, derives from the Greek word *dran*, which means not "to recite" or "to describe," but "to do," "to act.") The language of Greek tragedy, as noted in the second clause of the quotation, has considerable variety. Parts of the play are lyric, parts have musical accompaniment; other parts are rhetorical, others have the structure of a formal debate, and still others have the rapid-fire quality of *stichomythia* (a portion of dialogue in which two actors alternately speak one line of verse). The final clause of the passage quoted above deals with the tragic *catharsis*, the most common general

---

[1] Gerald F. Else, *The Origin and Early Form of Greek Tragedy* (Cambridge: Harvard University Press, 1965).

interpretation of which is that members of the audience, by watching events embodying pity and fear, themselves experience these emotions (pity for the character's suffering and sympathetic fear for him), gaining thereby an emotional release and balance.

Comedy, like tragedy, is also said to have had a choral origin: phallic songs in which revelers, possibly wearing animal costumes, engaged in ribald merriment. Athenian comedy, as seen in the plays of Aristophanes, contains a debate, an address to the audience on a current topic, satire directed against living people (using their actual names)—with wit, obscenity, and bawdiness mixed in varying proportions. In the plays of Aristophanes, Athenian democracy is lampooned, political figures satirized, other playwrights derided, the gods made fun of, and the comic aspects of sex fully exploited. *The Frogs*, for example, opens with Dionysos and Heracles discussing defecation. The message of *Lysistrata* may be summarized by the slogan, "Make love, not war"; the two activities are presented as mutually exclusive, for the women have a sex strike to persuade their husbands to stop the war.

Eventually, Greek comedy became less socially satiric and less ribald, dealing with ordinary people and their problems—chiefly, love and money, two themes which have characterized comedy ever since. Characters, subject matter, language, and outcome of plot are the major traditional distinctions between tragedy and comedy. Although exceptions to these distinctions can be found, tragedy usually deals with heroic personages, comedy with ordinary citizens; tragedy with events of magnitude on which hinge the fate of kingdoms, comedy with domestic concerns; tragedy using lofty language, comedy ordinary speech; tragedy ending in catastrophe, comedy in marriage.

While these distinctions generally hold in the post-Grecian theater as well as in the Attic theater, drama—in common with other literary forms—changed. After the fall of the Roman Empire, the Catholic Church tried to suppress the drama. Theatrical activity, however, was not extinguished. Traveling troubadours, mimes, and actors practiced their art during the Dark Ages—often keeping one step ahead of the law, for edicts were passed which forbade them from performing. Actors were regarded as sinful, since their trade consisted of lies and deceit: they pretended to be what they were not.

Ironically the church, which had condemned actors, helped foster the drama, for it employed theatrical elements to make its teachings more vivid. The earliest church drama (liturgical drama) was not spoken but sung, not in the vernacular but in Latin. It was performed not by professional actors but by members of the clergy, not in a theater but in the church itself.

Various Biblical stories were produced in the church, often with elaborate theatrical elements. During the Easter service the arrival of the three Marys at Jesus' tomb was enacted. Upon their realization that Jesus had risen, the prior would sing the *Te Deum laudamus*, at which point all of the cathedral bells would begin to chime. During the Christmas service the Magi would arrive at the altar bringing gold, frankincense, and myrrh to the newly born Jesus. On other occasions, scenes depicted the angel with the flaming sword; Jesus, Mary, and Joseph fleeing into Egypt; and the Slaughter of the Innocents (played by the entire choir).

The shape of the medieval cathedral influenced the shape of the medieval theater. Platforms—called *mansions, houses,* or *sedes*—were set up inside the church, each mansion representing a different, specific locale: the manger, Nazareth, the tomb, Hell, Heaven, and so forth. Between the mansions was an open space called the *platea*—an indefinite, unlocalized area which could be "anywhere." The multiscenic drama of the medieval theater was enacted by means of *simultaneous staging*: several locales on view at the same time, the actors moving from one to another as required by the text. When the religious drama moved outside the church into the town square, the multiple settings were retained, for the form of the drama was retained.

These multiscenic dramas, far different from the single setting, box-set play squeezed behind a proscenium arch, which so often is the setting for today's plays, were not primitive but were sophisticated and even spectacular. *The Play of Adam,* for example, a twelfth-century French drama, not only had lavish costumes but also lively scenic effects as devils thrust Adam and Eve into Hell, which belched out smoke and emitted sounds of chaos (made by clashing pots and kettles).

Plays were based on events in the Old and New Testaments (*mystery plays*), on the passion of Christ (*passion plays*), on incidents in the lives of the saints (*miracle plays*). In the fourteenth century a still more complex drama emerged, the *morality play*. An allegorical drama based on Christian teaching but not on Biblical stories, the morality play was a parable whose characters personified abstract ideas or characteristics (for example, mankind, beauty, virtue, vice). *Everyman* is perhaps the most famous of these morality plays.

The Elizabethan theater—William Shakespeare's theater—derived in large part from the medieval stage. Like the medieval theater, Shakespeare's was a multiscenic drama with rapid succession of scenes. A *platform stage* thrust into the audience allowed a more intimate relationship between actor and spectator than today's proscenium arch theater provides. Shakespeare's stage did not use realistic scenery to give a representational background to the action. The poet's words provided the scenery. "This castle hath a pleasant seat," says Duncan (*Macbeth,* I, vi), and the audience is before Macbeth's castle. The dramatist's words also provided stage lighting. Although the plays were performed in daylight, the poet could by his language transform the stage into night. "The moon is down," says Fleance (*Macbeth,* II, i). "And she goes down at twelve," adds Banquo, who, examining the daylight sky, remarks that thrifty heaven has extinguished its candles (stars). Thus, the actual time of day notwithstanding, night is created. Shakespeare's theater, like the medieval, was a theater not of realistic representation but of poetic conventions.

Shakespeare's theater was similar to Sophocles' in that both were theaters of presentation rather than of representation, of convention rather than of verisimilitude. Unlike the earlier theater, however, Shakespeare's had no chorus (on some occasions, a character was called "Chorus," but the resemblance is in name only: Shakespeare's chorus was a narrator), did not use either masks or exaggerated costumes (since the auditorium was considerably smaller, there was no need to exaggerate the features or the clothes of the performers), did not restrict itself to three actors on stage at the same time, and was not troubled by corpses on stage.

According to the German philosopher Georg Wilhelm Friedrich Hegel a fundamental distinction between Sophoclean and Shakespearean tragedy is the latter's greater complexity of character. The hero of a Greek tragedy exemplifies an ethical conception and a universal subject. The hero of a Shakespearean tragedy might also do so, but ethics and universals are little more than background for the individual, whose personality has greater relative importance. Although the heroes of Greek tragedy are not types or abstractions, they are less complex than Shakespeare's.

While Shakespeare's theater was far more concerned with the individual personality than was the Greek theater, today's theater is even more so. August Strindberg sounded the modern note when, in his preface to *Miss Julie*, he decried the conception of *character* as signifying a one-dimensional, unchanging individual, characterized entirely by a word ("drunk" or "melancholy," for instance), by a single defect (obesity or dipsomania), or by a set phrase that the character repeats. The Swedish playwright called for the abolition of the simple, one-dimensional stage character (the miser, the dolt, the brute, the jealous lover, and the like) and his replacement by complex personages in whom both virtue and vice are mixed. A miser, for example, might also be an excellent financier and a good father. Realistically drawn characters, Strindberg maintained, are not simple types but are conglomerates of many diverse characteristics—so many powerful influences that it is impossible to determine where one leaves off and the other begins. In the modern theater—as in *Miss Julie*—psychological, sociological, physical, and environmental motivations should replace caricatures. In the same preface, Strindberg boasted that his dialogue was untraditional in that his characters did not ask questions merely to receive a clever reply. Avoiding symmetrical, mathematical discourse, he has allowed his characters' dialogue to wander, as it does in real life where, during a conversation, a topic is dropped and later picked up, repeated, and developed. This type of characterization and of dialogue typifies a large part of the modern theater and may be found in plays like *Miss Julie* and in Tennessee Williams' *The Glass Menagerie* (though not in Strindberg's nonrealistic *A Dream Play*).

Like the dialogue, scenic practices in the modern theater generally aim at verisimilitude. Actors do not usually wear enormous headdresses or chant their dialogue in unison with fourteen others. Actors perform within —not in front of—settings that aim to convince the audience that they are real, trying to persuade the spectators that they are eavesdropping on events which occur before their eyes. The staple scenic device in the modern theater—the *box set*—consists of three visible walls of a room, the fourth removed in order to allow the audience to see what happens in that room. Lighting simulates the appropriate locale and time of day, properties are recognizably accurate, and make-up is so disguised that the audience is unaware of it. A production of *Pygmalion* following Bernard Shaw's design would typify this realistic scenic milieu.

Since much realistic scenery is commonplace, ugly, or drab, however, scene designers and playwrights sometimes attempt to achieve a more beautiful stage picture by such means as spacial arrangement, simplification, selectivity, and lighting. Although the results may be different from real life (for example, a blue tint to a scene, a wall-less doorway symbolizing an entire room), the particular properties used are frequently realistic enough to permit the audience to accept the scene as real. A production of *The Glass Menagerie* following the author's design would contain both realistic and unrealistic scenic elements.

The Glass Menagerie typifies another development in modern drama: the concern with characters in lower income brackets. Commoners figure prominently in some tragedies of Sophocles and Shakespeare, to be sure— the Sentry in *Antigonê*, the Porter in *Macbeth*—but such characters are not made central figures of a noncomic play. In our age of democracy, the stage is democratic. "Attention must be paid," in the words of Arthur Miller, to common, ordinary people and their problems. In today's theater, attention *is* paid. The Sentry and the drunken Porter today stand in the center of the stage.

In contemporary theater many traditional attitudes and practices have broken down. This disintegration reflects a world whose assumptions and values have been shattered. Playwrights are trying to create new forms that might directly express a sense of fragmentation and of spiritual dislocation, of man trapped in an incomprehensible and indifferent universe. A *Dream Play* is an effort to find a new form that is reflective of its subject matter. This play anticipates by half a century the "theater of the absurd," whose playwrights—chiefly, Samuel Beckett, Eugene Ionesco, and Harold Pinter —dramatize the absurdity of the human condition. These dramatists neither discuss a philosophy nor employ a conventionally linear plot. Instead, as in *A Dream Play*, such practices are discarded in favor of theme-centered juxtaposition of scenes; cyclic arrangements of futile efforts (the circularity directly expressive of the futility since it has neither beginning nor end); disintegrated, fragmented, and abstracted personality; a form that is an outgrowth and an embodiment of a particular poetic image, created anew by the subject matter of the individual work. The transitional and influential *A Dream Play* stands between the familiar forms and the new forms, retaining—partly by its comprehensible framework—elements of traditional dramatic structure while at the same time looking forward to newer, untraditional forms.

�֎ *Techniques of Theater*

Since the drama is a literary genre, several of the devices used in analyzing other literary genres may also be used to analyze the drama: theme; protagonist and antagonist in conflict; complications, climax, and resolution; images, connotations, and denotations. It is unnecessary, therefore, to dwell on them here. Instead, the reader is urged to consult "The Devices of Fiction" in the introduction to the short story (pages 22-28) and the discussion of language in the introduction to poetry (pages 375-379).

Unlike other literary genres, however, drama is not solely a literary art: It is also (and primarily) part of the art of the theater. Short stories, novels, and most poems are intended for the reader. Although the drama may be read, enjoyed, and analyzed as the other genres are, drama is intended for the *viewer*. Characters are not described for the audience but are embodied before the viewers by living representatives whom they see and hear, in milieus they themselves observe. They are not told about the events: they see them occurring. Plays, in other words, are written to be performed by actors upon a stage. The reader must remember this.

Living actors who are placed before an audience enact their scenes in what Thornton Wilder calls "a perpetual present time." This, says Wilder, distinguishes a play from a novel: "The novel is a past reported in the present. On the stage it is always now." [2] Even when the playwright uses a narrator—as Williams does in *The Glass Menagerie*—the audience sees the events that are enacted. Although the narrator tells the viewer that these events occurred in the past, he sees them occurring now, for the framework dissolves and the past is placed before him in the present.

In the drama, moreover, no one character speaks with the author's voice. The audience is not told by an impartial voice what attitude to take or what "truth" to believe. Sometimes a character may describe his

[2] Thornton Wilder, "Some Thoughts on Playwriting," in *Aspects of the Drama*, ed. Sylvan Barnet, Morton Berman, and William Burto (Boston: Little, Brown, 1962), pp. 9–10.

or another's state of mind; the author cannot. Shakespeare does not himself or through another character tell us that Lady Macbeth must drink in order to steel herself to assist in the murder of Duncan. She herself provides the information: "That which hath made them [Duncan's grooms] drunk hath made me bold: / What hath quench'd them hath given me fire" (II, ii). But neither the author nor the characters themselves nor other characters comment on the inner states of Macbeth and Lady Macbeth when they appear in public after the murder of Duncan (II, iii). Shakespeare reveals their inner states by such indirect means as the rhythms of the characters' language, their fluency or nonfluency, etc.

The warning not to confuse the narrator of a short story with the author of that story applies, _mutatis mutandis,_ to the drama. Even when a character may hold some of the author's views, it is a mistake to regard that character as a mouthpiece of the author. Nor, when a play employs a narrator, should one assume that the narrator is or speaks for the author. Although Tom, in _The Glass Menagerie_, writes at night after having worked all day in a shoe factory (as did Williams) and although he bears the author's real first name (Williams was christened Thomas Lanier), he has only a limited and biased comprehension of the other characters (his mother, for example). This admonition applies also to the chorus in a Greek tragedy, for it should not be taken as _fully_ representative of the author's views. Not only do the chorus' views change as the play progresses and it learns more of the true situation, but its members are not portrayed as intelligent or insightful enough to compare with the protagonist, let alone the author. The chorus might more properly be regarded as a link between ourselves and the heroic personages, a bridge between ourselves and characters greater than ourselves.

In the drama, even when a narrator or chorus is employed, all voices are partial. All statements emanate from a character, whose point of view and motives must be taken into account. The viewer is presented not with a known, credible voice but with the very problem of credibility, a question of what to believe. Compare, in this regard, Shaw's nondramatic epilogue to _Pygmalion_ with the dramatic ending the audience sees in the theater. In the epilogue the author explicitly tells us what happens. In the play a character tells us what he thinks will happen. He may be right; but he is not necessarily right.

In the theater, information, attitudes, and points of view can be given more objectively than in fiction. This characteristic of the drama is both a disadvantage and an advantage. It is a disadvantage because the author cannot be certain that his audience will receive the impressions he wishes them to receive, an advantage because the objectivity (the words and deeds of the characters themselves) create complexities and ambiguities that descriptive statements might diminish.

In examining the verbal fabric of the play, one must go beyond traditional linguistic analysis, for one needs to consider that the language is spoken aloud. Because of this, words tend to transmit a greater sense of urgency and potency than they otherwise might. Although verbal impact is not limited to the shock created by obscenity, taboo words illustrate the greater power of the spoken than of the read word. Of the plays in this volume, *Pygmalion* offers perhaps the most striking example. To imagine the impact of Eliza Doolittle's "Not bloody likely" when these words were first uttered in a London theater in 1914 today's viewer or reader would have to imagine, in place of the now mild but then obscene "bloody," one of today's taboo words, such as what may euphemistically be called "the eff word" (which is still potent enough to be taboo in many places). More powerful than language that is merely read, spoken language—with its pauses and inflexions, its emphases and rhythms, as well as the timbre of the voices producing the sounds—is an important factor in theatrical analysis.

Since living actors are placed before the viewer—embodying the characters engaged in activities and events the author has dramatized—his attitude toward the characters and the events is largely determined by the look of the stage. Theater addresses itself to our eyes as well as to our ears. The scenic environment of the action, its shape and color, the degree in which it resembles reality—these are important considerations. Important too are the groupings of the actors on stage, their composition, their movements, the colors of their costumes. The movements of the chorus in *Antigonê*—fifteen bearded Theban elders in beautiful costumes!—create visual rhythms and harmonies which vitally influence our understanding of the play. The very fact that fifteen voices chant the choral verses gives a power to these lyrics that is far different from that of a single voice. The various actors who might be cast as, say, Creon or Lady Macbeth can each find different aspects of the character to stress. The result will be not the author's character but the author's character as interpreted by the physical presence and personality of the actor in relation to the physical presence and personalities of the other actors. How much shorter than Macbeth is Lady Macbeth? Is a youthful or a middle-aged actress to play her? an attractive or unattractive actress? In a purely literary analysis of the play, such questions need not arise. When one considers the play as a blueprint for stage production, such questions must arise. Aside from differences in temperament, interpretation, etc., the very bodies and voices of Vivien Leigh, Judith Anderson, and Simone Signoret, all of whom have played Lady Macbeth, result in different Lady Macbeths. In a production of *Pygmalion*, how attractive or unattractive (which is not the same as handsome or ugly) an actor will play Higgins? This will make a difference in whether the audience wants Liza to marry him. In *The Glass Menagerie*, is Jim O'Connor to look handsome and vital, or will an actor be chosen who looks ordinary and run-down? One actress may stress the narrowness, blindness, and pettiness of Amanda Wingfield, another her warmth and her desire to help her daughter; another may attempt to achieve a balance.

The audiences who come to see the play will see one of these Jims, one of these Amandas, one of these *Menageries*. Audiences *have* seen the Jim O'Connors of Anthony Ross, Kirk Douglas, and Pat Hingle—all different from each other in important respects—and the Amanda Wingfields of Laurette Taylor, Helen Hayes, and Gertrude Lawrence—again, all different from each other in important respects. Unlike a novel, short story, or poem, in which no one stands between the author and the reader, a play has numerous people standing between the author and the audience: it is through them that one grasps the work.

In reading a play, one must do more than analyze the verbal structure. He must create for himself the visual pattern: the movement of Everyman as he goes from one mansion to another, the battles of *Macbeth*, the hat business following Mrs. Higgins' first speech in the third act of *Pygmalion*. When one sees the play in the theater, this will have been done for him; when he reads the play, he must do it himself. More than with any other literary form, the drama requires the reader to use his mind's eye to see the play. The reader needs to create in his imagination the production of that play, for the author intended his work primarily to be seen and heard on a stage rather than to be read at home or in a library. Shakespeare's drunken Porter (*Macbeth*, II, iii) has numerous comic lines, but he does not merely stand still and recite them. How does he deliver such an apparently simple line as, "Knock, knock, knock"? His appearance, his dress, what he does while speaking his lines and between his lines are all significant. Shakespeare, the anonymous author of *Everyman*, and the Greeks did not provide elaborate stage directions to help us visualize the play on stage. Modern authors, however, embellish the dialogue of their plays with such stage directions partly to help the reader imagine the theatrical enactment of the printed dialogue and partly to convey their intentions more precisely to the actors and directors who produce their plays. Shaw and Williams are among those who provide stage directions that help the reader visualize the action. When Shaw tells us that Henry Higgins stares after Eliza *"in sincere surprise"* and that he *"impatiently"* speaks a line, when Williams writes that Tom *"springs up"* to get an ugly, bulky coat and that Amanda *"closes the door hesitantly and with a troubled but faintly hopeful expression,"* these authors help us see the actors in our minds' eyes.

In examining the drama, then, one must bear the theater in mind. The play is a literary form that is enacted by performers on a stage. To concentrate on one factor to the neglect of the other would result in an incomplete picture and thus an incomplete experience. In the words of the scene designer Gordon Craig,

> . . . the Art of the Theatre is neither acting nor the play, it is not scene nor dance, but it consists of all the elements of which these things are composed: action, which is the very spirit of acting; words, which are the

body of the play; line and colour, which are the very heart of the scene; rhythm, which is the very essence of dance.[3]

Although different people might emphasize different elements of this art of the theater, all of these elements are vital, and all must be considered by the sensitive reader.

[3] Edward Gordon Craig, *On the Art of the Theatre* (New York: Theatre Arts Books, 1960), p. 138. Craig is usually referred to without his first name.

Sophocles § 496–405 B.C.

Aeschylus, Sophocles, and Euripides are the only three Attic trage-dians whose work has come down to us. Although we know virtually nothing of Sophocles' life, we do know that he wrote approximately 120 plays. Of these, only seven are extant: Ajax, Electra, Philoctetes, The Women of Trachis, *and three tragedies about Oedipus and his children. In story sequence they are:* Oedipus the King *(c. 429),* Oedipus at Colonus *(produced posthumously, 401), and* Antigonê *(c. 442). Aristotle, in his* Poetics, *frequently praises Sophocles' technical mastery, particularly in* Oedipus the King. *He admires Sophocles' treatment of the Chorus as an integral part of the action rather than as an interlude and approvingly reports the statement that whereas Euripides portrayed men as they are, Sophocles por-trayed them as they ought to be. Sophocles' theatrical innovations are said to include the addition of a third actor in tragedy, the abandonment of the trilogy for three independent and self-contained tragedies, the invention of scene painting, and the addition of three members to the Chorus, raising it in number from twelve to fifteen.*

Antigonê

TRANSLATED BY DUDLEY FITTS AND ROBERT FITZGERALD

PERSONS REPRESENTED

ANTIGONE
ISMENE
EURYDICE
CREON
HAIMON
TEIRESIAS
A SENTRY
A MESSENGER
CHORUS

SCENE: *Before the palace of* CREON, *King of Thebes. A central double door, and two lateral doors. A platform extends the length of the façade, and from this platform three steps lead down into the "orchestra," or chorus-ground.* TIME: *dawn of the day after the repulse of the Argive army from the assault on Thebes.*

§ PROLOGUE

ANTIGONE *and* ISMENE *enter from the central door of the Palace.*

ANTIGONE: Ismenê, dear sister,
   You would think that we had already suffered enough
   For the curse on Oedipus.
   I cannot imagine any grief
   That you and I have not gone through. And now—
   Have they told you of the new decree of our King Creon?
ISMENE: I have heard nothing: I know
   That two sisters lost two brothers, a double death
   In a single hour; and I know that the Argive army
   Fled in the night; but beyond this, nothing.   10
ANTIGONE: I thought so. And that is why I wanted you
   To come out here with me. There is something we must do.
ISMENE: Why do you speak so strangely?
ANTIGONE: Listen, Ismenê:
   Creon buried our brother Eteoclês
   With military honors, gave him a soldier's funeral,
   And it was right that he should; but Polyneicês,
   Who fought as bravely and died as miserably, —
   They say that Creon has sworn
   No one shall bury him, no one mourn for him,   20
   But his body must lie in the fields, a sweet treasure
   For carrion birds to find as they search for food.
   That is what they say, and our good Creon is coming here
   To announce it publicly; and the penalty—
   Stoning to death in the public square!
                                        There it is,

---

   1. 3. *Oedipus:* Father of Antigonê and Ismenê, Oedipus was destined to murder his father (Laïos) and marry his mother (Iocastê), which he did, but without knowing that they were his parents. These crimes brought a plague upon the city of Thebes, which he ruled. Upon learning the truth about his deeds, Oedipus blinded himself and went into self-imposed exile, leaving Creon, his brother-in-law, to govern Thebes. See Sophocles' play, *Oedipus the King.*
   1. 8. *two brothers:* Eteoclês and Polyneicês, sons of Oedipus, were to rule Thebes alternately, one year at a time. When Eteoclês, the first to rule, refused to step down, Polyneicês gathered an army from Argos and made war on Thebes. The two brothers met in combat and killed each other. Creon then became king. See Aeschylus' play, *The Seven Against Thebes.*

And now you can prove what you are:
A true sister, or a traitor to your family.
ISMENE: Antigonê, you are mad! What could I possibly do?
ANTIGONE: You must decide whether you will help me or not.
ISMENE: I do not understand you. Help you in what? 30
ANTIGONE: Ismenê, I am going to bury him. Will you come?
ISMENE: Bury him! You have just said the new law forbids it.
ANTIGONE: He is my brother. And he is your brother, too.
ISMENE: But think of the danger! Think what Creon will do!
ANTIGONE: Creon is not strong enough to stand in my way.
ISMENE: Ah sister!
Oedipus died, everyone hating him
For what his own search brought to light, his eyes
Ripped out by his own hand; and Iocastê died,
His mother and wife at once: she twisted the cords 40
That strangled her life; and our two brothers died,
Each killed by the other's sword. And we are left:
But oh, Antigonê,
Think how much more terrible than these
Our own death would be if we should go against Creon
And do what he has forbidden! We are only women,
We cannot fight with men, Antigonê!
The law is strong, we must give in to the law
In this thing, and in worse. I beg the Dead
To forgive me, but I am helpless: I must yield 50
To those in authority. And I think it is dangerous business
To be always meddling.
ANTIGONE: If that is what you think,
I should not want you, even if you asked to come.
You have made your choice, you can be what you want to be.
But I will bury him; and if I must die,
I say that this crime is holy: I shall lie down
With him in death, and I shall be as dear
To him as he to me.
It is the dead,
Not the living, who make the longest demands:
We die for ever . . .
You may do as you like, 60
Since apparently the laws of the gods mean nothing to you.
ISMENE: They mean a great deal to me; but I have no strength
To break laws that were made for the public good.
ANTIGONE: That must be your excuse, I suppose. But as for me,
I will bury the brother I love.
ISMENE: Antigonê,
I am so afraid for you!

ANTIGONE: You need not be:
   You have yourself to consider, after all.
ISMENE: But no one must hear of this, you must tell no one!
   I will keep it a secret, I promise!
ANTIGONE: Oh tell it! Tell everyone!
   Think how they'll hate you when it all comes out   70
   If they learn that you knew about it all the time!
ISMENE: So fiery! You should be cold with fear.
ANTIGONE: Perhaps. But I am doing only what I must.
ISMENE: But can you do it? I say that you cannot.
ANTIGONE: Very well: when my strength gives out, I shall do no more.
ISMENE: Impossible things should not be tried at all.
ANTIGONE: Go away, Ismenê:
   I shall be hating you soon, and the dead will too,
   For your words are hateful. Leave me my foolish plan:
   I am not afraid of the danger; if it means death,   80
   It will not be the worst of deaths—death without honor.
ISMENE: Go then, if you feel that you must.
   You are unwise,
   But a loyal friend indeed to those who love you.
           Exit into the Palace. ANTIGONE *goes off, L.*

       Enter the CHORUS.

§ PÁRADOS

STROPHE 1

CHORUS: Now the long blade of the sun, lying
   Level east to west, touches with glory
   Thebes of the Seven Gates. Open, unlidded
   Eye of golden day! O marching light
   Across the eddy and rush of Dircê's stream,
   Striking the white shields of the enemy
   Thrown headlong backward from the blaze of morning!
CHOREGOS: Polyneicês their commander
   Roused them with windy phrases,
   He the wild eagle screaming   10
   Insults above our land,

   1. 5. *Dircê's stream:* A spring near Thebes. Dircê was the wife of Lycos, who usurped the Theban throne. The children of the rightful rulers revenged themselves by killing Lycos and tying Dircê by her hair to a bull who dragged her about until she died. They then threw her into the stream which later bore her name.
   1. 8. *Chorêgos:* While the word here means "leader of the Chorus" it is also used to indicate the wealthy Athenian citizen who paid for the training and costuming of the Chorus, the musicians, and the supernumeraries—the man we might call the "angel." The word *coryphaios* is also used to signify "leader of the Chorus."

His wings their shields of snow,
His crest their marshalled helms.

ANTISTROPHE 1

CHORUS: Against our seven gates in a yawning ring
    The famished spears came onward in the night;
    But before his jaws were sated with our blood,
    Or pinefire took the garland of our towers,
    He was thrown back; and as he turned, great Thebes—
    No tender victim for his noisy power—
    Rose like a dragon behind him, shouting war.   20
CHOREGOS: For God hates utterly
    The bray of bragging tongues;
    And when he beheld their smiling,
    Their swagger of golden helms,
    The frown of his thunder blasted
    Their first man from our walls.

STROPHE 2

CHORUS: We heard his shout of triumph high in the air
    Turn to a scream; far out in a flaming arc
    He fell with his windy torch, and the earth struck him.
    And others storming in fury no less than his   30
    Found shock of death in the dusty joy of battle.
CHOREGOS: Seven captains at seven gates
    Yielded their clanging arms to the god
    That bends the battle-line and breaks it.
    These two only, brothers in blood,
    Face to face in matchless rage,
    Mirroring each the other's death,
    Clashed in long combat.

ANTISTROPHE 2

CHORUS: But now in the beautiful morning of victory
    Let Thebes of the many chariots sing for joy!   40
    With hearts for dancing we'll take leave of war:
    Our temples shall be sweet with hymns of praise,
    And the long night shall echo with our chorus.

§ SCENE I

CHOREGOS: But now at last our new King is coming:
    Creon of Thebes, Menoikeus' son.
    In this auspicious dawn of his reign
    What are the new complexities

1. 26. *Their first man:* Capaneus attacked one of the seven gates of Thebes, boasting that not even the gods could prevent him from achieving victory. Zeus, angered by his impiety, struck him down with a thunderbolt.

That shifting Fate has woven for him?
What is his counsel? Why has he summoned
The old men to hear him?

Enter CREON *from the Palace, C. He addresses the* CHORUS
from the top step.

CREON: Gentlemen: I have the honor to inform you that our Ship of
State, which recent storms have threatened to destroy, has come
safely to harbor at last, guided by the merciful wisdom of Heaven.   10
I have summoned you here this morning because I know that I
can depend upon you: your devotion to King Laïos was absolute;
you never hesitated in your duty to our late ruler Oedipus; and
when Oedipus died, your loyalty was transferred to his children.
Unfortunately, as you know, his two sons, the princes Eteoclês
and Polyneicês, have killed each other in battle; and I, as the next
in blood, have succeeded to the full power of the throne.
I am aware, of course, that no Ruler can expect complete loyalty
from his subjects until he has been tested in office. Nevertheless,
I say to you at the very outset that I have nothing but contempt   20
for the kind of Governor who is afraid, for whatever reason, to
follow the course that he knows is best for the State; and as for
the man who sets private friendship above the public welfare,—I
have no use for him, either. I call God to witness that if I saw my
country headed for ruin, I should not be afraid to speak out
plainly; and I need hardly remind you that I would never have
any dealings with an enemy of the people. No one values friendship more highly than I; but we must remember that friends
made at the risk of wrecking our Ship are not real friends at all.
These are my principles, at any rate, and that is why I have made   30
the following decision concerning the sons of Oedipus: Eteoclês,
who died as a man should die, fighting for his country, is to be
buried with full military honors, with all the ceremony that is
usual when the greatest heroes die; but his brother Polyneicês,
who broke his exile to come back with fire and sword against his
native city and the shrines of his fathers' gods, whose one idea was
to spill the blood of his blood and sell his own people into slavery
—Polyneicês, I say, is to have no burial: no man is to touch him
or say the least prayer for him; he shall lie on the plain, unburied;
and the birds and the scavenging dogs can do with him whatever   40
they like.
This is my command, and you can see the wisdom behind it. As
long as I am King, no traitor is going to be honored with the loyal
man. But whoever shows by word and deed that he is on the side
of the State,—he shall have my respect while he is living, and my
reverence when he is dead.

CHOREGOS: If that is your will, Creon son of Menoikeus,
    You have the right to enforce it: we are yours.
CREON: That is my will. Take care that you do your part.
CHOREGOS: We are old men: let the younger ones carry it out.   50
CREON: I do not mean that: the sentries have been appointed.
CHOREGOS: Then what is it that you would have us do?
CREON: You will give no support to whoever breaks this law.
CHOREGOS: Only a crazy man is in love with death!
CREON: And death it is; yet money talks, and the wisest
    Have sometimes been known to count a few coins too many.

Enter SENTRY *from L.*

SENTRY: I'll not say that I'm out of breath from running, King, be-
    cause every time I stopped to think about what I have to tell you,
    I felt like going back. And all the time a voice kept saying, "You
    fool, don't you know you're walking straight into trouble?"; and   60
    then another voice: "Yes, but if you let somebody else get the
    news to Creon first, it will be even worse than that for you!" But
    good sense won out, at least I hope it was good sense, and here I
    am with a story that makes no sense at all; but I'll tell it anyhow,
    because, as they say, what's going to happen's going to happen,
    and—
CREON: Come to the point. What have you to say?
SENTRY: I did not do it. I did not see who did it. You must not punish
    me for what someone else has done.
CREON: A comprehensive defense! More effective, perhaps,   70
    If I knew its purpose. Come: what is it?
SENTRY: A dreadful thing . . . I don't know how to put it—
CREON: Out with it!
SENTRY: Well, then:
    The dead man—
                  Polyneicês—
Pause. The SENTRY *is overcome, fumbles for words.* CREON *waits
impassively.*
                    out there—
                        someone,—
    New dust on the slimy flesh!
Pause. No sign from CREON
    Someone has given it burial that way, and
    Gone . . .
Long pause. CREON *finally speaks with deadly control.*
CREON: And the man who dared do this?
SENTRY: I swear I
    Do not know! You must believe me!
                  Listen:

The ground was dry, not a sign of digging, no,   80
Not a wheeltrack in the dust, no trace of anyone.
It was when they relieved us this morning: and one of them,
The corporal, pointed to it.
                              There it was,
The strangest—
              Look:
The body, just mounded over with light dust: you see?
Not buried really, but as if they'd covered it
Just enough for the ghost's peace. And no sign
Of dogs or any wild animal that had been there.

And then what a scene there was! Every man of us
Accusing the other: we all proved the other man did it,   90
We all had proof that we could not have done it.
We were ready to take hot iron in our hands,
Walk through fire, swear by all the gods,
It was not I!
I do not know who it was, but it was not I!
creon's *rage has been mounting steadily, but the* sentry *is too
intent upon his story to notice it.*
And then, when this came to nothing, someone said
A thing that silenced us and made us stare
Down at the ground: you had to be told the news,
And one of us had to do it! We threw the dice,
And the bad luck fell to me. So here I am,   100
No happier to be here than you are to have me:
Nobody likes the man who brings bad news.
CHOREGOS: I have been wondering, King: can it be that the gods have
    done this?
CREON (*furiously*): Stop!
    Must you doddering wrecks
Go out of your heads entirely? "The gods!"
Intolerable!
The gods favor this corpse? Why? How had he served them?
Tried to loot their temples, burn their images,   110
Yes, and the whole State, and its laws with it!
Is it your senile opinion that the gods love to honor bad men?
A pious thought!—
                  No, from the very beginning
There have been those who have whispered together,
Stiff-necked anarchists, putting their heads together,
Scheming against me in alleys. These are the men,
And they have bribed my own guard to do this thing.
Money!

Sententiously
There's nothing in the world so demoralizing as money.
Down go your cities,   120
Homes gone, men gone, honest hearts corrupted,
Crookedness of all kinds, and all for money!
To SENTRY

                                             But you—!
I swear by God and by the throne of God,
The man who has done this thing shall pay for it!
Find that man, bring him here to me, or your death
Will be the least of your problems: I'll string you up
Alive, and there will be certain ways to make you
Discover your employer before you die;
And the process may teach you a lesson you seem to have missed:
The dearest profit is sometimes all too dear: 130
That depends on the source. Do you understand me?
A fortune won is often misfortune.

SENTRY: King, may I speak?
CREON: Your very voice distresses me.
SENTRY: Are you sure that it is my voice, and not your conscience?
CREON: By God, he wants to analyze me now!
SENTRY: It is not what I say, but what has been done, that hurts you.
CREON: You talk too much.
SENTRY: Maybe; but I've done nothing.
CREON: Sold your soul for some silver: that's all you've done.
SENTRY: How dreadful it is when the right judge judges wrong!
CREON: Your figures of speech   140
May entertain you now; but unless you bring me the man,
You will get little profit from them in the end.

                                      Exit CREON *into the Palace.*

SENTRY: "Bring me the man"—!
I'd like nothing better than bringing him the man!
But bring him or not, you have seen the last of me here.
At any rate, I am safe!

                                                      Exit SENTRY.

§ ODE I

CHORUS: Numberless are the world's wonders, but none
More wonderful than man; the stormgray sea
Yields to his prows, the huge crests bear him high;
Earth, holy and inexhaustible, is graven

With shining furrows where his plows have gone
Year after year, the timeless labor of stallions.

ANTISTROPHE 1

The lightboned birds and beasts that cling to cover,
The lithe fish lighting their reaches of dim water,
All are taken, tamed in the net of his mind;
The lion on the hill, the wild horse windy-maned,   10
Resign to him; and his blunt yoke has broken
The sultry shoulders of the mountain bull.

STROPHE 2

Words also, and thought as rapid as air,
He fashions to his good use; statecraft is his,
And his the skill that deflects the arrows of snow,
The spears of winter rain: from every wind
He has made himself secure—from all but one:
In the late wind of death he cannot stand.

ANTISTROPHE 2

O clear intelligence, force beyond all measure!
O fate of man, working both good and evil!   20
When the laws are kept, how proudly his city stands!
When the laws are broken, what of his city then?
Never may the anárchic man find rest at my hearth,
Never be it said that my thoughts are his thoughts.

§ SCENE II

Re-enter SENTRY *leading* ANTIGONE.

CHOREGOS: What does this mean? Surely this captive woman
    Is the Princess, Antigonê. Why should she be taken?
SENTRY: Here is the one who did it! We caught her
    In the very act of burying him.—Where is Creon?
CHOREGOS: Just coming from the house.

Enter CREON, C.

CREON: What has happened?
    Why have you come back so soon?
SENTRY (*expansively*):   O King,
    A man should never be too sure of anything:
    I would have sworn
    That you'd not see me here again: your anger

Frightened me so, and the things you threatened me with;   10
But how could I tell then
That I'd be able to solve the case so soon?

No dice-throwing this time: I was only too glad to come!

Here is this woman. She is the guilty one:
We found her trying to bury him.
Take her, then; question her; judge her as you will.
I am through with the whole thing now, and glád óf it.
CREON: But this is Antigonê! Why have you brought her here?
SENTRY: She was burying him, I tell you!
CREON (severely):   Is this the truth?
SENTRY: I saw her with my own eyes. Can I say more?   20
CREON: The details: come, tell me quickly!
SENTRY: It was like this:
After those terrible threats of yours, King,
We went back and brushed the dust away from the body.
The flesh was soft by now, and stinking,
So we sat on a hill to windward and kept guard.
No napping this time! We kept each other awake.
But nothing happened until the white round sun
Whirled in the center of the round sky over us:
Then, suddenly,
A storm of dust roared up from the earth, and the sky   30
Went out, the plain vanished with all its trees
In the stinging dark. We closed our eyes and endured it.
The whirlwind lasted a long time, but it passed;
And then we looked, and there was Antigonê!
I have seen
A mother bird come back to a stripped nest, heard
Her crying bitterly a broken note or two
For the young ones stolen. Just so, when this girl
Found the bare corpse, and all her love's work wasted,
She wept, and cried on heaven to damn the hands   40
That had done this thing.
                              And then she brought more dust
And sprinkled wine three times for her brother's ghost.

We ran and took her at once. She was not afraid,
Not even when we charged her with what she had done.
She denied nothing.
                              And this was a comfort to me,
And some uneasiness: for it is a good thing
To escape from death, but it is no great pleasure

To bring death to a friend.
Yet I always say
There is nothing so comfortable as your own safe skin!
CREON (*slowly, dangerously*): And you, Antigonê,   50
　　You with your head hanging,—do you confess this thing?
ANTIGONE: I do. I deny nothing.
CREON (*to* SENTRY):　　　　　You may go.

Exit SENTRY.

　　To ANTIGONE
　　Tell me, tell me briefly:
　　Had you heard my proclamation touching this matter?
ANTIGONE: It was public. Could I help hearing it?
CREON: And yet you dared defy the law.
ANTIGONE:　　　　　I dared.
　　It was not God's proclamation. That final Justice
　　That rules the world below makes no such laws.

　　Your edict, King, was strong,
　　But all your strength is weakness itself against
　　The immortal unrecorded laws of God.   60
　　They are not merely now: they were, and shall be,
　　Operative for ever, beyond man utterly.

　　I knew I must die, even without your decree:
　　I am only mortal. And if I must die
　　Now, before it is my time to die,
　　Surely this is no hardship: can anyone
　　Living, as I live, with evil all about me,
　　Think Death less than a friend? This death of mine
　　Is of no importance; but if I had left my brother
　　Lying in death unburied, I should have suffered.   70
　　Now I do not.
You smile at me. Ah Creon,
　　Think me a fool, if you like; but it may well be
　　That a fool convicts me of folly.
CHOREGOS: Like father, like daughter: both headstrong, deaf to reason!
　　She has never learned to yield.
CREON:　　　　　She has much to learn.
　　The inflexible heart breaks first, the toughest iron
　　Cracks first, and the wildest horses bend their necks
　　At the pull of the smallest curb.
Pride? In a slave?
　　This girl is guilty of a double insolence,
　　Breaking the given laws and boasting of it.   80
　　Who is the man here,

She or I, if this crime goes unpunished?
Sister's child, or more than sister's child,
Or closer yet in blood—she and her sister
Win bitter death for this!
To servants

Go, some of you,
Arrest Ismenê. I accuse her equally.
Bring her: you will find her sniffling in the house there.

Her mind's a traitor: crimes kept in the dark
Cry for light, and the guardian brain shudders;
But how much worse than this   90
Is brazen boasting of barefaced anarchy!
ANTIGONE: Creon, what more do you want than my death?
CREON: Nothing.
That gives me everything.
ANTIGONE: Then I beg you: kill me.
This talking is a great weariness: your words
Are distasteful to me, and I am sure that mine
Seem so to you. And yet they should not seem so:
I should have praise and honor for what I have done.
All these men here would praise me
Were their lips not frozen shut with fear of you.
Bitterly
Ah the good fortune of kings,   100
Licensed to say and do whatever they please!
CREON: You are alone here in that opinion.
ANTIGONE: No, they are with me. But they keep their tongues in leash.
CREON: Maybe. But you are guilty, and they are not.
ANTIGONE: There is no guilt in reverence for the dead.
CREON: But Eteoclês—was he not your brother too?
ANTIGONE: My brother too.
CREON: And you insult his memory?
ANTIGONE (*softly*): The dead man would not say that I insult it.
CREON: He would: for you honor a traitor as much as him.
ANTIGONE: His own brother, traitor or not, and equal in blood.   110
CREON: He made war on his country. Eteoclês defended it.
ANTIGONE: Nevertheless, there are honors due all the dead.
CREON: But not the same for the wicked as for the just.
ANTIGONE: Ah Creon, Creon,
Which of us can say what the gods hold wicked?
CREON: An enemy is an enemy, even dead.
ANTIGONE: It is my nature to join in love, not hate.
CREON (*finally losing patience*): Go join them, then; if you must have
your love,

Find it in hell!

CHOREGOS: But see, Ismenê comes: 120

Enter ISMENE, *guarded.*

Those tears are sisterly, the cloud

That shadows her eyes rains down gentle sorrow.

CREON: You too, Ismenê,

    Snake in my ordered house, sucking my blood

    Stealthily—and all the time I never knew

    That these two sisters were aiming at my throne!

                                Ismenê,

Do you confess your share in this crime, or deny it?

Answer me.

ISMENE: Yes, if she will let me say so. I am guilty.

ANTIGONE (*coldly*): No, Ismenê. You have no right to say so.   130

    You would not help me, and I will not have you help me.

ISMENE: But now I know what you meant; and I am here

    To join you, to take my share of punishment.

ANTIGONE: The dead man and the gods who rule the dead

    Know whose act this was. Words are not friends.

ISMENE: Do you refuse me, Antigonê? I want to die with you:

    I too have a duty that I must discharge to the dead.

ANTIGONE: You shall not lessen my death by sharing it.

ISMENE: What do I care for life when you are dead?

ANTIGONE: Ask Creon. You're always hanging on his opinions.   140

ISMENE: You are laughing at me. Why, Antigonê?

ANTIGONE: It's a joyless laughter, Ismenê.

ISMENE: But can I do nothing?

ANTIGONE: Yes. Save yourself. I shall not envy you.

    There are those who will praise you; I shall have honor, too.

ISMENE: But we are equally guilty!

ANTIGONE: No more, Ismenê.

    You are alive, but I belong to Death.

CREON (*to the* CHORUS): Gentlemen, I beg you to observe these girls:

    One has just now lost her mind; the other,

    It seems, has never had a mind at all.

ISMENE: Grief teaches the steadiest minds to waver, King.   150

CREON: Yours certainly did, when you assumed guilt with the guilty!

ISMENE: But how could I go on living without her?

CREON: You are.

    She is already dead.

ISMENE: But your own son's bride!

CREON: There are places enough for him to push his plow.

    I want no wicked women for my sons!

ISMENE: O dearest Haimon, how your father wrongs you!

CREON: I've had enough of your childish talk of marriage!
CHOREGOS: Do you really intend to steal this girl from your son?
CREON: No; Death will do that for me.
CHOREGOS: Then she must die?
CREON (*ironically*): You dazzle me.

—But enough of this talk!   160

To Guards
You, there, take them away and guard them well:
For they are but women, and even brave men run
When they see Death coming.

Exeunt ISMENE, ANTIGONE, *and Guards.*

§ ODE II

STROPHE 1

CHORUS: Fortunate is the man who has never tasted God's vengeance!
Where once the anger of heaven has struck, that house is shaken
For ever: damnation rises behind each child
Like a wave cresting out of the black northeast,
When the long darkness under sea roars up
And bursts drumming death upon the windwhipped sand.

ANTISTROPHE 1

I have seen this gathering sorrow from time long past
Loom upon Oedipus' children: generation from generation
Takes the compulsive rage of the enemy god.
So lately this last flower of Oedipus' line   10
Drank the sunlight! but now a passionate word
And a handful of dust have closed up all its beauty.

STROPHE 2

What mortal arrogance
Transcends the wrath of Zeus?
Sleep cannot lull him, nor the effortless long months
Of the timeless gods: but he is young for ever,
And his house is the shining day of high Olympos.
All that is and shall be,
And all the past, is his.
No pride on earth is free of the curse of heaven.   20

ANTISTROPHE 2

The straying dreams of men
May bring them ghosts of joy:
But as they drowse, the waking embers burn them;

Or they walk with fíxed éyes, as blind men walk.
But the ancient wisdom speaks for our own time:
    Fate works most for woe
    With Folly's fairest show.
Man's little pleasure is the spring of sorrow.

§ SCENE III

CHOREGOS: But here is Haimon, King, the last of all your sons.
    Is it grief for Antigonê that brings him here,
    And bitterness at being robbed of his bride?

Enter HAIMAN.

CREON: We shall soon see, and no need of diviners.
                            —Son,
    You have heard my final judgment on that girl:
    Have you come here hating me, or have you come
    With deference and with love, whatever I do?
HAIMON: I am your son, father. You are my guide.
    You make things clear for me, and I obey you.
    No marriage means more to me than your continuing wisdom.   10
CREON: Good. That is the way to behave: subordinate
    Everything else, my son, to your father's will.
    This is what a man prays for, that he may get
    Sons attentive and dutiful in his house,
    Each one hating his father's enemies,
    Honoring his father's friends. But if his sons
    Fail him, if they turn out unprofitably,
    What has he fathered but trouble for himself
    And amusement for the malicious?
                        So you are right
    Not to lose your head over this woman.   20
    Your pleasure with her would soon grow cold, Haimon,
    And then you'd have a hellcat in bed and elsewhere.
    Let her find her husband in Hell!
    Of all the people in this city, only she
    Has had contempt for my law and broken it.

    Do you want me to show myself weak before the people?
    Or to break my sworn word? No, and I will not.
    The woman dies.
    I suppose she'll plead "family ties." Well, let her.
    If I permit my own family to rebel,   30
    How shall I earn the world's obedience?

Show me the man who keeps his house in hand,
He's fit for public authority.

                I'll have no dealings
With law-breakers, critics of the government:
Whoever is chosen to govern should be obeyed—
Must be obeyed, in all things, great and small,
Just and unjust! O Haimon,
The man who knows how to obey, and that man only,
Knows how to give commands when the time comes.
You can depend on him, no matter how fast   40
The spears come; he's a good soldier, he'll stick it out.

Anarchy, anarchy! Show me a greater evil!
This is why cities tumble and the great houses rain down,
This is what scatters armies!

No, no: good lives are made so by discipline.
We keep the laws then, and the lawmakers,
And no woman shall seduce us. If we must lose,
Let's lose to a man, at least! Is a woman stronger than we?
CHOREGOS: Unless time has rusted my wits,
    What you say, King, is said with point and dignity.   50
HAIMON (boyishly earnest): Father:
    Reason is God's crowning gift to man, and you are right
To warn me against losing mine. I cannot say—
I hope that I shall never want to say!—that you
Have reasoned badly. Yet there are other men
Who can reason, too; and their opinions might be helpful.
You are not in a position to know everything
That people say or do, or what they feel:
Your temper terrifies them—everyone
Will tell you only what you like to hear.   60
But I, at any rate, can listen; and I have heard them
Muttering and whispering in the dark about this girl.
They say no woman has ever, so unreasonably,
Died so shameful a death for a generous act:
"She covered her brother's body. Is this indecent?
She kept him from dogs and vultures. Is this a crime?
Death?—She should have all the honor that we can give her!"

This is the way they talk out there in the city.

You must believe me:
Nothing is closer to me than your happiness.   70
What could be closer? Must not any son

Value his father's fortune as his father does his?
I beg you, do not be unchangeable:
Do not believe that you alone can be right.
The man who thinks that,
The man who maintains that only he has the power
To reason correctly, the gift to speak, the soul—
A man like that, when you know him, turns out empty.

It is not reason never to yield to reason!

In flood time you can see how some trees bend,   80
And because they bend, even their twigs are safe,
While stubborn trees are torn up, roots and all.
And the same thing happens in sailing:
Make your sheet fast, never slacken,—and over you go,
Head over heels and under: and there's your voyage.
Forget you are angry! Let yourself be moved!
I know I am young; but please let me say this:
The ideal condition
Would be, I admit, that men should be right by instinct;
But since we are all too likely to go astray,   90
The reasonable thing is to learn from those who can teach.
CHOREGOS: You will do well to listen to him, King,
If what he says is sensible. And you, Haimon,
Must listen to your father.—Both speak well.
CREON: You consider it right for a man of my years and experience
To go to school to a boy?
HAIMON: It is not right
If I am wrong. But if I am young, and right,
What does my age matter?
CREON: You think it right to stand up for an anarchist?
HAIMON: Not at all. I pay no respect to criminals.   100
CREON: Then she is not a criminal?
HAIMON: The City would deny it, to a man.
CREON: And the City proposes to teach me how to rule?
HAIMON: Ah. Who is it that's talking like a boy now?
CREON: My voice is the one voice giving orders in this City!
HAIMON: It is no City if it takes orders from one voice.
CREON: The State is the King!
HAIMON: Yes, if the State is a desert.
    Pause
CREON: This boy, it seems, has sold out to a woman.
HAIMON: If you are a woman: my concern is only for you.
CREON: So? Your "concern"! In a public brawl with your father!   110
HAIMON: How about you, in a public brawl with justice?

CREON: With justice, when all that I do is within my rights?
HAIMON: You have no right to trample on God's right.
CREON (*completely out of control*): Fool, adolescent fool! Taken in
   by a woman!
HAIMON: You'll never see me taken in by anything vile.
CREON: Every word you say is for her!
HAIMON (*quietly, darkly*):   And for you.
  And for me. And for the gods under the earth.
CREON: You'll never marry her while she lives.
HAIMON: Then she must die.—But her death will cause another.
CREON: Another?   120
  Have you lost your senses? Is this an open threat?
HAIMON: There is no threat in speaking to emptiness.
CREON: I swear you'll regret this superior tone of yours!
  You are the empty one!
HAIMON: If you were not my father,
  I'd say you were perverse.
CREON: You girlstruck fool, don't play at words with me!
HAIMON: I am sorry. You prefer silence.
CREON: Now, by God—!
  I swear, by all the gods in heaven above us,
  You'll watch it, I swear you shall!
  To the Servants

          Bring her out!
  Bring the woman out! Let her die before his eyes!   130
  Here, this instant, with her bridegroom beside her!
HAIMON: Not here, no; she will not die here, King.
  And you will never see my face again.
  Go on raving as long as you've a friend to endure you.

               Exit HAIMON.

CHOREGOS: Gone, gone.
  Creon, a young man in a rage is dangerous!
CREON: Let him do, or dream to do, more than a man can.
  He shall not save these girls from death.
CHOREGOS: These girls?
  You have sentenced them both?
CREON: No, you are right.
  I will not kill the one whose hands are clean.   140
CHOREGOS: But Antigonê?
CREON (*somberly*):   I will carry her far away
  Out there in the wilderness, and lock her
  Living in a vault of stone. She shall have food,
  As the custom is, to absolve the State of her death.
  And there let her pray to the gods of hell:
  They are her only gods:

Perhaps they will show her an escape from death,
Or she may learn,
> though late,
That piety shown the dead is pity in vain.

Exit CREON.

§ ODE III

CHORUS: Love, unconquerable
Waster of rich men, keeper
Of warm lights and all-night vigil
In the soft face of a girl:
Sea-wanderer, forest-visitor!
Even the pure Immortals cannot escape you,
And mortal man, in his one day's dusk,
Trembles before your glory.

Surely you swerve upon ruin
The just man's consenting heart,   10
As here you have made bright anger
Strike between father and son—
And none has conquered but Love!
A girl's glánce wórking the will of heaven:
Pleasure to her alone who mocks us,
Merciless Aphrodîtê.

§ SCENE IV

CHOREGOS (*as* ANTIGONE *enters guarded*): But I can no longer stand
> in awe of this,
Nor, seeing what I see, keep back my tears.
Here is Antigonê, passing to that chamber
Where all find sleep at last.

ANTIGONE: Look upon me, friends, and pity me
Turning back at the night's edge to say
Good-by to the sun that shines for me no longer;
Now sleepy Death
Summons me down to Acheron, that cold shore:

l. 16. *Aphrodîtê:* Goddess of love and beauty.
l. 9. *Acheron:* The river of woe, one of five rivers separating the underworld from the world above. The others are Cocytos, the river of lamentation; Lethe, the river of forgetfulness; Styx, the river of the unbreakable oath; and Phlegethon, the river of fire.

There is no bridesong there, nor any music. 10
CHORUS: Yet not unpraised, not without a kind of honor,
　　　You walk at last into the underworld;
　　　Untouched by sickness, broken by no sword.
　　　What woman has ever found your way to death?

ANTISTROPHE 1

ANTIGONE: How often I have heard the story of Niobê,
　　　Tantalos' wretched daughter, how the stone
　　　Clung fast about her, ivy-close: and they say
　　　The rain falls endlessly
　　　And sifting soft snow; her tears are never done.
　　　I feel the loneliness of her death in mine. 20
CHORUS: But she was born of heaven, and you
　　　Are woman, woman-born. If her death is yours,
　　　A mortal woman's, is this not for you
　　　Glory in our world and in the world beyond?

STROPHE 2

ANTIGONE: You laugh at me. Ah, friends, friends,
　　　Can you not wait until I am dead? O Thebes,
　　　O men many-charioted, in love with Fortune,
　　　Dear springs of Dircê, sacred Theban grove,
　　　Be witnesses for me, denied all pity,
　　　Unjustly judged! and think a word of love 30
　　　For her whose path turns
　　　Under dark earth, where there are no more tears.
CHORUS: You have passed beyond human daring and come at last
　　　Into a place of stone where Justice sits.
　　　I cannot tell
　　　What shape of your father's guilt appears in this.

ANTISTROPHE 2

ANTIGONE: You have touched it at last: that bridal bed
　　　Unspeakable, horror of son and mother mingling:
　　　Their crime, infection of all our family!
　　　O Oedipus, father and brother! 40
　　　Your marriage strikes from the grave to murder mine.
　　　I have been a stranger here in my own land:
　　　All my life
　　　The blasphemy of my birth has followed me.
CHORUS: Reverence is a virtue, but strength
　　　Lives in established law: that must prevail.
　　　You have made your choice,
　　　Your death is the doing of your conscious hand.

l. 15. *Niobê:* For boasting that she was superior to the gods and ordering her people to refrain from worshiping them, Apollo and Artemis killed the children of the Theban queen Niobê and, as she grieved over their bodies, turned her to stone.

ANTIGONE: Then let me go, since all your words are bitter,
 And the very light of the sun is cold to me.   50
 Lead me to my vigil, where I must have
 Neither love nor lamentation; no song, but silence.
 CREON *interrupts impatiently.*
CREON: If dirges and planned lamentations could put off death,
 Men would be singing for ever.
 To the Servants
          Take her, go!
 You know your orders: take her to the vault
 And leave her alone there. And if she lives or dies,
 That's her affair, not ours: our hands are clean.
ANTIGONE: O tomb, vaulted bride-bed in eternal rock,
 Soon I shall be with my own again
 Where Persephonê welcomes the thin ghosts underground: 60
 And I shall see my father again, and you, mother,
 And dearest Polyneicês—
        dearest indeed
 To me, since it was my hand
 That washed him clean and poured the ritual wine:
 And my reward is death before my time!

 And yet, as men's hearts know, I have done no wrong,
 I have not sinned before God. Or if I have,
 I shall know the truth in death. But if the guilt
 Lies upon Creon who judged me, then, I pray,
 May his punishment equal my own.
CHOREGOS: O passionate heart,   70
 Unyielding, tormented still by the same winds!
CREON: Her guards shall have good cause to regret their delaying.
ANTIGONE: Ah! That voice is like the voice of death!
CREON: I can give you no reason to think you are mistaken.
ANTIGONE: Thebes, and you my fathers' gods,
 And rulers of Thebes, you see me now, the last
 Unhappy daughter of a line of kings,
 Your kings, led away to death. You will remember
 What things I suffer, and at what men's hands,
 Because I would not transgress the laws of heaven.   80

---

 1. 60. *Persephonê*: Wife of Hades (Pluto) and Queen of the Dead.
 1. 65. *And . . . time*: At this point, the translators have deleted sixteen lines which, they note, have "been bracketed as spurious, either in whole or in part, by the best critics. . . . [The passage] is dismal stuff. Antigonê is made to interrupt her lamentation by a series of limping verses whose sense is as discordant as their sound." The sense of the passage is that Antigonê would not have committed her deed for either a husband or a child since either could be replaced.

To the Guards, simply
Come: let us wait no longer.

Exit ANTIGONE, *L., guarded.*

§ ODE IV

STROPHE 1

CHORUS: All Danaê's beauty was locked away
In a brazen cell where the sunlight could not come:
A small room, still as any grave, enclosed her.
Yet she was a princess too,
And Zeus in a rain of gold poured love upon her.
O child, child,
No power in wealth or war
Or tough sea-blackened ships
Can prevail against untiring Destiny!

ANTISTROPHE 1

10

And Dryas' son also, that furious king,
Bore the god's prisoning anger for his pride:
Sealed up by Dionysos in deaf stone,
His madness died among echoes.
So at the last he learned what dreadful power
His tongue had mocked:
For he had profaned the revels,
And fired the wrath of the nine
Implacable Sisters that love the sound of the flute.

STROPHE 2

And old men tell a half-remembered tale
Of horror done where a dark ledge splits the sea
And a double surf beats on the gráy shóres:
How a king's new woman, sick
With hatred for the queen he had imprisoned,
Ripped out his two sons' eyes with her bloody hands

20

1. 1. *Danaê:* King Acrisios of Argos imprisoned his beautiful daughter because it was prophesied that she would bear a son who would kill him. Zeus came to her as golden rain and fathered her son Perseus, who fulfilled the prophecy.

1. 10. *Dryas' son:* Lycurgos, who opposed the worship of Dionysos. The god revenged himself by imprisoning Lycurgos in a rocky cave. Zeus, father of Dionysos, took more drastic revenge: he blinded Lycurgos.

1. 22. *a King:* Phineus, king of Salmydessos, in Thrace, married Cleopatra, daughter of Boreas (the North Wind) and Orithyia (daughter of Erechtheos, legendary king of Athens), who bore him two sons. Phineus later imprisoned Cleopatra and married Idaea (sometimes called Dia, Eurytia, or Idothea), who told him that his sons attempted to rape her and persuaded him to blind them. Because of this, the gods blinded him.

While grinning Arês watched the shuttle plunge
Four times: four blind wounds crying for revenge,

Crying, tears and blood mingled.—Piteously born,
Those sons whose mother was of heavenly birth!
Her father was the god of the North Wind
And she was cradled by gales,   30
She raced with young colts on the glittering hills
And walked untrammeled in the open light:
But in her marriage deathless Fate found means
To build a tomb like yours for all her joy.

§ SCENE V

Enter blind TEIRESIAS, *led by a Boy. The opening speeches of*
TEIRESIAS *should be in singsong contrast to the realistic lines of*
CREON.

TEIRESIAS: This is the way the blind man comes, Princes, Princes,
     Lock-step, two heads lit by the eyes of one.
CREON: What new thing have you to tell us, old Teiresias?
TEIRESIAS: I have much to tell you: listen to the prophet, Creon.
CREON: I am not aware that I have ever failed to listen.
TEIRESIAS: Then you have done wisely, King, and ruled well.
CREON: I admit my debt to you. But what have you to say?
TEIRESIAS: This, Creon: you stand once more on the edge of fate.
CREON: What do you mean? Your words are a kind of dread.
TEIRESIAS: Listen, Creon: 10
     I was sitting in my chair of augury, at the place
     Where the birds gather about me. They were all a-chatter,
     As is their habit, when suddenly I heard
     A strange note in their jangling, a scream, a
     Whirring fury; I knew that they were fighting,
     Tearing each other, dying
     In a whirlwind of wings clashing. And I was afraid.
     I began the rites of burnt-offering at the altar,
     But Hephaistos failed me: instead of bright flame,
     There was only the sputtering slime of the fat thigh-flesh   20
     Melting: the entrails dissolved in gray smoke,
     The bare bone burst from the welter. And no blaze!

     This was a sign from heaven. My boy described it,
     Seeing for me as I see for others.

l. 25. *Arês:* God of war.
l. 19. *Hephaistos:* God of fire.

I tell you, Creon, you yourself have brought
This new calamity upon us. Our hearths and altars
Are stained with the corruption of dogs and carrion birds
That glut themselves on the corpse of Oedipus' son.
The gods are deaf when we pray to them, their fire
Recoils from our offering, their birds of omen   30
Have no cry of comfort, for they are gorged
With the thick blood of the dead.

                                   O my son,
These are no trifles! Think: all men make mistakes,
But a good man yields when he knows his course is wrong,
And repairs the evil. The only crime is pride.

Give in to the dead man, then: do not fight with a corpse—
What glory is it to kill a man who is dead?
Think, I beg you:
It is for your own good that I speak as I do.
You should be able to yield for your own good.   40
CREON: It seems that prophets have made me their especial province.
All my life long
I have been a kind of butt for the dull arrows
Of doddering fortune-tellers!

                         No, Teiresias:
If your birds—if the great eagles of God himself
Should carry him stinking bit by bit to heaven,
I would not yield. I am not afraid of pollution:
No man can defile the gods.

                       Do what you will,
Go into business, make money, speculate
In India gold or that synthetic gold from Sardis,   50
Get rich otherwise than by my consent to bury him.
Teiresias, it is a sorry thing when a wise man
Sells his wisdom, lets out his words for hire!
TEIRESIAS: Ah Creon! Is there no man left in the world—
CREON: To do what?—Come, let's have the aphorism!
TEIRESIAS: No man who knows that wisdom outweighs any wealth?
CREON: As surely as bribes are baser than any baseness.
TEIRESIAS: You are sick, Creon! You are deathly sick!
CREON: As you say: it is not my place to challenge a prophet.
TEIRESIAS: Yet you have said my prophecy is for sale.   60
CREON: The generation of prophets has always loved gold.
TEIRESIAS: The generation of kings has always loved brass.
CREON: You forget yourself! You are speaking to your King.
TEIRESIAS: I know it. You are a king because of me.
CREON: You have a certain skill; but you have sold out.

TEIRESIAS: King, you will drive me to words that—
CREON: Say them, say them!
　Only remember: I will not pay you for them.
TEIRESIAS: No, you will find them too costly.
CREON: No doubt. Speak:
　Whatever you say, you will not change my will.
TEIRESIAS: Then take this, and take it to heart!　　　　　　70
　The time is not far off when you shall pay back
　Corpse for corpse, flesh of your own flesh.
　You have thrust the child of this world into living night,
　You have kept from the gods below the child that is theirs:
　The one in a grave before her death, the other,
　Dead, denied the grave. This is your crime:
　And the Furies and the dark gods of Hell
　Are swift with terrible punishment for you.

　Do you want to buy me now, Creon?

　　　　　　　　　　　　　　Not many days,
　And your house will be full of men and women weeping,　　80
　And curses will be hurled at you from far
　Cities grieving for sons unburied, left to rot
　Before the walls of Thebes.

　These are my arrows, Creon: they are all for you.
　But come, child: lead me home.
　To Boy
　Let him waste his fine anger upon younger men.
　Maybe he will learn at last
　To control a wiser tongue in a better head.

　　　　　　　　　　　　　　　　Exit TEIRESIAS.

CHOREGOS: The old man has gone, King, but his words
　Remain to plague us. I am old, too,　　　　　　　　　90
　But I cannot remember that he was ever false.
CREON: That is true. . . . It troubles me.
　Oh it is hard to give in! but it is worse
　To risk everything for stubborn pride.
CHOREGOS: Creon: take my advice.
CREON: What shall I do?
CHOREGOS: Go quickly: free Antigonê from her vault
　And build a tomb for the body of Polyneicês.
CREON: You would have me do this?
CHOREGOS: Creon, yes!

l. 77. *Furies:* Goddesses of vengeance who pursued evildoers. See Aeschylus' **play.**
The Eumenides.

And it must be done at once: God moves
Swiftly to cancel the folly of stubborn men.   100
CREON: It is hard to deny the heart! But I
  Will do it: I will not fight with destiny.
CHOREGOS: You must go yourself, you cannot leave it to others.
CREON: I will go.
          —Bring axes, servants:
Come with me to the tomb. I buried her, I
Will set her free.
          Oh quickly!
My mind misgives—
The laws of the gods are mighty, and a man must serve them
To the last day of his life!

                                         Exit CREON.

§ PÆAN

                                         STROPHE 1

CHOREGOS: God of many names
CHORUS: O Iacchos
                         son
of Kadmeian Sémelê
                  O born of the Thunder!
Guardian of the West
                Regent
of Eleusis' plain
               O Prince of maenad Thebes
and the Dragon Field of rippling Ismenos:

                                    ANTISTROPHE 1

CHOREGOS: God of many names
CHORUS: the flame of torches
  flares on our hills
         the nymphs of Iacchos
dance at the spring of Castalia:

l. 1. *Iacchos:* One of the names of Dionysos.
l. 2. *Sémelê:* Dionysos' mother, was Kadmos' daughter.
l. 4. *Eleusis' plain:* At Eleusis, a small town near Athens, a temple was built to worship Demeter, goddess of the corn. Dionysos, god of the vine, also came to be worshiped there.
       maenad: The frenzied worshipers of Dionysos (whom the Romans named Bacchus) were called Maenads or Bacchantes. In their madness, they would tear apart and devour the wild animals they met. See Euripides' play, usually translated as *The Bacchae*.
l. 6. *Ismenos:* Theban river sacred to Apollo, where Kadmos, founder of Thebes, killed a dragon and then sowed its teeth into the earth. From them, a crop of men arose and battled each other. Five survived and joined Kadmos in building Thebes.
l. 9. *spring of Castalia:* A spring on Parnasos, a mountain sacred to Apollo and the Muses.

from the vine-close mountain
$$\text{come ah come in ivy:} \qquad 10$$
Evohé evohé! sings through the streets of Thebes

CHOREGOS: God of many names
CHORUS: Iacchos of Thebes
    heavenly Child
            of Sémelê bride of the Thunderer!
The shadow of plague is upon us:
                       come
with clement feet
          oh come from Parnasos
   down the long slopes
            across the lamenting water

CHOREGOS: Iô Fire! Chorister of the throbbing stars!
   O purest among the voices of the night!
   Thou son of God, blaze for us!
CHORUS: Come with choric rapture of circling Maenads   20
   Who cry *Iô Iacche!*
           God of many names!

§ EXODOS

Enter MESSENGER, L.

MESSENGER: Men of the line of Kadmos, you who live
   Near Amphion's citadel:
                 I cannot say
Of any condition of human life "This is fixed,
This is clearly good, or bad." Fate raises up,
And Fate casts down the happy and unhappy alike:
No man can foretell his Fate.
                 Take the case of Creon:
Creon was happy once, as I count happiness:
Victorious in battle, sole governor of the land,
Fortunate father of children nobly born.
And now it has all gone from him! Who can say   10
That a man is still alive when his life's joy fails?
He is a walking dead man. Grant him rich,
Let him live like a king in his great house:

l. 13. *the Thunderer:* Zeus.
   l. 2. *Amphion:* Son of Zeus and husband of Niobê (see note p. 638), Amphion,
a musician, and his brother Zethos, an athlete, fortified Thebes with a wall. Amphion so
charmed the stones with music from his lyre that they formed themselves into a wall.

If his pleasure is gone, I would not give
So much as the shadow of smoke for all he owns.
CHOREGOS: Your words hint at sorrow: what is your news for us?
MESSENGER: They are dead. The living are guilty of their death.
CHOREGOS: Who is guilty? Who is dead? Speak!
MESSENGER: Haimon.
    Haimon is dead; and the hand that killed him
    Is his own hand.
CHOREGOS: His father's? or his own?   20
MESSENGER: His own, driven mad by the murder his father had done.
CHOREGOS: Teiresias, Teiresias, how clearly you saw it all!
MESSENGER: This is my news: you must draw what conclusions you
        can from it.
CHOREGOS: But look: Eurydicê, our Queen:
    Has she overheard us?

Enter EURIDICE *from the Palace, C.*

EURYDICE: I have heard something, friends:
    As I was unlocking the gate of Pallas' shrine,
    For I needed her help today, I heard a voice
    Telling of some new sorrow. And I fainted
    There at the temple with all my maidens about me.   30
    But speak again: whatever it is, I can bear it:
    Grief and I are no strangers.
MESSENGER: Dearest Lady,
    I will tell you plainly all that I have seen.
    I shall not try to comfort you: what is the use,
    Since comfort could lie only in what is not true?
    The truth is always best.
                              I went with Creon
    To the outer plain where Polyneicês was lying,
    No friend to pity him, his body shredded by dogs.
    We made our prayers in that place to Hecatê
    And Pluto, that they would be merciful. And we bathed   40
    The corpse with holy water, and we brought
    Fresh-broken branches to burn what was left of it,
    And upon the urn we heaped up a towering barrow
    Of the earth of his own land.
                                  When we were done, we ran
    To the vault where Antigonê lay on her couch of stone.
    One of the servants had gone ahead,

l. 27. *Pallas:* Athenê, goddess of wisdom.
l. 39. *Hecatê:* Goddess of darkness.
l. 40. *Pluto:* God of the underworld.

And while he was yet far off he heard a voice
Grieving within the chamber, and he came back
And told Creon. And as the King went closer,
The air was full of wailing, the words lost,   50
And he begged us to make all haste. "Am I a prophet?"
He said, weeping, "And must I walk this road,
The saddest of all that I have gone before?
My son's voice calls me on. Oh quickly, quickly!
Look through the crevice there, and tell me
If it is Haimon, or some deception of the gods!"

We obeyed; and in the cavern's farthest corner
We saw her lying:
She had made a noose of her fine linen veil
And hanged herself. Haimon lay beside her,   60
His arms about her waist, lamenting her,
His love lost under ground, crying out
That his father had stolen her away from him.

When Creon saw him the tears rushed to his eyes
And he called to him: "What have you done, child? Speak to me.
What are you thinking that makes your eyes so strange?
O my son, my son, I come to you on my knees!"
But Haimon spat in his face. He said not a word,
Staring—
                    And suddenly drew his sword
And lunged. Creon shrank back, the blade missed; and the boy,   70
Desperate against himself, drove it half its length
Into his own side, and fell. And as he died
He gathered Antigonê close in his arms again,
Choking, his blood bright red on her white cheek.
And now he lies dead with the dead, and she is his
At last, his bride in the houses of the dead.

Exit EURYDICE *into the Palace.*

CHOREGOS: She has left us without a word. What can this mean?
MESSENGER: It troubles me, too; yet she knows what is best,
Her grief is too great for public lamentation,
And doubtless she has gone to her chamber to weep   80
For her dead son, leading her maidens in his dirge.
CHOREGOS: It may be so: but I fear this deep silence
Pause
MESSENGER: I will see what she is doing. I will go in.

Exit MESSENGER *into the Palace.*

Enter CREON *with attendants, bearing* HAIMON's *body.*

CHOREGOS: But here is the King himself: oh look at him,
   Bearing his own damnation in his arms.
CREON: Nothing you say can touch me any more.
   My own blind heart has brought me
   From darkness to final darkness. Here you see
   The father murdering, the murdered son—
   And all my civic wisdom!   90

Haimon my son, so young, so young to die,
   I was the fool, not you; and you died for me.
CHOREGOS: That is the truth; but you were late in learning it.
CREON: This truth is hard to bear. Surely a god
   Has crushed me beneath the hugest weight of heaven.
   And driven me headlong a barbaric way
   To trample out the thing I held most dear.

The pains that men will take to come to pain!

Enter MESSENGER *from the Palace.*

MESSENGER: The burden you carry in your hands is heavy,
   But it is not all: you will find more in your house.   100
CREON: What burden worse than this shall I find there?
MESSENGER: The Queen is dead.
CREON: O port of death, deaf world,
   Is there no pity for me? And you, Angel of evil,
   I was dead, and your words are death again.
   Is it true, boy? Can it be true?
   Is my wife dead? Has death bred death?
MESSENGER: You can see for yourself.
   The doors are opened, and the body of EURYDICE *is disclosed within.*
CREON: Oh pity!
   All true, all true, and more than I can bear!   110
   O my wife, my son!
MESSENGER: She stood before the altar, and her heart
   Welcomed the knife her own hand guided,
   And a great cry burst from her lips for Megareus dead,
   And for Haimon dead, her sons; and her last breath
   Was a curse for their father, the murderer of her sons.
   And she fell, and the dark flowed in through her closing eyes.
CREON: O God, I am sick with fear.

---

1. 114. *Megareus:* Other son of Creon and Eurydicê, who died defending Thebes.
See Aeschylus' play, *The Seven Against Thebes.*

Are there no swords here? Has no one a blow for me?

MESSENGER: Her curse is upon you for the deaths of both.   120

CREON: It is right that it should be. I alone am guilty.

I know it, and I say it. Lead me in,

Quickly, friends.

I have neither life nor substance. Lead me in.

CHOREGOS: You are right, if there can be right in so much wrong.

The briefest way is best in a world of sorrow.

CREON: Let it come,

Let death come quickly, and be kind to me.

I would not ever ever see the sun again.

CHOREGOS: All that will come when it will; but we, meanwhile,   130

Have much to do. Leave the future to itself.

CREON: All my heart was in that prayer!

CHOREGOS: Then do not pray any more: the sky is deaf.

CREON: Lead me away. I have been rash and foolish.

I have killed my son and my wife.

I look for comfort; my comfort lies here dead.

Whatever my hands have touched has come to nothing.

Fate has brought all my pride to a thought of dust.

As CREON *is being led into the house, the* CHOREGOS *advances and*
speaks directly to the audience.

CHOREGOS: There is no happiness where there is no wisdom;

No wisdom but in submission to the gods.   140

Big words are always punished,

And proud men in old age learn to be wise.

§ FOR COMMENT

What is the theme of *Antigonê*? Does the view expressed by the chorus in
the play's last four lines belong also to the playwright? Do these words
apply to Antigonê? to Creon? How is the theme dramatized through plot
and character?

The conflict in *Antigonê* has been described in such terms as the
demands of the state *versus* those of the family, human law *versus* divine
law, etc. Antigonê, claiming that her obligation to bury her brother
transcends all political considerations, is put to death for her deed. Because of this, is Creon a villain, persecuting a heroine who dies for her
principles? What reasons does Creon give for his position? Some critics
claim that Antigonê is the tragic heroine; others, because Creon's suffering
is one of the play's principal concerns, call him the tragic hero. Find reasons for and against each interpretation, and tell which ones you find more
convincing. If you believe Antigonê to be the tragic heroine, account for
her absence during the last portion of the play. If you select Creon, explain

why the play is called *Antigonê*. If Sophocles did not wish to have a single tragic hero, how should we regard that play? If neither character alone is the central figure, how are the actions and sufferings of each related to those of the other? How is this relationship manifested in conflict and in plot structure?

The German philosopher Hegel regarded *Antigonê* as a type of tragedy in which two ethical forces stand in conflict, each making demands that are incompatible with those of the other. What the family demands, the state forbids; and *vice versa*. Although the obligation to each is "right" and although neither is immoral, according to Hegel, the exclusiveness of each claim makes "wrong." The tragic character caught in this dilemma is torn between the two claims but identifies himself wholly with one. This is true of both Antigonê and Creon. Do you accept this interpretation of *Antigonê*? If so, does it explain the tragic force or account for the focus of the play? Justify your answers.

The tragic hero is often discussed in terms of a "tragic flaw," a major defect in an otherwise admirable character. In Greek tragedy, this flaw is usually *hubris* (excessive pride). Does this conception apply to the tragic hero or heroes of *Antigonê*? If so, how does *hubris* help account for the action?

Both Antigonê and Creon portray themselves as upholding a necessary law which must be obeyed. Their motives, they claim, are unselfish. Is this entirely the case? Neither Antigonê nor Creon were forced to act as they do. Each could have made other decisions. Why didn't they, and what do their choices of action reveal? What is the attitude of each character toward the other characters? Do Antigonê and Creon resemble each other in this or in any other respect? If so, what do such resemblances reveal of Sophocles' theme?

Understanding a character comes in part from what the character does, what he says, and what other characters say about him. In the last two matters, the characters' knowledge and motives must be taken into account. Analyze Antigonê, Creon, Ismenê, Haimon, and Teiresias from these three aspects. Does what one character says about another character conflict with what the latter does and/or says about himself? If so, what does this discrepancy reveal?

What dramatic function is served by these characters: the Sentry, Ismenê, Haimon, Teiresias, and Eurydicê? Do they resemble each other in any way? Cite any similarities between the various characters with whom Creon and Antigonê are in conflict. What conflict does each scene dramatize? How is this conflict resolved? Analyze and evaluate the position of each character and the manner in which he argues that position. Cite any similarities you find between the conflicts in the various scenes. Chart the conflicts, resolutions, and revelations of character in each scene. Do you detect a pattern to the action?

Aeschylus, it is said, added a second actor to tragedy and Sophocles a third actor. Examine the two-character and the three-character scenes. How does Sophocles employ the third character?

Antigonê was written to be performed in an outdoor theater, during the day, utilizing such conventions as the chorus. How does the chorus' presence affect the action and the behavior of the characters? If the play were rewritten for an indoor theater, with the scenic appurtenances of to-day's stage, what changes might be made? How would they affect the drama?

Aristotle advised the playwright to treat the chorus "as one of the actors; it should be an integral part of the whole, and share in the action, in the manner not of Euripides but of Sophocles." Did Sophocles treat the chorus in *Antigonê* as "one of the actors"? If so, describe the "character" of the chorus. What is its relationship to the plot? Does it influence the action? Does it enter into dramatic conflict with another character? What is the chorus' position regarding the conflict between Antigonê and Creon? Is this position constant or does it change?

One function of the choral odes is to separate the dramatic episodes. What other functions does the chorus perform? Are the choral passages digressions, or are they related to the preceding and/or succeeding scenes? Give reasons.

Analyze the different types of language used in the play. The dialogue between Haimon and Creon, for example, resembles a debate. Locate those passages that are rhetorical, lyric, realistic, etc. Examine the methods by which language is used to characterize. What do the tone and choice of words of Creon's first speech reveal of the man? What does the language of Antigonê's speech in the opening scene with Ismenê reveal of the former's character? How similar or different is the language of the various characters?

Everyman § *Anonymous*

First produced in England during the latter half of the fifteenth century, Everyman, *whose author may have been a monk or clerk, is a morality play. Unlike mystery plays, passion plays, and miracle plays, which derive from Biblical or canonical sources (see the introduction to this section), morality plays are invented stories. Their fictional frameworks, however, clothe moral truths which are consonant with Catholic doctrine, for their authors aimed at teaching audiences lessons in Christian living and salvation. The characters, often personifications of good and evil, are usually involved in a struggle for a man's soul. Like its author, the source of* Everyman *is unknown. It may be based on a Dutch play,* Elckerlyc; *its source may be entirely English; or both plays may derive from a Latin work,* Homulus. *Frequently produced throughout the United States and England since its highly acclaimed London revival by William Poel in 1901,* Everyman *is today one of the most well-known medieval plays. Hugo von Hofmannsthal's* Jedermann, *based on* Everyman, *was performed annually at the Salzburg (Austria) Festival from 1920 to 1937 when the Nazis prohibited its production; in 1946, the year following Hitler's defeat, annual productions were resumed.*

Everyman

CHARACTERS

MESSENGER
GOD
DEATH
EVERYMAN
FELLOWSHIP
KINDRED
COUSIN
GOODS
GOOD DEEDS
KNOWLEDGE

CONFESSION
BEAUTY
STRENGTH
DISCRETION
FIVE WITS
ANGEL
DOCTOR

Here beginneth a treatise how the High Father of Heaven sendeth Death to summon every creature to come and give account of their lives in this world, and is in manner of a moral play.

[*Enter* MESSENGER *to speak Prologue.*]

MESSENGER: I pray you all give your audience,
    And hear this matter with reverence,
    By figure a moral play—
    The Summoning of Everyman called it is—
    That of our lives and ending shows
    How transitory we be all day.
    This matter is wondrous precious,
    But the intent of it is more gracious,
    And sweet to bear away.
    The story saith, Man, in the beginning,   10
    Look well, and take good heed to the ending,
    Be you never so gay!
    Ye think sin in the beginning full sweet,
    Which in the end causeth the soul to weep,
    When the body lieth in clay.
    Here shall you see how Fellowship and Jollity,
    Both Strength, Pleasure, and Beauty,
    Will fade from thee as flower in May.
    For ye shall hear how our Heaven King
    Calleth Everyman to a general reckoning: 20
    Give audience, and hear what he doth say.

[*Exit* MESSENGER.]

[*Enter* GOD, *who speaks.*]

GOD: I perceive, here in my majesty,
    How that all creatures be to me unkind,
    Living without dread in worldly prosperity:
    Of ghostly sight the people be so blind,

l. 3. *figure:* In form.
l. 6. *all day:* All of our days.
l. 8. *intent . . . gracious:* Its moral is more devout.
l. 23. *unkind:* Ungrateful.
l. 25. *ghostly:* Spiritual.

Drowned in sin, they know me not for their God.
In worldly riches is all their mind,
They fear not my rightwiseness, the sharp rod;
My law that I showed when I for them died
They forget clean, and shedding of my blood red; 30
I hanged between two, it cannot be denied;
To get them life I suffered to be dead;
I healed their feet, with thorns hurt was my head.
I could do no more than I did, truly,
And now I see the people do clean forsake me:
They use the seven deadly sins damnable,
As pride, covetise, wrath, and lechery,
Now in the world be made commendable;
And thus they leave of angels the heavenly company.
Every man liveth so after his own pleasure, 40
And yet of their life they be nothing sure.
I see the more that I them forbear
The worse they be from year to year;
All that liveth appaireth fast.
Therefore I will in all the haste
Have a reckoning of every man's person,
For, and I leave the people thus alone
In their life and wicked tempests,
Verily they will become much worse than beasts;
For now one would by envy another up eat, 50
Charity they all do clean forget.
I hoped well that every man
In my glory should make his mansion,
And thereto I had them all elect;
But now I see, like traitors deject,
They thank me not for the pleasure that I to them meant,
Nor yet for their being that I them have lent.
I proffered the people great multitude of mercy,
And few there be that asketh it heartily;
They be so cumbered with worldly riches, 60
That needs on them I must do justice,
On every man living without fear.
Where art thou, Death, thou mighty messenger?

[*Enter* DEATH.]

DEATH: Almighty God, I am here at your will,
  Your commandment to fulfill.
GOD: Go thou to Everyman,

l. 37. *covetise*: Covetousness.
l. 44. *appaireth*: Degenerates.

And show him in my name
A pilgrimage he must on him take,
Which he in no wise may escape;
And that he bring with him a sure reckoning   70
Without delay or any tarrying.

DEATH: Lord, I will in the world go run over all,
And cruelly out search both great and small.

[*Exit* GOD.]

Every man will I beset that liveth beastly,
Out of God's laws, and dreadeth not folly;
He that loveth riches I will strike with my dart,
His sight to blind, and from heaven to depart,
Except that alms be his good friend,
In hell for to dwell, world without end.

[*Enter* EVERYMAN.]

Lo, yonder I see Everyman walking;   80
Full little he thinketh on my coming;
His mind is on fleshly lusts and his treasure,
And great pain it shall cause him to endure
Before the Lord Heaven King.
Everyman, stand still! Whither are thou going
Thus gaily? Hast thou thy Maker forgot?

EVERYMAN: Why asketh thou?
Would'st thou wete?

DEATH: Yea, sir, I will show you.
In great haste I am sent to thee   90
From God out of His Majesty.

EVERYMAN: What, sent to me?

DEATH: Yea, certainly!
Though thou have forgot him here,
He thinketh on thee in the heavenly sphere,
As, ere we depart, thou shalt know.

EVERYMAN: What desireth God of me?

DEATH: That shall I show thee:
A reckoning he will needs have
Without any longer respite.   100

EVERYMAN: To give a reckoning, longer leisure I crave;
This blind matter troubleth my wit.

DEATH: On thee thou must take a long journey.

l. 69. *in no wise:* In no way.
l. 72. *over all:* Everywhere.
l. 77. *depart:* Separate.
l. 88. *wete:* Know.
l. 102. *blind:* Dark, unclear.

Therefore thy book of count with thee thou bring—
For turn again thou can not by no way.
And look thou be sure of thy reckoning,
For before God thou shalt answer and show
Thy many bad deeds, and good but a few,
How thou hast spent thy life, and in what wise,
Before the Chief Lord of paradise.   110
Have ado that we were in that way,
For, wete thou well, thou shalt make none attorney.
EVERYMAN: Full unready I am such reckoning to give.
I know thee not. What messenger art thou?
DEATH: I am Death, that no man dreadeth.
For every man I rest, and no man spareth;
For it is God's commandment
That all to me should be obedient.
EVERYMAN: O Death, thou comest when I had thee least in mind!
In thy power it lieth me to save.   120
Yet of my good will I give thee, if thou will be kind—
Yea, a thousand pound shalt thou have
And defer this matter till another day.
DEATH: Everyman, it may not be, by no way;
I set not by gold, silver, nor riches,
Nor by pope, emperor, king, duke, nor princes.
For, and I would receive gifts great,
All the world I might get;
But my custom is clean contrary:
I give thee no respite. Come hence and not tarry.   130
EVERYMAN: Alas! Shall I have no longer respite?
I may say, Death giveth no warning.
To think on thee, it maketh my heart sick,
For all unready is my book of reckoning.
But twelve year and I might have abiding,
My counting-book I would make so clear,
That my reckoning I should not need to fear.
Wherefore, Death, I pray thee, for God's mercy,
Spare me till I be provided of remedy.
DEATH: Thee availeth not to cry, weep, and pray;   140

l. 104. *count:* Accounts.
l. 105. *turn again:* Turn back.
l. 111. *Have . . . way:* Let us be on our way.
l. 112. *make . . . attorney:* You will make no one your attorney; i.e., you will not
be able to employ a lawyer.
l. 115. *that . . . dreadeth:* Who has dread of no man.
l. 116. *rest:* Arrest.
l. 125. *set not by:* I set no store by.
l. 135. *twelve . . . abiding:* If I might have but twelve years to live.

But haste thee lightly that thou were gone that journey,
And prove thy friends if thou can.
For wete thou well the tide abideth no man,
And in the world each living creature
For Adam's sin must die of nature.
EVERYMAN: Death, if I should this pilgrimage take,
And my reckoning surely make,
Show me, for saint charity,
Should I not come again shortly?
DEATH: No, Everyman; and thou be once there,   150
Thou mayst never more come here—
Trust me verily!
EVERYMAN: O gracious God, in the high seat celestial,
Have mercy on me in this most need;
Shall I have no company from this vale terrestrial
Of mine acquaintance that way me to lead?
DEATH: Yea, if any be so hardy
That would go with thee and bear thee company!
Hie thee that thou were gone to God's magnificence,
Thy reckoning to give before his presence.   160
What, weenest thou thy life is given thee,
And thy worldly goods also?
EVERYMAN: I had wend so, verily.
DEATH: Nay, nay; it was but lent thee;
For, as soon as thou art go,
Another a while shall have it, and then go therefro
Even as thou hast done.
Everyman, thou art mad! Thou hast thy wits full five,
And here on earth will not amend thy life;
For suddenly I do come.   170
EVERYMAN: O wretched caitiff, whither shall I flee
That I might 'scape endless sorrow!
Now, gentle Death, spare me till tomorrow,
That I may amend me
With good advisement.
DEATH: Nay, thereto I will not consent,
Nor no man will I respite,
But to the heart suddenly I shall smite
Without any advisement.
And now out of thy sight I will me hie.   180

l. 141. *lightly*: Quickly.
l. 143. *time abideth*: Time waits for.
l. 145. *of nature*: In the course of nature.
l. 161. *weenest*: Do you think? (Past participle is *wend*.)

See thou make thee ready shortly,
For thou mayst say, this is the day
That no man living may 'scape away.

[*Exit* DEATH.]

EVERYMAN: Alas! I may well weep with sighs deep.
Now have I no manner of company
To help me in my journey and me to keep,
And also my writing is full unready.
How shall I do now for to excuse me?
I would to God I had never be get!
To my soul a full great profit it had be,   190
For now I fear pains huge and great.
The time passeth; Lord, help, that all wrought.
For though I mourn it availeth nought.
The day passeth, and is almost ago.
I wot not well what for to do.
To whom were I best my complaint to make?
What and I to Fellowship thereof spake,
And showed him of this sudden chance!
For in him is all mine affiance;
We have in the world so many a day   200
Been good friends in sport and play.
I see him yonder, certainly;
I trust that he will bear me company;
Therefore to him will I speak to ease my sorrow.

[*Enter* FELLOWSHIP.]

Well met, good Fellowship, and good morrow!
FELLOWSHIP: Everyman, good morrow, by this day!
Sir, why lookest thou so piteously?
If any thing be amiss, I pray thee me say,
That I may help to remedy.
EVERYMAN: Yea, good Fellowship, yea,   210
I am in great jeopardy.
FELLOWSHIP: My true friend, show to me your mind.
I will not forsake thee to my life's end
In the way of good company.
EVERYMAN: That was well spoken, and lovingly.
FELLOWSHIP: Sir, I must needs know your heaviness;
I have pity to see you in any distress;

l. 186. *keep:* Protect.
l. 187. *writing:* Book of accounts.
l. 189. *be get:* Been born (begotten).
l. 195. *wot:* Know.
l. 197. *and:* If.
l. 199. *is . . . affiance:* Is my complete trust.

If any have you wronged, ye shall revenged be,
Though I on the ground be slain for thee,
Though that I know before that I should die. 220
EVERYMAN: Verily, Fellowship, gramercy.
FELLOWSHIP: Tush! by thy thanks I set not a straw:
Show me your grief, and say no more.
EVERYMAN: If I my heart should to you break,
And then you to turn your mind from me,
And would not me comfort when you hear me speak,
Then should I ten times sorrier be.
FELLOWSHIP: Sir, I say as I will do in deed.
EVERYMAN: Then be you a good friend at need.
I have found you true here before. 230
FELLOWSHIP: And so ye shall evermore;
For, in faith, and thou go to hell,
I will not forsake thee by the way.
EVERYMAN: Ye speak like a good friend. I believe you well.
I shall deserve it, and I may.
FELLOWSHIP: I speak of no deserving, by this day.
For he that will say and nothing do
Is not worthy with good company to go;
Therefore show me the grief of your mind,
As to your friend most loving and kind. 240
EVERYMAN: I shall show you how it is:
Commanded I am to go a journey,
A long way, hard and dangerous,
And give a strait count without delay
Before the high judge, Adonai.
Wherefore, I pray you bear me company,
As ye have promised, in this journey.
FELLOWSHIP: That is matter indeed! Promise is duty,
But, and I should take such a voyage on me,
I know it well, it should be to my pain. 250
Also it maketh me afeared, certain.
But let us take counsel here as well as we can,
For your words would fear a strong man.
EVERYMAN: Why, ye said if I had need
Ye would me never forsake, quick ne dead,
Though it were to hell, truly.
FELLOWSHIP: So I said, certainly,
But such pleasures be set aside, the sooth to say;

l. 224. *break*: Break open.
l. 225. *and. . . to*: If you were to.
l. 235. *I shall . . . may*: I shall repay you if I am able to do so.
l. 244. *strait count*: Strict account.
l. 253. *fear*: Frighten.

And also, if we took such a journey,
When should we come again?　　　　　　　　　　　260
EVERYMAN: Nay, never again till the day of doom.
FELLOWSHIP: In faith, then will not I come there!
Who hath you these tidings brought?
EVERYMAN: Indeed, Death was with me here.
FELLOWSHIP: Now, by God That all hath bought,
If Death were the messenger,
For no man that is living today
I will not go that loath journey—
Not for the father that begat me!
EVERYMAN: Ye promised otherwise, pardie.　　　　　270
FELLOWSHIP: I wot well I said so, truly;
And yet if thou wilt eat and drink, and make good cheer,
Or haunt to women the lusty company,
I would not forsake you while the day is clear,
Trust me verily!
EVERYMAN: Yea, thereto ye would be ready.
To go to mirth, solace, and play,
Your mind will sooner apply
Than to bear me company in my long journey.
FELLOWSHIP: Now, in good faith, I will not that way.　　　280
But and thou wilt murder, or any man kill,
In that I will help thee with a good will!
EVERYMAN: O, that is a simple advice indeed!
Gentle fellow, help me in my necessity;
We have loved long, and now I need,
And now, gentle Fellowship, remember me.
FELLOWSHIP: Whether ye have loved me or no,
By Saint John, I will not with thee go.
EVERYMAN: Yet I pray thee: take the labour, and do so much for me
To bring me forward, for saint charity,　　　　　290
And comfort me till I come without the town.
FELLOWSHIP: Nay, and thou would give me a new gown,
I will not a foot with thee go;
But, and thou had tarried, I would not have left thee so.
And as now God speed thee in thy journey,
For from thee I will depart as fast as I may.
EVERYMAN: Whither away, Fellowship? Will you forsake me?
FELLOWSHIP: Yea, by my fay, to God I betake thee.

l. 265. *That . . . bought:* Who has redeemed all of mankind.
l. 270. *pardie:* By God (*par Dieu*).
l. 273. *Or . . . company:* Or habitually spend your time in the company of lusty women.
l. 290. *bring me forward:* To go forth with me.
l. 298. *betake:* Commend.

EVERYMAN: Farewell, good Fellowship. For thee my heart is sore;
    Adieu for ever! I shall see thee no more. 300
FELLOWSHIP: In faith, Everyman, farewell now at the end!
    For you I will remember that parting is mourning.

                                            [Exit FELLOWSHIP.]

EVERYMAN: Alack! shall we thus depart indeed
    (Ah, Lady, help!) without any more comfort?
    Lo, Fellowship forsaketh me in my most need.
    For help in this world whither shall I resort?
    Fellowship here before with me would merry make;
    And now little sorrow for me doth he take.
    It is said, In prosperity men friends may find,
    Which in adversity be full unkind. 310
    Now whither for succor shall I flee,
    Sith that Fellowship hath forsaken me?
    To my kinsmen I will, truly,
    Praying them to help me in my necessity;
    I believe that they will do so,
    For kind will creep where it may not go.
    I will go say, for yonder I see them go.
    Where be ye now, my friends and kinsmen?

            [Enter KINDRED and COUSIN.]

KINDRED: Here be we now, at your commandment.
    Cousin, I pray you show us your intent 320
    In any wise, and do not spare.
COUSIN: Yea, Everyman, and to us declare
    If ye be disposed to go any whither,
    For, wete you well, we will live and die together.
KINDRED: In wealth and woe we will with you hold,
    For over his kin a man may be bold.
EVERYMAN: Gramercy, my friends and kinsmen kind.
    Now shall I show you the grief of my mind:
    I was commanded by a messenger,
    That is a high king's chief officer;
    He bade me go a pilgrimage, to my pain, 330
    And I know well I shall never come again;
    Also I must give a reckoning straight,
    For I have a great enemy that hath me in wait,
    Which intendeth me for to hinder.

l. 312. *sith:* Since.
l. 316. *kind . . . go:* I.e., blood is thicker than water.
l. 317. *Say:* Try (essay).
l. 326. *For . . . bold:* A man may speak without fear before his kin.
l. 334. *in wait:* In attendance.
l. 335. *for to hinder:* To prevent me from returning.

KINDRED: What account is that which ye must render?
　　That would I know.
EVERYMAN: Of all my works I must show
　　How I have lived, and my days spent;
　　Also of ill deeds that I have used　　　　　　　　　　340
　　In my time, sith life was me lent;
　　And of all virtues that I have refused.
　　Therefore I pray you go thither with me,
　　To help to make mine account, for saint charity.
COUSIN: What, to go thither? Is that the matter?
　　Nay, Everyman, I had liefer fast bread and water
　　All this five year and more.
EVERYMAN: Alas, that ever I was bore!
　　For now shall I never be merry
　　If that you forsake me.　　　　　　　　　　　　　350
KINDRED: Ah, sir, what ye be a merry man!
　　Take good heart to you, and make no moan.
　　But one thing I warn you, by Saint Anne,
　　As for me, ye shall go alone.
EVERYMAN: My Cousin, will you not with me go?
EVERYMAN: No, by our Lady! I have the cramp in my toe
　　Trust not to me, for, so God me speed,
　　I will deceive you in your most need.
KINDRED: It availeth not us to tice.
　　Ye shall have my maid with all my heart;　　　　360
　　She loveth to go to feasts, there to be nice,
　　And to dance, and abroad to start;
　　I will give her leave to help you in that journey,
　　If that you and she may agree.
EVERYMAN: Now show me the very effect of your mind.
　　Will you go with me, or abide behind?
KINDRED: Abide behind! Yea, that will I, and I may!
　　Therefore, farewell till another day.

　　　　　　　　　　　　　　　　　　　[*Exit* KINDRED.]

EVERYMAN: How should I be merry or glad?
　　For fair promises men to me make,　　　　　　　370
　　But when I have most need, they me forsake.
　　I am deceived: that maketh me sad.
COUSIN: Cousin Everyman, farewell now,
　　For verily I will not go with you;

l. 340. *used:* Committed.
l. 348. *bore:* Born.
l. 359. *tice:* Entice.
l. 361. *nice:* Wanton.
l. 362. *abroad to start:* To travel abroad.
l. 365. *effect:* Tenor.

Also of mine own life an unready reckoning
I have to account; therefore I make tarrying.
Now God keep thee, for now I go.

[*Exit* COUSIN.]

EVERYMAN: Ah, Jesus, is all come hereto?
   Lo, fair words maketh fools fain;
   They promise and nothing will do, certain.   380
   My kinsmen promised me faithfully
   For to abide with me steadfastly;
   And now fast away do they flee:
   Even so Fellowship promised me.
   What friend were best me of to provide?
   I lose my time here longer to abide.
   Yet in my mind a thing there is:
   All my life I have loved riches.
   If that my Goods now help me might,
   He would make my heart full light.   390
   I will speak to him in this distress.
   Where art thou, my Goods and riches?
GOODS [*calls from within*]: Who calleth me? Everyman? What, hast
      thou haste?
   I lie here in corners, trussed and piled so high,
   And in chests I am locked so fast,
   Also sacked in bags. Thou mayest see with thine eye
   I cannot stir; in packs low I lie.
   What would ye have? Lightly me say.
EVERYMAN: Come hither, Goods, in all the haste thou may,
   For of counsel I must desire thee.   400

[*Enter* GOODS.]

GOODS: Sir, and ye in the world have sorrow or adversity,
   That can I help you to remedy shortly.
EVERYMAN: It is another disease that grieveth me;
   In this world it is not, I tell thee so.
   I am sent for another way to go,
   To give a straight count general
   Before the highest Jupiter of all.
   And all my life I have had joy and pleasure in thee,
   Therefore I pray thee go with me,
   For, peradventure, thou mayst before God Almighty   410
   My reckoning help to clean and purify;
   For it is said ever among

l. 379. *fain:* Content.
l. 385. *me of to provide:* To provide myself with (for the journey).
l. 412. *For . . . ever:* It is frequently said.

That money maketh all right that is wrong.
GOODS: Nay, Everyman, I sing another song;
    I follow no man in such voyages,
    For, and I went with thee,
    Thou shouldst fare much the worse for me;
    For because on me thou did set thy mind,
    Thy reckoning I have made blotted and blind,
    That thine account thou cannot make truly;   420
    And that hast thou for the love of me.
EVERYMAN: That would grieve me full sore
    When I should come to that fearful answer.
    Up, let us go thither together.
GOODS: Nay, not so! I am too brittle, I may not endure;
    I will follow no man one foot, be ye sure.
EVERYMAN: Alas, I have thee loved, and had great pleasure
    All my life-days on goods and treasure.
GOODS: That is to thy damnation, without lesing
    For my love is contrary to the love everlasting;   430
    But if thou had me loved moderately during,
    As to the poor to give part of me,
    Then shouldst thou not in this dolour be,
    Nor in this great sorrow and care.
EVERYMAN: Lo, now was I deceived ere I was ware,
    And all I may wyte my spending of time.
GOODS: What, weenest thou that I am thine?
EVERYMAN: I had wend so.
GOODS: Nay, Everyman, I say no;
    As for a while I was lent thee—   440
    A season thou hast had me in prosperity.
    My condition is man's soul to kill;
    If I save one, a thousand I do spill;
    Weenest thou that I will follow thee?
    Nay, not from this world, verily!
EVERYMAN: I had wend otherwise.
GOODS: Therefore to thy soul Goods is a thief
    For when thou art dead, this is my guise:
    Another to deceive in the same wise
    As I have done thee, and all to his soul's reprief.   450

l. 429. *without lesing:* Without lying.
l. 431. *during:* During your lifetime.
l. 435. *ware:* Aware.
l. 436. *all . . . time:* I may blame everything on how I spent my time.
l. 442. *condition:* Nature.
l. 443. *spill:* Destroy.
l. 448. *guise:* Practice.
l. 450. *reprief:* Censure (reproof).

EVERYMAN: O false Goods, cursed may thou be!
    Thou traitor to God, that hast deceived me
    And caught me in thy snare.
GOODS: Marry, thou brought thyself in care,
    Whereof I am right glad.
    I must needs laugh: I cannot be sad.
EVERYMAN: Ah, Goods, thou hast had long my heartly love;
    I gave thee that which should be the Lord's above.
    But wilt thou not go with me indeed?
    I pray thee truth to say.   460
GOODS: No, so God me speed!
    Therefore farewell, and have good day.

                                  [*Exit* GOODS.]

EVERYMAN: O, to whom shall I make my moan
    For to go with me in that heavy journey?
    First, Fellowship said he would with me gone;
    His words were very pleasant and gay,
    But afterward he left me alone.
    Then spake I to my kinsmen, all in despair,
    And also they gave me words fair.
    They lacked no fair speaking,   470
    But all forsook me in the ending.
    Then went I to my Goods, that I loved best,
    In hope to have comfort; but there had I least,
    For my Goods sharply did me tell
    That he bringeth many into Hell.
    Then of myself I was ashamed,
    And so I am worthy to be blamed;
    Thus may I well myself hate.
    Of whom shall I now counsel take?
    I think that I shall never speed   480
    Till that I go to my Good Deeds.
    But alas, she is so weak
    That she can neither go nor speak.
    Yet will I venture on her now.
    My Good Deeds, where be you?
    [GOOD DEEDS *speaks from the ground.*]
GOOD DEEDS: Here I lie, cold in the ground;
    Thy sins hath me sore bound,
    That I cannot stir.
EVERYMAN: O Good Deeds, I stand in fear!
    I must you pray of counsel,   490
    For help now should come right well.

l. 483. *go:* Walk.
l. 491. *come right well:* Would be most welcome.

GOOD DEEDS: Everyman, I have understanding
    That ye be summoned account to make
    Before Messias, of Jerusalem King;
    And you do by me, that journey with you will I take.
EVERYMAN: Therefore I come to you my moan to make;
    I pray you that ye will go with me.
GOOD DEEDS: I would full fain, but I cannot stand—verily!
EVERYMAN: Why, is there anything on you fall?
GOOD DEEDS: Yea, sir, I may thank you of all;   500
    If ye had perfectly cheered me,
    Your book of count full ready had be.
    [*Shows him the Book of Account.*]
    Look, the books of your works and deeds eke.
    Oh, see how they lie under the feet,
    To your soul's heaviness.
EVERYMAN: Our Lord Jesus help me!
    For one letter here I can not see.
GOOD DEEDS: There is a blind reckoning in time of distress!
EVERYMAN: Good Deeds, I pray you, help me in this need,
    Or else I am for ever damned indeed!   510
    Therefore help me to make my reckoning
    Before the Redeemer of all thing,
    That King is, and was, and ever shall.
GOOD DEEDS: Everyman, I am sorry of your fall,
    And fain would I help you, and I were able.
EVERYMAN: Good Deeds, your counsel I pray you give me.
GOOD DEEDS: That shall I do verily;
    Though that on my feet I may not go,
    I have a sister that shall with you also,
    Called Knowledge, which shall with you abide,   520
    To help you to make that dreadful reckoning.

           [*Enter* KNOWLEDGE.]

KNOWLEDGE: Everyman, I will go with thee, and be thy guide,
    In thy most need to go by thy side.
EVERYMAN: In good condition I am now in every thing,
    And am whole content with this good thing;
    Thanked be God my Creator.

    l. 495. *And . . . me:* If you do as I say.
    l. 499. *is . . . fall:* Is there anything that has befallen you?
    l. 500. *of all:* For all (that has befallen me).
    l. 501. *cheered:* Cared for.
    l. 503. *eke:* Also.
    l. 508. *There . . . distress:* When a sinner is in trouble, he has difficulty in reading (i.e., reckoning, making an account of) his good deeds.
    l. 520. *Knowledge:* Knowledge of sin.

GOOD DEEDS: And when she hath brought you there,
 Where thou shalt heal thee of thy smart,
 Then go you with your reckoning and your Good Deeds together
 For to make you joyful at heart   530
 Before the blessed Trinity.
EVERYMAN: My Good Deeds, gramercy:
 I am well content, certainly,
 With your words sweet.
KNOWLEDGE: Now go we together lovingly
 To Confession, that cleansing river.
EVERYMAN: For joy I weep; I would we were there!
 But, I pray you, give me cognition
 Where dwelleth that holy man, Confession.
KNOWLEDGE: In the house of salvation: 540
 We shall find him in that place,
 That shall us comfort, by God's grace.
 [KNOWLEDGE *brings* EVERYMAN *to* CONFESSION.]
 Lo, this is Confession. Kneel down and ask for mercy,
 For he is in good conceit with God Almighty.
 [EVERYMAN *kneels.*]
EVERYMAN: O glorious fountain, that all uncleanness doth clarify,
 Wash from me the spots of vice unclean,
 That on me no sin may be seen.
 I come with Knowledge for my redemption,
 Redempt with hearty and full contrition;
 For I am commanded a pilgrimage to take,   550
 And great accounts before God to make.
 Now, I pray you, Shrift, mother of salvation,
 Help my Good Deeds for my piteous exclamation.
CONFESSION: I know your sorrow well, Everyman.
 Because with Knowledge ye come to me,
 I will you comfort as well as I can,
 And a precious jewel I will give thee,
 Called penance, voider of adversity.
 Therewith shall your body chastised be
 With abstinence and perseverance in God's service.   560
 Here shall you receive that scourge of me,
 [*Gives a scourge to* EVERYMAN.]
 Which is penance strong that ye must endure
 To remember thy Saviour was scourged for thee
 With sharp scourges and suffered it patiently;

l. 528. *smart:* Pain.
l. 544. *in good conceit:* In high esteem.
l. 549. *Redempt . . . full:* Redeemed by sincere and complete.
l. 552. *Shrift:* Confession.
l. 553. *for:* In reply to.

So must thou, ere thou scape that painful pilgrimage.
Knowledge, keep him in this voyage,
And by that time Good Deeds will be with thee.
But in any wise, be siker of mercy,
For your time draweth fast, and ye will saved be,
Ask God mercy, and He will grant truly.   570
When with the scourge of penance man doth him bind,
The oil of forgiveness then shall he find.

[*Exit* CONFESSION.]

EVERYMAN: Thanked be God for his gracious work!
　　For now I will my penance begin;
　　This hath rejoiced and lighted my heart,
　　Though the knots be painful and hard within.
KNOWLEDGE: Everyman, look your penance that ye fulfil,
　　What pain that ever it to you be,
　　And Knowledge shall give you counsel at will.
　　How your account ye shall make clearly.   580
EVERYMAN: O eternal God, O heavenly figure,
　　O way of rightwiseness, O goodly vision,
　　Which descended down in a virgin pure
　　Because he would Everyman redeem,
　　Which Adam forfeited by his disobedience!
　　O blessed Godhead, elect and high divine,
　　Forgive my grievous offence;
　　Here I cry thee mercy in this presence.
　　O ghostly treasure, O ransomer and redeemer,
　　Of all the world hope and conductor,   590
　　Mirror of joy, and founder of mercy,
　　Which illumineth heaven and earth thereby,
　　Hear my clamorous complaint, though it late be!
　　Receive my prayers, unworthy in thy benignity.
　　Though I be a sinner most abominable,
　　Yet let my name be written in Moses' table!
　　O Mary, pray to the Maker of all thing,
　　Me for to help at my ending,
　　And save me from the power of my enemy,
　　For Death assaileth me strongly!   600
　　And, Lady, that I may by means of thy prayer
　　Of your Son's glory to be partner,
　　By the means of his passion I it crave.

l. 566. *voyage:* Path.
l. 568. *But* . . . *siker:* But in any case, be a seeker.
l. 569. *draweth fast:* Comes quickly to an end.
l. 579. *at will:* When you wish it.
　　l. 596. *Moses' table:* Moses' tablets, containing an account of those who have done penance and been saved.

I beseech you, help my soul to save.
[EVERYMAN *rises*.]
Knowledge, give me the scourge of penance;
My flesh therewith shall give acquaintance.
I will now begin, if God give me grace.
KNOWLEDGE: Everyman, God give you time and space:
    Thus I bequeath you in the hands of our Saviour.
    Now may you make your reckoning sure.   610
EVERYMAN: In the name of the Holy Trinity,
    My body sore punished shall be.
    [*He scourges himself*.]
    Take this, body, for the sin of the flesh;
    Also thou delightest to go gay and fresh,
    And in the way of damnation thou did me bring;
    Therefore suffer now strokes of punishing.
    Now of penance I will wade the water clear,
    To save me from purgatory, that sharp fire.
    [GOOD DEEDS *rises*.]
GOOD DEEDS: I thank God, now I can walk and go,
    And am delivered of my sickness of woe.   620
    Therefore with Everyman I will go, and not spare;
    His good works I will help him to declare.
KNOWLEDGE: Now, Everyman, be merry and glad!
    Your Good Deeds cometh now; ye may not be sad.
    Now is your Good Deeds whole and sound,
    Going upright upon the ground.
EVERYMAN: My heart is light, and shall be evermore;
    Now will I smite faster than I did before.
GOOD DEEDS: Everyman, pilgrim, my special friend,
    Blessed be thou without end;   630
    For thee is prepared the eternal glory.
    Ye have me made whole and sound,
    Therefore I will bide by thee in every stound.
EVERYMAN: Welcome, my Good Deeds; now I hear thy voice,
    I weep for very sweetness of love.
KNOWLEDGE: Be no more sad, but ever rejoice;
    God seeth thy living in his throne above.
    Put on this garment to thy behoof,
    Which is wet with your tears,
    Or else before God you may it miss,   640
    When you to your journey's end come shall.

l. 614. *gay and fresh*: Lavishly attired.
l. 633. *stound*: Trial.
l. 637. *thy living*: Your manner of living.
l. 638. *behoof*: Advantage.

EVERYMAN [*taking the robe*]: Gentle Knowledge, what do ye it call?
KNOWLEDGE: It is the garment of sorrow:
    From pain it will you borrow;
    Contrition it is
    That getteth forgiveness;
    It pleaseth God passing well.
GOOD DEEDS: Everyman, will you wear it for your heal?
[EVERYMAN *puts on the robe.*]
EVERYMAN: Now blessed be Jesu, Mary's Son,
    For now have I on true contrition!   650
    And let us go now without tarrying;
    Good Deeds, have we clear our reckoning?
GOOD DEEDS: Yea, indeed I have it here.
EVERYMAN: Then I trust we need not fear;
    Now, friends, let us not part in twain.
KNOWLEDGE: Nay, Everyman, that will we not, certain.
GOOD DEEDS: Yet must thou lead with thee
    Three persons of great might.
EVERYMAN: Who should they be?
GOOD DEEDS: Discretion and Strength they hight,   660
    And thy Beauty may not abide behind.
KNOWLEDGE: Also ye must call to mind
    Your Five Wits as for your counsellors.
GOOD DEEDS: You must have them ready at all hours.
EVERYMAN: How shall I get them hither?
KNOWLEDGE: You must call them all together,
    And they will hear you incontinent.
EVERYMAN: My friends, come hither and be present:
    Discretion, Strength, my Five Wits, and Beauty.

[*Enter* DISCRETION, STRENGTH, FIVE WITS, *and* BEAUTY.]

BEAUTY: Here, at your will, we be all ready.   670
    What will ye that we should do?
GOOD DEEDS: That ye would with Everyman go,
    And help him in his pilgrimage.
    Advise you, will ye with him or not in that voyage?
STRENGTH: We will bring him all thither,
    To his help and comfort, ye may believe me.
DISCRETION: So will we go with him all together.

l. 644. *borrow:* Release.
l. 647. *passing well:* Very much.
l. 648. *heal:* Salvation.
l. 660. *Discretion:* Judgment.
    hight: Are called.
l. 663. *Wits:* Senses.
l. 667. *incontinent:* Immediately.

EVERYMAN: Almighty God, loved may thou be!
    I give thee laud that I have hither brought
    Strength, Discretion, Beauty, and Five Wits—lack I naught.   680
    And my Good Deeds, with Knowledge clear,
    All be in company at my will here;
    I desire no more to my business.
STRENGTH: And I, Strength, will by you stand in distress,
    Though thou would in battle fight on the ground.
FIVE WITS: And though it were through the world round,
    We will not depart for sweet ne sour.
BEAUTY: No more will I unto death's hour,
    Whatsoever thereof befall.
DISCRETION: Everyman, advise you first of all,   690
    Go with a good advisement and deliberation;
    We all give you virtuous monition
    That all shall be well.
EVERYMAN: My friends, hearken what I will tell:
    I pray God reward you in his heavenly sphere.
    Now hearken, all that be here,
    For I will make my testament
    Here before you all present.
    In alms half my goods I will give with my hands twain
    In the way of charity, with good intent,   700
    And the other half still shall remain
    In queth to be returned there it ought to be.
    This I do in despite of the fiend of Hell,
    To go quite out of his peril
    Ever after and this day.
KNOWLEDGE: Everyman, hearken what I say;
    Go to Priesthood, I you advise,
    And receive of him in any wise
    The holy sacrament and ointment together;
    Then shortly see ye him again hither;   710
    We will all abide you here.
FIVE WITS: Yea, Everyman, hie you that ye ready were.
    There is no emperor, king, duke, nor baron
    That of God hath commission
    As hath the least priest in the world being;

l. 679. *laud:* Praise.
l. 687. *ne:* Nor.
l. 692. *monition:* Forewarning.
l. 702. *queth:* Bequest.
      there: Where.
l. 704. *To . . . peril:* To escape imperilment by him.
l. 709. *sacrament and ointment:* Communion and Extreme Unction.
l. 715. *hath . . . being:* That lives.

For of the blessed sacraments pure and benign
He beareth the keys, and thereof hath the cure
For man's redemption—it is ever sure—
Which God for our soul's medicine
Gave us out of his heart with great pain,   720
Here in this transitory life, for thee and me;
The blessed sacraments seven there be:
Baptism, confirmation, with priesthood good,
And the sacrament of God's precious flesh and blood,
Marriage, the holy extreme unction, and penance;
These seven be good to have in remembrance,
Gracious sacraments of high divinity.

EVERYMAN: Fain would I receive the holy body
And meekly to my ghostly father I will go.

FIVE WITS: Everyman, that is the best that ye can do.   730
God will you to salvation bring,
For priesthood exceedeth all other thing;
To us Holy Scripture they do teach,
And converteth man from sin, Heaven to reach;
God hath to them more power given,
Than to any angel that is in heaven.
With five words he may consecrate
God's body in flesh and blood to make,
And handleth his Maker between his hands.
The priest bindeth and unbindeth all bands   740
Both in earth and in heaven.
Thou ministers all the sacraments seven;
Though we kissed thy feet, thou wert worthy;
Thou art the surgeon that cureth sin deadly:
No remedy we find under God,
But all only priesthood.
Everyman, God gave priests that dignity
And setteth them in his stead among us to be.
Thus be they above angels, in degree.
  [Exit EVERYMAN *to receive the final sacraments from the priest.*]

KNOWLEDGE: If priests be good, it is so, surely.   750
But when Jesus hanged on the cross with great smart,
There he gave, out of his blessed heart,
The same sacrament in great torment.
He sold them not to us, that Lord omnipotent.

l. 717. *cure:* Charge.
l. 728. *holy body:* The Eucharist.
l. 737. *five words: Hoc est enim corpus meum* (For this is my body).
l. 740. *bands:* Bonds.
l. 746. *But . . . priesthood:* Except as we receive them from the priesthood.
l. 751. *smart:* Pain.

Therefore Saint Peter the Apostle doth say
That Jesu's curse hath all they
Which God their Saviour do buy or sell,
Or they for any money do take or tell.
Sinful priests giveth the sinners example bad;
Their children sitteth by other men's fires, I have heard;   760
And some haunteth women's company
With unclean life, as lusts of lechery.
These be with sin made blind.

FIVE WITS: I trust to God no such may we find;
Therefore let us priesthood honour,
And follow their doctrine for our souls' succour.
We be their sheep, and they shepherds be
By whom we all be kept in surety.
Peace! for yonder I see Everyman come,
Which hath made true satisfaction.   770

GOOD DEEDS: Methinketh it is he indeed.

[*Enter* EVERYMAN]

EVERYMAN: Now Jesu be your alder speed.
I have received the sacrament for my redemption,
And then mine extreme unction:
Blessed be all they that counseled me to take it!
And now, friends, let us go without longer respite;
I thank God that ye have tarried so long.
Now set each of you on this rood your hand,
And shortly follow me.
I go before, there I would be: God be our guide.   780

STRENGTH: Everyman, we will not from you go
Till ye have done this voyage long.

DISCRETION: I, Discretion, will bide by you also.

KNOWLEDGE: And though this pilgrimage be never so strong,
I will never part you fro.
Everyman, I will be as sure by thee
As ever I did by Judas Maccabee.
[*They cross to the grave.*]

EVERYMAN: Alas, I am so faint I may not stand.
My limbs under me do fold.
Friends, let us not turn again to this land,   790
Not for all the world's gold;
For into this cave must I creep

l. 758. *tell:* Count out.
l. 772. *Now . . . speed:* Now Jesus help all of you.
l. 778. *rood:* Cross.
l. 785. *you fro:* From you.

And turn to earth and there to sleep.

BEAUTY: What, into this grave? Alas!

EVERYMAN: Yea, there shall ye consume, more and less.

BEAUTY: And what, should I smother here?

EVERYMAN: Yea, by my faith, and never more appear;
In this world live no more we shall,
But in Heaven before the highest Lord of all.

BEAUTY: I cross out all this; adieu, by Saint John!   800
I take my cap in my lap and am gone.

EVERYMAN: What, Beauty, whither will ye?

BEAUTY: Peace, I am deaf! I look not behind me,
Not and thou would give me all the gold in thy chest.

[*Exit* BEAUTY.]

EVERYMAN: Alas, whereto may I trust?
Beauty goeth fast away from me.
She promised with me to live and die.

STRENGTH: Everyman, I will thee also forsake and deny.
Thy game liketh me not at all.

EVERYMAN: Why, then ye will forsake me all?   810
Sweet Strength, tarry a little space.

STRENGTH: Nay, sir, by the rood of grace!
I will hie me from thee fast,
Though thou wep till thy heart to-brast.

EVERYMAN: Ye would ever bide by me, ye said.

STRENGTH: Yea, I have you far enough conveyed;
Ye be old enough, I understand,
Your pilgrimage to take on hand;
I repent me that I hither came.

EVERYMAN: Strength, you to displease I am to blame;   820
Yet promise is debt: this ye well wot.

STRENGTH: In faith, I care not!
Thou art but a fool to complain!
You spend your speech and waste your brain.
Go, thrust thee into the ground.

[*Exit* STRENGTH.]

EVERYMAN: I had wend surer I should you have found.
He that trusteth in his Strength,
She him deceiveth at the length.
Both Strength and Beauty forsaketh me,
Yet they promised me fair and lovingly.   830

l. 795. *there . . . less:* There you will completely decay.
l. 800. *I . . . this:* I.e., I cancel all my promises to you.
l. 801. *I . . . lap:* I.e., I remove my cap and hold it so low that it is by my lap.
l. 814. *to-brast:* Breaks.
l. 820. *you . . . blame:* I am to blame for having displeased you.

DISCRETION: Everyman, I will after Strength be gone;
    As for me, I will leave you alone.
EVERYMAN: Why, Discretion, will ye forsake me?
DISCRETION: Yea, in faith, I will go from thee;
    For when Strength goeth before,
    I follow after evermore.
EVERYMAN: Yet, I pray thee, for the love of the Trinity,
    Look in my grave once piteously.
DISCRETION: Nay, so nigh will I not come.
    Farewell, every one!   840

[Exit DISCRETION.]

EVERYMAN: O all thing faileth, save God alone!
    Beauty, Strength, and Discretion—
    For when Death bloweth his blast,
    They all run from me full fast.
FIVE WITS: Everyman, my leave now of thee I take;
    I will follow the other, for here I thee forsake.
EVERYMAN: Alas! then may I wail and weep,
    For I took you for my best friend.
FIVE WITS: I will no longer thee keep;
    Now farewell, and there an end.   850

[Exit FIVE WITS.]

EVERYMAN: O Jesu, help! All hath forsaken me!
GOOD DEEDS: Nay, Everyman, I will bide with thee.
    I will not forsake thee indeed;
    Thou shalt find me a good friend at need.
EVERYMAN: Gramercy, Good Deeds! Now may I true friends see.
    They have forsaken me, every one;
    I loved them better than my Good Deeds alone.
    Knowledge, will ye forsake me also?
KNOWLEDGE: Yea, Everyman, when ye to death shall go;
    But not yet, for no manner of danger.   860
EVERYMAN: Gramercy, Knowledge, with all my heart.
KNOWLEDGE: Nay, yet I will not from hence depart
    Till I see where ye shall be come.
EVERYMAN: Methink, alas, that I must be gone
    To make my reckoning and my debts pay,
    For I see my time is nigh spent away.
    Take example, all ye that this do hear or see,
    How they that I loved best do forsake me,
    Except my Good Deeds that bideth truly.
GOOD DEEDS: All earthly things is but vanity: 870
    Beauty, Strength, and Discretion do man forsake,

l. 838. *piteously:* With pity.

Foolish friends and kinsmen, that fair spake,
All fleeth save Good Deeds, and that am I.
EVERYMAN: Have mercy on me, God most mighty;
And stand by me, thou Mother and Maid, holy Mary!
GOOD DEEDS: Fear not, I will speak for thee.
EVERYMAN: Here I cry God mercy!
GOOD DEEDS: Short our end and minish our pain.
Let us go and never come again.
EVERYMAN: Into thy hands, Lord, my soul I commend.   880
Receive it, Lord, that it be not lost.
As thou me boughtest, so me defend,
And save me from the fiend's boast,
That I may appear with that blessed host
That shall be saved at the day of doom.
"*In manus tuas*," of might's most,
For ever "*commendo spiritum meum*."
[EVERYMAN *and* GOOD DEEDS *go to the grave.*]
KNOWLEDGE: Now hath he suffered that we all shall endure;
The Good Deeds shall make all sure;
Now hath he made ending.   890
Methinketh that I hear angels sing
And make great joy and melody
Where Everyman's soul received shall be.

[*Exit* KNOWLEDGE. *Enter an* ANGEL.]

ANGEL: Come, excellent elect spouse to Jesu!
Here above thou shalt go
Because of thy singular virtue.
Now the soul is taken the body fro,
Thy reckoning is crystal clear.
Now shalt thou into the heavenly sphere,
Unto the which all ye shall come   900
That liveth well before the day of doom.

[*Enter* DOCTOR *to speak Epilogue.*]

DOCTOR: This moral men may have in mind;
Ye hearers, take it of worth, old and young,
And forsake Pride, for he deceiveth you in the end,
And remember Beauty, Five Wits, Strength, and Discretion,
They all at the last do Everyman forsake,
Save his Good Deeds there doth he take.

l. 878. *Short:* Make short.
  minish: Diminish.
l. 887. *For . . . meum*": "*Into Thy hands*," most Mighty, "*forever I commend
my spirit*."—Luke, 23:46.
l. 903. *take it of worth:* Value it.

But beware, and they be small,
Before God he hath no help at all.
None excuse may be there for Everyman.   910
Alas, how shall he do then?
For after death amends may no man make,
For then mercy and pity do him forsake.
If his reckoning be not clear when he doth come,
God will say, "*Ite, maledicti, in ignem æternum.*"
And he that hath his account whole and sound,
High in heaven he shall be crowned.
Unto which place God bring us all thither,
That we may live body and soul together.
Thereto help the Trinity!   920
Amen, say ye, for saint charity.

Thus endeth this moral play of EVERYMAN.

§ FOR COMMENT

A prime example of the morality play, *Everyman* uses personification to help convey its didactic theme. State this theme. How is the play's message dramatized by characters, conflict, and plot? Does the didactic purpose make the play a drama of ideas? Why does *Everyman*, written in a framework of medieval Catholicism, still exert an appeal to twentieth-century non-Catholics?

How are the different characters individualized? Why do Beauty, Five Wits, Strength, and Discretion accompany Everyman to the grave but go no further? Why is Knowledge the *sister* of Good Deeds and not the friend or mother? Why does Knowledge, rather than Good Deeds, take Everyman to Confession? Why is Confession called the "mother of salvation"? When or how is Good Deeds cured? Who alone joins Everyman in the grave? Why does not Knowledge accompany him there?

Is there a reason for the particular sequence of scenes? Can the sequences be altered without affecting the continuity or the building to a climax?

Unlike twentieth-century plays, *Everyman* contains no directions for costumes, settings, and the like. What type of production should the play be given today? Describe how it might be costumed and what type of setting it might have. Should the production strive to reenact the original staging methods utilizing mansions and *platea*? If so, what mansions are required? Should the production attempt to recreate the medieval atmosphere in terms of today's theater? How might it do so?

l. 915. "Ite . . . æternum": "*Depart from me, ye cursed, into everlasting fire.*"
—*Matthew*, 25:41.

William Shakespeare § 1564–1616

Usually considered the greatest playwright in the English language, Shakespeare excelled in tragedy, comedy, chronicle history, tragicomedy, and nondramatic poetry. Born in the small town of Stratford-on-Avon, he went to London in 1587 or 1588. By 1594 he was a member of the Lord Chamberlain's Men, an acting company which James I placed under his patronage in 1603, renaming it the King's Men. Shakespeare was not only a playwright for this company but also an actor, probably in small roles, such as the Ghost in Hamlet. In 1599 he became a partner in the company's new Globe Theatre. Generally, the dates of composition of Shakespeare's plays can be determined only approximately, on the basis of references by contemporaries, entries in the Stationers' Register for later publication, allusions in the plays to historical events which can be dated, and differences in style and versification (the amount of rhyme, blank verse, and prose). For convenience, however, his plays are usually divided into four groups. The first (c. 1590–1593), an apprenticeship period, contains various types of plays, including two of Roman derivation, the Plautine Comedy of Errors *and the Senecan* Titus Andronicus. *The second period (c. 1594–1600), sometimes called his lyrical period, includes many of his best comedies and chronicle plays, such as* A Midsummer Night's Dream, Twelfth Night, *and* Henry IV, *Parts 1 and 2. The third period (c. 1600–1608) includes his greatest tragedies (*Hamlet, Othello, King Lear, *and* Macbeth) *and tragicomedies, such as* Measure for Measure. *The final period (c. 1609–1613) includes such romances as* The Winter's Tale.

Macbeth, based on Raphael Holinshed's Chronicles of England, Scotland, and Ireland *(1577), is thought to have been completed in 1606. Important actors who have performed the title role include David Garrick, John Philip Kemble, Edmund Kean, Sir Henry Irving, Edwin Booth, Maurice Evans, and Sir Laurence Olivier. Actresses who have played Lady Macbeth include Sarah Siddons, Adelaide Ristori, Lillah McCarthy, Vivien Leigh, and Dame Judith Anderson.*

The Tragedy of Macbeth

EDITED BY KENNETH MUIR

DRAMATIS PERSONAE

DUNCAN, King of Scotland

DONALBAIN, ⎫
MALCOLM, ⎭ His Sons

MACBETH, ⎫
BANQUO, ⎭ Generals of the King's Army

MACDUFF, ⎫
LENOX, ⎪
ROSSE, ⎪
MENTETH, ⎬ Noblemen of Scotland
ANGUS, ⎪
CATHNESS, ⎭

FLEANCE, Son to Banquo

SIWARD, Earl of Northumberland, General of the English Forces

YOUNG SIWARD, his Son

SEYTON, an Officer attending on Macbeth

BOY, Son to Macduff

AN ENGLISH DOCTOR

A SCOTTISH DOCTOR

A SOLDIER

A PORTER

AN OLD MAN

LADY MACBETH

LADY MACDUFF

GENTLEWOMAN attending on Lady Macbeth

[HECATE]

THREE WITCHES

Lords, Gentlemen, Officers, Soldiers, Murderers, Attendants, and Messengers.

The Ghost of Banquo, and other Apparitions.

SCENE: *In the end of the Fourth Act, in England; through the rest of the play, in Scotland.*

§ ACT I

SCENE I

An open place.

Thunder and lightning. Enter three WITCHES.

1 WITCH: When shall we three meet again?
    In thunder, lightning, or in rain?
2 WITCH: When the hurlyburly's done,
    When the battle's lost and won.
3 WITCH: That will be ere the set of sun.
1 WITCH: Where the place?
2 WITCH: Upon the heath.
3 WITCH: There to meet with Macbeth.
1 WITCH: I come, Graymalkin!
2 WITCH: Paddock calls.
3 WITCH: Anon!   10
ALL: Fair is foul, and foul is fair:
    Hover through the fog and filthy air.

                                               Exeunt.

SCENE II

A camp.

Alarum within. Enter KING DUNCAN, MALCOLM, DONALBAIN, LENOX,
    with Attendants, meeting a bleeding CAPTAIN.

DUNCAN: What bloody man is that? He can report,
    As seemeth by his plight, of the revolt
    The newest state.
MALCOLM: This is the Sergeant,
    Who, like a good and hardy soldier, fought
    'Gainst my captivity.—Hail, brave friend!
    Say to the King the knowledge of the broil,
    As thou didst leave it.
CAPTAIN: Doubtful it stood;
    As two spent swimmers, that do cling together
    And choke their art. The merciless Macdonwald
    (Worthy to be a rebel, for to that   10

l. 3. *hurlyburly:* Tumult.
l. 8. *Graymalkin:* A gray cat. Like the toad, a common associate of witches.
l. 9. *Paddock:* A toad.
l. 10. *Anon:* Immediately.
l. 6. *broil:* Battle.

The multiplying villainies of nature
Do swarm upon him) from the western isles
Of Kernes and Gallowglasses is supplied;
And Fortune, on his damned quarrel smiling,
Show'd like a rebel's whore: but all's too weak;
For brave Macbeth (well he deserves that name),
Disdaining Fortune, with his brandish'd steel,
Which smok'd with bloody execution,
Like Valour's minion, carv'd out his passage,
Till he fac'd the slave;   20
Which ne're shook hands, nor bade farewell to him,
Till he unseam'd him from the nave to th' chops,
And fix'd his head upon our battlements.
DUNCAN: O valiant cousin! worthy gentleman!
CAPTAIN: As whence the sun 'gins his reflection,
Shipwracking storms and direful thunders break,
So from that spring, whence comfort seem'd to come,
Discomfort swells. Mark, King of Scotland, mark:
No sooner justice had, with valour arm'd,
Compell'd these skipping Kernes to trust their heels,   30
But the Norweyan Lord, surveying vantage,
With furbish'd arms, and new supplies of men,
Began a fresh assault.
DUNCAN: Dismay'd not this
Our captains, Macbeth and Banquo?
CAPTAIN: Yes;
As sparrows eagles, or the hare the lion.
If I say sooth, I must report they were
As cannons overcharg'd with double cracks;
So they
Doubly redoubled strokes upon the foe:
Except they meant to bathe in reeking wounds,   40
Or memorize another Golgotha,
I cannot tell—
But I am faint, my gashes cry for help.
DUNCAN: So well thy words become thee, as thy wounds:
They smack of honour both.—Go, get him surgeons.
                                        Exit CAPTAIN, *attended.*

l. 13. *Of . . . supplied:* Is supplied with light-armed Irish foot soldiers and Irish
horsemen armed with sharp axes.
    l. 19. *minion:* Favorite.
    l. 22. *nave to th' chops:* The navel to the jaws.
    l. 24. *cousin:* A term of address from a sovereign to a nobleman; also, Duncan and
Macbeth were actually cousins.
    l. 41. *memorize:* Make memorable.

Enter ROSSE *and* ANGUS.

Who comes here?

MALCOLM: The worthy Thane of Rosse.

LENOX: What a haste looks through his eyes! So should he look
That seems to speak things strange.

ROSSE: God save the King!

DUNCAN: Whence cam'st thou, worthy Thane?

ROSSE: From Fife, great King,
Where the Norweyan banners flout the sky,   50
And fan our people cold. Norway himself,
With terrible numbers,
Assisted by that most disloyal traitor,
The Thane of Cawdor, began a dismal conflict;
Till that Bellona's bridegroom, lapp'd in proof,
Confronted him with self-comparisons,
Point against point, rebellious arm 'gainst arm,
Curbing his lavish spirit: and, to conclude,
The victory fell on us;—

DUNCAN: Great happiness!

ROSSE: That now   60
Sweno, the Norways' King, craves composition;
Nor would we deign him burial of his men
Till he disbursed at Saint Colme's Inch
Ten thousand dollars to our general use.

DUNCAN: No more that Thane of Cawdor shall deceive
Our bosom interest.—Go pronounce his present death,
And with his former title greet Macbeth.

ROSSE: I'll see it done.

DUNCAN: What he hath lost, noble Macbeth hath won.

Exeunt.

SCENE III

A heath.

Thunder. Enter the three WITCHES.

1 WITCH: Where hast thou been, Sister?

2 WITCH: Killing swine.

l. 51. *Norway himself:* The King of Norway.
l. 55. *Bellona's bridegroom:* Macbeth (Belonna is the Roman goddess of war).
        lapp'd in proof: Wearing armor.
l. 56. *self-comparisons:* As an equal.
l. 58. *lavish:* Impertinent.
l. 61. *composition:* Peace terms.
l. 63. *Saint Colme's Inch:* Now called Inchcolm, an island near Edinburgh.

3 WITCH: Sister, where thou?

1 WITCH: A sailor's wife had chestnuts in her lap,
 And mounch'd, and mounch'd, and mounch'd: "Give me,"
  quoth I:
 "Aroynt thee, witch!" the rump-fed ronyon cries.
 Her husband's to Aleppo gone, master o' th' *Tiger*:
 But in a sieve I'll thither sail,
 And like a rat without a tail;
 I'll do, I'll do, and I'll do.   10

2 WITCH: I'll give thee a wind.

1 WITCH: Th' art kind.

3 WITCH: And I another.

1 WITCH: I myself have all the other;
 And the very ports they blow,
 All the quarters that they know
 I' th' shipman's card.
 I'll drain him dry as hay:
 Sleep shall neither night nor day
 Hang upon his penthouse lid;   20
 He shall live a man forbid.
 Weary sev'n-nights nine times nine,
 Shall he dwindle, peak, and pine:
 Though his bark cannot be lost,
 Yet it shall be tempest-tost.
 Look what I have.

2 WITCH: Show me, show me.

1 WITCH: Here I have a pilot's thumb,
 Wrack'd, as homeward he did come.
 Drum within

3 WITCH: A drum! a drum!   30
 Macbeth doth come.

ALL: The Weïrd Sisters, hand in hand,
 Posters of the sea and land,
 Thus do go about, about:
 Thrice to thine, and thrice to mine,
 And thrice again, to make up nine.
 Peace!—the charm's wound up.

 l. 6. *Aroynt thee*: Begone.
   rump-fed: May mean fed on offal or may mean pampered.
   ronyon: Mangy creature.
 l. 14. *all the other*: All the other winds.
 l. 17. *shipman's card*: Compass.
 l. 20. *penthouse lid*: Eyelid.
 l. 21. *man forbid*: Like a man under a curse.
 l. 32. *Weïrd Sisters*: Sisters of Fate.
 l. 33. *Posters*: Travelers.

Enter MACBETH *and* BANQUO.

MACBETH: So foul and fair a day I have not seen.

BANQUO: How far is't call'd to Forres?—What are these,
So wither'd and so wild in their attire,   40
That look not like th' inhabitants o' th' earth,
And yet are on't? Live you? or are you aught
That man may question? You seem to understand me,
By each at once her choppy finger laying
Upon her skinny lips: you should be women,
And yet your beards forbid me to interpret
That you are so.

MACBETH: Speak, if you can:—what are you?

1 WITCH: All hail, Macbeth! hail to thee, Thane of Glamis!

2 WITCH: All hail, Macbeth! hail to thee, Thane of Cawdor!

3 WITCH: All hail, Macbeth! that shalt be King hereafter.   50

BANQUO: Good Sir, why do you start, and seem to fear
Things that do sound so fair?—I' th' name of truth,
Are ye fantastical, or that indeed
Which outwardly ye show? My noble partner
You greet with present grace, and great prediction
Of noble having, and of royal hope,
That he seems rapt withal: to me you speak not.
If you can look into the seeds of time,
And say which grain will grow, and which will not,
Speak then to me, who neither beg, nor fear,   60
Your favours nor your hate.

1 WITCH: Hail!

2 WITCH: Hail!

3 WITCH: Hail!

1 WITCH: Lesser than Macbeth, and greater.

2 WITCH: Not so happy, yet much happier.

3 WITCH: Thou shalt get kings, though thou be none:
So all hail, Macbeth and Banquo!

1 WITCH: Banquo and Macbeth, all hail!

MACBETH: Stay, you imperfect speakers, tell me more.   70
By Sinel's death I know I am Thane of Glamis;
But how of Cawdor? the Thane of Cawdor lives,
A prosperous gentleman; and to be King
Stands not within the prospect of belief,
No more than to be Cawdor. Say from whence

l. 44. *choppy:* Chapped.
l. 53. *fantastical:* Imaginary.
l. 56. *having:* Possessions.
l. 67. *get:* Beget.
l. 71. *Sinel:* Macbeth's father.

You owe this strange intelligence? or why
Upon this blasted heath you stop our way
With such prophetic greeting?—Speak, I charge you.

WITCHES *vanish.*

BANQUO: The earth hath bubbles, as the water has,
    And these are of them.—Whither are they vanish'd? 80
MACBETH: Into the air; and what seem'd corporal,
    Melted as breath into the wind. Would they had stay'd!
BANQUO: Were such things here, as we do speak about,
    Or have we eaten on the insane root,
    That takes the reason prisoner?
MACBETH: Your children shall be kings.
BANQUO: You shall be King.
MACBETH: And Thane of Cawdor too; went it not so?
BANQUO: To th' selfsame tune, and words. Who's here?

Enter ROSSE *and* ANGUS.

ROSSE: The King hath happily recciv'd, Macbeth,
    The news of thy success; and when he reads 90
    Thy personal venture in the rebels' fight,
    His wonders and his praises do contend,
    Which should be thine, or his: silenc'd with that,
    In viewing o'er the rest o' th' selfsame day,
    He finds thee in the stout Norweyan ranks,
    Nothing afeard of what thyself didst make,
    Strange images of death. As thick as hail,
    Came post with post; and every one did bear
    Thy praises in his kingdom's great defence,
    And pour'd them down before him.
ANGUS: We are sent, 100
    To give thee from our royal master thanks;
    Only to herald thee into his sight,
    Not pay thee.
ROSSE: And, for an earnest of a greater honour,
    He bade me, from him, call thee Thane of Cawdor:
    In which addition, hail, most worthy Thane,
    For it is thine.
BANQUO: What! can the Devil speak true?
MACBETH: The Thane of Cawdor lives: why do you dress me
    In borrow'd robes?
ANGUS: Who was the Thane, lives yet;
    But under heavy judgment bears that life 110
    Which he deserves to lose. Whether he was combin'd

l. 81. *corporal:* Corporeal.
l. 84. *Or . . . root:* Have we eaten the root which causes insanity?

With those of Norway, or did line the rebel
With hidden help and vantage, or that with both
He labour'd in his country's wrack, I know not;
But treasons capital, confess'd and prov'd,
Have overthrown him.

MACBETH (*aside*): Glamis, and Thane of Cawdor:
The greatest is behind.

    To ROSSE *and* ANGUS

                        Thanks for your pains.—

    To BANQUO

Do you not hope your children shall be kings
When those that gave the Thane of Cawdor to me
Promis'd no less to them?

BANQUO: That, trusted home,   120
Might yet enkindle you unto the crown,
Besides the Thane of Cawdor. But 'tis strange:
And oftentimes, to win us to our harm,
The instruments of Darkness tell us truths;
Win us with honest trifles, to betray's
In deepest consequence.—
Cousins, a word, I pray you.

MACBETH (*aside*):   Two truths are told,
As happy prologues to the swelling act
Of the imperial theme.—I thank you, gentlemen.—
(*aside*) This supernatural soliciting   130
Cannot be ill; cannot be good:—
If ill, why hath it given me earnest of success,
Commencing in a truth? I am Thane of Cawdor:
If good, why do I yield to that suggestion
Whose horrid image doth unfix my hair,
And make my seated heart knock at my ribs,
Against the use of nature? Present fears
Are less than horrible imaginings.
My thought, whose murther yet is but fantastical,
Shakes so my single state of man,   140
That function is smother'd in surmise,
And nothing is, but what is not.

BANQUO: Look, how our partner's rapt.

MACBETH (*aside*): If Chance will have me King, why, Chance may
        crown me,
Without my stir.

l. 120. *home:* Thoroughly.
l. 137. *use:* Custom.
l. 145. *Without my stir:* Without my having to stir, i.e., without my having to do
anything about it.

BANQUO: New honours come upon him,
Like our strange garments, cleave not to their mould,
But with the aid of use.
MACBETH (*aside*): Come what come may,
Time and the hour runs through the roughest day.
BANQUO: Worthy Macbeth, we stay upon your leisure.
MACBETH: Give me your favour: my dull brain was wrought 150
With things forgotten. Kind gentlemen, your pains
Are register'd where every day I turn
The leaf to read them.—Let us toward the King.—
To BANQUO
Think upon what hath chanc'd; and at more time,
The Interim having weigh'd it, let us speak
Our free hearts each to other.
BANQUO: Very gladly.
MACBETH: Till then, enough.—Come, friends.

Exeunt.

SCENE IV

Forres. A room in the palace.

Flourish. Enter DUNCAN, MALCOLM, DONALBAIN, LENOX, *and At*
tendants.

DUNCAN: Is execution done on Cawdor? Or not
Those in commission yet return'd?
MALCOLM: My Liege,
They are not yet come back; but I have spoke
With one that saw him die: who did report,
That very frankly he confess'd his treasons,
Implor'd your Highness' pardon, and set forth
A deep repentance. Nothing in his life
Became him like the leaving it: he died
As one that had been studied in his death,
To throw away the dearest thing he ow'd, 10
As 'twere a careless trifle.
DUNCAN: There's no art
To find the mind's construction in the face:

l. 146. *strange:* New.
l. 150. *favour:* Pardon.
       wrought: Bothered.
   l. 155. *Interim . . . it:* At a later time, after having considered it during the interim.
   l. 9. *studied in his death:* Well rehearsed in dying.
   l. 10. *ow'd:* Owned.
   l. 11. *careless:* Uncared for.

He was a gentleman on whom I built
An absolute trust—

Enter MACBETH, BANQUO, ROSSE, *and* ANGUS.

         O worthiest cousin!
The sin of my ingratitude even now
Was heavy on me. Thou art so far before,
That swiftest wing of recompense is slow
To overtake thee: would thou hadst less deserv'd,
That the proportion both of thanks and payment
Might have been mine! only I have left to say,   20
More is thy due than more than all can pay.
MACBETH: The service and the loyalty I owe,
 In doing it, pays itself. Your Highness' part
 Is to receive our duties: and our duties
 Are to your throne and state, children and servants;
 Which do but what they should, by doing everything
 Safe toward your love and honour.
DUNCAN: Welcome hither:
 I have begun to plant thee, and will labour
 To make thee full of growing.—Noble Banquo,
 That hast no less deserv'd, nor must be known   30
 No less to have done so, let me infold thee,
 And hold thee to my heart.
BANQUO: There if I grow,
 The harvest is your own.
DUNCAN: My plenteous joys,
 Wanton in fulness, seek to hide themselves
 In drops of sorrow.—Sons, kinsmen, Thanes,
 And you whose places are the nearest, know,
 We will establish our estate upon
 Our eldest, Malcolm; whom we name hereafter
 The Prince of Cumberland: which honour must
 Not unaccompanied invest him only,   40
 But signs of nobleness, like stars, shall shine
 On all deservers.—From hence to Inverness,
 And bind us further to you.
MACBETH: The rest is labour, which is not us'd for you:
 I'll be myself the harbinger, and make joyful
 The hearing of my wife with your approach;

  ll. 18–20. *would . . . mine:* I wish you had deserved less, so that I would be
capable of thanking you and rewarding you in proportion to what you deserve.
  l. 34. *Wanton:* Unrestrained.
  l. 45. *harbinger:* The king's officer who goes in advance to arrange lodging for the
monarch.

So, humbly take my leave.

DUNCAN: My worthy Cawdor!

MACBETH (*aside*): The Prince of Cumberland!—That is a step
On which I must fall down, or else o'erleap,
For in my way it lies. Stars, hide your fires! 50
Let not light see my black and deep desires;
The eye wink at the hand; yet let that be,
Which the eye fears, when it is done, to see.

Exit.

DUNCAN: True, worthy Banquo: he is full so valiant,
And in his commendations I am fed;
It is a banquet to me. Let 's after him,
Whose care is gone before to bid us welcome:
It is a peerless kinsman.

Flourish. Exeunt.

SCENE V

Inverness. A room in MACBETH's *castle.*

Enter LADY MACBETH, *reading a letter.*

LADY MACBETH: "They met me in the day of success; and I have learn'd
by the perfect'st report, they have more in them than mortal
knowledge. When I burn'd in desire to question them further,
they made themselves air, into which they vanish'd. Whiles I
stood rapt in the wonder of it, came missives from the King, who
all-hail'd me, 'Thane of Cawdor', by which title, before, these
Weïrd Sisters saluted me, and referr'd me to the coming on of time,
with 'Hail, King that shalt be!' This have I thought good to deliver thee (my dearest partner of greatness) that thou might'st not
lose the dues or rejoicing, by being ignorant of what greatness is 10
promis'd thee. Lay it to thy heart, and farewell."
Glamis thou art, and Cawdor; and shalt be
What thou art promis'd.—Yet do I fear thy nature:
It is too full o' th' milk of human kindness,
To catch the nearest way. Thou wouldst be great;
Art not without ambition, but without
The illness should attend it: what thou wouldst highly,
That wouldst thou holily; wouldst not play false,
And yet wouldst wrongly win; thou'dst have, great Glamis,
That which cries, "Thus thou must do," if thou have it; 20

l. 52. *eye . . . hand:* Let the eye pretend not to see what the hand is doing.
l. 17. *illness:* Evil or unscrupulousness.

And that which rather thou dost fear to do,
Than wishest should be undone. Hie thee hither,
That I may pour my spirits in thine ear,
And chastise with the valour of my tongue
All that impedes thee from the golden round,
Which fate and metaphysical aid doth seem
To have thee crown'd withal.

Enter a MESSENGER.

                            What is your tidings?
MESSENGER: The King comes here to-night.
LADY MACBETH: Thou'rt mad to say it.
Is not thy master with him? who, were't so,
Would have inform'd for preparation.   30
MESSENGER: So please you, it is true: our Thane is coming;
One of my fellows had the speed of him,
Who, almost dead for breath, had scarcely more
Than would make up his message.
LADY MACBETH: Give him tending:
He brings great news.

                                      Exit MESSENGER.
                       The raven himself is hoarse,
That croaks the fatal entrance of Duncan
Under my battlements. Come, you Spirits
That tend on mortal thoughts, unsex me here,
And fill me, from the crown to the toe, top-full
Of direst cruelty! make thick my blood,   40
Stop up th' access and passage to remorse;
That no compunctious visitings of Nature
Shake my fell purpose, nor keep peace between
Th' effect and it! Come to my woman's breasts,
And take my milk for gall, you murth'ring ministers,
Wherever in your sightless substances
You wait on Nature's mischief! Come, thick Night,
And pall thee in the dunnest smoke of Hell,
That my keen knife see not the wound it makes,
Nor Heaven peep through the blanket of the dark,   50
To cry, "Hold, hold!"

l. 25. *golden round:* Crown.
l. 26. *metaphysical:* Supernatural.
l. 33. *had . . . him:* Got here more quickly than he.
l. 38. *mortal:* Deadly.
l. 41. *remorse:* Compassion.
l. 45. *take . . . gall:* Take my milk and put gall in its place.
l. 46. *sightless:* Invisible.
l. 48. *pall:* Wrap.

Enter MACBETH.

Great Glamis! worthy Cawdor!
Greater than both, by the all-hail hereafter!
Thy letters have transported me beyond
This ignorant present, and I feel now
The future in the instant.

MACBETH: My dearest love,
Duncan comes here to-night.

LADY MACBETH: And when goes hence?

MACBETH: To-morrow, as he purposes.

LADY MACBETH: O! never
Shall sun that morrow see!
Your face, my Thane, is as a book, where men
May read strange matters. To beguile the time,   60
Look like the time; bear welcome in your eye,
Your hand, your tongue: look like th' innocent flower,
But be the serpent under't. He that's coming
Must be provided for; and you shall put
This night's great business into my dispatch;
Which shall to all our nights and days to come
Give solely sovereign sway and masterdom.

MACBETH: We will speak further.

LADY MACBETH: Only look up clear;
To alter favour ever is to fear.
Leave all the rest to me.   70

Exeunt.

SCENE VI

The same. Before the castle.

Hautboys and torches. Enter DUNCAN, MALCOLM, DONALBAIN,
BANQUO, LENOX, MACDUFF, ROSSE, ANGUS, *and Attendants.*

DUNCAN: This castle hath a pleasant seat; the air
Nimbly and sweetly recommends itself
Unto our gentle senses.

BANQUO: This guest of summer,
The temple-haunting martlet, does approve,
By his loved mansionry, that the heaven's breath

l. 72. *favour:* Countenance.
direction. *Hautboys:* Oboes.
l. 4. *martlet:* Martin.
      approve: Prove.
l. 5. *mansionry:* Residence.

Smells wooingly here: no jutty, frieze,
Buttress, nor coign of vantage, but this bird
Hath made his pendent bed, and procreant cradle:
Where they most breed and haunt, I have observ'd
The air is delicate.

Enter LADY MACBETH.

DUNCAN: See, see! our honour'd hostess.— 10
The love that follows us sometime is our trouble,
Which still we thank as love. Herein I teach you,
How you shall bid God 'ild us for your pains,
And thank us for your trouble.
LADY MACBETH: All our service,
In every point twice done, and then done double,
Were poor and single business, to contend
Against those honours deep and broad, wherewith
Your Majesty loads our house: for those of old,
And the late dignities heap'd up to them,
We rest your hermits.
DUNCAN: Where's the Thane of Cawdor? 20
We cours'd him at the heels, and had a purpose
To be his purveyor: but he rides well;
And his great love, sharp as his spur, hath holp him
To his home before us. Fair and noble hostess,
We are your guest to-night.
LADY MACBETH: Your servants ever
Have theirs, themselves, and what is theirs, in compt,
To make their audit at your Highness' pleasure,
Still to return your own.
DUNCAN: Give me your hand;
Conduct me to mine host: we love him highly,
And shall continue our graces towards him.
By your leave, hostess. 30
Exeunt.

l. 6. *jutty:* Projection.
l. 7. *coign of vantage:* Convenient corner.
l. 13. *'ild:* Reward.
l. 16. *single:* Weak.
l. 20. *We . . . hermits:* We remain your hermits (to pray for you).
l. 26. *in compt:* Subject to account.

SCENE VII

The same. A room in the castle.

> *Hautboys and torches. Enter, and pass over the stage, a Sewer, and*
> *divers Servants with dishes and service. Then enter* MACBETH.

MACBETH: If it were done, when 'tis done, then 'twere well
It were done quickly: if th' assassination
Could trammel up the consequence, and catch
With his surcease success; that but this blow
Might be the be-all and the end-all—here,
But here, upon this bank and shoal of time,
We'd jump the life to come.—But in these cases,
We still have judgment here; that we but teach
Bloody instructions, which, being taught, return
To plague th' inventor: this even-handed Justice   10
Commends th' ingredience of our poison'd chalice
To our own lips. He's here in double trust:
First, as I am his kinsman and his subject,
Strong both against the deed; then, as his host,
Who should against his murtherer shut the door,
Not bear the knife myself. Besides, this Duncan
Hath borne his faculties so meek, hath been
So clear in his great office, that his virtues
Will plead like angels, trumpet-tongu'd, against
The deep damnation of his taking-off;   20
And Pity, like a naked new-born babe,
Striding the blast, or heaven's Cherubins, hors'd
Upon the sightless couriers of the air,
Shall blow the horrid deed in every eye,
That tears shall drown the wind.—I have no spur
To prick the sides of my intent, but only
Vaulting ambition, which o'erleaps itself
And falls on th' other—

> *Enter* LADY MACBETH.

How now! what news?
LADY MACBETH: He has almost supp'd. Why have you left the chamber?
MACBETH: Hath he ask'd for me?
LADY MACBETH: Know you not, he has?   30
MACBETH: We will proceed no further in this business:

direction. *Sewer:* Chief servant.
l. 3. *trammel up:* Entangle.
l. 4. *surcease:* Death.
l. 7. *jump:* Risk.
l. 17. *faculties:* Prerogatives and powers.

He hath honour'd me of late; and I have bought
Golden opinions from all sorts of people,
Which would be worn now in their newest gloss,
Not cast aside so soon.
LADY MACBETH: Was the hope drunk,
Wherein you dress'd yourself? Hath it slept since?
And wakes it now, to look so green and pale
At what it did so freely? From this time
Such I account thy love. Art thou afeard
To be the same in thine own act and valour,   40
As thou art in desire? Would'st thou have that
Which thou esteem'st the ornament of life,
And live a coward in thine own esteem,
Letting "I dare not" wait upon "I would,"
Like the poor cat i' th' adage?
MACBETH: Pr'ythee, peace.
I dare do all that may become a man;
Who dares do more, is none.
LADY MACBETH: What beast was't then,
That made you break this enterprise to me?
When you durst do it, then you were a man;
And, to be more than what you were, you would   50
Be so much more the man. Nor time, nor place,
Did then adhere, and yet you would make both:
They have made themselves, and that their fitness now
Does unmake you. I have given suck, and know
How tender 'tis to love the babe that milks me:
I would, while it was smiling in my face,
Have pluck'd my nipple from his boneless gums,
And dash'd the brains out, had I so sworn
As you have done to this.
MACBETH: If we should fail?
LADY MACBETH: We fail?   60
But screw your courage to the sticking-place,
And we'll not fail. When Duncan is asleep
(Whereto the rather shall his day's hard journey
Soundly invite him), his two chamberlains
Will I with wine and wassail so convince,
That memory, the warder of the brain,
Shall be a fume, and the receipt of reason
A limbeck only: when in swinish sleep

---

l. 45. *cat i' th' adage:* The adage about the cat who wished to eat fish but did not
want to wet her feet.
l. 65. *convince:* Overpower.
l. 68. *limbeck:* Alembic (a vessel used in distilling).

Their drenched natures lie, as in a death,
What cannot you and I perform upon   70
Th' unguarded Duncan? what not put upon
His spongy officers, who shall bear the guilt
Of our great quell?
MACBETH: Bring forth men-children only!
For thy undaunted mettle should compose
Nothing but males. Will it not be receiv'd,
When we have mark'd with blood those sleepy two
Of his own chamber, and us'd their very daggers,
That they have done't?
LADY MACBETH: Who dares receive it other,
As we shall make our griefs and clamour roar
Upon his death?
MACBETH: I am settled, and bend up   80
Each corporal agent to this terrible feat.
Away, and mock the time with fairest show:
False face must hide what the false heart doth know.

Exeunt.

§ ACT II

SCENE I

The same. Court within the castle.

Enter BANQUO, *and* FLEANCE, *with a torch before him.*

BANQUO: How goes the night, boy?
FLEANCE: The moon is down; I have not heard the clock.
BANQUO: And she goes down at twelve.
FLEANCE: I take 't, 'tis later, Sir.
BANQUO: Hold, take my sword.—There's husbandry in heaven;
Their candles are all out.—Take thee that too.
A heavy summons lies like lead upon me,
And yet I would not sleep: merciful Powers!
Restrain in me the cursed thoughts that nature
Gives way to in repose!—Give me my sword.

Enter MACBETH, *and a Servant with a torch.*

Who's there?   10
MACBETH: A friend.

l. 72. *spongy:* Drunken, i.e., "soaked."
l. 73. *quell:* Murder.
l. 78. *other:* Otherwise.
l. 4. *husbandry:* Thrift.

BANQUO: What, Sir! not yet at rest? The King's a-bed:
    He hath been in unusual pleasure, and
    Sent forth great largess to your offices.
    This diamond he greets your wife withal,
    By the name of most kind hostess, and shut up
    In measureless content.
MACBETH: Being unprepar'd,
    Our will became the servant to defect,
    Which else should free have wrought.
BANQUO: All's well.
    I dreamt last night of the three Weïrd Sisters: 20
    To you they have show'd some truth.
MACBETH: I think not of them:
    Yet, when we can entreat an hour to serve,
    We would spend it in some words upon that business,
    If you would grant the time.
BANQUO: At your kind'st leisure.
MACBETH: If you shall cleave to my consent, when 'tis,
    It shall make honour for you.
BANQUO: So I lose none
    In seeking to augment it, but still keep
    My bosom franchis'd, and allegiance clear,
    I shall be counsell'd.
MACBETH: Good repose, the while!
BANQUO: Thanks, Sir: the like to you.   30
                      Exeunt BANQUO *and* FLEANCE.
MACBETH: Go, bid thy mistress, when my drink is ready,
    She strike upon the bell. Get thee to bed.—

                           Exit Servant.

    Is this a dagger, which I see before me,
    The handle toward my hand? Come, let me clutch thee:—
    I have thee not, and yet I see thee still.
    Art thou not, fatal vision, sensible
    To feeling, as to sight? or art thou but
    A dagger of the mind, a false creation,
    Proceeding from the heat-oppressed brain?
    I see thee yet, in form as palpable   40
    As this which now I draw.
    Thou marshall'st me the way that I was going;
    And such an instrument I was to use.—
    Mine eyes are made the fools o' th' other senses,

l. 14. *offices*: Servants' quarters.
l. 25. *If . . . consent*: If you support me when the time comes.
l. 28. *franchis'd*: Free from guilt.
l. 36. *sensible*: Perceptible through the senses.

Or else worth all the rest: I see thee still;
And on thy blade, and dudgeon, gouts of blood,
Which was not so before.—There's no such thing.
It is the bloody business which informs
Thus to mine eyes.—Now o'er the one half-world
Nature seems dead, and wicked dreams abuse   50
The curtain'd sleep: Witchcraft celebrates
Pale Hecate's off'rings; and wither'd Murther,
Alarum'd by his sentinel, the wolf,
Whose howl's his watch, thus with his stealthy pace,
With Tarquin's ravishing strides, towards his design
Moves like a ghost.—Thou sure and firm-set earth,
Hear not my steps, which way they walk, for fear
Thy very stones prate of my where-about,
And take the present horror from the time,
Which now suits with it.—Whiles I threat, he lives: 60
Words to the heat of deeds too cold breath gives.

A bell rings.

I go, and it is done: the bell invites me.
Hear it not, Duncan; for it is a knell
That summons thee to Heaven, or to Hell.

                                                                    Exit.

SCENE II

The same.

Enter LADY MACBETH.

LADY MACBETH: That which hath made them drunk hath made me
            bold:
    What hath quench'd them hath given me fire.—Hark!
            —Peace!
    It was the owl that shriek'd, the fatal bellman,
    Which gives the stern'st good-night. He is about it.
    The doors are open; and the surfeited grooms
    Do mock their charge with snores: I have drugg'd their possets,
    That Death and Nature do contend about them,

l. 46. *gouts:* Drops.
l. 48. *informs:* Assumes shape.
l. 52. *Hecate:* Goddess of the infernal regions, associated with witchcraft. Here the name is disyllabic.
l. 54. *watch:* Watchword or signal.
l. 55. *Tarquin's . . . strides:* Tarquin ravished Lucrece.
l. 6. *possets:* Drinks of milk, ale or sack, sugar, eggs, and other ingredients boiled together.

Whether they live, or die.

MACBETH (*within*): Who's there?—what, ho!

LADY MACBETH: Alack! I am afraid they have awak'd,   10
　　And 'tis not done:—th' attempt and not the deed
　　Confounds us.—Hark!—I laid their daggers ready;
　　He could not miss 'em.—Had he not resembled
　　My father as he slept, I had done't.—My husband!

Enter MACBETH.

MACBETH: I have done the deed.—Didst thou not hear a noise?

LADY MACBETH: I heard the owl scream, and the crickets cry.
　　Did not you speak?

MACBETH:　　　　　　　　When?

LADY MACBETH:　　　　　　　　　　Now.

MACBETH:　　　　　　　　　　　　　　As I descended?

LADY MACBETH: Ay.

MACBETH: Hark!
　　Who lies i' th' second chamber?

LADY MACBETH:　　　　　　　　　　Donalbain.   20

MACBETH: This is a sorry sight.

LADY MACBETH: A foolish thought to say a sorry sight.

MACBETH: There's one did laugh in's sleep, and one cried, "Murther!"
　　That they did wake each other: I stood and heard them;
　　But they did say their prayers, and address'd them
　　Again to sleep.

LADY MACBETH:　　　　There are two lodg'd together.

MACBETH: One cried, "God bless us!" and, "Amen," the other,
　　As they had seen me with these hangman's hands.
　　List'ning their fear, I could not say, "Amen,"
　　When they did say, "God bless us."

LADY MACBETH:　　　　　　　　Consider it not so deeply.   30

MACBETH: But wherefore could not I pronounce "Amen"?
　　I had most need of blessing, and "Amen"
　　Stuck in my throat.

LADY MACBETH:　　　　These deeds must not be thought
　　After these ways: so, it will make us mad.

MACBETH: Methought, I heard a voice cry, "Sleep no more!
　　Macbeth does murther Sleep,"—the innocent Sleep;
　　Sleep, that knits up the ravell'd sleave of care,
　　The death of each day's life, sore labour's bath,
　　Balm of hurt minds, great Nature's second course,
　　Chief nourisher in life's feast;—

LADY MACBETH:　　　　　　　　What do you mean?   40

l. 28. *As:* As if.
l. 39. *second course:* At dinner, the second course was the main course.

MACBETH: Still it cried, "Sleep no more!" to all the house:
"Glamis hath murther'd Sleep, and therefore Cawdor
Shall sleep no more, Macbeth shall sleep no more!"
LADY MACBETH: Who was it that thus cried? Why, worthy Thane,
You do unbend your noble strength, to think
So brainsickly of things. Go, get some water,
And wash this filthy witness from your hand.—
Why did you bring these daggers from the place?
They must lie there: go, carry them, and smear
The sleepy grooms with blood.
MACBETH: I'll go no more: 50
I am afraid to think what I have done;
Look on't again I dare not.
LADY MACBETH: Infirm of purpose!
Give me the daggers. The sleeping, and the dead,
Are but as pictures; 'tis the eye of childhood
That fears a painted devil. If he do bleed,
I'll gild the faces of the grooms withal,
For it must seem their guilt.

                                        Exit.—Knocking within.
MACBETH: Whence is that knocking?—
How is't with me, when every noise appals me?
What hands are here? Ha! they pluck out mine eyes.
Will all great Neptune's ocean wash this blood   60
Clean from my hand? No, this my hand will rather
The multitudinous seas incarnadine,
Making the green one red.

                    Re-enter LADY MACBETH.

LADY MACBETH: My hands are of your colour; but I shame
To wear a heart so white.
Knock
                    I hear a knocking
At the south entry:—retire we to our chamber.
A little water clears us of this deed:
How easy is it then! Your constancy
Hath left you unattended.—
Knock
                    Hark! more knocking.
Get on your night-gown, lest occasion call us,   70
And show us to be watchers.—Be not lost
So poorly in your thoughts.
MACBETH: To know my deed, 'twere best not know myself.

l. 70. *night-gown:* Dressing gown.

Knock

Wake Duncan with thy knocking: I would thou couldst!

Exeunt.

SCENE III

The same.

Enter a PORTER.

Knocking within

PORTER: Here's a knocking, indeed! If a man were Porter of Hell Gate, he should have old turning the key. (*Knocking*) Knock, knock, knock. Who's there, i' th' name of Belzebub?—Here's a farmer, that hang'd himself on th' expectation of plenty: come in, time-server; have napkins enow about you; here you'll sweat for't. (*Knocking*) Knock, knock. Who's there, i' th' other devil's name? —Faith, here's an equivocator, that could swear in both the scales against either scale; who committed treason enough for God's sake, yet could not equivocate to heaven: O! come in, equivocator. (*Knocking*) Knock, knock, knock. Who's there?—Faith, here's an   10 English tailor come hither for stealing out of a French hose: come in, tailor; here you may roast your goose. (*Knocking*) Knock, knock. Never at quiet! What are you?—But this place is too cold for Hell. I'll devil-porter it no further: I had thought to have let in some of all professions, that go the primrose way to th' everlasting bonfire. (*Knocking*) Anon, anon: I pray you, remember the Porter.

Opens the gate.

Enter MACDUFF *and* LENOX.

MACDUFF: Was it so late, friend, ere you went to bed,

That you do lie so late?

PORTER: Faith, Sir, we were carousing till the second cock; and drink,   20 Sir, is a great provoker of three things.

MACDUFF: What three things does drink especially provoke?

PORTER: Marry, Sir, nose-painting, sleep, and urine. Lechery, Sir, it provokes, and unprovokes: it provokes the desire, but it takes away the performance. Therefore, much drink may be said to be an equivocator with lechery: it makes him, and it mars him; it sets him on, and it takes him off; it persuades him, and disheartens

l. 2. *old:* Much.

l. 4. *hang'd . . . plenty:* Expecting a famine, a farmer stored his grain, which would then fetch high prices. When a rich harvest brought down the price of grain, the farmer was ruined and hanged himself.

l. 5. *napkins enow:* Enough handkerchiefs.

l. 20. *second cock:* Three in the morning.

him; makes him stand to, and not stand to: in conclusion, equi-
vocates him in a sleep, and, giving him the lie, leaves him.

MACDUFF: I believe, drink gave thee the lie last night.   30

PORTER: That it did, Sir, i' the very throat on me: but I requited him
for his lie; and (I think) being too strong for him, though he took
up my legs sometime, yet I made a shift to cast him.

MACDUFF: Is thy master stirring?

Enter MACBETH.

Our knocking has awak'd him; here he comes.

LENOX: Good morrow, noble Sir!

MACBETH: Good morrow, both!

MACDUFF: Is the King stirring, worthy Thane?

MACBETH: Not yet.

MACDUFF: He did command me to call timely on him:
I have almost slipp'd the hour.

MACBETH: I'll bring you to him.

MACDUFF: I know, this is a joyful trouble to you;   40
But yet 'tis one.

MACBETH: The labour we delight in physics pain.
This is the door.

MACDUFF: I'll make so bold to call,
For 'tis my limited service.

                                                        Exit.

LENOX: Goes the King hence to-day?

MACBETH: He does:—he did appoint so.

LENOX: The night has been unruly: where we lay,
Our chimneys were blown down; and, as they say,
Lamentings heard i' th' air; strange screams of death,
And, prophesying with accents terrible
Of dire conbustion, and confus'd events,   50
New hatch'd to th' woeful time, the obscure bird
Clamour'd the livelong night: some say, the earth
Was feverous, and did shake.

MACBETH: 'Twas a rough night.

LENOX: My young remembrance cannot parallel
A fellow to it.

Re-enter MACDUFF.

MACDUFF: O horror! horror! horror!
Tongue nor heart cannot conceive, nor name thee!

l. 33. *yet . . . him:* A pun meaning he managed to throw him (in wrestling),
and managed to vomit.
l. 42. *physics:* Cures.
l. 44. *limited:* Appointed.
l. 50. *combustion:* Tumult.

MACBETH, LENOX: What's the matter?
MACDUFF: Confusion now hath made his masterpiece!
    Most sacrilegious Murther hath broke ope
    The Lord's anointed Temple, and stole thence   60
    The life o' th' building!
MACBETH: What is 't you say? the life?
LENOX: Mean you his Majesty?
MACDUFF: Approach the chamber, and destroy your sight
    With a new Gorgon.—Do not bid me speak:
    See, and then speak yourselves.—

                      Exeunt MACBETH *and* LENOX.
                    Awake! awake!—
Ring the alarum-bell.—Murther, and treason!
Banquo, and Donalbain! Malcolm, awake!
Shake off this downy sleep, death's counterfeit,
And look on death itself!—up, up, and see
The great doom's image!—Malcolm! Banquo!   70
As from your graves rise up, and walk like sprites,
To countenance this horror!
Bell rings

              Enter LADY MACBETH.

LADY MACBETH: What's the business,
    That such a hideous trumpet calls to parley
    The sleepers of the house? speak, speak!
MACDUFF: O gentle lady,
    'Tis not for you to hear what I can speak:
    The repetition, in a woman's ear,
    Would murther as it fell.

              Enter BANQUO.

              O Banquo! Banquo!
Our royal master's murther'd!
LADY MACBETH: Woe, alas!
    What! in our house?
BANQUO: Too cruel, anywhere.
Dear Duff, I pr'ythee, contradict thyself,   80
And say, it is not so.

           Re-enter MACBETH *and* LENOX.

    l. 58. *Confusion:* Destruction.
    l. 64. *Gorgon:* The Gorgons, of which Medusa was one, were women with snakes for hair, huge claws, and teeth like swine. To look on a Gorgon would turn the beholder to stone.
    l. 72. *countenance:* Befit.

MACBETH: Had I but died an hour before this chance,
I had liv'd a blessed time; for, from this instant,
There's nothing serious in mortality;
All is but toys: renown, and grace, is dead;
The wine of life is drawn, and the mere lees
Is left this vault to brag of.

Enter MALCOLM *and* DONALBAIN.

DONALBAIN: What is amiss?
MACBETH: You are, and do not know't:
The spring, the head, the fountain of your blood
Is stopp'd; the very source of it is stopp'd.   90
MACDUFF: Your royal father's murther'd.
MALCOLM: O! by whom?
LENOX: Those of his chamber, as it seem'd, had done 't:
Their hands and faces were all badg'd with blood;
So were their daggers, which, unwip'd, we found
Upon their pillows: they star'd, and were distracted;
No man's life was to be trusted with them.
MACBETH: O! yet I do repent me of my fury,
That I did kill them.
MACDUFF: Wherefore did you so?
MACBETH: Who can be wise, amaz'd, temperate and furious,
Loyal and neutral, in a moment? No man: 100
Th' expedition of my violent love
Outrun the pauser, reason.—Here lay Duncan,
His silver skin lac'd with his golden blood;
And his gash'd stabs look'd like a breach in nature
For ruin's wasteful entrance: there, the murtherers,
Steep'd in the colours of their trade, their daggers
Unmannerly breech'd with gore. Who could refrain,
That had a heart to love, and in that heart
Courage, to make's love known?
LADY MACBETH: Help me hence, ho!
MACDUFF: Look to the Lady.   110
MALCOLM (*aside to* DONALBAIN): Why do we hold our tongues, that
    most may claim
This argument for ours?
DONALBAIN (*aside to* MALCOLM): What should be spoken
Here, where our fate, hid in an auger-hole,
May rush, and seize us? Let's away:

l. 101. *expedition:* Haste.
l. 107. *breech'd:* Covered.
l. 112. *argument:* Subject.

Our tears are not yet brew'd.

MALCOLM (*aside to* DONALBAIN):   Nor our strong sorrow
  Upon the foot of motion.

BANQUO: Look to the Lady:—

                                 LADY MACBETH *is carried out.*

  And when we have our naked frailties hid,
  That suffer in exposure, let us meet,
  And question this most bloody piece of work,
  To know it further. Fears and scruples shake us: 120
  In the great hand of God I stand; and thence
  Against the undivulg'd pretence I fight
  Of treasonous malice.

MACDUFF: And so do I.

ALL: So all.

MACBETH: Let's briefly put on manly readiness,
  And meet i' th' hall together.

ALL: Well contented.

               Exeunt all but MALCOLM *and* DONALBAIN.

MALCOLM: What will you do? Let's not consort with them:
  To show an unfelt sorrow is an office
  Which the false man does easy. I'll to England.

DONALBAIN: To Ireland, I: our separated fortune
  Shall keep us both the safer; where we are,   130
  There's daggers in men's smiles: the near in blood,
  The nearer bloody.

MALCOLM: This murtherous shaft that's shot
  Hath not yet lighted, and our safest way
  Is to avoid the aim: therefore, to horse;
  And let us not be dainty of leave-taking,
  But shift away. There's warrant in that theft
  Which steals itself, when there's no mercy left.

                                      Exeunt.

SCENE IV

Without the castle.

Enter ROSSE *and an* OLD MAN.

OLD MAN: Threescore and ten I can remember well;
  Within the volume of which time I have seen

l. 124. *briefly:* Quickly.
ll. 131–132. *near . . . bloody:* The nearer in blood-ties to Duncan, the nearer
we are to being killed.
l. 133. *lighted:* Alighted.
l. 136. *shift away:* Slip away.

Hours dreadful, and things strange, but this sore night
Hath trifled former knowings.
ROSSE: Ha, good Father,
Thou seest the heavens, as troubled with man's act,
Threatens his bloody stage: by th' clock 'tis day,
And yet dark night strangles the travelling lamp.
Is 't night's predominance, or the day's shame,
That darkness does the face of earth entomb,
When living light should kiss it?
OLD MAN: 'Tis unnatural,   10
Even like the deed that's done. On Tuesday last,
A falcon, towering in her pride of place,
Was by a mousing owl hawk'd at, and kill'd.
ROSSE: And Duncan's horses (a thing most strange and certain)
Beauteous and swift, the minions of their race,
Turn'd wild in nature, broke their stalls, flung out,
Contending 'gainst obedience, as they would make
War with mankind.
OLD MAN: 'Tis said, they eat each other.
ROSSE: They did so; to th' amazement of mine eyes,
That look'd upon 't.

Enter MACDUFF.

Here comes the good Macduff.   20
How goes the world, Sir, now?
MACDUFF: Why, see you not?
ROSSE: Is 't known, who did this more than bloody deed?
MACDUFF: Those that Macbeth hath slain.
ROSSE: Alas, the day!
What good could they pretend?
MACDUFF: They were suborn'd.
Malcolm, and Donalbain, the King's two sons,
Are stol'n away and fled; which puts upon them
Suspicion of the deed.
ROSSE: 'Gainst nature still:
Thriftless Ambition, that will ravin up
Thine own life's means!—Then 'tis most like
The sovereignty will fall upon Macbeth.   30
MACDUFF: He is already nam'd, and gone to Scone
To be invested.

l. 4. *trifled former knowings:* Has made previous experiences seem of little value.
l. 7. *travelling lamp:* The sun.
l. 24. *pretend:* Intend.
        suborn'd: Secretly incited.
l. 28. *ravin up:* Ravenously eat up.
l. 31. *Scone:* The place where Scottish kings were crowned.

ROSSE: Where is Duncan's body?
MACDUFF: Carried to Colme-kill,
    The sacred storehouse of his predecessors,
    And guardian of their bones.
ROSSE: Will you to Scone?
MACDUFF: No cousin; I'll to Fife.
ROSSE: Well, I will thither.
MACDUFF: Well, may you see things well done there:—adieu!—
    Lest our old robes sit easier than our new!
ROSSE: Farewell, Father.
OLD MAN: God's benison go with you; and with those   40
    That would make good of bad, and friends of foes!

                                                    Exeunt.

§ ACT III

SCENE I

Forres. A room in the palace.

Enter BANQUO.

BANQUO: Thou hast it now, King, Cawdor, Glamis, all,
    As the Weïrd Women promis'd; and, I fear,
    Thou play'dst most foully for't; yet it was said,
    It should not stand in thy posterity;
    But that myself should be the root and father
    Of many kings. If there come truth from them
    (As upon thee, Macbeth, their speeches shine),
    Why, by the verities on thee made good,
    May they not be my oracles as well,
    And set me up in hope? But, hush; no more.   10

Sennet sounded. Enter MACBETH *as* King; LADY MACBETH, *as*
        Queen; LENOX, ROSSE, *Lords and Attendants.*

MACBETH: Here's our chief guest.
LADY MACBETH: If he had been forgotten,
    It had been as a gap in our great feast,
    And all-thing unbecoming.
MACBETH: To-night we hold a solemn supper, Sir,
    And I'll request your presence.
BANQUO: Let your Highness

---

l. 33. *Colme-kill:* The place where Scottish kings were buried.
direction. *Sennet sounded:* A call on a trumpet or cornet.
l. 13. *all-thing:* Totally.
l. 14. *solemn:* Formal.

Command upon me, to the which my duties
Are with a most indissoluble tie
For ever knit.
MACBETH: Ride you this afternoon?
BANQUO: Ay, my good Lord.
MACBETH: We should have else desir'd your good advice   20
(Which still hath been both grave and prosperous)
In this day's council; but we'll take to-morrow.
Is't far you ride?
BANQUO: As far, my Lord, as will fill up the time
'Twixt this and supper: go not my horse the better,
I must become a borrower of the night,
For a dark hour, or twain.
MACBETH: Fail not our feast.
BANQUO: My Lord, I will not.
MACBETH: We hear, our bloody cousins are bestow'd
In England, and in Ireland; not confessing   30
Their cruel parricide, filling their hearers
With strange invention. But of that to-morrow,
When, therewithal, we shall have cause of State,
Craving us jointly. Hie you to horse: adieu,
Till you return at night. Goes Fleance with you?
BANQUO: Ay, my good Lord: our time does call upon 's.
MACBETH: I wish your horses swift, and sure of foot;
And so I do commend you to their backs.
Farewell.—

                                                Exit BANQUO.
Let every man be master of his time   40
Till seven at night;
To make society the sweeter welcome,
We will keep ourself till supper-time alone:
While then, God be with you.
                        Exeunt all except MACBETH *and a* SERVANT.
                        Sirrah, a word with you.
Attend those men our pleasure?
SERVANT: They are, my Lord,
Without the palace gate.
MACBETH: Bring them before us.
                                                Exit SERVANT.

To be thus is nothing, but to be safely thus:
Our fears of Banquo
Stick deep, and in his royalty of nature

l. 21. *still*: Always.
        prosperous: Profitable.
l. 44. *While*: Until.

Reigns that which would be fear'd: 'tis much he dares;   50
And, to that dauntless temper of his mind,
He hath a wisdom that doth guide his valour
To act in safety. There is none but he
Whose being I do fear: and under him
My Genius is rebuk'd; as, it is said,
Mark Antony's was by Cæsar. He chid the Sisters.
When first they put the name of King upon me,
And bade them speak to him; then, prophet-like,
They hail'd him father to a line of kings:
Upon my head they plac'd a fruitless crown,   ·   60
And put a barren sceptre in my gripe,
Thence to be wrench'd with an unlineal hand,
No son of mine succeeding. If 't be so,
For Banquo's issue have I fil'd my mind;
For them the gracious Duncan have I murther'd;
Put rancours in the vessel of my peace,
Only for them; and mine eternal jewel
Given to the common Enemy of man,
To make them kings, the seed of Banquo kings!
Rather than so, come, fate, into the list,   70
And champion me to th' utterance!—Who's there?—

Re-enter SERVANT, *with two* MURDERERS.

Now, go to the door, and stay there till we call.

Exit SERVANT.

Was it not yesterday we spoke together?
1 MURDERER: It was, so please your Highness.
MACBETH: Well then, now
Have you consider'd of my speeches?—know
That it was he, in the times past, which held you
So under fortune, which you thought had been
Our innocent self? This I made good to you
In our last conference; pass'd in probation with you,
How you were borne in hand; how cross'd; the instruments;   80
Who wrought with them; and all things else, that might,
To half a soul, and to a notion craz'd,
Say, "Thus did Banquo."

l. 62. *with . . . hand:* By one who is not my heir.
l. 64. *fil'd:* Defiled.
l. 67. *eternal jewel:* Immortal soul.
l. 68. *Enemy of man:* The devil.
l. 71. *to th' utterance:* To the utmost extremity, i.e., death.
l. 79. *pass'd . . . you:* Proved to you.
l. 80. *borne in hand:* Deluded.
l. 82. *notion:* Mind.

1 MURDERER:　　　　　　　You made it known to us.

MACBETH:　I did so; and went further, which is now
　　Our point of second meeting. Do you find
　　Your patience so predominant in your nature,
　　That you can let this go? Are you so gospell'd,
　　To pray for this good man, and for his issue,
　　Whose heavy hand hath bow'd you to the grave,
　　And beggar'd yours for ever?

1 MURDERER:　　　　　　　We are men, my Liege.　　　　90

MACBETH:　Ay, in the catalogue ye go for men;
　　As hounds, and greyhounds, mongrels, spaniels, curs,
　　Shoughs, water-rugs, and demi-wolves, are clept
　　All by the name of dogs: the valu'd file
　　Distinguishes the swift, the slow, the subtle,
　　The housekeeper, the hunter, every one
　　According to the gift which bounteous Nature
　　Hath in him clos'd; whereby he does receive
　　Particular addition, from the bill
　　That writes them all alike; and so of men.　　　　100
　　Now, if you have a station in the file,
　　Not i' th' worst rank of manhood, say 't;
　　And I will put that business in your bosoms,
　　Whose execution takes your enemy off,
　　Grapples you to the heart and love of us,
　　Who wear our health but sickly in his life,
　　Which in his death were perfect.

2 MURDERER:　　　　　　　I am one, my Liege,
　　Whom the vile blows and buffets of the world
　　Hath so incens'd, that I am reckless what
　　I do, to spite the world.

1 MURDERER:　　　　　　　And I another,　　　　110
　　So weary with disasters, tugg'd with fortune,
　　That I would set my life on any chance,
　　To mend it, or be rid on 't.

MACBETH:　　　　　　　Both of you
　　Know, Banquo was your enemy.

2 MURDERER:　　　　　　　True, my Lord.

MACBETH:　So is he mine; and in such bloody distance,
　　That every minute of his being thrusts

l. 93. *Shoughs:* Shaggy dogs.
　　water-rugs: hairy water dogs.
　　clept: Called.
l. 94. *valu'd file:* List indicating the value.
l. 96. *housekeeper:* Watchdog.
l. 98. *Hath in him clos'd:* Has enclosed within him.
l. 115. *distance:* Enmity.

Against my near'st of life: and though I could
With bare-fac'd power sweep him from my sight,
And bid my will avouch it, yet I must not,
For certain friends that are both his and mine,   120
Whose loves I may not drop, but wail his fall
Who I myself struck down: and thence it is
That I to your assistance do make love,
Masking the business from the common eye,
For sundry weighty reasons.

2 MURDERER: We shall, my Lord,
    Perform what you command us.
1 MURDERER: Though our lives—
MACBETH: Your spirits shine through you. Within this hour, at most,
    I will advise you where to plant yourselves,
    Acquaint you with the perfect spy o' th' time,
    The moment on't; for't must be done to-night,   130
    And something from the palace; always thought,
    That I require a clearness: and with him
    (To leave no rubs nor botches in the work),
    Fleance his son, that keeps him company,
    Whose absence is no less material to me
    Than is his father's, must embrace the fate
    Of that dark hour. Resolve yourselves apart;
    I'll come to you anon.
2 MURDERER: We are resolv'd, my Lord.
MACBETH: I'll call upon you straight: abide within.—

                                     Exeunt MURDERERS.

    It is concluded: Banquo, thy soul's flight,   140
    If it find Heaven, must find it out to-night.

                                       Exit.

SCENE II

The same. Another room.

           Enter LADY MACBETH *and a* SERVANT.

LADY MACBETH: Is Banquo gone from court?
SERVANT: Ay, Madam, but returns again to-night.
LADY MACBETH: Say to the King, I would attend his leisure
    For a few words.
SERVANT: Madam, I will.

                                     Exit.

l. 117. *near'st of life:* Most vital parts.
l. 129. *perfect . . . time:* The best time.
l. 132. *require a clearness:* It must always be kept in mind that I be free of suspicion.

LADY MACBETH: Nought's had, all's spent,
Where our desire is got without content:
'Tis safer to be that which we destroy,
Than by destruction dwell in doubtful joy.

Enter MACBETH.

How now, my Lord? why do you keep alone,
Of sorriest fancies your companions making,
Using those thoughts, which should indeed have died   10
With them they think on? Things without all remedy
Should be without regard: what's done is done.
MACBETH: We have scorch'd the snake, not kill'd it:
She'll close, and be herself; whilst our poor malice
Remains in danger of her former tooth.
But let the frame of things disjoint, both the worlds suffer,
Ere we will eat our meal in fear, and sleep
In the affliction of these terrible dreams,
That shake us nightly. Better be with the dead,
Whom we, to gain our peace, have sent to peace,   20
Than on the torture of the mind to lie
In restless ecstasy. Duncan is in his grave;
After life's fitful fever he sleeps well;
Treason has done his worst: nor steel, nor poison,
Malice domestic, foreign levy, nothing
Can touch him further!
LADY MACBETH: Come on:
Gentle my Lord, sleek o'er your rugged looks;
Be bright and jovial among your guests to-night.
MACBETH: So shall I, Love; and so, I pray, be you.
Let your remembrance apply to Banquo: 30
Present him eminence, both with eye and tongue:
Unsafe the while, that we
Must lave our honours in these flattering streams,
And make our faces vizards to our hearts,
Disguising what they are.
LADY MACBETH: You must leave this.
MACBETH: O! full of scorpions is my mind, dear wife!
Thou know'st that Banquo, and his Fleance, lives.
LADY MACBETH: But in them Nature's copy's not eterne.
MACBETH: There's comfort yet; they are assailable:
Then be thou jocund. Ere the bat hath flown   40

l. 11. *without all remedy:* That cannot be remedied.
l. 16. *let . . . disjoint:* Let the universe come apart.
l. 32. *Unsafe . . . that:* Since we are unsafe.
l. 34. *vizards:* Masks.
l. 38. *But . . . eterne:* But they will not live forever.

His cloister'd flight; ere to black Hecate's summons
The shard-born beetle, with his drowsy hums,
Hath rung Night's yawning peal, there shall be done
A deed of dreadful note.
LADY MACBETH: What's to be done?
MACBETH: Be innocent of the knowledge, dearest chuck,
Till thou applaud the deed. Come, seeling Night,
Scarf up the tender eye of pitiful Day,
And, with thy bloody and invisible hand,
Cancel, and tear to pieces, that great bond
Which keeps me pale!—Light thickens; and the crow   50
Makes wings to th' rooky wood;
Good things of Day begin to droop and drowse,
Whiles Night's black agents to their preys do rouse.
Thou marvell'st at my words: but hold thee still;
Things bad begun make strong themselves by ill.
So, pr'ythee, go with me.

                                           Exeunt.

SCENE III

The same. A park, with a road leading to the palace.

Enter three MURDERERS.

1 MURDERER: But who did bid thee join with us?
3 MURDERER: Macbeth.
2 MURDERER: He needs not our mistrust; since he delivers
Our offices, and what we have to do,
To the direction just.
1 MURDERER: Then stand with us.
The west yet glimmers with some streaks of day;
Now spurs the lated traveller apace,
To gain the timely inn; and near approaches
The subject of our watch.
3 MURDERER: Hark! I hear horses.
BANQUO (*within*): Give us a light there, ho!
2 MURDERER: Then 'tis he: the rest
That are within the note of expectation,   10
Already are i' th' court.

l. 42. *shard-born:* Born in excrement.
l. 45. *chuck:* A term of endearment.
l. 49. *that great bond:* Banquo's bond of life.
ll. 2–4. *He needs . . . just:* The Second Murderer speaks to the First Murderer:
We need not distrust him (the Third Murderer) since he brings our assignments and
exact instructions (from Macbeth) regarding what we must do.
l. 6. *lated:* Belated.

1 MURDERER: His horses go about.
3 MURDERER: Almost a mile; but he does usually,
So all men do, from hence to the palace gate
Make it their walk.

Enter BANQUO, *and* FLEANCE, *with a torch.*

2 MURDERER: A light, a light!
3 MURDERER: 'Tis he.
1 MURDERER: Stand to 't.
BANQUO: It will rain to-night.
1 MURDERER: Let it come down.

The FIRST MURDERER *strikes out the light, while the others assault*
BANQUO.

BANQUO: O, treachery! Fly, good Fleance, fly, fly, fly!
Thou may'st revenge—O slave!

Dies. FLEANCE *escapes.*

3 MURDERER: Who did strike out the light?
1 MURDERER: Was't not the way?
3 MURDERER: There's but one down: the son is fled.
2 MURDERER: We have lost
Best half of our affair.   20
1 MURDERER: Well, let's away,
And say how much is done.

Exeunt.

SCENE IV

A room of state in the palace.

A banquet prepared. Enter MACBETH, LADY MACBETH, ROSSE,
LENOX, *Lords, and Attendants.*

MACBETH: You know your own degrees, sit down: at first
And last, the hearty welcome.
LORDS: Thanks to your Majesty.
MACBETH: Ourself will mingle with society,
And play the humble host.
Our hostess keeps her state; but, in best time,
We will require her welcome.
LADY MACBETH: Pronounce it for me, Sir, to all our friends;
For my heart speaks, they are welcome.

Enter FIRST MURDERER, *to the door.*

MACBETH: See, they encounter thee with their hearts' thanks.
Both sides are even: here I'll sit i' th' midst.   10

l. 5. *keeps her state:* Remains seated in her chair of state.

Be large in mirth; anon, we'll drink a measure
 The table round.
 Goes to door.
 There's blood upon thy face.
MURDERER: 'Tis Banquo's then.
MACBETH: 'Tis better thee without, than he within.
 Is he dispatch'd?
MURDERER: My Lord, his throat is cut;
 That I did for him.
MACBETH: Thou art the best o' th' cut-throats;
 Yet he's good that did the like for Fleance:
 If thou didst it, thou are the nonpareil.
MURDERER: Most royal Sir . . . Fleance is scap'd.
MACBETH: Then comes my fit again: I had else been perfect;   20
 Whole as the marble, founded as the rock,
 As broad and general as the casing air:
 But now, I am cabin'd, cribb'd, confin'd, bound in
 To saucy doubts and fears.—But Banquo's safe?
MURDERER: Ay, my good Lord, safe in a ditch he bides,
 With twenty trenched gashes on his head;
 The least a death to nature.
MACBETH: Thanks for that.—
 There the grown serpent lies; the worm, that's fled,
 Hath nature that in time will venom breed,
 No teeth for th' present.—Get thee gone; to-morrow   30
 We'll hear ourselves again.

                                                                                         Exit MURDERER.
LADY MACBETH: My royal Lord,
 You do not give the cheer: the feast is sold,
 That is not often vouch'd, while 'tis a-making,
 'Tis given with welcome: to feed were best at home;
 From thence, the sauce to meat is ceremony;
 Meeting were bare without it.
MACBETH: Sweet remembrancer!—
 Now, good digestion wait on appetite,
 And health on both!
LENOX: May it please your Highness sit?
MACBETH: Here had we now our country's honour roof'd,
 Were the grac'd person of our Banquo present;   40

l. 14. *'Tis . . . within:* It is better on you than in him.
l. 18. *nonpareil:* The one without peer.
l. 22. *casing:* Surrounding.
l. 31. *hear ourselves:* Speak to one another.
ll. 32–33. *You . . . vouch'd:* Without words of welcome a feast was considered
a business transaction.

The Ghost of BANQUO *enters, and sits in* MACBETH's *place.*

Who may I rather challenge for unkindness,
Than pity for mischance!

ROSSE: His absence, Sir,
Lays blame upon his promise. Please 't your Highness
To grace us with your royal company?

MACBETH: The table's full.

LENOX: Here is a place reserv'd, Sir.

MACBETH: Where?

LENOX: Here, my good Lord. What is't that moves your Highness?

MACBETH: Which of you have done this?

LORDS: What, my good Lord?

MACBETH: Thou canst not say, I did it: never shake
Thy gory locks at me.   50

ROSSE: Gentlemen, rise; his Highness is not well.

LADY MACBETH: Sit, worthy friends. My Lord is often thus,
And hath been from his youth: pray you, keep seat;
The fit is momentary; upon a thought
He will again be well. If much you note him,
You shall offend him, and extend his passion;
Feed, and regard him not.—Are you a man?

MACBETH: Ay, and a bold one, that dare look on that
Which might appal the Devil.

LADY MACBETH: O proper stuff!
This is the very painting of your fear: 60
This is the air-drawn dagger, which, you said,
Led you to Duncan. O! these flaws and starts
(Impostors to true fear), would well become
A woman's story at a winter's fire,
Authoris'd by her grandam. Shame itself!
Why do you make such faces? When all's done,
You look but on a stool.

MACBETH: Pr'ythee, see there!
Behold! look! lo! how say you?
Why, what care I? If thou canst nod, speak too.—
If charnel-houses and our graves must send   70
Those that we bury, back, our monuments
Shall be the maws of kites.

                                                Ghost disappears.

LADY MACBETH: What! quite unmann'd in folly?

l. 54. *upon a thought*: In an instant.
l. 56. *passion*: Suffering.
l. 59. *proper stuff*: Absolute nonsense.
l. 62. *flaws*: Bursts of passion.

MACBETH: If I stand here, I saw him.

LADY MACBETH: Fie! for shame!

MACBETH: Blood hath been shed ere now, i' th' olden time,
  Ere humane statute purg'd the gentle weal;
  Ay, and since too, murthers have been perform'd
  Too terrible for the ear: the time has been,
  That, when the brains were out, the man would die,
  And there an end; but now, they rise again,
  With twenty mortal murthers on their crowns,   80
  And push us from our stools. This is more strange
  Than such a murther is.

LADY MACBETH: My worthy Lord,
  Your noble friends do lack you.

MACBETH: I do forget.—
  Do not muse at me, my most worthy friends,
  I have a strange infirmity, which is nothing
  To those that know me. Come, love and health to all;
  Then, I'll sit down.—Give me some wine: fill full:—
  I drink to th' general joy o' th' whole table,
  And to our dear friend Banquo, whom we miss;
  Would he were here!

Re-enter Ghost.

                 To all, and him, we thirst,   90
  And all to all.

LORDS: Our duties, and the pledge.

MACBETH: Avaunt! and quit my sight! let the earth hide thee!
  Thy bones are marrowless, thy blood is cold;
  Thou hast no speculation in those eyes,
  Which thou dost glare with.

LADY MACBETH: Think of this, good Peers,
  But as a thing of custom: 'tis no other;
  Only it spoils the pleasure of the time.

MACBETH: What man dare, I dare:
  Approach thou like the rugged Russian bear,
  The arm'd rhinoceros, or th' Hyrcan tiger;   100
  Take any shape but that, and my firm nerves
  Shall never tremble: or, be alive again,
  And dare me to the desert with thy sword;
  If trembling I inhabit then, protest me

l. 76. *murthers:* Wounds.
l. 84. *muse:* Wonder.
l. 100. *arm'd:* Armored.
ll. 104–105. *If . . . girl:* If I continue to tremble, then call me a baby girl.

The baby of a girl. Hence, horrible shadow!
Unreal mock'ry, hence!—

Ghost disappears.

Why, so;—being gone,
I am a man again.—Pray you, sit still.

LADY MACBETH: You have displac'd the mirth, broke the good
    meeting
With most admir'd disorder.

MACBETH: Can such things be,
And overcome us like a summer's cloud,   110
Without our special wonder? You make me strange
Even to the disposition that I owe,
When now I think you can behold such sights,
And keep the natural ruby of your cheeks,
When mine is blanch'd with fear.

ROSSE: What sights, my Lord?

LADY MACBETH: I pray you, speak not; he grows worse and worse;
Question enrages him At once, good night:—
Stand not upon the order of your going,
But go at once.

LENOX: Good night, and better health
Attend his Majesty!

LADY MACBETH: A kind good night to all!   120

Exeunt Lords and Attendants.

MACBETH: It will have blood, they say: blood will have blood:
Stones have been known to move, and trees to speak;
Augures, and understood relations, have
By magot pies, and choughs, and rooks, brought forth
The secret'st man of blood.—What is the night?

LADY MACBETH. Almost at odds with morning, which is which.

MACBETH: How say'st thou, that Macduff denies his person,
At our great bidding?

LADY MACBETH: Did you send to him, Sir?

MACBETH: I heard it by the way; but I will send.
There's not a one of them, but in his house   130
I keep a servant fee'd. I will to-morrow
(And betimes I will) to the Weïrd Sisters:
More shall they speak; for now I am bent to know,
By the worst means, the worst. For mine own good,
All causes shall give way: I am in blood

l. 109. *admir'd:* Wondrous.
l. 110. *overcome:* Pass over.
l. 112. *owe:* Own, possess.
l. 124. *magot-pies:* Magpies.
        choughs: Jackdaws.

Stepp'd in so far, that, should I wade no more,
Returning were as tedious as go o'er.
Strange things I have in head, that will to hand,
Which must be acted, ere they may be scann'd.
LADY MACBETH: You lack the season of all natures, sleep.   140
MACBETH: Come, we'll go to sleep. My strange and self-abuse
 Is the initiate fear, that wants hard use:
 We are yet but young in deed.

                Exeunt.

SCENE V

The heath.

Thunder. Enter the three WITCHES, *meeting* HECATE.

1 WITCH: Why, how now, Hecate? you look angerly.
HECATE: Have I not reason, beldams as you are,
 Saucy, and overbold? How did you dare
 To trade and traffic with Macbeth,
 In riddles, and affairs of death;
 And I, the mistress of your charms,
 The close contriver of all harms,
 Was never call'd to bear my part,
 Or show the glory of our art?
 And, which is worse, all you have done   10
 Hath been but for a wayward son,
 Spiteful, and wrathful; who, as others do,
 Loves for his own ends, not for you.
 But make amends now: get you gone,
 And at the pit of Acheron
 Meet me i' th' morning: thither he
 Will come to know his destiny.
 Your vessels, and your spells, provide,
 Your charms, and everything beside.
 I am for th' air; this night I'll spend   20
 Unto a dismal and a fatal end:
 Great business must be wrought ere noon.
 Upon the corner of the moon
 There hangs a vap'rous drop profound;
 I'll catch it ere it come to ground:
 And that, distill'd by magic sleights,

l. 141. *self-abuse:* Self-delusion.
l. 142. *initiate fear:* Fear of the novice.
  l. 15. *pit of Acheron:* The River of Woe in Hades, over which Charon ferried the
dead.

Shall raise such artificial sprites,
As, by the strength of their illusion,
Shall draw him on to his confusion.
He shall spurn fate, scorn death, and bear   30
His hopes 'bove wisdom, grace, and fear;
And you all know, security
Is mortals' chiefest enemy.
Song within: "Come away, come away," etc.
Hark! I am call'd: my little spirit, see,
Sits in a foggy cloud, and stays for me.

                                                    Exit.

1 WITCH: Come, let's make haste: she'll soon be back again.

                                                    Exeunt.

SCENE VI

Somewhere in Scotland.

Enter LENOX *and another* LORD.

LENOX: My former speeches have but hit your thoughts,
    Which can interpret farther: only, I say,
    Things have been strangely borne. The gracious Duncan
    Was pitied of Macbeth:—marry, he was dead:—
    And the right-valiant Banquo walk'd too late;
    Whom, you may say (if't please you) Fleance kill'd,
    For Fleance fled. Men must not walk too late.
    Who cannot want the thought, how monstrous
    It was for Malcolm, and for Donalbain,
    To kill their gracious father? damned fact!   10
    How it did grieve Macbeth! did he not straight,
    In pious rage, the two delinquents tear,
    That were the slaves of drink, and thralls of sleep?
    Was not that nobly done? Ay, and wisely too;
    For 'twould have anger'd any heart alive
    To hear the men deny 't. So that, I say,
    He has borne all things well: and I do think,
    That, had he Duncan's sons under his key
    (As, and 't please Heaven, he shall not), they should find
    What 'twere to kill a father; so should Fleance.   20
    But, peace!—for from broad words, and 'cause he fail'd
    His presence at the tyrant's feast, I hear,
    Macduff lives in disgrace. Sir, can you tell
    Where he bestows himself?
LORD: The son of Duncan,

1. 21. *broad:* Plain.

From whom this tyrant holds the due of birth,
Lives in the English court; and is receiv'd
Of the most pious Edward with such grace,
That the malevolence of fortune nothing
Takes from his high respect. Thither Macduff
Is gone to pray the holy King, upon his aid   30
To wake Northumberland, and warlike Siward;
That, by the help of these (with Him above
To ratify the work), we may again
Give to our tables meat, sleep to our nights,
Free from our feasts and banquets bloody knives,
Do faithful homage, and receive free honours,
All which we pine for now. And this report
Hath so exasperate the King, that he
Prepares for some attempt of war.

LENOX: Sent he to Macduff?

LORD: He did: and with an absolute "Sir, not I,"   40
The cloudy messenger turns me his back,
And hums, as who should say, "You'll rue the time
That clogs me with this answer."

LENOX: And that well might
Advise him to a caution, t' hold what distance
His wisdom can provide. Some holy Angel
Fly to the court of England, and unfold
His message ere he come, that a swift blessing
May soon return to this our suffering country
Under a hand accurs'd!

LORD: I'll send my prayers with him.

Exeunt.

§ ACT IV

SCENE I

A dark cave. In the middle, a boiling cauldron.

Thunder. Enter the three WITCHES.

1 WITCH: Thrice the brinded cat hath mew'd.
2 WITCH: Thrice, and once the hedge-pig whin'd.
3 WITCH: Harpier cries:—'Tis time, 'tis time.
1 WITCH: Round about the cauldron go;
        In the poison'd entrails throw.—

l. 1. *brinded:* Branded with fire, i.e., streaked with a different hue.
l. 3. *Harpier:* Possibly a misspelling or corruption of Harpy (a monster with a woman's head and a bird's body).

Toad, that under cold stone
Days and nights has thirty-one
Swelter'd venom, sleeping got,
Boil thou first i' th' charmed pot.
ALL: Double, double toil and trouble: 10
    Fire, burn; and, cauldron, bubble.
2 WITCH: Fillet of a fenny snake,
    In the cauldron boil and bake;
    Eye of newt, and toe of frog,
    Wool of bat, and tongue of dog,
    Adder's fork, and blind-worm's sting,
    Lizard's leg, and howlet's wing,
    For a charm and powerful trouble,
    Like a hell-broth boil and bubble.
ALL: Double, double toil and trouble: 20
    Fire, burn; and, cauldron, bubble.
3 WITCH: Scale of dragon, tooth of wolf;
    Witches' mummy; maw, and gulf,
    Of the ravin'd salt-sea shark;
    Root of hemlock, digg'd i' th' dark;
    Liver of blaspheming Jew;
    Gall of goat, and slips of yew,
    Sliver'd in the moon's eclipse;
    Nose of Turk, and Tartar's lips;
    Finger of birth-strangled babe,   30
    Ditch-deliver'd by a drab,
    Make the gruel thick and slab:
    Add thereto a tiger's chaudron,
    For th' ingredience of our cauldron.
ALL: Double, double toil and trouble:
    Fire, burn; and, cauldron, bubble.
2 WITCH: Cool it with a baboon's blood:
    Then the charm is firm and good.

       Enter HECATE, *and the other three* WITCHES.

HECATE: O, well done! I commend your pains,
    And every one shall share i' th' gains.   40
    And now about the cauldron sing,

  l. 8. *Swelter'd:* Sweated.
  l. 12. *fenny:* From the marshes.
  l. 16. *fork:* Forked tongue.
      blind-worm's: Lizard's.
  l. 17. *howlet's:* Owl's.
  l. 23. *gulf:* Stomach.
  l. 24. *ravin'd:* Ravenous.
  l. 31. *drab:* Prostitute.
  l. 33. *chaudron:* Entrails.

Like elves and fairies in a ring,
Enchanting all that you put in.
Music and a song, "Black spirits," *etc.*

Exeunt HECATE *and the three other* WITCHES.

2 WITCH: By the pricking of my thumbs,
Something wicked this way comes.—
Knocking.
Open, locks,
Whoever knocks.

Enter MACBETH.

MACBETH: How now, you secret, black, and midnight hags!
What is't you do?

ALL: A deed without a name.

MACBETH: I conjure you, by that which you profess,   50
Howe'er you come to know it, answer me:
Though you untie the winds, and let them fight
Against the Churches; though the yesty waves
Confound and swallow navigation up;
Though bladed corn be lodg'd, and tree blown down;
Though castles topple on their warders' heads;
Though palaces, and pyramids, do slope
Their heads to their foundations; though the treasure
Of Nature's germens tumble all together,
Even till destruction sicken, answer me   60
To what I ask you.

1 WITCH: Speak.

2 WITCH: Demand.

3 WITCH: We'll answer.

1 WITCH: Say, if thou'dst rather hear it from our mouths,
Or from our masters?

MACBETH: Call 'em; let me see 'em.

1 WITCH: Pour in sow's blood, that hath eaten
Her nine farrow; grease, that's sweaten
From the murderer's gibbet, throw
Into the flame.

ALL: Come, high, or low;
Thyself and office deftly show.

Thunder. FIRST APPARITION, *an armed head.*

MACBETH: Tell me, thou unknown power,—

1 WITCH: He knows thy thought:
Hear his speech, but say thou nought.   70

l. 53. *yesty:* Foamy.
l. 59. *germens:* Seeds.
l. 65. *farrow:* Litter of nine.

1 APPARITION: Macbeth! Macbeth! Macbeth! beware Macduff;
  Beware the Thane of Fife.—Dismiss me.—Enough.

Descends.

MACBETH: Whate'er thou art, for thy good caution, thanks:
  Thou hast harp'd my fear aright.—But one word more:—
1 WITCH: He will not be commanded. Here's another,
  More potent than the first.

Thunder. SECOND APPARITION, *a bloody child.*

2 APPARITION: Macbeth! Macbeth! Macbeth!—
MACBETH: Had I three ears, I'd hear thee.
2 APPARITION: Be bloody, bold, and resolute: laugh to scorn
  The power of man, for none of woman born   80
  Shall harm Macbeth.

Descends.

MACBETH: Then live, Macduff: what need I fear of thee?
  But yet I'll make assurance double sure,
  And take a bond of Fate: thou shalt not live;
  That I may tell pale-hearted fear it lies,
  And sleep in spite of thunder.—

Thunder. THIRD APPARITION, *a child crowned with a tree in
his hand.*

                What is this,
  That rises like the issue of a king;
  And wears upon his baby brow the round
  And top of sovereignty?
ALL: Listen, but speak not to 't.
3 APPARITION: Be lion-mettled, proud, and take no care   90
  Who chafes, who frets, or where conspirers are:
  Macbeth shall never vanquish'd be, until
  Great Birnam wood to high Dunsinane hill
  Shall come against him.

Descends.

MACBETH: That will never be:
  Who can impress the forest; bid the tree
  Unfix his earth-bound root? Sweet bodements! good!
  Rebellious dead, rise never, till the wood
  Of Birnam rise; and our high-plac'd Macbeth
  Shall live the lease of Nature, pay his breath
  To time, and mortal custom.—Yet my heart   100
  Throbs to know one thing: tell me (if your art
  Can tell so much), shall Banquo's issue ever

l. 96. *bodements:* Bodings.
l. 100. *mortal custom:* Die a natural death.

Reign in this kingdom?

ALL: Seek to know no more.

MACBETH: I will be satisfied: deny me this,
 And an eternal curse fall on you! Let me know.—
 Why sinks that cauldron? and what noise is this?
 (*Hautboys.*)

1 WITCH: Show!

2 WITCH: Show!

3 WITCH: Show!

ALL: Show his eyes, and grieve his heart;   110
 Come like shadows, so depart.

 A *show of eight Kings, the last with a glass in his hand;*
   BANQUO *following.*

MACBETH: Thou art too like the spirit of Banquo: down!
 Thy crown does sear mine eye-balls:—and thy hair,
 Thou other gold-bound brow, is like the first:—
 A third is like the former:—filthy hags!
 Why do you show me this?—A fourth?—Start, eyes!
 What! will the line stretch out to th' crack of doom?
 Another yet?—A seventh?—I'll see no more:—
 And yet the eighth appears, who bears a glass,
 Which shows me many more; and some I see,   120
 That two-fold balls and treble sceptres carry.
 Horrible sight!—Now, I see, 'tis true;
 For the blood-bolter'd Banquo smiles upon me,
 And points at them for his.—What! is this so?

1 WITCH: Ay, Sir, all this is so:—but why
 Stands Macbeth thus amazedly?—
 Come, sisters, cheer we up his sprites,
 And show the best of our delights.
 I'll charm the air to give a sound,
 While you perform your antic round;   130
 That this great King may kindly say,
 Our duties did his welcome pay.

        Music. The WITCHES *dance, and vanish.*

MACBETH: Where are they? Gone?—Let this pernicious hour
 Stand aye accursed in the calendar!—
 Come in, without there!

       Enter LENOX.

LENOX: What's your Grace's will?

MACBETH: Saw you the Weïrd Sisters?

  direction. *glass:* Mirror.
  l. 130. *antic round:* Grotesque dance.

LENOX: No, my Lord.
MACBETH: Came they not by you?
LENOX: No, indeed, my Lord.
MACBETH: Infected by the air whereon they ride;
    And damn'd all those that trust them!—I did hear
    The galloping of horse: who was't came by?   140
LENOX: 'Tis two or three, my Lord, that bring you word,
    Macduff is fled to England.
MACBETH: Fled to England?
LENOX: Ay, my good Lord.
MACBETH (*aside*): Time, thou anticipat'st my dread exploits:
    The flighty purpose never is o'ertook,
    Unless the deed go with it. From this moment,
    The very firstlings of my heart shall be
    The firstlings of my hand. And even now,
    To crown my thoughts with acts, be it thought and done:
    The castle of Macduff I will surprise;   150
    Seize upon Fife; give to th' edge o' th' sword
    His wife, his babes, and all unfortunate souls
    That trace him in his line. No boasting like a fool;
    This deed I'll do, before this purpose cool:
    But no more sights!—Where are these gentlemen?
    Come, bring me where they are.
                                      Exeunt.

SCENE II

Fife. A room in MACDUFF's *castle.*

Enter LADY MACDUFF, *her* SON, *and* ROSSE.

LADY MACDUFF: What had he done, to make him fly the land?
ROSSE: You must have patience, Madam.
LADY MACDUFF: He had none:
    His flight was madness: when our actions do not,
    Our fears do make us traitors.
ROSSE: You know not,
    Whether it was his wisdom, or his fear.
LADY MACDUFF: Wisdom! to leave his wife, to leave his babes,
    His mansion, and his titles, in a place
    From whence himself does fly? He loves us not:
    He wants the natural touch; for the poor wren,

l. 144. *thou anticipat'st:* You prevent.
l. 153. *trace:* Follow.
l. 7. *titles:* Properties.

The most diminitive of birds, will fight,   10
Her young ones in her nest, against the owl.
All is the fear, and nothing is the love;
As little is the wisdom, where the flight
So runs against all reason.
ROSSE: My dearest coz,
I pray you, school yourself: but, for your husband,
He is noble, wise, judicious, and best knows
The fits o' th' season. I dare not speak much further:
But cruel are the times, when we are traitors,
And do not know ourselves; when we hold rumour
From what we fear, yet know not what we fear,   20
But float upon a wild and violent sea
Each way, and move—I take my leave of you:
Shall not be long but I'll be here again.
Things at the worst will cease, or else climb upward
To what they were before.—My pretty cousin,
Blessing upon you!
LADY MACDUFF: Father'd he is, and yet he's fatherless.
ROSSE: I am so much a fool, should I stay longer,
It would be my disgrace, and your discomfort:
I take my leave at once.

                                                   Exit.
LADY MACDUFF: Sirrah, your father's dead: 30
And what will you do now? How will you live?
SON: As birds do, mother.
LADY MACDUFF: What, with worms and flies?
SON: With what I get, I mean; and so do they.
LADY MACDUFF: Poor bird! thou'dst never fear the net, nor lime,
The pit-fall, nor the gin.
SON: Why should I, mother?
Poor birds they are not set for.
My father is not dead, for all your saying.
LADY MACDUFF: Yes, he is dead: how wilt thou do for a father?
SON: Nay, how will you do for a husband?
LADY MACDUFF: Why, I can buy me twenty at any market.   40
SON: Then you'll buy 'em to sell again.
LADY MACDUFF: Thou speak'st with all thy wit;
And yet, i' faith, with wit enough for thee.
SON: Was my father a traitor, mother?

l. 10. *diminitive*: Diminutive.
l. 17. *fits o' th' season*: The violent disorders of the times.
l. 20. *It . . . discomfort*: I would disgrace myself by weeping and thereby make
you uncomfortable.
l. 34. *lime*: Used to catch birds.
l. 35. *gin*: Snare.

LADY MACDUFF: Ay, that he was.

SON: What is a traitor?

LADY MACDUFF: Why, one that swears and lies.

SON: And be all traitors that do so?

LADY MACDUFF: Every one that does so is a traitor, and must be
    hang'd.   50

SON: And must they all be hang'd that swear and lie?

LADY MACDUFF: Every one.

SON: Who must hang them?

LADY MACDUFF: Why, the honest men.

SON: Then the liars and swearers are fools; for there are liars and
    swearers enow to beat the honest men, and hang up them.

LADY MACDUFF: Now God help thee, poor monkey! But how wilt thou
    do for a father?

SON: If he were dead, you'd weep for him: if you would not, it were
    a good sign that I should quickly have a new father.   60

LADY MACDUFF: Poor prattler, how thou talk'st!

Enter a MESSENGER

MESSENGER: Bless you, fair dame! I am not to you known,
    Though in your state of honour I am perfect.
    I doubt, some danger does approach you nearly:
    If you will take a homely man's advice,
    Be not found here; hence, with your little ones.
    To fright you thus, methinks, I am too savage;
    To do worse to you were fell cruelty,
    Which is too nigh your person. Heaven preserve you!
    I dare abide no longer.

                                     Exit.

LADY MACDUFF: Whither should I fly?   70

    I have done no harm. But I remember now
    I am in this earthly world, where, to do harm
    Is often laudable; to do good, sometime
    Accounted dangerous folly: why then, alas!
    Do I put up that womanly defence,
    To say, I have done no harm? What are these faces!

Enter MURDERERS.

MURDERERS: Where is your husband?

LADY MACDUFF: I hope, in no place so unsanctified,
    Where such as thou may'st find him.

MURDERERS: He's a traitor.

l. 63. *in . . . perfect:* I have complete knowledge of your rank of honor.
l. 64. *doubt:* Fear.
l. 65. *homely:* Humble.

SON: Thou liest, thou shag-hair'd villain!

MURDERERS: What, you egg!   80

> *Stabbing him.*

Young fry of treachery!

SON: He has kill'd me, mother:

Run away, I pray you!

>   *Dies.*
>
> *Exit* LADY MACDUFF, *crying "Murther!" and pursued by the*
>   MURDERERS.

SCENE III

England. A room in the King's palace.

> *Enter* MALCOLM *and* MACDUFF.

MALCOLM: Let us seek out some desolate shade, and there

Weep our sad bosoms empty.

MACDUFF: Let us rather

Hold fast the mortal sword, and like good men

Bestride our downfall birthdom. Each new morn,

New widows howl, new orphans cry; new sorrows

Strike heaven on the face, that it resounds

As if it felt with Scotland, and yell'd out

Like syllable of dolour.

MALCOLM: What I believe, I 'll wail;

What know, believe; and what I can redress,

As I shall find the time to friend, I will.   10

What you have spoke, it may be so, perchance.

This tyrant, whose sole name blisters our tongues,

Was once thought honest: you have lov'd him well;

He hath not touch'd you yet. I am young; but something

You may deserve of him through me, and wisdom

To offer up a weak, poor, innocent lamb,

T' appease an angry god.

MACDUFF: I am not treacherous.

MALCOLM: But Macbeth is.

A good and virtuous nature may recoil,

In an imperial charge. But I shall crave your pardon: 20

That which you are my thoughts cannot transpose:

Angels are bright still, though the brightest fell:

l. 4. *Bestride . . . birthdom:* Defend our downfallen fatherland.
l. 10. *to friend:* Propitious.
l. 12. *sole:* Mere.
ll. 14–15. *something . . . me:* If you betrayed me, he might reward you.
l. 21. *transpose:* Transform.

Though all things foul would wear the brows of grace,
Yet Grace must still look so.
MACDUFF: I have lost my hopes.
MALCOLM: Perchance even there where I did find my doubts.
   Why in that rawness left you wife and child
   (Those precious motives, those strong knots of love),
   Without leave-taking?—I pray you,
   Let not my jealousies be your dishonours,
   But mine own safeties: you may be rightly just,   30
   Whatever I shall think.
MACDUFF: Bleed, bleed, poor country!
   Great tyranny, lay thou thy basis sure,
   For goodness dare not check thee! wear thou thy wrongs;
   The title is affeer'd!—Fare thee well, Lord:
   I would not be the villain that thou think'st
   For the whole space that's in the tyrant's grasp,
   And the rich East to boot.
MALCOLM: Be not offended:
   I speak not as in absolute fear of you.
   I think our country sinks beneath the yoke;
   It weeps, it bleeds; and each new day a gash   40
   Is added to her wounds: I think, withal,
   There would be hands uplifted in my right;
   And here, from gracious England, have I offer
   Of goodly thousands: but, for all this,
   When I shall tread upon the tyrant's head,
   Or wear it on my sword, yet my poor country
   Shall have more vices than it had before,
   More suffer, and more sundry ways than ever,
   By him that shall succeed.
MACDUFF: What should he be?
MALCOLM: It is myself I mean; in whom I know   50
   All the particulars of vice so grafted,
   That, when they shall be open'd, black Macbeth
   Will seem as pure as snow; and the poor State
   Esteem him as a lamb, being compar'd
   With my confineless harms.
MACDUFF: Not in the legions
   Of horrid Hell can come a devil more damn'd
   In evils, to top Macbeth.

l. 26. *rawness:* Undefended state.
l. 29. *jealousies:* Suspicions.
l. 34. *affeer'd:* Confirmed.
l. 55. *confineless harms:* Boundless vices.

MALCOLM: I grant him bloody,
  Luxurious, avaricious, false, deceitful,
  Sudden, malicious, smacking of every sin
  That has a name; but there's no bottom, none,   60
  In my voluptuousness: your wives, your daughters,
  Your matrons, and your maids, could not fill up
  The cistern of my lust; and my desire
  All continent impediments would o'erbear,
  That did oppose my will: better Macbeth,
  Than such an one to reign.
MACDUFF: Boundless intemperance
  In nature is a tyranny; it hath been
  Th' untimely emptying of the happy throne,
  And fall of many kings. But fear not yet
  To take upon you what is yours: you may   70
  Convey your pleasures in a spacious plenty,
  And yet seem cold—the time you may so hoodwink:
  We have willing dames enough; there cannot be
  That vulture in you, to devour so many
  As will to greatness dedicate themselves,
  Finding it so inclin'd.
MALCOLM: With this, there grows
  In my most ill-compos'd affection such
  A staunchless avarice, that, were I King,
  I should cut off the nobles for their lands;
  Desire his jewels, and this other's house: 80
  And my more-having would be as a sauce
  To make me hunger more; that I should forge
  Quarrels unjust against the good and loyal,
  Destroying them for wealth.
MACDUFF: This avarice
  Sticks deeper, grows with more pernicious root
  Than summer-seeming lust; and it hath been
  The sword of our slain kings: yet do not fear;
  Scotland hath foisons to fill up your will,
  Of your mere own. All these are portable,
  With other graces weigh'd.   90
MALCOLM: But I have none: the king-becoming graces,
  As Justice, Verity, Temp'rance, Stableness,
  Bounty, Perseverance, Mercy, Lowliness,
  Devotion, Patience, Courage, Fortitude,

l. 59. *Sudden:* Violent.
l. 77. *affection:* Disposition.
l. 78. *staunchless:* Insatiable.
l. 88. *foisons:* Plenty.
l. 89. *your mere own:* Completely yours.

I have no relish of them; but abound
In the division of each several crime,
Acting it many ways. Nay, had I power, I should
Pour the sweet milk of concord into Hell,
Uproar the universal peace, confound
All unity on earth.

MACDUFF: O Scotland! Scotland!   100

MALCOLM: If such a one be fit to govern, speak:
I am as I have spoken.

MACDUFF: Fit to govern?
No, not to live.—O nation miserable!
With an untitled tyrant bloody-scepter'd,
When shalt thou see thy wholesome days again,
Since that the truest issue of thy throne
By his own interdiction stands accus'd,
And does blaspheme his breed? Thy royal father
Was a most sainted King: the Queen, that bore thee,
Oft'ner upon her knees than on her feet,   110
Died every day she liv'd. Fare thee well!
These evils thou repeat'st upon thyself
Hath banish'd me from Scotland.—O my breast,
Thy hope ends here!

MALCOLM: Macduff, this noble passion,
Child of integrity, hath from my soul
Wip'd the black scruples, reconcil'd my thoughts
To thy good truth and honour. Devilish Macbeth
By many of these trains hath sought to win me
Into his power, and modest wisdom plucks me
From over-credulous haste: but God above   120
Deal between thee and me! for even now
I put myself to thy direction, and
Unspeak mine own detraction; here abjure
The taints and blames I laid upon myself,
For strangers to my nature. I am yet
Unknown to woman, never was forsworn;
Scarcely have coveted what was mine own;
At no time broke my faith: would not betray
The Devil to his fellow; and delight
No less in truth, than life: my first false speaking 130
Was this upon myself. What I am truly,
Is thine, and my poor country's, to command:
Whither, indeed, before thy here-approach,

l. 95. *relish:* Trace.
l. 96. *division:* Variation.
l. 118. *trains:* Devices, artifices.

Old Siward, with ten thousand warlike men,
Already at a point, was setting forth.
Now we'll together, and the chance of goodness
Be like our warranted quarrel. Why are you silent?
MACDUFF: Such welcome and unwelcome things at once,
    'Tis hard to reconcile.

Enter a DOCTOR.

MALCOLM: Well, more anon.
    Comes the King forth, I pray you?   140
DOCTOR: Aye, Sir; there are a crew of wretched souls,
    That stay his cure: their malady convinces
    The great assay of art; but at his touch,
    Such sanctity hath Heaven given his hand,
    They presently amend.
MALCOLM: I thank you, Doctor.

Exit DOCTOR.

MACDUFF: What's the disease he means?
MALCOLM: 'Tis call'd the Evil:
    A most miraculous work in this good King,
    Which often, since my here-remain in England,
    I have seen him do. How he solicits Heaven,
    Himself best knows; but strangely-visited people,   150
    All swoln and ulcerous, pitiful to the eye,
    The mere despair of surgery, he cures;
    Hanging a golden stamp about their necks,
    Put on with holy prayers: and 'tis spoken,
    To the succeeding royalty he leaves
    The healing benediction. With this strange virtue,
    He hath a heavenly gift of prophecy;
    And sundry blessings hang about his throne,
    That speak him full of grace.

Enter ROSSE.

MACDUFF: See, who comes here.
MALCOLM: My countryman; but yet I know him not.   160
MACDUFF: My ever-gentle cousin, welcome hither.
MALCOLM: I know him now. Good God, betimes remove
    The means that makes us strangers!
ROSSE: Sir, amen.
MACDUFF: Stands Scotland where it did?

    l. 135. *at a point*: Prepared.
    l. 142. *That . . . cure*: That wait for him to cure them.
          convinces: Defeats.
    l. 143. *assay of art*: Effort of medical skill.
    l. 152. *mere*: Complete.

ROSSE: Alas, poor country!
   Almost afraid to know itself. It cannot
   Be call'd our mother, but our grave; where nothing,
   But who knows nothing, is once seen to smile;
   Where sighs, and groans, and shrieks that rent the air
   Are made, not mark'd; where violent sorrow seems
   A modern ecstasy: the dead man's knell   170
   Is there scarce ask'd for who; and good men's lives
   Expire before the flowers in their caps,
   Dying or ere they sicken.
MACDUFF: O relation,
   Too nice, and yet too true!
MALCOLM: What's the newest grief?
ROSSE: That of an hour's age doth hiss the speaker;
   Each minute teems a new one.
MACDUFF: How does my wife?
ROSSE: Why, well.
MACDUFF: And all my children?
ROSSE: Well too.
MACDUFF: The tyrant has not batter'd at their peace?
ROSSE: No; they were well at peace, when I did leave 'em.
MACDUFF: Be not a niggard of your speech: how goes't?   180
ROSSE: When I came hither to transport the tidings,
   Which I have heavily borne, there ran a rumour
   Of many worthy fellows that were out;
   Which was to my belief witness'd the rather,
   For that I saw the tyrant's power afoot.
   Now is the time of help. Your eye in Scotland
   Would create soldiers, make our women fight,
   To doff their dire distresses.
MALCOLM: Be 't their comfort,
   We are coming thither. Gracious England hath
   Lent us good Siward, and ten thousand men;   190
   An older, and a better soldier, none
   That Christendom gives out.
ROSSE: Would I could answer
   This comfort with the like! But I have words,
   That would be howl'd out in the desert air,
   Where hearing should not latch them.
MACDUFF: What concern they?
   The general cause? or is it a fee-grief,

l. 166. *nothing:* Nobody.
l. 167. *once:* Ever.
l. 170. *ecstasy:* A commonplace disturbance of mind.
l. 196. *fee-grief:* An individual sorrow.

Due to some single breast?

ROSSE: No mind that's honest
But in it shares some woe, though the main part
Pertains to you alone.

MACDUFF: If it be mine,
Keep it not from me; quickly, let me have it.   200

ROSSE: Let not your ears despise my tongue for ever,
Which shall possess them with the heaviest sound,
That ever yet they heard.

MACDUFF: Humh! I guess at it.

ROSSE: Your castle is surpris'd; your wife, and babes,
Savagely slaughter'd: to relate the manner,
Were, on the quarry of these murther'd deer,
To add the death of you.

MALCOLM: Merciful Heaven!—
What, man! ne'er pull your hat upon your brows:
Give sorrow words; the grief, that does not speak,
Whispers the o'er-fraught heart, and bids it break.   210

MACDUFF: My children too?

ROSSE: Wife, children, servants, all
That could be found.

MACDUFF: And I must be from thence!
My wife kill'd too?

ROSSE: I have said.

MALCOLM: Be comforted:
Let's make us med'cines of our great revenge,
To cure this deadly grief.

MACDUFF: He has no children.—All my pretty ones?
Did you say all?—O Hell-kite!—All?
What, all my pretty chickens, and their dam,
At one fell swoop?

MALCOLM: Dispute it like a man.

MACDUFF: I shall do so;   220
But I must also feel it as a man:
I cannot but remember such things were,
That were most precious to me.—Did Heaven look on,
And would not take their part? Sinful Macduff!
They were all struck for thee. Naught that I am,
Not for their own demerits, but for mine,
Fell slaughter on their souls: Heaven rest them now!

MALCOLM: Be this the whetstone of your sword: let grief
Convert to anger; blunt not the heart, enrage it.

MACDUFF: O! I could play the woman with mine eyes,   230
And braggart with my tongue.—But, gentle Heavens,

l. 225. *Naught:* Wicked.

Cut short all intermission; front to front,
Bring thou this fiend of Scotland, and myself;
Within my sword's length set him; if he 'scape,
Heaven forgive him too!
MALCOLM: This tune goes manly.
Come, go we to the King: our power is ready;
Our lack is nothing but our leave. Macbeth
Is ripe for shaking, and the Powers above
Put on their instruments. Receive what cheer you may;
The night is long that never finds the day.   240

Exeunt.

§ ACT V

SCENE I

Dunsinane. A room in the castle.

Enter a DOCTOR *of Physic and a Waiting* GENTLEWOMAN.

DOCTOR: I have two nights watch'd with you, but can perceive no truth
in your report. When was it she last walk'd?

GENTLEWOMAN: Since his Majesty went into the field, I have seen her
rise from her bed, throw her night-gown upon her, unlock her
closet, take forth paper, fold it, write upon't, read it, afterwards
seal it, and again return to bed; yet all this while in a most fast
sleep.

DOCTOR: A great perturbation in nature, to receive at once the benefit
of sleep, and do the effects of watching! In this slumbery agitation,
besides her walking and other actual performances, what, at any   10
time, have you heard her say?

GENTLEWOMAN: That, Sir, which I will not report after her.

DOCTOR: You may, to me; and 'tis most meet you should.

GENTLEWOMAN: Neither to you, nor any one; having no witness to
confirm my speech.

Enter LADY MACBETH, *with a taper.*

Lo you! here she comes. This is her very guise; and, upon my life,
fast asleep. Observe her: stand close.

DOCTOR: How came she by that light?

GENTLEWOMAN: Why, it stood by her: she has light by her continually;
'tis her command.   20

DOCTOR: You see, her eyes are open.

GENTLEWOMAN: Ay, but their sense are shut.

1. 9. *do . . . watching:* Behave as though awake.

DOCTOR: What is it she does now? Look, how she rubs her hands.

GENTLEWOMAN: It is an accustom'd action with her, to seem thus washing her hands. I have known her continue in this a quarter of an hour.

LADY MACBETH: Yet here's a spot.

DOCTOR: Hark! she speaks. I will set down what comes from her, to satisfy my remembrance the more strongly.

LADY MACBETH: Out, damned spot! out, I say!—One; two: why, then 30
'tis time to do't.—Hell is murky.—Fie, my Lord, fie! a soldier, and afeard?—What need we fear who knows it, when none can call our power to accompt?—Yet who would have thought the old man to have had so much blood in him?

DOCTOR: Do you mark that?

LADY MACBETH: The Thane of Fife had a wife: where is she now?—What, will these hands ne'er be clean?—No more o' that, my Lord, no more o' that: you mar all with this starting.

DOCTOR: Go to, go to: you have known what you should not.

GENTLEWOMAN: She has spoke what she should not, I am sure of that: 40
Heaven knows what she has known.

LADY MACBETH: Here's the smell of the blood still: all the perfumes of Arabia will not sweeten this little hand. Oh! oh! oh!

DOCTOR: What a sigh is there! The heart is sorely charg'd.

GENTLEWOMAN: I would not have such a heart in my bosom, for the dignity of the whole body.

DOCTOR: Well, well, well.

GENTLEWOMAN: Pray God it be, sir.

DOCTOR: This disease is beyond my practice: yet I have known those which have walk'd in their sleep, who have died holily in their 50
beds.

LADY MACBETH: Wash your hands, put on your night-gown; look not so pale.—I tell you yet again, Banquo's buried: he cannot come out on's grave.

DOCTOR: Even so?

LADY MACBETH: To bed, to bed: there's knocking at the gate. Come, come, come, come, give me your hand. What's done cannot be undone. To bed, to bed, to bed.

Exit.

DOCTOR: Will she go now to bed?

GENTLEWOMAN: Directly. 60

DOCTOR: Foul whisp'rings are abroad. Unnatural deeds
Do breed unnatural troubles: infected minds
To their deaf pillows will discharge their secrets.
More needs she the divine than the physician.—
God, God forgive us all! Look after her;

Remove from her the means of all annoyance,
And still keep eyes upon her.—So, good night:
My mind she has mated, and amaz'd my sight.
I think, but dare not speak.
GENTLEWOMAN: Good night, good Doctor.

Exeunt.

SCENE II

The country near Dunsinane.

Enter, with drums and colours, MENTETH, CATHNESS, ANGUS, LENOX,
and Soldiers.

MENTETH: The English power is near, led on by Malcolm,
His uncle Siward, and the good Macduff.
Revenges burn in them; for their dear causes
Would, to the bleeding and the grim alarm,
Excite the mortified man.
ANGUS: Near Birnam wood
Shall we well meet them: that way are they coming.
CATHNESS: Who knows if Donalbain be with his brother?
LENOX: For certain, Sir, he is not. I have a file
Of all the gentry: there is Siward's son,
And many unrough youths, that even now   10
Protest their first of manhood.
MENTETH: What does the tyrant?
CATHNESS: Great Dunsinane he strongly fortifies.
Some say he's mad; others, that lesser hate him,
Do call it valiant fury: but, for certain,
He cannot buckle his distemper'd cause
Within the belt of rule.
ANGUS: Now does he feel
His secret murthers sticking on his hands;
Now minutely revolts upbraid his faith-breach:
Those he commands move only in command,
Nothing in love: now does he feel his title   20
Hang loose about him, like a giant's robe
Upon a dwarfish thief.
MENTETH: Who then shall blame

l. 66. *annoyance:* Doing violence or harm to herself.
l. 68. *mated:* Bewildered.
l. 4. *bleeding . . . alarm:* Bloody and grim battle.
l. 5. *mortified:* Dead.
l. 10. *unrough:* Beardless.
l. 18. *minutely:* Occurring every minute.

His pester'd senses to recoil and start,
When all that is within him does condemn
Itself, for being there?
CATHNESS: Well; march we on,
To give obedience where 'tis truly ow'd:
Meet we the med'cine of the sickly weal;
And with him pour we, in our country's purge,
Each drop of us.
LENOX: Or so much as it needs
To dew the sovereign flower, and drown the weeds.   30
Make we our march towards Birnam.

Exeunt, marching.

SCENE III

Dunsinane. A room in the castle.

Enter MACBETH, DOCTOR, *and Attendants.*

MACBETH: Bring me no more reports; let them fly all:
Till Birnam wood remove to Dunsinane,
I cannot taint with fear. What's the boy Malcolm?
Was he not born of woman? The spirits that know
All mortal consequence have pronounc'd me thus:
"Fear not, Macbeth; no man that's born of woman
Shall e'er have power upon thee."—Then fly, false Thanes,
And mingle with the English epicures:
The mind I sway by, and the heart I bear,
Shall never sag with doubt, nor shake with fear.   10

Enter a SERVANT.

The devil damn thee black, thou cream-fac'd loon!
Where gott'st thou that goose look?
SERVANT: There is ten thousand—
MACBETH: Geese, villain?
SERVANT: Soldiers, Sir.
MACBETH: Go, prick thy face, and over-red thy fear,
Thou lily-liver'd boy. What soldiers, patch?
Death of thy soul! those linen cheeks of thine
Are counsellors to fear. What soldiers, whey-face?
SERVANT: The English force, so please you.
MACBETH: Take thy face hence.

Exit SERVANT.

l. 15. *patch:* Fool.

—Seyton!—I am sick at heart,
When I behold—Seyton, I say!—This push   20
Will cheer me ever, or disseat me now.
I have liv'd long enough: my way of life
Is fall'n into the sere, the yellow leaf;
And that which should accompany old age,
· As honour, love, obedience, troops of friends,
I must not look to have; but in their stead,
Curses, not loud, but deep, mouth-honour, breath,
Which the poor heart would fain deny, and dare not.
Seyton!—

Enter SEYTON.

SEYTON: What's your gracious pleasure?
MACBETH: What news more?   30
SEYTON: All is confirm'd, my Lord, which was reported.
MACBETH: I'll fight, till from my bones my flesh be hack'd.
Give me my armour.
SEYTON: 'Tis not needed yet.
MACBETH: I'll put it on.
Send out moe horses, skirr the country round;
Hang those that talk of fear. Give me mine armour.—
How does your patient, Doctor?
DOCTOR: Not so sick, my Lord,
As she is troubled with thick-coming fancies,
That keep her from her rest.
MACBETH: Cure her of that:
Canst thou not minister to a mind diseas'd,   40
Pluck from the memory a rooted sorrow,
Raze out the written troubles of the brain,
And with some sweet oblivious antidote
Cleanse the stuff'd bosom of that perilous stuff
Which weighs upon the heart?
DOCTOR: Therein the patient
Must minister to himself.
MACBETH: Throw physic to the dogs; I'll none of it.—
Come, put mine armour on; give me my staff.—
Seyton, send out—Doctor, the Thanes fly from me.—
Come, sir, despatch.—If thou couldst, Doctor, cast   50

ll. 20–21. *This push . . . now:* This attack will either put me in my throne
forever or else dethrone me immediately.
l. 35. *moe:* More.
  skirr: Scour.
l. 43. *oblivious:* Causing oblivion.
l. 48. *staff:* Lance.

The water of my land, find her disease,
And purge it to a sound and pristine health,
I would applaud thee to the very echo,
That should applaud again.—Pull 't off, I say.—
What rhubarb, cyme or what purgative drug,
Would scour these English hence?—Hear'st thou of them?
DOCTOR: Ay, my good Lord: your royal preparation
Makes us hear something.
MACBETH: Bring it after me.—
I will not be afraid of death and bane,
Till Birnam forest come to Dunsinane.   60

Exit.

DOCTOR (*aside*): Were I from Dunsinane away and clear,
Profit again should hardly draw me here.

Exeunt.

SCENE IV

Country near Dunsinane. A wood in view.

Enter, with drum and colours, MALCOLM, *old* SIWARD, *and his Son,*
MACDUFF, MENTETH, CATHNESS, ANGUS, LENOX, ROSSE, *and Soldiers, marching.*

MALCOLM: Cousins, I hope the days are near at hand,
That chambers will be safe.
MENTETH: We doubt it nothing.
SIWARD: What wood is this before us?
MENTETH: The wood of Birnam.
MALCOLM: Let every soldier hew him down a bough,
And bear't before him: thereby shall we shadow
The numbers of our host, and make discovery
Err in report of us.
SOLDIER: It shall be done.
SIWARD: We learn no other but the confident tyrant
Keeps still in Dunsinane, and will endure
Our setting down before 't.
MALCOLM: 'Tis his main hope;   10
For where there is advantage to be gone,
Both more and less have given him the revolt,
And none serve with him but constrained things,
Whose hearts are absent too.
MACDUFF: Let our just censures

ll. 50–51. *cast . . . land:* Diagnose the urine.
l. 11. *advantage to be gone:* Opportunity to desert.
l. 12. *more and less:* High and low, i.e., noblemen and commoners.

Attend the true event, and put we on
Industrious soldiership.
SIWARD: The time approaches,
That will with due decision make us know
What we shall say we have, and what we owe.
Thoughts speculative their unsure hopes relate,
But certain issue strokes must arbitrate;   20
Towards which advance the war.

Exeunt, marching.

SCENE V

Dunsinane. Within the castle.

Enter, with drum and colours, MACBETH, SEYTON, *and Soldiers.*

MACBETH: Hang out our banners on the outward walls;
The cry is still, "They come!" Our castle's strength
Will laugh a siege to scorn: here let them lie,
Till famine and the ague eat them up.
Were they not forc'd with those that should be ours,
We might have met them dareful, beard to beard,
And beat them backward home. What is that noise?
A cry within, of women.
SEYTON: It is the cry of women, my good Lord.

Exit.

MACBETH: I have almost forgot the taste of fears.
The time has been, my senses would have cool'd   10
To hear a night-shriek; and my fell of hair
Would at a dismal treatise rouse, and stir,
As life were in't. I have supp'd full with horrors:
Direness, familiar to my slaughterous thoughts,
Cannot once start me.

Re-enter SEYTON.

                        Wherefore was that cry?
SEYTON: The Queen, my Lord, is dead.
MACBETH: She should have died hereafter:
There would have been a time for such a word.—
To-morrow, and to-morrow, and to-morrow,
Creeps in this petty pace from day to day,   20

ll. 14–16. *Let our . . . soldiership:* Let us delay our opinions about the defections from Macbeth's army until after the actual battle, and meanwhile act like industrious soldiers.
Sc. V, l. 5. *forc'd:* Reinforced.
l. 15. *Cannot . . . me:* Can never again startle me.

To the last syllable of recorded time;
And all our yesterdays have lighted fools
The way to dusty death. Out, out, brief candle!
Life's but a walking shadow; a poor player,
That struts and frets his hour upon the stage,
And then is heard no more: it is a tale
Told by an idiot, full of sound and fury,
Signifying nothing.

Enter a MESSENGER.

Thou com'st to use thy tongue; thy story quickly.
MESSENGER: Gracious my Lord,   30
    I should report that which I say I saw,
    But know not how to do't.
MACBETH: Well, say, sir.
MESSENGER: As I did stand watch upon the hill,
    I look'd toward Birnam, and anon, methought,
    The wood began to move.
MACBETH: Liar, and slave!
MESSENGER: Let me endure your wrath, if 't be not so.
    Within this three mile may you see it coming;
    I say, a moving grove.
MACBETH: If thou speak'st false,
    Upon the next tree shalt thou hang alive,
    Till famine cling thee: if thy speech be sooth,   40
    I care not if thou dost for me as much.—
    I pull in resolution; and begin
    To doubt th' equivocation of the fiend,
    That lies like truth: "Fear not, till Birnam wood
    Do come to Dunsinane";—and now a wood
    Comes toward Dunsinane.—Arm, arm, and out!—
    If this which he avouches does appear,
    There is nor flying hence, nor tarrying here.
    I 'gin to be aweary of the sun,
    And wish th' estate o' th' world were now undone.—   50
    Ring the alarum bell!—Blow, wind! come, wrack!
    At least we'll die with harness on our back.

Exeunt.

l. 40. *cling:* Wither.
       sooth: The truth.
l. 52. *harness:* Armor.

SCENE VI

The same. A plain before the castle.

Enter, with drum and colours, MALCOLM, *old* SIWARD, MACDUFF,
etc., and their army, with boughs.

MALCOLM: Now, near enough: your leavy screens throw down,
And show like those you are.—You, worthy uncle,
Shall, with my cousin, your right noble son,
Lead our first battle: worthy Macduff, and we,
Shall take upon 's what else remains to do,
According to our order.
SIWARD: Fare you well.—
Do we but find the tyrant's power to-night,
Let us be beaten, if we cannot fight.
MACDUFF: Make all our trumpets speak; give them all breath,
Those clamorous harbingers of blood and death.   10

Exeunt. Alarums continued.

SCENE VII

The same. Another part of the plain.

Enter MACBETH.

MACBETH: They have tied me to a stake: I cannot fly,
But, bear-like, I must fight the course.—What's he,
That was not born of woman? Such a one
Am I to fear, or none.

Enter young SIWARD.

YOUNG SIWARD: What is thy name?
MACBETH: Thou 'lt be afraid to hear it.
YOUNG SIWARD: No; though thou call'st thyself a hotter name
Than any is in hell.
MACBETH: My name's Macbeth.
YOUNG SIWARD: The devil himself could not pronounce a title
More hateful to mine ear.
MACBETH: No, nor more fearful.
YOUNG SIWARD: Thou liest, abhorred tyrant: with my sword   10
I'll prove the lie thou speak'st.
They fight, and young SIWARD *is slain.*
MACBETH: Thou wast born of woman:—

l. 1. *leavy:* Leafy.
l. 2. *bear-like . . . course:* Like a bear tied to a stake in a bear-baiting arena, I
must fight it out.

But swords I smile at, weapons laugh to scorn,
Brandish'd by man that's of a woman born.

Exit.

Alarums. Enter MACDUFF.

MACDUFF: That way the noise is.—Tyrant, show thy face:
If thou be'st slain, and with no stroke of mine,
My wife and children's ghosts will haunt me still.
I cannot strike at wretched Kernes, whose arms
Are hir'd to bear their staves: either thou, Macbeth,
Or else my sword, with an unbatter'd edge,
I sheathe again undeeded. There thou shouldst be;   20
By this great clatter, one of greatest note
Seems bruited. Let me find him, Fortune!
And more I beg not.

Exit. Alarum.

Enter MALCOLM *and old* SIWARD.

SIWARD: This way, my Lord;—the castle's gently render'd:
The tyrant's people on both sides do fight;
The noble Thanes do bravely in the war.
The day almost itself professes yours,
And little is to do.
MALCOLM: We have met with foes
That strike beside us.
SIWARD: Enter, Sir, the castle.

Exeunt. Alarum.

SCENE VIII

Another part of the field.

Enter MACBETH.

MACBETH: Why should I play the Roman fool, and die
On mine own sword? whiles I see lives, the gashes
Do better upon them.

Re-enter MACDUFF.

MACDUFF: Turn, Hell-hound, turn!
MACBETH: Of all men else I have avoided thee:
But get thee back, my soul is too much charg'd
With blood of thine already.
MACDUFF: I have no words;

l. 22. *bruited:* Announced.
l. 29. *strike beside us:* Deliberately miss us.

My voice is in my sword: thou bloodier villain
Than terms can give thee out!
They fight.
MACBETH: Thou losest labour:
As easy may'st thou the intrenchant air
With thy keen sword impress, as make me bleed: 10
Let fall thy blade on vulnerable crests;
I bear a charmed life; which must not yield
To one of woman born.
MACDUFF: Despair thy charm;
And let the Angel, whom thou still hast serv'd,
Tell thee, Macduff was from his mother's womb
Untimely ripp'd.
MACBETH: Accursed be that tongue that tells me so,
For it hath cow'd my better part of man:
And be these juggling fiends no more believ'd,
That palter with us in a double sense;   20
That keep the word of promise to our ear,
And break it to our hope.—I 'll not fight with thee.
MACDUFF: Then yield thee, coward,
And live to be the show and gaze o' th' time:
We 'll have thee, as our rarer monsters are,
Painted upon a pole, and underwrit,
"Here may you see the tyrant."
MACBETH: I will not yield,
To kiss the ground before young Malcolm's feet,
And to be baited with the rabble's curse.
Though Birnam wood be come to Dunsinane,   30
And thou oppos'd, being of no woman born,
Yet I will try the last: before my body
I throw my warlike shield: lay on, Macduff;
And damn'd be him that first cries, "Hold, enough!"
          Exeunt, fighting. Alarums. Re-enter fighting, and MACBETH *slain.*

SCENE IX

Within the castle.

Retreat. Flourish. Enter, with drum and colours, MALCOLM, *old*
      SIWARD, ROSSE, *Thanes, and Soldiers.*

MALCOLM: I would the friends we miss were safe arriv'd.
SIWARD: Some must go off; and yet, by these I see,

l. 9. *intrenchant:* Uncuttable.
l. 20. *palter:* Equivocate.
l. 2. *go off:* Die.

So great a day as this is cheaply bought.

MALCOLM: Macduff is missing, and your noble son.

ROSSE: Your son, my Lord, has paid a soldier's debt:
He only liv'd but till he was a man;
The which no sooner had his prowess confirm'd,
In the unshrinking station where he fought,
But like a man he died.

SIWARD: Then he is dead?

ROSSE: Ay, and brought off the field. Your cause of sorrow   10
Must not be measur'd by his worth, for then
It hath no end.

SIWARD: Had he his hurts before?

ROSSE: Ay, on the front.

SIWARD: Why then, God's soldier be he!
Had I as many sons as I have hairs,
I would not wish them to a fairer death:
And so, his knell is knoll'd.

MALCOLM: He's worth more sorrow,
And that I'll spend for him.

SIWARD: He's worth no more;
They say he parted well and paid his score:
And so, God be with him!—Here comes newer comfort.

Re-enter MACDUFF, *with* MACBETH's *head.*

MACDUFF: Hail, King! for so thou art. Behold, where stands   20
Th' usurper's cursed head: the time is free.
I see thee compass'd with thy kingdom's pearl,
That speak my salutation in their minds;
Whose voices I desire aloud with mine,—
Hail, King of Scotland!

ALL: Hail, King of Scotland!

Flourish

MALCOLM: We shall not spend a large expense of time,
Before we reckon with your several loves,
And make us even with you. My Thanes and kinsmen,
Henceforth be Earls; the first that ever Scotland
In such an honour nam'd. What's more to do,   30
Which would be planted newly with the time,—
As calling home our exil'd friends abroad,
That fled the snares of watchful tyranny;
Producing forth the cruel ministers
Of this dead butcher, and his fiend-like Queen,
Who, as 'tis thought, by self and violent hands

l. 8. *unshrinking station:* The place where he did not shrink.
l. 36. *self:* Her own.

Took off her life;—this, and what needful else
That calls upon us, by the grace of Grace,
We will perform in measure, time, and place.
So thanks to all at once, and to each one,   40
Whom we invite to see us crown'd at Scone.

Flourish. Exeunt.

§ FOR COMMENT

Examining the broad aspects of *Macbeth*, one can see that the first part is concerned with the rise of Macbeth's power, the second with its decline. Between the two parts, almost midway through the play, are the escape of Fleance and the visit of Banquo's ghost. Analyze the structure of the play in more detail. What precipitates the major action? What resolves it? Chart the most significant events, act by act. Show the relationship of these climactic events to the play's theme, then chart the most significant events or major purposes of the various scenes and show their relationship to the act.

In the very first scene, all three Witches exclaim, "Fair is foul, and foul is fair." This line, with its coupling of opposites, can be taken as one of the play's leitmotifs, for its variants are found in every scene. Trace the leitmotif as it occurs in every scene of the play. Show how it affects the mood of the scene and how its repetition creates tension or suspense.

Macbeth is rewarded by the title Thane of Cawdor, an ironically appropriate name, for he, like the former bearer of the title, will be a traitor to Duncan. Find other instances of the use of irony.

Is there a pattern to the sequence of Macbeth's murders? What do they reveal about Macbeth? Although Macbeth commits a number of evil deeds, the audience does not stop pitying him. Why? Does it continue to admire him as well? Why?

What is Lady Macbeth's analysis of Macbeth's character? How accurate is it? What does this analysis reveal of Lady Macbeth? How perceptive is Macbeth in analyzing his own motives for wanting to kill Duncan? How does the language reflect character and situation? In each of Macbeth's soliloquies, explain how language is used to reveal character and situation. Do these soliloquies reflect a change within Macbeth? Explain how revelation of character through soliloquy differs from revelation of character through dialogue. Find examples to demonstrate these differences.

Compare and contrast the characters of Macbeth and Lady Macbeth. Trace their development throughout the play. Show how the development of each is different from that of the other. Are the later stages of their development foreshadowed by events or speeches in the early part of the play?

Since Macbeth has no heirs, and since the Witches stated that Banquo would not be King, ambition plays no role in Macbeth's decision to murder Banquo and his son. Why then does he decide to kill them? Although Banquo suspects Macbeth of having murdered Duncan in order to become King ("I fear," he says to himself, "Thou play'dst most foully for't"), he does not oppose Macbeth. Has Banquo kept silent because of ambition for his son? If not, why does he not oppose Macbeth? List the number of ways in which Banquo is employed as a foil to Macbeth. Is he a foil in the matter of ambition as well? Can you reconcile this with his silence?

Explain the use of Lady Macduff as a foil to Lady Macbeth. Why is not Macduff developed more fully as a foil to Macbeth? Shakespeare could have done so by giving him more scenes early in the play. Why didn't he?

Obviously, the drunken Porter episode serves as a separation scene: separating two scenes concerning the same characters, it gives Lady Macbeth time to smear the blood on the grooms and the performers playing Macbeth and his wife time to change costume. However, a well written separation scene is usually not noticeable as a time-filler because it performs other dramatic functions. Cite other dramatic purposes the drunken Porter episode fulfills. Find other separation scenes in this play, and tell what other dramatic functions each fulfills.

Banquo describes the Witches as "So wither'd and so wild in their attire, / That look not like th' inhabitants o' th' earth." Their fingers, he says, are chapped, their lips skinny, and their chins bearded. This describes the desired effect of the Witches' costumes and make-up. What other costume and make-up suggestions does Shakespeare provide?

August Strindberg § 1849–1912

*Acknowledged as Sweden's foremost playwright, Strindberg is also
known for his novels, short stories, essays, and poems. His theatrical
output covers a vast range of subjects and styles, including the psychological (The Father, 1887), the naturalistic (Miss Julie, 1888),
the historical (Erik XIV, 1899), and the expressionistic (A Dream
Play, 1902; Prologue, 1906). An important influence on both the
realistic and the nonrealistic drama, Strindberg's plays have historical as well as intrinsic value. In such realistic dramas as The Dance
of Death (Part I, 1900; Part II, 1901) his unflinching explorations
of passions and repressions, his incisive portrayals of the proximity
of love and hatred, against a background of class attitudes and
antagonisms, combine a feeling of verisimilitude with a bristling
theatricality. In such nonrealistic works as The Ghost Sonata
(1907) he achieves a freedom from the restraints of conventional,
linear drama, making him a forerunner of and an influence on the
Surrealists and the Absurdists. Such major figures as Ibsen and Shaw
recognized Strindberg's importance, and Eugene O'Neill—one of
the many modern playwrights influenced by Strindberg—called him
"the precursor of all modernity in our present theatre" and "the
greatest genius of all modern dramatists."*

A Dream Play

TRANSLATED BY ELIZABETH SPRIGGE

AUTHOR'S NOTE

In this dream play, as in his former dream play *To Damascus*, the
Author has sought to reproduce the disconnected but apparently logical form of a dream. Anything can happen; everything is possible and
probable. Time and space do not exist; on a slight groundwork of
reality, imagination spins and weaves new patterns made up of memories, experiences, unfettered fancies, absurdities and improvisations.

The characters are split, double and multiply; they evaporate, crystallise, scatter and converge. But a single consciousness holds sway over them all—that of the dreamer. For him there are no secrets, no incongruities, no scruples and no law. He neither condemns nor acquits, but only relates, and since on the whole, there is more pain than pleasure in the dream, a tone of melancholy, and of compassion for all living things, runs through the swaying narrative. Sleep, the liberator, often appears as a torturer, but when the pain is at its worst, the sufferer awakes—and is thus reconciled with reality. For however agonising real life may be, at this moment, compared with the tormenting dream, it is a joy.

DRAMATIS PERSONÆ[1]

(The voice of) FATHER INDRA [2]
INDRA'S DAUGHTER [3]
THE GLAZIER
THE OFFICER
THE FATHER
THE MOTHER
LINA
THE DOORKEEPER
THE BILLSTICKER
THE PROMPTER
THE POLICEMAN
THE LAWYER
THE DEAN OF PHILOSOPHY
THE DEAN OF THEOLOGY
THE DEAN OF MEDICINE
THE DEAN OF LAW
THE CHANCELLOR
KRISTIN
THE QUARANTINE MASTER
THE ELDERLY FOP
THE COQUETTE
THE FRIEND
THE POET
HE
SHE (doubles with Victoria's voice)
THE PENSIONER
UGLY EDITH

[1] Dramatis Personæ: There is no list of characters in the original. [Translator's note]
[2] Father Indra: Indra, the principal Vedic god, is associated with the sky and air, with thunder, lightning, and rain.
[3] Indra's Daughter: A character invented by Strindberg. In Hindu mythology, Indra does not have a daughter.

EDITH'S MOTHER
THE NAVAL OFFICER
ALICE
THE SCHOOLMASTER
NILS
THE HUSBAND
THE WIFE
THE BLIND MAN
1ST COAL HEAVER
2ND COAL HEAVER
THE GENTLEMAN
THE LADY
Singers and Dancers (Members of the Opera Company)
Clerks, Graduates, Maids, Schoolboys, Children, Crew, Righteous People.

§ PROLOGUE

An impression of clouds, crumbling cliffs, ruins of castles and fortresses. The constellations Leo, Virgo and Libra are seen, with the planet Jupiter shining brightly among them.

On the highest cloud-peak stands the DAUGHTER *of* INDRA. INDRA'S VOICE *is heard from above.*

INDRA'S VOICE: *Where art thou, Daughter?*
DAUGHTER: *Here, Father, here!*
INDRA'S VOICE: *Thou hast strayed, my child.*
   Take heed, thou sinkest.
   How cam'st thou here?
DAUGHTER: *Borne on a cloud, I followed the lightning's*
   blazing trail from the ethereal heights,
   But the cloud sank, and still is falling.
   Tell me, great Father Indra, to what region
   am I come? The air's so dense, so hard to breathe.
INDRA'S VOICE: *Leaving the second world thou camest to the third.*
   From Cucra, Star of the Morning,
   Far art thou come and enterest
   Earth's atmosphere. Mark there
   The Sun's Seventh House that's called the Scales.[4]
   The Morning Star is at the autumn weighing,
   When day and night are equal.
DAUGHTER: *Thou speak'st of Earth. Is that the dark*
   and heavy world the moon lights up?

[4] *the Scales:* Libra, the seventh sign of the zodiac, is represented as a pair of scales. The constellation Libra is said to resemble a pair of scales.

INDRA'S VOICE: *It is the darkest and the heaviest*
of all the spheres that swing in space.
DAUGHTER: *Does not the sun shine there?*
INDRA'S VOICE: *It shines, but not unceasingly.*
DAUGHTER: *Now the clouds part, and I can see . . .*
INDRA'S VOICE: *What see'st thou, child?*
DAUGHTER: *I see . . . that Earth is fair . . . It has green woods,*
blue waters, white mountains, yellow fields.
INDRA'S VOICE: *Yes, it is fair, as all that Brahma[5] shaped,*
yet in the dawn of time
was fairer still. Then came a change,
a shifting of the orbit, maybe of more.
Revolt followed by crime which had to be suppressed.
DAUGHTER: *Now I hear sounds arising . . .*
What kind of creatures dwell down there?
INDRA'S VOICE: *Go down and see. The Creator's children I*
would not decry,
but it's their language that thou hearest.
DAUGHTER: *It sounds as if . . . it has no cheerful ring.*
INDRA'S VOICE: *So I believe. Their mother-tongue*
is called Complaint. Truly a discontented,
thankless race is this of Earth.
DAUGHTER: *Ah, say not so! Now I hear shouts of joy,*
and blare and boom. I see the lightning flash.
Now bells are pealing and the fires are lit.
A thousand thousand voices rise,
singing their praise and thanks to heaven.

Pause

Thy judgment is too hard on them, my Father.
INDRA: *Descend and see, and hear, then come again*
and tell me if their lamentations
and complaint are justified.
DAUGHTER: *So be it. I descend. Come with me, Father!*
INDRA: *No. I cannot breathe their air.*
DAUGHTER: *Now the cloud sinks. It's growing dense. I suffocate!*
This is not air, but smoke and water that I breathe,
so heavy that it drags me down and down.
And now I clearly feel its reeling!
This third is surely not the highest world.
INDRA: *Neither the highest, truly, nor the lowest.*

[5] *Brahma:* In Hinduism, the universal, supreme soul, the primal source and final goal of being. Later in the play (p. 796) Indra's Daughter calls Brahma "the divine primal force."

It is called Dust, and whirls with all the rest,
And so at times its people, struck with dizziness,
live on the borderline of folly and insanity . . .
Courage, my child, for this is but a test!
DAUGHTER (*on her knees as the cloud descends*): I am sinking!

[*The curtain rises on* THE GROWING CASTLE.]

The background shows a forest of giant hollyhocks in bloom: white, pink, crimson, sulphur-yellow and violet. Above this rises the gilded roof of a castle with a flower-bud crowning its summit. Under the walls of the castle lie heaps of straw and stable-muck.

On each side of the stage are stylised representations of interiors, architecture and landscape which remain unchanged throughout the play.

The GLAZIER *and the* DAUGHTER *enter together.*

DAUGHTER: The castle keeps on growing up out of the earth. Do you see how it has grown since last year?

GLAZIER (*to himself*): I've never seen that castle before—and I've never heard of a castle growing . . . but . . . (*To the* DAUGHTER *with conviction*) Yes, it's grown six feet, but that's because they've manured it. And if you look carefully, you'll see it's put out a wing on the sunny side.

DAUGHTER: Ought it not to blossom soon? We are already halfway through the summer.

GLAZIER: Don't you see the flower up there?

DAUGHTER (*joyfully*): Yes, I see it. Father, tell me something. Why do flowers grow out of dirt?

GLAZIER: They don't like the dirt, so they shoot up as fast as they can into the light—to blossom and to die.

DAUGHTER: Do you know who lives in the castle?

GLAZIER: I used to know, but I've forgotten.

DAUGHTER: I believe there is a prisoner inside, waiting for me to set him free.

GLAZIER: What will you get if you do?

DAUGHTER: One does not bargain about what one has to do. Let us go into the castle.

GLAZIER: Very well, we will.

They go towards the background which slowly vanishes to the sides, disclosing a simple bare room with a table and a few chairs. A screen cuts the stage in two [the other half unlighted]. A YOUNG OFFICER *in an unconventional modern uniform sits rocking his chair and striking the table with his sword.*

[*The* DAUGHTER *and the* GLAZIER *enter.*]

She goes up to the OFFICER *and gently takes the sword from his hands.*

DAUGHTER: No, no, you mustn't do that.

OFFICER: Please, Agnes, let me keep my sword.

DAUGHTER: But you are cutting the table to pieces. (*To the* GLAZIER) Father, you go down to the harness room and put in that window pane, and we will meet later.

Exit GLAZIER.

DAUGHTER: You are a prisoner in your own room. I have come to set you free.

OFFICER: I have been waiting for this, but I wasn't sure you would want to.

DAUGHTER: The castle is strong—it has seven walls—but it shall be done. Do you want to be set free—or not?

OFFICER: To tell the truth, I don't know. Either way I'll suffer. Every joy has to be paid for twice over with sorrow. It's wretched here, but I'd have to endure three times the agony for the joys of freedom . . . Agnes, I'll bear it, if only I may see you.

DAUGHTER: What do you see in me?

OFFICER: The beautiful, which is the harmony of the universe. There are lines in your form which I have only found in the movement of the stars, in the melody of strings, in the vibrations of light. You are a child of heaven.

DAUGHTER: So are you.

OFFICER: Then why do I have to groom horses, clean stables and have the muck removed?

DAUGHTER: So that you may long to get away.

OFFICER: I do. But it's so hard to pull oneself out of it all.

DAUGHTER: It is one's duty to seek freedom in the light.

OFFICER: Duty? Life has not done its duty by me.

DAUGHTER: You feel wronged by life?

OFFICER: Yes. It has been unjust. . . .

Voices are now heard from behind the dividing screen, which is drawn aside [*as the lights go up on the other set: a homely living-room.*] *The* OFFICER *and the* DAUGHTER *stand watching, gestures and expression held. The* MOTHER, *an invalid, sits at a table. In front of her is a lighted candle, which from time to time she trims with snuffers. On the table are piles of new underclothing, which she is marking with a quill pen. Beyond is a brown cupboard.*

The FATHER *brings her a silk shawl.*

FATHER (*gently*): I have brought you this.

MOTHER: What use is a silk shawl to me, my dear, when I am going to die so soon?

FATHER: You believe what the doctor says?

MOTHER: What he says too, but most of all I believe the voice that speaks within me.

FATHER (*sorrowfully*): Then it really is grave . . . And you are thinking of your children, first and last.

MOTHER: They were my life, my justification, my happiness, and my sorrow.

FATHER: Kristina, forgive me . . . for everything.

MOTHER: For what? Ah, my dear, forgive *me!* We have both hurt each other. Why, we don't know. We could not do otherwise . . . However, here is the children's new linen. See that they change twice a week—on Wednesdays and Sundays, and that Louisa washes them— all over . . . Are you going out?

FATHER: I have to go to the school at eleven.

MOTHER: Before you go ask Alfred to come.

FATHER (*pointing to the* OFFICER): But, dear heart, he is here.

MOTHER: My sight must be going too . . . Yes, it's getting so dark. (*Snuffs candle.*) Alfred, come!

The FATHER *goes out through the middle of the wall, nodding goodbye. The* OFFICER *moves forward to the* MOTHER.

MOTHER: Who is that girl?

OFFICER (*whispering*): That's Agnes.

MOTHER: Oh, is it Agnes? Do you know what they are saying? That she is the daughter of the God Indra, who begged to come down to Earth so as to know what it is really like for human beings. But don't say anything.

OFFICER: She *is* a child of the Gods.

MOTHER (*raising her voice*): Alfred, my son, I shall soon be leaving you and your brothers and sisters. I want to say one thing—for you to remember all your life.

OFFICER (*sadly*): What is it, Mother?

MOTHER: Only one thing: never quarrel with God.

OFFICER: What do you mean, Mother?

MOTHER: You must not go on feeling you have been wronged by life.

OFFICER: But I've been treated so unjustly.

MOTHER: You're still harping on the time you were unjustly punished for taking that money which was afterwards found.

OFFICER: Yes. That piece of injustice gave a twist to the whole of my life.

MOTHER: I see. Well now, you just go over to that cupboard . . .

OFFICER (*ashamed*): So you know about that. The . . .

MOTHER: "The Swiss Family Robinson" which . . .

OFFICER: Don't say any more . . .

MOTHER: Which your brother was punished for . . . when it was *you* who had torn it to pieces and hidden it.

OFFICER: Think of that cupboard still being there after twenty years. We have moved so many times—and my mother died ten years ago.

MOTHER: Yes. What of it? You are always questioning everything, and so spoiling the best of life for yourself . . . Ah, here's Lina!

Enter LINA.

LINA: Thank you very much all the same, Ma'am, but I can't go to the christening.
MOTHER: Why not, child?
LINA: I've got nothing to wear.
MOTHER: You can borrow this shawl of mine.
LINA: Oh no, Ma'am, you're very kind, but that would never do.
MOTHER: I can't see why not. I shan't be going to any more parties.
OFFICER: What will Father say? After all, it's a present from him.
MOTHER: What small minds!
FATHER (*putting his head in*): Are you going to lend my present to the maid?
MOTHER: Don't talk like that! Remember I was in service once myself. Why should you hurt an innocent girl?
FATHER: Why should you hurt me, your husband?
MOTHER: Ah, this life! If you do something good, someone else is sure to think it bad; if you are kind to one person, you're sure to harm another. Ah, this life!

She snuffs the candle so that it goes out. The room grows dark and the screen is drawn forward again.

DAUGHTER: Human beings are to be pitied.
OFFICER: Do you think so?
DAUGHTER: Yes, life is hard. But love conquers everything. Come and see.

They withdraw and the background disappears. The OFFICER *vanishes and the* DAUGHTER *comes forward alone.*

The new scene shows an old derelict wall. In the middle of the wall a gate opens on an alley leading to a green plot where a giant blue monkshood is growing. To the left of the gate is the door-window of the Stage DOORKEEPER'*s lodge. The Stage* DOORKEEPER *is sitting with a grey shawl over her head and shoulders, crocheting a star-patterned coverlet. On the right is an announcement-board which the* BILLSTICKER *is washing. Near him is a fishnet with a green handle and a green fish box. Further right the cupboard [from the previous set] has become a door with an air-hole shaped like a four-leafed clover. To the left is a small lime tree with a coal-black stem and a few pale green leaves.*

The DAUGHTER *goes up to the* DOORKEEPER.

DAUGHTER: Isn't the star coverlet finished yet?
DOORKEEPER: No, my dear. Twenty-six years is nothing for such a piece of work.
DAUGHTER: And your sweetheart never came back?

DOORKEEPER: No, but it wasn't his fault. He *had* to take himself off, poor fellow. That was thirty years ago.

DAUGHTER (*to* BILLSTICKER): She was in the ballet, wasn't she? Here—at the Opera.

BILLSTICKER: She was the prima ballerina, but when *he* went away, it seems he took her dancing with him . . . so she never got any more parts.

DAUGHTER: All complain—with their eyes, and with their voices too.

BILLSTICKER: I haven't much to complain of—not now I've got my net and a green fish box.

DAUGHTER: Does that make you happy?

BILLSTICKER: Yes, very happy. That was my dream when I was little, and now it's come true. I'm all of fifty now, you know.

DAUGHTER: Fifty years for a fishnet and a box!

BILLSTICKER: A *green* box, a *green* one . . .

DAUGHTER (*to* DOORKEEPER): Let me have that shawl now, and I'll sit here and watch the children of men. But you must stand behind and tell me about them.

The DAUGHTER *puts on the shawl and sits down by the gate.*

DOORKEEPER: This is the last day of the Opera season. They hear now if they've been engaged for the next.

DAUGHTER: And those who have not?

DOORKEEPER: Lord Jesus, what a scene! I always pull my shawl over my head.

DAUGHTER: Poor things!

DOORKEEPER: Look, here's one coming. She's not been engaged. See how she's crying!

The SINGER *rushes in from the right and goes through the gate with her handkerchief to her eyes. She pauses a moment in the alley beyond and leans her head against the wall, then goes quickly out.*

DAUGHTER: Human beings are to be pitied.

DOORKEEPER: But here comes one who seems happy enough.

The OFFICER *comes down the alley, wearing a frock-coat and top hat. He carries a bouquet of roses and looks radiantly happy.*

DOORKEEPER: He's going to marry Miss Victoria.

OFFICER (*downstage, looks up and sings*): Victoria!

DOORKEEPER: The young lady will be down in a minute.

WOMAN'S VOICE (*from above, sings*): I am here!

OFFICER (*pacing*): Well, I am waiting.

DAUGHTER: Don't you know me?

OFFICER: No, I know only one woman—Victoria! Seven years I have come here to wait for her—at noon when the sun reaches the chimneys, and in the evening as darkness falls. Look at the paving. See? Worn by the steps of the faithful lover? Hurrah! She is mine. (*Sings.*) Victoria! (*No answer.*) Well, she's dressing now. (*To the* BILLSTICKER) Ah, a fishnet I see! Everyone here at the Opera is crazy about fishnets—or rather about fish. Dumb fish—because they cannot sing . . . What does a thing like that cost?

BILLSTICKER: It's rather dear.

OFFICER (*sings*): Victoria! . . . (*Shakes the lime tree.*) Look, it's budding again! For the eighth time. (*Sings.*) Victoria! . . . Now she's doing her hair . . . (*To* DAUGHTER) Madam, kindly allow me to go up and fetch my bride.

DOORKEEPER: Nobody's to go on the stage.

OFFICER: Seven years I've walked up and down here. Seven times three hundred and sixty-five I make two thousand five hundred and fifty-five. (*Stops and pokes the door with the clover-shaped hole.*) Then this door I've seen two thousand five hundred and fifty-five times and I still don't know where it leads to. And this clover leaf to let in the light. Who does it let the light in for? Is anyone inside? Does anybody live there?

DOORKEEPER: I don't know. I've never seen it open.

OFFICER: It looks like a larder door I saw when I was four years old, when I went out one Sunday afternoon with the maid—to see another family and other maids. But I only got as far as the kitchen, where I sat between the water barrel and the salt tub. I've seen so many kitchens in my time, and the larders are always in the passage, with round holes and a clover leaf in the door. But the Opera can't have a larder as it hasn't got a kitchen. (*Sings.*) Victoria! (*To* DAUGHTER) Excuse me, Madam, she can't leave by any other way, can she?

DOORKEEPER: No, there is no other way.

OFFICER: Good. Then I'm bound to meet her.

> *Members of the Opera Company swarm out of the building, scrutinised by the* OFFICER. *They go out by the gate.*

She's sure to come. (*To* DAUGHTER) Madam, that blue monkshood out there—I saw it when I was a child. Is it the same one? I remember it in a rectory garden when I was seven—with two doves, blue doves, under the hood. Then a bee came and went into the hood, and I thought: "Now I've got you," so I grabbed the flower, but the bee stung through it, and I burst into tears. However, the rector's wife came and put moist earth on it—and then we had wild strawberries and milk for supper . . . I believe it's growing dark already. Where are you off to, Billsticker?

BILLSTICKER: Home to my supper.

> [*Exit with fishnet and box.*]

OFFICER (*rubbing his eyes*): Supper? At this time of day? . . . (*To* DAUGHTER) Excuse me, may I just step inside a moment and telephone to the Growing Castle?

DAUGHTER: What do you want to say to them?

OFFICER: I want to tell the glazier to put in the double windows. It will be winter soon and I'm so dreadfully cold.

The OFFICER *goes into the* DOORKEEPER'S *Lodge.*

DAUGHTER: Who is Miss Victoria?

DOORKEEPER: She is his love.

DAUGHTER: A true answer. What she is to us or others doesn't matter to him. Only what she is to *him*, that's what she *is*.

It grows dark suddenly.

DOORKEEPER (*lighting the lantern*): Dusk falls quickly today.

DAUGHTER: To the gods a year is as a minute.

DOORKEEPER: While to human beings a minute may be as long as a year.

The OFFICER *comes out again. He looks shabbier, and the roses are withered.*

OFFICER: Hasn't she come yet?

DOORKEEPER: No.

OFFICER: She's sure to come. She'll come. (*Paces up and down.*) But all the same . . . perhaps it would be wiser to cancel that luncheon . . . as it's now evening. Yes, that's what I'll do. (*Goes in and telephones.*)

DOORKEEPER (*to* DAUGHTER): May I have my shawl now?

DAUGHTER: No, my friend. You rest and I'll take your place, because I want to know about human beings and life—to find out if it really is as hard as they say.

DOORKEEPER: But you don't get any sleep on this job. Never any sleep, night or day.

DAUGHTER: No sleep at night?

DOORKEEPER: Well, if you can get any with the bell wire on your arm, because the night watchmen go up on the stage and are changed every three hours . . .

DAUGHTER: That must be torture.

DOORKEEPER: So you think, but we others are glad enough to get such a job. If you knew how much I'm envied.

DAUGHTER: Envied? Does one envy the tortured?

DOORKEEPER: Yes. But I'll tell you what's worse than night-watching and drudgery and draughts and cold and damp. That's having to listen, as I do, to all their tales of woe. They all come to me. Why? Perhaps they read in my wrinkles the runes of suffering, and that makes them talk. In that shawl, my dear, thirty years of torment's hidden—my own and others.

DAUGHTER: That's why it is so heavy and stings like nettles.

DOORKEEPER: Wear it if you like. When it gets too heavy, call me and I'll come and relieve you of it.

DAUGHTER: Goodbye. What you can bear, surely I can.

DOORKEEPER: We shall see. But be kind to my young friends and put up with their complaining.

The DOORKEEPER *disappears down the alley. The stage is blacked out. When light returns, the lime tree is bare, the blue monkshood withered, and the green plot at the end of the alley has turned brown.*

The OFFICER *enters. His hair is grey and he has a grey beard. His clothes are ragged; his collar soiled and limp. He still carries the bouquet of roses, but the petals have dropped.*

OFFICER (*wandering round*): By all the signs, summer is over and autumn at hand. I can tell that by the lime tree—and the monkshood. (*Pacing*) But autumn is *my* spring, for then the theatre opens again. And then she is bound to come. (*To* DAUGHTER) Dear lady, may I sit on this chair for a while?

DAUGHTER: Do, my friend. I can stand.

OFFICER (*sitting*): If only I could sleep a little it would be better.

He falls asleep for a moment, then starts up and begins walking again. He stops by the clover-leaf door and pokes it.

OFFICER: This door—it gives me no peace. What is there behind it? Something must be. (*Soft ballet music is heard from above.*) Ah, the rehearsals have begun! (*The lights come and go like a lighthouse beam.*) What's this? (*Speaking in time with the flashes*) Light and darkness; light and darkness.

DAUGHTER (*with the same timing*): Day and night; day and night. A merciful providence wants to shorten your waiting. And so the days fly, chasing the nights.

The light is now constant. The BILLSTICKER *enters with his net and his implements.*

OFFICER: Here's the Billsticker with his net. How was the fishing?

BILLSTICKER: Not too bad. The summer was hot and a bit long . . . the net was all right, but not quite what I had in mind.

OFFICER: "Not quite what I had in mind." Excellently put. Nothing ever is as one imagined it—because one's mind goes further than the act, goes beyond the object. (*He walks up and down striking the bouquet against the walls until the last leaves fall.*)

BILLSTICKER: Hasn't she come down yet?

OFFICER: No, not yet, but she'll come soon. Do you know what's behind that door, Billsticker?

BILLSTICKER: No, I've never seen it open.

OFFICER: I'm going to telephone to a locksmith to come and open it. (*Goes *into the Lodge. The* BILLSTICKER *pastes up a poster and moves away*.)

DAUGHTER: What was wrong with the fishnet?

BILLSTICKER: Wrong? Well, there wasn't anything wrong exactly. But it wasn't what I'd had in mind, and so I didn't enjoy it *quite* as much . . .

DAUGHTER: How did you imagine the net?

BILLSTICKER: How? I can't quite tell you . . .

DAUGHTER: Let me tell you. In your imagination it was different—green but not *that* green.

BILLSTICKER: You understand, Madam. You understand everything. That's why they all come to you with their troubles. Now if you'd only listen to me, just this once . . .

DAUGHTER: But I will, gladly. Come in here and pour out your heart. (*She goes into the Lodge. The* BILLSTICKER *stays outside and talks to her through the window.*)

The stage is blacked out again, then gradually the lights go up. The lime tree is in leaf; the monkshood in bloom; the sun shines on the greenery at the end of the alley. The BILLSTICKER *is still at the window and the* DAUGHTER *can be seen inside.*

The OFFICER *enters from the Lodge. He is old and white-haired; his clothes and shoes are in rags. He carries the stems of the bouquet. He totters backwards and forwards slowly like a very old man, and reads the poster.*

A BALLET GIRL [*comes out of the Theatre*].

OFFICER: Has Miss Victoria gone?

BALLET GIRL: No, she hasn't.

OFFICER: Then I'll wait. Will she come soon?

BALLET GIRL (*gravely*): Yes, she's sure to.

OFFICER: Don't go—then you'll be able to see what's behind that door. I've sent for the locksmith.

BALLET GIRL: That will be really interesting to see this door opened. The door and the Growing Castle. Do you know the Growing Castle?

OFFICER: Do I? Wasn't I imprisoned there?

BALLET GIRL: Really, was that you? But why did they have so many horses there?

OFFICER: It was a stable castle, you see.

BALLET GIRL (*distressed*): How silly of me not to have thought of that.

[*Moves towards the Lodge. A* CHORUS GIRL *comes out of the Theatre.*]

OFFICER: Has Miss Victoria gone?

CHORUS GIRL (*gravely*): No, she hasn't gone. She never goes.

OFFICER: That's because she loves me. No, you mustn't go before the locksmith comes. He's going to open this door.

CHORUS GIRL: Oh, is the door going to be opened? Really? What fun! I just want to ask the Doorkeeper something.

[*She joins the* BILLSTICKER *at the window. The* PROMPTER *comes out of the Theatre.*]

OFFICER: Has Miss Victoria gone?

PROMPTER: Not so far as I know.

OFFICER: There you are! Didn't I say she was waiting for me? No, don't go. The door's going to be opened.

PROMPTER: Which door?

OFFICER: Is there more than one door?

PROMPTER: Oh, I see—the one with the clover-leaf! Of course I'll stay. I just want to have a few words with the Doorkeeper.

[*He joins the group at the window. They all speak in turn to the* DAUGHTER.] *The* GLAZIER *comes through the gate.*

OFFICER: Are you the locksmith?

GLAZIER: No, the locksmith had company. But a glazier's just as good.

OFFICER: Yes, indeed . . . indeed. But . . . er . . . have you brought your diamond with you?

GLAZIER: Of course. A glazier without a diamond—what good would that be?

OFFICER: None. Let's get to work then. (*He claps his hands. All group themselves in a circle round the door.* MALE CHORUS *in costumes of* Die Meistersinger,[6] *and* GIRL DANCERS *from* Aïda[7] *come out of the theatre and join them.*) Locksmith—or Glazier—do your duty! (*The* GLAZIER *goes towards the door holding out his diamond.*) A moment such as this does not recur often in a lifetime. Therefore, my good friends, I beg you to reflect seriously upon . . .

[*During the last words the* POLICEMAN *has entered by the gate.*]

POLICEMAN: In the name of the law I forbid the opening of this door.

OFFICER: Oh God, what a fuss there is whenever one wants to do anything new and great! Well—we shall take proceedings . . . To the lawyer then, and we will see if the law holds good. To the lawyer!

Without any lowering of the curtain the scene changes to the LAWYER's *office. The gate has now become the gate in an office railing stretching across the stage. The* DOORKEEPER's *Lodge is a recess for the* LAWYER's *desk, the lime tree, leafless, a coat-and-hat stand. The announcement-board is covered with proclamations and Court decrees and the clover-door is a document cupboard. The* LAWYER *in frock coat and white tie is sitting on the left inside the railing of the gate, at this high desk covered with papers. His*

---

[6] Opera by Richard Wagner (1813–1883).
[7] Opera by Giuseppi Verdi (1813–1901).

appearance bears witness to unspeakable suffering. His face is chalk-white, furrowed and purple-shadowed. He is hideous; his face mirrors all the crime and vice with which, through his profession, he has been involved.

Of his two clerks one has only one arm; the other a single eye. The people, who had gathered to witness the opening of the door, are now clients waiting to see the LAWYER, *and look as if they have always been there.*

The DAUGHTER, *wearing the shawl, and the* OFFICER *are in front. The* OFFICER *looks curiously at the cupboard door and from time to time pokes it.*

The LAWYER *goes up to the* DAUGHTER.

LAWYER: If you let me have that shawl, my dear, I'll hang it here until the stove is lighted and then I'll burn it with all its griefs and miseries.

DAUGHTER: Not yet, my friend. I must let it get quite full first, and I want above all to gather *your* sufferings up in it, the crimes you have absorbed from others, the vices, swindles, slanders, libel . . .

LAWYER: My child, your shawl would not be big enough. Look at these walls! Isn't the wall-paper stained as if by every kind of sin? Look at these documents in which I write records of evil! Look at me! . . . Nobody who comes here ever smiles. Nothing but vile looks, bared teeth, clenched fists, and all of them squirt their malice, their envy, their suspicions over me. Look, my hands are black and can never be clean! See how cracked they are and bleeding! I can never wear my clothes for more than a few days because they stink of other people's crimes. Sometimes I have the place fumigated with sulphur, but that doesn't help. I sleep in the next room and dream of nothing but crime. I have a murder case in Court now—that's bad enough—but do you know what's worst of all? Separating husbands and wives. Then earth and heaven seem to cry aloud, to cry treason against primal power, the source of good, against love! And then, do you know, after reams of paper have been filled with mutual accusations, if some kindly person takes one or other of the couple aside and asks them in a friendly sort of way the simple question—"What have you really got against your husband—or your wife?"—then he, or she, stands speechless. They don't know. Oh, once it was something to do with a salad, another time about some word. Usually it's about nothing at all. But the suffering, the agony! All this I have to bear. Look at me! Do you think, marked as I am by crime, I can ever win a woman's love? Or that anyone wants to be the friend of a man who has to enforce payment of all the debts of the town? It's misery to be human.

DAUGHTER: Human life is pitiable!

LAWYER: It is indeed. And what people live on is a mystery to me. They marry with an income of two thousand crowns when they need four. They borrow, to be sure, they all borrow, and so scrape along somehow by the skin of their teeth until they die. Then the estate is always insolvent. Who has to pay up in the end? Tell me that.

DAUGHTER: He who feeds the birds.

LAWYER: Well, if He who feeds the birds would come down to earth and see the plight of the unfortunate children of men, perhaps He would have some compassion . . .

DAUGHTER: Human life is pitiful.

LAWYER: Yes, that's the truth. (*To the* OFFICER) What do you want?

OFFICER: I only want to ask if Miss Victoria has gone.

LAWYER: No, she hasn't. You can rest assured of that. Why do you keep poking my cupboard?

OFFICER: I thought the door was so very like . . .

LAWYER: Oh, no, no, no!

Church bells ring.

OFFICER: Is there a funeral in the town?

LAWYER: No, it's Graduation—the conferring of Doctors' degrees. I myself am about to receive the degree of Doctor of Law. Perhaps you would like to graduate and receive a laurel wreath?

OFFICER: Why not? It would be a little distraction.

LAWYER: Then perhaps we should proceed at once to the solemn rites. But you must go and change.

Exit OFFICER.

The stage is blacked out and changes to the interior of the Church.

The barrier now serves as the chancel rail. The announcement-board shows the numbers of the hymns. The lime-tree hatstand has become a candelabra, the LAWYER's *desk is the* CHANCELLOR's *lectern, and the Clover-door leads to the vestry. The Chorus from Die Meistersinger are ushers with wands. The dancers carry the laurel wreaths. The rest of the people are the congregation.*

The new background shows only a gigantic organ, with a mirror over the keyboard.

Music is heard. At the sides stand the four Deans of the Faculties Philosophy, Theology, Medicine and Law. For a moment there is no movement, then:

The USHERS *come forward from the right.*[8]

The Dancers follow, holding laurel wreaths in their outstretched hands.

Three Graduates come in from the left, are crowned in turn by the

[8] This scene follows exactly the normal ceremony in a Swedish university when Doctors' degrees are conferred. As each Graduate has the wreath put on his head, a gun outside is fired. The Chancellor and the Faculties bow. Then the new doctor bows to them.

One of the Graduates should be the Officer and another the Schoolmaster of the later scene. [Translator's note]

Dancers and go out to the right.
The LAWYER *advances to receive his wreath.*
The Dancers turn away, refusing to crown him, and go out.
The LAWYER, *greatly agitated, leans against a pillar.*
Everyone disappears. The LAWYER *is alone.*
The DAUGHTER *enters with a white shawl over her head and*
shoulders.

DAUGHTER: Look, I have washed the shawl. But what are you doing here? Didn't you get your laurels?

LAWYER: No. I was discredited.

DAUGHTER: Why? Because you have defended the poor, said a good word for the sinner, eased the burden of the guilty, obtained reprieve for the condemned? Woe to mankind! Men are not angels, but pitiable creatures.

LAWYER: Do not judge men harshly. It is my business to plead for them.

DAUGHTER (*leaning against the organ*): Why do they strike their friends in the face?

LAWYER: They know no better.

DAUGHTER: Let us enlighten them—you and I together. Will you?

LAWYER: There can be no enlightenment for them. Oh that the gods in heaven might hear our woe!

DAUGHTER: It shall reach the throne. (*Sits at the organ.*) Do you know what I see in this mirror? The world as it should be. For as it is it's wrong way up.

LAWYER: How did it come to be wrong way up?

DAUGHTER: When the copy was made.

LAWYER: Ah! You yourself have said it—the copy! I always felt this must be a poor copy, and when I began to remember its origin nothing satisfied me. Then they said I was cynical and had a jaundiced eye, and so forth.

DAUGHTER: It is a mad world. Consider these four Faculties. Organized society subsidizes all four: Theology, the doctrine of Divinity, continually attacked and ridiculed by Philosophy claiming wisdom for itself; and Medicine always giving the lie to Philosophy and discounting Theology as one of the sciences, calling it superstition. And there they sit together on the Council, whose function is to teach young men respect for the University. Yes, it's a madhouse. And woe to him who first recovers his senses!

LAWYER: The first to discover it are the theologians. For their preliminary studies they take Philosophy, which teaches them that Theology is nonsense, and then they learn from Theology that Philosophy is nonsense. Madness.

DAUGHTER: Then there's Law, serving all but its servants.

LAWYER: Justice, to the just unjust. Right so often wrong.

DAUGHTER: Thus you have made it, O Children of Men! Child, come! You shall have a wreath from me . . . one more fitting. (*She puts a crown of thorns on his head.*)⁹ Now I will play to you. (*She sits at the organ and plays a Kyrie, but instead of the organ, voices are heard singing. The last note of each phrase is sustained.*)

CHILDREN'S VOICES: Lord! Lord!

WOMEN'S VOICES: Be merciful!

MEN'S VOICES (*tenor*): Deliver us for Thy mercy's sake.

MEN'S VOICES (*bass*): Save Thy children, O Lord, and be not wrathful against us.

ALL: Be merciful! Hear us! Have compassion for mortals. Are we so far from Thee? Out of the depths we call. Grace, Lord! Let not the burden be too heavy for Thy children. Hear us! Hear us!

The stage darkens as the DAUGHTER *rises and approaches the*
LAWYER.
By means of lighting the organ is changed to the wall of a grotto.
The sea seeps in between basalt pillars with a harmony of waves
and wind.

LAWYER: Where are we?

DAUGHTER: What do you hear?

LAWYER: I hear drops falling.

DAUGHTER: Those are the tears of mankind weeping. What more do you hear?

LAWYER: A sighing . . . a moaning . . . a wailing.

DAUGHTER: The lamentation of mortals has reached so far, no further. But why this endless lamentation? Is there no joy in life?

LAWYER: Yes. The sweetest which is also the bitterest—love! Marriage and a home. The highest and the lowest.

DAUGHTER: Let me put it to the test.

LAWYER: With me?

DAUGHTER: With you. You know the rocks, the stumbling stones. Let us avoid them.

LAWYER: I am poor.

DAUGHTER: Does that matter if we love one another? And a little beauty costs nothing.

LAWYER: My antipathies may be your sympathies.

DAUGHTER: They can be balanced.

LAWYER: Supposing we tire?

DAUGHTER: Children will come, bringing ever new interests.

LAWYER: You? You will take me, poor, ugly, despised, discredited?

DAUGHTER: Yes. Let us join our destinies.

---

⁹ In Molander's production, as the Daughter put the crown of thorns on the Lawyer's head he knelt, facing the audience, his arms outstretched in the form of a crucifix. [Translator's note]

Olaf Molander, a Swedish director, has staged several productions of A *Dream Play* in Scandinavia.

LAWYER: So be it.

The scene changes to a very simple room adjoining the LAWYER'S
*office. On the right is a large curtained double bed, close to it a
window with double panes; on the left a stove and kitchen utensils.
At the back an open door leads to the office, where a number of
poor people can be seen awaiting admission.* KRISTIN, *the maid,
is pasting strips of paper along the edges of the inner window.
The* DAUGHTER, *pale and worn, is at the stove.*

KRISTIN: I paste, I paste.

DAUGHTER: You are shutting out the air. I am suffocating.

KRISTIN: Now there's only one small crack left.

DAUGHTER: Air, air! I cannot breathe.

KRISTIN: I paste, I paste.

LAWYER (*from the office*): That's right, Kristin. Warmth is precious.

KRISTIN *pastes the last crack.*

DAUGHTER: Oh, it's as if you are glueing up my mouth!

LAWYER (*coming to the doorway with a document in his hand*): Is the
child asleep?

DAUGHTER: Yes, at last.

LAWYER (*mildly*): That screaming frightens away my clients.

DAUGHTER (*gently*): What can be done about it?

LAWYER: Nothing.

DAUGHTER: We must take a bigger flat.

LAWYER: We have no money.

DAUGHTER: May I open the window, please? This bad air is choking me.

LAWYER: Then the warmth would escape, and we should freeze.

DAUGHTER: It's horrible! Can't we at least scrub the place?

LAWYER: You can't scrub—neither can I, and Kristin must go on pasting.
She must paste up the whole house, every crack in floor and walls and
ceiling.

[*Exit* KRISTIN, *delighted.*]

DAUGHTER: I was prepared for poverty, not dirt.

LAWYER: Poverty is always rather dirty.

DAUGHTER: This is worse than I dreamt.

LAWYER: We haven't had the worst. There's still food in the pot.

DAUGHTER: But what food!

LAWYER: Cabbage is cheap, nourishing and good.

DAUGHTER: For those who like cabbage. To me it's repulsive.

LAWYER: Why didn't you say so?

DAUGHTER: Because I loved you. I wanted to sacrifice my taste.

LAWYER: Now I must sacrifice my taste for cabbage. Sacrifices must be
mutual.

DAUGHTER: Then what shall we eat? Fish? But you hate fish.

LAWYER: And it's dear.

DAUGHTER: This is harder than I believed.

LAWYER (*gently*): You see how hard it is. And the child which should be our bond and blessing is our undoing.

DAUGHTER: Dearest! I am dying in this air, in this room with its backyard view, with babies screaming through endless sleepless hours, and those people out there wailing and quarrelling and accusing . . . Here I can only die.

LAWYER: Poor little flower, without light, without air.

DAUGHTER: And you say there are others worse off.

LAWYER: I am one of the envied of the neighbourhood.

DAUGHTER: None of it would matter, if only I could have some beauty in our home.

LAWYER: I know what you're thinking of—a plant, a heliotrope to be exact; but that costs as much as six quarts of milk or half a bushel of potatoes.

DAUGHTER: I would gladly go without food to have my flower.

LAWYER: There is one kind of beauty that costs nothing. Not to have it in his home is sheer torture for a man with any sense of beauty.

DAUGHTER: What is that?

LAWYER: If I tell you, you will lose your temper.

DAUGHTER: We agreed never to lose our tempers.

LAWYER: We agreed. Yes. All will be well, Agnes, if we can avoid those sharp hard tones. You know them—no, not yet.

DAUGHTER: We shall never hear those.

LAWYER: Never, if it depends on me.

DAUGHTER: Now tell me.

LAWYER: Well, when I come into a house, first I look to see how the curtains are hung. (*Goes to the window and adjusts the curtain.*) If they hang like a bit of string or rag, I soon leave. Then I glance at the chairs. If they are in their places, I stay. (*Puts a chair straight against the wall.*) Next I look at the candlesticks. If the candles are crooked, then the whole house is askew. (*Straightens a candle on the bureau.*) That you see, my dear, is the beauty which costs nothing.

DAUGHTER (*bowing her head*): Not that sharp tone, Axel!

LAWYER: It wasn't sharp.

DAUGHTER: Yes it was.

LAWYER: The devil take it!

DAUGHTER: What kind of language is that?

LAWYER: Forgive me, Agnes. But I have suffered as much from your untidiness as you do from the dirt. And I haven't dared straighten things myself, because you would have been offended and thought I was reproaching you. Oh, shall we stop this?

DAUGHTER: It is terribly hard to be married, harder than anything. I think one has to be an angel.

LAWYER: I think one has.

DAUGHTER: I am beginning to hate you after all this.

LAWYER: Alas for us then! But let us prevent hatred. I promise never to mention untidiness again, although it is torture to me.

DAUGHTER: And I will eat cabbage, although that is torment to me.

LAWYER: And so—life together is a torment. One's pleasure is the other's pain.

DAUGHTER: Human beings are pitiful.

LAWYER: You see that now?

DAUGHTER: Yes. But in God's name let us avoid the rocks, now that we know them so well.

LAWYER: Let us do that. We are tolerant, enlightened people. Of course we can make allowances and forgive.

DAUGHTER: Of course we can smile at trifles.

LAWYER: We, only we can do it. Do you know, I read in the paper this morning . . . By the way, where is the paper?

DAUGHTER (*embarrassed*): Which paper?

LAWYER (*harshly*): Do I take more than one newspaper?

DAUGHTER: Smile—and don't speak harshly! I lit the fire with your newspaper.

LAWYER (*violently*): The devil you did!

DAUGHTER: Please smile. I burnt it because it mocked what to me is holy.

LAWYER: What to me is unholy! Huh! (*Striking his hands together, beside himself.*) I'll smile, I'll smile till my back teeth show. I'll be tolerant and swallow my opinions and say yes to everything and cant and cringe. So you've burnt my paper, have you? (*Pulls the bed curtains.*) Very well. Now I'm going to tidy up until you lose your temper . . . Agnes, this is quite impossible!

DAUGHTER: Indeed it is.

LAWYER: Yet we must stay together. Not for our vows' sake, but for the child's.

DAUGHTER: That's true—for the child's sake. Yes, yes, we must go on.

LAWYER: And now I must attend to my clients. Listen to them muttering. They can't wait to tear one another to pieces, to get each other fined and imprisoned. Benighted souls!

Enter KRISTIN *with pasting materials.*

DAUGHTER: Wretched, wretched beings! And all this pasting! (*She bows head in dumb despair.*)

KRISTIN: I paste, I paste!

The LAWYER *standing by the door, nervously fingers the handle.*

DAUGHTER: Oh how that handle squeaks! It is as if you were twisting my heart-strings.

LAWYER: I twist, I twist!

DAUGHTER: Don't!

LAWYER: I twist . . .

DAUGHTER: No!

LAWYER: I . . .

The OFFICER *[now middle-aged] takes hold of the handle from inside the office.*

OFFICER: May I?

LAWYER (*letting go of the handle*): Certainly. As you have got your degree.

OFFICER (*entering*): The whole of life is now mine. All paths are open to me. I have set foot on Parnassus, the laurels are won. Immortality, fame, all are mine!

LAWYER: What are you going to live on?

OFFICER: Live on?

LAWYER: You'll need a roof surely, and clothes and food?

OFFICER: Those are always to be had, as long as there's someone who cares for you.

LAWYER: Fancy that now, fancy that! Paste, Kristin, paste! Until they cannot breathe.

Goes out backwards, nodding.

KRISTIN: I paste, I paste! Until they cannot breathe.

OFFICER: Will you come now?

DAUGHTER: Oh quickly! But where to?

OFFICER: To Fairhaven, where it is summer and the sun is shining. Youth is there, children and flowers, singing and dancing, feasting and merry-making.

[Exit KRISTIN.]

DAUGHTER: I would like to go there.

OFFICER: Come!

LAWYER (*entering*): Now I shall return to my first hell. This one was the second—and worst. The sweetest hell is the worst. Look, she's left hairpins all over the floor again! (*Picks one up.*)

OFFICER: So he has discovered the hairpins too.

LAWYER: Too? Look at this one. There are two prongs but one pin. Two and yet one. If I straighten it out, it becomes one single piece. If I bend it, it is two, without ceasing to be one. In other words the two are one. But if I break it—like this—(*Breaks it in half*)—then the two are two. (*He throws away the pieces.*)

OFFICER: So much he has seen. But before one can break it, the prongs must diverge. If they converge, it holds.

LAWYER: And if they are parallel, they never meet. Then it neither holds nor breaks.

OFFICER: The hairpin is the most perfect of all created things. A straight line which is yet two parallel lines.

LAWYER: A lock that closes when open.

OFFICER: Closes open—a plait of hair loosed while bound.

LAWYER: Like this door. When I close it, I open the way out, for you, Agnes.

Goes out, closing the door.

DAUGHTER: And now?

*The scene changes. The bed with its hangings is transformed into
a tent, the stove remaining. The new background shows a beautiful
wooded shore, with beflagged landing stages and white boats,
some with sails set. Among the trees are little Italianesque villas,
pavilions, kiosks and marble statues.*

In the middle distance is a strait.

*The foreground presents a sharp contrast with the background.
Burnt hillsides, black and white tree stumps as after a forest fire,
red heather, red pigsties and outhouses. On the right is an open-air
establishment for remedial exercises, where people are being treated
on machines resembling instruments of torture.*

*On the left is part of the Quarantine Station; open sheds with fur-
naces, boilers and pipes.*

[*The* DAUGHTER *and the* OFFICER *are standing as at the end of the
previous scene.*]

The QUARANTINE MASTER, *dressed as a blackamoor, comes along the
shore.*

OFFICER (*going up and shaking hands with the* QUARANTINE MASTER):
What? You here, old Gasbags? [10]

QUARANTINE MASTER: Yes, I'm here.

OFFICER: Is this place Fairhaven?

QUARANTINE MASTER: No, that's over there. [*Points across the strait.*] This
is Foulstrand.

OFFICER: Then we've come wrong.

QUARANTINE MASTER: We! Aren't you going to introduce me?

OFFICER: It wouldn't do. (*Low.*) That is the Daughter of Indra.

QUARANTINE MASTER: Of India? I thought it must be Varuna[11] himself.
Well, aren't you surprised to find me black in the face?

OFFICER: My dear fellow, I am over fifty, at which age one ceases to be
surprised. I assumed at once that you were going to a fancy dress ball
this afternoon.

QUARANTINE MASTER: Quite correct. I hope you'll come with me.

OFFICER: Certainly, for there doesn't seem to be any attraction in this place.
What kind of people live here?

QUARANTINE MASTER: The sick live here, and the healthy over there.

OFFICER: But surely only the poor here?

QUARANTINE MASTER: No, my boy, here you have the rich. [*Indicates the
gymnasium.*] Look at that man on the rack. He's eaten too much
pâté-de-foie-gras with truffles, and drunk so much Burgundy that his
feet are knotted.

---

[10] *Gasbags:* Original "Ordström," meaning "Stream of Words." [Translator's note]
[11] *Varuna:* In Hindu mythology, the supreme god of heaven, the all-seeing creator
and ruler.

OFFICER: Knotted?

QUARANTINE MASTER: He's got knotted feet, and that one lying on the guillotine has drunk so much brandy that his backbone's got to be mangled.

OFFICER: That's not very pleasant either.

QUARANTINE MASTER: What's more here on this side live all those who have some misery to hide. Look at this one coming now, for instance.

An elderly fop is wheeled on to the stage in a bath chair, accompanied by a gaunt and hideous coquette of sixty, dressed in the latest fashion and attended by the "Friend," a man of forty.

OFFICER: It's the Major! Our schoolfellow.

QUARANTINE MASTER: Don Juan! You see, he's still in love with the spectre at his side. He doesn't see that she has grown old, that she is ugly, faithless, cruel.

OFFICER: There's true love for you. I never would have thought that flighty fellow had it in him to love so deeply and ardently.

QUARANTINE MASTER: That's a nice way of looking at it.

OFFICER: I've been in love myself—with Victoria. As a matter of fact I still pace up and down the alley, waiting for her.

QUARANTINE MASTER: So you're the fellow who waits in the alley?

OFFICER: I am he.

QUARANTINE MASTER: Well, have you got that door open yet?

OFFICER: No, we're still fighting the case. The Billsticker is out with his fishnet, you see, which delays the taking of evidence. Meanwhile, the Glazier has put in window-panes at the castle, which has grown half a story. It has been an unusually good year this year—warm and damp.

QUARANTINE MASTER (*pointing to the sheds*): But you've certainly had nothing like the heat of my place there.

OFFICER: What's the temperature of your furnaces then?

QUARANTINE MASTER: When we're disinfecting cholera suspects, we keep them at sixty degrees.

OFFICER: But is there cholera about again?

QUARANTINE MASTER: Didn't you know?

OFFICER: Of course I know. But I so often forget what I know.

QUARANTINE MASTER: And I so often wish I could forget—especially myself. That's why I go in for masquerades, fancy dress, theatricals.

OFFICER: Why. What's the matter with you?

QUARANTINE MASTER: If I talk, they say I'm bragging. If I hold my tongue they call me a hypocrite.

OFFICER: Is that why you blacked your face?

QUARANTINE MASTER: Yes. A shade blacker than I am.

OFFICER: Who's this coming?

QUARANTINE MASTER: Oh, he's a poet! He's going to have his mud bath.

The POET *enters, looking at the sky and carrying a pail of mud.*

OFFICER: But, good heavens, he ought to bathe in light and air!

QUARANTINE MASTER: No, he lives so much in the higher spheres that he gets homesick for the mud. It hardens his skin to wallow in the mire, just as it does with pigs. After his bath he doesn't feel the gadflies stinging.

OFFICER: What a strange world of contradictions!

POET (*ecstatically*): Out of clay the god Ptah[12] fashioned man on a potter's wheel, a lathe (*Mockingly*), or some other damned thing . . . (*Ecstatically*) Out of clay the sculptor fashions his more or less immortal masterpieces (*Mockingly*), which are usually only rubbish. (*Ecstatically*) Out of clay are formed those objects, so domestically essential bearing the generic name of pots and pans. (*Mockingly*) Not that it matters in the least to me what they're called. (*Ecstatically*) Such is clay! When clay is fluid, it is called mud. *C'est mon affaire!* (*Calls.*) Lina!

Enter LINA *with a bucket.*

POET: Lina, show yourself to Miss Agnes. She knew you ten years ago when you were a young, happy, and, let me add, pretty girl. (*To* DAUGHTER) Look at her now! Five children, drudgery, squalling, hunger, blows. See how beauty has perished, how joy has vanished in the fulfillment of duties which should give that inner contentment which shows in the harmonious lines of a face, in the tranquil shining of the eyes . . .

QUARANTINE MASTER (*putting a hand to the* POET's *lips*): Shut up! Shut up!

POET: That's what they all say. But if you are silent, they tell you to talk. How inconsistent people are!

Distant dance music is heard.

DAUGHTER (*going up to* LINA): Tell me your troubles.

LINA: No, I daren't. I'd catch it all the worse if I did.

DAUGHTER: Who is so cruel?

LINA: I daren't talk about it. I'll be beaten.

POET: May be, but I shall talk about it even if the Blackamoor knocks my teeth out. I shall talk about all the injustice there is here. Agnes, Daughter of the Gods, do you hear that music up on the hill? Well, that's a dance for Lina's sister, who has come home from town—where she went astray, you understand. Now they are killing the fatted calf, while Lina, who stayed at home, has to carry the swill pail and feed the pigs.

DAUGHTER: There is rejoicing in that home because the wanderer has forsaken the path of evil, not only because she has come home. Remember that.

---

12 *Ptah:* An Egyptian god, worshiped as the creative force which shaped the world and fathered gods as well as men.

POET: Then give a ball and a supper every evening for this blameless servant who has never gone astray. Do that for her—they never do. On the contrary, when Lina is free, she has to go to prayer meetings where she's reprimanded for not being perfect. Is that justice?

DAUGHTER: Your questions are difficult to answer, because there are so many unknown factors.

POET: The Caliph, Harun the Just, was of the same opinion. Sitting quietly on his exalted throne he could never see how those below were faring. Presently complaints reached his lofty ear, so one fine day he stepped down in disguise and walked unobserved among the crowd to watch the workings of justice.

DAUGHTER: You do not think I am Harun the Just, do you?

OFFICER: Let's change the subject. Here are newcomers.

A white boat, shaped like a dragon, glides into the Strait. It has a light blue silken sail on a gilded yard, and a golden mast with a rose-red pennon. At the helm, with their arms round each other's waists, sit HE *and* SHE.

There you see perfect happiness, utter bliss, the ecstasy of young love. *The light grows stronger.* HE *stands up in the boat and sings.*

HE:
>Hail fairest bay!
>Where I passed youth's spring tide,
>where I dreamed its first roses,
>I come now again,
>no longer alone.
>Forests and havens,
>heaven and sea,
>greet her!
>My love, my bride,
>my sun, my life!

The flags on Fairhaven dip in salute. White handkerchiefs wave from villas and shores. The music of harps and violins sound over the strait.

POET: See how light streams from them! And sound rings across the water! Eros!

OFFICER: It is Victoria.

QUARANTINE MASTER: Well, if it is . . .

OFFICER: It is his Victoria. I have my own, and mine no one will ever see. Now hoist the quarantine flag while I haul in the catch.

The QUARANTINE MASTER *waves a yellow flag. The* OFFICER *pulls on a line which causes the boat to turn in towards Foulstrand.*

Hold hard there!

HE *and* SHE *become aware of the dreadful landscape and show their horror.*

QUARANTINE MASTER: Yes, yes, it's hard lines, but everyone has to land here, everyone coming from infectious areas.

POET: Think of being able to speak like that—to behave like that when you see two human beings joined in love. Do not touch them! Do not lay hands on love—that is high treason. Alas, alas! All that is most lovely will now be dragged down, down into the mud.

HE and SHE come ashore, shamed and sad.

HE: What is it? What have we done? [13]

QUARANTINE MASTER: You don't have to do anything in order to meet with life's little discomforts.

SHE: How brief are joy and happiness!

HE: How long must we stay here?

QUARANTINE MASTER: Forty days and forty nights.

SHE: We would rather throw ourselves into the sea.

HE: Live here—among burnt hills and pigsties?

POET: Love can overcome everything, even sulphur fumes and carbolic acid.[14]

The QUARANTINE MASTER goes into a shed. Blue sulphurous vapour pours out.

QUARANTINE MASTER *(coming out)*: I'm burning the sulphur. Will you kindly step inside.

SHE: Oh, my blue dress will lose its colour!

QUARANTINE MASTER: And turn white. Your red roses will turn white too.

HE: So will your cheeks, in forty days.

SHE *(to the OFFICER)*: That will please you.

OFFICER: No, it won't. True, your happiness was the source of my misery, but . . . that's no matter. [HE *and* SHE *go into the shed.*] [*To* DAUGHTER] I've got my degree now, and a job as tutor over there. [*Indicates Fairhaven.*] Heigho! And in the fall I'll get a post in a school, teaching the boys the same lessons I learnt myself, all through my childhood, all through my youth. Teach them the same lessons I learnt all through my manhood and finally all through my old age. The same lessons! What is twice two? How many times does two go into four without remainder? Until I get a pension and have nothing to do but wait for meals and the newspapers, until in the end I'm carried out to the crematorium and burnt to ashes. (*To* QUARANTINE MASTER *as he comes out of the shed*) Have you no pensioners here? To be a pensioner is the worst fate after twice two is four, going to school again when one's taken one's degree, asking the same questions until one dies . . .

An elderly man walks past with his hands behind his back.

Look, there goes a pensioner waiting for his life to ebb. A Captain, probably, who failed to become a Major, or a Clerk to the Court who

[13] Literally "woe to us." [Translator's note]
[14] The Poet does not speak again and is not mentioned until the end of the later quayside scene, so perhaps here he goes out. [Translator's note]

was never promoted. Many are called, but few are chosen. He's just walking about, waiting for breakfast.

PENSIONER: No, for the paper, the morning paper!

OFFICER: And he is only fifty-four. He may go on for another twenty-five years, waiting for meals and the newspaper. Isn't that dreadful?

PENSIONER: What is not dreadful? Tell me that. Tell me that.

OFFICER: Yes. Let him tell who can.

Exit PENSIONER.

Now I shall teach boys twice two is four. How many times does two go into four without remainder? (*He clutches his head in despair.*)

Enter HE *and* SHE *from the shed. Her dress and roses are white, her face pale. His clothes are also bleached.*

And Victoria whom I loved, for whom I desired the greatest happiness on earth, she has her happiness now, the greatest happiness she can know, while I suffer, suffer, suffer!

SHE: Do you think I can be happy, seeing your suffering? How can you believe that? Perhaps it comforts you to know that I shall be a prisoner here for forty days and forty nights. Tell me, does it comfort you?

OFFICER: Yes and no. I cannot have pleasure while you have pain. Oh!

HE: And do you think my happiness can be built on your agony?

OFFICER: We are all to be pitied—all of us.

All lift their hands to heaven. A discordant cry of anguish breaks from their lips.

ALL: Oh!

DAUGHTER: O God, hear them! Life is evil! Mankind is to be pitied.

ALL (*as before*): Oh!

The stage is blacked out and the scene changes.
The whole landscape is in winter dress with snow on the ground and on the leafless trees. Foulstrand is in the background, in shadow.
The strait is still in the middle distance. On the near side is a landing stage with white boats and flags flying from flagstaffs. In the strait a white warship, a brig with gunports, is anchored.
The foreground presents Fairhaven, in full light.
On the right is a corner of the Assembly Rooms with open windows through which are seen couples dancing.
On a box outside stand three Maids, their arms round each other's waists, watching the dancing.
On the steps is a bench on which UGLY EDITH *is sitting, bareheaded and sorrowful, with long dishevelled hair, before on open piano.*
On the left is a yellow wooden house outside which two Children in summer dresses are playing ball.

The DAUGHTER *and* OFFICER *enter.*

DAUGHTER: Here is peace and happiness. Holiday time. Work over, every day a festival, everyone in holiday attire. Music and dancing even in the morning. (*To the Maids*) Why don't you go in and dance, my dears?

SERVANTS: Us?

OFFICER: But they are servants.

DAUGHTER: True. But why is Edith sitting there instead of dancing?

> EDITH *buries her face in her hands.*

OFFICER: Don't ask her! She has been sitting there for three hours without being invited to dance.

> *He goes into the yellow house.*

DAUGHTER: What cruel pleasure!

> The MOTHER, *in a décolleté dress, comes out of the Assembly*
> *Rooms and goes up to* EDITH.

MOTHER: Why don't you go in as I told you?

EDITH: Because . . . because I can't be my own partner. I know I'm ugly and no one wants to dance with me, but I can avoid being reminded of it. (*She begins to play Bach's* Toccata con Fuga, No. 10.)
The waltz at the ball is heard too, first faintly, then growing louder
as if in competition with the Toccata. *Gradually* EDITH *overcomes*
it and reduces it to silence. Dance couples appear in the doorway,
> *and everyone stands reverently listening.*

> A NAVAL OFFICER *seizes* ALICE, *one of the guests, by the waist.*

NAVAL OFFICER: Come, quick! (*He leads her down to the landing stage.*
EDITH *breaks off, rises and watches them in despair. She remains stand-*
ing as if turned to stone.)
The front wall of the yellow house vanishes. Boys are sitting on
forms, among them the OFFICER *looking uncomfortable and wor-*
ried. In front of them stands the SCHOOLMASTER, *wearing spectacles*
> *and holding chalk and a cane.*

SCHOOLMASTER (*to the* OFFICER): Now, my boy, can you tell me what twice two is?
The OFFICER *remains seated, painfully searching his memory with-*
> *out finding an answer.*

You must stand up when you are asked a question.

OFFICER (*rising anxiously*): Twice two . . . let me see . . . That makes two twos.

SCHOOLMASTER: Aha! So you have not prepared your lesson.

OFFICER (*embarrassed*): Yes, I have, but . . . I know what it is, but I can't say it.

SCHOOLMASTER: You're quibbling. You know the answer, do you? But you can't say it. Perhaps I can assist you. (*Pulls the* OFFICER'S *hair.*)

OFFICER: Oh, this is dreadful, really dreadful!

SCHOOLMASTER: Yes, it is dreadful that such a big boy should have no ambition.

OFFICER (*agonised*): A *big* boy. Yes, I certainly am big, much bigger than these others. I am grown up, I have left school . . . (*As if waking*) I have even graduated. Why am I sitting here then? Haven't I got my degree?

SCHOOLMASTER: Certainly. But you have got to stay here and mature. Do you see? You must mature. Isn't that so?

OFFICER (*clasping his head*): Yes, that's so, one must mature . . . Twice two—is two, and this I will demonstrate by analogy, the highest form of proof. Listen! Once one is one, therefore twice two is two. For that which applies to the one must also apply to the other.

SCHOOLMASTER: The proof is perfectly in accord with the laws of logic, but the answer is wrong.

OFFICER: What is in accord with the laws of logic cannot be wrong. Let us put it to the test. One into one goes once, therefore two into two goes twice.

SCHOOLMASTER: Quite correct according to analogy. But what then is once three?

OFFICER: It is three.

SCHOOLMASTER: Consequently twice three is also three.

OFFICER (*pondering*): No, that can't be right . . . It can't be, for if so . . . (*Sits down in despair.*) No, I am not mature yet . . .

SCHOOLMASTER: No, you are not mature by a long way.

OFFICER: Then how long shall I have to stay here?

SCHOOLMASTER: How long? Here? You believe that time and space exist? Assuming time does exist, you ought to be able to say what time is. What is time?

OFFICER: Time . . . (*Considers.*) I can't say, although I know what it is. Ergo, I may know what twice two is without being able to say it. Can you yourself say what time is?

SCHOOLMASTER: Certainly I can.

ALL THE BOYS: Tell us then!

SCHOOLMASTER: Time? . . . Let me see. (*Stands motionless with his finger to his nose.*) While we speak, time flies. Consequently time is something which flies while I am speaking.

BOY (*rising*): You're speaking now, sir, and while you're speaking, I fly. Consequently I am time. (*Flies.*)

SCHOOLMASTER: That is quite correct according to the laws of logic.

OFFICER: Then the laws of logic are absurd, for Nils, though he did fly, can't be time.

SCHOOLMASTER: That is also quite correct according to the laws of logic, although it is absurd.

OFFICER: Then logic is absurd.

SCHOOLMASTER: It really looks like it. But if logic is absurd, then the whole world is absurd . . . and I'll be damned if I stay here and teach you absurdities! If anyone will stand us a drink, we'll go and bathe.

OFFICER: That's a *posterus prius*, a world back to front, for it's customary to bathe first and have one's drink afterwards. You old fossil!

SCHOOLMASTER: Don't be so conceited, Doctor.

OFFICER: Captain, if you please. I am an officer, and I don't understand why I should sit here among a lot of schoolboys and be insulted.

SCHOOLMASTER (*wagging his finger*): We must mature!

Enter QUARANTINE MASTER.

QUARANTINE MASTER: The quarantine period has begun.

OFFICER: So there you are. Fancy this fellow making me sit here on a form, when I've taken my degree.

QUARANTINE MASTER: Well, why don't you go away?

OFFICER: Go away? That's easier said than done.

SCHOOLMASTER: So I should think. Try!

OFFICER (*to* QUARANTINE MASTER): Save me! Save me from his eyes!

QUARANTINE MASTER: Come on then! Come and help us dance. We must dance before the plague breaks out. We must.

OFFICER: Will the ship sail then?

QUAANTINE MASTER: The ship will sail first. A lot of tears will be shed of course.

OFFICER: Always tears; when she comes in and when she sails. Let's go.

They go out.

The SCHOOLMASTER *continues to give his lesson in mime.*
The Maids, who were standing at the window of the ballroom,
walk sadly down to the quay. EDITH, *until then motionless beside*
the piano, follows them.

DAUGHTER (*to* OFFICER): Isn't there one happy person in this paradise?

OFFICER: Yes, here comes a newly wed couple. Listen to them.

The Newly Wed Couple enter.

HUSBAND (*to* WIFE): My happiness is so complete that I wish to die.

WIFE: But why to die?

HUSBAND: In the midst of happiness grows a seed of unhappiness. Happiness consumes itself like a flame. It cannot burn for ever, it must go out, and the presentiment of its end destroys it at its very peak.

WIFE: Let us die together, now at once.

HUSBAND: Die! Yes, let us die. For I fear happiness, the deceiver.

They go towards the sea and disappear.

DAUGHTER (*to the* OFFICER): Life is evil. Human beings are to be pitied!

OFFICER: Look who's coming now. This is the most envied mortal in the place. (*The* BLIND MAN *is led in.*) He is the owner of these hundreds of Italian villas. He owns all these bays and creeks and shores and woods, the fish in the water, the birds in the air and the game in the woods. These thousands of people are his tenants, and the sun rises over his sea and sets over his lands.

DAUGHTER: And does he complain too?

OFFICER: Yes, with good cause, as he cannot see.

QUARANTINE MASTER: He is blind.

DAUGHTER: The most envied of all!

OFFICER: Now he's going to see the ship sail with his son aboard.

BLIND MAN: I do not see, but I hear. I hear the fluke of the anchor tearing the clay bed, just as when the hook is dragged out of a fish and the heart comes up too through the gullet. My son, my only child, is going to journey to strange lands across the great sea. Only my thoughts can go with him . . . Now I hear the chain clanking . . . and there's something flapping and lashing like washing on a clothes line . . . Wet handkerchiefs perhaps . . . And I hear a sound of sighing . . . or sobbing . . . like people crying . . . Maybe the plash of small waves against the hull, or maybe the girls on the quay, the abandoned, the inconsolable. I once asked a child why the sea was salt, and the child, whose father was on a long voyage, replied at once: "The sea is salt because sailors cry so much." "But why do sailors cry so much?" "Well," he said, "because they keep going away . . . And so they're always drying their handkerchiefs up on the masts." "And why do people cry when they're sad?" I asked. "Oh," said he, "that's because the eye window must be washed sometimes, so we can see better." *The brig has set sail and glided away. The girls on the quay alternately wave their handkerchiefs and dry their eyes. Now on the topmast is hoisted the signal "Yes," a red ball on a white ground.*

ALICE *waves a triumphant reply.*

DAUGHTER (*to* OFFICER): What does that flag mean?

OFFICER: It means "yes." It is the lieutenant's "yes" in red, red as heart's blood, written on the blue cloth of the sky.

DAUGHTER: Then what is "no" like?

OFFICER: Blue as tainted blood in blue veins. Look how elated Alice is.

DAUGHTER: And how Edith is weeping.

BLIND MAN: Meeting and parting, parting and meeting. That's life. I met his mother, then she went away. My son was left; now he has gone.

DAUGHTER: But he will come back.

BLIND MAN: Who is speaking to me? I have heard that voice before. In my dreams, in boyhood when summer holidays began, in early married life when my child was born. Whenever life smiled, I heard that voice, like the whisper of the South wind, like the sounds of a heavenly harp, like the angels' greeting, as I imagine it, on Christmas Eve.

The LAWYER *enters, goes up to the* BLIND MAN *and whispers.*

Really?

LAWYER: Yes, it's a fact. (*Goes across to the* DAUGHTER.) You have seen most things now, but you have not yet experienced the worst thing of all.

DAUGHTER: What can that be?

LAWYER: Repetitions, reiterations. Going back. Doing one's lessons again . . . Come!

DAUGHTER: Where to?

LAWYER: To your duties.

DAUGHTER: What are they?

LAWYER: Everything you abominate. Everything you least want to do, and yet must. They are to abstain and renounce, to go without, to leave behind. They are everything that is disagreeable, repulsive, painful.

DAUGHTER: Are there no pleasant duties?

LAWYER: They become pleasant when they are done.

DAUGHTER: When they no longer exist. So duty is altogether unpleasant. What then can one enjoy?

LAWYER: What one enjoys is sin.

DAUGHTER: Sin?

LAWYER: Which is punished. Yes. If I enjoy myself one day, one evening, the next day I have a bad conscience and go through the torments of hell.

DAUGHTER: How strange!

LAWYER: I wake in the morning with a headache, and then the repetition begins, but it is a distorted repetition, so that everything which was charming and witty and beautiful the night before appears in memory ugly, stupid, repulsive. Pleasure stinks, and enjoyment falls to pieces. What people call success is always a step towards the next failure. The successes in my life have been my downfall. Men have an instinctive dread of another's good fortune. They feel it's unjust that fate should favour any one man, so try to restore the balance by rolling boulders across his path. To have talent is to be in danger of one's life—one may so easily starve to death. However, you must go back to your duties, or I shall take proceedings against you, and we shall go through all three Courts, first, second, third.

DAUGHTER: Go back? To the stove and the cabbage and the baby clothes?

LAWYER: Yes. And it's washing day—the big wash when all the handkerchiefs have to be done.

DAUGHTER: Oh, must I do that again?

LAWYER: The whole of life is only repetition. Look at the schoolmaster there. Yesterday he took his doctor's degree, was crowned with laurels, scaled Parnassus, was embraced by the monarch. Today he is back at school, asking what twice two is . . . and that's what he will go on doing until he dies. But come now, back to your home.

DAUGHTER: I would rather die.

LAWYER: Die? One can't do that. To begin with taking one's own life is so dishonourable that even one's corpse is dishonoured. And to add to that one is damned, for it is a mortal sin.

DAUGHTER: It is not easy to be human.

ALL: Hear, hear!

DAUGHTER: I will not go back with you to humiliation and dirt. I shall return to the place from which I came. But first the door must be opened, so that I may know the secret. I wish the door to be opened.

Enter the POET.

LAWYER: Then you must retrace your steps, go back the way you came, and put up with all the horrors of a lawsuit; the repetitions, the redraftings, the reiterations.

DAUGHTER: So be it. But first I shall seek solitude in the wilderness to find myself. We shall meet again. (*To the* POET) Come with me.

A distant cry of lamentation rises.

VOICES: Oh, oh! oh!

DAUGHTER: What was that?

LAWYER: The doomed at Foulstrand.

DAUGHTER: Why do they wail so today?

LAWYER: Because here the sun is shining, here is music and dance and youth. This makes them suffer more.

DAUGHTER: We must set them free.

LAWYER: Try! Once a deliverer came, but he was hanged upon a cross.

DAUGHTER: By whom?

LAWYER: By all the righteous.

DAUGHTER: Who are they?

LAWYER: Don't you know the righteous? Well, you will.

DAUGHTER: Was it they who refused you your degree?

LAWYER: Yes.

DAUGHTER: Then I do know them.

The scene changes to a Mediterranean resort. In the background are villas, a Casino with a terrace, and a blue strip of sea. In the foreground is a white wall over which hang branches of orange trees in fruit. Below this to one side a huge heap of coal and two wheel barrows.

The DAUGHTER *and the* LAWYER *come on to the terrace.*

DAUGHTER: This is paradise.

1ST COAL HEAVER: This is hell.

2ND COAL HEAVER: A hundred and twenty in the shade.

1ST COAL HEAVER: Shall we get into the sea?

2ND COAL HEAVER: Then the police'd come: "You mustn't bathe here!"

1ST COAL HEAVER: Can't we have a bit of fruit off that tree?

2ND COAL HEAVER: No. The police would come.

1ST COAL HEAVER: One can't work in this heat. I'm going to chuck it.[15]

2ND COAL HEAVER: Then the police will come and take you up. (*Pause*) Besides, you'll have nothing to eat.

1ST COAL HEAVER: Nothing to eat! We, who do the most work, get the least food. And the rich, who do nothing, get it all. Might one not, without taking liberties with the truth, call this unjust? What has the Daughter of the Gods up there to say about it?

DAUGHTER: I have no answer. But, tell me, what have you done to get so black and have so hard a lot?

1ST COAL HEAVER: What have we done? Got ourselves born of poor and pretty bad parents. Been sentenced a couple of times maybe.

DAUGHTER: Sentenced?

1ST COAL HEAVER: Yes. The ones that don't get caught sit up there in the Casino eating eight course dinners with wine.

DAUGHTER (*to* LAWYER): Can this be true?

LAWYER: More or less, yes.

DAUGHTER: Do you mean that everyone at some time or other deserves imprisonment?

LAWYER: Yes.

DAUGHTER: Even you?

LAWYER: Yes.

DAUGHTER: Is it true those poor men aren't allowed to bathe in that sea?

LAWYER: No, not even with their clothes on. Only those who try to drown themselves avoid paying. And they are more than likely to get beaten up at the police station.

DAUGHTER: Can't they go and bathe outside the town—in the country?

LAWYER: There is no country. It's all fenced in.

DAUGHTER: I mean where it is open and free.

LAWYER: Nothing is free. Everything is owned.

DAUGHTER: Even the sea, the vast, wide . . . ?

LAWYER: Everything. You can't go out in a boat, nor can you land, without it all being booked and paid for. It's marvellous.

DAUGHTER: This is not paradise.

LAWYER: I promise you that.

DAUGHTER: Why don't people do anything to improve conditions?

LAWYER: They certainly do. But all reformers end in prison or the madhouse.

DAUGHTER: Who puts them in prison?

LAWYER: All the righteous, all the respectable.

DAUGHTER: Who puts them in the madhouse?

LAWYER: Their own despair when they see the hopelessness of the struggle.

DAUGHTER: Has it occurred to anyone that there may be unknown reasons for this state of things?

LAWYER: Yes, the well-off always think that is so.

[15] *chuck it*: Stop it, i.e., stop working.

DAUGHTER: That there is nothing wrong with things as they are?

1ST COAL HEAVER: And yet we are the foundation of society. If there's no coal, the kitchen stove goes out and the fire on the hearth too. The machines in the factory stop working; the lights in streets and shops and homes all go out. Darkness and cold descend on you. That's why we sweat like hell carrying filthy coal. What do you give us in return?

LAWYER (*to* DAUGHTER): Help them. (*Pause*) I know things can't be exactly the same for everybody, but why should there be such inequality?

The GENTLEMAN *and the* LADY *cross the terrace.*

LADY: Are you coming to play cards?

GENTLEMAN: No, I must go for a little walk to get an appetite for dinner.
Exeunt.

1ST COAL HEAVER: To *get* an appetite!

2ND COAL HEAVER: To *get* . . . !

Children enter. When they catch sight of the black workers they scream with terror [and run off].

1ST COAL HEAVER: They scream when they see us. They scream!

2ND COAL HEAVER: Curse it! We'd better get out the scaffolds soon and execute this rotten body.

1ST COAL HEAVER: Curse it, I say too!

LAWYER (*to* DAUGHTER): It's all wrong. It's not the people who are so bad, but . . .

DAUGHTER: But?

LAWYER: The system.

DAUGHTER (*hiding her face in her hands*): This is not paradise.

1ST COAL HEAVER: No. This is hell, pure hell.

The scene changes to [the earlier set of] Fingal's Cave. Long green billows roll gently into the cave. A red bell-buoy rocks upon the waves, but gives no sound until later. Music of the winds. Music of the waves.

The DAUGHTER *is with the* POET.

POET: Where have you brought me?

DAUGHTER: Far from the murmur and wailing of the children of men. To this grotto at the ends of the oceans to which we give the name *Indra's Ear*, for here, it is said, the King of Heaven listens to the lamentations of mortals.

POET: Why here?

DAUGHTER: Do you not see that this cave is shaped like a shell? Yes, you see it. Do you not know that your ear is shaped like a shell? You know, but you have given it no thought. (*She picks up a shell.*) As a child, did you never hold a shell to your ear and listen to the whisper of your heart's blood, to the humming of thoughts in your brain, to the parting of a thousand little worn-out tissues in the fabric of your body? All this you can hear in a small shell. Think then what may be heard in this great one.

POET (*listening*): I hear nothing but the sighing of the wind.

DAUGHTER: Then I will be its interpreter. Listen to the lamentation of the winds. (*She speaks to soft music.*)

> *Born under heaven's clouds,*
> *chased were we by Indra's fires*
> *down to the crust of earth.*
> *The mould of acres soiled our feet,*
> *we had to bear*
> *the dust of roads and city smoke,*
> *the kitchen's reek and fumes of wine.*
> *Out to these spacious seas we blew,*
> *to air our lungs,*
> *to shake our wings*
> *and bathe our feet.*
> *Indra, Lord of Heaven,*
> *hear us!*
> *Listen to our sighing!*
> *Earth is not clean,*
> *life is not just,*
> *men are not evil*
> *nor are they good.*
> *They live as best they may*
> *from one day to another,*
> *Sons of dust in dust they walk,*
> *born of the dust,*
> *dust they become.*
> *Feet they have to trudge,*
> *no wings.*
> *Dust-soiled they grow.*
> *Is the fault theirs*
> *or Thine?*

POET: So I heard once . . .

DAUGHTER: Hush! The winds are still singing.

> *Continues to soft music.*

> *We, the winds, the sons of air,*
> *bear man's lamentation.*
> *Thou hast heard us*
> *on autumn eves in the chimney stack,*
> *in the stove-pipe's vent,*
> *in the window cracks,*

as the rain wept on the tiles.
Or on winter nights,
mid the pine-wood's snows,
or on the stormy ocean,
hast heard the moaning and the whine,
of rope and sail.
That is us, the winds,
the sons of air,
who from human breasts
we pierced ourselves,
these sounds of suffering learnt.
In sickroom, on the battlefield,
and most where the newborn lie,
screaming, complaining,
of the pain of being alive.
It is we, we, the winds
who whine and whistle,
woe! woe! woe!

POET: It seems to me that once before . . .
DAUGHTER: Hush! The waves are singing.

Speaks to soft music.

It is we, we the waves,
that rock the winds
to rest.
Green cradling waves,
wet are we and salt.
Like flames of fire,
wet flames we are.
Quenching, burning,
cleansing, bathing,
generating, multiplying.
We, we the waves,
that rock the winds
to rest.

False waves and faithless. Everything on earth that is not burned is drowned by those waves. Look there! (*She points to the wreckage.*) Look what the sea has stolen and destroyed! All that remains of those sunken ships is their figureheads . . . and the names—Justice, Friendship, Golden Peace, and Hope. That's all that's left of hope, treacherous hope. Spars, rowlocks, bailers. And see! The lifebuoy which saved itself, letting those in need perish.

POET (*searching the wreckage*): Here is the name of the ship Justice. This is the ship which sailed from Fairhaven with the Blind Man's son on board. So she sank. And Alice's sweetheart was in her too, Edith's hopeless love.

DAUGHTER: The blind man? Fairhaven? Surely that I dreamt. Alice's sweetheart, ugly Edith, Foulstrand and the quarantine, the sulphur and carbolic, graduation in the church, the lawyer's office, the alley and Victoria. The Growing Castle and the Officer . . . These things I dreamt.

POET: Of these things I once made poetry.

DAUGHTER: You know then what poetry is?

POET: I know what dreams are. What is poetry?

DAUGHTER: Not reality, but more than reality. Not dreams, but waking dreams.

POET: Yet the children of men believe that poets merely play—invent and fabricate.

DAUGHTER: It is just as well, my friend, or else the world would be laid waste from lack of endeavour. All men would lie upon their backs, gazing at the heavens; no hand would be lifted to plough or spade, or plane or axe.

POET: Do you speak thus, Daughter of Indra? You, who are half of heaven?

DAUGHTER: You are right to reproach me. I have lived too long down here, and like you have bathed in mud. My thoughts can no longer fly. Clay is on their wings and soil about their feet. And I myself (*She raises her arms.*) I am sinking, sinking! Help me, Father, God of Heaven! (*Silence*) No longer can I hear His answer. The ether no longer carries the sound of His lips to the shell of my ear . . . the silver thread has snapped. Alas, I am earthbound!

POET: Do you mean then soon—to go?

DAUGHTER: As soon as I have burnt this earthly matter, for the waters of the ocean cannot cleanse me. Why do you ask?

POET: I have a prayer—a petition.

DAUGHTER: A petition?

POET: A petition from mankind to the ruler of the universe, drawn up by a dreamer.

DAUGHTER: Who is to present it?

POET: Indra's Daughter.

DAUGHTER: Can you speak the words?

POET: I can.

DAUGHTER: Speak them then.

POET: It is better that you should.

DAUGHTER: Where shall I read them?

POET: In my thoughts—or here. (*He gives her a scroll.*)

DAUGHTER: So be it. I will speak them. (*She takes the scroll but does not read.*)

"Why with anguish are you born?
Why do you hurt your mother so,

Child of man, when bringing her
the joy of motherhood,
joy beyond all other joys?
Why wake to life,
why greet the light
with a cry of fury and of pain,
Child of man, when to be glad
should be the gift of life?
Why are we born like animals?
We who stem from God and man,
whose souls are longing to be clothed
in other than this blood and filth.
Must God's own image cut its teeth?"

Speaking her own thoughts.

Silence! No more! The work may not condemn the master. Life's
riddle still remains unsolved.

Continuing the POET's *bitter words.*

"And then the journey's course begins,
over thistles, thorns and stones.
If it should touch a beaten track,
comes at once the cry: 'Keep off!'
Pluck a flower, straight you'll find
the bloom you picked to be another's.
If cornfields lie across your path
and you must pursue your way,
trampling on another's crops,
others then will trample yours
that your loss may equal theirs.
Every pleasure you enjoy
brings to all your fellows sorrow,
yet your sorrow gives no gladness.
So sorrow, sorrow upon sorrow
on your way—until you're dead
and then, alas, give others bread.

Her own thought.

Is it thus, O son of dust,
You seek to win the ear of God?

POET: *How may son of dust find words,*
so pure, so light, so luminous,
that they can rise up from the earth?
Child of the Gods, translate for me,

> *this lamentation into speech*
> *fit for Immortal ears.*

DAUGHTER: I will.

POET (*pointing*): What is floating there—a buoy?

DAUGHTER: Yes.

POET: It is like a lung with a windpipe.

DAUGHTER: It is the watchman of the sea. When danger is abroad, it sings.

POET: It seems to me that the sea is rising, and the waves beginning to . . .

DAUGHTER: You are not mistaken.

POET: Alas, what do I see? A ship—on the rocks.

DAUGHTER: What ship can it be?

POET: I believe it is the ghost-ship.

DAUGHTER: What is that?

POET: The Flying Dutchman.[16]

DAUGHTER: He? Why is he punished so cruelly, and why does he not come ashore?

POET: Because he had seven unfaithful wives.

DAUGHTER: Shall he be punished for that?

POET: Yes. All righteous men condemned him.

DAUGHTER: Incomprehensible world! How can he be freed from this curse?

POET: Freed? One would beware of freeing him.

DAUGHTER: Why?

POET: Because . . . No, that is not the Dutchman. It is an ordinary ship in distress. Then why does the buoy not sound? Look how the sea is rising! The waves are towering, and soon we shall be imprisoned in this cave. Now the ship's bell is ringing. Soon there will be another figure-head in here. Cry out buoy! Watchman, do your duty!

> *The buoy sounds a four-part chord in fifths and sixths, like fog-*
> *horns.*

The crew is waving to us . . . but we ourselves perish.

DAUGHTER: Do you not want to be set free?

POET: Yes, yes I do! But not now . . . and not by water!

THE CREW (*singing four-part*): Christ Kyrie![17]

POET: They are calling and the sea is calling. But no one hears.

CREW (*singing as before*): Christ Kyrie!

DAUGHTER: Who is it coming there?

POET: Walking upon the water! Only One walks upon the water. It is not Peter, the rock, for he sank like a stone.

> *A white light appears over the sea.*

CREW (*as before*): Christ Kyrie!

---

[16] *The Flying Dutchman:* Refers both to the fabled ghost ship and its captain, who is condemned to sail the seas until Judgment Day.

[17] *Christ Kyrie:* Lord Christ! An embellishment of the *Kyrie eleison* (Lord, have mercy upon us), the first part of the mass and the last relic of the use of Greek in the early Roman liturgy.

DAUGHTER: Is it He?

POET: It is He, the crucified.

DAUGHTER: Why, tell me why He was crucified.

POET: Because He wished to set men free.

DAUGHTER: Who—I have forgotten—who crucified Him?

The cave grows darker.

POET: All righteous men.

DAUGHTER: This incomprehensible world!

POET: The sea is rising. Darkness is falling on us. The storm is growing wilder.

The CREW *shriek.*

The crew are screaming with horror because they have seen their Saviour . . . and now . . . they are throwing themselves overboard in terror of the Redeemer.

The CREW *shriek again.*

Now they are screaming because they are going to die. They were born screaming and they die screaming.

The mounting waves threaten to drown them in the cave. The light begins to change.

DAUGHTER: If I were sure it was a ship . . .

POET: Indeed, I do not think it is a ship. It's a two storied house, with trees round it . . . and a telephone tower—a tower reaching to the skies. It's the modern Tower of Babel, sending up its wires to communicate with those above.

DAUGHTER: Child, man's thought needs no wires for its flight. The prayers of the devout penetrate all worlds. That is surely no Tower of Babel. If you wish to storm the heavens, storm them with your prayers.

POET: No, it's not a house . . . not a telephone tower. Do you see?

DAUGHTER: What do you see?

During the following speech, the scene changes to the alley of the Opera House.

POET: I see a snow-covered heath . . . a parade ground. The winter sun is shining behind a church on the hill, so that the tower casts its long shadow on the snow. Now a troop of soldiers comes marching over the heath. They march on the tower and up the spire . . . Now they are on the cross, and I seem to know that the first to tread on the weather-cock must die . . . They are drawing near it. It's the Corporal at their head who . . . Ah! A cloud is sailing over the heath, across the sun . . . Now everything has gone. The moisture of the cloud has put out the fire of the sun. The sunlight created a shadowy image of the tower, but the shadow of the cloud smothered the image of the tower.

[*It is springtime. The tree and the monkshood are in bud. The Stage* DOORKEEPER *sits in her old place. The* DAUGHTER *enters, followed by the* POET.]

DAUGHTER (*to* DOORKEEPER): Has the Chancellor arrived yet?

DOORKEEPER: No.

DAUGHTER: Nor the Deans?

DOORKEEPER: No.

DAUGHTER: You must send for them at once. The door is going to be opened.

DOORKEEPER: Is it so urgent?

DAUGHTER: Yes. It's thought that the answer to the riddle of the universe is locked up in there. So send for the Chancellor and the Deans of the four Faculties. (*The* DOORKEEPER *blows a whistle.*) And don't forget the Glazier and his diamond, or nothing can be done.

The personnel of the Opera pour from the building as in the earlier scene.

The OFFICER [*young again*], *in morning coat and top hat, comes through the gate, carrying a bouquet of roses and looking radiantly happy.*

OFFICER (*singing*): Victoria!

DOORKEEPER: The young lady will be down in a minute.

OFFICER: Good. The carriage is waiting, the table is laid, the champagne is on the ice . . . Let me embrace you, Madam. (*Embraces the* DOORKEEPER.) Victoria!

WOMAN'S VOICE (*from above, singing*): I am here.

OFFICER (*pacing*): Well, I am waiting.

POET: I seem to have lived through all this before.

DAUGHTER: I too.

POET: Perhaps I dreamt it.

DAUGHTER: Or made a poem of it.

POET: Or made a poem.

DAUGHTER: You know then what poetry is.

POET: I know what dreaming is.

DAUGHTER: I feel that once before, somewhere else, we said these words.

POET: Then soon you will know what reality is.

DAUGHTER: Or dreaming.

POET: Or poetry.

Enter the CHANCELLOR *and the* DEANS OF THEOLOGY, PHILOSOPHY, MEDICINE *and* LAW, [*followed by the* GLAZIER *and a group of Righteous People*].

CHANCELLOR: It's all a question of the door, you understand. What does the Dean of Theology think about it?

DEAN OF THEOLOGY: I don't think—I believe. Credo.

DEAN OF PHILOSOPHY: I think.

DEAN OF MEDICINE: I know.

DEAN OF LAW: I doubt—until I have heard the evidence and witnesses.

CHANCELLOR: Now they will quarrel again. Well then, first what does Theology believe?

DEAN OF THEOLOGY: I believe that this door ought not to be opened, as it conceals dangerous truths.

DEAN OF PHILOSOPHY: The truth is never dangerous.

DEAN OF MEDICINE: What is truth?

DEAN OF LAW: Whatever can be proved by two witnesses.

DEAN OF THEOLOGY: Anything can be proved by two false witnesses—if you're a pettifogger.

DEAN OF PHILOSOPHY: Truth is wisdom, and wisdom and knowledge are philosophy itself. Philosophy is the science of sciences, the knowledge of knowledge. All other sciences are its servants.

DEAN OF MEDICINE: The only science is natural science. Philosophy is not science. It is mere empty speculation.

DEAN OF THEOLOGY: Bravo!

DEAN OF PHILOSOPHY (*to* DEAN OF THEOLOGY): You say bravo. And what, may I ask, are you? The arch enemy of knowledge, the antithesis of science. You are ignorance and darkness.

DEAN OF MEDICINE: Bravo!

DEAN OF THEOLOGY (*to* DEAN OF MEDICINE): And you say bravo—you who can't see further than the end of your own nose in a magnifying glass. You who believe in nothing but your deceptive senses—in your eyes, for instance, which may be long-sighted, short-sighted, blind, purblind, squinting, one-eyed, colour-blind, red-blind, green-blind . . .

DEAN OF MEDICINE: Blockhead!

DEAN OF THEOLOGY: Ass!

They fight.

CHANCELLOR: Enough! Birds of a feather shouldn't peck each other's eyes out.

DEAN OF PHILOSOPHY: Had I to choose between these two, Theology and Medicine, I should choose—neither.

DEAN OF LAW: And if I had to sit in judgment over you three, I should condemn—every one of you . . . You can't agree upon a single point, and never have been able to. Let's get back to the matter in hand. What's your opinion, Chancellor, of this door and the opening of it?

CHANCELLOR: Opinion? I don't have opinions. I am merely appointed by the Government to see you don't break each other's arms and legs in the Senate in the course of educating the young. Opinions? No, I take good care not to have any. I had a few once, but they were soon exploded. Opinions always are exploded—by opponents, of course. Perhaps we had better have the door opened now, even at the risk of it concealing dangerous truths.

DEAN OF LAW: What is truth? What is the truth?

DEAN OF THEOLOGY: I am the Truth and the Life . . .

DEAN OF PHILOSOPHY: I am the knowledge of knowledge.

DEAN OF MEDICINE: I am exact knowledge . . .

DEAN OF LAW: I doubt.

They fight.

DAUGHTER: Shame on you, teachers of youth!

DEAN OF LAW: Chancellor, as delegate of the Government and head of the teaching staff, denounce this woman. She has cried "shame on you" which is contumely, and she has ironically referred to you as "teachers of youth," which is slander.

DAUGHTER: Poor youth!

DEAN OF LAW: She pities youth, and that's tantamount to accusing us. Chancellor, denounce her!

DAUGHTER: Yes, I accuse you—all of you—of sowing the seeds of doubt and dissension in the minds of the young.

DEAN OF LAW: Listen to her! She herself is raising doubts in the young as to our authority, yet she is accusing us of raising doubts. I appeal to all righteous men. Is this not a criminal offence?

ALL THE RIGHTEOUS: Yes, it is criminal.

DEAN OF LAW: The righteous have condemned you. Go in peace with your gains. Otherwise . . .

DAUGHTER: My gains? Otherwise what?

DEAN OF LAW: Otherwise you will be stoned.

POET: Or crucified.

DAUGHTER (*to the* POET): I am going. Come with me and learn the answer to the riddle.

POET: Which riddle?

DAUGHTER: What does he mean by my "gains"?

POET: Probably nothing at all. That's what we call idle chatter. He was just chattering.

DAUGHTER: But that hurt me more than anything else.

POET: That's why he said it. Human beings are like that.

The GLAZIER *opens the door and looks inside.*

ALL THE RIGHTEOUS: Hurrah! The door is open.

The DEANS *look inside.*

CHANCELLOR: What was concealed behind that door?

GLAZIER: I can't see anything.

CHANCELLOR: He can't see anything. Well, I'm not surprised. Deans! What was concealed behind that door?

DEAN OF THEOLOGY: Nothing. That is the solution of the riddle of the universe. Out of nothing in the beginning God created heaven and earth.

DEAN OF PHILOSOPHY: Out of nothing comes nothing.

DEAN OF MEDICINE: Bosh! That is nothing.

DEAN OF LAW: I doubt everything. And there's some swindle here. I appeal to all righteous men.

DAUGHTER (*to* POET): Who are these righteous?

POET: Let him tell you who can. All the righteous are often just one person.

Today they are me and mine, tomorrow you and yours. One is nominated for the post, or rather, one nominates oneself.

ALL THE RIGHTEOUS: We have been swindled.

CHANCELLOR: Who has swindled you?

ALL THE RIGHTEOUS: The Daughter!

CHANCELLOR: Will the Daughter kindly inform us what her idea was in having the door opened.

DAUGHTER: No, my friends. If I told you, you would not believe it.

DEAN OF MEDICINE: But there's nothing there.

DAUGHTER: What you say is correct. But you have not understood it.

DEAN OF MEDICINE: What she says is bosh.

ALL: Bosh!

DAUGHTER (*to* POET): They are to be pitied.

POET: Do you mean that seriously?

DAUGHTER: Very seriously.

POET: Do you think the righteous are to be pitied too?

DAUGHTER: They most of all perhaps.

POET: And the four Faculties?

DAUGHTER: They too, and not least. Four heads and four minds with a single body. Who created such a monster?

ALL: She does not answer.

CHANCELLOR: Then stone her!

DAUGHTER: This is the answer.

CHANCELLOR: Listen! She is answering.

ALL: Stone her! She is answering.

Enter LAWYER.

DAUGHTER: If she answers, or if she does not answer, stone her! (*To* POET) Come, you Seer, and I will answer the riddle, but far from here, out in the wilderness, where none can hear us, none can see us. For . . .
The LAWYER *interrupts by taking hold of her arm.*

LAWYER: Have you forgotten your duties?

DAUGHTER: God knows I have not. But I have higher duties.

LAWYER: But your child?

DAUGHTER: My child? Yes?

LAWYER: Your child is calling you.

DAUGHTER: My child! Alas, I am earthbound! And this anguish in my breast, this agony, what is it?

LAWYER: Don't you know?

DAUGHTER: No.

LAWYER: It is the pangs of conscience.

DAUGHTER: The pangs of conscience?

LAWYER: Yes. They come after every neglected duty, after every pleasure, however innocent—if there is such a thing as an innocent pleasure, which is doubtful. And they also come every time one causes pain to one's neighbour.

DAUGHTER: Is there no remedy?

LAWYER: Yes, but only one. To do one's duty instantly.

DAUGHTER: You look like a devil when you say the word "duty." But when one has, as I, two duties?

LAWYER: Fulfil first one and then the other.

DAUGHTER: The higher first. Therefore, you look after my child, and I will do my duty.

LAWYER: Your child is unhappy without you. Can you let another suffer on your account?

DAUGHTER: There is conflict in my soul. It is pulled this way and that until it is torn in two.

LAWYER: These, you see, are life's little trials.

DAUGHTER: Oh, how they tear one!

POET: You would have nothing to do with me, if you knew what misery I have caused through following my vocation—yes, my vocation, which is the highest duty of all.

DAUGHTER: What do you mean?

POET: I had a father, whose hopes were centred in me, his only son. I was to have carried on his business, but I ran away from the Commercial College.[18] Worry brought my father to his grave. My mother wanted me to be religious. I couldn't be religious. She disowned me. I had a friend who helped me when I was desperate, but that friend turned out to be a tyrant to the very people whose cause I upheld. So to save my soul I had to strike down my friend and benefactor. Since that time I have had no peace. I am considered base, contemptible, the scum of the earth. Nor do I get any comfort from my conscience when it tells me I did right, for the next moment it assures me I did wrong. That is the way of life.

DAUGHTER: Come with me, out into the wilderness.

LAWYER: Your child!

DAUGHTER (*indicating all present*): These are my children. Each one of them is good, but as soon as they are together they fight and turn into devils. Farewell!

[*Blackout. When the lights go up the scene has changed to*] Outside the Castle.

The set is the same as the earlier one, except that now the ground is covered with blue monkshood, aconite and other flowers. The chrysanthemum bud at the top of the tower is on the point of bursting. The Castle windows are lit with candles. [In the foreground is a fire.]

DAUGHTER: The hour is at hand when with the aid of fire I shall ascend

18 *Commercial College*: Business School.

again into the ether. This is what you call death and approach with so much fear.

POET: Fear of the unknown.

DAUGHTER: Which yet you know.

POET: Who knows it?

DAUGHTER: Mankind. Why do you not believe your prophets?

POET: Prophets have never been believed. Why is that? If they truly speak with the voice of God, why then do men not believe? His power to convince should be irresistible.

DAUGHTER: Have you always doubted?

POET: No, I have had faith many times, but after a while it drifted away, like a dream when one awakens.

DAUGHTER: To be mortal is not easy.

POET: You understand this now?

DAUGHTER: Yes.

POET: Tell me, did not Indra once send his son down to earth to hear man's complaint?

DAUGHTER: He did. And how was he received?

POET: How did he fulfil his mission?—to answer with a question.

DAUGHTER: To answer with another—was not the state of mankind bettered by his visit to the earth? Answer truly.

POET: Bettered? Yes, a little, a very little. Now, instead of further questions, will you tell me the answer to the riddle?

DAUGHTER: What purpose would that serve? You would not believe me.

POET: I shall believe you, for I know who you are.

DAUGHTER: Then I will tell you. In the dawn of time, before your sun gave light, Brahma, the divine primal force let himself be seduced by Maya, the World Mother, that he might propagate. This mingling of the divine element with the earthly was the Fall from heaven. This world, its life and its inhabitants are therefore only a mirage, a reflection, a dream image.

POET: My dream!

DAUGHTER: A true dream. But, in order to be freed from the earthly element, the descendants of Brahma sought renunciation and suffering. And so you have suffering as the deliverer. But this yearning for suffering comes into conflict with the longing for joy, for love. Now you understand what love is; supreme joy in the greatest suffering, the sweetest is the most bitter. Do you understand now what woman is? Woman, through whom sin and death entered into life.

POET: I understand. And the outcome?

DAUGHTER: What you yourself know. Conflict between the pain of joy and the joy of pain, between the anguish of the penitent and the pleasure of the sensual.

POET: And the conflict?

DAUGHTER: The conflict of opposites generates power, as fire and water create the force of steam.

POET: But peace? Rest?

DAUGHTER: Hush! You must ask no more, nor may I answer. The altar is decked for the sacrifice, the flowers keep vigil, the candles are lighted, the white sheet hangs in the window, the threshold is strewn with pine.[19]

POET: How calmly you speak! As if suffering did not exist for you.

DAUGHTER: Not exist? I suffered all your sufferings a hundred fold because my sensibilities were finer.

POET: Tell me your sorrows.

DAUGHTER: Poet, could you tell your own with utter truth? Could your words ever once convey your thoughts?

POET: You are right. No. To myself I have always seemed a deaf mute, and while the crowd was acclaiming my song, to me it seemed a jangle. And so, you see, I was always ashamed when men paid me homage.

DAUGHTER: And yet you wish me to speak? Look into my eyes.

POET: I cannot endure your gaze.

DAUGHTER: How then will you endure my words, if I speak in my own language?

POET: Even so, before you go, tell me from what you suffered most down here.

DAUGHTER: From living. From feeling my vision dimmed by having eyes, my hearing dulled by having ears, and my thought, my airy, luminous thought, bound down in a labyrinth of fat. You have seen a brain. What twisting channels, what creeping ways!

POET: Yes, and that is why the minds of the righteous are twisted.

DAUGHTER: Cruel, always cruel, each one of you.

POET: How can we be otherwise?

DAUGHTER: Now first I shake the dust from my feet, the earth, the clay. (*She takes off her shoes and puts them in the fire.*)

[*One after another the following characters come in, put their contributions on the fire, cross the stage and go out, while the* POET *and the* DAUGHTER *stand watching.*]

DOORKEEPER: Perhaps I may burn my shawl too?

OFFICER: And I my roses, of which only the thorns are left.

BILLSTICKER: The posters can go, but my fishnet never.

GLAZIER: Farewell to the diamond that opened the door.

LAWYER: The report of the proceedings in the High Court touching the Pope's beard or the diminishing water supply in the sources of the Ganges.

---

[19] *The altar . . . with pine:* Signs of mourning in Sweden. [Translator's note]

QUARANTINE MASTER: A small contribution in the shape of the black mask which turned me into a blackamoor against my will.

VICTORIA [SHE]: My beauty—my sorrow.

EDITH: My ugliness—my sorrow.

BLINDMAN (*putting his hand in the fire*): I give my hand which is my sight.

DON JUAN *is pushed in in the bathchair [accompanied by the CO-QUETTE and the FRIEND].*

DON JUAN: Make haste, make haste! Life is short.

POET: I have read that when a life is nearing its end, everything and everyone pass by in a single stream. Is this the end?

DAUGHTER: For me, yes. Farewell!

POET: Say a parting word!

DAUGHTER: No, I cannot. Do you think your language can express our thoughts?

Enter the DEAN OF THEOLOGY, *raging.*

DEAN OF THEOLOGY: I am disowned by God; I am persecuted by men; I am abandoned by the Government, and scorned by my colleagues. How can I have faith when no one else has faith? How can I defend a God who does not defend His own people? It's all bosh!

He throws a book on the fire and goes out. The POET *snatches the book from the flames.*

POET: Do you know what this is? A Book of Martyrs, a calendar with a martyr for each day of the year.

DAUGHTER: A martyr?

POET: Yes, one who was tortured and put to death for his faith. Tell me why. Do you believe all who are tortured suffer, all who are put to death feel pain? Surely suffering is redemption and death deliverance.

KRISTIN *enters with her paste and strips of paper.*

KRISTIN: I paste, I paste, till there is nothing left to paste.

POET: If heaven itself cracked open, you would try to paste it up: Go away!

KRISTIN: Are there no inner windows in the Castle?

POET: No, none there.

KRISTIN: I'll go then, I'll go.

Exit.

[*As the* DAUGHTER *speaks her last lines the flames rise until the Castle is on fire.*]

DAUGHTER: *The parting time has come; the end draws near.*
Farewell, you child of man, dreamer,
poet, who knows best the way to live.
Above the earth on wings you hover,
plunging at times to graze the dust,
but not to be submerged.

Now I am going, now the hour has come
to leave both friend and place,
how sharp the loss of all I loved,
how deep regret for all destroyed!
Ah, now I know the whole of living's pain!
This then it is to be a human being—
ever to miss the thing one never prized
and feel remorse for what one never did,
to yearn to go, yet long to stay.
And so the human heart is split in two,
emotions by wild horses torn—
conflict, discord and uncertainty.
Farewell! Tell all on earth I shall remember them.
Where I am going, and in your name
carry their lamentations to the throne.
Farewell!

She goes into the Castle. Music is heard. The background is
lighted up by the burning Castle, and now shows a wall of hu-
man faces, questioning, mourning, despairing. While the Castle
is burning, the flower-bud on the roof bursts into a giant chry-
santhemum.

§ FOR COMMENT

The Daughter's statement, "Human beings are to be pitied," is often taken to be a major theme of A *Dream Play*. Is this play a wail of despair? Does the play indicate that man's pitiful condition is permanent, or is there a ray of hope? If optimistic elements exist, tell how they are presented. Do you agree with Strindberg's prefatory statement that there is neither condemnation nor acquittal of mankind in the play but only a depiction of life?

In his prefatory note Strindberg states his intention of reproducing "the disconnected but apparently logical form of a dream," where anything may happen, where time and space no longer matter, where characters may split or multiply, etc. With this announcement, and especially with the play itself, Strindberg tries to break sharply with such familiar dramaturgical devices as the illusion of external reality, suspense, a linear plot progression, and the psychology of human beings in verisimilar relationships. Why does he attempt to abandon such traditional conceptions? Does he completely break with them? Might one trace a plot of sorts concerning Indra's Daughter who makes a journey to and from Earth, going from innocence and ignorance to experience and knowledge? Reread the play, tracing her journey. In what sense is this similar to the traditional treatment of plot? In what sense is it different? Are there other "plots"—

or at least threads—in this play? Do such threads suggest that one should, in examining plays like this, acquire a new view of the use of plot in a play? If so, explain this new view.

Notice how cycles are utilized. Setting aside the prologue, one can see that the play proper begins and ends before the Castle. The Officer repeatedly goes to school. What do such cycles represent? What other cycles do you find in the play? How are they related to each other? Sometimes Strindberg uses parallel actions rather than cycles. An example of this would be the Daughter rescuing the Officer from the Castle and the Officer later rescuing her from the Lawyer. What other patterns can you find? Why does Strindberg construct such patterns? Do they offset the cyclic movement? How do they and the cycles reflect the theme?

Strindberg tries to convey both the content and the form of a dream. By what symbols, actions, and events are the workings of the subconscious made manifest in this play? Does the play's form truly follow that of a dream? Find those places wherein the laws of causality are suspended, wherein "normal" relationships of events are bypassed. What is substituted for them? Is there any sort of logic in the play's sequence of scenes? If not, can the scenes be rearranged without damaging the fabric? Justify your rearrangement. If the scenes cannot be rearranged, explain their relationship to each other and to the play as a whole. Can any scene be omitted? Justify your answer. Do you agree with Strindberg's statement that a single consciousness, the dreamer's, holds sway over all the play's elements? Is there a sleep-to-waking pattern? How is the presence of the dreamer made evident in the work?

Because of its formal characteristics *A Dream Play* has been called expressionist. *Expressionism* presents an outward, external manifestation of that which is essentially internal. In expressionist plays time is shattered. The Officer, for example, changes from youth to old age in the course of just a few minutes. Find other examples of the dissolution of the normal course of time. In expressionism, the personality is fragmented into many parts, each of which becomes a separate personage. In *A Dream Play* the four major male figures—the Officer, the Lawyer, the Quarantine Master, and the Poet—are commonly thought to be aspects of a single character. Define these aspects. Show how they are related to each other and to the Daughter. How might a production of the play suggest their relationship?

Other features of expressionism include the abstraction of the social environment (not its absence, which is quite different), the fragmentation instead of concentration of scenes, unrealistic linguistic devices, unrealistic scenic devices, and general distortion and exaggeration of emotions and thoughts. How are these manifested in this play?

When *A Dream Play* was written, painted drops and back cloths were used in the theater. Strindberg's original stage directions include references to the backdrop rising and coming down. The translator's substitution of less dated terms (for example, "the scene changes") is in harmony, however, with Strindberg's desires. In the play's first Stockholm production in 1907 scenery was projected by a lighting instrument. Although the result disappointed the author in this particular case, he was eager to explore the possibilities of setting the stage by means of projections and lighting. He intended a permanent setting (probably of side wings and borders that would remain unchanged throughout the play) that could suggest various locales, plus a background that would change when required. A production of this play, he felt, should go all the way to reproduce the fluidity of the script. He once suggested the use of red plush curtains with differently colored lights playing on them, creating backgrounds of different colors, and a few scenic accessories to suggest the separate locales (a blackboard for the school, a few statues for Fairhaven, large seashells to suggest the closeness of the sea, etc.). What scenic arrangements do you think might best accomplish Strindberg's purposes of abstraction and fluidity? Explain how your choice might facilitate the movement from one scene to another. How might projected scenery be used? Do you think this play could be produced more effectively as a motion picture? In what scenes might close-ups, long shots, and dissolves help achieve the desired qualities? Or would a motion picture prove to be too realistic a medium for the effective presentation of this play?

Bernard Shaw § 1856–1950

Shaw, who was born in Ireland and moved to England in 1876, was christened George Bernard but preferred not to use his first name. A prominent member of the Fabian Society, he wrote and edited numerous essays and tracts on socialism. His first collection of plays is called Plays Unpleasant *since he tells the audience unpleasant truths about itself, including its guilt in creating and profiting from prostitution* (Mrs. Warren's Profession, 1894). *His second volume is by contrast called* Plays Pleasant *since he emphasizes not society's crimes but its romantic follies, including its idealistic attitudes toward love and war* (Arms and the Man, 1894). *In successive plays (including* Man and Superman, 1903, *and* Major Barbara, 1905) *Shaw's religious concerns become as important as his socialist ethic. Dramatizing the doctrines of the life force and creative evolution, he posits not an anthropomorphic God but an evolutionary force within the universe, striving to perfect itself but making mistakes as it does so. Shaw's ideal Life Force hero is both a philosopher and a man of action acting unselfishly for the benefit of mankind as he tries first to discover the world's "inner will," then to find means of accomplishing that will, and next to help accomplish it.*

In addition to writing and directing plays, Shaw wrote drama criticism (The Quintessence of Ibsenism, 1891), *theater reviews* (1895–1898), *music reviews* (1876–1894), *novels (including* Love Among the Artists, 1881), *and screenplays (including* Pygmalion, 1938).

Pygmalion[1]

A ROMANCE IN FIVE ACTS

CHARACTERS

ELIZA DOOLITTLE
HENRY HIGGINS
ALFRED DOOLITTLE
COLONEL PICKERING
MRS. HIGGINS
MRS. PEARCE
FREDDY EYNSFORD HILL
MRS. EYNSFORD HILL
CLARA EYNSFORD HILL
A PARLOR-MAID
SEVERAL BYSTANDERS

NOTE FOR TECHNICIANS

A complete representation of the play as printed in this edition is technically possible only on the cinema screen or on stages furnished with exceptionally elaborate machinery. For ordinary theatrical use the scenes separated by rows of asterisks are to be omitted.

In the dialogue an e upside down[2] indicates the indefinite vowel, sometimes called obscure or neutral, for which, though it is one of the commonest sounds in English speech, our wretched alphabet has no letter.

§ ACT I

London at 11.15 *p.m. Torrents of heavy summer rain. Cab whistles blowing frantically in all directions. Pedestrians running for shelter into the portico of St. Paul's church (not Wren's[3] cathedral but Inigo Jones's[4] church in Covent Garden vegetable market), among them a lady and her daughter in evening dress. All are peering out gloomily at the rain, except one man with his back turned to the rest, wholly preoccupied with a notebook in which he is writing.*

The church clock strikes the first quarter.

[1] *Pygmalion:* In *Metamorphoses,* Ovid tells of Pygmalion, a mythical sculptor, who vowed never to marry but to devote himself entirely to his art. Pygmalion created a statue of a beautiful woman, whom he named Galatea, and fell in love with her. In answer to his prayer, the goddess Venus gave the statue life. Pygmalion and Galatea married.

[2] ə: Pronounced as the second vowel in *other*.

[3] *Wren:* Sir Christopher Wren (1632–1723), British architect.

[4] *Jones:* Inigo Jones (1573–1652), British architect and scene-designer.

THE DAUGHTER (*in the space between the central pillars, close to the one on her left*): I'm getting chilled to the bone. What can Freddy be doing all this time? He's been gone twenty minutes.

THE MOTHER (*on her daughter's right*): Not so long. But he ought to have got us a cab by this.

A BYSTANDER (*on the lady's right*): He wont[5] get no cab not until half-past eleven, missus, when they come back after dropping their theatre fares.

THE MOTHER: But we must have a cab. We cant stand here until half-past eleven. It's too bad.

THE BYSTANDER: Well, it ain't my fault, missus.

THE DAUGHTER: If Freddy had a bit of gumption, he would have got one at the theatre door.

THE MOTHER: What could he have done, poor boy?

THE DAUGHTER: Other people got cabs. Why couldnt he?

Freddy rushes in out of the rain from the Southampton Street side, and comes between them closing a dripping umbrella. He is a young man of twenty, in evening dress, very wet round the ankles.

THE DAUGHTER: Well, havnt you got a cab?

FREDDY: Theres not one to be had for love or money.

THE MOTHER: Oh, Freddy, there must be one. You cant have tried.

THE DAUGHTER: It's too tiresome. Do you expect us to go and get one ourselves?

FREDDY: I tell you theyre all engaged. The rain was so sudden: nobody was prepared; and everybody had to take a cab. Ive been to Charing Cross[6] one way and nearly to Ludgate Circus the other; and they were all engaged.

THE MOTHER: Did you try Trafalgar Square?

FREDDY: There wasn't one at Trafalgar Square.

THE DAUGHTER: Did you try?

FREDDY: I tried as far as Charing Cross Station. Did you expect me to walk to Hammersmith?

THE DAUGHTER: You havnt tried at all.

THE MOTHER: You really are very helpless, Freddy. Go again; and dont come back until you have found a cab.

FREDDY: I shall simply get soaked for nothing.

THE DAUGHTER: And what about us? Are we to stay here all night in this draught, with next to nothing on? You selfish pig—

FREDDY: Oh, very well: I'll go, I'll go. (*He opens his umbrella and dashes*

---

[5] *wont:* This is not a typographical error but an instance of Shaw's punctuation and spelling anomalies. Shaw omitted apostrophes from such words as *won't* and *isn't*, while retaining them in other words, e.g., *I'm* and *it's*. He spells the verb *show*, which rhymes with *sew*, as *shew*, but he spells the noun *show*. Instead of using *italics* for emphasis, Shaw uses s p a c e s between letters.

[6] *Charing Cross:* This and other names, unless otherwise noted, are streets, squares, sections, or places in London.

*off Strandwards,[7] but comes into collision with a flower girl who is
hurrying in for shelter, knocking her basket out of her hands. A blinding flash of lightning, followed instantly by a rattling peal of thunder,
orchestrates the incident.)*

THE FLOWER GIRL: Nah then, Freddy: look wh' y' gowin, deah.

FREDDY: Sorry. (*He rushes off.*)

THE FLOWER GIRL (*picking up her scattered flowers and replacing them in
the basket*): Theres menners f' yer! Tə-oo banches o voylets trod into
the mad. (*She sits down on the plinth of the column, sorting her
flowers, on the lady's right. She is not at all a romantic figure. She is
perhaps eighteen, perhaps twenty, hardly older. She wears a little sailor
hat of black straw that has long been exposed to the dust and soot of
London and has seldom if ever been brushed. Her hair needs washing
rather badly: its mousy color can hardly be natural. She wears a shoddy
black coat that reaches nearly to her knees and is shaped to her waist.
She has a brown skirt with a coarse apron. Her boots are much the
worse for wear. She is no doubt as clean as she can afford to be; but
compared to the ladies she is very dirty. Her features are no worse than
theirs; but their condition leaves something to be desired; and she
needs the services of a dentist.*)

THE MOTHER: How do you know that my son's name is Freddy, pray?

THE FLOWER GIRL: Ow, eez yə-ooa san, is e? Wal, fewd dan y' də-ooty
bawmz a mathre should, eed now bettern to spawl a pore gel's flahrzn
than run awy athaht pyin. Will ye-oo py me f'them? (*Here, with apolo-
gies, this desperate attempt to represent her dialect without a phonetic
alphabet must be abandoned as unintelligible outside London.*)

THE DAUGHTER: Do nothing of the sort, mother. The idea!

THE MOTHER: Please allow me, Clara. Have you any pennies?

THE DAUGHTER: No. Ive nothing smaller than sixpence.

THE FLOWER GIRL (*hopefully*): I can give you change for a tanner,[8] kind
lady.

THE MOTHER (*to Clara*): Give it to me. (*Clara parts reluctantly.*) Now
(*To the girl*) This is for your flowers.

THE FLOWER GIRL: Thank you kindly, lady.

THE DAUGHTER: Make her give you the change. These things are only a
penny a bunch.

THE MOTHER: Do hold your tongue, Clara. (*To the girl*) You can keep the
change.

THE FLOWER GIRL: Oh, thank you, lady.

THE MOTHER: Now tell me how you know that young gentleman's name.

THE FLOWER GIRL: I didnt.

THE MOTHER: I heard you call him by it. Dont try to deceive me.

---

[7] *Strandwards:* Toward The Strand (a street).

[8] *tanner:* Six pence.

THE FLOWER GIRL (*protesting*): Who's trying to deceive you? I called him Freddy or Charlie same as you might yourself if you was talking to a stranger and wished to be pleasant.

THE DAUGHTER: Sixpence thrown away! Really, mamma, you might have spared Freddy that. (*She retreats in disgust behind the pillar.*)

An elderly gentleman of the amiable military type rushes into the shelter, and closes a dripping umbrella. He is in the same plight as Freddy, very wet about the ankles. He is in evening dress, with a light overcoat. He takes the place left vacant by the daughter.

THE GENTLEMAN: Phew!

THE MOTHER (*to the gentleman*): Oh, sir, is there any sign of its stopping?

THE GENTLEMAN: I'm afraid not. It started worse than ever about two minutes ago. (*He goes to the plinth beside the flower girl; puts up his foot on it; and stoops to turn down his trouser ends.*)

THE MOTHER: Oh dear! (*She retires sadly and joins her daughter.*)

THE FLOWER GIRL (*taking advantage of the military gentleman's proximity to establish friendly relations with him*): If it's worse, it's a sign it's nearly over. So cheer up, Captain; and buy a flower off a poor girl.

THE GENTLEMAN: I'm sorry. I havnt any change.

THE FLOWER GIRL: I can give you change, Captain.

THE GENTLEMAN: For a sovereign?[9] Ive nothing less.

THE FLOWER GIRL: Garn! Oh do buy a flower off me, Captain. I can change half-a-crown.[10] Take this for tuppence.[11]

THE GENTLEMAN: Now dont be troublesome: theres a good girl. (*Trying his pockets*) I really havnt any change—Stop: heres three hapence,[12] if thats any use to you. (*He retreats to the other pillar.*)

THE FLOWER GIRL (*disappointed, but thinking three half-pence better than nothing*): Thank you, sir.

THE BYSTANDER (*to the girl*): You be careful: give him a flower for it. Theres a bloke[13] here behind taking down every blessed word youre saying. (*All turn to the man who is taking notes.*)

THE FLOWER GIRL (*springing up terrified*): I aint done nothing wrong by speaking to the gentleman. Ive a right to sell flowers if I keep off the kerb. (*Hysterically*) I'm a respectable girl: so help me, I never spoke to him except to ask him to buy a flower off me.

General hubbub, mostly sympathetic to the flower girl, but deprecating her excessive sensibility. Cries of: Dont start hollerin. Who's hurting you? Nobody's going to touch you. Whats the good of

---

[9] *sovereign:* One pound (twenty shillings make a pound).
[10] *half-a-crown:* Two shillings, six pence (twelve pence, or pennies, make a shilling).
[11] *tuppence:* Two pence.
[12] *hapence:* Half pennies (the first syllable, which is accented, is pronounced *hey*).
[13] *bloke:* Man.

fussing? Steady on. Easy easy, etc., *come from the elderly staid spectators, who pat her comfortingly. Less patient ones bid her shut her head, or ask her roughly what is wrong with her. A remoter group, not knowing what the matter is, crowd in and increase the noise with question and answer:* Whats the row? Whatshe do? Where is he? A tec taking her down. What! him? Yes: him over there: Took money off the gentleman, etc.

THE FLOWER GIRL (*breaking through them to the gentleman, crying wildly*): Oh, sir, dont let him charge me. You dunno what it means to me. Theyll take away my character and drive me on the streets for speaking to gentlemen. They—

THE NOTE TAKER (*coming forward on her right, the rest crowding after him*): There! there! there! there! who's hurting you, you silly girl? What do you take me for?

THE BYSTANDER: It's aw rawt: e's a gentleman: look at his bə-oots. (*Explaining to the note taker*) She thought you was a copper's nark, sir.

THE NOTE TAKER (*with quick interest*): Whats a copper's nark?

THE BYSTANDER (*inapt at definition*): It's a—well, it's a copper's nark, as you might say. What else would you call it? A sort of informer.

THE FLOWER GIRL (*still hysterical*): I take my Bible oath I never said a word—

THE NOTE TAKER (*overbearing but good-humored*): Oh, shut up, shut up. Do I look like a policeman?

THE FLOWER GIRL (*far from reassured*): Then what did you take down my words for? How do I know whether you took me down right? You just shew me what youve wrote about me. (*The note taker opens his book and holds it steadily under her nose, though the pressure of the mob trying to read it over his shoulders would upset a weaker man.*) Whats that? That aint proper writing. I cant read that.

THE NOTE TAKER: I can. (*Reads, reproducing her pronunciation exactly.*) "Cheer ap, Keptin; n' baw ya flahr orf a pore gel."

THE FLOWER GIRL (*much distressed*): It's because I called him Captain. I meant no harm. (*To the gentleman*) Oh, sir, dont let him lay a charge agen me for a word like that. You—

THE GENTLEMAN: Charge! I make no charge. (*To the note taker*) Really, sir, if you are a detective, you need not begin protecting me against molestation by young women until I ask you. Anybody could see that the girl meant no harm.

THE BYSTANDERS GENERALLY (*demonstrating against police espionage*): Course they could. What business is it of yours? You mind your own affairs. He wants promotion, he does. Taking down people's words! Girl never said a word to him. What harm if she did? Nice thing a girl cant shelter from the rain without being insulted, etc., etc., etc. (*She is conducted by the more sympathetic demonstrators back to her plinth, where she resumes her seat and struggles with her emotion.*)

THE BYSTANDER: He aint a tec.[14] He's a blooming busybody: thats what he is. I tell you, look at his bə-oots.

THE NOTE TAKER (*turning on him genially*): And how are all your people down at Selsey? [15]

THE BYSTANDER (*suspiciously*): Who told you my people come from Selsey?

THE NOTE TAKER: Never you mind. They did. (*To the girl*) How do you come to be up so far east? You were born in Lisson Grove.

THE FLOWER GIRL (*appalled*): Oh, what harm is there in my leaving Lisson Grove? It wasnt fit for a pig to live in; and I had to pay four-and-six a week. (*In tears*) Oh, boo—hoo—oo—

THE NOTE TAKER: Live where you like; but stop that noise.

THE GENTLEMAN (*to the girl*): Come, come! he cant touch you: you have a right to live where you please.

A SARCASTIC BYSTANDER (*thrusting himself between the note taker and the gentleman*): Park Lane, for instance. I'd like to go into the Housing Question with you, I would.

THE FLOWER GIRL (*subsiding into a brooding melancholy over her basket, and talking very low-spiritedly to herself*): I'm a good girl, I am.

THE SARCASTIC BYSTANDER (*not attending to her*): Do you know where I come from?

THE NOTE TAKER (*promptly*): Hoxton.

Titterings. Popular interest in the note taker's performance increases.

THE SARCASTIC ONE (*amazed*): Well, who said I didn't? Bly me! you know everything, you do.

THE FLOWER GIRL (*still nursing her sense of injury*): Aint no call to meddle with me, he aint.

THE BYSTANDER (*to her*): Of course he aint. Dont you stand it from him. (*To the note taker*) See here: what call have you to know about people what never offered to meddle with you?

THE FLOWER GIRL: Let him say what he likes. I dont want to have no truck[16] with him.

THE BYSTANDER: You take us for dirt under your feet, dont you? Catch you taking liberties with a gentleman!

THE SARCASTIC BYSTANDER: Yes: tell him where he come from if you want to go fortune-telling.

THE NOTE TAKER: Cheltenham,[17] Harrow,[18] Cambridge,[19] and India.

THE GENTLEMAN: Quite right.

[14] *tec*: Detective.

[15] *Selsey*: A city in Sussex.

[16] *truck*: Dealings.

[17] *Cheltenham*: A city in Gloucestershire.

[18] *Harrow*: A famous public school (what we in the United States would call a private school) for boys, in Middlesex.

[19] *Cambridge*: The university, also public (private), in Cambridgeshire.

Great laughter. Reaction in the note taker's favor. Exclamations of: He knows all about it. Told him proper. Hear him tell the toff [20] where he come from? etc.

THE GENTLEMAN: May I ask, sir, do you do this for your living at a music hall?

THE NOTE TAKER: I've thought of that. Perhaps I shall some day.
The rain has stopped; and the persons on the outside of the crowd begin to drop off.

THE FLOWER GIRL (*resenting the reaction*): He's no gentleman, he aint, to interfere with a poor girl.

THE DAUGHTER (*out of patience, pushing her way rudely to the front and displacing the gentleman, who politely retires to the other side of the pillar*): What on earth is Freddy doing? I shall get pneumownia if I stay in this draught any longer.

THE NOTE TAKER (*to himself, hastily making a note of her pronunciation of "monia"*): Earlscourt.

THE DAUGHTER (*violently*): Will you please keep your impertinent remarks to yourself.

THE NOTE TAKER: Did I say that out loud? I didnt mean to. I beg your pardon. Your mother's Epsom,[21] unmistakeably.

THE MOTHER (*advancing between the daughter and the note taker*): How very curious! I was brought up in Largelady Park, near Epsom.

THE NOTE TAKER (*uproariously amused*): Ha! ha! What a devil of a name! Excuse me. (*To the daughter*) You want a cab, do you?

THE DAUGHTER: Dont dare speak to me.

THE MOTHER: Oh please, please, Clara. (*Her daughter repudiates her with an angry shrug and retires haughtily.*) We should be so grateful to you, sir, if you found us a cab. (*The note taker produces a whistle.*) Oh, thank you. (*She joins her daughter.*)

The note taker blows a piercing blast.

THE SARCASTIC BYSTANDER: There! I knowed he was a plainclothes copper.

THE BYSTANDER: That aint a police whistle: thats a sporting whistle.

THE FLOWER GIRL (*still preoccupied with her wounded feelings*): He's no right to take away my character. My character is the same to me as any lady's.

THE NOTE TAKER: I don't know whether youve noticed it; but the rain stopped about two minutes ago.

THE BYSTANDER: So it has. Why didn't you say so before? and us losing our time listening to your silliness! (*He walks off towards the Strand.*)

THE SARCASTIC BYSTANDER: I can tell where you come from. You come from Anwell. Go back there.

THE NOTE TAKER (*helpfully*): Hanwell.

[20] *toff*: Gentleman.
[21] *Epsom*: In Surrey.

THE SARCASTIC BYSTANDER (*affecting great distinction of speech*): Thenk you, teacher. Haw haw! So long. (*He touches his hat with mock respect and strolls off.*)

THE FLOWER GIRL: Frightening people like that? How would he like it himself?

THE MOTHER: It's quite fine now, Clara. We can walk to a motor bus. Come. (*She gathers her skirts above her ankles and hurries off towards the Strand.*)

THE DAUGHTER: But the cab—(*Her mother is out of hearing.*) Oh, how tiresome! (*She follows angrily.*)

> All the rest have gone except the note taker, the gentleman, and the flower girl, who sits arranging her basket, and still pitying herself in murmurs.

THE FLOWER GIRL: Poor girl! Hard enough for her to live without being worrited and chivied.[22]

THE GENTLEMAN (*returning to his former place on the note taker's left*): How do you do it, if I may ask?

THE NOTE TAKER: Simply phonetics. The science of speech. Thats my profession: also my hobby. Happy is the man who can make a living by his hobby! You can spot an Irishman or a Yorkshireman by his brogue. I can place any man within six miles. I can place him within two miles in London. Sometimes within two streets.

THE FLOWER GIRL: Ought to be ashamed of himself, unmanly coward!

THE GENTLEMAN: But is there a living in that?

THE NOTE TAKER: Oh yes. Quite a fat one. This is an age of upstarts. Men begin in Kentish Town with £80 a year, and end in Park Lane with a hundred thousand. They want to drop Kentish Town; but they give themselves away every time they open their mouths. Now I can teach them—

THE FLOWER GIRL: Let him mind his own business and leave a poor girl—

THE NOTE TAKER (*explosively*): Woman: cease this detestable boohooing instantly; or else seek the shelter of some other place of worship.

THE FLOWER GIRL (*with feeble defiance*): Ive a right to be here if I like, same as you.

THE NOTE TAKER: A woman who utters such depressing and disgusting sounds has no right to be anywhere—no right to live. Remember that you are a human being with a soul and the divine gift of articulate speech: that your native language is the language of Shakespeare and Milton and The Bible; and dont sit there crooning like a bilious pigeon.

THE FLOWER GIRL (*quite overwhelmed, looking up at him in mingled wonder and deprecation without daring to raise her head*): Ah-ah-ah-ow-ow-ow-oo!

THE NOTE TAKER (*whipping out his book*): Heavens! what a sound! (*He

---

[22] *worrited and chivied*: Worried and harassed.

writes; *then holds out the book and reads, reproducing her vowels exactly.*) Ah-ah-ah-ow-ow-ow-oo!

THE FLOWER GIRL (*tickled by the performance, and laughing in spite of herself*): Garn!

THE NOTE TAKER: You see this creature with her kerbstone English: the English that will keep her in the gutter to the end of her days. Well, sir, in three months I could pass that girl off as a duchess at an ambassador's garden party. I could even get her a place as lady's maid or shop assistant, which requires better English.

THE FLOWER GIRL: What's that you say?

THE NOTE TAKER: Yes, you squashed cabbage leaf, you disgrace to the noble architecture of these columns, you incarnate insult to the English language: I could pass you off as the Queen of Sheba. (*To the Gentleman*) Can you believe that?

THE GENTLEMAN: Of course I can. I am myself a student of Indian dialects; and—

THE NOTE TAKER (*eagerly*): Are you? Do you know Colonel Pickering, the author of Spoken Sanscrit?

THE GENTLEMAN: I am Colonel Pickering. Who are you?

THE NOTE TAKER: Henry Higgins, author of Higgins's Universal Alphabet.

PICKERING (*with enthusiasm*): I came from India to meet you.

HIGGINS: I was going to India to meet you.

PICKERING: Where do you live?

HIGGINS: 27A Wimpole Street. Come and see me tomorrow.

PICKERING: I'm at the Carlton.[23] Come with me now and lets have a jaw over some supper.

HIGGINS: Right you are.

THE FLOWER GIRL (*to Pickering, as he passes her*): Buy a flower, kind gentleman. I'm short for my lodging.

PICKERING: I really havnt any change. I'm sorry. (*He goes away.*)

HIGGINS (*shocked at the girl's mendacity*): Liar. You said you could change half-a-crown.

THE FLOWER GIRL (*rising in desperation*): You ought to be stuffed with nails, you ought. (*Flinging the basket at his feet*) Take the whole blooming basket for sixpence.

The church clock strikes the second quarter.

HIGGINS (*hearing in it the voice of God, rebuking him for his Pharisaic want of charity to the poor girl*): A reminder. (*He raises his hat solemnly; then throws a handful of money into the basket and follows Pickering.*)

THE FLOWER GIRL (*picking up a half-crown*): Ah-ow-ooh! (*Picking up a couple of florins*)[24] Aaah-ow-ooh! (*Picking up several coins*) Aaaaah-ow-ooh! (*Picking up a half-sovereign*) Aaaaaaaaaaaah-ow-ooh!!!

[23] *Carlton*: A London hotel.
[24] *florin*: A florin is worth two shillings.

FREDDY (*springing out of a taxicab*): Got one at last. Hallo! (*To the girl*) Where are the two ladies that were here?

THE FLOWER GIRL: They walked to the bus when the rain stopped.

FREDDY: And left me with a cab on my hands! Damnation!

THE FLOWER GIRL (*with grandeur*): Never mind, young man. I'm going home in a taxi. (*She sails off to the cab. The driver puts his hand behind him and holds the door firmly shut against her. Quite understanding his mistrust, she shews him her handful of money.*) A taxi fare aint no object to me, Charlie. (*He grins and opens the door.*) Here. What about the basket?

THE TAXIMAN: Give it here. Tuppence extra.

LIZA: No: I dont want nobody to see it. (*She crushes it into the cab and and gets in, continuing the conversation through the window.*) Goodbye, Freddy.

FREDDY (*dazedly raising his hat*): Goodbye.

TAXIMAN: Where to?

LIZA: Bucknam Pellis (Buckingham Palace).

TAXIMAN: What d'ye mean—Bucknam Pellis?

LIZA: Dont you know where it is? In the Green Park, where the King lives. Goodbye, Freddy. Dont let me keep you standing there. Goodbye.

FREDDY: Goodbye. (*He goes.*)

TAXIMAN: Here? Whats this about Bucknam Pellis? What business have you at Bucknam Pellis?

LIZA: Of course I havnt none. But I wasn't going to let him know that. You drive me home.

TAXIMAN: And wheres home?

LIZA: Angel Court, Drury Lane, next Meiklejohn's oil shop.

TAXIMAN: That sounds more like it, Judy. (*He drives off.*)

*   *   *   *   *   *   *   *

Let us follow the taxi to the entrance to Angel Court, a narrow little archway between two shops, one of them Meiklejohn's oil shop. When it stops there, Eliza gets out, dragging her basket with her.

LIZA: How much?

TAXIMAN (*indicating the taximeter*): Cant you read? A shilling.

LIZA: A shilling for two minutes!!

TAXIMAN: Two minutes or ten: it's all the same.

LIZA: Well, I dont call it right.

TAXIMAN: Ever been in a taxi before?

LIZA (*with dignity*): Hundreds and thousands of times, young man.

TAXIMAN (*laughing at her*): Good for you, Judy. Keep the shilling, darling, with best love from all at home. Good luck! (*He drives off.*)

LIZA (*humiliated*): Impidence!

She picks up the basket and trudges up the alley with it to her lodging: *a small room with very old wall paper hanging loose in the damp places. A broken pane in the window is mended with paper. A portrait of a popular actor and a fashion plate of ladies' dresses, all wildly beyond poor Eliza's means, both torn from news-papers, are pinned up on the wall. A birdcage hangs in the window; but its tenant died long ago: it remains as a memorial only.*

These are the only visible luxuries: the rest is the irreducible minimum of poverty's needs: a wretched bed heaped with all sorts of coverings that have any warmth in them, a draped packing case with a basin and jug on it and a little looking glass over it, a chair and table, the refuse of some suburban kitchen, and an American alarum clock on the shelf above the unused fireplace: the whole lighted with a gas lamp with a penny in the slot meter. Rent: four shillings a week.

Here Eliza, chronically weary, but too excited to go to bed, sits, counting her new riches and dreaming and planning what to do with them, until the gas goes out, when she enjoys for the first time the sensation of being able to put in another penny without grudging it. This prodigal mood does not extinguish her gnawing sense of the need for economy sufficiently to prevent her from calculating that she can dream and plan in bed more cheaply and warmly than sitting up without a fire. So she takes off her shawl and skirt and adds them to the miscellaneous bedclothes. Then she kicks off her shoes and gets into bed without any further change.

§ ACT II

Next day at 11 a.m. Higgins's laboratory in Wimpole Street. It is a room on the first floor, looking on the street, and was meant for the drawing room. The double doors are in the middle of the back wall; and persons entering find in the corner to their right two tall file cabinets at right angles to one another against the walls. In this corner stands a flat writing table, on which are a phonograph, a laryngoscope, a row of tiny organ pipes with a bellows, a set of lamp chimneys for singing flames with burners attached to a gas plug in the wall by an indiarubber tube, several tuning-forks of different sizes, a life-size image of half a human head, shewing in section the vocal organs, and a box containing a supply of wax cylinders for the phonograph.

Further down the room, on the same side, is a fireplace, with a comfortable leather-covered easy-chair at the side of the hearth nearest the door, and a coal-scuttle. There is a clock on the mantlepiece. Between the fireplace and the phonograph table is a stand for newspapers.

On the other side of the central door, to the left of the visitor, is a cabinet of shallow drawers. On it is a telephone and the telephone directory. The corner beyond, and most of the side wall, is occupied by a grand piano, with the keyboard at the end furthest from the door, and a bench for the players extending the full length of the keyboard. On the piano is a dessert dish heaped with fruit and sweets, mostly chocolates.

The middle of the room is clear. Besides the easy-chair, the piano bench, and two chairs at the phonograph table, there is one stray chair. It stands near the fireplace. On the walls, engravings: mostly Piranesis[25] and mezzotint portraits. No paintings.

Pickering is seated at the table, putting down some cards and a tuning-fork which he has been using. Higgins is standing up near him, closing two or three file drawers which are hanging out. He appears in the morning light as a robust, vital, appetizing sort of man of forty or thereabouts, dressed in a professional-looking black frock-coat with a white linen collar and black silk tie. He is of energetic, scientific type, heartily, even violently interested in everything that can be studied as a scientific subject, and careless about himself and other people, including their feelings. He is, in fact, but for his years and size, rather like a very impetuous baby "taking notice" eagerly and loudly, and requiring almost as much watching to keep him out of unintended mischief. His manner varies from genial bullying when he is in a good humor to stormy petulance when anything goes wrong; but he is so entirely frank and void of malice that he remains likeable even in his least reasonable moments.

HIGGINS (*as he shuts the last drawer*): Well, I think thats the whole show.

PICKERING: It's really amazing. I havnt taken half of it in, you know.

HIGGINS: Would you like to go over any of it again?

PICKERING (*rising and coming to the fireplace, where he plants himself with his back to the fire*): No, thank you: not now. I'm quite done up for this morning.

HIGGINS (*following him, and standing beside him on his left*): Tired of listening to sounds?

PICKERING: Yes. It's a fearful strain. I rather fancied myself because I can pronounce twenty-four distinct vowel sounds; but your hundred and thirty beat me. I cant hear a bit of difference between most of them.

HIGGINS (*chuckling, and going over to the piano to eat sweets*): Oh, that comes with practice. You hear no difference at first; but you keep on listening, and presently you find theyre all as different as A from B. (*Mrs Pearce looks in: she is Higgins's housekeeper.*) Whats the matter?

MRS PEARCE (*hesitating, evidently perplexed*): A young woman asks to see you, sir.

HIGGINS: A young woman! What does she want?

---

[25] *Piranesi:* Gian Battista Piranesi (1720–1728), Venetian engraver and scene-designer.

MRS PEARCE: Well, sir, she says youll be glad to see her when you know what she's come about. She's quite a common girl, sir. Very common indeed. I should have sent her away, only I thought perhaps you wanted her to talk into your machines. I hope Ive not done wrong; but really you see such queer people somctimes—youll excuse me, I'm sure, sir—

HIGGINS: Oh, thats all right, Mrs Pearce. Has she an interesting accent?

MRS PEARCE: Oh, something dreadful, sir, really. I dont know how you can take an interest in it.

HIGGINS (*to Pickering*): Lets have her up. Shew her up, Mrs Pearce. (*He rushes across to his working table and picks out a cylinder to use on the phonograph.*)

MRS PEARCE (*only half resigned to it*): Very well, sir. It's for you to say. (*She goes downstairs.*)

HIGGINS: This is rather a bit of luck. I'll shew you how I make records. We'll set her talking; and I'll take it down first in Bell's Visible Speech;[26] then in broad Romic;[27] and then we'll get on the phonograph so that you can turn her on as often as you like with the written transcript before you.

MRS PEARCE (*returning*): This is the young woman, sir.

The flower girl enters in state. She has a hat with three ostrich feathers, orange, sky-blue, and red. She has a nearly clean apron, and the shoddy coat has been tidied a little. The pathos of this deplorable figure, with its innocent vanity and consequential air, touches Pickering, who has already straightened himself in the presence of Mrs Pearce. But as to Higgins, the only distinction he makes between men and women is that when he is neither bullying nor exclaiming to the heavens against some feather-weight cross, he coaxes women as a child coaxes its nurse when it wants to get anything out of her.

HIGGINS (*brusquely, recognizing her with unconcealed disappointment, and at once, babylike, making an intolerable grievance of it*): Why, this is the girl I jotted down last night. She's no use: I've got all the records I want of the Lisson Grove lingo; and I'm not going to waste another cylinder on it. (*To the girl*) Be off with you: I dont want you.

THE FLOWER GIRL: Dont you be so saucy. You aint heard what I come for yet. (*To Mrs Pearce, who is waiting at the door for further instructions*) Did you tell him I come in a taxi?

MRS PEARCE: Nonsense, girl! what do you think a gentleman like Mr Higgins cares what you came in?

THE FLOWER GIRL: Oh, we are proud! he aint above giving lessons, not him:

[26] *Bell's Visible Speech:* A method of transcribing sounds, devised by Alexander Melville Bell (1819–1905), father of Alexander Graham Bell (1847–1922), inventor of the telephone.

[27] *Romic:* A method of phonetic notation invented by Henry Sweet (1845–1912), a philologist and linguist, on whom Higgins is partly based.

I heard him say so. Well, I aint come here to ask for any compliment; and if my money's not good enough I can go elsewhere.

HIGGINS: Good enough for what?

THE FLOWER GIRL: Good enough for yə-oo. Now you know, dont you? I've come to have lessons, I am. And to pay for em tə-oo: make no mistake.

HIGGINS (*stupent*): Well!!! (*Recovering his breath with a gasp*) What do you expect me to say to you?

THE FLOWER GIRL: Well, if you was a gentleman, you might ask me to sit down, I think. Dont I tell you I'm bringing you business?

HIGGINS: Pickering: shall we ask this baggage to sit down, or shall we throw her out of the window?

THE FLOWER GIRL (*running away in terror to the piano, where she turns at bay*): Ah-ah-oh-ow-ow-ow-oo! (*Wounded and whimpering*) I wont be called a baggage when Ive offered to pay like any lady.
Motionless, the two men stare at her from the other side of the room, amazed.

PICKERING (*gently*): But what is it you want?

THE FLOWER GIRL: I want to be a lady in a flower shop stead of sellin at the corner of Tottenham Court Road. But they wont take me unless I can talk more genteel. He said he could teach me. Well, here I am ready to pay him—not asking any favor—and he treats me zif I was dirt.

MRS PEARCE: How can you be such a foolish ignorant girl as to think you could afford to pay Mr Higgins?

THE FLOWER GIRL: Why shouldnt I? I know what lessons cost as well as you do; and I'm ready to pay.

HIGGINS: How much?

THE FLOWER GIRL (*coming back to him, triumphant*): Now youre talking! I thought youd come off it when you saw a chance of getting back a bit of what you chucked at me last night. (*Confidentially*) Youd had a drop in, hadnt you?

HIGGINS (*peremptorily*): Sit down.

THE FLOWER GIRL: Oh, if youre going to make a compliment of it—

HIGGINS (*thundering at her*): Sit down.

MRS PEARCE (*severely*): Sit down, girl. Do as youre told.

THE FLOWER GIRL: Ah-ah-ah-ow-ow-oo! (*She stands, half rebellious, half bewildered.*)

PICKERING (*very courteous*): Wont you sit down? (*He places the stray chair near the hearthrug between himself and Higgins.*)

LIZA (*coyly*): Dont mind if I do. (*She sits down. Pickering returns to the hearthrug.*)

HIGGINS: Whats your name?

THE FLOWER GIRL: Liza Doolittle.

HIGGINS (*declaiming gravely*):
> Eliza, Elizabeth, Betsy and Bess,
> They went to the woods to get a bird's nes':

PICKERING: They found a nest with four eggs in it:

HIGGINS: They took one apiece, and left three in it.

They laugh heartily at their own fun.

LIZA: Oh, dont be silly.

MRS PEARCE (*placing herself behind Eliza's chair*: You mustnt speak to the gentleman like that.

LIZA: Well, why wont he speak sensible to me?

HIGGINS: Come back to business. How much do you propose to pay me for the lessons?

LIZA: Oh, I know whats right. A lady friend of mine gets French lessons for eighteenpence an hour from a real French gentleman. Well, you wouldnt have the face[28] to ask me the same for teaching me my own language as you would for French; so I wont give more than a shilling. Take it or leave it.

HIGGINS (*walking up and down the room, rattling his keys and his cash in his pockets*): You know, Pickering, if you consider a shilling, not as a simple shilling, but as a percentage of this girl's income, it works out as fully equivalent to sixty or seventy guineas from a millionaire.

PICKERING: How so?

HIGGINS: Figure it out. A millionaire has about £150 a day. She earns about half-a-crown.

LIZA (*haughtily*): Who told you I only—

HIGGINS (*continuing*): She offers me two-fifths of her day's income for a lesson. Two-fifths of a millionaire's income for a day would be somewhere about £60. It's handsome. By George, it's enormous! it's the biggest offer I ever had.

LIZA (*rising, terrified*): Sixty pounds! What are you talking about? I never offered you sixty pounds. Where would I get—

HIGGINS: Hold your tongue.

LIZA (*weeping*): But I aint got sixty pounds. Oh—

MRS PEARCE: Dont cry, you silly girl. Sit down. Nobody is going to touch your money.

HIGGINS: Somebody is going to touch you, with a broomstick, if you dont stop snivelling. Sit down.

LIZA (*obeying slowly*): Ah-ah-ah-ow-oo-o! One would think you was my father.

HIGGINS: If I decide to teach you, I'll be worse than two fathers to you. Here! (*He offers her his silk handkerchief.*)

LIZA: Whats this for?

HIGGINS: To wipe your eyes. To wipe any part of your face that feels moist. Remember: thats your handkerchief; and thats your sleeve. Dont mistake the one for the other if you wish to become a lady in a shop.

Liza, utterly bewildered, stares helplessly at him.

MRS PEARCE: It's no use talking to her like that, Mr Higgins: she doesnt

[28] *face*: Boldness.

understand you. Besides, youre quite wrong: she doesnt do it that way at all. (*She takes the hankerchief.*)

LIZA (*snatching it*): Here! You give me that handkerchief. He gev it to me, not to you.

PICKERING (*laughing*): He did. I think it must be regarded as her property, Mrs Pearce.

MRS PEARCE (*resigning herself*): Serve you right, Mr Higgins.

PICKERING: Higgins: I'm interested. What about the ambassador's garden party? I'll say youre the greatest teacher alive if you make that good. I'll bet you all the expenses of the experiment you cant do it. And I'll pay for the lessons.

LIZA: Oh, you are real good. Thank you, Captain.

HIGGINS (*tempted, looking at her*): It's almost irresistible. She's so deliciously low—so horribly dirty—

LIZA (*protesting extremely*): Ah-ah-ah-ah-ow-ow-oo-oo!!! I aint dirty: I washed my face and hands afore I come, I did.

PICKERING: Youre certainly not going to turn her head with flattery, Higgins.

MRS PEARCE (*uneasy*): Oh, dont say that, sir: theres more ways than one of turning a girl's head; and nobody can do it better than Mr Higgins, though he may not always mean it. I do hope, sir, you wont encourage him to do anything foolish.

HIGGINS (*becoming excited as the idea grows on him*): What is life but a series of inspired follies? The difficulty is to find them to do. Never lose a chance: it doesnt come every day. I shall make a duchess of this draggletailed guttersnipe.

LIZA (*strongly deprecating this view of her*): Ah-ah-ah-ow-ow-oo!

HIGGINS (*carried away*): Yes: in six months—in three if she has a good ear and a quick tongue—I'll take her anywhere and pass her off as anything. We'll start today: now! this moment! Take her away and clean her, Mrs Pearce. Monkey Brand,[29] if it wont come off any other way. Is there a good fire in the kitchen?

MRS PEARCE (*protesting*): Yes; but—

HIGGINS (*storming on*): Take all her clothes off and burn them. Ring up Whitely[30] or somebody for new ones. Wrap her up in brown paper til they come.

LIZA: Youre no gentleman, youre not, to talk of such things. I'm a good girl, I am; and I know what the like of you are, I do.

HIGGINS: We want none of your Lisson Grove prudery here, young woman. Youve got to learn to behave like a duchess. Take her away, Mrs Pearce. If she gives you any trouble, wallop her.

LIZA (*springing up and running between Pickering and Mrs Pearce for protection*): No! I'll call the police, I will.

[29] *Monkey Brand:* Trade name of a scouring soap.
[30] *Whitely:* A large store in London.

MRS PEARCE: But Ive no place to put her.

HIGGINS: Put her in the dustbin.[31]

LIZA: Ah-ah-ah-ow-ow-oo!

PICKERING: Oh come, Higgins! be reasonable.

MRS PEARCE (*resolutely*): You must be reasonable, Mr Higgins: really you must. You cant walk over everybody like this.

Higgins, thus scolded, subsides. The hurricane is succeeded by a zephyr of amiable surprise.

HIGGINS (*with professional exquisiteness of modulation*): I walk over everybody! My dear Mrs Pearce, my dear Pickering, I never had the slightest intention of walking over anyone. All I propose is that we should be kind to this poor girl. We must help her to prepare and fit herself for her new station in life. If I did not express myself clearly it was because I did not wish to hurt her delicacy, or yours.

Liza, reassured, steals back to her chair.

MRS PEARCE (*to Pickering*): Well, did you ever hear anything like that, sir?

PICKERING (*laughing heartily*): Never, Mrs Pearce: never.

HIGGINS (*patiently*): Whats the matter?

MRS PEARCE: Well, the matter is, sir, that you cant take a girl up like that as if you were picking up a pebble on the beach.

HIGGINS: Why not?

MRS PEARCE: Why not! But you dont know anything about her. What about her parents? She may be married.

LIZA: Garn!

HIGGINS: There! As the girl very properly says, Garn! Married indeed! Dont you know that a woman of that class looks a worn out drudge of fifty a year after she's married?

LIZA: Whood marry me?

HIGGINS (*suddenly resorting to the most thrillingly beautiful low tones in his best elocutionary style*): By George, Eliza, the streets will be strewn with the bodies of men shooting themselves for your sake before Ive done with you.

MRS PEARCE: Nonsense, sir. You mustnt talk like that to her.

LIZA (*rising and squaring herself determinedly*): I'm going away. He's off his chump,[32] he is. I dont want no balmies teaching me.

HIGGINS (*wounded in his tenderest point by her insensibility to his elocution*): Oh, indeed! I'm mad, am I? Very well, Mrs Pearce: you neednt order the new clothes for her. Throw her out.

LIZA (*whimpering*): Nah-ow. You got no right to touch me.

MRS PEARCE: You see now what comes of being saucy. (*Indicating the door*) This way, please.

LIZA (*almost in tears*): I didnt want no clothes. I wouldnt have taken them. (*She throws away the handkerchief.*) I can buy my own clothes.

31 *dustbin:* Garbage can.
32 *off his chump:* Out of his mind.

HIGGINS (*deftly retrieving the handkerchief and intercepting her on her reluctant way to the door*): Youre an ungrateful wicked girl. This is my return for offering to take you out of the gutter and dress you beautifully and make a lady of you.

MRS PEARCE: Stop, Mr Higgins. I wont allow it. It's you that are wicked. Go home to your parents, girl; and tell them to take better care of you.

LIZA: I aint got no parents. They told me I was big enough to earn my own living and turned me out.

MRS PEARCE: Wheres your mother?

LIZA: I aint got no mother. Her that turned me out was my sixth stepmother.[33] But I done without them. And I'm a good girl, I am.

HIGGINS: Very well, then, what on earth is all this fuss about? The girl doesnt belong to anybody—is no use to anybody but me. (*He goes to Mrs Pearce and begins coaxing.*) You can adopt her, Mrs Pearce: I'm sure a daughter would be a great amusement to you. Now dont make any more fuss. Take her downstairs; and—

MRS PEARCE: But whats to become of her? Is she to be paid anything? Do be sensible, sir.

HIGGINS: Oh, pay her whatever is necessary: put it down in the housekeeping book. (*Impatiently*) What on earth will she want with money? She'll have her food and her clothes. She'll only drink if you give her money.

LIZA (*turning on him*): Oh you are a brute. It's a lie: nobody ever saw the sign of liquor on me. (*To Pickering*) Oh, sir: youre a gentleman: dont let him speak to me like that.

PICKERING (*in good-humored remonstrance*): Does it occur to you, Higgins, that the girl has some feelings?

HIGGINS (*looking critically at her*): Oh no, I dont think so. Not any feelings that we need bother about. (*Cheerily*) Have you, Eliza?

LIZA: I got my feelings same as anyone else.

HIGGINS (*to Pickering, reflectively*): You see the difficulty?

PICKERING: Eh? What difficulty?

HIGGINS: To get her to talk grammar. The mere pronunciation is easy enough.

LIZA: I dont want to talk grammar. I want to talk like a lady in a flower-shop.

MRS PEARCE: Will you please keep to the point, Mr Higgins. I want to know on what terms the girl is to be here. Is she to have any wages? And what is to become of her when youve finished your teaching? You must look ahead a little.

HIGGINS (*impatiently*): Whats to become of her if I leave her in the gutter? Tell me that, Mrs Pearce.

MRS PEARCE: Thats her own business, not yours, Mr Higgins.

---

[33] *sixth stepmother:* Euphemism for the sixth woman Eliza's father lived with since he and Eliza's mother separated.

HIGGINS: Well, when Ive done with her, we can throw her back into the gutter; and then it will be her own business again; so thats all right.

LIZA: Oh, youve no feeling heart in you: you dont care for nothing but yourself. (*She rises and takes the floor resolutely.*) Here! Ive had enough of this. I'm going. (*Making for the door*) You ought to be ashamed of yourself, you ought.

HIGGINS (*snatching a chocolate cream from the piano, his eyes suddenly beginning to twinkle with mischief*): Have some chocolates, Eliza.

LIZA (*halting, tempted*): How do I know what might be in them? Ive heard of girls being drugged by the like of you.
Higgins whips out his penknife; cuts a chocolate in two; puts one half into his mouth and bolts it; and offers her the other half.

HIGGINS: Pledge of good faith, Eliza. I eat one half: you eat the other. (*Liza opens her mouth to retort: he pops the half chocolate into it.*) You shall have boxes of them, barrels of them, every day. You shall live on them. Eh?

LIZA (*who has disposed of the chocolate after being nearly choked by it*): I wouldnt have ate it, only I'm too ladylike to take it out of my mouth.

HIGGINS: Listen, Eliza. I think you said you came in a taxi.

LIZA: Well, what if I did? Ive as good a right to take a taxi as anyone else.

HIGGINS: You have, Eliza; and in future you shall have as many taxis as you want. You shall go up and down and round the town in a taxi every day. Think of that, Eliza.

MRS PEARCE: Mr Higgins: youre tempting the girl. It's not right. She should think of the future.

HIGGINS: At her age! Nonsense! Time enough to think of the future when you havnt any future to think of. No, Eliza: do as this lady does: think of other people's futures; but never think of your own. Think of chocolates, and taxis, and gold, and diamonds.

LIZA: No: I dont want no gold and no diamonds. I'm a good girl, I am. (*She sits down again, with an attempt at dignity.*)

HIGGINS: You shall remain so, Eliza, under the care of Mrs Pearce. And you shall marry an officer in the Guards, with a beautiful moustache: the son of a marquis, who will disinherit him for marrying you, but will relent when he sees your beauty and goodness—

PICKERING: Excuse me, Higgins; but I really must interfere. Mrs Pearce is quite right. If this girl is to put herself in your hands for six months for an experiment in teaching, she must understand thoroughly what she's doing.

HIGGINS: How can she? She's incapable of understanding anything. Besides, do any of us understand what we are doing? If we did, would we ever do it?

PICKERING: Very clever, Higgins; but not to the present point. (*To Eliza*) Miss Doolittle—

LIZA (*overwhelmed*): Ah-ah-ow-oo!

HIGGINS: There! Thats all youll get out of Eliza. Ah-ah-ow-oo! No use explaining. As a military man you ought to know that. Give her her orders: thats enough for her. Eliza: you are to live here for the next six months, learning how to speak beautifully, like a lady in a florist's shop. If youre good and do whatever youre told, you shall sleep in a proper bedroom, and have lots to eat, and money to buy chocolates and take rides in taxis. If youre naughty and idle you will sleep in the back kitchen among the black beetles, and be walloped by Mrs Pearce with a broomstick. At the end of six months you shall go to Buckingham Palace in a carriage, beautifully dressed. If the King finds out youre not a lady, you will be taken by the police to the Tower of London, where your head will be cut off as a warning to other presumptuous flower girls. If you are not found out, you shall have a present of seven-and-sixpence to start life with as a lady in a shop. If you refuse this offer you will be a most ungrateful wicked girl; and the angels will weep for you. (*To Pickering*) Now are you satisfied, Pickering? (*To Mrs Pearce*) Can I put it more plainly and fairly, Mrs Pearce?

MRS PEARCE (*patiently*): I think youd better let me speak to the girl properly in private. I dont know that I can take charge of her or consent to the arrangement at all. Of course I know you dont mean her any harm; but when you get what you call interested in people's accents, you never think or care what may happen to them or you. Come with me, Eliza.

HIGGINS: That's all right. Thank you, Mrs Pearce. Bundle her off to the bath-room.

LIZA (*rising reluctantly and suspiciously*): Youre a great bully, you are. I wont stay here if I dont like. I wont let nobody wallop me. I never asked to go to Bucknam Palace, I didnt. I was never in trouble with the police, not me. I'm a good girl—

MRS PEARCE: Dont answer back, girl. You dont understand the gentleman. Come with me. (*She leads the way to the door, and holds it open for Eliza.*)

LIZA (*as she goes out*): Well, what I say is right. I wont go near the King, not if I'm going to have my head cut off. If I'd known what I was letting myself in for, I wouldnt have come here. I always been a good girl; and I never offered to say a word to him; and I dont owe him nothing; and I dont care; and I wont be put upon; and I have my feelings the same as anyone else—

Mrs Pearce shuts the door; and Eliza's plaints are no longer audible.

* * * * * * * *

Eliza is taken upstairs to the third floor greatly to her surprise; for she expected to be taken down to the scullery. There Mrs Pearce opens a door and takes her into a spare bedroom.

MRS PEARCE: I will have to put you here. This will be your bedroom.

LIZA: O-h, I couldnt sleep here, missus. It's too good for the likes of me. I should be afraid to touch anything. I aint a duchess yet, you know.

MRS PEARCE: You have got to make yourself as clean as the room: then you wont be afraid of it. And you must call me Mrs Pearce, not missus. (*She throws open the door of the dressingroom, now modernized as a bathroom.*)

LIZA: Gawd! whats this? Is this where you wash clothes? Funny sort of copper I call it.

MRS PEARCE: It is not a copper.[34] This is where we wash ourselves, Eliza, and where I am going to wash you.

LIZA: You expect me to get into that and wet myself all over! Not me. I should catch my death. I knew a woman did it every Saturday night; and she died of it.

MRS PEARCE: Mr Higgins has the gentleman's bathroom downstairs; and he has a bath every morning, in cold water.

LIZA: Ugh! He's made of iron, that man.

MRS PEARCE: If you are to sit with him and the Colonel and be taught you will have to do the same. They wont like the smell of you if you dont. But you can have the water as hot as you like. There are two taps: hot and cold.

LIZA (*weeping*): I couldnt. I dursnt. Its not natural: it would kill me. Ive never had a bath in my life: not what youd call a proper one.

MRS PEARCE: Well, dont you want to be clean and sweet and decent, like a lady? You know you cant be a nice girl inside if youre a dirty slut outside.

LIZA. Boohoo!!!!

MRS PEARCE: Now stop crying and go back into your room and take off all your clothes. Then wrap yourself in this (*Taking down a gown from its peg and handing it to her*) and come back to me. I will get the bath ready.

LIZA (*all tears*): I cant. I wont. I'm not used to it. Ive never took off all my clothes before. It's not right: it's not decent.

MRS PEARCE: Nonsense, child. Dont you take off all your clothes every night when you go to bed?

LIZA (*amazed*): No. Why should I? I should catch my death. Of course I take off my skirt.

MRS PEARCE: Do you mean that you sleep in the underclothes you wear in the daytime?

LIZA: What else have I to sleep in?

[34] *copper:* A large iron boiler used for washing clothes.

MRS PEARCE: You will never do that again as long as you live here. I will get you a proper nightdress.

LIZA: Do you mean change into cold things and lie awake shivering half the night? You want to kill me, you do.

MRS PEARCE: I want to change you from a frowzy slut to a clean respectable girl fit to sit with the gentlemen in the study. Are you going to trust me and do what I tell you or be thrown out and sent back to your flower basket?

LIZA: But you dont know what the cold is to me. You dont know how I dread it.

MRS PEARCE: Your bed won't be cold here: I will put a hot water bottle in it. (*Pushing her into the bedroom*) Off with you and undress.

LIZA: Oh, if only I'd known what a dreadful thing it is to be clean I'd never have come. I didnt know when I was well off. I— (*Mrs Pearce pushes her through the door, but leaves it partly open lest her prisoner should take to flight.*)

Mrs Pearce puts on a pair of white rubber sleeves, and fills the bath, mixing hot and cold, and testing the result with the bath thermometer. She perfumes it with a handful of bath salts and adds a palmful of mustard. She then takes a formidable looking long handled scrubbing brush and soaps it profusely with a ball of scented soap.

Eliza comes back with nothing on but the bath gown huddled tightly round her, a piteous spectacle of abject terror.

MRS PEARCE: Now come along. Take that thing off.

LIZA: Oh I couldnt, Mrs Pearce: I reely couldnt. I never done such a thing.

MRS PEARCE: Nonsense. Here: step in and tell me whether its hot enough for you.

LIZA: Ah-oo! Ah-oo! It's too hot.

MRS PEARCE (*deftly snatching the gown away and throwing Eliza down on her back*): It wont hurt you. (*She sets to work with the scrubbing brush.*)

Eliza's screams are heartrending.

*   *   *   *   *   *   *   *

Meanwhile the Colonel has been having it out with Higgins about Eliza. Pickering has come from the hearth to the chair and seated himself astride of it with his arms on the back to cross-examine him.

PICKERING: Excuse the straight question, Higgins. Are you a man of good character where women are concerned?

HIGGINS (*moodily*): Have you ever met a man of good character where women are concerned?

PICKERING: Yes: very frequently.

HIGGINS (*dogmatically, lifting himself on his hands to the level of the piano, and sitting on it with a bounce*): Well, I havn't. I find that the moment I let a woman make friends with me, she becomes jealous, exacting, suspicious, and a damned nuisance. I find that the moment I let myself make friends with a woman, I become selfish and tyrannical. Women upset everything. When you let them into your life, you find that the woman is driving at one thing and youre driving at another.

PICKERING: At what, for example?

HIGGINS (*coming off the piano restlessly*): Oh, Lord knows! I suppose the woman wants to live her own life; and the man wants to live his; and each tries to drag the other on to the wrong track. One wants to go north and the other south; and the result is that both have to go east, though they both hate the east wind. (*He sits down on the bench at the keyboard.*) So here I am, a confirmed old bachelor, and likely to remain so.

PICKERING (*rising and standing over him gravely*): Come, Higgins! You know what I mean. If I'm to be in this business I shall feel responsible for that girl. I hope it's understood that no advantage is to be taken of her position.

HIGGINS: What! That thing! Sacred, I assure you. (*Rising to explain*) You see, she'll be a pupil; and teaching would be impossible unless pupils were sacred. I've taught scores of American millionairesses how to speak English: the best looking women in the world. I'm seasoned. They might as well be blocks of wood. *I* might as well be a block of wood. It's—

Mrs Pearce *opens the door. She has Eliza's hat in her hand. Pickering retires to the easy-chair at the hearth and sits down.*

HIGGINS (*eagerly*): Well, Mrs Pearce: is it all right?

MRS PEARCE (*at the door*): I just wish to trouble you with a word, if I may, Mr Higgins.

HIGGINS: Yes, certainly. Come in. (*She comes forward.*) Dont burn that, Mrs Pearce. I'll keep it as a curiosity. (*He takes the hat.*)

MRS PEARCE: Handle it carefully, sir, please. I had to promise her not to burn it; but I had better put it in the oven for a while.

HIGGINS (*putting it down hastily on the piano*): Oh! thank you. Well, what have you to say to me?

PICKERING: Am I in the way?

MRS PEARCE: Not in the least, sir. Mr Higgins: will you please be very particular what you say before the girl?

HIGGINS (*sternly*): Of course. I'm always particular about what I say. Why do you say this to me?

MRS PEARCE (*unmoved*): No, sir: youre not at all particular when youve mislaid anything or when you get a little impatient. Now it doesnt matter before me: I'm used to it. But you really must not swear before the girl.

HIGGINS (*indignantly*): I swear! (*Most emphatically*) I never swear. I detest the habit. What the devil do you mean?

MRS PEARCE (*stolidly*): Thats what I mean, sir. You swear a great deal too much. I dont mind your damning and blasting, and what the devil and where the devil and who the devil—

HIGGINS: Mrs Pearce: this language from your lips! Really!

MRS PEARCE (*not to be put off*): —but there is a certain word I must ask you not to use. The girl used it herself when she began to enjoy the bath. It begins with the same letter as bath.[35] She knows no better: she learnt it at her mother's knee. But she must not hear it from your lips.

HIGGINS (*loftily*): I cannot charge myself with having ever uttered it, Mrs Pearce. (*She looks at him steadfastly. He adds, hiding an uneasy conscience with a judicial air*) Except perhaps in a moment of extreme and justifiable excitement.

MRS PEARCE: Only this morning, sir, you applied it to your boots, to the butter, and to the brown bread.

HIGGINS: Oh, that! Mere alliteration, Mrs Pearce, natural to a poet.

MRS PEARCE: Well, sir, whatever you choose to call it, I beg you not let the girl hear you repeat it.

HIGGINS: Oh, very well, very well. Is that all?

MRS PEARCE: No, sir. We shall have to be very particular with this girl as to personal cleanliness.

HIGGINS: Certainly. Quite right. Most important.

MRS PEARCE: I mean not to be slovenly about her dress or untidy in leaving things about.

HIGGINS (*going to her solemnly*): Just so. I intended to call your attention to that. (*He passes on to Pickering, who is enjoying the conversation immensely.*) It is these little things that matter, Pickering. Take care of the pence and the pounds will take care of themselves is as true of personal habits as of money. (*He comes to anchor on the hearthrug, with the air of a man in an unassailable position.*)

MRS PEARCE: Yes, sir. Then might I ask you not to come down to breakfast in your dressing-gown, or at any rate not to use it as a napkin to the extent you do, sir. And if you would be so good as not to eat everything off the same plate, and to remember not to put the porridge saucepan out of your hand on the clean tablecloth, it would be a better example to the girl. You know you nearly choked yourself with a fishbone in a jam only last week.

HIGGINS (*routed from the hearthrug and drifting back to the piano*): I may do these things sometimes in absence of mind; but surely I dont do them habitually. (*Angrily*) By the way: my dressing-gown smells most damnably of benzine.

[35] *same . . . bath*: The word is *bloody*, then considered a taboo word.

MRS PEARCE: No doubt it does, Mr. Higgins. But if you will wipe your fingers—

HIGGINS (*yelling*): Oh very well, very well: I'll wipe them in my hair in future.

MRS PEARCE: I hope youre not offended, Mr Higgins.

HIGGINS (*shocked at finding himself thought capable of an unamiable sentiment*): Not at all, not at all. Youre quite right, Mrs Pearce: I shall be particularly careful before the girl. Is that all?

MRS PEARCE: No, sir. Might she use some of those Japanese dresses you brought from abroad? I really cant put her back into her old things.

HIGGINS: Certainly. Anything you like. Is that all?

MRS PEARCE: Thank you, sir. Thats all. (*She goes out.*)

HIGGINS: You know, Pickering, that woman has the most extraordinary ideas about me. Here I am, a shy, diffident sort of man. Ive never been able to feel really grown-up and tremendous, like other chaps. And yet she's firmly persuaded that I'm an arbitrary overbearing bossing kind of person. I cant account for it.

Mrs Pearce returns.

MRS PEARCE: If you please, sir, the trouble's beginning already. Theres a dustman[36] downstairs, Alfred Doolittle, wants to see you. He says you have his daughter here.

PICKERING (*rising*): Phew! I say!

HIGGINS (*promptly*): Send the blackguard up.

MRS PEARCE: Oh, very well, sir. (*She goes out.*)

PICKERING: He may not be a blackguard, Higgins.

HIGGINS: Nonsense. Of course he's a blackguard.

PICKERING: Whether he is or not, I'm afraid we shall have some trouble with him.

HIGGINS (*confidently*): Oh no: I think not. If theres any trouble he shall have it with me, not I with him. And we are sure to get something interesting out of him.

PICKERING: About the girl?

HIGGINS: No. I mean his dialect.

PICKERING: Oh!

MRS PEARCE (*at the door*): Doolittle, sir. (*She admits Doolittle and retires.*)

Alfred is an elderly but vigorous dustman, clad in the costume of his profession, including a hat with a back brim covering his neck and shoulders. He has well marked and rather interesting features, and seems equally free from fear and conscience. He has a remarkably expressive voice, the result of a habit of giving vent to his feelings without reserve. His present pose is that of wounded honor and stern resolution.

[36] *dustman:* Garbage collector.

DOOLITTLE (*at the door, uncertain which of the two gentlemen is his man*):
Professor Iggins?

HIGGINS: Here. Good morning. Sit down.

DOOLITTLE: Morning, Governor.[37] (*He sits down magisterially.*) I come about a very serious matter, Governor.

HIGGINS (*to Pickering*): Brought up in Hounslow. Mother Welsh, I should think. (*Doolittle opens his mouth, amazed. Higgins continues.*) What do you want, Doolittle?

DOOLITTLE (*menacingly*): I want my daughter: thats what I want. See?

HIGGINS: Of course you do. Youre her father, arnt you? You dont suppose anyone else wants her, do you? I'm glad to see you have some spark of family feeling left. She's upstairs. Take her away at once.

DOOLITTLE (*rising, fearfully taken aback*): What?

HIGGINS: Take her away. Do you suppose I'm going to keep your daughter for you?

DOOLITTLE (*remonstrating*): Now, now, look here, Governor. Is this reasonable? Is it fairity to take advantage of a man like this? The girl belongs to me. You got her. Where do I come in? (*He sits down again.*)

HIGGINS: Your daughter had the audacity to come to my house and ask me to teach her how to speak properly so that she could get a place in a flower-shop. This gentleman and my housekeeper have been here all the time. (*Bullying him*) How dare you come here and attempt to blackmail me? You sent her here on purpose.

DOOLITTLE (*protesting*): No, Governor.

HIGGINS: You must have. How else could you possibly know that she is here?

DOOLITTLE: Don't take a man up like that, Governor.

HIGGINS: The police shall take you up. This is a plant—a plot to extort money by threats. I shall telephone for the police. (*He goes resolutely to the telephone and opens the directory.*)

DOOLITTLE: Have I asked you for a brass farthing? [38] I leave it to the gentleman here: have I said a word about money?

HIGGINS (*throwing the book aside and marching down on Doolittle with a poser*): What else did you come for?

DOOLITTLE (*sweetly*): Well, what would a man come for? Be human, Governor.

HIGGINS (*disarmed*): Alfred: did you put her up to it?

DOOLITTLE: So help me, Governor, I never did. I take my Bible oath I aint seen the girl these two months past.

HIGGINS: Then how did you know she was here?

DOOLITTLE ("*most musical, most melancholy*"):[39] I'll tell you, Governor, if

---

[37] *Governor:* Sir.

[38] *farthing:* A fourth of a penny (half a hapenny).

[39] "*most . . . melancholy*": From John Milton's *Il Penseroso* (1632).

youll only let me get a word in. I'm willing to tell you. I'm wanting to tell you. I'm waiting to tell you.

HIGGINS: Pickering: this chap has a certain natural gift of rhetoric. Observe the rhythm of his native woodnotes wild.[40] "I'm willing to tell you: I'm wanting to tell you: I'm waiting to tell you." Sentimental rhetoric! thats the Welsh strain in him. It also accounts for his mendacity and dishonesty.

PICKERING: Oh, please, Higgins: I'm west country myself. (*To Doolittle*) How did you know the girl was here if you didnt send her?

DOOLITTLE: It was like this, Governor. The girl took a boy in the taxi to give him a jaunt. Son of her landlady, he is. He hung about on the chance of her giving him another ride home. Well, she sent him back for her luggage when she heard you was willing for her to stop here. I met the boy at the corner of Long Acre and Endell Street.

HIGGINS: Public house. Yes?

DOOLITTLE: The poor man's club, Governor: why shouldnt I?

PICKERING: Do let him tell his story, Higgins.

DOOLITTLE: He told me what was up. And I ask you, what was my feelings and my duty as a father? I says to the boy, "You bring me the luggage," I says—

PICKERING: Why didnt you go for it yourself?

DOOLITTLE: Landlady wouldnt have trusted me with it, Governor. She's that kind of woman: you know. I had to give the boy a penny afore he trusted me with it, the little swine. I brought it to her just to oblige you like, and make myself agreeable. Thats all.

HIGGINS: How much luggage?

DOOLITTLE: Musical instrument, Governor. A few pictures, a trifle of jewelry, and a bird-cage. She said she didnt want no clothes. What was I to think from that, Governor? I ask you as a parent what was I to think?

HIGGINS: So you came to rescue her from worse than death,[41] eh?

DOOLITTLE (*appreciatively: relieved at being so well understood*): Just so, Governor. Thats right.

PICKERING: But why did you bring her luggage if you intended to take her away?

DOOLITTLE: Have I said a word about taking her away? Have I now?

HIGGINS (*determinedly*): Youre going to take here away, double quick. (*He crosses to the hearth and rings the bell.*)

DOOLITTLE (*rising*): No, Governor. Dont say that. I'm not the man to stand in my girl's light. Heres a career opening for her, as you might say; and—

[40] *woodnotes wild:* From John Milton's *L'Allegro* (1632): "sweetest Shakespeare, Fancy's child,/Warble[s] his native woodnotes wild."

[41] *worse . . . death:* Short for "a fate worse than death," i.e. rape.

Mrs Pearce opens the door and awaits orders.

HIGGINS: Mrs Pearce: this is Eliza's father. He has come to take her away. Give her to him. (*He goes back to the piano, with an air of washing his hands of the whole affair.*)

DOOLITTLE: No. This is a misunderstanding. Listen here—

MRS PEARCE: He cant take her away, Mr Higgins: how can he? You told me to burn her clothes.

DOOLITTLE: Thats right. I cant carry the girl through the streets like a blooming[42] monkey, can I? I put it to you.

HIGGINS: You have put it to me that you want your daughter. Take your daughter. If she has no clothes go out and buy her some.

DOOLITTLE (*desperate*): Wheres the clothes she come in? Did I burn them or did your missus here?

MRS PEARCE: I am the housekeeper, if you please. I have sent for some clothes for your girl. When they come you can take her away. You can wait in the kitchen. This way, please.

Doolittle, much troubled, accompanies her to the door; then hesitates; finally turns confidentially to Higgins.

DOOLITTLE: Listen here, Governor. You and me is men of the world, aint we?

HIGGINS: Oh! Men of the world, are we? Youd better go, Mrs Pearce.

MRS PEARCE: I think so, indeed, sir. (*She goes, with dignity.*)

PICKERING: The floor is yours, Mr Doolittle.

DOOLITTLE (*to Pickering*): I thank you, Governor. (*To Higgins, who takes refuge on the piano bench, a little overwhelmed by the proximity of his visitor; for Doolittle has a professional flavour of dust about him.*) Well, the truth is, I've taken a sort of fancy to you, Governor; and if you want the girl, I'm not so set on having her back home again but what I might be open to an arrangement. Regarded in the light of a young woman, she's a fine handsome girl. As a daughter she's not worth her keep; and so I tell you straight. All I ask is my rights as a father; and youre the last man alive to expect me to let her go for nothing; for I can see youre one of the straight sort, Governor. Well, whats a five-pound note to you? and whats Eliza to me? (*He turns to his chair and sits down judicially.*)

PICKERING: I think you ought to know, Doolittle, that Mr Higgins's intentions are entirely honorable.

DOOLITTLE: Course they are, Governor. If I thought they wasn't, I'd ask fifty.

HIGGINS (*revolted*): Do you mean to say that you would sell your daughter for £50?

DOOLITTLE: Not in a general way I would; but to oblige a gentleman like you I'd do a good deal, I do assure you.

PICKERING: Have you no morals, man?

---

[42] *blooming:* An acceptable variant of "bloody."

DOOLITTLE (*unabashed*): Cant afford them, Governor. Neither could you if you was as poor as me. Not that I mean any harm, you know. But if Liza is going to have a bit out of this, why not me too?

HIGGINS (*troubled*): I dont know what to do, Pickering. There can be no question that as a matter of morals it's a positive crime to give this chap a farthing. And yet I feel a sort of rough justice in his claim.

DOOLITTLE: Thats it, Governor. Thats all I say. A father's heart, as it were.

PICKERING: Well, I know the feeling; but really it seems hardly right—

DOOLITTLE: Dont say that, Governor. Dont look at it that way. What am I, Governors both? I ask you, what am I? I'm one of the undeserving poor: thats what I am. Think of what that means to a man. It means that he's up agen middle class morality all the time. If theres anything going, and I put in for a bit of it, it's always the same story: "Youre undeserving; so you cant have it." But my needs is as great as the most deserving widow's that ever got money out of six different charities in one week for the death of the same husband. I dont need less than a deserving man: I need more. I dont eat less hearty than him; and I drink a lot more. I want a bit of amusement, cause I'm a thinking man. I want cheerfulness and a song and a band when I feel low. Well, they charge me just the same for everything as they charge the deserving. What is middle class morality? Just an excuse for never giving me anything. Therefore, I ask you, as two gentlemen, not to play that game on me. I'm playing straight with you. I aint pretending to be deserving. I'm undeserving; and I mean to go on being undeserving. I like it; and thats the truth. Will you take advantage of a man's nature to do him out of the price of his own daughter what he's brought up and fed and clothed by the sweat of his brow until she's growed big enough to be interesting to you two gentlemen? Is five pounds unreasonable? I put it to you; and I leave it to you.

HIGGINS (*rising, and going over to Pickering*): Pickering: if we were to take this man in hand for three months, he could choose between a seat in the Cabinet and a popular pulpit in Wales.

PICKERING: What do you say to that, Doolittle?

DOOLITTLE: Not me, Governor, thank you kindly. Ive heard all the preachers and all the prime ministers—for I'm a thinking man and game for politics or religion or social reform same as all the other amusements—and I tell you it's a dog's life any way you look at it. Undeserving poverty is my line. Taking one station in society with another, it's—it's—well, it's the only one that has any ginger in it, to my taste.

HIGGINS: I suppose we must give him a fiver.

PICKERING: He'll make a bad use of it, I'm afraid.

DOOLITTLE: Not me, Governor, so help me I wont. Dont you be afraid that I'll save it and spare it and live idle on it. There wont be a penny of it left by Monday: I'll have to go to work same as if I'd never had it. It wont pauperize me, you bet. Just one good spree for myself and the missus, giving pleasure to ourselves and employment to others, and satisfaction to you to think it's not been throwed away. You couldnt spend it better.

HIGGINS (*taking out his pocket book and coming between Doolittle and the piano*): This is irresistible. Lets give him ten. (*He offers two notes to the dustman.*)

DOOLITTLE: No, Governor. She wouldnt have the heart to spend ten; and perhaps I shouldnt neither. Ten pounds is a lot of money: it makes a man feel prudent like; and then goodbye to happiness. You give me what I ask you, Governor: not a penny more, and not a penny less.

PICKERING: Why dont you marry that missus of yours? I rather draw the line at encouraging that sort of immorality.

DOOLITTLE: Tell her so, Governor: tell her so. I'm willing. It's me that suffers by it. Ive no hold on her. I got to be agreeable to her. I got to give her presents. I got to buy her clothes something sinful. I'm a slave to that woman, Governor, just because I'm not her lawful husband. And she knows it too. Catch her marrying me! Take my advice, Governor: marry Eliza while she's young and dont know no better. If you dont you'll be sorry for it after. If you do, she'll be sorry for it after; but better her than you, because youre a man, and she's only a woman and dont know how to be happy anyhow.

HIGGINS: Pickering: if we listen to this man another minute, we shall have no convictions left. (*To Doolittle*) Five pounds I think you said.

DOOLITTLE: Thank you kindly, Governor.

HIGGINS: Youre sure you wont take ten?

DOOLITTLE: Not now. Another time, Governor.

HIGGINS (*handing him a five-pound note*): Here you are.

DOOLITTLE: Thank you, Governor. Good morning. (*He hurries to the door, anxious to get away with his booty. When he opens it he is confronted with a dainty and exquisitely clean young Japanese lady in a simple blue cotton kimono printed cunningly with small white jasmine blossoms. Mrs Pearce is with her. He gets out of her way deferentially and apologizes.*) Beg pardon, miss.

THE JAPANESE LADY: Garn! Dont you know your own daughter?

DOOLITTLE	*exclaiming*	Bly me! it's Eliza!
HIGGINS	*simul-*	Whats that? This!
PICKERING	*taneously*	By Jove!

LIZA: Dont I look silly?

HIGGINS: Silly?

MRS PEARCE (*at the door*): Now, Mr Higgins, please dont say anything to make the girl conceited about herself.

HIGGINS (*conscientiously*): Oh! Quite right, Mrs Pearce. (*To Eliza*) Yes: damned silly.

MRS PEARCE: Please, sir.

HIGGINS (*correcting himself*): I mean extremely silly.

LIZA: I should look all right with my hat on. (*She takes up her hat; puts it on; and walks across the room to the fireplace with a fashionable air.*)

HIGGINS: A new fashion, by George! And it ought to look horrible!

DOOLITTLE (*with fatherly pride*): Well, I never thought she'd clean up as good looking as that, Governor. She's a credit to me, ain't she?

LIZA: I tell you, it's easy to clean up here. Hot and cold water on tap, just as much as you like, there is. Woolly towels, there is; and a towel horse[43] so hot, it burns your fingers. Soft brushes to scrub yourself, and a wooden bowl of soap smelling like primroses. Now I know why ladies is so clean. Washing's a treat for them. Wish they could see what it is for the like of me!

HIGGINS: I'm glad the bathroom met with your approval.

LIZA: It didnt: not all of it; and I dont care who hears me say it. Mrs Pearce knows.

HIGGINS: What was wrong, Mrs Pearce?

MRS PEARCE (*blandly*): Oh, nothing, sir. It doesn't matter.

LIZA: I had a good mind to break it. I didn't know which way to look. But I hung a towel over it, I did.

HIGGINS: Over what?

MRS PEARCE: Over the looking-glass, sir.

HIGGINS: Doolittle: you have brought your daughter up too strictly.

DOOLITTLE: Me! I never brought her up at all, except to give her a lick of a strap[44] now and again. Dont put it on me, Governor. She aint accustomed to it, you see: thats all. But she'll soon pick up your free-and-easy ways.

LIZA: I'm a good girl, I am; and I wont pick up no free and easy ways.

HIGGINS: Eliza: if you say again that youre a good girl, your father shall take you home.

LIZA: Not him. You dont know my father. All he come here for was to touch you for some money to get drunk on.

DOOLITTLE: Well, what else would I want money for? To put into the plate in church, I suppose. (*She puts out her tongue at him. He is so incensed by this that Pickering presently finds it necessary to step between them.*) Dont you give me none of your lip;[45] and dont let me hear you giving this gentleman any of it neither, or youll hear from me about it. See?

HIGGINS: Have you any further advice to give her before you go, Doolittle? Your blessing, for instance.

DOOLITTLE: No, Governor: I aint such a mug[46] as to put up my children

---

[43] *towel horse:* A wooden stand on which towels are hung.
[44] *lick of a strap:* A beating.
[45] *Dont . . . lip:* Don't talk back to me.
[46] *mug:* Dupe.

to all I know myself. Hard enough to hold them in without that. If you want Eliza's mind improved, Governor, you do it yourself with a strap. So long, gentlemen. (*He turns to go.*)

HIGGINS (*impressively*): Stop. Youll come regularly to see your daughter. It's your duty, you know. My brother is a clergyman; and he could help you in your talks with her.

DOOLITTLE (*evasively*): Certainly, I'll come, Governor. Not just this week, because I have a job at a distance. But later on you may depend on me. Afternoon, gentlemen. Afternoon, maam. (*He touches his hat to Mrs Pearce, who disdains the salutation and goes out. He winks at Higgins, thinking him probably a fellow-sufferer from Mrs Pearce's difficult disposition, and follows her.*)

LIZA: Dont you believe the old liar. He'd as soon you set a bulldog on him as a clergyman. You wont see him again in a hurry.

HIGGINS: I dont want to, Eliza. Do you?

LIZA: Not me. I dont want never to see him again, I dont. He's a disgrace to me, he is, collecting dust, instead of working at his trade.

PICKERING: What is his trade, Eliza?

LIZA: Talking money out of other people's pockets into his own. His proper trade's a navvy; and he works at it sometimes too—for exercise—and earns good money at it. Aint you going to call me Miss Doolittle any more?

PICKERING: I beg your pardon, Miss Doolittle. It was a slip of the tongue.

LIZA: Oh, I dont mind; only it sounded so genteel. I should just like to take a taxi to the corner of Tottenham Court Road and get out there and tell it to wait for me, just to put the girls in their place a bit. I wouldnt speak to them, you know.

PICKERING: Better wait til we get you something really fashionable.

HIGGINS: Besides, you shouldnt cut your old friends now that you have risen in the world. Thats what we call snobbery.

LIZA: You dont call the like of them my friends now, I should hope. Theyve took it out on me often enough with their ridicule when they had the chance; and now I mean to get a bit of my own back. But if I'm to have fashionable clothes, I'll wait. I should like to have some. Mrs Pearce says youre going to give me some to wear in bed at night different to what I wear in the daytime; but it do seem a waste of money when you could get something to shew. Besides, I never could fancy changing into cold things on a winter night.

MRS PEARCE (*coming back*): Now, Eliza. The new things have come for you to try on.

LIZA: Ah-ow-oo-ooh! (*She rushes out.*)

MRS PEARCE (*following her*): Oh, dont rush about like that, girl. (*She shuts the door behind her.*)

HIGGINS: Pickering: we have taken on a stiff job.

PICKERING (*with conviction*): Higgins: we have.

*   *   *   *   *   *   *   *

There seems to be some curiosity as to what Higgins's lessons to Eliza were like. Well, here is a sample: the first one.

Picture Eliza, in her new clothes, and feeling her inside put out of step by a lunch, dinner, and breakfast of a kind to which it is unaccustomed, seated with Higgins and the Colonel in the study, feeling like a hospital out-patient at a first encounter with the doctors.

Higgins, constitutionally unable to sit still, discomposes her still more by striding restlessly about. But for the reassuring presence and quietude of her friend the Colonel she would run for her life, even back to Drury Lane.

HIGGINS: Say your alphabet.

LIZA: I know my alphabet. Do you think I know nothing? I dont need to be taught like a child.

HIGGINS (*thundering*): Say your alphabet.

PICKERING: Say it, Miss Doolittle. You will understand presently. Do what he tells you; and let him teach you in his own way.

LIZA: Oh well, if you put it like that—Ahyee, bəyee, cəyee, dəyee—

HIGGINS (*with the roar of a wounded lion*): Stop. Listen to this, Pickering. This is what we pay for as elementary education. This unfortunate animal has been locked up for nine years in school at our expense to teach her to speak and read the language of Shakespear and Milton. And the result is Ahyee, Bə-yee, Cə-yee, Dəyee. (*To Eliza*) Say A, B, C, D.

LIZA (*almost in tears*): But I'm sayin it. Ahyee, Bəyee, Cəyee—

HIGGINS: Stop. Say a cup of tea.

LIZA: A cappətə-ee.

HIGGINS: Put your tongue forward until it squeezes against the top of your lower teeth. Now say cup.

LIZA: C-c-c—I cant. C-Cup.

PICKERING: Good. Splendid, Miss Doolittle.

HIGGINS: By Jupiter, she's done it the first shot. Pickering: we shall make a duchess of her. (*To Eliza*) Now do you think you could possibly say tea? Not tə-yee, mind: if you ever say bə-yee cə-yee də-yee again you shall be dragged round the room three times by the hair of your head. (*Fortissimo*) T, T, T, T.

LIZA (*weeping*): I cant hear no difference cep that it sounds more genteel-like when you say it.

HIGGINS: Well, if you can hear that difference, what the devil are you crying for? Pickering: give her a chocolate.

PICKERING: No, no. Never mind crying a little, Miss Doolittle: you are doing very well; and the lessons wont hurt. I promise you I wont let him drag you round the room by your hair.

HIGGINS: Be off with you to Mrs Pearce and tell her about it. Think about it. Try to do it by yourself: and keep your tongue well forward in your mouth instead of trying to roll it up and swallow it. Another lesson at half-past four this afternoon. Away with you.

Eliza, still sobbing, rushes from the room.

*   *   *   *   *   *   *   *

And that is the sort of ordeal poor Eliza has to go through for months before we meet her again on her first appearance in London society of the professional class.

§ ACT III

It is Mrs Higgins's at-home day. Nobody has yet arrived. Her drawing room, in a flat on Chelsea Embankment, has three windows looking on the river; and the ceiling is not so lofty as it would be in an older house of the same pretension. The windows are open, giving access to a balcony with flowers in pots. If you stand with your face to the windows, you have the fireplace on your left and the door in the right-hand wall close to the corner nearest the windows.

Mrs Higgins was brought up on Morris[47] and Burne Jones;[48] and her room, which is very unlike her son's room in Wimpole Street, is not crowded with furniture and little tables and nicknacks. In the middle of the room there is a big ottoman; and this, with the carpet, the Morris wall-papers, and the Morris chintz window curtains and brocade covers of the ottoman and its cushions, supply all the ornament, and are much too handsome to be hidden by odds and ends of useless things. A few good oil-paintings from the exhibitions in the Grosvenor Gallery thirty years ago (the Burne Jones, not the Whistler[49] side of them) are on the walls. The only land-scape is a Cecil Lawson[50] on the scale of a Rubens.[51] There is a portrait of Mrs Higgins as she was when she defied the fashion in her youth in one of the beautiful Rossettian costumes[52] which, when caricatured by people who did not understand, led to the absurdities of popular estheticism in the eighteen-seventies.

In the corner diagonally opposite the door Mrs Higgins, now over sixty

[47] *Morris*: William Morris (1834–1896), English socialist, poet, and artist, who designed and made such products as fabrics, wallpaper, and furniture.
[48] *Burne Jones*: Sir Edward Coley Burne-Jones (1833–1898), English painter and designer.
[49] *Whistler*: James Abbott McNeill Whistler (1834–1903), American painter and etcher.
[50] *Lawson*: Cecil Lawson (1851–1882), English painter.
[51] *Rubens*: Peter Paul Rubens (1577–1640), Flemish painter.
[52] *Rossettian costumes*: Costumes like those in the pictures of Dante Gabriel Rossetti (1828–1882), English painter and poet.

and long past taking the trouble to dress out of the fashion, sits writing at an elegantly simple writing-table with a bell button within reach of her hand. There is a Chippendale chair further back in the room between her and the window nearest her side. At the other side of the room, further forward, is an Elizabethan chair roughly carved in the taste of Inigo Jones. On the same side a piano in a decorated case. The corner between the fire-place and the window is occupied by a divan cushioned in Morris chintz.

It is between four and five in the afternoon.

The door is opened violently; and Higgins enters with his hat on.

MRS HIGGINS (*dismayed*): Henry! (*Scolding him*) What are you doing here today? It is my at-home day:[53] you promised not to come. (*As he bends to kiss her, she takes his hat off, and presents it to him.*

HIGGINS: Oh bother! (*He throws the hat down on the table.*)

MRS HIGGINS: Go home at once.

HIGGINS (*kissing her*): I know, mother. I came on purpose.

MRS HIGGINS: But you mustnt. I'm serious, Henry. You offend all my friends: they stop coming whenever they meet you.

HIGGINS: Nonsense! I know I have no small talk; but people dont mind. (*He sits on the settee.*)

MRS HIGGINS: Oh! dont they? Small talk indeed! What about your large talk? Really, dear, you mustnt stay.

HIGGINS: I must. Ive a job for you. A phonetic job.

MRS HIGGINS: No use, dear. I'm sorry; but I cant get round your vowels; and though I like to get pretty postcards in your patent shorthand, I always have to read the copies in ordinary writing you so thoughtfully send me.

HIGGINS: Well, this isnt a phonetic job.

MRS HIGGINS: You said it was.

HIGGINS: Not your part of it. Ive picked up a girl.

MRS HIGGINS: Does that mean that some girl has picked you up?

HIGGINS: Not at all. I dont mean a love affair.

MRS HIGGINS: What a pity!

HIGGINS: Why?

MRS HIGGINS: Well, you never fall in love with anyone under forty-five. When will you discover that there are some rather nice-looking young women about?

HIGGINS: Oh, I cant be bothered with young women. My idea of a lovable woman is somebody as like you as possible. I shall never get into the way of seriously liking young women: some habits lie too deep to be changed. (*Rising abruptly and walking about, jingling his money and his keys in his trouser pockets*) Besides, theyre all idiots.

MRS HIGGINS: Do you know what you would do if you really loved me, Henry?

HIGGINS. Oh bother! What? Marry, I suppose.

[53] *at-home day:* A day in which the host or hostess receives guests.

MRS HIGGINS: No. Stop fidgeting and take your hands out of your pockets. (*With a gesture of despair, he obeys and sits down again.*) Thats a good boy. Now tell me about the girl.

HIGGINS: She's coming to see you.

MRS HIGGINS: I dont remember asking her.

HIGGINS: You didnt. *I* asked her. If youd known her you wouldnt have asked her.

MRS HIGGINS: Indeed! Why!

HIGGINS: Well, it's like this. She's a common flower girl. I picked her off the kerbstone.

MRS HIGGINS: And invited her to my at-home!

HIGGINS (*rising and coming to her to coax her*): Oh, thatll be all right. I've taught her to speak properly; and she has strict orders as to her behavior. She's to keep to two subjects: the weather and everybody's health—Fine day and How do you do, you know—and not to let herself go on things in general. That will be safe.

MRS HIGGINS: Safe! To talk about our health! about our insides! perhaps about our outsides! How could you be so silly, Henry?

HIGGINS (*impatiently*): Well, she must talk about something. (*He controls himself and sits down again.*) Oh, she'll be all right: dont you fuss. Pickering is in it with me. Ive a sort of bet on that I'll pass her off as a duchess in six months. I started on her some months ago; and she's getting on like a house on fire. I shall win my bet. She has a quick ear; and she's easier to teach than my middle-class pupils because she'd had to learn a complete new language. She talks English almost as you talk French.

MRS HIGGINS: Thats satisfactory, at all events.

HIGGINS: Well, it is and it isnt.

MRS HIGGINS: What does that mean?

HIGGINS: You see, Ive got her pronunciation all right; but you have to consider not only how a girl pronounces, but what she pronounces; and that's where—

They are interrupted by the parlor-maid, announcing guests.

THE PARLOR-MAID: Mrs and Miss Eynsford Hill. (*She withdraws.*)

HIGGINS: Oh Lord! (*He rises; snatches his hat from the table; and makes for the door; but before he reaches it his mother introduces him.*)

Mrs and Miss Eynsford Hill are the mother and daughter who sheltered from the rain in Covent Garden. The mother is well bred, quiet, and has the habitual anxiety of straitened means. The daughter has acquired a gay air of being very much at home in society: the bravado of genteel poverty.

MRS EYNSFORD HILL (*to Mrs Higgins*): How do you do? (*They shake hands.*)

MISS EYNSFORD HILL: How d'you do? (*She shakes.*)

MRS HIGGINS (*introducing*): My son Henry.

MRS EYNSFORD HILL: Your celebrated son! I have so longed to meet you, Professor Higgins.

HIGGINS (*glumly, making no movement in her direction*): Delighted. (*He backs against the piano and bows brusquely.*)

MISS EYNSFORD HILL (*going to him with confident familiarity*): How do you do?

HIGGINS (*staring at her*): Ive seen you before somewhere. I havnt the ghost of a notion where; but Ive heard your voice. (*Drearily*) It doesnt matter. Youd better sit down.

MRS HIGGINS: I'm sorry to say that my celebrated son has no manners. You mustnt mind him.

MISS EYNSFORD HILL (*gaily*): I don't. (*She sits in the Elizabethan chair.*)

MRS EYNSFORD HILL (*a little bewildered*): Not at all. (*She sits on the ottoman between her daughter and Mrs Higgins, who has turned her chair away from the writing-table.*)

HIGGINS: Oh, have I been rude? I didnt mean to be.

He goes to the central window, through which, with his back to the company, he contemplates the river and the flowers in Battersea Park on the opposite bank as if they were a frozen desert.

The parlor-maid returns, ushering in Pickering.

THE PARLOR-MAID: Colonel Pickering. (*She withdraws.*)

PICKERING: How do you do, Mrs Higgins?

MRS HIGGINS: So glad youve come. Do you know Mrs Eynsford Hill—Miss Eynsford Hill? (*Exchange of bows. The Colonel brings the Chippendale chair a little forward between Mrs Hill and Mrs Higgins, and sits down.*)

PICKERING: Has Henry told you what weve come for?

HIGGINS (*over his shoulder*): We were interrupted: damn it!

MRS HIGGINS: Oh Henry, Henry, really!

MRS EYNSFORD HILL (*half rising*): Are we in the way?

MRS HIGGINS (*rising and making her sit down again*): No, no. You couldnt have come more fortunately: we want you to meet a friend of ours.

HIGGINS (*turning hopefully*): Yes, by George! We want two or three people. You'll do as well as anybody else.

The parlor-maid returns, ushering Freddy.

THE PARLOR-MAID: Mr Eynsford Hill.

HIGGINS (*almost audibly, past endurance*): God of Heaven! another of them.

FREDDY (*shaking hands with Mrs Higgins*): Ahdedo? [54]

MRS HIGGINS: Very good of you to come. (*Introducing*) Colonel Pickering.

FREDDY (*bowing*): Ahdedo?

MRS HIGGINS: I dont think you know my son, Professor Higgins.

[54] *Ahdedo:* How do you do?

FREDDY (*going to Higgins*): Ahdedo?

HIGGINS (*looking at him much as if he were a pickpocket*): I'll take my oath Ive met you before somewhere. Where was it?

FREDDY: I dont think so.

HIGGINS (*resignedly*): It dont matter, anyhow. Sit down.

He shakes Freddy's hand, and almost slings him on to the ottoman with his face to the window; then comes round to the other side of it.

HIGGINS: Well, here we are, anyhow! (*He sits down on the ottoman next* MRS EYNSFORD HILL, *on her left.*) And now, what the devil are we going to talk about until Eliza comes?

MRS HIGGINS: Henry: you are the life and soul of the Royal Society's[55] soirées; but really youre rather trying on more commonplace occasions.

HIGGINS: Am I? Very sorry. (*Beaming suddenly*) I suppose I am, you know. (*Uproariously*) Ha, ha!

MISS EYNSFORD HILL (*who considers Higgins quite eligible matrimonially*): I sympathize. I havent any small talk. If people would only be frank and say what they really think!

HIGGINS (*relapsing into gloom*): Lord forbid!

MRS EYNSFORD HILL (*taking up her daughter's cue*): But why?

HIGGINS: What they think they ought to think is bad enough, Lord knows; but what they really think would break up the whole show. Do you suppose it would be really agreeable if I were to come out now with what I really think?

MISS EYNSFORD HILL (*gaily*): Is it so very cynical?

HIGGINS: Cynical! Who the dickens said it was cynical? I mean it wouldn't be decent.

MRS EYNSFORD HILL (*seriously*): Oh! I'm sure you dont mean that, Mr Higgins.

HIGGINS: You see, we're all savages, more or less. We're supposed to be civilized and cultured—to know all about poetry and philosophy and art and science, and so on; but how many of us know even the meanings of these names? (*To Miss Hill*) What do you know of poetry? (*To Mrs Hill*) What do you know of science? (*Indicating Freddy*) What does he know of art or science or anything else? What the devil do you imagine I know of philosophy?

MRS HIGGINS (*warningly*): Or of manners, Henry?

THE PARLOR-MAID (*opening the door*): Miss Doolittle. (*She withdraws.*)

HIGGINS (*rising hastily and running to Mrs Higgins*): Here she is, mother. (*He stands on tiptoe and makes signs over his mother's head to Eliza to indicate to her which lady is her hostess.*)

Eliza, who is exquisitely dressed, produces an impression of such remarkable distinction and beauty as she enters that they all rise,

[55] *Royal Society:* English organization of scientists.

quite fluttered. Guided by Higgins's signals, she comes to Mrs. Higgins with studied grace.

LIZA (*speaking with pedantic correctness of pronunciation and great beauty of tone*): How do you do, Mrs Higgins? (*She gasps slightly in making sure of the H in Higgins, but is quite successful.*) Mr Higgins told me I might come.

MRS HIGGINS (*cordially*): Quite right: I'm very glad indeed to see you.

PICKERING: How do you do, Miss Doolittle?

LIZA (*shaking hands with him*): Colonel Pickering, is it not?

MRS EYNSFORD HILL: I feel sure we have met before, Miss Doolittle. I remember your eyes.

LIZA: How do you do? (*She sits down on the ottoman gracefully in the place just left vacant by Higgins.*)

MRS EYNSFORD HILL (*introducing*): My daughter Clara.

LIZA: How do you do?

CLARA (*impulsively*): How do you do? (*She sits down on the ottoman beside Eliza, devouring her with her eyes.*)

FREDDY (*coming to their side of the ottoman*): Ive certainly had the pleasure.

MRS EYNSFORD HILL (*introducing*): My son Freddy.

LIZA: How do you do?

Freddy bows and sits down in the Elizabethan chair, infatuated.

HIGGINS (*suddenly*): By George, yes: it all comes back to me! (*They stare at him.*) Covent Garden! (*Lamentably*) What a damned thing!

MRS HIGGINS: Henry, please! (*He is about to sit on the edge of the table.*) Dont sit on my writing-table: youll break it.

HIGGINS (*sulkily*): Sorry.

He goes to the divan, stumbling into the fender and over the fire-irons on his way; extricating himself with muttered imprecations; and finishing his disastrous journey by throwing himself so impatiently on the divan that he almost breaks it. Mrs Higgins looks at him, but controls herself and says nothing.

A long and painful pause ensues.

MRS HIGGINS (*at last, conversationally*): Will it rain, do you think?

LIZA: The shallow depression in the west of these islands is likely to move slowly in an easterly direction. There are no indications of any great change in the barometrical situation.

FREDDY: Ha! ha! how awfully funny!

LIZA: What is wrong with that, young man? I bet I got it right.

FREDDY: Killing!

MRS EYNSFORD HILL: I'm sure I hope it wont turn cold. Theres so much influenza about. It runs right through our whole family regularly every spring.

LIZA (*darkly*): My aunt died of influenza: so they said.

MRS EYNSFORD HILL (*clicks her tongue sympathetically*): !!!

LIZA (*in the same tragic tone*): But it's my belief they done the old woman in.

MRS HIGGINS (*puzzled*): Done her in?

LIZA: Ye-e-e-e-es, Lord love you! Why should she die of influenza? She come through diphtheria right enough the year before. I saw her with my own eyes. Fairly blue with it, she was. They all thought she was dead; but my father he kept ladling gin down her throat till she came to so sudden that she bit the bowl off the spoon.

MRS EYNSFORD HILL (*startled*): Dear me!

LIZA (*piling up the indictment*): What call would a woman with that strength in her have to die of influenza? What become of her new straw hat that should have come to me? Somebody pinched it; and what I say is, them as pinched it done her in.

MRS EYNSFORD HILL (*hastily*): What does doing her in mean?

HIGGINS (*hastily*): Oh, thats the new small talk. To do a person in means to kill them.

MRS EYNSFORD HILL (*to Eliza, horrified*): You surely dont believe that your aunt was killed?

LIZA: Do I not! Them she lived with would have killed her for a hat-pin, let alone a hat.

MRS EYNSFORD HILL: But it cant have been right for your father to pour spirits down her throat like that. It might have killed her.

LIZA: Not her. Gin was mother's milk to her. Besides, he'd poured so much down his own throat that he knew the good of it.

MRS EYNSFORD HILL: Do you mean that he drank?

LIZA: Drank! My word! Something chronic.

MRS EYNSFORD HILL: How dreadful for you!

LIZA: Not a bit. It never did him no harm what I could see. But then he did not keep it up regular. (*Cheerfully*) On the burst, as you might say, from time to time. And always more agreeable when he had a drop in. When he was out of work, my mother used to give him four-pence and tell him to go out and not come back until he'd drunk himself cheerful and loving-like. Theres lots of women has to make their husbands drunk to make them fit to live with. (*Now quite at her ease*) You see, it's like this. If a man has a bit of conscience, it always takes him when he's sober; and then it makes him low-spirited. A drop of booze just takes that off and makes him happy. (*To Freddy, who is in convulsions of suppressed laughter*) Here! what are you sniggering at?

FREDDY: The new small talk. You do it so awfully well.

LIZA: If I was doing it proper, what was you laughing at? (*To Higgins*) Have I said anything I oughtnt?

MRS HIGGINS (*interposing*): Not at all, Miss Doolittle.

LIZA: Well, thats a mercy, anyhow. (*Expansively*) What I always say is—

HIGGINS (*rising and looking at his watch*): Ahem!

LIZA (*looking round at him; taking the hint; and rising*): Well: I must go. (*They all rise. Freddy goes to the door.*) So pleased to have met you. Goodbye. (*She shakes hands with Mrs Higgins.*)

MRS HIGGINS: Goodbye.

LIZA: Goodbye, Colonel Pickering.

PICKERING: Goodbye, Miss Doolittle. (*They shake hands.*)

LIZA (*nodding to the others*): Goodbye, all.

FREDDY (*opening the door for her*): Are you walking across the Park, Miss Doolittle? If so—

LIZA (*with perfectly elegant diction*): Walk! Not bloody likely. (*Sensation*) I am going in a taxi. (*She goes out.*)

 Pickering gasps and sits down. Freddy goes out on the balcony to catch another glimpse of Eliza.

MRS EYNSFORD HILL (*suffering from shock*): Well, I really cant get used to the new ways.

CLARA (*throwing herself discontentedly into the Elizabethan chair*): Oh, it's all right, mamma, quite right. People will think we never go anywhere or see anybody if you are so old fashioned.

MRS EYNSFORD HILL: I daresay I am very old-fashioned; but I do hope you wont begin using that expression, Clara. I have got accustomed to hear you talking about men as rotters, and calling everything filthy and beastly; though I do think it horrible and unlady like. But this last is really too much. Dont you think so, Colonel Pickering?

PICKERING: Dont ask me. Ive been away in India for several years; and manners have changed so much that I sometimes dont know whether I'm at a respectable dinnertable or in a ship's forecastle.

CLARA: It's all a matter of habit. Theres no right or wrong in it. Nobody means anything by it. And it's so quaint, and gives such a smart emphasis to things that are not in themselves very witty. I find the new small talk delightful and quite innocent.

MRS EYNSFORD HILL (*rising*): Well, after that, I think it's time for us to go.

 Pickering and Higgins rise.

CLARA (*rising*): Oh yes: we have three at-homes to go to still. Goodbye, Mrs Higgins. Goodbye, Colonel Pickering. Goodbye, Professor Higgins.

HIGGINS (*coming grimly at her from the divan, and accompanying her to the door*): Goodbye. Be sure you try on that small talk at the three at-homes. Dont be nervous about it. Pitch it in strong.

CLARA (*all smiles*): I will. Goodbye. Such nonsense, all this early Victorian prudery!

HIGGINS (*tempting her*): Such damned nonsense!

CLARA: Such bloody nonsense!

MRS EYNSFORD HILL (*convulsively*): Clara!

CLARA: Ha! ha! (*She goes out radiant, conscious of being thoroughly up to date, and is heard descending the stairs in a stream of silvery laughter.*)

FREDDY (*to the heavens at large*): Well, I ask you— (*He gives it up, and comes to Mrs Higgins.*) Goodbye.

MRS HIGGINS (*shaking hands*): Goodbye. Would you like to meet Miss Doolittle again?

FREDDY (*eagerly*): Yes, I should, most awfully.

MRS HIGGINS: Well, you know my days.

FREDDY: Yes, Thanks awfully. Goodbye. (*He goes out.*)

MRS EYNSFORD HILL: Goodbye, Mr Higgins.

HIGGINS: Goodbye. Goodbye.

MRS EYNSFORD HILL (*to Pickering*): It's no use. I shall never be able to bring myself to use that word.

PICKERING: Dont. It's not compulsory, you know. Youll get on quite well without it.

MRS EYNSFORD HILL: Only, Clara is so down on me if I am not positively reeking with the latest slang. Goodbye.

PICKERING: Goodbye. (*They shake hands.*)

MRS EYNSFORD HILL (*to Mrs Higgins*): You mustnt mind Clara. (*Pickering, catching from her lowered tone that this is not meant for him to hear, discreetly joins Higgins at the window.*) We're so poor! and she gets so few parties, poor child! She doesnt quite know. (*Mrs Higgins, seeing that her eyes are moist, takes her hand sympathetically and goes with her to the door.*) But the boy is nice. Dont you think so?

MRS HIGGINS: Oh, quite nice. I shall always be delighted to see him.

MRS EYNSFORD HILL: Thank you, dear. Goodbye. (*She goes out.*)

HIGGINS (*eagerly*): Well? Is Eliza presentable? (*He swoops on his mother and drags her to the ottoman, where she sits down in Eliza's place with her son on her left.*)

Pickering returns to his chair on her right.

MRS HIGGINS: You silly boy, of course she's not presentable. She's a triumph of your art and of her dressmaker's; but if you suppose for a moment that she doesn't give herself away in every sentence she utters, you must be perfectly cracked about her.

PICKERING: But dont you think something might be done? I mean something to eliminate the sanguinary element from her conversation.

MRS HIGGINS: Not as long as she is in Henry's hands.

HIGGINS (*aggrieved*): Do you mean that my language is improper?

MRS HIGGINS: No, dearest: it would be quite proper—say on a canal barge; but it would not be proper for her at a garden party.

HIGGINS (*deeply injured*): Well I must say—

PICKERING (*interrupting him*): Come, Higgins: you must learn to know yourself. I havent heard such language as yours since we used to review the volunteers in Hyde Park twenty years ago.

HIGGINS (*sulkily*): Oh, well, if you say so, I suppose I dont always talk like a bishop.

MRS HIGGINS (*quieting Henry with a touch*): Colonel Pickering: will you tell me what is the exact state of things in Wimpole Street?

PICKERING (*cheerfully: as if this completely changed the subject*): Well, I have come to live there with Henry. We work together at my Indian Dialects; and we think it more convenient—

MRS HIGGINS: Quite so. I know all about that: it's an excellent arrangement. But where does this girl live?

HIGGINS: With us, of course. Where should she live?

MRS HIGGINS: But on what terms? Is she a servant? If not, what is she?

PICKERING (*slowly*): I think I know what you mean, Mrs Higgins.

HIGGINS: Well, dash me if *I* do! Ive had to work at the girl every day for months to get her to her present pitch. Besides, she's useful. She knows where my things are, and remembers my appointments and so forth.

MRS HIGGINS: How does your housekeeper get on with her?

HIGGINS: Mrs Pearce? Oh, she's jolly glad to get so much taken off her hands; for before Eliza came, she used to have to find things and remind me of my appointments. But she's got some silly bee in her bonnet about Eliza. She keeps saying "You dont think, sir": doesnt she, Pick?

PICKERING: Yes: thats the formula. "You dont think, sir." Thats the end of every conversation about Eliza.

HIGGINS: As if I ever stop thinking about the girl and her confounded vowels and consonants. I'm worn out, thinking about her, and watching her lips and her teeth and her tongue, not to mention her soul, which is the quaintest of the lot.

MRS HIGGINS: You certainly are a pretty pair of babies, playing with your live doll.

HIGGINS: Playing! The hardest job I ever tackled: make no mistake about that, mother. But you have no idea how frightfully interesting it is to take a human being and change her into a quite different human being by creating a new speech for her. It's filling up the deepest gulf that separates class from class and soul from soul.

PICKERING (*drawing his chair closer to Mrs Higgins and bending over to her eagerly*): Yes: it's enormously interesting. I assure you, Mrs Higgins, we take Eliza very seriously. Every week—every day almost—there is some new change. (*Closer again*) We keep records of every stage—dozens of gramophone disks and photographs—

HIGGINS (*assailing her at the other ear*): Yes, by George: it's the most absorbing experiment I ever tackled. She regularly fills our lives up: doesnt she, Pick?

PICKERING: We're always talking Eliza.

HIGGINS: Teaching Eliza.

PICKERING: Dressing Eliza.

MRS HIGGINS: What!

HIGGINS: Inventing new Elizas.

HIGGINS	*(speaking together)*	You know, she has the most extraordinary quickness of ear:
PICKERING		I assure you, my dear Mrs Higgins, that girl
HIGGINS		just like a parrot. Ive tried her with every
PICKERING		is a genius. She can play the piano quite beautifully.
HIGGINS		possible sort of sound that human being can make—
PICKERING		We have taken her to classical concerts and to music
HIGGINS		Continental dialects, African dialects, Hottentot
PICKERING		halls; and it's all the same to her: she plays everything
HIGGINS		clicks, things it took me years to get hold of; and
PICKERING		she hears right off when she comes home, whether it's
HIGGINS		she picks them up like a shot, right away, as if she had
PICKERING		Beethoven[56] and Brahms[57] or Lehar[58] and Lionel Moncktan;[59]
HIGGINS		been at it all her life.
PICKERING		though six months ago, she'd never as much as touched a piano—

MRS HIGGINS *(putting her fingers in her ears, as they are by this time shouting one another down with intolerable noise)*: Sh-sh-sh—sh! (*They stop.*)

PICKERING: I beg your pardon. (*He draws his chair back apologetically.*)

HIGGINS: Sorry. When Pickering starts shouting nobody can get a word in edgeways.

MRS HIGGINS: Be quiet, Henry. Colonel Pickering: dont you realize that when Eliza walked in Wimpole Street, something walked in with her?

PICKERING: Her father did. But Henry soon got rid of him.

MRS HIGGINS: It would have been more to the point if her mother had. But as her mother didnt something else did.

PICKERING: But what?

[56] *Beethoven:* Ludwig van Beethoven (1770–1827), German composer.
[57] *Brahms:* Johannes Brahms (1833–1897), German composer.
[58] *Lehar:* Franz Lehar (1870–1948), Hungarian composer of operettas.
[59] *Monckton:* Lionel Monckton (1861–1924), English composer of musical comedies.

MRS HIGGINS (*unconsciously dating herself by the word*): A problem.

PICKERING: Oh, I see. The problem of how to pass her off as a lady.

HIGGINS: I'll solve that problem. Ive half solved it already.

MRS HIGGINS: No, you two infinitely stupid male creatures: the problem of what is to be done with her afterwards.

HIGGINS: I dont see anything in that. She can go her own way, with all the advantages I have given her.

MRS HIGGINS: The advantages of that poor woman who was here just now! The manners and habits that disqualify a fine lady from earning her own living without giving her a fine lady's income! Is that what you mean?

PICKERING (*indulgently, being rather bored*): Oh, that will be all right, Mrs Higgins. (*He rises to go.*)

HIGGINS (*rising also*): We'll find her some light employment.

PICKERING: She's happy enough. Dont you worry about her. Goodbye. (*He shakes hands as if he were consoling a frightened child, and makes for the door.*)

HIGGINS: Anyhow, theres no good bothering now. The thing's done. Good-bye, mother. (*He kisses her, and follows Pickering.*)

PICKERING (*turning for a final consolation*): There are plenty of openings. We'll do whats right. Goodbye.

HIGGINS (*to Pickering as they go out together*): Lets take her to the Shake-spear exhibition at Earls Court.

PICKERING: Yes: lets. Her remarks will be delicious.

HIGGINS: She'll mimic all the people for us when we get home.

PICKERING: Ripping.[60] (*Both are heard laughing as they go downstairs.*)

MRS HIGGINS (*rises with an impatient bounce, and returns to her work at the writing-table. She sweeps a litter of disarranged papers out of the way; snatches a sheet of paper from her stationery case; and tries reso-lutely to write. At the third time she gives it up; flings down her pen; grips the table angrily and exclaims*): Oh, men! men!! men!!!

✻   ✻   ✻   ✻   ✻   ✻   ✻   ✻

Clearly Eliza will not pass as a duchess yet; and Higgins's bet re-mains unwon. But the six months are not yet exhausted; and just in time Eliza does actually pass as a princess. For a glimpse of how she did it imagine an Embassy in London one summer evening after dark. The hall door has an awning and a carpet across the sidewalk to the kerb, because a grand reception is in progress. A small crowd is lined up to see the guests arrive.

A Rolls-Royce car drives up. Pickering in evening dress, with medals and orders, alights, and hands out Eliza, in opera cloak, evening dress, diamonds, fan, flowers and all accessories. Higgins

[60] *Ripping:* Excellent, splendid.

follows. The car drives off; and the three go up the steps and into the house, the door opening for them as they approach.

Inside the house they find themselves in a spacious hall from which the grand staircase rises. On the left are the arrangements for the gentlemen's cloaks. The male guests are depositing their hats and wraps there.

On the right is a door leading to the ladies' cloakroom. Ladies are going in cloaked and coming out in splendor. Pickering whispers to Eliza and points out the ladies' room. She goes into it. Higgins and Pickering take off their overcoats and take tickets for them from the attendant.

One of the guests, occupied in the same way, has his back turned. Having taken his ticket, he turns round and reveals himself as an important looking young man with an astonishingly hairy face. He has an enormous moustache, flowing out into luxuriant whiskers. Waves of hair cluster on his brow. His hair is cropped closely at the back, and glows with oil. Otherwise he is very smart. He wears several worthless orders. He is evidently a foreigner, guessable as a whiskered Pandour[61] from Hungary; but in spite of the ferocity of his moustache he is amiable and genially voluble.

Recognizing Higgins, he flings his arms wide apart and approaches him enthusiastically.

WHISKERS: Maestro, maestro. (*He embraces Higgins and kisses him on both cheeks.*) You remember me?

HIGGINS: No I dont. Who the devil are you?

WHISKERS: I am your pupil: your first pupil, your best and greatest pupil. I am little Nepommuck,[62] the marvellous boy.[63] I have made your name famous throughout Europe. You teach me phonetic. You cannot forget ME.

HIGGINS: Why dont you shave?

NEPOMMUCK: I have not your imposing appearance, your chin, your brow.

---

[61] *Pandour:* One of a group of brutal, marauding soldiers in eighteenth-century Croatia.

[62] *Nepommuck:* Shaw may have had in mind Saint John of Nepomuck (c. 1345–1393), who was martyred because he refused to speak of what was told him in the confessional. The introit of the mass of Saint John of Nepomuck (May 16) is "The Lord endowed me with the gift of speech: with it I shall praise Him [*Ecclesiasticus,* 51:30]. I said, I will live watchfully, and never use my tongue amiss [*Psalms,* 38:2]." Both references are to the Catholic Bible. Shaw may also have had in mind the Hungarian composer Johann Nepomuk Hummel (1778–1837), who studied under Mozart and was inferior to his teacher.

[63] *marvelous boy:* In *Resolution and Independence* (1802), William Wordsworth called Thomas Chatterton "the marvellous Boy,/ The sleepless Soul that perished in his pride." Chatterton (1752–1770), author of a number of poems based on fourteenth- and fifteenth-century English, which he ascribed to a fictitious fifteenth-century priest, Thomas Rowley, committed suicide at the age of eighteen.

Nobody notice me when I shave. Now I am famous: they call me Hairy Faced Dick.

HIGGINS: And what are you doing here among all these swells?

NEPOMMUCK: I am interpreter. I speak 32 languages. I am indispensable at these international parties. You are great cockney specialist: you place a man anywhere in London the moment he open his mouth. I place any man in Europe.

A footman hurries down the grand staircase and comes to Nepommuck.

FOOTMAN: You are wanted upstairs. Her Excellency cannot understand the Greek gentleman.

NEPOMMUCK: Thank you, yes, immediately.

The footman goes and is lost in the crowd.

NEPOMMUCK (*to Higgins*): This Greek diplomatist pretends he cannot speak nor understand English. He cannot deceive me. He is the son of a Clerkenwell watchmaker. He speaks English so villainously that he dare not utter a word of it without betraying his origin. I help him to pretend; but I make him pay through the nose. I make them all pay. Ha ha! (*He hurries upstairs.*)

PICKERING: Is this fellow really an expert? Can he find out Eliza and blackmail her?

HIGGINS: We shall see. If he finds her out I lose my bet.

Eliza comes from the cloakroom and joins them.

PICKERING: Well, Eliza, now for it. Are you ready?

LIZA: Are you nervous, Colonel?

PICKERING: Frightfully. I feel exactly as I felt before my first battle. It's the first time that frightens.

LIZA: It is not the first time for me, Colonel. I have done this fifty times— hundreds of times—in my little piggery in Angel Court in my daydreams. I am in a dream now. Promise me not to let Professor Higgins wake me; for if he does I shall forget everything and talk as I used to in Drury Lane.

PICKERING: Not a word, Higgins. (*To Eliza*) Now, ready?

LIZA: Ready.

PICKERING: Go.

They mount the stairs, Higgins last. Pickering whispers to the footman on the first landing.

FIRST LANDING FOOTMAN: Miss Doolittle, Colonel Pickering, Professor Higgins.

SECOND LANDING FOOTMAN: Miss Doolittle, Colonel Pickering, Professor Higgins.

At the top of the staircase the Ambassador and his wife, with Nepommuck at her elbow, are receiving.

HOSTESS (*taking Eliza's hand*): How d'ye do?

HOST (*same play*): How d'ye do? How d'ye do, Pickering?

LIZA (*with a beautiful gravity that awes her hostess*): How do you do? (*She passes on to the drawingroom.*)

HOSTESS: Is that your adopted daughter, Colonel Pickering? She will make a sensation.

PICKERING: Most kind of you to invite her for me. (*He passes on.*)

HOSTESS (*to Nepommuck*): Find out all about her.

NEPOMMUCK (*bowing*): Excellency—(*He goes into the crowd.*)

HOST: How d'ye do, Higgins? You have a rival here tonight. He introduced himself as your pupil. Is he any good?

HIGGINS: He can learn a language in a fortnight—knows dozens of them. A sure mark of a fool. As a phonetician, no good whatever.

HOSTESS: How d'ye do, Professor?

HIGGINS: How do you do? Fearful bore for you this sort of thing. Forgive my part in it. (*He passes on.*)

In the drawingroom and its suite of salons the reception is in full swing. Eliza passes through. She is so intent on her ordeal that she walks like a somnambulist in a desert instead of a débutante in a fashionable crowd. They stop talking to look at her, admiring her dress, her jewels, and her strangely attractive self. Some of the younger ones at the back stand on their chairs to see.

The Host and Hostess come in from the staircase and mingle with their guests. Higgins, gloomy and contemptuous of the whole business, comes into the group where they are chatting.

HOSTESS: Ah, here is Professor Higgins: he will tell us. Tell us all about the wonderful young lady, Professor.

HIGGINS (*almost morosely*): What wonderful young lady?

HOSTESS: You know very well. They tell me there has been nothing like her in London since people stood on their chairs to look at Mrs Langtry.[64]

Nepommuck joins the group, full of news.

HOSTESS: Ah, here you are at last, Nepommuck. Have you found out all about the Doolittle lady?

NEPOMMUCK: I have found out all about her. She is a fraud.

HOSTESS: A fraud! Oh no.

NEPOMMUCK: YES, yes. She cannot deceive me. Her name cannot be Doolittle.

HIGGINS: Why?

NEPOMMUCK: Because Doolittle is an English name. And she is not English.

HOSTESS: Oh, nonsense! She speaks English perfectly.

NEPOMMUCK: Too perfectly. Can you shew me any English woman who speaks English as it should be spoken? Only foreigners who have been taught to speak it speak it well.

[64] *Mrs Langtry:* Lily Langtry (1852–1929), beautiful English actress, known as "the Jersey Lily."

HOSTESS: Certainly she terrified me by the way she said How d'ye do. I had a schoolmistress who talked like that; and I was mortally afraid of her. But if she is not English what is she?

NEPOMMUCK: Hungarian.

ALL THE REST: Hungarian!

NEPOMMUCK: Hungarian. And of royal blood. I am Hungarian. My blood is royal.

HIGGINS: Did you speak to her in Hungarian?

NEPOMMUCK: I did. She was very clever. She said "Please speak to me in English: I do not understand French." French! She pretend not to know the difference between Hungarian and French. Impossible: she knows both.

HIGGINS: And the blood royal? How did you find that out?

NEPOMMUCK: Instinct, maestro, instinct. Only the Magyar races can produce that air of the divine right, those resolute eyes. She is a princess.

HOST: What do you say, Professor?

HIGGINS: I say an ordinary London girl out of the gutter and taught to speak by an expert. I place her in Drury Lane.

NEPOMMUCK: Ha ha ha! Oh, maestro, maestro, you are mad on the subject of cockney dialects. The London gutter is the whole world for you.

HIGGINS (to the Hostess): What does your Excellency say?

HOSTESS: Oh, of course I agree with Nepommuck. She must be a princess at least.

HOST: Not necessarily legitimate, of course. Morganatic perhaps. But that is undoubtedly her class.

HIGGINS: I stick to my opinion.

HOSTESS: Oh, you are incorrigible.

The group breaks up, leaving Higgins isolated. Pickering joins him.

PICKERING: Where is Eliza? We must keep an eye on her.

Eliza joins them.

LIZA: I dont think I can bear much more. The people all stare so at me. An old lady has just told me that I speak exactly like Queen Victoria. I am sorry if I have lost your bet. I have done my best; but nothing can make me the same as these people.

PICKERING: You have not lost it, my dear. You have won it ten times over.

HIGGINS: Let us get out of this. I have had enough of chattering to these fools.

PICKERING: Eliza is tired; and I am hungry. Let us clear out and have supper somewhere.

§ ACT IV

The Wimpole Street laboratory. Midnight. Nobody in the room. The clock on the mantelpiece strikes twelve. The fire is not alight: it is a summer night.

Presently Higgins and Pickering are heard on the stairs.

HIGGINS (*calling down to Pickering*): I say, Pick: lock up, will you? I shant be going out again.

PICKERING: Right. Can Mrs Pearce go to bed? We dont want anything more, do we?

HIGGINS: Lord, no!

Eliza opens the door and is seen on the lighted landing in all the finery in which she has just won Higgins's bet for him. She comes to the hearth, and switches on the electric lights there. She is tired: her pallor contrasts strongly with her dark eyes and hair; and her expression is almost tragic. She takes off her cloak; puts her fan and gloves on the piano; and sits down on the bench, brooding and silent. Higgins, in evening dress, with overcoat and hat, comes in, carrying a smoking jacket which he has picked up downstairs. He takes off the hat and overcoat; throws them carelessly on the newspaper stand; disposes of his coat in the same way; puts on the smoking jacket; and throws himself wearily into the easy-chair at the hearth. Pickering, similarly attired, comes in. He also takes off his hat and overcoat, and is about to throw them on Higgins's when he hesitates.

PICKERING: I say: Mrs Pearce will row if we leave these things lying about in the drawing room.

HIGGINS: Oh, chuck them over the bannisters into the hall. She'll find them there in the morning and put them away all right. She'll think we were drunk.

PICKERING: We are, slightly. Are there any letters?

HIGGINS: I didnt look. (*Pickering takes the overcoats and hats and goes downstairs. Higgins begins half singing half yawning an air from La Fanciulla del Golden West.[65] Suddenly he stops and exclaims.*) I wonder where the devil my slippers are!

Eliza looks at him darkly; then rises suddenly and leaves the room.

Higgins yawns again, and resumes his song.

Pickering returns, with the contents of the letter-box in his hand.

PICKERING: Only circulars, and this coroneted billet-doux for you. (*He throws the circulars into the fender, and posts himself on the hearth-rug, with his back to the grate.*)

---

[65] *La . . . West: The Girl of the Golden West*, an opera (1910) by Giacomo Puccini, based on the play of the same name (1905) by David Belasco.

HIGGINS (*glancing at the billet-doux*): Money-lender. (*He throws the letter after the circulars.*)

Eliza returns with a pair of large down-at-heel slippers. She places them on the carpet before Higgins, and sits as before without a word.

HIGGINS (*yawning again*): Oh Lord! What an evening! What a crew! What a silly tomfoolery! (*He raises his shoe to unlace it, and catches sight of the slippers. He stops unlacing and looks at them as if they had appeared there of their own accord.*) Oh! theyre there, are they?

PICKERING (*stretching himself*): Well, I feel a bit tired. It's been a long day. The garden party, a dinner party, and the reception! Rather too much of a good thing. But youve won your bet, Higgins. Eliza did the trick, and something to spare, eh?

HIGGINS (*fervently*): Thank God it's over!

Eliza flinches violently; but they take no notice of her; and she recovers herself and sits stonily as before.

PICKERING: Were you nervous at the garden party? I was. Eliza didn't seem a bit nervous.

HIGGINS: Oh, she wasnt nervous. I knew she'd be all right. No: it's the strain of putting the job through all these months that has told on me. It was interesting enough at first, while we were at the phonetics; but after that I got deadly sick of it. If I hadnt backed myself to do it I should have chucked the whole thing up two months ago. It was a silly notion: the whole thing has been a bore.

PICKERING: Oh come! the garden party was frightfully exciting. My heart began beating like anything.

HIGGINS: Yes, for the first three minutes. But when I saw we were going to win hands down, I felt like a bear in a cage, hanging about doing nothing. The dinner was worse: sitting gorging there for over an hour, with nobody but a damned fool of a fashionable woman to talk to! I tell you, Pickering, never again for me. No more artificial duchesses. The whole thing has been simple purgatory.

PICKERING: Youve never been broken in properly to the social routine. (*Strolling over to the piano*) I rather enjoy dipping into it occasionally myself: it makes me feel young again. Anyhow, it was a great success: an immense success. I was quite frightened once or twice because Eliza was doing it so well. You see, lots of the real people cant do it at all: theyre such fools that they think style comes by nature to people in their position; and so they never learn. Theres always something professional about doing a thing superlatively well.

HIGGINS: Yes: thats what drives me mad: the silly people dont know their own silly business. (*Rising*) However, it's over and done with; and now I can go to bed at last without dreading tomorrow.

Eliza's beauty becomes murderous.

PICKERING: I think I shall turn in too. Still, it's been a great occasion: a triumph for you. Goodnight. (*He goes.*)

HIGGINS (*following him*): Goodnight. (*Over his shoulder, at the door*) Put out the lights, Eliza; and tell Mrs Pearce not to make coffee for me in the morning: I'll take tea. (*He goes out.*)

Eliza tries to control herself and feel indifferent as she rises and walks across to the hearth to switch off the lights. By the time she gets there she is on the point of screaming. She sits down in Higgins's chair and holds on hard to the arms. Finally she gives way and flings herself furiously on the floor, raging.

HIGGINS (*in despairing wrath outside*): What the devil have I done with my slippers? (*He appears at the door.*)

LIZA (*snatching up the slippers, and hurling them at him one after the other with all her force*): There are your slippers. And there. Take your slippers; and may you never have a day's luck with them!

HIGGINS (*astounded*): What on earth—! (*He comes to her.*) Whats the matter? Get up. (*He pulls her up.*) Anything wrong?

LIZA (*breathless*): Nothing wrong—with you. Ive won your bet for you, havnt I? Thats enough for you. *I* dont matter, I suppose.

HIGGINS: *You* won *my* bet! You! Presumptuous insect! *I* won it. What did you throw those slippers at me for?

LIZA: Because I wanted to smash your face. I'd like to kill you, you selfish brute. Why didnt you leave me where you picked me out of—in the gutter? You thank God it's all over, and that now you can throw me back again there, do you? (*She crisps her fingers frantically.*)

HIGGINS (*looking at her in cool wonder*): The creature is nervous, after all.

LIZA (*gives a suffocated scream of fury, and instinctively darts her nails at his face*): !!

HIGGINS (*catching her wrists*): Ah! would you? Claws in, you cat. How dare you shew your temper to me? Sit down and be quiet. (*He throws her roughly into the easy-chair.*)

LIZA (*crushed by superior strength and weight*): Whats to become of me? Whats to become of me?

HIGGINS: How the devil do I know whats to become of you? What does it matter what becomes of you?

LIZA: You dont care. I know you dont care. You wouldnt care if I was dead. I'm nothing to you—not so much as them slippers.

HIGGINS (*thundering*): Those slippers.

LIZA (*with bitter submission*): Those slippers. I didnt think it made any difference now.

A pause. Eliza hopeless and crushed. Higgins a little uneasy.

HIGGINS (*in his loftiest manner*): Why have you begun going on like this? May I ask whether you complain of your treatment here?

LIZA: No.

HIGGINS: Has anybody behaved badly to you? Colonel Pickering? Mrs Pearce? Any of the servants?

LIZA: No.

HIGGINS: I presume you dont pretend that *I* have treated you badly?

LIZA: No.

HIGGINS: I am glad to hear it. (*He moderates his tone.*) Perhaps youre tired after the strain of the day. Will you have a glass of champagne? (*He moves towards the door.*)

LIZA: No. (*Recollecting her manners*) Thank you.

HIGGINS (*good-humored again*): This has been coming on you for some days. I suppose it was natural for you to be anxious about the garden party. But thats all over now. (*He pats her kindly on the shoulder. She writhes.*) Theres nothing more to worry about.

LIZA: No. Nothing more for you to worry about. (*She suddenly rises and gets away from him by going to the piano bench, where she sits and hides her face.*) Oh God! I wish I was dead.

HIGGINS (*staring after her in sincere surprise*): Why? In heaven's name, why? (*Reasonably, going to her*) Listen to me, Eliza. All this irritation is purely subjective.

LIZA: I dont understand. I'm too ignorant.

HIGGINS: It's only imagination. Low spirits and nothing else. Nobody's hurting you. Nothing's wrong. You go to bed like a good girl and sleep it off. Have a little cry and say your prayers: that will make you comfortable.

LIZA: I heard your prayers. "Thank God it's all over!"

HIGGINS (*impatiently*): Well, dont you thank God it's all over? Now you are free and can do what you like.

LIZA (*pulling herself together in desperation*): What am I fit for? What have you left me fit for? Where am I to go? What am I to do? Whats to become of me?

HIGGINS (*enlightened, but not at all impressed*): Oh, thats whats worrying you, is it? (*He thrusts his hands into his pockets, and walks about in his usual manner, rattling the contents of his pockets, as if condescending to a trivial subject out of pure kindness.*) I shouldnt bother about it if I were you. I should imagine you wont have much difficulty in settling yourself somewhere or other, though I hadnt quite realized that you were going away. (*She looks quickly at him: he does not look at her, but examines the dessert stand on the piano and decides that he will eat an apple.*) You might marry, you know. (*He bites a large piece out of the apple and munches it noisily.*) You see, Eliza, all men are not confirmed old bachelors like me and the Colonel. Most men are the marrying sort (poor devils!); and youre not bad-looking: it's quite a pleasure to look at you sometimes—not now, of course, because youre crying and looking as ugly as the very devil; but when youre all right and quite yourself, youre what I should call attractive. That is, to the people in the marrying line, you understand. You go to bed and have a good nice rest; and then get up and look at yourself in the glass; and you wont feel so cheap.

Eliza again looks at him, speechless, and does not stir. The look is quite lost on him: he eats his apple with a dreamy expression of happiness, as it is quite a good one.

HIGGINS (*a genial afterthought occurring to him*): I daresay my mother could find some chap or other who would do very well.

LIZA: We were above that at the corner of Tottenham Court Road.

HIGGINS (*waking up*): What do you mean?

LIZA: I sold flowers. I didnt sell myself. Now youve made a lady of me I'm not fit to sell anything else. I wish youd left me where you found me.

HIGGINS (*slinging the core of the apple decisively into the grate*): Tosh, Eliza. Dont you insult human relations by dragging all this cant about buying and selling into it. You neednt marry the fellow if you dont like him.

LIZA: What else am I to do?

HIGGINS: Oh, lots of things. What about your old idea of a florist's shop? Pickering could set you up in one: he has lots of money. (*Chuckling*) He'll have to pay for all those togs[66] you have been wearing today; and that, with the hire of the jewellery, will make a big hole in two hundred pounds. Why, six months ago you would have thought it the millennium to have a flower shop of your own. Come! youll be all right. I must clear off to bed: I'm devilish sleepy. By the way, I came down for something: I forgot what it was.

LIZA: Your slippers.

HIGGINS: Oh yes, of course. You shied them at me. (*He picks them up, and is going out when she rises and speaks to him.*)

LIZA: Before you go, sir—

HIGGINS (*dropping the slippers in his surprise at her calling him Sir*): Eh?

LIZA: Do my clothes belong to me or to Colonel Pickering?

HIGGINS (*coming back into the room as if her question were the very climax of unreason*): What the devil use would they to be Pickering?

LIZA: He might want them for the next girl you pick up to experiment on.

HIGGINS (*shocked and hurt*): Is that the way you feel towards us?

LIZA: I dont want to hear anything more about that. All I want to know is whether anything belongs to me. My own clothes were burnt.

HIGGINS: But what does it matter? Why need you start bothering about that in the middle of the night?

LIZA: I want to know what I may take away with me. I dont want to be accused of stealing.

HIGGINS (*now deeply wounded*): Stealing! You shouldnt have said that, Eliza. That shews a want of feeling.

[66] *togs:* Clothes.

LIZA: I'm sorry. I'm only a common ignorant girl; and in my station I have to be careful. There cant be any feelings between the like of you and the like of me. Please will you tell me what belongs to me and what doesnt?

HIGGINS (*very sulky*): You may take the whole damned houseful if you like. Except the jewels. Theyre hired. Will that satisfy you? (*He turns on his heel and is about to go in extreme dudgeon.*)

LIZA (*drinking in his emotion like nectar, and nagging him to provoke a further supply*): Stop, please. (*She takes off her jewels.*) Will you take these to your room and keep them safe? I dont want to run the risk of their being missing.

HIGGINS (*furious*): Hand them over. (*She puts them into his hands.*) If these belonged to me instead of to the jeweller, I'd ram them down your ungrateful throat. (*He perfunctorily thrusts them into his pockets, unconsciously decorating himself with the protruding ends of the chains.*)

LIZA (*taking a ring off*): This ring isnt the jeweller's: it's the one you bought me in Brighton.[67] I dont want it now. (*Higgins dashes the ring violently into the fireplace, and turns on her so threateningly that she crouches over the piano with her hands over her face, and exclaims.*) Dont you hit me.

HIGGINS: Hit you! You infamous creature, how dare you accuse me of such a thing? It is you who have hit me. You have wounded me to the heart.

LIZA (*thrilling with hidden joy*): I'm glad. Ive got a little of my own back, anyhow.

HIGGINS (*with dignity, in his finest professional style*): You have caused me to lose my temper: a thing that has hardly ever happened to me before. I prefer to say nothing more tonight. I am going to bed.

LIZA (*pertly*): Youd better leave a note for Mrs Pearce about the coffee; for she wont be told by me.

HIGGINS (*formally*): Damn Mrs Pearce; and damn the coffee; and damn you; and (*Wildly*) damn my own folly in having lavished my hard-earned knowledge and the treasure of my regard and intimacy on a heartless guttersnipe. (*He goes out with impressive decorum, and spoils it by slamming the door savagely.*)

Eliza goes down on her knees on the hearthrug to look for the ring. When she finds it she considers for a moment what to do with it. Finally she flings it down on the dessert stand and goes upstairs a tearing rage.

* * * * * * * *

The furniture of Eliza's room has been increased by a big wardrobe and a sumptuous dressing-table. She comes in and switches

[67] *Brighton:* A seaside resort in southern England.

on the electric light. She goes to the wardrobe; opens it; and pulls out a walking dress, a hat, and a pair of shoes, which she throws on the bed. She takes off her evening dress and shoes; then takes a padded hanger from the wardrobe; adjusts it carefully in the evening dress; and hangs it in the wardrobe, which she shuts with a slam. She puts on her walking shoes, her walking dress, and hat. She takes her wrist watch from the dressing-table and fastens it on. She pulls on her gloves; takes her vanity bag; and looks into it to see that her purse is there before hanging it on her wrist. She makes for the door. Every movement expresses her furious resolution.

She takes a last look at herself in the glass.

She suddenly puts out her tongue at herself; then leaves the room, switching off the electric light at the door.

Meanwhile, in the street outside, Freddy Eynsford Hill, lovelorn, is gazing up at the second floor, in which one of the windows is still lighted.

The light goes out.

FREDDY: Goodnight, darling, darling, darling.

Eliza comes out, giving the door a considerable bang behind her.

LIZA: Whatever are you doing here?

FREDDY: Nothing. I spend most of my nights here. It's the only place where I'm happy. Dont laugh at me, Miss Doolittle.

LIZA: Dont you call me Miss Doolittle, do you hear? Liza's good enough for me. (*She breaks down and grabs him by the shoulders.*) Freddy: you dont think I'm a heartless guttersnipe, do you?

FREDDY: Oh no, no, darling: how can you imagine such a thing? You are the loveliest, dearest—

He loses all self-control and smothers her with kisses. She, hungry for comfort responds. They stand there in one another's arms.

An elderly police constable arrives.

CONSTABLE (*scandalized*): Now then! Now then!! Now then!!!

They release one another hastily.

FREDDY: Sorry, constable. Weve only just become engaged.

They run away.

The constable shakes his head, reflecting on his own courtship and on the vanity of human hopes. He moves off in the opposite direction with slow professional steps.

The flight of the lovers takes them to Cavendish Square. There they halt to consider their next move.

LIZA (*out of breath*): He didnt half give me a fright, that copper. But you answered him proper.

FREDDY: I hope I havent taken you out of your way. Where were you going?

LIZA: To the river.

FREDDY: What for?

LIZA: To make a hole in it.

FREDDY (*horrified*): Eliza, darling. What do you mean? What's the matter?

LIZA: Never mind. It doesnt matter now. There's nobody in the world now but you and me, is there?

FREDDY: Not a soul.

They indulge in another embrace, and are again surprised by a much younger constable.

SECOND CONSTABLE: Now then, you two! What's this? Where do you think you are? Move along here, double quick.

FREDDY: As you say, sir, double quick.

They run away again, and are in Hanover Square before they stop for another conference.

FREDDY: I had no idea the police were so devilishly prudish.

LIZA: It's their business to hunt girls off the streets.

FREDDY: We must go somewhere. We cant wander about the streets all night.

LIZA: Cant we? I think it'd be lovely to wander about for ever.

FREDDY: Oh, darling.

They embrace again, oblivious of the arrival of a crawling taxi.
It stops.

TAXIMAN: Can I drive you and the lady anywhere, sir?

They start asunder.

LIZA: Oh, Freddy, a taxi. The very thing.

FREDDY: But, damn it, I've no money.

LIZA: I have plenty. The Colonel thinks you should never go out without ten pounds in your pocket. Listen. We'll drive about all night; and in the morning I'll call on old Mrs Higgins and ask her what I ought to do. I'll tell you all about it in the cab. And the police wont touch us there.

FREDDY: Righto! Ripping. (*To the Taximan*) Wimbledon Common. (*They drive off.*)

§ ACT V

Mrs Higgins's drawing room. She is at her writing-table as before. The parlormaid comes in.

THE PARLORMAID (*at the door*): Mr Henry, maam, is downstairs with Colonel Pickering.

MRS HIGGINS: Well, shew them up.

THE PARLORMAID: Theyre using the telephone, maam. Telephoning to the police, I think.

MRS HIGGINS: What!

THE PARLORMAID (*coming further in and lowering her voice*): Mr Henry is in a state, maam. I thought I'd better tell you.

MRS HIGGINS: If you had told me that Mr Henry was not in a state it would have been more surprising. Tell them to come up when theyve finished with the police. I suppose he's lost something.

THE PARLORMAID: Yes, maam. (*Going.*)

MRS HIGGINS: Go upstairs and tell Miss Doolittle that Mr. Henry and the Colonel are here. Ask her not to come down til I send for her.

THE PARLORMAID: Yes, maam.

    Higgins bursts in. He is, as the parlormaid has said, in a state.

HIGGINS: Look here, mother: heres a confounded thing!

MRS HIGGINS: Yes, dear. Good morning. (*He checks his impatience and kisses her, whilst the parlormaid goes out.*) What is it?

HIGGINS: Eliza's bolted.

MRS HIGGINS (*calmly continuing her writing*): You must have frightened her.

HIGGINS: Frightened her! nonsense! She was left last night, as usual, to turn out the lights and all that; and instead of going to bed she changed her clothes and went right off: her bed wasnt slept in. She came in a cab for her things before seven this morning; and that fool Mrs Pearce let her have them without telling me a word about it. What am I to do?

MRS HIGGINS: Do without, I'm afraid, Henry. The girl has a perfect right to leave if she chooses.

HIGGINS (*wandering distractedly across the room*): But I cant find anything. I dont know what appointments Ive got. I'm—(*Pickering comes in. Mrs Higgins puts down her pen and turns away from the writing-table.*)

PICKERING (*shaking hands*): Good morning, Mrs Higgins. Has Henry told you? (*He sits down on the ottoman.*)

HIGGINS: What does that ass of an inspector say? Have you offered a reward?

MRS HIGGINS (*rising in indignant amazement*): You dont mean to say you have set the police after Eliza.

HIGGINS: Of course. What are the police for? What else could we do? (*He sits in the Elizabethan chair.*)

PICKERING: The inspector made a lot of difficulties. I really think he suspected us of some improper purpose.

MRS HIGGINS: Well, of course he did. What right have you to go to the police and give the girl's name as if she were a thief, or a lost umbrella, or something? Really! (*She sits down again, deeply vexed.*)

HIGGINS: But we want to find her.

PICKERING: We cant let her go like this, you know, Mrs Higgins. What were we to do?

MRS HIGGINS: You have no more sense, either of you, than two children. Why—

The parlormaid comes in and breaks off the conversation.

THE PARLORMAID: Mr. Henry: a gentleman wants to see you very particular. He's been sent on from Wimpole Street.

HIGGINS: Oh, bother! I cant see anyone now. Who is it?

THE PARLORMAID: A Mr Doolittle, sir.

PICKERING: Doolittle! Do you mean the dustman?

THE PARLORMAID: Dustman! Oh no, sir: a gentleman.

HIGGINS (*springing up excitedly*): By George, Pick, it's some relative of hers that she's gone to. Somebody we know nothing about. (*To the parlormaid*) Send him up, quick.

THE PARLORMAID: Yes, sir. (*She goes.*)

HIGGINS (*eagerly, going to his mother*): Genteel relatives! now we shall hear something. (*He sits down in the Chippendale chair.*)

MRS HIGGINS: Do you know any of her people?

PICKERING: Only her father: the fellow we told you about.

THE PARLORMAID (*announcing*): Mr Doolittle. (*She withdraws.*)

Doolittle enters. He is resplendently dressed as for a fashionable wedding, and might, in fact, be the bridegroom. A flower in his buttonhole, a dazzling silk hat, and patent leather shoes complete the effect. He is too concerned with the business he has come on to notice Mrs Higgins. He walks straight to Higgins, and accosts him with vehement reproach.

DOOLITTLE (*indicating his own person*): See here! Do you see this? You done this.

HIGGINS: Done what, man?

DOOLITTLE: This, I tell you. Look at it. Look at this hat. Look at this coat.

PICKERING: Has Eliza been buying you clothes?

DOOLITTLE: Eliza! not she. Why would she buy me clothes?

MRS HIGGINS: Good morning, Mr Doolittle. Wont you sit down?

DOOLITTLE (*taken aback as he becomes conscious that he has forgotten his hostess*): Asking your pardon, maam. (*He approaches her and shakes her proffered hand.*) Thank you. (*He sits down on the ottoman, on Pickering's right.*) I am that full of what has happened to me that I cant think of anything else.

HIGGINS: What the dickens has happened to you?

DOOLITTLE: I shouldnt mind if it had happened to me: anything might happen to anybody and nobody to blame but Providence, as you might say. But this is something that you done to me: yes, you, Enry Iggins.

HIGGINS: Have you found Eliza?

DOOLITTLE: Have you lost her?

HIGGINS: Yes.

DOOLITTLE: You have all the luck, you have. I aint found her; but she'll find me quick enough now after what you done to me.

MRS HIGGINS: But what has my son done to you, Mr Doolittle?

DOOLITTLE: Done to me! Ruined me. Destroyed my happiness. Tied me up and delivered me into the hands of middle class morality.

HIGGINS (*rising intolerantly and standing over Doolittle*): Youre raving. Youre drunk. Youre mad. I gave you five pounds. After that I had two conversations with you, at half-a-crown an hour. Ive never seen you since.

DOOLITTLE: Oh! Drunk am I? Mad am I? Tell me this. Did you or did you not write a letter to an old blighter[68] in America that was giving five millions to found Moral Reform Societies all over the world, and that wanted you to invent a universal language for him?

HIGGINS: What! Ezra D. Wannafeller! He's dead. (*He sits down again carelessly.*)

DOOLITTLE: Yes: he's dead; and I'm done for. Now did you or did you not write a letter to him to say that the most original moralist at present in England, to the best of your knowledge, was Alfred Doolittle, a common dustman?

HIGGINS: Oh, after your first visit I remember making some silly joke of the kind.

DOOLITTLE: Ah! you may well call it a silly joke. It put the lid on me right enough. Just give him the chance he wanted to shew that Americans is not like us: that they reckonize and respect merit in every class of life, however humble. Them words is in his blooming will, in which, Henry Higgins, thanks to your silly joking, he leaves me a share in his Pre-digested Cheese Trust worth four thousand a year on condition that I lecture for his Wannafeller Moral Reform World League as often as they ask me up to six times a year.

HIGGINS: The devil he does! Whew! (*Brightening suddenly*) What a lark!

PICKERING: A safe thing for you, Doolittle. They wont ask you twice.

DOOLITTLE: It aint the lecturing I mind. I'll lecture them blue in the face, I will, and not turn a hair. It's making a gentleman of me that I object to. Who asked him to make a gentleman of me? I was happy. I was free. I touched pretty nigh everybody for money when I wanted it, same as I touched you, Enry Iggins. Now I am worrited; tied neck and heels; and everybody touches me for money. It's a fine thing for you, says my solicitor. Is it? says I. You mean it's a good thing for you, I says. When I was a poor man and had a solicitor once when they found a pram in the dust cart, he got me off, and got shut of me and got me shut of him as quick as he could. Same with the doctors: used to shove me out of the hospital before I could hardly stand on my

---

[68] *blighter*: Mildly derogatory slang term, meaning *fellow*.

legs, and nothing to pay. Now they finds out that I'm not a healthy man and cant live unless they looks after me twice a day. In the house I'm not let do a hand's turn for myself: somebody else must do it and touch me for it. A year ago I hadnt a relative in the world except two or three that wouldnt speak to me. Now Ive fifty, and not a decent week's wages among the lot of them. I have to live for others and not for myself: thats middle class morality. You talk of losing Eliza. Dont you be anxious: I bet she's on my doorstep by this: she that could support herself easy by selling flowers if I wasnt respectable. And the next one to touch me will be you, Enry Iggins. I'll have to learn to speak middle class language from you, instead of speaking proper English. Thats where youll come in; and I darcsay thats what you done it for.

MRS HIGGINS: But, my dear Mr Doolittle, you need not suffer all this if you are really in earnest. Nobody can force you to accept this bequest. You can repudiate it. Isnt that so, Colonel Pickering?

PICKERING: I believe so.

DOOLITTLE (*softening his manner in deference to her sex*): Thats the tragedy of it, maam. It's easy to say chuck it; but I havent the nerve. Which of us has? We're all intimidated. Intimidated, maam: thats what we are. What is there for me if I chuck it but the workhouse in my old age? I have to dye my hair already to keep my job as a dustman. If I was one of the deserving poor, and had put by a bit, I could chuck it; but then why should I, acause the deserving poor might as well be millionaires for all the happiness they ever has. They dont know what happiness is. But I, as one of the undeserving poor, have nothing between me and the pauper's uniform but this here blasted four thousand a year that shoves me into the middle class. (Excuse the expression, maam; youd use it yourself if you had my provocation.) Theyve got you every way you turn: it's a choice between the Skilly of the workhouse and the Char Bydis[69] of the middle class; and I havnt the nerve for the workhouse. Intimidated: thats what I am. Broke. Bought up. Happier men than me will call for my dust, and touch me for their tip; and I'll look on helpless, and envy them. And thats what your son has brought me to. (*He is overcome by emotion.*)

MRS HIGGINS: Well, I'm very glad youre not going to do anything foolish, Mr Doolittle. For this solves the problem of Eliza's future. You can provide for her now.

DOOLITTLE (*with melancholy resignation*): Yes, maam: I'm expected to provide for everyone now, out of four thousand a year.

---

[69] *Skilly . . . Bydis:* The phrase "between Scylla and Charybdis" means between two dangers, either of which is difficult to avoid without risking destruction by the other. The term derives from Homer's *The Odyssey*, wherein Odysseus must sail safely between a dangerous rock (Scylla) and a whirlpool (Charybdis).

HIGGINS (*jumping up*): Nonsense! he cant provide for her. He shant provide for her. She doesnt belong to him. I paid him five pounds for her. Doolittle: either youre an honest man or a rogue.

DOOLITTLE (*tolerantly*): A little of both, Henry, like the rest of us: a little of both.

HIGGINS: Well, you took that money for the girl; and you have no right to take her as well.

MRS HIGGINS: Henry: dont be absurd. If you want to know where Eliza is, she is upstairs.

HIGGINS (*amazed*): Upstairs!!! Then I shall jolly soon fetch her downstairs. (*He makes resolutely for the door.*)

MRS HIGGINS (*rising and following him*): Be quiet, Henry. Sit down.

HIGGINS: I—

MRS HIGGINS: Sit down, dear; and listen to me.

HIGGINS: Oh very well, very well, very well. (*He throws himself ungraciously on the ottoman, with his face towards the windows.*) But I think you might have told us this half an hour ago.

MRS HIGGINS: Eliza came to me this morning. She told me of the brutal way you two treated her.

HIGGINS (*bounding up again*): What!

PICKERING (*rising also*): My dear Mrs Higgins, she's been telling you stories. We didnt treat her brutally. We hardly said a word to her; and we parted on particularly good terms. (*Turning on Higgins*) Higgins: did you bully her after I went to bed?

HIGGINS: Just the other way about. She threw my slippers in my face. She behaved in the most outrageous way. I never gave her the slightest provocation. The slippers came bang into my face the moment I entered the room—before I had uttered a word. And used perfectly awful language.

PICKERING (*astonished*): But why? What did we do to her?

MRS HIGGINS: I think I know pretty well what you did. The girl is naturally rather affectionate, I think. Isnt she, Mr Doolittle?

DOOLITTLE: Very tender-hearted, maam. Takes after me.

MRS HIGGINS: Just so. She had become attached to you both. She worked very hard for you, Henry. I dont think you quite realize what anything in the nature of brain work means to a girl of her class. Well, it seems that when the great day of trial came, and she did this wonderful thing for you without making a single mistake, you two sat there and never said a word to her, but talked together of how glad you were that it was all over and how you had been bored with the whole thing. And then you were surprised because she threw your slippers at you! *I* should have thrown the fire-irons at you.

HIGGINS: We said nothing except that we were tired and wanted to go to bed. Did we, Pick?

PICKERING (*shrugging his shoulders*): That was all.

MRS HIGGINS (*ironically*): Quite sure?

PICKERING: Absolutely. Really, that was all.

MRS HIGGINS: You didnt thank her, or pet her, or admire her, or tell her how splendid she'd been.

HIGGINS (*impatiently*): But she knew all about that. We didnt make speeches to her, if thats what you mean.

PICKERING (*conscience stricken*): Perhaps we were a little inconsiderate. Is she very angry?

MRS HIGGINS (*returning to her place at the writing-table*): Well, I'm afraid she won't go back to Wimpole Street, especially now that Mr Doolittle is able to keep up the position you have thrust on her; but she says she is quite willing to meet you on friendly terms and to let bygones be bygones.

HIGGINS (*furious*): Is she, by George? Ho!

MRS HIGGINS: If you promise to behave yourself, Henry, I'll ask her to come down. If not, go home; for you have taken up quite enough of my time.

HIGGINS: Oh, all right. Very well. Pick: you behave yourself. Let us put on our best Sunday manners for this creature that we picked out of the mud. (*He flings himself sulkily into the Elizabethan chair.*)

DOOLITTLE (*remonstrating*): Now, now, Enry Iggins! Have some consideration for my feelings as a middle class man.

MRS HIGGINS: Remember your promise, Henry. (*She presses the bell-button on the writing-table.*) Mr Doolittle: will you be so good as to step out on the balcony for a moment. I dont want Eliza to have the shock of your news until she has made it up with these two gentlemen. Would you mind?

DOOLITTLE: As you wish, lady. Anything to help Henry to keep her off my hands. (*He disappears through the window.*)

The parlormaid answers the bell. Pickering sits down in Doolittle's place.

MRS HIGGINS: Ask Miss Doolittle to come down, please.

THE PARLORMAID: Yes, maam. (*She goes out.*)

MRS HIGGINS: Now, Henry: be good.

HIGGINS: I am behaving myself perfectly.

PICKERING: He is doing his best, Mrs Higgins.

A pause. Higgins throws back his head; stretches out his legs; and begins to whistle.

MRS HIGGINS: Henry, dearest, you dont look at all nice in that attitude.

HIGGINS (*pulling himself together*): I was not trying to look nice, mother.

MRS HIGGINS: It doesnt matter, dear. I only wanted to make you speak.

HIGGINS: Why?

MRS HIGGINS: Because you cant speak and whistle at the same time.

Higgins groans. Another very trying pause.

HIGGINS (*springing up, out of patience*): Where the devil is that girl? Are we to wait here all day?

Eliza enters, sunny, self-possessed, and giving a staggeringly convincing exhibition of ease of manner. She carries a little workbasket, and is very much at home. Pickering is too much taken aback to rise.

LIZA: How do you do, Professor Higgins? Are you quite well?

HIGGINS (*choking*): Am I— (*He can say no more.*)

LIZA: But of course you are: you are never ill. So glad to see you again, Colonel Pickering. (*He rises hastily; and they shake hands.*) Quite chilly this morning, isn't it? (*She sits down on his left. He sits beside her.*)

HIGGINS: Dont you dare try this game on me. I taught it to you; and it doesnt take me in. Get up and come home; and dont be a fool.

Eliza takes a piece of needlework from her basket, and begins to stitch at it, without taking the least notice of this outburst.

MRS HIGGINS: Very nicely put, indeed, Henry. No woman could resist such an invitation.

HIGGINS: You let her alone, mother. Let her speak for herself. You will jolly soon see whether she has an idea that I havnt put into her head or a word that I havent put into her mouth. I tell you I have created this thing out of the squashed cabbage leaves of Covent Garden; and now she pretends to play the fine lady with me.

MRS HIGGINS (*placidly*): Yes, dear; but youll sit down, wont you?

Higgins sits down again, savagely.

LIZA (*to Pickering, taking no apparent notice of Higgins, and working away deftly*): Will you drop me altogether now that the experiment is over, Colonel Pickering?

PICKERING: Oh dont. You mustnt think of it as an experiment. It shocks me, somehow.

LIZA: Oh, I'm only a squashed cabbage leaf—

PICKERING (*impulsively*): No.

LIZA (*continuing quietly*): —but I owe so much to you that I should be very unhappy if you forgot me.

PICKERING: It's very kind of you to say so, Miss Doolittle.

LIZA: It's not because you paid for my dresses. I know you are generous to everybody with money. But it was from you that I learnt really nice manners; and that is what makes one a lady, isn't it? You see it was so very difficult for me with the example of Professor Higgins always before me. I was brought up to be just like him, unable to control myself, and using bad language on the slightest provocation. And I should never have known that ladies and gentlemen didnt behave like that if you hadnt been there.

HIGGINS: Well!!

PICKERING: Oh, thats only his way, you know. He doesnt mean it.

LIZA: Oh, *I* didnt mean it either, when I was a flower girl. It was only my way. But you see I did it; and thats what makes the difference after all.

PICKERING: No doubt. Still, he taught you to speak; and I couldnt have done that, you know.

LIZA (*trivially*): Of course: that is his profession.

HIGGINS: Damnation!

LIZA (*continuing*): It was just like learning to dance in the fashionable way: there was nothing more than that in it. But do you know what began my real education?

PICKERING: What?

LIZA (*stopping her work for a moment*): Your calling me Miss Doolittle that day when I first came to Wimpole Street. That was the beginning of self-respect for me. (*She resumes her stitching.*) And there were a hundred little things you never noticed, because they came naturally to you. Things about standing up and taking off your hat and opening doors—

PICKERING: Oh, that was nothing.

LIZA: Yes: things that shewed you thought and felt about me as if I were something better than a scullery-maid; though of course I know you would have been just the same to a scullery-maid if she had been let into the drawing room. You never took off your boots in the dining room when I was there.

PICKERING: You mustnt mind that. Higgins takes off his boots all over the place.

LIZA: I know. I am not blaming him. It is his way, isn't it? But it made such a difference to me that you didnt do it. You see, really and truly, apart from the things anyone can pick up (the dressing and the proper way of speaking, and so on), the difference between a lady and a flower girl is not how she behaves, but how she's treated. I shall always be a flower girl to Professor Higgins, because he always treats me as a flower girl, and always will; but I know I can be a lady to you, because you always treat me as a lady, and always will.

MRS HIGGINS: Please dont grind your teeth, Henry.

PICKERING: Well, this is really very nice of you, Miss Doolittle.

LIZA: I should like you to call me Eliza, now, if you would.

PICKERING: Thank you. Eliza, of course.

LIZA: And I should like Professor Higgins to call me Miss Doolittle.

HIGGINS: I'll see you damned first.

MRS HIGGINS: Henry! Henry!

PICKERING (*laughing*): Why dont you slang back at him? Dont stand it. It would do him a lot of good.

LIZA: I cant. I could have done it once; but now I cant go back to it. You told me, you know, that when a child is brought to a foreign country, it picks up the language in a few weeks, and forgets its own. Well, I am a child in your country. I have forgotten my own language, and can speak nothing but yours. Thats the real break-off with the corner of Tottenham Court Road. Leaving Wimpole Street finishes it.

PICKERING (*much alarmed*): Oh! but youre coming back to Wimpole Street, arnt you? Youll forgive Higgins?

HIGGINS (*rising*): Forgive! Will she, by George! Let her go. Let her find out how she can get on without us. She will relapse into the gutter in three weeks without me at her elbow.

> Doolittle appears at the centre window. With a look of digni- fied reproach at Higgins, he comes slowly and silently to his daughter, who, with her back to the window, is unconscious of his approach.

PICKERING: He's incorrigible, Eliza. You wont relapse, will you?

LIZA: No: not now. Never again. I have learnt my lesson. I dont believe I could utter one of the old sounds if I tried. (*Doolittle touches her on the left shoulder. She drops her work, losing her self-possession utterly at the spectacle of her father's splendor.*) A-a-a-a-ah-ow-ooh!

HIGGINS (*with a crow of triumph*): Aha! Just so. A-a-a-a-ahowooh! A-a-a-a-ahowooh! A-a-a-a-ahowooh! Victory! Victory! (*He throws himself on the divan, folding his arms, and spraddling arrogantly.*)

DOOLITTLE: Can you blame the girl? Dont look at me like that, Eliza. It aint my fault. Ive come into some money.

LIZA: You must have touched a millionaire this time, dad.

DOOLITTLE: I have. But I'm dressed something special today. I'm going to St George's, Hanover Square. Your stepmother is going to marry me.

LIZA (*angrily*): Youre going to let yourself down to marry that low common woman!

PICKERING (*quietly*): He ought to, Eliza. (*To Doolittle*) Why has she changed her mind?

DOOLITTLE (*sadly*): Intimidated, Governor. Intimidated. Middle class morality claims its victim. Wont you put on your hat, Liza, and come and see me turned off?

LIZA: If the Colonel says I must, I—I'll (*almost sobbing*) I'll demean myself. And get insulted for my pains, like enough.

DOOLITTLE: Dont be afraid: she never comes to words with anyone now, poor woman! respectability has broke all the spirit out of her.

PICKERING (*squeezing Eliza's elbow gently*): Be kind to them, Eliza. Make the best of it.

LIZA (*forcing a little smile for him through her vexation*): Oh well, just to shew theres no ill feeling. I'll be back in a moment. (*She goes out.*)

DOOLITTLE (*sitting down beside Pickering*): I feel uncommon nervous about the ceremony, Colonel. I wish youd come and see me through it.

PICKERING: But youve been through it before, man. You were married to Eliza's mother.

DOOLITTLE: Who told you that, Colonel?

PICKERING: Well, nobody told me. But I concluded—naturally—

DOOLITTLE: No: that aint the natural way, Colonel: it's only the middle class way. My way was always the undeserving way. But dont say nothing to Eliza. She dont know: I always had a delicacy about telling her.

PICKERING: Quite right. We'll leave it so, if you dont mind.

DOOLITTLE: And youll come to the church, Colonel, and pull me through straight?

PICKERING: With pleasure. As far as a bachelor can.

MRS HIGGINS: May I come, Mr Doolittle? I should be very sorry to miss your wedding.

DOOLITTLE: I should indeed be honored by your condescension, maam; and my poor old woman would take it as a tremenjous compliment. She's been very low, thinking of the happy days that are no more.

MRS HIGGINS (*rising*): I'll order the carriage and get ready. (*The men rise, except Higgins.*) I shant be more than fifteen minutes. (*As she goes to the door Eliza comes in, hatted and buttoning her gloves.*) I'm going to the church to see your father married, Eliza. You had better come in the brougham with me. Colonel Pickering can go on with the bridegroom.

Mrs Higgins goes out. Eliza comes to the middle of the room between the centre window and the ottoman. Pickering joins her.

DOOLITTLE: Bridegroom. What a word! It makes a man realize his position, somehow. (*He takes up his hat and goes towards the door.*)

PICKERING: Before I go, Eliza, do forgive Higgins and come back to us.

LIZA: I dont think dad would allow me. Would you, dad?

DOOLITTLE (*sad but magnanimous*): They played you off very cunning, Eliza, them two sportsmen. If it had been only one of them, you could have nailed him. But you see, there was two; and one of them chaperoned the other, as you might say. (*To Pickering*) It was artful of you, Colonel; but I bear no malice: I should have done the same myself. I been the victim of one woman after another all my life, and I dont grudge you two getting the better of Liza. I shant interfere. It's time for us to go, Colonel. So long, Henry. See you in St George's, Eliza. (*He goes out.*)

PICKERING (*coaxing*): Do stay with us, Eliza. (*He follows Doolittle.*)

Eliza goes out on the balcony to avoid being alone with Higgins. He rises and joins her there. She immediately comes back into the room and makes for the door; but he goes along the balcony and gets his back to the door before she reaches it.

HIGGINS: Well, Eliza, youve had a bit of your own back, as you call it. Have you had enough? and are you going to be reasonable? Or do you want any more?

LIZA: You want me back only to pick up your slippers and put up with your tempers and fetch and carry for you.

HIGGINS: I havnt said I wanted you back at all.

LIZA: Oh, indeed. Then what are we talking about?

HIGGINS: About you, not about me. If you come back I shall treat you just as I have always treated you. I cant change my nature; and I dont intend to change my manners. My manners are exactly the same as Colonel Pickering's.

LIZA: Thats not true. He treats a flower girl as if she was a duchess.

HIGGINS: And I treat a duchess as if she was a flower girl.

LIZA: I see. (*She turns away composedly, and sits on the ottoman, facing the window.*) The same to everybody.

HIGGINS: Just so.

LIZA: Like father.

HIGGINS (*grinning, a little taken down*): Without accepting the comparison at all points, Eliza, it's quite true that your father is not a snob, and that he will be quite at home in any station of life to which his eccentric destiny may call him. (*Seriously*) The great secret, Eliza, is not having bad manners or good manners or any other particular sort of manners, but having the same manner for all human souls: in short, behaving as if you were in Heaven, where there are no third-class carriages, and one soul is as good as another.

LIZA: Amen. You are a born preacher.

HIGGINS (*irritated*): The question is not whether I treat you rudely, but whether you ever heard me treat anyone else better.

LIZA (*with sudden sincerity*): I dont care how you treat me. I dont mind your swearing at me. I shouldnt mind a black eye: Ive had one before this. But (*standing up and facing him*) I wont be passed over.

HIGGINS: Then get out of my way; for I wont stop for you. You talk about me as if I were a motor bus.

LIZA: So you are a motor bus: all bounce and go, and no consideration for anyone. But I can do without you: dont think I cant.

HIGGINS: I know you can. I told you you could.

LIZA (*wounded, getting away from him to the other side of the ottoman with her face to the hearth*): I know you did, you brute. You wanted to get rid of me.

HIGGINS: Liar.

LIZA: Thank you. (*She sits down with dignity.*)

HIGGINS: You never asked yourself, I suppose, whether I could do without you.

LIZA (*earnestly*): Dont you try to get round me. Youll have to do without me.

HIGGINS (*arrogant*): I can do without anybody. I have my own soul: my own spark of divine fire. But (*with sudden humility*) I shall miss you, Eliza. (*He sits down near her on the ottoman.*) I have learnt something from your idiotic notions: I confess that humbly and gratefully. And I have grown accustomed to your voice and appearance. I like them, rather.

LIZA: Well, you have both of them on your gramophone and in your book of photographs. When you feel lonely without me, you can turn the machine on. It's got no feelings to hurt.

HIGGINS: I cant turn your soul on. Leave me those feelings; and you can take away the voice and the face. They are not you.

LIZA: Oh, you are a devil. You can twist the heart in a girl as easy as some could twist her arms to hurt her. Mrs Pearce warned me. Time and again she has wanted to leave you; and you always got round her at the last minute. And you dont care a bit for her. And you dont care a bit for me.

HIGGINS: I care for life, for humanity; and you are a part of it that has come my way and been built into my house. What more can you or anyone ask?

LIZA: I wont care for anybody that doesnt care for me.

HIGGINS: Commercial principles, Eliza. Like (*reproducing her Covent Garden pronunciation with professional exactness*) s'yollin voylets [selling violets], isnt it?

LIZA: Dont sneer at me. It's mean to sneer at me.

HIGGINS: I have never sneered in my life. Sneering doesnt become either the human face or the human soul. I am expressing my righteous contempt for Commercialism. I dont and wont trade in affection. You call me a brute because you couldnt buy a claim on me by fetching my slippers and finding my spectacles. You were a fool: I think a woman fetching a man's slippers is a disgusting sight: did I ever fetch your slippers? I think a good deal more of you for throwing them in my face. No use slaving for me and then saying you want to be cared for: who cares for a slave? If you come back, come back for the sake of good fellowship; for youll get nothing else. Youve had a thousand times as much out of me as I have out of you; and if you dare to set up your little dog's tricks of fetching and carrying slippers against my creation of a Duchess Eliza, I'll slam the door in your silly face.

LIZA: What did you do it for if you didnt care for me?

HIGGINS (*heartily*): Why, because it was my job.

LIZA: You never thought of the trouble it would make for me.

HIGGINS: Would the world ever have been made if its maker had been afraid of making trouble? Making life means making trouble. Theres only one way of escaping trouble; and thats killing things. Cowards, you notice, are always shrieking to have troublesome people killed.

LIZA: I'm no preacher: I dont notice things like that. I notice that you dont notice me.

HIGGINS (*jumping up and walking about intolerantly*): Eliza: youre an idiot. I waste the treasures of my Miltonic mind by spreading them before you. Once for all, understand that I go my way and do my work without caring twopence what happens to either of us. I am not intimidated, like your father and your stepmother. So you can come back or go to the devil: which you please.

LIZA: What am I to come back for?

HIGGINS (*bouncing up on his knees on the ottoman and leaning over it to her*): For the fun of it. Thats why I took you on.

LIZA (*with averted face*): And you may throw me out tomorrow if I dont do everything you want me to?

HIGGINS: Yes; and you may walk out tomorrow if I dont do everything you want me to.

LIZA: And live with my stepmother?

HIGGINS: Yes, or sell flowers.

LIZA: Oh! if I only could go back to my flower basket! I should be independent of both you and father and all the world! Why did you take my independence from me? Why did I give it up? I'm a slave now, for all my fine clothes.

HIGGINS: Not a bit. I'll adopt you as my daughter and settle money on you if you like. Or would you rather marry Pickering?

LIZA (*looking fiercely round at him*): I wouldnt marry you if you asked me; and youre nearer my age than what he is.

HIGGINS (*gently*): Than he is: not "than what he is."

LIZA (*losing her temper and rising*): I'll talk as I like. Youre not my teacher now.

HIGGINS (*reflectively*): I dont suppose Pickering would, though. He's as confirmed an old bachelor as I am.

LIZA: Thats not what I want; and dont you think it. I've always had chaps enough wanting me that way. Freddy Hill writes to me twice and three times a day, sheets and sheets.

HIGGINS (*disagreeably surprised*): Damn his impudence! (*He recoils and finds himself sitting on his heels.*)

LIZA: He has a right to if he likes, poor lad. And he does love me.

HIGGINS (*getting off the ottoman*): You have no right to encourage him.

LIZA: Every girl has a right to be loved.

HIGGINS: What! By fools like that?

LIZA: Freddy's not a fool. And if he's weak and poor and wants me, maybe he'd make me happier than my betters that bully me and dont want me.

HIGGINS: Can he make anything of you? Thats the point.

LIZA: Perhaps I could make something of him. But I never thought of us making anything of one another; and you never think of anything else. I only want to be natural.

HIGGINS: In short, you want me to be as infatuated about you as Freddy? Is that it?

LIZA: No I dont. Thats not the sort of feeling I want from you. And dont you be too sure of yourself or of me. I could have been a bad girl if I'd liked. Ive seen more of some things than you, for all your learning. Girls like me can drag gentlemen down to make love to them easy enough. And they wish each other dead the next minute.

HIGGINS: Of course they do. Then what in thunder are we quarrelling about?

LIZA (*much troubled*): I want a little kindness. I know I'm a common ignorant girl, and you a book-learned gentleman; but I'm not dirt under your feet. What I done (*correcting herself*) what I did was not for the dresses and the taxis: I did it because we were pleasant together and I come—came—to care for you; not to want you to make love to me, and not forgetting the difference between us, but more friendly like.

HIGGINS: Well, of course. Thats just how I feel. And how Pickering feels. Eliza: youre a fool.

LIZA: Thats not a proper answer to give me. (*She sinks on the chair at the writing table in tears.*)

HIGGINS: It's all youll get until you stop being a common idiot. If youre going to be a lady, youll have to give up feeling neglected if the men you know dont spend half their time snivelling over you and the other half giving you black eyes. If you cant stand the coldness of my sort of life, and the strain of it, go back to the gutter. Work til youre more a brute than a human being; and then cuddle and squabble and drink til you fall asleep. Oh, it's a fine life, the life of the gutter. It's real: it's warm: it's violent: you can feel it through the thickest skin: you can taste it and smell it without any training or any work. Not like Science and Literature and Classical Music and Philosophy and Art. You find me cold, unfeeling, selfish, dont you? Very well: be off with you to the sort of people you like. Marry some sentimental hog or other with lots of money, and a thick pair of lips to kiss you with and a thick pair of boots to kick you with. If you cant appreciate what youve got, youd better get what you can appreciate.

LIZA (*desperate*): Oh, you are a cruel tyrant. I cant talk to you: you turn everything against me: I'm always in the wrong. But you know very well all the time that youre nothing but a bully. You know I cant go back to the gutter, as you call it, and that I have no real friends in the world but you and the Colonel. You know well I couldnt bear to live with a low common man after you two; and it's wicked and cruel of you to insult me by pretending I could. You think I must go back to Wimpole Street because I have nowhere else to go but my father's. But dont you be too sure that you have me under your feet to be trampled on and talked down. I'll marry Freddy, I will, as soon as I'm able to support him.

HIGGINS (*thunderstruck*): Freddy!!! that young fool! That poor devil who couldnt get a job as an errand boy even if he had the guts to try for it! Woman: do you not understand that I have made you a consort for a king?

LIZA: Freddy loves me: that makes him king enough for me. I dont want him to work: he wasnt brought up to it as I was. I'll go and be a teacher.

HIGGINS: Whatll you teach, in heaven's name?

LIZA: What you taught me. I'll teach phonetics.

HIGGINS: Ha! ha! ha!

LIZA: I'll offer myself as an assistant to that hairyfaced Hungarian.

HIGGINS (*rising in a fury*): What! That imposter! that humbug! that toadying ignoramus! Teach him my methods! my discoveries! You take one step in his direction and I'll wring your neck. (*He lays hands on her.*) Do you hear?

LIZA (*defiantly non-resistant*): Wring away. What do I care? I knew youd strike me some day. (*He lets her go, stamping with rage at having forgotten himself, and recoils so hastily that he stumbles back into his seat on the ottoman.*) Aha! Now I know how to deal with you. What a fool I was not to think of it before! You cant take away the knowledge you gave me. You said I had a finer ear than you. And I can be civil and kind to people, which is more than you can. Aha! (*Purposely dropping her aitches to annoy him*) Thats done you, Enry Iggins, it az. Now I dont care that (*Snapping her fingers*) for your bullying and your big talk. I'll advertize it in the papers that your duchess is only a flower girl that you taught, and that she'll teach anybody to be a duchess just the same in six months for a thousand guineas. Oh, when I think of myself crawling under your feet and being trampled on and called names, when all the time I had only to lift up my finger to be as good as you, I could just kick myself.

HIGGINS (*wondering at her*): You damned impudent slut, you! But it's better than snivelling; better than fetching slippers and finding spectacles, isnt it? (*Rising*) By George, Eliza, I said I'd make a woman of you; and I have. I like you like this.

LIZA: Yes: you turn round and make up to me now that I'm not afraid of you, and can do without you.

HIGGINS: Of course I do, you little fool. Five minutes ago you were like a millstone round my neck. Now youre a tower of strength: a consort battleship. You and I and Pickering will be three old bachelors instead of only two men and a silly girl.

    Mrs Higgins returns, dressed for the wedding. Eliza instantly becomes cool and elegant.

MRS HIGGINS: The carriage is waiting, Eliza. Are you ready?

LIZA: Quite. Is the Professor coming?

MRS HIGGINS: Certainly not. He cant behave himself in church. He makes remarks out loud all the time on the clergyman's pronunciation.

LIZA: Then I shall not see you again, Professor. Goodbye. (*She goes to the door.*)

MRS HIGGINS (*coming to Higgins*): Goodbye, dear.

HIGGINS: Goodbye, mother. (*He is about to kiss her, when he recollects something.*) Oh, by the way, Eliza, order a ham and a Stilton cheese, will you? And buy me a pair of reindeer gloves, number eights, and a tie to match that new suit of mine. You can choose the color. (*His cheerful, careless, vigorous voice shews that he is incorrigible.*)

LIZA (*disdainfully*): Number eights are too small for you if you want them lined with lamb's wool. You have three new ties that you have forgotten in the drawer of your washstand. Colonel Pickering prefers double Gloucester to Stilton; and you dont notice the difference. I telephoned Mrs Pearce this morning not to forget the ham. What you are to do without me I cannot imagine. (*She sweeps out.*)

MRS HIGGINS: I'm afraid youve spoilt that girl, Henry. I should be uneasy about you and her if she were less fond of Colonel Pickering.

HIGGINS: Pickering! Nonsense: she's going to marry Freddy. Ha ha! Freddy! Freddy!! Ha ha ha ha ha!!!!! (*He roars with laughter as the play ends.*)

*   *   *   *   *   *   *   *

The rest of the story need not be shewn in action, and indeed, would hardly need telling if our imaginations were not so enfeebled by their lazy dependence on the ready-mades and reach-me-downs of the ragshop in which Romance keeps its stock of "happy endings" to misfit all stories. Now, the history of Eliza Doolittle, though called a romance because the transfiguration it records seems exceedingly improbable, is common enough. Such transfigurations have been achieved by hundreds of resolutely ambitious young women since Nell Gwynne[70] set them the example by playing queens and fascinating kings in the theatre in which she began by selling oranges. Nevertheless, people in all directions have assumed, for no other reason than that she became the heroine of a romance, that she must have married the hero of it. This is unbearable, not only because her little drama, if acted on such a thoughtless assumption, must be spoiled, but because the true sequel is patent to anyone with a sense of human nature in general, and of feminine instinct in particular.

Eliza, in telling Higgins she would not marry him if he asked her, was not coquetting: she was announcing a well-considered decision. When a bachelor interests, and dominates, and teaches, and becomes important to a spinster, as Higgins with Eliza, she always, if she has character enough to be capable of it, considers very seriously indeed whether she will play for becoming that bachelor's wife, especially if he is so little interested in marriage that a determined and devoted woman might capture him if she set herself resolutely to do it. Her decision will depend a good deal on whether she is really free to choose; and that, again, will depend on her age and income. If she is at the end of her youth, and has no security for her livelihood, she will marry him because she must marry anybody who will provide for her. But at Eliza's age a good-looking girl does not feel that pressure: she feels free to pick and choose. She is therefore guided by

---

[70] *Gwynne:* Also spelled Nell Gwyn (1650–1687), English orange girl and actress who became one of Charles II's mistresses.

her instinct in the matter. Eliza's instinct tells her not to marry Higgins. It does not tell her to give him up. It is not in the slightest doubt as to his remaining one of the strongest personal interests in her life. It would be very sorely strained if there was another woman likely to supplant her with him. But as she feels sure of him on that last point, she has no doubt at all as to her course, and would not have any, even if the difference of twenty years in age, which seems so great to youth, did not exist between them.

As our own instincts are not appealed to by her conclusion, let us see whether we cannot discover some reason in it. When Higgins excused his indifference to young women on the ground that they had an irresistible rival in his mother, he gave the clue to his inveterate old-bachelordom. The case is uncommon only to the extent that remarkable mothers are uncommon. If an imaginative boy has a sufficiently rich mother who has intelligence, personal grace, dignity of character without harshness, and a cultivated sense of the best art of her time to enable her to make her house beautiful, she sets a standard for him against which very few women can struggle, besides effecting for him a disengagement of his affections, his sense of beauty, and his idealism from his specifically sexual impulses. This makes him a standing puzzle to the huge number of uncultivated people who have been brought up in tasteless homes by commonplace or disagreeable parents, and to whom, consequently, literature, painting, sculpture, music, and affectionate personal relations come as modes of sex if they come at all. The word passion means nothing else to them; and that Higgins could have a passion for phonetics and idealize his mother instead of Eliza, would seem to them absurd and unnatural. Nevertheless, when we look round and see that hardly anyone is too ugly or disagreeable to find a wife or a husband if he or she wants one, whilst many old maids and bachelors are above the average in quality and culture, we cannot help suspecting that the disentanglement of sex from the associations with which it is so commonly confused, a disentanglement which persons of genius achieve by sheer intellectual analysis, is sometimes produced or aided by parental fascination.

Now, though Eliza was incapable of thus explaining to herself Higgins's formidable powers of resistance to the charm that prostrated Freddy at the first glance, she was instinctively aware that she could never obtain a complete grip of him, or come between him and his mother (the first necessity of the married woman). To put it shortly, she knew that for some mysterious reason he had not the makings of a married man in him, according to her conception of a husband as one to whom she would be his nearest and fondest and warmest interest. Even had there been no mother-rival, she would still have refused to accept an interest in herself that was secondary to philosophic interests. Had Mrs Higgins died, there would still have been Milton and the Universal Alphabet. Landor's[71] re-

71 *Landor:* Walter Savage Landor (1775–1864), English writer.

mark that to those who have the greatest power of loving, love is a second-ary affair, would not have recommended Landor to Eliza. Put that along with her resentment of Higgins's domineering superiority, and her mistrust of his coaxing cleverness in getting round her and evading her wrath when he had gone too far with his impetuous bullying, and you will see that Eliza's instinct had good grounds for warning her not to marry her Pyg-malion.

And now, whom did Eliza marry? For if Higgins was a predestinate old bachelor, she was most certainly not a predestinate old maid. Well, that can be told very shortly to those who have not guessed it from the indications she has herself given them.

Almost immediately after Eliza is stung into proclaiming her con-sidered determination not to marry Higgins, she mentions the fact that young Mr Frederick Eynsford Hill is pouring out his love for her daily through the post. Now Freddy is young, practically twenty years younger than Higgins: he is a gentleman (or, as Eliza would qualify him, a toff), and speaks like one. He is nicely dressed, is treated by the Colonel as an equal, loves her unaffectedly, and is not her master, nor ever likely to domi-nate her in spite of his advantage of social standing. Eliza has no use for the foolish romantic tradition that all women love to be mastered, if not actually bullied and beaten. "When you go to women" says Nietzsche[72] "take your whip with you." Sensible despots have never confined that pre-caution to women: they have taken their whips with them when they have dealt with men, and been slavishly idealized by the men over whom they have flourished the whip much more than by women. No doubt there are slavish women as well as slavish men; and women, like men, admire those that are stronger than themselves. But to admire a strong person and to live under that strong person's thumb are two different things. The weak may not be admired and hero-worshipped; but they are by no means dis-liked or shunned; and they never seem to have the least difficulty in marry-ing people who are too good for them. They may fail in emergencies; but life is not one long emergency: it is mostly a string of situations for which no exceptional strength is needed, and with which even rather weak people can cope if they have a stronger partner to help them out. Accordingly, it is a truth everywhere in evidence that strong people, masculine or femi-nine, not only do not marry stronger people, but do not shew any prefer-ence for them in selecting their friends. When a lion meets another with a louder roar "the first lion thinks the last a bore." The man or woman who feels strong enough for two, seeks for every other quality in a partner than strength.

The converse is also true. Weak people want to marry strong people who do not frighten them too much; and this often leads them to make the mistake we describe metaphorically as "biting off more than they can chew." They want too much for too little; and when the bargain is un-

[72] *Nietzsche:* Friedrich Wilhelm Nietzsche (1844–1900), German philosopher.

reasonable beyond all bearing, the union becomes impossible: it ends in the weaker party being either discarded or borne as a cross, which is worse. People who are not only weak, but silly or obtuse as well, are often in these difficulties.

This being the state of human affairs, what is Eliza fairly sure to do when she is placed between Freddy and Higgins? Will she look forward to a lifetime of fetching Higgins's slippers or to a lifetime of Freddy fetching hers? There can be no doubt about the answer. Unless Freddy is biologically repulsive to her, and Higgins biologically attractive to a degree that overwhelms all her other instincts, she will, if she marries either of them, marry Freddy.

And that is just what Eliza did.

Complications ensued; but they were economic, not romantic. Freddy had no money and no occupation. His mother's jointure, a last relic of the opulence of Largelady Park, had enabled her to struggle along in Earlscourt with an air of gentility, but not to procure any serious secondary education for her children, much less give the boy a profession. A clerkship at thirty shillings a week was beneath Freddy's dignity, and extremely distasteful to him besides. His prospects consisted of a hope that if he kept up appearances somebody would do something for him. The something appeared vaguely to his imagination as a private secretaryship or a sinecure of some sort. To his mother it perhaps appeared as a marriage to some lady of means who could not resist her boy's niceness. Fancy her feelings when he married a flower girl who had become disclassed under extraordinary circumstances which were now notorious!

It is true that Eliza's situation did not seem wholly ineligible. Her father, though formerly a dustman, and now fantastically disclassed, had become extremely popular in the smartest society by a social talent which triumphed over every prejudice and every disadvantage. Rejected by the middle class, which he loathed, he had shot up at once into the highest circles by his wit, his dustmanship (which he carried like a banner), and his Nietzschean transcendence of good and evil. At intimate ducal dinners he sat on the right hand of the Duchess; and in country houses he smoked in the pantry and was made much of by the butler when he was not feeding in the dining room and being consulted by cabinet ministers. But he found it almost as hard to do all this on four thousand a year as Mrs Eynsford Hill to live in Earlscourt on an income so pitiably smaller that I have not the heart to disclose its exact figure. He absolutely refused to add the last straw to his burden by contributing to Eliza's support.

Thus Freddy and Eliza, now Mr and Mrs Eynsford Hill, would have spent a penniless honeymoon but for a wedding present of £500 from the Colonel to Eliza. It lasted a long time because Freddy did not know how to spend money, never having had any to spend, and Eliza, socially trained by a pair of old bachelors, wore her clothes as long as they held together and looked pretty, without the least regard to their being many months out of fashion. Still, £500 will not last two young people for ever; and they both knew, and Eliza felt as well, that they must shift for themselves in the end. She could quarter herself on Wimpole Street because it had come to be her home; but she was quite aware that she ought not to quarter Freddy there, and that it would not be good for his character if she did.

Not that the Wimpole Street bachelors objected. When she consulted them, Higgins declined to be bothered about her housing problem when that solution was so simple. Eliza's desire to have Freddy in the house with her seemed of no more importance than if she had wanted an extra piece of bedroom furniture. Pleas as to Freddy's character, and the moral obligation on him to earn his own living, were lost on Higgins. He denied that Freddy had any character, and declared that if he tried to do any useful work some competent person would have the trouble of undoing it: a procedure involving a net loss to the community, and great unhappiness to Freddy himself, who was obviously intended by Nature for such light work as amusing Eliza, which, Higgins declared, was a much more useful and honorable occupation than working in the city. When Eliza referred again to her project of teaching phonetics, Higgins abated not a jot of his violent opposition to it. He said she was not within ten years of being qualified to meddle with his pet subject; and as it was evident that the Colonel agreed with him, she felt she could not go against them in this grave matter, and that she had no right, without Higgins's consent, to exploit the knowledge he had given her; for his knowledge seemed to her as much his private property as his watch: Eliza was no communist. Besides, she was superstitiously devoted to them both, more entirely and frankly after her marriage than before it.

It was the Colonel who finally solved the problem, which had cost him much perplexed cogitation. He one day asked Eliza, rather shyly, whether she had quite given up her notion of keeping a flower shop. She replied that she had thought of it, but had put it out of her head, because the Colonel had said, that day at Mrs Higgins's, that it would never do. The Colonel confessed that when he said that, he had not quite recovered from the dazzling impression of the day before. They broke the matter to Higgins that evening. The sole comment vouchsafed by him very nearly led to a serious quarrel with Eliza. It was to the effect that she would have in Freddy an ideal errand boy.

Freddy himself was next sounded on the subject. He said he had been thinking of a shop himself; though it had presented itself to his pennilessness as a small place in which Eliza should sell tobacco at one counter whilst he sold newspapers at the opposite one. But he agreed that it would be extraordinarily jolly to go early every morning with Eliza to Covent Garden and buy flowers on the scene of their first meeting: a sentiment which earned him many kisses from his wife. He added that he had always been afraid to propose anything of the sort, because Clara would make an awful row about a step that must damage her matrimonial chances, and his mother could not be expected to like it after clinging for so many years to that step of the social ladder on which retail trade is impossible.

This difficulty was removed by an event highly unexpected by Freddy's mother. Clara, in the course of her incursions into those artistic circles which were the highest within her reach, discovered that her conversational qualifications were expected to include a grounding in the novels of Mr H. G. Wells.[73] She borrowed them in various directions so energetically that she swallowed them all within two months. The result was a conversion of a kind quite common today. A modern Acts of the Apostles[74] would fill fifty whole Bibles if anyone were capable of writing it.

Poor Clara, who appeared to Higgins and his mother as a disagreeable and ridiculous person, and to her own mother as in some inexplicable way a social failure, had never seen herself in either light; for, though to some extent ridiculed and mimicked in West Kensington like everybody else there, she was accepted as a rational and normal—or shall we say inevitable?—sort of human being. At worst they called her The Pusher; but to them no more than to herself had it ever occurred that she was pushing the air, and pushing it in a wrong direction. Still, she was not happy. She was growing desperate. Her one asset, the fact that her mother was what the Epsom greengrocer called a carriage lady, had no exchange value, apparently. It had prevented her from getting educated, because the only education she could have afforded was education with the Earlscourt greengrocer's daughter. It had led her to seek the society of her mother's class; and that class simply would not have her, because she was much poorer than the greengrocer, and, far from being able to afford a maid, could not afford even a housemaid, and had to scrape along at home with an illiberally treated general servant. Under such circumstances nothing could give her an air of being a genuine product of Largelady Park. And yet its tradition made her regard a marriage with anyone within her reach as an unbearable humiliation. Commercial people and professional people in a small way were odious to her. She ran after painters and novelists; but she did not charm them; and her bold attempts to pick up and practice artistic and literary talk irritated them. She was, in short, an utter failure, an ignorant, incompetent, pretentious, unwelcome, penniless, useless little snob; and though she did not admit these disqualifications (for nobody ever faces unpleasant truths of this kind until the possibility of a way out dawns on them) she felt their effects too keenly to be satisfied with her position.

Clara had a startling eyeopener when, on being suddenly wakened to enthusiasm by a girl of her own age who dazzled her and produced in her a gushing desire to take her for a model, and gain her friendship, she discovered that this exquisite apparition had graduated from the gutter in a few months time. It shook her so violently, that when Mr H. G. Wells lifted her on the point of his puissant pen, and placed her at the angle of

[73] *Wells*: Herbert George Wells (1866–1946), English novelist and socialist.
[74] *Acts of the Apostles*: One of the books of the New Testament.

view from which the life she was leading and the society to which she clung appeared in its true relation to real human needs and worthy social structure, he effected a conversion and a conviction of sin comparable to the most sensational feats of General Booth [75] or Gypsy Smith.[76] Clara's snobbery went bang. Life suddenly began to move with her. Without knowing how or why, she began to make friends and enemies. Some of the acquaintances to whom she had been a tedious or indifferent or ridiculous affliction, dropped her: others became cordial. To her amazement she found that some "quite nice" people were saturated with Wells, and that this accessibility to ideas was the secret of their niceness. People she had thought deeply religious, and had tried to conciliate on that tack with disastrous results, suddenly took an interest in her, and revealed a hostility to conventional religion which she had never conceived possible except among the most desperate characters. They made her read Galsworthy;[77] and Galsworthy exposed the vanity of Largelady Park and finished her. It exasperated her to think that the dungeon in which she had languished for so many unhappy years had been unlocked all the time, and that the impulses she had so carefully struggled with and stifled for the sake of keeping well with society, were precisely those by which alone she could have come into any sort of sincere human contact. In the radiance of these discoveries, and the tumult of their reaction, she made a fool of herself as freely and conspicuously as when she so rashly adopted Eliza's expletive in Mrs Higgins's drawing room; for the new-born Wellsian had to find her bearings almost as ridiculously as a baby; but nobody hates a baby for its ineptitudes, or thinks the worse of it for trying to eat the matches; and Clara lost no friends by her follies. They laughed at her to her face this time; and she had to defend herself and fight it out as best she could.

When Freddy paid a visit to Earlscourt (which he never did when he could possibly help it) to make the desolating announcement that he and his Eliza were thinking of blackening the Largelady scutcheon by opening a shop, he found the little household already convulsed by a prior announcement from Clara that she also was going to work in an old furniture shop in Dover Street, which had been started by a fellow Wellsian. This appointment Clara owed, after all, to her old social accomplishment of Push. She had made up her mind that, cost what it might, she would see Mr Wells in the flesh; and she had achieved her end at a garden party. She had better luck than so rash an enterprise deserved. Mr Wells came up to her expectations. Age had not withered him, nor could custom stale his infinite variety in half an hour. His pleasant neatness and compactness, his small hands and feet, his teeming ready brain, his unaffected accessibility, and a certain fine apprehensiveness which stamped him as susceptible from

[75] *General Booth*: William Booth (1829–1912) founded the Salvation Army in 1865.

[76] *Gypsy Smith*: Rodney Smith (1860–1947), English evangelist known as "Gipsy Smith."

[77] *Galsworthy*: John Galsworthy (1867–1933), English novelist and playwright.

his topmost hair to his tipmost toe, proved irresistible. Clara talked of nothing else for weeks and weeks afterwards. And as she happened to talk to the lady of the furniture shop, and that lady also desired above all things to know Mr Wells and sell pretty things to him, she offered Clara a job on the chance of achieving that end through her.

And so it came about that Eliza's luck held, and the expected opposition to the flower shop melted away. The shop is in the arcade of a railway station not very far from the Victoria and Albert Museum; and if you live in that neighbourhood you may go there any day and buy a buttonhole from Eliza.

Now here is a last opportunity for romance. Would you not like to be assured that the shop was an immense success, thanks to Eliza's charms and her early business experience in Covent Garden? Alas! the truth is the truth: the shop did not pay for a long time, simply because Eliza and her Freddy did not know how to keep it. True, Eliza had not to begin at the very beginning: she knew the names and prices of the cheaper flowers; and her elation was unbounded when she found that Freddy, like all youths educated at cheap, pretentious, and thoroughly inefficient schools, knew a little Latin. It was very little, but enough to make him appear to her a Porson[78] or Bentley,[79] and to put him at his ease with botanical nomenclature. Unfortunately he knew nothing else; and Eliza, though she could count money up to eighteen shillings or so, and had acquired a certain familiarity with the language of Milton from her struggles to qualify herself for winning Higgins's bet, could not write out a bill without utterly disgracing the establishment. Freddy's power of stating in Latin that Balbus built a wall and that Gaul was divided into three parts did not carry with it the slightest knowledge of accounts or business: Colonel Pickering had to explain to him what a cheque book and a bank account meant. And the pair were by no means easily teachable. Freddy backed up Eliza in her obstinate refusal to believe that they could save money by engaging a bookkeeper with some knowledge of the business. How, they argued, could you possibly save money by going to extra expense when you already could not make both ends meet? But the Colonel, after making the ends meet over and over again, at last gently insisted; and Eliza, humbled to the dust by having to beg from him so often, and stung by the uproarious derision of Higgins, to whom the notion of Freddy succeeding at anything was a joke that never palled, grasped the fact that business, like phonetics, has to be learned.

On the piteous spectacle of the pair spending their evenings in shorthand schools and polytechnic classes, learning bookkeeping and typewriting with incipient junior clerks, male and female, from the elementary schools, let me not dwell. There were even classes at the London School of Economics, and a humble personal appeal to the director of that institution

[78] *Porson:* Richard Porson (1759–1808), English scholar.
[79] *Bentley:* Richard Bentley (1662–1742), English clergyman and scholar.

to recommend a course bearing on the flower business. He, being a humorist, explained to them the method of the celebrated Dickensian essay on Chinese Metaphysics by the gentleman who read an article on China and an article on Metaphysics and combined the information. He suggested that they should combine the London School with Kew Gardens.[80] Eliza, to whom the procedure of the Dickensian gentleman seemed perfectly correct (as in fact it was) and not in the least funny (which was only her ignorance), took the advice with entire gravity. But the effort that cost her the deepest humiliation was a request to Higgins, whose pet artistic fancy, next to Milton's verse, was caligraphy, and who himself wrote a most beautiful Italian hand, that he would teach her to write. He declared that she was congenitally incapable of forming a single letter worthy of the least of Milton's words; but she persisted; and again he suddenly threw himself into the task of teaching her with a combination of stormy intensity, concentrated patience, and occasional bursts of interesting disquisition on the beauty and nobility, the august mission and destiny, of human handwriting. Eliza ended by acquiring an extremely uncommercial script which was a positive extension of her personal beauty, and spending three times as much on stationery as anyone else because certain qualities and shapes on paper became indispensable to her. She could not even address an envelope in the usual way because it made the margins all wrong.

Their commercial schooldays were a period of disgrace and despair for the young couple. They seemed to be learning nothing about flower shops. At last they gave it up as hopeless, and shook the dust of the shorthand schools, and the polytechnics, and the London School of Economics from their feet for ever. Besides, the business was in some mysterious way beginning to take care of itself. They had somehow forgotten their objections to employing other people. They came to the conclusion that their own way was the best, and that they had really a remarkable talent for business. The Colonel, who had been compelled for some years to keep a sufficient sum on current account at his bankers to make up their deficits, found that the provision was unnecessary: the young people were prospering. It is true that there was not quite fair play between them and their competitors in trade. Their week-ends in the country cost them nothing, and saved them the price of their Sunday dinners; for the motor car was the Colonel's; and he and Higgins paid the hotel bills. Mr F. Hill, florist and greengrocer (they soon discovered that there was money in asparagus; and asparagus led to other vegetables), had an air which stamped the business as classy; and in private life he was still Frederick Eynsford Hill, Esquire. Not that there was any swank about him: nobody but Eliza knew that he had been christened Frederick Challoner. Eliza herself swanked like anything.

That is all. That is how it has turned out. It is astonishing how much Eliza still manages to meddle in the housekeeping at Wimpole Street in

[80] *Kew Gardens:* Large botanical collection at Kew in Surrey.

spite of the shop and her own family. And it is notable that though she never nags her husband, and frankly loves the Colonel as if she were his favorite daughter, she has never got out of the habit of nagging Higgins that was established on the fatal night when she won his bet for him. She snaps his head off on the faintest provocation, or on none. He no longer dares to tease her by assuming an abysmal inferiority of Freddy's mind to his own. He storms and bullies and derides; but she stands up to him so ruthlessly that the Colonel has to ask her from time to time to be kinder to Higgins; and it is the only request of his that brings a mulish expression into her face. Nothing but some emergency or calamity great enough to break down all likes and dislikes, and throw them both back on their common humanity—and may they be spared any such trial!—will ever alter this. She knows that Higgins does not need her, just as her father did not need her. The very scrupulousness with which he told her that day that he had become used to having her there, and dependent on her for all sorts of little services, and that he should miss her if she went away (it would never have occurred to Freddy or the Colonel to say anything of the sort) deepens her inner certainty that she is "no more to him than them slippers"; yet she has a sense, too, that his indifference is deeper than the infatuation of commoner souls. She is immensely interested in him. She has even secret mischievous moments in which she wishes she could get him alone, on a desert island, away from all ties and with nobody else in the world to consider, and just drag him off his pedestal and see him making love like any common man. We all have private imaginations of that sort. But when it comes to business, to the life that she really leads as distinguished from the life of dreams and fancies, she likes Freddy and she likes the Colonel; and she does not like Higgins and Mr Doolittle. Galatea never does quite like Pygmalion: his relation to her is too godlike to be altogether agreeable.

§ FOR COMMENT

Boasting that *Pygmalion* was a didactic play about phonetics, Shaw asserted that great art can never be anything but didactic. Some critics agree with Shaw's contention, variously interpreting *Pygmalion* as a plea for a phonetic alphabet or a sermon on the breaking of class barriers. To others the play is pure entertainment, a fairy tale devoid of social purpose. Examine the case for each of these points of view. Which is more convincing? What do you think is the place of didacticism in drama? in literature in general?

How is the Doolittle subplot related thematically to the main plot about Eliza and Higgins? How is the exposition concerning the Eynsford Hills related to the Eliza-Higgins story? Who is the play's central character: Pygmalion or Galatea, Higgins or Eliza?

Shaw could have begun *Pygmalion* in the second act, conveying the earlier action by exposition. Why did he choose to do otherwise? Why is the crowd scene necessary? In the first act, Clara's admonitions to her mother about the cost of the flowers foreshadows the later revelation about the Eynsford Hills' financial circumstances. What other foreshadowings does the first act contain regarding Eliza, Higgins, and Pickering? How does the first act anticipate the play's plot and theme?

In the postscript to the play, Shaw says that Eliza will not marry Higgins. Does the author convince you that Eliza will marry Freddy instead? Based on the evidence in the play itself, do you think Eliza will return to Higgins? Why did Shaw decide against bringing Freddy on stage and dramatizing Eliza's decision? Why is the play subtitled "A Romance"? Doolittle tells Eliza that if either Higgins or Pickering had not been present she might have married the other, but as it was, each of the men chaperoned the other. Is Doolittle's assertion true? Was Eliza thinking of marriage?

Analyze the interpolated film sequences. Explain what they add to the work. Is the play weaker because it lacks the ballroom scene?

How do Higgins and Doolittle perceive themselves? To what extent is their self-judgment accurate? What, in addition to her role in the main plot, is Mrs. Higgins' dramatic function? How do Pickering and Freddy serve as foils for Higgins?

How is language used to characterize? Why is the language of each character appropriate only to him?

When *Pygmalion* was first produced in England, audiences were shocked by the taboo word "bloody." Although it is easy for today's audiences to accept this word, would they accept its replacement by one of today's obscenities? Could you justify such a replacement? Should obscenity be condoned or condemned in the theater?

Shaw said that his comedy was based on the truth, which he called the funniest thing in the world. In Act V Eliza declares that she will marry Freddy as soon as she is able to support him. Does this reversal of the usual phraseology make the statement funny? Does it make the statement true? Locate examples of comic lines and situations that might support Shaw's contention. What similar reversals or other comic devices does Shaw use?

Examine the descriptions of Eliza's costumes. What do they tell us of character and theme? Examine the costume descriptions of the other characters, answering the same questions.

Based on Shaw's stage directions, draw a *ground plan* (a view of the stage from above) of the settings and, using coins or similar objects, follow Shaw's *blocking* (movement) of the characters, attempting as you do so to visualize the stage picture. Try to invent additional movement and business to help convey the attitudes of the characters and the ideas of the play.

Tennessee Williams § 1911–

One of the United States' most prominent playwrights, Williams—christened Thomas Lanier and born in Mississippi—has also written poetry, short stories, a novel, and screenplays. In his plays Williams explores the emotions of fragile individuals confronting an inhumane, savage society. These weak, defenseless creatures, with whom he usually sympathizes, are frequently victims not only of a hostile world but also of their own neuroses. Williams is probably best known for his portrayal of hypersensitive, lonely Southern women, clutching at life while trying to keep alive their memories of a romantic past. The clash between the sensitive, frail, poetic victims and the callous, cruel, and vulgar brutes often results in violence, a major characteristic of Williams, whose plays abound in rape, cannibalism, and castration.

The Glass Menagerie (1944) won the New York Drama Critics' Circle Award as the best American play for that season. A Streetcar Named Desire (1947), Cat on a Hot Tin Roof (1955), and The Night of the Iguana (1962) also earned Williams awards from the Drama Critics' Circle. He won a Pulitzer Prize for A Streetcar Named Desire and again for Cat on a Hot Tin Roof.

The Glass Menagerie

CHARACTERS

AMANDA WINGFIELD, the mother. A little woman of great but confused vitality clinging frantically to another time and place. Her characterization must be carefully created, not copied from type. She is not paranoiac, but her life is paranoia. There is much to admire in Amanda, and as much to love and pity as there is to laugh at. Certainly she has endurance and a kind of heroism, and though her foolishness makes her unwittingly cruel at times, there is tenderness in her slight person.

LAURA WINGFIELD, her daughter. Amanda, having failed to establish contact with reality, continues to live vitally in her illusions, but Laura's situation is even graver. A childhood illness has left her crippled, one leg slightly shorter than the other, and held in a brace. This defect need not be more

than suggested on the stage. Stemming from this, Laura's separation increases till she is like a piece of her own glass collection, too exquisitely
fragile to move from the shelf.

TOM WINGFIELD, her son. And the narrator of the play. A poet with a job in a
warehouse. His nature is not remorseless, but to escape from a trap he has
to act without pity.

JIM O'CONNOR, the gentleman caller. A nice, ordinary, young man.

SCENES

SCENE   *An Alley in St. Louis.*
PART I   *Preparation for a Gentleman Caller*
PART II   *The Gentleman Calls*
TIME   *Now [c. 1944] and the Past.*

THE AUTHOR'S PRODUCTION NOTES

Being a "memory play," *The Glass Menagerie* can be presented with
unusual freedom of convention. Because of its considerably delicate or
tenuous material, atmospheric touches and subtleties of direction play
a particularly important part. Expressionism and all other unconventional techniques in drama have only one valid aim, and that is a closer
approach to truth. When a play employs unconventional techniques, it
is not, or certainly shouldn't be, trying to escape its responsibility of
dealing with reality, or interpreting experience, but is actually or
should be attempting to find a closer approach, a more penetrating and
vivid expression of things as they are. The straight realistic play with
its genuine frigidaire and authentic ice-cubes, its characters that speak
exactly as its audience speaks, corresponds to the academic landscape
and has the same virtue of a photographic likeness. Everyone should
know nowadays the unimportance of the photographic in art: that
truth, life, or reality is an organic thing which the poetic imagination
can represent or suggest, in essence, only through transformation,
through changing into other forms than those which were merely
present in appearance.

These remarks are not meant as a preface only to this particular
play. They have to do with a conception of a new, plastic theatre
which must take the place of the exhausted theatre of realistic conventions if the theatre is to resume vitality as a part of our culture.

THE SCREEN DEVICE

There is only one important difference between the original and acting
version of the play and that is the omission in the latter of the device
which I tentatively included in my original script. This device was the
use of a screen on which were projected magic-lantern slides bearing
images or titles. I do not regret the omission of this device from the
present Broadway production. The extraordinary power of Miss Taylor's performance made it suitable to have the utmost simplicity in
the physical production. But I think it may be interesting to some

readers to see how this device was conceived. So I am putting it into the published manuscript. These images and legends, projected from behind, were cast on a section of wall between the front-room and dining-room areas, which should be indistinguishable from the rest when not in use.

The purpose of this will probably be apparent. It is to give accent to certain values in each scene. Each scene contains a particular point (or several) which is structurally the most important. In an episodic play, such as this, the basic structure or narrative line may be obscured from the audience; the effect may seem fragmentary rather than architectural. This may not be the fault of the play so much as a lack of attention in the audience. The legend or image upon the screen will strengthen the effect of what is merely allusion in the writing and allow the primary point to be made more simply and lightly than if the entire responsibility were on the spoken lines. Aside from this structural value, I think the screen will have a definite emotional appeal, less definable but just as important. An imaginative producer or director may invent many other uses for this device than those indicated in the present script. In fact the possibilities of the device seem much larger to me than the instance of this play can possibly utilize.

THE MUSIC

Another extra-literary accent in this play is provided by the use of music. A single recurring tune, "The Glass Menagerie," is used to give emotional emphasis to suitable passages. This tune is like circus music, not when you are on the grounds or in the immediate vicinity of the parade, but when you are at some distance and very likely thinking of something else. It seems under those circumstances to continue almost interminably and it weaves in and out of your preoccupied consciousness; then it is the lightest, most delicate music in the world and perhaps the saddest. It expresses the surface vivacity of life with the underlying strain of immutable and inexpressible sorrow. When you look at a piece of delicately spun glass you think of two things: how beautiful it is and how easily it can be broken. Both of those ideas should be woven into the recurring tune, which dips in and out of the play as if it were carried on a wind that changes. It serves as a thread of connection and allusion between the narrator with his separate point in time and space and the subject of his story. Between each episode it returns as reference to the emotion, nostalgia, which is the first condition of the play. It is primarily Laura's music and therefore comes out most clearly when the play focuses upon her and the lovely fragility of glass which is her image.

THE LIGHTING

The lighting in the play is not realistic. In keeping with the atmosphere of memory, the stage is dim. Shafts of light are focused on selected areas or actors, sometimes in contradistinction to what is the apparent center. For instance, in the quarrel scene between Tom and Amanda, in which Laura has no active part, the clearest pool of light is on her figure. This is also true of the supper scene, when her silent figure on the sofa should remain the visual center. The light upon Laura should be distinct from the others, having a peculiar pristine clarity such as light used in early religious portraits of female saints or madonnas. A certain correspondence to light in religious paintings, such as El Greco's, where the figures are radiant in atmosphere that is relatively dusky, could be effectively used throughout the play. (It will also permit a more effective use of the screen.) A free, imaginative use light can be of enormous value in giving a mobile, plastic quality to plays of a more or less static nature.

§ SCENE I

The Wingfield apartment is in the rear of the building, one of those vast hive-like conglomerations of cellular living-units that flower as warty growths in overcrowded urban centers of lower middle-class populations and are symptomatic of the impulse of this largest and fundamentally enslaved section of American society to avoid fluidity and differentiation and to exist and function as one interfused mass of automatism.

The apartment faces an alley and is entered by a fire escape, a structure whose name is a touch of accidental poetic truth, for all of these huge buildings are always burning with the slow and implacable fires of human desperation. The fire escape is included in the set—that is, the landing of it and steps descending from it.

The scene is memory and is therefore nonrealistic. Memory takes a lot of poetic license. It omits some details; others are exaggerated, according to the emotional value of the articles it touches, for memory is seated predominantly in the heart. The interior is therefore rather dim and poetic.

At the rise of the curtain, the audience is faced with the dark, grim rear wall of the Wingfield tenement. This building, which runs parallel to the footlights, is flanked on both sides by dark, narrow alleys which run into murky canyons of tangled clotheslines, garbage cans, and the sinister latticework of neighboring fire escapes. It is up and down these side alleys that exterior entrances and exits are made, during the play. At the end of TOM'S *opening commentary, the dark tenement wall slowly reveals (by the means of a transparency) the interior of the ground floor Wingfield apartment.*

Downstage is the living room, which also serves as a sleeping room for LAURA, *the sofa unfolding to make her bed. Upstage, center, and divided by a wide arch or second proscenium with transparent faded portieres (or second curtain), is the dining room. In an old-fashioned what-not in the living room are seen scores of transparent glass animals. A blown-up photograph of the father hangs on the wall of the living room, facing the audience, to the left of the archway. It is the face of a very handsome young man in a doughboy's[1] First World War cap. He is gallantly smiling, ineluctably smiling, as if to say, "I will be smiling forever."*

The audience hears and sees the opening scene in the dining room through both the transparent fourth wall of the building and the transparent gauze portieres of the dining-room arch. It is during this revealing scene that the fourth wall slowly ascends, out of sight. This transparent exterior wall is not brought down again until the very end of the play, during TOM's *speech.*

The narrator is an undisguised convention of the play. He takes whatever license with dramatic convention is convenient to his purposes.

TOM *enters dressed as a merchant sailor from alley, stage left, and strolls across the front of the stage to the fire escape. There he stops and lights a cigarette. He addresses the audience.*

TOM: Yes, I have tricks in my pocket, I have things up my sleeve. But I am the opposite of a stage magician. He gives you illusion that has the appearance of truth. I give you truth in the pleasant disguise of illusion.

To begin with, I turn back time. I reverse it to that quaint period, the thirties, when the huge middle class of America was matriculating in a school for the blind. Their eyes had failed them, or they had failed their eyes, and so they were having their fingers pressed forcibly down on the fiery Braille alphabet of a dissolving economy.

In Spain there was revolution. Here there was only shouting and confusion.

In Spain there was Guernica.[2] Here there were disturbances of labor, sometimes pretty violent, in otherwise peaceful cities such as Chicago, Cleveland, Saint Louis . . .

This is the social background of the play.

Music

The play is memory.

Being a memory play, it is dimly lighted, it is sentimental, it is not realistic.

In memory everything seems to happen to music. That explains the fiddle in the wings.

I am the narrator of the play, and also a character in it.

---

[1] American infantryman.
[2] During the Spanish Civil War the city of Guernica was heavily bombarded by Franco's forces.

The other characters are my mother, Amanda, my sister, Laura, and a gentleman caller who appears in the final scenes.

He is the most realistic character in the play, being an emissary from a world of reality that we were somehow set apart from.

But since I have a poet's weakness for symbols, I am using this character also as a symbol; he is the long delayed but always expected something that we live for.

There is a fifth character in the play who doesn't appear except in this larger-than-life-size photograph over the mantel.

This is our father who left us a long time ago.

He was a telephone man who fell in love with long distances; he gave up his job with the telephone company and skipped the light fantastic out of town . . .

The last we heard of him was a picture post-card from Mazatlan, on the Pacific coast of Mexico, containing a message of two words— "Hello— Good-bye!" and no address.

I think the rest of the play will explain itself. . . .

AMANDA'S *voice becomes audible through the portieres.*

Legend on screen: "Où Sont Les Neiges." [3]

He divides the portieres and enters the upstage area.

AMANDA *and* LAURA *are seated at a drop-leaf table. Eating is indicated by gestures without food or utensils.* AMANDA *faces the audience,* TOM *and* LAURA *are seated in profile. The interior has lit up softly and through the scrim we see* AMANDA *and* LAURA *seated at the table in the upstage area.*

AMANDA (*calling*): Tom?

TOM: Yes, Mother.

AMANDA: We can't say grace until you come to the table!

TOM: Coming, Mother. (*He bows slightly and withdraws, reappearing a few moments later in his place at the table.*)

AMANDA (*to her son*): Honey, don't *push* with your *fingers*. If you have to push with something, the thing to push with is a crust of bread. And chew—chew! Animals have sections in their stomachs which enable them to digest food without mastication, but human beings are supposed to chew their food before they swallow it down. Eat food leisurely, son, and really enjoy it. A well-cooked meal has lots of delicate flavors that have to be held in the mouth for appreciation. So chew your food and give your salivary glands a chance to function!

TOM *deliberately lays his imaginary fork down and pushes his chair back from the table.*

---

[3] "Where are the snows [of yesteryear]?" From François Villon's "Ballade of Dead Ladies."

TOM: I haven't enjoyed one bite of this dinner because of your constant directions on how to eat it. It's you that make me rush through meals with your hawk-like attention to every bite I take. Sickening—spoils my appetite—all this discussion of—animals' secretion—salivary glands —mastication!

AMANDA (*lightly*): Temperament like a Metropolitan star! (*He rises and crosses downstage.*) You're not excused from the table.

TOM: I'm getting a cigarette.

AMANDA: You smoke too much.

LAURA *rises.*

LAURA: I'll bring in the blanc mange.

He remains standing with his cigarette by the portieres during the following.

AMANDA (*rising*): No, sister, no, sister—you be the lady this time and I'll be the darky.

LAURA: I'm already up.

AMANDA: Resume your seat, little sister—I want you to stay fresh and pretty—for gentlemen callers!

LAURA: I'm not expecting any gentlemen callers.

AMANDA (*crossing out to kitchenette. Airily*): Sometimes they come when they are least expected! Why, I remember one Sunday afternoon in Blue Mountain— (*Enters kitchenette.*)

TOM: I know what's coming!

LAURA: Yes. But let her tell it.

TOM: Again?

LAURA: She loves to tell it.

AMANDA *returns with bowl of dessert.*

AMANDA: One Sunday afternoon in Blue Mountain—your mother received —seventeen!—gentlemen callers! Why, sometimes there weren't chairs enough to accommodate them all. We had to send the nigger over to bring in folding chairs from the parish house.

TOM (*remaining at portieres*): How did you entertain those gentlemen callers?

AMANDA: I understood the art of conversation!

TOM: I bet you could talk.

AMANDA: Girls in those days *knew* how to talk, I can tell you.

TOM: Yes?

Image: AMANDA *as a girl on a porch, greeting callers*

AMANDA: They knew how to entertain their gentlemen callers. It wasn't enough for a girl to be possessed of a pretty face and a graceful figure

—although I wasn't slighted in either respect. She also needed to have a nimble wit and a tongue to meet all occasions.

TOM: What did you talk about?

AMANDA: Things of importance going on in the world! Never anything coarse or common or vulgar. (*She addresses* TOM *as though he were seated in the vacant chair at the table though he remains by portieres. He plays this scene as though he held the book.*) My callers were gentlemen—all! Among my callers were some of the most prominent young planters of the Mississippi Delta—planters and sons of planters!

TOM *motions for music and a spot of light on* AMANDA.

Her eyes lift, her face glows, her voice becomes rich and elegiac.

Screen legend: "Où Sont Les Neiges."

There was young Champ Laughlin who later became vice-president of the Delta Planters Bank.

Hadley Stevenson who was drowned in Moon Lake and left his widow one hundred and fifty thousand in Government bonds.

There were the Cutrere brothers, Wesley and Bates. Bates was one of my bright particular beaux! He got in a quarrel with that wild Wainwright boy. They shot it out on the floor of Moon Lake Casino. Bates was shot through the stomach. Died in the ambulance on his way to Memphis. His widow was also well-provided for, came into eight or ten thousand acres, that's all. She married him on the rebound —never loved her—carried my picture on him the night he died!

And there was that boy that every girl in the Delta had set her cap for! That beautiful, brilliant young Fitzhugh boy from Greene County!

TOM: What did he leave his widow?

AMANDA: He never married! Gracious, you talk as though all of my old admirers had turned up their toes to the daisies!

TOM: Isn't this the first you've mentioned that still survives?

AMANDA: That Fitzhugh boy went North and made a fortune—came to be known as the Wolf of Wall Street! He had the Midas touch, whatever he touched turned to gold!

And I could have been Mrs. Duncan J. Fitzhugh, mind you! But —I picked your *father!*

LAURA (*rising*): Mother, let me clear the table.

AMANDA: No, dear, you go in front and study your typewriter chart. Or practice your shorthand a little. Stay fresh and pretty!—It's almost time for our gentlemen callers to start arriving. (*She flounces girlishly toward the kitchenette.*) How many do you suppose we're going to entertain this afternoon?

TOM *throws down the paper and jumps up with a groan.*

LAURA (*alone in the dining room*): I don't believe we're going to receive any, Mother.

AMANDA (*reappearing, airily*): What? No one—not one? You must be joking! (LAURA *nervously echoes her laugh. She slips in a fugitive manner through the half-open portieres and draws them gently behind her. A shaft of very clear light is thrown on her face against the faded tapestry of the curtains. Music: "The Glass Menagerie" under faintly. Lightly*) Not one gentleman caller? It can't be true! There must be a flood, there must have been a tornado!

LAURA: It isn't a flood, it's not a tornado, Mother. I'm just not popular like you were in Blue Mountain. . . . (TOM *utters another groan.* LAURA *glances at him with a faint, apologetic smile. Her voice catching a little*) Mother's afraid I'm going to be an old maid.

The Scene Dims Out with "Glass Menagerie" Music.

§ SCENE II

"Laura, Haven't You Ever Liked Some Boy?"

On the dark stage the screen is lighted with the image of blue roses.

Gradually LAURA'S *figure becomes apparent and the screen goes out.*

The music subsides.

LAURA *is seated in the delicate ivory chair at the small clawfoot table.*

She wears a dress of soft-violet material for a kimono—her hair tied back from her forehead with a ribbon.

She is washing and polishing her collection of glass.

AMANDA *appears on the fire-escape steps. At the sound of her ascent,* LAURA *catches her breath, thrusts the bowl of ornaments away and seats herself stiffly before the diagram of the typewriter keyboard as though it held her spellbound.*

Something has happened to AMANDA. *It is written in her face as she climbs to the landing: a look that is grim and hopeless and a little absurd.*

She has on one of those cheap or imitation velvety-looking cloth coats with imitation fur collar. Her hat is five or six years old, one of those dreadful cloche hats that were worn in the late twenties and she is clasping an enormous black patent-leather pocketbook with nickel clasps and initials. This is her full-dress outfit, the one she usually wears to the D.A.R.[4]

Before entering she looks through the door.

She purses her lips, opens her eyes very wide, rolls them upward and shakes her head.

Then she slowly lets herself in the door. Seeing her mother's expression LAURA *touches her lips with a nervous gesture.*

LAURA: Hello, Mother, I was— (*She makes a nervous gesture toward the chart on the wall.* AMANDA *leans against the shut door and stares at* LAURA *with a martyred look.*)

AMANDA: Deception? Deception? (*She slowly removes her hat and gloves, continuing the sweet suffering stare. She lets the hat and gloves fall on the floor—a bit of acting.*)

LAURA (*shakily*): How was the D.A.R. meeting? (AMANDA *slowly opens her purse and removes a dainty white handkerchief which she shakes out delicately and delicately touches to her lips and nostrils.*) Didn't you go to the D.A.R. meeting, Mother?

AMANDA (*faintly, almost inaudibly*): —No—No. (*Then more forcibly*) I did not have the strength—to go to the D.A.R. In fact, I did not have the courage! I wanted to find a hole in the ground and hide myself in it forever! (*She crosses slowly to the wall and removes the diagram of the typewriter keyboard. She holds it in front of her for a second, staring at it sweetly and sorrowfully—then bites her lips and tears it in two pieces.*)

LAURA (*faintly*): Why did you do that, Mother? (AMANDA *repeats the same procedure with the chart of the Gregg Alphabet.*) Why are you—

AMANDA: Why? Why? How old are you, Laura?

LAURA: Mother, you know my age.

AMANDA: I thought that you were an adult; it seems that I was mistaken. (*She crosses slowly to the sofa and sinks down and stares at* LAURA.)

LAURA: Please don't stare at me, Mother. (AMANDA *closes her eyes and lowers her head. Count ten.*)

AMANDA: What are we going to do, what is going to become of us, what is the future? (*Count ten.*)

LAURA: Has something happened, Mother? (AMANDA *draws a long breath and takes out the handkerchief again. Dabbing process*) Mother, has —something happened?

[4] Daughters of the American Revolution.

AMANDA: I'll be all right in a minute, I'm just bewildered— (*Count five.*) —by life. . . .

LAURA: Mother, I wish that you would tell me what's happened!

AMANDA: As you know, I was supposed to be inducted into my office at the D.A.R. this afternoon. (*Image: A Swarm of Typewriters*) But I stopped off at Rubicam's Business College to speak to your teachers about your having a cold and ask them what progress they thought you were making down there.

LAURA: Oh. . . .

AMANDA: I went to the typing instructor and introduced myself as your mother. She didn't know who you were. Wingfield, she said. We don't have any such student enrolled at the school!

I assured her she did, that you had been going to classes since early in January.

"I wonder," she said, "if you could be talking about that terribly shy little girl who dropped out of school after only a few days' attendance?"

"No," I said, "Laura, my daughter, has been going to school every day for the past six weeks!"

"Excuse me," she said. She took the attendance book out and there was your name, unmistakably printed, and all the dates you were absent until they decided that you had dropped out of school.

I still said, "No, there must have been some mistake! There must have been some mix-up in the records!"

And she said, "No—I remember her perfectly now. Her hands shook so that she couldn't hit the right keys! The first time we gave a speed-test, she broke down completely—was sick at the stomach and almost had to be carried into the wash-room! After that morning she never showed up any more. We phoned the house but never got any answer"—while I was working at Famous and Barr, I suppose, demonstrating those— Oh!

I felt so weak I could barely keep on my feet!

I had to sit down while they got me a glass of water!

Fifty dollars' tuition, all of our plans—my hopes and ambitions for you—just gone up the spout, just gone up the spout like that.

> LAURA *draws a long breath and gets awkwardly to her feet. She crosses to the victrola and winds it up.*

What are you doing?

LAURA: Oh! (*She releases the handle and returns to her seat.*)

AMANDA: Laura, where have you been going when you've gone out pretending that you were going to business college?

LAURA: I've just been going out walking.

AMANDA: That's not true.

LAURA: It is. I just went walking.

AMANDA: Walking? Walking? In winter? Deliberately courting pneumonia in that light coat? Where did you walk to, Laura?

LAURA: All sorts of places—mostly in the park.

AMANDA: Even after you'd started catching that cold?

LAURA: It was the lesser of two evils, Mother. (*Image: Winter Scene in Park*) I couldn't go back up. I—threw up—on the floor!

AMANDA: From half past seven till after five every day you mean to tell me you walked around in the park, because you wanted to make me think that you were still going to Rubicam's Business College?

LAURA: It wasn't as bad as it sounds. I went inside places to get warmed up.

AMANDA: Inside where?

LAURA: I went in the art museum and the bird-houses at the Zoo. I visited the penguins every day! Sometimes I did without lunch and went to the movies. Lately I've been spending most of my afternoons in the Jewel-box, that big glass house where they raise the tropical flowers.

AMANDA: You did all this to deceive me, just for deception? (LAURA *looks down.*) Why?

LAURA: Mother, when you're disappointed, you get that awful suffering look on your face, like the picture of Jesus' mother in the museum!

AMANDA: Hush!

LAURA: I couldn't face it.

Pause. A whisper of strings

Legend: "The Crust of Humility."

AMANDA (*hopelessly fingering the huge pocketbook*): So what are we going to do the rest of our lives? Stay home and watch the parades go by? Amuse ourselves with the glass menagerie, darling? Eternally play those worn-out phonograph records your father left as a painful reminder of him?

We won't have a business career—we've given that up because it gave us nervous indigestion! (*Laughs wearily.*) What is there left but dependency all our lives? I know so well what becomes of unmarried women who aren't prepared to occupy a position. I've seen such pitiful cases in the South—barely tolerated spinsters living upon the grudging patronage of sister's husband or brother's wife!—stuck away in some little mouse-trap of a room—encouraged by one in-law to visit another —little birdlike women without any nest—eating the crust of humility all their life!

Is that the future that we've mapped out for ourselves?

I swear it's the only alternative I can think of!

It isn't a very pleasant alternative, is it?

Of course—some girls *do marry.*

LAURA *twists her hands nervously.*

Haven't you ever liked some boy?

LAURA: Yes. I liked one once. (*Rises*.) I came across his picture a while ago.

AMANDA (*with some interest*): He gave you his picture?

LAURA: No, it's in the year-book.

AMANDA (*disappointed*): Oh—a high-school boy.

Screen image: Jim as High-school Hero Bearing a Silver Cup.

LAURA: Yes. His name was Jim. (LAURA *lifts the heavy annual from the clawfoot table*.) Here he is in *The Pirates of Penzance*.

AMANDA (*absently*): The what?

LAURA: The operetta the senior class put on. He had a wonderful voice and we sat across the aisle from each other Mondays, Wednesdays, and Fridays in the Aud. Here he is with the silver cup for debating! See his grin?

AMANDA (*absently*): He must have had a jolly disposition.

LAURA: He used to call me—Blue Roses.

Image: Blue Roses

AMANDA: Why did he call you such a name as that?

LAURA: When I had that attack of pleurosis—he asked me what was the matter when I came back. I said pleurosis—he thought that I said Blue Roses! So that's what he always called me after that. Whenever he saw me, he'd holler, "Hello, Blue Roses!" I didn't care for the girl that he went out with. Emily Meisenbach. Emily was the best-dressed girl at Soldan. She never struck me, though, as being sincere. . . . It says in the Personal Section—they're engaged. That's—six years ago! They must be married by now.

AMANDA: Girls that aren't cut out for business careers usually wind up married to some nice man. (*Gets up with a spark of revival*.) Sister, that's what you'll do!

LAURA *utters a startled, doubtful laugh. She reaches quickly for a piece of glass.*

LAURA: But, Mother—

AMANDA: Yes? (*Crossing to photograph*)

LAURA (*in a tone of frightened apology*): I'm—crippled!

Image: Screen

AMANDA: Nonsense! Laura, I've told you never, never to use that word. Why, you're not crippled, you just have a little defect—hardly noticeable, even! When people have some slight disadvantage like that, they cultivate other things to make up for it—develop charm—and vivacity

—and—*charm!* That's all you have to do! (*She turns again to the photograph.*)

One thing your father had *plenty of*—was *charm!*

TOM *motions to the fiddle in the wings.*

The Scene Fades Out with Music.

§ SCENE III

Legend on screen: "After the Fiasco—"

TOM *speaks from the fire-escape landing.*

TOM: After the fiasco at Rubicam's Business College, the idea of getting a gentleman caller for Laura began to play a more and more important part in Mother's calculations.

It became an obsession. Like some archetype of the universal unconscious, the image of the gentleman caller haunted our small apartment. . . .

Image: Young Man at Door with Flowers

An evening at home rarely passed without some allusion to this image, this specter, this hope. . . .

Even when he wasn't mentioned, his presence hung in Mother's preoccupied look and in my sister's frightened, apologetic manner—hung like a sentence passed upon the Wingfields!

Mother was a woman of action as well as words.

She began to take logical steps in the planned direction.

Late that winter and in the early spring—realizing that extra money would be needed to properly feather the nest and plume the bird—she conducted a vigorous campaign on the telephone, roping in subscribers to one of those magazines for matrons called *The Homemaker's Companion,* the type of journal that features the serialized sublimations of ladies of letters who think in terms of delicate cuplike breasts, slim, tapering waists, rich, creamy thighs, eyes like wood-smoke in autumn, fingers that soothe and caress like strains of music, bodies as powerful as Etruscan sculpture.

Screen Image: Glamor Magazine Cover.

AMANDA *enters with phone on long extension cord. She is spotted in the dim stage.*

AMANDA: Ida Scott? This is Amanda Wingfield!
We *missed* you at the D.A.R. last Monday!

I said to myself: She's probably suffering with that sinus condition! How is that sinus condition?

Horrors! Heaven have mercy!—You're a Christian martyr, yes, that's what you are, a Christian martyr!

Well, I just now happened to notice that your subscription to the *Companion's* about to expire! Yes, it expires with the next issue, honey! —just when that wonderful new serial by Bessie Mae Hopper is getting off to such an exciting start. Oh, honey, it's something that you can't miss! You remember how *Gone With the Wind* took everybody by storm? You simply couldn't go out if you hadn't read it. All everybody *talked* was Scarlett O'Hara. Well, this is a book that critics already compare to *Gone With the Wind*. It's the *Gone With the Wind* of the post-World War generation!—What?—Burning?—Oh, honey, don't let them burn, go take a look in the oven and I'll hold the wire! Heavens—I think she's hung up!

Dim out.

Legend on screen: "You Think I'm in Love with Continental Shoemakers?"

Before the stage is lighted, the violent voices of TOM *and* AMANDA *are heard.*

They are quarreling behind the portieres. In front of them stands LAURA *with clenched hands and panicky expression.*

A clear pool of light on her figure throughout this scene.

TOM: What in Christ's name am I—
AMANDA (*shrilly*): Don't you use that—
TOM: Supposed to do!
AMANDA: Expression! Not in my—
TOM: Ohhh!
AMANDA: Presence! Have you gone out of your senses?
TOM: I have, that's true, *driven* out!
AMANDA: What is the matter with you, you—big—big—*idiot!*
TOM: Look!—I've got *no thing*, no single thing—
AMANDA: Lower your voice!
TOM: In my life here that I can call my *own!* Everything is—
AMANDA: Stop that shouting!
TOM: Yesterday you confiscated my books! You had the nerve to—
AMANDA: I took that horrible novel back to the library—yes! That hideous book by that insane Mr. Lawrence.[5] (TOM *laughs wildly.*) I cannot control the output of diseased minds or people who cater to them—

---

[5] D. H. Lawrence (1885–1930), English novelist, author of *Lady Chatterley's Lover*, and other novels.

(TOM *laughs still more wildly.*) BUT I WON'T ALLOW SUCH FILTH BROUGHT INTO MY HOUSE! No, no, no, no, no!

TOM: House, house! Who pays rent on it, who makes a slave of himself to—

AMANDA (*fairly screeching*): Don't you DARE to—

TOM: No, no, I mustn't say things! *I've* got to just—

AMANDA: Let me tell you—

TOM: I don't want to hear any more! (*He tears the portieres open. The upstage area is lit with a turgid smoky red glow.*)

AMANDA'S *hair is in metal curlers and she wears a very old bathrobe, much too large for her slight figure, a relic of the faithless Mr.Wingfield. An upright typewriter and a wild disarray of manuscripts is on the drop-leaf table. The quarrel was probably precipitated by* AMANDA'S *interruption of his creative labor. A chair lying overthrown on the floor. Their gesticulating shadows are cast on the ceiling by the fiery glow.*

AMANDA: You *will* hear more, you—

TOM: No, I won't hear more, I'm going out!

AMANDA: You come right back in—

TOM: Out, out, out! Because I'm—

AMANDA: Come back here, Tom Wingfield! I'm not through talking to you!

TOM: Oh, go—

LAURA (*desperately*): —Tom!

AMANDA: You're going to listen, and no more insolence from you! I'm at the end of my patience!

He comes back toward her.

TOM: What do you think I'm at? Aren't I supposed to have any patience to reach the end of, Mother? I know, I know. It seems unimportant to you, what I'm *doing*—what I *want* to do—having a little *difference* between them! You don't think that—

AMANDA: I think you've been doing things that you're ashamed of. That's why you act like this. I don't believe that you go every night to the movies. Nobody goes to the movies night after night. Nobody in their right minds goes to the movies as often as you pretend to. People don't go to the movies at nearly midnight, and movies don't let out at two A.M. Come in stumbling. Muttering to yourself like a maniac! You get three hours' sleep and then go to work. Oh, I can picture the way you're doing down there. Moping, doping, because you're in no condition!

TOM (*wildly*): No, I'm in no condition!

AMANDA: What right have you got to jeopardize your job? Jeopardize the security of us all? How do you think we'd manage if you were—

TOM: Listen! You think I'm crazy *about the warehouse?* (*He bends fiercely toward her slight figure.*) You think I'm in love with the Continental Shoemakers? You think I want to spend fifty-five *years* down there in that—*celotex interior!* with—*fluorescent—tubes!* Look! I'd rather somebody picked up a crowbar and battered out my brains—than go back mornings! I *go!* Every time you come in yelling that God damn "*Rise and Shine!*" "*Rise and Shine!*" I say to myself, "How *lucky dead* people are!" But I get up. I *go!* For sixty-five dollars a month I give up all that I dream of doing and being *ever!* And you say self —*self's* all I ever think of. Why, listen, if self is what I thought of, Mother, I'd be where he is—GONE! (*Pointing to father's picture*) As far as the system of transportation reaches! (*He starts past her. She grabs his arm.*) Don't grab at me, Mother!

AMANDA: Where are you going?

TOM: I'm going to the *movies!*

AMANDA: I don't believe that lie!

TOM (*crouching toward her, overtowering her tiny figure. She backs away, gasping*): I'm going to opium dens! Yes, opium dens, dens of vice and criminals' hang-outs, Mother. I've joined the Hogan gang, I'm a hired assassin, I carry a tommy-gun in a violin case! I run a string of cat-houses in the Valley! They call me Killer, Killer Wingfield, I'm leading a double-life, a simple, honest warehouse worker by day, by night a dynamic *czar* of the *underworld, Mother.* I go to gambling casinos, I spin away fortunes on the roulette table! I wear a patch over one eye and a false mustache, sometimes I put on green whiskers. On those occasions they call me—*El Diablo!* Oh, I could tell you things to make you sleepless! My enemies plan to dynamite this place. They're going to blow us all sky-high some night! I'll be glad, very happy, and so will you! You'll go up, up on a broomstick, over Blue Mountain with seventeen gentlemen callers! You ugly—babbling old—*witch.* . . . (*He goes through a series of violent, clumsy movements, seizing his overcoat, lunging to the door, pulling it fiercely open. The women watch him, aghast. His arm catches in the sleeve of the coat as he struggles to pull it on. For a moment he is pinioned by the bulky garment. With an outraged groan he tears the coat off again, splitting the shoulder of it, and hurls it across the room. It strikes against the shelf of* LAURA's *glass collection, there is a tinkle of shattering glass.* LAURA *cries out as if wounded.*)

Music. Legend: "The Glass Menagerie"

LAURA (*shrilly*): My glass!—menagerie. . . . (*She covers her face and turns away.*)

But AMANDA *is still stunned and stupefied by the "ugly witch" so that she barely notices this occurrence. Now she recovers her speech.*

AMANDA (*in an awful voice*): I won't speak to you—until you apologize! (*She crosses through portieres and draws them together behind her.* TOM *is left with* LAURA. LAURA *clings weakly to the mantel with her face averted.* TOM *stares at her stupidly for a moment. Then he crosses to shelf. Drops awkwardly on his knees to collect the fallen glass, glancing at* LAURA *as if he would speak but couldn't.*)

"*The Glass Menagerie*" *Steals in as the Scene Dims Out.*

§ SCENE IV

The interior is dark. Faint light in the alley.

A deep-voiced bell in a church is tolling the hour of five as the scene commences.

TOM *appears at the top of the alley. After each solemn boom of the bell in the tower, he shakes a little noise-maker or rattle as if to express the tiny spasm of man in contrast to the sustained power and dignity of the Almighty. This and the unsteadiness of his advance make it evident that he has been drinking.*

As he climbs the few steps to the fire-escape landing light steals up inside. LAURA *appears in nightdress, observing* TOM's *empty bed in the front room.*

TOM *fishes in his pockets for door key, removing a motley assortment of articles in the search, including a perfect shower of movie-ticket stubs and an empty bottle. At last he finds the key, but just as he is about to insert it, it slips from his fingers. He strikes a match and crouches below the door.*

TOM (*bitterly*): One crack—and it falls through!

LAURA *opens the door.*

LAURA: Tom, Tom, what are you doing?
TOM: Looking for a door key.
LAURA: Where have you been all this time?
TOM: I have been to the movies.
LAURA: All this time at the movies?
TOM: There was a very long program. There was a Garbo picture and a Mickey Mouse and a travelogue and a newsreel and a preview of coming attractions. And there was an organ solo and a collection for the milk-fund—simultaneously—which ended up in a terrible fight between a fat lady and an usher!
LAURA (*innocently*): Did you have to stay through everything?
TOM: Of course! And, oh, I forgot! There was a big stage show. The head-

liner on this stage show was Malvolio the Magician. He performed wonderful tricks, many of them, such as pouring water back and forth between pitchers. First it turned to wine and then it turned to beer and then it turned to whiskey. I know it was whiskey it finally turned into because he needed somebody to come up out of the audience to help him, and I came up—both shows! It was Kentucky Straight Bourbon. A very generous fellow, he gave souvenirs. (*He pulls from his back pocket a shimmering rainbow-colored scarf.*) He gave me this. This is his magic scarf. You can have it, Laura. You wave it over a canary cage and you get a bowl of gold-fish. You wave it over the gold-fish bowl and they fly away canaries. . . . But the wonderfullest trick of all was the coffin trick. We nailed him into a coffin and he got out of the coffin without removing one nail. (*He has come inside.*) There is a trick that would come in handy for me—get me out of this 2 by 4 situation! (*Flops onto bed and starts removing shoes.*)

LAURA: Tom—Shhh!

TOM: What're you shushing me for?

LAURA: You'll wake up Mother.

TOM: Goody, goody! Pay 'er back for all those "Rise an' Shines." (*Lies down, groaning.*) You know it don't take much intelligence to get yourself into a nailed-up coffin, Laura. But who in hell ever got himself out of one without removing one nail?

> As if in answer, the father's grinning photograph lights up.

Scene Dims Out

Immediately following: The church bell is heard striking six. At the sixth stroke the alarm clock goes off in AMANDA's *room, and after a few moments we hear her calling: "Rise and Shine! Rise and Shine! Laura, go tell your brother to rise and shine!"*

TOM (*sitting up slowly*): I'll rise—but I won't shine.

> The light increases.

AMANDA: Laura, tell your brother his coffee is ready.

> LAURA *slips into front room.*

LAURA: Tom!—It's nearly seven. Don't make Mother nervous. (*He stares at her stupidly. Beseechingly*) Tom, speak to Mother this morning. Make up with her, apologize, speak to her!

TOM: She won't to me. It's her that started not speaking.

LAURA: If you just say you're sorry she'll start speaking.

TOM: Her not speaking—is that such a tragedy?

LAURA: Please—please!

AMANDA (*calling from kitchenette*): Laura, are you going to do what I asked you to do, or do I have to get dressed and go out myself?

LAURA: Going, going—soon as I get on my coat! (*She pulls on a shapeless felt hat with nervous, jerky movement, pleadingly glancing at* TOM. *Rushes awkwardly for coat. The coat is one of* AMANDA's, *inaccurately made-over, the sleeves too short for* LAURA.) Butter and what else?

AMANDA (*entering upstage*): Just butter. Tell them to charge it.

LAURA: Mother, they make such faces when I do that.

AMANDA: Sticks and stones can break our bones, but the expression on Mr. Garfinkel's face won't harm us! Tell your brother his coffee is getting cold.

LAURA (*at door*): Do what I asked you, will you, will you, Tom?

He looks sullenly away.

AMANDA: Laura, go now or just don't go at all!

LAURA (*rushing out*): Going—going! (*A second later she cries out.* TOM *springs up and crosses to door.* AMANDA *rushes anxiously in.* TOM *opens the door.*)

TOM: Laura?

LAURA: I'm all right. I slipped, but I'm all right.

AMANDA (*peering anxiously after her*): If anyone breaks a leg on those fire-escape steps, the landlord ought to be sued for every cent he possesses! (*She shuts door. Remembers she isn't speaking and returns to other room.*)

As TOM *enters listlessly for his coffee, she turns her back to him and stands rigidly facing the window on the gloomy gray vault of the areaway. Its light on her face with its aged but childish features is cruelly sharp, satirical as a Daumier print.*[6]

Music under: "*Ave Maria*"

TOM *glances sheepishly but sullenly at her averted figure and slumps at the table. The coffee is scalding hot; he sips it and gasps and spits it back in the cup. At his gasp,* AMANDA *catches her breath and half turns. Then catches herself and turns back to window.*

TOM *blows on his coffee, glancing sidewise at his mother. She clears her throat.* TOM *clears his. He starts to rise. Sinks back down again, scratches his head, clears his throat again.* AMANDA *coughs.* TOM *raises his cup in both hands to blow on it, his eyes staring over the rim of it at his mother for several moments. Then he slowly sets the cup down and awkwardly and hesitantly rises from the chair.*

TOM (*hoarsely*): Mother. I—I apologize, Mother. (AMANDA *draws a quick, shuddering breath. Her face works grotesquely. She breaks into child-*

6 Honoré Daumier (1808–1879), French painter and caricaturist.

like tears.) I'm sorry for what I said, for everything that I said, I didn't mean it.

AMANDA (*sobbingly*): My devotion has made me a witch and so I make myself hateful to my children!

TOM: No, you *don't*.

AMANDA: I worry so much, don't sleep, it makes me nervous!

TOM (*gently*): I understand that.

AMANDA: I've had to put up a solitary battle all these years. But you're my right-hand bower! Don't fall down, don't fail!

TOM (*gently*): I try, Mother.

AMANDA (*with great enthusiasm*): Try and you will SUCCEED! (*The notion makes her breathless.*) Why, you—you're just *full* of natural endowments! Both my children—they're *unusual* children! Don't you think I know it? I'm so—*proud!* Happy and—feel I've—so much to be thankful for but—Promise me one thing, Son!

TOM: What, Mother?

AMANDA: Promise, Son, you'll—never be a drunkard!

TOM (*turns to her grinning*): I will never be a drunkard, Mother.

AMANDA: That's what frightened me so, that you'd be drinking! Eat a bowl of Purina!

TOM: Just coffee, Mother.

AMANDA: Shredded wheat biscuit?

TOM: No. No, Mother, just coffee.

AMANDA: You can't put in a day's work on an empty stomach. You've got ten minutes—don't gulp! Drinking too-hot liquids makes cancer of the stomach. . . . Put cream in.

TOM: No, thank you.

AMANDA: To cool it.

TOM: No! No, thank you, I want it black.

AMANDA: I know, but it's not good for you. We have to do all that we can to build ourselves up. In these trying times we live in, all that we have to cling to is—each other. . . . That's why it's so important to—Tom, I—I sent out your sister so I could discuss something with you. If you hadn't spoken I would have spoken to you. (*Sits down.*)

TOM (*gently*): What is it, Mother, that you want to discuss?

AMANDA: *Laura!*

TOM *puts his cup down slowly.*

Legend on screen: *"Laura"*

Music: *"The Glass Menagerie"*

TOM: —Oh—Laura . . .

AMANDA (*touching his sleeve*): You know how Laura is. So quiet but—still water runs deep! She notices things and I think she—broods about them. (TOM *looks up*.) A few days ago I came in and she was crying.

TOM: What about?

AMANDA: You.

TOM: Me?

AMANDA: She has an idea that you're not happy here.

TOM: What gave her that idea?

AMANDA: What gives her any idea? However, you do act strangely. I—I'm not criticizing, understand *that!* I know your ambitions do not lie in the warehouse, that like everybody in the whole wide world—you've had to—make sacrifices, but—Tom—Tom—life's not easy, it calls for —Spartan endurance! There's so many things in my heart that I cannot describe to you! I've never told you but I—*loved* your father. . . .

TOM (*gently*): I know that, Mother.

AMANDA: And you—when I see you taking after his ways! Staying out late—and—well, you *had* been drinking the night you were in that— terrifying condition! Laura says that you hate the apartment and that you go out nights to get away from it! Is that true, Tom?

TOM: No. You say there's so much in your heart that you can't describe to me. That's true of me, too. There's so much in my heart that I can't describe to *you!* So let's respect each other's—

AMANDA: But, why—*why*, Tom—are you always so *restless?* Where do you go to, nights?

TOM: I—go to the movies.

AMANDA: Why do you go to the movies so much, Tom?

TOM: I go to the movies because—I like adventure. Adventure is something I don't have much of at work, so I go to the movies.

AMANDA: But, Tom, you go to the movies *entirely* too *much!*

TOM: I like a lot of adventure.

AMANDA *looks baffled, then hurt. As the familiar inquisition resumes he becomes hard and impatient again.* AMANDA *slips back into her querulous attitude toward him.*

Image on screen: Sailing Vessel with Jolly Roger

AMANDA: Most young men find adventure in their careers.

TOM: Then most young men are not employed in a warehouse.

AMANDA: The world is full of young men employed in warehouses and offices and factories.

TOM: Do all of them find adventure in their careers?

AMANDA: They do or they do without it! Not everybody has a craze for adventure.

TOM: Man is by instinct a lover, a hunter, a fighter, and none of those instincts are given much play at the warehouse!

AMANDA: Man is by instinct! Don't quote instinct to me! Instinct is something that people have got away from! It belongs to animals! Christian adults don't want it!

TOM: What do Christian adults want, then, Mother?

AMANDA: Superior things! Things of the mind and the spirit! Only animals have to satisfy instincts! Surely your aims are somewhat higher than theirs! Than monkeys—pigs—

TOM: I reckon they're not.

AMANDA: You're joking! However, that isn't what I wanted to discuss.

TOM (*rising*): I haven't much time.

AMANDA (*pushing his shoulders*): Sit down.

TOM: You want me to punch in red at the warehouse, Mother?

AMANDA: You have five minutes. I want to talk about Laura.

Legend: "Plans and Provisions"

TOM: All right! What about Laura?

AMANDA: We have to be making some plans and provisions for her. She's older than you, two years, and nothing has happened. She just drifts along doing nothing. It frightens me terribly how she just drifts along.

TOM: I guess she's the type that people call home girls.

AMANDA: There's no such type, and if there is, it's a pity! That is, unless the home is hers, with a husband!

TOM: What?

AMANDA: Oh, I can see the handwriting on the wall as plain as I see the nose in front of my face! It's terrifying!

More and more you remind me of your father! He was out all hours without explanation!—Then *left! Good-bye!*

And me with the bag to hold. I saw that letter you got from the Merchant Marine. I know what you're dreaming of. I'm not standing here blindfolded.

Very well, then. Then *do* it!

But not till there's somebody to take your place.

TOM: What do you mean?

AMANDA: I mean that as soon as Laura has got somebody to take care of her, married, a home of her own, independent—why, then you'll be free to go wherever you please, on land, on sea, whichever way the wind blows you!

But until that time you've got to look out for your sister. I don't say me because I'm old and don't matter! I say for your sister because she's young and dependent.

I put her in business college—a dismal failure! Frightened her so it made her sick at the stomach.

I took her over to the Young People's League at the church. Another fiasco. She spoke to nobody, nobody spoke to her. Now all she does is fool with those pieces of glass and play those worn-out records. What kind of a life is that for a girl to lead?

TOM: What can I do about it?

AMANDA: Overcome selfishness!

Self, self, self is all that you ever think of!

TOM *springs up and crosses to get his coat. It is ugly and bulky.*
He pulls on a cap with earmuffs.

Where is your muffler? Put your wool muffler on!

He snatches it angrily from the closet and tosses it around his
neck and pulls both ends tight.

Tom! I haven't said what I had in mind to ask you.

TOM: I'm too late to—

AMANDA (*catching his arm—very importunately. Then shyly*): Down at
the warehouse, aren't there some—nice young men?

TOM: No!

AMANDA: There *must* be—*some* . . .

TOM: Mother—(*Gesture*)

AMANDA: Find out one that's clean-living—doesn't drink and—ask him out
for sister!

TOM: What?

AMANDA: For *sister*! To *meet*! Get *acquainted*!

TOM (*stamping to door*): Oh, my go-osh!

AMANDA: Will you? (*He opens door. Imploringly*) Will you? (*He starts
down.*) Will you? *Will* you, dear?

TOM (*calling back*): Yes!

AMANDA *closes the door hesitantly and with a troubled but faintly*
hopeful expression.

Screen image: Glamor Magazine Cover

Spot AMANDA *at phone.*

AMANDA: Ella Cartwright? This is Amanda Wingfield!

How are you, honey?

How is that kidney condition? (*Pause*)

Horrors! (*Pause*)

You're a Christian martyr, yes, honey, that's what you are, a
Christian martyr!

Well, I just now happened to notice in my little red book that
your subscription to the *Companion* has just run out! I knew that you
wouldn't want to miss out on the wonderful serial starting in this new
issue. It's by Bessie Mae Hopper, the first thing she's written since
Honeymoon for Three.

Wasn't that a strange and interesting story? Well, this one is
even lovelier, I believe. It has a sophisticated, society background. It's
all about the horsey set on Long Island!

Fade Out.

§ SCENE V

Legend on screen: "Annunciation" Fade with music.

It is early dusk of a spring evening. Supper has just been finished in the Wingfield apartment. AMANDA and LAURA in light-colored dresses are removing dishes from the table, in the upstage area, which is shadowy, their movements formalized almost as a dance or ritual, their moving forms as pale and silent as moths.

TOM, in white shirt and trousers, rises from the table and crosses toward the fire-escape.

AMANDA (as he passes her): Son, will you do me a favor?

TOM: What?

AMANDA: Comb your hair! You look so pretty when your hair is combed! (TOM slouches on sofa with evening paper. Enormous caption "Franco Triumphs") There is only one respect in which I would like you to emulate your father.

TOM: What respect is that?

AMANDA: The care he always took of his appearance. He never allowed himself to look untidy. (He throws down the paper and crosses to fire-escape.) Where are you going?

TOM: I'm going out to smoke.

AMANDA: You smoke too much. A pack a day at fifteen cents a pack. How much would that amount to in a month? Thirty times fifteen is how much, Tom? Figure it out and you will be astounded at what you could save. Enough to give you a night-school course in accounting at Washington U! Just think what a wonderful thing that would be for you, Son!

TOM is unmoved by the thought.

TOM: I'd rather smoke. (He steps out on landing, letting the screen door slam.)

AMANDA (sharply): I know! That's the tragedy of it. . . . (Alone, she turns to look at her husband's picture.)

Dance music: "All the World Is Waiting for the Sunrise!"

TOM (to the audience): Across the alley from us was the Paradise Dance Hall. On evenings in spring the windows and doors were open and the music came outdoors. Sometimes the lights were turned out except for a large glass sphere that hung from the ceiling. It would turn slowly about and filter the dusk with delicate rainbow colors. Then the orchestra played a waltz or a tango, something that had a slow and sensuous rhythm. Couples would come outside, to the relative privacy of the alley. You could see them kissing behind ash-pits and telephone poles.

This was the compensation for lives that passed like mine, without any change or adventure.

Adventure and change were imminent in this year. They were waiting around the corner for all these kids.

Suspended in the mist over Berchtesgaden,[7] caught in the folds of Chamberlain's umbrella—[8]

In Spain there was Guernica!

But here there was only hot swing music and liquor, dance halls, bars, and movies, and sex that hung in the gloom like a chandelier and flooded the world with brief, deceptive rainbows. . . .

All the world was waiting for bombardments!

AMANDA *turns from the picture and comes outside.*

AMANDA (*sighing*): A fire-escape landing's a poor excuse for a porch. (*She spreads a newspaper on a step and sits down, gracefully and demurely as if she were settling into a swing on a Mississippi veranda.*) What are you looking at?

TOM: The moon.

AMANDA: Is there a moon this evening?

TOM: It's rising over Garfinkel's Delicatessen.

AMANDA: So it is! A little silver slipper of a moon. Have you made a wish on it yet?

TOM: Um-hum.

AMANDA: What did you wish for?

TOM: That's a secret.

AMANDA: A secret, huh? Well, I won't tell mine either. I will be just as mysterious as you.

TOM: I bet I can guess what yours is.

AMANDA: Is my head so transparent?

TOM: You're not a sphinx.

AMANDA: No, I don't have secrets. I'll tell you what I wished for on the moon. Success and happiness for my precious children! I wish for that whenever there's a moon, and when there isn't a moon, I wish for it, too.

TOM: I thought perhaps you wished for a gentleman caller.

AMANDA: Why do you say that?

TOM: Don't you remember asking me to fetch one?

AMANDA: I remember suggesting that it would be nice for your sister if you brought home some nice young man from the warehouse. I think that I've made that suggestion more than once.

TOM: Yes, you have made it repeatedly.

---

7 Adolf Hitler's retreat in the Bavarian Mountains.

8 Neville Chamberlain, England's Prime Minister before World War II, made several efforts to appease Hitler—an appeasement that came to be symbolized by the umbrella he always carried with him.

AMANDA: Well?

TOM: We are going to have one.

AMANDA: *What?*

TOM: A gentleman caller!

The Annunciation Is Celebrated with Music.

AMANDA *rises.*

Image on screen: Caller with Bouquet

AMANDA: You mean you have asked some nice young man to come over?

TOM: Yep. I've asked him to dinner.

AMANDA: You really did?

TOM: I did!

AMANDA: You did, and did he—*accept?*

TOM: He did!

AMANDA: Well, well—well, well! That's—lovely!

TOM: I thought that you would be pleased.

AMANDA: It's definite then?

TOM: Very definite.

AMANDA: Soon?

TOM: Very soon.

AMANDA: For heaven's sake, stop putting on and tell me some things, will you?

TOM: What things do you want me to tell you?

AMANDA: *Naturally* I would like to know when he's *coming!*

TOM: He's coming tomorrow.

AMANDA: *Tomorrow?*

TOM: Yep. Tomorrow.

AMANDA: But, Tom!

TOM: Yes, Mother?

AMANDA: Tomorrow gives me no time!

TOM: Time for what?

AMANDA: Preparations! Why didn't you phone me at once, as soon as you asked him, the minute that he accepted? Then, don't you see, I could have been getting ready!

TOM: You don't have to make any fuss.

AMANDA: Oh, Tom, Tom, Tom, of course I have to make a fuss! I want things nice, not sloppy! Not thrown together. I'll certainly have to do some fast thinking, won't I?

TOM: I don't see why you have to think at all.

AMANDA: You just don't know. We can't have a gentleman caller in a pig-sty! All my wedding silver has to be polished, the monogrammed table linen ought to be laundered! The windows have to be washed and fresh curtains put up. And how about clothes? We have to *wear* something, don't we?

TOM: Mother, this boy is no one to make a fuss over!

AMANDA: Do you realize he's the first young man we've introduced to your sister?

It's terrible, dreadful, disgraceful that poor little sister has never received a single gentleman caller! Tom, come inside! (*She opens the screen door.*)

TOM: What for?

AMANDA: I want to ask you some things.

TOM: If you're going to make such a fuss, I'll call it off, I'll tell him not to come!

AMANDA: You certainly won't do anything of the kind. Nothing offends people worse than broken engagements. It simply means I'll have to work like a Turk! We won't be brilliant, but we will pass inspection. Come on inside. (TOM *follows, groaning.*) Sit down.

TOM: Any particular place you would like me to sit?

AMANDA: Thank heavens I've got that new sofa! I'm also making payments on a floor lamp I'll have sent out! And put the chintz covers on, they'll brighten things up! Of course I'd hoped to have these walls repapered. . . . What is the young man's name?

TOM: His name is O'Connor.

AMANDA: That, of course, means fish—tomorrow is Friday! I'll have that salmon loaf—with Durkee's dressing! What does he do? He works at the warehouse?

TOM: Of course! How else would I—

AMANDA: Tom, he—doesn't drink?

TOM: Why do you ask me that?

AMANDA: Your father *did*!

TOM: Don't get started on that!

AMANDA: He *does* drink, then?

TOM: Not that I know of!

AMANDA: Make sure, be certain! The last thing I want for my daughter's a boy who drinks!

TOM: Aren't you being a little bit premature? Mr. O'Connor has not yet appeared on the scene!

AMANDA: But will tomorrow. To meet your sister, and what do I know about his character? Nothing! Old maids are better off than wives of drunkards!

TOM: Oh, my God!

AMANDA: Be still!

TOM (*leaning forward to whisper*): Lots of fellows meet girls whom they don't marry!

AMANDA: Oh, talk sensibly, Tom—and don't be sarcastic! (*She has gotten a hairbrush.*)

TOM: What are you doing?

AMANDA: I'm brushing that cow-lick down!

What is this young man's position at the warehouse?

TOM (*submitting grimly to the brush and the interrogation*): This young man's position is that of a shipping clerk, Mother.

AMANDA: Sounds to me like a fairly responsible job, the sort of job *you* would be in if you just had more *get-up*.

What is his salary? Have you any idea?

TOM: I would judge it to be approximately eighty-five dollars a month.

AMANDA: Well—not princely, but—

TOM: Twenty more than I make.

AMANDA: Yes, how well I know! But for a family man, eighty-five dollars a month is not much more than you can just get by on. . . .

TOM: Yes, but Mr. O'Connor is not a family man.

AMANDA: He might be, mightn't he? Some time in the future?

TOM: I see. Plans and provisions.

AMANDA: You are the only young man that I know of who ignores the fact that the future becomes the present, the present the past, and the past turns into everlasting regret if you don't plan for it!

TOM: I will think that over and see what I can make of it.

AMANDA: Don't be supercilious with your mother! Tell me some more about this—what do you call him?

TOM: James D. O'Connor. The D. is for Delaney.

AMANDA: Irish on *both* sides! *Gracious!* And doesn't drink?

TOM: Shall I call him up and ask him right this minute?

AMANDA: The only way to find out about those things is to make discreet inquiries at the proper moment. When I was a girl in Blue Mountain and it was suspected that a young man drank, the girl whose attentions he had been receiving, if any girl *was*, would sometimes speak to the minister of his church, or rather her father would if her father was living, and sort of feel him out on the young man's character. That is the way such things are discreetly handled to keep a young woman from making a tragic mistake!

TOM: Then how did you happen to make a tragic mistake?

AMANDA: That innocent look of your father's had everyone fooled!

He *smiled*—the world was *enchanted*!

No girl can do worse than put herself at the mercy of a handsome appearance!

I hope that Mr. O'Connor is not too good-looking.

TOM: No, he's not too good-looking. He's covered with freckles and hasn't too much of a nose.

AMANDA: He's not right-down homely, though?

TOM: Not right-down homely. Just medium homely, I'd say.

AMANDA: Character's what to look for in a man.

TOM: That's what I've always said, Mother.

AMANDA: You've never said anything of the kind and I suspect you would never give it a thought.

TOM: Don't be so suspicious of me.

AMANDA: At least I hope he's the type that's up and coming.

TOM: I think he really goes in for self-improvement.

AMANDA: What reason have you to think so?

TOM: He goes to night school.

AMANDA (*beaming*): Splendid! What does he do, I mean study?

TOM: Radio engineering and public speaking!

AMANDA: Then he has visions of being advanced in the world!

Any young man who studies public speaking is aiming to have an executive job some day!

And radio engineering? A thing for the future!

Both of these facts are very illuminating. Those are the sort of things that a mother should know concerning any young man who comes to call on her daughter. Seriously or—not.

TOM: One little warning. He doesn't know about Laura. I didn't let on that we had dark ulterior motives. I just said, why don't you come and have dinner with us? He said okay and that was the whole conversation.

AMANDA: I bet it was! You're eloquent as an oyster.

However, he'll know about Laura when he gets here. When he sees how lovely and sweet and pretty she is, he'll thank his lucky stars he was asked to dinner.

TOM: Mother, you mustn't expect too much of Laura.

AMANDA: What do you mean?

TOM: Laura seems all those things to you and me because she's ours and we love her. We don't even notice she's crippled any more.

AMANDA: Don't say crippled! You know that I never allow that word to be used!

TOM: But face facts, Mother. She is and—that's not all—

AMANDA: What do you mean "not all"?

TOM: Laura is very different from other girls.

AMANDA: I think the difference is all to her advantage.

TOM: Not quite all—in the eyes of others—strangers—she's terribly shy and lives in a world of her own and those things make her seem a little peculiar to people outside the house.

AMANDA: Don't say peculiar.

TOM: Face the facts. She is.

The dance-hall music changes to a tango that has a minor and somewhat ominous tone.

AMANDA: In what way is she peculiar—may I ask?

TOM (*gently*): She lives in a world of her own—a world of—little glass ornaments, Mother. . . . (*Gets up.* AMANDA *remains holding brush, looking at him, troubled.*) She plays old phonograph records and—

that's about all— (*He glances at himself in the mirror and crosses to door.*)

AMANDA (*sharply*): Where are you going?

TOM: I'm going to the movies. (*Out screen door*)

AMANDA: Not to the movies, every night to the movies! (*Follows quickly to screen door.*) I don't believe you always go to the movies! (*He is gone.* AMANDA *looks worriedly after him for a moment. Then vitality and optimism return and she turns from the door. Crossing to portieres*) Laura! Laura! (LAURA *answers from kitchenette.*)

LAURA: Yes, Mother.

AMANDA: Let those dishes go and come in front! (LAURA *appears with dish towel. Gaily*) Laura, come here and make a wish on the moon!

Screen image: Moon

LAURA (*entering*): Moon—moon?

AMANDA: A little silver slipper of a moon.
Look over your left shoulder, Laura, and make a wish!

LAURA *looks faintly puzzled as if called out of sleep.* AMANDA *seizes her shoulders and turns her at an angle by the door.*

Now!
Now, darling, *wish!*

LAURA: What shall I wish for, Mother?

AMANDA (*her voice trembling and her eyes suddenly filling with tears*): Happiness! Good fortune!

The violin rises and the stage dims out.

The Curtain Falls.

§ SCENE VI

Image: High-school Hero

TOM: And so the following evening I brought Jim home to dinner. I had known Jim slightly in high school. In high school Jim was a hero. He had tremendous Irish good nature and vitality with the scrubbed and polished look of white chinaware. He seemed to move in a continual spotlight. He was a star in basketball, captain of the debating club, president of the senior class and the glee club, and he sang the male lead in the annual light operas. He was always running or bounding, never just walking. He seemed always at the point of defeating the law of gravity. He was shooting with such velocity through his adolescence that you would logically expect him to arrive at nothing short of the White House by the time he was thirty. But Jim apparently ran into more interference after his graduation from Soldan. His speed had definitely slowed. Six years after he left high school he was holding a job that wasn't much better than mine.

Image: Clerk

He was the only one at the warehouse with whom I was on friendly terms. I was valuable to him as someone who could remember his former glory, who had seen him win basketball games and the silver cup in debating. He knew of my secret practice of retiring to a cabinet of the wash-room to work on poems when business was slack in the warehouse. He called me Shakespeare. And while the other boys in the warehouse regarded me with suspicious hostility, Jim took a humorous attitude toward me. Gradually his attitude affected the others, their hostility wore off and they also began to smile at me as people smile at an oddly fashioned dog who trots across their path at some distance.

I knew that Jim and Laura had known each other at Soldan, and I had heard Laura speak admiringly of his voice. I didn't know if Jim remembered her or not. In high school Laura had been as unobtrusive as Jim had been astonishing. If he did remember Laura, it was not as my sister, for when I asked him to dinner, he grinned and said, "You know, Shakespeare, I never thought of you as having folks!"

He was about to discover that I did. . . .

Light up stage.

Legend on screen: "The Accent of a Coming Foot"

Friday evening. It is about five o'clock of a late spring evening which comes "scattering poems in the sky."

A delicate lemony light is in the Wingfield apartment.

Amanda has worked like a Turk in preparation for the gentleman caller. The results are astonishing. The new floor lamp with its rose-silk shade is in place, a colored paper lantern conceals the broken light fixture in the ceiling, new billowing white curtains are at the windows, chintz covers are on chairs and sofa, a pair of new sofa pillows make their initial appearance.

Open boxes and tissue paper are scattered on the floor.

LAURA *stands in the middle with lifted arms while* AMANDA *crouches before her, adjusting the hem of the new dress, devout and ritualistic. The dress is colored and designed by memory. The arrangement of* LAURA's *hair is changed; it is softer and more becoming. A fragile, unearthly prettiness has come out in* LAURA: *she is like a piece of translucent glass touched by light, given a momentary radiance, not actual, not lasting.*

AMANDA (*impatiently*): Why are you trembling?

LAURA: Mother, you've made me so nervous!

AMANDA: How have I made you nervous?

LAURA: By all this fuss! You make it seem so important!

AMANDA: I don't understand you, Laura. You couldn't be satisfied with just sitting home, and yet whenever I try to arrange something for you, you seem to resist it.

She gets up.

Now take a look at yourself.

No, wait! Wait just a moment—I have an idea!

LAURA: What is it now?

AMANDA *produces two powder puffs which she wraps in handker-chiefs and stuffs in* LAURA's *bosom*

LAURA: Mother, what are you doing?

AMANDA: They call them "Gay Deceivers"!

LAURA: I won't wear them!

AMANDA: You will!

LAURA: Why should I?

AMANDA: Because, to be painfully honest, your chest is flat.

LAURA: You make it seem like we were setting a trap.

AMANDA: All pretty girls are a trap, a pretty trap, and men expect them to be.

Legend: "A Pretty Trap"

Now look at yourself, young lady. This is the prettiest you will ever be.

I've got to fix myself now! You're going to be surprised by your mother's appearance. (*She crosses through portieres, humming gaily.*)

LAURA *moves slowly to the long mirror and stares solemnly at herself.*

A wind blows the white curtains inward in a slow, graceful motion and with a faint, sorrowful sighing.

AMANDA (*off stage*): It isn't dark enough yet. (*She turns slowly before the mirror with a troubled look.*)

Legend on screen: "This Is My Sister: Celebrate Her with Strings!" Music

AMANDA (*laughing, off*): I'm going to show you something. I'm going to make a spectacular appearance!

LAURA: What is it, Mother?

AMANDA: Possess your soul in patience—you will see! Something I've resurrected from that old trunk! Styles haven't changed so terribly much after all. . . .

She parts the portieres.

Now just look at your mother!

She wears a girlish frock of yellowed voile with a blue silk sash. She carries a bunch of jonquils—the legend of her youth is nearly revived. Feverishly

This is the dress in which I led the cotillion. Won the cakewalk twice at Sunset Hill, wore one spring to the Governor's ball in Jackson! See how I sashayed around the ballroom, Laura?

She raises her skirt and does a mincing step around the room.

I wore it on Sundays for my gentlemen callers! I had it on the day I met your father—

I had malaria fever all that spring. The change of climate from East Tennessee to the Delta—weakened resistance—I had a little temperature all the time—not enough to be serious—just enough to make me restless and giddy!—Invitations poured in—parties all over the Delta!—"Stay in bed," said Mother, "you have fever!"—but I just wouldn't—I took quinine but kept on going, going!—Evenings, dances! —Afternoons, long, long rides! Picnics—lovely!—So lovely, that country in May—All lacy with dogwood, literally flooded with jonquils!— That was the spring I had the craze for jonquils. Jonquils became an absolute obsession. Mother said, "Honey, there's no more room for jonquils." And still I kept on bringing in more jonquils. Whenever, wherever I saw them, I'd say, "Stop! Stop! I see jonquils!" I made the young men help me gather the jonquils! It was a joke, Amanda and her jonquils! Finally there were no more vases to hold them, every available space was filled with jonquils. No vases to hold them? All right, I'll hold them myself! And then I—(*She stops in front of the picture. Music*) met your father!

Malaria fever and jonquils and then—this—boy. . . .

She switches on the rose-colored lamp.

I hope they get here before it starts to rain.

She crosses upstage and places the jonquils in bowl on table.

I gave your brother a little extra change so he and Mr. O'Connor could take the service car home.

LAURA (*with altered look*): What did you say his name was?
AMANDA: O'Connor.
LAURA: What is his first name?
AMANDA: I don't remember. Oh, yes, I do. It was—Jim!

LAURA sways slightly and catches hold of a chair.

Legend on screen: "Not Jim!"

LAURA (*faintly*): Not—Jim.

AMANDA: Yes, that was it, it was Jim! I've never known a Jim that wasn't nice!

Music: Ominous

LAURA: Are you sure his name is Jim O'Connor?

AMANDA: Yes. Why?

LAURA: Is he the one that Tom used to know in high school?

AMANDA: He didn't say so. I think he just got to know him at the warehouse.

LAURA: There was a Jim O'Connor we both knew in high school—(*Then, with effort*) If that is the one that Tom is bringing to dinner—you'll have to excuse me, I won't come to the table.

AMANDA: What sort of nonsense is this?

LAURA: You asked me once if I'd ever liked a boy. Don't you remember I showed you this boy's picture?

AMANDA: You mean the boy you showed me in the year book?

LAURA: Yes, that boy.

AMANDA: Laura, Laura, were you in love with that boy?

LAURA: I don't know, Mother. All I know is I couldn't sit at the table if it was him!

AMANDA: It won't be him! It isn't the least bit likely. But whether it is or not, you will come to the table. You will not be excused.

LAURA: I'll have to be, Mother.

AMANDA: I don't intend to humor your silliness, Laura. I've had too much from you and your brother, both!

So just sit down and compose yourself till they come. Tom has forgotten his key so you'll have to let them in, when they arrive.

LAURA (*panicky*): Oh, Mother—*you* answer the door!

AMANDA (*lightly*): I'll be in the kitchen—busy!

LAURA: Oh, Mother, please answer the door, don't make me do it!

AMANDA (*crossing into kitchenette*): I've got to fix the dressing for the salmon. Fuss, fuss—silliness!—over a gentleman caller!

Door swings shut. LAURA is left alone.

Legend: "Terror!"

She utters a low moan and turns off the lamp—sits stiffly on the edge of the sofa, knotting her fingers together.

Legend on screen: "The Opening of a Door!"

TOM *and* JIM *appear on the fire-escape steps and climb to landing.
Hearing their approach,* LAURA *rises with a panicky gesture. She
retreats to the portieres.*

The doorbell. LAURA *catches her breath and touches her throat.
Low drums*

AMANDA (*calling*): Laura, sweetheart! The door!

LAURA *stares at it without moving.*

JIM: I think we just beat the rain.

TOM: Uh-huh. (*He rings again, nervously.* JIM *whistles and fishes for a
cigarette.*)

AMANDA (*very, very gaily*): Laura, that is your brother and Mr. O'Connor!
Will you let them in, darling?

LAURA *crosses toward kitchenette door.*

LAURA (*breathlessly*): Mother—you go to the door!

AMANDA *steps out of kitchenette and stares furiously at* LAURA.
She points imperiously at the door.

LAURA: Please, please!

AMANDA (*in a fierce whisper*): What is the matter with you, you silly
thing?

LAURA (*desperately*): Please, you answer it, *please!*

AMANDA: I told you I wasn't going to humor you, Laura. Why have you
chosen this moment to lose your mind?

LAURA: Please, please, please, you go!

AMANDA: You'll have to go to the door because I can't!

LAURA (*despairingly*): I can't either!

AMANDA: *Why?*

LAURA: I'm *sick!*

AMANDA: I'm sick, too—of your nonsense! Why can't you and your brother
be normal people? Fantastic whims and behavior!

TOM *gives a long ring.*

Preposterous goings on! Can you give me one reason—(*Calls out
lyrically.*) COMING! JUST ONE SECOND!—why you should be afraid to
open a door? Now you answer it, Laura!

LAURA: Oh, oh, oh . . . (*She returns through the portieres. Darts to the
victrola and winds it frantically and turns it on.*)

AMANDA: Laura Wingfield, you march right to that door!

LAURA: Yes—yes, Mother!

*A faraway, scratchy rendition of "Dardanella" softens the air and
gives her strength to move through it. She slips to the door and
draws it cautiously open.*

Tom enters with the caller, JIM O'CONNOR.

TOM: Laura, this is Jim. Jim, this is my sister, Laura.

JIM (*stepping inside*): I didn't know that Shakespeare had a sister!

LAURA (*retreating stiff and trembling from the door*): How—how do you do?

JIM (*heartily extending his hand*): Okay!

LAURA *touches it hesitantly with hers.*

JIM: Your hand's *cold,* Laura!

LAURA: Yes, well—I've been playing the victrola. . . .

JIM: Must have been playing classical music on it! You ought to play a little hot swing music to warm you up!

LAURA: Excuse me—I haven't finished playing the victrola. . . .

She turns awkwardly and hurries into the front room. She pauses a second by the victrola. Then catches her breath and darts through the portieres like a frightened deer.

JIM (*grinning*): What was the matter?

TOM: Oh—with Laura? Laura is—terribly shy.

JIM: Shy, huh? It's unusual to meet a shy girl nowadays. I don't believe you ever mentioned you had a sister.

TOM: Well, now you know. I have one. Here is the *Post Dispatch.* You want a piece of it?

JIM: Uh-huh.

TOM: What piece? The comics?

JIM: Sports! (*Glances at it.*) Ole Dizzy Dean[9] is on his bad behavior.

TOM (*disinterest*): Yeah? (*Lights cigarette and crosses back to fire-escape door.*)

JIM: Where are *you* going?

TOM: I'm going out on the terrace.

JIM (*goes after him*): You know, Shakespeare—I'm going to sell you a bill of goods!

TOM: What goods?

JIM: A course I'm taking.

TOM: Huh?

JIM: In public speaking! You and me, we're not the warehouse type.

TOM: Thanks—that's good news.

But what has public speaking got to do with it?

JIM: It fits you for—executive positions!

TOM: Awww.

JIM. I tell you it's done a helluva lot for me.

Image: Executive at Desk

[9] Baseball pitcher for the St. Louis Cardinals.

TOM: In what respect?

JIM: In every! Ask yourself what is the difference between you an' me and men in the office down front? Brains?—No!—Ability?—No! Then what? Just one little thing—

TOM: What is that one little thing?

JIM: Primarily it amounts to—social poise! Being able to square up to people and hold your own on any social level!

AMANDA (*off stage*): Tom?

TOM: Yes, Mother?

AMANDA: Is that you and Mr. O'Connor?

TOM: Yes, Mother.

AMANDA: Well, you just make yourselves comfortable in there.

TOM: Yes, Mother.

AMANDA: Ask Mr. O'Connor if he would like to wash his hands.

JIM: Aw, no—no—thank you—I took care of that at the warehouse. Tom—

TOM: Yes?

JIM: Mr. Mendoza was speaking to me about you.

TOM: Favorably?

JIM: What do you think?

TOM: Well—

JIM: You're going to be out of a job if you don't wake up.

TOM: I am waking up—

JIM: You show no signs.

TOM: The signs are interior.

Image on screen: The Sailing Vessel with Jolly Roger Again

TOM: I'm planning to change. (*He leans over the rail speaking with quiet exhilaration. The incandescent marquees and signs of the first-run movie houses light his face from across the alley. He looks like a voyager.*) I'm right at the point of committing myself to a future that doesn't include the warehouse and Mr. Mendoza or even a night-school course in public speaking.

JIM: What are you gassing about?

TOM: I'm tired of the movies.

JIM: Movies!

TOM: Yes, movies! Look at them— (*A wave toward the marvels of Grand Avenue.*) All of those glamorous people—having adventures—hogging it all, gobbling the whole thing up! You know what happens? People go to the *movies* instead of *moving*! Hollywood characters are supposed to have all the adventures for everybody in America, while everybody in America sits in a dark room and watches them have them! Yes, until there's a war. That's when adventure becomes available to the masses! *Everyone's* dish, not only Gable's! [10] Then the

[10] Clark Gable, popular movie star.

people in the dark room come out of the dark room to have some adventures themselves—Goody, goody!—It's our turn now, to go to the South Sea Island—to make a safari—to be exotic, far-off!—But I'm not patient. I don't want to wait till then. I'm tired of the *movies* and I am *about* to *move!*

JIM (*incredulously*): Move?

TOM: Yes.

JIM: When?

TOM: Soon!

JIM: Where? Where?

Theme three music seems to answer the question, while TOM *thinks it over. He searches among his pockets.*

TOM: I'm starting to boil inside. I know I seem dreamy, but inside—well, I'm boiling!—Whenever I pick up a shoe, I shudder a little thinking how short life is and what I am doing!—Whatever that means, I know it doesn't mean shoes—except as something to wear on a traveler's feet! (*Finds paper.*) Look—

JIM: What?

TOM: I'm a member.

JIM (*reading*): The Union of Merchant Seamen.

TOM: I paid my dues this month, instead of the light bill.

JIM: You will regret it when they turn the lights off.

TOM: I won't be here.

JIM: How about your mother?

TOM: I'm like my father. The bastard son of a bastard! See how he grins? And he's been absent going on sixteen years!

JIM: You're just talking, you drip. How does your mother feel about it?

TOM: Shhh!—Here comes Mother! Mother is not acquainted with my plans!

AMANDA (*enters portieres*): Where are you all?

TOM: On the terrace, Mother.

They start inside. She advances to them. TOM *is distinctly shocked at her appearance. Even* JIM *blinks a little. He is making his first contact with girlish Southern vivacity and in spite of the night-school course in public speaking is somewhat thrown off the beam by the unexpected outlay of social charm.*

Certain responses are attempted by JIM *but are swept aside by* AMANDA's *gay laughter and chatter.* TOM *is embarrassed but after the first shock* JIM *reacts very warmly, grins and chuckles, is alto-gether won over.*

Image: Amanda as a Girl

AMANDA (*coyly smiling, shaking her girlish ringlets*): Well, well, well, so this is Mr. O'Connor. Introductions entirely unnecessary. I've heard so much about you from my boy. I finally said to him, Tom—good gracious!—why don't you bring this paragon to supper? I'd like to meet this nice young man at the warehouse!—Instead of just hearing him sing your praises so much!

I don't know why my son is so stand-offish—that's not Southern behavior!

Let's sit down and—I think we could stand a little more air in here! Tom, leave the door open. I felt a nice fresh breeze a moment ago. Where has it gone to?

Mmm, so warm already! And not quite summer, even. We're going to burn up when summer really gets started.

However, we're having—we're having a very light supper. I think light things are better fo' this time of year. The same as light clothes are. Light clothes an' light food are what warm weather calls fo'. You know our blood gets so thick during th' winter—it takes a while fo' us to *adjust* ou'selves—when the season changes . . .

It's come so quick this year. I wasn't prepared. All of a sudden—heavens! Already summer!—I ran to the trunk an' pulled out this light dress— Terribly old! Historical almost! But feels so good—so good an' co-ol, y' know. . . .

TOM: Mother—

AMANDA: Yes, honey?

TOM: How about—supper?

AMANDA: Honey, you go ask Sister if supper is ready! You know that Sister is in full charge of supper!

Tell her you hungry boys are waiting for it.

To Jim

Have you met Laura?

JIM: She—

AMANDA: Let you in? Oh, good, you've met already! It's rare for a girl as sweet an' pretty as Laura to be domestic! But Laura is, thank heavens, not only pretty but also very domestic. I'm not at all. I never was a bit. I never could make a thing but angel-food cake. Well, in the South we had so many servants. Gone, gone, gone. All vestige of gracious living! Gone completely! I wasn't prepared for what the future brought me. All of my gentlemen callers were sons of planters and so of course I assumed that I would be married to one and raise my family on a large piece of land with plenty of servants. But man proposes—and woman accepts the proposal!—To vary that old, old saying a little bit—I married no planter! I married a man who worked for the telephone company!—That gallantly smiling gentleman over there! (*Points to the picture.*) A telephone man who—fell in love with long-

distance!—Now he travels and I don't even know where!—But what
am I going on for about my—tribulations?

Tell me yours—I hope you don't have any!

Tom?

TOM (*returning*): Yes, Mother?

AMANDA: Is supper nearly ready?

TOM: It looks to me like supper is on the table.

AMANDA: Let me look— (*She rises prettily and looks through portieres.*)
Oh, lovely!—But where is Sister?

TOM: Laura is not feeling well and she says that she thinks she'd better
not come to the table.

AMANDA: What?—Nonsense!—Laura? Oh, Laura!

LAURA (*off stage, faintly*): Yes, Mother.

AMANDA: You really must come to the table. We won't be seated until
you come to the table!

Come in, Mr. O'Connor. You sit over there, and I'll—

Laura? Laura Wingfield!

You're keeping us waiting, honey! We can't say grace until you
come to the table!

The back door is pushed weakly open and LAURA *comes in. She is
obviously quite faint, her lips trembling, her eyes wide and staring.
She moves unsteadily toward the table.*

Legend: "Terror!"

*Outside a summer storm is coming abruptly. The white curtains
billow inward at the windows and there is a sorrowful murmur
and deep blue dusk.*

LAURA *suddenly stumbles—she catches at a chair with a faint
moan.*

TOM: Laura!

AMANDA: Laura!

There is a clap of thunder.

Legend: "Ah!"

Despairingly

Why, Laura, you *are* sick, darling! Tom, help your sister into the
living room, dear!

Sit in the living room, Laura—rest on the sofa.

Well!

To the gentleman caller

Standing over the hot stove made her ill!—I told her that it was
just too warm this evening, but—

TOM comes back in. LAURA is on the sofa.

Is Laura all right now?

TOM: Yes.

AMANDA: What *is* that? Rain? A nice cool rain has come up!

She gives the gentleman caller a frightened look.

I think we may—have grace—now. . . .

TOM looks at her stupidly.

Tom, honey—you say grace!

TOM: Oh . . .

"For these and all thy mercies—"

*They bow their heads, AMANDA stealing a nervous glance at JIM.
In the living room LAURA, stretched on the sofa, clenches her hand
to her lips, to hold back a shuddering sob.*

God's Holy Name be praised—

The Scene Dims Out.

§ SCENE VII

A Souvenir

*Half an hour later. Dinner is just being finished in the upstage area which
is concealed by the drawn portieres.*

*As the curtain rises LAURA is still huddled upon the sofa, her feet drawn
under her, her head resting on a pale blue pillow, her eyes wide and mysteriously watchful. The new floor lamp with its shade of rose-colored silk
gives a soft, becoming light to her face, bringing out the fragile, unearthly
prettiness which usually escapes attention. There is a steady murmur of
rain, but it is slackening and stops soon after the scene begins; the air outside becomes pale and luminous as the moon breaks out.*

*A moment after the curtain rises, the lights in both rooms flicker and go
out.*

JIM: Hey, there, Mr. Light Bulb!

AMANDA laughs nervously.

Legend: "Suspension of a Public Service"

AMANDA: Where was Moses when the lights went out? Ha-ha. Do you
know the answer to that one, Mr. O'Connor?

JIM: No, Ma'am, what's the answer?
AMANDA: In the dark!

JIM *laughs appreciatively.*

Everybody sit still. I'll light the candles. Isn't it lucky we have them on the table? Where's a match? Which of you gentlemen can provide a match?
JIM: Here.
AMANDA: Thank you, sir.
JIM: Not at all, Ma'am!
AMANDA: I guess the fuse has burnt out. Mr. O'Connor, can you tell a burnt-out fuse? I know I can't and Tom is a total loss when it comes to mechanics.

Sound: Getting up. Voices recede a little to kitchenette.

Oh, be careful you don't bump into something. We don't want our gentleman caller to break his neck. Now wouldn't that be a fine howdy-do?
JIM: Ha-ha!
Where is the fuse-box?
AMANDA: Right here next to the stove. Can you see anything?
JIM: Just a minute.
AMANDA: Isn't electricity a mysterious thing?
Wasn't it Benjamin Franklin who tied a key to a kite?
We live in such a mysterious universe, don't we? Some people say that science clears up all the mysteries for us. In my opinion it only creates more!
Have you found it yet?
JIM: No, Ma'am. All these fuses look okay to me.
AMANDA: Tom!
TOM: Yes, Mother?
AMANDA: That light bill I gave you several days ago. The one I told you we got the notices about?

Legend: "Ha!"

TOM: Oh—Yeah.
AMANDA: You didn't neglect to pay it by any chance?
TOM: Why, I—
AMANDA: Didn't! I might have known it!
JIM: Shakespeare probably wrote a poem on that light bill, Mrs. Wingfield.
AMANDA: I might have known better than to trust him with it! There's such a high price for negligence in this world!
JIM: Maybe the poem will win a ten-dollar prize.

AMANDA: We'll just have to spend the remainder of the evening in the nineteenth century, before Mr. Edison made the Mazda lamp!

JIM: Candlelight is my favorite kind of light.

AMANDA: That shows you're romantic! But that's no excuse for Tom.

Well, we got through dinner. Very considerate of them to let us get through dinner before they plunged us into everlasting darkness, wasn't it, Mr. O'Connor?

JIM: Ha-ha!

AMANDA: Tom, as a penalty for your carelessness you can help me with the dishes.

JIM: Let me give you a hand.

AMANDA: Indeed you will not!

JIM: I ought to be good for something.

AMANDA: Good for something? (*Her tone is rhapsodic.*) *You?* Why, Mr. O'Connor, nobody, *nobody's* given me this much entertainment in years—as you have!

JIM: Aw, now, Mrs. Wingfield!

AMANDA: I'm not exaggerating, not one bit! But Sister is all by her lonesome. You go keep her company in the parlor!

I'll give you this lovely old candelabrum that used to be on the altar at the Church of the Heavenly Rest. It was melted a little out of shape when the church burnt down. Lightning struck it one spring. Gypsy Jones was holding a revival at the time and he intimated that the church was destroyed because the Episcopalians gave card parties.

JIM: Ha-ha!

AMANDA: And how about you coaxing Sister to drink a little wine? I think it would be good for her! Can you carry both at once?

JIM: Sure. I'm Superman!

AMANDA: Now, Thomas, get into this apron!

The door of kitchenette swings closed on AMANDA's *gay laughter;*
the flickering light approaches the portieres.

LAURA *sits up nervously as he enters. Her speech at first is low and*
breathless from the almost intolerable strain of being alone with
a stranger.

The legend: "I Don't Suppose You Remember Me at All!"

In her first speeches in this scene, before Jim's warmth overcomes
her paralyzing shyness, LAURA's *voice is thin and breathless as*
though she has just run up a steep flight of stairs.

JIM's *attitude is gently humorous. In playing this scene it should*
be stressed that while the incident is apparently unimportant, it
is to LAURA *the climax of her secret life.*

JIM: Hello, there, Laura.

LAURA (*faintly*): Hello. (*She clears her throat.*)

JIM: How are you feeling now? Better?

LAURA: Yes. Yes, thank you.

JIM: This is for you. A little dandelion wine. (*He extends it toward her with extravagant gallantry.*)

LAURA: Thank you.

JIM: Drink it—but don't get drunk!

He laughs heartily. LAURA *takes the glass uncertainly; laughs shyly.*

Where shall I set the candles?

LAURA: Oh—oh, anywhere . . .

JIM: How about here on the floor? Any objections?

LAURA: No.

JIM: I'll spread a newspaper under to catch the drippings. I like to sit on the floor. Mind if I do?

LAURA: Oh, no.

JIM: Give me a pillow?

LAURA: What?

JIM: A pillow!

LAURA: Oh . . . (*Hands him one quickly.*)

JIM: How about you? Don't you like to sit on the floor?

LAURA: Oh—yes.

JIM: Why don't you, then?

LAURA: I—will.

JIM: Take a pillow! (LAURA *does. Sits on the other side of the candelabrum.* JIM *crosses his legs and smiles engagingly at her.*) I can't hardly see you sitting way over there.

LAURA: I can—see you.

JIM: I know, but that's not fair, I'm in the limelight. (LAURA *moves her pillow closer.*) Good! Now I can see you! Comfortable?

LAURA: Yes.

JIM: So am I. Comfortable as a cow! Will you have some gum?

LAURA: No, thank you.

JIM: I think that I will indulge, with your permission. (*Musingly unwraps it and holds it up.*) Think of the fortune made by the guy that invented the first piece of chewing gum. Amazing, huh? The Wrigley Building is one of the sights of Chicago—I saw it summer before last when I went up to the Century of Progress.[11] Did you take in the Century of Progress?

LAURA: No, I didn't.

JIM: Well, it was quite a wonderful exposition. What impressed me most was the Hall of Science. Gives you an idea of what the future will be in America, even more wonderful than the present time is! (*Pause.*

[11] Chicago World's Fair, 1933–1934.

Smiling at her) Your brother tells me you're shy. Is that right, Laura?

LAURA: I—don't know.

JIM: I judge you to be an old-fashioned type of girl. Well, I think that's a pretty good type to be. Hope you don't think I'm being too personal —do you?

LAURA (*hastily, out of embarrassment*): I believe I *will* take a piece of gum, if you—don't mind. (*Clearing her throat*) Mr. O'Connor, have you—kept up with your singing?

JIM: Singing? Me?

LAURA: Yes. I remember what a beautiful voice you had.

JIM: When did you hear me sing?

Voice off stage in the pause

VOICE (*off stage*):

> O blow, ye winds, heigh-ho,
> A-roving I will go!
> I'm off to my love
> With a boxing glove—
> Ten thousand miles away!

JIM: You say you've heard me sing?

LAURA: Oh, yes! Yes, very often. . . . I—don't suppose—you remember me—at all?

JIM (*smiling doubtfully*): You know I have an idea I've see you before. I had that idea soon as you opened the door. It seemed almost like I was about to remember your name. But the name that I started to call you wasn't a name! And so I stopped myself before I said it.

LAURA: Wasn't it—Blue Roses?

JIM (*springs up. Grinning*): Blue Roses!—My gosh, yes—Blue Roses! That's what I had on my tongue when you opened the door!

Isn't it funny what tricks your memory plays? I didn't connect you with high school somehow or other.

But that's where it was; it was high school. I didn't even know you were Shakespeare's sister!

Gosh, I'm sorry.

LAURA: I didn't expect you to. You—barely knew me!

JIM: But we did have a speaking acquaintance, huh?

LAURA: Yes, we—spoke to each other.

JIM: When did you recognize me?

LAURA: Oh, right away!

JIM: Soon as I came in the door?

LAURA: When I heard your name I thought it was probably you. I knew that Tom used to know you a little in high school. So when you came in the door—Well, then I was—sure.

JIM: Why didn't you *say* something, then?

LAURA (*breathlessly*): I didn't know what to say, I was—too surprised!

JIM: For goodness' sakes! You know, this sure is funny!

LAURA: Yes! Yes, isn't it, though . . .

JIM: Didn't we have a class in something together?

LAURA: Yes, we did.

JIM: What class was that?

LAURA: It was—singing—Chorus!

JIM: Aw!

LAURA: I sat across the aisle from you in the Aud.

JIM: Aw.

LAURA: Mondays, Wednesdays, and Fridays.

JIM: Now I remember—you always came in late.

LAURA: Yes, it was so hard for me, getting upstairs. I had that brace on my leg—it clumped so loud!

JIM: I never heard any clumping.

LAURA (*wincing at the recollection*): To me it sounded like—thunder!

JIM: Well, well, well, I never even noticed.

LAURA: And everybody was seated before I came in. I had to walk in front of all those people. My seat was in the back row. I had to go clumping all the way up the aisle with everyone watching!

JIM: You shouldn't have been self-conscious.

LAURA: I know, but I was. It was always such a relief when the singing started.

JIM: Aw, yes, I've placed you now! I used to call you Blue Roses. How was it that I got started calling you that?

LAURA: I was out of school a little while with pleurosis. When I came back you asked me what was the matter. I said I had pleurosis—you thought I said Blue Roses. That's what you always called me after that!

JIM: I hope you didn't mind.

LAURA: Oh, no—I liked it. You see, I wasn't acquainted with many— people. . . .

JIM: As I remember you sort of stuck by yourself.

LAURA: I—I—never have had much luck at—making friends.

JIM: I don't see why you wouldn't.

LAURA: Well, I—started out badly.

JIM: You mean being—

LAURA: Yes, it sort of—stood between me—

JIM: You shouldn't have let it!

LAURA: I know, but it did, and—

JIM: You were shy with people!

LAURA: I tried not to be but never could—

JIM: Overcome it?

LAURA: No, I—I never could!

JIM: I guess being shy is something you have to work out of kind of gradually.

LAURA (*sorrowfully*): Yes—I guess it—

JIM: Takes time!

LAURA: Yes.

JIM: People are not so dreadful when you know them. That's what you have to remember! And everybody has problems, not just you, but practically everybody has got some problems.

> You think of yourself as having the only problems, as being the only one who is disappointed. But just look around you and you will see lots of people as disappointed as you are. For instance, I hoped when I was going to high school that I would be further along at this time, six years later, than I am now—You remember that wonderful write-up I had in *The Torch*?

LAURA: Yes! (*She rises and crosses to table.*)

JIM: It said I was bound to succeed in anything I went into! (LAURA *returns with the annual.*) Holy Jeez! *The Torch!* (*He accepts it reverently. They smile across it with mutual wonder.* LAURA *crouches beside him and they begin to turn through it.* LAURA's *shyness is dissolving in his warmth.*)

LAURA: Here you are in *The Pirates of Penzance!*

JIM (*wistfully*): I sang the baritone lead in that operetta.

LAURA (*raptly*): So—*beautifully!*

JIM (*protesting*): Aw—

LAURA: Yes, yes—beautifully—beautifully!

JIM: You heard me?

LAURA: All three times!

JIM: No!

LAURA: Yes!

JIM: All three performances?

LAURA (*looking down*): Yes.

JIM: Why?

LAURA: I—wanted to ask you to—autograph my program.

JIM: Why didn't you ask me to?

LAURA: You were always surrounded by your own friends so much that I never had a chance to.

JIM: You should have just—

LAURA: Well, I—thought you might think I was—

JIM: Thought I might think you was—what?

LAURA: Oh—

JIM (*with reflective relish*): I was beleaguered by females in those days.

LAURA: You were terribly popular!

JIM: Yeah—

LAURA: You had such a—friendly way—

JIM: I was spoiled in high school.

LAURA: Everybody—liked you!

JIM: Including you?

LAURA: I—yes, I—I did, too— (*She gently closes the book in her lap.*)

JIM: Well, well, well!—Give me that program, Laura. (*She hands it to him. He signs it with a flourish.*) There you are—better late than never!

LAURA: Oh, I—what a—surprise!

JIM: My signature isn't worth very much right now.

But some day—maybe—it will increase in value!

Being disappointed is one thing and being discouraged is something else. I am disappointed but I am not discouraged.

I'm twenty-three years old.

How old are you?

LAURA: I'll be twenty-four in June.

JIM: That's not old age!

LAURA: No, but—

JIM: You finished high school?

LAURA (*with difficulty*): I didn't go back.

JIM: You mean you dropped out?

LAURA: I made bad grades in my final examinations. (*She rises and replaces the book and the program. Her voice strained.*) How is—Emily Meisenbach getting along?

JIM: Oh, that kraut-head!

LAURA: Why do you call her that?

JIM: That's what she was.

LAURA: You're not still—going with her?

JIM: I never see her.

LAURA: It said in the Personal Section that you were—engaged!

JIM: I know, but I wasn't impressed by that—propaganda!

LAURA: It wasn't—the truth?

JIM: Only in Emily's optimistic opinion!

LAURA: Oh—

Legend: "What Have You Done Since High School?"

JIM *lights a cigarette and leans indolently back on his elbows, smiling at* LAURA *with a warmth and charm which lights her inwardly with altar candles. She remains by the table and turns in her hands a piece of glass to cover her tumult.*

JIM (*after several reflective puffs on a cigarette*): What have you done since high school? (*She seems not to hear him.*) Huh? (LAURA *looks up.*) I said what have you done since high school, Laura?

LAURA: Nothing much.

JIM: You must have been doing something these six long years.

LAURA: Yes.

JIM: Well, then, such as what?

LAURA: I took a business course at business college—

JIM: How did that work out?

LAURA: Well, not very—well—I had to drop out, it gave me—indigestion—

JIM *laughs gently.*

JIM: What are you doing now?

LAURA: I don't do anything—much. Oh, please don't think I sit around doing nothing! My glass collection takes up a good deal of time. Glass is something you have to take good care of.

JIM: What did you say—about glass?

LAURA: Collection I said—I have one—(*She clears her throat and turns away again, acutely shy.*)

JIM (*abruptly*): You know what I judge to be the trouble with you? Inferiority complex! Know what that is? That's what they call it when someone low-rates himself!

I understand it because I had it, too. Although my case was not so aggravated as yours seems to be. I had it until I took up public speaking, developed my voice, and learned that I had an aptitude for science. Before that time I never thought of myself as being outstanding in any way whatsoever!

Now I've never made a regular study of it, but I have a friend who says I can analyze people better than doctors that make a profession of it. I don't claim that to be necessarily true, but I can sure guess a person's psychology. Laura! (*Takes out his gum.*) Excuse me, Laura. I always take it out when the flavor is gone. I'll use this scrap of paper to wrap it in. I know how it is to get it stuck on a shoe.

Yep—that's what I judge to be your principal trouble. A lack of confidence in yourself as a person. You don't have the proper amount of faith in yourself. I'm basing that fact on a number of your remarks and also on certain observations I've made. For instance that clumping you thought was so awful in high school. You say that you even dreaded to walk into class. You see what you did? You dropped out of school, you gave up an education because of a clump, which as far as I know was practically nonexistent! A little physical defect is what you have. Hardly noticeable even! Magnified thousands of times by imagination!

You know what my strong advice to you is? Think of yourself as *superior* in some way!

LAURA: In what way would I think?

JIM: Why, man alive, Laura! Just look about you a little. What do you see? A world full of common people! All of 'em born and all of 'em going to die!

Which of them has one-tenth of your good points! Or mine! Or anyone else's, as far as that goes—Gosh!

Everybody excels in some one thing. Some in many!

Unconsciously glances at himself in the mirror.

All you've got to do is discover in *what!*

Take me, for instance.

He adjusts his tie at the mirror.

My interest happens to lie in electro-dynamics. I'm taking a course in radio engineering at night school, Laura, on top of a fairly responsible job at the warehouse. I'm taking that course and studying public speaking.

LAURA: Ohhhh.

JIM: Because I believe in the future of television.

Turning back to her

I wish to be ready to go up right along with it. Therefore I'm planning to get in on the ground floor. In fact I've already made the right connections and all that remains is for the industry itself to get under way! Full steam—

His eyes are starry.

Knowledge—Zzzzzp! Money—Zzzzzzp!—Power! That's the cycle democracy is built on!

His attitude is convincingly dynamic. LAURA *stares at him, even her shyness eclipsed in her absolute wonder. He suddenly grins.*

I guess you think I think a lot of myself!

LAURA: No—o-o-o, I—

JIM: Now how about you? Isn't there something you take more interest in than anything else?

LAURA: Well, I do—as I said—have my—glass collection—

A peal of girlish laughter from the kitchen

JIM: I'm not right sure I know what you're talking about. What kind of glass is it?

LAURA: Little articles of it, they're ornaments mostly!

Most of them are little animals made out of glass, the tiniest little animals in the world. Mother calls them a glass menagerie!

Here's an example of one, if you'd like to see it!

This one is one of the oldest. It's nearly thirteen.

Music: "The Glass Menagerie"
He stretches out his hand.

Oh, be careful—if you breathe, it breaks!

JIM: I'd better not take it. I'm pretty clumsy with things.

LAURA: Go on, I trust you with him!

Places it in his palm.

There now—you're holding him gently!

Hold him over the light, he loves the light! You see how the light shines through him?

JIM: It sure does shine!

LAURA: I shouldn't be partial, but he is my favorite one.

JIM: What kind of a thing is this one supposed to be?

LAURA: Haven't you noticed the single horn on his forehead?

JIM: A unicorn, huh?

LAURA: Mmm-hmmm!

JIM: Unicorns, aren't they extinct in the modern world?

LAURA: I know!

JIM: Poor little fellow, he must feel sort of lonesome.

LAURA (*smiling*): Well, if he does he doesn't complain about it. He stays on a shelf with some horses that don't have horns and all of them seem to get along nicely together.

JIM: How do you know?

LAURA (*lightly*): I haven't heard any arguments among them!

JIM (*grinning*): No arguments, huh? Well, that's a pretty good sign! Where shall I set him?

LAURA: Put him on the table. They all like a change of scenery once in a while!

JIM (*stretching*): Well, well, well, well—

Look how big my shadow is when I stretch!

LAURA: Oh, oh, yes—it stretches across the ceiling!

JIM (*crossing to door*): I think it's stopped raining. (*Opens fire-escape door.*) Where does the music come from?

LAURA: From the Paradise Dance Hall across the alley.

JIM: How about cutting the rug a little, Miss Wingfield?

LAURA: Oh, I—

JIM: Or is your program filled up? Let me have a look at it. (*Grasps imaginary card.*) Why, every dance is taken! I'll just have to scratch some out. (*Waltz music: "La Golondrina"*) Ahhh, a waltz! (*He executes some sweeping turns by himself then holds his arms toward* LAURA.)

LAURA (*breathlessly*): I—can't dance!

JIM: There you go, that inferiority stuff!

LAURA: I've never danced in my life!

JIM: Come on, try!

LAURA: Oh, but I'd step on you!

JIM: I'm not made out of glass.

LAURA: How—how—how do we start?

JIM: Just leave it to me. You hold your arms out a little.

LAURA: Like this?

JIM: A little bit higher. Right. Now don't tighten up, that's the main thing about it—relax.

LAURA (*laughing breathlessly*): It's hard not to.

JIM: Okay.

LAURA: I'm afraid you can't budge me.

JIM: What do you bet I can't. (*He swings her into motion.*)

LAURA: Goodness, yes, you can!

JIM: Let yourself go, now, Laura, just let yourself go.

LAURA: I'm—

JIM: Come on!

LAURA: Trying!

JIM: Not so stiff— Easy does it!

LAURA: I know but I'm—

JIM: Loosen th' backbone! There now, that's a lot better.

LAURA: Am I?

JIM: Lots, lots better! (*He moves her about the room in a clumsy waltz.*)

LAURA: Oh, my!

JIM: Ha-ha!

LAURA: Oh, my goodness!

JIM: Ha-ha-ha! (*They suddenly bump into the table.* JIM *stops.*) What did we hit on?

LAURA: Table.

JIM: Did something fall off it? I think—

LAURA: Yes.

JIM: I hope it wasn't the little glass horse with the horn!

LAURA: Yes.

JIM: Aw, aw, aw. Is it broken?

LAURA: Now it is just like all the other horses.

JIM: It's lost its—

LAURA: Horn!

It doesn't matter. Maybe it's a blessing in disguise.

JIM: You'll never forgive me. I bet that that was your favorite piece of glass.

LAURA: I don't have favorites much. It's no tragedy, Freckles. Glass breaks so easily. No matter how careful you are. The traffic jars the shelves and things fall off them.

JIM: Still I'm awfully sorry that I was the cause.

LAURA (*smiling*): I'll just imagine he had an operation. The horn was removed to make him feel less—freakish!

They both laugh.

Now he will feel more at home with the other horses, the ones that don't have horns. . . .

JIM: Ha-ha, that's very funny!

Suddenly serious

I'm glad to see that you have a sense of humor.
You know—you're—well—very different!
Surprisingly different from anyone else I know!

His voice becomes soft and hesitant with a genuine feeling.

Do you mind me telling you that?

LAURA *is abashed beyond speech.*

I mean it in a nice way. . . .

LAURA *nods shyly, looking away.*

You make me feel sort of—I don't know how to put it!
I'm usually pretty good at expressing things, but—
This is something that I don't know how to say!

LAURA *touches her throat and clears it—turns the broken unicorn
in her hands.*

Even softer

Has anyone ever told you that you were pretty?

Pause: Music

LAURA *looks up slowly, with wonder, and shakes her head.*

Well, you are! In a very different way from anyone else.
And all the nicer because of the difference, too.

His voice becomes low and husky. LAURA *turns away, nearly faint
with the novelty of her emotions.*

I wish that you were my sister. I'd teach you to have some confidence in yourself. The different people are not like other people, but
being different is nothing to be ashamed of. Because other people are
not such wonderful people. They're one hundred times one thousand.
You're one times one! They walk all over the earth. You just stay here.
They're common as—weeds, but—you—well, you're—*Blue Roses!*

Image on screen: Blue Roses

Music changes.

LAURA: But blue is wrong for—roses. . . .
JIM: It's right for you!—You're—pretty!
LAURA: In what respect am I pretty?
JIM: In all respects—believe me! Your eyes—your hair—are pretty! Your
hands are pretty!

He catches hold of her hand.

You think I'm making this up because I'm invited to dinner and have to be nice. Oh, I could do that! I could put on an act for you, Laura, and say lots of things without being very sincere. But this time I am. I'm talking to you sincerely. I happened to notice you had this inferiority complex that keeps you from feeling comfortable with people. Somebody needs to build your confidence up and make you proud instead of shy and turning away and—blushing—
Somebody—ought to—
Ought to—*kiss* you, Laura!

His hands slips slowly up her arm to her shoulder.

Music swells tumultuously.

He suddenly turns her about and kisses her on the lips.

When he releases her, LAURA *sinks on the sofa with a bright, dazed look.*

JIM *backs away and fishes in his pocket for a cigarette.*

Legend on screen: "Souvenir"

Stumble-john!

He lights the cigarette, avoiding her look.

There is a peal of girlish laughter from AMANDA *in the kitchen.*

LAURA *slowly raises and opens her hand. It still contains the little broken glass animal. She looks at it with a tender, bewildered expression.*

Stumble-john!
I shouldn't have done that— That was way off the beam. You don't smoke, do you?

She looks up, smiling, not hearing the question.

He sits beside her a little gingerly. She looks at him speechlessly —waiting.

He coughs decorously and moves a little farther aside as he considers the situation and senses her feelings, dimly, with perturbation.

Gently

Would you—care for a—mint?

She doesn't seem to hear him but her look grows brighter even.

Peppermint—Life-Saver?
My pocket's a regular drug store—wherever I go . . .

*He pops a mint in his mouth. Then gulps and decides to make a
clean breast of it. He speaks slowly and gingerly.*

Laura, you know, if I had a sister like you, I'd do the same thing
as Tom. I'd bring out fellows and—introduce her to them. The right
type of boys of a type to—appreciate her.
Only—well—he made a mistake about me.
Maybe I've got no call to be saying this. That may not have been
the idea in having me over. But what if it was?
There's nothing wrong about that. The only trouble is that in my
case—I'm not in a situation to—do the right thing.
I can't take down your number and say I'll phone.
I can't call up next week and—ask for a date.
I thought I had better explain the situation in case you—mis-
understood it and—hurt your feelings.

Pause

Slowly, very slowly, LAURA's *look changes, her eyes returning
slowly from his to the ornament in her palm.*

AMANDA *utters another gay laugh in the kitchen.*

LAURA (*faintly*): You—won't—call again?
JIM: No, Laura, I can't.

He rises from the sofa.

As I was just explaining, I've—got strings on me.
Laura, I've—been going steady!
I go out all of the time with a girl named Betty.
She's a home-girl like you, and Catholic, and Irish, and in a great
many ways we—get along fine.
I met her last summer on a moonlight boat trip up the river to
Alton, on the *Majestic.*
Well—right away from the start it was—love!

Legend: Love!

LAURA *sways slightly forward and grips the arm of the sofa. He
fails to notice, now enrapt in his own comfortable being.*

Being in love has made a new man of me!

Leaning stiffly forward, clutching the arm of the sofa, LAURA *struggles visibly with her storm. But* JIM *is oblivious, she is a long way
off.*

The power of love is really tremendous!
Love is something that—changes the whole world, Laura!

The storm abates a little and LAURA *leans back. He notices her
again.*

It happened that Betty's aunt took sick, she got a wire and had to
go to Centralia. So Tom—when he asked me to dinner—I naturally
just accepted the invitation, not knowing that you—that he—that I—

He stops awkwardly.

Huh—I'm a stumble-john!

He flops back on the sofa.

The holy candles in the altar of LAURA's *face have been snuffed
out. There is a look of almost infinite desolation.*

JIM *glances at her uneasily.*

I wish that you would—say something.

*She bites her lip which was trembling and then bravely smiles.
She opens her hand again on the broken glass ornament. Then
she gently takes his hand and raises it level with her own. She
carefully places the unicorn in the palm of his hand, then pushes
his fingers closed upon it.*

What are you—doing that for? You want me to have him?—
Laura?

She nods.

What for?
LAURA: A—souvenir . . .

She rises unsteadily and crouches beside the victrola to wind it up.

*Legend on screen: "Things Have a Way of Turning Out So
Badly!"*

Or image: "Gentleman Caller Waving Good-bye!—Gaily"

At this moment AMANDA *rushes brightly back in the front room.
She bears a pitcher of fruit punch in an old-fashioned cut-glass
pitcher and a plate of macaroons. The plate has a gold border and
poppies painted on it.*

AMANDA: Well, well, well! Isn't the air delightful after the shower? I've
made you children a little liquid refreshment.

Turns gaily to the gentleman caller.

Jim, do you know that song about lemonade?

> "Lemonade, lemonade
> Made in the shade and stirred with a spade—
> Good enough for any old maid!"

JIM (*uneasily*): Ha-ha! No—I never heard it.

AMANDA: Why, Laura! You look so serious!

JIM: We were having a serious conversation.

AMANDA: Good! Now you're better acquainted!

JIM (*uncertainly*): Ha-ha! Yes.

AMANDA: You modern young people are much more serious-minded than my generation. I was so gay as a girl!

JIM: You haven't changed, Mrs. Wingfield.

AMANDA: Tonight I'm rejuvenated! The gaiety of the occasion, Mr. O'Connor!

> *She tosses her head with a peal of laughter. Spills lemonade.*

Oooo! I'm baptizing myself!

JIM: Here—let me—

AMANDA (*setting the pitcher down*): There now. I discovered we had some maraschino cherries. I dumped them in, juice and all!

JIM: You shouldn't have gone to that trouble, Mrs. Wingfield.

AMANDA: Trouble, trouble? Why, it was loads of fun!

Didn't you hear me cutting up in the kitchen? I bet your ears were burning! I told Tom how outdone with him I was for keeping you to himself so long a time! He should have brought you over much, much sooner! Well, now that you've found your way, I want you to be a very frequent caller! Not just occasional but all the time.

Oh, we're going to have a lot of gay times together! I see them coming!

Mmm, just breathe that air! So fresh, and the moon's so pretty!

I'll skip back out—I know where my place is when young folks are having a— serious conversation!

JIM: Oh, don't go out, Mrs. Wingfield. The fact of the matter is I've got to be going.

AMANDA: Going, now? You're joking! Why, it's only the shank of the evening, Mr. O'Connor!

JIM: Well, you know how it is.

AMANDA: You mean you're a young workingman and have to keep workingmen's hours. We'll let you off early tonight. But only on the condition that next time you stay later.

What's the best night for you? Isn't Saturday night the best night for you workingmen?

JIM: I have a couple of time-clocks to punch, Mrs. Wingfield. One at morning, another one at night!

AMANDA: My, but you *are* ambitious! You work at night, too?

JIM: No, Ma'am, not work but—Betty! (*He crosses deliberately to pick up his hat. The band at the Paradise Dance Hall goes into a tender waltz.*)

AMANDA: Betty? Betty? Who's—Betty!

There is an ominous cracking sound in the sky.

JIM: Oh, just a girl. The girl I go steady with! (*He smiles charmingly. The sky falls.*)

Legend: "The Sky Falls"

AMANDA (*a long-drawn exhalation*): Ohhhh . . . Is it a serious romance, Mr. O'Connor?

JIM: We're going to be married the second Sunday in June.

AMANDA: Ohhhh—how nice!

Tom didn't mention that you were engaged to be married.

JIM: The cat's not out of the bag at the warehouse yet.

You know how they are. They call you Romeo and stuff like that.

He stops at the oval mirror to put on his hat. He carefully shapes the brim and the crown to give a discreetly dashing effect.

It's been a wonderful evening, Mrs. Wingfield. I guess this is what they mean by Southern hospitality.

AMANDA: It really wasn't anything at all.

JIM: I hope it don't seem like I'm rushing off. But I promised Betty I'd pick her up at the Wabash depot, an' by the time I get my jalopy down there her train'll be in. Some women are pretty upset if you keep 'em waitin.

AMANDA: Yes, I know— The tyranny of women!

Extends her hand.

Good-bye, Mr. O'Connor.

I wish you luck—and happiness—and success! All three of them, and so does Laura!—Don't you, Laura?

LAURA: Yes!

JIM (*taking her hand*): Good-bye, Laura. I'm certainly going to treasure that souvenir. And don't you forget the good advice I gave you.

Raises his voice to a cheery shout.

So long, Shakespeare!

Thanks again, ladies—Good night!

He grins and ducks jauntily out.

Still bravely grimacing, AMANDA *closes the door on the gentleman caller. Then she turns back to the room with a puzzled expression.*

She and LAURA *don't dare to face each other.* LAURA *crouches
beside the victrola to wind it.*

AMANDA (*faintly*): Things have a way of turning out so badly.
I don't believe that I would play the victrola.
Well, well—well—
Our gentleman caller was engaged to be married!
Tom!

TOM (*from back*): Yes, Mother?

AMANDA: Come in here a minute. I want to tell you something awfully
funny.

TOM (*enters with macaroon and a glass of the lemonade*): Has the gentleman caller gotten away already?

AMANDA: The gentleman caller has made an early departure.
What a wonderful joke you played on us!

TOM: How do you mean?

AMANDA: You didn't mention that he was engaged to be married.

TOM: Jim? Engaged?

AMANDA: That's what he just informed us.

TOM: I'll be jiggered! I didn't know about that.

AMANDA: That seems very peculiar.

TOM: What's peculiar about it?

AMANDA: Didn't you call him your best friend down at the warehouse?

TOM: He is, but how did I know?

AMANDA: It seems extremely peculiar that you wouldn't know your best
friend was going to be married!

TOM: The warehouse is where I work, not where I know things about
people!

AMANDA: You don't know things anywhere! You live in a dream; you
manufacture illusions!

He crosses to door.

Where are you going?

TOM: I'm going to the movies.

AMANDA: That's right, now that you've had us make such fools of ourselves. The effort, the preparations, all the expense! The new floor
lamp, the rug, the clothes for Laura! All for what? To entertain some
other girl's fiancé!
Go to the movies, go! Don't think about us, a mother deserted,
an unmarried sister who's crippled and has no job! Don't let anything
interfere with your selfish pleasure!
Just go, go, go—to the movies!

TOM: All right, I will! The more you shout about my selfishness to me
the quicker I'll go, and I won't go to the movies!

AMANDA: Go, then! Then go to the moon—you selfish dreamer!

TOM *smashes his glass on the floor. He plunges out on the fire escape, slamming the door.* LAURA *screams—cut by door.*

Dance-hall music up. TOM *goes to the rail and grips it desperately, lifting his face in the chill white moonlight penetrating the narrow abyss of the alley.*

Legend on screen: "And So Good-bye . . ."

TOM's *closing speech is timed with the interior pantomime. The interior scene is played as though viewed through sound-proof glass.* AMANDA *appears to be making a comforting speech to* LAURA *who is huddled upon the sofa. Now that we cannot hear the mother's speech, her silliness is gone and she has dignity and tragic beauty.* LAURA's *dark hair hides her face until at the end of the speech she lifts it to smile at her mother.* AMANDA's *gestures are slow and graceful, almost dancelike, as she comforts the daughter. At the end of her speech she glances a moment at the father's picture—then withdraws through the portieres. At close of* TOM's *speech,* LAURA *blows out the candles, ending the play.*

TOM: I didn't go to the moon, I went much further—for time is the longest distance between two places—

Not long after that I was fired for writing a poem on the lid of a shoe-box.

I left Saint Louis. I descended the steps of the fire escape for a last time and followed, from then on, in my father's footsteps, attempting to find in motion what was lost in space—

I traveled around a great deal. The cities swept about me like dead leaves, leaves that were brightly colored but torn away from the branches.

I would have stopped, but I was pursued by something.

It always came upon me unawares, taking me altogether by surprise. Perhaps it was a familiar bit of music. Perhaps it was only a piece of transparent glass—

Perhaps I am walking along a street at night, in some strange city, before I have found companions. I pass the lighted window of a shop where perfume is sold. The window is filled with pieces of colored glass, tiny transparent bottles in delicate colors, like bits of a shattered rainbow.

Then all at once my sister touches my shoulder. I turn around and look into her eyes . . .

Oh, Laura, Laura, I tried to leave you behind me, but I am more faithful than I intended to be!

I reach for a cigarette, I cross the street, I run into the movies or a bar, I buy a drink, I speak to the nearest stranger—anything that can blow your candles out!

LAURA *bends over the candles.*

—for nowadays the world is lit by lightning! Blow out your candles, Laura—and so good-bye. . . .

She blows the candles out.

The scene dissolves.

§ FOR COMMENT

Tennessee Williams is usually thought of not as a reflector of social injustices but as an explorer of the emotional turmoil of fragile people threatened by a hostile environment. Although this is true, the social environment is not absent from Williams' work. How does *The Glass Menagerie* reflect the Depression of the 1930's? In what way is the social picture of the times related to the psychological problems of the characters?

Williams' work usually contrasts the realistic and the romantic temperaments, frequently in hostile opposition to each other. How does this play dramatize such a contrast? Do individual characters embody one or the other trait, or do they have aspects of both?

Do any of the three Wingfields change from the beginning to the end of the play? Explain your answer. One of the play's major conflicts is between Amanda and Tom. How much should we sympathize with either party? with Laura and Jim? Find other elements of conflict which are developed and resolved. Amanda sees herself as the formerly genteel lady of the South; Tom sees himself as a sensitive poet. How do Laura and Jim see themselves? To what extent should we accept each character's self-valuation?

Jean Cocteau once distinguished between poetry *in* the theater and poetry *of* the theater. The former is composed of language, the latter of theatrical elements (scenery, lighting, etc.). Although Williams employs both types of poetry, he does not eschew realism. Identify the realistic and nonrealistic elements in this play. Do they clash or complement each other? Examine both scenic effects and language to find the nonrealistic or poetic elements. See the author's production notes and stage directions, indicating music, legends on a screen, and special lighting effects. The original production of *The Glass Menagerie* and most professional revivals of this play in the United States have not followed the production notes. Do you think they should be followed in a production of the play? What qualities might they contribute that are otherwise lacking? Or do you think they underscore the obvious?

The Glass Menagerie is called "a memory play." Is the label accurate? Are the events shown from Tom's point of view, or is the memory framework merely a literary device an excuse for a flashback, that does not color the events we see? Support your answers by references to the play. Can you think of other plays, short stories, or novels in which the story is told as a memory? In what respects are they similar to and/or different from *The Glass Menagerie?*

Symbolic of Laura's isolation and fragility is her glass menagerie, perhaps the most prominent symbolic element of the setting. How do other elements of the production (for example, the fire escape, the dance hall music) reinforce the play's moods and themes? Does each of the characters have a "glass menagerie" of his own, that is, a symbol of his own retreat from reality? If so, what are they? Why is Laura's emphasized by the title?

How successful is the effort of each character to cope with reality? Account for his success and/or failure. What are the objectives of each character regarding himself and the others? How selfish is the concern of each? To what degree does each indulge in self-deception?

Explore the dialogue to find patterns of words and phrases. For example, Tom frequently uses the word "adventure," Amanda keeps calling Tom a "dreamer," and the Gentleman Caller very often uses the pronoun "I." These and other words function as leitmotifs. What do they reveal of the character? of the character's understanding of himself? of his understanding of another character? Examine the relationship of language to characterization. Compare, for example, Amanda's speech about her past (Scene One) with Jim's speech about what he did after high school (Scene Seven). Why is the dialogue idiosyncratic to the character who speaks it? Find examples of idiosyncratic dialogue in the shorter speeches of these characters, as well as in speeches of Laura and Tom.

The play builds to the arrival of the Gentleman Caller as a means of saving Laura. What does his departure mean from Laura's point of view? from Amanda's? from his own? What might have been the result of his staying? Why is it impossible for this particular character to have stayed?

Appendix

❇️ *Writing About Literature*

Literary analysis is the process of examining and gathering data from a piece of literature to support a thesis concerning it. The thesis might be as broad as a total interpretation of meaning or as limited as the discussion of the function of a mark of punctuation. The end product of literary analysis might be a book, an article, a short theme handed in as a class assignment; or it might form the basis of a literary discussion. Except that more attention is paid to formal composition, writing about literature is not essentially different from talking about literature. In both cases a thesis is advanced and supported by means of relevant details.

Nor is writing about literature different from ordinary expository writing. One goes through much the same kind of process whether he marshalls evidence to support his position that a local bond issue should be passed, that his television set needs repair, or that the setting of John Steinbeck's "Flight" is functional in the story, or that a knowledge of Katherine Mansfield's *Journal* is beneficial to an understanding of her stories. The difference lies in the places one seeks the corroborating data, not in the process used. One uses a combination of personal observations and the observations of authorities in the field. A person's own observations gathered from a careful reading of "Flight" become the starting point, the *primary source* of his analysis. The observations of others are *secondary sources* used to help corroborate the thesis.

But whatever the thesis or the sources used for evidence to support the thesis, or whether the thesis is to be presented orally through discussion or in print, the thesis must be clearly stated and supported by a sufficient number of details marshalled in a convincing manner.

In this discussion we will be specifically concerned with the writing of literary papers. The student might be asked to write a paper based solely upon his own observations, or he might be asked to write what is known as a research paper, in which he combines his own observations with the observations of authorities in the field.

Let us begin with a discussion of the former, a paper that the student is to write based entirely upon his own observations without the assistance of secondary sources. In choosing a subject his first concern should be to find one that he is equipped to handle, and his second concern should be that its breadth and depth are appropriate to the assignment. It would be nonsensical for a student to choose to write a paper on Gerard Manley Hopkins' prosody if he had no knowledge of Hopkins' poetic theory, the limited evidence of a few poems to be found in a text such as this, and a 1,000-word limit to his assignment. This kind of subject demands extensive knowledge and a convincing array of evidence before any thesis derived from it could be persuasive. It would be equally nonsensical and foolhardy for a student to choose to write a complete interpretation of meaning of "A Hunger Artist," even if he felt competent to do so and had the text before him, since the complexity of the story demands fuller treatment than could be handled in a 1,000-word paper. It would be far better for him to limit his subject to a discussion of one aspect of the story relevant to its interpretation. A discussion of the function of the tone of the story or of the role of the impresario is more limited and thus better suited to the requirements of a short paper. A 2,000-word paper would allow the student more scope and he might consider a comparison: the function of tone in "A Hunger Artist" as compared with the function of tone in "The Black Prince," or the role of the impresario in "A Hunger Artist" as compared with the role of the impresario in "The Infant Prodigy."

Once the student has found a subject, he will need to gather the available evidence relevant to it and form a thesis based on that evidence. He must be sure to gather all the evidence, because if he does not he can be accused of distorting and mishandling, and his thesis will be open to serious question.

One way to form a thesis concerning a subject is to pose a question: What is the function of the setting in "Flight"? An examination of the setting in that story will provide data that point to a conclusion, and the conclusion can then become the thesis: "In 'Flight' the setting functions to help to reveal both characters and situation, to foreshadow the events in the story, to create mood, and to embody symbolically the conflict in the story." Once the thesis is clearly stated, the organization that the paper will take should also be clearly defined, for it follows that if the setting functions in four ways, a discussion of these four ways will provide the body of the paper.

Thus:

Setting in "Flight" helps to:
1. reveal both characters and situation
2. foreshadow events
3. create mood
4. symbolize the conflict

When the student has progressed this far, he is ready to organize his data under the four headlines and to begin writing his paper. It is essential that the paper conform to the requirements of a well organized composition, that it be unified around a central thesis, that it have a logical and orderly development, that it flow smoothly from one point to the next, and that it be free from deviations from standard usage and grammar.

The paper will probably take the following form:

1. an introduction, leading to a statement of thesis
2. paragraphs of development, including the presentation of the supporting evidence
3. a conclusion

§ THE INTRODUCTION

An introductory paragraph should capture the reader's interest as well as introduce the subject of the paper. For this reason it is well to avoid a thesis statement at the beginning of the introductory paragraph. Placed here it is sometimes too abrupt, too jarring. The reader is usually not psychologically ready for it. The thesis statement is best placed at the end of the introductory paragraph. The movement of the paragraph should be from the general to the particular. The reader needs to be led into the paper gently; he needs to be prepared for the statement of thesis.

Analyze the following introductory paragraphs taken from student papers. Notice that in each one some attempt is made to involve the reader in the subject before the thesis is presented.

The obvious conflict in the story "Flight" by John Steinbeck generates from Pepé's attempt to flee an unseen pursuer. Pepé has killed a man and seeks to escape. On the surface the plot movement of the story can be said to be simply causative. Pepé kills and flees. But there is a more complex struggle underlying the surface of the story. From the opening description of the rugged, weather-beaten coastline where Pepé grew up, to the desolate mountain wasteland where he died, there is illustrated the cycle of nature and the part Pepé plays in it. In this story nature can be said to be the antagonist, for from the beginning of the story to the end, there is a complete cycle from which Pepé issues, fights with, and returns to nature.

Araby, the land of mystery, casts a spell on its namesake's story. The person and mind of the protagonist operate in its half-darkness. When he goes to play it is dusk, and the nether light and chilly air play on him and his senses until his body glows. The light turns familiar things into secret places. The lanes, the gardens, the stables, are all dark and appealing. The shadows become hiding places from familiar life and duties.

A mere surface reading of a volume of short stories by Anton Chekhov reveals two important things: 1) Plot is not emphasized, and 2) exposition in the form of pure narration is rather limited. Thus the stories depend for their effect neither on a series of happenings nor on a recitation of facts and events. A detailed examination of the stories reveals that their effect depends on Chekhov's ability to delineate character and to establish and maintain mood as he indicates that one or two isolated events symbolize a life and time composite.

Thomas Hardy has blended characters and environment so skillfully in certain scenes in *Tess of the d'Urbervilles* that the scenes become vivid and unforgettable images. But they are not just pictorial. They all have symbolic significance relating to the whole novel. I have selected certain of what I feel are the most important of these scenes, and in this paper I shall attempt to discuss their function in relation to the total structure of the novel.

§ DEVELOPMENT

In a composition unity is essential and is achieved by constant but varied reference to the central point. Every paragraph of development must be closely related to the thesis and every sentence in every paragraph should be closely related to the main point of that paragraph. Thus:

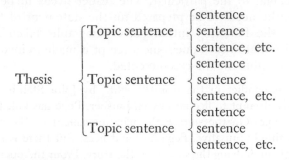

Paragraphs should be arranged in some kind of logical order, building one upon the other until the conclusion is reached. A smooth flow of paragraphs is achieved by attention to transitions. The topic sentence of paragraph 2 for example might read: "Not only does the setting function to create mood (topic of first paragraph), it also helps to reveal both characters and situations (topic of second paragraph)." By mentioning the topic of the preceding paragraph while announcing the topic of the present paragraph the student is able to achieve an orderly flow of ideas. Other ways to achieve good transitions not only between paragraphs but also between sentences are the use of such transition words as "nevertheless," "however," "on the other hand," and so forth; repetition of key words and phrases; and the parallel construction of sentences and phrases.

Examine the following student paper, paying particular attention to the means by which a smooth flow of ideas is achieved.

On the Physics of Teeter-Totters and May Poles

E. E. Cummings' poem "if everything happens that can't be done" captures the singsong feeling of children playing. It is an endorsement of the wonder in life, which is, unfortunately, usually lost, forgotten, or denied after childhood. Cummings' poem has that special awe that children communicate to those around them by their innocence and their unjaded responses and acceptance of themselves and their environments. It is also an indictment of academic learning and the stifled approach to life which is often the result of academic educations. Cummings' poem achieves this effect to a great extent through its technical structure.

The technical structure of the poem is both very tight and very loose, with particular use being made of contrasts in meter, rhyme scheme, arrangement of lines, punctuation, and vocabulary.

The poem consists of five stanzas of five lines each. The second and fourth verses of each stanza are placed on three lines on the page while the other three verses occupy one line each. The rhyme scheme is *aabba*, with slight variations where the rhyme is half or suspended. All of these rhymes are masculine. There is also use of internal rhyme and alliteration. The meter is primarily anapestic tetrameter with the last two lines of each stanza being anapestic trimeter. There is much use of substitution in the meter.

This is the basic structure of the poem as a whole. From this uniformity of the stanzas as to rhyme, meter, and line arrangement comes the poem's basic flow and continuity of movement, which is extremely important to the general feeling of the complete poem.

The unity within the stanzas is likewise very tightly built. The lines of each stanza are linked and interlinked like pretzeled strings of sausages, in much the same manner as are the stanzas themselves. The first, second and third lines of each stanza are linked, as was mentioned above, by uniformly having four feet in each line. The fourth and fifth lines are likewise linked by each having three metric feet. The rhyme scheme links the first, second and fifth lines and also links the third and fourth lines. The second and fourth lines are linked by the punctuating parentheses that join them, both in each stanza and from one stanza to the next, as poetic "asides," or perhaps as stage whispers to the reader. This also acts to link the first, third and fifth lines of each particular stanza and to link them from stanza to stanza throughout the poem.

Thus, the structure of the poem is very tightly knit, both within each particular stanza and in the poem as a solitary unit. This tightness is of primary importance to the success of the poem because it acts as a contrasting background that brings out and intensifies the free childlike exuberance of the poem's statement. For into this closely restricted structure, Cummings places many rhythmic substitutions, line variations and other technical changes of pace which intensify his message and at the same time seem subtle and unobtrusive because of the flow and continuity of the tight foundation.

Although the basic rhythm is anapestic, each line except the fourth in each stanza begins with an iamb. This has the effect of giving the line a starting flip which is carried into a skipping rhythm by the following anapests. Iambs are scattered throughout the poem to give jerks to the rhythm making it suggest a child skipping and changing the order in which his feet hit the ground. Also, and necessary for the effect, each lines ends in a skiplike accent.

The effect of this rhythm is compounded by Cummings' choice of language. Most of the words Cummings chooses are short words that begin with hard skipping sounds and/or words that end in vowel sounds that have a feeling of flying or being in the air when skipping: ". . . can't be done," ". . . is a my," ". . . is a bough."

Besides this aid to the rhythm, Cummings' choice of language also suggests the language of children in its grammar and order. Even the words are all simple compounds and words of the most general nature, i.e., "every-anything," etc. Forms such as "stupidest," ". . . who's we," or inversions such as "which around" suggest again children. Cummings' use of abstract words also suggests his theme of the child and his awe. ". . . and deep in the high that does nothing but fall." There is this suggestion because of a child's acceptance of the words' meanings without need for a specifically defined context for the words to describe.

The total effect of these things, the use of words and the skipping rhythm, is childlike like a child's imagination that has yet to learn where it may not go and like sliding down a slide and rushing up the small incline at the slide's bottom, or like whirling around to stop on roller skates or like any or all of the infinite other childhood actions that do not stop, but instead jump up in the air at the end.

This is the strongest single effect of the poem, the effect of children's exuberant accelerated play. It is mirrored also in the line arrangement of the poem. As was mentioned, the second and fourth lines of each stanza are surrounded by parentheses. These lines are also more irregular in rhythm than the other lines. In each stanza the second line has more iambs than the other lines and the fourth lines are the only totally ana-pestic lines. These lines are also broken down into three lines on the page. The effect, when reading from the end of a long line through three clipped irregular length lines to another long line, is like whirling around and around in a spiral and then stopping suddenly and the world seems to be moving in the other direction. In the moment of stopping there is the effect of the slide again or of a swing just about to descend from its arc.

Another effect coming from the combination of these things plus the separate nature in meaning of these lines is that of an "aside," as was formerly said, where Cummings allies himself with children against "creeping academia" and academic pedantry such as this paper has become, just as children ally themselves against other children. It is somewhat like telling important secrets only to your best friends.

And so, by using all of these ways, the firm tight base, the rhythms, the language, the placement, the rhyme, the punctuation, and much more which is not the technical part of writing a poem, Cummings asks his readers to let themselves feel the wonder of life as simply as do children. He asks this, not directly, but by writing in a manner, a style, that suggests children and the awesome affirmation of life that is where children live. He does not ask that they bind themselves to a child's lack of knowledge, also, but that they seek knowledge with a reverence for life which means only a simple acceptance and awareness that life is here, now.

Individual paragraphs may be ordered in various ways, depending on the needs of the topic. Details may be arranged in a chronological order according to the plot movement of the story or in some kind of logical order, as, for example, from the least important to the most important. Ideas may be contrasted or compared; analogies may be used or examined. Probably for most literary papers, the paragraphs will be developed by means of enumeration of details derived from the text. In presenting material from the text the student should avoid what is known as the "patchwork quilt," that is, an arrangement of quotations placed one after another with little or no interpretation or comment.

The following paragraphs illustrate how quotations and references to the text can be combined with interpretation and comment to avoid the appearance of the patchwork quilt:

In the first stanza of "Sailing to Byzantium" it is the young people and the ordinary birds of Ireland who are "at their song" and "caught in that sensual music." It is a song of today, of this life, of pleasures of the body ("sensual"), but also a song of death, because the physicality celebrated is fated to be "begotten, born, and die." The song is sung by the young who are vital and pleased with the enjoyments of youth but who are not yet concerned with aging and disillusionment and death. In the second stanza it is the old man's soul that must "clap its hands and sing, and louder sing." It is a song celebrating the magnificence of the monuments of Byzantium. The soul sings to protect against the old man's label, "a tattered coat upon a stick," singing that there is more to life than Ireland—there is the "holy city of Byzantium." In the third stanza the sages of Byzantium are the singers. It is a song of purgation of the soul through fire, a song of eternity. The old man beseeches the sages to become "the singing masters of my soul" because his soul is trapped in a dying body, and he knows there is a higher existence for the soul in eternity. In the last stanza it is the old man, his soul regenerated, who sings. It is a song of the artificial art of the

Grecian goldsmiths, of everything that is supernatural, non-physical. The poet sits "upon a golden bough" to sing joyfully about eternal Byzantium, and about the past, the present, and the future.

A third way Steinbeck uses animal and inanimate imagery in "Flight" is to depict man's condition in his natural habitat—the world of nature. As an embryo, Pepé, "a foolish chicken," lives in a world where ". . . the sea below the cliff was glinting and blue and the white surf creamed on the reef, when even the stone mountains looked kindly. . . ." Yet his mother can foresee his initiation into the adult world, for she says, "Yes, thou art a man, my poor little Pepé. . . . I have seen it coming on thee." She tells the children, "Pepé goes on a journey. . . . He has a man's thing to do." And while the moonlight thins, reaching toward the sea, Pepé sets out on his journey, and the mournful death wail follows after him.

§ Conclusion

The conclusion of the literary paper summarizes the main points and reiterates the thesis.

Araby does turn out to be a place of darkness and mystery, but it has none of the Eastern enchantment the boy had imagined. It is in reality no farther east than where a cockney accent originates. At the bazaar he finds a very unmysterious girl bantering with two young men and when she speaks to the boy it is only out of duty and with little concern. When the light is out and there is finally total darkness, the boy sees what half-light had hidden: that however blind and brown the world is, this is, nevertheless, its true condition, and it must be seen and accepted as such.

These four stories, "The Huntsman," "The Kiss," "The Lady with the Pet Dog," and "The Darling," as well as those referred to briefly in the opening paragraphs of this paper, illustrate Chekhov's general tendency to create effect in his stories by relying on his ability to delineate character and to establish and maintain mood while indicating that isolated situations are suggestive of an entire composite of events in human experience. In some of the stories, plot and exposition are more important than in others, but they are never the dominant elements.

§ Some Stylistic Notes

1. Literary papers range from formal to semiformal in style. Do not use contractions, colloquialisms, or slang.
2. Write your paper as though you were addressing it to someone who is reasonably familiar with the text of the piece (or pieces) you are discussing. It is not necessary to do extensive summary or paraphrase. What you would say to another class member is a suitable standard.

3. Use the present tense consistently in literary analysis. The literary work is considered to exist in the present. Say, "the narrator expresses" (not "expressed"). Say, "Steinbeck uses" (not "used").

4. Titles of short pieces are set in quotation marks. Titles of long pieces are italicized. "The Raven," "Flight," *The Great Gatsby, Macbeth.*

5. Do not apologize. An apology will subvert your efforts. If you do not know enough about a subject, you should not write on it.

6. Keep your paper balanced. Spend equal amounts of time in discussions of items having equal importance.

7. Quotations of less than five lines should be run into the body of your text. Longer quotations are set in.

8. Make an appropriate title for your paper. Do not simply use the title of the piece you are writing about: The Function of the Setting in "Flight," The Role of the Impresario in "A Hunger Artist," Images in "Ars Poetica."

§ Using Secondary Sources

Secondary sources are used to supplement your own observations. They are incorporated into your paper to lend the weight of professional judgment to the support of your thesis. If your writing assignment is to include the use of secondary sources, you must locate the findings of critics and scholars relevant to your thesis. You will, of course, be looking for opinions that help to support your thesis, but you cannot ignore opinions that are contrary. Such opinions make up an opposition stand that must be admitted and then dismissed on some logical basis. It might be possible to destroy the opposition stand by suggesting that material facts have been ignored or by attacking the logic of the argument. But whatever the method of attack, the opposition must be dismissed before you can proceed with your thesis.

In a paper using secondary sources, a good place to handle the opposition is at the beginning of the paper. Opinions of professionals in the field may be summarized in such a way as to show a division of critical judgment making pertinent further discussion which your paper purports to do. Examine the following introductory paragraphs of a student paper that skillfully summarize differing opinions and dispose of the opposition before moving to the defense of the thesis.

The Implicit Mode of Hemingway

In his fiction, Ernest Hemingway makes use of the implicit rather than the explicit to present his comments on man; and the power and distinctiveness of his fiction is a result of his use of irony, symbolism, and understatement.

Hemingway's devotion to the implicit has brought a shower of abuse from his detractors who insist that he is too limited. They say his characters are uncomplicated; his "action" circles are narrowly limited; his style has stripped so much away that little is left but "a group of clevernesses"; and his code is a crude, simple outlook that cannot be compared to the profound Stoicism that it is sometimes thought to resemble.[1] Hemingway's defenders, on the other hand, insist that these limitations are a strength rather than a weakness. They say that his characters, while appearing overtly as simple primitives, are heroic figures whose real battle is to be found within themselves and whose primitivism is a complicated barrier made up of ritual, legend, sacraments, and symbols; he has succeeded in making the violent world of his stories a moral equivalent of life; his spare economical style of writing is a precise instrument of implication; and his code is a broadly relevant one that gives meaning to a world where love and religion are absent. That Hemingway knew what he was doing when he placed these limitations on himself is shown in this comment on his aims, "Prose, he once said, is not interior decoration but architecture, and the Baroque is over." [2]

Hemingway's unique style is derived from his days as a reporter and news correspondent. In the hard school of the newspaper world, he learned that "Pure objective writing is the only true form of storytelling." [3] Hemingway later said that he was "enormously excited to learn that the English language yields to simplicity through brevity." [4] Through his long apprenticeship with the newspaper world, the young Hemingway gradually developed the style that is often referred to as iceberg imagery, a reference to Hemingway's own statement: "The dignity of movement of an iceberg is due to only one-eighth of it being above water." [5] Thus he effectively characterizes the immense power of the unsaid and goes on to demonstrate this power in his works.

To make use of secondary sources it is, of course, necessary to locate them first. Their usual repository is the library where the card catalogue can lead you to books on your subject or possibly to special bibliographies that have already been prepared. Periodical indexes are helpful for both books and articles, and one source can often lead to others. Once you have located a list of promising sources, examine them and take notes on any pertinent ones. Careful note-taking will greatly facilitate your effort. Be sure to keep a careful record of the source of every note since any material you use must be cited by footnote reference, and every source, whether paraphrased or quoted, will need to be recorded in a bibliography.

If you use secondary sources, you must tell your reader why the source

---

[1] Robert P. Weeks, "Introduction," Hemingway, A Collection of Critical Essays (Englewood Cliffs, N.J.: Prentice-Hall, 1964), p. 1.

[2] Weeks, p. 1.

[3] Charles A. Fenton, The Apprenticeship of Ernest Hemingway (New York: Farrar, Straus and Young, 1954), p. 41.

[4] Fenton, pp. 42–43.

[5] Quoted in Weeks, p. 6.

is pertinent, exactly what it is, whose finding it is, and where it is to be found. Your reader should never be confused about whether a stated opinion is yours or someone else's; be careful to take credit for what is yours and to give credit for what is another's. Sometimes in giving credit you may use the name of that author and the title of his work in the body of your paper, but if you do not, then this information, as well as information that will help your reader locate the source, must be cited in a footnote.

In writing literary papers there are certain conventions of documentation which need to be followed just as there are conventions of punctuation or usage. The first reference to any secondary source should be cited in a footnote that contains the name of the author (if it is not given in the body of your paper), the title of the work from which you took the reference (if it is not given in the body of the paper), the place of publication, the publisher, the date of publication, and the specific page number where the reference may be located.

For books by single authors the footnote entry takes the following form:

1 Charles A. Fenton, *The Apprenticeship of Ernest Hemingway* (New York: Farrar, Straus and Young, 1954), p. 41.

Any items used in the body of your paper are omitted from the footnote entry. If, for example, you have made specific reference in your paper to the name of the author and the title of the book, then the footnote entry would read:

1 (New York: Farrar, Straus and Young, 1954), p. 41.

Nothing needs to be repeated. After you have once made reference to a given source, further reference to the same source may be cited as:

2 Fenton, p. 46.

In the unusual case that you are citing works by two different men named Fenton, you will need to add more information to your footnote, perhaps a short title:

2 Fenton, *Apprenticeship*, p. 46.

For books having two authors, the footnote entry takes the following form:

1 Harry Modean Campbell and Ruel E. Foster, *William Faulkner* (Norman, Oklahoma: University of Oklahoma Press, 1951), p. 71.

Books having more than two authors may be cited as:

1 Albert C. Baugh, *et al.*, *A Literary History of England* (New York: Appleton-Century-Crofts, 1948), p. 57.

Anthologies which are compiled by an editor take the following form:

1 William E. Buckler and Arnold B. Sklare, eds., *Stories from Six Authors* (New York: McGraw-Hill, 1960), p. 58.

References to articles appearing in collections take the following form:

1 E. M. Halliday, "Hemingway's Ambiguity: Symbolism and Irony," *Hemingway, A Collection of Critical Essays*, ed. Robert P. Weeks (Englewood Cliffs, N.J.: Prentice-Hall, 1964), p. 57.

References to articles appearing in journals take the following form:

¹ Seymour L. Gross, "Hawthorne's 'My Kinsman, Major Molineux': History as Moral Adventure," *Nineteenth Century Fiction*, XII (1957–1958), 97.

For a fuller discussion of footnoting, see any good handbook, or *The MLA Style Sheet*, accepted as standard usage by nearly all professionals in the field.

Any work cited in a footnote must appear in a bibliography at the end of your paper. The bibliography may also include general sources when no specific reference is used. You should be careful, however, to cite in a bibliography only those sources that you have used; do not pad your bibliography.

The bibliographical entry consists of three parts: the author with his last name placed first, since bibliographies are alphabetized; the title of the work; and the facts of publication, including the place of publication, publisher, and the date of publication. For journal articles, the volume number, date, and page reference are also included.

The following sample bibliography gathers together the examples cited above and includes the kinds of sources you will most often use. For unusual situations, you should again refer to a fuller treatment of documentation either in a handbook or in *The MLA Style Sheet*.

§ BIBLIOGRAPHY

Baugh, Albert C., *et al. A Literary History of England* (New York: Appleton-Century-Crofts, 1948).

Buckler, William E., and Arnold B. Sklare, eds. *Stories from Six Authors* (New York: McGraw-Hill, 1960).

Campbell, Harry Modean, and Ruel E. Foster. *William Faulkner* (Norman, Oklahoma: University of Oklahoma Press, 1951).

Fenton, Charles A. *The Apprenticeship of Ernest Hemingway* (New York: Farrar, Straus and Young, 1954).

Halliday, E. M. "Hemingway's Ambiguity: Symbolism and Irony," *Hemingway, A Collection of Critical Essays*, ed. Robert P. Weeks (Englewood Cliffs, N.J.: Prentice-Hall, 1964).

Gross, Semour L. "Hawthorne's 'My Kinsman, Major Molineux': History as Moral Adventure," *Nineteenth Century Fiction*, XII (1957–58), 97–109.

Bear in mind that secondary sources in the kinds of papers discussed above may become primary sources in other kinds of papers. A student interested in writing a paper on the subject of how contemporary reviewers reacted to William Faulkner's *The Sound and the Fury* would have to locate these reviews, and they would become primary sources for his paper, while another student might use the same reviews as secondary sources for a paper discussing the function of Benjy in the novel.

Suggestions for Writing

I. Topics appropriate for analysis of individual works. (The student should be aware that each of the following topics, if applied to another literary work, can lead to another paper. It is possible, for example, to analyze the function of setting in any of the stories, novels, or plays and in many of the poems. Papers can also be developed from many of the questions asked in the comments following the various stories, poems, and plays, and the discussions of the novels.)

A. The function of the setting in "Flight"
B. Use of point of view in "The Egg"
C. Characterization in "The Black Prince"
D. Relevance of tone in "A Hunger Artist"
E. Use of symbols in *The Trial*
F. The role of stanzas in the structure of "Sailing to Byzantium"
G. Imagery in Longfellow's "A Psalm of Life"
H. Role of sound in "Ulalume"
I. Movement in *Antigonê*
J. Dramatization of the past in *The Glass Menagerie*
K. Speech used to reveal inner state, attitudes, and values, seen in *Macbeth*
L. Scenery used to reveal theme and create atmosphere in *Pygmalion*

II. Topics for papers of comparison

A. Devices

1. A comparison of the use of point of view in "The Black Prince" and "A Hunger Artist"
2. Setting as symbol in "The Secret Sharer" and "Petrified Man"
3. Closed couplets in *Mac Flecknoe* and *The Rape of the Lock*
4. Nature imagery in "Fern Hill" and "After Apple-Picking"
5. Rhyme in "Pied Beauty" and "I Heard a Fly Buzz"
6. The use of irony in *Antigonê* and *Everyman*
7. Stage business in *Pygmalion* and *Macbeth*

8. Scenery used to reveal theme and create atmosphere in *The Glass Menagerie* and *A Dream Play*

B. Structure
1. Elements of the fairy tale in "Hop-Frog" and "The Black Prince"
2. Dream imagery in "My Kinsman, Major Molineux" and "A Hunger Artist"
3. The Oedipal pattern in "My Oedipus Complex" and "The Rocking-Horse Winner"
4. Pastoralism in "Lycidas" and *The Deserted Village*
5. Sonnet form in "It Is a Beauteous Evening" and "God's Grandeur"
6. Ballad stanza in "Sir Patrick Spens" and "O What Is That Sound Which So Thrills the Ear"
7. Plot in *Everyman* and *A Dream Play*
8. Foreshadowing in *Macbeth* and *Pygmalion*
9. Dream imagery in *A Dream Play* and "My Kinsman, Major Molineux"

C. Theme
1. The concept of evil in "A Good Man Is Hard to Find" and "Benito Cereno"
2. The initiation theme in "Araby" and "Flight"
3. Love in Marvell's "The Definition of Love" and Shakespeare's "Shall I Compare Thee to a Summer's Day"
4. Idea of nature in "Design" and "I Wandered Lonely as a Cloud"
5. Elegiac elements in Auden's "In Memory of W. B. Yeats" and Tate's "Winter Mask: To the Memory of W. B. Yeats"
6. Money in *Everyman* and *Pygmalion*
7. Power in *Antigonê* and *Macbeth*
8. Retribution in *Antigonê* and *Everyman*

III. Topics for research papers. (Any of the above topics, if used in conjunction with secondary sources, can become research papers. The following topics can suggest other possibilities.)

A. A summary of the given interpretations of any story, poem, play, or novel
1. Critical controversy over "Benito Cereno"
2. Permanence of *The Great Gatsby*, a review of the criticism
3. Contemporary reviews of *Tess of the d'Urbervilles*
4. Helen of Troy in Yeats' poetry
5. Critical appraisals of Keats' "Ode on a Grecian Urn"
6. A comparison of the interpretation of *Macbeth* presented by

Samuel Taylor Coleridge, William Hazlitt, Thomas de Quincy, and Samuel Johnson or by A. C. Bradley, John Dover Wilson, E. K. Chambers, G. Wilson Knight, Lily B. Campbell, and Irving Ribner

7. The interpretations of *Macbeth* by Lionel Barrymore, Sir John Gielgud, Sir Laurence Olivier, Maurice Evans, Alec Guinness
8. The permanence of *Pygmalion*, a review of the criticism

B. A comparison of any poem, play, story, or novel printed in this anthology with another or others to be found outside of the anthology

1. The idea of a double in Conrad's "The Secret Sharer" and Poe's "William Wilson"
2. A comparison of the theme of darkness in "Benito Cereno" and Conrad's "Heart of Darkness"
3. The portrait of the southern aristocrat in Faulkner's *Absalom, Absalom!* and *The Sound and the Fury*
4. Pastoralism in *The Deserted Village* and *The Vicar of Wakefield*
5. Frost's conception of nature
6. A comparison of Strindberg's treatment of character in *A Dream Play* with his treatment of character in *Miss Julie*
7. A comparison of Ovid's treatment of the Pygmalion myth in *The Metamorphoses* with Shaw's treatment in *Pygmalion*
8. A comparison of Shaw's *Pygmalion* with the musical comedy derived from it, *My Fair Lady*

Glossary of Literary Terms

This glossary does not pretend to be either complete or exhaustive. It is a collection of critical terms used within the book. Page references are to the fuller discussions in which the various terms occur.

Alexandrine: a six-stress iambic line. See p. 380.

Allegory: the limited, particular use of a symbol or group of symbols so that instead of representing a complex of meanings a single meaning or pattern of meanings is presented. See p. 610.

Alliteration: the repetition of the initial sounds of words. See pp. 383–384.

Allusion: a reference, either explicit, implicit, or to a context outside that of the work of literature. Allusions may be literary, historical, religious, etc. See pp. 539–541.

Ambiguity: the condition existing when more than one meaning is present in a word or syntax. Also less commonly called **plurisignification.** See pp. 46–47, 346–351.

Anapest: a metrical foot consisting of two unstressed syllables and one stressed syllable. See p. 380.

Antagonist: the character with whom the **protagonist** is involved in conflict. See p. 23.

Assonance: repetition of vowel sounds. See p. 384.

Atmosphere: the predominant mood of a story. See p. 25.

Blocking: moving the actor from one area of the stage to another, usually devised by the director. See p. 885.

Box set: realistic theater setting, displaying three visible walls of a room, the fourth wall removed in order to allow the audience to see what happens in the room. See p. 612.

Cadence: the organization of speech rhythms into the highly organized pattern more commonly called **meter.** See p. 379.

Caesura: a pause within a line of poetry. See p. 382.

Central observer: that character through whose sensibility events and scenes are presented in **limited third person narration.** See p. 26.

Character: a person in a story, play, or poem. See pp. 23, 610.

Characterization: the process by which an author creates character, the devices by which he makes us believe a character is the particular type of person he is. See p. 23.

Climax: the turning point of the action after which only one outcome is possible. Also called **crisis.** See p. 24.

Closed couplet: two lines of verse in which the sense is carried on through the two lines but not beyond. Also called **end-stopped.** See p. 382.

Comedy: See p. 609.

Conceit: an elaborate or startling image or comparison in which many points of similarity between two things usually considered unrelated are pointed out. See Donne's "The Flea," p. 404, and "A Valediction: Forbidding Mourning," p. 405.

Conflict: the struggle which occurs between the **protagonist** and the **antagonist,** fate or environment, or within the **protagonist** or with conflicting value systems. Also called **complication.** See p. 23.

Connotative meaning: the suggestions aroused by a word. See pp. 376–377.

Consonance: repetition of consonant sounds. See p. 384.

Couplet: any two lines of verse, but usually used to mean two lines of verse rhyming consecutively. See p. 382.

Crisis: See **climax.**

Dactyl: a metrical foot composed of one stressed syllable followed by two unstressed syllables. See p. 380.

Denotative meaning: the "ordinary" meaning of a word, the dictionary meaning. See p. 376.

Dimeter: a line of poetry containing two feet or two stresses. See p. 381.

Direct characterization: explicit description of character traits, physical appearance, moral attributes or degree of sensitivity. See p. 23.

Dithyramb: choral song about incidents in the life of a god or hero. See p. 607.

Dramatic characterization: presentation of a character's traits through his speeches or his actions so that from these the reader infers the existence of certain character traits. See pp. 23, 613.

Elegy: a poem mourning the death of a person, often using the **pastoral** convention. See pp. 423–424.

Elizabethan sonnet: See **Shakespearean sonnet.**

Enjambement: carrying over the sense from one line of poetry to another without pause. Also called **run-on.** See p. 383.

Exposition: information which the author provides to the reader to make clear the **conflict** which will be presented. See p. 24.

Expressionism: an outward, external representation of that which is essentially internal or abstract, often involving dislocations or fragmentations of time, personality, and the social environment, and general distortions of emotions and thought. See p. 800.

Fairy tale: a story set in a realm outside ordinary reality, containing miraculous adventures, violent actions, usually with a happy ending. See p. 38.

Feminine rhyme: rhyming of unstressed syllables. See p. 383.

First person narration: a narrative in which the teller of the story speaks in his own voice and manner. See p. 25.

Flat characters: those which exhibit one predominant character trait. See p. 23.

Floor plan: See **ground plan.**

Foot: a unit of meter containing at least one stressed syllable and at least one other syllable, either stressed or unstressed. See p. 380.

Foreshadowing: hints of what is to come. See p. 24.

Ground plan: a drawing of the stage as seen from above. Also called **floor plan.** See p. 885.

Heptameter: a line of poetry composed of seven feet or seven stresses. See p. 381.

Heroic couplet: two five-stress iambic lines rhyming consecutively, usually restricted to such couplets which are end-stopped. See p. 384.

Hexameter: a line of poetry composed of six feet or six stresses. Also called an **Alexandrine.** See p. 381.

Houses: See **mansions.**

Iamb: a metrical foot consisting of one unstressed and one stressed syllable. See p. 380.

Imperfect rhyme: less than exact repetition of terminal sounds. Various kinds of imperfect rhyme are **half rhyme, eye rhyme,** and **slant rhyme.** See p. 383.

Intentional fallacy: the theory that literary criticism consists of judging the success with which an author has carried out his intentions in a work of literature. See p. 8.

Irony: a literary device in which the superficial meaning contrasts, usually incongruously, with the intended meaning. In verbal irony, the intended meaning of words contrasts with the literal meaning, as when a fat person is called "Slim" or a clumsy one, "Grace." Other kinds of irony are dramatic irony, which depends upon the entire structure of the play or literary work. Situational irony presents a contrast between what is expected and what actually occurs, i.e., it concerns actions rather than words alone. Irony is one of the most important of all literary devices. It is one of the chief methods by which a writer may hold contrasting or opposite emotions, ideas, or attitudes in tension and thus express the complexity, contradiction, and even disorder to be found in life itself. See p. 46.

Italian sonnet: See **Petrarchan sonnet.**

Leitmotif: details or images in a literary work that recur so frequently that their repetition constitutes a significant pattern. See p. 746.

Limited third person narration: that which employs a **central observer** through whose mind all events and scenes are presented. See p. 26.

Line: a unit of verse, composed of one or more kinds of metrical feet. See p. 381.

Macrocosm: the larger world of human existence. See p. 176.

Mansions: in medieval drama, platforms which represent different specific locales. Also called **stations, sedes,** or **houses.** See p. 610.

Märchen: See **fairy tale.**

Masculine rhyme: rhyming of stressed syllables. See p. 383.

Metaphor: broadly, any figurative language. In a more limited sense, an unstated comparison. See p. 377.

Meter: regular, patterned rhythm, usually either accentual (based on the number of accents or stresses in a given line) or syllabic (based on the number of syllables in a given line), or sometimes a combination of accentual and syllabic. See p. 379.

Microcosm: a little world which reflects the larger world. See p. 176.

Miracle play: a play based on incidents in the life of a saint. See p. 610.

Monometer: a line of poetry consisting of one foot or containing one stressed syllable. See p. 381.

Morality play: an allegorical drama based on Christian teaching but not on Biblical stories, in which the characters represent abstract ideas or characteristics. See pp. 610, 677.

Mystery play: a play based on events in the Old or New Testament. See p. 610.

Myth: a body of information, traditional or deliberately created, used to explain questions and problems often considered unanswerable. The truth or untruth of myth is usually considered irrelevant. See pp. 10–12.

Narrative: any story involving persons who act out in a particular time and place some kind of **conflict**. See pp. 22–23.

Octave: the first eight lines of a **sonnet**. Also called the **octet**. See p. 385.

Onomatopoeia: a device in which the sounds of words imitate their meaning. See p. 384.

Orchestra: the circular area in the Greek theater in front of the **skene**, used by the Chorus as a dancing place. In today's theater, the main floor, used as a seating area for the spectators. See p. 607.

Ottava rima: an eight-line stanza rhyming *abababcc*. See pp. 384–385.

Paradox: a statement which at first glance seems obviously false, but upon closer consideration is seen to contain truth. See pp. 46–47.

Passion play: a play dealing with the sufferings of Christ. See p. 610.

Pastoral: a kind of literature that uses the relatively restricted world of shepherds to comment on the larger, more complex world of ordinary life. See pp. 397, 423–424.

Pentameter: a line of poetry containing five feet or five stresses. See p. 381.

Persona: originally the mask used by Roman actors. Now used to describe a character who speaks directly in a literary work but who may or may not represent the author's ideas and attitudes. See p. 25.

Petrarchan sonnet: a sonnet in which the first eight lines rhyme *abbaabba* and the last six lines may be rhymed in a variety of ways. Also called an **Italian sonnet**. See p. 385.

Platea: in medieval drama, an indefinite, unlocalized place. See p. 610.

Platform stage: a stage which extends into the auditorium and which is surrounded on all but one side by the audience. Shakespeare's stage was a platform stage. See p. 610.

Plot: the pattern of action constructed by the author, usually involving some indication of causation. See p. 23.

Point of view: the particular vantage point from which a story is told, but usually either first person or third person. See p. 25.

Primary source: an original work of literature. See p. 951.

Proscenium arch: the "picture frame" dividing the stage from the audience. Through this frame, the audience sees the action. See p. 610.

Protagonist: the most important character in a work of literature, the central character, the one to whom all the events have relevance. See p. 23.

Quatrain: a four-line stanza. See p. 384.

Resolution: the solution of the conflict of the plot, often involving recognition or discovery by the **protagonist** or the reader. Also called **falling action** and **denouement.** See p. 24.

Rhyme: the repetition of the terminal sounds of words. See p. 383.

Rhyme royal: a seven-line stanza rhyming *ababbcc.* See p. 384.

Rising action: the section of the **plot** leading to the presentation of the **conflict.** See p. 24.

Round characters: those which reveal many character traits. See p. 23.

Run-on: See **enjambement.**

Satire: a kind of literature which holds ideas, attitudes, and behavior up to ridicule. Usually satire is stronger than **irony.** See p. 428.

Secondary source: observations about an original work of literature, usually by other writers but possibly by the author. See pp. 951, 958.

Sedes: See **mansions.**

Sentimentality: the demand on the part of an author for a greater emotional response than is warranted by the situation he has created, usually considered a serious flaw in literature. Sometimes, though, an author may present a character who is sentimental, even when the over-all effect of the story is not.

Sestet: the last six lines of a sonnet. Also called **sextet.** See p. 385.

Setting: the particular time and place in which a work of literature occurs. See pp. 23, 24–25.

Shakespearean sonnet: a sonnet consisting of three quatrains rhymed *abab, cdcd, efef,* concluded by a couplet, *gg.* Also called an **Elizabethan sonnet.** See p. 386.

Simile: a stated comparison, usually with *like* or *as.* See pp. 377–378.

Simultaneous staging: several locales on view at the same time, the actors moving from one to another as required by the play. See p. 610.

Skene: the scene building in the ancient Greek theater. It had three doors, through which the actors entered and left the stage, and was scenic background for the action. See p. 607.

Sonnet: a fourteen-line poem written in five-stress iambic lines. The two main kinds of sonnets are the **Italian sonnet,** in which the first eight lines always rhyme *abbaabba* and in which the last six lines may be rhymed in a variety of ways; and the **Shakespearean** or **Elizabethan sonnet,** consisting of three quatrains rhymed *abab, cdcd, efef,* concluded by a couplet, *gg.* See pp. 385–386.

Spenserian stanza: a nine-line stanza rhyming *ababbcbcc,* with the last an **Alexandrine** or six-stress iambic line. See p. 385.

Spondee: a metrical foot composed of two stressed syllables. See p. 380.

Stanza: a combination of lines of poetry to form a pattern which is repeated throughout a poem. See p. 382.

Stations: See **mansions.**

Stichomythia: dialogue in which two actors alternately speak one line of verse. See pp. 608–609.

Stream of consciousness: an attempt by an author to represent thoughts and sensations which flow without apparent logic. See p. 26.

Style: the language used by an author, his vocabulary and syntax. See p. 26.

Suspense: the expectancy an author creates concerning events yet to come in a literary work. See p. 24.

Symbolic action: action which suggests a meaning beyond the merely literal, sometimes achieving the symbolic dimension through repetition. See p. 24.

Symbolism: the use of one thing to stand for another thing, feeling, idea, or complex of any of these things. See pp. 14–16.

Tercet: a three-line stanza. See p. 384.

Tetrameter: a line of poetry containing four feet or four stresses. See p. 381.

Theme: the central idea or point of a story, poem, play, or novel. See p. 22.

Third person narration: presentation of a story from the point of view of omniscience, or from that of a **central observer,** through whose sensibility all events and scenes are reported. See p. 26.

Tone: the voice or attitude of the author which emerges from the work. See pp. 26–27.

Tragedy: See pp. 608–609.

Trimeter: a line of poetry containing three feet or three stresses. See p. 381.

Triplet: three-line stanza, but also three lines of verse rhyming consecutively. See p. 384.

Trochee: a metrical foot composed of a stressed syllable followed by an unstressed syllable. See p. 380.

True rhyme: exact repetition of terminal sounds. See p. 383.

Universality: the wide prevalence of ideas, attitudes, etc. A literary work is said to possess universality when its meaning and value transcend any one particular time or place. See p. 5.

Index of Authors' Names, Titles, and First Lines of Poems